Winner's Electoral College Vote %	Winner's Popular Vote %	Congress	House Majority Party	House Minority Party	Majority Party	Minority Party
**	No popular vote	1st	38 Admin †	26 Opp	17 Admin	9 Opp
		2nd	37 Fed ††	33 Dem-R	16 Fed	13 Dem-R
**	No popular vote	3rd	57 Dem-R	48 Fed	17 Fed	13 Dem-R
		4th	54 Fed	52 Dem-R	19 Fed	13 Dem-R
**	No popular vote	5th	58 Fed	48 Dem-R	20 Fed	12 Dem-R
		6th	64 Fed	42 Dem-R	19 Fed	13 Dem-R
HR**	No popular vote	7th	69 Dem-R	36 Fed	18 Dem-R	13 Fed
		8th	402 Dem-R	39 Fed	25 Dem-R	9 Fed
92.0	No popular vote	9th	116 Dem-R	25 Fed	27 Dem-R	7 Fed
		10th	118 Dem-R	24 Fed	28 Dem-R	6 Fed
69.7	No popular vote	11th	94 Dem-R	48 Fed	28 Dem-R	6 Fed
		12th	108 Dem-R	36 Fed	30 Dem-R	6 Fed
59.0	No popular vote	13th	112 Dem-R	68 Fed	27 Dem-R	9 Fed
		14th	117 Dem-R	65 Fed	25 Dem-R	11 Fed
84.3	No popular vote	15th	141 Dem-R	42 Fed	34 Dem-R	10 Fed
		16th	156 Dem-R	27 Fed	35 Dem-R	7 Fed
99.5	No popular vote	17th	158 Dem-R	25 Fed	44 Dem-R	4 Fed
		18th	187 Dem-R	26 Fed	44 Dem-R	4 Fed
HR	39.1 †††	19th	105 Admin	97 Dem-J	26 Admin	20 Dem-J
		20th	119 Dem-J	94 Admin	28 Dem-J	20 Admin
68.2	56.0	21st	139 Dem	74 Nat R	26 Dem	22 Nat R
		22nd	141 Dem	58 Nat R	25 Dem	21 Nat R
76.6	54.5	23rd	147 Dem	53 AntiMas	20 Dem	20 Nat R
		24th	145 Dem	98 Whig	27 Dem	25 Whig
57.8	50.9	25th	108 Dem	107 Whig	30 Dem	18 Whig
		26th	124 Dem	118 Whig	28 Dem	22 Whig
79.6	52.9					
–	52.9	27th	133 Whig	102 Dem	28 Whig	22 Dem
		28th	142 Dem	79 Whig	28 Whig	25 Dem
61.8	49.6	29th	143 Dem	77 Whig	31 Dem	25 Whig
		30th	115 Whig	108 Dem	36 Dem	21 Whig
56.2	47.3	31st	112 Dem	109 Whig	35 Dem	25 Whig
–	–	32nd	140 Dem	88 Whig	35 Dem	24 Whig
85.8	50.9	33rd	159 Dem	71 Whig	38 Dem	22 Whig
		34th	108 Rep	83 Dem	40 Dem	15 Rep
58.8	45.6	35th	118 Dem	92 Rep	36 Dem	20 Rep
		36th	114 Rep	92 Dem	36 Dem	26 Rep
59.4	39.8	37th	105 Rep	43 Dem	31 Rep	10 Dem
		38th	102 Rep	75 Dem	36 Rep	9 Dem
91.0	55.2					
–	–	39th	149 Union	42 Dem	42 Union	10 Dem
		40th	143 Rep	49 Dem	42 Rep	11 Dem
72.8	52.7	41st	149 Rep	63 Dem	56 Rep	11 Dem
		42nd	134 Rep	104 Dem	52 Rep	17 Dem
81.9	55.6	43rd	194 Rep	92 Dem	49 Rep	19 Dem
		44th	169 Rep	109 Dem	45 Rep	29 Dem
50.1	47.9 †††	45th	153 Dem	140 Rep	39 Rep	36 Dem
		46th	149 Dem	130 Rep	42 Dem	33 Rep
58.0	48.3	47th	147 Rep	135 Dem	37 Rep	37 Dem
–	–	48th	197 Dem	118 Rep	38 Rep	36 Dem
54.6	48.5	49th	183 Dem	140 Rep	43 Rep	34 Dem
		50th	169 Dem	152 Rep	39 Rep	37 Dem

Source for election data: Svend Peterson, *A Statistical History of American Presidential Elections.* New York: Frederick Ungar Publishing, 1963. Updates: Richard Scammon, *America Votes* 19. Washington D.C.: Congressional Quarterly, 1991; *Congressional Quarterly Weekly Report*, Nov. 7, 1992, p. 3552.

Abbreviations:

Admin = Administration supporters
AntiMas = Anti-Masonic
Dem = Democratic
Dem-R = Democratic-Republican
Fed = Federalist
Dem-J = Jacksonian Democrats
Nat R = National Republican
Opp = Opponents of administration
Rep = Republican
Union = Unionist

American Government

SIXTH EDITION

American Government

SIXTH EDITION

SUSAN WELCH
THE PENNSYLVANIA STATE UNIVERSITY

JOHN GRUHL
MICHAEL STEINMAN
JOHN COMER
UNIVERSITY OF NEBRASKA—LINCOLN

SUSAN M. RIGDON
UNIVERSITY OF ILLINOIS AT URBANA-CHAMPAIGN

WEST PUBLISHING COMPANY
Minneapolis/St. Paul New York Los Angeles San Francisco

West's Commitment to the Environment

In 1906, West Publishing Company began recycling materials left over from the production of books. This began a tradition of efficient and responsible use of resources. Today, 100% of our legal bound volumes are printed on acid-free, recycled paper consisting of 50% new paper pulp and 50% paper that has undergone a de-inking process. We also use vegetable-based inks to print all of our books. West recycles nearly 27,700,000 pounds of scrap paper annually—the equivalent of 229,300 trees. Since the 1960s, West has devised ways to capture and recycle waste inks, solvents, oils, and vapors created in the printing process. We also recycle plastics of all kinds, wood, glass, corrugated cardboard, and batteries, and have eliminated the use of polystyrene book packaging. We at West are proud of the longevity and the scope of our commitment to the environment.

West pocket parts and advance sheets are printed on recyclable paper and can be collected and recycled with newspapers. Staples do not have to be removed. Bound volumes can be recycled after removing the cover.

Production Credits

Interior Design: Roslyn M. Stendahl
Copyediting: Sheryl Rose
Proofreading: James Bohen
Artwork: Randy Miyake
Composition: Carlisle Communications
Cover Image: Tony Stone Worldwide
Index: E. Virginia Hobbs

Production, Prepress, Printing and Binding by West Publishing Company.

Printed with Printwise
Environmentally Advanced Water Washable Ink

Printed in the United States of America
03 02 01 00 99 98 97 96 8 7 6 5 4 3 2 1 0

Library of Congress Cataloging-in-Publication Data

American government / Susan Welch ... [et al.].—6th ed.
p. cm.
Includes bibliographical references and index.
ISBN: 0-314-06119-3 (hard : alk. paper)
1. United States—Politics and government.
I. Welch, Susan.
JK274.A54754 1996
320.973—dc20 95-45307
CIP

Photo Credits

1 (top) Joseph Kossuth Dixon, Courtesy Library of Congress; **1** (bottom) Schapiro, Liaison International; **2** AP/Wide World Photos; **4** Tomas Muscionico/Contact Press; **5** Brown Brothers; **6** Sebastiao Slagado; **22** Courtesy of Winterthur Museum; **24** Dennis Brack Ltd./Black Star; **27** The Metropolitan Museum of Art, Bequest of Charles Allen Munn, 1924 (24-90-35); **28** Historical Society of Pennsylvania; **41** The Granger Collection; **46** Roland Freeman/Magnum Photos, Inc.; **50** Sygma; **53** The Bettmann Archives; **60** U.S. Dept. of Agriculture; **61** AP/Wide World Photos; **63** Bettmann; **70** © 1988, J. B. Diederich, Contact Press Images, Inc.; **75** (top) Woodfin Camp & Associates; **75** (bottom) Brown Brothers; **76** Robb Kendrik Photography; **80** Black Star; **87** From the Collections of the St. Louis Mercantile Library Association; **108** Washington D.C. Fencer's Club, © Neal Slavin Studio, Inc.; **111** © 1986 Ken Heinen; **115** Donna Binder/Impact Visuals; **118** Gotham Book Mart, New York, N.Y.; **119** Michael Salas; **121** The Bettmann Archives; **122** Courtesy of Christian Coalition; **124** © 1989 Shelly Katz/Black Star; **125** Lynn Johnson; **126** Alex Quesada, Matrix; **132** Pierre Gleizes/Greenpeace; **135** AP/Wide World Photos; **140** Andy Levin; **142** P. F. Bentley/Time Magazine; **144** The Granger Collection; **146** (left) The Granger Collection; **146** (right) The Granger Collection; **147** Courtesy of the New York Historical Society; **162** Newsweek—Wally McNamee; **168** Newsweek—Wally McNamee; **171** The Granger Collection; **173** UPI/Bettmann Newsphotos; **176** Brown Brothers; **177** AP/Wide World Photos; **180** Courtesy of Smithsonian Institute; **182** Courtesy of Smithsonian Institute; **184** Courtesy of Smithsonian Institute; **185** Tracey Litt/Impact Visuals; **186** Bettmann; **189** Courtesy of Smithsonian Institute; **190** AP/Wide World Photos; **192** Bettmann; **194** Courtesy of Smithsonian Institute; **195** Steve Leonard/Black Star; **199** UPI/Bettmann; **200** Dan Lamant/Matrix; **208** Ira Wyman/Sygma; **212** Alex Webb/Magnum Photos, Inc.; **214** Jodi Buren/Time Magazine; **216** (left) Dane Penland; **216** (right) The Bettmann Archives; **220** Phil Huber/Black Star; **222** (top) Dan Adams/George Eastman House; **222** (bottom) Cynthia Johnson/Liaison International; **224** JB Pictures LTD/Stephen Terry; **227** Bettmann; **230** Time Magazine; **231** Time Magazine; **252** Alex Webb/Magnum Photos, Inc.; **255** The Granger Collection; **256** The Byron Collection, Museum of the City of New York; **271** UPI/Bettmann Newsphotos; **273** The Granger Collection; **278** AP/Wide World Photos; **283** (top) Reuters/Bettmann; **283** (bottom left) Laura Pedrick; **283** (bottom right) Reuters/Bettmann; **284** Terry Ashe/Time Magazine; **286** John Ficara; **301** Courtesy of Ailes Communications; **304** Mark Hess Illustration; **307** Engraving by Whitechurch, copyright 1855; courtesy of Library of Congress; **308** George Tames, New York Times Pictures;

—Continued following index

BRIEF CONTENTS

PART ONE

The American System 1

CHAPTER 1 AMERICAN DEMOCRACY 2

CHAPTER 2 THE CONSTITUTION 22

CHAPTER 3 FEDERALISM AND THE GROWTH OF GOVERNMENT 50

PART TWO

Links Between People and Government 75

CHAPTER 4 PUBLIC OPINION 76

CHAPTER 5 INTEREST GROUPS 108

CHAPTER 6 POLITICAL PARTIES 140

CHAPTER 7 ELECTIONS 168

CHAPTER 8 THE MEDIA 212

CHAPTER 9 MONEY AND POLITICS 252

PART THREE

Institutions 283

CHAPTER 10 CONGRESS 284

CHAPTER 11 THE PRESIDENCY 328

CHAPTER 12 THE BUREAUCRACY 364

CHAPTER 13 THE JUDICIARY 396

PART FOUR

Civil Liberties and Rights 429

CHAPTER 14 CIVIL LIBERTIES 430

CHAPTER 15 CIVIL RIGHTS 470

PART FIVE

Public Policies 521

CHAPTER 16 SOCIAL WELFARE POLICY 522

CHAPTER 17 ECONOMIC POLICY 554

CHAPTER 18 REGULATION AND ENVIRONMENTAL POLICY 586

CHAPTER 19 FOREIGN POLICY 620

CONTENTS

Preface xiv

PART ONE

The American System 1

CHAPTER 1
AMERICAN DEMOCRACY 2

YOU ARE THERE: Is Politics Necessary? 3
AMERICAN DIVERSITY 5
Ethnic and Economic Diversity 5
NEW POPULISM 8
Diversity and the Public Interest 9
NEW POPULISM: Controlling Immigration 11
Characteristics of Democracy 13
Value of the Individual 13
Political Equality 13
Majority Rule 14
Minority Rights 14
Direct and Indirect Democracy 14
Classical Democracy 14
Contemporary Theories of American Democracy 15
Pluralism 16
Elitism 16
Current Views 17
Conclusion: Is Government Responsive? 18
EPILOGUE: Politics, Representation, and Democratic Government 19
Key Terms 20
Further Readings 20
Notes 20

CHAPTER 2
THE CONSTITUTION 22

YOU ARE THERE: The Case of the Confidential Tapes 23
The Articles of Confederation 25
National Government Problems 25
State Government Problems 26
The Constitution 26
The Constitutional Convention 26
AMERICAN DIVERSITY: Founding Mothers 27
Features of the Constitution 31
Motives of the Founders 34
AMERICAN DIVERSITY: Did the Iroquois Influence the Founders? 35
Ratification of the Constitution 38
Changing the Constitution 40
Conclusion: Is The Constitution Responsive? 42
SYMBOLIC SOLUTIONS FOR COMPLEX PROBLEMS: Making English the Official National Language 43
EPILOGUE: The President Complies 46
Key Terms 47
Further Readings 47
Notes 47

CHAPTER 3
FEDERALISM AND THE GROWTH OF GOVERNMENT 50

YOU ARE THERE: Can Uncle Sam Help Baby-Sit? 51
Federal and Other Systems 53
Federal Systems 53
Unitary Systems 54
Confederal Systems 54
The Political Bases of Federalism 54
The Constitutional Bases of Federalism 55
Major Features of the System 55
Interpretations of Federalism 56
Federalism and the Growth of Government 58
Early Nationalist Period 58
Pre-Civil War Period 59
The Civil War to the New Deal 60
The New Deal 61
From the New Deal to the Great Society 62
NEW POPULISM: A New Western Saga: Cowboys versus the Government? 64
New Federalism 64
Contemporary Federalism 65
Federal-State Relations 65
Interstate Relations 67

SYMBOLIC SOLUTIONS FOR COMPLEX PROBLEMS: Should the Federal Government Turn Welfare Over to the States? 68

State-Local Relations 70

Conclusion: Is Federalism Responsive? 70

EPILOGUE: Ros-Lehtinen Supported the Bill 71

Key Terms 72

Further Readings 72

Notes 72

PART TWO

Links Between People and Government 75

CHAPTER 4

PUBLIC OPINION 76

YOU ARE THERE: The President Considers the Nation's Rising Concern over Crime 77

Nature of Public Opinion 78

Formation of Public Opinion 79

Agents of Political Socialization 80

Impact of Political Socialization 84

Measuring Public Opinion 84

Early Polling Efforts 84

Emergence of Scientific Polling 85

Polling Problems 86

Accuracy of Polls 86

Uses of Polls 87

NEW POPULISM: Teledemocracy: If Politicians Can't Do the Job, Can We? 88

Impact of Polls 89

How Informed Is Public Opinion? 92

Public Opinion 93

Ideology 93

Social Welfare and the Proper Role of Government 94

Social Issues 95

Race 96

Political Tolerance 98

Trust in Government 99

AMERICAN DIVERSITY: If Women Were in Charge, a Kinder and Gentler Nation? 102

Conclusion: Is Government Responsive to Public Opinion? 103

EPILOGUE: The President Followed the Polls 104

Key Terms 104

Further Readings 104

Notes 104

CHAPTER 5

INTEREST GROUPS 108

YOU ARE THERE: The NAACP Debates the Thomas Nomination 109

Group Formation 111

Why Groups Form 111

Why People Join 112

Who Joins? 113

Types of Interest Groups 113

Private Interest Groups 113

NEW POPULISM: The Angriest White Males 114

Public Interest Groups 120

Tactics of Interest Groups 126

Direct Lobbying Techniques 126

Indirect Lobbying Techniques 129

Protest and Civil Disobedience 132

Success of Interest Groups 133

Resources 133

Competition and Goals 134

Conclusion: Do Interest Groups Help Make Government Responsive? 136

EPILOGUE: The NAACP Opposed the Thomas Nomination 137

Key Terms 137

Further Readings 137

Notes 137

CHAPTER 6

POLITICAL PARTIES 140

YOU ARE THERE: Should the Republicans Offer the Voters a "Contract"? 141

What Are Political Parties? 143

Development and Change in the Party System 144

Preparty Politics: The Founders' Views of Political Parties 145

First Party Systems: Development of Parties 146

Second Party Systems: Rise of the Democrats 146

Third Party Systems: Rise of the Republicans 147

Fourth Party System: Republican Dominance 148

Fifth Party Systems: Democratic Dominance 148
Has the Fifth Party System Realigned? 149
The Parties Today 151
Characteristics of the Party System 152
Two Parties 152
Fragmentation 152
Moderation 153
NEW POPULISM: Do We Need a Third Party? 154
Minor Parties in American Politics 155
Party in the Electorate 155
Party Identification 155
Characteristics of Democrats and Republicans 156
Party in Government 156
Party Organization 158
National Party Organization 158
State and Local Party Organizations 160
Big-City Party Organizations 160
The Nominating Process 161
Caucuses 161
Conventions 161
Primaries 161
Conclusion: Do Political Parties Make Government More Responsive? 164
EPILOGUE: The Republicans Adopt a Contract 164
Key Terms 166
Further Readings 166
Notes 166

CHAPTER 7
ELECTIONS 168

The American Electorate 171
Early Limits on Voting Rights 171
Blacks and the Right to Vote 171
AMERICAN DIVERSITY: Blacks and Hispanics in Office 172
The Voting Rights Act 173
Women and the Right to Vote 175
Other Expansions of the Electorate 176
AMERICAN DIVERSITY: Women in Office 177
Voter Turnout 178
Political Activism in the Nineteenth Century 178
Progressive Reforms 178
Recent Turnout 178
Who Does Not Vote? 179
Why Turnout is Low 179
SYMBOLIC SOLUTIONS FOR COMPLEX PROBLEMS? Same Day Voter Registration 181
Other Campaign Participation 184
Presidential Nominating Campaigns 186
Who Runs for President and Why? 186
How a Candidate Wins the Nomination 187
AMERICAN DIVERSITY: Can an African American Be Elected President? 188
Presidential Caucuses and Conventions 190
Presidential Primaries 190
Reforming the Nomination Process 191
The National Conventions 192
Independent and Third-Party Nominees 195
The General Election Campaign 195
Campaign Organizations 195
Images and Issues 196
The Electoral College 196
Campaign Strategies 197
The Media Campaign 199
Campaign Funding 203
Voting 203
Party Loyalties 203
Candidate Evaluations 204
NEW POPULISM: The Angry White Male 205
Parties, Candidates, and Issues 206
Conclusion: Do Elections Make Government Responsive? 206
EPILOGUE: The Package Works 207
Key Terms 208
Further Readings 209
Notes 209

CHAPTER 8
THE MEDIA 212

YOU ARE THERE: Should You Pull Him Out of "the Closet"? 213
The Media State 215
Roles of the Media 215
Concentration of the Media 216
Atomization of the Media 217
NEW POPULISM: Talk Radio 218
Relationship Between the Media and Politicians 220
Symbiotic Relationship 221
Adversarial Relationship 224

Relationship between the Media and Recent Administrations 226
Relationship between the Media and Congress 230

Bias of the Media 230
Political Bias 231
Commercial Bias 234

Impact of the Media on Politics 238
Impact on the Public Agenda 239
Impact on Political Parties and Elections 240
Impact on Public Opinion 242

Conclusion: Are the Media Responsive? 243

EPILOGUE: Signorile Revealed Official's Homosexuality 244
Key Terms 245
Further Readings 245
Notes 245

CHAPTER 9
MONEY AND POLITICS 252

YOU ARE THERE: Quid Pro Quo? Or No? 253

The Development of Laws to Regulate Money and Politics 255
Money in Nineteenth-Century American Politics 255
Early Reforms 256

The Role of Money in Election Campaigns 257
Campaign Finance Laws 257
Loopholes in the Reforms 258
How the System Works 259

The Impact of Campaign Money 263
Does the Campaign Finance System Deter Good Candidates? 263
Does Money Win Elections? 264
Does Money Buy Favorable Policies? 266

Reforming the Campaign Money System 269

Conflicts of Interest 271
Conflict-of-Interest Reforms 271

SYMBOLIC SOLUTIONS FOR COMPLEX PROBLEMS? Public Funding for Congressional Campaigns 272
Congress 273
The Executive Branch 275

Conclusion: Does the Influence of Money Make Government Less Responsive? 276

EPILOGUE: DeConcini Intervenes 277
Key Terms 279
Further Readings 279
Notes 279

PART THREE

Institutions 283

CHAPTER 10
CONGRESS 284

YOU ARE THERE: Should You Risk Your Career? 285

Members and Constituencies 288
Members 288
Constituencies 289

SYMBOLIC SOLUTIONS FOR COMPLEX PROBLEMS? Term Limits 290

Congressional Campaigns and Elections 292
The Advantage of Incumbency 292

AMERICAN DIVERSITY: Women in Congress 295
Unsafe at Any Margin? 296
Challengers 296

NEW POPULISM: The 1994 Congressional Elections 298
Campaigns 300
Voting for Congress 301

The Representative on the Job 302
Informal Norms 302
Working Privately and "Going Public" 302
Voting by Members 303

How Congress Is Organized 305
How Congressional Organization Evolved 306
Leaders 307
Committees 308
Staff 313

What Congress Does 313
Lawmaking 313

AMERICAN DIVERSITY: Black Power in Congress 312
Overseeing the Federal Bureaucracy 317
Budget Making 319

Conclusion: Is Congress Responsive? 320

EPILOGUE: Margolies-Mezvinsky Supports the President and Loses Her Job 322
Key Terms 323
Further Readings 323
Notes 324

CHAPTER 11
THE PRESIDENCY 328

YOU ARE THERE: Retreat Again? 329

Presidential Job Description 331

Qualifications 331

Tenure 331

Succession 331

Rewards 332

Growth of the Modern Presidency 332

The Presidency Before the New Deal 332

Development of the Personal Presidency 334

Presidential Power 336

Persuading the Washingtonians 337

Persuading the Public 339

Presidential Popularity 341

Limits of Presidential Power 342

Roles of the President 343

Growth of Presidential Staff 343

Administrative Leadership 345

SYMBOLIC SOLUTIONS FOR COMPLEX PROBLEMS? Line-item Veto 346

Domestic Policy Leadership 349

Foreign Policy Leadership 350

Military Leadership 354

Symbolic Leadership 357

Party Leadership 358

Conclusion: Is The Presidency Responsive? 359

EPILOGUE: The President Stands Firm 360

Key Terms 361

Further Readings 361

Notes 361

CHAPTER 12
THE BUREAUCRACY 364

YOU ARE THERE: Attacking AIDS 365

Bureaucracy 367

Nature of Bureaucracy 367

Public and Private Bureaucracies 367

SYMBOLIC SOLUTIONS FOR COMPLEX PROBLEMS? Slashing the Bureaucracy 370

Federal Bureaucracy 371

Growth of the Bureaucracy 371

Why the Bureaucracy Has Grown 372

Types of Bureaucracy 374

Bureaucratic Functions 376

Making Policy 377

AMERICAN DIVERSITY: Women and Minorities in the Civil Service 378

Administering Policy 382

Other Functions 383

Expectations About the Federal Bureaucracy 384

Responsiveness 384

Neutral Competence 384

Controlling the Bureaucracy 387

President 387

AMERICAN DIVERSITY: Presidential Administrative Appointments 388

Congress 388

Courts 389

Interest Groups and Individuals 389

Conclusion: Is the Bureaucracy Responsive? 391

EPILOGUE: Neutral Competence and AIDS 392

Key Terms 393

Further Readings 393

Notes 393

CHAPTER 13
THE JUDICIARY 396

YOU ARE THERE: Friend or Foe? 397

Development of the Courts' Role in Government 398

Founding to the Civil War 399

Civil War to the Depression 401

Depression to the Present 402

Courts 404

Structure of the Courts 404

Jurisdiction of the Courts 404

Judges 405

Selection of Judges 405

AMERICAN DIVERSITY: Do Women Judges Make a Difference? 407

Tenure of Judges 411

Qualifications of Judges 412

Independence of Judges 412

Access to the Courts 412
Wealth Discrimination in Access 413
Interest Group Help in Access 413
Restrictions on Access 413
Proceeding Through the Courts 415
Deciding Cases 415
Interpreting Statutes 415
Interpreting the Constitution 416
Restraint and Activism 418
Following Precedents 419
Making Law 419
The Power of the Courts 420
Use of Judicial Review 420
Use of Political Checks Against the Courts 421
Conclusion: Are the Courts Responsive? 424
EPILOGUE: Exclusion of Japanese Upheld 425
Key Terms 426
Further Readings 426
Notes 426

PART FOUR
Civil Liberties and Rights 429

CHAPTER 14
CIVIL LIBERTIES 430

YOU ARE THERE: Does Religious Liberty Include Animal Sacrifice? 431
The Constitution and the Bill of Rights 432
Individual Rights in the Constitution 432
The Bill of Rights 433
Freedom or Expression 434
Freedom of Speech 434
Freedom of the Press 439
Libel and Obscenity 441
Freedom of Religion 444
AMERICAN DIVERSITY: Can They Be "As Nasty as They Wanna Be"? 446
Rights of Criminal Defendants 452
Search and Seizure 452
Self-Incrimination 453
Counsel 454
Jury Trial 454
Cruel and Unusual Punishment 454
Rights in Theory and in Practice 456
Right to Privacy 456
Birth Control 456
Abortion 456
SYMBOLIC SOLUTIONS FOR COMPLEX PROBLEMS? Capitol Punishment 458
Homosexuality 462
Right to Die 463
Conclusion: Are the Courts Responsive in Interpreting Civil Liberties? 464
EPILOGUE: The First Amendment Protects Animal Sacrifice 464
Key Terms 465
Further Readings 465
Notes 465

CHAPTER 15
CIVIL RIGHTS 470

YOU ARE THERE: Compromise or Continue to Fight? 471
Race Discrimination 473
Discrimination Against African Americans 473
AMERICAN DIVERSITY: Black Masters 475
Overcoming Discrimination Against African Americans 477
Continuing Discrimination Against African Americans 485
Discrimination Against Hispanics 490
Discrimination Against Native Americans 493
Sex Discrimination 496
Discrimination Against Women 496
Discrimination Against Men 503
Affirmative Action 504
NEW POPULISM: Opposition to Affirmative Action 507
Are Civil Rights Enough? 511
Conclusion: Is Government Responsive in Granting Civil Rights? 513
EPILOGUE: Hamer Continues to Fight 514
Key Terms 515
Further Readings 515
Notes 516

PART FIVE

Public Policies 521

CHAPTER 16

SOCIAL WELFARE POLICY 522

YOU ARE THERE: Can This Bill Be Saved? 523

What Are Social Welfare Policies? 526

Evolution of Social Welfare Policies 526

Social Welfare for Everyone 527

How Social Security Works 527

Problems with the Program 527

The Future of Social Security 528

Federal Health Care Programs 529

Health Care Reforms 530

Social Welfare for the Poor 534

How Many are Poor? 534

Who is Poor? 535

The Cause of Poverty 536

Basic Programs for the Poor 538

Reforming Welfare for the Poor 539

SYMBOLIC SOLUTIONS FOR COMPLEX PROBLEMS?
Cutting Off Welfare Benefits 544

Social Welfare for the Well-Off 546

Tax Breaks 546

Farm Subsidies 546

Other Programs for the Rich 547

Conclusions: Are Social Welfare Programs Responsive? 548

EPILOGUE: Health Care Reform Dies 549

Key Terms 551

Further Reading 551

Notes 551

CHAPTER 17

ECONOMIC POLICY 554

YOU ARE THERE: Stand by Your Man? 555

Types of Economic Systems 556

Capitalism 556

Socialism and Communism 556

Mixed Economies 556

Economics Systems and Political Systems 557

Regulating the Economy 558

Economic Problems 558

Government's Economic Tools 560

Managing the Economy for Political Purposes 563

The Budget in the Economy 565

Our Tax Burden 565

Income Tax Policy 566

Where the Money Goes 569

Discretionary and Mandatory Spending 569

Budget Forecasting 570

Deficits and Debt 571

SYMBOLIC SOLUTIONS FOR COMPLEX PROBLEMS?
Balancing the Budget by Constitutional Amendment? 572

Government and the Economy in the 21st Century 575

The American Quarter Century 575

Age of Diminished Expectations 577

What Can Government Do? 580

Conclusion: Is Our Economic Policy Responsive? 582

EPILOGUE: Kerrey Opposes the President 583

Key Terms 583

Further Reading 583

Notes 584

CHAPTER 18

REGULATION AND ENVIRONMENTAL POLICY 586

YOU ARE THERE: Endangered Species or Endangered Jobs? 587

Development of Regulation 589

Reasons for Regulation 589

Kinds of Regulation 591

Writing Regulations 592

Enforcing Regulations 594

Cycles of Regulation 595

Deregulation 596

Reregulation 598

Deregulation: The Cycle Continues 599

SYMBOLIC SOLUTIONS FOR COMPLEX PROBLEMS?
Deregulating to "Get Government Off Our Backs" 600

Regulatory Politics and Environmental Protection 602

Evolution of Government's Role 603

Implementing Environmental Regulations 605
Reforming Environmental Regulation 610
Benefits and Costs of Regulation 614
Conclusion: Is Regulation Responsive? 615
EPILOGUE: At Loggerheads 615
Key Terms 616
Further Reading 616
Notes 617

CHAPTER 19
FOREIGN POLICY 620

YOU ARE THERE: Trade Rights, or Trading Rights for Jobs 621
Foreign Policy Goals 623
Making Foreign Policy in a Democracy 624
The Inner Circle 624
Specialists 626
Congress 626
Interest Groups and Lobbyists 628
Public Opinion 629
Changing Approaches to U.S. Foreign Policy 630
Isolationism 630
The Cold War 631
Containment in the Nuclear Age 633
Vietnam 633
Detente 637
Cold War Revival 638
End of the Cold War 638
Merchant Diplomacy and Multilateralism 641
Military Instruments of Foreign Policy 642
NEW POPULISM: The Return of "Isolationism" 640
Military Intervention 643
Military Alliances 645
Military Aid 647
Economic Instruments of Foreign Policy 648
Trade 648
Economic Sanctions 651
Foreign Aid 653
Conclusion: Is Our Foreign Policy Responsive? 658
EPILOGUE: Pelosi Goes Along 658
Key Terms 659
Further Reading 659
Notes 660
Appendix A: The Declaration of Independence 663
Appendix B: Constitution of the United States 665
Appendix C: Federalist Paper #10 677
Appendix D: Federalist Paper #51 681
Glossary 685
Name Index 691
Subject Index 703
Presidents, Elections and Congresses 1789–present inside front and back covers

PREFACE

The sixth edition of our text, *American Government*, tries, as did the previous editions, to interest students in learning about the exciting, important, and controversial issues in American public life. We believe an introductory course succeeds if most students develop an understanding of major ideas, an interest in learning more about American government, and an ability to begin to understand and evaluate the news they hear about American political issues. Although a firm grounding in the essential "nuts and bolts" of American government is crucial, other approaches are helpful in motivating students' interest in government.

We offer the essential "nuts and bolts" of American government, but we also want the student to understand why (and sometimes how) these important features have evolved, their impact on government and individuals, and why they are controversial (if they are) and worth learning. For example, we prefer students to leave the course remembering why campaign finance laws were created and why they have the impact they do than to memorize specific dollar limitations on giving for different types of candidates from different types of organizations. The latter will change or will soon be forgotten, but understanding the "whys" will help the student understand the campaign finance issue long after the course is over.

We have also tried to interest students by describing and discussing the impact of various features of government. For example, students who do not understand why learning about voter registration laws is important may "see the light" when they understand the link between such laws and low voter turnout. Therefore, a particular emphasis throughout the book is on the *impact* of government: how individual features of government affect its responsiveness to different groups (in Lasswell's terms, "Who gets what and why?"). We realize that nothing in American politics is simple; rarely does one feature of government produce, by itself, a clear outcome. Nevertheless, we think that students will be more willing to learn about government if they see some relationships between how government operates and the impact it has on them as citizens of America.

Changes in the Sixth Edition

This edition contains a wealth of new material. Over the past several years, voter anger with government and politicians has grown. Along with that is increasing public support for new laws that limit the power of government or elected officials, such as term limits, the balanced budget amendment, and limits on taxing power. In two new features found in most chapters, we focus on helping students understand and evaluate the anger and the policies sometimes suggested by those who claim to be "fed up" with government and politics. One of these features, *The New Populism*, examines the roots and manifestations of discontent with government, comparing today's unrest with the populist movement of the late nineteenth century. For example, in Chapter 3 we examine the discontent of many westerners with federal government control of western lands; in Chapter 7 we focus on the "angry white male"; and in Chapter 8 we explore "talk" radio as a manifestation of new populism.

A second feature, *Symbolic Solutions for Complex Problems?*, again found in most chapters, analyzes policy suggestions to see if they would likely help solve the problems they are directed toward or whether they are merely symbolic solutions, ideas that sound good but would have little impact. Symbolic Solutions boxes focus on popular idea such as term limits (Chapter 10), public financing of campaigns (Chapter 9), the line item veto (Chapter 11), slashing the bureaucracy (Chapter 12), and turning welfare over to the states (Chapter 3).

In addition to these new features, we have extensively revised the entire text. In Chapter 1, we explore the suggestion that Americans, though vastly proud of the American system in general, do not like the manifestations of democracy they see in their political institutions, particularly Congress—disagreement, lobbying, negotiation, and delay. We return to that paradox in later chapters as we discuss the seemingly growing anger toward and impatience with government.

In Chapters 6, 7, and 10, we have integrated much material about the new Republican-dominated Congress, and the factors that led to the recent stunning reversal of partisan fortunes. Written in mid-1995, the text also provides more analysis of the Clinton administration, especially in Chapters 11, 12, and 16 through 19. The impact of new technology on politics receives more consideration in this edition, especially in Chapters 4 and 8.

The changing direction of the Supreme Court is reflected in considerable revisions in Chapters 13 and 14. Chapter 15 contains an expanded and revised discussion of affirmative action, as well as updated material on the status of blacks, Hispanics, and Native Americans.

As always, the policy chapters are substantially revised to reflect current issues and debates. Beyond that, both Chapter 18 on regulation and the environment and Chapter 19 on foreign policy have been thoroughly revised and reorganized.

We are delighted to have the opportunity to write a sixth edition and to improve the text further in ways suggested by our students and readers. We have been extremely pleased by the reaction of instructors and students to our first five editions. We were especially gratified twice to have won the American Government Textbook Award from the Women's Caucus for Political Science of the American Political Science Association.

Special Features

Student interest and analytic abilities grow when confronted with a clash of views about important issues. Today there is much discussion about how to stimulate the critical thinking abilities of students. Beginning with the first edition, our text has provided features especially designed to do this by involving students in the controversies—and excitement—of American politics.

YOU ARE THERE. Each chapter opens with a scenario called "You Are There." In a page or two the student reads about a real-life political dilemma faced by a public official or a private citizen involved in a controversial issue. Students are asked to put themselves in that individual's shoes, to weigh the pros and cons, and to decide what should be done. The instructor may want to poll the entire class and use the "You Are There" as a basis for class discussion. In the "Epilogue" at the end of the chapter, we reveal the actual decision and discuss it in light of the ideas presented in the chapter.

One-third of the *You Are There* features in this edition are new. They feature such timely topics as the development of the Republicans' "Contract with America" (Chapter 6), the demise of the Clinton health care proposals (Chapter 16), and the Henry Foster nomination for Surgeon General (Chapter 11).

AMERICAN DIVERSITY. In many chapters, American Diversity boxes illustrate the impact of the social diversity of the American population on political life. The boxes help students understand how diversity of backgrounds and attitudes shape views of politics and positions on issues.

THE NEW POPULISM. This new feature, described above, analyzes why voters are angry, and some of the manifestations of that anger. These boxes help explain the complexity and diversity of public opinion.

SYMBOLIC SOLUTIONS FOR COMPLEX PROBLEMS? Another new feature, already described, helps students evaluate whether commonly discussed solutions to complex public problems might work, or whether some might be only symbolic or actually might make the problem worse.

BOXES. In each chapter several boxes highlighting interesting aspects of American politics draw the students into the material. Many illustrate how government and politics really work in a particular situation—how a corporation lobbies for government benefits, how a seemingly powerless group is able to organize for political action, how interest groups solicit money by mail, and how political polls are done—while others highlight features of government that may be of particular interest to students—what standard of risk should government use in regulating acne medication, how ethnicity shapes voting behavior, and the impact of federal programs on students.

Several other features help students organize their study:

OUTLINE. Each chapter begins with an outline of its contents.

KEY TERMS. Key terms are boldfaced within the text and listed at the end of each chapter.

FURTHER READING. A brief, annotated list of further readings contains works that might be useful to a student doing research or looking for further reading.

GLOSSARY. A glossary at the end of the book defines terms that may be unfamiliar to students.

The Organization and Contents of the Book

While the basic organization of American government books is fairly standard, our text has a unique chapter on money and politics and a half chapter on environmental politics. Other features include a civil rights chapter that integrates a thorough treatment of constitutional issues concerning minorities and women, a discussion of the civil rights and women's rights movements, and contemporary research on the political status of these groups. We include in this chapter the special legal problems of Hispanics and Indians.

Substantive policy chapters reinforce the emphasis on the impact of government action. Our social welfare policy chapter is unique in its treatment of social welfare programs for the middle income and wealthy as well as the poor. A chapter on economic policymaking complements the section on budgeting found in the chapter on Congress. The treatment of economic policy highlights the relationship between politics and the economy, and should help the student better understand issues such as the deficit, inflation, and unemployment. The chapter on regulation emphasizes the underlying rationale for regulation and its problems and benefits, with special emphasis on environmental regulation. The chapter on foreign policy places current foreign policy issues in the context of the history of our foreign policy aims, especially since World War II, and features new issues arising in the post–Cold War world.

Some instructors will prefer not to use any of the policy chapters. The book stands as a whole without them, as many policy examples are integrated into the rest of the text. Different combinations of the policy chapters may also be used, as each chapter is independent.

The organization of the book is straightforward. After material on democracy, the Constitution, and federalism, the book covers linkages, including money and politics, then institutions, and finally policy. Civil liberties and rights are treated after the chapter on the judiciary. But the book is flexible enough that instructors can modify the order of the chapters. Some instructors will prefer to cover institutions before process. Others may prefer to discuss civil liberties and rights when discussing the Constitution. Still others may wish to integrate some of the policy chapters into the treatment of institutions. For example, the economic policy chapter could be used in conjunction with the section in the Congress chapter on the budget. The social welfare chapter complements the chapters on public opinion and interest groups. The foreign policy chapter fits nicely with the treatment of the presidency. The chapter on regulation could serve as a case study following the chapter on bureaucracy.

Supplementary Materials

The supplementary materials complement the book.

INSTRUCTOR'S MANUAL. Written by Jeff Walz, the instructor's manual provides lectures, lecture suggestions, and in-class exercises for each chapter. Suggestions for out-of-class papers and projects are also provided. A student questionnaire is included to allow instructors to collect student data that can be used in class throughout the semester as a comparison with national poll data presented in the book.

INSTRUCTIONAL MATERIALS ON DISKETTES. The lectures and other material in the instructor's manual are provided on computer diskettes. So is the student questionnaire, which will spare instructors the trouble of having it retyped or re-entered on computer disks.

STUDENT STUDY GUIDE. An excellent Student Guide, written by Susan Rigdon, provides students with exercises emphasizing the major points of each chapter. Chapter objectives and key terms are reviewed. Practice multiple choice questions are provided. Unlike many such guides, this one also helps the students learn to write essays, thus emphasizing the improvement of analytic skills. Essay writing tips are given, then illustrated in each chapter.

VIDEODISC. Developed to support concepts in the book, our disk combines use of video clips, charts, and graphs. It is approximately 50 minutes long and is comprised of 4- to 6-minute segments that can be used to enhance lectures.

VIDEOTAPES. Qualified adopters are entitled to choose from West's Political Science Video Library. A list of tapes is available upon request. In addition, the *Government by Consent* video collection and the *Equal Justice Under the Law* series are available.

TRANSPARENCY ACETATES. Fifty full-color acetates of important maps and illustrations from the text are offered to adopters.

ACKNOWLEDGMENTS

We would like to thank the many people who have aided and sustained us during the lengthy course of this project. Our current and former University of Nebraska and Penn State colleagues have been most tolerant and helpful. We thank them all. In particular, we appreciate the assistance of John Hibbing, Philip Dyer, Robert Miewald, Beth Theiss-Morse, Louis Picard, John Peters, David Rapkin, Peter Maslowski, David Forsythe, W. Randy Newell, and Steven Daniels who provided us with data, bibliographic information, and other insights that we have used here. We are especially grateful to Philip Dyer, Alan Booth, Louis Picard, Robert Miewald, and John Hibbing who read one or more chapters and saved us from a variety of errors.

We are also grateful to the many other readers of our draft manuscript. Without their assistance the book would have been less accurate, complete, and lively.

Reviewers include:

Alan Abramowitz, State University of New York at Stony Brook.
Larry Adams, Baruch College-City University of New York
Danny M. Adkison, Oklahoma State University
James Alt, Harvard University
Margery Marzahn Ambrosius, Kansas State University
Kevin Bailey, North Harris Community College
Kennette M. Benedict, Northwestern University
Timothy Bledsoe, Wayne State University
Jon Bond, Texas A&M University
Paul R. Brace, New York University
Joseph V. Brogan, La Salle University
James R. Brown, Jr., Central Washington University
Chalmers Brumbaugh, Elon College
Richard G. Buckner, Jr., Santa Fe Community College
Ronald Busch, Cleveland State University
Carl D. Cavalli, Memphis State University
Richard A. Champagne, University of Wisconsin, Madison
Michael Connelly, Southwestern Oklahoma State University
Gary Copeland, University of Oklahoma
George H. Cox, Jr., Georgia Southern College
Paige Cubbison, Miami-Dade University
Landon Curry, Southwest Texas State University
Jack DeSario, Case Western Reserve University
Robert E. DiClerico, West Virginia University
Ernest A. Dover, Jr., Midwestern State University
Georgia Duerst-Lahti, Beloit College
Ann H. Elder, Illinois State University
Ghassan E. El-Eid, Butler University
C. Lawrence Evans, College of William and Mary
Murray Fischel, Kent State University
Bobbe Fitzhugh, Eastern Wyoming College
Marianne Fraser, University of Utah
Jarvis Gamble, Owens Community College
David Garrison, Collin County Community College
Phillip L. Gianos, California State University—Fullerton
Doris A. Graber, University of Illinois—Chicago
Ruth M. Grubel, University of Wisconsin—Whitewater
Stefan D. Haag, Austin Community College
Larry M. Hall, Belmont University
Edward Harpham, University of Texas—Dallas
Peter O. Haslund, Santa Barbara City College
Richard P. Heil, Fort Hays State University
Peggy Heilig, University of Illinois at Urbana
Craig Hendricks, Long Beach City College
Marjorie Hershey, Indiana University
Samuel B. Hoff, Delaware State College
Robert D. Holsworth, Virginia Commonwealth University
Jesse C. Horton, San Antonio College
Gerald Houseman, Indiana University
Jerald Johnson, University of Vermont
Loch Johnson, University of Georgia
Evan M. Jones, St. Cloud State University
Henry C. Kenski, University of Arizona
Matt Kerbel, Villanova University
Marshall R. King, Maryville College
Orma Lindford, Kansas State University
Peter J. Longo, University of Nebraska—Kearney
Roger C. Lowery, University of North Carolina—Wilmington
H. R. Mahood, Memphis State University
Jarol B. Manheim, The George Washington University

A. NICK MINTON, University of Massachusetts—Lowell
MATTHEW MOEN, University of Maine
MICHAEL NELSON, Vanderbilt University
BRUCE NESMITH, Coe College
WALTER NOELKE, Angelo State University
THOMAS PAYETTE, Henry Ford Community College
THEODORE B. PEDELISKI, University of North Dakota
JERRY PERKINS, Texas Tech University
TONI PHILLIPS, University of Arkansas
C. HERMAN PRITCHETT, University of California—Santa Barbara
CHARLES PRYSBY, University of North Carolina—Greensboro
SANDRA L. QUINN-MUSGROVE, Our Lady of the Lake University
DONALD R. RANISH, Antelope Valley Community College
LINDA RICHTER, Kansas State University
JERRY SANDVICK, North Hennepin Community College
JAMES RICHARD SAUDER, University of New Mexico
ELEANOR A. SCHWAB, South Dakota State University
EARL SHERIDAN, University of North Carolina—Wilmington
EDWARD SIDLOW, Northwestern University
CYNTHIA SLAUGHTER, Angelo State University
JOHN SQUIBB, Lincolnland Community College
M. H. TAJALLI-TEHRANI, Southwest Texas State University
KRISTINE A. THOMPSON, Moorehead State University
R. MARK TILLER, Austin Community College
GORDON J. TOLLE, South Dakota State University
SUSAN TOLLESON-RINEHART, Texas Tech University
BERNADYNE WEATHERFORD, Rowan College of New Jersey
RICHARD UNRUH, Fresno Pacific College
JAY VAN BRUGGEN, Clarion University of Pennsylvania
KENNY WHITBY, University of South Carolina
CLIFFORD J. WIRTH, University of New Hampshire
ANN WYNIA, North Hennepin Community College
MARY D. YOUNG, Southwestern Michigan College

We are also grateful to those instructors who have used the book and relayed their comments and suggestions to us. Our students at the University of Nebraska have also provided invaluable reactions to the previous editions.

Others too have been of great assistance to us. Margery M. Ambrosius generously helped gather information for several tables. Jeff Walz, Staci Beavers, and Michael Moore provided essential service and help in producing the ancillary materials for the book.

Several people at West Publishing also deserve our thanks. Clark Baxter has been a continual source of encouragement and optimism from the beginning of the first edition through the last decision on the sixth. We are greatly in debt to David Farr, who designed and produced the first edition of the book, and to Michelle McAnelly, who produced this edition.

Finally, the contribution of our spouses—Nancy Comer, Linda Steinman, and Alan Booth—can hardly be summarized in a sentence or two. But we are very appreciative that they were supportive all the time and patient most of the time.

ABOUT THE AUTHORS

SUSAN WELCH received her A.B. and Ph.D. degrees from the University of Illinois at Urbana-Champaign. She is currently Dean of the College of the Liberal Arts and Professor of Political Science at The Pennsylvania State University. Her teaching and research areas include legislatures, state and urban politics, and women and minorities in politics. She has edited the *American Politics Quarterly.*

JOHN GRUHL, a Professor of Political Science, received his A.B. from DePauw University in Greencastle, Indiana and his Ph.D. from the University of California at Santa Barbara. Since joining the University of Nebraska faculty in 1976, he has taught and done research in the areas of judicial process, criminal justice, and civil rights and liberties. He won University of Nebraska campus wide distinguished teaching awards in 1979 and 1986 for excellence in undergraduate teaching, and became a charter member of the University's Academy of Distinguished Teachers in 1995.

MICHAEL STEINMAN graduated from George Washington University with a B.A. in 1964. His M.A. and Ph.D. degrees are from the University of Chicago. An Associate Dean of the College of Arts and Sciences and Professor of Political Science at the University of Nebraska-Lincoln, he teaches courses in public administration and does research in policing and domestic violence. In 1984 he won a campus wide distinguished teaching award for his development and implementation of a Keller Plan Introduction to American Government course.

JOHN COMER is a Professor of Political Science at the University of Nebraska. He received his A.B. in political science from Miami University of Ohio in 1965, and his Ph.D. from the Ohio State University in 1971. His teaching and research focus on interest groups, public opinion, voting behavior, and political parties.

SUSAN RIGDON received A.B. and Ph.D. degrees in political science from the University of Illinois in 1966 and 1971. She has taught American Government at several institutions in the U.S. and China, and has other teaching and research interests in foreign policy, comparative government, and political development. She is a Research Associate in Anthropology at the University of Illinois at Urbana-Champaign.

PART ONE

The American System

Italian immigrants arrive at Ellis Island, New York, in 1910 (right). Elementary students in Brentwood, California, where the multicultural present looks like America's future (below).

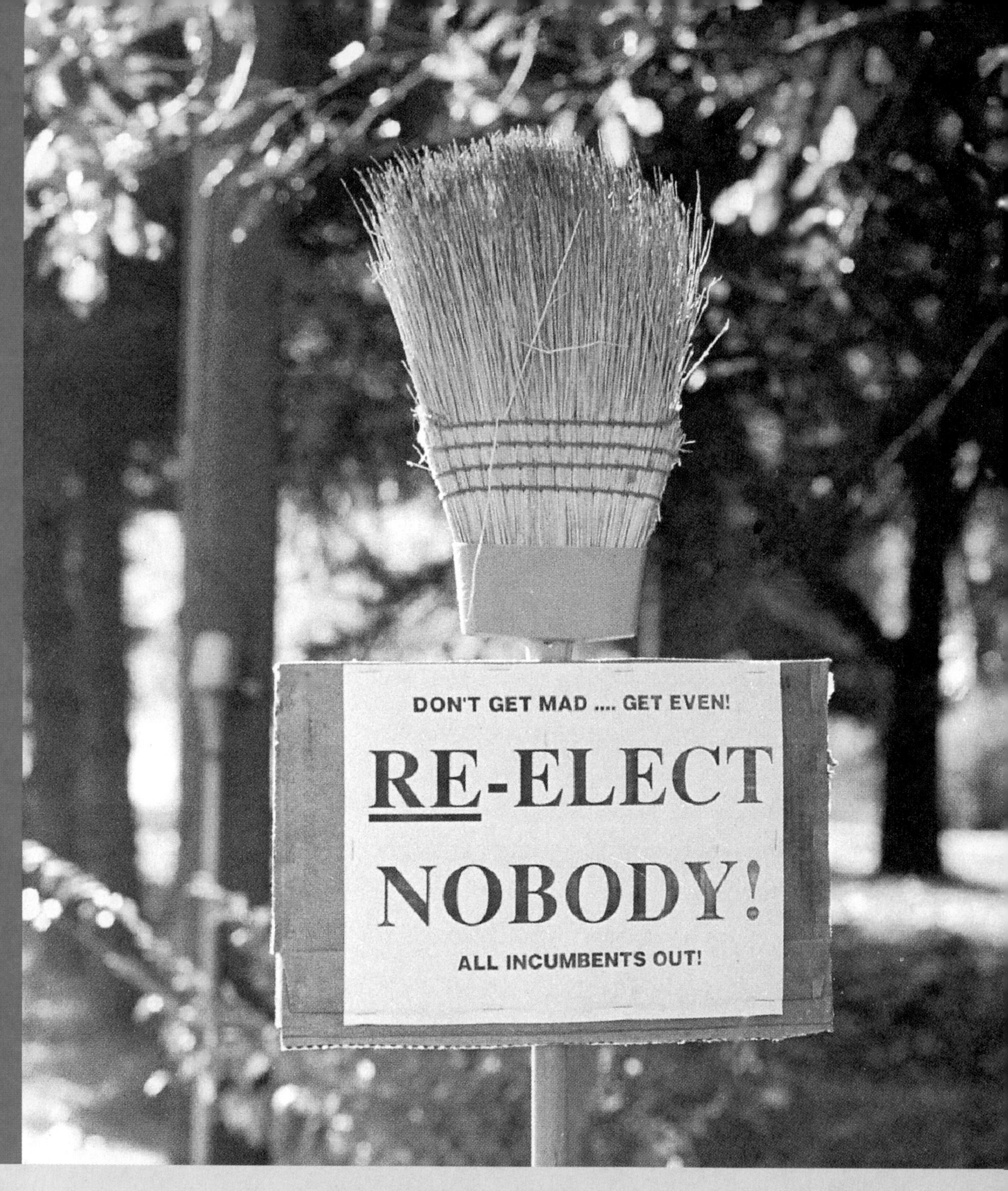
DON'T GET MAD .... GET EVEN!
RE-ELECT
NOBODY!
ALL INCUMBENTS OUT!

1 American Democracy

You Are There

Is Politics Necessary?

It is November, 1992. You are a 21-year-old first-time voter and must make a choice from among George Bush, Bill Clinton, and Ross Perot. You consider yourself an independent and are skeptical about what the candidates are saying. You are not sure if they are talking about the things most Americans care about.

Like many Americans, you do not really trust government and politicians. You have heard about the Vietnam War and the Watergate and Iran-contra scandals. You do not know much about them, but do know that they involved many government officials who were not always honest with the public. You also know that the taxpayers are footing the bill for the recent collapse of many banks and savings and loans, and that many members of the House of Representatives overdrew their checking accounts in the House bank, some more than 100 times, without any consequences. President Bush criticized them but he had already broken his promise not to raise taxes. You wonder whether these politicians are working for most Americans or for the "special interests."

Then too, you know that times are not good. The economy is stagnant and the cities are crumbling. Many people are out of work and you worry about getting a good job after you graduate. Like most other Americans, you feel that the country is headed in the wrong direction. And what are the politicians doing about it? Not much, at least that you can see. The president blames Congress while Congress blames the president. Republicans blame Democrats while Democrats blame Republicans. Maybe, you think, politics is just mudslinging rather than solving problems.

The two major party candidates seem to promise more of the same. Republican candidate and incumbent George Bush has been a politician most of his life. People joked that he had "the longest resume in Washington" even before he became president. As president, he does not appear to have much vision or interest in tackling our domestic problems. While Democratic candidate and Arkansas governor Bill Clinton is an "outsider" to Washington politics, he has wanted to be president for a long time and is a "career politician" who shades the truth to avoid offending voters. You still do not know how he avoided the draft during the Vietnam War and whether he has cheated on his wife, though you are not sure these things are all that important anyway. His admission that he tried marijuana without inhaling seems to justify his nickname, "Slick Willie."

There is a third candidate, Ross Perot, a multi-billionaire Texas businessman. In an appearance on the "Larry King Live" television show, Perot declared that he would run for president if volunteers could get his name on the ballot in all 50 states. Minutes later, phone lines were jammed as thousands called to volunteer their help.

Perot's message resonates with you and other Americans fed up with government as usual. He promises quick fixes to America's problems, fixes that could be devised by smart people sitting around a table. Running as a sort of national "Roto-Rooter candidate,"[1] Perot drills home the idea that Americans must come to grips with the reality of the budget deficit and the sinking economy. He argues that he can fix these problems along with the entire laborious political process. He claims he will "have the House and Senate dancing like Ginger Rogers and Fred Astaire." Appealing to a public fed up with politicians and stalemate, Perot's ratings soared. His informal down-to-

CONTINUED 

OUTLINE

American Diversity
- Ethnic and Economic Diversity
- Diversity and the Public Interest

Characteristics of Democracy
- Value of the Individual
- Political Equality
- Majority Rule
- Minority Rights
- Direct and Indirect Democracy

Classical Democracy

Contemporary Theories of American Democracy
- Pluralism
- Elitism
- Current Views

Conclusion: Is Government Responsive?

earth style on talk shows is a striking contrast to the other candidates and their handlers.

One of Perot's favorite lines is "It's that simple." But you wonder if it *is* that simple. Many of Perot's positions are undefined. Most are one-liners. The media, reflecting as well as stimulating public concern, are looking for more information about Perot to determine how he would fix national problems. And, after some digging, the media found some information that was not flattering. For example, Perot has a penchant for hiring investigators to look into the backgrounds and lifestyles of his employees. At times in his career, he simply quit whatever he was doing when the going got rough. He left the Navy early because he did not get along with his commander and left the board of directors of General Motors when it did not support his view of what GM policies should be.

Moreover, Perot's behavior seems unpredictable. He hired Hamilton Jordan, Jimmy Carter's White House chief of staff, and Ed Rollins, Ronald Reagan's 1984 presidential campaign manager, to run his campaign. But Perot then seemed unhappy about "selling out" to professional politicians. Jordan and Rollins urged him to have a full-fledged campaign with extensive advertising in the media, many public appearances, and position papers. However, growing uncertain about whether he wanted to spend the millions it would take to do all this and becoming fed up with what he thought were personal attacks against him, he soon fired Jordan and Rollins. Later, he withdrew from the race on the day of Bill Clinton's acceptance speech at the Democratic Convention. But he even hedged doing this. After weeks of hesitating, he said he would take a poll to see if he should reenter the race. After polling his own volunteers, he reentered the race on October 1, 1992.

Ross Perot is caught in a flood of media attention.

These moves make you wonder if Perot has the temperament to be president. He is used to being the boss in his businesses. In fact, bumper stickers proclaim "Ross for Boss." He tells his employees what to do and can fire them if they do not obey or if they do not move fast enough to please him. But politicians in our government of shared powers and checks and balances cannot order each other around. They have to persuade each other to work together. The president has to persuade members of Congress to pass the laws and the budgets he wants. Then he has to persuade bureaucratic agencies to implement the laws the way he wants them implemented. We get impatient when politicians take what seems like an infinite amount of time to do something. But in a diverse society, there are always competing interests that want politicians to do contradictory things.

You do not know whether Perot has the temperament to persuade rather than order. During the campaign, he showed a short temper dealing with the press, snapping at reporters who asked reasonable questions. Perhaps more significantly, Perot did not have the ability, or willingness, to persuade others when he served on GM's board. Although economists concede that he knew what he was talking about regarding GM's problems, he could not bring about changes in GM because he did not forge alliances with other board members or key executives. He quit after his complaints got nowhere. Would he behave this way as president?

Perot says he knows what we need. A vote for him may be a vote to give politics a backseat. But can he really get government to work? Is his lack of political experience going to benefit the nation? Can we really take politics out of governing, and would we be better off if we did?

How do you vote?

Inconsistencies dominate American politics. Americans cherish the symbols of democracy, but deplore its realities.[2] We visit Washington to marvel at the Washington Monument, the Jefferson and Lincoln Memorials, the Capitol, and the White House. We show these symbols of our democracy to our children, hoping they will revere them. We cherish the Declaration of Independence and the Constitution.

But at the same time that we prize these symbols of democracy, we condemn the reality of democracy. We define debates over issues as quarrels or "bickering"; we call compromises "selling out"; we label conflict as mere self-interest; we tag interest groups and political parties as "special interests." We have no tolerance for the slow pace of government's dealing with the nation's problems. In other words, we love the concept of democracy, but hate the rough and tumble, the give and take, and the conflict that is democracy in action.[3]

America has a split political personality in other ways too. Most people have a low opinion of Congress, yet we reelect most of its members. We love the idea that the average person has a say in government, yet half of us do not vote, even in presidential elections. We criticize big government while complaining that it does not do very much.

Why do we act as if we dislike democracy in action? Has government failed? Are the laws it enacts not what the people want? Is it the fault of the media, emphasizing mostly the negative side of government? Are average citizens actually shut out of the process? Or is the problem really the fault of citizens, and not government at all?

We can begin to answer these questions by exploring the reasons why American government is characterized by conflict and compromise. One major reason is, of course, that Americans do not agree on either the nature of the problems that confront us, or their solutions. If we all agreed, there would be no need for debate, bargaining, compromise, or delays. The other major reason is that we have chosen a representative democracy as our form of government. Most Americans, even those highly dissatisfied with the way government actually works, do not want a king, a dictator, or an emperor to make decisions for us.

In this chapter we will look at some of the differences among Americans, and we will examine democracy as a form of government. In later chapters we will explore some specifics about our political processes and institutions that have led Americans to distrust and dislike the workings of our political system.

American Diversity

"Here is not merely a nation but a teeming Nation of nations."[4] Poet Walt Whitman's statement tells us a lot about our country and its politics. America is a diverse nation, peopled by individuals from all over the world. We are a conglomeration of different religions, races, ethnic groups, cultural traditions, and socioeconomic groups.

Ethnic and Economic Diversity

Diversity exists because all of us are immigrants or descendants of immigrants. Even those we call native Americans crossed a land bridge from Asia about 50,000 years ago. The next major wave of immigration occurred in the early 1600s with people from Britain, Holland, France, and Spain. These first European colonists came for a variety of reasons, some to find a place to practice their religion, others to escape political tyranny, and still others to make their fortunes. British culture and the English language soon became dominant. Although all immigrants have had to adapt to this culture, succeeding generations have helped modify it into a unique, American culture.

The immigration of Africans began in 1619 and continued through the early 1800s. Unlike other immigrant groups, most blacks did not come freely. They were brought in chains as slaves. This fact has had a profound impact on American culture and politics.

A fourth major wave of immigration occurred in the mid-1800s. It included millions of people from

These 1910 immigrants from Bohemia and Bulgaria illustrate the European character of most early twentieth century immigration. Meals served at Ellis Island around this time featured beef stew, boiled potatoes, rye bread with herring for Jews, and crackers and milk for women and children.

Russian emigrants wait at Moscow Airport for their flight to America.

Ireland fleeing the potato famine and Germans escaping political turmoil. Most immigrants since then also came for economic, religious, and political reasons. Starting in the late 1800s and continuing until World War I, another influx included many Chinese and Japanese laborers and millions of Italians, Poles, and Jews.

Beginning in the 1970s, the latest major wave has included Vietnamese, Cambodians, Russian Jews, and Latin Americans. Most are Asians and Mexicans. The entry of 6 million legal and at least 2 million illegal immigrants in the 1980s accounted for over one-third of the nation's growth in that decade. By 1995, immigration rose to an estimated 1,100,000 newcomers annually, over 800,000 of whom enter the country legally.[5] Immigration has fueled the growth of Sunbelt states like California, Texas, and Florida and has ensured that industrial states such as New York and Illinois would not lose population.[6]

The Statue of Liberty welcomes newcomers by proclaiming, "Give me your tired, your poor, your huddled masses yearning to breathe free. . . ." Nevertheless, "old Americans," worried about threats to what they regard as the American "character," do not always share this sentiment. Native Americans resisted the first European immigrants and with good reason. The "Know-Nothings" won popularity in the 1840s by spreading fear of a Catholic takeover. Patriotic fervor during World War I produced hostility toward Americans of German birth or descent. For example, in 1918, Iowa's governor required all groups of two or more people to speak only English, even when using the telephone.[7] From 1924 to 1965, federal law limited immigration from most areas outside western Europe. As indicated in the New Populism box, the debate continues about whether today's immigrants are an asset or a problem for our society.

Although each generation of immigrants has faced resentment from preceding generations, each has contributed to the building of America. Early European immigrants settled the eastern seaboard and pushed west to open the frontier. African immigrants helped build the South's economy with their slave labor. Germans helped develop the Midwest into an agricultural heartland, while Irish, Italian, Polish, and Russian newcomers provided labor for America's industrial revolution and turned many cities into huge metropolises. In 1910, 40% of New York City's population was foreign born, and another 40% had foreign-born parents. In many other major cities, including Chicago, Cleveland, and Boston, at least half of the population was foreign born or had parents who were.[8] Chinese immigrants helped build the transcontinental railroad linking East and West, and Japanese and Hispanics helped California become our top food producer. All immigrant groups have gone on from their initial roles to play a fuller part in American life.

There is evidence that America is a melting pot for millions. Among white ethnic groups, so much intermarriage has occurred that many people cannot identify their ancestry. In the 1990 census, 100 million Americans could name no specific ancestry or reported multiple ancestries.[9] This blending continues. For example, although more than 90% of Italian-Americans age 65 and over have two parents of Italian ancestry, only 18% of Italian-American children under 5 have. Jews, who as recently as 35 years ago were restricted by quotas from enrolling at universities and joining private clubs and were discriminated against in hiring by many universities, banks, and corporations, are now blending into the melting pot partly through intermarriage and partly through the reduction of discrimination. Today, the efficiency of the melting pot means that for many Americans of white, European ancestry, the most common "ethnic experience" is eating ethnic foods.[10]

However, for many others whose skin color or language mark them as different, integration into America's melting pot has been much slower. For example, comprising 12% of the population, blacks were Americans long before the ancestors of most whites. Yet they have experienced the most consistent and severe discrimination.

Hispanics (including several diverse groups of Spanish origin, primarily Mexican-Americans, Cuban-Americans, and Puerto Ricans) comprise about 9% of the population. Like blacks, Hispanics tend to be less educated and have lower incomes than other white Americans. Although they also face discrimination, Hispanics are growing in number and integrating into the larger society faster than blacks.

Asian-Americans, the fastest growing minority, are about 3% of the population. They have achieved considerable economic success despite harsh discrimination in the past and more subtle forms today. For example, although Asian-Americans are represented far beyond their population share at most top universities, many suspect that some universities have set informal admissions quotas to limit their numbers.

Despite the discrimination still faced by many Americans whose ancestry is not European, racial boundaries are beginning to erode. For example, one government study showed that 6 percent of people considering themselves black, one-third who considered themselves Asian, and 70 percent of those who considered themselves American Indian were thought to be white by survey researchers. A study of infant deaths showed that many infants were classified by a different race at death than on their birth certificates. A quarter of those who identified themselves as American Indian to the Census did not claim American Indian ancestry. Interracial marriages and interracial children are becoming increasingly common. More than half the births to an American Indian parent and one-third of the births to an Asian-American parent had one parent of a different race. One-fourth of the children born to a Hispanic parent had a non-Hispanic other parent.[11]

Despite the important fact that white America has resisted the assimilation of blacks much more than of Asians or Hispanics, even these racial barriers are beginning to erode slightly. The number of black-white marriages has tripled and the number of births of babies with one black and one white parent has quintupled in the past twenty years.

All of these examples indicate that once seemingly clear notions of "race" as either black or white are

New Populism

Americans are fed up. Majorities think the country is in "deep and serious trouble," believe the American dream will be difficult to achieve for their children, are suspicious of the press, schools, and religious and business leaders, think society is too tolerant of people who misbehave, and are angry at leaders who "say one thing and do another." Reflecting this concern, one journalist noted "a tidal wave of discontent," and an author titled his recent book *Why Americans Hate Politics.*[1]

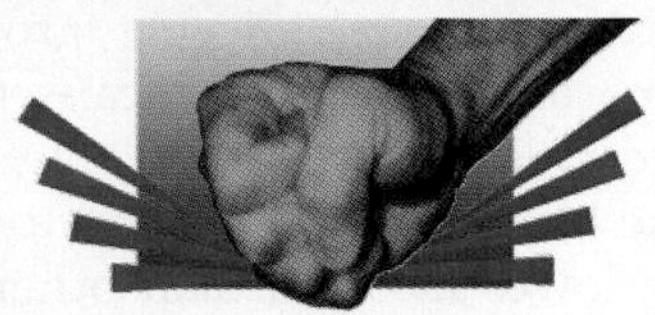

In short, many Americans are frustrated and angry, especially with government, believing the country is going in the wrong direction and our leaders do not see or care. An expanding economy and falling unemployment have not convinced most Americans that the country is on the right path. Frustrated with George Bush, the Republican president, voters threw him out in 1992. Not satisfied with that change, and equally frustrated with a Congress controlled by Democrats, voters threw many of them out in 1994, giving Republicans control of both houses of Congress for the first time since the Eisenhower Administration. Indeed, many Americans are so angry at Congress and the president, they would like to make laws themselves through national referenda.[2]

None of this is new in American history. We have a long tradition of distrust and anger directed at government and other powerful institutions. After all, in 1776, we revolted against the British government because many Americans thought it was remote and unrepresentative of our interests. Andrew Jackson became president in 1828 by running as a frontiersman opposed to the power of the eastern elites.

What we call the *populist movement* began in the late 1800s in the rural Midwest, when many Americans, especially farmers and small business owners, believed the national government to be the pawn of big interests (then called "trusts") such as big business, the railroads, and banks. In the view of the populists, these interests worked against the common people. In general *populism* describes movements that celebrate "the people" in contrast with the greed or immorality of the powerful. Because populism is characterized by resentment toward elites and often by faith in a popular leader,[3] it is different than simply an affirmation of the democratic right of all to participate.

The populist movement of the late 1800s, led by the great orator and Democratic leader William Jennings Bryan, combined religious conservatism with economic radicalism. Although Bryan was narrowly defeated for president all three times he ran (in 1896, 1900, and 1908), he made a mark on American history with his mobilization of the common people against the business elites of the time and in favor of moral traditonalism (such as outlawing the sale of liquor and fighting the teaching of evolution in the schools). Populist calls for regulation of big business presaged some of the regulations passed in this century and their concerns with moral issues are reflected in our current debates over prayer in the schools, abortion, and other such issues.

CONTINUED 

becoming confused as we become an increasingly multiracial society. In the 1990 Census, 75 multiracial categories were named, along with 600 American Indian tribes and 70 categories of Hispanics. One survey showed that one-third of African Americans believe that blacks are not a single race, and almost half of both black and white respondents believed that government should not collect information on race at all.[12]

Ethnic and racial diversity is not the only cleavage in society, though it has been the most controversial one in the past decade. (and many times before in American history). Religious differences certainly exist, and sometimes spill over into politics. For example, many Catholics and fundamentalist Protestants are against abortion, while many mainline Protestants are pro-choice.

Economic diversity also divides our nation. Though we think of ourselves as a land of opportunity, most people who are born poor stay poor. Opportunities knock harder and more often for those who are born into the upper and middle classes. And, although our society is not as class conscious as many others, our personal economic situations play an important part in shaping our views toward politics and our role in it. In 1992, for example, most poor Americans did not vote and most who did voted for Bill Clinton. Most well-off Americans did vote, and voted for George Bush.

Regional and residential differences can also be important, especially when they are intertwined with economic interests. Midwestern farmers, who produce the food we eat, have quite different views on farm bills than big-city dwellers who are interested in

Populists also distrusted the institutions of government and representative democracy, such as legislatures and political parties, believing that these were controlled by powerful interests working against the common people. Early in this century, some of these beliefs underpinned successful efforts in many states to allow citizens to make laws themselves through initiatives (proposals put on the ballot by groups of individuals) or referenda (proposals put on the ballot by a vote of the legislature) and to remove officials in recall elections.

In the last decade, the label "populist" has again become fashionable.[4] Most politicians call themselves populists, trying to portray themselves as representatives of the average citizen. One recent author wrote about contemporary populism by using Jesse Jackson (champion of the liberal Democrats) and Pat Robertson (champion of the conservative Christian Republicans) as examples.[5] Ross Perot is often cited as a new populist, and both Bill Clinton and Newt Gingrich are sometimes called populists too. Indeed, even businesses use the populist label: Banana Republic has a line of men's trousers called "Populist pants . . . for the individual in every man."[6]

Today, the moral and religious emphasis of populism is more likely to be found among Republicans, while the economic emphasis is found among Democrats. Thus Republican populists are most likely to emphasize returning to the traditional moral and cultural values of this society, while Democratic populists are more likely to emphasize improving the standard of living for the average person and curbing big business.

Because populism has been an important part of American history and has recently reemerged as a major theme, and because populist ideals underlie discussions over many contemporary issues, throughout the book we will discuss the ideas of New Populism as they pertain to specific problems. As we will see in these boxes, the term *populism* means many things to many people, but underlying each use is a resentment that government and others (such as business or media elites) who hold great power in society are not acting in a way to promote the best interests of "ordinary" people.

1. See E. J. Dionne, Jr., *Why Americans Hate Politics* (New York: Simon and Schuster, 1991).
2. The poll results are from "Opinion Outlook," *National Journal,* February 4, 1995, p. 324; and Kevin Phillips, "The Voters Are Already Tapping Their Feet," *Washington Post National Weekly Edition,* November 21–27, 1994, p. 24.
3. See Allen D. Hertzke, *Echoes of Discontent: Jesse Jackson, Pat Robertson, and the Resurgence of Populism* (Washington, D.C.: CQ Press, 1993).
4. See the following for comprehensive recent studies of the populist tradition: Michael Kazin, *The Populist Persuasion* (New York: Basic Books, 1995) and Christopher Lasch, *The Revolt of the Elites and the Betrayal of Democracy* (New York: W. W. Norton, 1995).
5. Hertzke, *Echoes of Discontent.*
6. David Oshinsky, "The Last Refuge of Everybody," *New York Times Book Review,* February 12, 1995, p. 14.

buying food at a cheap price. Suburban dwellers in affluent communities and residents of decaying urban areas usually have quite different notions of whether the government should help local schools.

Despite a sometimes overwhelming diversity, most Americans share some common goals and values. Indeed, these goals and values are often what attracts new immigrants. We idealize our nation's Founders and the reasons they fought a revolution. Most Americans support our form of government[13] and believe that America is a land of opportunity for those willing to work hard.

Shared values reduce the strains produced by our differences. They also allow us to compete intensely on some issues but cooperate on others. For example, Protestant fundamentalists and Catholic leaders disagree strongly about aid to parochial schools but agree on opposing abortion. Rich and poor differ over the role government should play in reducing unemployment but largely agree about protecting the environment. Jews and blacks sometimes disagree over the use of quotas, but both tend to favor more public spending for social programs. Majorities of American of all ancestries who have been in the United States a generation want to tighten immigration laws but disagree how to do it. Thus, although most Americans share some basic beliefs, our "nation of nations" is cross-cut with cleavages.

Diversity and the Public Interest

Diversity produces different perceptions of the world. As a result, people tend to define society's problems differently and have conflicting views about what government should do about them. This means that, although government officials typically justify their actions in terms of the "public interest," that interest is usually impossible to define to everyone's satisfaction. Thus, whether a policy will further the public interest is almost always a matter for political debate.

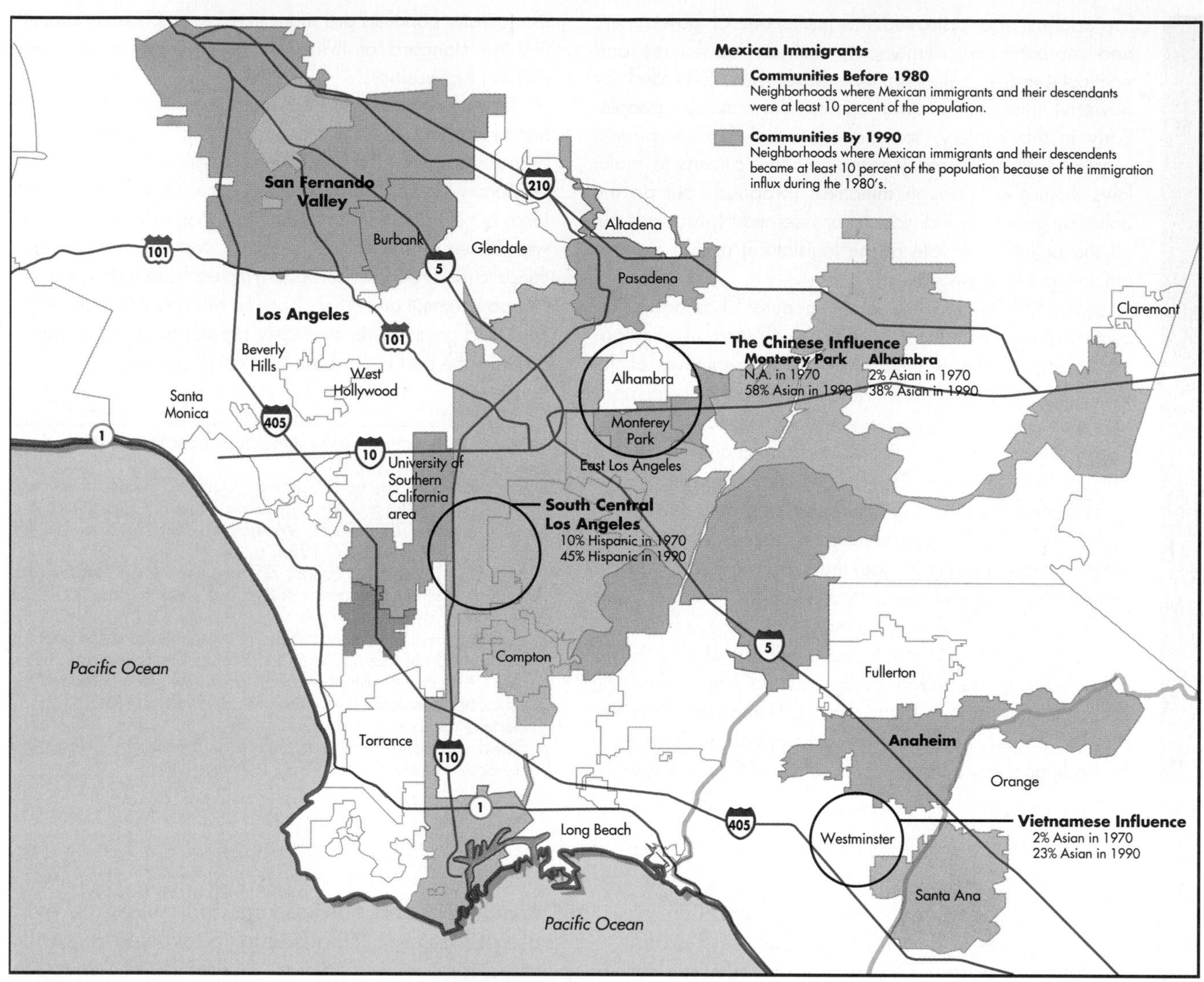

The huge influx of immigrants in the 1980s, especially from Mexico, changed the face of the Los Angeles area.
SOURCE: Based on Gallup Polls via *The New York Times,* Sunday, September 18, 1994, pp. E4–5.

People disagree about what government should do and whether government is responsive because they have different views of their own interests and those of society.

The existence of disagreement leads to **politics,** the competition to shape government's impact on society's problems and goals. Government can coerce us to do things because it is supposed to represent the public interest.[14] Politics, though, entails not only conflict but cooperation. It brings people together when they realize that cooperation is the only way to address problems. For some issues, they discover that their shared values are more important than their differences.

While the conflict in politics gives us reason to be skeptical about individuals' and groups' claims that they seek the public interest, cooperation in politics gives us reason to accept the possibility that the public interest can be achieved. Thus, the Greek philosopher Aristotle wrote 2,000 years ago that politics is the most noble thing in which people can engage, partly because it helps them to know themselves and partly because it forces them to relate to others. Individuals have their own needs, but they have to consider other citizens' needs too.

The conflict and cooperation in politics are channeled through government. We call our form of government a "democracy."

New Populism

Controlling Immigration

Immigration, and the seeming inability of government to control it, is one of the issues about which many Americans are angry. Substantial majorities, believing that immigrants cost taxpayers money because of their use of welfare, public schools, and hospitals, would like to see immigration limited. This anger is particularly strong in states where immigrants are concentrated; about 72 percent of America's immigrants live in California, Florida, Illinois, New Jersey, New York, and Texas. There the pressure on public services is most acute and the resentment against immigrants most pronounced (and conversely, some states are barely touched by immigration; for example, in 1992 when California had over 330,000 new immigrants, Wyoming had 281).[1]

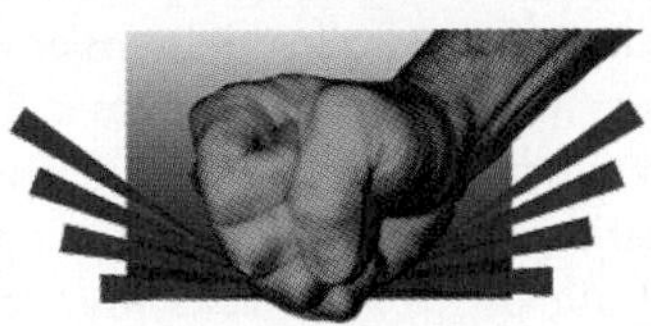

Dislike of immigrants and a variety of other kinds of minorities is part of the populist tradition, though the targets of hostility have varied over time. Around the turn of the century, populists opposed immigration because a large proportion of immigrants were Catholics or Jews coming from southern and eastern Europe, a mix that seemed threatening to the dominant Anglo-Saxon, Protestant group. In the 1930s, Father Charles Coughlin appealed to a mass following by arguing that a Jewish conspiracy ran the government. In 1968 Governor George Wallace (D-Ala.) won a substantial following among white working-class voters in his race for president by running on the race issue (Governor Wallace had stood "in the schoolhouse door" to try to prevent blacks from attending the University of Alabama.)

Today, the dramatic influx of new residents has triggered resentment similar to earlier anti-immigration feelings. In the last twenty years, America has experienced the second largest wave of immigration in its history (the largest since the 1910s and 1920s). Most of today's immigrants are Asians or Latin Americans, and relatively few are from Europe. In 1992, for example, about 15% of the nearly 1,000,000 legal immigrants were from Europe, over one-third from Asia (the largest groups being Vietnamese, Filipino, Chinese, and Indian), nearly 40 percent from Mexico and Central America, and the remainder from the rest of the world.[2] Illegal immigrants presumably come largely from Mexico and Central America.

The size of this immigration flood (over 7 million arrived during the 1980s) triggered a number of negative responses. One that most Americans believe is that immigrants take jobs away from permanent residents. California, Florida, New Jersey, and Texas do have jobless rates well above the national average, which exacerbates concern over the impact of immigrants on unemployment. However, the evidence that immigrants deprive permanent residents of jobs is not clear. Immigrants, particularly illegal ones, do take some low-paying, unskilled jobs, especially in restaurants, food processing plants, and other traditional low-wage industries. They also take very low paying seasonal farm work jobs, which most other Americans do not want. Most legal immigrants, many of whom are well educated and skilled, do not deprive other residents of jobs. In fact, they increase total employment and generate more economic activity and benefits.[3]

In states with large immigrant populations, people are concerned that immigrants do not pay taxes but use a disproportionate share of public services. Of course, everyone pays sales taxes. However, many illegals do not pay income tax or contribute to Social Security through payroll deductions. They are often hired on a cash basis and avoid these taxes (as do some citizens and legal aliens). Newcomers increase demand for state and local public services, particularly health care and education. In New York City, for example, some schools are so crowded, largely because of immigration, that one out of 11 students lacks a desk or a chair, and some classes are held in hallways, on staircases, and even in closets. Such conditions force the schools to seek more tax revenues from an already unhappy public.[4] Although federal funds help to pay for many of these services, this assistance is shrinking as the federal government cuts funding to the states.

Part of the concern about immigration reflects noneconomic issues. Some native-born Americans fear non-English languages, different cultural traditions and religious practices, and nonwhite skin colors. In 1991, Republican presidential candidate Patrick Buchanan complained that immigration is about to "submerge" our "predominantly Caucasian Western society" and warned about a "dilution" of our European heritage.[5] A newspaper criticized immigrants who "bring with them their non-Christian Third World cultures, poverty-mindedness and a tendency toward crime."[6]

This does not mean that everyone who opposes immigration is racist. Some people just do not like change, or are afraid of so much change at a time when our economy is performing sluggishly and when the country faces so many problems related to poverty and crime.

What does the public want done about immigration? Most (about 60%) would like to see tighter controls on legal

CONTINUED 

immigration and more effort to curb illegal immigration. Federal legislation in 1986 and 1990 did try to make it more difficult to enter the country illegally by imposing significant penalties for employers who hire illegal workers. However, our long, thinly patrolled borders make it extremely difficult to keep people out. Employer penalties have proven less than completely effective because illegals can buy forged Social Security cards and other papers, and because some employers are willing to risk penalties in order to hire cheap labor (obviously, illegal workers cannot complain to the government about less than minimum wages or safety standards). Though the public wants greater controls over illegals, and 65% say they are willing to spend federal tax money to patrol the Mexican border more thoroughly, only half favor a national identity card, which could help control illegal immigration.[7]

Citizens in some states are taking action on their own. For example, in 1994 60% of the voters in California (which has about 40% of the nation's illegal immigrants) voted for Proposition 187, the "Save Our State" initiative. Challenged in the courts as unconstitutional, it seeks to deny most state and local services, including public education and nonemergency health care, to illegal immigrants and their children.[8] Citizens are making efforts to put similar propositions on the ballots in other states, and a number of states have filed lawsuits arguing that Washington is responsible for higher state and local spending necessitated by the failure of its immigration policies. A number of proposals in Congress call for eliminating or reducing welfare and other services for illegal, and sometimes even legal, immigrants. Even liberals such as Senator Ted Kennedy of Massachusetts and former member of Congress Barbara Jordan have argued for more aggressive efforts to control immigration.

Populism has always been a "people's movement" with a focus on resentment of political, social, or economic elites. But historically populism has always included a resentment and dislike of those of "the people" who were different and weaker, including immigrants, Catholics and Jews, blacks and Asians. Today, one focus of this resentment is immigrants. Yet, in the case of immigration, it is easier to resent and dislike than it is to make dramatic changes in the status quo. In fact, despite the rhetoric so prevalent in discussions of immigration, Americans have very mixed feelings about what to do about it. Almost all Americans want to reduce illegal immigration, and a solid majority wants to reduce legal immigration too. But only about half believe we should stop providing government health and education benefits to immigrants (even legal ones) and their children. About half also believe we should deny American citizenship to children born here to immigrants who have not become U.S. citizens themselves.

Despite the anger over immigration, it appears likely that anti-immigrant legislation is more likely to pass in states where the most immigrants live. National opinion patterns are divided, suggesting that stringent new legislation might be difficult to pass nationally. On the other hand, there seems clear support for limiting immigration, even if there are no clear views on how to treat new residents once they are here.

Source: Drawing by D. Reilly; © 1994 The New Yorker Magazine, Inc.

"Yet, even as we give thanks for the blessings we've secured for ourselves and our program, we must be mindful of the danger of everybody and his brother lining up to grab the next ship over."

---

1. *Statistical Abstract of the United States, 1994.* Table 10.
2. *Statistical Abstract of the United States, 1994.* Table 8.
3. "Illegal Aliens Depress Wages for Some in US," *New York Times,* March 20, 1988, p. 16; Thomas Muller and Thomas Espenshade, *The Fourth Wave: California's Newest Immigrants* (Washington, D.C.: Urban Institute Press, 1985), pp. 101–22; Philip Martin, "Labor Intensive Agriculture," *Scientific American 249* (October 1983), p. 57; Leon Bouvier and Robert Gardner, "Immigration to the U.S.: The Unfinished Story," *Population Bulletin 41* (November 1986): pp. 28–31; Peter Passell, "So Much for Assumptions about Immigration and Jobs," *New York Times,* April 15, 1990, p. 4E; K. F. McCarthy and R. B. Valdez. *Current and Future Effects of Mexican Immigration in California* (Santa Monica, Calif.: The Rand Corporation, 1986).
4. "Students Without Desks," *New York Times,* February 6, 1995, p. E16.
5. George F. Will, "Buchanan Takes Aim," *Washington Post National Weekly Edition,* December 16–22, 1991, p. 28.
6. This quote from the *Christian American* is reported in Dick Kirschten, "Building Blocs," *National Journal,* September 26, 1992, p. 2173.
7. Information in this paragraph is from Dick Kirschten, "Immigration: Second Thoughts," *National Journal,* January 21, 1995, pp. 150–151.
8. Survey data are reported in Bruce Nelan, "Not Quite So Welcome Anymore," *Time* (Special Issue on the New Face of America; Fall, 1993), pp. 10–13.

➤ Characteristics of Democracy

Democracy was invented by ancient Greek city-states (the term *democracy,* meaning authority of the people, is a Greek term). The principles that shape our democracy are also rooted in the Judeo-Christian tradition and in British history.

Value of the Individual

Democracy emphasizes the value of the individual.[15] This principle has roots in the Judeo-Christian belief that every individual is equal and has worth before God. It also shaped the works of the British philosophers Thomas Hobbes and John Locke. Briefly, they wrote that individuals give some of their rights to government so it can protect them from each other. Individuals then use their remaining liberties to pursue their individually defined visions of the good life. These ideas are part of social contract theory, which we discuss in Chapter 2.

Influenced by these ideas, early Americans emphasized liberty over other goals of government. This is reflected in the Declaration of Independence and the Constitution and Bill of Rights. James Madison, for example, justified the Constitution by writing that government's job is to protect the "diversity" of interests and abilities that exists among individuals. Liberty is also reflected in our long tradition of rights, deriving from Britain's. Usually these are rights against the government—for example, government shall not deny freedom of assembly, and government shall not engage in unreasonable searches and seizures. Essentially, this means the overall right to be left alone by the government. Such individualistic values have molded popular expectations. Immigrants often came and still come to America to be their own bosses: to farm their own farms, manufacture or sell their own products, and worship their own way. Although the opportunities for many individuals to get ahead in America are limited by prejudice and poverty, living in a society with an explicit commitment to individual worth can be exciting and liberating.

Political Equality

Although the Judeo-Christian belief that all people are equal in the eyes of God reflects one type of equality, it led logically to other types, such as political equality. The ancient Greek emphasis on the opportunity and responsibility of all citizens to participate in ruling their city-states also contributed to our notion of political equality. Thus, the Declaration of Independence proclaimed that "all men are created equal." This did not mean that all people are born with equal virtues or abilities. It meant that all (at the time excluding male slaves and all women) are born with equal standing before government and entitled to equal rights.

Inevitably, some people use their virtues or abilities to amass more wealth and power than others and

"We can't come to an agreement about how to fix your car, Mr. Simons. Sometimes that's the way things happen in a democracy."

Source: Drawing by Handelsman; © 1987 The New Yorker Magazine, Inc.

have more influence over government. The ancient Greeks feared that democracy could not tolerate extremes of wealth and poverty. They thought a wealthy minority, out of smugness, and an impoverished minority, out of desperation, would try to act independently of the rest of the people and consequently disregard the public interest. Early Americans worried less about this. They thought they could create a government that would protect individual diversity and still survive (as we will discuss more fully in Chapter 2).

Americans have always considered themselves relatively equal politically and socially if not economically. Alexis de Tocqueville, a perceptive Frenchman who traveled through the Untied States in the 1830s, observed that Americans felt more equal than Europeans did. De Tocqueville attributed this feeling to the absence of a hereditary monarchy and aristocracy in this country. There was no tradition in America of looking up to kings and queens and aristocrats as one's "betters."

A belief in political equality leads to **popular sovereignty,** or rule by the people. Abraham Lincoln expressed this concept when he spoke of "government of the people, by the people and for the people." If individuals are equal, no one person or small group has the right to rule others. Instead, the people collectively rule themselves. Of course, not all the people can be a president, a member of Congress, or a judge. But these officials are not the rulers; they are the representatives of the people, who together have authority as the rulers.

Majority Rule

Commitments to the principles of individual worth and political equality lead to majority rule. That is, when there are disagreements over policies, majorities rather than minorities decide. If individuals are equal, then policies should be determined according to the desires of the greater number. Otherwise, some individuals would be bestowed with more authority than others.

Majority rule helps provide the support necessary to control the governed. Those in the minority go along because they accept this principle and expect to be in the majority on other issues. At a minimum, the minority expects those in the majority to respect their basic rights. If these expectations are not fulfilled, the minority is less likely to accept majority rule and tolerate majority decisions. Thus, majority rule necessarily entails minority rights.

Minority Rights

While majority rule is important, it sometimes conflicts with minority rights. Majorities make decisions *for* "the people" but in doing so do not *become* "the people." "The people" includes members of the majority *and* members of the minority. As a result, majorities that harm minority rights diminish everyone's rights. Sadly, as James Madison and other writers of the Constitution feared, majorities in the United States have sometimes forgotten this and denied minorities their rights. For example, the government put Americans of Japanese descent into special camps during World War II. At other times, blacks were slaves; religious minorities could not practice their beliefs; those with unpopular opinions lost basic rights; and women could not vote.

Thus, democratic principles sometimes contradict each other. These principles are goals more than depictions of reality. Americans have struggled for two centuries to reconcile practice with democratic aims and to perfect a system of government that was revolutionary for its time and remains the envy of many around the world.

Direct and Indirect Democracy

Our description of democracy must include one additional refinement. Democracies may be either direct or indirect. A **direct democracy** permits citizens to vote on most issues. The best example of a direct democracy is the town meeting, which has been the traditional government of many New England towns for over 350 years. Although town meetings today are often attended by relatively small numbers of citizens, they still offer one of the few opportunities people have to rule themselves directly. Citizens attending them make their own laws (e.g., whether to put parking meters on the main street) and elect officers to enforce them (such as the police chief and city clerk).

Our national government is an **indirect democracy,** or a **republic.** Citizens have an indirect impact on government because they select policymakers to make decisions for them. Thus, members of Congress, not rank-and-file citizens, vote bills into law.

Classical Democracy

Democratic principles come alive when individuals participate in government. The ancient Greek philosopher Aristotle concluded that there were three types of government in the city-states of his day: democracies, societies ruled by the many; monarchies, societies ruled by one person—kings, queens, or emperors; and aristocracies, societies ruled by a few elites. Aristotle's definition of democracy emphasized the importance of citizen participation in government through debating, voting, and holding office. We call this vision **classical democracy.**

In a classical democracy, citizens are committed to learning about and participating in government. They are well informed, discuss public affairs regularly, tell public officials what they think, and vote. Some political theorists think that, compared to individuals who do not take their roles as democratic citizens seriously, those who do are more likely to see the complexities in issues and, while disagreeing with each other, still share common goals and work together to accomplish them.[16]

Political scientists initially accepted the classical democratic view as a fairly accurate picture of American politics. However, by the 1940s and using information from surveys and voter turnout records, they discovered that many fewer citizens take advantage of their democratic rights than classical democratic theory predicts. For example, voting is a routine political activity. It is the easiest way to participate in politics and the least costly in terms of time and energy. Yet only one-half of Americans vote in presidential elections and only one-third have voted in recent congressional elections. Even fewer vote in purely local elections. Instead of being motivated to participate in politics as in a classical democracy, most citizens are little involved. In fact, one-fifth of the electorate does nothing at all political, not even discussing politics.[17]

Only about one-tenth of the population takes full advantage of opportunities to participate. These activists, the "gladiators" of politics, give money to candidates, make phone calls, distribute leaflets, write letters to legislators, attend meetings or join neighbors to work for a common end (such as neighborhood preservation).

Why does the reality of political participation fall short of classical democratic expectations? One recent analysis argues that many Americans do not participate because they are turned off by, among other things, long political campaigns in which sound bites and negative campaigning replace meaningful dialogue about issues.[18] Another and more enduring explanation is that political participation is class-based: People who participate tend to have more money and education. The American working class and lower class, unlike their counterparts in many European countries, lack strong trade unions and political parties to represent them. American trade unions involve mostly the middle and better-off classes. American political parties appeal more to middle-class than working-class interests too. Thus, the poor do not have strong organizations to promote their political participation.

The poor also tend to belong to fewer organizations of any kind (civic groups, labor unions, or issue-oriented groups) than the middle or upper classes. As a result, they have fewer opportunities to be drawn into political action through such associations.

In addition, political participation requires both time and money. Many poor adults are single heads of families with little spare time for political activity or resources for transportation and babysitters.

Race and ethnicity explain political participation too, but not as well. Blacks and Hispanics participate less than others, but this is due primarily to their average lower education and income levels. At each education and income level, blacks and Hispanics participate at about the same rates.

Age also explains participation in politics. Young people participate much less than their elders. The middle-aged—the highest participators—are more apt to be established in a career and family life and have more time and money to devote to political activities. They are also less apt to be infirm than older people.

Thus, American government is not a classical democracy. Only a small minority of citizens fully participates in politics. Majorities cannot rule when most people do not take advantage of their rights by voting or trying to influence government or each other.[19] Furthermore, those who do participate are not representative of the whole population in class and other social characteristics. This can have an important impact on the kind of public policy we have. Elected officials chosen by people with more money and education are unlikely to have the same perspectives as those chosen by people with less money and education.

➤Contemporary Theories of American Democracy

Revelations of low levels of participation prompted political scientists to find other ways to explain the workings of American democracy.

Pluralism

In the 1950s, many political scientists thought they knew how American democracy operated. In a theory called **pluralism,** they sought to reconcile democratic principles with the evidence that most people do not participate actively in politics.

Pluralists maintain that government is responsive to groups of citizens working together to promote their common interests.[20] Individuals join others with like beliefs to influence government.

The pluralist view maintains that enough people belong to enough interest groups that government ultimately hears everyone. This produces, according to pluralist theory, a kind of balance in which no group loses so often that it stops competing. As a result, no group or small number of groups can dominate government. This encourages people to continue to "play the game" by finding ways to compromise with each other. It also leads government to avoid major policy changes to maintain the balance and the popular support that comes with it.

Pluralist theory is attractive because it says democracy can "work" without everyone participating in politics. Actual participation is by group leaders and paid staff who represent rank-and-file members to government. There is some validity to this theory. Thousands of interest groups in Washington employ experts to represent them in congressional corridors, bureaucratic agencies, and courtrooms.

As Chapter 5 shows, however, many people and issues fall through the cracks of interest group representation. The poor are especially unlikely to be organized and to have many resources to fight political battles. Groups do not represent them well or at all. In addition, intense competitions between well-organized groups on some issues—such as abortion—do not always make compromise possible.

Groups may not always even represent the interests of their members. In 1915, Robert Michels formulated the "iron law of oligarchy."[21] This "law" says that effective power in a group, no matter what its size, usually goes to a few, an oligarchy or an elite. In fact, groups create elites by electing officers and hiring staffs. As they spend more time on group affairs and develop ties to public officials, group leaders may come to see group interests differently than do many members.

Elitism

Problems with pluralist theory, especially its failure to acknowledge the limited power of citizens with average or below-average incomes, led some political scientists to search for another explanation of how American democracy works. A second school of thought gained considerable support in the 1960s. This theory, called **elitism,** stated that American democracy was much less democratic than pluralists believed.

Elite theory maintains that the holders of a few top jobs in key parts of the society rule. They are the leaders of major corporations (such as IBM, Exxon, General Motors, and AT&T), major universities (such as Harvard, Chicago, and Stanford), major foundations (Ford, Rockefeller, and Johnson) and major media outlets (the *New York Times, Washington Post,* CBS, NBC, and ABC). Elite jobs are also found in important parts of government, such as the Defense Department.

One political scientist identified 7,314 key jobs in major organizations such as these.[22] Some especially important jobs led to memberships on the boards of directors of other organizations. In addition, he found that about 4,300 elite business leaders controlled well over 50% of America's corporate wealth and that almost 40% of them had once held a government post. If this is right, relatively few people share the most powerful jobs and make some of the most important decisions in America.

Shared backgrounds help tie many elite members together. This was a major conclusion of one of the most famous elite theorists, the sociologist C. Wright Mills.[23] He noted that many elite members had gone to the same prep schools and universities and belonged to the same church denominations. Having like backgrounds and heading key organizations, they developed similar views about how government should work.

Elite theory does not limit elite membership to those with elite backgrounds, however. One does not

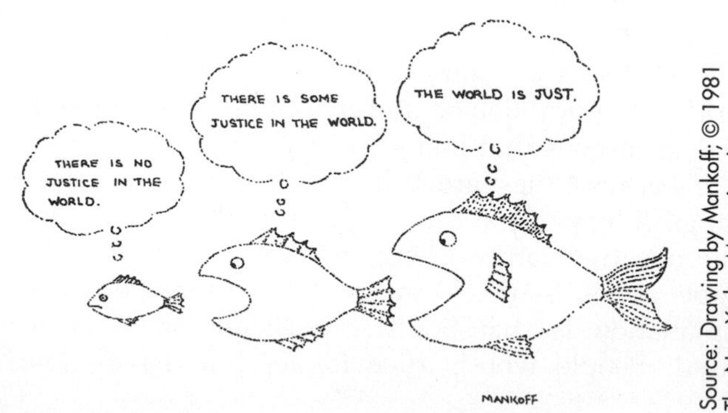

Source: Drawing by Mankoff; © 1981 The New Yorker Magazine, Inc.

have to attend a prep school like Choate, graduate from Princeton, and be an Episcopalian. Anyone committed to elite views who rises to the top of a major organization can belong. Elite theory includes important labor leaders among the chosen few even if their backgrounds do not include silver spoons.

Elite theorists acknowledge that elite members compete with each other. However, they see intra-elite competition as jockeying for more benefits rather than as a major threat to elite cohesion. Thus, some elite members want to cut military spending to lower the budget deficit, which they think hurts the economy; others in defense industries disagree. Although the two sides may not agree on this issue, they agree about most things and deal with their differences in a noncombative way.

Most elite members agree about equating the public interest with protecting the status quo. From an elite perspective, this is not selfish. Like many people, elite members define the nation's well-being in terms of their own. President Eisenhower's defense secretary, Charles Wilson, a former executive at General Motors, replied to charges that his corporate background might bias his public performance by saying, "What is good for the country is good for General Motors, and what's good for General Motors is good for the country."

Elite theory is believable. A 1990 survey reported that 77% of a large sample believed that government is run by "a few big intersts."[24] It is often hard to know what is *really* going on in Washington, and easy to be frustrated when the process yields outcomes we do not like. Elite theory offers a plausible explanation: "They" have met in posh, smoke-filled rooms to cut a deal. Anyone who knows anything about tax law has probably had such thoughts.

It is misleading, however, to think that a few powerful people determine everything. America's diversity produces too many different interests and opinions to permit this. Elite members do not always get what they want. For example, environmentalists have won big victories over major oil and utility companies. In the face of industry opposition, consumer groups and conservationists have gotten government to require automobile safety and fuel efficiency standards. In 1988, voters in California passed an initiative proposal to cut auto insurance rates by 20%. The insurance industry spent $43 million opposing the proposal while supporters spent only $300,000. Nevertheless, elite theory is still useful. It reminds us that tremendous inequalities of resources exist, enabling some parts of society to influence government more than others.

Current Views

Political scientists have had spirited debates about whether pluralism or elitism is the best explanation of American politics. Gradually, most have come to see that neither explains everything. Interest groups do not represent everyone, especially the poor, the working class, and the apathetic. Elites do not decide everything and sometimes lose important battles. Sometimes policy reveals a mix of influences. For example, President Bush's energy program of drilling for more oil, fighting to preserve access to Persian Gulf oil, and promoting nuclear power reflected elite views in the energy business. But it is also likely that most Americans preferred this approach to changing their lifestyles to lower energy consumption and dependence on foreign resources. Thus, both elite and pluralist theory can be used to explain Bush's energy program.

Current perspectives on how government works stress the "veto" many interest groups have in issues affecting them. Some political scientists have labeled this **hyperpluralism,** suggesting a pluralist system run wild. With so many interests, it is difficult to find common ground to work out solutions to problems. The close ties of many interests to congressional committees and subcommittees considering legislation allow them to stop policy ideas they dislike. And modern technology heightens their impact. A witness to congressional hearings on tax reform reported that lobbyists used cellular phones to produce floods of protest by phone or fax the instant anyone "even *thought*" about something they opposed.[25] So many powerful groups have clout that attempts to alter the status quo or change national priorities are extremely difficult. Presidents Carter, Reagan, and Clinton found this out when they tried to produce major changes in energy, budget, and health care policy, respectively. The Clinton White House tried to work with over 1,100 interest groups on health care reform, to no avail.[26] Efforts to bring about major changes in national domestic priorities are extremely difficult.

The difficulties created by interest group vetoes often contribute to gridlock and what one observer calls the "blame game."[27] Gridlock occurs when policies are not enacted or administered effectively because the president and Congress cannot agree on what to do. Politicians representing different interests often blame each other for this inaction, or play the "blame game," when they see that gridlock is likely to keep them from getting what they want. For example, although they agreed privately that cuts were needed, Democrats in Congress accused Republicans of hurting the elderly by supporting Social Security cuts to lower the budget deficit; and congressional Republicans blame President Clinton for budget deficits, though his are smaller than his Republican predecessors. The blame game encourages elected officials to distrust each other and furthers public cynicism about government's responsiveness and effectiveness.

Given the presence of many strong groups and their veto opportunities, passing a law means fashioning compromises out of competing group views.[28] In addition to being slow, it often leads to vaguely worded laws giving actual policymaking authority to bureaucrats who work less visibly with interest group help. In effect, agencies and interest groups, not Congress, often legislate. Thus, chemical industry lobbyists help write regulations on hazardous waste, and military contractors help the Pentagon write weapons contracts.

The growth of bureaucratic policymaking makes our democracy more indirect than the writers of the Constitution intended. Most citizens cannot monitor and influence the actions of a president, 535 members of Congress organized into over 300 committees and subcommittees, *and* bureaucratic agencies. The leaders of major interest groups can, and this gives them considerable power. The possibility that these leaders may be relatively independent of their rank-and-file memberships makes them even more important.

These views challenge both pluralism and elitism by concluding that government responds to many but not all groups. This suggests a hybrid explanation of American government stressing the clout of more powerful groups, whose leaders may belong to a larger, more diversified elite.

➤Conclusion: Is Government Responsive?

In America, these days, few people seem pleased with their government. Does that mean that government is not responsive to them? This is a difficult question to answer. Let us look, for example, at the health care debate that occupied the political landscape during much of 1994. President Clinton proposed a major reform of the health care system (we will discuss more details of that system in Chapter 16), and the public overwhelmingly appeared to agree that a dramatic overhaul was necessary and important. By the time the debate in Congress was over and interest groups had lobbied both the public and the Congress, public opinion had shifted to a very divided and not very enthusiastic stance toward health care reform. Congress killed Clinton's bill. Is this an example of elite power or pluralist democracy? Is this an example of a responsive government or an unresponsive one? Clearly the lack of public support for the health care bill by the end of the debate was reflected in congressional action, and in that sense government was responsive. On the other hand, special interests with a financial stake in the existing system were responsible for the change in public opinion, and that suggests an elitist interpretation of events and a government not very responsive to the "real" desires of the public. Whichever interpretation we choose, however, it is clear that the entire process contributed to public frustration with government. The president and Congress attacked an important issue with great fanfare, spent months debating the issue, and ended up doing nothing. The fact that the lack of passage of a bill was congruent with public opinion is lost in the larger focus on government as ineffective.

Democracy assumes that majorities control government. Indirect democracy assumes that people control their representatives. Most people, of course, do not try to control government directly or the organizations and leaders who say they represent them. Nonetheless, in contemporary American government, the number of organized interests and their effectiveness in making their views known have both multiplied, so that government officials are besieged by a cacophony of views. And this has happened in an era when the workings of government are increasingly in public view. The result has been a feeling by most people that government is out of their control and unrepresentative of their interests.

We have argued that much of this is a necessary component of a democratic system in a large and diverse nation. Nonetheless, to say we must live with debate, compromise, and slowness in our system does not mean we cannot improve and speed the workings of government. In the next eleven chapters, we will examine carefully the major institutions and processes of our democracy to see if we can shed light on how they contribute to public dissatisfaction and how they might be improved.

EPILOGUE

Politics, Representation, and Democratic Government

Like 44% of the other young voters who went to the polls, you decided to vote for Bill Clinton. Ross Perot received 19% of the total popular vote, higher than any third-party candidate in this century except Teddy Roosevelt in 1912. Perot did especially well among independents, garnering about 30% of their vote. His vote among younger voters was about 23%, only slightly higher than among the public as a whole.

The lack of fit between the personal characteristics needed to be a successful business leader and those needed to be a successful politician illustrates why Perot was attractive to millions of disillusioned Americans. This lack of fit also illustrates why he was not an especially good presidential candidate. Millions of Americans were looking for a decisive, independent leader to break the policy deadlock in Washington. Perot was decisive in business and had, at many points, moved quickly to end commitments that were not working to his advantage. But one needs patience to be successful in politics. As a business owner, a person may be able to achieve quick results by telling employees what to do and accepting their resignations if they do not want to do it. In politics, one can be successful only to the extent that one can negotiate. There are many competing interests at stake in most political decisions. Majority coalitions built by persuasion, patience, and correct perceptions of other interests are the keys to political success.

Building coalitions by reconciling diverse interests is what politics is. At its worst, the political process can lead to gridlock when no leader, party, or other force is able to bring diverse interests together. At its best, this process can bring people and interests together and produce decisions that benefit most if not all. Politics occurs because people almost always disagree. In democratic systems, a variety of institutions have evolved over the centuries that seek to ensure the representation of different interests in society when political decisions are made. Political parties, interest groups, and elections are examples of such institutions. Their often cumbersome nature reflects the difficulty of reconciling diverse interests in a complex society and the structures of our own government, designed to make sure most interests are heard.

Like many other frustrated citizens, Perot expressed disdain for much of the political process, including parties and interest groups. Like most Americans, he finds the democratic process, with its compromises and delays, messy and unpalatable. Perhaps not surprisingly, the party he created to sustain his candidacy, United We Stand America, has been plagued by internal dissension and has lost much of its strength. Some former state and local party officers charge that Perot, in the words of one, wants a party of "automatons who are out there as window dressing."[29] By 1995, Perot's popularity had fallen so low that no one in a national survey volunteered his name as someone to support for president in 1996.[30]

Nevertheless, the conditions that fueled Perot's candidacy in 1992 have not changed. Most Americans still think that government does not work very well. In addition, for all their anger with government over the years, many Americans are not well informed about it, nor do most participate in it. This includes college-age voters. A recent survey found that only 16% of those entering college in 1994 said they "discuss politics" often; only 32% called "keeping up with political affairs" important.[31] That many Americans are not well informed about government helps to explain the public's attraction to quick fixes and seemingly easy solutions. Thus, many Americans continue to demand tax cuts, but oppose spending cuts that affect them (half of our households receive some sort of federal financial payment).[32] They want democracy but no arguments or compromises.

So the political ground remains fertile for candidates who use the rhetoric that made Perot a national

POOR SUSAN, SHE MARRIED A MEMBER OF A RIGHT-WING PARAMILITARY GROUP.

figure. Quick fixes look good to those who are poorly informed about government and who resent the debating, compromises, and slowness of democracy. But quick fixes and free lunches have much in common. There is no such thing as either. Politics is necessary to govern a democratic society. Ignoring politics and the institutions we have to represent ourselves, such as political parties and interest groups, will not eliminate politics. Rather, it would eliminate the most effective ways yet developed for the public to influence government's decisions.

➤Key Terms

populism
politics
popular sovereignty
direct democracy
indirect democracy
republic
classical democracy
pluralism
elitism
hyperpluralism

➤Further Reading

John E. Chubb and Paul E. Peterson, *Can the Government Govern?* (Washington, D.C.: Brookings Institution, 1989). *A collection of case studies showing how the public interest often suffers when elected officials and bureaucrats avoid hard policy choices by playing the blame game with each other and "special interests."*

Marilyn P. Davis, *Mexican Voices/American Dreams: An Oral History of Mexican Immigration to the United States* (New York: Owl/Holt, 1990). *The author describes the Mexican immigrant experience in the words of the immigrants themselves.*

William Greider, *Who Will Tell the People: The Betrayal of American Democracy* (New York: Simon & Schuster, 1992). *A populist perspective that views Washington politics as a "grand bazaar" where wealthy interest groups exchange favors with public officials who want to maintain their power.*

Alan D. Hertzke, *Echoes of Discontent: Jesse Jackson, Pat Robertson, and the Resurgence of Populism* (Washington, D.C.: CQ Press, 1993), *Hertzke examines two contemporary examples of populism, while providing a good historical context for this important phenomenon in American politics.*

John R. Hibbing and Beth Theiss-Morse, *Congress as Public Enemy: Public Attitudes toward American Political Institutions* (Cambridge: Cambridge University Press, 1995). *The authors argue that the public is fed up with Congress because Congress is where the internal workings of democracy—the debates, appeals to self, partisan, and group interest, compromises, and inefficiencies—are most obvious.*

Harold Lasswell, *Politics: Who Gets What, When, How* (New York: New World Publishing, 1958). *A classic treatment of some very practical political problems.*

Michael Pertschuk, *Giant Killers* (New York: W. W. Norton, 1986). *A public interest lobbyist describes several major congressional battles in the 1980s showing that the side with money and status does not always win.*

Hedrick Smith, *The Power Game: How Washington Works* (New York: Random House, 1988). *A Pulitzer Prize winning journalist's account of the colorful personalities and complex alliances that shape national policymaking. Loaded with good anecdotes.*

➤Notes

1. A label given to Perot by analyst Kevin Phillips. See Howard Fineman, "Running Scared," *Newsweek*, November 2, 1992, p. 47.
2. See John Hibbing and Beth Theiss-Morse, *Congress as Public Enemy: Public Attitudes toward American Political Institutions.* (Cambridge: Cambridge University Press, 1995); Hibbing and Theiss-Morse, "Civics Is Not Enough; Teaching Barbarics in K-12," forthcoming in *PS*; Gabriel A. Almond and Sidney Verba, *The Civic Culture* (Boston: Little, Brown, 1965), p. 64.
3. Hibbing and Morse, *ibid.*
4. Walt Whitman, *Leaves of Grass and Selected Prose*, Lawrence Buell, ed. (New York: Random House, 1981), p. 449.
5. Tom Morganthau, "What Color Is Black?" *Newsweek*, February 13, 1995, p. 65.
6. The data in this paragraph are from Barbara Vobejda, "The Land of the Immigrant and the Home of Diversity." *Washington Post National Weekly Edition*, March 18-24, 1991, p. 34; and Dick Kirschten, "Second Thoughts," *National Journal*, December 21, 1995, p. 151.
7. Robert Reinhold, "Resentment Against New Immigrants," *New York Times*, October 26, 1986, p. 6E.
8. Susan Welch and Timothy Bledsoe, *Urban Reform and Its Consequences* (Chicago: University of Chicago Press, 1988), p. 2.
9. Bureau of the Census, *General Social and Economy Characteristics: U.S. Summary* (Washington, D.C.: U.S. Government Printing Office, 1990), Part 1, Table 12.
10. Richard D. Alba, "The Twilight of Ethnicity Among Americans of European Ancestry: The Case of Italians," in Richard Alba, ed., *Ethnicity and Race in the U.S.A.: Toward the Twenty-First Century* (London: Routledge & Kegan Paul, 1985), pp. 134–58. Discussed in David Brinkerhoff and Lynn White, *Sociology*, 2d ed. (St. Paul, Minn.: West Publishing, 1988), p. 259.
11. Antonio McDaniel, "The Dynamic Racial Composition of the United States," *Daedalus* (Winter 1995), pp. 179–198; Lawrence Wright, "One Drop of Blood," *New Yorker* (July 25, 1994), pp. 46–55.
12. Reported in Morganthau, "What Color Is Black?" p. 64. Data on black-white intermarriage is found in Susan Kalish "Interracial Baby Boomlet in Progress?" *Population Today* 20 (December 1992), pp. 1–2.

13. Ronald Inglehart, "The Renaissance of Political Culture," *American Political Science Review 82* (December 1988); p. 1213.

14. H. H. Gerth and C. Wright Mills, trans. and eds., *From Max Weber: Essays in Sociology* (New York: Oxford University Press, 1958), p. 78.

15. Louis Hartz, *The Liberal Tradition in America* (New York: Harcourt, Brace, 1955).

16. For a discussion of this see Mark Warren, "Democratic Theory and Self-Transformation," *American Political Science Review 86* (March, 1992), pp. 8–23.

17. This discussion draws on Sidney Verba and Norman Nie, *Participation in America* (New York: Harper & Row, 1972); and Stephen Earl Bennett and Linda L. M. Bennett, "Political Participation," in Samuel Long, ed., *Annual Review of Political Science* (Norwood, N.J.: Ablex Publishing Group, 1986).

18. E. J. Dionne, Jr., *Why Americans Hate Politics* (New York: Simon & Schuster, 1991).

19. Robert A. Dahl, *A Preface to Democratic Theory* (Chicago: University of Chicago Press, 1956), p. 142.

20. See Arthur F. Bentley, *The Process of Government* (Chicago: University of Chicago Press, 1908); and David Truman, *The Governmental Process* (New York: A. A. Knopf, 1951).

21. Robert Michels, *Political Parties* (New York: Collier Books, 1915).

22. Thomas R. Dye, *"Who's Running America? The Bush Era* (Englewood Cliffs, N.J.: Prentice-Hall, 1990), p. 12.

23. C. Wright Mills, *The Power Elite* (New York: Oxford University Press, 1956).

24. Cited in Allen D. Hertzke, *Echoes of Discontent: Jesse Jackson, Pat Robertson, and the Resurgence of Populism.* (Washington, DC: CQ Press, 1993) p. 235.

25. Reported in Robert Wright, "Hyper Democracy," *Time,* January 23, 1995, p. 18.

26. David S. Broder, "Can We Govern?" *Washington Post National Weekly Edition,* January 31–February 6, 1994, p. 23.

27. Hedrick Smith, *The Power Game: How Washington Works* (New York: Random House, 1988), chapter 17.

28. For example, see Theodore J. Lowi, *The End of Liberalism,* 2d ed. (New York: W. W. Norton, 1979).

29. Dan Balz, "Turf War Among the Grass Roots," *Washington Post National Weekly Edition,* May 2–8, 1994, p. 12.

30. "Opinion Outlook," *National Journal,* January 21, 1995, p. 194.

31. Rene Sanchez, "Don't Know Much About Politics," *Washington Post National Weekly Edition,* January 16–22, 1995, p. 37.

32. Michael Wines, "Taxpayers Are Angry. They're Expensive, Too," *New York Times,* November 20, 1994, p. E5.

2 The Constitution

You Are There

The Case of the Confidential Tapes

In June 1972, a security guard for the Watergate building in Washington, D.C., noticed that tape had been placed across the latch of a door to keep it from locking. The guard peeled off the tape. When he made his rounds later, he noticed that more tape had been placed across the latch. He called the police.

The police encountered five burglars in the headquarters of the Democratic National Committee. Wearing surgical gloves and carrying tear gas guns, photographic equipment, and electronic gear, they had been installing wiretaps on the Democratic party's phones.

No one expected this break-in to lead to the White House. The *Washington Post* assigned two young reporters who usually covered local matters to the story. But the unlikely pair of Bob Woodward, a Yale graduate, and Carl Bernstein, a college dropout, were ambitious, and they uncovered a series of bizarre connections. The burglars had links with President Richard Nixon's Committee to Reelect the President (CREEP).

The administration dismissed the break-in as the work of overzealous underlings. Even the press called it a "caper." Indeed, it was hard to imagine that high officials in the administration could be responsible. In public opinion polls, Nixon enjoyed an enormous lead, almost 20%, over the various Democrats vying for their party's nomination to challenge him in the fall election. Risky tactics seemed unnecessary.

But Woodward and Bernstein discovered that White House staff members had engaged in other criminal and unethical actions to sabotage the Democrats' campaign. They had forged letters accusing some of the Democrats' candidates of homosexual acts. Later they had obtained and publicized psychiatric records, causing the Democrats' vice presidential nominee to resign.

Nixon won reelection handily, but the revelations forced his two top aides to resign and prompted the Senate to establish a special committee to investigate what was being called the **Watergate scandal.** When investigators happened to ask the president's appointment secretary if there was a taping device in the Oval Office, he said, "I was hoping you fellows wouldn't ask me about that." Then he revealed what only a handful of aides had known—that Nixon had secretly tape-recorded conversations in nine locations in the White House, the Executive Office Building across the street, and Camp David in Maryland. Nixon had intended to create a comprehensive record of his presidency to demonstrate his greatness.[1]

The tapes could confirm or refute charges of White House complicity in the break-in and cover-up, but Nixon refused to release them. Special Prosecutor Archibald Cox filed suit to force Nixon to do so, and federal trial court Judge John Sirica ordered him to do so. After the federal appeals court affirmed the trial court's decision, Nixon demanded his attorney general fire Cox. The attorney general and deputy attorney general both refused and resigned in protest. Then the third-ranking official in the Justice Department, Robert Bork, fired the special prosecutor. (Bork later would be nominated to the Supreme Court by President Reagan.)

The public furor over this "Saturday Night Massacre" was so intense that Nixon finally did release some tapes. But one crucial tape contained a mysterious 18-minute gap that a presidential aide speculated was caused by "some sinister force."

CONTINUED 

OUTLINE

The Articles of Confederation
- National Government Problems
- State Government Problems

The Constitution
- The Constitutional Convention
- Features of the Constitution
- Motives of the Founders
- Ratification of the Constitution
- Changing the Constitution

Conclusion: Is the Constitution Responsive?

To mollify critics Nixon appointed a new special prosecutor, Leon Jaworski. After his investigation, Jaworski presented evidence to a grand jury that indicted seven of the president's aides for the cover-up, specifically for obstruction of justice, and even named the president as an "unindicted coconspirator."

The House Judiciary Committee considered impeaching the president, and Jaworski subpoenaed more tapes. Nixon issued edited transcripts of the conversations but not the tapes themselves. As a compromise he proposed that one person listen to the tapes—a senator who was 72 years old and hard of hearing. Frustrated, Jaworski went to court, where Judge Sirica ordered Nixon to release the tapes. When Nixon refused, Jaworski appealed directly to the Supreme Court.

You are Chief Justice Warren Burger, appointed to the Court by President Nixon in 1969 partly because of your calls for more law and order. Three of your brethren also were appointed by Nixon. In the case of *United States v. Nixon,* you are faced with a question that could lead to a grave constitutional showdown with the president. Special Prosecutor Jaworski claims he needs the tapes because they contain evidence pertaining to the upcoming trial of the president's aides indicted for the cover-up. Without all relevant evidence, which possibly could vindicate the aides, the trial court might not convict them.

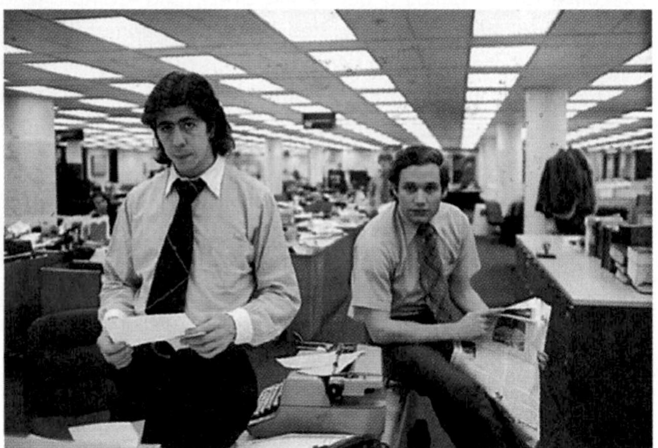
Washington Post reporters Carl Bernstein (left) and Bob Woodward uncovered the Watergate scandal.

President Nixon claims he has **executive privilege**—authority to withhold information from the courts and Congress. Although the Constitution does not mention such a privilege, Nixon claims the privilege is inherent in the powers of the presidency. Without it presidents could not guarantee confidentiality in conversations with other officials or even foreign leaders. This could make it difficult for them to govern.

There are few precedents to guide you. Many past presidents exercised executive privilege when pressed for information by Congress. In these instances, Congress ordinarily acquiesced rather than sue for the information, so the courts did not rule on the existence of the privilege. Once, in 1953, the Eisenhower administration invoked the privilege, and the Supreme Court upheld the claim. However, this case involved national security.[2]

In addition to considering the merits of the opposing sides, you also need to consider the extent of the Court's power. The Court lacks strong means to enforce its rulings. It has to rely on its authority as the highest interpreter of the law in the country. Therefore, if the Court orders Nixon to relinquish the tapes and Nixon refuses, there would be little the Court could do. The refusal would show future officials they could disregard your orders with impunity.

In this high-stakes contest, do you and your brethren on the Court order Nixon to turn over the tapes, or do you accept his claim of executive privilege?

Early settlers came to America for many reasons. Some came to escape religious persecution, others to establish their own religious orthodoxy. Some came to get rich, others to avoid debtors' prison. Some came to enrich their families or companies in the Old World, others to flee the closed society of that world. Some came as free persons, others as indentured servants or slaves. Few came to practice self-government. Yet the desire for self-government was evident from the beginning.[3] The settlers who arrived in Jamestown in 1607 established the first representative assembly in America. The pilgrims who reached Plymouth in 1620 drew up the Mayflower Compact in which they vowed to "solemnly & mutually in the presence of God, and one of another, covenant and combine our selves together into a civill body politick." They pledged to establish laws for "the generall good of the colonie" and in return promised "all due submission and obedience."[4]

During the next century and a half, the colonies adopted constitutions and elected representative assemblies. Of course, the colonies lived under British rule; they had to accept the appointment of royal governors and the presence of British troops. But a vast ocean separated the two continents. At such a distance, Britain could not wield the control it might at closer reach. Consequently, it granted the colonies a measure of autonomy, with which they practiced a degree of self-government.

These early efforts toward self-government led to conflict with the mother government. In 1774 the colonies established the Continental Congress to coordinate their action. Within months the conflict reached flashpoint, and the Congress urged the colonies to form their own governments. In 1776 the Congress adopted the Declaration of Independence.

After six years of war, the Americans accepted the British surrender. At the time it seemed they had met their biggest test. Yet they would find fomenting a revolution easier than fashioning a government and drafting a declaration of independence easier than crafting a constitution.

➤The Articles of Confederation

Even before the war ended, the Continental Congress passed a constitution, and in 1781 the states ratified it. This first constitution, the **Articles of Confederation,** formed a "league of friendship" among the states. As a confederation, it allowed each state to retain its "sovereignty" and "independence." That is, it made the states supreme over the national government.

Under the Articles, however, Americans would face problems with both their national and state governments.

National Government Problems

The Articles established a Congress, with one house in which each state had one vote. But the Articles strictly limited the powers that Congress could exercise, and they provided no executive or judicial branch.

The Articles reflected the colonial experience under the British government. The leaders feared a powerful central government with a powerful executive like a king. They thought such a government would be too strong and too distant to guarantee individual liberty. Additionally, the Articles reflected a lack of national identity among the people. Most did not view themselves as Americans yet. As Edmund Randolph remarked, "I am not really an American, I am a Virginian."[5] Consequently, the leaders established a very decentralized government that left most authority to the states.

The Articles satisfied many people. Most people were small farmers and, although many of them sank into debt during the depression that followed the war, they felt they could influence the state governments to help them. They realized they could not influence a distant central government as readily.

But the Articles frustrated bankers, merchants, manufacturers, and others in the upper classes. They envisioned a great commercial empire rather than the agricultural society the country had. More than local trade, they wanted national and even international trade. For this they needed uniform laws, stable money, sound credit, and enforceable debt collection. They needed a strong central government that could protect them against debtors and against state governments sympathetic to debtors. The Articles provided neither the foreign security nor the domestic climate necessary to nourish these requisites of a commercial empire.

After the war the army disbanded, leaving the country vulnerable to hostile forces surrounding it. Britain maintained outposts with troops in the Northwest Territory (now the Midwest), in violation of the peace treaty, and an army in Canada. Spain, which had occupied Florida and California for a long time and had claimed the Mississippi River Valley as a result of a treaty before the war, posed a threat. Barbary pirates from northern Africa seized American ships and sailors.

Congress could not raise an army, because it could not draft individuals directly, or finance an army, because it could not tax individuals directly. Instead, it had to ask the states for soldiers and money. The states, however, were not always sympathetic to the problems of the distant government. And although Congress could make treaties with foreign countries, the states made, or broke, treaties independently of Congress. Without the ability to establish a credible army or negotiate a binding treaty, the government could not get the British troops out of the country. Neither could it get the British government to ease restrictions on shipping or the Spanish government to permit navigation on the Mississippi River.

In addition to an inability to confront foreign threats, the Articles demonstrated an inability to cope with domestic crises. The country bore a heavy war debt that brought the government close to bankruptcy. Since Congress could not tax individuals directly, it could not shore up the shaky government.

The states competed with each other for commercial advantage. As independent governments, they imposed tariffs on goods from other states. The tariffs slowed the growth of businesses.

In short, the government under the Articles seemed too decentralized to ensure either peace or prosperity. The Articles, one leader concluded, gave Congress the privilege of asking for everything, while reserving to each state the prerogative of granting nothing.[6] A similar situation exists today in the United Nations, which must rely on member countries to furnish troops for its peacekeeping forces and dues for its operating expenses.

State Government Problems

There were other conflicts closer to home. State constitutions adopted during the Revolution made the state legislatures more representative than the colonial legislatures had been. And most state legislatures began to hold elections every year. The result was heightened interest among candidates and turnover among legislators. In the eyes of national leaders, there was much pandering to voters and horsetrading by politicians as various factions vied for control. The process seemed up for grabs. According to the Vermont Council of Censors, laws were "altered—realtered—made better—made worse; and kept in such a fluctuating position that persons in civil commission scarce know what is law."[7] In short, state governments were experiencing more democracy than any other governments in the world at the time. National leaders, stunned by the changes in the few years since the Revolution, considered this development an "excess of democracy."

Moreover, state constitutions made the legislative branch the most powerful. Some state legislatures began to dominate the other branches, and national leaders called them "tyrannical."

The national leaders, most of whom were wealthy and many of whom were creditors, pointed to the laws passed in some states that relieved debtors of some of their obligations. The farmers who were in debt pressed the legislatures for relief that would slow or shrink the payments owed to their creditors. Some legislatures granted such relief.

While these laws worried the leaders, **Shays's Rebellion** in western Massachusetts in 1786 and 1787 scared them. Boston merchants who had loaned Massachusetts money during the war insisted on being repaid in full so they could trade with foreign merchants. The state levied steep taxes that many farmers could not pay during the hard times. The law authorized foreclosure—sale of the farmers' property for the taxes—and jail for the debtors. The law essentially transfered wealth from the farmers to the merchants. The farmers protested the legislature's refusal to grant any relief from the law. Bands of farmers blocked entrances to courthouses where judges were scheduled to hear cases calling for foreclosure and jail. Led by Daniel Shays, some marched to the Springfield arsenal to seize weapons. Although they were defeated by the militia, their sympathizers were victorious in the next election and the legislature did provide some relief from the law.

Both the revolt and the legislature's change in policy frightened the wealthy. To them it raised the specter of "mob rule." Nathaniel Gorham, the president of the Continental Congress and a prominent merchant, wrote Prince Henry of Prussia, announcing "the failure of our free institutions" and asking if the prince would agree to become king of America. (The prince declined.)[8] Just months after the uprising, the Congress approved a convention for "the sole and express purpose of revising the Articles of Confederation."

To a significant extent, then, the debate at the time reflected a conflict between two competing visions of the future American political economy—agricultural or commercial.[9] Most leaders espoused the latter, and the combination of national problems and state problems prompted them to push for a new government.

➤The Constitution

The Constitutional Convention

The Setting

The **Constitutional Convention** convened in Philadelphia, then the country's largest city, in 1787. That year the Industrial Revolution was continuing to sweep Europe and beginning to reach this continent. The first American cotton mill opened in Massachusetts and the first American steamboat plied the Delaware River.[10]

State legislatures chose 74 delegates to the convention; 55 attended. They met at the Pennsylvania State House—now Independence Hall—in the same room where some of them had signed the Declaration of Independence 11 years before.

American Diversity

Founding Mothers

Charles Francis Adams, a grandson of President John Adams and Abigail Adams, declared in 1840, "The heroism of the females of the Revolution has gone from memory with the generation that witnessed it, and nothing, absolutely nothing remains upon the ear of the young of the present day."[1] That statement is still true today; in the volumes written about the revolutionary and Constitution-making eras, much is said of the "founding fathers" and very little about the "founding mothers." Although no women were at the Constitutional Convention, in many other ways women contributed significantly to the political ferment of the time. The political role of women during the Constitution-making era was probably greater than it would be again for a century.

Before the Revolutionary War, women were active in encouraging opposition to the British. Groups of women, some called the "daughters of liberty," led boycotts of British goods as part of the protest campaign against taxation without representation. A few women were political pamphleteers, helping to increase public sentiment for independence. One of those pamphlet writers, Mercy Otis Warren, of Massachusetts, was thought to be the first person to urge the Massachusetts delegates to the Continental Congress to vote for separation from England.[2] Throughout the period before and after the Revolution, Warren shared her political ideas in personal correspondence with leading statesmen of the time, such as John Adams and Thomas Jefferson. Later she wrote a three-volume history of the American Revolution.

Many women were part of the American army during the battles for independence. Most filled traditional women's roles as cooks, sewers, and nurses, but some disguised themselves as men (this was before a military bureaucracy mandated preenlistment physical exams) and fought in battle. One such woman, wounded in action in 1776, is the only Revolutionary War veteran buried at West Point. Still other women fought to defend their homes using hatchets, farm implements, and pots of boiling lye in addition to muskets.

Following independence, some women continued an active political role. Mercy Warren, for example, campaigned against the proposed Constitution because she felt it was not democratic enough.

Independence did not bring any improvement in the political rights of women. In fact, after the Constitution was adopted, some rights that women had held before were gradually lost, such as the right of some women to vote. It was to be another century before the rights of women became a full-fledged part of our national political agenda.

1. Quoted in Linda Grant DePauw and Conover Hunt, *Remember the Ladies* (New York: Viking Press, 1976), p. 9.
2. Alice Felt Tyler, *Freedom's Ferment* (New York: Harper & Row, 1962).

This English political cartoon satirizes a gathering of leading women in North Carolina who drew up a resolution to boycott taxed English goods and tea.

Delegates came from every state except Rhode Island. That state was controlled by farmers and debtors who feared that the convention would weaken states' powers to relieve debtors of their debts.

The delegates were distinguished by their education, experience, and enlightenment. Benjamin Franklin, of Pennsylvania, was the best-known American in the world. He had been a printer, scientist, and diplomat. At 81 he was the oldest delegate. George Washington, of Virginia, was the most respected American in the country. As the commander of the revolutionary army, he was a national hero. He was chosen to preside over the convention. The presence of men like Franklin and Washington gave the convention legitimacy.

The delegates quickly determined that the Articles were hopeless. Rather than revise them, as instructed by Congress, the delegates decided to start over and draft a new constitution.[11] But what would they substitute for the Articles?

The Predicament

The delegates came to the convention because they suffered under a government that was too weak. Yet previously Americans had fought a revolution because they chafed under a government that was too strong. "The nation lived in a nearly constant alternation of fears that it would cease being a nation altogether or become too much of one."[12] People feared both anarchy and tyranny.

This predicament was made clear by the diversity of opinions among the leaders. At one extreme was Patrick Henry, of Virginia, who had been a firebrand of the Revolution. He felt the country would become too strong, perhaps even become a monarchy, in reaction to the current problems with the Articles. Although chosen as a delegate to the convention, he said he "smelt a rat" and did not attend. At the other extreme was Alexander Hamilton, of New York, who had been an aide to General Washington during the war and had seen the government's inability to supply and pay its own troops. Since then he had called for a stronger national government. He wanted one that could veto the laws of the state governments. And he wanted one person to serve as chief executive for life and others to serve as senators for life. He did attend the convention but, finding little agreement with his proposals, participated infrequently.

In between were those like James Madison, of Virginia, who was a nationalist but less extreme than Hamilton. Small and frail, timid and self-conscious as a speaker, he was nonetheless intelligent, savvy, and audacious. He had been instrumental behind the scenes in convening the convention and securing George Washington's attendance. (He publicized that Washington would attend without asking Washington first. Washington, who was in retirement, did not plan to attend but reluctantly agreed to because of the expectation that he would.)[13] Drawing upon his study of governments in history to learn why many had failed, Madison had secretly drafted a plan for a new government that was a total departure from the Articles. Madison's ideas set the agenda for the convention. In the end, his views, more than anyone

This plan of a slave ship shows the overcrowding that led to inhumane conditions, rampant disease, and high mortality.

else's, would prevail, and he would be called the Father of the Constitution.[14]

Consensus

Despite disagreements, the delegates did see eye to eye on the most fundamental issues. They agreed that the government should be a republic—an indirect democracy—in which people could vote for at least some of the officials who would represent them. This was the only form of government they seriously considered. They also agreed that the national government should be supreme over the state governments. At the same time, they thought the government should be limited, with checks to prevent it from exercising too much power.

They agreed that the national government should have three separate branches—legislative, executive, and judicial—to exercise separate powers. They thought both the legislative and executive branches should be strong.

Conflict

Although there was considerable agreement over the fundamental principles and elemental structure of the new government, the delegates quarreled about the specific provisions concerning representation, slavery, and trade.

REPRESENTATION There was sharp conflict between delegates from large states and small states. Large states sought a strong central government that they could control; small states feared a government that would control them.

When the convention began, Edmund Randolph introduced the Virginia Plan drafted by Madison. According to this plan, the central government would be strong. The legislature would have more power than under the Articles, and a national executive and national judiciary also would have considerable power. The legislature would be divided into two houses, with representation based on population in each.

But delegates from the small states calculated that the three largest states—Pennsylvania, Virginia, and Massachusetts—would have a majority of the representatives and could control the legislature. These delegates countered with the New Jersey Plan, introduced by William Paterson. According to this plan, the central government would be relatively strong, although not as strong as under the Virginia Plan. But the primary difference was that the legislature would be one house, with representation by states, which would have one vote each. This was exactly the same as the structure of Congress under the Articles, also designed to prevent the large states from controlling the legislature.

The convention deadlocked. George Washington wrote that he almost despaired of reaching agreement. To ease tensions Benjamin Franklin suggested that the delegates begin each day with a prayer, but they could not agree on this either; Alexander Hamilton insisted they did not need "foreign aid."

Faced with the possibility that the convention would disband without a constitution, the delegates compromised. Delegates from Connecticut and other states proposed a plan in which the legislature would have two houses. In one, representation would be based on population, and members would be elected by voters. In the other, representation would be by states, and members would be selected by state legislatures. Presumably the large states would dominate the former, the small states the latter. The delegates narrowly approved this **Great Compromise,** or Connecticut Compromise. Delegates from the large states still objected, but those from the small states made it clear that such a compromise was necessary for their agreement and, in turn, their states' ratification. The large states, though, did extract a concession that all taxing and spending bills must originate in the house in which representation was based on population. This provision would allow the large states to take the initiative on these important measures.

The compromise was "great" in that it not only resolved this critical issue but paved the way for resolution of other issues.

SLAVERY In addition to conflict between large states and small states over representation, there was conflict between northern states and southern states over slavery, trade, and taxation.

With representation in one house based on population, the delegates had to decide how to apportion the seats. They agreed that Indians would not count as part of the population but differed about slaves. Delegates from the South, where slaves were one-third of the population, wanted slaves to count fully in order to boost their number of representatives. They argued that their use of slaves produced wealth that benefited the entire nation. Delegates from the North, where most states had outlawed slavery or at least the slave trade after the Revolution, did not want slaves to count at all. Gouverneur Morris, of

Pennsylvania, said the southerners' position "... comes to this: that the inhabitant of Georgia and South Carolina who goes to the coast of Africa, and in defiance of the most sacred laws of humanity tears away his fellow creatures from their dearest connections and damns them to the most cruel bondages, shall have more votes in a government instituted for the protection of the rights of mankind than the citizen of Pennsylvania or New Jersey who views with a laudable horror so nefarious a practice."[15] Others pointed out that slaves were not considered persons when it came to rights such as voting. Nevertheless, southerners asserted that they would not support a constitution if slaves were not counted at least partially. In the **Three-fifths Compromise,** the delegates agreed that three-fifths of the slaves would be counted in apportioning the seats.

As a result the votes of southern whites would be worth more than those of northerners in electing members to the House of Representatives and presidents (because the Electoral College would be based on membership in Congress). Between 1788 and 1860, nine of the 15 presidents, including all five who served two terms, were slaveowners.[16]

Although northerners had to accept this compromise in order for southerners to support the Constitution, northerners apparently did not contest two other provisions addressing slavery. Southerners pushed through one provision forbidding Congress to ban the importation of slaves before 1808 and another requiring free states to return any escaped slaves to their owners in slave states. In these provisions southerners won most of what they wanted; even the provision permitting Congress to ban the slave trade in 1808 was hardly a limitation because by then planters would have enough slaves to fulfill their needs by natural population increases rather than importation. In return, northerners, representing most shippers, got authority for Congress to regulate commerce by a simple majority rather than a two-thirds majority. Thus, northerners conceded two provisions reinforcing slavery in order to benefit shippers.[17]

Yet the framers were embarrassed by the hypocrisy of claiming to have been enslaved by the British while allowing enslavement of blacks. The framers' embarrassment is reflected in their language. The three provisions reinforcing slavery never mention "slavery" or "slaves"; one gingerly refers to "free persons" and "other persons."

The unwillingness to tackle the slavery issue more directly has been called the "Greatest Compromise" by one political scientist.[18] But an attempt to abolish slavery would have led the five southern states to refuse to ratify the Constitution.

TRADE AND TAXATION Slavery also underlay a compromise on trade and taxation. With a manufacturing economy, northerners sought protection for their businesses. In particular, they wanted a tax on manufactured goods imported from England. Without a tax, these goods would be cheaper than northern goods; but with a tax, northern goods would be more competitive—and prices for southern consumers more expensive. With an agricultural economy, southerners sought free trade for their plantations. They wanted a guarantee that there would be no tax on agricultural products exported to England. Such a tax would make their products less competitive abroad and, they worried, amount to an indirect tax on slavery—the labor responsible for the products. The delegates compromised by allowing Congress to tax imported goods but not exported ones. Tariffs on imported goods would become a point of controversy between the North and South in the years leading up to the Civil War.

With all issues resolved, a committee was appointed to write the final draft. Gouverneur Morris was the member of the committee most responsible for the polished style of the document. He was also largely responsible for the stirring preamble. In earlier drafts the preamble had not referred to "the people" but had listed the states. Morris's change signaled a shift in emphasis from the states to the people directly.

After 17 weeks of debate, the Constitution was ready. On September 17, 1787, 39 of the original 55 delegates signed it. Some delegates had left when they saw the direction the convention was taking, and 3 others refused to sign, feeling that the Constitution gave too much authority to the national government. Most of the rest were not entirely happy with the result—even Madison, who was most responsible for the content of the document, was despondent that his plan for a national legislature was compromised by having one house with representation by states—but they thought it was the best they could do. Benjamin Franklin had some qualms, but he was more optimistic. Referring to the sun painted on the back of George Washington's chair, he remarked that throughout the proceedings he had wondered whether it was a rising or setting sun. "But now ... I have the happiness to know that it is a rising and not a setting sun."

The Founders and the People

Democracy is "the worst of all political evils."
—Elbridge Gerry

"[T]he people have ever been and ever will be unfit to retain the exercise of power in their own hands."
—William Livingston

"[T]he people [should] have as little to do as may be about the government."
—Roger Sherman

"Notwithstanding the oppression and injustice experienced among us from democracy, the genius of the people is in favor of it, and the genius of the people must be consulted."
—George Mason

"It seems indispensable that the mass of citizens should not be without a voice in making the laws which they are to obey, in choosing the magistrates who are to administer them."
—James Madison

In part these statements reflect the Founders' support for republicanism and opposition to democracy, as they defined the terms. But in a more general sense, these statements reflect the Founders' ambivalence about "the people." Rationally they believed in popular sovereignty, but emotionally they feared it. Perhaps no statement illustrates this ambivalence more than the one by New England clergyman Jeremy Belknap: "Let it stand as a principle that government originates from the people; but let the people be taught . . . that they are not able to govern themselves."

SOURCE: Richard Hofstadter, *The American Political Tradition and the Men Who Made It* (New York: Vintage, 1948), pp. 3–17.

Features of the Constitution

William Gladstone, a British prime minister in the nineteenth century, said the American Constitution was "the most wonderful work ever struck off at a given time by the brain and purpose of man."[19] To see why it was unique, it is necessary to examine its major features.

A Written Constitution

The Founders established the idea of a written constitution, first in the Articles of Confederation and then more prominently in the Constitution itself. Other Western countries had constitutions that served as their supreme law, but these constitutions were not written or, if written, not as a single document. For example, the British constitution, which consisted of various customs, declarations, acts of Parliament, and precedents of courts, was partly unwritten and partly written. To Americans this was no constitution at all. They felt that a constitution should be a fundamental law above all other laws—not a mixture of customs and laws.

This belief is reflected in Americans' use of social contract theory. A **social contract,** not a literal contract like a business contract, is an implied agreement between the people and their government. The people give up part of their liberty to the government, which in exchange protects the remainder of their liberty. The Mayflower Compact was a very general form of social contract, whereas the written Constitution, stipulating the powers and limits of government, was a more specific form of social contract.

A Republic

As explained in Chapter 1, the Founders distinguished between a **republic** and a **democracy.** They created a republic. Also called an "indirect democracy," this form of government is one in which people vote for representatives who make decisions for them.

The Founders opposed a "direct democracy" in which the will of the people becomes law. Some city-states of ancient Greece and medieval Europe had direct democracies but could not sustain them. The Founders thought a large country would have even less ability to do so because people could not be brought together in one place in order to act. The Founders also believed human nature was such that people could not withstand the passions of the moment and would be swayed by a demagogue to take unwise action. Eventually, democracy would collapse into tyranny. "Remember," John Adams wrote, "democracy never lasts long. It soon wastes, exhausts, and murders itself. There never was a democracy yet that did not commit suicide."[20]

The Founders favored a republic because they firmly believed the people should have some voice in government for it to be based on the consent of the governed. So the Founders provided that the people could elect representatives to the House and that the state legislators, themselves elected by the people, could select senators and members of the Electoral College, who would choose the president. In this way the people would have a voice but one filtered through their presumably wiser representatives.

The Founders considered a democracy radical and a republic only slightly less radical. Because they believed the country could not maintain a democracy, they worried that it might not be able to maintain a republic either. When the Constitutional Convention closed, Benjamin Franklin was approached by a woman who asked, "Well, Doctor, what have we got, a republic or a monarchy?" Franklin responded, "A republic, madam, if you can keep it."

Fragmentation of Power

Other countries assumed that government must have a concentration of power to be strong enough to govern. However, when the Founders made our national government more powerful than it had been under the Articles, they feared they also had made it more capable of oppression, and therefore they fragmented its power.

The Founders believed people were selfish, coveting more and more property, and that leaders lusted after more and more power. They assumed such human nature was unchangeable. Madison speculated, "If men were angels, no government would be necessary." But, alas, Madison said, men are not angels. Therefore, "In framing a government which is to be administered by men over men, the great difficulty lies in this: you must first enable the government to control the governed; and in the next place oblige it to control itself."[21] The Founders decided the way to oblige government to control itself was to structure it to prevent any one leader, group of leaders, or factions of people from exercising power over more than a small part of it. Thus, the Founders fragmented government's power. This is reflected in three concepts they built into the structure of government—federalism, separation of powers, and checks and balances.

FEDERALISM The first division of power was between the national government and the state governments. This division of power is called **federalism.** Foreign governments had been "unitary"; that is, the central government wielded all authority. At the other extreme, the U.S. government under the Articles had been "confederal," which meant that although there was some division of power, the state governments wielded almost all authority. The Founders wanted a strong national government, but they also wanted, or at least realized they would have to accept, reasonably strong state governments as well. They invented a federal system as a compromise between the unitary and confederal systems.

SEPARATION OF POWERS The second division of power was within the national government. The power to make, administer, and judge the laws was split into three branches—legislative, executive, and judicial (see Figure 1). In the legislative branch, the power was split further into two houses. This **separation of powers** contrasts with the British parliamentary system in which its legislature, Parliament, is supreme. Both executive and judicial officials are drawn from it and responsible to it. Madison expressed the American view of such an arrangement when he said that "the accumulation of all powers, legislative, executive, and judiciary, in the same hands . . . may justly be pronounced the very definition of tyranny."[22]

FIGURE 1
Separation of Powers

Branch:	**Legislative Congress** House	Senate	**Executive Presidency** President	**Judicial Federal Courts** Judges
Officials chosen by:	People	People, (originally, state legislatures)	Electoral College, whose members are chosen by the people (originally, by state legislatures)	President, with advice and consent of Senate
For term of:	2 years	6 years	4 years	Life
To represent primarily:	Common people Large states	Wealthy people Small states	All people	Constitution

Separation of powers, as envisioned by the Founders, means not only that government functions are to be performed by different branches, but also that officials of these branches are to be chosen by different people, for different terms, and to represent different constituencies.

To reinforce the separation of powers, officials of the three branches were chosen by different means. Representatives were elected by the people (at that time mostly white men who owned property), senators were selected by the state legislatures, and the president was selected by the Electoral College, whose members were selected by the states. Only federal judges were chosen by officials in the other branches. They were nominated by the president and confirmed by the Senate. Once appointed, however, they were allowed to serve for "good behavior"—essentially life—so they had much independence. (Since the Constitution was written, the Seventeenth Amendment has provided for election of senators by the people, and the state legislatures have provided for election of members of the Electoral College by the people.)

Officials of the branches were also chosen at different times. Representatives were given a two-year term, senators a six-year term (with one-third of them up for reelection every two years), and the president a four-year term. These staggered terms would make it less likely that temporary passions in society would bring about a massive switch of officials or policies.

The Senate was designed to act as a conservative brake on the House, due to senators' selection by state legislatures and their longer terms. After returning from France, Thomas Jefferson met with George Washington over breakfast. Jefferson protested the establishment of a legislature with two houses. Washington supposedly asked, "Why did you pour that coffee into your saucer?" "To cool it," Jefferson replied. Similarly, Washington explained, "We pour legislation into the senatorial saucer to cool it."[23]

CHECKS AND BALANCES To guarantee separation of powers, the Founders built in overlapping powers called **checks and balances** (see Figure 2). Madison suggested that "the great security against a gradual concentration of the several powers in the same department consists in giving those who administer each department the necessary constitutional means and personal motives to resist encroachments by the others. . . . *Ambition must be made to counteract ambition.*"[24] To that end, each branch was given some authority over the others. If one branch abused its power, the others could use their checks to thwart it.

Thus, rather than a simple system of separation of powers, ours is a complex, even contradictory, system of both separation of powers and checks and balances. The principle of separation of powers gives each branch its own sphere of authority, but the system of checks and balances allows each branch to intrude into

■ FIGURE 2
Checks and Balances

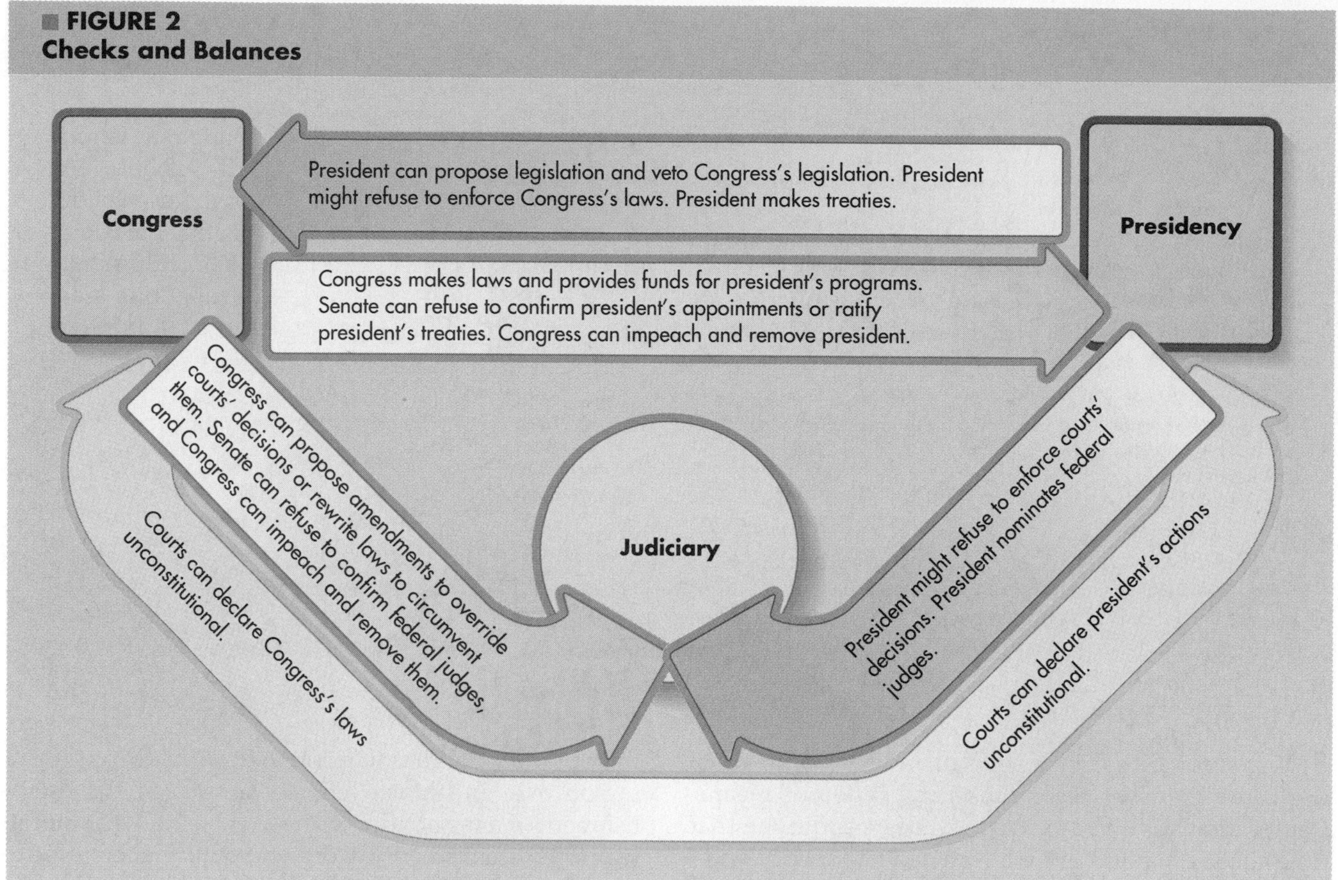

Congress
Presidency
President can propose legislation and veto Congress's legislation. President might refuse to enforce Congress's laws. President makes treaties.
Congress makes laws and provides funds for president's programs. Senate can refuse to confirm president's appointments or ratify president's treaties. Congress can impeach and remove president.
Judiciary
Congress can propose amendments to override courts' decisions or rewrite laws to circumvent them. Senate can refuse to confirm federal judges, and Congress can impeach and remove them.
Courts can declare Congress's laws unconstitutional.
President might refuse to enforce courts' decisions. President nominates federal judges.
Courts can declare president's actions unconstitutional.

Most of the major checks and balances between the three branches are explicit in the Constitution, though some are not. For example, the courts' power to declare congressional laws or presidential actions unconstitutional—their power of "judicial review"—is not mentioned. And the president's power to refuse to enforce congressional laws or judicial decisions is not mentioned or even implied. In fact, it contradicts the Constitution, but sometimes it is asserted by the president nonetheless.

the other branches' spheres. For example, because of separation of powers, Congress makes the laws, but due to checks and balances, the president can veto them and the courts can rule them unconstitutional. In these ways all three branches are involved in legislating. One political scientist calls ours "a government of separated institutions sharing powers."[25]

With federalism, separation of powers, and checks and balances, the Founders expected conflict. They invited the parts of government to struggle against each other in order to limit each other's ability to dominate all. At the same time, the Founders hoped for "balanced government." The national and state governments would represent different interests, and the branches within the national government would represent different interests. The House would represent the "common" people and the large states, the Senate the wealthy people and the small states, the president all the people, and the Supreme Court the Constitution. The parts of government would have to compromise to get anything accomplished. Although each part would struggle for more power, it could not accumulate enough to dominate the others. Eventually its leaders would have to compromise and adopt policies in the interest of all of the parts and their constituencies. Paradoxically, then, the Founders expected narrow conflict to produce broader harmony.

■ Motives of the Founders

To understand the Constitution better, it is useful to consider the motives of the Founders. Were they selfless patriots, sharing their wisdom and experience? Or

American Diversity

Did the Iroquois Influence the Founders?

For many years popular writers portrayed Native Americans as simple savages. To some they were "bloodthirsty savages." To others they were "noble savages." But to almost all writers, Indians were so preoccupied by surviving that they had little time for anything but hunting and fighting. Yet these Native Americans had far more sophisticated societies than most writers, until recently, gave them credit for.

Although most Americans are aware that the colonists adopted the tactics of Indian warfare—the forerunner of modern guerrilla warfare—to defeat the British in the Revolutionary War, few Americans realize that the colonists mirrored several other Indian practices in founding the country. In fact, the colonists used some similar concepts to those of the Iroquois in the Declaration of Independence, Articles of Confederation, and Constitution.

The Iroquois, who inhabited what is now New York State, included the Cayugas, Mohawks, Oneidas, Onondagas, and Senecas. (After the early 1700s they also included the Tuscaroras, who migrated from the Carolinas.) After generations of bloody warfare, the "Five Nations" formed the **Iroquois Confederacy** sometime between 1000 and 1450, according to various estimates.[1]

Iroquois Government

The Confederacy adopted a constitution called the "Great Law of Peace." Although some provisions were not written, others were recorded on "wampum belts," constructed of shells sewn in intricate patterns on hides. Few white Americans realized that the Iroquois' constitution was partly written until it was transcribed into English in the late nineteenth century.

The Great Law provided for a union with federalism, checks and balances, restrictions on the power of the leaders, opportunities for participation by the people, and some natural rights and equality for the people.

Federalism was most apparent. Each of the Five Nations essentially was a state within a state. Each was allowed to govern its internal affairs. (Even non-Iroquois nations conquered by the Iroquois were allowed to keep their form of government as long as they did not make war on other nations.)

Checks and balances were incorporated in several ways. The Confederacy established a system of clans that overlapped the boundaries of the nations. Members of clans were considered relatives despite living in different nations. Thus, the system of clans was designed to operate like the system of checks and balances in the U.S. Constitution: Where checks and balances were intended to prevent the dominance of one branch of government, or one faction that got control of a branch of government, clans were intended to prevent the dominance of one nation in the Confederacy.

The Confederacy used governing procedures that also entailed checks and balances. The "older brothers"—Mohawks and Senecas—were on "one side of the house." The "younger brothers"—Cayugas and Oneidas—were on the "opposite side of the house." The "firekeepers"—Onondagas—would break the tie if the two sides disagreed. If the two sides agreed, the "firekeepers" could veto the measure, but then the two sides could override the veto. Thus, the governing council was analogous to a two-house legislature and an executive with a limited veto.

The Great Law had elaborate provisions for the selection and obligations of the chiefs who sat on the governing council. Most chiefs were selected by women from extended families that had hereditary power. Thus, these women were permitted to participate in making these important political decisions, although they themselves were not permitted to serve on the council.

The chiefs were obligated to communicate with the people—send messages to them and consider requests from them. The chiefs were expected to tolerate anger and criticism by the people and to reflect "endless patience" and "calm deliberation." The chiefs were to be the people's servants rather than their masters. As such, they were not supposed to accumulate more wealth than the people. (In fact, there was some pressure to give away their material possessions, so they would be poorer than the people.) If the chiefs failed to follow these rules, they could be recalled or impeached.

The Great Law also provided for some natural rights and equality. There was significant separation of church and state. There was no state religion, and the duties of the civil chiefs were distinct from those of the religious leaders. The Great Law upheld freedom of expression in religious and political matters, and it reflected tolerance of different races and national origins. For example, its adoption rules included no restrictions on the basis of race or national origin. Even some Anglo-Americans received full citizenship in the Confederacy.

Thus, in various ways the Iroquois government, unlike the Indian civilizations in Central and South America, reflected characteristics we consider democratic.[2] As one historian concluded, "all these things were part of the American way of life before Columbus landed."[3]

Iroquois Influence on American Government?

In colonial times the Iroquois occupied land between the English on the Atlantic Coast and the French in what is now southern Canada. The Iroquois controlled the only level mountain pass and the best communication and trade route between the English and the French. The Iroquois were the balance of power between these settlers, whose nations were at war with each other.

Britain tried to forge an alliance with the Iroquois. Colonial envoys and Indian chiefs held treaty councils to establish the alliance. As early as 1744 one chief, Canassatego, advised the colonies to unite, as the Iroquois had, for the colonists' protection (and for the Indians' convenience—to reduce the confusion of dealing with separate colonies). Benjamin Franklin, who served as an envoy and as the printer of the proceedings of the councils, was fascinated by the Iroquois and seemed influenced by Canassatego's advice. He too urged the colonies to unite, and he proposed a plan very similar to the Iroquois Confederacy. But the plan was not adopted by the colonies, who fretted that it would deny their individual independence. It was not accepted by the Crown either, who feared that it would establish the colonies' joint independence from the mother country. The colonies would not unite until the Crown imposed the Stamp Act and other measures two decades later.

Many colonists were intrigued by Iroquois ways. Franklin found a market eager for his accounts of the treaty councils. He printed accounts of 13 councils in 26 years. An official in New York's colonial government published a systematic description of Iroquois government in 1727 and expanded it in 1747. Other officials asked the Iroquois for information about their confederacy's structure.

Over the years there was much intermingling between European and Native American cultures. (At least one colonial official was adopted by the Mohawks, and another was allowed to serve on their councils and even lead their war parties at times.) And some Founders admired certain Indian practices and ideas. Besides Franklin, Thomas Jefferson and Thomas Paine, for example, were attracted to the Iroquois' emphasis on natural rights and their restrictions on their leaders' power and wealth. Thus, "the American frontier became a laboratory for democracy precisely at a time when colonial leaders were searching for alternatives to what they regarded as European tyranny and class stratification."[4]

Historians debate whether the Iroquois actually influenced the Founders. The parallels between the Iroquois government and our Declaration of Independence, Articles of Confederation, and Constitution could be coincidental. Political ideas can take root in more than one society simultaneously. But the parallels are striking and the possibilities are intriguing. The roots of our political ideas might be more numerous and complex than we have assumed.[5]

SOURCE: Bruce E. Johansen, *Forgotten Founders* (Ipswich, Mass.: Gambit, 1982). Additional sources are cited, especially in Chapter 1.

1. Johansen, p. 22.
2. Johansen, pp. 17-18.
3. Felix Cohen, quoted in Johansen, p. 13.
4. Johansen, p. xv.
5. At least fragments of evidence suggest that Native Americans influenced European philosophers, such as Locke, Montesquieu, and Rousseau, who in turn influenced the colonists. Some Iroquois chiefs had been to Europe, and the Europeans were as intrigued by their ways as the colonists were. Johansen, pp. 14, 52.

were they selfish property owners, protecting their interests? To answer these questions it is necessary to look at the philosophical ideas, political experience, and economic interests that influenced these men.

Philosophical Ideas

The Founders were exceptionally well educated intellectuals who incorporated philosophical ideas into the Constitution. At a time when the average person did not dream of going to college, a majority of the Founders graduated from college. As learned men, they shared a common library of writers and philosophers.

The framers of the Constitution reflected the ideals of the Enlightenment, a pattern of thought emphasizing the use of reason, rather than tradition or religion, to solve problems; they studied past governments to determine why they had failed in the hope they could apply these lessons to the present.

From all accounts they engaged in a level of debate at the convention that was rare in politics, citing philosophers ranging from the ancient Greeks to the modern British and French. Even when they did not mention them explicitly, their comments seemed to reflect the writings of particular philosophers.

The views of John Locke, a seventeenth-century English philosopher, underlay many of the ideas of the Founders. In fact, his views permeate the Declaration of Independence and Constitution more than those of any other single person.

Locke, like some previous philosophers, believed people had **natural rights.** These rights were inherent; they existed from the moment people were born. And they were inalienable; they were given by God so they could not be taken away. One of the most important was the right to property. When people worked the land, clearing it and planting it, they mixed their labor with it. This act, according to Locke, made the land their property. Some people, due to more work or luck, would accumulate more property than others. Thus, the right to property would result in inequality of wealth. Yet he thought it would lead to greater productivity for society. This view of property appealed to Americans who saw an abundance of land in the new country.

Locke wrote that people came together to form government through a social contract that established a **limited government,** strong enough to protect their rights but not too strong to threaten these rights. This government should not act without the consent of the governed. To make its decisions, this government should follow majority rule. (Locke never resolved the conflict between majority rule and natural rights—that is, between majority rule and minority rights for those who disagree with the majority.)

The views of Charles de Montesquieu, an eighteenth-century French philosopher, also influenced the debate at the convention and the provisions of the Constitution itself. Others had suggested separation of powers before, but Montesquieu refined the concept and added that of checks and balances. The Founders, referring to him as "the celebrated Montesquieu," cited him more than any other thinker.[26] (Presumably they cited him more than Locke because by this time Locke's views had so permeated American society that the Founders considered them just "common sense.")[27]

The principles of the system of mechanics formulated by Isaac Newton, an eighteenth-century British mathematician, also pervaded the provisions of the Constitution. As Newton viewed nature as a machine, so the Founders saw the constitutional structure as a machine, with different parts having different functions and balancing each other. Newton's principle of action and reaction is manifested in the Founders' system of checks and balances. The natural environment and the constitutional structure both were viewed as self-regulating systems.[28]

Political Experience

Although the Founders were intellectuals, they were also practical politicians. According to one interpretation, they were "first and foremost superb democratic politicians" and the convention was "a nationalist reform caucus which had to operate with great delicacy and skill in a political cosmos full of enemies."[29]

The Founders brought extensive political experience to the convention: 8 had signed the Declaration of Independence; 39 had served in Congress; 7 had been governors; many had held other state offices; some had helped write their state constitutions. The framers drew upon this experience. For example, while they cited Montesquieu in discussing separation of powers, they also referred to the experience of colonial and state governments that already had some separation of powers.

As practical politicians, "no matter what their private dreams might be, they had to take home an acceptable package and defend it—and their own political futures—against predictable attack."[30] So they compromised the difficult issues and ducked the stickiest ones. Ultimately, they pieced together a Constitution that allowed each delegate to go home and announce that his state won something.

Economic Interests

Historian Charles Beard sparked a lively debate when he published *An Economic Interpretation of the Constitution* in 1913.[31] Beard argued that those with money and investments in manufacturing and shipping dominated the Constitutional Convention and state ratification conventions and that they produced a document that would increase their wealth. (After Beard published his conclusions, an Ohio newspaper proclaimed, "Scavengers, hyena-like, desecrate the graves of the dead patriots we revere.")[32] Later scholars questioned Beard's facts and interpretations, pointing out that support for the Constitution was not based strictly on wealth; Elbridge Gerry, one of the richest men in the country, opposed the Constitution, whereas Hamilton and Madison, both of more modest means, supported it.[33]

Source: Drawing by Donald Reilly; © 1974 The New Yorker Magazine, Inc.

"Religious freedom is my immediate goal, but my long range plan is to go into real estate."

Although some of Beard's specific points do not hold up, his underlying position that the Founders represented an elite that sought to protect its property from the masses seems more valid. The delegates to the Constitutional Convention were an elite. They included prosperous planters, manufacturers, shippers, and lawyers. About one-third were slaveowners. Most came from families of prominence and married into other families of prominence. Not all were wealthy, but most were at least well-to-do. Only one, a delegate from Georgia, was a yeoman farmer like most men in the country. In short, "this was a convention of the well-bred, the well-fed, the well-read, and the well-wed."[34]

The Founders supported the right to property. The promise of land and perhaps riches enticed most immigrants to come to America.[35] A desire for freedom from arbitrary taxes and trade restrictions spurred some colonists to fight in the Revolution.[36] And the inability of the government under the Articles to provide a healthy economy prompted the Founders to convene the Constitutional Convention. They probably agreed with Madison that "the first object of government" is to protect property.[37]

The Founders' emphasis on property was not as elitist as it might seem, however. Land was plentiful and, with westward expansion, even more would be available. Already most men were middle-class farmers who owned some property. Many who owned no property could foresee the day when they would, so most Americans wanted to protect property.

The Founders diverged from the farmers in their desire to protect other property in addition to land, such as wealth and credit. Of the 55 delegates, 40 were owners of government bonds that had depreciated under the Articles, and 24 were moneylenders.[38] So the delegates included provisions to protect commerce, including imports and exports, contracts, and debts, and provisions to regulate currency, bankruptcy, and taxes.

Political scientists and historians disagree about which of these three influences on the Founders—philosophical, political, or economic—was most important. Actually the influences are difficult to separate because they reinforce each other; the framers' ideas point to the same sort of constitution that their political experience and economic interests do.[39]

Ratification of the Constitution

The Constitution specified that ratification would occur through conventions in the states and that the document would take effect with approval of conventions in 9 of the 13 states. The framers purposely did not provide for approval by the state legislatures because they feared that some legislatures would reject it because it reduced their power. Too, the framers wanted the broader base of support for the new government that ratification conventions would provide.

Technically the procedures for ratification were illegal. According to the Articles of Confederation, which were still in effect, any changes had to be approved by all 13 states. However, the framers suspected that they would not find support in all states.

Indeed, ratification was uncertain. Many people opposed the Constitution, and there was a lively campaign against it in newspapers, pamphlets, and mass meetings. And although the procedures required ratification by only 9 states, the framers realized they needed support from all of the largest states and much of the public to lend legitimacy to the new government.

Constitutional Provisions Protecting Property

"The Times, Places and Manner of holding Elections for Senators and Representatives, shall be prescribed in each State by the Legislature thereof."	Allows state to set property qualifications to vote.
"The Congress shall have Power . . . To coin Money."	Centralizes currency.
"No State shall . . . emit bills of credit."	Prevents states from printing paper money.
"Congress shall have Power . . . To establish uniform Laws on the subject of Bankruptcies."	Allows Congress to prevent states from relieving debtors of obligation to pay.
"No State shall . . . pass any . . . Law impairing the Obligation of Contracts."	Prevents states from relieving debtors of obligation to pay.
"The United States shall guarantee to every State [protection] against domestic Violence."	Protects states from debtor uprisings.
"Congress shall have Power . . . To provide for calling forth the Militia to execute the Laws of the Union, suppress insurrections."	Protects creditors from debtor uprisings.

Knowing opponents would charge them with setting up a national government to dominate the state governments, those who supported the Constitution ingeniously adopted the name **Federalists** to emphasize a real division of power between the national and state governments. They dubbed their opponents **Antifederalists** to imply that they did not want a division of power between the governments.

The Antifederalists faulted the Constitution for lacking a bill of rights. The Constitution did contain some protection for individual rights, such as the provision that the writ of habeas corpus, which protects against arbitrary arrest and detention, cannot be suspended except during rebellion or invasion, and the provision that a criminal defendant has a right to a jury trial. But the framers made no effort to include most of the rights people believed they had, because most states already had a bill of rights in their own constitutions. They also thought that by fragmenting power no branch could become strong enough to deny individual rights. Yet critics demanded provisions protecting various rights of criminal defendants and freedom of the press. In response, the Federalists promised to propose amendments guaranteeing these rights as soon as the government began.

The Antifederalists criticized the Constitution for other reasons. Localists at heart, they were wary of entrusting power to officials far away; they correctly claimed that republics historically worked only in small geographical areas where the population was more homogeneous and the officials were closer to the people. They worried that the central government, to function effectively, would accumulate too much power and the presidency would become a monarchy or Congress an aristocracy. One delegate to the Massachusetts convention blasted the Federalists:

> These lawyers, and men of learning and moneyed men, that talk so finely, and gloss over matters so smoothly, to make us poor illiterate people swallow down the pill, expect to get into Congress themselves; they expect to . . . get all the power and all the money into their own hands, and then they will swallow up all us little folks . . . just as the whale swallowed up Jonah![40]

But the Antifederalists had no alternative plan. They were divided; some wanted to amend the Articles, while others wanted to reject both the Articles and the Constitution in favor of some yet undetermined form of government. Their lack of unity on an alternative was instrumental in their inability to win support.[41]

Ratification was quick in some states, a bitter struggle in others. Within three months after the Constitutional Convention, Delaware became the first state to ratify, and six months later New Hampshire became the necessary ninth. Virginia and New York followed but they ratified only by narrow margins. Indeed, New York ratified only by three votes after New York City threatened to secede from the state if the state did not ratify. So the Constitution took effect and the new government began in 1788, with George Washington becoming president. Within one year, North Carolina and Rhode Island, both of which initially rejected the Constitution, became the last states to approve it.

Changing the Constitution

The framers expected their document to last; Madison wrote, "We have framed a constitution that will probably be still around when there are 196 million people."[42] Yet because the framers realized it would need some changes, they drafted a Constitution that can be changed either formally by constitutional amendment or informally by judicial interpretation or political practice. In doing so, they left a legacy for later governments. "The example of changing a Constitution, by assembling the wise men of the state, instead of assembling armies," Jefferson noted, "will be worth as much to the world as the former examples we had given them."[43]

By Constitutional Amendment

That the Articles of Confederation could be amended only by a unanimous vote of the states posed an almost insurmountable barrier to any amendment at all. The framers of the Constitution made sure this experience would not repeat itself. On the other hand, they did not make amendment easy; although the procedures do not require unanimity, they do require widespread agreement.

PROCEDURES The procedures for amendment entail action by both the national government and the state governments. Amendments can be proposed in either of two ways—by a two-thirds vote of both houses of Congress or by a national convention called by Congress at the request of two-thirds of the state legislatures. Congress then specifies which way amendments must be ratified—either by three-fourths of the state legislatures or by ratifying conventions in three-fourths of the states. Among these avenues, the usual route has been proposal by Congress and ratification by state legislatures (see Figure 3).

FIGURE 3
Avenues for Constitutional Amendment

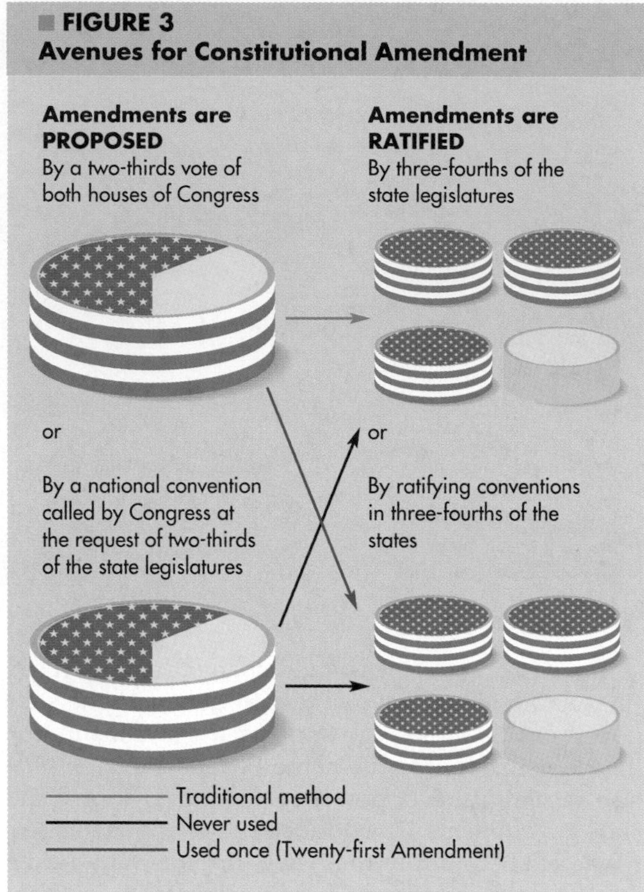
Amendments are PROPOSED
By a two-thirds vote of both houses of Congress
or
By a national convention called by Congress at the request of two-thirds of the state legislatures
Amendments are RATIFIED
By three-fourths of the state legislatures
or
By ratifying conventions in three-fourths of the states
Traditional method
Never used
Used once (Twenty-first Amendment)

AMENDMENTS In the first Congress under the Constitution, the Federalists fulfilled their promise to support a bill of rights. Madison drafted the amendments, Congress proposed them, and the states ratified 10 of them in 1791. This **Bill of Rights** includes freedom of expression—speech, press, assembly, and religion (First Amendment). It also includes numerous rights for those accused of crimes—protection against unreasonable searches and seizures (Fourth), protection against compulsory self-incrimination (Fifth), guarantee of due process of law (Fifth), the right to counsel and a jury trial in criminal cases (Sixth), and protection against excessive bail and fines, and cruel and unusual punishment (Eighth). It also includes a jury trial in civil cases (Seventh).

In addition to these major rights, the Bill of Rights includes two amendments that grew out of the colonial experience with Great Britain—the right to bear arms for a militia (Second) and the right not to have soldiers quartered in homes during peacetime (Third). The Bill of Rights also includes two general amendments—a statement that the listing of these rights does not mean these are the only ones people have (Ninth) and a statement that the powers not given to the national government are reserved to the states (Tenth).

The Federalist Papers

Out of the great debate over ratification came a series of essays considered the premier example of American political philosophy. Titled the **Federalist Papers,** these essays were written by Alexander Hamilton (*left*), James Madison (*center*), and John Jay. At the urging of Hamilton,[1] the authors wrote 85 essays that appeared in New York newspapers during the ratification debates there. The authors tried to convince delegates to the convention to vote for ratification.

In the fashion of the time, the papers were published anonymously—by "Publius" (Latin for "Public Man"). They were so unified in approach that few of the authors' contemporaries could discern their pens at work. Given the arguments and compromises at the Constitutional Convention, one political scientist speculated that the framers who read the essays "must have discovered with some surprise what a coherent and well-thought-out document they had prepared."[2]

Despite the unity of the papers, political scientists have identified the authors of individual ones. Hamilton wrote most of those describing the defects of the Articles, Madison most of those explaining the structure of the new government, including the famous #10 and #51 (reprinted at the back of this book). Before he became sick, Jay, who was secretary of foreign affairs, wrote a few concerning foreign policy.

Actually there is little evidence that the essays swayed any of the delegates. Yet they have endured because readers see them as an original source of political thinking and as one of the best guides to the intentions of the Framers.

1. Although Hamilton worried that the Constitution would not establish a strong enough government, he thought it was preferable to the Articles, which he despised.

2. John P. Roche, ed., *Origins of American Political Thought* (New York: Harper & Row, 1967), p. 163.

Among the other 17 amendments to the Constitution, the strongest theme is the expansion of citizenship rights:

- Abolition of slavery (Thirteenth, 1865)
- Equal protection, due process of law (Fourteenth, 1868)
- Right to vote for black men (Fifteenth, 1870)
- Direct election of senators (Seventeenth, 1913)
- Right to vote for women (Nineteenth, 1920)
- Right to vote in presidential elections for District of Columbia residents (Twenty-third, 1960)
- Abolition of poll tax in federal elections (Twenty-fourth, 1964)
- Right to vote for persons eighteen and older (Twenty-sixth, 1971)

Another theme is the increase of federal power. Many amendments, notably those regarding voting, take authority away from the states and authorize Congress to enforce these rights by "appropriate legislation."

Most amendments proposed by Congress were ratified by the states, although some were not. Recently, two proposed amendments were not ratified. One would have provided equal rights for women (this amendment will be discussed in Chapter 15), and the other would have given congressional representation to the District of Columbia, as though it were a state.

These and other recent amendments have had time limits for ratification—usually seven years—set by Congress. But an amendment preventing members of Congress from giving themselves a midterm pay raise, written by Madison and passed by Congress in 1789, had no time limit. Once Michigan ratified it in 1992, it reached the three-fourths mark and became the Twenty-seventh Amendment.

Although the Constitution expressly provides for change by amendment, its ambiguity about some subjects and silence about others virtually guarantee change by interpretation and practice as well.

By Judicial Interpretation

If there is disagreement about what the Constitution means, who is to interpret it? Although the Constitution does not say, the judicial branch has taken on this role. To decide disputes brought to them, the courts must determine what the relevant provisions of the Constitution mean. By saying the provisions mean one thing rather than another, the courts can, in effect, change the Constitution. Woodrow Wilson called the Supreme Court "a constitutional convention in continuous session." The Court has acted as a safety valve, diffusing pressure for new amendments by interpreting the Constitution in such a way as to bring about the same results as new amendments.

By Political Practice

Political practice has accounted for some very important changes. These include the rise of political parties and the demise of the Electoral College as an independent body. They also include the development of the cabinet to advise the president and the development of the committee system to operate the two houses of Congress.

The Founders would be surprised to learn that only 17 amendments, aside from the Bill of Rights, have been adopted in about 200 years. In part this is due to their wisdom, but in part it is due to changes in judicial interpretation and political practice, which have combined to create a "living Constitution."

Conclusion: Is the Constitution Responsive?

Soon after ratification, the Constitution became accepted by the people. It took on the aura of a secular Bible. People embraced it, consulted it for guidance, cited it for support, and debated the meaning of its provisions.

The Constitution has proven to be so popular that many countries have copied parts of it. Almost all of the 170-plus nations in the world today have a constitution written as a single document. Many have provisions similar to those in our Constitution. The Kenyan constitution speaks of "freedom of expression," the Costa Rican gives the "right to petition," and the German says that "all persons shall be equal before the law." And officials and groups in, of all unlikely places, South Africa and Russia, are considering provisions in our Constitution as they change theirs.[44]

But the brevity of our Constitution remains unique; with just 89 sentences, it is far shorter than those of other nations. Because it is short, it is necessarily general; because it is general, it is necessarily ambiguous; because it is ambiguous, it is necessarily open to interpretation. This provides succeeding generations the opportunity to adapt the Constitution to

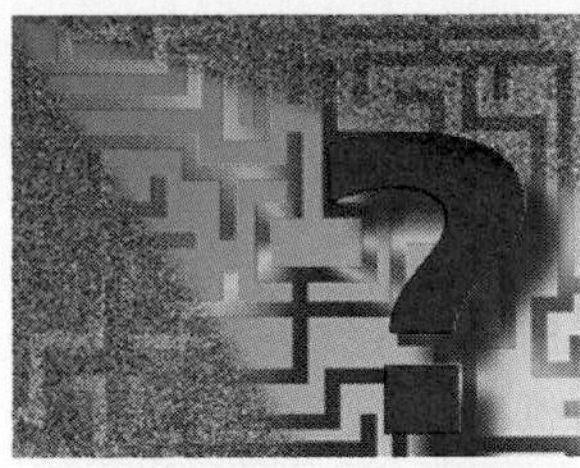

Symbolic Solutions for Complex Problems?

Making English the Official National Language

In some chapters we have a box examining what we consider largely a symbolic solution for what is actually a complex problem. The proposal is symbolic in that it appears to address the problem, but because of the complexity of the problem, the solution is not likely to solve the problem or, possibly, even ameliorate it.

The symbolic solution tends to be a simple solution—we could title these boxes "Simple Solutions for Complex Problems?"—and a simple solution is not likely to solve a complex problem. (There might, of course, be exceptions, as there are to other generalizations.)

People tell pollsters they favor many of these ideas. But we want students to recognize that these ideas, so appealing at first glance, are more symbolic than substantive. We want students to recognize that politicians, political parties, and interest groups might urge adoption of these ideas because they are trying to rally people to their side for other reasons. They might see these ideas as ways to gain support in an election campaign or in a policy fight. At a time when national problems seem intractable, it is tempting for politicians to claim they can solve them, even if they cannot. And it is tempting for politicians to claim they can solve them quickly, as most of these proposals imply, even when they cannot. Or proponents might see these as ways to advance some hidden agenda. (For example, before the 1994 elections Republicans called for term limits for members of Congress at least in part because they saw term limits as a way to oust entrenched Democrats from Congress.)

Our belief is that citizens should demand real solutions for real problems and that they should not allow themselves to be manipulated or appeased by proposals that merely pretend to address the problems. Symbolic actions can be useful, especially as protests in the early stages of controversies, but they must give way to substantive efforts if problems are to be resolved.

We do need to emphasize, however, that reasonable people can disagree and some readers might want to adopt these proposals even if they are largely symbolic. Other readers might want them for other reasons. We will elaborate in individual boxes.

In this chapter we focus on the proposal for a constitutional amendment making English the official national language. This proposal is a reaction to the influx of immigrants in recent decades. Some native-born Americans are sincerely worried about the tide of immigrants, as Chapter 1 explained, while other native-born Americans are simply annoyed by the inability of many immigrants to speak English.

Of course, the U.S. has had waves of immigrants before. However, most waves have not been as large and have not included as diverse a group of people as now. In the past, most immigrants were Europeans. Now, many are Latin Americans, many are Asians, and some are Middle Easterners as well. Los Angeles offers election ballots in Spanish, Chinese, Japanese, Vietnamese, Korean, and Tagalog. Its county courts provide interpreters for about 80 languages. (Even so, confusion occurs. A police officer testified that he had read a suspect his Miranda rights in the Tai-shan dialect of Chinese, but the judge discovered that the man understood only the Cantonese dialect, so he had to disregard the confession.)[1]

Groups like *U.S. English* and *English First* have sounded the alarm: "If this continues, the next American president could well be elected by people who can't read or speak English!" Seventeen states have passed laws making English their official language, and some members of Congress have proposed a constitutional amendment for the entire country.

It is not clear what effect the amendment would have. Election ballots and other forms now printed in various languages probably would be printed only in English, and bilingual education programs in public schools probably would be scaled back. The amendment would not restrict private, religious, or ceremonial use of foreign languages.

But no doubt there would be different interpretations of the amendment by different branches of the government in different parts of the country. When California made English its official language in the 1980s, one city council fired librarians for buying foreign language books and subscribing to foreign language magazines. In some cities teachers forbade students from speaking foreign languages among themselves, and hospitals forbade employees from speaking any language but English. One official reprimanded a worker who spoke Spanish to a co-worker in the hallway, and another fired workers who spoke Filipino to patients who spoke that language.[2]

Despite uncertainty about the interpretation of an amendment, might one nonetheless prompt people who do not speak English to learn the language?

The underlying assumption is that immigrants are taking longer to learn English than in the past and that some are refusing to learn it at all. It is true that some immigrant communities are so large that people can survive without learning English. Some Mexican immigrants in parts of the Southwest and some Cuban immigrants in parts of Florida speak Spanish alone. Contrary to some perceptions, however, most immigrants feel pressure to learn English. It helps them land jobs and function in the broader society. Their children, who grow up and attend schools in this society, learn English and put more pressure on them.

A survey of Hispanics in 40 cities found that more than 90% thought U.S. citizens and residents should learn English.[3] A survey of Hispanics in South Florida found that 98% thought it was important for their children to read and write "perfect English."[4] And their children apparently agree. More than four-fifths of immigrant children in south Florida and more than two thirds of those in San Diego prefer English to their familial language.[5]

Another study of immigrants underscored the value they put on succeeding in school. These families are more likely to have rules about doing homework and maintaining grades (including rules limiting television) than they are to have requirements about performing household chores or part-time jobs.[6] Their efforts to succeed in school as a way to make it in society reflect similar efforts by past immigrants.

It should not be surprising, then, that current immigrants are mastering English. Of 17.3 million Spanish speakers in the United States, less than 10% do not speak English.[7] Cuban-Americans are learning it as fast or faster than any previous group in history.[8] Mexican-Americans are learning it as they stay longer in the U.S. Although most of those who come for work and plan to return to Mexico do not speak English or do not speak it well, most of those who plan to remain in the U.S. learn to speak more English and almost all of their children learn to speak fluent English.[9] Thus, the process takes time, but it does work.

Consequently, a constitutional amendment making English the official national language would be little more than a symbolic solution. Immigrants already are learning English.

Some advocates of an amendment acknowledge that it would be a symbol—a symbol of national unity at a time when there is more diversity than ever before. To this extent, the debate is not just about prodding immigrants to learn English; it is also about persuading them to assimilate—to shed their foreign ways and adopt our "American ways." Yet it is hard to see what an amendment would accomplish beyond what learning English and adapting to society already are accomplishing. And if the fear is of too much immigration, changing immigration laws is a much more direct solution.

In fact, an amendment might be counterproductive. It could encourage more xenophobia—fear of foreigners—and more intolerance of diversity. It could result in more discrimination against even legal immigrants. Abolition of bilingual ballots might disfranchise some, and abolition of bilingual forms might make it difficult for some to receive government services for which they are eligible. An amendment also would restrict freedom of speech. A federal court struck down Arizona's law as a violation of the First Amendment.

1. Otto Friedrich, "The Changing Face of America," *Time,* July 8, 1985, p. 29.
2. Eloise Salholz, "Say It in English," *Newsweek,* February 20, 1989, p. 23; Margaret Carlson, "Only English Spoken Here," *Time,* December 5, 1988, p. 29; Elaine Elinson, "On the Job, English Only Rules Are on the Rise," *Civil Liberties* (Fall, 1990), p. 5.
3. Lynne Duke, "English Spoken Here," *Washington Post National Weekly Edition,* December 21–27, 1992, p. 37.
4. Salholz, "Say It in English," p. 23.
5. Joel Kotkin, "Can the Melting Pot Be Reheated?" Washington Post National Weekly Edition, July 11-17, 1994, p. 23.
6. Nathan Caplan, Marcella H. Choy, and John K. Whitmore, *Children of the Boat People: A Study of Educational Success* (Ann Arbor: University of Michigan Press, 1992).
7. 1990 Census of the Population, Social and Economic Characteristics, Part I, Table 13; Less than 5% of Asian-language speakers and less than 2% of other language speakers do not speak English.
8. Thomas Boswell and James Curtis, *The Cuban American Experience* (Totowa, N.J.: Rowman & Allanheld, 1983), p. 191.
9. Kevin F. McCarthy and R. Burciaga Valdez, *Current and Future Effects of Mexican Immigration in California—Executive Summary* (Santa Monica: Rand Corporation, 1985), p. 27.

---

changing times. The longer, more detailed, and less flexible constitutions of other nations become outdated and periodically need complete revision.

In 1987 our Constitution celebrated its bicentennial as the oldest written constitution in the world. During the same 200 years, France, for example, had 10 distinct constitutional orders, including five republics, two empires, one monarchy, one plebiscitary dictatorship, and one puppet dictatorship during World War II.

Although our Constitution, and the institutions it established, have been responsive enough to survive, are they responsive enough to allow us to solve our problems? Can a constitution written by a small circle of men whose fastest mode of travel was horseback continue to serve masses of diverse people, some of whom have traveled by spaceship?

Intended to construct a government responsive to the masses of people to a limited extent, the Constitution set up a republic, which allowed the people to elect some representatives who would make their laws. This gave the people more say in government than people in other countries enjoyed at the time.

But the Constitution was intended to construct a government unresponsive to the masses of people to a large extent. It was expected to filter the public's passions and purify their selfish desires. Consequently, the Founders limited participation in government, allowing people to vote only for members of the House of Representatives—not for members of the Senate or the president.

Moreover, the Founders fragmented the power of government. Federalism, separation of powers, and checks and balances combine to make it difficult for any one group to capture all of government. Instead,one faction might control one branch, another faction another branch, and so on, with the result a standoff. Then the factions must compromise to accomplish anything.

Since the time of the founding, changes in the Constitution, whether by amendment, interpretation, or practice, have expanded opportunities for participation in government. But the changes have done little to modify the fragmentation of power, which remains the primary legacy of the Founders.

This structure has prevented many abuses of power, though it has not always worked. During the Vietnam War, for example, one branch—the presidency—exercised vast power while the others acquiesced. This structure also has provided the opportunity for one branch to pick up the slack when the others became sluggish. The overlapping of powers ensured by checks and balances allows every branch to act on virtually every issue it chooses to. In the 1950s President Eisenhower and Congress were reluctant to push for civil rights for blacks, but the Supreme Court did so by declaring segregation unconstitutional in a series of cases.

But the system's very advantage has become its primary disadvantage. In their efforts to fragment power so that no branch could accumulate too much, the Founders divided power to the point where the branches sometimes cannot wield enough. In their efforts to build a government that requires a national majority to act, they built one that allows a small minority to block action. This problem has become increasingly acute as society has become increasingly complex. Like a mechanical device that operates only when all of its parts function in harmony, the system moves only when there is consensus or compromise. Consensus is rare in a large heterogeneous society; compromise is common, but it requires a long time as well as the realization by competing interests that they cannot achieve much of what they want without compromise. Even then, compromise often results in only a partial solution.

At best the system moves inefficiently and incrementally. At worst it moves hardly at all; the Constitution has established a government that is slow to respond to change. Characterized by one political scientist as a "negative, do-nothing system,"[45] the government is most likely to respond to the status quo and the groups that want to maintain it.

Yet some political scientists believe the American people actually prefer this arrangement. Because the people are suspicious of government, they may be reluctant to let one party dominate it and use it to advance that party's policies. In surveys many people say they think it is good for one party to control the presidency and the other to control Congress. In presidential and congressional elections, typically half or more of the voters split their ticket between the two major parties. As a result, between 1968 and 1996 opposing parties controlled the executive and legislative branches for all but six years.

During the election of 1992, rising voices complained of "gridlock," and voters elected a Democratic president and a Democratic Congress. But the Democratic Congress itself was split between northerners and southerners and between members who most wanted to solve social problems they thought had been neglected and those who most wanted to reduce the deficit. Therefore, Clinton did not have a working majority. Then in the congressional elections in 1994, voters elected Republican majorities in both houses of Congress. Thus, voters who complained of gridlock just two years before cast their ballots in a way to produce more gridlock.

EPILOGUE

The President Complies

Chief Justice Warren Burger announced the unanimous decision in the case of *United States v. Nixon:* The president must turn over the tapes.[46] The Court acknowledged the existence of executive privilege in general but rejected it in this situation because another court needed the information for an upcoming trial and because the information did not relate to national security.

The Court emphasized that courts would determine the legitimacy of claims of executive privilege, not presidents, as Nixon wanted. Because of separation of powers, Nixon argued, neither the judicial nor legislative branch should involve itself in this executive decision. However, this president, who as a high school student in Whittier, California, had won a prize from the Kiwanis Club for the best oration on the Constitution, ignored the system of checks and balances, which limits separation of powers. In this case, checks and balances authorized the courts to conduct criminal trials of the president's aides and Congress to conduct impeachment proceedings against the president. To do so, the courts and Congress needed the information on the tapes.

Richard Nixon, after submitting his resignation as president, prepares to leave Washington.

Within days of the Court's decision, the House Judiciary Committee passed three articles of impeachment. These charged Nixon with obstruction of justice, by covering up a crime; defiance of the committee's subpoenas for the tapes; and abuse of power. Nevertheless, some Republicans maintained there was no "smoking gun"—that is, no clear evidence of crimes. They said the impeachment effort was strictly political.

Regardless, Nixon's support in Congress dwindled, and he found himself caught between a rock and a hard spot: Releasing the tapes would furnish more evidence for impeachment, but not releasing them would spur impeachment. He reportedly considered disregarding the decision but, after 12 days of weighing his options, complied with the order.

Releasing the tapes did reveal a smoking gun. Although the tapes did not show that Nixon participated in planning the break-in, they did show that he participated in covering it up. When the burglars blackmailed the administration, Nixon approved paying them hush money. He ordered the head of his reelection committee to "stonewall it" and "cover up." He and an aide formulated a plan to have the CIA thwart the FBI in its investigation of the scandal. When his top aides were subpoenaed to appear before the grand jury, he encouraged them to lie.

In addition to this evidence of crimes, the tapes revealed much vulgarity and profanity in Nixon's conversations. Such language undercut the public's positive image of Nixon.

The tapes, printed as a book that became an instant best-seller, repelled the public. When it became clear that public opinion would force the House to impeach him and the Senate to remove him, Nixon decided to resign. On August 9, 1974, he became the first American president to do so. Vice President Gerald Ford became the new president.

Although the smoking gun had been found, some people still thought the crimes relatively minor and the punishment excessively harsh. But Nixon was not driven from office solely or even primarily because of the break-in. Rather, he lost the public's trust because of the cover-up. He had campaigned for president on a "law and order" platform and had sworn an oath of office "to take care that the laws be faithfully executed." During the cover-up, he had repeatedly proclaimed that he was innocent of any wrongdoing. As the evidence came to light, the hypocrisy and lying became too much for the public to stomach. Ultimately, Nixon could not lead the public he had misled for so long.

Despite depression and cynicism about the scandal, many people saw that the system had worked as it was supposed to. The Founders had divided power to make it difficult for any one branch to amass too much power. In the face of the president's efforts to exercise vast power, the courts, with their orders to turn over the tapes, and Congress, with its Senate Watergate Committee hearings and House Judiciary Committee impeachment proceedings, checked the president's abuse of power. In addition, the media, with its extensive publicity, first prompted and then reinforced the actions of the courts and Congress.

However, although the system worked, it worked slowly. More than two years elapsed between the break-in and the resignation. For more than half the length of a presidential term, the president and many of his aides were so preoccupied with Watergate they could not devote sufficient attention to other problems facing the country.

When the affair was over, 21 of the president's men were convicted and sentenced to prison for their Watergate crimes. Except for one, a burglar who was most uncooperative and who served 52 months, the men served from 4 to 12 months. Nixon, who could have and probably would have been prosecuted after leaving office, received a pardon in advance from President Ford.

Nine years after the resignation, the security guard who discovered the break-in was convicted for shoplifting in Augusta, Georgia. Unemployed, he had stolen a pair of shoes for his son. Unlike the president's men, he received the maximum sentence—12 months for the $12 shoes.

Yet the story is not over. Congress passed a law mandating that other, unreleased tapes and documents be turned over to the National Archives, which was to make public any that related to Watergate or had "general historic significance." However, the Archives, prodded by Nixon's team of lawyers, has delayed releasing all but a handful of tapes.[47] In one of these, Nixon is heard remarking to his chief of staff, "I always wondered about that taping equipment, but I'm damn glad we have it, aren't you?"[48]

➤Key Terms

- Watergate scandal
- executive privilege
- Articles of Confederation
- Shays's Rebellion
- Constitutional Convention
- Great Compromise
- Three-fifths Compromise
- social contract
- republic
- democracy
- federalism
- separation of powers
- checks and balances
- natural rights
- limited government
- Iroquois Confederacy
- Federalists
- Antifederalists
- *Federalist Papers*
- Bill of Rights
- Gettysburg Address

➤Further Reading

Leonard W. Levy, ed., *Essays on the Making of the Constitution* (New York: Oxford University Press, 1969). *Essays that address the question, Was the Constitution an undemocratic document framed and ratified by an undemocratic minority for an undemocratic society?*

Clinton Rossiter, 1787: *The Grand Convention* (New York: Macmillan, 1966). *A lively account of the Constitutional Convention and the ratification campaign.*

Theodore H. White, *Breach of Faith* (New York: Atheneum, 1975). *A chronicle of the Watergate scandal as a Greek tragedy in which actors on both sides behaved in such ways as to fulfill their destinies.*

Bob Woodward and Carl Bernstein, *All the President's Men* (New York: Simon and Schuster, 1974). *Riveting account of journalistic sleuthing by the two reporters who broke the Watergate story.*

➤Notes

1. Nixon thought he might be considered an American Disraeli. (Benjamin Disraeli, a British prime minister in the nineteenth century, was a Tory who had progressive ideas.) Nixon praised

Robert Blake's biography of Disraeli, and one cabinet secretary remarked, in 1971, "The similarities are great, Mr. President, but what a pity that Blake could not quote Disraeli's conversation." Nixon did not destroy the tapes, even after they became a liability, apparently for this reason. Sidney Blumenthal, "The Longest Campaign," *The New Yorker,* August 8, 1994, p. 37.

2. *United States v. Reynolds,* 345 U.S. 1 (1953).

3. The Indians, of course, had their own governments, and the Spanish might have established St. Augustine, Florida, or Santa Fe, New Mexico, before the English established Jamestown. These Spanish settlements were extensions of Spanish colonization of Mexico and were governed by Spanish officials in Mexico City.

4. This is not to suggest that the Pilgrims believed in democracy. Apparently they were motivated to draft the compact by threats from some on the Mayflower that when the ship landed they would "use their owne libertie; for none had power to command them." Thus, the compact was designed to bind them to the laws of the colony. Richard Shenkman, *"I Love Paul Revere, Whether He Rode or Not"* (New York: Harper Collins, 1991), pp. 141-42.

5. David Hawke, *A Transaction of Free Men* (New York: Scribner's, 1964), p. 209.

6. Louis Fisher, *President and Congress* (New York: Free Press, 1972), p. 14.

7. Gordon S. Wood, "The Origins of the Constitution," *This Constitution: A Bicentennial Chronicle* (Summer 1987), pp. 10-11.

8. Eric Black, *Our Constitution* (Boulder, Colo.: Westview Press, 1988), p. 6. Shays, eventually pardoned by Massachusetts, settled in New York and became a staunch Federalist (Black, p. 8).

9. For development of this idea, see Kenneth M. Dolbeare and Linda J. Medcalf, "The Political Economy of the Constitution," *This Constitution: A Bicentennial Chronicle* (Spring 1987), pp. 4-10.

10. Black, *Our Constitution,* p. 59.

11. The Constitution, however, would reflect numerous aspects of the Articles. See Donald S. Lutz, "The Articles of Confederation as the Background to the Federal Republic," *Publius,* 20 (Winter 1990), pp. 55-70.

12. Robert McCloskey, *The American Supreme Court* (Chicago: University of Chicago Press, 1960), p. 29.

13. Fred Barbash, "James Madison: A Man for the '80s," *Washington Post National Weekly Edition,* March 30, 1987, p. 23.

14. According to a poll in 1987, the bicentennial of the Constitution, only 1% of the public identified Madison as the one who played the biggest role in creating the Constitution. Most—31%—said Thomas Jefferson, who was a diplomat in France during the convention. Black, *Our Constitution,* p. 15.

15. Paul Finkelman, "Slavery at the Philadelphia Convention," *This Constitution: A Bicentennial Chronicle* (1987), pp. 25-30.

16. Finkelman, "Slavery at the Philadelphia Convention," p. 29.

17. Finkelman, "Slavery at the Philadelphia Convention.

18. Theodore J. Lowi, *American Government* (Hinsdale, Ill.: Dryden Press, 1976), p. 97.

19. C. Herman Pritchett, *Constitutional Law of the Federal System* (Englewood Cliffs, N.J.: Prentice-Hall, 1984), p. xi.

20. Richard Hofstadter, *The American Political Tradition and the Men Who Made It* (New York: Random House, 1948), p. 13.

21. *Federalist Paper #51.*

22. *Federalist Paper #47.*

23. Max Farrand, *The Framing of the Constitution of the United States* (New Haven: Yale University Press, 1913).

24. *Federalist Paper #51.*

25. Richard E. Neustadt, *Presidential Power and the Modern Presidents* (New York: Macmillan, 1990), p. 29.

26. Donald S. Lutz, "The Relative Influence of European Writers on Later Eighteenth-Century American Political Thought," *American Political Science Review 78* (March 1984), pp. 139-97.

27. Alpheus T. Mason and Richard H. Leach, *In Quest of Freedom: American Political Thought and Practice,* 2nd ed. (Englewood Cliffs, N.J.: Prentice-Hall, 1973), p. 51.

28. For development of this idea, see Martin Landau, "A Self-Correcting System: The Constitution of the United States," *This Constitution: A Bicentennial Chronicle* (Summer 1986), pp. 4-10.

29. John P. Roche, "The Founding Fathers: A Reform Caucus in Action," *American Political Science Review 56* (March 1962), pp. 799-816.

30. Ibid.

31. Charles Beard, *An Economic Interpretation of the Constitution* (New York: Macmillan, 1913).

32. Ellen Nore, "Charles A. Beard's Economic Interpretation of the Origins of the Constitution," *This Constitution* (Winter 1987), p. 39.

33. R. E. Brown, *Charles Beard and the Constitution* (Princeton: Princeton University Press, 1956); Forrest MacDonald, *We the People* (Chicago: University of Chicago Press, 1976).

34. James MacGregor Burns, *The Vineyard of Liberty* (New York: Alfred A. Knopf, 1982), p. 33.

35. Bernard Bailyn, *Voyagers to the West* (New York: Alfred Knopf, 1986), p. 20.

36. The Boston Tea Party, contrary to myth, was not prompted by higher taxes on British tea. Parliament lowered the taxes to give the British East India Company, facing bankruptcy, an advantage in the colonial market. This threatened American shippers who smuggled tea from Holland and controlled about three-fourths of the market. The shippers resented Parliament's attempt to manipulate the economy from thousands of miles away. Shenkman, *"I Love Paul Revere, Whether He Rode or Not,"* p. 155.

37. *Federalist Paper #10.*

38. Black, *Our Constitution,* p. 21.

39. Calvin C. Jillson and Cecil L. Eubanks, "The Political Structure of Constitution Making," *American Journal of Political Science* 29 (August 1984), pp. 435–58.

40. Jonathan Elliot, *The Debates in the Several State Conventions on the Adoption of the Federal Constitution as Recommended by the General Convention at Philadelphia, in 1787,* 2nd ed., 5 vols. (Philadelphia, 1896), vol. II, p. 102; as quoted in Cecilia M. Kenyon, "Men of Little Faith," in John P. Roche, ed., *Origins of American Political Thought* (New York: Harper & Row, 1967), pp. 197-98.

41. For Antifederalist thinking, see W. B. Allen and Gordon Lloyd, eds., *The Essential Antifederalist* (Lanham, Md.: University Press of America, 1985).

42. "A Fundamental Contentment," *This Constitution: A Bicentennial Chronicle* (Fall 1984), p. 44.

43. Charles Warren, *The Making of the Constitution* (Boston: Little, Brown, 1928), p. xiv.

44. "South Africa Looks at U.S. Constitution," *Lincoln Sunday Journal-Star (New York Times),* October 7, 1990; David Remnick, " 'We, the People,' from the Russian," *Washington Post National Weekly Edition,* September 10-16, 1990, p. 11.

45. Harold J. Spaeth, *Supreme Court Policy Making* (San Francisco: W. H. Freeman, 1979), p. 13.

46. 418 U.S. 683 (1974).

47. Seymour M. Hersh, "Nixon's Last Cover-up: The Tapes He Wants the Archives To Suppress," *The New Yorker,* Dec. 14, 1992, pp. 76-95.

48. "Tapes Confirm Nixon Approved Hush Money," *Lincoln Journal* (AP), June 5, 1991.

3 Federalism and the Growth of Government

You Are There

Can Uncle Sam Help Baby-Sit?

It is 1990. You are Ileana Ros-Lehtinen, Republican member of the House of Representatives from Florida. The first Hispanic woman elected to Congress, you won your seat only last year in a bitter special election. Although your Miami-centered district contains significant numbers of blacks and Jews, a majority of your constituents, like you, are Cuban-American, conservative, and strongly attached to the Republican Party. During your first few months in office, you have voted strongly conservative, winning a perfect score from some conservative interest groups who rate voting patterns of members of Congress.[1]

You are facing a choice concerning a package of legislation relating to children. The bill would give $2.5 billion to the states to increase existing grant programs for child care, begin funding state programs for before-and-after-school day care for "latch key" children, help poor and lower-middle income families pay for child care, and require states to set quality, health, and safety standards for child-care providers.

Support for the bill is broad. More than 100 organized groups have endorsed the legislation. Over 60% of the public, including those who are not parents as well as those who are, believe the federal government should do something to make child care more available and affordable.[2] Both parties are seeking to show the public that they are concerned about children.

There is much to be concerned about. One out of five children is poor. Nineteen percent of all white children, 30% of all Hispanic children, and 54% of all black children live in homes with only one parent.[3] The census projects that only 39% of all newborns will live with both parents until they are 18. Growing numbers of children, many of them children of cocaine addicts, live with neither parent. And every night, 100,000 children are among the nation's homeless.[4]

To make matters worse, teenage pregnancy, higher than in any other industrial nation in the world, is increasing, bringing a new cycle of poverty-stricken and often one-parent families. Children born into such homes are themselves likely to be poor, suffer ill health, bear children early, drop out of school, and end up on welfare or in prison.

Contributing to these woes, the Reagan administration cut back many programs designed to help children, including programs to provide nutrition and health care for low-income pregnant women and their babies, vaccinations, Head Start, school breakfasts and lunches, and food stamps. But now, people are becoming concerned. As Jesse Jackson argued, "We can either fund Head Start and child care and day care on the front side of life, or welfare and jail care on the back side of life."[5] Conservatives and business people, normally against federal involvement in family life, have also decided that the problem of America's children can no longer be ignored. They realize that our society will not be able to function in the future, let alone be competitive in the international economic arena, with a generation of ill-fed, ill-educated, ill-trained young people outside the mainstream of society. A recent report of a group of major corporate executives called for drastic increases for funding early childhood programs.

Among the many needs of America's children and their families is quality day care. Over half of the women with children under 3 and almost three-quarters of women with

CONTINUED 

OUTLINE

Federal and Other Systems
- Federal Systems
- Unitary Systems
- Confederal Systems

The Political Bases of Federalism

The Constitutional Bases of Federalism
- Major Features of the System
- Interpretations of Federalism

Federalism and the Growth of Government
- Early Nationalist Period
- Pre–Civil War Period
- The Civil War to the New Deal
- The New Deal
- From the New Deal to the Great Society
- New Federalism

Contemporary Federalism
- Federal-State Relations
- Interstate Relations
- State-Local Relations

Conclusion: Is Federalism Responsive?

children from 3 to 17 work in the paid labor force. And the number of working women increases each year as economic pressures force families to work harder to stay afloat. But many parents cannot afford day care and do not have trustworthy friends and relatives to baby-sit. Some go on welfare so they can stay home with their children, others leave their children in dirty or dangerous environments, and others worry constantly about tenuous day-care arrangements. And even families that can afford day care cannot always find quality arrangements.

The child-care bill tries to increase the supply of day-care centers, increase their health and safety standards, and help families pay for them. President Bush dislikes this bill and has threatened to veto it. The bill is also opposed by conservatives in the Republican party, one of whom thundered that it would "Sovietize the American family by warehousing babies."[6] The alternative offered by two conservative legislators, and supported by many Republicans, would authorize less money for grant programs, require no standards for the quality of child care, and offer nothing for latchkey children.

How should you vote? On the one hand, you are in favor of the goals of the bill. You are a former teacher and know the problems faced by parents who cannot find adequate child care. On the other hand, you are concerned about the contents of the bill. It is costly. It sets up federal standards that you oppose. You believe such involvement will increase the size of the federal bureaucracy and cause problems for day-care providers. You are not much in favor of the federal government getting more involved in family life and encroaching on areas left to the states, and you would like to support your fellow Republicans. What do you decide?

Most Americans claim to believe that state governments are more responsive to them than the federal government, (Table 1), but over the past 60 years have asked the federal government to get involved in almost every policy issue imaginable. Many Americans decry the growth of big government, and yet few realize that over the past 25 years, the size of state governments has doubled while the federal government has grown hardly at all. Most Americans want small government, but they also want a government powerful enough to keep the peace abroad and maintain peace and prosperity at home.

These issues of the size and scope of the federal government relative to the states are not new. They are the same issues that the Founders debated at the Constitutional Convention in 1787. The issue of whether the states or the national government should have the final say in political decisions was the central conflict in the Civil War (1861-1865), which ultimately determined that the national government, not the states, was supreme.

Because of this outcome, and because of the tasks we ask government to do, we live in a nation with a strong central government. Yet we vigorously disagree about just how strong that government should be. Critics accuse the national government and its programs of being too large, too expensive, and too intrusive on the rights of the states and the people. Yet when members of Congress suggest cutting programs severely or transferring responsibilities back to the states, the public outcry is vociferous. And even though our system of powers at both the national and state levels contributes to the messiness of democracy that the public dislikes, there is little support for streamlining or centralizing powers at the national level.

These contradictions are perhaps endemic to a federal system. In this chapter we will examine the nature of American federalism and how it has changed as government has grown.

TABLE 1 The Public Trusts the States More

	STATE	FEDERAL
Which government do you trust to:		
do a better job running things	70%	27%
establish rules about who can receive welfare	70	25
set rules for workplace safety	55	42
set Medicare and Medicaid regulations	52	43
set environmental rules for clean air and clean water	51	47
protect civil rights	35	61

SOURCE: Washington Post–ABC Poll, reported in Richard Morin, "Power to the States," *Washington Post National Weekly Edition*, March 27–April 2, 1995, p. 37.

Federalism is the only domestic issue in the United States over which several million Americans fought and 500,000 died. This photograph shows the remains of Richmond, Virginia after a Civil War battle.

➤Federal and Other Systems

Federal Systems

The term **federalism** describes a system in which power is constitutionally divided between a central government and subnational or local governments (in the United States the subnational governments are the states). Both levels of government receive their grants of power from a higher authority—the will of the people as expressed in a constitution, for example. Each level can deal directly with individuals to tax, regulate, or provide benefits.

Power granted to each level is not necessarily exclusive. In fact, in the United States only one power is left solely to the states, and that is the power to determine whether they shall exist. States cannot be abolished or altered without their own consent.

Nearly 90% of all nations are unitary systems, but several large nations are federal systems—for example, Germany, Canada, India, and Brazil. Federal systems vary greatly in their basic economic and political characteristics; they are similar only in the fact that each has a written constitution allocating some powers to the national and some to the subnational governments.

Unitary Systems

In contrast to the federal system, in a **unitary system** the national government creates subnational governments and gives them what power it wishes. Thus, the national government is supreme. In Britain, for example, the national government can give or take away any power of the subnational governments or can even abolish them, as it did with some counties several years ago. And, in unitary Sweden, the national parliament abolished 90% of its local governments from 1952 to 1975.

In the United States, the 50 states are each unitary with respect to their local governments; cities, counties, and school districts can be altered or even eliminated by state governments.

The distinction between unitary and federal is not at all related to the distinction between democracy and authoritarianism. Some unitary systems are among the most democratic in the world (Britain and Sweden); others are authoritarian (Egypt and Ghana). Nor are only federal systems decentralized. All modern governments have to decentralize power because a central government, even in a unitary system, cannot run every local service or deal with every local problem.

Confederal Systems

The third arrangement between central and subnational governments is confederal. In a **confederal system** the central government has only those powers given to it by the subnational governments; it cannot act directly on citizens. Two examples of confederal systems are the United States under the Articles of Confederation and the United Nations. The lack of central authority in such systems makes them basically unworkable in modern nations.

The Political Bases of Federalism

Why do some nations choose a federal form of government while others do not? The Founders of the United States chose federalism as one means of limiting governmental power. Another reason for choosing federalism was that it could help deal with national diversity. Federal systems are often, though not always, ethnically, linguistically, religiously, or racially diverse. We in the United States are not as diverse as peoples in India, for example, but we are a nation of many ethnic groups, races, religions, and political traditions.

Our states also reflect this diversity. Despite our national media networks, franchises and chains bringing the same stores to all parts of the country, and transportation systems that carry us across the nation in only a few hours, there are still significant differences among us, and not just in whether we prefer Texas chili or New England clam chowder. In different states and regions, we have developed somewhat different political styles and attitudes. Most governors of Pennsylvania, for example, could never be elected in Idaho, and vice versa. Ways of looking at politics, partisan preferences, ideology, appropriate ways of organizing for political action, and other political features vary greatly across our nation.

Distinctive ways of looking at, and participating in, politics are called **political cultures.**[7] In the United States, three cultures predominate, each having a regional and, to some extent, ethnic base (see Figure 1).

One is the *moralistic* political culture, found in states of the upper Midwest and New England that are populated by Scandinavians or descendants of the Yankee Puritans who arrived from England. In this culture, politics is seen as a way of improving life, and people have a strong sense that they should participate. Politics is relatively free of corruption.

A second type is the *individualistic* political culture, most typical in the large band of industrial states of the Midwest and East populated by immigrant groups from Eastern and Southern Europe and from Ireland. In these states, the ultimate objective of politics is not so much to create a better public life but rather to get things for yourself and your group. The traditional machine politics of many large cities are good examples of the individualistic political culture.

In a *traditionalistic* culture, still present in some of the South, politics is left to a small elite. Politics is not seen as a way to further the public good but as a way to maintain the status quo. Louisiana politics offers an example: There it has been said that "a politician's first obligation is to entertain, his second not to get caught stealing, and his third to govern."[8]

In some areas, immigration patterns of this century have blurred cultural patterns; the West, for example, is populated by a mix of people from all three cultures.

Although these cultural patterns are regional, there are cultural differences within regions. The political corruption and shady political dealing tolerated by

FIGURE 1
Political Cultures

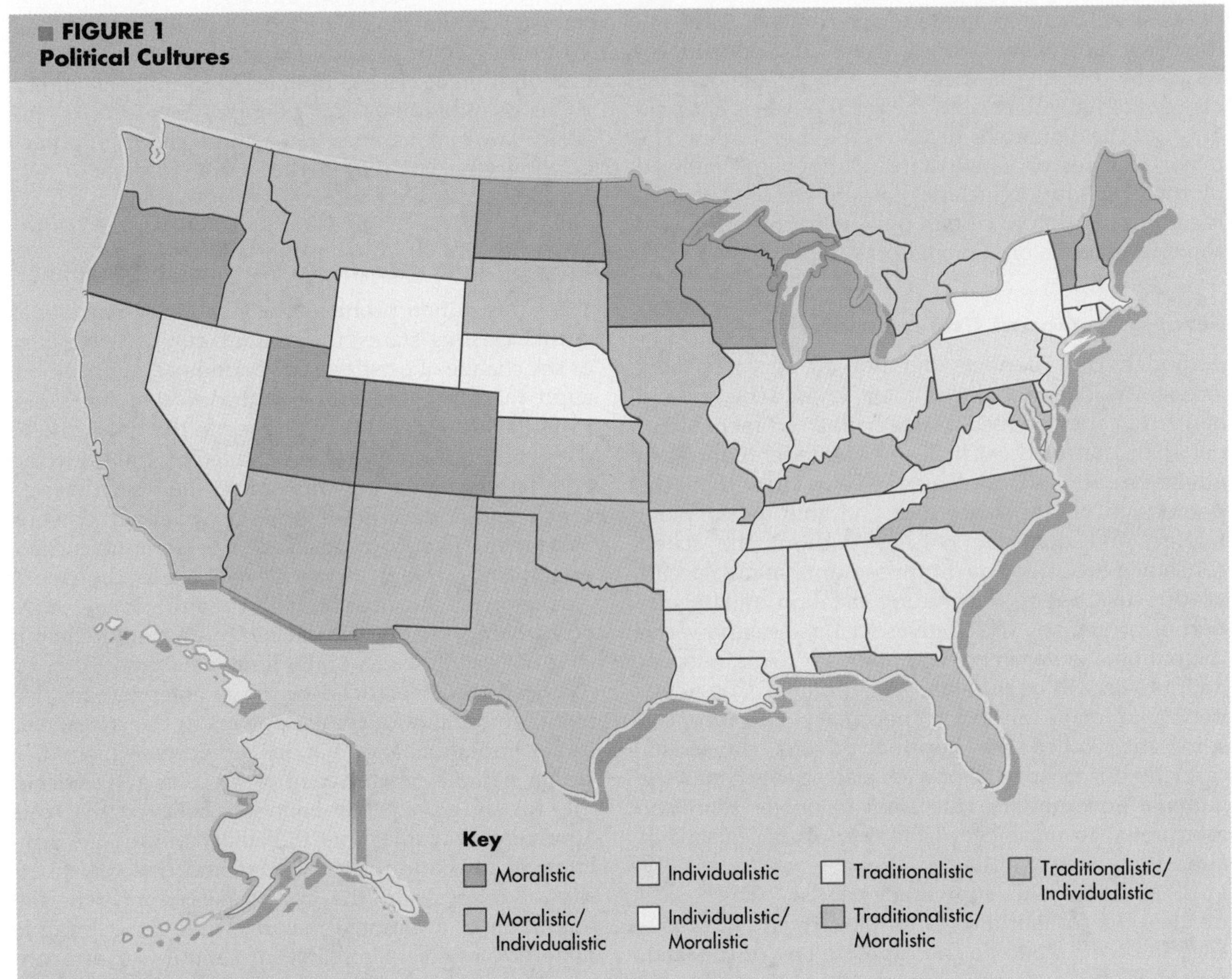

SOURCE: Daniel Elazar, *American Federalism: A View from the States*, 3rd ed. (New York: Harper & Row, 1984), p. 135.

Illinoisians would never be accepted by Minnesotans. Nevada and Utah share a common border but very different political cultures.

In addition to cultural and ethnic differences, states are diverse in their economic well-being. For example, despite the growth in the southern economy since the 1950s, residents of most southern states still lag behind the rest of the United States in income and education.

Thus, state boundaries mean something beyond identifying the government to which state taxes are paid. In policy areas as diverse as economic development, welfare, and regulation of personal morality (such as gambling and prostitution), states vary widely. Federalism, even with a strong national government, does provide some autonomy for states to adopt and maintain policies consistent with their own political cultures.

➤The Constitutional Bases of Federalism

Major Features of the System

As we saw in Chapter 2, the Founders were unsure how to solve the problem of national versus state powers. All wanted limited government. Although they saw federalism as one way to limit government power by dividing it, there was little debate over the concept of federalism, and the main outlines emerged only as the Founders dealt with other issues. The major features of nation-state relationships outlined by the Constitution include a strong national government, prohibition of certain powers to the states, and some limitations on national powers.

Strong National Government

Although the Founders did not all agree on how strong the national government should be, all did agree that they wanted a national government stronger than that of the Articles of Confederation. They wanted a national government able to tax without the permission of the states, and one able to carry out foreign and domestic policies without the states' consent. Thus, the Constitution grants many specific powers to Congress, including taxation and regulation of commerce, which gives tremendous power to the national government and allows it to be independent of the will of the state governments. Congress's power to make all laws **"necessary and proper,"** sometimes called the **implied powers clause,** for carrying out its specific powers also strengthened the national government. This grant of power soon was interpreted to mean that Congress could legislate in almost any area it wished.

In addition, the **supremacy clause,** which says treaties, the Constitution, and "laws made in pursuance thereof" are to be the supreme law of the land, contributed to a strong national government.

Although it was a compromise decision, a president independent of Congress and the state legislatures also strengthened the national government. The president's power to be commander in chief and to execute the laws of the United States further enlarged national powers.

Prohibition of Certain Powers to the States

The Constitution forbids states to undertake actions that might conflict with the power of the national government; they cannot enter into treaties, keep troops or navies, make war, print or coin money, or levy import or export taxes on goods. These prohibitions reaffirmed that the national government was to be supreme in making foreign policy and regulating interstate commerce. Under the Articles, the national government was limited in both these areas. The new Constitution also forbade states to infringe on certain rights of individuals. For example, a state could not pass a law making an action a crime and then punish citizens who committed the "crime" before it was made illegal (called an *ex post facto* law).

Some Limitations on National Powers

The Constitution prohibits the creation of new states within existing states, the combination of two states, or the change of existing state boundaries without the approval of the legislatures of the affected states.

The Tenth Amendment granted to the states and to the people those powers not granted by the Constitution to the national government. At the time, this was considered a significant limit on national powers. Since then, the broad construction of Congress's "necessary and proper" powers has made the Tenth Amendment inconsequential. Recently there have been attempts to breathe life into this amendment, but thus far they have had only limited success.[9]

These three features—a strong national government, prohibition of certain powers to the states, and some limitations on national powers—ensured a strong national government as well as a significant role for the states. The Founders believed that this arrangement would limit the ability of any one government to tyrannize its citizens and that the diversity of interests in the system would prevent the formation of a national majority that could trample minority rights. Similarly, a central government would ensure that states could protect the rights of their citizens against arbitrary local majorities. Many believed that the primary virtue of a federal system was that the authority of government was limited because it was divided between two levels.

Interpretations of Federalism

The Founders left the exact details of the nation-state relationship vague because they could not agree on specifics. It is not surprising that different views of federalism emerged.[10]

Nation-Centered Federalism

In *The Federalist Papers,* Alexander Hamilton clearly articulated the view that national power was to be supreme. This nation-centered view of federalism rests on the assumption that the Constitution is a document ratified by the people. The states have many powers, but the national government has the ultimate responsibility for preserving the nation and the viability of the states as well. Nation-centered federalism was the view held by northerners in justifying a war to prevent the southern states from seceding in 1861.

State-Centered Federalism

Another view, later used by southerners to justify their defiance of the central government before the Civil War, held that the Constitution is a product of state action. In this view, the states created the union. State-centered federalists argue that the grant of powers to Congress is limited to those items specifically mentioned in Article I. Madison said, "The powers delegated . . . to the federal government are few and defined. Those which are to remain in the state governments are numerous and indefinite."[11] In this view, any attempt by Congress to go beyond these explicitly listed powers violates state authority.

Dual Federalism

Dual federalism is the idea that the Constitution created a system in which nation and state each have separate grants of power, with each supreme in its own sphere. In this view, the two levels of government are essentially equal. Their differences derive from their different jurisdictions, not from any inequality.

Cooperative Federalism

The term **cooperative federalism** refers to the continuing cooperation among federal, state, and local officials in carrying out the business of government. The term encompasses the relationship of federal and state officials when distributing payments to farmers, providing welfare services, planning highways, organizing centers for the elderly, and carrying out all the functions that the national and state governments jointly fund and organize. It also refers to informal cooperation in locating criminals, tracking down mysterious diseases, and many other activities. A person speaking of cooperative federalism is not evaluating the legalistic relationship of national and state governments but rather referring to day-to-day joint activities.

Federalism and the "Mischiefs of Faction"

Probably the most influential work of American political theory was written by James Madison in *Federalist Paper* #10 (reprinted in the appendix to this book). This work helps explain the attraction of a federalist system for Madison and many of the other Founders.

In *Federalist* #10, Madison asserted that it is inevitable that factions—groups of citizens seeking some goal contrary to the rights of other citizens or to the well-being of the whole country—will threaten the stability of nations. To cure the "**mischiefs of faction**" Madison said government had either to remove the causes of faction or to control its effects.

Madison believed the government could never remove the causes of faction because this would require changing selfish human nature, which he thought impossible. It also would require taking away freedom by outlawing opinions and strictly regulating behavior. People would inevitably have different ideas and beliefs, and government, he thought, should not try to prevent this.

Because one could not remove the causes of faction without too greatly inhibiting freedom, Madison recommended that a properly constructed government should control its effects. If a faction were less than a majority, Madison believed it could be controlled through majority rule, the majority defeating the minority faction. However, if the faction were a majority, then a greater problem arose, but one for which Madison had an answer.

To control a majority faction, one had only to limit the ability of a majority to carry out its wishes. Madison believed this was impossible in a small democracy, where there is little check on a majority determined to do something. But in a large federalist system, there are many checks on a majority faction—more interests competing with each other and large distances to separate those who might scheme to deprive others of liberty. As Madison noted, "The influence of factious leaders may kindle a flame within their particular States, but will be unable to spread a general conflagration through the other States." Having many states and having them spread over a large territory were, in Madison's view, major checks against majority tyranny.

➤Federalism and the Growth of Government

In 200 years, our national government has grown from a few hundred people with relatively limited impact on the residents of 13 small states to a government employing millions, affecting the daily lives of most of the population of more than 260 million people. This transformation is closely related to the changing way in which Americans understand the federal system.

Over the years, the dominant interpretations of federalism have shifted among the nation-centered, state-centered, and dual views. Changing interpretations have reflected court opinions, pressing economic needs, the philosophies of those in the executive and legislative branches, and changing public demands. The most general trend has been away from state-centered and toward nation-centered federalism, but there have been significant shorter-term trends in the opposite direction. Moreover, the term cooperative federalism has come into use, since World War II, to describe everyday relations between national and state officials.

Early Nationalist Period

Very soon after the Constitution was ratified, the federal courts became the arbiters of the Constitution. (Note that we are using "federal" to mean "national," a confusing but common usage. "Federal government" normally means "national government.") John Marshall, chief justice of the United States from 1801 to 1835, was a firm nationalist, and the decisions of his court emphasized the need for a strong national government. The Marshall-led Supreme Court not only held that decisions of the state courts could be overturned by the federal courts, it also, in the case of *McCulloch v. Maryland,* gave approval to the broad interpretation of Congress's implied powers in the Constitution.

McCulloch v. Maryland

The broad interpretation of the clause giving Congress the right to make all laws "necessary and proper" to carry out the powers that the Constitution gives it, grew out of a case involving the establishment of a national bank.

Ironically, it was John Calhoun, later to become the leading states' rights advocate, who introduced a bill to charter a Bank of the United States (B.U.S.). The bill passed, and in 1817 the bank went into business, setting up branches in cities across the country. However, it was immediately unpopular because it competed with smaller banks operating under state laws and because some of its branches engaged in reckless and even fraudulent practices.

In an attempt to diminish the competition from the B.U.S., the government of Maryland levied a tax on the notes issued by the Baltimore branch of the bank. The B.U.S. refused to pay, but the Maryland state courts upheld the right of Maryland to tax the bank. The case then went to the Supreme Court.

In *McCulloch v. Maryland,* John Marshall wrote one of his most influential decisions.[12] Pronouncing the tax unconstitutional, Marshall wrote that "the power to tax involves the power to destroy." The states should not have the power to destroy the bank, he stated, because the bank was "necessary and proper" to carry out Congress's powers to collect taxes, borrow money, regulate commerce, and raise an army. Marshall argued that if the goal of the legislation is legitimate and constitutional, "all means which are appropriate, which are plainly adapted to that end, which are not prohibited, but consistent with the letter and spirit of the Constitution, are constitutional."

Thus, Marshall interpreted "necessary" quite loosely. The bank was probably not necessary, but it was "useful." This interpretation of the implied powers clause allowed Congress to wield much more authority than the Constitution gave it explicitly.

Although there was some negative reaction—"a deadly blow has been struck at the sovereignty of the states," cried one Baltimore newspaper—the Court maintained its strongly nationalistic position as long as Marshall was chief justice.

Early Growth of Government

At the same time the courts were interpreting national powers broadly, the national government was exercising its powers on a rather small scale. The federal government had only 1,000 employees in the administration of George Washington, and this number had increased to 33,000 during the presidency of James Buchanan 70 years later. It raised relatively little revenue. But state governments were also small and had limited functions. There were only a few federal-state cooperative activities. For example, the federal government gave land to the states to support education and participated in joint federal-state-private ventures, such as canal-building projects initiated by the states.

Are States Really Closer to the People?

Much of today's rhetoric suggests that many federal government programs, such as health care, welfare, education, and environmental protection, for example, should be turned over to the states because the states are "closer to the people." But what does that mean?

Those who argue that states are closer to the people point to the relative smallness of states. The United States has 257 million residents. Although 7 states have over 10 million people, and California has over 30 million, most (32) states have less than 5 million residents. Thus, it should be possible for individuals to have more say in state government than national. Moreover, states are, on the whole, more homogeneous in their cultures than the nation, and these state cultures lead to different policy preferences: Residents of traditionalistic states, on average, have different views of desirable government action than residents of individualistic or moralistic states. Thus, leaving policy-making to the states means that public policy can be more sensitive to the preferences of state communities. Being closer to the people may also mean that state governments can respond more quickly to changes in the public mood; state legislators are closer to the grassroots than national legislators. Finally, smaller government should be more efficient.

However, reality is not always as simple as a slogan. Except in a few very small states, where town meetings still prevail, it is difficult for individuals to have much say in their state government as well as their national government. States are not small entities, even if they are a lot smaller than the federal government. In fact, states have more employees than the federal government and are growing faster (see figure). Moreover, most people know a lot more about what is going on in Washington than they do about what is going on in Lincoln, Springfield, Sacramento, or Harrisburg, to name a few state capitals, and in that sense have more tools to make the federal government responsive than they do the state government. (How many talk shows or CNN clones focus on what is going on in the statehouse?) There is also evidence that being "closer to the people" also means being more susceptible to the pressures of big money, and the relative homogeneity of state populations may make it easier to steamroller the rights of small groups. Finally, there is no evidence that state governments are less corrupt or more efficient than the federal government.[1] Indeed, federal pressure has been a major influence on professionalizing of state bureaucracies.

These problems with state governments do not mean that turning some federal programs back to the states is necessarily a bad idea. The problems do suggest, though, that we need to look beyond slogans to the reality of politics, national and state.

Number of Employees in the Federal and State Governments, 1975–1991

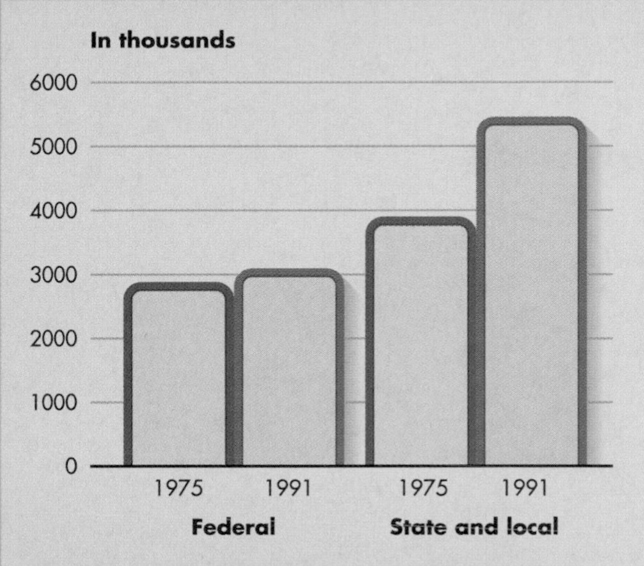

SOURCE: *Statistical Abstract of the United States, 1994,* Tables 527 and 495.

1. See for recent discussions, Richard Cohen, "States Aren't Saints Either," *Washington Post National Weekly Edition,* April 3–9, 1995, p. 28; R. W. Apple, "You Say You Want a Devolution," *New York Times,* January 29, 1995, Section 4, p. 1.

Thus, the early nationalist period was characterized by the growth of nation-centered federalism in legal doctrine, by small-scale state and national government, and by a few intergovernmental cooperative activities responding to the needs of an expanding nation.

Pre-Civil War Period

In 1836, the Court began to interpret the Tenth Amendment as a strict limitation on federal powers, holding that powers to provide for public health,

In a spirit of optimism amidst the turmoil of the Civil War, Congress in 1862 established federal support for the land grant colleges, a striking example of intergovernmental cooperation in the nineteenth century. Today many of these institutions are among our finest universities. Here, students plow on the campus of The Pennsylvania State University, one of the first land grant colleges.

safety, and order were *exclusively* powers of the state government, not of the national government. This dual federalism interpretation eroded some of the nation-centered federal interpretations of the Marshall Court while continuing to uphold the rights of the federal courts to interpret the Constitution.

At the same time, champions of the state-centered view of federalism were gaining ascendance in the South. Southern leaders feared that the federal government, dominated by the increasingly populous North, would regulate or even abolish slavery. John Calhoun, one of the leading proponents for the state-centered view, even went so far as to say that a state could nullify laws of Congress (the doctrine of nullification). According to Calhoun, a state could withdraw from the Union if it wished. When the South did secede from the Union in 1861, it called itself the Confederate States of America, emphasizing the supremacy of the states embedded in a confederal system.

After the Civil War, the vision of state-centered federalism largely lost its credibility. Some southern segregationists tried to revive the idea in the 1950s and 1960s as a protest against federal laws and actions to further the civil rights of blacks; the Alabama legislature even passed a nullification resolution in 1950. However, most people thought the idea was absurd.

The Civil War to the New Deal

After the Civil War, vast urbanization and industrialization took place throughout the United States. Living and working conditions for many city dwellers were appalling. Adults as well as children who moved into the cities often took jobs in sweatshops—factories where they worked long hours in unsafe conditions for low pay.

Spurred by revelations of these unsafe and degrading conditions, states and sometimes Congress tried to regulate working conditions, working hours, and pay through such means as child labor and industrial safety laws. Beginning in the 1880s, a conservative Supreme Court used the dual federalism doctrine to rule unconstitutional many of these attempts. It often decided that Congress and the states had overstepped their powers. From 1874 to 1937, the Supreme Court found 50 federal and 400 state laws unconstitutional.[13] Before the Civil War, in contrast, the Court overturned only 2 congressional and 60 state laws.

At the same time that the Court was limiting both state and national action in regulating business and industry, both levels of government were slowly expanding. The revenues of both grew—the United States through an income tax finally ratified in 1913, the states and localities through gasoline and cigarette taxes, higher property taxes, and some state income taxes. Federal support for state programs also grew through land and case grants given by the federal government to the states.[14] By the late 1920s, however, most governmental functions still rested primarily in state and local hands. The states were clearly the dominant partner in providing most services, from health and sanitation to police and fire protection. The federal government provided few direct services to individuals, nor did it regulate their behavior. The Great Depression signaled a dramatic shift in this arrangement.

The New Deal

To grasp the scope of the changes that have taken place in our federal structure between 1930 and today, consider the report of a sociologist who studied community life in Muncie, Indiana.[15] In 1924 the federal government in Muncie was symbolized by little more than the post office and the American flag. Today, two-thirds of the households in Muncie depend in part on federal funds—federal employment, Social Security, welfare payments, food stamps, veterans benefits, student scholarships and loans, Medicare and Medicaid, and many other smaller programs.

In large part, the Great Depression brought about these changes. During the stock market crash of 1929, wealthy people became poor overnight. In the depths of the Depression one-fourth of the work force was unemployed, and banks failed daily.

Unlike today, there was no systematic national program of relief for the unemployed then—no unemployment compensation, no food stamps, no welfare, nothing to help put food on the table and pay the rent. Millions were hungry, homeless, and hopeless. States and localities, which had the responsibility for providing relief to the poor, were overwhelmed; they did not have the funds or organizational resources to cope with the millions needing help. And private charities did not have enough resources to even begin to assume the burden.

The magnitude of the economic crisis led to the election of a Democrat, Franklin Delano Roosevelt, in 1932. He formulated, and Congress passed, a program called the **New Deal.** Its purpose was to stimulate economic recovery and aid the victims of the depression who were unemployed, hungry, and often in ill health. New Deal legislation regulated many activities of business and labor, set up a welfare system for the first time, and began a large scale federal-state cooperation in funding and administering programs through federal **grants-in-aid.** These grants-in-aid provided federal money to states (and occasionally to local governments) to set up programs to help people—for example, the aged poor or the unemployed.

These measures had strong political support, although they were opposed by many business and conservative groups and initially by the Supreme Court, which was still following the dual federalism doctrine. But after the reelection of Roosevelt in 1936, the Court became more favorable toward New Deal legislation, and later resignations of two conservative judges ensured that the Court would be sympathetic to the New Deal (see Chapter 13 for more on the Court and the New Deal.)

The Court decisions approving New Deal legislation were, in a sense, a return to the nation-centered

President Roosevelt's confidence, along with the hopes people had in his New Deal programs, led to public support for the expansion of the role of the federal government.

federalism of John Marshall's day. But although the Supreme Court ratified much of the New Deal, it also approved more sweeping *state* regulations of business and labor than had the more conservative pre-New Deal Court. Thus, the change in court philosophy did not enlarge the federal role at the expense of the powers of the state. *It enlarged the powers of both state and federal government.* In doing so, it responded to preferences on the part of taxpayers for a more active government to cope with the tragedy of the Depression. The limited government desired by the Founders became less limited as both state and national government grew.

Changes in patterns of taxing and spending soon reflected the green light given to federal involvement with the states and localities. As Figure 2 indicates, the federal share of spending for domestic needs (omitting spending for the military) nearly tripled from 17% in 1929, before the New Deal, to 47% in 1939, a decade later. The state share stayed constant while the local share dropped dramatically. Local governments did not spend less, but the state and federal governments spent more. Likewise state spending increased, but not as much as federal spending. The federal government raised more revenue and in turn gave much of it to the states and localities in the form of grants-in-aid to carry out programs such as unemployment compensation, free school lunches, emergency welfare relief, farm surpluses to the needy, and other programs.

The New Deal brought a dramatic change in the relationship of the national government to its citizens. Before this, when the national government directly touched the lives of citizens, it usually was to give or sell them something, such as land for settlers or subsidies for businesses helping develop the frontier.[16] With New Deal programs the federal government directly affected the lives of its citizens through its regulations (of banks and working conditions, for example) and its redistributive policies designed to protect the poor (such as Social Security and Aid to Dependent Children).

FIGURE 2
The New Deal Increased Federal and State Spending More Than Local

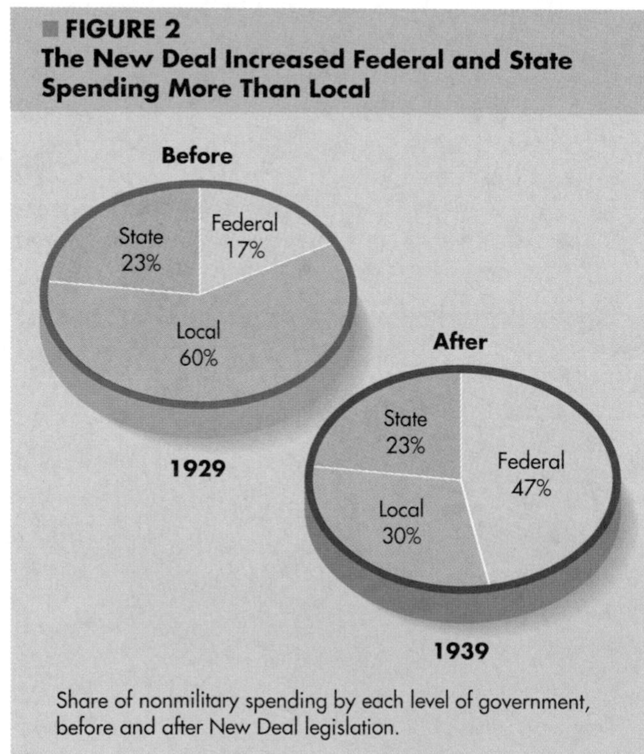

Share of nonmilitary spending by each level of government, before and after New Deal legislation.

SOURCE: "Significant Features of Fiscal Federalism," *Advisory Commission on Intergovernmental Relations* (Washington, D.C.: U.S. Government Printing Office, 1979), p. 7.

From the New Deal to the Great Society

During the years that followed the initiation of the New Deal, federal aid to states increased steadily but not dramatically. But federal support to the states carried conditions. For example, local administrators of Aid to Dependent Children programs had to be hired through a merit system, not because of political or personal connections. Construction funds for highways could be spent only on highways whose designs met professional standards. Thus, federal "strings" accompanied federal money.

The Great Depression ended with the beginning of U.S. involvement in World War II in 1941. The federal government continued to expand during the war, fueled by the growth of the military and the need to mobilize the civilian economy for war. Although the size of the military shrunk somewhat after the war, the military establishment never receded to pre-war levels (although when the Pentagon—the headquarters of the military—was being designed during the war, President Roosevelt had suggested that it should be designed to be converted to a storage facility after the war). The Cold War conflict with the Soviet Union and its allies provided a continuing stimulus for a strong national government.

By the 1950s, some public officials became uneasy about the growing size of the federal goverment and

New Deal Legislation Passed During Roosevelt's First Term

March 9, 1933	Emergency Banking Act
March 31, 1933	Civilian Conservation Corps created
May 12, 1933	Agricultural Adjustment Act
May 12, 1933	Federal Emergency Relief Act
May 18, 1933	Tennessee Valley Authority created
June 5, 1933	Nation taken off gold standard
June 13, 1933	Home Owners Loan Corporation created
June 16, 1933	Federal Deposit Insurance Corporation created
June 16, 1933	Farm Credit Administration created
June 16, 1933	National Industrial Recovery Act
January 30, 1934	Dollar devalued
June 6, 1934	Securities and Exchange Commission authorized
June 12, 1934	Reciprocal Tariff Act
June 19, 1934	Federal Communications Commission created
June 27, 1934	Railroad Retirement Act
June 28, 1934	Federal Housing Administration authorized
April 8, 1935	Works Progress Administration created
July 5, 1935	National Labor Relations Act
August 14, 1935	Social Security Act
August 26, 1935	Federal Power Commission created
August 30, 1935	National Bituminous Coal Conservation Act
February 19, 1936	Soil Conservation and Domestic Allotment Act

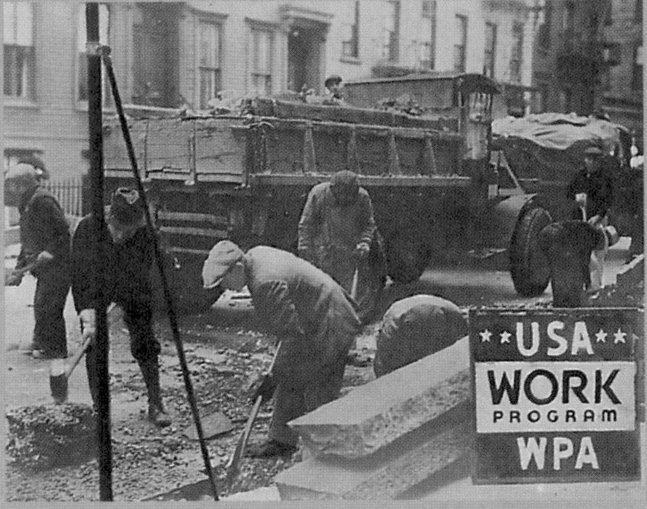

Franklin Roosevelt took office on March 4, 1933. He immediately sent to Congress a group of legislative proposals, many of which Congress passed within 100 days. Roosevelt's program, known as the New Deal, enlarged the role of the federal government. Shown in the photo are civilians employed in the Works Progress Administration (WPA), a New Deal agency that built the schools, roads, airports, and post offices in many towns in the late 1930s. Though the term "boondoggle" was coined in reference to some WPA projects, the agency was successful in putting millions to work and improving the nation's public buildings, roads, and bridges.

SOURCE: List compiled by Lee Epstein and Thomas Walker, *Constitutional Law for a Changing America: Institutional Powers and Constraints* (Washington, DC: CQ Press, 1992), p. 283.

its involvement in so many state and local programs. Yet under President Eisenhower, a Republican concerned about the growth of federal involvement, many new federal grants-in-aid to the states were added, ranging from the massively expensive interstate highway program to collegiate programs in science, engineering, and languages. Federal grants-in-aid spending nearly tripled during his administration (1952-1960).

The 1960s witnessed an explosion in federal programs. Mostly a consequence of President Lyndon Johnson's Great Society, new programs of federal aid mushroomed both in number and in cost. Federal support for state and local activities extended to

New Populism

A New Western Saga: Cowboys versus the Government?

Midwestern and prairie farmers battled big railroads, big business, and big government in the first populist movement of the late nineteenth century. Today, some populist themes are echoed in the battle by western farmers and ranchers against big government.

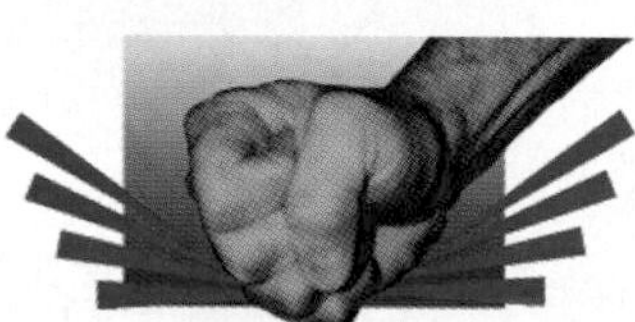

Several key issues have recently inflamed simmering controversies. Many westerners are angry that the federal government controls huge amounts of land in most western states. In most nonwestern states, the government owns less than 5 percent of land; in several western states (Alaska, Idaho, Oregon, Utah), the government owns over 50 percent.[1] In Nevada, it owns 87 percent. The federal government owns this land in part to protect natural resources considered valuable for the entire country (lumber, minerals, and places of great scenic beauty such as the Grand Tetons and the Grand Canyon). As the landowner, the federal government, through the Bureau of Land Management (BLM) and the Forest Service, places restrictions on how the land can be used. It limits the number of cattle that can graze the land, how much timber can be cut from forested lands, and, in some areas, what kind of vehicles can drive on the land. It places other restrictions on land use in order to protect endangered species. Although the government tries to balance the interests of farmers and ranchers with environmental concerns, any regulation creates angry protests. As one irate state legislator noted, "The federal government has a stranglehold on the rural West."[2]

The antagonism of many westerners to the federal regulations is growing. Although the BLM has canceled grazing permits of some ranchers, defiance is common. And, as one BLM official notes, "We can't protect the resource because we are afraid our employees will be shot."[3] Another claims that "Folks are taking the law into their own hands. We're going to have anarchy and chaos in eastern Nevada."[4]

At the same time, of course, the federal government provides farmers and ranchers with grazing rights, water rights, and mining subsidies far below market costs. When the Clinton administration tried to increase the price to farmers and ranchers for these goods, that too raised a storm of protest.[5] Thus, some farmers and ranchers who want to be free of federal regulations are nonetheless willing to accept federal handouts.

Land is not the only issue igniting controversy. Gun restrictions and even the income tax are sparking opposition. In some western states, protesters have turned to violence. Most, however, are trying to fight the federal government by organizing groups to push local land control, to elect representatives sympathetic with western interests, and to use the courts to fight the federal government.

These developments are hardly new to American history. The West may have been "won" by hardy pioneers seeking to escape the confines of the cities, but government financed much of its exploration and settlement. Thus, the conflict between the wish for freedom from government and the desire for aid from it has strong roots in western history.

1. *Statistical Abstract of the United States, 1994* (Washington, D.C.: U.S. Government Printing Office, 1994), Table 354.
2. Christopher John Farley, "The West Is Wild Again," *Time* (March 20, 1995), p. 46.
3. Tom Kenworthy, "Dueling with the Forest Service," *Washington Post National Weekly Edition,* February 27–March 5, 1995, p. 31.
4. Ibid.
5. Farley, "The West Is Wild Again," p. 46.

almost every area imaginable, including former state and local preserves such as local law enforcement, urban mass transit, and public education.

A new feature of the Great Society era was an increasing number of grants going directly to localities. Because they believed the state legislatures were unresponsive to their interests, urban and other local governments now demanded, and got, direct federal support that bypassed states.

The vast increase in programs and the multiplying requirements and conditions of the grants made federal aid ever more complex. State and local officials felt hamstrung by the increasingly burdensome regulations.

New Federalism

The continuing expansion of the federal government during the 1950s and its explosive growth in the

1960s led to a reaction in the 1970s. Alarmed at the growth of the national government, elected officials of both parties called for reevaluation of the scope of federal activity. Republican leaders were especially vocal in their belief that the national government was becoming too large and that many federal activities could be better handled by the states.

Both President Nixon (1968–1974) and President Reagan (1980–1988) advocated a **new federalism.** Their definitions were quite different.

President Nixon proposed two important innovations: **general revenue sharing** and **block grants.** General revenue sharing funded every state and city (and a few other types of local government) according to a specified formula. These governments could spend the money as they saw fit, subject to only a few conditions (for example, the money could not be used to support activities that discriminated on the basis of race, age, or sex). Block grants, another innovation, were given for a special purpose, such as to promote community development. They were a compromise between the nearly total discretion given to states and localities under revenue sharing and the rigidities of the earlier grants. Block grants enabled Congress and the president to set priorities for spending while giving states and localities flexibility in determining exactly how to spend the money.

Though Jimmy Carter began to decrease federal spending on grants to states and localities, it was Ronald Reagan who made curbing the growth of the federal government a main theme of his administration. Using a dual federalist rhetoric, Reagan articulated a vision of a smaller federal government and more powerful states.[17] He suggested that he would propose radical changes in the relationships between the federal government and the states. But in fact he did little of that. Though he persuaded Congress to drop a few grants, consolidate other grants, and eliminate general revenue sharing, Reagan's major impact on nation-state relationships was through his budget priorities. By massively increasing military spending and running huge deficits requiring ever larger interest payments, the amount of money available for domestic spending shrank. Money spent on federal grants-in-aid declined substantially relative to overall spending during the 1980s.

Thus, whereas the centerpiece of Nixon's "new federalism" was to provide *more* unrestricted or minimally restricted federal funds to states and localities, Reagan's "new federalism" was directed toward dramatically *reducing* federal support to the states. State and localities were told to support new programs with their own resources.

Despite Republican control of the White House throughout most of the 1970s and 1980s, the federal government continued to grow. State activity also increased. Many states modernized and expanded their tax systems and were then able to take advantage of the economic boom in the 1980s. With these resources, the states enacted hundreds of new programs in many areas, especially education, child care and child protection, and economic development. Moreover, as the federal government has backed away from increased regulations, state regulation increased in areas as diverse as the insurance industry, environmental protection, and consumer affairs.

Today, however, cuts in federal aid to states mean cuts in state support for services such as education, housing, and Medicaid. In the 1980s and 1990s, cuts in that aid are reflected in increasing homelessness and hunger, program cuts and higher tuition in public universities, and the growing number of people without adequate medical care or medical insurance.

➤Contemporary Federalism

Today's federalism is a mixture of cooperation and conflict. One expert calls it "competitive federalism," because states and the federal government are competing for leadership of the nation's domestic policy.[18] In this section, we will review some of the major features of today's federalism, and then return to some of the areas of conflict and contention that are the subject of current debate.

Federal-State Relations

Cooperation

Much federal-state activity is cooperative. Given the large number of governments in the United States, it is essential that they cooperate. And they do. States and the federal government work together in a myriad of activities in almost every area of policy. One example of informal but intensive cooperation is the National Disease Control Center, which helps state and local governments with health emergencies. National and state police and other crime-fighting agencies share data on crimes and criminals. Another area of cooperation is joint regulatory activity. The federal government and the states jointly regulate some businesses and industry. The federal government sets standards, and each state decides whether to enforce the standard itself or let the federal government do it. Joint activity is found in several areas, including occupational safety and environmental regulation.

Another important area of federal-state cooperation is federal grants to states. The federal government gives funds to states to cope with problems that do not stop at state borders. Federal grant-in-aid programs represent a compromise between those who want a nationally administered program and those who want to keep a program at the state or local level. Unemployment compensation, administered by the states under federal regulation and funding, is a good example. Moreover, despite some examples of inefficiency, major federal programs have succeeded in helping state and local governments meet real needs and, along the way, they have increased the professionalism of state and local bureaucrats.

Federal programs often serve the interests of state and local officials, who would rather have programs paid for by federal taxes than state and local taxes. And the system greatly benefits many different kinds of interest groups that demand national action when they are spurned by the states. Groups of all ideological stripes pragmatically seek federal aid. For example, both conservatives and liberals supported a federal grant program helping states collect child support money from nonpaying divorced or unmarried fathers.

States and Localities as Lobbyists

A crucial part of the relationship of the states to the federal government concerns lobbying. The importance of federal money to states and localities and the need for coordination between federal and state bureaucracies have stimulated the organization of groups of state and local officials, such as the National Conference of State Legislatures, the National League of Cities, and the American Public Welfare Association. These groups lobby for favorable legislation for states and localities and work with federal agencies to ensure that new regulations are implemented in a way acceptable to the states. Most of these organizations have multimillion-dollar budgets and employ a sizable staff of lobbyists and researchers. Many individual states and cities have their own Washington lobbyists, and these lobbyists appear to have some positive effect on increasing federal aid.[19]

Conflict

Current federal-state relations are also characterized by conflict. One of the sharpest clashes concerns the so-called **unfunded mandates.** These are federal laws requiring states to do something, usually to regulate. Often the federal government transfers money to the states to cover part of the cost of the activity, but not always. For example, the federal government requires the states to deduct child support from the wages of parents who fall behind on payments. The state is also to deduct payments automatically from paychecks of fathers of children whose mothers are on welfare.[20] States that fail to carry out these mandates risk losing the federal contributions to their welfare funds.

Environmental regulations are, overall, the most expensive federal mandates. Meeting federal standards for clean air and water is projected to cost billions. Other recent federal regulations include a mandate that states and localities provide for the education of illegal immigrants and one that requires,

TABLE 2 Number of Government Units in the United States

Part of the reason that intergovernmental relations in the United States are so complex is that there are so many governments. Though the number of school districts has decreased dramatically in the last forty years, and the number of townships has declined slowly, the number of "special districts"–created for a single purpose, such as parks, airports, or flood control management–continues to grow.

	STATES	COUNTIES	MUNICIPALITIES	TOWNSHIPS AND TOWNS	SCHOOL DISTRICTS	SPECIAL DISTRICTS
1942	48	3,050	16,220	18,919	108,579	8,299
1992	50	3,043	19,296	16,666	14,556	33,131

SOURCE: *Statistical Abstract of the United States*, 1993 (Washington, D.C.: U.S. Government Printing Office, 1993), Table 468.

■ **FIGURE 3**
What Does the Federal Government Give the States Money to Do?

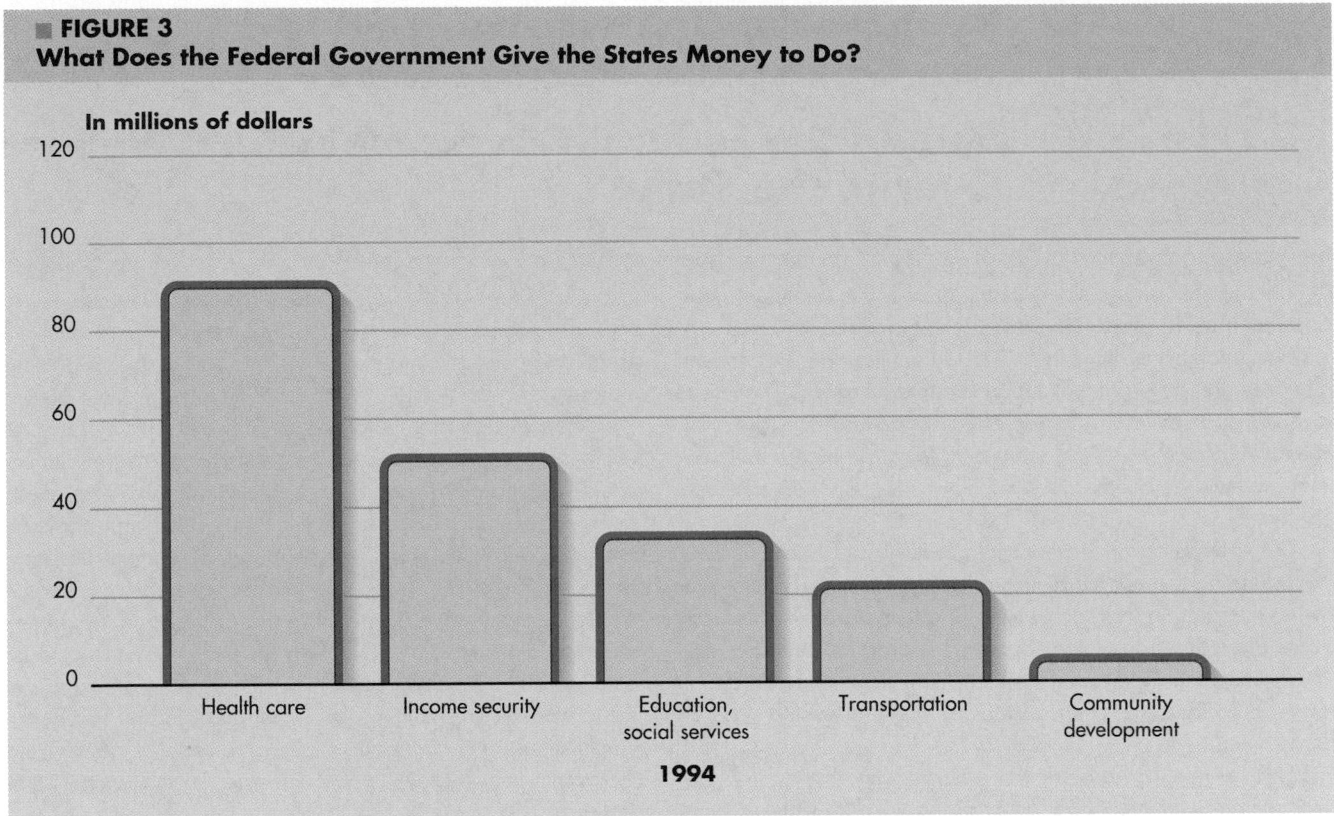

SOURCE: *Statistical Abstract of the United States,* Washington, D.C.: U.S. Government Printing office, 1994, Table 468.

among other things, public buildings, sidewalks, and transportation to be accessible to the handicapped.

The burdens of these and other mandates led to a plank in the Republicans' 1994 "Contract with America" calling for legislation to reduce such mandates. Some conservatives would like to abolish unfunded mandates completely. Others believe that unfunded mandates are sometimes beneficial, but that their costs should be made more public at the time legislation is passed. Still others believe the attack on unfunded mandates is really an attack on all regulatory action by the federal government. This group believes that expecting states to enact significant regulations in some areas is impracticable.

Another area of conflict is more basic. Some favor a radical shift in federal-state responsibilities, with a return to some form of dual federalism. States would handle many more programs than they do now, and the federal government would shrink in size, scope, and cost.

Proponents of this view do not all have the same assumptions. Some believe that government has a role to play in solving societal problems, and the states are capable of handling that role. Others believe that government has no role, and that turning programs over to the states will kill them.

Even though most people agree there are some areas that the federal government should leave to the states, the problem is there is little consensus on what those areas are. For example, some argue that the federal government should leave health care to the states but centralize welfare programs at the federal level. Others believe exactly the opposite.

■ Interstate Relations

Constitutional Requirements

The Constitution established rules governing states' relationships with each other. One important provision is the **full faith and credit clause,** which requires states to recognize contracts. If you marry in Ohio, Pennsylvania must recognize your marriage. The Constitution also provides that if a fugitive from

Symbolic Solutions for Complex Problems?

Should the Federal Government Turn Welfare Over to the States?

Americans are angry at government, and one of the favorite specific objects of public wrath is the welfare program. A particular object of hostility is Aid to Families with Dependent Children, the program that supports a total of almost 14 million people: poor children, their mothers, and sometimes their fathers.[1] Although most Americans believe government should do more to help the poor, most also believe we spend too much for welfare.[2]

The AFDC program is now a joint federal and state program. Most funding is provided by the federal government, which also writes the rules under which welfare is administered. States have some discretion in how they operate the program, but are very much limited by the federal rules. Many state leaders believe they could run the programs better than does the federal government.

One of the current popular reform ideas is to give the responsibility for the AFDC program back to the states. Given the political climate, it is not surprising that many members of Congress, along with state officials, believe that welfare could be given to the states to administer.

Welfare reform, long demanded by politicians of both parties, was a plank in the Republicans' "Contract with America," and was incorporated in the Republicans' welfare reform bill introduced early in the 1995 congressional session. (In Chapter 16, we will discuss more specifics about welfare and other reform proposals.) One of its key provisions was to consolidate federal support for AFDC and many other antipoverty programs (such as food stamps and food aid to women, infants, and children) into block grants to be paid to the states. The states, in turn, could decide how much money they wanted to spend, declare eligibility standards for those who receive the money, and set priorities among different programs. Different states, then, could have different standards and programs. The federal government could withdraw from these programs.

But is turning welfare over to the states a real solution or only symbolic? The answer to that question, in turn, depends on the definition of the problem the proposal is designed to solve.

Some believe that the problem with welfare is that it is too expensive. Turning the program over to the states would not, in itself, reduce the costs of welfare. Congress could cut the welfare budget whether or not the program is turned over to the states. In fact, many governors are reluctant to support a block grant approach to welfare unless Congress declared that states would get a fixed level of funding for each recipient. They are fearful that, if block grants are adopted, the federal government will shrink the amount of funds it puts into this program, leaving states holding the bag.

Others believe that the problem with welfare is that it is not responsive to local needs and conditions. States, in theory, could respond more quickly and efficiently to evolving needs. Some states might discover they did not need one particular program, but would need more support for another program. Being smaller, states should be able to run programs with less red tape. Many governors believe that if they had the money, they would know what to do with the welfare system. On the other hand, larger states have the same diversity of interests as the nation as a whole—huge urban areas and small rural communities, rich and poor, black and white. It is likely that the same controversies would emerge in the states as in Congress.

Still others believe that the problem with the welfare program is that it is too complex, with too many regulations and too many overlapping programs for the poor. At first blush, the block grant solution seems a real solution to complexity. States could get federal funds without conditions. Said one state representative, "Send us the unfettered authority. We'll do it. That's our job."[3] If that happened, the federal government would leave it to individual states to decide who is eligible for aid. Yet some of those most committed to the idea of letting the states run the welfare system also favor limiting access to welfare by, for example, noncitizens and teenagers who have babies. If the federal government attaches strings to its aid, prohibiting states from denying aid to these or other groups, we might soon see a system little different from today's, with the states having to follow hundreds of federal regulations. Many Republicans, as well as Democrats, are reluctant, however, to turn the administration of the program entirely over to the states.

Indeed a system of block grants might even increase complexity in the system. Individuals might be eligible for welfare assistance in one state and not another (under the existing system, there is a uniform standard of eligibility, though monthly payments vary greatly from one state to another). States differ in their capacity to raise money, too, and the poorest states have less capacity and more demand. The current system tries to remedy this by giving larger amounts of assistance to poorer states.

Source: Oliphant © 1995 Universal Press Syndicate.

Still others say that the problem with welfare is that it encourages immorality by offering cash benefits for having babies whether or not a person is able to care for and support children. There is little evidence that individuals do have children just because of welfare, but even if it were true, turning the system over to the states without other changes in the system is not likely to change the incentive structures. Incentives for having babies, for holding jobs, for living in a two-parent household could be changed whether or not the system is run by the federal government or by the states. The problem is that there is no agreement on just how the incentives *should* be changed.

The solution of turning welfare over to the states seems to be mostly symbolic if it is targeted to the problems of cost, incentives, or simplicity. It might be a partial real solution to the problems of allowing different communities and regions to deal with welfare in different ways. It seems unlikely, though, that such a solution will really get at the basic dilemmas at the heart of the system: we want to be generous to the children, but not so generous that it encourages their parents to stay on welfare. And, we would like to help the adults on welfare make something of themselves so they can hold jobs, but we do not want to spend money on job training, health benefits, and child care that would enable more of them to have a reasonable chance of doing this. Balancing these disparate objectives is difficult whether the program is run by the federal government or the states.

1. *Statistical Abstract of the United States, 1994* (Washington, DC: U.S. Government Printing Office, 1994), Table 577.
2. Richard Morin, "What the Public Really Wants," *Washington Post National Weekly Edition*, January 9–15, 1995, p. 37; Jeffrey L. Katz with Alissa Rubin and Peter MacPherson, "Major Aspects of Welfare Bill Approved by Subcommittee," *CQ* (February 18, 1995), p. 525.
3. Rochelle L. Stanfield, "The New Federalism," *National Journal* (January 28, 1995), p. 229.

justice flees from one state to another, he or she is supposed to be extradited, that is, sent back to the state with jurisdiction.

Voluntary Cooperation

Most state-to-state interaction is informal and voluntary, with state officials consulting with officials in other states about common problems and states borrowing ideas from one another. Sometimes states enter into formal agreements, called interstate compacts, to deal with a common problem—operating a port or allocating water from a river basin, for example.

Interstate Competition

Changing economic patterns and an overall loss of economic competitiveness by the United States in the world market have stimulated vigorous competition among the states to attract new businesses and jobs. They advertise the advantages of their states to prospective new businesses: low taxes, good climate, a skilled workforce, low wages, and little government regulation. This growing competition prompts states to give tax advantages and other financial incentives to businesses willing to relocate there.

Critics believe that these offers serve mostly to erode a state's tax base and have little impact on most business relocation decisions. Evidence indicates that low taxes are not the primary reason for business relocation.[21] Nevertheless, without some special break for business, states now feel at a competitive disadvantage in recruiting them. Business interests pressure states to adopt legislation more favorable to business.

Who, Me? Students as Recipients of Federal Aid

All college students are direct or indirect recipients of federal grant dollars. Your college or university was probably built in part by federal funds, some of your faculty were supported by federal funds during their training, and the federal government helps hundreds of thousands of college students each year through grants and low-interest loans. If you are less than 60 years old, it is likely that part of your elementary or secondary education (including your school lunches) also was paid for by federal money, even if you went to a private school.

If you live in a city with a municipal bus or subway system, your bus fare is lowered by as much as half because it is partially supported by federal dollars. Even if you do not ride a bus or subway, the federal government has paid for part of your transportation—whatever it is—by contributing to the funding of many streets and roads. If you drive to another city during your school holidays, you drive over highways for which Uncle Sam has paid up to 90% of the cost. If you fly, you fly into airports that are partially paid for by the federal government.

If you or your parents have been unemployed, your unemployment compensation is paid in part by the federal government through a grant program. If one of your parents died while you were a youngster, you probably received Social Security benefits, and if you have lived in poverty, you may have received AFDC (Aid to Families with Dependent Children).

If you feel that you have been affected by none of these grants, here is a final example. If you have a flush toilet, it is probably connected to a sewer paid for by, you guessed it, Uncle Sam, who has spent hundreds of millions in grants to local communities for sewer construction.

State-Local Relations

Another important feature of contemporary federalism is the relationship of states to their localities—counties, cities, and special districts. These relationships are defined by state constitutions; they are not dealt with in the federal constitution. States differ in the autonomy they grant to their localities. In some states, **home rule** charters give local governments considerable autonomy in such matters as setting tax rates, regulating land use, and choosing their form of local government. In many states, cities of different sizes have different degrees of autonomy. Although localities are creatures of their states, whereas states exist independently of the national government, some of the same problems that affect national-state relations also affect state-local relations. City and county officials often wish for more authority and fewer mandates from the state.

A little-known example of federal-state-local cooperation is firefighting in wilderness areas. In 1988, more than 15,000 firefighters converged to fight summer fires in Yellowstone and surrounding areas. Led by members of the U.S. Forest Service and other federal agencies, the firefighters were sent by state and local governments of every state.

Conclusion: Is Federalism Responsive?

Across the United States, our beliefs in democracy, freedom, and equality bind us together. In many ways we are becoming more alike, as rapid transportation, television and other forms of instant communication, fast-food franchises, hotel chains, and other nationwide businesses bring about an increasing similarity in what we think about, our tastes in culture and food, and even political activities. But to say that Alabama is more like New York than it used to be is certainly not to say they are alike. Our federal system helps us accommodate this diversity by allowing both state and federal governments a role in making policy.

Our Founders probably did not foresee a federal system like the one we have now; the federal government has surpassed the states in power and scope of action. Yet one of the paradoxes of our system is that as the national government has gained extraordinary power, so have the states and localities. All levels of government are stronger than in the eighteenth century. Federal power *and* state power have grown hand in hand.

It is probably foolish to pretend to know how the Founders might deal with our complex federal system. However, many of them were quite astute politicians who would undoubtedly recognize that our system evolved because various groups over time demanded national action. Yet we continue to believe in local control and grassroots government. Our system is a logical outcome of our contradictory impulses for national solutions and local control.

Is such a complex system responsive? It is very responsive in that groups and individuals making a demand that is rejected at one level of government can go to another level. The federal system creates multiple points of access, each with power to satisfy political demands. Yet the system is less responsive in that the same multiple levels and points of access also block demands. Civil rights groups, for example, were able to win voting rights for blacks in most states before the 1960s. But they were still blocked in several states until the national government acted. Thus federalism creates opportunities for influence, but it also creates possibilities for roadblocks to achieving national political action. This, of course, is what Madison foresaw.

Does this complex federal system contribute toward the anger many Americans feel toward their government? Although hard evidence is not available, it certainly seems that the multiple points of access, and the ability to stop action at many levels, contributes to Americans' sense that their government is out of the control of the people.

Source: Jack Ohman. Tribune Media Services

EPILOGUE

Ros-Lehtinen Supported the Bill

Representative Ros-Lehtinen was one of only 47 Republicans who supported the child-care bill (119 voted no). But most Democrats supported it, so it passed 265-145. Later in 1990, the Senate and House agreed on a version of the bill, which was signed by President Bush. The bill became the first significant child-care legislation in 19 years.

Those who might otherwise resist the expansion of federal power into the area of child care and family life voted for this bill because they believe that

America's children need help. It is probably not coincidental that, though a large majority of Republicans voted against the bill, a large majority of Republican *women* voted for it.

Although the funds spent in this bill are not large by federal budget standards, the decision to fund the program in a time of budgetary scarcity illustrates why and how federal programs have grown over the years. Conservatives as well as liberals often see the federal government as the appropriate agent to carry out what they believe are worthy policies. Resistance to a bigger federal government takes second place to a desired policy objective. In this light, big government is bad only when it wants to do something you do not want it to do.

Key Terms

federalism
unitary system
confederal system
political culture
"necessary and proper"
implied powers clause
supremacy clause
dual federalism
cooperative federalism
"mischiefs of faction"
McCulloch v. Maryland
New Deal
grants-in-aid
new federalism
general revenue sharing
block grants
unfunded mandates
home rule
full faith and credit clause

Further Reading

Daniel Elazar, *American Federalism: A View from the States,* 3rd ed. (New York: Harper & Row, 1984). *Explores the development of intergovernmental relations and examines American political cultures.*

Paul Peterson, Barry Rabe, and Kenneth Wong, *When Federalism Works* (Washington, D.C.: Brookings Institute, 1986). *Challenges prevailing wisdom to argue that most federal grant programs work.*

Jeffrey Pressman and Aaron Wildavsky, *Implementation* (Berkeley, Calif.: University of California Press, 1973). *The difficulties of translating federal laws into working programs when dealing with a multiplicity of state and local governments.*

Alice Rivlin, *Reviving the American Dream: The Economy, the States, and the Federal Government* (Washington, D.C.: Brookings Institute, 1992). *An analysis of the fiscal relations between the federal government and the states by Clinton's budget director.*

David Walker, *The Rebirth of Federalism* (Chatham, N.J.: Chatham House, 1995). *A recent look at contemporary trends.*

John Steinbeck, *The Grapes of Wrath* (New York: Viking, 1939). *A novel portraying the conditions facing the country that set the stage for the New Deal.*

Notes

1. Grant Ujifusa and Michael Barone, "Almanac of American Politics 1990," Washington, D.C.: *National Journal,* 1991, pp. 288-90.

2. *Congressional Quarterly Weekly Report,* July 2, 1988, p. 1834.

3. Spencer Rich, "More Kids Live in One-Parent Household," *Washington Post National Weekly Edition,* March 20-26, 1989, pp. 2934-39.

4. See Julie Kosterlitz, "Not Just Kid Stuff," *National Journal,* November 19, 1988, pp. 2934-29; Calvin Tomkins, "A Sense of Urgency," *New Yorker,* March 27, 1989, pp. 48-74; Ellen Goodman, "Tough Look at Spending on Children," *Lincoln Star,* March 21, 1989, p. 8.

5. "The Emerging Child Care Issue," *Time,* May 16, 1988, p. 42.

6. Antifeminist Phyllis Schlafly, quoted in "The Emerging Child Care Issue."

7. Daniel Elazar, *American Federalism: A View from the States,* 3rd ed. (New York: Harper & Row, 1984).

8. Paul Taylor, "End of the Louisiana Hayride," *Washington Post National Weekly Edition,* March 18, 1985, p. 13.

9. A 1976 Supreme Court decision used the Tenth Amendment as a reason to forbid the federal government to extend minimum wage and hour laws to state and local government employees. See *National League of Cities v. Usery,* 426 U.S. 833 (1976). This decision was partially overruled in 1985. See *Garcia v. San Antonio Metropolitan Transit Authority,* 83 L.Ed. 2d 1016 (1985).

10. The following discussion is drawn from Richard Leach, *American Federalism* (New York: W. W. Norton, 1970), chapter 1. See also Christopher Hamilton and Donald Wells, *Federalism, Power and Political Economy: A New Theory of Federalism's Impact on American Life* (Englewood Cliffs, N.J.: Prentice Hall, 1990).

11. James Madison, Alexander Hamilton, and John Jay, *The Federalist Papers,* # 45. Several editions.

12. *McCulloch v. Maryland,* 4 Wheat. 316 (1819).

13. Alfred Kelly and Winfred Harbeson, *The American Constitution: Its Origins and Development* (New York: W. W. Norton, 1976).

14. Daniel Elazar, *The American Partnership* (Chicago: University of Chicago Press, 1962).

15. Perhaps because he is a sociologist (!), Theodore Caplan did not fully appreciate the extent of federal involvement in Muncie, even in 1924—the support of veterans, schools, roads, and hospitals by federal land grants. Nevertheless, his major point is valid: The federal presence there was nothing compared to now. Caplan is quoted in Daniel Walker, *Toward a Functioning Federalism* (Cambridge, Mass.: Winthrop, 1981), pp. 3-4.

16. Theodore Lowi, *The Personal President* (Ithaca, N.Y.: Cornell University Press, 1985).

17. Paul Peterson, Barry Rabe, and Kenneth Wong, *When Federalism Works* (Washington, D.C.: Brookings Institute, 1986). See also John Schwartz, *America's Hidden Success,* 2nd ed. (New York: W. W. Norton, 1988); David Walker, *The Rebirth of Federalism: Slouching toward Washington* (Chatham, N.J.: Chatham House, 1995).

18. Alice Rivlin, *Reviving the American Dream: The Economy, the States and the Federal Government* (Washington, D.C.: Brookings Institute).

19. Neil Berch, "Why Do Some States Play the Federal Aid Game Better than Others?" *American Politics Quarterly,* 20 (July, 1992) pp. 366-377.

20. See Mary Ann Glendon, *Abortion and Divorce in Western Law* (Cambridge, Mass.: Harvard University Press, 1987), pp. 87-88; see also Susan Welch, Sue Thomas, and Margery Ambrosius, "Family Policy," in Virginia Gray and Herbert Jacob, *State Politics and Policy,* 5th ed. (Boston: Little, Brown, 1995).

21. Enid F. Beaumont and Harold Hovey, "State, Local and Federal Development Policies: New Federalism Patterns, Chaos, or What?" *Public Administration Review* 45 (March/April 1985), pp. 327-32; Barry Rubin and C. Kurt Zorn, "Sensible State and Local Development," *Public Administration Review* 45 (March/April 1985), pp. 333-39.

PART TWO

Links Between People and Government

Journalists fill the Los Angeles Coliseum for the 1984 Olympics (top). Teddy Roosevelt called the presidency a "bully pulpit" at which he could speak, through the press, to the people to persuade them to support his programs (below).

4 Public Opinion

that fail to consider the specifics of each case often result in jail terms when a less severe penalty would save the taxpayers money and open prison space for more violent criminals. Imprisonment for minor crimes like drug possession often leads to more violent crimes once a person is released.

Moreover, even the most violent criminals usually do not continue their violent behavior as they get older. Thus, the "three strikes" law would require the government to pay hundreds of thousands of dollars to confine inmates well beyond the years when they are likely to commit crimes. Finally, crime is largely a matter handled by state and local governments. Most criminals have violated state laws and are punished by the states. It is unlikely that a federal "three strikes" law will have a significant impact on crime.

Weighing these factors, do you support "three strikes and you're out," and win favor with the public as well as undermine the Republicans on the issue? Or do you try to educate the public by informing them of the costs and limitations of building more prisons and putting more and more people behind bars? Or perhaps you do nothing, and hope that when the media turn their attention to another issue, the concern with crime will diminish.[3]

Our feelings about public opinion are contradictory. On the one hand, in a democracy we want leaders to be responsive to public opinion. Yet often we complain that our elected officials do not lead but simply follow the latest trends in public opinion polls. And these public opinion polls are contradictory, too. Many Americans are angry with government. They do not trust it; they think it is too big and spends too much money. At the same time, they like the services government provides them, and very few Americans are willing to cut spending so drastically as to eliminate their favorite service or program.

In this chapter we will explore public opinion to better understand these contradictions. We will describe how public opinion is formed and measured and discuss the pattern of public opinion on some important issues. For example, are Americans really as angry and mistrustful as the media portray? Finally, we will assess the extent to which government is responsive to public opinion. Because political science is primarily interested in opinions that affect government, the focus of this chapter is public opinion about political issues, personalities, institutions, and events.

➤Nature of Public Opinion

We can define **public opinion** as the collection of individual opinions toward issues or objects of general interest, that is, those that concern a significant number of people. Public opinion can be described in terms of direction, intensity, and stability. Direction refers to whether public opinion is positive or negative. Generally it is mixed: Some individuals have a positive opinion, others negative. Intensity refers to the strength of opinion. Intense opinions are more likely to be the basis for behavior. Gun enthusiasts strongly opposed to gun control are likely to act on their opinions and vote against members of Congress who support gun registration.

Most public issues are not of interest to most people. Individuals may feel intensely about one or two issues that directly affect them, but not everyone, or even a majority, is intense about the same issues. The relative absence of severe economic and social divisions in the United States explains the lack of intense opinions. With the possible exception of the racial and states' rights issues that almost destroyed the nation in the 1860s, there has been nothing like the long-standing, divisive class and religious conflicts of many European nations.

Opinions also differ in stability. An opinion is more likely to change when an individual lacks intensity or information about an issue. The opinions of citizens toward the country are more stable than their opinions of presidential candidates. For example, polls following the party nominating conventions in 1992 showed Bill Clinton's margins over George Bush seesawing back and forth from day to day (Figure 1). At this stage of the campaign, many voters were undecided. Some opposed Bush but did not know enough about Clinton to support him firmly. They would see something on television or read something in the press favorable to Clinton and report a preference for him, and then see something unfavorable and shift to Bush.[4]

You Are There

The President Considers the Nation's Rising Concern over Crime

It is January 1994 and you are President Clinton, about to speak to the nation in your annual State of the Union address. The speech will identify the issues you want Congress to consider in the coming year, and help mobilize the public behind your program. You need something to demonstrate to the American people that you are not out of step with moderate middle America but a "new kind of Democrat" who is sympathetic to the needs and wants of average citizens. A tough anticrime bill might be such a policy.

Republicans have called you another "tax and spend Democrat." In your first year in office you pushed through an economic plan that boosted taxes on the wealthy but also increased gas taxes that will affect the middle class. You supported the North American Free Trade Agreement (NAFTA). In the long run it should help the economy, but in the short run it might prompt some U.S. corporations to relocate their factories in Mexico, costing some blue collar workers their jobs. You have been criticized on noneconomic issues, too. Some believe your positions on abortion, gays in the military, and other social issues are too liberal.

You are looking for a policy that will counter the perception that you are always on the liberal side of issues. You realized early in your career that it is beneficial to be "tough on crime." After losing your first election for governor of Arkansas to an opponent who ran on a law-and-order platform, you came out in favor of capital punishment, setting execution dates for 26 prisoners.[1] Even in the midst of the hectic presidential campaign, you rushed back to Arkansas to deny clemency to a condemned murderer who was so brain-damaged that he seemed unaware what was going on. You said, "I can be nicked on a lot, but no one can say I'm soft on crime.[2]

Americans are increasingly concerned with crime. Public opinion polls show that one in five Americans, more than on any other issue including the economy, report crime is the main problem facing the nation, a rise of 15% since June. Even though the crime rate has declined recently, it is higher than a decade ago, and public concern is triggered by news stories of violent crime, such as the murder of a twelve-year-old in California and the shooting of passengers on a New York City railway train.

A crime bill is now working its way through Congress. One provision is dubbed "three strikes and you're out." It has an appealing sound and means life imprisonment for anyone convicted of three serious crimes. Taking a tough position on crime is likely to gain approval with the public and outflank the Republicans who would otherwise use the issue against you and your party in the next election. Moreover, you genuinely believe that repeat violent offenders have to be put away permanently so they will be unable to commit other crimes.

On the other hand, you recognize that "three strikes and you're out" is an oversimplified response to a difficult issue. First, most crime is caused by lack of jobs, family breakdown, and drugs. Putting criminals behind bars will not affect these conditions. Second, longer sentences will only stress the nation's prison system, which is so overcrowded that many convicts already serve less time than they should. Mandatory sentences

CONTINUED 

OUTLINE

Nature of Public Opinion

Formation of Public Opinion

- Agents of Political Socialization
- Impact of Political Socialization

Measuring Public Opinion

- Early Polling Efforts
- Emergence of Scientific Polling
- Polling Problems
- Accuracy of Polls
- Uses of Polls
- Impact of Polls

How Informed is Public Opinion?

Public Opinion

- Ideology
- Social Welfare and the Proper Role of Government
- Social Issues
- Race
- Political Tolerance
- Trust in Government

Conclusion: Is Government Responsive to Public Opinion?

FIGURE 1
The Presidential "Poller Coaster"

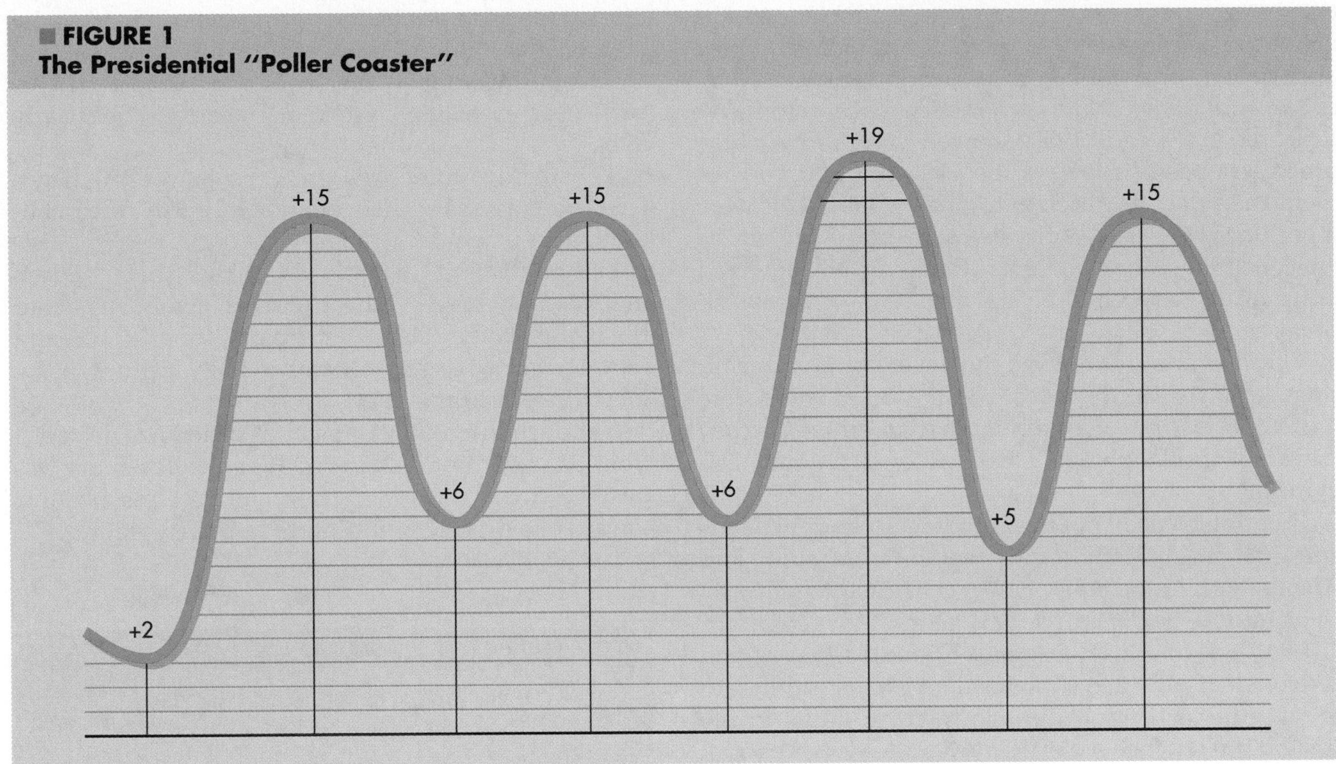

Clinton's margins over Bush rose and fell dramatically early in the 1992 campaign. *Source: USA Today,* October 3, 1992. Polls taken August 20–September 2, 1992. The term "poller coaster" was coined by Richard Morin, "The Ups and Downs of Political Poll-Taking," *Washington Post National Weekly Edition,* October 5, 1992, p. 37.

FORMATION OF PUBLIC OPINION

People have opinions about issues and objects because they learn them in a process called **political socialization.**

As with other types of learning, individuals learn about politics by being exposed to new information from parents, peers, schools, the media, political leaders, and the community. These sources are referred to as **agents of political socialization.** Individuals also can learn about politics through direct personal experience.

Political learning begins at an early age and continues through life. Reasoning capacity as well as the demands placed upon an individual influence what is learned.[5] Very young children are unable to distinguish the political from the nonpolitical world. If fact, young children have difficulty separating political figures from cartoon characters. Some confuse the political with the religious. Twenty-five percent of a sample of five- and six-year-olds reported that the president takes his orders directly from God.[6] By first grade, however, children begin to see government as distinct and unique.[7]

The inability to understand abstract concepts or complex institutions means the child's conception of government is limited. Most identify government with the president.[8] Children can recognize the president—they see him on television—and understand that he is a leader of the nation much as the parent is a leader of the family. In general, experiences with parents and other adult figures provide children with a basis for understanding remote authority figures such as the president.[9] Positive feelings toward parents are also responsible for positive feelings toward the president. Children describe the president as good and helpful[10] and view him as more powerful than he really is.[11]

With age, children develop greater capacity to learn, and greater demands are placed upon them. They are introduced to political ideas and institutions by parents, teachers, and peers. Their conception of government broadens to include Congress and such things as voting, freedom, and democracy. The idealization of the president gives way to a more complex and realistic image. The process can be accelerated by events and parental and community reaction to them. Research in the early 1970s showed that children were much less positive toward the president and government than they had been in the 1960s. The 1970s were a period when support for government among adults was declining. The Watergate scandal in 1973 lowered both adults' and children's evaluations of the president.[12]

These effects did not last, however. Although children socialized in the late 1960s and early 1970s were more cynical toward government than others, as they matured their opinions changed and became less cynical.[13]

In adolescence, political understanding expands still further. Children discuss politics with family and friends. Political activity, however limited, begins. By their middle teens, individuals begin to develop consistent positions on issues.[14] Some fifteen- and sixteen-year-olds have political opinions similar to many adults'. They begin to recognize faults in the system but still believe the United States is better than other countries. They rate the country low in limiting violence and fostering political morality, but they rate it high in providing educational opportunities, a good standard of living, and science and technology.[15] For most, the positive feelings toward American government learned earlier are reinforced.

In adulthood, opinions toward specific policies and personalities develop, and political activity becomes more serious. Most Americans have not developed a critical perspective, and few are asked or pushed to criticism by the schools, press, political parties, or political institutions. Although disillusionment with government in general increases, it is basically passive and directed toward political leaders rather than institutions.[16] In the absence of a major upheaval, depression or war, for most, the positive feelings developed toward government early in life are likely to remain and perhaps even cushion the impact of such events if they occur.[17]

Agents of Political Socialization

Family

Children are not born little Republicans and Democrats. Most learn these allegiances from the family. Individuals are influenced by the family throughout life. Families are particularly important in shaping the opinions of children, however, because of the strong emotional ties among members and because of parents' near exclusive control of their children's early lives.

The family influences opinions in several ways. First, parents share their opinions directly with children, who may adopt them.

Second, parents say or do things that children imitate. They may overhear parents' comments about the Republican or Democratic party, for example, and repeat what they hear. Many initially learn a party identification in this way.

Third, children may transfer or generalize opinions from parents to other objects. When children are less positive toward parents, they are also less positive toward the president and other authority figures.[18]

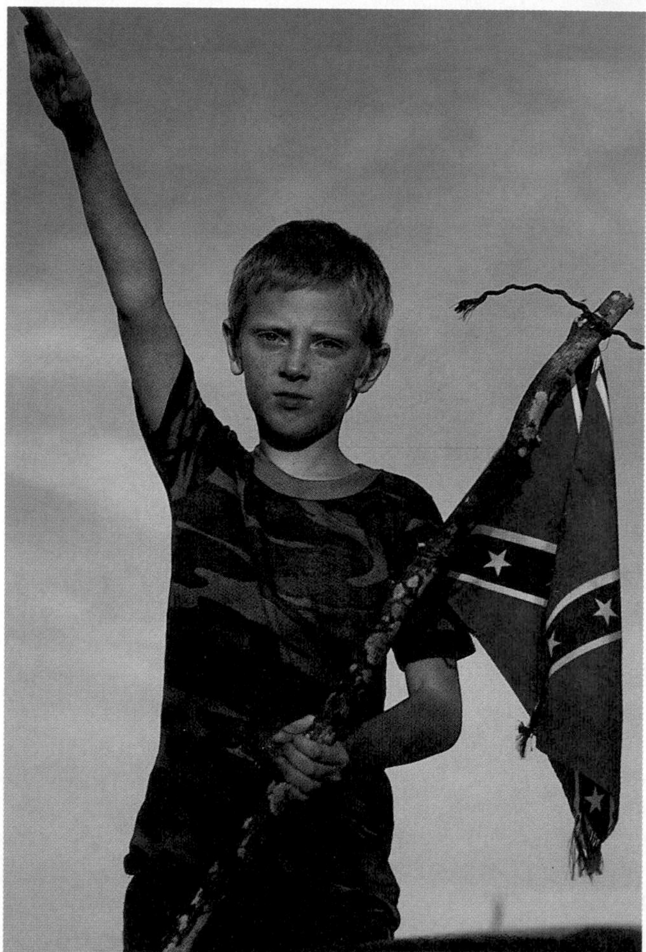

This boy, at a white supremacist rally, likely was socialized in these views by his parents.

Fourth, the family shapes the personality of the child. This may affect the child's political opinions. For example, the family contributes to self-image. Individuals who are self-confident are more likely to participate in politics than others.

Fifth, the family places children in a network of social and economic relationships that influences how they view the world and how the world views them. White children who live in a middle-class suburb will likely view themselves and the world around them differently than black children who live in a large city ghetto.

The influence of the family is strongest when children clearly perceive what the parents' opinion is and that the matter is important to the parents. In the case of party identification, cues are frequent and unambiguous. In one study, 72% of a sample of high school seniors could identify their parents' party identification, whereas no more than 36% could identify their parents' opinion on any other issue.[19]

Today, however, the family has less opportunity to influence the child. Parents no longer have exclusive control during a child's preschool years, and the number of households with both parents working or with a single parent who works means that children have fewer daily contact hours with parents. Consequently, other agents of socialization are becoming more influential. For example, we turn more often to the schools to deal with problems the family dealt with in the past.

School

A child of our acquaintance who came to the United States at the age of five could not speak English and did not know the name of his new country. After a few months of kindergarten, he knew that George Washington and Abraham Lincoln were good presidents, he was able to recount stories of the Pilgrims, he could draw the flag, and he felt strongly that the United States was the best country in the world. This child illustrates strikingly the importance of the school in political socialization and how values and symbols of government are explicitly taught in American schools, as they are in schools in all nations.[20]

Schools promote patriotic rituals, such as beginning each day with the Pledge of Allegiance, and include patriotic songs and programs in many activities. In the lower grades, children celebrate national holidays such as Presidents' Day and Thanksgiving and learn the history and symbols associated with them. Such exercises foster awe and respect for government.

In the upper grades, mock conventions, elections, Girls' and Boys' State, and student government introduce students to the operation of government. School clubs often operate with democratic procedures and reinforce the concepts of voting and majority rule. The state of Illinois even let the state's elementary school children vote to select the official state animal, fish, and tree, conveying the message that voting is the way we decide things.

Curricula and textbooks also foster commitment to government; civics or government courses are offered in most schools and in many places are required of all students. Textbooks, particularly those used in elementary grades, emphasize compliance with authority and the need to be "good" citizens and appear to foster these traits. They are less successful in teaching political participation skills and support for democratic values. Even textbooks in advanced grades often present idealized versions of the way government works and exaggerated views of the responsiveness of government to citizen participation.

Nor does the curriculum make much difference. Civics instruction has only a modest impact on knowledge of and interest in politics, sense of political efficacy (feelings that one can influence government), levels of tolerance, and political trust.[21] Nor do teachers generally have much impact, though there is evidence that they have more impact if they are believable.[22] Consequently, only a minority of a sample of 17-year-olds could list four or more ways to influence politics. Sixty percent of a sample of high school seniors favored allowing the police and other groups to censor books and movies.[23]

The failure of the schools to develop participation skills and commitment to democratic values often is attributed to the "hidden curriculum."[24] Schools are run by teachers and administrators with little input from students. In such an environment, it is not surprising that students fail to develop participation skills and democratic values.

Education—the skills that it provides and experiences it represents—does make a difference, however. People who have more years of formal education are generally more interested in and knowledgeable about politics.[25] They are also more likely to participate in politics and to be politically tolerant. But educated Americans are no more likely than others to appreciate that democratic politics and government involves disagreements, arguments, bargaining, and compromise—in other words, to understand the reality of politics in a democratic society.

The major impact of schooling is that it helps create "good" citizens. Citizens are taught to accept political authority and the institutions of government and to channel political activity in legitimate and supportive ways. Thus, the schools provide a valuable function for the state.

Studies have shown the liberalizing influence of a college education. Many go to college to get a job that pays a high salary. Some attend to expand their knowledge and understanding of the world. Others enroll because their parents want them to or simply because everyone else does. Probably no one goes to become more liberal in his or her opinions. But becoming more liberal is often the result.[26]

College students are more liberal than the population as a whole, and the longer they are in college the more liberal they become. Seniors are more liberal than freshmen, and graduates are more liberal than undergraduates.

Why does college lead to liberal opinions? One explanation is that a college education leads to greater self-confidence. As a result, college graduates are less likely to feel threatened by changes in society and more likely to accept them. Support for change is a component of liberalism.

Another explanation is that college leads to a broadened perspective on the world. Individuals begin to look beyond their immediate environment and see themselves as part of a larger world community. This leads to an increased tolerance of different opinions and an awareness of the conditions that are faced by the less fortunate and by those in other parts of the world; all are components of liberalism.

Still another explanation is that liberal college professors indoctrinate students. A Carnegie Commission survey showed that 64% of the social science faculty in the nation's colleges identified themselves as liberal and only 20% regarded themselves as conservative. Faculty in other disciplines are much less likely to be liberal, however. For example, 30% of the business and 55% of the natural science faculty identified themselves as liberal. Although the potential for influence exists, and college professors, no doubt, affect some students, their impact is probably not great. The broadened outlook that leads to greater tolerance of ideas is likely to make students more resistant to indoctrination.

Evidence also suggests that students' attitudes vary over time. During the height of the Vietnam War, 1968–1971, students were more likely to identify themselves as liberal in outlook than were students before and after. (Liberal attitudes are discussed more fully later in the chapter.) In recent years, college students have moved to the center. For example, 24% of college freshmen identified themselves as liberal in 1990 compared to 38% in 1970. Over the same time period, however, there was only a 2% shift to conservatism. Thus, the big change was from liberal identification to middle of the road. At the same time, college faculty changed very little. Thus, students are not simply a reflection of their college classroom teachers. At large universities, where the largest percentage of students attend college, the environment is sufficiently diverse to reinforce all points of view.

Although students are more conservative than they were in the late 1960s, they remain predominantly liberal. They are much more likely to be pro-choice on the abortion issue, for example, than the general public. A comparison of college and noncollege youth also revealed substantial differences. Eighteen percent of college youth agreed that money is very important, compared to 40% of the noncollege youth. Thirty-six percent of the college students responded that abortion is morally wrong; 64% of the noncollege youth took that position.

Still another explanation for the liberalizing influence of college is that it attracts those who are more liberal in the first place. Some evidence suggests that this may be true for some issues. Whereas 68% of 1990 college freshmen thought the courts treat criminals too leniently, 83% of the public thought so. Fifty-six percent of college freshmen favored busing to achieve racial balance in the schools, whereas only 33% of the adult population favored it.

The most distinctive characteristic of college freshmen in 1994 was their lack of interest in politics. Only 16% said that they frequently discuss politics and only 32% considered it important to keep up with political affairs. These figures, which have been declining since the late 1960s, represent an all-time low.[27]

Although some liberals attend college and have their opinions reinforced, and others are influenced by college faculty, liberal opinions most likely result from increased political awareness and a broadened world perspective.

Peers

In many instances, peers simply reinforce the opinions of the family or school. When there is a conflict between peer and parental socialization, peers sometimes win but only on issues of special relevance to youth. For example, peer influence is more important than family influence on the issue of whether 18-year-olds should be allowed to vote, but parental influence appears to be more significant with respect to partisanship and vote choice.[28] Peers have the most influence when the peer group is attractive to the individual and when the individual spends more time with the group.

Opinions on Abortion

Issues that involve moral questions have the greatest potential to be divisive. Slavery was a moral issue that almost destroyed the nation. In the first decades of this century, prohibition—banning the sale of alcoholic beverages—was a divisive moral issue. In 1992, whether gays should be permitted to serve in the military emerged as another divisive moral issue.

Abortion is the most contentious such issue. In the 1970s, abortion emerged as a moral issue. There are two dimensions to public opinion on this issue. One involves the health and safety of the mother or child. The vast majority of Americans endorse legal abortion when the mother's health may be endangered, the child is likely to have a serious defect, or the pregnancy is the result of rape or incest. This pattern of opinion has been reasonably stable over the past decade.

The other dimension relates to the personal preferences of the mother. Americans are divided on whether a legal abortion is acceptable when the family has a low income and does not want any more children or when the mother is unmarried and does not want to marry the father.

Although the accompanying tables do not reveal intensity, the patterns in boxes a, b, and c show agreement, or consensus, whereas boxes d, e, and f reveal disagreement, or conflict.

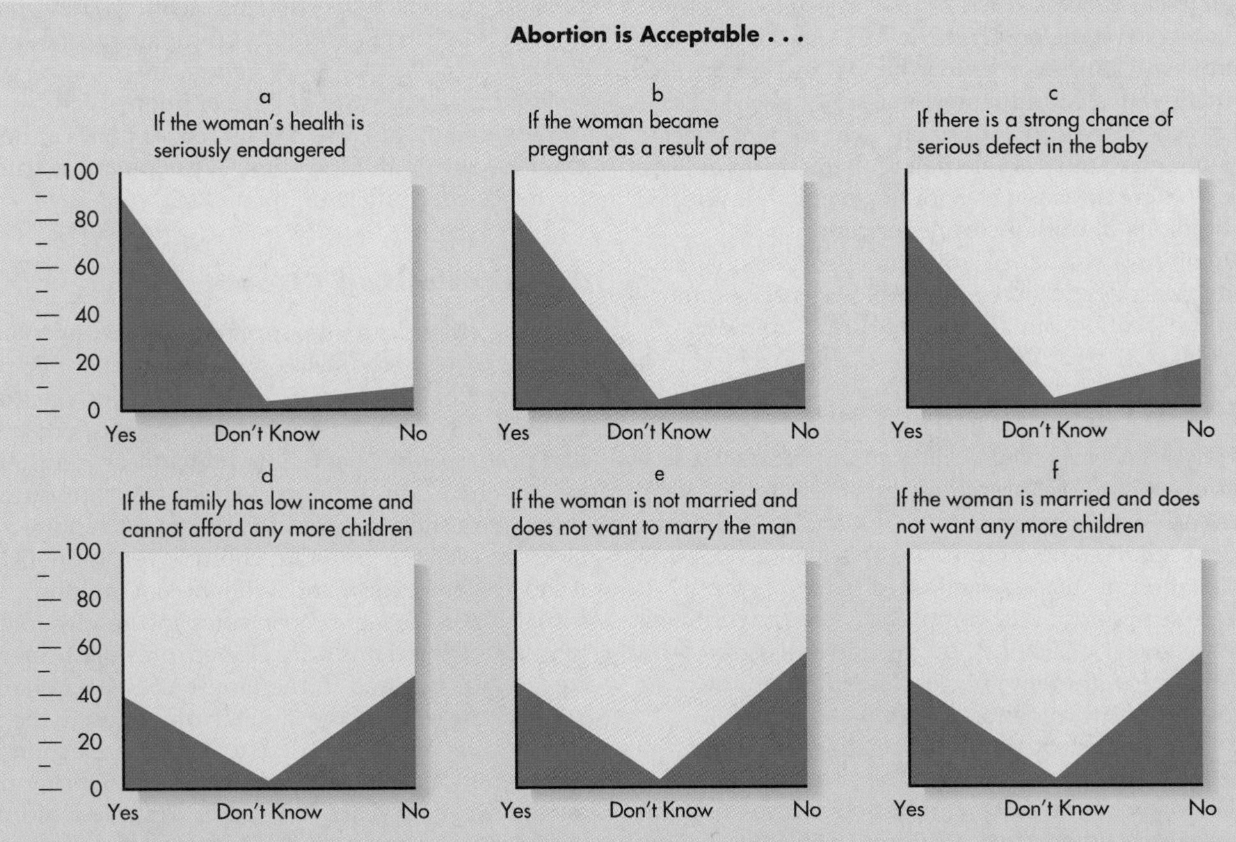

SOURCE: Surveys by the National Opinion Research Center, General Social Surveys, 1993.

Mass Media

The primary effect of the media on children is to increase their level of information about politics. For adults the media primarily influence what people think about, that is, the issues, events, and personalities they pay attention to,[29] but the media also influence opinions about issues and individuals. Research shows that changes in public opinion tend to follow sentiments expressed by television news commentators.[30] We will examine the impact of the media in more detail in Chapter 8.

Adult Socialization

Not all political socialization occurs in childhood. It is a lifelong process; opinions change as we have new experiences.

Citizens' encounters with government have the potential to change their opinions about politics. Many Americans who were particularly hard hit by the Great Depression, for example, became active in the political process for the first time. Most of these new voters voted Democratic in 1932, and many have voted Democratic ever since. The war in Vietnam was another event that influenced masses of people. Some took to the streets to protest the war; others rejected their country and traveled to Canada to avoid the draft. Watergate was yet another event that affected the opinions of millions of Americans.

Opinions also change with changed personal situations. Marriage, divorce, unemployment, or a move to a new location can all affect political opinions.[31]

Impact of Political Socialization

Each new generation of Americans is socialized to a large extent by the preceding generations. In many ways each new generation will look and act much like the one that came before. In this sense, political socialization is biased against change. Typically it leads to support for and compliance with government and the social order. Although many disagree with particular government policies, few question the basic structure of government.

Yet the impact of political socialization is not the same for all groups of people. The socialization experiences of poor minority children are different from those of rich white ones. Children from low-income families are more cynical about government; black children feel less able to influence government and are less inclined to trust it.[32]

Measuring Public Opinion

Public opinion typically is measured by asking individuals to answer questions in a survey. If done properly, this is the most accurate way to measure public opinion. Before the use of polls, other techniques were employed: Elected officials relied on opinions of people who wrote or talked to them; journalists tried to gauge public opinion by talking selectively to individuals; letters written to newspaper editors or newspaper editorials were thought to reflect public opinion.

These techniques can lead to distortions. Letters to public officials and newspapers are more likely to come from people with extreme opinions[33] or from those with writing skills, that is, people with more education. Nor will opinions culled from a few conversations match the pattern of opinion for the nation as a whole. Editorial opinion is even less likely to provide an accurate picture of public opinion because most newspaper publishers tend to be conservative, which often is reflected in their editorials. In most presidential elections in this century, newspapers have favored the Republican candidate by about three to one.[34]

Polling to measure public opinion is an obvious improvement, but the result of a poll cannot be equated with public opinion. A poll is an instrument for measuring public opinion.

Early Polling Efforts

The first attempts to measure popular sentiments on a large scale were the **straw polls** (or unscientific polls) developed by newspapers in the nineteenth century.[35] In 1824, the *Harrisburg Pennsylvanian,* in perhaps the first poll assessing candidate preferences, sent reporters to check on support for the four presidential contenders that year. In July, the paper reported that Jackson was the popular choice over John Quincy Adams, Henry Clay, and William H. Crawford. Jackson also received the most votes in the election, but John Quincy Adams was elected president after the contest was decided in the House of Representatives. Toward the end of the nineteenth century, the *New York Herald* regularly tried to forecast election outcomes in local, state, and national races. During presidential election years, the paper collected estimates from reporters and political leaders across the country and predicted the Electoral College vote by state.

Straw polls are still employed today. Some newspapers have interviewers who ask adults at shopping

Words Do Make a Difference

A major problem for public opinion pollsters is designing questions that accurately measure what the public believes about issues. "It's not the case that a few words don't make a lot of difference in a poll question." What? Get the picture? Poorly worded questions, such as those with double negatives, can confuse the public and lead pollsters to draw the wrong conclusions.

This was illustrated recently in a poll sponsored by the American Jewish Committee to find out the proportion of Americans who doubt that the Holocaust (the mass murder of millions of Jews by the Nazis in World War II) happened. The survey asked the following question: "As you know, the term Holocaust usually refers to the killing of millions of Jews in Nazi death camps during World War II. Does it seem possible or does it seem impossible to you that the Nazi extermination of the Jews never happened?" The results: 22% said it was possible that the Holocaust never happened: another 12% were not sure. The conclusion: About one-third of the country either doubted the truth of the Holocaust or was uncertain.

Since no reputable historian or anyone with the slightest knowledge of world affairs denies that the Holocaust happened, this "finding" was shocking. Commentators reflected on how the public could be so ignorant of one of the major events, not just of twentieth century history, but of all recorded history. On further investigation, however, it seems that the question wording influenced the responses.

Another version of the question asked "Does it seem possible to you that the Nazi extermination of Jews never happened, or do you feel certain that it happened?" This time only 1% said it was possible the Holocaust never happened. Eight percent were unsure, and 90% said they were certain the Holocaust happened.

Why the difference? A study of 13 polls with estimates of Holocaust doubters from 1% to 46% found that studies with high estimates used double-negative wording. For example, to express that the Holocaust happened, one had to respond "impossible" that it "never happened." Such wording often results in a response that is exactly the opposite of what is intended.

What do Americans really know about the Holocaust? Nine of 10 have heard of the Holocaust; however, only two-thirds are able to correctly explain the Holocaust. In 1992, knowledge of the Holocaust increased with publicity surrounding the opening of the Holocaust Museum in Washington and the release of the Academy Award–winning movie *Schindler's List.*

SOURCE: Richard Morin, "From Confusing Questions, Confusing Answers," *Washington Post National Weekly Edition,* July 18–24, 1994, p. 37.

centers and other locations their voting preferences. Some have readers return coupons printed in the papers. Television and radio stations often ask questions and provide two telephone numbers for listeners to call—one for yes, one for no. The votes then are electronically recorded.

The major problem with straw polls is that there is no way to ensure that the sample of individuals giving opinions is representative of the larger population. Generally speaking, they are not.

The famed *Literary Digest* poll is a good example. This magazine conducted polls of presidential preferences between 1916 and 1936. As many as 18 million ballots were mailed out to persons drawn from telephone directories and automobile registration lists. Although the purpose was less to measure public opinion than to boost subscriptions, the *Digest* did have a pretty good record. It predicted the winners in 1924, 1928, and 1932. However, in 1936, the magazine predicted Alfred Landon would win, but Franklin Delano Roosevelt won by a landslide. The erroneous prediction ended the magazine's polling, and in 1938 the *Digest* went out of business.

A bias in the *Digest*'s polling procedure that the editors failed to consider led to erroneous results. At the time, owners of telephones and automobiles were disproportionately middle- and high-income individuals who could afford a telephone or car in the depths of the Depression; these people were much more likely to vote for Landon (a Republican) than were lower-income people.[36] Since the survey was drawn from telephone directories and auto registrations, lower income people were disproportionately excluded from the poll.

Emergence of Scientific Polling

Scientific polling began after World War I, inspired by the new field of business known as marketing research. After the war, demand for consumer goods rose, and American business, no longer engaged in the production of war materials, turned to satisfying consumer demand. Businesses used marketing research to identify what consumers wanted and, perhaps more important, how products would be packaged so consumers would buy them. For example, the American Tobacco Company changed from a green to a white package during World War II because it found that a white package was more attractive to women smokers.[37]

Also important to the development of scientific polling was the application of mathematical prin-

Source: Drawing by M. Stevens; © 1989 The New Yorker Magazine, Inc.

"One final question: Do you now own or have you ever owned a fur coat?"

ciples of probability. To check the rates of defects in manufactured products, random or spot inspections of a few items, called a sample, were made. From these, projections of defects among the entire group of items could be made. From this use of sampling, it was a small step to conclude that sampling a small number of individuals could provide information about a larger population.

In the early 1930s, George Gallup and several others, using probability-based sampling techniques, began polling opinions on a wide scale. In 1936, Gallup predicted that the *Literary Digest* would be wrong and that Roosevelt would be reelected with 55.7% of the vote. Roosevelt received 62.5%.

Increasingly, polls were used by government. In 1940, Roosevelt became the first president to use polls on a regular basis, employing a social scientist to measure trends in public opinion about the war in Europe. Most major American universities have a unit that does survey research, and there are hundreds of commercial marketing research firms, private pollsters, and newspaper polls.

Polling Problems

Lying and opinion change can affect the accuracy of public opinion polls. Although the practice is not widespread, individuals may lie, especially if one of the response alternatives is more socially desirable than the others. For example, many people claim to have voted in an election when they did not, and a few falsely claim to have voted for the winning candidate in a presidential election.[38]

Another problem is opinion change. If opinions change between the time a poll is taken and the announcement of its results, the poll will not be accurate. In 1948, most pollsters predicted that Thomas Dewey would beat Harry Truman in the presidential election. Of course Truman won. The flawed prediction resulted from the failure of pollsters to poll right up to election day. Within two weeks of the election, when most pollsters ceased polling, many undecided voters decided to vote for Truman, and many voters who intended to vote for Dewey shifted to Truman. While today's pollsters poll up until the day before the election, many voters decide at literally the last minute. Polls cannot capture these last-minute decisions.

Increasing numbers of respondents—as many as one-half in some polls—who refuse to be interviewed over the telephone are another problem.[39] Many refuse because they believe they will be asked to spend money. With the growth of the telemarketing industry, most people have been called and asked to buy a product or donate to an organization. Others simply do not want to spend the time to answer pollsters' questions. For polls to provide an accurate picture of public opinion, pollsters need to minimize nonrespondents, those who are a part of the sample but who cannot be interviewed either because they refuse or cannot be reached. A nonresponse rate of 10% is probably acceptable; however, recent polls have nonresponse rates of 20 to 30%. Those who are underrepresented are men, the young, whites, and the wealthy. They are the most difficult to reach and may be more likely to refuse to respond.[40]

Determining who will and who will not vote is also a problem in election polling. Simply asking people whether they intend to vote inflates voting estimates because some people are ashamed to admit they will not vote. To overcome this, pollsters have developed some elaborate, though imperfect, procedures to measure voting,[41] such as having persons mark a ballot.

Accuracy of Polls

Although polls sometimes miss, as in 1948, they predicted the 1992 presidential election almost ex-

SLOP Surveys Are Sloppy Surveys

SLOP is an acronym for self-selected listener opinion polls. SLOP surveys are telephone call-in polls used increasingly by radio and television stations and even by newspapers. Why attach such a negative label to call-in polls? The answer is simple: The results are meaningless because those who call in do not reflect the views of the general public.

An example was CBS's survey to gauge public reaction to President Bush's 1992 State of the Union address. The program allowed viewers to dial and then respond to a series of recorded questions by pushing buttons on their telephone. The views of more than 300,000 respondents were recorded. In an effort to measure representativeness, CBS, at the same time, conducted a survey of 1,241 adults. A comparison of the two polls revealed that the results differed by 10% or more on seven of the nine questions. One question asked whether respondents were better off or worse off than four years ago. In the call-in poll, 54% said they were worse off, compared to 32% in the scientific survey. Viewers who felt they were worse off called in greater proportions than viewers who felt they were better off. In other words, viewers who are more angered or concerned may be more likely to use their telephones to express their opinions.

Another problem with call-in polls is that people can call in more than once. *Parade* magazine conducted a call-in poll on abortion and received more than 300,000 responses. It later acknowledged that 21 percent of the callers may have voiced their opinion more than once. Obviously, if the views of some people are counted two or more times, the results will not be representative of the general public.

Despite these problems, SLOP surveys are likely to continue. As one pollster put it, ". . . it's a good show. And who's going to give up a good show just for the truth?"

SOURCES: Richard Morin, "Another Contribution to SLOPpy Journalism," *Washington Post National Weekly Edition*, February 10, 1992, p. 38. Richard Morin, "Numbers from Nowhere: The Hoax of the Call-in 'Polls,' " *Washington Post*, February 9, 1992, p. B3.

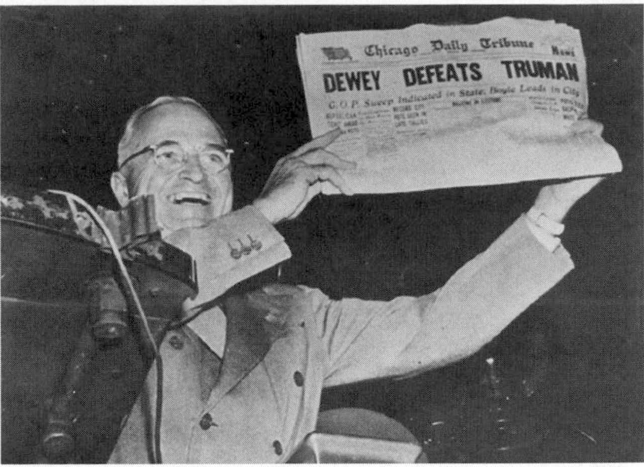

Harry Truman exults in incorrect headlines, based on poll results and early returns, the morning after the 1948 election.

actly. The average of the final results of six major polls was 44% for Clinton, 37% for Bush, and 15% for Perot. The outcome of the election was 43% for Clinton, 38% for Bush, and 19% for Perot.[42] All the polls underrepresented Perot's vote. Many of his voters may have been excluded in pollsters' estimates of likely voters because they had not voted in recent elections. Others may have been unwilling to tell pollsters who they were supporting because of the stigma attached to third-party candidates. Or some others may have shifted to Perot at the last minute because of his election eve media blitz.[43]

Uses of Polls

Polls can be used in different ways. Journalists use them to satisfy the public's curiosity and to make reading about the election more interesting and exciting.

Political scientists, sociologists, and psychologists use polls to test hypotheses about political and social behavior, for example, to find out why people vote for particular candidates or why they vote at all.

Polls also provide information for elected officials, candidates for office and their strategists, political parties, public administrators, and others involved in politics. Elected officials use polls to provide valuable information about the opinions of constituents.

Candidates for public office use them to assess their chances of winning and to help them decide whether to run. Once this decision is made, polls provide information that helps candidates direct limited campaign resources to those groups in the population that support them or might be persuaded to do so. Candidates also use polls to help determine which issues they need to emphasize and which they should ignore.

New Populism

Teledemocracy: If Politicians Can't Do the Job, Can We?

Many Americans believe that politicians are out of touch with the realities of today's world. Working and middle-class people with jobs feel they are working harder but falling further behind. Men with high school educations are, on average, less well off than their parents' generation. White men resent affirmative action and the opportunities it offers, but women and minorities know that despite affirmative action they still have not attained equality in the workplace. Families need two incomes, and maybe more, to stay even with increasing demands. The poor are falling further behind. "Being middle class used to mean you were comfortable. Today being middle class means you're scared."[1]

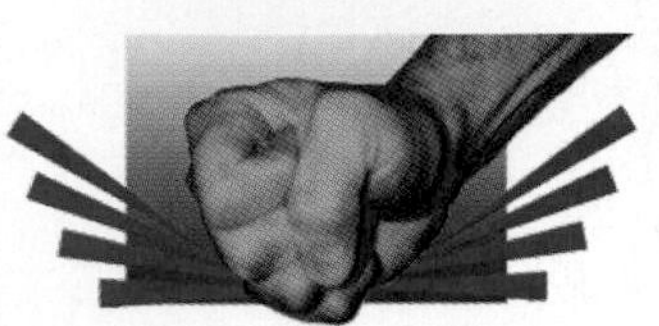

These feelings have several political manifestations. In 1992, they stimulated Ross Perot to run for president and enabled Bill Clinton to win. In 1994, they helped the Republicans take over Congress. They lend support to calls for term limits. And they have encouraged consideration of "teledemocracy," which is a name for many different versions of electronic town meetings. Teledemocracy is a new populist idea because it assumes that we would be better off if we bypassed our political leaders and made government decisions ourselves. Indeed, as one commentator argues, "nostalgia is growing for a high-tech update of Athenian democracy or of . . . townspeople gathered around a cast-iron stove in rural Vermont."[2]

Town meetings have indeed been a tradition of many New England towns for 350 years. They are an exercise in direct democracy: Citizens in a local community come together to discuss public issues and make local laws.

During the 1992 presidential election campaign, Ross Perot talked about the possibility of an electronic town meeting in which everyone in the nation could be part of a discussion and preference vote on some policy. His idea was to link Americans electronically. During the campaign, he had a satellite broadcast that linked rallies in six different states. Participants could hear one another cheer as Perot spoke to them from Florida. President Clinton employed a similar format when he participated in a televised question-and-answer session with citizens in four cities. Citizens in television studios in Atlanta, Miami, and Seattle could interact directly with the president in a Detroit studio.

"Teledemocracy" would go a long way toward transforming our representative democracy into a direct democracy. The president, or perhaps the leadership of Congress or the political parties, would identify a problem such as the deficit or health care reform. Then the president, the Cabinet secretaries, members of Congress, policy experts, or even ordinary citizens would lay out the arguments, pro and con, and ask Americans to register their preferences by pushing a button. Although their preferences would not be binding, elected politicians would probably feel tremendous pressure to follow them as though they were.

If the technology existed to do it—which it does not yet—would teledemocracy be a good idea? Perot—and

Polls enable candidates and parties to evaluate the campaign and to assess their own and the opposition's strengths and weaknesses. Candidates will sometimes commission private polls and leak favorable results to the press to try to manipulate opinion. For example, they will cite polls showing them ahead, or gaining, in order to help raise money and maintain campaign staff morale.[44]

Polls have become a major tool of candidates running for office at all levels. The proliferation of polling firms and the ability of candidates to raise money to buy their services means polling is within the reach of most candidates. Candidates for national office, who can raise substantial campaign sums, are especially likely to poll. The need for polling is driven in part by the desire of candidates to shape their campaign image or that of their opponent in a way that will win votes. Knowing what the voters will respond to is the key. Presidential campaigns poll almost continuously throughout the campaign. There were close to 200 polls (a conservative estimate) in the 1992 presidential campaign.

Administrators sometimes use opinion surveys to assess public reaction to proposed policies. For example, the Internal Revenue Service sponsored polls to determine whether public confidence in the tax

Newt Gingrich too—envisions it as a cure to government gridlock and the influence of special interests. The idea that citizens might bypass the machinery of representative democracy and directly influence government decisions has a gut-level appeal, especially if government is not responding quickly to problems facing the country. Teledemocracy appeals to those Americans who are displeased by the processes of modern democracy, including lobbying and compromise. However, most issues that cause gridlock do so because they are difficult and complex and have no easy solutions. There are not just two options, for example, to solving our health care problems. Dozens or more decisions need to be made, each involving complex options. How could these be explained in a short television program? Legislative bills are often hundreds of pages long with many complex provisions.

The Founders' fear of a tyrannical majority moved by passion led them to create a representative democracy with checks and balances to ensure that decisions would be filtered and made deliberately rather than hastily. Checks and balances guard against popular whims and demagoguery while protecting minority rights. A long process of writing, rewriting, and amending legislation contributes, in many cases, to better legislation that takes into account the complex interests of society. Bills passed without taking account of minority viewpoints or complex issues can be very bad bills. As one political scientist notes, "Look at history. The reality of human experience is that emotional responses have turned to utter tragedy time and time again." It was Hitler, after all, who pioneered the electronic referendum, using radio broadcasts to drum up votes to support his rise to power.

Proponents like Perot and Gingrich believe that teledemocracy would increase participation. It could stimulate interest and get people to think about alternatives and trade-offs involved in choosing one policy rather than another.

Yet rates of participation were low in an early experiment with electronic democracy at the local level. It is likely that the same interested, educated people who participate in politics now would be the major participants in teledemocracy. And of course, not everyone has a computer to participate in teledemocracy. There is now about one computer for every ten adults,[3] a figure likely to grow substantially. Still, the poor are clearly at a disadvantage in this sort of voting system.

This vision of an electronic national referendum is perhaps extreme. However, in other respects, direct democracy is already here. Citizens are wired to Washington through public opinion polls, talk radio, faxes, phones, and e-mail. From C-SPAN's studios just off Capitol Hill, lawmakers chat with callers live—including those who have been monitoring lawmakers' activities via the C-SPAN cameras. More messages pass through the Beltway barrier than ever before, and politicians pay attention to them.

Judging from what we already have, more direct democracy is unlikely to moderate middle-class anger. It may make it worse. Intensely held opinions unfiltered by the political process lead to dubious laws that do not address real issues. For example, "three strikes and you're out" was created by talk radio and won support in the White House and Congress through telephone polls, talk shows, and faxes. It is unlikely to affect crime, but is likely to further frustrate citizens with government when they find that in spite of "three strikes" laws crime is still a major problem.

1. "Why Are We So Angry," *U.S. News and World Report* (November 7, 1994), p. 31.
2. Kevin Phillips, "Virtual Washington," *Time,* Spring 1995, p. 60.
3. Ibid., p. 65.

system was eroding. Evidence from those polls was a factor in persuading Congress to reform the tax system.

Impact of Polls

Polls have a major impact on American politics. Most Americans (75%) think that polls work for the best interests of the public.[45] Polls provide public officials with a continuous and accurate sense of what the public wants.[46] If the direct democracy of the New England town meeting is the ideal, the use of public opinion polls is about as close as the modern state is likely to get to this ideal. Polls provide some public input into policymaking processes often dominated by interest groups.

Polls also help interpret the meaning of elections. When voters cast their ballots for one candidate over another, all anyone knows for sure is that a majority of voters preferred one candidate. Polls reveal what elections mean and thus help make the political process more responsive to voters. For example, Reagan interpreted his election and reelection to mean voters wanted less government. The polls, however, suggested that voters simply lacked confidence in Carter and Mondale; there was little evidence that voters wanted less government or more conservative policies, except that they wanted (in 1980) to spend

Focus Groups: Measuring or Manipulating Public Opinion?

Ever wonder where the ideas for political ads come from? Many come from people like you, meeting in focus groups. A focus group is a dozen or so ordinary people who are brought together to share their opinions on everything from grocery products to television sitcoms. They are also used by political candidates to examine voters' attitudes. Focus group leaders ask questions such as, "If George Bush came to your house for dinner, what would you talk about?" or "If the candidate were a color, what would he be?" Sessions are taped and consultants spend hours poring over every word and gesture in an effort to find out what is on voters' minds.

Unlike in public opinion polls, the samples are not drawn scientifically, nor is a great deal of time spent ensuring that questions used to measure opinions are fair and unbiased. The only requirement is that participants feel comfortable enough with each other to share their thoughts. It is considered risky to mix people of different social characteristics, for example blue- with white-collar workers, blacks with whites, even men with women. According to Bill Clinton's pollster, "The key to a focus group is homogeneity. The more homogeneity, the more revealing."

A 1985 episode from Macomb County, Michigan, a region of predominantly white suburbs with many "Reagan Democrats," illustrates the point. After years of winning elections, the Democrats hired a pollster to conduct focus groups to find out why, in the 1980s, they began losing. He found white, middle-class Democrats turning away from the party because of race. These Democratic defectors saw hiring preferences for blacks as a threat to their own livelihoods and the black-majority city of Detroit as a "sinkhole" for their tax dollars. Each group listened to a quotation from Robert Kennedy exhorting whites to honor their "special obligation" to blacks. Virtually every participant reacted angrily. One said, "I can't go along with that." Another remarked, "No wonder they killed him."

The findings are somewhat unexpected because public opinion polls reflect a different picture. The hostility toward affirmative action and spending for minorities would not have been revealed in a mixed group, nor is it likely that the depth of feeling would have been reflected in a public opinion poll. Yes–no–I don't know answers in public opinion polls reveal the substance but not the texture of public opinion. Feelings censored from public comments often rise to the surface in focus groups. These feelings are likely to come into play when people vote.

The 1992 presidential campaigns used more focus groups than ever. Every ad was tested with a focus group. The Clinton campaign began holding focus groups in New Hampshire even before the candidate announced. Personal responsibility and welfare reform, centrist themes from Clinton's earlier days, bombed when tested in focus groups. With high unemployment and depressed real estate values, New Hampshire residents did not want to hear about personal responsibility. And instead of viewing welfare recipients as freeloaders, they recognized them as people who lost their jobs to the recession and could no longer make it—people very much like themselves. In response to this information, Clinton abandoned his message and developed a new one, tailored to New Hampshire.

Between New Hampshire and the convention, the Clinton campaign convened focus groups at every major crisis. When Paul Tsongas challenged him, focus groups directed the campaign to contrast Tsongas's theme of sacrifice with Clinton's "people first" message. When Jerry Brown rose in the polls, focus groups revealed that the campaign should confront him on the issues rather than on his image as "Governor Moonbeam." Focus groups were behind the idea to profile Clinton's humble beginnings at the Democratic National Convention. His Georgetown, Yale, and Oxford education had given many voters the impression that he was a Bush-style blue-blood.

On the Republican side, focus groups pushed the campaign to capitalize on voters' image of Clinton as a "slick politician." Focus groups revealed Barbara Bush as one of Bush's positives, so she was profiled during the Republican National Convention.

Focus group participants invariably come away with a sense of empowerment, a feeling that someone is genuinely interested in their opinions. Most forget what they suspected at the beginning, that they are being used for the $50 fee. To be sure, politicians are interested in their opinions, but not to make the system more responsive to them. Rather, politicians use their opinions to produce a potent message that will influence their vote. As a former Perot pollster put it, "They're the guinea pigs allowing us to exploit the electorate."

SOURCE: Elizabeth Kolbert, "Test-Marketing a President," *The New York Times Magazine,* August 30, 1992, p. 18.

more on the military. The Republicans claimed their victory in the 1994 congressional elections was an indication that voters supported the party's "Contract with America," but polls showed most Americans had never heard of it (see You Are There, Chapter 6).

Polls also contribute to the selection of political candidates who take a middle position on issues. Because extremist candidates generally are not accepted by large numbers of voters and do not do well in the polls, they are seldom treated as serious candidates by either the political parties or the electorate. It is no accident that presidential elections are often contests between two moderates.

Unfortunately, polls also have a negative impact on politics. Politicians have come to rely heavily on them and sacrifice judgment and leadership to them.

Richard Nixon was obsessed with his standing in the polls. When he resigned the presidency in 1974, those who cleaned out his desk found stacks of papers tracking opinions about him in polls dating back to 1952 when he ran for vice president with Dwight Eisenhower.[47] Lyndon Johnson carried clippings of polls demonstrating popular support, or so he claimed, for the war in Vietnam, and waved them at reporters who questioned his policies in news conferences.

No one argues that public opinion should be ignored by politicians, but it does not always reflect the most desirable policy. Officials who follow it blindly may do the public and the nation a disservice.

The increasing reliance on polls by politicians has resulted in an increase in the number of pollsters, and this has had some negative effects. Drawn to polling because of its potential for financial rewards and access to political power, pollsters entering the profession in the past decade are less likely to be formally trained and committed to professional standards than those entering earlier. Today, many pollsters come from political consulting backgrounds and poll exclusively for members of one political party. This may result in a greater commitment to the political success of their clients and a lesser commitment to providing an accurate portrait of public opinion. The credibility of all polls is threatened when the goal is manipulating rather than monitoring public opinion.[48]

An example of manipulation is the so-called "push poll." A pollster asks whether the person being called is for John Jones, Mary Smith, or undecided in the upcoming congressional election. If the answer is Smith or undecided, the person is asked: "If you were told that Smith's hobby is driving a high-powered sports car at dangerous speeds through residential neighborhoods and seeing how many children and pets she can run over, would that make a difference in your vote?" You are asked your preference again. The idea is to see if certain "information" can "push" voters away from the opposition candidate or a neutral opinion and toward support for the candidate favored by those doing the poll.[49] Learning the weaknesses of the opposition candidate has always been a part of politics, but push polls seek to manipulate, rarely focus on a candidate's issue positions, and often distort a candidate's record and the facts.

An even more vicious tactic is pumping thousands of calls into a district under the guise of conducting a poll, with the intent of spreading false information about a candidate. This technique is increasingly used by candidates in both political parties.[50] Both the push poll and the phony poll are corruptions of the political process as well as violations of survey ethics.

Polls also may affect some political candidates adversely. Preelection polls often show the well-known candidate ahead, which can discourage others from running or staying in the race. Polls also affect a candidate's ability to raise money and recruit campaign workers; no one likes to contribute money to a candidate who is likely to lose.[51]

Some argue that polls influence voters not only indirectly but directly by creating a bandwagon effect, causing voters to support the candidate who is ahead.[52] Others argue that polls create an underdog effect, causing voters to rally around the candidate who is behind. Neither the bandwagon nor the underdog effect inevitably occurs. One polling expert claimed that "both do occur, under some circumstances and to some very small degree and they largely cancel each other out."[53] Critics also have charged that polling may lead to decreased voter participation. After hearing the results of dozens of polls before an election, some voters may believe they do not need to vote. As polls become more numerous, they will be more likely to have this effect. On the other hand, the increased number of polls, both good and bad ones, may diminish their importance for the public as well as those who want the information they provide. A leading pollster points out that when something is in such great supply, its value goes down.[54]

➤How Informed Is Public Opinion?

Many Americans are ignorant of elementary aspects of American government. For example, in a 1978 poll, more than half did not know that two senators were elected from each state.[55] In 1989, over 50% could not identify the first ten amendments to the Constitution as the Bill of Rights.[56] Forty percent did not know which party had the most members in the House of Representatives in 1992.[57] (See Table 1.)

Many Americans are also unable to identify prominent political personalities. In 1986, six years after George Bush was elected to the vice presidency, 23% could not identify him. More people can identify the judge on the television show "The People's Court" than can identify the chief justice of the United States.[58] Moreover, in spite of increases in education, levels of knowledge have not changed much since the 1940s.[59]

Only a small percentage of Americans can identify a single piece of legislation passed by Congress.[60] Prior to the 1994 elections more than one-half knew nothing about the well-publicized "Contract with America."[61] In House and Senate elections, most Americans are unaware of candidates' stands on issues.[62] For example, in the nationally publicized Virginia Senate race between incumbent Senator Charles Robb and Oliver North, six out of ten did not know the candidates' positions on gun control and school prayer, despite the voters identifying these issues as important. Eight out of ten did not know their positions on term limits, and four out of ten did not know their positions on social security. Overall, two out of three did not know any of the candidates' positions.[63]

TABLE 1 Political Ignorance of the Public

	PERCENTAGE UNABLE TO IDENTIFY
Vice president (1992)	12
Supreme Court as final interpreter of Constitution (1992)	28
Party with most members in the House before election (1988)	40
Party with most members in the Senate before election (1988)	46
Number of senators elected from each state (1978)	48
State candidates for the Senate (1992)	50
Leader of Russian Republic (1992)	55
Local candidates for the House (1992)	61
Speaker of the House (1992)	74
Chief Justice of the United States (1992)	92

SOURCE: Center for Political Studies, American National Election Studies, 1978, 1988, 1992.

Many Americans are uninformed about current issues. For example, seven out of ten feel that the country spends too much on foreign aid, and two out of three say we should cut spending on foreign aid. However, these sentiments are based on the perception that the U.S. spends vastly more than it does. Asked to estimate how much of the federal budget is spent on foreign aid, a recent poll found the median estimate to be 15%, 15 times greater than the actual amount spent. Asked what an appropriate amount would be, the average response was 8%. Thus, 70 percent of the population thinks we spend too much on foreign aid but many of them would support an amount substantially above what the country currently spends.[64]

A large number have no opinion on many issues.[65] Evidence suggests that from 15% to 25% of the population have not thought enough about most issues to venture an opinion when asked. Others often volunteer responses but have no real opinions. A recent poll asked whether or not the 1975 Public Affairs Act should be repealed. Twenty-four percent agreed that it should be; another 19% disagreed. The problem is that there is no such thing as the 1975 Public Affairs Act. Forty-three percent had an opinion on something that did not exist.[66]

Individuals tend to think most about those issues that are important to them, such as family and work. Most people view politics as irrelevant to their personal concerns and therefore not very important. The lack of public concern often leads government to be responsive to special interests at the expense of the public.

Before we conclude that the public is incompetent, however, we need to consider the standard by which the public should be judged.

Some political scientists argue that individual citizens know in general what they like and dislike and can make sound political judgments on this basis.[67] It is probably unreasonable to expect most people to have an opinion on all issues. Those who have the greatest stake in an issue will be most likely to have an opinion on it.

We also need to consider the failure of public officials to educate the public on many issues. Politicians often do not like to discuss issues, especially controversial ones. When they do, public awareness does increase. After former President Reagan made an issue of American support for the Nicaraguan contras, awareness of the issue and the side the United States was supporting jumped from 25% to 59%.[68]

➤Public Opinion

Public opinion polls cover virtually every aspect of American life. Polls have reported the number of California drivers with paraphernalia hanging from their rearview mirrors and Iowans with ornaments on their lawns. Political polls examine opinions about political issues and political candidates, whether the American people are liberal or conservative, and whether this influences their positions on issues and preferences for political candidates. While it is important to know how Americans stand on current issues and how they feel about political candidates, it is also important to know what they think about government: its founding principles, political institutions, and political leaders. This is especially true in a time when the media are filled with discussions of voter anger at government.

We begin by discussing ideology, what it is, what the labels liberal and conservative mean, and whether Americans identify themselves as liberal or conservative. We then look at how ideology relates to opinions on specific issues such as social welfare, social issues, and race. We also explore how ideology is related to political tolerance, whether Americans are willing to extend rights and liberties to individuals who do not share their opinions. Finally, we look at trust in government: Do Americans trust their government to do the right thing, and are liberals more trusting than conservatives?

Ideology

The term **ideology** refers to a highly organized and coherent set of opinions. In the extreme, one who is ideological takes a position on all issues consistent with his or her ideology. Liberalism and conservatism are terms used to describe the current major ideologies in American politics. Liberals are sometimes identified by the label "left," and conservatives by the label "right."

A **liberal** is someone who believes in a national government active in domestic policies, providing help to individuals and communities in areas such as health, education, and welfare. In the New Deal era of Roosevelt, liberalism was seen as a way to use government authority to expand opportunities and improve the quality of life for all. With this as their platform, the Democrats came to power in the 1930s and dominated American politics through the 1960s. Since the 1960s, liberalism has been identified with some less popular policies, particularly the civil rights policies of the Democrats. These policies threatened the white-dominated social order in the South and white ethnic communities in the North. Blacks increased their support of the Democratic Party, and many whites, especially in the South, increased their support of the Republican Party. The term was also linked to the anti-Vietnam protests and to Supreme Court decisions that expanded the rights of persons accused of crimes, legalized abortion, and barred mandatory prayers in public schools.

A **conservative** is someone who believes that the domestic role of government should be minimized and that individuals are responsible for their own well-being. However, conservatives often support increases in military spending and recently, the label has also been attached to those, often affiliated with fundamentalist religions, who favor government action banning abortions and approving mandatory school prayers.

To what extent are Americans ideological? Do the ideological labels liberal and conservative describe the opinions of the American people? One way to find out whether a person is liberal or conservative is to ask. The greatest percentage of Americans opt for the middle, identifying themselves as moderate or centrist. Comparing the percentage of liberals to conservatives reveals conservatives to be slightly more numerous. These distributions have changed very little in the past 15 years.

Self-identifications are helpful, but one cannot be sure that individuals actually know what the label means or that they support the positions identified with the label. To determine whether the labels distinguish Americans in terms of issue positions, we need to look at specific issues.

On a number of issues liberals and conservatives take different positions. However, on most issues a majority of liberals and conservatives take the same position. On social welfare issues, for example, most liberals and conservatives endorse increased spending for health care, education, the environment, and to combat drugs. Majorities of liberals and conservatives have similar feelings on issues of race and are supportive of civil liberties for all Americans whether or not they share their views. Both tend to agree on the failings of the government. All of this means that most Americans are not very ideological. While many call themselves liberals and conservatives, these groups do not represent cohesive blocs of citizens with opposing issue positions seeking to control the government to enact their position into law.

Why aren't Americans more ideological? First, we are not very interested in politics. Much of what we find important in life falls outside of politics. We are concerned about our families and jobs, which for most are not directly and immediately affected by government. Lack of interest leads to lack of intensity. Even where majorities of liberals and conservatives disagree—as, for example, on abortion, prayer in school, and busing—feelings of most are not very intense, perhaps because most are not touched by these issues.

Second, political candidates and parties do not usually mobilize their followings with ideological or issue appeals. Both candidates and parties try to be all things to all people, for reasons we will discuss more fully in Chapter 6, and often blunt the ideological or issue content of their message in order to attract support from both the right and the left.

Nonetheless, our political leaders of both parties are more ideological than the rank and file. Obviously political leaders are more interested in politics, and this contributes to the intensity of their feelings. And while a few years ago scholars talked of "the end of ideology," today they remark on its increase in American political debates.

Social Welfare and the Proper Role of Government

Government programs to help individuals deal with economic hardship started during the Great Depression in the 1930s. These included programs to provide aid for the elderly (Social Security), unemployed, and poor (Aid to Dependent Children). Most Americans supported government assistance of this kind in the 1930s and support it today.

Still, Americans have mixed feelings about social welfare spending (see Figure 2). Support is high for Social Security and for helping the poor. About half feel that the nation is spending too little to assist the poor and poor children, and slightly fewer think wespend too little on Social Security.[69] Nearly 85% favored provisions of the Clinton health care plan that would have subsidized medical costs for the low-income and unemployed.

On the other hand, support for "welfare," especially Aid to Dependent Children, is much lower.

FIGURE 2
Self-Identified Liberals and Conservatives Differ on Spending for Social Services

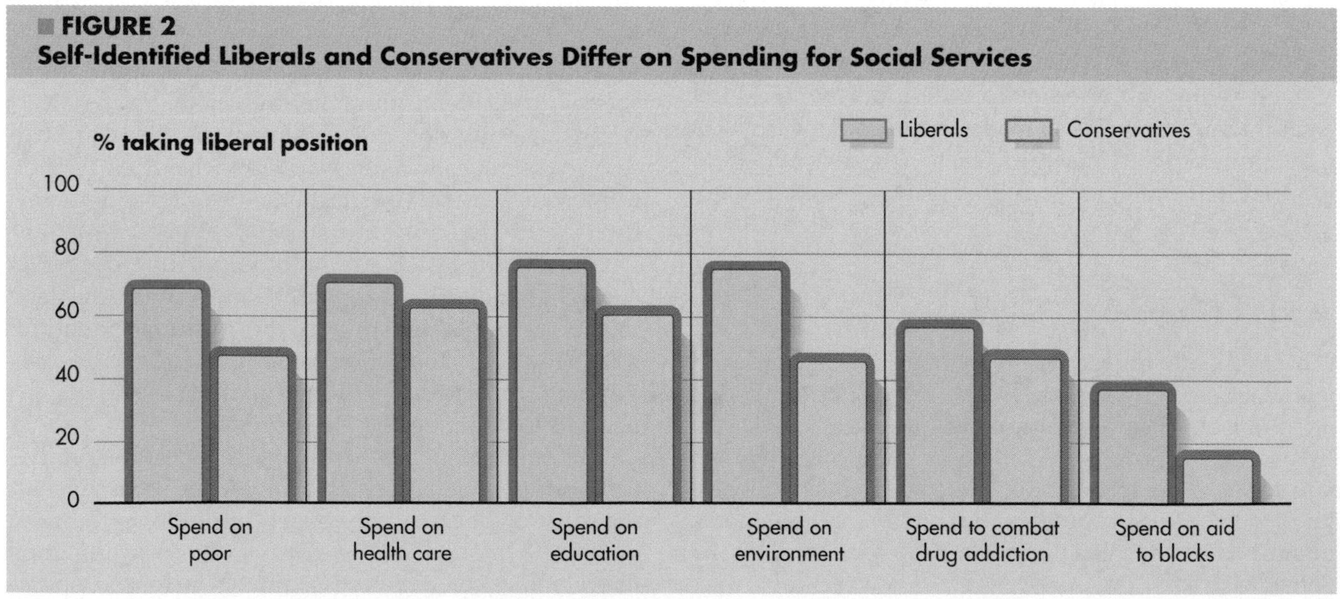

SOURCE: 1993 General Social survey.

Polls show most (60% to 80%) support reforms that would require persons on welfare to work and get off welfare after two years. Over 50% feel, however, that it is unfair for the government to cut off payments after two years if there is no other source of income. Most Americans (75%) believe the answer to welfare is job training and are willing to pay more in the short term to provide it.

We might summarize by noting that Americans appear to favor helping the poor, but they do not like "welfare," which for decades has been the target of both government officials and the media. (We will discuss this system and opinions about it in Chapter 16.) They believe that requiring work and training for jobs is the key to welfare reform and their eyes glaze over when officials and commentators discuss problems with these approaches.

Americans approve increased spending for education, health care, the environment, drug rehabilitation, and crime and law enforcement. For example, two-thirds favor increased spending for improving and protecting the nation's health. Although less than a majority, sizable numbers favor increases in spending for the nation's highways and bridges, mass transportation, and parks and recreation. Only small minorities, less than 10%, oppose additional funding in these areas.

In spite of these sentiments, Americans think their taxes are too high. Seventy-six percent favor a middle-class tax cut. Forty-one percent prefer fewer services to reduce taxes, while only 20% say the government should provide more services and increase taxes.

Consistent with Republican goals to devolve functions of government from the national to state levels, 75% want the states to take over many of the responsibilities performed by the national government.[70] Only 12% say that the national government does the best job of spending tax dollars in an efficient and constructive manner. Thirty-two percent say that state governments do the best job.

The preference for state over national government is linked to lack of confidence in the national government. Complaints include that the government wastes money, spends too much on the wrong things, takes too long to solve problems, and offers ineffective solutions to problems. It is possible (indeed likely) that the greater visibility of the national government compared to state governments in turn leads to this relative lack of confidence. If our state legislatures were covered by television to the extent that Congress is, it is probable the evaluations by the public would be quite different. It is possible (indeed likely) that the greater visibility of the national government compared to state governments in turn leads to this relative lack of confidence. If our state legislatures were covered by television to the extent that Congress is, it is probable that the evaluations by the public would be quite different.

Americans have not, however, given up on the national government. They want it managed better and want to see better performance from government employees. Few want to see the government made smaller by cutting spending and programs.

Social Issues

Beginning in the 1960s, so-called social issues have been important sources of political debate. These issues generally relate to family, school, and church. More specifically, they include opinions on abortion, prayer in public schools, restrictions on pornography, tolerance of homosexuals, crime, and the role of women in society.

Social issues have led to a clash of values between those seeking to preserve traditional moral standards and those seeking to establish new ones. Many Americans feel that government policy has encouraged the decline in moral standards and increased permissiveness. Spurred by a rising crime rate in the 1960s and 1970s, Americans felt increasingly that the courts were not being severe enough with criminals. Forty-eight percent responded that the courts were not harsh enough with criminals in 1965; 86% felt this way in 1993.[71] Increasing numbers of Americans, 59% in 1993, were also willing to endorse the death penalty for murder.[72]

The position of liberals and conservatives on social issues is opposite of what it is on social welfare. On social welfare issues, liberals are likely to support government action, but on social issues they are more likely to reject government involvement. Liberals generally prefer to leave questions of religious belief and sexual morality to individuals to decide for themselves, while conservatives are more willing to call upon government to enforce particular standards of behavior.

Conservatives, for example, are more likely to favor a ban on abortion and to require prayer in public schools (see Figure 3). They are more willing to support capital punishment. Conservatives are considerably more likely than liberals to respond that homosexual relations are always wrong and somewhat more likely to subscribe to the traditional roles for women. For example, conservatives are more

■ FIGURE 3
Self-Identified Liberals and Conservatives Differ on Social Issues

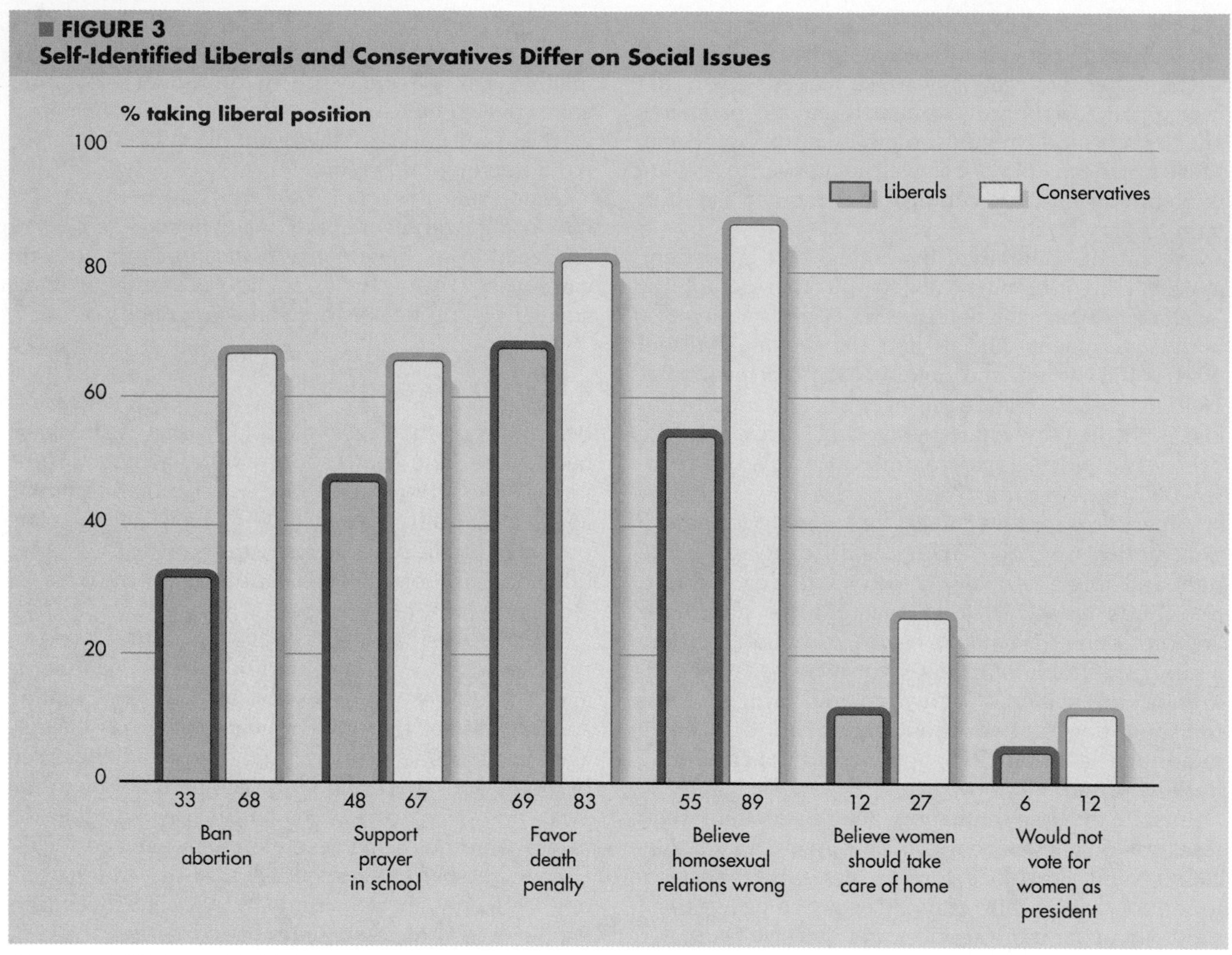

SOURCE: 1993 General Social Survey.

likely to feel that women should take care of the home and leave running the country to men.

Liberals and conservatives do not differ on all social issues, however. They are similar in their attitudes about whether they would vote for a woman president; a high percentage of both liberals and conservatives say they would. Nor is there much difference between them in their strong support for the death penalty.

■ Race

Public opinion has influenced as well as responded to the progress of the black struggle for equality. Although the historical record extends to colonial times, the polling record begins in the 1940s. It shows white America increasingly opposed to discrimination and segregation, at least in principle.[73] In fact, the change might be characterized as revolutionary. For example, whereas only one-third accepted the idea of black and white children going to the same schools in 1942, in the 1980s more than 90% approved. The percentage believing that whites do not have a right to keep blacks out of their neighborhood has nearly doubled since 1963, and a 1989 survey found that only one-third of white Americans live in all-white neighborhoods, and two-thirds claim they have a fairly close friend who is black (80% of blacks claim they have a fairly close white friend).[74] Thirty-eight percent were against laws forbidding intermarriage in 1963; 79% were opposed in 1990.[75]

Only 37% expressed a willingness to vote for a black candidate for president in 1958; in 1986, 86% expressed such willingness. These findings suggest that white America is becoming much more tolerant of racial diversity. Although the North continues to be more supportive of black rights than the South, whites in both regions show increased acceptance of blacks.

Public opinion can change because individuals change or because older individuals with one set of opinions are replaced by a new generation with a different set. Changes in whites' racial opinions through 1960 occurred for both reasons. In the 1970s, most changes occurred because of replacement. Difference in socialization between those born in the 1920s and 1930s and those born in the 1950s and 1960s has led to much greater support for racial integration.

There is, however, another side to the issue. White America has been much slower to accept government initiatives to achieve racial equality. For example, 38% approved the federal government's ensuring fair treatment for blacks in jobs in 1964; the same number endorsed the idea in the 1970s. Busing to achieve racial balance in schools has never had much appeal to whites. Thirteen percent endorsed the idea in 1972, and 25% did in 1986.

Unwillingness to endorse government initiatives to end segregation sometimes reflects racist feelings.[76] For example, most whites believe that blacks are more likely than whites to prefer living on welfare, to be lazy, and to be less intelligent.[77] Nonetheless, lack of white support for government action to deal with race issues may also reflect an objection to government's telling people what to do. Some evidence that more than racism is involved is that blacks too are far less supportive of busing, for example, than they are of school integration. The gap between support for integration and support for busing is not as large among blacks as among whites, but it is substantial.[78]

There are other indications that whites are not necessarily motivated by racism when they will not support government initiatives to end segregation. Since 1966, 90% or more of whites have indicated a willingness to send their children to a school where a few blacks attend, and 80% have been willing to send their children to a school where half of the students are black, a substantial increase since 1958, when only 50% were willing. Most white Americans have no objection to a black living next door or to a family member bringing a black guest to dinner (see Figure 4). Although a small minority still find it difficult to accept blacks and be close to them, by most measures a majority of white Americans do not have this problem. Even where whites would be a minority—a school or neighborhood with mostly blacks—half report it would not bother them.[79]

A third reason that white Americans are reluctant to accept government intervention is that most have closed their eyes to the racial prejudice that still exists. Less than one-fourth of whites see the discrimination in education and housing. Only a small majority of whites recognize the discrimination in hiring and promotion, and they overwhelmingly reject racial preferences (even without quotas) to redress this discrimination.[80] Three out of four Americans oppose affirmative action programs that give preference to minorities and women to make up for past and current discrimination. A majority of whites believe affirmative action hurts white men.[81] It is not only Republicans and conservatives who oppose racial preferences, but Democrats and liberals as well.[82] This may explain President Clinton's pledge to examine the government's affirmative action policies and make changes where necessary (we will explore affirmative action in more detail in Chapter 15).

Blacks see things quite differently. About a third believe that there is discrimination in education, about half believe discrimination exists in housing and getting an unskilled job, and about two-thirds see discrimination in getting a skilled job or managerial position and equal pay.[83] The average black American sees discrimination in three or four of these areas. Thus, blacks and whites differ markedly in their perceptions that racism exists.

Moreover, given the lack of progress in fighting ills that beset poor blacks, many blacks have adopted conspiratorial views to explain problems in the black community. For example, a 1990 survey of New Yorkers found that 60% of blacks compared to 16% of whites believe that government may be responsible for making drugs easily available in black neighborhoods in order to harm the black community; 29% of blacks believe it is possible that AIDS was deliberately created in order to infect blacks. And a large majority believed it is possible that government singles out black elected officials for investigation. These views may seem amazing to most whites, but they are probably no more amazed than blacks are when they note that substantial numbers of whites believe there is no racial discrimination in America.

What do blacks believe should be done about race discrimination? Although the polling record for

■ **FIGURE 4**
Whites Have Grown More Accepting of Neighborhood Integration

Residential segregation is the lynchpin of racial separation in America. Such segregation influences the quality and nature of schools, employment opportunities, and the amenities of daily life. In the past twenty years, American cities have become somewhat less segregated, stimulated in part by whites changing attitudes about residential segregation.

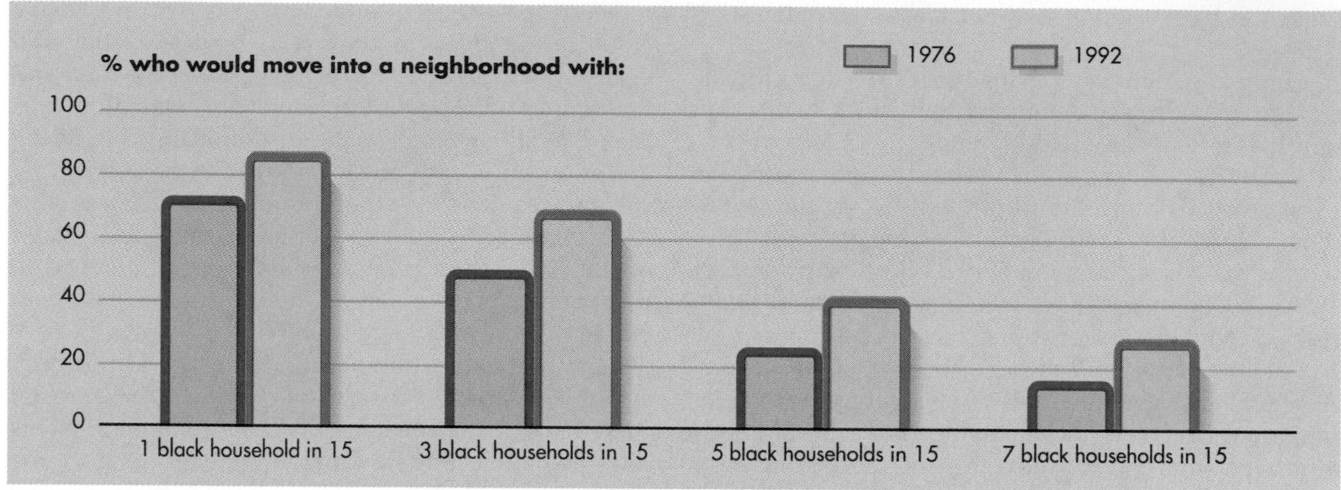

SOURCE: Douglas Massey and Nance Denton, *American Apartheid* (Cambridge: Harvard University Press, 1993).

blacks does not extend as far back as it does for whites, blacks have overwhelmingly endorsed integration. Nearly all blacks have responded consistently that blacks and whites should go to the same schools and that blacks have a right to live anywhere they want to. Intermarriage is approved by three of four blacks.

Like whites, blacks have become somewhat less supportive of government initiatives. In 1964, 92% thought the national government should ensure blacks fair treatment in jobs; in 1974, 82% did. Support for government assistance in school integration has varied considerably, although in 1986 about the same proportion approved it as in 1964 (more than 80%). Some blacks fear that government initiatives will only antagonize whites. Others believe government aid hurts blacks by making them too dependent. Still others believe government is ineffective in bringing about an end to discrimination.

Self-identified liberals and conservatives also differ on race issues. Liberals are somewhat more likely to oppose laws that ban racial intermarriage, to disagree that whites have a right to keep blacks out of their neighborhood, and to accept sending their children to a school where most are a different race. They are also more likely to endorse busing and say they would vote for a black candidate for president. However, these differences are fairly small (except for attitudes toward busing they range from 5 to 9 percentage points), and majorities of both liberals and conservatives favor the proequality stance in all instances except busing.

■ Political Tolerance

Political tolerance is the willingness of individuals to extend procedural rights and liberties to people with whom they disagree. Tolerance is important because it embodies many elements essential to democratic government, such as freedom of speech and assembly.

J. William Fulbright, former senator from Arkansas, once said, "Americans believe in the right to free speech until someone tries to exercise it." In other words, people are tolerant in the abstract but not when called upon to support speakers they disagree with. More than 85% of Americans claim to believe in free speech for all,[84] yet a 1954 nationwide survey found that only 37% of the respondents would allow a person opposed to churches and religion to speak in their communities.[85] Even fewer would permit an admitted communist to speak. More highly educated people were more tolerant than those with less edu-

TABLE 2 Political Tolerance Has Increased Toward Some Things

	PERCENTAGE AGREEING	
A person should be allowed to speak who. . .	**1954**	**1993**
Is an admitted Communist	28%	71%
Opposes all churches and religion	38	73
Favors government ownership of all the railroads and large industries	65	78*
Advocates doing away with elections and letting the military run the country	†	66
Claims blacks are inferior	†	62
Is an admitted homosexual	†	81

*Data from 1982 General Social Survey.
† Question not asked.

SOURCES: 1954 data are from Samual Stouffer, *Communism, Conformity, and Civil Liberties* (New York: John Wiley and Sons, 1954). 1993 data are from National Opinion Research Center, General Social Survey, 1993.

cation, and political elites were more tolerant than the general public.

At first the finding that elites were more tolerant than the general public was reassuring. After all, many elites are in a position to deprive people of rights, and elites help shape public opinion. But later studies revealed that elites are more tolerant than the general public largely because they are better educated. There is no "elite" distinction apart from education.[86] Elites, however, do influence the opinions of the general public on civil liberties. When elites agree among themselves, the general public is more likely to reflect this consensus.[87]

More recent studies suggest that Americans have become substantially more tolerant of communists, socialists, and atheists (see Table 2).[88] However, overall levels of tolerance may not have increased quite as much as some people think.

In the 1950s, people perceived communists and socialists as a major threat. As the perception of the threat diminished, so did people's fears. Research on tolerance, therefore, has first asked people which groups they dislike and then assessed their tolerance toward those groups.[89] Two-thirds or more thought that members of their least-liked group should be banned from being president and from teaching in the public schools. Many responded that the group should be outlawed, indicating a high degree of intolerance. On the other hand, in the 1970s, the public was more willing to allow their least-liked group to speak and teach than they were to allow communists to do so in 1954.[90] This suggests that tolerance may have increased. Thus, although intolerance remains, it seems that the public has grown more tolerant since the 1950s.

While increased levels of political tolerance since the 1950s are a reason to be positive, job insecurity and declining real wages have helped promote negative feelings toward minorities and immigrants and others outside the mainstream. A majority of whites, for example, agree that equal rights for racial minorities have gone too far. Eighty-two percent agree that people coming to live in the U.S. should be restricted and controlled more than they are now.[91] Such sentiments are not likely to lead to a loss of civil liberties unless political elites direct citizens' fears in an attempt to gain political advantage.

In general, liberals tend to be more tolerant than conservatives, at least toward communists, atheists, racists, and those who would support a military government. For example, in 1990, 74% of those who identified themselves as liberals in a national survey indicated a willingness to allow a communist to speak in their community; 66% of the conservatives took this position.[92]

Trust in Government

An important dimension of public opinion is the trust or support citizens have for their government, its institutions, its officials, and fellow citizens. With high levels of trust, citizens might do everything government demands. They would pay their taxes and, if called upon to do so, defend the government. They might also gullibly accept anything officials tell them. At low levels of trust, citizens would be more skeptical; they may even disobey the law. At the lowest levels, they might try to overthrow the government or commit violent acts against it, as with the Oklahoma City bombing. Thus, democratic government "depends on a fine balance between trust and distrust."[93]

Public trust of government has declined significantly in the last 30 years. In the early sixties, Americans were supportive of the government. A comparison of five nations—the United States, Britain, West Germany, Italy, and Mexico—found Americans to be the most positive about the responsiveness and performance of government; 95% of the Americans sampled pointed to the government when asked what aspects of the nation they were proud of.[94] The picture that emerged was one of trust and confidence.

The pattern, however, changed sometime in the mid-1960s. Trust in government declined after 1964 and continued to decline through 1980 (see Figure 5). The pattern was characteristic not only of opinions toward government but of opinions toward all major institutions in society, including the medical profession, business, labor, and the press (see Figure 6). Government responsiveness also was rated less positively during the 1960s and 1970s.

Why have levels of trust and confidence declined? One answer is the performance of government itself. In the mid to late 1960s, the nation was divided over a number of issues, including what to do about the war in Vietnam and the civil rights demands of blacks. Many people wanted the government to do everything possible to win the war in Vietnam, whereas others wanted an immediate withdrawal of U.S. forces; the Johnson and Nixon policies of limited and prolonged war were unresponsive to both sides.

The civil rights struggle also divided the nation. Some wanted government to do more to speed the progress of blacks and other minorities, whereas others thought government was moving too fast. Once more, government chose a middle course responsive to neither side.[95]

Following on the heels of these seemingly intractable problems, the early 1970s brought news of Watergate and corruption in government, and after 1973 the nation experienced economic problems, inflation, high interest rates, and unemployment. The government was little more successful in dealing with these than it was with the problems of the 1960s. Levels of trust again declined.

Between 1980 and 1984, levels of trust and confidence in government increased modestly. People seemed to respond to what appeared to be an improved economy and a few foreign policy successes. Reagan's personal popularity seemed to inspire confidence on the part of the American people.

Reagan's involvement in the Iran-contra scandal, a sense that his administration lacked compassion, and popular dissatisfaction with domestic and foreign policy diminished his appeal, however, and no doubt contributed to a decline in trust between 1984 and 1986.[96] In the 1990s, trust has continued to fall and in 1994 was at a record low.[97] Congress and the president (both Bush and Clinton) have been deadlocked over crucial issues, from health care reform to budget deficits.

This brief overview suggests that policy failure is responsible for declining trust. Citizens have become increasingly oriented to government in terms of the services (jobs and high standard of living) they expect government to provide. When performance falls short of expectations, trust in government also falls.[98] One study documents the link between confidence in government and the state of the economy. Between 1966 and 1980, every percentage increase in unemployment lowered confidence in government by almost 3%.[99]

However, others theorize that declining trust can be traced not to policy but to process.[100] This viewpoint holds that declining trust is highly correlated with the increasing visibility of government. As Americans see more of their federal government on a day-to-day basis, through C-SPAN and newscasts,

FIGURE 5
Trust in Government Declined During the 1960s and 1970s

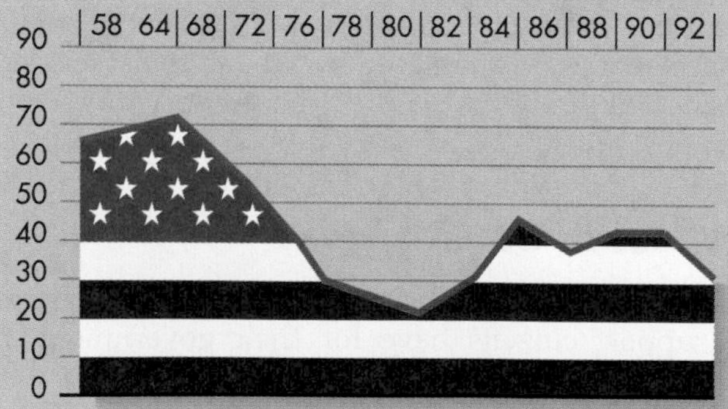

Percentage saying can trust government to do what is right "most of the time" or "all of the time."

SOURCE: National Election Studies, the Center for Political Studies.

FIGURE 6
Confidence in American Institutions Has Declined Since the 1960s

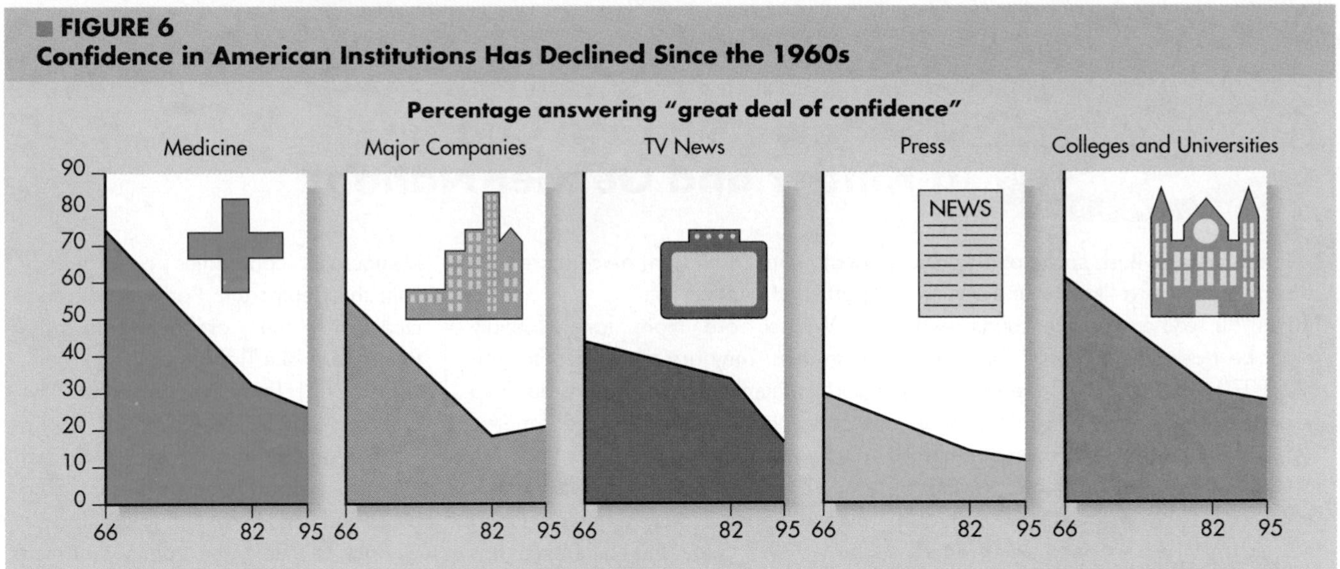

SOURCE: The Harris Surveys, 1990.

they like it less and trust it less. Talk radio and television interpret what are normal parts of the democratic process—lobbying, bargaining, negotiating, and compromise—as cynical acts done only for the self-interest of an individual, interest group, or political party. Of course, there is plenty of self-interest in politics, as in any other form of human endeavor, but compromise and negotiation are a necessary part of a democratic process. Since most Americans seem neither to understand nor like that part of the process, the more exposure the process gets to the public eye, the less the public likes it.

Probably both policy and process have contributed to declining trust of government. Moreover, the two reinforce each other. Policy deadlock contributes to negative reactions to process, but even when the process yields significant policies, the public visibility of the mechanics of the policy process, with its negotiations and deals, still contributes to cynicism and mistrust.

Levels of trust among liberals and conservatives are frequently influenced by the party that occupies the White House. During Republican administrations, liberals tend to be less trusting; when Democrats hold office, liberals are more trusting.[101] Extremists are distrustful regardless of who occupies the White House. Americans who join militias and talk about government as an alien force are clearly examples of those having high levels of distrust. These Americans no longer believe that government sometimes makes mistakes or is simply too big to be effective; they have come to believe that it is directed by a force out of control of ordinary Americans (foreigners, communists, Jews, "the New World Order," and others are favorite suspects).

Those holding these extreme beliefs are a small fraction of the population. Most Americans generally believe that government is good, if sometimes misguided. However, if trust continues to decline, more Americans may be open to the arguments of those who believe that government is the enemy.

The pattern of low trust of government by the public is not unique to the United States.[102] In America a recent poll showed 8 out of 10 thought the country was going in the wrong direction. Seventy percent responded this way in Canada, and 44% in Japan. Large numbers do not trust their government to do what is right. Moreover, many see a bleak future ahead. Forty percent of Americans respond that future generations of Americans will be worse off than people today. In Canada, more than 50% respond this way. To a large extent, this reflects the economic uncertainty that global competition and technological change are producing, particularly among the less skilled and educated, and the inability of governments to do much about it. Countries have less power than ever in controlling their economies. Companies can move operations and individuals can transfer capital across national boundaries at will. While this creates economic opportunity, it also creates anxiety. Individuals are unclear what they need or should do to protect themselves and their families.

American Diversity

If Women Were in Charge, a Kinder and Gentler Nation?

In 1988, George Bush spoke of his goal to be president of a "kinder and gentler nation." If women ran the country we might be closer to that goal. Since the mid-1970s, public opinion polls have consistently shown women to be more supportive than men of government efforts to help the less fortunate. Women are more likely to endorse spending for the elderly, handicapped, sick, and poor. They are also more likely to support efforts to improve the conditions of minorities.

The nation would also be tougher on crime if women were in charge. More women than men think the government should make the war on crime a top priority. They are more likely to support stronger action against drunk driving, drug dealing, rape, and spouse abuse, but they are less likely to endorse the death penalty and are much more supportive of gun control.

Women are more family-friendly than men. They are more likely to support a number of programs to help working parents, including paid maternity leave and child care.

While women were less likely than men to support military spending during the 1980s, today this difference has disappeared. With the end of the Cold War and with pressing domestic problems, support for military spending among men has declined. However, women (26%) were more likely than men (15%) to favor staying out of the Persian Gulf War.

Differences in opinions have also led women and men to support different candidates and political parties. Women are more likely to vote for Democratic candidates and identify with the Democratic Party. Men, especially white men, are becoming more Republican (see The Angry White Male, Chapter 7.) Forty-five percent of the women voted for Bill Clinton in 1992, 42% of the men did. Women were less likely to support George Bush (38 to 39%) and Ross Perot (17 to 21%).

Prior to 1970, the opinions of men and women on most issues were the same. The gender gap emerged with the growth of the women's movement in the 1970s and is likely to remain as long as the economic position of women in society trails that of men.

SOURCE: "The Gender Gap Revisited," *Washington Post National Weekly Edition*, May 25, 1992, p. 37; Clyde Wilcox. *The Latest American Revolution?* (New York: St Martin's, 1995), p. 19.

Examples of the Gender Gap

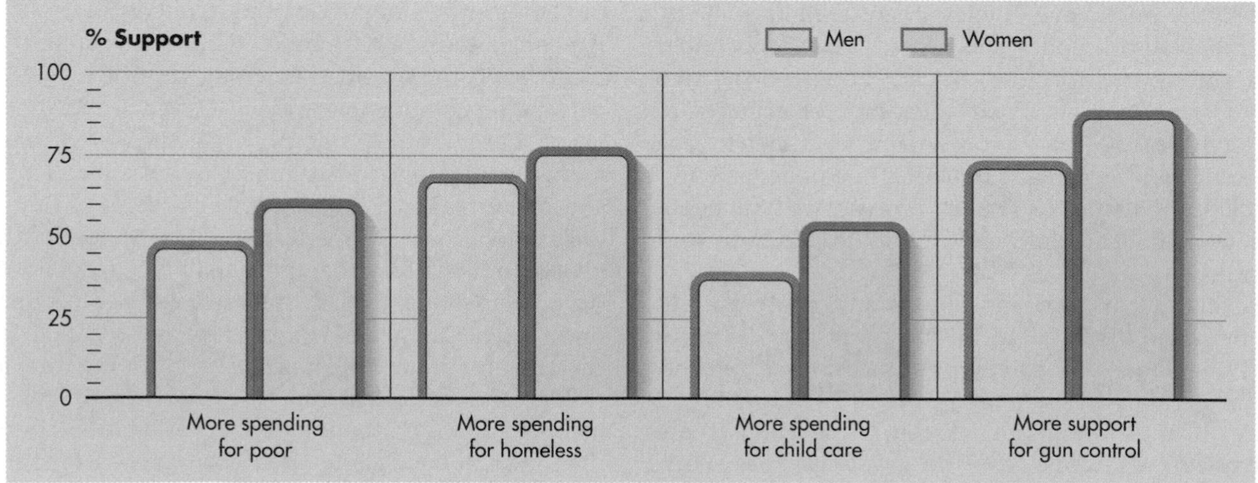

SOURCE: 1993 General Social Survey and 1992 CPS National Election Study.

At the same time, however, Americans as well as citizens in other industrialized countries report that they are contented with the lives they lead. Citizens' negative response to government and their concern for the future may result from what they read and see in the news and the political rhetoric of politicians as much as it does their personal situation.[103] Thus, the declining levels of trust might be due to the expanding scope of the media in developed countries.

"My third felony was a smart move. Folks on the outside are still waiting for health care."

Source: Drawing by Handelsman. © 1994. The New Yorker Magazine, Inc.

➤Conclusion: Is Government Responsive to Public Opinion?

Our interest in public opinion stems in part from the belief that in a democracy government should be responsive to the wishes of the people. But is it? Political scientists have had only limited success answering this question because of the difficulty in measuring influence.

The most direct way to assess whether public policy is responsive to public opinion is to compare changes in policy with changes in opinion. The largest study of this type examined several hundred public opinion surveys done between 1935 and 1979. From these surveys, the researchers culled hundreds of questions, each of which dealt with a particular policy and had been asked more than one time. On more than 300 of these questions, public opinion had changed. The authors of the study compared changes in these 300 opinions with changes, if any, in public policy. They found congruence between opinion and policy changes in more than two-thirds of the opinions. Congruence was most likely when the opinion change was large and stable and when the opinion moved in a liberal direction.

The authors acknowledged that in about one-half of the cases, the policy change may have caused the opinion change, but in the other half the opinion change probably caused the policy change or they both affected each other. Although in many instances policy was not congruent with public opinion, on important issues, when changes in public opinion were clear-cut, policy usually became consistent with opinion.[104]

Although policy usually changes with changes in opinions, sometimes it does not. One reason is that reelection does not rest with the entire public but with the voting public, and those who vote often differ in their policy preferences from those who do not.[105] To the extent that elected public officials are responsive to voters, and voters differ from nonvoters, public policy will not reflect public opinion.

Then too, elected public officials must not only pay attention to the direction of public opinion but also to its intensity. It may be advantageous for an elected official to vote in support of a minority opinion that is intensely held. A minority with intense feelings is more likely to vote against a candidate who does not support its position than is a group with weak preferences. When elected officials are confronted with an intense minority—for example, the gun lobby—public policy may not reflect public opinion.

Moreover, public opinion is not the only influence on public policy, nor is it necessarily the most important. Interest groups, political parties, other institutions of government, and public officials' own preferences also influence policy, and they may or may not agree with public opinion. Where the preferences of the various influences do not agree, policy generally will reflect a compromise among them.

Finally, there is nothing sacred about public opinion. Even when a majority of the public favors a course of action, one should not assume that this is the most desirable course; the public can be wrong. This possibility led the Founders to establish a government that was partially insulated from the influence of public opinion. In other words, we do not have complete and immediate correspondence between opinion and policy because the Founders did not want instant government responsiveness. They built a federal system with separation of powers and many checks and balances to ensure that the majority could not steamroll the minority. Thus one should not expect public policy to reflect public opinion perfectly. The fact that policy usually comes to reflect large and stable majorities does indicate, however, that government is eventually responsive on important issues. Indeed, some observers think politicians pay too much attention to public opinion, to the point that leaders are fearful of leading or of offending the competing groups pulling in opposite directions. The result is more gridlock.

EPILOGUE

The President Followed the Polls

Driven by growing public sentiment that crime was the number one problem facing the nation, in his State of the Union address the president called on Congress to pass a "strong, smart, tough crime bill," including "three strikes and you're out." He was rewarded with his longest standing ovation (22 seconds) of the speech. He also called for 100,000 more police officers, a ban on semiautomatic weapons, boot camps for young offenders, and drug treatment for prison inmates. Although he argued for tougher penalties for those who commit violent crimes, he also called for more job training and national service that could provide jobs and strengthen families and thus help in the fight against crime.

This support at least temporarily pulled the rug out from under Republicans who have traditionally been the hard-liners on crime. Months later, when asked which party they thought could best handle the crime problem, the public gave the Democrats a slight edge, 39–32%, reversing a traditional Republican advantage and an indication that this aspect of Clinton's "new Democrat" politics are paying off.[106]

➤Key Terms

public opinion
political socialization
agents of political socialization
straw polls
ideology
liberal
conservative
political tolerance

➤Further Reading

Herbert Asher, *Polling and the Public: What Every Citizen Should Know* (Washington, D.C.: CQ Press, 1988). *An introduction to polling methodology and the influence of polls on American politics as well as advice to citizens on how to evaluate polls.*

P. Brace and B. Hinckley, *Follow the Leader: Opinion Polls and the Modern President* (New York: Basic Books, 1992). *A survey of how recent presidents have allowed the results of public opinion polls to influence their position on issues.*

B. I. Page and R. Y. Shapiro, *The Rational Public: Fifty Years of Trends in American's Policy Preferences* (Chicago: University of Chicago Press, 1992). *An examination of the influence of public opinion on public policy using public opinion polling information generated over the past fifty years.*

T. E. Mann and G. R. Orren, eds. *Media Polls and American Politics* (Washington, D.C.: Brookings, 1992). *Several essays focusing on the influence of media-conducted polls on American political institutions and elections.*

Celinda Lake, *Public Opinion Polling: A Handbook for Public Interest and Citizen Advocacy Groups* (Washington, D.C.: Island Press, 1987). *A step-by-step treatment for lay audiences on how to conduct a public opinion poll.*

➤Notes

1. Michael Kramer, "Frying Them Isn't the Answer," *Time* (March 14, 1994), p. 34.
2. *Ibid.*
3. Material is drawn from: Richard Morin, "Public Enemy No. 1: Crime," *Washington Post National Weekly Edition* (January 24–30,

1994), p. 37; Richard Lacayo, "Lock 'Em Up," *Time* (February 7, 1994), pp. 51–59; Michael Kramer, "Tough, But Smart?" *Time* (February 7, 1994), p. 29.

4. Richard Morin, "The Ups and Downs of Political Poll-Taking," *Washington Post National Weekly Edition* (October 5, 1992), p. 37.

5. T. E. Cook, "The Bear Market in Political Socialization and the Costs of Misunderstood Psychological Theories," *American Political Science Review* 79 (December 1985), pp. 1079–93.

6. S. W. Moore et al., "The Civic Awareness of Five and Six Year Olds," *Western Political Quarterly* 29 (August 1976), pp. 418.

7. R. W. Connell, *The Child's Construction of Politics* (Carlton, Victoria: Melbourne University Press, 1971).

8. F. I. Greenstein, *Children and Politics* (New Haven, Conn.: Yale University Press, 1965), p. 122; see also F. I. Greenstein, "The Benevolent Leader Revisited: Children's Images of Political Leaders in Three Democracies," *American Political Science Review* 69 (December 1975), pp. 1317–98; R. D. Hess and J. V. Torney, *The Development of Attitudes in Children* (Chicago: Aldine, 1967).

9. Hess and Torney, *Development of Attitudes in Children;* Connell, *Child's Construction of Politics.*

10. Greenstein, *Children and Politics;* Greenstein, "The Benevolent Leader"; and Hess and Torney, *Development of Attitudes in Children.*

11. Connell, *Child's Construction of Politics.*

12. F. C. Arterton, "The Impact of Watergate on Children's Attitudes toward the President," *Political Science Quarterly* 89 (June 1974), pp. 269–88; also F. Haratwig and C. Tidmarch, "Children and Political Reality: Changing Images of the President," paper presented at the 1974 Annual Meeting of the Southern Political Science Association; J. Dennis and C. Webster, "Children's Images of the President and Government in 1962 and 1974," *American Politics Quarterly* 4 (October 1975), pp. 386–405; R. P. Hawkins, S. Pingree, and D. Roberts, "Watergate and Political Socialization," *American Politics Quarterly* 4 (October 1975), pp. 406–36.

13. M. A. Delli Carpini, *Stability and Change in American Politics: The Coming of Age of the Generation of the 1960s* (New York: New York University Press, 1986), pp. 86–89.

14. R. Merelman, *Political Socialization and Educational Climates* (New York: Holt, Rinehart and Winston, 1971), p. 54.

15. R. Sigel and M. Hoskin, *The Political Involvement of Adolescents* (New Brunswick, N.J.: Rutgers University Press, 1981).

16. J. Citrin, "Comment: The Political Relevance of Trust in Government," *American Political Science Review* 68 (September 1974), pp. 973–1001; J. Citrin and D. P. Green, "Presidential Leadership and the Resurgence of Trust in Government," *British Journal of Political Science* 16 (1986), pp. 431–53.

17. It is plausible to assume that the content of early political socialization influences what is learned later, but the assumption has not been adequately tested. Thus, we might expect the positive opinions toward government and politics developed early in childhood to condition the impact of traumatic events later in life. D. Easton and J. Dennis, *Children and the Political System: Origins of Regime Legitimacy* (New York: McGraw-Hill, 1969); R. Weissberg, *Political Learning, Political Choice and Democratic Citizenship* (Englewood Cliffs, N.J.: Prentice-Hall, 1974). See also D. D. Searing, J. J. Schwartz, and A. E. Line, "The Structuring Principle: Political Socialization and Belief System," *American Political Science Review* 67 (June 1973), pp. 414–32.

18. D. Jaros, H. Hirsch, and F. Fleron, Jr., "The Malevolent Leader: Political Socialization in an American Subculture," *American Political Science Review* 62 (June 1968), pp. 564–75.

19. K. Tedin, "The Influence of Parents on the Political Attitudes of Adolescents," *American Political Science Review* 68 (December 1974), pp. 1579–92.

20. On the impact of the public schools and teachers on political socialization, particularly in the area of loyalty and patriotism, see Hess and Torney, *Development of Attitudes in Children.*

21. K. Langton and M. K. Jennings, "Political Socialization and the High School Civics Curriculum," *American Political Science Review* 62 (September 1968), pp. 852–77.

22. D. Goldenson, "An Alternative View about the Role of the Secondary School in Political Socialization: A Field Experimental Study of the Development of Civil Liberties Attitudes," *Theory and Research in Social Education* 6 (March 1978), pp. 44–72.

23. The study of 17-year-olds is reported by E. Shantz, "Sideline Citizens," in Byron Massiales, ed., *Political Youth, Traditional Schools* (Englewood Cliffs, N.J.: Prentice-Hall, 1972), pp. 69–70; the study of high school seniors is reported by H. H. Remmers and R. D. Franklin, "Sweet Land of Liberty," in H. H. Remmers, ed., *Anti-Democratic Attitudes in American Schools* (Evanston, Ill.: Northwestern University Press, 1963), p. 62.

24. R. Merelman, "Democratic Politics and the Culture of American Education," *American Political Science Review* 74 (June 1980), pp. 319–32.

25. G. Almond and S. Verba, *Civic Culture* (Boston: Little, Brown, 1965); John R. Hibbing and Elizabeth Theiss-Morse, "Civics Is Not Enough: Teaching Barbarics in K-12," forthcoming, *P.S.*

26. Material for this section is drawn from E. C. Ladd and S. M. Lipset, *The Divided Academy* (New York: McGraw-Hill, 1975); C. Kesler, "The Movement of Student Opinion," *The National Review* (November 23) 1979, p. 29; E. L. Boyer, *College: The Undergraduate Experience in America* (New York: Harper & Row, 1986); "Fact File: Attitudes and Characteristics of This Year's Freshman," *The Chronicle of Higher Education* (January 11, 1989) pp. A33–A34; General Social Survey, National Opinion Research Center, 1984, p. 87.

27. Rene Sanchez, "Don't Know Much About Politics," *Washington Post National Weekly Edition,* January 16, 1995, p. 37.

28. M. K. Jennings and R. G. Niemi, *The Political Character of Adolescence* (Princeton, N.J.: Princeton University Press, 1974), p. 243.

29. M. McCombs and D. Shaw, "The Agenda Setting Function of the Media," *Public Opinion Quarterly* 36 (Summer 1972), pp. 176–87.

30. B. I. Page, R. Shapiro, and G. R. Dempsey, "What Moves Public Opinion?" *American Political Science Review* 81 (March 1987), pp. 23–44.

31. H. Weissberg, "Marital Differences in Voting," *Public Opinion Quarterly 51* (1987), pp. 335–43.

32. P. R. Abramson, *Political Attitudes in America* (San Francisco: Freeman, 1983), pp. 150, 213; see also Paul R. Abramson, *The Political Socialization of Black Americans* (New York: Free Press, 1977).

33. P. E. Converse, A. R. Clausen, and W. Miller, "Electoral Myth and Reality," *American Political Science Review* 59 (1965), pp. 321–26.

34. J. P. Robinson, "The Press as Kingmaker: What Surveys Show from the Last Five Campaigns," *Journalism Quarterly* 49 (Summer 1974), p. 592.

35. For a review of the history of polling, see Hennessy, *Public Opinion,* pp. 42–44, 46–50. See also C. Roll and A. Cantril, *Polls: Their Use and Misuse in Politics* (New York: Basic Books, 1972), pp. 3–16.

36. P. Squire, "The 1936 Literary Digest Poll," *Public Opinion Quarterly* 52 (1988), pp. 125–33; see also Don Cahalan, "The Digest Poll Rides Again," *Public Opinion Quarterly* 53 (1989), pp. 107–13.

37. Hennessy, *Public Opinion,* p. 46.

38. I. A. Lewis and W. Schneider, "Is the Public Lying to the Pollsters?" *Public Opinion Magazine* (April/May 1982), pp. 42–47. See also A. Clausen, "Response Validity and Vote Report," *Public Opinion Quarterly* 32 (1968), pp. 588–606.

39. "All Things Considered," National Public Radio, October 30, 1992.

40. Richard Morin, "A Pollster's Worst Nightmare: Declining Response Rates," *Washington Post National Weekly* (July 5–11, 1993), p. 37.

41. H. Asher, *Polling and the Public* (Washington, D.C.: CQ Press, 1988), pp. 113–14.

42. "Polls Came Close to Nailing Election," *Lincoln Journal* (November 11, 1992).

43. Many questioned the polls because some pollsters, Gallup in particular, showed Bush overcoming a substantial Clinton lead and closing to within two percentage points a week before the election. Some argued that this was not a real surge but resulted from a change by Gallup in reporting Bush's support among likely rather than registered voters the week before the election. R. Morin, "Surveying the Ups and Downs of Election '92," *Washington Post National Weekly Edition* (November 9, 1992), p. 37.

44. H. Mendelsohn and I. Crespi, *Polls, Television, and the New Politics* (Scranton, Penn.: Chandler, 1972), pp. 125–28.

45. B. Sussman, "In Pollsters We Trust," *Washington Post National Weekly Edition* (August 25, 1968), p. 37.

46. M. C. Shelley and H. Hwang, "The Mass Media and Public Opinion Polls in the 1988 Presidential Election," *American Politics Quarterly* 19 (January 1991), pp. 59–79.

47. "Nixon Memos Include Polls, Funeral Plan," *Lincoln Journal* (May 29, 1987).

48. R. Morin, "Surveying the Surveyors," *Washington Post National Weekly Edition* (March 2, 1992), p. 37.

49. David Broder, "Push Polls Plunge Politics to a New Low," *Lincoln Star* (October 9, 1994), p. 5E.

50. Ibid.

51. Roll and Cantril, *Polls: Their Use and Misuse in Politics,* p. 23; Mendelsohn and Crespi, *Polls, Television, and the New Politics,* p. 130.

52. Roll and Cantril, *Polls,* p. 24.

53. J. Klapper, quoted in B. Sussman, "Some Answers to the Polls' Critics," *Washington Post National Weekly Edition,* November 12, 1984, p. 37.

54. Richard Morin, "When the Method Becomes the Message," *Washington Post National Weekly Edition,* December 19–25, 1994, p. 33.

55. 1978 National Election Study, Center for Political Studies, University of Michigan.

56. Michael X. Delli Carpini and Scott Keeter, "U.S. Public Knowledge of Politics," *Public Opinion Quarterly* (Winter, 1991), pp. 583–612.

57. Richard Morin, "They Know Only What They Don't Like," *Washington Post National Weekly Edition,* October 3–9, 1994, p. 37.

58. 1986 National Election Study, Center for Political Studies, University of Michigan; "Wapner Top Judge in Recognition Poll," *Lincoln Star,* June 23, 1989, p. 1 (*Washington Post* syndication).

59. Delli Carpini, "U.S. Public Knowledge of Politics."

60. Morin, "They Know What They Don't Like."

61. New York Times/CBS News Poll, February 22–25, 1995.

62. Richard Morin, "With Scandal Aplenty, Who Cares About Issues?" *Washington Post National Weekly Edition,* October 17–23, 1994, p. 37.

63. Ibid.

64. Richard Morin, "Foreign Aid: Mired in Misunderstanding," *Washington Post National Weekly Edition,* March 20–26, 1995, p. 37.

65. M. J. Robinson and M. Clancey, "Teflon Politics," *Public Opinion* 7 (April/May 1984), pp. 14–18.

66. Richard Morin, "What Informed Public Opinion?" *Washington Post National Weekly Edition,* April 10–16, 1995, p. 36.

67. V. O. Key, *The Responsible Electorate* (Cambridge, Mass.: Harvard University Press, 1966); N. Nie, S. Verba, and J. R. Petrocik, *The Changing American Voter* (Cambridge, Mass.: Harvard University Press, 1976), chapter 18.

68. B. Sussman, "When Politicians Talk about Issues People Listen," *Washington Post National Weekly Edition,* August 18, 1986, p. 37.

69. Data in this section are summarized in *The Public Perspective* 6, no. 2 (February/March, 1995), pp. 39–46.

70. Data here are from Peter Hart Research Associates Survey for the Council for Excellence in Government, March 16–18, 1995.

71. Gallup Survey, December 16, 1993.

72. Ibid.

73. This section draws heavily on H. Schuman, C. Steeh, and L. Bobo, *Racial Attitudes in America* (Cambridge, Mass.: Harvard University Press, 1985); data summaries are drawn from the General Social Surveys of the National Opinion Research Center, University of Chicago, and National Elections Studies of CPS, University of Michigan; see also L. Sigelman and S. Welch, *Black Americans' Views of Racial Inequality* (Cambridge, Mass.: Cambridge University Press, 1991).

74. *Washington Post National Weekly Edition,* October 30, 1989, p. 37.

75. "Whites Retain Negative Views of Minorities, a Survey Finds," *New York Times, January 10, 1991,* p. C19; *M.* Jackman, "General and Applied Tolerance: Does Education Increase Commitment to Racial Inequality?" *American Journal of Political Science* 22 (1978), pp. 302–24; M. Jackman, "Education and Policy Commitment to Racial Equality," *American Journal of Political Science* 25 (1981), pp. 256–69; D. Kinder and D. Sears, "Prejudice and Politics," *Journal of Personality and Social Psychology* 40 (1981), pp. 414–31.

76. "Whites Retain Negative Views."

77. H. Schuman and L. Bobo, "Survey-Based Experiments on White Attitudes toward Residential Integration," *American Journal of Sociology* 94 (1988), pp. 272–94; W. R. Merriman and E. Carmines, "The Limits of Liberal Tolerance: The Case of Racial Politics," *Polity* 20 (1988), pp. 519–26; see also Schuman, Steeh, and Bobo, *Racial Attitudes.*

78. L. Sigelman and S. Welch, "A Dream Deferred: Black Attitudes toward Race and Inequality," unpublished manuscript, 1989. Almost all blacks support school integration, only 50% to 60% support busing.

79. 1990 General Social Survey.

80. ABC/*Washington Post* Poll, 1981.

81. Richard Morin, "No Place for Calm and Quiet Opinions," *Washington Post National Weekly Edition* (April 24–30, 1994), p. 34.

82. Martin Gilens and Paul Sniderman, "Affirmative Action and the Politics of Realignment." Paper presented at the Midwest Political Science Association Meeting, Chicago, Ill., 1995; Paul Sniderman and Thomas Piazza, *The Scar of Race* (Cambridge, Mass: Harvard University Press, 1993).

83. ABC/*Washington Post* Poll, 1981 and 1986.

84. J. Sullivan, G. Marcus, S. Feldman, and J. Pierson, "Sources of Political Tolerance: A Multivariate Analysis," *American Political Science Review* 75 (March 1981), pp. 92–106.

85. S. Stouffer, *Communism, Conformity, and Civil Liberties* (New York: John Wiley and Sons, 1954).

86. R. W. Jackman, "Political Elites, Mass Publics, and Support for Democratic Principles," *Journal of Politics* 34 (August 1972), p. 753.

87. H. McClosky and J. Zaller, *The American Ethos: Public Attitudes toward Capitalism and Democracy* (Cambridge, Mass.: Harvard University Press, 1986).

88. C. Z. Nunn, H. H. Crockett, Jr., and J. A. Williams, *Tolerance for Nonconformity* (San Francisco: Jossey-Bass, 1976).

89. J. Sullivan, J. Pierson, and G. Marcus, "An Alternative Conceptualization of Tolerance: Illusory Increases 1950s–1970s," *American Political Science Review* 73 (September 1979), pp. 781–94. For a critique of this study, see P. M. Sniderman, P. E. Tetlock, J. M. Glaser, D. P. Gress, and M. Hout, "Principled Tolerance and the American Mass Public," *British Journal of Political Science* 19 (January 1989), pp. 25–46.

90. P. Abramson, "Comments on Sullivan, Pierson, and Marcus," *American Political Science Review* 74 (June 1980): pp. 780–81.

91. "Polls Find Americans Angry, Anxious, Less Altruistic," *Lincoln Journal* (September 21, 1994), p. 9.

92. 1990 General Social Survey.

93. Judith Shklar, quoted in Paul Taylor, "In Watergate's Wake: The Good, the Bad, and the Ugly," *Washington Post National Weekly Edition,* June 22, 1992, p. 25.

94. Almond and Verba, *Civic Culture,* pp. 64–68.

95. A. Miller, "Political Issues and Trust in Government, 1964–1970," *American Political Science Review* 68 (September 1974), pp. 951–72.

96. S. M. Lipset and W. Schneider, *The Confidence Gap* (New York: Free Press, 1983), pp. 63–64.

97. "Clinton's High Victory Rate Conceals Disappointments," *Congressional Quarterly Weekly Report* (December 31, 1994), pp. 3619–3623.

98. A. Miller and S. Borrelli, "Confidence in Government During the 1980s," *American Politics Quarterly* 19 (April 1991), pp. 147–73.

99. T. J. Lowi, *The Personal President* (Ithaca, N.Y.: Cornell University Press, 1985), pp. 64–68.

100. Hibbing and Theiss-Morse, *Congress as Public Enemy: Public Attitudes Toward Political Institutions (Cambridge: Cambridge University Press, 1995).*

101. 1990 General Social Survey.

102. Richard Morin, "I'm OK; My Government's Not," *Washington Post National Weekly Edition* (July 26–August 1, 1993), p. 37.

103. Ibid.

104. Benjamin Page and Robert Shapiro, "Effects of Public Opinion on Policy," *American Political Science Review* 77 (March 1983), pp. 175–90.

105. Sidney Verba and Norman H. Nie, *Participation in America: Political Democracy and Social Equality* (New York: Harper & Row, 1972), chapter 15.

106. Dan Balz, "Taking a Positive View," *Washington Post National Weekly Edition* (March 7–13, 1994), p. 13.

5 Interest Groups

You Are There

The NAACP Debates the Thomas Nomination

It is August 1991 and you are Benjamin Hooks, executive director of the National Association for the Advancement of Colored People (NAACP). You and the organization are faced with one of the most difficult decisions in the organization's 80-year history.

President Bush has nominated Clarence Thomas, a black federal appeals court judge, to replace Thurgood Marshall on the Supreme Court. Marshall, the first African-American to serve on the Court, was the principal architect of the NAACP's efforts to attack segregation through the courts in the 1940s and '50s. Marshall represented the NAACP in *Brown v. Board of Education* in which the Supreme Court outlawed segregation in public schools in 1954. Appointed to the Court by President Johnson in 1967, Marshall became a spokesperson for black interests and liberal causes on the Court. With the shift of the Court to the right in the 1970s and 1980s, Marshall became one of the last liberal voices on a bench dominated by conservative appointees of Presidents Reagan and Bush. When age and illness prevented Marshall from continuing, Bush nominated Thomas to fill the vacancy.

Clarence Thomas was born into a poor family and raised by a grandfather who taught the values of hard work and discipline. He attended Catholic schools with income earned from the family's fuel business. Later he earned a scholarship to attend Holy Cross College, and then gained admission to Yale Law School through an affirmative action program.

Following law school, Thomas worked for Missouri State Attorney General John Danforth. After several years with Monsanto Corporation, he rejoined newly elected Senator Danforth in Washington. His rise as a black Republican continued with an appointment by President Reagan as Assistant Secretary of Education for Civil Rights and later chairman of the Equal Employment Opportunity Commission (EEOC). President Bush appointed Thomas to the Circuit Court of Appeals for the District of Columbia.

As a Reagan appointee, Thomas established his conservative credentials. During his years at the Office of Civil Rights, he failed to implement policies that would have funneled millions of dollars to black colleges. In sworn testimony, Thomas conceded his failure to implement the law. The effect was devastating on the educational opportunities of young blacks. While with the EEOC, he vigorously opposed affirmative action, rejecting a policy he had benefited from when he applied to law school. He also violated civil rights laws by failing to process thousands of age discrimination cases. Thomas and the Reagan Administration simply did not believe in affirmative action and civil rights laws and were lax about enforcing laws to implement them.

Thomas is one of a minority of black conservatives highly critical of the social welfare programs begun in the 1930s to pull the nation out of the Great Depression, and expanded in the 1960s and 1970s in an effort to help people out of poverty. While the programs of the 1930s improved the lot of most Americans, segregation and discrimination against blacks remained. And although some of the programs of the 1960s and 1970s were targeted directly at blacks, conservatives like Thomas view them as obstacles to black self-empowerment. Programs such as affirmative action that treat blacks as disadvantaged, they argue, hold blacks back and prevent them from achieving and moving ahead. They reject what they consider to

CONTINUED 

OUTLINE

Group Formation
- Why Groups Form
- Why People Join
- Who Joins?

Types of Interest Groups
- Private Interest Groups
- Public Interest Groups

Tactics of Interest Groups
- Direct Lobbying Techniques
- Indirect Lobbying Techniques
- Protest and Civil Disobedience

Success of Interest Groups
- Resources
- Competition and Goals

Conclusion: Do Interest Groups Help Make Government Responsive?

be the paternalism and racism of liberalism, which sees all blacks as ghetto dwellers, products of broken families, fugitives from the underclass, and deficient in mainstream culture. Their view is, "I made it on my own, so can you." Because they reject the liberal welfare state, the principal agent for black advancement for the past 60 years, they are separated from most black leaders and the black community as a whole.

So you are facing a dilemma. As a leader of one of the major civil rights groups, you think there should be a black on the Court and you know your fellow African Americans do too. Yet you are worried about Thomas's views. Not only has he questioned the value of social programs that you consider essential, but he has attacked civil rights groups. As Assistant Attorney General, he said these groups have done "nothing right," their leaders just "bitch, bitch, bitch, moan and whine." You wonder if he will harm the black cause more than help it. Only 43, he could sit on the high Court a long time.

Yet some black lawyers urge that Thomas be given a chance. They think that Thomas's impoverished childhood will lead him to feel empathy for poor people. And they maintain that once on the bench he would be subject to fewer partisan pressures than as a member of the Reagan Administration, so he might not vote the way conservatives expect. (His stint as an appeals court judge has been too short to indicate.)

You are beginning to realize how shrewd the nomination is. The president chose a black, as people would expect for this vacancy, yet he found one who seems to reject the policies that most black leaders support. Thus, the president is trying to split blacks and at the same time, trying to split the Democratic party coalition of blacks, liberals, women, and others. For not only does Thomas criticize civil rights policies, he also criticizes the Court's abortion rulings that most women's group leaders support. The president is trying to drive a wedge between black and other groups in the coalition.

Of course, Bush is not going to nominate exactly the type of person you would prefer. As a Republican, he is not going to choose a Democrat. As a conservative, feeling pressure from groups that are conservative, he is not going to choose a liberal or even a moderate.

You and the NAACP feel strong pressure to support a black nominee. However, if Thomas gets on the bench, he will probably be at odds with the black agenda supported by every major black political and social leader over the past 60 years. If, on the other hand, you oppose Thomas, it might mean sacrificing a black seat on the Court. Bush might turn to a Hispanic or even a conservative white for his choice.[1]

As director of the NAACP, which way do you direct the organization? Do you support the Thomas nomination and ensure a black on the Court for years to come, and in the process repudiate the policies of a lifetime that you and the NAACP have supported? Or do you oppose Thomas and run the risk of losing a black on the Court and a chance that Thomas might change his views after he is confirmed?

In the United States everything from fruits to nuts is organized. From apple growers to filbert producers, every interest has an organization to represent it. These organizations touch every aspect of our lives; members of the American College of Obstetrics and Gynecology bring us into the world, and members of the National Funeral Directors Association usher us out.

Organizations that try to achieve at least some of their goals with government assistance are called **interest groups.** Fruit and nut growers want government subsidies and protection from imported products; doctors and funeral directors want to be free of government controls. The efforts of interest groups to influence government are called **lobbying.** Lobbying may involve direct contact between a lobbyist, or consultant or lawyer, as they prefer to be called, and a government official; or it may involve indirect action, such as attempts to sway public opinion, which will in turn influence officials.

People organize and lobby because these are ways for them to enhance their influence. As one Washington lobbyist put it, "Democracy is not a spectator sport. If you want to have a hand in shaping the nation, you must get into it with more than your one vote on the Tuesday after the first Monday in November."[2] Or as another put it, somewhat more forcefully, "The modern government is huge, pervasive, intrusive into everybody's life. If you just let things take their course and don't get involved in the game, you get trampled on."[3]

The Founders feared the harmful effects of interest groups. Madison was intent on "curing the mischiefs of faction" through separation of powers, checks and balances, and federalism. Today, many people bemoan the "mischiefs of faction" or "special interests" because they seem to block government actions favoring the larger interests of society.[4] Sometimes it seems that everyone is represented in Washington but the people.

Do interest groups undermine the people's interests? Or do they make government more responsive by giving people greater representation in the political process? These are the difficult questions we explore in this chapter.

➤Group Formation

There are thousands of groups in the United States. Americans seem to be "joiners." As early as the 1830s, the Frenchman Alexis de Tocqueville, who traveled in America, noted the tendency of Americans to join groups: "In no country in the world has the principle of association been more successfully used or applied to a greater multitude of objects than in America."[5] Even now Americans are more likely than citizens in other countries to belong to groups.[6]

However, this pattern may be changing. Participation in community organizations is down. Labor unions, PTAs, women's clubs, fraternal organizations have seen membership fall off.[7] The change reflects less leisure time as well as growing suspicion and distrust of citizens toward each other. Between 1960 and 1993, the percentage of Americans saying that most people can be trusted fell by more than a third.[8]

The United States is especially fertile for the growth of groups. Compared to most other countries, it is racially, religiously, and ethnically diverse. These differences give rise to different interests and views on public issues and often lead to the formation of groups that express those views.[9]

Groups can organize because of the freedom to speak, assemble, and petition government, guaranteed in the First Amendment to the Constitution. Without such freedom, only groups favored by the government—or groups whose members are willing to be punished for their actions—could exist.

The federal structure also encourages the proliferation of groups. It is not enough to have a national organization. Because state and local governments have significant power, groups also must be organized at those levels to protect their interests.

Why Groups Form

The formation of groups occurs in waves.[10] In some periods formation is rapid and extensive, whereas at other times there is very little activity.

In 1773 a group of colonists organized to protest British taxes on tea by throwing tea into Boston Harbor. In 1989 groups organized to protest a congressional pay increase by sending teabags to their representatives in Washington.

Social and economic stress often account for these surges.[11] The stress of the Revolutionary War period activated groups for and against independence. The slavery controversy in the decades before the Civil War energized groups on both sides of the issue. After the war, rapid industrialization led to the formation of trade unions and business associations. Economic problems in agricultural areas spurred the development of farm groups.

The greatest surge in group formation occurred between 1900 and 1920. Stimulated by the shocks of industrialization, urbanization, immigration, and the government's response to them, groups such as the United States Chamber of Commerce, American Medical Association, American Farm Bureau Federation, National Association for the Advancement of Colored People (NAACP), Socialist and Communist parties, and countless others formed.[12]

The 1960s and 1970s witnessed an interest group explosion, directed primarily toward Washington. As the national government expanded in power and influence in the post-World War II period, it increasingly became the center of interest group efforts to satisfy demands for favorable public policy. Spurred by the success of civil rights and war protest movements in the 1960s, other groups representing racial minorities, women, consumers, the poor, the elderly, and the environment organized. Business lobbying surged in the late 1970s as a response to the success of

For Right to Undress, Nudists Flex Right to Redress

For those of you who get the urge to go skinny-dipping in the public pool or tan in the nude at the neighborhood park, the 17,000-member Naturalist Society, the nation's most politically active organization of nudists, is out to help.

While the National Park Service allows nude beaches in remote areas, conflicts occur at more accessible beaches. Members argue that they "are tired of always moving farther down the beach." To protect their right to clothing-optional recreation, as members call it, the organization retained a Washington lobbyist to make its case to Congress.

The first task of their newly hired lobbyist is to make the issue less attention grabbing. The strategy is to become just another pestering group in Washington. When the smirks fade from the faces of official Washington, the group believes it will be taken more seriously.

Politically, nudists are divided into conservative and liberal camps. Conservatives tend to join the Florida-based Sunbathing Association, which claims 36,000 members. They prefer to be left alone and gravitate toward private clubs. Liberals are more likely to join the Naturalist Society and use public beaches.

Besides beach access, nudists are addressing other issues as well, including child custody and jobs. Many have lost children and jobs because of their penchant for nude recreation.

SOURCE: "The Right to Undress," *Common Cause Magazine* (January/February 1991), pp. 6–7.

consumer and environmental groups in prompting government to increase the regulation of occupational safety and environmental standards.[13]

Technological changes also accelerate group formation. A national network of railroads and the telegraph contributed to the surge in the early 1900s. Computer-generated direct mail appeals, to solicit funds and mobilize members to action, as well as WATS lines (wide-area telephone service), increased the ability of groups to form and mobilize in the 1960s and 1970s. The number of groups increased by 60% between 1960 and 1980, and the number sending representatives to Washington doubled.[14] The spread of personal computers and the growing system of computer networks known as the Internet in the 1990s facilitates communication between persons with an endless variety of narrow interests. PCs and the Internet are particularly useful for persons who wish to organize citizens but who lack financial resources for more sophisticated approaches.[15] For example, members and sympathizers of militia groups are able to use the Internet to keep each other informed about group activities.

Group organizers also play a role in group formation.[16] These entrepreneurs often come from established groups. They gain experience and then strike out on their own. Many civil rights activists of the 1950s and early 1960s founded organizations in the late 1960s. Some used their skills to organize groups against the war in Vietnam and later to organize groups for women's rights and environmental causes.[17] Thus the formation of one group often opens the door to the formation of others.

The government is also important to group formation. Government attempts to deal with perceived problems often generate organized opposition groups, such as the increase in business lobbying in response to environmental lobbying. In addition, government provides direct financial assistance to some groups, particularly nonprofit organizations. Groups as diverse as the American Council of Education, the National Governors Association, and the National Council of Senior Citizens obtain a large percentage of their budgets through federal grants and contracts.[18]

Why People Join

Most people join groups voluntarily because of the benefits groups provide.[19] Some are attracted to groups for political or ideological reasons. Members of Common Cause join because they support the group's goals of campaign finance reform and ethics in government. The benefits are the psychological satisfaction of being identified with the cause and the prospect that the group will succeed. Some groups offer monetary benefits to members such as discounted prices for goods and services. The large nonfarm membership of the Farm Bureau often is attributed to the cut-rate insurance policies offered through the organization.[20] The American Association of Retired Persons (AARP) provides health, home, and auto insurance; a motor club; a travel service; investment counseling; discount drugs and medicines; and a magazine. These services attract members and generate millions of dollars for the organization. Two-thirds of AARP's revenue comes from business activities that provide discount services to members. Groups also provide social benefits. Some people join groups to make friends.

Because most groups seek to expand their membership and people join for different reasons, most groups provide a mix of benefits. The National Rifle Association (NRA) lobbies against gun regulation and control. Some people join for this reason. Others join to secure other NRA services: *The American Rifleman* (a monthly magazine), a hunter's information service, low-cost firearm insurance, membership in local gun clubs, and shooting competitions.[21] Still others join because they enjoy associating with fellow gun enthusiasts.

Some people join groups because they are coerced. For example, in many states lawyers must join the state bar association to practice law.

■ Who Joins?

Not all people are equally likely to join groups.[22] Those with higher incomes and education are more likely to belong. They can afford membership dues, have the leisure necessary to take part, and have the social and intellectual skills that facilitate group participation. They also appear more attractive to many groups and therefore are more apt to be recruited. Whites more often belong to groups than blacks, but mostly because of their higher average income and education.[23]

➤Types of Interest Groups

Interest groups come in all shapes and sizes. Some have large memberships, such as the American Federation of Labor-Congress of Industrial Organizations (AFL-CIO) with 13 million members. Others have small memberships, such as the Mushroom Growers Association with 14 members.

Two types of groups do not have any members.[24] Corporations do not have members but act as interest groups when they lobby government. Some Washington-based groups also do not have members. They lobby on behalf of specific interests and are funded by the government, private foundations, other groups, or fees from consulting. The Children's Defense Fund (CDF) is one such group. Founded in 1973, its staff of 90, funded entirely from private funds, lobbies on behalf of a broad range of issues involving children.[25]

Some groups have members, but their sole purpose is financial support. Supporters are "checkbook" members, and the group is simply the staff. Supporters' main links to the organization are occasional checks they send to it. They may receive a newsletter and requests to write their senator or representative, but they do not interact with other members nor participate in decision making. Some public interest groups, such as Congress Watch, Ralph Nader's organization, have this organizational structure. Many **political action committees (PACs)** do also. They raise money through direct mail and channel it to political candidates. How to spend the money, some of which goes to staff, is determined solely by the staff.

Some interest groups are formally organized, with appointed or elected leaders, regular meetings, and dues-paying members. Some are large corporations whose leaders are the corporate officers hired by boards of directors. Others have no leaders and few prescribed rules.

Thus, interest groups can be distinguished according to their membership and organizational structure. They also can be distinguished by their goals.

■ Private Interest Groups

Private interest groups pursue chiefly economic interests that benefit their members.

Business

Business organizations are the largest and most powerful interest groups (see Figure 1). Some have argued that the major cleavage in American politics is between business groups on the one hand and government and not-for-profit institutions on the other.[26] E. E. Schattschneider notes that "the struggle for power is largely a confrontation of two major power systems, government and business."[27]

However, throughout the 1980s and 1990s, government often supported the interests of business regardless of which party controlled the White House or Congress.[28] Republicans traditionally favor business, and Democrats recently have supported business more than in the past, due to contributions to Democrats by business and the election of more moderate and conservative Democrats. Under Clinton, business won major international trade agreements. It was able to secure "most favored nation" trade privileges for China in spite of human rights violations by that country. Despite courting by the Clinton administration, business lobbies defeated the administration's economic stimulus package and health care reform proposal, which would have required employers to provide employee health insurance. They also sty-

■ **FIGURE 1**
Business Interests Dominate the Contemporary Interest Group System

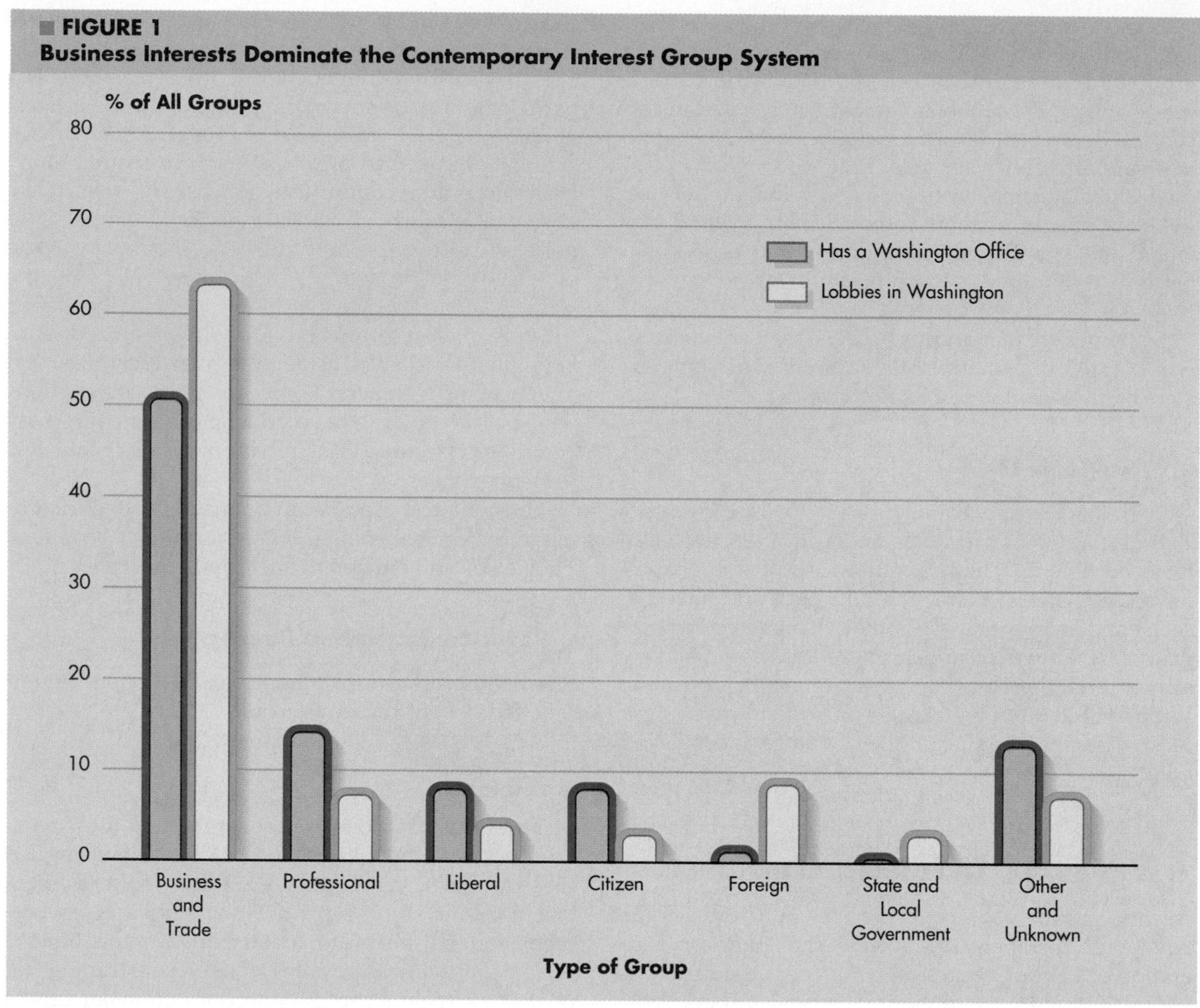

NOTE: Groups with a Washington office number 2,810, and 6,601 groups lobby there. "Liberal" groups are those representing women, minorities, the poor, labor, and the elderly. "Citizen" includes public interest groups such as Common Cause.
SOURCE: K. L. Schlozman and J. T. Tierney, *Organized Interests and American Democracy* (New York: Harper & Row, 1986), p. 67.

mied labor's goal of prohibiting permanent replacement of striking workers.

With Republican control of Congress in 1994, business can expect even more success.[29] Environmental regulations and product liability laws are likely to change in favor of business.

Business is not monolithic, however. The Chamber of Commerce, one of the most important business groups, represents a great range of different businesses. The National Association of Manufacturers and the Business Roundtable represent big business.

Other organizations represent small business: the National Federation of Independent Business and the National Small Business Association. These groups often, but not always, ally with big business.

In addition to these general groups, hundreds of trade associations represent single industries, such as builders, used-car salespeople, and restaurant owners. Many corporations also lobby in Washington.

Labor

Although there are more than 100 labor unions in the United States, the AFL-CIO is probably the most important politically. It is a confederation of 88 trade and industrial unions with 13 million members. It has

New Populism
The Angriest White Males

Although most interest groups seek to achieve their goals through lawful and democratic processes, a few of the angriest are going far beyond changing government by "throwing the rascals out" through the voting process. They are working to overthrow the government itself. Americans were shocked and horrified by the bombing of the federal building in Oklahoma City. While this was apparently the work of a few terrorists, whose enemy is the federal government, groups of militia have sprung up across the country who also despise the federal government.

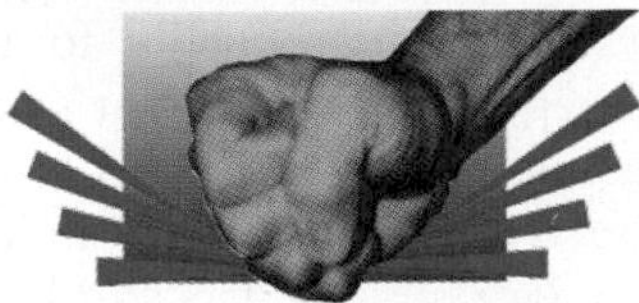

They live in a world of paranoia, hate, and fear. They believe that government has betrayed the people and subverted the Constitution. They believe that government has sold out to a mysterious "New World Order," a one-world government. They believe that "the nation is already under siege by troops hovering in black helicopters who have embedded interstate road signs with directional codes that only they can read."[1] Some groups also believe that Jews, blacks, or immigrants are trying to take over the government. And some even believe that bar codes in grocery stores are secret codes ordered by a foreign government, that bar codes on dollars allow government agents to drive by houses and determine how much money the occupants have, and that the government has installed electronic devices in car ignitions to stall autos on the day the "New World Order" takes over.[2]

Historians point out that the paranoid strain in American politics runs deep; only a few years ago, many people believed that it was the Communists who were about to take over America. With the demise of Communism, coupled with our own economic and social troubles, many people look closer to home to find an enemy.

Militias collect weapons, cache food, train in the woods, and await an invasion from a United Nations force. While their rage is, theoretically, against the forces of the "New World Order," in practice it is directed at federal agents and policies. Members have a particular hatred for gun control laws, believing that such laws are part of a plot by foreign agents to disarm America and take over. They are especially angry at the Bureau of Alcohol, Tobacco, and Firearms for its 1993 raid on the Branch Davidian religious sect at Waco, Texas (which ended in a mass suicide of the Davidians) and more generally because this agency enforces gun regulations.

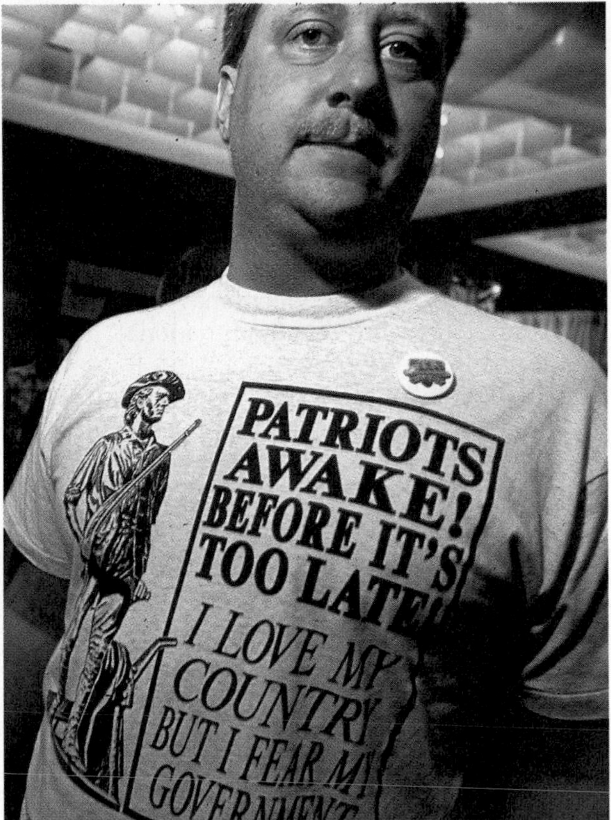

A small number of Americans are deeply suspicious of the government.

Of course, not all members of militia are males, and not all believe in all these conspiracy theories. Nor did most start out by believing any of these theories, but rather by being angry at government for being unresponsive to their concerns, whether they want to own assault weapons, think they should be able to graze their cattle on public lands, or believe that government has gone too far in protecting the rights of minorities.

Experts estimate that active members of the militia total less than 100,000 nationwide, but the concerns that fuel their hatred and fear resonate with many more Americans. In fact, a recent poll showed that four of ten Americans believe that the government threatens their freedom.[3]

---

1. "Inside the World of the Paranoid," *New York Times* (April 30, 1995), Section 4, p. 1.
2. Jill Smolowe, "Enemies of the State," *Time* (May 8, 1995), pp. 60–69.
3. Steven Thomma, "Poll Shows 4 of 10 Distrust Government," *Centre Daily Times* (April 29, 1995), p. 1. Another common set of conspiracy theories is found among urban blacks, some of whom believe that AIDs and drug traffic are white plots to destroy the black community.

a staff of 500 and includes some of the most skillful lobbyists in Washington. Through its Committee on Political Education (COPE), it provides substantial sums of money as well as a pool of campaign workers to candidates for public office, typically Democratic candidates. In recent years labor has lobbied hard to eliminate the right of employers to hire replacement workers for striking employees; to defeat the North American Free Trade Agreement between the U.S., Mexico, and Canada, which may mean a loss of American jobs; and to adopt national health care reform.

Although still significant, the political influence of labor unions has waned since the 1960s. One reason is that membership has declined. Only 16% of the nonagricultural work force belongs to unions (see Figure 2). Declining membership reflects changes in the economy. In the 1970s and 1980s, millions from the "baby boom" generation entered the job market but could not find jobs. Slowdowns in manufacturing, such as steel and auto production, added to unemployment. The oversupply of workers, along with a fear of inflation and presidents hostile to unions, created pressures to keep wages low. Labor's bargaining position with business weakened, and there was little reason for union workers to look to unions for help or for nonunion workers to join. Additionally, global competition robbed labor of its most powerful

FIGURE 2
Union Membership Has Decreased

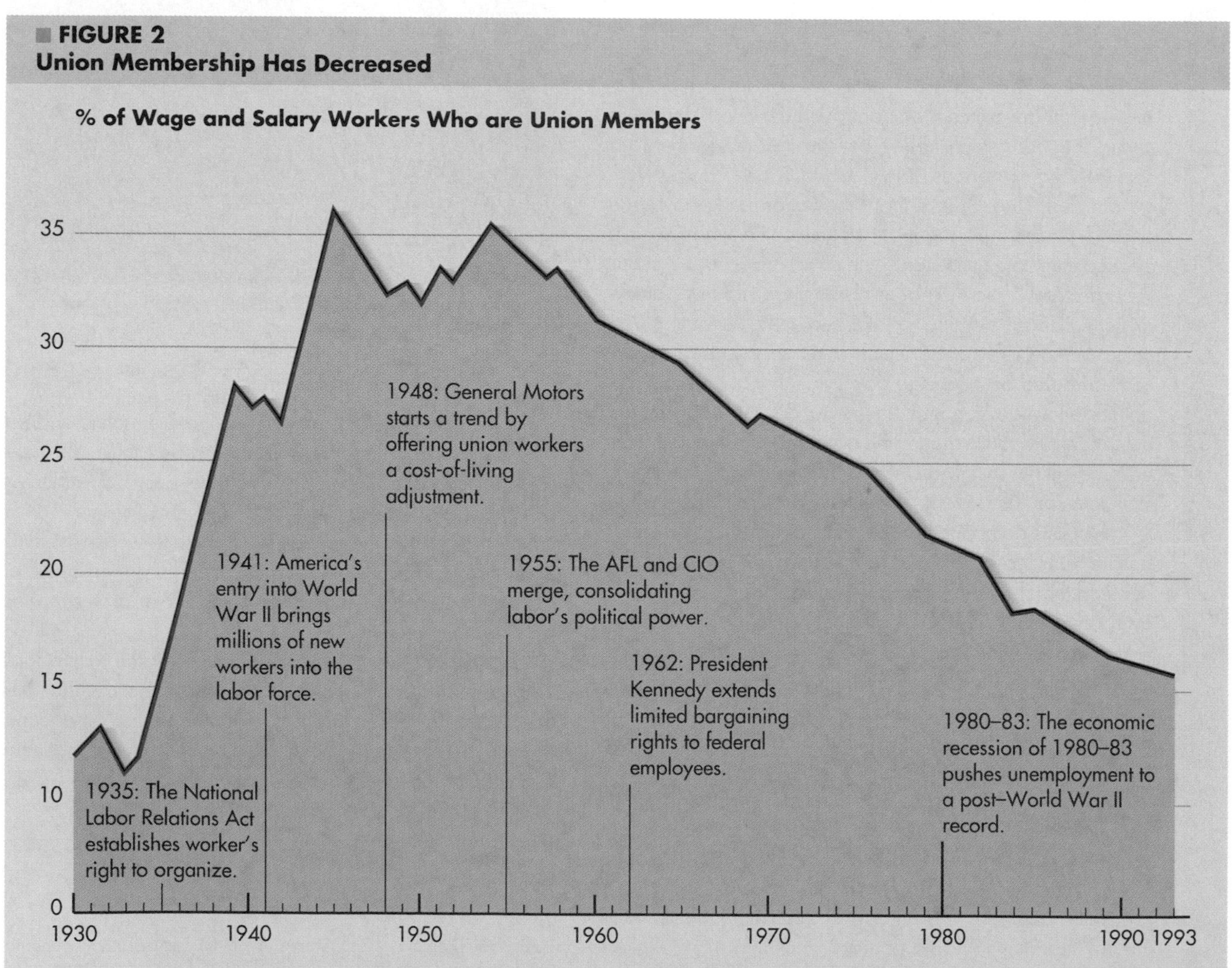
% of Wage and Salary Workers Who are Union Members
35
30
25
20
15
10
0
1930
1940
1950
1960
1970
1980
1990 1993
1935: The National Labor Relations Act establishes worker's right to organize.
1941: America's entry into World War II brings millions of new workers into the labor force.
1948: General Motors starts a trend by offering union workers a cost-of-living adjustment.
1955: The AFL and CIO merge, consolidating labor's political power.
1962: President Kennedy extends limited bargaining rights to federal employees.
1980–83: The economic recession of 1980–83 pushes unemployment to a post–World War II record.

SOURCES: Christoph Blumrich, *Newsweek*, September 5, 1983, p. 51; *Statistical Abstract of the United States*. 1990; *Lincoln Journal*, March 1993.

weapon—the strike. Fearful that they will be replaced or that their employers will suffer in the competitive marketplace, employees are unwilling to strike. In recent testimony, the AFL-CIO signaled its willingness to curb the right to strike if Congress would restrict the right of business to use replacement workers during a strike.[30]

Some businesses also frustrated union efforts to organize workers by opting for a "progressive management" approach to keep workers satisfied. Others threatened to fire pro-union employees or predicted dire consequences from unionization; both tactics are illegal. Such tactics have increased in the 1980s in part because Reagan, and to a lesser extent Bush, appointed only probusiness people to the National Labor Relations Board (NLRB), the agency that hears cases involving threats and intimidation against employees who support unionization.[31] Previous presidents had appointed representatives of both business and labor to the board.

Until recently unions have also been unwilling to appeal to nonmanufacturing sectors of the economy. With the exception of teachers and government employees, unions have shown little interest in organizing younger workers, women, and those in clerical and service occupations. In general, union organizing activity has decreased in recent years.[32] Labor's political influence has also declined because its membership

Corporate Lobbies: Big Winners in the Government Sweepstakes

When one thinks of special interests seeking special favors from the government, the image of disgruntled farmers or abortion activists marching on Washington comes to mind. President Reagan used the label to identify labor unions, teachers, and women's groups when he charged that Walter Mondale, the Democratic party nominee for president in 1984, was the candidate of special interests. However, if the term refers to groups that are the most powerful and successful in winning "goodies" from the federal government, it applies to America's biggest and wealthiest corporations.

Corporations lobby Congress and government agencies for a variety of benefits including subsidies and tax breaks. In 1994, business received $50 billion in direct subsidies and another $50 billion in tax breaks. One of the leading beneficiaries of government largess is agribusiness, which receives nearly $30 billion in subsidies. Large, profitable ranchers are allowed to graze their livestock on federal lands at a fraction of what it would cost on private property. One hundred million dollars is doled out by the government to companies to advertise their products abroad. Sunkist Growers, Inc., received $18 million to promote citrus products. The American Soybean Growers got $10 million, Gallo wines $5 million, and McDonalds $.5 million to push Chicken McNuggets.

Mining companies are permitted to extract minerals from public lands for nothing. The "biggest prize" went to a Toronto-based company that has mined $9 billion worth of gold from public lands since 1987. The founder of the company collected $32 million in salary in 1992.

Pharmaceutical companies are also big winners. U.S. taxpayers paid out $32 million dollars over 15 years to develop Taxol, an anticancer drug. Bristol-Myers Squibb was given exclusive rights to market the drug in 1991, at which time it charged $986 for a three-week supply. Estimates are that the company recouped eight times its production costs. Taxpayers paid once to develop the drug and again to use it.

These benefits are often justified on the grounds that they promote competitiveness with companies that enjoy unfair marketing advantages. For example, the $100 million provided firms to advertise their products overseas is supposed to help American firms overcome the advantages enjoyed by foreign companies that are subsidized by their governments. However, most of the firms are reaping huge profits, and subsidies and tax breaks are only a small part of the overall net worth of corporate America.

Programs like food stamps ($25 billion in 1994) and Aid to Families with Dependent Children ($15 billion in 1994) are often criticized as "giveaways" that should be cut in periods of tight budgets and deficits. Few call for elimination of corporate "giveaways." One reason is that corporations lobby effectively to keep them.

SOURCE: James P. Donahue, "The Corporate Welfare Kings," *Washington Post National Weekly Edition* (March 21–27, 1993), p. 24.

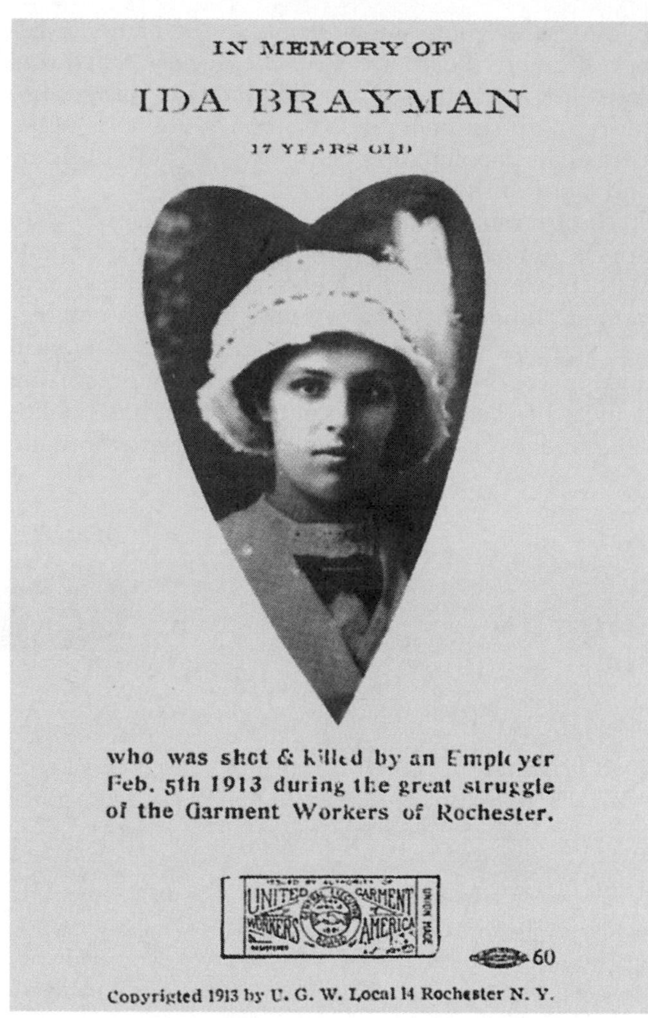

IN MEMORY OF
IDA BRAYMAN
17 YEARS OLD
who was shot & killed by an Employer Feb. 5th 1913 during the great struggle of the Garment Workers of Rochester.
UNITED GARMENT WORKERS AMERICA
UNION MADE
60
Copyrighted 1913 by U. G. W. Local 14 Rochester N. Y.

This postcard commemorates the death of a 17-year-old woman striking for recognition of her union, an eight-hour day, and extra pay for overtime and holidays.

is located primarily in the Northeast and Midwest, which are declining in population and losing representation in Congress. In the South and Southwest, where population is increasing, opposition to unions is strong and only a small percentage of the work force is unionized.

Union clout has also been weakened by an inability of union leaders to deliver the vote of rank-and-file members, particularly in presidential elections. Although leaders generally endorse Democratic candidates, rank-and-file members support both Democrats and Republicans. In 1984, despite a massive effort by union leaders to rally support for Walter Mondale, the Democratic presidential candidate, 45% of union households voted for Reagan. Forty-one percent voted for George Bush in 1988. However, only 24% supported Bush in 1992.

If an expected labor shortage materializes, conditions will be better for unionization. Providing more services to members, as done by interest groups such as AARP and NRA, may also make unionization more attractive to workers.[33] If not, labor's influence in American politics will continue to decline. (Although some expected union influence to grow in the Clinton White House, Clinton and the unions divided on the issue of NAFTA.)

Agriculture

Agricultural interests are represented by a variety of general and specialized groups. The American Farm Bureau Federation, the largest of the general agriculture interest groups, began when the federal government established the agricultural extension service with agents in rural locations to help farmers. To encourage cooperation with agents, the government offered grants to states that organized county farm bureaus. By 1919 a national organization was formed.

Despite its roots, the Farm Bureau today is staunchly opposed to government intervention in the economy, including subsidies to farmers. This reflects the conservative ideology of the large and wealthy farm interests that dominate the organization. Despite opposition to government subsidies, many members benefit from them.

The National Farmers' Union, which is considerably smaller than the Farm Bureau, represents small farming interests. It strongly supports government subsidies to farmers.

The American Agriculture Movement (AAM) began as a protest movement by farmers who were badly hurt by falling prices in the mid-1970s.[34] Dissatisfied with the position of both the Farm Bureau and the Farmers' Union, AAM called for a national farmer's strike until the government adopted a policy that included guaranteed income levels for farmers. Today AAM has a small, permanent lobbying staff in Washington and speaks out primarily on issues that benefit small farmers and ranchers.[35]

Along with the general interest groups, hundreds of commodity organizations promote specific products and operate much like business trade associations. Examples include cattle, cotton, milk, tobacco, and wool producers. Large agribusiness firms such as Cargill also have powerful lobbies in Washington.

Professionals

Most professions—occupations that require considerable specialized instruction or training, such as medicine, law, and teaching—have organizations to protect and promote their interests. Doctors have the powerful American Medical Association (AMA)[36] which has worked first to keep government out of medicine and then to shape Medicare and other government health programs in ways that benefit doctors. Although still influential, the AMA is no longer unchallenged; consumer and public interest groups, insurance companies, and national chains of hospitals and clinics are now highly involved in health-care issues.

The American Bar Association (ABA) represents the legal profession. The ABA supports the economic interests of lawyers and has promoted structural and procedural reforms of the courts.[37] The ABA also advises the president and Senate on the qualifications of those being considered for federal judgeships. The National Bar Association represents the nation's black lawyers. It deals with professional matters of particular interest to black lawyers and, like the ABA, passes judgment on the qualifications of federal judges. In the nomination of Clarence Thomas to the Supreme Court, the NBA narrowly voted to oppose his nomination 128–124.[38]

The National Education Association has a membership of 1.7 million teachers.[39] Perhaps its greatest national lobbying successes have been the establishment of the cabinet-level Department of Education in 1979 and defeating Reagan's attempts to dismantle it.

Even political scientists have a professional association, with 12,000 members. The American Political Science Association and other social science organizations also support an umbrella organization whose staff seeks to educate Congress and bureaucrats about the value of social science research.

Elderly

While the population of the nation as a whole has tripled since 1900, the number of elderly has increased eightfold. Today, persons over 65 are over 12% of the population. Several groups, sometimes called the "gray lobby," represent their interests.

Founded in 1958 to provide insurance to the elderly, the American Association of Retired Persons (AARP), with 33 million members, is the nation's largest and one of its most powerful interest groups. Recruited by direct mail and word of mouth, AARP attracts 8,000 new members a day. For $5, anyone over 50 can join and use the numerous benefits provided by the organization[40] (see Table 1).

AARP members review publications targeted for senior citizens.

With 1,300 employees and 18 lobbyists, AARP has become a potent political force. AARP's lobbying efforts are directed primarily at preserving and expanding government benefits to the elderly, which total about $14 billion each month.[41] The Reagan administration quickly dropped the idea of cutting cost-of-living increases in Social Security to reduce the nation's deficit when AARP and others protested. Reagan's budget director lamented, "These are people who have plenty of time on their hands, who are well organized, who vote regularly, and they are a massive political force."[42] Although programs for the elderly represent one-third of the budget, politicians are reluctant to touch them. Those who have suggested doing so have earned themselves the AARP label "granny-basher." Mindful of their political influence, Clinton got AARP to support reforming health care by including long-term nursing home care as part of his health care proposal.

TABLE 1 AARP is a Big Business

ACTIVITY	AARP'S 1987 REVENUE IN MILLIONS OF DOLLARS
Health insurance	$82.0
Magazine	34.0
Auto/home insurance	17.0
Travel service	2.0
Mutual funds	1.5
Pharmacy	1.0
Motor club	1.0

Influence is exercised primarily by a flood of correspondence to members of Congress from AARP members. There is no congressional district where the AARP is not 50,000 strong.[43]

To counterbalance the power of the gray lobby, a number of groups such as Americans for Generational Equity and the Children's Defense Fund have formed, but they are small by comparison.

Foreign Governments

Foreign interests also lobby in Washington. Mexico has a 16-member Washington office that geared up to support NAFTA. In addition to spending $1 million to polish the country's image, it distributed more than 100,000 pieces of mail, including state-by-state analyses of NAFTA's impact, to members of Congress. Most countries recruit lobbyists from the ranks of former members of Congress and the bureaucracy. Since 1974, 47% of former employees of the U.S. Office of Trade Assistance have worked for foreign governments, the most prominent for Japan. Though it happens frequently, most people consider it unethical for former government employees to leave government and take jobs with interest groups, corporations, or foreign governments and use their knowledge and skills to lobby government. Many officials of OTA helped draw up the rules for U.S. trade, then left and helped foreign governments beat the rules. As one writer put it, "No wonder we are losing the trade war."[44] The Clinton administration attempted to close the revolving door by requiring top political appointees to refrain from lobbying their agencies for five years after leaving government and from representing foreign governments forever.[45] However, two of his senior advisors left to take jobs with major lobbying firms. Both said they would not lobby government, but they were hired because of their contacts in the Clinton administration.

Public Interest Groups

Public interest groups, of which there are more than 2,500 with 40 million members,[46] lobby for benefits that cannot be limited or restricted to their members. The National Taxpayers Union lobbies for reduced taxes not only for themselves but for everyone who pays taxes. Amnesty International lobbies for the rights of political prisoners around the world even though none of its members are prisoners. Although nearly all groups think of themselves as pursuing the public interest, the label applies only to those working for other than personal or corporate interests. "Public interest" does not mean that a majority of the public necessarily favors the goals of these groups.

Public interest groups are not new, but their numbers and size increased dramatically during the late 1960s and early 1970s. Several factors account for this surge. Americans were becoming increasingly distrustful of government, which appeared to favor special interests over more general interests. The need for a balance between the two led many to join public interest groups. Many middle-class Americans also had the financial means to support public interest groups. The new technology mentioned earlier also made it possible to reach and mobilize large numbers of them.[47]

While many of the public interest groups that were established during the 1960s and 1970s were "shoestring" operations staffed by idealistic social reformers with few professional skills, the public interest organizations of today have larger budgets and memberships and a cadre of professionals—attorneys, management consultants, direct-mail fund-raisers, and communications directors—handling day-to-day operations and seeking to influence government with a variety of strategies and tactics.[48]

Multiple-Issue Groups

Some public interest groups are multiple-issue groups, involved with a broad range of issues. Others have a narrower focus and are often referred to as single-issue groups.

CONSUMER GROUPS One of the more famous consumer organizations is the network founded by Ralph Nader. Author of *Unsafe at Any Speed,* a book exposing safety defects in Corvair automobiles, Nader testified before Congress, which was considering the 1965 Auto Safety Act. Nader became famous practically overnight when the press revealed that General Motors had hired a private detective to try to collect evidence that could discredit him. Greatly embarrassed when this ploy became known, GM had to pay Nader an out-of-court settlement for harassment. No "dirt" was ever found—Nader then and now lives a Spartan life and is apparently totally devoted to his work.

With the settlement and funds from book royalties and lecture tours, Nader founded a wide variety of public interest organizations, the most famous of which is called Public Citizen. Nader's staff members, called "Nader's Raiders" to characterize their zeal, are willing to accept low wages and work long hours. Their reward is the chance to influence government to pass and enforce laws protecting consumers and workers and reducing government waste.

Nader's organizations research and publicize problems and lobby in Congress. Current causes include problems in the nuclear industry, costs of health care, consumer protection, and congressional campaign finances.

Although consumer groups achieved many of their objectives in the 1960s and 1970s, since then they have had less success. Their main target, business, reasserted its political dominance.

WOMEN'S GROUPS Groups advocating women's equality have mushroomed in the past two decades and range from large, mass-based organizations with a broad agenda, such as the National Organization for Women (NOW), to much smaller groups with very specific interests such as women's athletics or women's election to office.

NOW is the largest women's group with 150,000 members in all 50 states.[49] With a national board made up of regional representatives and national salaried officers, NOW is well organized. It has field representatives and organizers, researchers, lobbyists, and specialists in various policy areas such as reproductive freedom and economic rights.

NOW is funded largely from membership dues but has actively solicited funds by mail. It also receives income from subscriptions and selling such things as T-shirts and posters. Private foundations interested in promoting women's rights also provide significant funding.

Although NOW began as a protest movement, today its focus is on lobbying at the national, state, and local levels. It provides leadership training and education for local and state groups and works with a shifting coalition of other women's rights groups.

In recent years the women's movement has divided between groups pushing an ideological agenda, like NOW, which continues to see abortion as a major concern, and more pragmatic groups such as the National Women's Political Caucus, which sees its task as electing women to public office regardless of their stands on the issues.

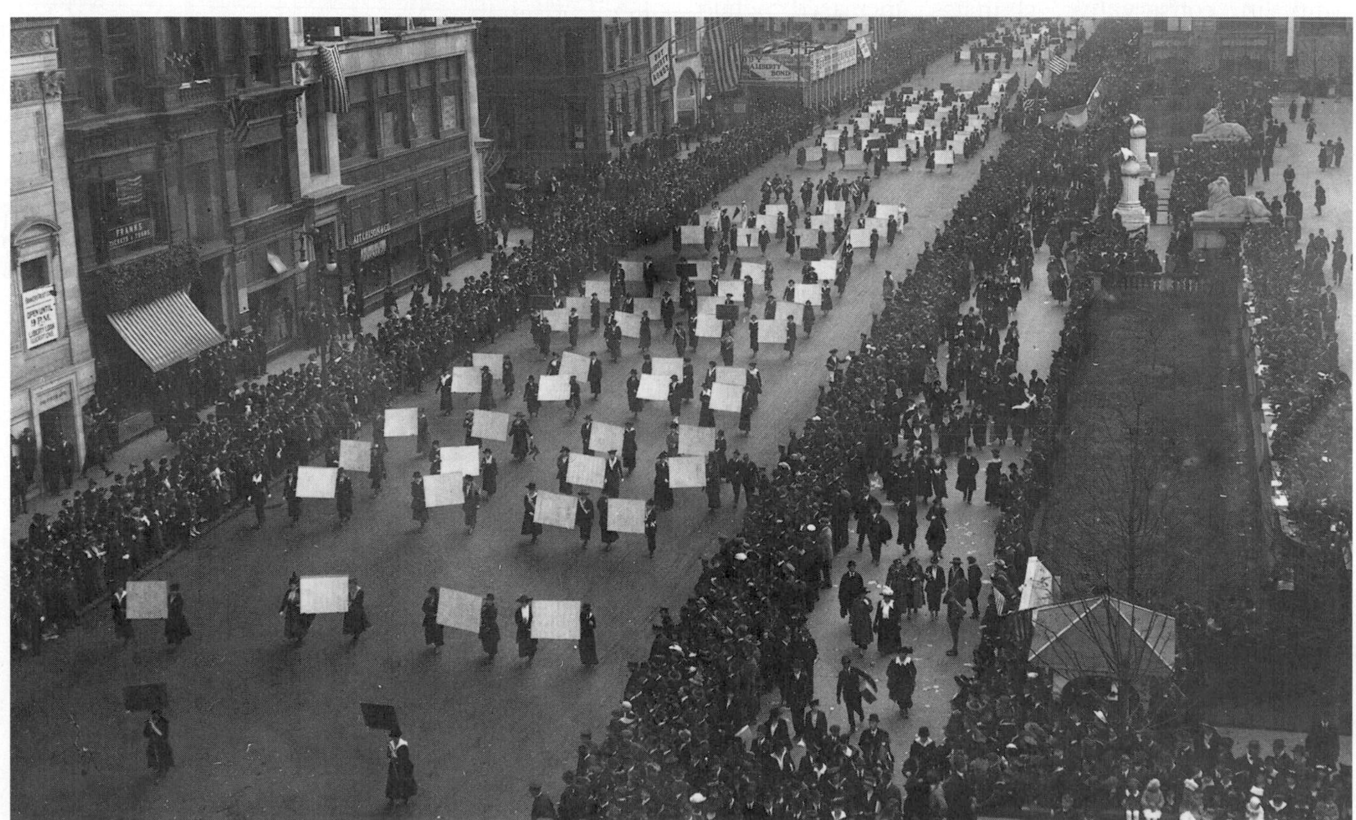

The first wave of women's organizations campaigned for women's right to vote. Here, some of 20,000 marchers parade for women's rights in New York City in 1917.

RELIGIOUS GROUPS Religious groups often lobby on political issues. The National Council of Churches, representing liberal Protestant denominations, has spoken out on civil rights, human rights, and other social issues. Catholic groups have been active in both antiabortion and antinuclear movements. Jewish groups have been involved in lobbying for liberal issues, such as the rights of workers and minorities.

Jewish groups have been particularly active in lobbying for Israel. Since its beginning in 1951, the pro-Israel lobby has lost on only three key decisions, all involving the sale of U.S. arms to Egypt and Saudi Arabia. The success of Jewish groups in lobbying for Israel reflects their commitment, organization, and political skill, and an opposition Arab lobby that is weak by comparison.[50]

Identified by a "born again" experience, a desire to win converts to Jesus Christ, and a literal interpretation of the Bible, members of the Christian right, sometimes called fundamentalists, spurred by what they saw as a decline in traditional values, became active in politics in the 1970s.[51] The National Association of Evangelicals, representing conservative Protestant denominations, gained in visibility and prestige as the membership in conservative churches increased while membership in mainline churches declined.[52]

Opposed to abortion, divorce, homosexuality, and women's rights, conservative Christians were the major force behind the effort of television evangelist Pat Robertson to win the Republican presidential nomination in 1988. Local churches worked to secure names on endorsing petitions and funds. Although he did not win the nomination, Robertson did win a number of delegates to the Republican National Convention.

Following his loss of the nomination, Robertson converted a mailing list of two million names into the Christian Coalition under the leadership of Ralph Reed. Unlike the religious right groups of the 1980s, which were primarily concerned with spreading their message through television and radio, the Coalition runs training seminars at which participants are taught how to win control of the Republican party from the ground up. Operating quietly in the early 1990s, Reed cautioned his followers never to mention the Christian Coalition among Republicans. By 1992, the organization had gained dominance or leverage in twenty state parties.[53]

The Coalition has 1.2 million members, half of which pay $15 annual dues. Each state has a chapter and nineteen states have full-time field staffs who raise their own salary. The Coalition has emerged as a political powerhouse that includes schools, newspapers, magazines, radio and television stations, and thousands of politically mobilized churches. The organization is seen by religious right leaders as a counterweight to a "liberal establishment," which Robertson believes is controlled by "secular humanists who are exerting every effort to debase and eliminate Bible-based Christianity from our society."[54]

'94 Christian Coalition

VOTER  GUIDE

WASHINGTON
Congressional
District 5

Tom Foley (D)	ISSUES	George Nethercutt (R)
Opposes	Term Limits for Congress	Supports
Opposes	Balanced Budget Amendment	Supports
Supports	Taxpayer Funding of Abortion	Opposes
Opposes	Parental Choice in Education (Vouchers)	Supports
No Response*	Voluntary Prayer in Public Schools	Supports
No Response*	Homosexuals in the Military	Opposes
Supports	Banning Ownership of Legal Firearms	Opposes
No Response*	Capital Punishment for Murder	Supports
Supports	Federal Government Control of Health Care	Opposes
Supports	Raising Federal Income Taxes	Opposes

*Each candidate was sent a 1994 Federal Issues Survey by certified mail or facsimile machine. When possible, positions of candidates on issues were verified or determined using voting records and/or public statements.

Paid for and authorized by the Christian Coalition; Post Office Box 1990; Chesapeake, Virginia 23327-1990. The Christian Coalition is a pro-family citizen action organization. This voter guide is provided for educational purposes only and is not to be construed as an endorsement of any candidate or political party.

★ Vote on November 8 ★

Voter guides were distributed to churches on the Sunday before the election in 1994.

The network involved itself heavily in political campaigns in 1992 and 1994. The Coalition raised money, registered voters, ran phone banks, and graded legislators.[55] In the 1994 congressional elections, the group distributed 33 million voter guides, many through churches on the Sunday before the election, which compared Republicans and Democrats on several "key" issues.[56] Opponents of the Coalition charged the guides were biased against

Democrats, claiming, for example, that support of the Clinton health care plan was identified in the guide as support for "Federal Government Control of Health Care." Sixty percent or more of the candidates supported by the Coalition won.[57]

Now the most powerful organization in the Republican party, the Coalition hopes to broaden its appeal. If, however, it moves any distance to the left, it may lose the enthusiasm and support of its supporters on the right. Already some supporters have become agitated by efforts to merge family and social issues with the traditional economic concerns of the Republican party. On the other hand, unwillingness to compromise on issues such as abortion, feminism, and church-state relations runs the risk of dividing the party.[58]

A church network also provided Jesse Jackson with needed support during his campaign for the Democratic presidential nomination in 1988. Black ministers endorsed his candidacy, urged their members to vote for him, and raised funds. Black churches throughout the nation served as the basic political units for the Jackson effort, particularly during the early stages of the campaign.[59]

GAYS AND LESBIANS Gay rights organizations have a shorter history than most other major political groups. The first groups formed after World War II in an era when, on the rare occasions when gays came to public attention, they were labeled as deviates. For example, in 1954, after a raid of a bar where gay men congregated, a Miami newspaper headline noted, "Perverts Seized in Bar Raids." Early gay and lesbian groups focused largely on sharing information about how to survive and how to fight police repression.[60]

In the middle 1960s, a few gays followed the example of the civil rights movements and organized small public demonstrations. Other gays argued that such public demonstrations undermined the safety and well-being of the homosexual subculture, which by then existed underground in many large cities. Nonetheless, during the '60s the gay rights movement became more radical and visible. Like Vietnam War protestors, women's rights advocates, and civil rights activists, many gays embarked upon active protests to challenge the status quo. News of a violent confrontation between gays and the police after a 1969 police raid of a gay bar in New York City helped fuel this new "gay liberation" movement. Street protests became common in large cities. Gays began forming clubs on campuses. By 1972, the issue of civil rights for gays began to be discussed in presidential campaigns, and in 1973 the American Psychiatric Association removed homosexuality from its lists of mental disorders.

Although some states decriminalized homosexual acts, many barriers remained. In some states, homosexual acts remained criminal. Gays and lesbians could be dismissed from the military if discovered. Being gay often meant losing a job, being evicted, or losing custody of a child, if divorced.

The AIDS epidemic, which began in 1981, opened a new chapter in the fight for rights of gays and lesbians. The media attention on AIDS and its impact on the gay community led to new discussions about discrimination against gays. It also revealed that many entertainers and other celebrities were gay.

Today, some gays and lesbians mostly want freedom from discrimination in jobs and other areas of life. Others want recognition of same-sex marriages. Not surprisingly, the goals of gay rights groups also differ. Some work reasonably comfortably within the mainstream; for example, the Human Rights Campaign Fund is a political action group that raised more than $4 million for candidates in the 1992 election. Others focus on specific issues, such as the Gay Men's Health Crisis, which seeks to support those with AIDS. Groups like Act Up or Queer Nation are oriented toward dramatic political action. Though most gays and lesbians vote Democratic, the Log Cabin Federation is a group of gay Republicans.

Evidence accumulates that lobbying by gay and lesbian groups is paying off. In a recent poll, 70% agreed that gays should have equal rights in hiring and firing; 78% favored increasing efforts for AIDS research, prevention, and care; and 57% supported a bill to ban workplace discrimination against gays.[61] However, the public is less supportive of lifestyle changes such as legalizing gay marriages.

ENVIRONMENTAL GROUPS Environmental groups are another example of multiple issue groups. Earth Day 1970 marked the beginning of the environmental movement in the United States. Spurred by an oil spill in California, what was to be a "teach-in" on college campuses mushroomed into a day of national environmental awareness with an estimated 20 million Americans taking part. A minority movement in the 1970s, the environmental lobby today is large and active and its values are supported by most Americans.[62]

Some environmental groups, such as the National Audubon Society, Sierra Club, and the Natural Resources Defense Council, have permanent offices in Washington with highly skilled professionals who carry out a full range of lobbying activities. All experienced substantial growth in membership and finances during the 1980s, when the Reagan administration threatened to undo the environmental gains of the 1970s.[63]

The so-called "Greens" are environmental groups that shun conventional lobbying approaches and are more confrontational. Groups like Greenpeace, Earth First!, and the Sea Shepherds seek a "green cultural revolution." Local citizen groups have also organized in support of local environmental concerns such as the location of toxic or nuclear waste dumps. Citizens, skeptical of government and corporate claims that such facilities are safe, want them located elsewhere.[64]

OTHER MULTIPLE-ISSUE INTEREST GROUPS Common Cause, a multiple-issue group established in 1970 by John Gardner, attracted nearly 100,000 members in the first six months of its existence. Much of the group's lobbying program has been directed toward improving the accountability of government. The group successfully lobbied for the 1974 Campaign Reform Act, which placed stricter rules on reporting campaign expenditures and contributions and provided public financing for presidential elections. The organization also supports further finance reform, including public funding of congressional elections.

A new organization, The Fair Government Foundation, founded after the 1994 elections by Republican Senator Paul Coverdell of Georgia, sees itself as a counterweight to Common Cause. Although small by comparison—it has a budget of $300,000 and two fulltime staff—it opposes public funding of elections and views any limits on spending as a violation of the First Amendment.[65]

Other multiple-issue interest groups include the American Civil Liberties Union, concerned with protecting the constitutional rights of citizens; the League of Women Voters, concerned with government reform and expanding women's roles and participation; and the Children's Defense Fund, concerned with protecting the nation's children.

Single-Issue Groups

Single-issue groups pursue public interest goals but are distinguished by their intense concern for a single issue and their reluctance to compromise. Members of the National Rifle Association (NRA) passionately oppose most forms of government control of firearms. For years, in spite of a majority of Americans who support gun control, the NRA has successfully lobbied Congress to prevent significant gun control. The group has members in every congressional district and is well organized to mobilize them. It spent a great deal of money in a losing battle to defeat the Brady Act, which requires a five-day waiting period in order to purchase a gun. It also failed to prevent a ban on sales of assault weapons.

While the NRA remains a major political force, antigun sentiment is growing as more and more Americans respond to increasing gun violence that touches cities, suburbs, and small towns. The result is an increase in the political influence of antigun groups such as Handgun Control and politicians more willing to take on the NRA. The image of the NRA has been damaged by its unwillingness to accept reasonable gun control measures. To restore its image, the group has shifted emphasis from guns to criminal justice. Its Crime Strike division has made a point of calling for tougher sentences, more prisons, and a crackdown on drug crimes. Its image was tarnished even more, however, when a fund-raising letter at the time of the bombing of the federal building in Oklahoma City referred to federal law enforcement officers as "jackbooted government thugs, wearing black, armed to the teeth, who break down a door, open fire with an automatic weapon and kill or maim law-abiding citizens." The jackboot reference, which is associated with Nazi stormtroopers, led former president George Bush (a longtime NRA member and

Pressure on Congress and state legislatures from the National Rifle Association has meant that even guns like these are readily available in most states.

supporter) to resign his membership. The organization lost more than 300,000 members in 1995.

The abortion controversy has generated a number of single-issue groups. The National Right to Life Committee seeks a constitutional amendment banning all abortions. The committee works to elect candidates who favor such an amendment and defeat those who do not. After the 1989 and 1992 Supreme Court decisions allowing more state regulation of abortion, pro-life groups turned their attention to state legislators. They pushed for laws requiring informed consent, waiting periods, and parental consent for minors.

Operation Rescue is a confrontational antiabortion group that attempts to prevent women seeking abortions access to abortion clinics. Many "rescuers" have been arrested and jailed because of their activities. The group graduated its first class of abortion protesters from its military-style boot camp in Florida. The 22 men and women, ranging in age from 16 to 67, learned a number of skills to assist them in their fight against abortion. From a private detective, they learned how to obtain information about people, for example, that license plates can be used to obtain home addresses. The purpose is to identify people who perform abortions: to pray or picket in front of their homes, confront them in the supermarket, and identify them as "murderers" to their neighbors and children.

A lawyer lectured on how to file lawsuits against local officials, police, abortion doctors, and activists in an effort to bog them down in paperwork. Students were instructed in how to infiltrate abortion clinics. One scenario has a man and woman stage an argument in the waiting area, one pleading with the other not to go through with the abortion. In another, a student uses a borrowed urine sample from a pregnant woman and goes through all the steps of obtaining an abortion up to reclining on the operating table. The purpose is to disrupt clinic operations. Students also learn the art of phone taps and long-distance surveillance. Graduates are expected to return home and teach others what they have learned. These tactics, including the murder of two doctors by deranged right-to-lifers have limited access to abortion because many physicians do not wish to be harassed and simply refuse to perform abortions.[66] The application of federal racketeering laws to those who disrupt clinic activities may limit these tactics in the future.

Anti-abortion activists picked up considerable support in Congress following the 1994 elections, but abortion issues were set aside during the first session in favor of issues identified in the "Contract with America" (see You Are There, Chapter 6). Abortion is likely to be an important issue in the 1996 presidential election. Anti-abortion religious activists, likely to have a major impact on the Republican nomination, have indicated they will not support a candidate who is not pro-life, thus offering the possibility of a split within the Republican party.[67]

Members of the national Abortion Rights Action League and Planned Parenthood are fervently committed to protecting women's right to abortion. Planned Parenthood is the oldest, largest, best-financed, and most powerful single advocate of reproductive freedom for women, including birth control and abortion.

Since 1988, the organization has mounted a major effort to win policymakers to the pro-choice point of view. Using the theme that Americans want abortion to be safe and legal, ads were placed in national newspapers. Testimony was provided by physicians who treated botched abortions in the days when abortion was illegal, by clergy involved in counseling, and by women who underwent illegal abortion because they had no choice. Three months before the 1989 Supreme Court decision allowing state regulation of abortion (for more on this see Chapter 14), 300,000 pro-choice activists staged a march in Washington. Calling the event the "March for Women's Lives," the goal was to recast the issue in terms of freedom and choice rather than abortion. The march slogan, "Who Decides, You or Them?" became the rallying cry in several state elections in 1989. The

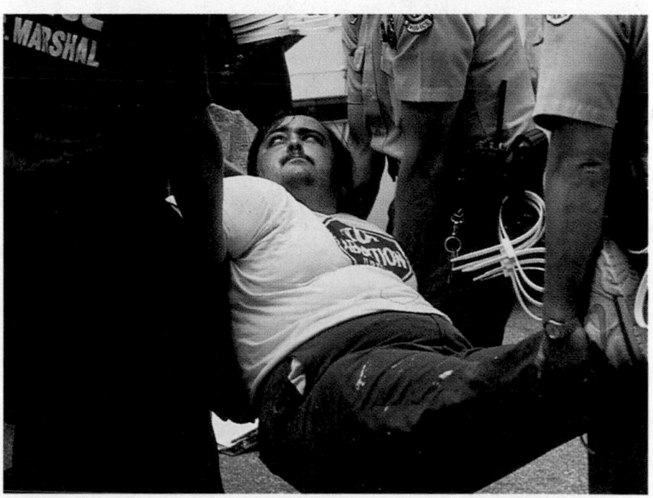

The right-to-life movement is considered a single-issue group.

three-day event received substantial publicity and demonstrated to members of Congress that the movement could mobilize a large number of supporters.[68] A major lobbying effort is currently underway to include abortion coverage in any health care reform enacted by Congress.

Single-issue groups have increased in number since the mid-1960s. Some view this with alarm, because when groups clash over a highly emotional issue and are unwilling to compromise, government cannot resolve the issue.[69] The issue commands excessive time and energy of policy makers at the expense of broader issues that may be more important.

On the other hand, single-issue groups have always been part of politics.[70] These groups may even be beneficial because they represent interests that may not be well represented in Congress. Fears about single-issue groups may result from the groups' own exaggerated claims of influence, their heavy media coverage, and in the case of some anti-abortion groups, their resort to violence.

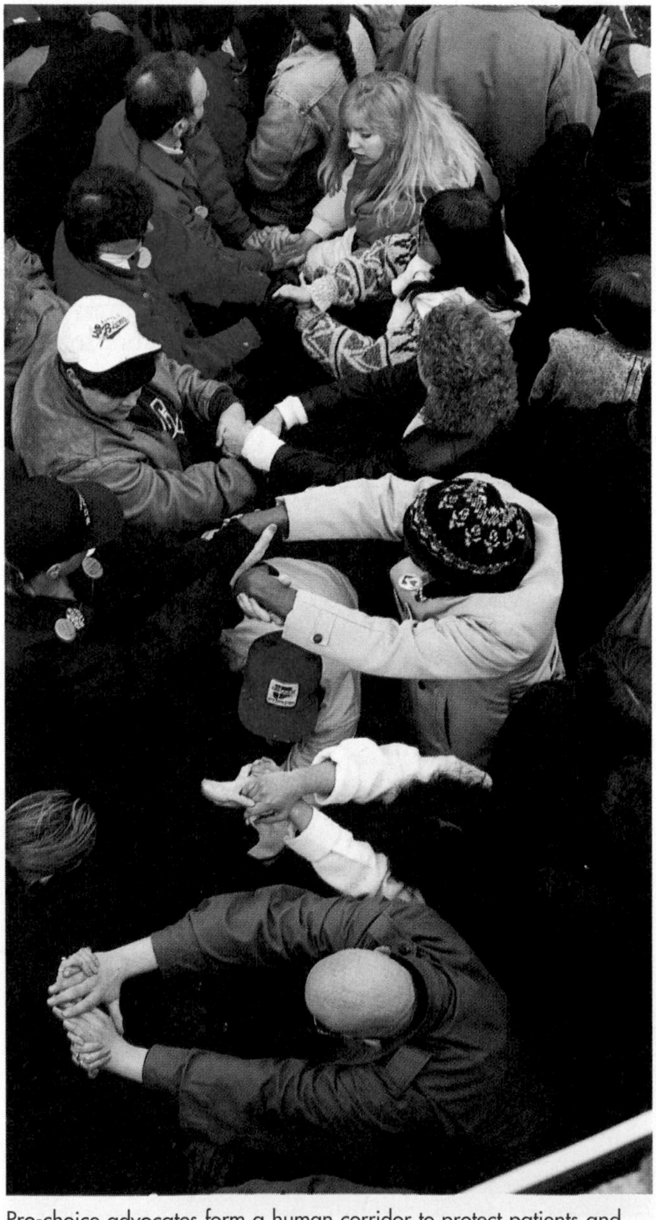

Pro-choice advocates form a human corridor to protect patients and workers entering a clinic in Buffalo.

➤Tactics of Interest Groups

Interest groups engage in a variety of tactics to secure their goals. Some try to influence policymakers directly, whereas others seek to mold public opinion and influence policymakers indirectly. Sometimes interest groups form broad coalitions or engage in protest activity, both of which involve direct and indirect techniques.

■ Direct Lobbying Techniques

Direct lobbying techniques involve personal encounters between lobbyists and public officials. Some lobbyists are volunteers; others are permanent, salaried employees of the groups they represent; and others are contract lobbyists, "hired guns" who represent any individual or group willing to pay for the service. Contract lobbyists include the numerous Washington lawyers affiliated with the city's most prestigious law firms. Many have worked for government, so they can boast of contacts in government and access to policymakers to plead their clients' cases. Most firms recruit from the ranks of both Republicans and Democrats to assure access regardless of which party controls government.

Making Personal Contacts

Making personal contacts, in an office or in a more informal setting, is the most effective lobbying technique. Compared to other forms of lobbying, direct personal contact is relatively inexpensive, and it minimizes problems of misinterpretation by allowing questions to be answered on the spot.

Lobbyists know that contacting every legislator is unnecessary, whereas contacting key legislators, those who sit on the committees having jurisdiction over

The Ten Commandments of Lobbying

I Thou shalt speak only the truth, and speak it clearly and succinctly; on two pages and in 15-second sound bites.

II Thou shalt translate the rustle of thy grassroots into letters, phone calls, and personal visits.

III Thou shalt not underestimate thy opponent, for he surely packeth a rabbit punch.

IV Help thy friends with reelection; but in victory, dwelleth not on the power of thy PAC.

V Thou shalt know thy issue and believe in it, but be ready to compromise; half a loaf will feed some of thy people.

VI Runneth not out of patience. If thou can not harvest this year, the next session may be bountiful.

VII Love thy neighbor; thou wilst need him for a coalition.

VIII Study arithmetic, that thou may count noses. If thou can count 51, rejoice. Thou shalt win in the Senate.

IX Honor the hard-working staff, for they prepare the position papers for the members.

X Be humble in victory, for thy bill may yet be vetoed.

SOURCE: Ernest Wittenberg and Elisabeth Wittenberg, *How to Win in Washington* (Cambridge, Mass.: Blackwell, 1989), p. 16.

matters of interest to the lobbyists, and staff serving those committees, is critical.[71] Conventional wisdom also suggests that only those legislators who support a group's position or who are known to be undecided should be contacted directly.[72] Putting undue pressure on known opponents may jeopardize prospects for working together in the future on other issues.

To a large extent lobbying is building relationships based on friendship. As Leon Panetta, when he was chair of the House Budget Committee, put it, "The most effective lobbyists here are the ones you don't think of as lobbyists." Referring to one prominent Washington lobbyist, Panetta said, "I don't think of him as a lobbyist. He's almost a constituent, or a friend." Barbara Boxer, then a Democratic representative from California, referring to the same gentleman, described him as "a lovely, wonderful guy. In the whole time I've known him, he's never asked me to vote for anything." At a gathering she joked, he's almost "a member of the family."[73]

Providing Expertise

Some lobbying groups do research and present their findings to public officials. One of the major strengths of Ralph Nader's organization, and the public interest movement in general, is the ability to provide public officials, particularly Congress, with accurate and reliable information.

Lobbyists often have a great deal of knowledge and expertise that is useful in drafting legislation. A legislator may ask a lobbyist to draft a bill or both may work together in drafting legislation. Sometimes interest groups themselves draft legislation and ask a sympathetic legislator to introduce it. General Electric drafted a tax reform measure that saved it millions in taxes. There is nothing illegal about this.

Testifying at Hearings

Testifying at congressional hearings is designed to establish a group's credentials as a "player" in the policy area as well as to convince its own constituents that it is doing its job. A member of a prominent Washington law firm with responsibility at his firm for prepping witnesses to testify identified the Boy Scout motto, "Be Prepared," as the most important principle to follow in getting ready for a hearing. Beyond that, he offers a few other tips: Keep it short. Time is at a premium in Washington. No one has an hour to listen to you. Don't read your statement. Good salespeople don't have prepared statements. They know the product and can talk to you about it. Don't be arrogant. Some witnesses are short with members because they believe committee members don't understand their business. Too bad. Most members of Congress don't care about your business; they are going to make a decision based on what they hear. Don't guess. If you don't know the answer to a question, say so and promise to supply the answer later. Don't be hokey, but illustrate whenever possible. It is easier to focus on a wrecked fender in a hearing room than to visualize a set of statistics.[74]

Another advantage of testifying is that it provides free publicity. Staging sometimes occurs. A lobbyist might request a sympathetic legislator to ask certain questions that the lobbyist is prepared to answer or to indicate in advance what questions will be asked. Sometimes celebrities are invited to testify. In a not unprecedented but certainly rare move, Mrs. Clinton, the principal player in developing the president's health care reform, testified before several congressional committees. This White House effort prompted a former Reagan aid to quip, they "do PR the way (former chair of the Joint Chiefs) Colin Powell does war: maximum use of force."[75]

Giving Money

Lobbyists try to ensure access to legislators, and giving money is one way to guarantee this. Justin Dart, a longtime financial backer of Ronald Reagan, once said that having a dialogue with a politician is fine, "but with a little money they hear you better."[76] One Democrat commented in a similar vein, "Who do members of Congress see? They'll certainly see the one who gives the money. It's hard to say no to someone who gives you $5,000."[77]

The primary way groups channel money to legislators is through campaign contributions. Groups, including businesses and unions, may set up political action committees (PACS) to give money to campaigns of political candidates.

The number of PACs has grown dramatically in the past decade as has the amount of money they have contributed. (We discuss PACs more fully in Chapter 9).

Lobbying the Bureaucracy

For lobbyists, the battle is not over when a bill is passed. Lobbyists also must influence bureaucrats who implement policy. For example, regulations outlawing sex discrimination in educational institutions were drafted largely in the Department of Education with only broad guidelines from Congress. Both women's rights groups and interests opposing them lobbied for years to influence the regulations.

In influencing bureaucrats, interest groups use most of the tactics already described. They also try to influence who gets appointed to bureaucratic positions. Someone opposed by the major agricultural interest groups is not likely to be appointed secretary of agriculture. Nor is someone unsympathetic to labor apt to be appointed head of the Labor Department. The auto industry vetoed a number of Clinton's nominees to head the National Highway Traffic Safety Administration. While consumer groups want someone interested in promoting automobile safety, the industry is looking for someone more sympathetic to their interests and concerns. Of course, groups do not always succeed in their opposition. President Reagan appointed as heads of several agencies persons strongly opposed by interest groups sympathetic to the agency's activities. He appointed a secretary of the interior opposed to many governmental efforts to protect public land and an Environmental Protection Agency head who opposed most government efforts to protect the environment.

The influence of groups in the appointment process is especially crucial in the case of appointments to regulatory agencies such as the Food and Drug Administration. By influencing appointments to an agency, the regulated industry can improve its prospects of favorable treatment.

GREAT! MY PANEL OF EXPERT ADVISORS IS READY FOR YOU!
Congressman Spin
Health Plan
DOCS LOBBY
INSURANCE LOBBY
DRUG LOBBY

Cartoonists and Writers Syndicate
Source: By Wilkinson for the Philadelphia Daily News.

Lobbying the Courts

Like bureaucrats, judges also make policy. Some interest groups try to achieve their goals by getting involved in cases and persuading courts to rule in their favor. Although most groups do not initiate litigation, some use it as their primary tactic. Litigation has been employed extensively by civil liberties organizations, particularly the American Civil Liberties Union (ACLU), civil rights organizations such as the NAACP, environmental groups such as the Sierra Club, and public interest groups such as Common Cause. Litigation often is used by groups that lack influence in Congress and the bureaucracy.

Groups can file civil suits, represent defendants in criminal cases, or file friend of the court briefs, which are written arguments asking the court to decide a case a particular way.[78]

Some groups use the courts to make their opponents negotiate with them. Environmental groups frequently challenge developers who threaten the environment in order to force them to bear the costs of defending themselves and to delay the project. The next time, developers may be more willing to make concessions to avoid lengthy and costly litigation.

Groups try to influence the courts indirectly by lobbying the Senate to support or oppose judicial nominees.

Indirect Lobbying Techniques

Traditionally, lobbyists employed tactics of direct persuasion almost exclusively—providing information, advice, and occasionally pressure. More recently, interest groups are going public, that is, mobilizing their activists and molding and activating public opinion. A recent study of 175 lobbying groups found that most were doing more of all kinds of lobbying activity, but the largest increases were in going public.[79] Talking with the media increased the most, and mobilizing the grass roots to send letters and telegrams and make telephone calls was second.

Washington's "Super Lobbyist"

There are thousands of lobbyists or, as they prefer to be called, political consultants, in Washington, but the label "super lobbyist" applies to only a small number. Thomas H. Boggs, of the Washington law firm of Patton, Boggs, and Blow, is one. The firm has more than eighty lawyers, but it is referred to as "Boggs's firm." Boggs, son of the late Democratic Majority Leader Hale Boggs and former Democratic Representative Lindy Boggs of Louisiana,, is reputed to be one of the capital's most powerful lobbyists.

Like most successful lobbyists, Boggs is intelligent and personable. He is also cunning and calculating. His approach is soft-sell rather than hard-line pressure. He understands the political process, especially in the House of Representatives, and has a keen sense of what motivates politicians. A few years ago he was able to win over liberal Representative Charles Rangel, a Harlem Democrat, to retain import duties on steel because some of the imported steel would come from apartheid South Africa. He convinced the late Representative William Ketchum, a conservative Republican, to retain the import duties because the company Boggs represented was located in Ketchum's district and would be hurt by competition with a foreign steel maker. Boggs points with pride to his ability to build coalitions comprising both liberals and conservatives and notes this ability as one reason he is successful.

While Boggs is a Democrat, most on his client list—one of the longest in Washington with nearly 500 names—are corporations. Being a Democrat, however, is not a handicap. It means he has access to Democratic members of Congress who are most likely to oppose business. Republicans typically vote with business. As one corporate lobbyist put it, "Republicans usually vote with you anyway. So Tommy knows he has most of them, and every time he gets a Democrat, particularly a liberal, that's icing on the cake."

As do most lobbying firms in Washington, Patton, Boggs, and Blow employ both Republicans and Democrats. The bipartisan approach and the mix of clients who are occasionally on opposite ends of issues smacks of conflict of interest. This leaves Boggs and his firm open to the charge that they are driven chiefly by money rather than moral purpose. As a lobbyist for Ralph Nader's organization put it, "Some attorneys and lobbyists have a reputation of trying to persuade their clients to do the right thing. Nobody ever says that about Tommy Boggs." Boggs is uncomfortable when conversations turn to what he hopes to contribute to society or about his political philosophy. He simply responds, "I enjoy playing the game."

And Boggs knows how to play the game. During a policy strategy session at the Carter White House, Boggs suddenly walked in. The ploy enabled him to brag about his access to the White House and added credibility to his claim that he could advise his business clients on what the "opposition" was up to. While Boggs has had some notable successes over the years—for example, he gets much of the credit for the Chrysler bailout—he does not win all the time. However, he convinces people that he can make things happen. Even if the belief in his power and influence is exaggerated, it does not matter to Boggs, as long as his clients and would-be clients hold this belief.

Boggs's chief asset is his ability to raise money for congressional candidates. He contributes himself, generally the $25,000 maximum allowed by law. More important, he gets his clients to contribute. Boggs also calls upon a network of Washington lobbyists to contribute. "I hit these guys," he says, "and I know they'll come back and hit me up."

While very important to his success, fund-raising is only part of Boggs's job. He can be seen prowling the corridors of Congress, talking with members, and picking up whatever political information he can. Like any well-connected lobbyist, he attends as many as ten receptions per week, two or more some evenings. The schedule is hectic and no one claims Boggs does not work hard for his clients.

SOURCES: A. R. Hunt, "The Washington Power Brokers," ed. P. Woll, *Behind the Scenes of American Government*, 6th ed. (Little, Brown and Company: Boston, Mass., 1987); *National Journal* (September 14, 1985).

Mobilizing the Grass Roots

The constituency of an interest group—the group's members or those whom the group serves—can help communicate the group's position to public officials. The National Rifle Association is effective in mobilizing its members. The NRA can generate thousands of letters within a few days. As one senator remarked, "I'd rather be a deer in hunting season than run afoul of the NRA crowd."[80]

Conservative Christian minister Jerry Falwell activated his "gospel grapevine" to flood the White House and Congress in opposition to the president's plan to lift the ban on homosexuals in the military. Warning of a new radical homosexual rights agenda, he urged viewers of his "Old Time Gospel Hour" to call and register their opinions.

Grassroots lobbying was the hallmark of the effort to derail or modify health care reform. Industries affected by the proposed change lined up their own supporters. Cigarette companies rallied tobacco growers to oppose increases in the cigarette taxes. The Pharmaceutical Manufacturers Association had the presidents of 26 drug companies write letters to 600,000 workers asking them to write Congress warning of dangers in price controls. Insurance agents provided their clients with a booklet called "A Citizen's Guide to Health Care Reform" and urged them to contact their representatives. The AMA sent 660,000 physicians and 48,000 medical students a questionnaire marked "For Patients" with 10 questions on Clinton's health care proposal. The chief lobbyist for the National Federation of Independent Business, which also opposed the Clinton plan, says "You use the people back home to sensitize members of Congress and staff. I get listened to on the Hill because they know I have 600,000 small businessmen behind me back home. The grass roots gives me standing."[81]

Appeals to write or phone policymakers often exaggerate the severity of the problem and the strength of the opposition. Only the threat of imminent failure or a monstrous adversary with superior resources is sufficient to move most members. Because of the difficulty in mobilizing members and the cost in time and money, grassroots efforts are typically a last resort. Besides, as one lobbyist put it, members of Congress "hate it when you call in the dogs."[82]

To be successful, mass letter writing and phone calls must look sincere and spontaneous. Groups often send members sample letters to help them know what to write, but letters that appear unique are most effective. Campaigns producing thousands of postcards generally are not effective unless representatives do not hear from the other side.

Sometimes grassroots lobbying involves more than phoning or writing letters. A lobbyist for the nation's hospitals opposed to the Clinton plan for health care reform encouraged hospital administrators across the nation to get acquainted with their representative, work with the member to organize town meetings to discuss issues, and guide the member on a tour of the local hospital to point out how many people are

Caps Off to the Beer Lobby

Do you like to have a beer now and then? If so, perhaps membership in the Beer Drinkers of America is for you. But then again maybe it is not. While an organization for beer drinkers may seem slightly odd, an organization for beer producers and sellers seems quite likely.

A "fact sheet" put out by the organization says that the group has a membership of 700,000 beer drinkers. Their mission is to mobilize members to fight things such as taxes on beer, restrictions on advertising, and deposit laws, ostensibly on behalf of beer drinkers.

How did the group get started? One version is that a few fellow beer drinkers decided to oppose a proposed tax on beer on the ballot in New Mexico back in 1987. (We can visualize a couple of mad-as-hell couch potatoes sitting in a mobile home in the desert flinging empties at the TV and clamoring they weren't going to take it any more.) A more plausible version is that the group was the brainchild of a lobbyist trying to help a client beat back the beer tax. The lobbyist and a friend persuaded one beer company to put up some seed money and many beer retailers to spread the word. In less than a year, 4,000 signed on. Today, money comes from two beer companies and from beer wholesalers who pressure their employees to join. Of the 700,000, only 150,000, most of whom are employed by the beer industry, actually pay dues; the rest support the group by signing petitions and writing letters.

Unfortunately for all the real beer drinkers in the country, the organization is a tool of the industry. Why all the deception? The industry hopes to use the group to scare members of Congress. Members might vote against the industry but they don't want to go back to their districts having voted against "Joe Six Pack."

SOURCE: Sean Holton, "Beer Biz Leaves 1 Drinker Foaming," *Orlando Sentinel* (September 12, 1993), pp. 1A, 7A.

employed and what the hospital means to the local community. "If done well, the member summoned to the Oval Office can turn to the president and say 'I can't go with you on this, Mr. President, because I promised the people in my district.' "[83]

Molding Public Opinion

Groups use public relations techniques to shape public opinion through the media. Ads in newspapers, magazines, and on television supply the public with information, foster a positive image of the group, or promote a public policy. By themselves ads have little impact in moving policymakers to action or shifting public opinion dramatically in the short run. They are most effective in combination with other tactics.

Groups also may stage events such as rallies or pickets to attract media coverage to their cause. For example, those opposing racial segregation in South Africa have won considerable attention picketing and protesting outside the South African embassy in Washington, D.C. They were especially effective because they enlisted members of Congress, community leaders, and other celebrities in their protests. Arrests of members of Congress and other celebrities for trespassing kept the issue in the limelight for months.

Those arguing in favor of tort reform (limiting damages courts will award to those injured in auto accidents, air disasters, unsuccessful surgeries or other mishaps) focus on the few outrageous huge settlements for seemingly innocuous injuries. Those arguing against such changes focus on the poor widows left penniless after being permanently incapacitated by the rapacious behavior of a wealthy corporation.[84]

A tactic increasingly used by interest groups to influence public opinion is rating members of Congress. Groups may choose a number of votes crucial to their concerns such as, abortion, conservation, or consumer affairs. Or they may select many votes reflecting a liberal or conservative outlook. They then publicize the votes to their members with the ultimate objective of trying to defeat candidates who vote against their positions. The impact of these ratings is probably minimal unless they are used in a concerted effort to target certain members for defeat.

Coalition Building

Coalitions, networks of groups with similar concerns, help individual groups press their demands. Coalitions can be large and focused on many issues or small and very specific. For example, 7-Eleven stores, Kingsford charcoal, amusement parks, and lawn and garden centers joined the Daylight Saving Time Coalition to lobby Congress to extend daylight saving time. All wanted additional daylight hours to snack, grill, play, or till the soil, which would mean more money in their pockets.

Coalitions have formed around health care reform. The AFL-CIO, American Airlines, Chrysler Corp, the American College of Physicians and the League of Women Voters support health care reform, and the American Conservative Union, United Seniors Union, Citizens for a Sound Economy, and National Taxpayers have joined a coalition of Citizens Against Health Rationing. Similarly, more than 2,700 companies and trade associations were members of USA*NAFTA, a coalition supporting the trade agreement.[85]

Coalitions demonstrate broad support for an issue and also take advantage of the different strengths of groups. One group may be adept at grassroots lobbying, another at public relations. One may have lots of money, another lots of members.

The growth of coalitions in recent years reflects a number of changes in the policy process.[86] Issues have become increasingly complex. Legislation often affects a variety of interests, which makes it easier to form coalitions among groups representing the interests. In addition, changes in technology make it easier for groups to communicate with each other and with constituents. And the number of interest groups is larger than it used to be, especially the number of public interest groups. Many such groups have limited resources, and coalitions help them stretch their lobbying efforts. Some "black hat" business groups, with image problems, seek to associate themselves with "white hat" organizations ranging from labor unions to consumer groups.[87] The decentralization of Congress and the weakness of political parties also have led to coalition building to win needed majorities at the various stages of the policy process.

Coalitions vary in their duration—some are short-term, whereas others are permanent. Coalitions involved with the health care issue are likely to remain only until the issue is resolved. Coalitions supporting and opposing NAFTA ceased to exist when Congress approved the measure.

On the other hand, the Leadership Conference on Civil Rights is a permanent coalition of 185 civil rights, ethnic, religious and other groups (Elks, Actors Equity, YMCA, and the National Funeral Directors and Morticians Association). Unlike short-term coalitions, permanent ones need to be sensitive to how today's actions will affect future cooperation. Some issues may be avoided even though a majority of coalition members want to deal with them. When a coalition is unified, however, it can be formidable.

In elections, coordination among PACs in channeling money to political candidates is widespread. Business PACs, for example, take their lead from the Business-Industry Political Action Committee (BIPAC). Information is shared on candidates' issue positions, likelihood of winning, and need for funding.

Protest and Civil Disobedience

Groups that lack access or hold unpopular positions can protest. They can target policymakers directly or indirectly through public opinion. In recent years, issues as diverse as abortion, American support for the contras in Nicaragua, busing to promote school integration, nuclear weapons, and the poor farm economy in the Midwest have generated protest marches and rallies.

Peaceful but illegal protest activity, where those involved allow themselves to be arrested and punished, is called civil disobedience. Greenpeace is an environmental and peace group that practices civil disobedience. It started in 1971 when a group of environmentalists and peace activists sent two boats to Amchitka Island in the Aleutians to protest a U.S. underground nuclear weapon test. The boats were named *Greenpeace,* linking the environment and peace. Although the boats failed to reach the island, the publicity generated by the affair led Washington to cancel the test.

Throughout the 1970s and 1980s, Greenpeace staged a number of such protests. To protest dumping of toxic wastes and sewage in the ocean, 13 Greenpeace activists lowered themselves from a New York bridge and hung there for eight hours, preventing any sewage barges from carrying wastes out to sea. All were arrested. To protect endangered whales, members placed them-

Greenpeace attempts to influence public opinion with dramatic events. Here, Greenpeace protests dumping of nuclear waste at sea, while dumpers prepare to drop a barrel of waste on the Greenpeace protestors.

selves in the path of a harpoon, narrowly missing being struck. Others parachuted over coal-powered power plants to protest acid rain. Their goal was to generate publicity and dramatic photographs that would activate the general population.

Protest can generate awareness of an issue, but to be successful, it must influence mass or elite opinion. Often it is the first step in a long struggle that takes years to resolve. Sometimes the first result is hostility toward the group using it. Antiwar protest by college students in the 1960s and 1970s angered not only government officials, who targeted the leaders for harassment, but also many citizens. In the early years of the women's movement, the media labeled many female protestors "bra burners" even though it is not clear if any woman ever burned a bra.

Extended protests are difficult because they demand more skill by the leaders and sacrifices from the participants. Continued participation, essential to success, robs participants of a normal life. It can mean jail, physical harm, or even death and requires discipline to refrain from violence, even when violence is used against them.

The civil rights movement provides the best example of the successful use of extended protest and civil disobedience in twentieth-century America. By peacefully demonstrating against legalized segregation in the South, black and some white protestors drew the nation's attention to the discrepancy between the American values of equality and democracy and the southern laws that separated blacks from whites in every aspect of life. Protestors used tactics such as sit-ins, marches, and boycotts. Confrontations with authorities often won protestors national attention and public support, which eventually led to change.

All tactics can be effective, but some lend themselves better to some groups than others. For example, business groups with great financial resources can pay for skillful lobbyists and donate to political candidates. Labor unions have many members and can help candidates canvass and get out the vote. Public interest groups rely on activating public opinion and, where members are intensely committed to a cause, protest.

➤Success of Interest Groups

Although no interest group gets everything it wants from government, some are more successful than others. Politics is not a game of chance, where only luck determines winners and losers. Knowing what to do and how to do it—strategy and tactics—are important, as are resources, competition, and goals.

Resources

Although large size does not guarantee success, large groups have advantages. They can get the attention of public officials by claiming to speak for more people or by threatening to mobilize members against them.

The geographical distribution of members of a group is also important. Because organized labor is concentrated in the Northeast, its influence is less strong elsewhere. The Chamber of Commerce, on the other hand, has members and influence throughout the country.

Other things being equal, a group with well-educated members has an advantage because highly educated people are more likely than others to communicate with public officials and contribute to lobbying efforts.

Group cohesion and intensity are also advantages. Public officials are unlikely to respond to a group if it cannot agree on what it wants or if it does not appear to feel very strongly about its position. For example, in recent years the NAACP has suffered from deep splits within its leadership over tactics and allies. Such splits diminish the clout of a group. Selection of a new chair, Mrylie Evers-Williams, a successful businesswoman and widow of the civil rights martyr Medgar Evans was an attempt to bind the wounds and present a united face to the world.

A large **market share,** the number of members in a group compared to its potential membership, is another advantage. For years the American Medical Association enrolled a large percentage (70% or more) of the nation's doctors as members. As its member-

Source: Reprinted by permission: Tribune Media Services

ship (as a percentage of the total number of doctors) has declined, so too has its influence.

The more money a group has, the more successful it probably will be. Not only does money buy skilled lobbyists and access to elected officials, it is also necessary for indirect lobbying efforts.

Knowledge is a major resource too. If leaders of a group are experts in a policy area, they are more apt to get the attention of public officials. Knowledge of how things get done in Washington is also helpful, which is why many groups employ former members of Congress and the executive branch as lobbyists.

Finally, public image is important. A negative public image often troubles new, change-oriented groups, such as the animal rights movement. Many of the country's traditional interest groups, big business and organized labor, also suffer from a poor image, being viewed as too powerful and self-serving.

Few groups are blessed with all resources, but the more resources a group has, the better its chances of getting what it wants from government.

Competition and Goals

Success also depends on group competition and goals.

Many groups are successful because they face weak opponents. Supporters of gun control have public opinion on their side, but their main organization, the National Council to Control Handguns, has a membership of only 400,000 and a budget of $7.5 million, a fraction of the NRA's. Used-car dealers successfully lobbied against "the lemon law," which would have required them to tell customers of any defects in cars. Few lobbyists represented the other side. These mismatches between groups occur most often on highly technical issues where one

Organizing Protest: The Montgomery Bus Boycott

The 1955 Montgomery, Alabama, bus boycott was the first successful civil rights protest, and it brought its 26-year-old leader, Dr. Martin Luther King, Jr., to national prominence. Montgomery, like most southern cities, required blacks to sit in the back of public buses while whites sat in the front. The dividing line between the two was a "no man's land" where blacks could sit if there were no whites. If whites needed the seats, blacks had to give them up and move to the back.

One afternoon, Rosa Parks, a seamstress at a local department store and a leader in the local chapter of the National Association for the Advancement of Colored People (NAACP), boarded the bus to go home. The bus was filled and when a white man boarded, the driver called on the four blacks behind the whites to move to the back. Three got up and moved, but Mrs. Parks, tired from a long day and of the injustice of always having to move for white people, said she did not have to move because she was in "no man's land." Under a law that gave him the authority to enforce segregation, the bus driver arrested her.

That evening a group of black women professors at the black state college in Montgomery, led by Jo Ann Robinson, drafted a letter of protest. They called on blacks to stay off the buses on Monday to protest the arrest. They worked through the night making 35,000 copies of their letter to distribute to Montgomery's black residents. Fearful for their jobs and concerned that the state would cut funds to the black college if it became known they had used state facilities to produce the letter, they worked quickly and quietly.

The following day black leaders met and agreed to the boycott. More leaflets were drafted calling on blacks to stay off the buses on Monday. On Sunday, black ministers encouraged their members to support the boycott, and on Monday 90% of the blacks walked to work, rode in black-owned taxis, or shared rides in private cars.

The boycott inspired confidence and pride in the black community and signaled a subtle change in the opinions of blacks toward race relations. This was obvious when, as nervous white police looked on, hundreds of blacks jammed the courthouse to see that Rosa Parks was safely released after her formal conviction. And it was obvious later that evening at a mass rally when Martin Luther King cried out, "There comes a time when people get tired of being trampled over by the iron feet of oppression. There comes a time when people get tired of being pushed out of the glittering sunlight of life's July, and left standing amidst the piercing chill of an Alpine November." After noting that the glory of American democracy is the right to protest, King appealed to the strong religious faith of the crowd, "If we are wrong, God Almighty is wrong. . . . If we are wrong, Jesus of Nazareth was merely a utopian dreamer. . . . If we are wrong, justice is a lie." These words and this speech established King as a charismatic leader for the civil rights movement.

Each day of the boycott was a trial for blacks and their leaders. Thousands had to find a way to get to work and leaders struggled to keep a massive carpool going. However, each evening's rally built up morale for the next day's boycott. Later side has more expertise or the public has less interest.

When a group competes with other groups of nearly equal resources, the outcome is often a compromise or a stalemate. The Clean Air Act was not rewritten for years because the auto industry, which wanted a weaker law, and the environmental lobby, which wanted a tougher one, were about equal in strength. The increased clout of the environmental forces finally led to a strengthening of the law in 1990.

Groups that work to preserve the status quo are generally more successful than groups promoting change; it is usually easier to prevent government action than to bring it about. Separation of powers among the Congress, executive branch, and the courts; checks and balances within each branch; and division of authority between the states and national government provide interest groups with numerous points in the political process to exercise influence. Groups wishing to change policy have to persuade officials throughout the political process to go along; groups opposed to change only have to persuade officials at one point in the process. Groups promoting change must win over the House, Senate, White House, bureaucracy, and courts; groups against change need convince only one of them.

Groups are more likely to be successful in securing very narrow and specific benefits than they are in promoting broad policy changes. For example, corporations are concerned with broad policy issues, but they are more likely to be successful in obtaining exemptions from major policy initiatives than they are in winning or losing on the policy itself. The tax code is riddled with exemptions for corporations; the beneficiaries are rarely identified by name. The 1986 changes in the tax code contained an exemption for

Continued

the rallies became prayer services, as the black community prayed for strength to keep on walking, for courage to remain nonviolent, and for guidance to those who oppressed them.

The city bus line was losing money. City leaders urged more whites to ride the bus to make up lost revenue, but few did. Recognizing the boycott could not go on forever, black leaders agreed to end it if the rules regarding the seating of blacks in "no man's land" were relaxed. Thinking they were on the verge of breaking the boycott, the city leaders refused. Police began to harass carpoolers and issue bogus tickets for trumped-up violations. Then the city leaders issued an ultimatum: Settle or face arrest. A white grand jury indicted more than 100 boycott leaders for the alleged crime of organizing the protest. In the spirit of nonviolence, the black leaders, including King, surrendered.

The decision to arrest the leaders proved to be the turning point of the boycott. The editor of the local white paper said it was "the dumbest act that has ever been done in Montgomery."[1] With the mass arrests, the boycott finally received national attention. Reporters from all over the world streamed into Montgomery to cover the story. The publicity brought public and financial support. The arrests caused the boycott to become a national event and its leader, Martin Luther King, a national figure. A year later, the U.S. Supreme Court declared Alabama local and state laws requiring segregation in buses unconstitutional, and when the city complied with the Court's order, the boycott ended.

Rosa Parks became a hero of the civil rights movement. She has been honored many times since then, and millions saw her appearance at the 1988 Democratic National Convention.

Rosa Parks being fingerprinted after her arrest.

1. Taylor Branch, *Parting the Waters, America in the King Years* (New York: Simon and Schuster, 1988), p. 83.

SOURCES: Taylor Branch, *Parting the Waters*, chapters 4 and 5; and Juan Williams; *Eyes on the Prize* (New York: Viking Press, 1987).

Phillips Petroleum, identified in the bill as a "corporation incorporated on June 13, 1917, which has its principle place of business in Bartlesville, Oklahoma."[88] Phillips was not concerned about the basic tax changes because it was not affected by them. Such exemptions are unlikely to receive media attention and become controversial. In this way, politicians are able to satisfy a major interest group without risking a hostile public reaction.

➤Conclusion: Do Interest Groups Help Make Government Responsive?

Interest groups provide representation that helps make government more responsive. Although elected officials are representatives, they cannot adequately represent all interests in our diverse society. Interest groups pick up some of the slack by representing the views and opinions of their members and constituents and communicating these to political decision makers. This does not mean that all members agree with everything group leaders say or do, or that group leaders are accountable to their members. Group leaders often develop perspectives somewhat different from those of their members. In most instances, however, groups do represent and speak for at least some of the interests of their members. In voluntary organizations particularly, leaders are likely to reflect the interests of their members. If they do not, members can simply exercise their option to leave. Even "checkbook" members can withhold their support if they disagree with group leaders.

Interest groups do not represent, however, all interests or all interests equally. In 1960, E. E. Schattschneider described the pressure system as small in terms of members and biased toward business and the wealthy. At that time no more than 1,500 groups were included, and more than 50% represented either corporations or trade and business associations.[89] Few groups represented consumers, taxpayers, the environment, women, and minorities.

The pressure system has changed since Schattschneider wrote, but its bias remains. The number of interest groups exploded in the 1960s and 1970s, with many of the new groups representing consumers, environmentalists, minorities, and other nonbusiness interests, but these were more than offset by an increase in the number of corporations in the pressure system.

Business interests still dominate, as we saw earlier. Indeed, business had a greater presence in Washington in the 1980s than it did in the 1960s. Nearly two-thirds of the groups in Washington in the 1980s represented either corporations or trade associations. Groups representing minorities, women, the poor, and elderly are less than 10% of all groups with an office in Washington and only 5% of all groups that lobby.

This bias in the pressure system is a big advantage for business and wealthy interests, and it may be increasing. Over the past three decades, business groups have gained in numbers and influence relative to other groups. Labor unions and the Democratic party, strong supporters of legislation to improve the welfare of the working class, often in opposition to business and wealthy interests, have declined or shifted their focus. As one political analyst put it, "The nature of representative government in the U.S. has changed, so that more and more of the weight of influence in Washington comes from interest groups, not voters."[90] And interest groups are predominantly looking out for the interests of business. The declining level of prosperity of the middle and working classes is one reflection of this change.

Interest group strength is relevant to the debate between those who think our system reflects pluralism and those who think it is run by elites. People who argue that we have a pluralist system emphasize group competition and the ability of individuals to organize themselves to influence government. Those who think we have an elitist government point to the inequality of group competition. On some issues, such as those involving economic benefits for workers, there is competition among groups. On other issues, such as tax policy, there is little.

James Madison foresaw the inevitable development of interest groups and wanted to create a government that would hold them in check. That is, he wanted government to prevent one or more of them from doing harm to others or to the nation as a whole. Madison thought a system of checks and balances and competition among groups would accomplish this. Just as he thought, competing groups can slow the political process. In recent years, we have called this gridlock. But when there is no competition, the nation suffers. Similarly, it suffers when so many interests are involved in politics that it is difficult for government to take action. Government's capacity to do its job is limited by both the bias in the pressure system and the large number of interest groups. Moreover, the built-in checks and balances that Madison thought would preserve the system threaten it by allowing groups to block needed action.

How can we preserve the constitutional rights of interest groups to form and petition government and still keep government responsive to the needs of unorganized or poorly organized interests that lack the resources to press their demands? Recognizing and correcting imbalances in group strength is not simple or easy. Groups currently enjoying an advantage will fight to keep it.

EPILOGUE

The NAACP Opposed the Thomas Nomination

After long and careful deliberation, Hooks and the NAACP decided to oppose the Thomas nomination. Despite the eagerness to have an African-American on the Court, the negatives of Thomas's positions on the issues outweighed the positives of his race. The NAACP pointed to Thomas's insensitivity toward critical areas affecting African-Americans and his view that all are capable of lifting themselves by their bootstraps when, for many, there are no bootstraps. There was concern with his inconsistent views on civil rights, first accepting and then rejecting affirmative action remedies, and his unwillingness to enforce civil rights laws as an administrator in the Reagan administration. The organization did not consider allegations by Anita Hill, a former employee at EEOC, that she had been sexually harassed by Thomas when he headed the agency. The NAACP made its decision in August; Hill's charges did not become public until October.

Despite the NAACP's opposition, Thomas was confirmed. Thomas's tenure on the Court suggests that Hooks and the NAACP were right to oppose him. Thomas has joined Justices Scalia and Rehnquist to form a "hard core" of conservative thought on the Court. In some decisions, Thomas has demonstrated his hostility toward civil rights and individual liberties. His decisions prompted the Southern Christian Leadership Conference (SCLC), the only major civil rights organization to endorse his nomination, to unanimously record a vote of "no confidence" in him at its annual meeting in 1992. The resolution declared that Thomas failed to demonstrate "compassion, sensitivity, independence and intellectual courage."

➤Key Terms

interest groups
lobbying
political action committees (PACs)
private interest groups
public interest groups
single-issue groups
coalitions
market share

➤Further Reading

Jeffrey M. Berry, *The Interest Group Society*, 2nd ed. (Boston: Little, Brown, 1989). *A general survey of interest groups in American politics. It covers political action committees, lobbyists and lobbying, the internal dynamics of groups, and the problems that interest groups present to society.*

Jeffrey Birnbaum, *The Lobbyists: How Influence Peddlers Get Their Way in Washington* (New York: Times Books, 1993). *A study of lobbyists' activities surrounding major issues considered by Congress in the 1989–1990 session.*

Mark Green, *The Other Government* (New York: W. W. Norton, 1975). *An examination of the role of Washington lawyers in representing clients before the government.*

Michael Pertschuk, *Giant Killers* (New York: W. W. Norton, 1986). *How low-budget lobbies can sometimes defeat the big guys by superior organization, tactics, and luck.*

E. E. Schattschneider, *The Semi-Sovereign People* (New York: Henry Holt & Company, 1975). *A classical statement on how interest group politics benefit business and corporate interests by limiting the involvement of citizens in the political process.*

Ernest Wittenberg and Elisabeth Wittenberg, *How to Win in Washington: Very Practical Advice about Lobbying, the Grassroots and the Media* (Cambridge, Mass.: Basil Blackwell, 1989). *A "how to" book for average citizens.*

➤Notes

1. Most of the information here and in the Epilogue is drawn from *Court of Appeal: The Black Community Speaks Out on the Racial and Sexual Politics of Thomas vs. Hill,* ed. The Black Scholar (New York: Ballantine Books, 1992).

2. Ernest Wittenberg and Elisabeth Wittenberg, *How to Win in Washington* (Cambridge, Mass.: Blackwell, 1989), p. 24.

3. Jeffrey Birnbaum, *The Lobbyists* (New York: Times Books, 1992), p. 32.

4. M. A. Peterson and J. L. Walker, "Interest Group Responses to Partisan Change: The Impact of the Reagan Administration upon the National Interest Group System," in A. J. Cigler and B. A. Loomis, eds., *Interest Group Politics,* 2nd ed. (Washington, D.C.: CQ Press, 1987), p. 162.

5. A. de Tocqueville, *Democracy in America* (New York: Knopf, 1945), p. 191.

6. G. Almond and S. Verba, *Civil Culture* (Boston: Little, Brown, 1965), pp. 266–306.

7. David Broder, "Civility, Civic-Mindedness Great Investments for 1995," *Lincoln Journal-Star* (February 22, 1995), p. 2B; Robert D. Putnam, "Bowling Along: America's Declining Social Capital," *Journal of Democracy* (January, 1995), pp. 65–78.

8. Ibid.

9. D. Truman, *The Governmental Process* (New York: Knopf, 1964), pp. 25–26.

10. Ibid., p. 59.

11. Ibid., pp. 26–33.

12. J. Q. Wilson, *Political Organization* (New York: Basic Books, 1973), p. 198.

13. G. K. Wilson, *Interest Groups in America* (Oxford: Oxford University Press, 1981), chapter 5; see also G. K. Wilson, "American Business and Politics," in Cigler and Loomis, *Interest Group Politics,* pp. 221–35.

14. K. L. Schlozman and J. T. Tierney, "More of the Same: Washington Pressure Group Activity in a Decade of Change," *Journal of Politics* 45 (May 1983); pp. 335–56.

15. Christopher H. Foreman, Jr., "Grassroots Victim Organizations: Mobilizing for Personal and Public Health," in Allan J. Cigler and Burdett A. Loomis, *Interest Group Politics,* 4th ed. (Washington, D.C.: CQ Press, 1994), pp. 33–53.

16. R. H. Salisbury, "An Exchange Theory of Interest Groups," *Midwest Journal of Political Science* 13 (February 1969): 1–32.

17. J. M. Berry, *The Interest Group Society* (Boston: Little Brown, 1984), pp. 26–28.

18. J. L. Walker, "The Origins and Maintenance of Interest Groups in America," *American Political Science Review* 77 (June 1983), pp. 398–400; see also *National Journal* (August 1981), p. 1376.

19. Wilson, *Political Organization,* chapter 3.

20. C. Brown, "Explanations of Interest Group Membership Over Time," *American Politics Quarterly* 17 (January 1989), pp. 32–53.

21. C. Brown, "Explanations of Interest Group Membership." The National Rifle Association. Annual Meeting of Midwest P.S. Association, 1987.

22. National Opinion Research Center, General Social Surveys, 1987.

23. N. Babchuk and R. Thompson, "The Voluntary Associations of Negroes," *American Sociological Review* 27 (October 1962), pp. 662–65; see also P. Klobus-Edwards, J. Edwards, and D. Klemmach, "Differences in Social Participation of Blacks and Whites," *Social Forces,* 56 (1978), pp. 1035–52.

24. M. T. Hayes, "The New Group Universe" in Cigler and Loomis, *Interest Group Politics,* pp. 133–45.

25. C. Tomkins, "A Sense of Urgency," *New Yorker,* March 27, 1989, pp. 48–74.

26. Walker, "The Origins and Maintenance of Interest Groups in America."

27. E. E. Schattschneider, *Semi-Sovereign People* (New York: Holt, Rinehart, and Winston, 1960), p. 118.

28. David Broder and Michael Weisskopf, "Finding New Friends on the Hill," *Washington Post National Weekly Edition* (October 3–9, 1994), p. 11.

29. Peter Behr, "The Corporate Winning Streak," *Washington Post National Weekly Edition* (January 30–February 5, 1995), p. 24.

30. F. Swoboda, "Striking Out as a Weapon Against Management," *Washington Post National Weekly Edition* (July 13, 1992), p. 20.

31. P. E. Johnson, "Organized Labor in an Era of Blue Collar Decline," in A. J. Cigler and B. A. Loomis, eds. *Interest Group Politics,* 3rd ed. (Washington, D.C.: CQ Press, 1991), pp. 33–62.

32. Ibid., p. 47.

33. Ibid., p. 51.

34. A. J. Cigler and J. M. Hansen, "Group Formation Through Protest: The American Agriculture Movement," in A. J. Cigler and B. A. Loomis, eds., *Interest Group Politics* (Washington, D.C.: CQ Press, 1983), chapter 4.

35. A. J. Cigler, "Organizational Maintenance and Political Activity on the Cheap: The American Agriculture Movement," in Cigler and Loomis, *Interest Group Politics,* pp. 81–108.

36. On the AMA, see L. H. Zeigler and G. W. Peak, *Interest Groups in American Society,* 2nd ed. (Englewood Cliffs, N.J.: Prentice-Hall, 1972), pp. 225–58.

37. For a discussion of the ABA, see M. Green, "The ABA: The Rhetoric Has Changed But the Morality Lingers On," *Washington Monthly* (January 1974): 21–27.

38. G. Less, "Running Hard for a Place on the Bench," *Washington Post National Weekly Edition* (August 19, 1992), p. 12.

39. The education lobby is treated in R. Stanfield, "The Education Lobby Reborn," *National Journal,* August 9, 1983, pp. 1452–56.

40. J. Tierney, "Old Money, New Power," *New York Times Magazine,* October 23, 1988, p. 69.

41. "Grays on the Go," *Time,* February 22, 1988, p. 69.

42. "Gray Power," *Time,* January 4, 1988, p. 36.

43. "Our Footloose Correspondents," *New Yorker,* August 8, 1988, p. 70.

44. "Grapevine," *Time* (November 28, 1988, p. 24; see also D. Kaul, "Perot Raises Worthwhile Point Regarding Foreign Lobbyists," *Lincoln Journal-Star* (October 25, 1992), p. 5B.

45. *Congressional Quarterly Weekly Report* (December 12, 1992), p. 3792.

46. A. S. McFarland, *Common Cause* (Chatham, N.J.: Chatham House, 1984); see also A. S. McFarland, *Public Interest Lobbies: Decision Making on Energy* (Washington, D.C.: American Enterprise Institute, 1976).

47. R. G. Shaiko, "More Bang for the Buck: The New Era of Full Service Public Interest Groups," in Cigler and Loomis, *Interest Group Politics,* p. 109.

48. Ibid., p. 120.

49. For a discussion of the evolution of NOW and its success in lobbying Congress, see A. N. Costain and W. D. Costain, "The

Women's Lobby: Impact of a Movement on Congress," in Cigler and Loomis, *Interest Group Politics.*

50. E. M. Uslaner, "A Tower of Babel on Foreign Policy," in Cigler and Loomis, *Interest Group Politics,* p. 309.

51. K. Wald, *Religion and Politics* (New York: St. Martin's Press, 1985), pp. 182–212.

52. James L. Guth, John C. Green, Lyman A. Jellstedt, and Corwin E. Wmidt, "Onward Christian Soldiers: Religious Activist Groups in American Politics," *in* Cigler and Loomis, *Interest Group Politics,* p. 57.

53. Sidney Blumental, "Christian Soldiers," *New Yorker* (July 18, 1994), p. 36.

54. Ibid., p. 37.

55. David Von Drehle and Thomas B. Edsall, "The Religious Right Returns," *The Washington Post National Weekly Edition* (August 29–September 4, 1994), p. 6.

56. "Prodding Voters to the Right," *Time* (November 21, 1994), p. 62.

57. Ibid.

58. "Religious Right Returns," p. 6.

59. A. D. Hertzke, "The Role of Churches in Political Mobilization: The Presidential Campaigns of Jesse Jackson and Pat Robertson," in Cigler and Loomis, *Interest Group Politics,* pp. 180–85.

60. The source for most of the next paragraphs is Eric Marcus, *Making History: The Struggle for Gay and Lesbian Equal Rights 1945–1990* (New York: Harper-Collins, 1992). Also see Jeffrey Schmalz, "Gay Politics Goes Mainstream," *New York Times Magazine* (October 11, 1992), pp. 18ff.

61. Gabriel Rotello, "94 Was a Good Year for Gay Rights," *Lincoln Journal-Star* (January 7, 1995), p. 10.

62. C. J. Bosso, "Adaption and Change in the Environmental Movement" in Cigler and Loomis, *Interest Group Politics,* pp. 155–56.

63. Ibid., p. 162.

64. Ibid., p. 169.

65. Tim Curran, "Common Cause Gets Rival," *Roll Call* (February 6, 1995), p. 41.

66. Sarah Tippit-Melbourne and Nancy Traver, "Camp for Crusaders," *Time* (April 19, 1993), p. 40.

67. Spencer Rich, "Gaining Strength in Their Numbers," *Washington Post National Weekly Edition* (December 12–18, 1994), p. 14.

68. A. Rubin, "Interest Groups and Abortion Politics in the Post-Webster Era," in Cigler and Loomis, *Interest Group Politics,* pp. 249–251; *Congressional Quarterly Weekly Report* (March 27, 1993), pp. 755–57.

69. D. Broder, "Let 100 Single-Issue Groups Bloom," *Washington Post,* January 7, 1979, pp. C1–C2; see also D. Broder, *The Party's Over: The Failure of Politics in America* (New York: Harper & Row, 1972).

70. Wilson, *Interest Groups,* chapter 4.

71. P. M. Evans, "Lobbying the Committee: Interest Groups and the House Public Works and Transportation Committee, in the Post-Webster Era," in Cigler and Loomis, *Interest Group Politics,* pp. 257–76.

72. Berry, *Interest Group Society,* p. 188.

73. Jeffrey Birnbaum, *The Lobbyists* (New York: Times Books, 1992), p. 40.

74. Ernest Wittenberg and Elisabeth Wittenberg, *How to Win in Washington* (Cambridge, Massachusetts: Blackwell, 1989), p. 24.

75. David Broder and Spencer Rich, "The Health Care Battle Begins," *Washington Post National Weekly Edition* (September 27–October 3, 1993), p. 6.

76. E. Drew, *Politics and Money: The New Road to Corruption* (New York: Macmillan, 1983), p. 78.

77. Ibid.

78. For an article dealing with the success of interest group ligating at the district court level see L. Epstein and C. K. Rowland, "Debunking the Myth of Interest Group Invincibility in the Courts," *American Political Science Review* 85 (March 1991): 205–20.

79. S. Kernell, *Going Public* (Washington, D.C.: CQ Press, 1986), p. 34.

80. R. Harris, "If You Love Your Grass," *New Yorker,* April 20, 1968, p. 57.

81. Michael Weisskopf, "Letting No Grass Roots Grow Under Their Feet," *The Washington Post National Weekly Edition* (October 18–24, 1993), pp. 20–21.

82. Evans, "Lobbying the Committee," p. 269.

83. Sandra Boodman, "Health Care's Power Player," *Washington Post National Weekly Edition* (February 14–20, 1994), pp. 6–7.

84. Jeffrey Birnbaum, *The Lobbyists* (New York: Times Books, 1992), p. 40.

85. Dan Balz and David Broder, "Take Two Lobbyists and Call Me in the Morning," *The Washington Post National Weekly Edition* (October 18–24, 1993), pp. 10–11.

86. Much of the information in this section is taken from B. A. Loomis, "Coalitions of Interests: Building Bridges in the Balkanized State," in Cigler and Loomis, *Interest Group Politics,* 2nd ed., pp. 258–74.

87. Jeffrey Birnbaum, *The Lobbyists* (New York: Times Books, 1992), p. 83.

88. Dan Clawson, Alan Neustadtl, and Denise Scott, *Money Talks* (New York: Basic Books, 1992), p. 91.

89. Schattschneider, *Semi-Sovereign People,* chapter 2.

90. Kevin Phillips, "Fat City," *Time* (September 26, 1995), p. 51.

6 Political Parties

You Are There

Should the Republicans Offer the Voters a "Contract"?

You are Newt Gingrich, a Republican member of the House of Representatives from Georgia. Although it is early 1994, you sense that your party has a good chance to gain many congressional seats in the November elections, and an outside chance to become the majority party. Voter anger, coupled with the redistricting that changed many district lines in 1992, led a record number of House incumbents (48) to retire. Four other incumbents were defeated in primary elections, leaving 52 seats open. This offers a large opportunity for Republicans to take control of the House. If they do, you will likely become the Speaker of the House, the most powerful office in the House of Representatives.

You have been a key member of the Republican congressional party almost from your first day in Washington. You were one of the first to discover the potential of C-SPAN to get your messages to the public. Your political action committee, GOPAC, raises money from conservative business leaders and uses it to recruit and train Republican candidates who believe in your conservative message.[1] You even provide a list of words tested in focus groups that Republican candidates should use in the campaign: Democrats are to be associated with decay, sickness, stagnation, corruption and waste, and Republicans with change, truth, morality, courage, and family, for example. In the last election, 21 of 47 newly elected Republicans were GOPAC recruits.

Now you are focusing on the strategies and tactics that will ensure a successful 1994 congressional campaign. At a meeting with fellow Republican members of the House, Richard Armey (Texas), Bill Paxon (New York), Tom DeLay (Texas), and others, you discuss the possibility of offering voters a specific platform of actions that your party would take if elected.[2]

Such a possibility is unheard of in off-year (non–presidential election) congressional elections. During presidential election years, parties offer platforms of promises. Though often vague, these platforms distinguish the two major parties, and the winning presidential candidate usually will try to follow through on at least some of the more specific ideas. But congressional elections are generally much less focused on national party goals. These elections tend to be highly individual, with incumbents having great advantages, and both incumbents and challengers tend to focus on local and state issues.

In recent campaigns, candidates have waged highly negative campaigns, both responding to and fueling voter anger at politics and politicians. And during this election year, voters are even more angry than in 1992, when they spurned George Bush's bid for a second term. Fueled by radio and television talk show hosts, Americans said they were fed up with politics as usual: with politicians attuned more to special interest groups than voters, members of Congress who had been in Washington

CONTINUED 

What Are Political Parties?

Development and Change in the Party System

- Preparty Politics: The Founders' View of Political Parties
- First Party System: Development of Parties
- Second Party System: Rise of the Democrats
- Third Party System: Rise of the Republicans
- Fourth Party System: Republican Dominance
- Fifth Party System: Democratic Dominance
- Has the Fifth Party System Realigned?

The Parties Today

Characteristics of the Party System

- Two Parties
- Fragmentation
- Moderation
- Minor Parties in American Politics

Party in the Electorate

- Party Identification
- Characteristics of Democrats and Republicans

Party in Government

Party Organization

- National Party Organization
- State and Local Party Organizations
- Big-City Party Organizations

The Nominating Process

- Caucuses
- Conventions
- Primaries

Conclusion: Do Political Parties Make Government More Responsive?

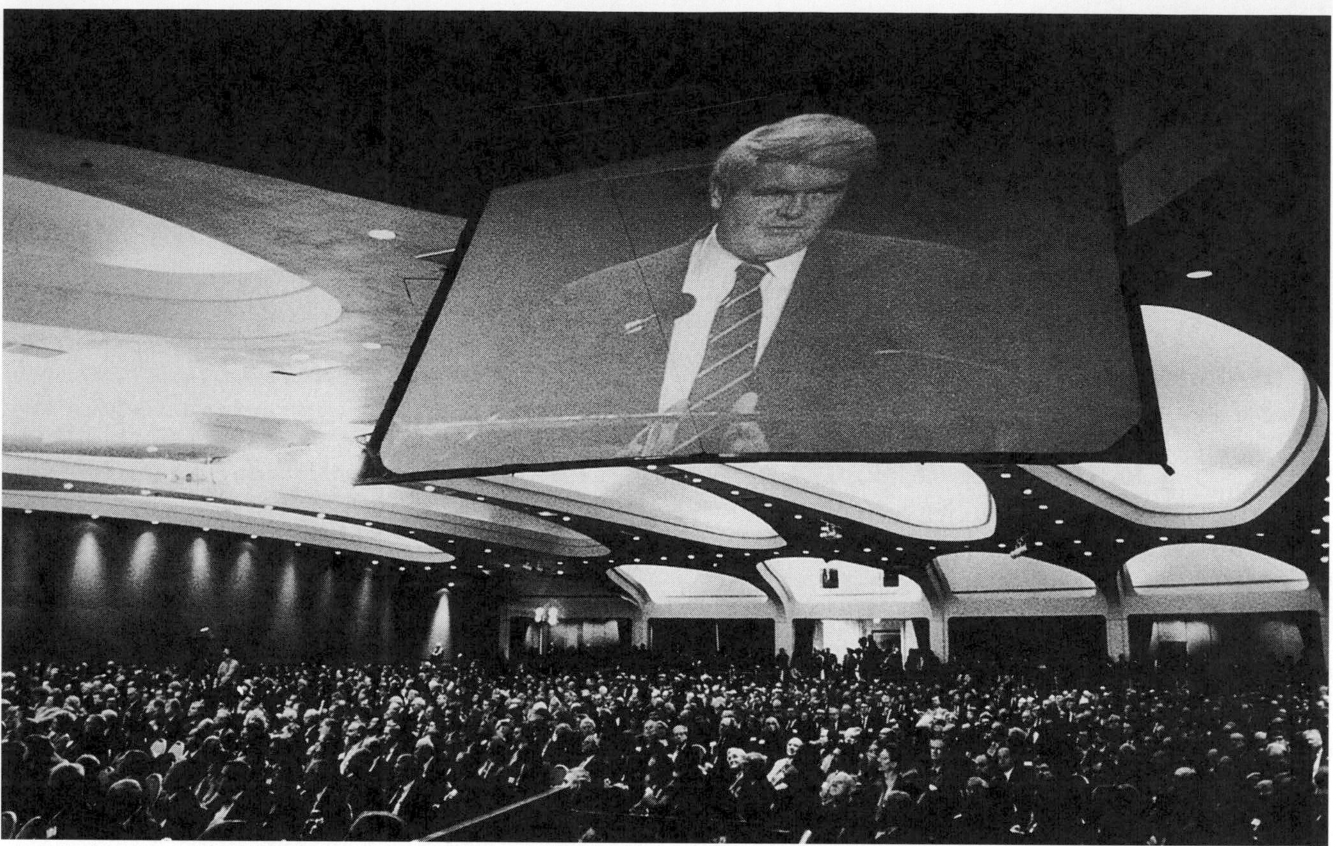

Newt Gingrich

so long they had forgotten the people back home, and elected officials who were unwilling to balance the federal budget. Americans were dubious about their economic futures, terrified of crime, and furious at the breakdown in morality. They blamed government for these problems, or at least for not doing something about them. They especially blamed Democrats, who had controlled Congress for forty years. Most of all, the public seemed to believe that government was no longer accountable to the people.

You think, however, that playing on the voters' negative feelings may not be quite enough to win the majority that you want. Negativism will win some votes, but you believe that the voters want something more positive. Providing a "platform" for this midyear election might be unique enough to draw voters' attention and give a focus to the campaign rhetoric of Republican candidates throughout the nation.

However, there are potential drawbacks to this idea. Exactly what should be part of such a platform? Like the Democrats, your party has significant divisions among its members, especially over issues of morality such as abortion rights and school prayer, and over budget issues too. Political parties in the U.S. are not tightly disciplined organizations characterized by shared values on all major issues. Drawing up a platform that everyone could agree on would not be an easy task, and a public fight among members over the terms of such a platform would negate any benefits of having one at all.

Moreover, if such a platform could be constructed, there would be a danger that Republicans would be labeled a failure if they could not carry out that platform. Being specific about what the party wanted to do might make it easier for Democrats and other skeptics to point to all the platform promises that were not accomplished. And the more specific the platform, the easier it would be to spot and criticize these failures.

What do you decide? Do you go ahead with a Republican platform, risking party division and possible failure to deliver on your promises? Or do you follow a more traditional approach, focusing almost entirely on what is wrong with the Clinton presidency and the Democratic Congress?

George Washington warned against the "baneful" effects of parties and described them as the people's worst enemies. More recently, a respected political scientist, E. E. Schattschneider, argued that "political parties created democracy and that democracy was impossible without them."[3] The public echoes these contradictory views. Many believe that parties create conflict where none exists, yet most identify with one of our two major parties.[4]

These same feelings exist among candidates for office. They often avoid political parties by establishing their own personal campaign organizations and raising their own funds. If elected, they often do not follow the party line. At the same time, candidates for national and state offices are nominated in the name of political parties, they rely on parties for assistance, and they have little chance of winning unless they are Democrats or Republicans.

In this chapter, we examine American political parties to see why they are important and why many observers believe that if they become less important and effective, our system of government may not work as well as it does.

➤What Are Political Parties?

Political parties are a major link between people and government. They provide a way for the public to have some say about who serves in government and what policies are chosen. Political parties generally are defined as organizations that seek to control government by recruiting, nominating, and electing their members to public office. They consist of three interrelated components: the **party in the electorate,** those who identify with the party; the **party in government,** those who are appointed or elected to office as members of a political party; and the formal **party organization,** the party "professionals" who run the party at the national, state, and local levels (see Figure 1).[5]

FIGURE 1
The Three Components of Political Parties

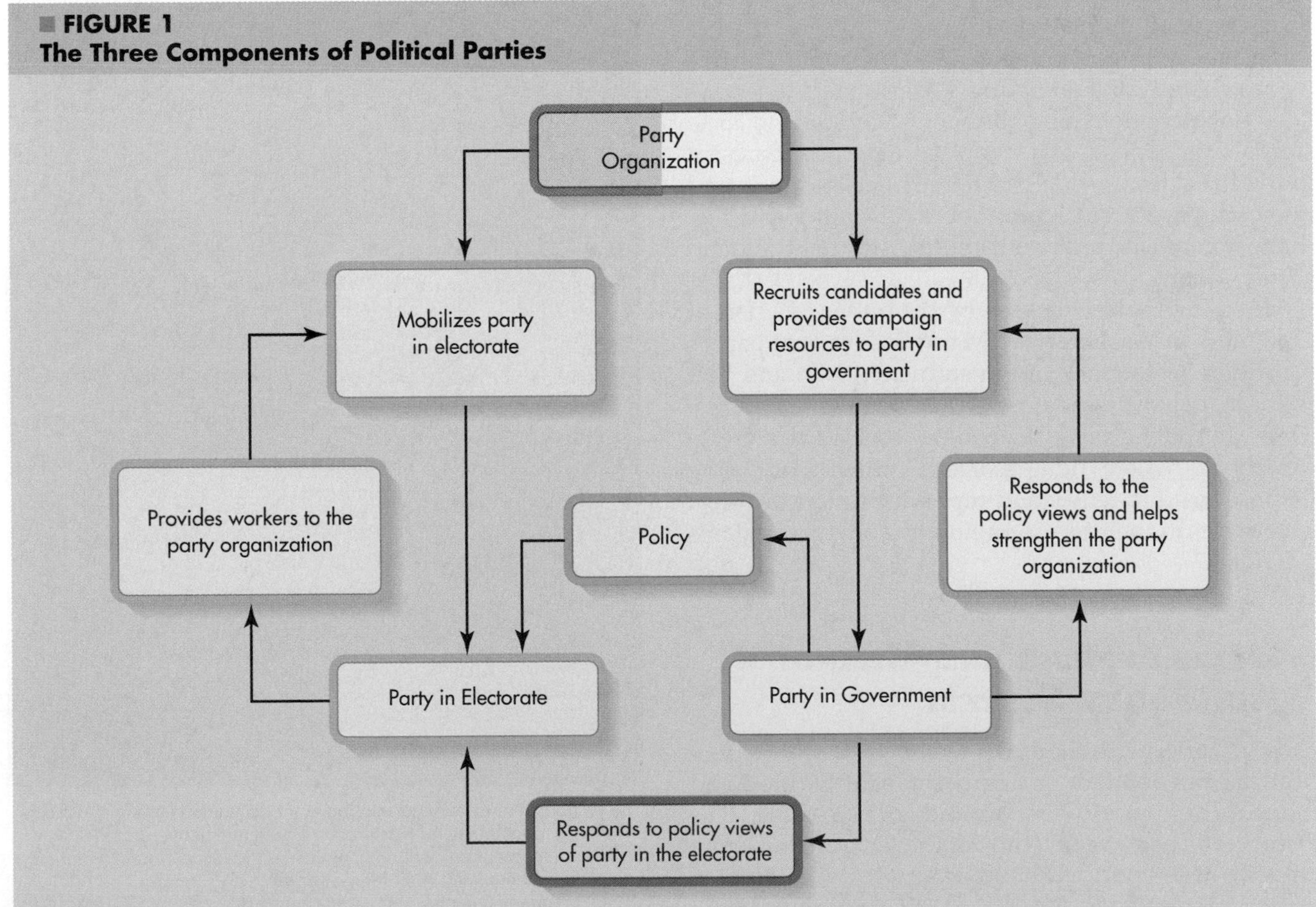

In linking the public and government policymakers, parties serve several purposes. They help select public officials by recruiting and screening candidates and then providing campaign resources. They help empower citizens by activating and interesting them in politics. Individually, citizens have little power, but collectively, through parties, they can influence government.

Many voters feel an attachment to a political party, an affiliation they acquire early in life and which aids them in deciding among competing candidates. Some voters simply vote their party identification, regardless of candidates or issues. But parties also help many people vote on the basis of issues. Parties are associated, however dimly, in the voters' minds with issues. In the recent past, the Democratic party has favored an expanded role for the national government in maintaining the economic well-being of Americans, whereas the Republican party has supported a more limited role. Most voters understand this difference. Knowing a candidate belongs to a particular party is a clue to the candidate's general stand on the issues, and voters therefore do not need to study each candidate's position in great detail.

The party in government plays an important role in organizing and operating government; it formulates policy options and ultimately decides which to support or oppose. When political parties represent individuals from widely different backgrounds and interests, parties aid society by aggregating and mediating conflicts and contributing to political and social stability.

However, parties are seen by the public as a part of the "mess in Washington." Many believe that parties contribute to the lack of government action and that partisan debates are mostly meaningless squabbles. Thus the public tends to believe that parties create differences where none existed, rather than being institutions that reflect and represent Americans' real differences in their views on how to solve the nation's problems.

Development and Change in the Party System

Most Americans think of the Democratic and Republican parties as more or less permanent fixtures, and indeed they have been around a long time. The Democratic party evolved from the Jacksonian Democrats in 1832, and the Republican party was founded in 1854. Nevertheless, the current party system is only one of five distinct party systems that have existed in American history (see Figure 2).

In tracing the development of these systems, we need to keep two things in mind. First, parties developed after the nation's founding, they grew to be very powerful in the late nineteenth century, and they have declined in influence since then.

Second, there have been periods of stability in the party system when one party has dominated American politics and won most elections. There have also been periods of transition and instability when neither party has dominated, and control of government has been divided between the parties or has shifted back and forth. In transition periods, issues emerge that are difficult to resolve, and voters establish new party loyalties based on them. The transition from one stable party system to another is called a **realignment.**

The factions that developed into the first political parties were already vying with each other in Washington's administration. Thomas Jefferson (*second from left*) and Alexander Hamilton (*fourth from left*) are pictured here with Washington (*right*).

FIGURE 2
The Five American Party Systems

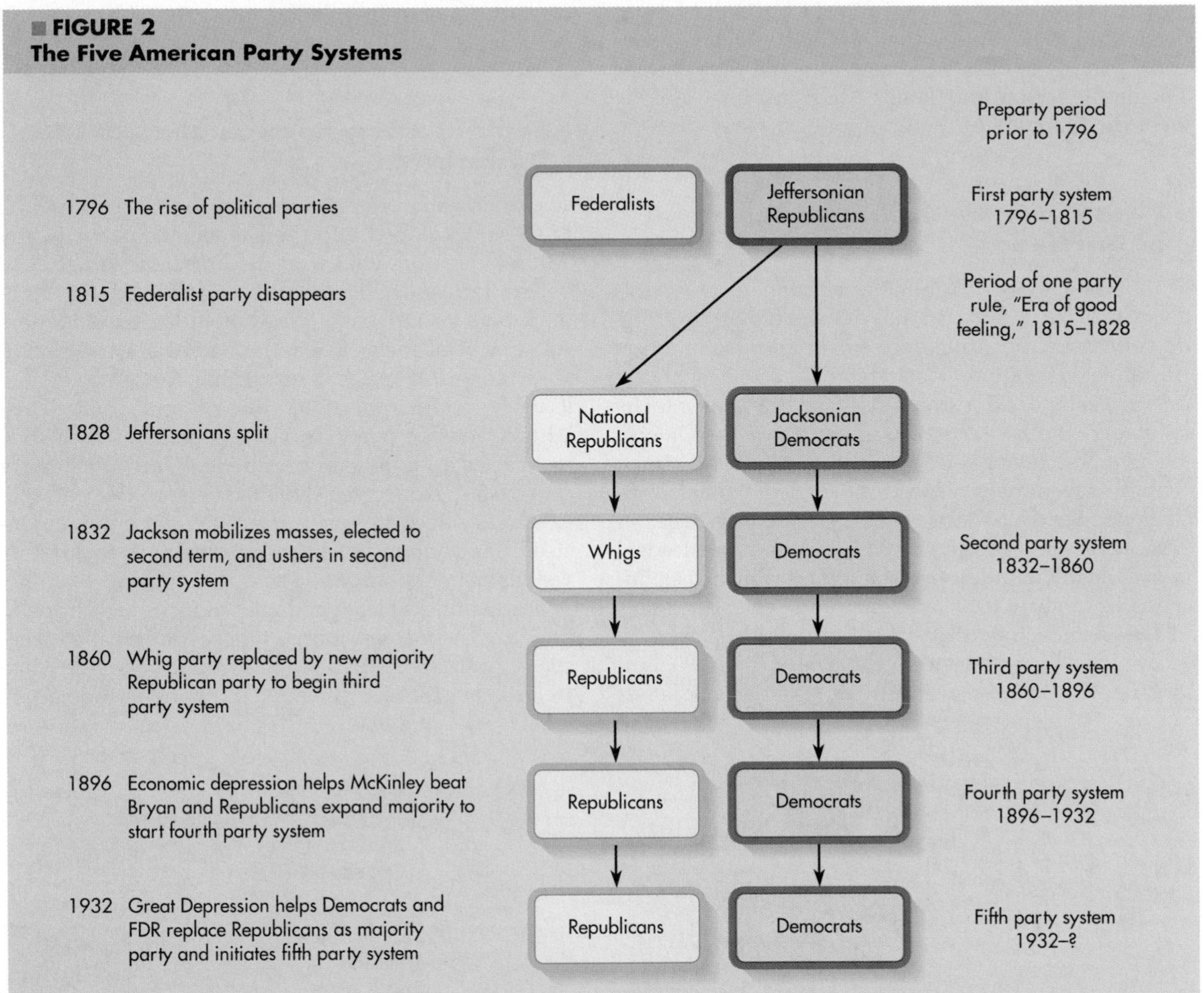
Preparty period
prior to 1796
1796 The rise of political parties
Federalists
Jeffersonian Republicans
First party system
1796–1815
1815 Federalist party disappears
Period of one party rule, "Era of good feeling," 1815–1828
1828 Jeffersonians split
National Republicans
Jacksonian Democrats
1832 Jackson mobilizes masses, elected to second term, and ushers in second party system
Whigs
Democrats
Second party system
1832–1860
1860 Whig party replaced by new majority Republican party to begin third party system
Republicans
Democrats
Third party system
1860–1896
1896 Economic depression helps McKinley beat Bryan and Republicans expand majority to start fourth party system
Republicans
Democrats
Fourth party system
1896–1932
1932 Great Depression helps Democrats and FDR replace Republicans as majority party and initiates fifth party system
Republicans
Democrats
Fifth party system
1932–?

Preparty Politics: The Founders' Views of Political Parties

Most of the Founders viewed political parties as dangerous to stable government. This antiparty feeling was rooted in three basic beliefs. First, the Founders thought parties created and exploited conflicts that undermined consensus on public policy. Second, they thought parties were instruments by which a small and narrow interest could impose its will on society. And third, they believed parties stifled independent thought and behavior.[6]

Madison feared political parties as much as interest groups because he felt both pursued selfish interests at the expense of the common good. He referred to both as "factions" in *Federalist #10.* John Adams dreaded what he considered the greatest political evil, the formation of rival political parties.

Therefore, it is not surprising that the Constitution does not mention political parties. Nevertheless, it created a system in which parties, or something like them, were inevitable. When the Founders established popular elections as the mechanism for selecting political leaders, an agency for organizing and mobilizing supporters of political candidates was needed. Indeed, despite their antiparty feelings, several of the Founders were active in the first parties. Thomas Jefferson and James Madison, for example, were the founders of the first political party.

First Party System: Development of Parties

With Washington's unanimous election to the presidency in 1788, it appeared the nation could be governed by consensus. But differences of opinion soon arose. Alexander Hamilton, Washington's secretary of the treasury, supported a strong national government. His following, the Federalists, were opposed by Thomas Jefferson, secretary of state, who feared a strong central government. The conflict led Jefferson to challenge Federalist John Adams for the presidency in 1796. Jefferson lost, but he then recruited able leaders in each state, founded newspapers, established political clubs, and in 1800 ran again and won. Jefferson's victory demonstrated the utility of political parties.

By Jefferson's second term, more than 90% of members of Congress were either Federalists or Jeffersonians (later called Jeffersonian Republicans) and consistently voted in support of their party.[7]

Second Party System: Rise of the Democrats

The Jeffersonian Republicans split into factions. One of these developed into the Democratic party, led by Andrew Jackson, who won the presidency in 1828.

The Jacksonian Democrats emphasized the common person and encouraged popular participation. As a result of their efforts, the vote was expanded to all white adult males. Presidential electors were selected in popular elections rather than by state legislatures, and the party convention became the instrument used to nominate presidential and other party candidates. No longer did members of the party in Congress select the party's presidential nominee. Instead, conventions opened up decisions to local as well as national party elites.

Many political leaders deplored Jackson's efforts to mobilize the masses. John Quincy Adams called Jackson a "barbarian." An Adams supporter referred to Jackson's victory as "the howl of raving Democracy."[8]

In 1828, opponents of Andrew Jackson called him a jackass. Political cartoonists and journalists began to use the donkey to symbolize Jackson and the Democratic Party. In the 1870s, Thomas Nast popularized the donkey as a symbol of the party in his cartoons and originated the elephant as a symbol of the Republican Party. His 1874 cartoon showed the Democratic donkey dressed as a lion frightening the other animals of the jungle, including the Republican elephant.

Jackson's popular appeal and the organizational effort of his party brought large numbers to the polls for the first time. By 1828, more than a million votes were cast for president. Building on the efforts of Jefferson, Jackson introduced a uniquely American idea, a mass-population-based party organization.

Third Party System: Rise of the Republicans

The conflict over slavery brought a new party alignment. Abolitionists and proslavery factions split the Whig party, which had been the primary opposition

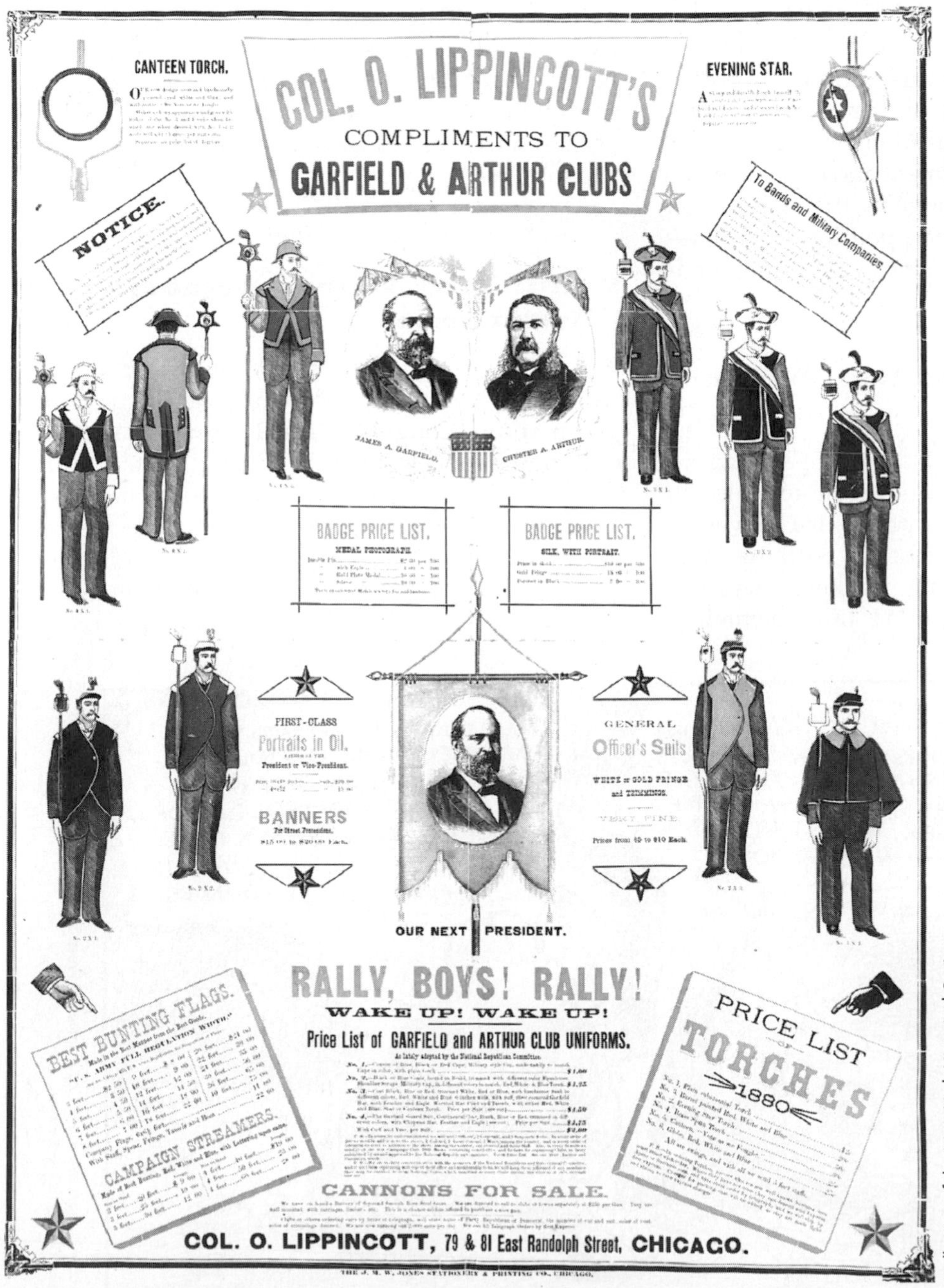

Collection of the New York Historical Society

Today, most citizens take part in political activities as "couch potatoes" watching television. During the third party era, most eligible voters (largely white males) participated actively. Torchlight parades and rallies were frequent, and businesses sprang up to supply the necessary torches, banners, flags, and uniforms.

to the Democrats. By 1860, the Whigs disappeared and a new party, the Republicans (not related to the Jeffersonian or National Republicans), emerged. The Republicans (also known as the GOP—Grand Old Party), reflecting abolitionist sentiment, nominated Abraham Lincoln for president. Northern Democrats who opposed slavery joined Republicans to form a new majority party.

After the Civil War, the Republicans usually won the presidency and controlled Congress. After 1876, however, elections were close and the parties evenly matched in Congress.

Parties were strong during this period. They controlled nominations for office and mobilized voters through extensive local organizations. Big-city political machines provided employment and other help for many new immigrants in exchange for their allegiance. Corruption—vote buying and political payoffs—linked poor immigrants, big business, and party leaders in strong party machines.

Fourth Party System: Republican Dominance

The election of 1896 ushered in another party alignment. Democrat William Jennings Bryan appealed to southerners and farmers of the plains. He played to their hostility toward the Northeast, with its large corporations and growing ethnic working class. His was a religious appeal too, pitting fundamentalists against Catholics. But his appeal was too narrow and the Democrats were soundly defeated.

During this period a third party, the Progressives, became popular. The Progressives championed political reform, especially of big-city machines. Although the Progressives did not win the presidency, their ideas eventually were enacted into law. These included voter registration and the secret ballot, which reduced election fraud; the direct primary, which allowed rank-and-file voters to nominate their party's candidates and reduce control by party bosses; and civil service reform, which reduced political patronage. These reforms, intended to check corruption, all weakened political parties. They gave parties, and their bosses, less control over elections and jobs.

Fifth Party System: Democratic Dominance

In the 1920s, the Republicans began to lose support in the cities. The party ignored the plight of poor immigrants and in Congress pushed through quotas limiting immigration from southern and eastern Europe. After the Depression hit in 1929, these immigrants, along with many women voting for the first time, joined traditional Democrats in the South to elect Franklin Roosevelt in 1932. This election reflected another party alignment.

Source: Oliphant copyright 1990 Universal Press Syndicate. Reprinted with permission. All rights reserved.

The **New Deal coalition,** composed of city dwellers, blue-collar workers, Catholic and Jewish immigrants, blacks, and southerners, elected Roosevelt to an unprecedented four terms. The coalition was an odd alliance of northern liberals and southern conservatives. It stuck together in the 1930s and 1940s because of Roosevelt's personality and skill and because northerners did not seriously challenge southern racial policies.

But the coalition came unglued after Roosevelt's death. The Republicans, by nominating a popular war hero, General Dwight D. Eisenhower, won the presidency in 1952 and 1956. Although the Democrats regained the White House in 1960, the civil rights movement and the Vietnam War divided them sharply, and they lost again in 1968 and 1972.[9] They won in 1976 by nominating a southerner—Jimmy Carter—and because the Republicans suffered from the Watergate scandal. Even though the Democrats dominated Congress until 1994, they had much less success in winning the presidency. Democrats have won the White House only twice since 1964, suggesting that the fifth party system may have ended.

Has the Fifth Party System Realigned?

The fifth party system has changed, but has a major realignment occurred? Many of the signs that preceded major realignments of the party system have been present for some time. **Ticket splitting,** voting for a member of one party for one office but a member of another party for a different one, is at a high level (see Figure 3). In the 1980s, ticket splitting was two to three times that in the 1950s.[10] This is most evident at the national level. The Republicans have occupied the White House and the Democrats have controlled Congress most of the time since 1968.

Another sign of change is the increased number of citizens who do not choose to identify with a political party. Many voters who became eligible to vote for the first time during the 1980s and 1990s have not been attracted to either party, and some older voters lack firm attachments to their party.

Realigning periods also are characterized by compelling issues that fracture the unity of the major parties.[11] In the years before 1860, slavery was such an issue. It divided the Democrats and destroyed the

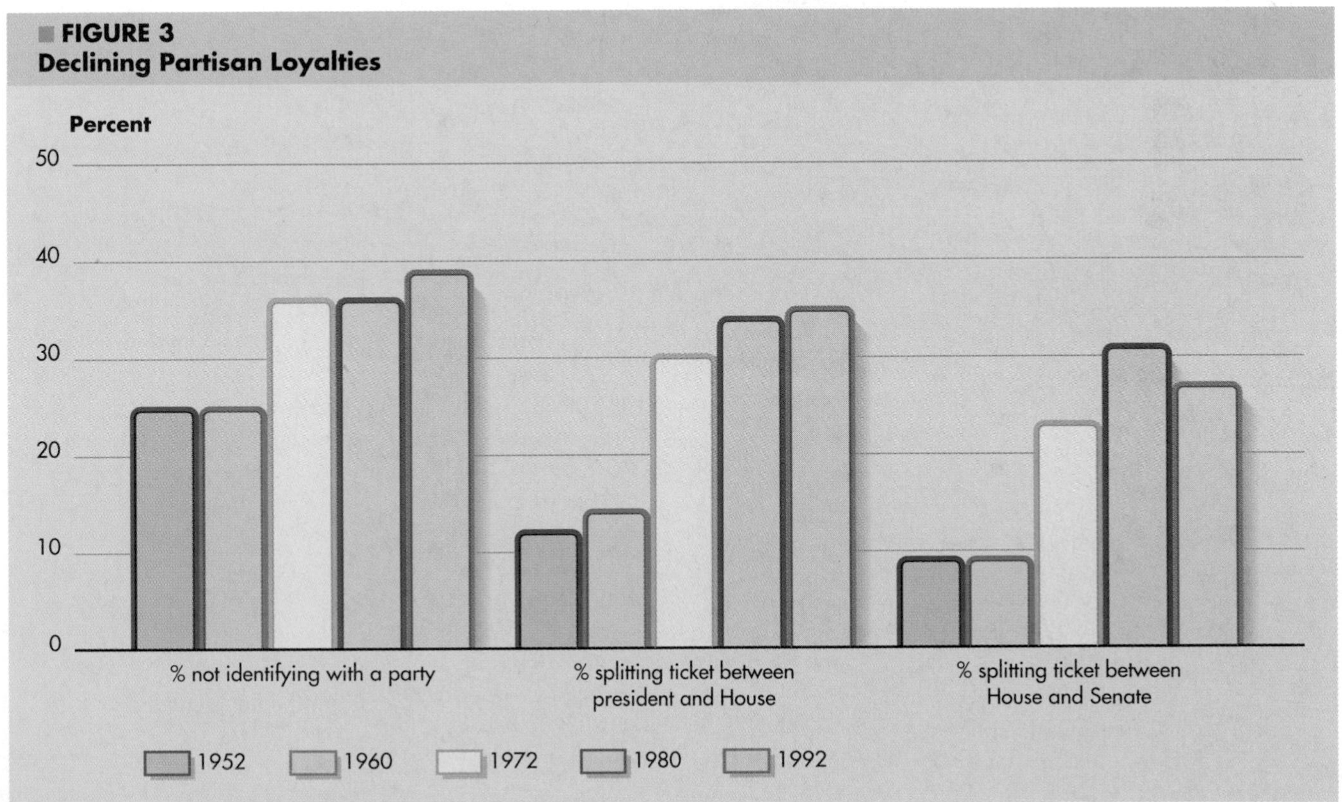

SOURCE: CPS National Election Studies.

Whigs. In 1932, economic issues led many Republicans away from their party to the Democrats. As memories of the Depression and influence of Depression-era economic issues fade, the potential exists for new issues to mobilize and realign voters.

While a major realignment has not occurred, the fifth party system has changed since the 1960s. Blue-collar ethnics and Catholics have found the Democrats much less attractive.[12] As New Deal policies succeeded, blue-collar workers became much less concerned with economic security and turned their attention to other issues. Many were upset with the party's promotion of civil rights. Divisions in the party over the Vietnam War pushed many who were

The Electorate of the 1990s

We have discussed the divisions within each of the two major parties. One survey organization has tried to describe these divisions more specifically by focusing on what different subgroups of the voting population really want. Though these sketches are necessarily to some extent superficial and time-bound, they do capture some of the complexity of the voting public.

Largely Republican

Enterprisers: 12% of registered voters, 74% Republican. Antigovernment, antiwelfare, probusiness. Largely male, white, middle-aged, affluent and college-educated. Key issue: Opposed to health care reform. Heroes: Ronald Reagan, Colin Powell, and Rush Limbaugh. Villains: Bill and Hillary Clinton, Ted Kennedy, and gay rights activists.

Moralists: 20% of registered voters, 65% Republican. Antigovernment, antiwelfare, and anti–big business. Religious and socially intolerant. White, middle-aged, average income and education. Key issues: Support for prayer in school and harsher sentences for criminals. Heroes: Ronald Reagan and Colin Powell. Villains: Gay rights activists.

Libertarians: 4% of registered voters, 54% Republican. Antigovernment, anti–social welfare, and probusiness. Tolerant but not religious. Male, white, highly educated and affluent. Key issues: Cutting taxes and welfare. Hero: Colin Powell. Villains: Ted Kennedy, Louis Farrakhan, Jerry Falwell.

Largely Independent

New Economy Independents: 19% of registered voters, 52% independent (27% Democratic). Strong environmentalists, but oppose government regulation. Pro–social welfare, but not sympathetic to blacks. Female, young and middle-aged, white-collar professionals and service workers, average income; 40% are working women. Key issues: Support for health care reform, stricter gun control, government spending for job training, and gay rights. No heroes. Villain: Jerry Falwell.

Bystanders: None of the registered voters, but 8% of the population, 52% independent. Environmentalist. Young, female, less education and income. Key issues: none. Heroes: none. Villains: Tobacco companies.

Embittered: 7% of registered voters, 39% independent, 36% Democrat; 25% African-American. Antigovernment, antipolitician, and antibusiness. Religious and socially intolerant. Believe discrimination is barrier to black progress. Low skill, low income. Support school prayer and oppose government-funded abortions. Hero: John Kennedy. Villains: Insurance companies, MTV, Rush Limbaugh.

Largely Democrat

Seculars: 10% of registered voters, 46% Democrat (31% independent who lean Democrat). Somewhat progovernment. Anticorporations. Strong commitment to environment. Tolerant. White, relatively young, highly educated and affluent. Favor government funding for abortion, gun control, and gay rights. Oppose school prayer. Hero: Hillary Clinton. Villains: Rush Limbaugh, Jerry Falwell, Oliver North, Louis Farrakhan, tobacco companies.

New Democrats: 8% registered voters, 62% Democrat, but most voted for Bush in 1988. Progovernment, proenvironment, more probusiness than other Democratic groups. Religious but not intolerant. Female, average income and education, high proportion of minorities, employed in social service and educational occupations. Key issues: Support for health care reform and job training. Heroes: Hillary Clinton and Colin Powell. Villain: Rush Limbaugh.

New Dealers: 8% registered voters, 82% Democrat. Faith in government, but distrust politicians and big business. Conservative on race and social welfare programs. Strongly religious, moderately tolerant. Oldest group: one-third over 65. Labor unions, low income, no college. Oppose government-funded abortions and support prayer in schools, health care reform, and use of military force. Heroes: Franklin Roosevelt, John Kennedy, Jimmy Carter, Al Gore. Villain: Jerry Falwell.

Partisan Poor: 8% registered voters, 89% Democrat. Progovernment, anti–big business; 41% nonwhite, blue collar, very poor. Favor government spending to help poor, job training, health care reform, and school prayer. Heroes: John Kennedy, Jimmy Carter, Bill and Hillary Clinton. Villain: Rush Limbaugh.

SOURCE: *The New Political Landscape.* Times Mirror Center for the People and the Press, October 1994.

in favor of the war, particularly union members, to the Republicans. Some objected to the Democratic party's positions on social issues such as opposition to capital punishment, prayer in schools, and support for abortion and the rights of criminal defendants.

However, in the 1980s, economic concerns returned. Today blue-collar workers find their standard of living eroding, and feel left behind and left out.[13] This has not moved them back to their Democratic roots, however. They feel resentful at what they believe to be the Democrats' favoritism toward minorities and policies that seem to free citizens of personal responsibility for their actions (for example, crime policies that some see as "coddling criminals"). The big-city machines that once mobilized workers to vote Democratic are gone, and the labor unions, which did the same, are dramatically weakened.

Other changes drove some voters to the Democratic party. Northern white Protestants and white-collar workers are somewhat less Republican than they used to be. Many of them are employed by government and more sympathetic to government's role in solving societal problems. The Democrats are also appealing increasingly to better-educated voters, who support Democratic initiatives such as health care reform, commitment to the environment, and abortion rights.[14]

In general, then, there has been some evidence of slight realignment focused on issues of government size and scope, with parties becoming slightly more homogeneous.[15] Although only a modest realignment has occurred nationally, a regional one, confined to the South, has certainly occurred. Long a bastion of Democratic party strength, the South began to drift away in the 1950s and showed major signs of change in 1964. For the first time in a century, the Republicans carried Alabama, Georgia, Louisiana, Mississippi, and South Carolina in the presidential election. Upset with the civil rights policies of the national Democratic party, many white southerners voted for Barry Goldwater, the Republican nominee.

Since 1968 Republicans have carried the South in all presidential elections, except for Jimmy Carter's election in 1976. Although the Georgian carried the region, a majority of white southerners voted for Ford. Carter won the region on the strength of the black vote. Clinton carried his home state, Arkansas, and that of his running mate, Tennessee. He also picked up Louisiana, but, like Carter, lost the majority of white Southerners.

White southerners increasingly vote for Republicans in congressional races too. In 1994 they cast the majority of their votes for Republicans.

Today the Republican party is competitive in the South in statewide races and, measured in terms of voter registration and party identification, is equal to the Democrats.[16]

The change in party identification among white southerners is the main reason that polls have shown a decline in Democratic loyalties nationwide. The shift of white southerners to the Republican party makes the South not only more Republican, but it makes the Republicans more conservative. The change also gives the party system a somewhat more ideological look. The southern Democrats who changed tend to be conservatives and are more ideologically compatible with policies of the Republican party.

The race issue, which spurred this realignment, continues to play a role. Where white southerners in the 1950s and 1960s claimed "betrayal" by the national Democratic party for its policies urging equality for blacks, they now say they object to its policies accepting affirmative action for minorities. The polarization between the races has sharpened the realignment between the parties to such an extent in some places that whites who are asked their party affiliation sometimes retort, "I'm white, aren't I?" meaning "I'm Republican."[17]

There also has been some **dealignment.**[18] More individuals have opted for independence as parties become less and less relevant. Increasing numbers say that there is nothing that they like or dislike about parties, suggesting that citizens are indifferent toward them. Similarly, the number who have something positive to say about one party and something negative to say about the other has declined, again suggesting that parties are not as important to citizens as they were in the 1950s and 1960s.[19] Candidates and issues have become more important.

The increasing tendency toward dealignment may stretch the length of time it takes for a realignment, or postpone a realignment altogether. That is, some people who might have switched parties do not care enough about them to switch. Some observers see a "rolling realignment" that has been moving the country to the right and toward the Republicans in fits and starts since the early 1970s.

➤The Parties Today

Generally each party is more ideologically homogenous than it used to be, with most Republicans considering themselves conservative. In fact, the Republican party represents an uneasy coalition of traditional conservatives, motivated primarily by a desire to minimize government intervention in the economy, and new conservatives, motivated primarily by a desire to institutionalize their religious and moral values. Called the religious right, the new conservatives want to increase government intervention in such areas as abortion, prayers in school, and pornography. In many states, the religious right controls the Republican party. Since the 1992 Republican National Convention, the right has avoided open confrontations with moderate Republicans, and national party leaders have stressed issues such as taxing and smaller government, on which both agree. With white born-again Christians 17% of the electorate, party success in 1996 and beyond may depend on keeping more divisive issues such as abortion in the background.

Class differences are also apparent among conservatives. Many traditional conservatives are upper-middle and upper class, while many new conservatives are lower-middle class. The two factions were united in their hate for communism and their support for Reagan. But now the disintegration of the Soviet Union and the Communist bloc and the retirement of Reagan leave them with less in common.[20]

The Democrats are also divided, however. Some want to strengthen the party's appeal to the working class and poor with more economically liberal spending policies but more socially conservative policies. Others want to target the angry middle class voters with more conservative economic policies, such as the balanced budget and cutting spending.

Despite the changing nature of the parties, and despite three Republican presidential election victories during the 1980s, more people still declare themselves Democrat than Republican. Until 1994, Democrats continued to control the House of Representatives and the Senate and to dominate state legislatures and gubernatorial offices. Even after the 1994 congressional elections, polls showed somewhat more Democrats than Republicans (41 to 35%).

Characteristics of the Party System

The American party system is characterized by some intriguing and even unique qualities.

Two Parties

First, the American party system is a **two-party system.** Only two parties win seats in Congress, and only two parties compete effectively for the presidency. The development and perpetuation of two parties is rare among the nations of the world.

In Western Europe, for example, **multiparty systems** are the rule. Italy has 9 national parties and several regional parties; France and Germany have 4. Great Britain, although a predominantly two-party system, now has at least 3 significant minor parties. Multiparty systems also are found in Canada, which has 3 parties, and Israel, which has more than 20.

Why do we have a two-party system? The most common explanation is the nature of our election system.[21] Public officials are elected from **single-member districts** under a **winner-take-all** arrangement. This means only one individual is elected from a district or state—the individual who receives the most votes. This contrasts with **proportional representation** election schemes, where seats in the national legislature go to political parties roughly according to the proportion of the popular vote the parties' candidates receive.

In single-member district, winner-take-all systems, only the major parties have much chance of winning legislative seats. Without much hope of developing a base to build on, minor parties tend to die off or merge with one of the major parties. However, this explanation might not account for the difference. It may be the party system that influences the election system rather than the reverse. Where only two parties exist, it is to their advantage to maintain an election system that undermines the development and growth of minor parties. For example, legislatures, controlled by the two parties, have tried to make it as difficult as possible for third parties to get on the ballot (though the courts have struck down much of this restrictive legislation). Where several parties exist, it is to their advantage to establish an election system that benefits many parties.[22]

Fragmentation

The federal system, with its fragmentation of power between state and national levels, leads to fragmentation within parties. State and local parties have their own resources and power bases separate from those of the national parties.

Power also is fragmented at each level. At the national level, power is shared among the president and members of Congress. No one controls the party. Presidents often have a difficult time winning support for their policies among their party members in Congress.

As parties have weakened, this problem has become more apparent. In 1992 House Republicans supported President Bush 71% of the time, Senate Republicans 73%. In 1993 House Democrats supported President Clinton 77% of the time, Senate Democrats 87%. Even on major issues, congressional Democrats broke with Clinton. For the North American Free Trade Agreement (NAFTA), two of the top three majority leaders in the House actually led the opposition and two of the top three majority leaders in the Senate joined the opposition. For a crime bill, three committee chairs and 17 subcommittee chairs in the two chambers sided with the opponents. These leaders, among congressional members, had the most to lose from a party breakdown and policy defeats. (As they later learned, to their sorrow. Congressional Democrats' failure to accomplish more contributed to the public's disgust and the Republicans' takeover in the 1994 elections.)

These defections illustrate members' independence from their party. To be reelected, they need to satisfy only a plurality of the voters in their district or state, not the president. When Clinton considered a gas tax increase to reduce the deficit, Democratic Senator Herbert Kohl (Wis.) told him the increase would be no more than 4.3 cents per gallon. Clinton had to accept this figure because the bill's outcome was in doubt and the senator's vote was crucial. Kohl, a multimillionaire, paid for his initial election campaign and could pay for a reelection bid, so he felt no obligation to his party. Such independence makes it difficult to forge a unified party.

Moderation

American political parties are moderate; there are no extremely liberal or extremely conservative major parties. One reason for this is that the people themselves are moderate (see Figure 4). To attract the most voters, the parties try to appear moderate.

FIGURE 4
Parties Aim Their Campaigns to the Middle, Where the Voters Are

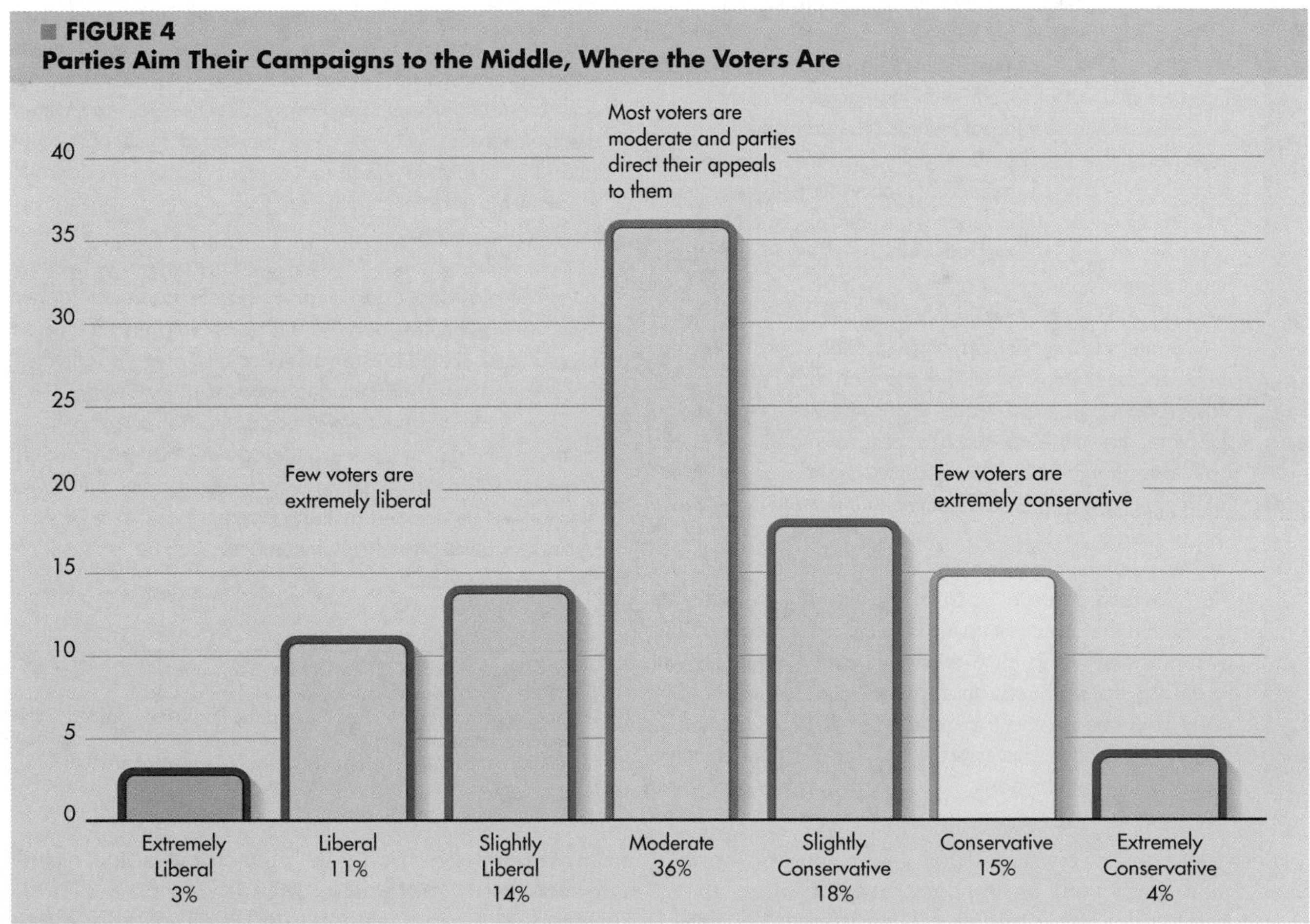

SOURCE: Data from 1990 General Social Survey, National Opinion Research Center. The labels (such as "liberal") were self-descriptions.

New Populism

Do We Need a Third Party?

Populist anger at politicians, big government, and existing institutions occasionally leads to a movement to start a new political party, one that will better represent the needs of the average voter. The populist tag was sometimes attached to the attempts to form a third party by Ross Perot and his movement in 1992 and George Wallace and his supporters in 1968.

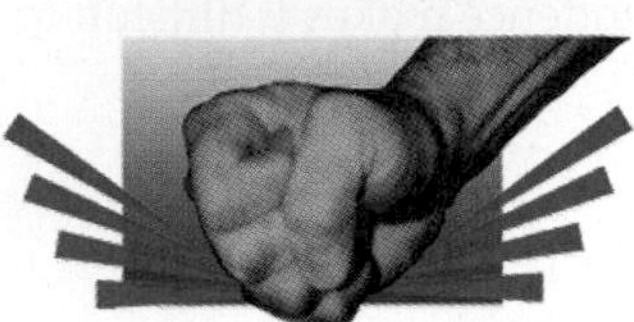

The populist argument that existing leaders and institutions have somehow been corrupted and separated from the wishes of the public fits well with the desire of third-party leaders to oust the existing political parties and their leaders. And in an era when the public seems to have lost its close allegiance to the existing parties, and is alienated from government in general, it would seem fairly easy for third-party candidates to be successful. Indeed, a recent poll indicated that 82% of the public believe that the parties are "pretty much out of touch" with the people.[1]

Other polls also suggest there is substantial support for a third party. Over half of those polled in 1994 indicated that a third major party is needed.[2] Support was highest among men, those under 30, independents, liberals, and those who are more educated. Over half of those polled in 1995, after Republicans took over control of Congress, still wanted a third party. Even 48% of Republicans did.[3]

Despite such sentiments, third parties have rarely had much success. Think of all the attention that Perot's candidacy received in 1992—but he garnered less than 20% of the vote. He certainly did his best to mobilize the disgruntled, angry voters into his camp. Yet he was unsuccessful in making the kind of impact he wanted. He did not even win one state.

Many voters might consider a third party an antidote to the "business as usual" politics in Washington. Yet when faced with the choice of voting against a candidate of their own party, or voting for a relatively unknown quantity with no ties to the party structure, many voters spurn the third party and choose the tried and true. Though their anger remains, it is often expressed with a vote for the nonincumbent of the major party. Thus, angry voters threw out George Bush in 1992 rather than electing Ross Perot, and the same angry voters threw out the Democratic Congress in 1994.

Although many issues calling for solutions remain, it is difficult to establish a new party. Not only are most voters in the habit of supporting one of the two major parties, but various laws favor the existence of the two-party system. These laws make it harder for third-party candidates to get on the ballot and give the existing parties the edge in public financing of presidential elections.

Most third parties in history have started on a small scale in one region. The 1948 Dixiecrat party had its roots in the South as a protest against the move by the Democrats toward more rights for blacks; the Populist party of 1892 was rooted in the Midwest. With the pervasiveness of the mass media today, it is easier for potential third parties to gain a national audience if they are well funded.

Forming a third party requires dynamic and energetic leaders with financial and organizational resources. Jesse Jackson and Ross Perot are two such forceful personalities. Both had substantial resources; Jackson's were his strength and visibility in the black community and in its network of churches. Perot was a billionaire, able to buy as much television time as he wanted. But even with his resources, Jackson did not form a third party, but chose to work within the Democratic party. Perot organized a third party, but after his failure to gain more votes in the presidential election, his party has sputtered.

Even if a new party began to develop, it is likely that one or both of the existing parties, seeing the appeal of the new party, would adopt some of its ideas to avoid further defections to the new party. The Prohibition party died when prohibition became law, and the Socialist party faded when Roosevelt's New Deal included new social legislation.

Thus, while the new wave of populism in the country is certainly stimulating discussions of a new third-party movement for 1996, if recent history is any guide, the 1996 election will be decided by the two major parties and not an upstart. Populists will throw incumbents out, but only within the two-party system.

1. Joel Kotkin, "Catching the Third Wave," *Washington Post National Weekly Edition* (February 6–12, 1995): 24.
2. Times Mirror Center for People and the Press, as reprinted in the *New York Times* (September 21, 1994): A21.
3. Laurence I. Barrett, "Party of Spoilers," *Time* (March 13, 1995): 91.

Because parties try to attract many voters, both have liberals as well as conservatives, though the Democratic party has more liberals and fewer conservatives than the Republican party. This combination prompts parties to moderate their appeals and nominate moderate candidates. When liberal or conservative candidates do get nominated, they usually move toward the middle on some issues or at least portray themselves as moderate. Reagan, when running for reelection, embraced a conciliatory stance toward the Soviet Union in contrast to his earlier "evil empire" posture. Bill Clinton became a "new kind" of Democrat. The implication is that, unlike those in the past who catered to minorities and special interests, he would deal with the problems of middle America.

Minor Parties in American Politics

Sometimes called "third parties," minor parties are as varied as the causes they represent. Some are one-issue parties, like the American Know-Nothing party (1856), which ran on a platform opposing immigrants and Catholics, and the Prohibition party (1869 to the present), which campaigns to ban the sale of liquor.

Other parties advocate radical change in the American political system. Economic protest parties, such as the Populist party of 1892, sometimes appear when economic conditions are especially bad and disappear when times improve. Since the 1920s, the Communist party has espoused the adoption of a Communist system.

Some parties are simply candidates who failed to receive their party's nomination and decided to go it alone. In 1968, Alabama Governor George Wallace split from the Democratic party to run for president as the candidate of the conservative American Independent Party. Failing to get the Republican nomination, John Anderson launched a third-party campaign in 1980. Though both Wallace and Anderson had significant public support, neither won a large number of votes nor had much influence on the election outcome.

Ross Perot's third-party candidacy in 1992 had no association with either party. He simply decided to run (see Chapter 7). Although he polled 19% of the vote, his candidacy did not influence the election's outcome.

Minor parties face many obstacles in trying to establish themselves. Because a sizable portion of the electorate is firmly attached to the existing parties, minor party candidates find it difficult to attract voter support and money and to develop lasting state and local organizations. Even voters who favor the ideas or candidates of a minor party often will not vote for them because in a close race between the major party candidates, a vote for a minor party is seen as a "wasted" vote. And most third-party movements die after their candidate's defeat. Perot was able to overcome some of these problems by drawing on his personal fortune to fund his "volunteer" organization and his campaign. He is also making an effort to keep his organization, United We Stand America, in place.

Party in the Electorate

The party in the electorate—those individuals who identify with a political party—are a party's grassroots supporters. **Party identification** is a psychological link between individuals and a party; no formal or organization membership is necessary. In contrast, European parties do have members; members pay dues and sign a pledge that they accept the basic principles of the party. The percentage of voters who are members ranges from 1 or 2% in some countries to over 40% in others.

Party Identification

A majority of Americans identify with a political party (see Table 1). In 1992, 36% said they were Democrats, 25% Republicans, and 38% independent.

In Chapter 4, we discussed how political socialization leads to party identification early in childhood. Political scientists used to think that changes in party identification after childhood were rare except for those that occurred during major party realignments. But in fact people change their party identification more often. This can happen because they change jobs or residence, or because they develop policy views that conflict with their original party. As we have seen, for example, the national Democratic party's increased support for civil rights and other liberal policies caused many white southerners to leave the party.

TABLE 1 Party Identification, 1960–1992

AFFILIATION	1960	1972	1980	1992
Strong Democrat	21	15	18	18
Weak Democrat	25	25	23	18
Independent Democrat*	8	11	11	14
Independent	8	13	13	12
Independent Republican*	7	11	10	12
Weak Republican	13	13	14	14
Strong Republican	14	10	9	11
Apolitical, do not know	4	2	2	0

*Independents who lean toward the Democrats or Republicans.

SOURCE: University of Michigan Survey Research Center CPS/NES.

Characteristics of Democrats and Republicans

Although people from all walks of life are found in each party, individuals with certain characteristics are more likely to be found in one than the other (see Table 2). Blacks and Hispanics are more likely than non-Hispanic whites to be Democrats. Jews and Catholics are more likely than Protestants to be Democrats.

High-income professionals and those in business are most apt to be Republicans; low-income blue-collar workers are most likely to be Democrats. Skilled blue-collar workers and white-collar workers are in between.

In Chapter 4 we called attention to the gender gap—differences between men and women on issues. The gap is reflected in party affiliation as well. Women are more likely than men to be Democrats.

Party in Government

Nationally, the party in government is the party's elected members of Congress and, for the party that occupies the White House, the president. The party in government links the party in the electorate to their government. The job of the party in government is to enact policies that party voters favor. This seems like a simple idea, but political scientists have waged great debates over how close the link between the party in government and the party in the electorate should be.

Proponents of a **responsible party government** believe parties should take clear and contrasting positions on issues and enforce them on their members. "Responsible" party government would be responsible in that

- voters would have a choice between parties advocating different programs;

TABLE 2 Characteristics of Republicans, Democrats, and Independents

	REPUBLICAN	DEMOCRAT	INDEPENDENT
Total	25%	36%	38%
Age 18–29	26	28	46
30–49	27	37	36
50 and over	28	44	28
Less than high school education	19	50	31
High school graduate	24	40	36
Some college education	28	34	37
College graduate	35	31	34
Men	30	31	39
Women	23	42	36
White	31	30	39
Black	4	70	26
Hispanic	29	21	50
Asian	50	25	25
Protestant	33	35	32
Catholic	21	43	35
Jewish	5	68	27
Professional and business	30	33	37
Other white collar	27	36	37
Blue collar	25	37	38
Under $15,000	19	46	36
$15,000–$24,999	22	44	34
$25,000 and over	32	33	35
Conservative	49	21	32
Middle of the road	26	36	39
Liberal	9	57	35

SOURCE: CPS/NES 1992.

- a party would make sure that its members in office vote for these programs;
- therefore, if a party had a majority, it would enact its program into law.

Under these conditions, voting for one party rather than another would have definite policy consequences. It would increase the prospects for popular control of government because a voter would know what a vote for one party means for public policy. Great Britain is an example of responsible party government. Political parties there are heavily involved in developing, articulating, and implementing public policy. If a party member defects too often from important policy positions, party leaders can deny him or her the right to stand for reelection as the party's candidate.

The American system is not a responsible party government. Political parties do not always offer clear and contrasting positions. When they do, party leaders are limited in authority to ensure that members support the "party," that is, the position of the president or party's leaders in Congress.

Although the American system is not a responsible party government, it has some elements of party responsibility. The party links presidents with the members of their party in Congress. Members of the president's party in Congress support his policies more often than members of the opposition. Parties also have important organizational and leadership functions in Congress. Party influence is visible in congressional voting.[23] Nearly two-thirds of all roll calls found a majority of one party opposed to a majority of the other in 1993, and the proportion of members voting with their party was 85% (see Figure 4).

Party loyalty in roll-call voting increased dramatically during the 1980s. This reflects, in large part, the realignment of the South. In the days before blacks were allowed to vote and before the Republicans offered real challenges in most Southern districts, the vast majority of Southern members of Congress were conservative Democrats, Democrats who voted like Republicans. As white conservatives have moved into the Republican party, districts with conservative white majorities are much more likely to elect Republicans rather than conservative Democrats. Districts with large numbers of black voters are more likely than before to elect blacks or moderate or liberal white Democrats. Thus voting patterns of representatives from the South are divided along party lines. The movement of parties and voters in the South was reflected in the nation as a whole in 1994, with Republican voters moving to the right and Democratic voters moving to the left. Eighty percent of self-identified conservatives voted Republican and 82% of self-identified liberals voted Democratic.[24]

Party leaders have been more forceful in imposing party discipline on members of Congress. The Democratic leadership increasingly used choice committee assignments and positions as incentives to vote with the party.

As a result, Democrats—both North and South—act and vote differently from Republicans. Levels of party unity rival those during the heights of the New Deal era.

Party unity increased in 1993. On issues where a majority of Democrats voted against a majority of Republicans, Democrats in both the House and Senate voted an average of 85% of the time with their party, while Republicans voted 84% of the time with their party. (See Figure 5). After 12 years of Republican control of the White House, Democrats felt some need to support a Democratic president. Many Republicans, hoping to embarrass Clinton and resentful of the Democrats' unwillingness to allow them much of a voice, voted as a bloc on many issues to defeat his policies. Forty-seven Republicans in the Senate held their ground and helped defeat Clinton's economic stimulus program in 1993, and House Republicans voted in a bloc in opposition to Clinton's 1993 budget. With the return of divided control in 1994, Clinton and the Democrats may have to be somewhat more accommodating to the Republicans if legislation is to

Source: Tony Auth, Universal Press Syndicate, Reprinted with permission.

FIGURE 5
Party Unity is on the Rise in Congress

The percentage of times the average Democrat or Republican in Congress voted with his or her party majority on votes where a majority of Democrats opposed a majority of Republicans.

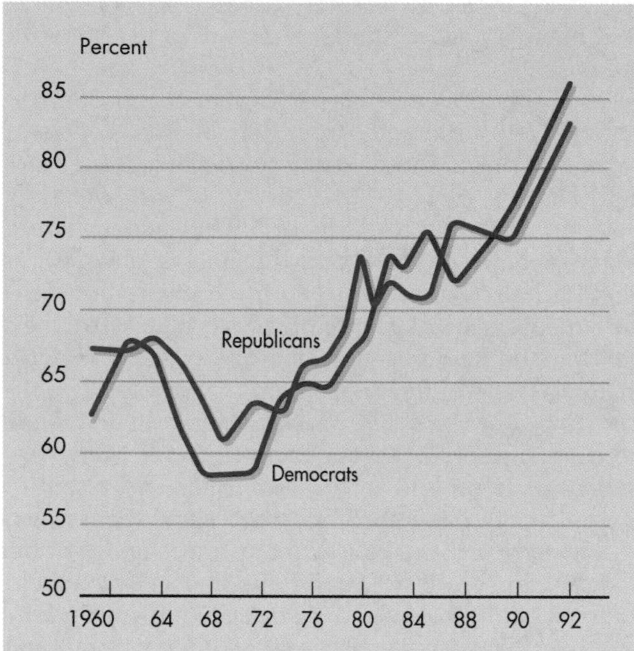

SOURCE: Party unity voting studies in *Congressional Quarterly Almanac* for the respective years, Washington, D.C.: Congressional Quarterly.

pass, and the threat of a veto could make the Republicans somewhat more cooperative with Clinton. The result may be less partisanship in voting.

Much higher levels of party voting would require major changes in the operation of government. Party leaders would have to be given more power to maintain party discipline in Congress. A greater tie between the president and Congress also would be required. This could be accomplished on a continuing basis only through a constitutional change providing for a parliamentary system similar to Britain's, in which Congress would elect the president. Such a change is unlikely.

Party Organization

The party organization is the third component of the political party. The major levels of party organization—national, state, and local—coincide with political units responsible for administering elections. Within the local parties there are further subdivisions. The smallest unit is usually the precinct-level organization. Several precincts comprise a ward or district; several wards comprise the city or county organization.

Although party organization seems hierarchical (organized from the top down), it is not. Party organization is a layered structure with each layer linked to, but independent of, the others. Higher levels cannot dictate to or impose penalties on lower levels to ensure compliance.

Party organization is only loosely connected with the party in government. This contrasts with the British system, in which the party leaders in Parliament try to maintain a tight grip on the party organization.

National Party Organization

The head of the party organization is the national chair. Although selected by the party's presidential nominee, the national chair is not a major political figure.

Responsibilities of the national party chair include managing the national headquarters, overseeing the national party apparatus, planning the national convention, and coordinating the presidential campaign efforts of the national organization with those of the nominee's personal organization. Fund-raising and promotion of the party also fall on the chair. The new chair of the Republican party built a television studio and launched GOP-TV, the Republican National Committee network that carries his weekly talk show; started a slick magazine; and founded the National Policy Forum, a quasi–think tank intended to develop Republican positions on issues. He also reduced the party's $4 million debt.[25]

Members of the **national committee** are selected by state party committees or conventions, and membership usually is awarded on the basis of service to the party. Duties of the committee are few but important: It chooses the site of the national convention and the formula for determining the number of delegates each state sends to it.

Both parties also have two national campaign committees that are growing in influence. In the 1980s both parties raised more money than ever from a variety of sources. Money came from PACs and large and small contributors. Both party organizations opened permanent headquarters and expanded their staffs.[26]

The national party organizations have become increasingly active in recruiting candidates to run for office. The Republicans' programs to help their candidates are better developed, but the Democrats' are catching up. Since 1984, the Republican organization has provided every female Senate primary candidate a $1,500 campaign contribution (once a similar amount has been raised by the candidate). Specific candidates have been encouraged to run. In an effort to convince a Nebraskan to run for the Senate, the Republican national organization invited her to Washington to tour the capital, dine with senators, and see what life in the Senate is like (she ran and lost). Occasionally, the organizations have discouraged individuals from running, especially where another candidate appeared to have a better chance of winning.

Training in managing a campaign is also available from the national party organizations. Both parties hold how-to seminars and help candidates design campaign strategies; they help research issues and write speeches; and they conduct polls and work with state and local party organizations to get out the vote.

National party organizations are heavily involved in campaign financing. They contribute directly to candidates and raise funds for them through direct mail and by encouraging PACs to contribute. They also assist candidates in raising their own funds.

While the national parties are not as powerful as they were a century ago, they are active. They play the role of intermediary between candidates and voters and between candidates and other political actors, such as campaign consultants and PAC leaders, who possess the skills and resources needed to communicate with the electorate.

The growing capacity of parties to offer candidates such help may be partly responsible for the increased party voting in Congress in recent years. National party organizations, however, are growing in power at the expense of state and local ones.[27] The national party's greater fund-raising capacity coupled with generous PAC donations means that members of Congress are less dependent on state and local parties than ever.

Divided We Stand?

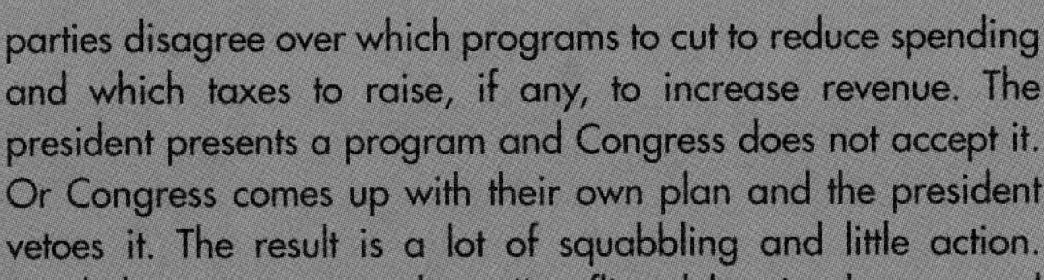

Since 1981, we have had **divided government.** For all but two years, one party controlled the White House and the other the Congress. The Founders made divided government possible by dividing authority between the executive and legislative branches and providing that members of each would be elected in different ways and for different terms. This contrasts with parliamentary systems, in which voters vote for members of the legislative branch and they in turn choose the executive leader of the nation.

In the first half of the twentieth century, divided government did not occur very often. From 1900 to 1950, only 4 of 26 presidential and midterm elections resulted in divided government. However, from 1952 to 1994, 14 of 22 elections did.[1] Even with Reagan's overwhelming victory in 1980, the Republicans failed to win control of the House of Representatives. While the party captured the Senate, their dominance lasted only until 1986, when the Democrats regained majority control. President Bush faced both a House and Senate controlled by the Democrats, and now President Clinton faces a Republican Congress.

Some believe that divided government is partially responsible for our failure to solve many of our important problems. The term *gridlock* has often been used to suggest this policy stalemate. The continuing attempt to reduce the federal deficit is a striking example. While nearly everyone agreed that the deficit was a significant problem, it continues to grow. The parties disagree over which programs to cut to reduce spending and which taxes to raise, if any, to increase revenue. The president presents a program and Congress does not accept it. Or Congress comes up with their own plan and the president vetoes it. The result is a lot of squabbling and little action. Divided government produces "conflict, delay, inadequate and ineffective policies or no policies at all."[2]

Gridlock, however, is also the result of responsiveness to the public. Gridlock can be a reflection of democracy. Perhaps gridlock accurately reflects the public's view. Most people do not want to cut programs—at least their programs—or increase taxes. Since we must do one or the other to reduce the deficit, inaction reflects public sentiment.

Moreover, united government will probably not eliminate gridlock. From 1946 to 1990, as many major laws passed during periods of divided government as in periods of united government. Adoption of policies that address major problems are usually the result of strong presidential leadership, significant events, and changes in public opinion rather than united government.[3]

1. M. Fiorina, *Divided Government* (New York: Macmillan, 1992), p. 7.
2. J. L. Sundquist, "Needed: A Political Theory for the New Era of Coalition Government in the United States." *Political Science Quarterly 103 (1988), p. 629.*
3. D. R. Mayhew, "Divided Party Control: Does It Make a Difference?" *PS: Political Science and Politics,* December 1991, pp. 637–40.

American Diversity

Do Republicans Differ from Democrats on Issues?

Republicans are often more conservative than Democrats. Independents are in between, though usually closer to the Democrats. On some issues, however, there is little difference.

	Republicans	Democrats	Independents	Difference Between Republicans and Democrats
			On Most Issues, Yes	
Government spending too little on:				
Poor	52%	79%	70%	27%
Health	68	81	73	13
Government spending too much on defense	35	45	55	10
Favor capital punishment	87	74	78	13
			On Some Issues, No	
Government spending too little on:				
Education	73	75	75	2
Environment	75	75	71	0

SOURCE: General Social Survey, 1990.

State and Local Party Organizations

Each state and local party has a chair and committee to direct the activities of their party activists. In some communities, parties may be so weak and unimportant that there is little party organization. Because of this, someone who wants to become active in the party organization only has to show up at party meetings and be willing to work.

Big-City Party Organizations

Unlike most local party organizations today, the **political machine,** which flourished in some of the nation's largest cities in the late nineteenth and early twentieth centuries, was strong and powerful. At the head of the machine was a boss, who often served as mayor and directed operations in such a way as to maintain control over the city and the organization.

The machine relied on the votes of the poor and working class, many of whom had only recently immigrated from Europe. Most accounts of machine politics are negative, dwelling on graft and corruption. However, the machine provided a number of valuable services. In a period when there were no welfare agencies, the machine provided jobs, food, and fuel for the thousands of immigrants who had no place else to turn. In return, party leaders expected individuals to vote for machine candidates.

Business also benefited from machines. The machine provided (for a fee) permits for business expansion, licenses, new roads, utilities, and police and fire protection.

The key to the machine's success was **patronage,** that is, giving jobs to party loyalists when the party controlled local government. An army of city employees, whose jobs depended on the political success of the machine, would dutifully bring family and friends to the polls on election day. One of the last of the big-city bosses, Mayor Richard Daley, head of the Chicago machine during the 1960s and 1970s, controlled 35,000 public jobs and, indirectly through public contracts, 10,000 private ones.[28]

Reformers disturbed by corruption and by lower-class control of city politics eventually passed laws making it difficult for machines to operate. Merit examinations for city jobs, nonpartisan elections, secret-ballots, and voter registration undercut the means that

Building a Modern-day Party Organization

With the decline of political parties and an increase in the number of candidates who are beholden mostly to themselves, it seemed impossible for anyone to develop a cadre of party officeholders with the party loyalty that characterized big city party organizations. However, new House Speaker Newt Gingrich has managed the impossible. Over the past 10 years, Gingrich has personally recruited, trained, and financed an army of new Republicans that are remarkably loyal to him and his agenda.

About half of the Republicans in Congress are recruits from his so-called "farm team." Gingrich's political action committee, GOPAC, is considered by some to be a more important party organ than the Republican National Committee. One of GOPAC's strategies is to recruit and train candidates who are enthusiastic about Gingrich's vision for America, a combination of cultural conservatism and economic freedom. Training sessions on campaign tactics are held across the country, and campaign manuals and tapes detail campaign "do's" and "don'ts". Word lists coach candidates on how to talk like Newt. Candidates can call in and talk to Gingrich himself.

The plan started when Gingrich was first elected to the House, where he joined like-minded Republicans to plan a strategy to make the Republicans the party of the future. Initially the movement relied on C-SPAN to get the message out. Even though the House chamber was empty, Gingrich could reach millions of cable watchers. Later, GOPAC was established to raise money for Republican candidates from conservative business leaders.

The organization decided to make the House bank scandal a major issue and blame it on the Democrats. They also decided to endorse term limits as a way to appeal to angry voters.

The most famous GOPAC document is "Language, a Key Mechanism of Control," in which Gingrich provides a list of words tested in focus groups to use in discussing the opposition. Democrats were to be associated with decay, sick, pathetic, stagnation, corrupt, waste, and traitors. Republicans were to be identified with share, change, truth, moral, courage, family, peace, and duty.

With each election, the Gingrich "farm team" boasted more winners. By 1992, 21 of the 47 Republicans elected to the House were GOPAC recruits, and nationwide the organization had 8,600 candidates running for office. By 1994, GOPAC had 33 new members in the House and 9,600 candidates across the nation. Moreover, Gingrich realized his dream, a Republican House majority.

The next step is to bring on the revolution.

SOURCE: Thomas B. Rosenstiel, "Gingrich created army," *Lincoln Star*, December 20, 1994, pp. 1 & 5.

machines had to secure voter loyalty. Political machines were dealt another blow when the federal government assumed responsibility for welfare needs in the 1930s; individuals no longer had to rely on the machine. And with a more educated population and greater employment opportunities, patronage jobs were no longer as desirable.

➤The Nominating Process

The major function of political parties is to nominate and elect candidates to office. Often many candidates of one party want to run for the same office. Parties have devised three ways—caucuses, conventions, and primaries—to choose among these contenders.

Caucuses

A **caucus** is a meeting. In the early eighteenth century, party candidates were nominated by a small number of party leaders and officeholders in a caucus. It was criticized by many because so few people actually participated.

Conventions

By 1830, the increased number of voters in elections and the desire of parties to win their continued support led to new procedures to involve more voters in nominations. Caucuses of local residents selected delegates to attend county, state, and national conventions. These conventions then nominated candidates for public office.

Party conventions usually were controlled by party leaders who decided what happened and who was nominated. The leaders often made decisions behind the scenes in "smoke-filled rooms."

Primaries

In the early 1900s Progressive reformers argued that nominating conventions ignored the rank-and-file voter. Because they believed that party leaders in their "smoke-filled rooms" were corrupt and not to be trusted, reformers established the **direct primary** to increase citizen participation and check the influence of party bosses in nominations. The primary allows the voters in an election to choose the party's candidates. Today all states use primary elections, sometimes in conjunction with caucuses and conventions, to nominate candidates.

Primaries vary from state to state according to who is eligible to vote in them. A **closed primary** limits participation to those who are registered with a party or declare a preference for a party. Thus only Democrats can vote in the Democratic party's primary. An **open primary** imposes no such limits; regardless of party registration, one may vote in either party's primary.

Party leaders and others favoring strong parties oppose open primaries. They argue that only voters who are party supporters should be permitted to vote in the party's primary. They fear that independents and opposition partisans will vote for candidates who are less sympathetic to the party's position on issues or who are less likely to win.

A Day in the Life of a Machine Politician

George Washington Plunkitt was a ward leader in the infamous Tammany Hall machine, the Democratic party organization that governed New York City for seven decades in the late nineteenth and early twentieth centuries. Although Plunkitt was on the city payroll, he did not have a free ride. The demands of his job were exhausting. Yet by providing needed services to his constituents he had many opportunities to build support for the party. Now government provides many of these services, thus making parties less vital. Entries from Plunkitt's diary illustrate the pervasive role of the party:

2:00 A.M. Aroused from sleep by a bartender who asked me to go to the police station and bail out a saloon keeper who had been arrested for violating the excise law. Furnished bail and returned to bed at three o'clock.

6:00 A.M. Awakened by fire engines. Hastened to the scene of the fire . . . found several tenants who had been burned out, took them to a hotel, supplied them with clothes, fed them, and arranged temporary quarters for them.

8:30 A.M. Went to the police court to secure the discharge of six "drunks," my constituents, by a timely word to the judge. Paid the fines of two.

9:00 A.M. Appeared in the municipal district court to direct one of my district captains to act as counsel for a widow about to be dispossessed. . . . Paid the rent of a poor family and gave them a dollar for food.

11:00 A.M. At home again. "Fixed" the troubles of four men waiting for me: one discharged by the Metropolitan Railway for neglect of duty; another wanted a job on the road; the third on the subway; and the fourth was looking for work with a gas company.

3:00 P.M. Attended the funeral of an Italian. Hurried back for the funeral of a Hebrew constituent. Went conspicuously to the front both in the Catholic church and the synagogue.

George Washington Plunkit holds forth in his unofficial office, a bootblack stand at the New York County Court House.

7:00 P.M. Went to district headquarters to preside over a meeting of election district captains, submitted lists of all the voters in their districts and told who were in need, who were in trouble, who might be won over [to Tammany] and how.

8:00 P.M. Went to a church fair. Took chances on everything, bought ice cream for the young girls and the children, kissed the little ones, flattered their mothers, and took the fathers out for something down at the corner.

9:00 P.M. At the clubhouse again. Spent $10 for a church excursion. Bought tickets for a baseball game. Listened to the complaints of a dozen pushcart peddlers who said they were being persecuted by the police. Promised to go to police headquarters in the morning and see about it.

10:30 P.M. Attended a Hebrew wedding reception and dance. Had previously sent a handsome wedding present to the bride.

12:00 P.M. In bed.

SOURCE: Alistair Cooke, *Alistair Cooke's America* (New York: Alfred A. Knopf, 1973), pp. 290–91; adapted from William L. Riordon, *Plunkitt of Tammany Hall* (New York: E. P. Dutton, 1963), pp. 91–93.

A minority of states use runoff primaries, which pit the two highest vote-getters in the primary against each other for the party's nomination. Over the years, the inability of the Republican party to compete effectively for office in the South meant that the winner of the Democratic party's primary was virtually assured of winning the general election. Due to the large number of Democratic candidates, sometimes the winner of the primary did not have a majority of the vote. In those cases, some southern states used a runoff election between the two highest vote-getters in the primary.

Although primaries have increased citizen participation in nominations, turnout in primaries is quite low and unrepresentative. Turnout reached record lows in the 1992 presidential primaries, when average turnout in Democratic primaries was 12% and in Republican primaries 8%. While Montana and New Hampshire had record high turnouts, 11 states recorded new lows.[29] Voters in primaries are unrepresentative of the public at large. Primary voters tend to have higher incomes and education and to be older, more interested in politics, and more partisan.[30]

Why Not Return to the "Smoke-Filled Rooms"?

In addition to attracting a small and unrepresentative group of voters to the ballot box, primaries have other flaws. In some ways, the primary process is less responsive to voters than party conventions, where candidates were once selected by a small group of party leaders meeting in smoke-filled hotel rooms.

Primaries do not necessarily provide voters with much choice. Many primaries are uncontested. Often the presence of an incumbent deters challengers, or at least strong challengers. In either case, incumbents are generally renominated.

Primaries also may make the general election less competitive. The minority party (that is, the party less likely to win the general election) often has no strong candidate who can mount an effective campaign in the general election. In preprimary days, party leaders generally made sure there were strong candidates running in the general election regardless of election prospects.

Another problem with primaries is that the electorate may nominate a candidate known by his or her party peers to be incompetent, difficult to work with, or lacking in character and integrity. Although the convention system does not guarantee that such candidates will be avoided, party leaders are more likely to know the real strengths and weaknesses of potential candidates than are voters, who must rely on the media for information. Indeed, voters have so little information about primary candidates that success often turns on name recognition.

Primaries hurt the most, however, by freeing candidates from supporting the party's program. It is nearly impossible for party leaders to withhold nominations from candidates who are party members in name only or who often vote with the other party. Thus, the party bonds are weakened and members can feel free to vote and act however they want.

This might seem desirable. But when candidates vote completely independent of their party, it is more difficult for voters to cast an informed vote. When parties offer a clear choice, voters know what they are voting for and can reward or punish the parties for what they do or plan to do in office. Thus, party voting can make government more responsive to the voters.

Some commentators have advocated returning to convention nominations. If we did so, the abuses that we associate with the smoke-filled rooms of a century ago are less likely to occur today because of the greater likelihood of exposure by the media and hostile voter reaction. In states and localities where the parties are competitive, it is likely that conventions would produce strong candidates. This would give voters a real choice in the general election. However, in locales dominated by one party, the convention system would not necessarily produce stronger candidates than a primary. At the presidential level, smoke-filled rooms produced the likes of Franklin Roosevelt and John Kennedy. Perhaps the greatest argument for smoke-filled rooms is Harry Truman. Although a product of machine politics, Truman was honest and incorruptible. Tapped to be FDR's vice president in 1944 by party bosses who knew Roosevelt would not live out his term, Truman became an excellent president.

Why haven't we returned to the convention system? Primaries are widely accepted. They *seem* more democratic because more people are involved than in conventions, where only party activists participate. But the sheer number of people involved is only one aspect of democracy and probably not the most important. Democracy also implies that those making the nominations are representative of the public; primary electorates are not. Moreover, a democratic process must offer some choice, and primaries adversely affect competition.

Although it is unlikely that we will abolish primaries and return to conventions, in recent years party leaders have asserted more control in some states through preprimary endorsements. Parties endorse candidates for nomination. The endorsed candidates are listed first on the primary ballot or are simply publicized as the "official" party candidate. Although on occasion the preferred candidate is defeated, the voters usually go along with the party's choice. Such arrangements promote party strength and ultimately responsiveness to voters.

7 Elections

You Are There

To Package or Not?

You are Bill Clinton. It is May 1992 and you are sure you will win the Democratic nomination for president, but unsure whether you can win the election. Your road to the nomination has been rocky; many people, including loyal Democrats, think you are a weak candidate. They fear you will drag the Democrats down to their fourth straight presidential election defeat. Now your campaign staff presents you with a plan that they think will lead to victory in November. But from your perspective the plan has significant problems.

You are one of six declared Democratic presidential candidates. None of you is well known; Paul Tsongas is a former U.S. senator from Massachusetts who dropped out of the Senate a decade earlier to battle cancer; Jerry Brown, a former governor of California; Tom Harkin, a U.S. senator from Iowa; Bob Kerrey, a U.S. senator and former governor of Nebraska; and Douglas Wilder, governor of Virginia, the first black ever to be elected governor. You and the others struggled for name recognition and votes in the snows of New Hampshire. Tsongas was predicted to win, since he had the advantage of being from neighboring Massachusetts. Your candidacy started strong, but soon floundered. Stories of your alleged womanizing flooded the media. The press gave extensive coverage to one woman, Gennifer Flowers, who claimed she had had a twelve-year affair with you. Fearing that your campaign would end soon after it began, you and your wife, Hillary, agreed to be on the television program "60 Minutes" to talk about these accusations and about your marriage. The show, which aired right after the Super Bowl, captured a huge audience. You denied having an affair with Flowers, admitted your marriage had had some hard times, but said you and Hillary had stuck together through good times and bad. The interview evoked sympathy for you. Polls showed that the scandal over Gennifer Flowers swayed only 11% of the voters, and 82% thought that enough had been said about your personal life.[1]

Just when you thought that crisis was over, *The Wall Street Journal* published a story on your draft record. Although many men your age had been drafted for the Vietnam War, many others avoided the draft, and you were one of them. The former ROTC head at the University of Arkansas claimed you had promised to join, but then changed your mind when you were no longer threatened by the draft. Your letter to the head, thanking him for "saving me from the draft," was a follow-up story that made the media rounds. A week before the New Hampshire primary, support for you in the polls dropped 17 points in 48 hours.[2] Polls indicated you could finish third behind both Tsongas and Kerrey.

Facing disaster, you spent the last week appearing on television night and day and meeting as many people as you could in malls and McDonald's restaurants. New Hampshire had only 125,000 voters, and you must have met most of them.

CONTINUED 

OUTLINE

The American Electorate
- Early Limits on Voting Rights
- Blacks and the Right to Vote
- The Voting Rights Act
- Women and the Right to Vote
- Other Expansions of the Electorate

Voter Turnout
- Political Activism in the Nineteenth Century
- Progressive Reforms
- Recent Turnout
- Who Does Not Vote?
- Why Turnout is Low

Other Campaign Participation

Presidential Nominating Campaigns
- Who Runs for President and Why?
- How a Candidate Wins the Nomination
- Presidential Caucuses and Conventions
- Presidential Primaries
- Reforming the Nomination Process
- The National Conventions
- Independent and Third-Party Nominations

The General Election Campaign
- Campaign Organization
- Images and Issues
- The Electoral College
- Campaign Strategies
- The Media Campaign
- Campaign Funding

Voting
- Party Loyalties
- Candidate Evaluations
- Issues
- Parties, Candidates, and Issues

Conclusion: Do Elections Make Government Responsive?

You finished second to Paul Tsongas, and promptly labeled yourself the winner—"the comeback kid."

After New Hampshire, Tsongas's campaign sputtered and died and you became the front runner. Yet throughout the primary season, voters never really were very enthusiastic about you.[3] Before the primary season was over, your campaign team assembled focus groups of voters and then prepared a report. It concluded that most voters did not really know much about you, but many did not like you anyway. You are viewed unfavorably by a large minority of Democratic voters and by about 40% of all general election voters. The report states that voters have a general impression that "[Clinton] will say what is necessary and that he does not 'talk straight.' " Moreover, you are in large part responsible for this image, your consultants inform you. They say that voters believe you are the ultimate politician: evasive, never gives a straight answer, always has handy lists and instant analysis. Moreover, voters say, "He's not real, he's privileged like the Kennedys, he can't stand up to special interests." The report concluded that people are discounting your messages because of their impression of you. And they do not like Hillary much either, perceiving her as unaffectionate and not interested in her family.[4] Indeed, many voters do not even know you and Hillary have a daughter, because Hillary has tried to shield her from the media.

Your consultants outline a comprehensive strategy to try to remake your image, to "reposition" you, to reflect your human qualities, and to show that you can stand up to special interests. They call for creating an image of an "honest, plain-folks idealist and his warm and loving wife."[5] To create this image, the plan suggests specific tactics, such as your appearances on television talk shows, playing your saxophone, making fun of yourself, and saying unpopular things to powerful groups in order to prove your independence. It also suggests ideas for making your family more prominent. It calls for "events where Bill and Hillary can go on dates with the American people." Finally, it suggests broad strategies, such as a populist message that would appeal to the middle class, calling for change and pointing out failures of government to bring about a secure economic future.

Your advisors believe that these messages work. In focus groups, people become much more favorable about you when they are given information about your coming from a small town, surviving your childhood with an alcoholic stepfather, working your way through Yale, and now asking for change in American society.

It angers you that voters do not know much about you. At a staff meeting, you give vent to these feelings: "So far as I'm concerned, we're at zero. . . . We don't exist in the national consciousness. . . . I don't think you can minimize how horrible I feel, having worked all my life to stand for things, having busted my butt for seven months and the American people don't know crap about it."[6] You want to inform people about your real background and beliefs, and you see that this is a well-thought-out plan to do that.

Yet you realize there's a risk to this strategy. One risk is that it will seem too much like a strategy. People already think you are a slick politician, and this plan seems so programmed, so, well, political. Voters may believe that any new image is just that: an image, not reality. Moreover, there is a risk that some of the activities suggested will not seem very presidential: appearances on TV talk shows, playing your sax, and "dates with the American people." Perhaps these kinds of activities will make you seem less presidential than Bush.

What do you decide? Adopt the plan or not?

Americans have fought and died in wars to preserve the rights of citizens to choose their leaders through democratic elections. Some have even died here at home, trying to exercise these rights. Despite this, most Americans take these important rights for granted; about half do not bother to vote, and even fewer participate in other ways.

Moreover, the process by which we choose our leaders, especially the president, has been sharply criticized in recent years. Critics charge that election campaigns are meaningless and offer little information to the voters, that candidates pander to the most ill-informed and mean-spirited citizens, and that public relations and campaign spending, not positions on issues or strength of character, determine the winners.

In this chapter, we analyze why voting is important to a democracy and why, despite its importance, so few do it. We then examine political campaigns and elections to see how they affect the kinds of leaders and policies we have. We will see that the lack of participation by many reinforces the government's responsiveness to those who do participate, especially those who are well organized.

➤THE AMERICAN ELECTORATE

During the more than two centuries since the Constitution was written, two important developments have altered the right to vote, termed **suffrage.** First, suffrage gradually has been extended to include almost all citizens aged 18 or over. Second, deciding who may vote now lies largely in the hands of the federal government. The electorate has been widened mostly through constitutional amendments, congressional acts, and Supreme Court decisions.

■ Early Limits on Voting Rights

Although the Declaration of Independence stated that "all men are created equal," at the time of the Constitution and shortly thereafter, the central political right of voting was denied to most Americans. States decided who would be granted suffrage. In some only an estimated 10% of the white males could vote, whereas in others 80% could.[7]

Controversial property qualifications for voting existed in many states. Some argued that only those with an economic stake in society should have a say in political life. But critics of the property requirement repeated a story of Tom Paine's:

> You require that a man shall have $60 worth of property, or he shall not vote. Very well . . . here is a man who today owns a jackass, and the jackass is worth $60. Today the man is a voter and he goes to the polls and deposits his vote. Tomorrow the jackass dies. The next day the man comes to vote without his jackass and he cannot vote at all. Now tell me, which was the voter, the man or the jackass?[8]

Because the Constitution gave states the power to regulate suffrage, the elimination of property requirements was a gradual process. By the 1820s, most were gone, although some lingered to mid-century.

In some states, religious tests also were applied. A voter had to be a member of the "established" church or could not be a member of certain religions (such as Roman Catholic or Jewish). However, religious tests disappeared even more quickly than property qualifications.

By the time of the Civil War, state action had expanded the rights of white men. However, neither slaves, Indians, nor southern free blacks could vote, although northern blacks could in a few states.[9] Women's voting rights were confined to local elections in a few states.[10]

■ Blacks and the Right to Vote

The Civil War began the long, slow, and often violent process of expanding the rights of blacks to full citizenship. Between 1865 and 1870, three amendments were passed to give political rights to former slaves and other blacks. One, the Fifteenth Amendment, prohibited the denial of voting rights on the basis of race and thus gave the right to vote to black men.

For a short time following this amendment, black rights were ensured by a northern military presence in the South and by close monitoring of southern politics. During this **Reconstruction** period, blacks voted and even were elected to office in those places where they were numerous (at that time 90% of the black population lived in the South, most in the Deep South states of Mississippi, Alabama, South Carolina, Louisiana, and Georgia). Two southern blacks were elected to the Senate and 14 were elected to the House between 1869 and 1877.

Although blacks did not dominate politics or even receive a proportional share of offices, whites saw blacks' political activities as a threat to their own dominance. White southerners began to prevent blacks from voting through intimidation that ranged from mob violence and lynchings to economic sanctions against blacks who attempted to vote.

THE FIRST COLORED SENATOR AND REPRESENTATIVES.
In the 41st and 42nd Congress of the United States.

During Reconstruction, blacks were elected to the United States Congress for the first time. Shown here are those elected to the Forty-first Congress in 1868.

American Diversity

Blacks and Hispanics in Office

Before the Voting Rights Act, few African Americans held major public office. Only a handful were members of Congress and few were state legislators, mayors of major cities, or other important political officers. Following the Voting Rights Act, southern blacks began to have the political clout to elect members of their own race to office for the first time. Progress, slow to be sure, has occurred; in 1968, there were only 23 black legislators in southern legislatures, but by 1993, there were nearly 250, including 42 in Mississippi. Virginia, the heart of the Confederacy,elected the nation's first black governor, Douglas Wilder. And 16 black members of Congress represent southern constituencies.

The number of northern black officeholders also has increased, reflecting heightened black political activity there too. Richard Hatcher, who became mayor of Gary, Indiana, in 1968, was the first black mayor of a major U.S. city. By 1993 there were 38 black mayors in northern and southern cities of 50,000 or more. This includes not only cities where blacks are a majority, such as New Orleans, Detroit, Baltimore, and Birmingham, but also cities where blacks are a minority, such as Seattle and Denver.

Nationally, the number of black officeholders has increased from an estimated 1,200 in 1969 to over 8,000 in 1993. Although this is far from proportional representation, it is a dramatic increase.

Hispanics too have improved their representation in political office. From a total of little more than 3,000 Hispanic public officials in 1985, their numbers have grown to nearly 5,200.

In sum, though progress seems slow, blacks and Hispanics, like other ethnic groups, are beginning to achieve political clout through elections.

SOURCES: *Statistical Abstract of the U.S. 1994* (Washington Government Printing Office, 1994), Tables 443 and 444. Joint Center for Political Studies. *National Roster of Black Elected Officials* (Washington, D.C., 1993).

These methods, both violent and nonviolent, were tolerated by the North, where the public and political leaders had lost interest in the fate of blacks or had simply grown tired of the struggle. The acquiescence of northern political leaders to the reestablishment of white supremacy in the South became clear in the wake of the disputed 1876 election, when southern Democrats agreed to support Republican Rutherford B. Hayes for president in return for an end to the northern military presence in the South and a hands-off policy toward activities there. This marked the end of Reconstruction.

By the end of the nineteenth century, blacks were effectively disfranchised in all of the South. The last black southern member of Congress served to 1901. Another would not be elected until 1972.

The loss of black voting rights was legitimized in southern constitutions and laws. **Literacy tests** were often required, supposedly to make sure voters could read and write and thus evaluate political information. Most blacks, who had been denied education, were illiterate. Many whites also were illiterate, but fewer were barred from voting. Local election registrars exercised much discretion in deciding who had to take the test and how to administer and evaluate it. Because the tests were used primarily to take away black voting rights, educated blacks often were asked for legal interpretations of obscure constitutional provisions, which few could provide.

Some laws had exemptions that whites were allowed to take advantage of. An "understanding clause" exempted those who could not read and write but who could explain sections of the federal or state constitution to the satisfaction of the examiner, and a "good moral character clause" exempted those with such character. Again, local election registrars exercised discretion in deciding who understood the Constitution and who had good character. Finally, the **grandfather clause** exempted those whose grandfathers had the right to vote before 1867, that is, before blacks could legally vote in the South.

The **poll tax** was another device used to deny black voting rights. The tax, though only a couple of dollars, was often a sizable proportion of one's monthly income and a burden on poor people. In some states individuals had to pay not only for the present election but for every past election in which they were eligible to vote but did not.

In the **white primary,** also used to deprive blacks of voting rights, blacks were barred from voting in primary elections, where party nominees were chosen. Because the Democrats always won the general elections, the real contests were in the Democratic primaries. The states justified doing this on the grounds that political parties were private, rather than governmental, organizations and thus could discriminate just as private clubs or individuals could.

Less formal means also were used to exclude blacks from voting. Registrars often closed their offices when blacks tried to register, or whites threatened blacks with the loss of jobs or housing if they tried to vote. Polling places were sometimes located far from black neighborhoods or were moved at the last minute without notifying potential voters. If these means failed, whites threatened or practiced violence. In one election in Mobile, whites wheeled a cannon to a polling place and aimed it at about 1,000 blacks lined up to vote.

The treatment of blacks by the southern establishment was summarized on the floor of the Senate by South Carolina Senator Benjamin ("Pitchfork Ben") Tillman, who served from 1895 to 1918. As he put it, "We took the government away. We stuffed ballot boxes. We shot them. We are not ashamed of it."

Over time, the Supreme Court and Congress outlawed the "legal" barriers to black voting in the South. The Court invalidated the grandfather clause in 1915 and the white primary in 1944. Through the Twenty-fourth Amendment, Congress abolished the poll tax for federal elections in 1964, and the Court invalidated the tax for state elections in 1966.[11] But threats of physical violence and economic reprisals still kept most southern blacks from voting. Although many blacks in the urban areas of the rim South (North Carolina, Florida, Texas, Tennessee) could and did vote, those in the rural South and most in the Deep South could not; in 1960, black registration ranged from 5% to 40% in southern states.[12]

■ The Voting Rights Act

Today black voting rates approach those of whites. In the deep South, much of this dramatic change was brought about by the passage of the **Voting Rights Act** (VRA) in 1965, which made it illegal to interfere with anyone's right to vote. The act suspended the

Blacks line up to vote in Peachtree, Alabama, after enactment of the Voting Rights Act of 1965.

Racial Gerrymandering

This North Carolina district (12), shown in purple on the maps, was drawn to create a black majority district. It consists of parts of 10 counties along the I-85 interstate and includes the predominantly black sections of Durham, Greensboro, Winston-Salem, and Charlotte. As one reporter noted, "In most electoral contests, candidates try to focus on finding out what the voters want. But in the 12th, the candidates face a challenge just *finding out who the voters are.*"[1]

The practice of drawing strangely shaped districts to fulfill political objectives, called "gerrymandering," is hardly new in American politics. The name originated in 1812 when the Massachusetts legislature carved out a district that historian John Fiske said had a "dragonlike contour." When painter Gilbert Stuart saw the misshapen district, he drew in a head, wings, and claws and exclaimed, "That will do for a salamander!" Editor Benjamin Russell replied, "Better say Gerrymander," after Elbridge Gerry, then governor of Massachusetts.[2] Since then gerrymandering has been widely used by politicians to benefit their own political parties.

The Supreme Court has ruled that racial gerrymandering, the drawing of district lines to concentrate racial minorities, is constitutionally suspect, and a variety of other cases on this issue are pending in state and federal courts.

Supporters of racial gerrymandering, under the Voting Rights Act amendments of 1982, believe it is the best way to increase minority representation. It allows members of a minority racial group to elect members of their own race. But others argue that low numbers of racial and ethnic minorities in Congress cannot appropriately be changed by the use of deliberate gerrymanders. Some also object to the creation of minority-dominant districts because they see the dangers of thereby creating other districts with fewer minorities. These other districts will be more white than before, with representatives who are less sensitive to the interests of minorities.

One possible reform that meets the objectives of both groups is cumulative voting. Under a system of **cumulative voting,** members of Congress would not be elected from single-member districts, but from at-large districts in which several members of Congress would be elected at the same time. Voters would each have a number of votes equal to the number of seats in the district. They could apportion their votes among the candidates in any way that they preferred.

If, for example, the district included six seats in the House of Representatives, each voter would have six votes. The voter could give all six to one candidate, give one to each of six different candidates, or use any other method to distribute the six votes.

Members of any group, including racial, ethnic, religious, political, or economic groups, could target their votes on the candidates most likely to represent the group's interests. In the case of minority voters, the preferred candidates might be members of the minority group but could also be sympathetic members of some other group.

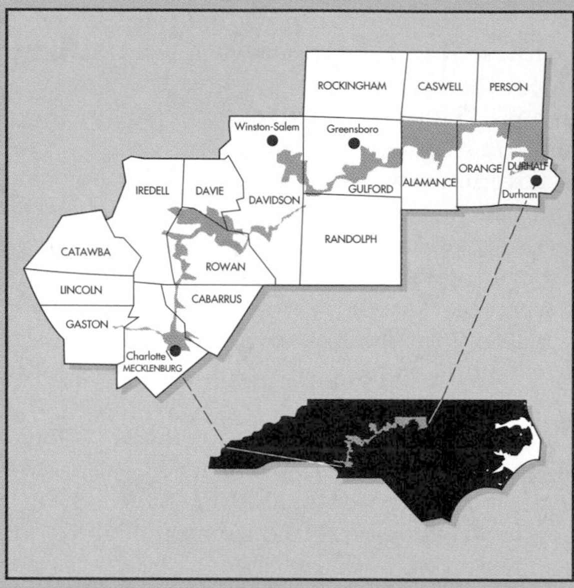

This election procedure could produce greater racial and ethnic diversity in representative bodies such as Congress without creating new districts on the basis of race or ethnicity. Cumulative voting has less potential for creating barriers between groups, since there would be no group basis for the creation of districts. This procedure is not totally new to the United States; it was used for many years in Illinois to elect members of their state's House of Representatives. Still, acceptance of cumulative voting for congressional districts seems remote.

---

1. Charles Mahtesian, "Blacks' Political Hopes Boosted by Newly Redrawn Districts," *Congressional Quarterly Weekly Report* (April 25, 1992), p. 1087.
2. *Guide to Congress,* 2nd ed. (Washington, D.C.: Congressional Quarterly, Inc., 1976), p. 563; *Congressional Quarterly, The Race to Capitol Hill,* (February 29, 1992), pp. 103–105.

OTHER SOURCES: Kenneth J. Cooper, "Wrong Turns on the Map?" *Washington Post National Weekly Edition,* January 31–February 6, 1994, p. 14; Bruce E. Cain, "Voting Rights and Democratic Theory Toward a Color-Blind Society?" *The Brookings Review,* Winter 1992, pp. 46–50; Carol M. Swain, "The Voting Rights Act: Some Unintended Consequences," *The Brookings Review,* Winter 1992, p. 51; George R. Will, "Districting by Pigmentation," *Newsweek,* July 12, 1993, p. 72; Lani Guinier, *The Tyranny of the Majority: Fundamental Fairness in Representative Democracy,* reviewed in David J. Garrow, "Lani Guinier in Her Own Words," *Washington Post National Weekly Edition,* April 4–10, 1994, p. 35; Douglas Amy, *Real Choices/New Voices: The Case for Proportional Representation Elections in the United States* (New York: Columbia University Press, 1993).

use of literacy tests and, most important, it sent federal voter registrars into counties where less than 50% of the voting age population (black and white) was registered. The premise of this requirement was that if so few had registered, there must be serious barriers to registration. All of Alabama, Mississippi, South Carolina, and Louisiana, substantial parts of North Carolina, and scattered counties in five northern states were included in the area covered by registrars.

Any changes in election procedures had to be approved by the Department of Justice or the U.S. District Court for the District of Columbia. States or counties had to show a clean record of not discriminating for ten years before they could escape this supervision. Those who sought to deter blacks from voting through intimidation now had to face the force of the federal government.

Though black registration had been increasing in the rim states of the South (Virginia, North Carolina, Texas, for example), due to voter registration and education projects, the impact of the VRA in the Deep South was dramatic.[13] Within a year after federal registrars were sent, hundreds of thousands of southern blacks were registered, radically changing the nature of southern politics. In the most extreme case, Mississippi registration of blacks zoomed from 7% to 41%. In Alabama the black electorate doubled in four years.

Due to these increases, not only have dozens of blacks been elected, but white politicians must now court black voters to get elected. Even George Wallace, the segregationist Alabama governor who had opposed the civil rights movement in the 1960s, eagerly sought black votes in the 1970s and 1980s. Control of the U.S. Senate returned to the Democrats in 1986 partially because black votes made the difference in the election of several Democratic southern senators. In these cases, the majority of whites voted for the Republicans, but a huge majority of blacks voted Democratic.

The Voting Rights Act was renewed and expanded in 1970, 1975, and 1982. It now covers more states and other minorities, such as Hispanics, Asians, Native Americans, and Eskimos, and thus serves as a basic protection for minority voting rights. For example, states must provide bilingual ballots in counties in which 5% or more of the population does not speak English.

The 1982 renewal and its subsequent judicial interpretation expanded the nature of the Voting Rights Act. In addition to protecting minorities' voting rights, the act now requires states with large minority populations to draw boundaries specifically to increase the probabilities that minorities will win seats. After the 1990 Census, eleven new congressional districts were created for blacks and six for Hispanics. All but one were actually won by blacks and Hispanics in the 1992 election. Partly as a result of this redistricting, blacks were elected to Congress for the first time since Reconstruction in Alabama, Florida, North Carolina, South Carolina, and Virginia. Hispanics were elected for the first time ever in Illinois and New Jersey. In all, 39 blacks and 19 Hispanics were elected to Congress, a dramatic increase from the 25 blacks and 10 Hispanics serving before the 1992 election.[14] Whether these gains will be maintained is likely to depend on the outcome of court challenges to these gerrymanders.

Women and the Right to Vote

When property ownership defined the right to vote, women property owners could vote in some places. When property requirements were removed, suffrage came to be seen as a male right only. Women's right to vote was reintroduced in the 1820s in Tennessee school board elections.[15] From that time on, women had the vote in some places, usually only at the local level or for particular kinds of elections.

The national movement for women's suffrage did not gain momentum until after the Civil War. Before and during that war, many women helped lead the campaign to abolish slavery and establish full political rights for blacks. When black men got the vote after the Civil War, some women saw the paradox in their working to enfranchise these men when they themselves lacked the right to vote. Led by Susan B. Anthony, Elizabeth Cady Stanton, and others, they lobbied Congress and the state legislatures for voting rights for women.

The first suffrage bill was introduced in Congress in 1868 and each year thereafter until 1893. Most members were strong in their condemnation of women as potential voters. One senator claimed that if women could hold political views different from their husbands it would make "every home a hell on earth."

When Wyoming applied to join the union in 1889, it already had granted women the right to vote. Congress initially tried to bar Wyoming for that reason but then relented when the Wyoming territorial legislature declared, "We will remain out of the Union 100 years rather than come in without the

commissioners, that many have no idea for whom or what they are voting. This proliferation of elective offices, thought by some to promote democracy and popular control, may promote only voter confusion and alienation. The problem is compounded because elections for different offices are held at different times. For example, most states have decided to hold elections for governor in nonpresidential election years. This decision probably reduces presidential election turnout by 7% and may reduce by one-third the number of those who vote for governor in those states.[29]

Primary elections are another problem. One estimate is that holding primary campaigns diminishes the general election turnout by 5%.[30]

By contrast, in Britain the time between calling an election (by the current government) and the actual election is only a month. In March, 1992, Prime Minister John Major called the election; in April it was held. All campaigning was done during that time. There are no primaries. Moreover, as in most other parliamentary democracies, British citizens vote only for their representative in parliament and (at one other time) for the local representative. Voters are not faced with choices for a myriad of offices they barely recognize.

Barriers to Registration

The necessity of registering has been a major impediment to voting. About one-quarter of nonvoters surveyed in 1990 indicated they did not vote because it was too difficult. As one commentator put it, "The United States is the only major democracy where government assumes no responsibility for helping citizens cope with voter registration procedures."[31] In many other nations, voter registrars go door to door to register voters, or voters are registered automatically when they pay taxes or receive public services. Difficult registration procedures have a special impact on low-income Americans, who were 17% less likely to vote in states with difficult registration procedures than in other states.[32]

Some states make it more convenient to register by having registration periods lasting up to election day (most states require registration at least 25 days before the election), registration in precincts or neighborhoods instead of one county office, registration by mail, registration offices open in the evenings and Saturday, and a policy of not purging voters who fail to vote from the registration lists.

In other jurisdictions, voter registrars try to hinder groups working to increase registration. They may refuse to allow volunteers to register voters outside the registration office or let only selected volunteers handle registration (for example, allowing members of the League of Women Voters or the Christian Right as volunteers but not the NAACP or organizations targeted toward registering lower-income groups).[33] One estimate is that voting turnout would be 9%

From this 1840 Whig campaign gimmick came the phrase "keep the ball rolling."

higher if all states' procedures were similar to those of states that try to facilitate voter registration.[34]

To try to increase registration, Congress recently passed a law to make registration easier; it allows people to register at public offices such as welfare offices and drivers' license bureaus (for this reason it is called the **"motor voter"** law.)[35] Similar plans have increased registration in the 30 or so states that had these policies before the federal government did.[36] Evidence after eight months of the law show the greatest expansion of voter registration in American history; five million new voters registered. Of course, the real test is how many of these registrants will actually vote.

A related proposal suggests that change of address cards filed with the post office be accompanied by cards that go to the voting registration offices in the voter's former residence and new residence. Registration in the new residence would be automatic. One estimate is that the mobility of our society reduces voting by as much as 9%. The proposal also would reduce election fraud by removing names of residents who move from voting rosters.[37]

Failures of Parties to Mobilize Voters

Traditionally political parties mobilized voters to turn out. As parties have declined in importance, they have become less effective in this role. The lack of effectiveness on the part of political parties in mobilizing millions of nonvoters, most of them working class or poor, is another reason for low voter turnout. Because of their low income, most of these nonvoters are Democrats. If mobilized, they would probably

Young People Vote Less

Ratification of the Twenty-sixth Amendment to the U.S. Constitution in 1971 gave 18–20 year olds the right to vote. Political observers expected that the campus activism of the Vietnam and civil rights era would be reflected in high voting turnouts among young people.

But in 1972, their first presidential election, less than half of young voters turned out, and even that small turnout has declined precipitously since. As the figure indicates, only 38% of 18–20 year olds voted in 1988, compared with over 60% of their elders.

Why the low vote? One might expect that young people are more alienated from politics than their elders, but this does not seem to be true. Young voters are more trusting and less cynical. Others attribute low voting turnout to the high degree of mobility of young adults; they change their residences frequently, and perhaps do not have time or do not take time to figure out how and where to register. Many young people are preoccupied with major life changes, going to college, leaving home, starting their first full-time job, getting married, starting a family. Then too, young people do not have the habit of voting.

In an attempt to encourage young adults to vote in 1992, MTV featured a number of conversations with the political candidates, as well as ads urging young people to vote: "Choose or Lose." Madonna, for example, warned the audience that if they did not vote, they were "going to get a spankie." So far, information is unavailable that would tell us if this "threat" had an impact.

SOURCE: Census Bureau, Richard L. Berke, "Is the Vote, Too, Wasted on Youth?" *New York Times* (June 30, 1991), p. 2.

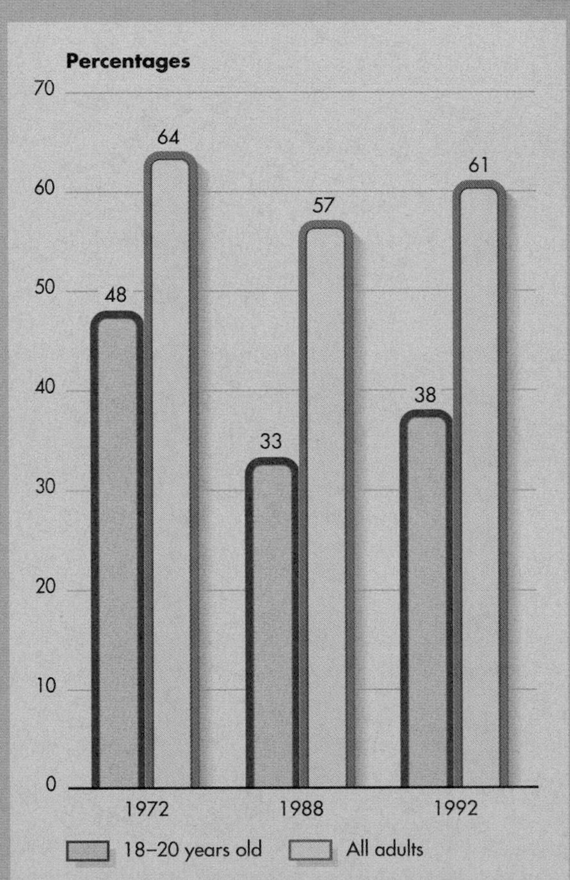

Current Population Reports, "Voting and Registration in the Election (various editions)," U.S. Census, series P20.

vote for Democrats, although in some elections the preferences of nonvoters have simply reflected the preferences of voters.[38]

Republicans are most fearful of this potential electorate. One conservative analyst wrote that a national registration plan, by tapping the voting power of the poor, "has the potential for altering the American party system."[39]

Even some Democrats are wary. The party has embraced social and economic reforms that attracted many middle-class and some business groups. The goals of these groups sometimes conflict with those of the poor, and the party's leaders do not want to threaten these constituencies. Moreover, in recent years the party has muted its appeals to the working class. This further reduces the incentives of working-class people to vote, and in turn decreases the incentive of Democrats to appeal to working class voters.[40] However, increasing voter turnout has now become a partisan issue with most Democrats backing attempts to increase turnout (such as the motor voter plan), and most Republicans opposing them.

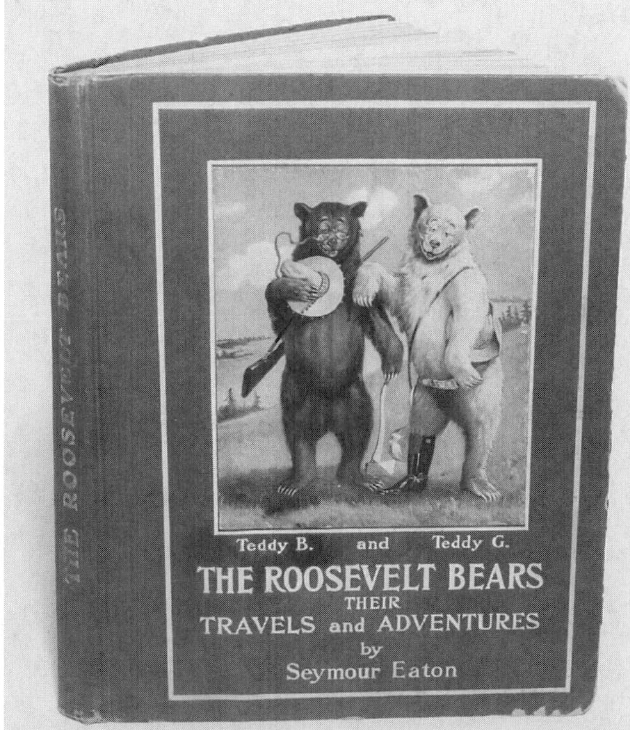

Voter turnout was higher in the days when campaigns were more fun and involved more people. Songs were often written about the candidates, and, here, a book about teddy bears reflects Theodore (Teddy) Roosevelt's popularity.

Voting as a Rational Calculation of Costs and Benefits

Nonvoting also may be the result of a rational calculation of the costs and benefits of voting. Economist Anthony Downs argues that people vote when they believe the perceived benefits of voting are greater than the costs.[41] If a voter sees a difference between the parties or candidates, and favors one party's position over the other, that voter has a reason to vote and can expect some benefit from doing so. For that reason, people who are highly partisan vote more than those less attached to a party, and people with a strong sense of political efficacy, the belief they can influence government, vote more than others.

Voters who see no difference between the candidates or parties, however, may believe that voting is not worth the effort it takes and that it is more rational to abstain. And in fact, 40% of nonvoters in 1990 gave only the excuse that they were "too busy," suggesting a large degree of apathy.[42] Nevertheless, some people will vote even if they think there is no difference between the candidates because they have a sense of civic duty, a belief that their responsibilities as citizens include voting. Most voters feel gratified that they have done their duties as citizens. In fact, more voters give this as an explanation for voting than any other reason, including the opportunity to influence policy.[43]

Downs assumes that the costs of voting are minimal, but, in reality, for many people the time, expense, and possible embarrassment of trying to register are greater than the perceived benefits of voting. This is especially true for lower-income people who perceive that neither party is attentive to their interests. Moreover, it is possible that the frequency, length, and media orientation of campaigns lower the perceived benefits of voting for people of all incomes by trivializing the election and emphasizing the negative.

➤Other Campaign Participation

We have seen that only about half of all Americans vote in presidential elections, and even fewer vote in off-year congressional races. Still fewer participate actively in political campaigns. For example, in a recent year, about one-quarter of the population said that they worked for a party or candidate. About an equal proportion claimed that they contributed money to a party or candidate. Smaller proportions attended political meetings or actually belonged to a political club.

Unlike voting, rates of participation in campaigns have not declined over the past 20 years. This suggests that people are not less political than they used to be, but that something about elections themselves has decreased voter turnout. Indeed, more people give money to candidates and parties than they used to, probably because, unlike 20 years ago, candidates and parties now use mass mailing techniques to solicit funds from supporters.[44] Hundreds of thou-

Gay Power

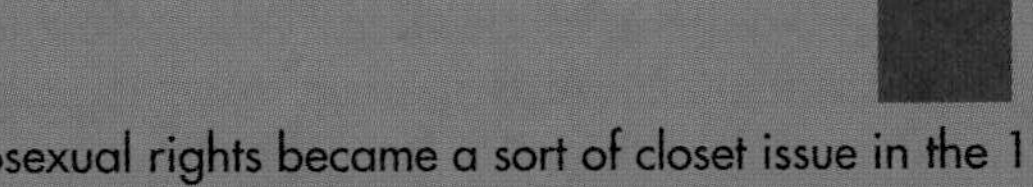

In recent years, homosexuals have become more politically active. Spurred by the crisis of AIDS among the gay community and the initially slow response of the federal government to the disease, gays have begun to organize to exercise political clout.

How much clout can gays have? Even the number of gays in the U.S. is a politically sensitive question. Many gay activists argue that 10% of the population is gay. Various recent surveys of sexual activity indicate the number may be considerably lower, perhaps as low as 1%. Sexual orientation is not a question asked in standard national surveys, and if it were, it might not elicit truthful answers, so that it is difficult to know the accuracy of the estimates. Whatever the numbers, homosexuals have been "coming out of the closet" in significant numbers in recent years.

Gay issues are now being openly considered in political campaigns. "Gay rights" includes a number of different things. Most discussed have been ending the ban on homosexuals in the military and giving homosexuals equal rights to jobs and housing. Some gay activists want legal recognition of same-sex marriages and a general acknowledgement of homosexuality as an acceptable lifestyle. The public overwhelmingly supports nondiscrimination in jobs and in the military but is not supportive of homosexual lifestyles and same-sex marriages.

Barney Frank (D-Mass), one of three openly gay members of Congress, at a fund-raiser.

Homosexual rights became a sort of closet issue in the 1992 elections. All the Democratic candidates courted the gay vote and all sought financial support from the gay community. These candidates, and Ross Perot, supported ending the ban on homosexuals in the military, for example. Clinton received strong support from the gay community; in some areas gays are a significant political force. In California, for example, perhaps as many as 10% of all voters are gay.

Most Republicans are less supportive of homosexual rights. Such rights are anathema to many fundamentalist Christians, who consider homosexuality a sin and refuse to think that it could be an acceptable lifestyle. These fundamentalists, and other conservatives, are an important part of the Republican constituency and are strongly opposed to extension of rights to gays. At the 1992 Republican convention, some speakers overtly attacked gays and gay rights. However, as one conservative political analyst remarked, "The gay-bashing turned people off."

President Bush, who had at least a dozen aides and officials who were gay, personally did not engage in direct gay-bashing. He and other top Republicans used more subtle attacks on gays and gay lifestyles, for example by calling for a return to "family values," a term that can mean almost anything but was intended to be a code word for traditional family values.

In 1994, a number of openly gay candidates were elected, including three members of Congress and state legislators in Arizona, California, Missouri, and Washington. These successes are coming at a time when the gay community is being weakened through the AIDS epidemic, which has already caused about 150,000 deaths, two-thirds gay men. But AIDS has been important in encouraging gays to come out of the closet, and possibly has been important in encouraging broader tolerance of gays. Twice as many people now say they know someone who is a homosexual than did so a decade ago. Even though there is no consensus on homosexual issues, it seems clear that gays are gaining legitimacy in the political process.

SOURCES: Jeffrey Schmalz, "Gay Politics Goes Mainstream," *New York Times Magazine* (October 11, 1992), p. 18ff. Much of this box is drawn from the Schmalz article; Bill McAllister and Michael Weisskopf, "Breaking Through the 'Lavender Ceiling,' " *Washington Post National Weekly Edition* (November 14–20, 1994), p. 14.

candidates emphasize mobilizing their own voters. Democrats have to work harder at this than Republicans because Democratic voters often do not vote and are more likely to vote for the other party than are Republicans.

Both parties must try to persuade independent voters because independents are the swing voters; their votes determine the outcome. In 1964, when Johnson trounced Republican Goldwater, 80% of Republicans voted for Goldwater. And in 1988, when

The Role of the Electoral College

Critics frequently suggest that the Electoral College, a complex and sometimes puzzling institution, should be reformed or abolished. One reform would keep the overall system but eliminate electors as individuals; electoral votes would automatically be cast according to a state's popular vote.

Abolishing the Electoral College in favor of a direct popular election is another reform idea that has some support. Votes would be counted nationwide; state totals would not matter. This proposal has been offered as a constitutional amendment in Congress several times but has never won approval. Even if passed in Congress, it probably would fail to obtain ratification by the necessary three-fourths of the state legislatures because large states would oppose it.

One reason that some argue for abolishing the Electoral College is that there are some undemocratic aspects to it, just as the Founders intended. The Electoral College makes it possible for the candidate with the most popular votes to lose the election. This has occurred three times: John Quincy Adams (1824), Rutherford B. Hayes (1876), and Benjamin Harrison (1888).

Critics of the Electoral College argue that these historical anomalies should not happen; in a democratic system, the person with the most votes should win. Further, the Electoral College often converts candidates with a plurality but not a majority of the popular vote into majority winners in the Electoral College. This may give a greater legitimacy to the winners. In 1960 John F. Kennedy won only 49.7% of the popular vote but a substantial 56% of the Electoral College vote. Significant margins of popular votes can be turned into the appearance of consensus too. For example, in 1984 President Reagan won 59% of the popular vote, but because he won in 49 states, he won 97% of the Electoral College vote.

Another undemocratic feature of the current system is the **faithless elector,** an elector who decides to cast a vote for a personal choice, not for that of his or her state's voters. Occasionally electors do stray from their pledge—in 1988 a West Virginia elector voted for Lloyd Bentsen for president and later said she wished she had voted for Kitty Dukakis. Even though the intent of the Founders was to allow electors to cast their votes any way they desired, many people believe that in our more democratic era electors should be bound by the wishes of the voters. However, no faithless elector has ever made a difference in the outcome of an election.

Some people favor abolishing the College because direct election is a more understandable system. However, there is a need to formulate rules to deal with situations where no candidate gets a majority and that makes the popular vote alternative more complicated than at first glance.

The major reason we retain the Electoral College system, though, is that in the current system, voters in large states receive more attention from candidates. A 1-vote margin in Pennsylvania yields the candidate 29 electoral votes, a 1-vote margin in North Dakota only 3 electoral votes. So it is more important to get that extra vote in Pennsylvania than in North Dakota. Rational candidates and parties will direct their resources and perhaps tailor their policy views accordingly.

Although political scientists have debated the actual extent of the large state bias in the current system, most believe it does exist and is significant.[1] Urbanites, especially central city residents, have more clout in the Electoral College system than they would have under a direct election system. Minority groups benefit too, because they are disproportionately located in urban areas. (However, one should not overstate this clout. The more liberal candidates, presumably those favored by the more urban interests, have lost most presidential elections since 1968.)

Supporters of the system argue that this urban bias is fair when viewed in the context of our other political institutions. The Senate, for example, overrepresents the interests of smaller, rural states because each state, regardless of population, has two votes. Many of the institutions of Congress, too, work in a way that gives an advantage to more conservative interests, often identified with rural America. The complex committee system and diffused power structure make dramatic changes in the status quo difficult.

Defenders of the Electoral College argue that to abolish it would remove a balance that exists in American politics: the conservative, rural bias of Congress on the one hand and the liberal, urban bias of the Electoral College on the other.

1. Lawrence Longley and James Dana, Jr., "New Empirical Estimates of the Biases of the Electoral College for the 1980s," *Western Political Quarterly* 37 (March 1984), pp. 157–75.

Dukakis was soundly beaten by Bush, 75% of Democrats voted for Dukakis. It was the independent voters who determined the outcomes.

The crucial strategic question is where to allocate resources of time and money: where to campaign, where to buy media time and how much to buy, and where to spend money helping local organizations. Candidates must always remember that they have to win a majority of the Electoral College vote. The most populous states, with the largest number of electoral votes, are vital. Prime targets are those large states that could go to either party, such as Illinois, Texas, California, and New York.

Candidates also have to expand their existing bases of support. Most of the western states have been solidly Republican in their presidential loyalties. Republicans have been able to build on their solid western base and their strength in the South. They only have to carry a few of the large industrial states to win.

Democrats have a strategic problem given the western Republican bloc. Between the end of Reconstruction and 1948, the South was solidly Democratic, but there have been no solidly Democratic states in presidential elections since then (although Washington, D.C., has been solidly Democratic). Since 1976, the Democrats have consistently lost the South. During the 1980s some strategists believed the Democrats should try to win back the South by choosing more conservative candidates. Others argued for a strategy to win without the South, aiming for the industrial states of the East and Midwest along with California and a few other states of the West. This was largely Clinton's strategy, though he did win his own home state and Gore's (Arkansas and Tennessee) and picked up Louisiana too. The non-southern strategy was used successfully by the Republicans between the 1870s and the 1920s, when they were able to capture the White House regularly without ever winning a southern state.

The Media Campaign

The media campaign consists of paid advertising, personal appearances on talk shows, debates, and coverage on news broadcasts and in print media. Candidates have the most control over paid advertising and the least over news coverage; but even there,

Families all across the country gathered in front of their TV to watch the first televised presidential debates in 1960, featuring Senator John F. Kennedy (D, Mass) and Vice President Richard Nixon (R, Cal).

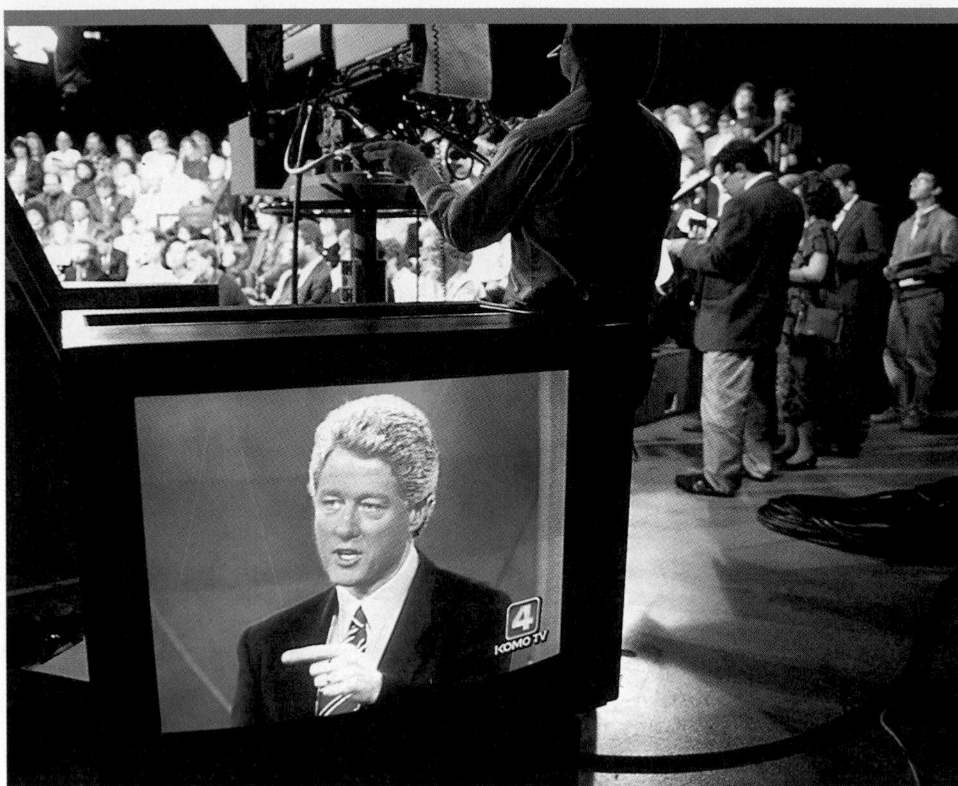

Few Americans see candidates in person anymore. Most see candidates only on TV. Here a studio audience is linked by satellite to Bill Clinton.

campaigns spend hundreds of hours devising strategies to show their candidates to best advantage.

Campaigns are expensive because they rely so heavily on the media to get the candidate's message to the voters. As one observer argued, "Today's presidential campaign is essentially a mass media campaign. It is not that the mass media entirely determine what happens.... But it is no exaggeration to say that, for the large majority of voters, the campaign has little reality apart from the media version.[58]

Impact of the Media

The media, through news coverage, personal appearances by candidates, and paid advertisements, help shape voters' opinions and choices in three ways. They inform, they help set the campaign agenda, and they help persuade voters.[59] In Chapter 8, we will discuss these effects.

Use of the Media

MEDIA EVENTS Candidates try to use the media to their advantage by staging media events that allow them to be photographed doing and saying noncontroversial things in front of enthusiastic crowds and patriotic symbols. As Bush campaign strategist Roger Ailes proclaimed 20 years ago, "This is the beginning of a whole new concept. This is the way they'll be elected forevermore. The next guys will have to be performers."[60]

Candidates and their advisers try to design settings that will encourage television reporters to focus their stories on the candidate and put his or her policies in the best light.[61] In 1988, George Bush almost literally wrapped himself in the flag, frequently "pledging allegiance," until negative media reaction led his advisers to decide that they were overdoing it.

Candidates spend most of their time going from media market to media market, hoping to get both national and local coverage.[62] Some candidates are much better than others at using the media. Gerald Ford was plagued by media coverage that seemed to emphasize his bumbling.

ADVERTISING Paid advertisements allow candidates to focus on points most favorable to their case or to portray their opponents in the most negative light. Most political ads are quite short, 30 or 60 seconds in length. Television ads were first used in the 1952 campaign. One, linking the Democratic Truman administration to the unpopular Korean War, showed two soldiers in combat talking about the futility of war. Then one of the soldiers is hit and dies. The other one deliberately exposes himself to the enemy and is also killed. The announcer's voice says, "Vote Republican."[63] Today's ads are perhaps less

Negative Campaigning in 1988 and 1992

Almost all observers agree that negative campaigning was a successful strategy in the 1988 presidential election. Over 60% of the public thought that Bush's campaign was dirty, but he won handily anyway. (Forty percent thought Dukakis's campaign was dirty.)[1] Bush successfully painted a picture of Dukakis as "not a patriot, no believer in law and order, no manly man, no lover of family . . . one of those loose lovers of 'them' and 'their' ways."[2] He did this in part by hitting Dukakis hard for vetoing a bill which would have made the Pledge of Allegiance mandatory in Massachusetts schools each day. Though Dukakis did this because he felt the bill was unconstitutional, Bush's campaign used the veto to challenge Dukakis's patriotism. And the Bush campaign linked Dukakis to Willie Horton, a convict who was furloughed from the Massachusetts prison system while Dukakis was governor. Horton, while on furlough, raped a woman and terrorized her and her fiance. Though 40 other states and the federal government had furlough programs, the Bush campaign used the Horton incident to portray Dukakis as soft on crime. The impact of this is illustrated by the fact that three years later, focus groups of voters remembered little about the 1988 election except the Horton ads.[3]

Election analysts feared that the success of negative advertising in 1988 would set the stage for even more in 1992. But, much to the surprise of many, negative campaigning did not work so well in 1992. By October, the Bush campaign, failing to find its own focus, was reduced simply to portraying Clinton as a taxer and spender, a liar and a coward, and even a possible Soviet sympathizer. In a truly desperate moment, Bush claimed, "My dog Millie knows more about foreign affairs than these two bozos!" (the bozos were Clinton and Gore). And, during the last week of the campaign, reporters at the *Washington Post* and other news organizations received messages from high-ranking Republican officials passing on rumors that Clinton was having an affair which was being covered up by the Secret Service. These calls urged the press to report the rumors.[4]

Why was this negative strategy less successful in 1992 than in 1988? One possibility is that Clinton was a better candidate than Dukakis. Indeed, recalling the fate of the Dukakis campaign, Clinton's team was ready to respond to any negative the Bush campaign could offer. For example, when the Clinton campaign caught wind of upcoming Bush television ads, they prepared counterattacks to launch immediately. And often they did get wind of one (both campaigns sometimes did this by intercepting satellite transmissions as ads were beamed to local stations or by getting a friendly television employee to play the ad). When the Bush campaign aired its "Night of the Living Dead" ad, which depicted Arkansas as a barren state populated by a lonely buzzard, Clinton's response was broadcast only 24 hours later.[5] During the Republican convention, James Carville, Clinton's campaign manager, ordered his staff to be ready to answer any line of the keynote address within an hour.

But the major difference between 1988 and 1992 may be that the voters were less receptive to negative campaigning because they were more concerned about real issues. A poor economy tends to focus voters' concerns. In 1992, the economy was sour and so were the voters. At several times in the campaign, voters indicated they were fed up with personal attacks. Early in the primary season, polls showed that voters were tired of hearing about Clinton's alleged womanizing. During the second presidential debate, the one with audience participation, both the moderator and a participant from the audience indicated they were annoyed with personal attacks and wanted to hear about the issues.

Edward Rollins, the Republican consultant who ran Ronald Reagan's 1984 campaign, summed up the 1992 campaign by noting, "It is not that negative campaigning does not work, it is that the voters this year did not want it. And George Bush talked about the draft about 200 times and his economic agenda about three times.[6] The lesson of the campaign may be, then, not that dirty campaigns do not work at all, but rather that there are some circumstances under which they will not work.

1. Richard Morin, "Relieved Rather than Elated," *Washington Post National Weekly Edition,* November 7–13, 1988, p. 42.
2. Gus Tyler, "After the Brawl Was Over," *New Leader,* November 28, 1988, p. 7.
3. Deborah Tannen, "Lies, Damned Lies, and Political Ads," *Washington Post National Weekly Edition,* September 21–27, 1992.
4. Ann Devroy, "The Low Road that Went Nowhere," *Washington Post National Weekly Edition* (November 9–15, 1992), p. 7.
5. Howard Kurtz, "In Advertising Give and Take, Clinton Camp Took and Responded," *Washington Post,* November 6, 1992, p. A10.
6. Devroy, "The Low Road . . .", p. 7.

supported Democratic congressional candidates, and they favored Clinton over Bush by 44% to 36%, only half voted for Dukakis and a majority voted for Reagan in 1980 and 1984.

Blacks are probably the most distinctive group politically. About 90% consistently vote Democratic, and this loyalty has increased over the past 25 years.

Hispanics who, like blacks, also have lower-than-average incomes, are not as universally Democratic as blacks and have voted Republican in significant numbers in recent elections. Although almost three-quarters voted Democratic in congressional elections, just about 60% voted for Dukakis in 1988 and Clinton in 1992.

Hispanics vote Republican more than they previously did for several reasons. One is that many Hispanics are moving into the middle class. Another is that Republicans have made a great effort to lure Hispanic voters. Moreover, a growing number are Cuban Americans, largely located in Florida, whose most intense political opinion is anticommunism. Cuban Americans are much more likely to be Republican than either Mexican Americans or Puerto Ricans.

White Protestants generally give a majority of their vote to the Republicans and have done so for decades. However, as for other groups, income differences are important in determining the vote of Protestants.

Ethnicity and religion are important in determining the vote because they are shorthand terms for many other factors influencing political behavior—class, historical treatment within the society, and basic culture and values. Jews are predominantly Democratic, for example, because as a persecuted minority throughout much of their history, they have learned to identify with the underdog, even when their own economic circumstances move them into the middle or upper class. Catholics were sometimes discriminated against too; this discrimination plus their working-class status propelled them to the party of Roosevelt. As Catholics have moved into the middle class and as tolerance toward Catholics has grown, Catholics, like Protestants, have tended to vote their income. Moreover, evangelical Protestants (such as Southern Baptist and Assembly of God) are much more likely to vote for Republicans than are mainline Protestants (such as Episcopalians or Presbyterians).

"This year I'm not getting involved in any complicated issues. I'm just voting my straight ethnic prejudices."

Source: Drawing by Whitney Darrow, Jr.; © 1970 The New Yorker Magazine, Inc.

Candidate Evaluations

Candidates' personalities and styles have had more impact as party influence has declined and as television has become voters' major source of information about elections. Reagan's popularity in 1984 is an example of the influence of a candidate and his personality. The perceived competence and integrity of candidates are other facets of candidate evaluation. Voters are less likely to support candidates who do not seem capable of handling the job, regardless of their issue positions. Jimmy Carter suffered in 1980 because of voter evaluations of his competence and leadership.

Issues

Issues are a third factor influencing the vote. Although Americans are probably more likely to vote on issues now than they were in the 1950s, issues only influence some voters some of the time. In 1984 and 1988, for example, voters' issue positions overall were closer to the positions of Mondale and Dukakis than to Reagan or Bush. And, in the 1992 election, 14% of those voters who considered themselves liberal voted for George Bush and 18% of those who considered themselves conservative voted for Bill Clinton.

Still, although other factors also influence voters, many do cast issue votes. To cast an issue vote, voters have to be informed about issues and have opinions. In recent elections, more than 80% of the public could take a position on issues such as government spending, military spending, women's rights, and relations with the Soviet Union.[75] Knowledge about these is-

New Populism
The Angry White Male

If 1992 was the year of the woman in politics, 1994 was the year of the "angry white male." Feeling "left behind and left out," white men turned in large numbers to the Republicans in that off-year election.[1] Sixty-two percent of white male voters voted for Republican House candidates, compared to only 55% of women, the largest gender gap ever reported.[2] In some key races, the split was even greater. In California, for example, 59% of white male voters supported conservative Republican nominee Michael Huffington compared to 41% of white women.[3]

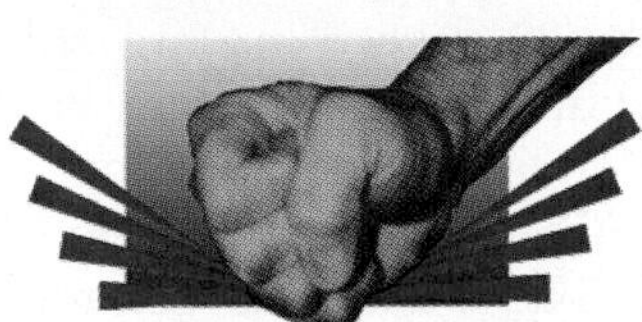

The term "angry white male" is not very precise. Obviously not all white males are angry. Moreover, middle and upper class white males have traditionally voted Republican, so no special explanations are needed for their 1994 vote. But consider the lower and working class white males, who traditionally have been loyal to the Democratic party. Why did they move toward the Republicans in 1994?

Some analysts argued that the issues of the 1994 campaign, such as taxes, spending, crime, gun control, were issues of particular importance to men and to Republicans. Others argue that the shift of white men to the Republican party was based on much broader issues of social and economic change. During the 1980s, the economic status of those with only high school educations declined. Although the economy was strong in the year before the 1994 election, many people face layoffs as American corporations "downsize" and jobs go elsewhere or nowhere. Men with high school educations can no longer expect to keep high-paying jobs throughout their career, or expect to have jobs that pay more than their fathers earned. Indeed, during the 1980s, the median hourly wage for men fell 10%.[4]

Partly as a consequence, the world of the one-earner, male-centered family has also declined. Most families need two earners to achieve or even aspire to a middle-class existence. Most women are increasingly in the workforce and have an increasing amount of power within families.

Even though the economic declines in the fortunes of those with high school educations occurred mostly during the 1980s, under a Republican administration, many white males blame the Democrats. Partly this is because of the cultural changes. Many white men feel pushed aside by the demands of minority groups and women pursuing their agendas of equality. Although white men receive higher wages than any other group and control most businesses, educational institutions, legislative bodies, and other centers of power in America, working class men do not share in this power.[5] They are sliding downhill in their own economic power, as high-paying, skilled, blue-collar jobs move overseas or disappear altogether. But they believe that others are moving ahead. They see gains made by women and minorities in getting better jobs and access to higher education.

As one survey of white working class Detroiters found, "These white Democratic defectors express a profound distaste for blacks, a sentiment that pervades almost everything they think about government and politics. . . . Blacks constitute the explanation for [the whites'] vulnerability and for almost everything that has gone wrong in their lives."[6]

Angry white males are also angry with women, especially their increasing economic and political power. In 1994, white males who voted Republican were twice as likely as other white men to think it unimportant that women be elected to office, for example.[7]

Working class white males believe that public policies, especially affirmative action, are working to move women and minorities ahead, but not them. They overestimate how effective these policies are. They are angry with the Democrats since it is the party that has most strongly supported civil rights laws since the 1960s.

Angry white males, then, seem caught between two forces. Predominantly working class, their economic fortunes are not rosy. The rich are getting richer, but the working class is not. Because they are white males, no government policies seem to be directed toward helping them. Indeed, many minorities and women view them as oppressors or at the least, beneficiaries of the existing system, not people who also need help. The resentment generated by these forces, then, propelled many "angry white males" to pull the Republican lever in the 1994 election. Whether this anger will remain directed at the Democrats for their support of affirmative action and civil rights, or whether it will turn on Republicans whose economic policies encourage increasing economic divisions between rich and poor, remains to be seen.

---

1. Thomas B. Edsall, "The Democrats' Gender and Class Gap," *Washington Post National Weekly Edition* (June 6, 1994), p. 12.
2. Richard Morin and Barbara Vobejda, "It Was the Year of the Angry (White) Man," *Washington Post National Weekly Edition* (November 11–20, 1994), p. 37; "Portrait of the Electorate: Who Voted for Whom in the House," *New York Times* (November 13, 1994), p. 24.
3. Ibid.
4. Thomas Edsall, "The U.S. Male, Caught in a Cultural Shift," *Washington Post National Weekly Edition* (May 8–14, 1995), p. 25.
5. Ibid.
6. Herbert Hill, "Black Workers, Organized Labor, and Title VII of the 1964 Civil Rights Act," in Herbert Hill and James Jones, ed. *Race in America.* (Madison: University of Wisconsin Press, 1993), p. 329.
7. Richard Morin, "And How Did the Voters Judge the Media?" *Washington Post National Weekly Edition* (December 5–11, 1994), p. 37.

sues may have been vague, but individuals were able to understand the issues enough to define their own general positions.

Also, for voters to cast issue votes, candidates must have detectable policy differences. A substantial minority of voters are able to detect some differences among presidential candidates. In recent elections the percentages able to identify correctly general differences between the major party candidates varied between 36 and 62%.[76]

In the 1972 through 1988 elections, more than 70% of those who could correctly identify the positions of the candidates as well as their own position on an important issue cast a vote consistent with their own position.[77] We call this issue voting. Issues with the highest proportion of issue voting were those that typically divided Republicans and Democrats, such as government spending, military spending, and government aid to the unemployed and minorities. However, because only one-third to two-thirds of the electorate was able to define both their own and the candidates' positions on each issue, the proportion of the total electorate that can be said to cast an "issue vote" is usually less than 40%, and for some issues it is much less.[78]

Some scholars have suggested that issue voting is really more of an evaluation of the current incumbents. If voters like the way incumbents, or the incumbent's party, have handled the job in general or in certain areas—the economy or foreign policy, for example—they will vote accordingly, even without much knowledge about the specifics of the issues.

Voting on the basis of past performance is called **retrospective voting.** There is good evidence that many people do this, especially according to economic conditions.[79] Voters support incumbents if national income is growing in the months preceding the election. Since World War II, the incumbent party has won a presidential election only once when the growth rate was less than 3% (Eisenhower in 1956) and lost only once when it was more than 3% (Ford in 1976). Unemployment and inflation seem to have less consistent effects on voting, and economic conditions two or three years before the election have little impact on voting.[80] The recession in the early Reagan years hurt Republicans in the congressional elections of 1982, but the recovery helped Reagan get reelected in 1984 and helped put Bush in the White House in 1988.

Parties, Candidates, and Issues

All three factors—parties, candidates, and issues—clearly matter. Party loyalties are especially important because they help shape our views about issues and candidates. However, if issues and candidates did not matter, the Democrats would have won every presidential election since the New Deal. Republican victories suggest that they often have had more attractive candidates (as in 1952, 1956, 1980, and 1984) or issue positions (in 1972 and in some respects in 1980). However, , the Democrat's partisan advantage shrank throughout the 1980s. Though there are still more Democrats than Republicans, the margin is modest and the number of independents is growing.

Party loyalties have been even more important in congressional voting. The Democrats controlled the House continuously between 1954 and 1994, and controlled the Senate most of those years. However, the Democratic lock on the House was broken in the 1994 election which found the Republicans winning control in a sweeping victory. Clearly, issues overcame traditional partisan habits in that election. Exactly which issues, however, were less than clear.

Conclusion: Do Elections Make Government Responsive?

Although election campaigns are far less successful in mobilizing voters and ensuring a high turnout today than they were in the past century, in a democracy, we expect elections to allow us to control government. Through them we can "throw the rascals out" and bring in new faces with better ideas, or so we think. But other than to change the party that controls government, do elections make a difference?

In the popular press, we hear a lot about "mandates." A president with a **mandate** is one who is clearly directed by the voters to take some particular course of action—reduce taxes or begin arms control talks, for example. George Bush had a substantial majority in his 1988 victory. But did he have a mandate? If so, what for? The campaign hardly talked about the budget deficit even though the election-day polls showed that this was the issue of concern to the largest group of voters. They, in turn, gave an overwhelming majority of *their* votes to Dukakis. On other issues, such as protecting the environment, Bush portrayed himself as a liberal. On many issues, ranging from abortion to day care to defense policy, the two candidates clearly differed. But did Bush's victory mean that he was to limit abortions, leave it to the states to fund day care, or continue the Reagan defense policy? Did he have a mandate on any of these issues?

Like most things in politics, the answer is not simple. Sometimes elections have an effect on policy, but often their effects are not clear-cut. In 1992, some voters chose a candidate on the basis of the economy, others the budget deficit issue, others on health care, and so on. Only one issue (the economy) was the primary concern of even a quarter of the voters.

In the surprising 1994 election, specific policy issues appeared to have little impact. Instead, voters appeared to be expressing their negative views about government generally. Though Republicans presented a "Contract with America," it is not clear which, if any, of the points of that contract, including a balanced budget amendment, term limits, cutting back welfare, spending cuts, and increasing military spending, have majority support.

Typically, even presidents are given a very vague mandate. Reagan's huge election victory in 1984 did not mean that the public agreed more with him than with Mondale on the issues, but mainly that they liked him and approved of the upturn in the economy. Still, over time a rough agreement develops between public attitudes and policies.[81]

It is primarily political parties that translate the mix of various issues into government action because voters' issue positions influence their party loyalties and their evaluations of candidates. A vote for the candidate of one's own party is usually a reflection of agreement on at least some important issues.[82] Once in office, the party in government helps sort out the issues for which there is a broad public mandate from those for which there is not.

Elections that appear to be mandates can become "mandates for disaster." More than one observer has pointed out that every twentieth-century president who has won election by 60% or more of the popular vote soon encountered serious political trouble. After his landslide in 1920, Warren Harding had his Teapot Dome scandal involving government corruption. Emboldened by his 1936 triumph, Franklin Roosevelt tried to pack the Supreme Court and was resoundingly defeated on that issue. Lyndon Johnson won by a landslide in 1964 and was soon mired in Vietnam. Richard Nixon smashed George McGovern in 1972 but then had to resign because of Watergate. Ronald Reagan's resounding victory in 1984 (a shade less than 60%) was followed by the blunders of the Iran-contra affair. Of these presidents, only Roosevelt was able to recover fully from his political misfortune. Reagan regained his personal popularity but seemed to have little influence on policy after Iran-contra. One recent observer has argued that these disasters come because "the euphoria induced by overwhelming support at the polls evidently loosens the president's grip on reality."[83]

Elections can point out new directions for government and allow citizens to make it responsive to their needs, but the fact that many individuals do not vote means that the new directions may not reflect either the needs or wishes of the public. If election turnout falls too far, the legitimacy of elections may be threatened. People may come to believe that election results do not reflect the wishes of the majority. For this reason, it was a healthy thing for our democratic system that election turnout increased in 1992, halting a slow and steady decline. If elections promote government responsiveness to those who participate in them, higher turnouts help increase responsiveness.

EPILOGUE

The Package Works

Clinton decided to follow the blueprint laid out in his campaign team's report. Between the end of the primaries and the convention, Clinton worked hard getting free media coverage and beginning the process of redefining his image. Avid TV viewers saw him on the "Today" show, "MTV," "Good Morning America," "Larry King Live," and "Arsenio Hall," where he put on his sunglasses and played "Heartbreak Hotel" on his sax. The print press quickly picked up on the new themes. *U.S. News and World Report* discussed "The Bill Clinton Nobody Knows," while readers of *People* magazine were treated to a cover story, "At Home with the Clinton Family."

From dead last in the three-way race in April, he began to gain strength in the polls. In a tie with his opponents before the Democratic convention, by the end of the convention, he was 24 points ahead.[84]

And after the convention, instead of lowering his profile as candidates often do between the convention and Labor Day, the traditional beginning of the fall

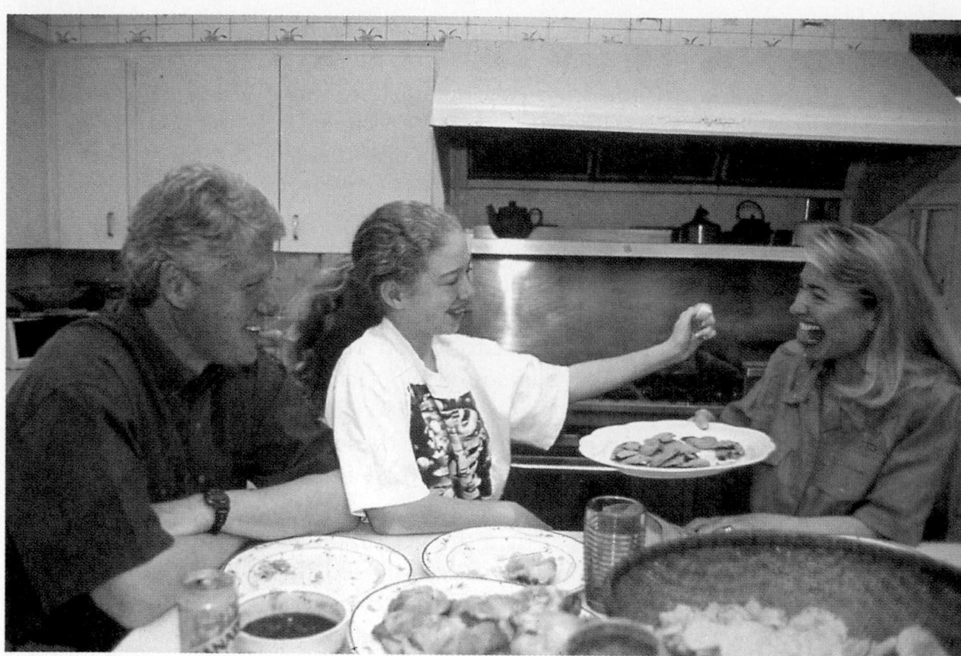

The Clinton family became more prominent in Clinton's campaign after his campaign team discovered the public knew little about them.

campaign, Clinton and Gore took to the heartland in a bus caravan. Clinton's team recalled the fate of Michael Dukakis in 1988. Dukakis had a lead over George Bush in midsummer and stayed out of the public eye until Labor Day. His lead evaporated. The Clinton and Gore bus tour, on the other hand, kept the campaign in the public eye, offered numerous photo opportunities of Bill and Hillary practically every day, got Clinton and Gore on local media throughout the Midwest, and helped solidify the image of Clinton as an average, likable guy.

It is probably true that Republican focus groups and surveys identified Clinton's weaknesses just as accurately as did Clinton's own surveys. Indeed, a major part of President Bush's message was attacks on Clinton's family values, integrity, and trustworthiness. Bush and some of his campaign aides clearly thought this strategy would work in 1992, as it did in 1988 against Michael Dukakis. Though voters and analysts decried this negative strategy, it was successful in 1988. Because of the draft avoidance and womanizing charges, Clinton seemed to be an even better target than Dukakis.

But the Bush strategy failed for several reasons. Voters were more concerned about the fate of the economy than about alleged character flaws. Indeed, in the second presidential debate, which included audience participation, one woman complained that "the amount of time the candidates have spent in this campaign trashing their opponents' character and their programs is depressingly large."[85] Second, the Clinton team learned from the Dukakis debacle. They answered every attack Bush made, but at the same time they stayed focused on their own campaign message. And third, the image modification brought about by the Clinton team had changed the basic impressions that the public had of Clinton, making him more impervious to attack. As one journalist reported, "By the time Mr. Clinton and Mr. Gore took to the highways on bus trips with their wives—double dates with the American people—the old Clinton image was so faded it hardly remained."[86]

➤Further Reading

Lucius Barker, *Our Time Has Come: A Delegate's Diary of Jesse Jackson's 1984 Presidential Campaign* (Urbana, Ill.: University of Illinois Press, 1988); Adolph Reed, *The Jesse Jackson Phenomenon* (New Haven: Yale University Press, 1986). *Barker provides a unique account of Jackson's 1984 campaign from his viewpoint as a political scientist and Jackson delegate. Reed's account of Jackson is relatively unsympathetic.*

Taylor Branch, *Parting the Waters: America in the King Years* (New York: Simon & Schuster, 1988). *An excellent, readable account that illustrates the impact of political protest in changing America's race laws and to a considerable extent its attitudes about race.*

Robert Darcy, Susan Welch, and Janet Clark. *Women, Elections, and Representation* (Lincoln, Neb.: University of Nebraska Press, 1994). *An examination of the potential barriers faced by women candidates.*

Kathleen Hall Jamieson, *Packaging the Presidency* (New York: Oxford University Press, 1984). *The history and impact of presidential campaign advertising. Jamieson's followup,* Dirty Politics *(New York: Oxford University Press, 1992) argues that the media encourage negative and dishonest campaigning by their focus on the horse race.*

Allan Lichtman and Ken De Cell, *The Thirteen Keys to the Presidency.* (Madison Books, 1990). *Focusing on 13 factors—"Keys"—that help explain presidential election outcomes, these authors correctly predict every election since 1860.*

Frances Fox Piven and Richard Cloward, *Why Americans Don't Vote* (New York: Pantheon, 1988). *The authors attribute nonvoting to restrictive registration laws and the disinterest of parties in mobilizing the working class.*

Theodore H. White, *The Making of the President,* 4 vols. (New York: Atheneum Publishers, 1961, 1965, 1969, 1973). *Journalistic accounts of presidential elections from 1960 to 1972. White was the first journalist to travel with the candidates and give an inside view of campaign strategy.*

➤Key Terms

suffrage
Reconstruction
literacy tests
grandfather clause
poll tax
white primary
Voting Rights Act
cumulative voting
Progressive reforms
motor voter law
presidential preference primaries
Super Tuesday
Electoral College
faithless elector
retrospective voting
mandate

➤Notes

1. "The Specter of Scandal," *Newsweek* (November/December 1992), p. 34.
2. *Newsweek,* July 20, 1992, p. 25.
3. Michael Kelly, "The Making of a First Family: A Blueprint," *New York Times* (November 14, 1992), p. lff.
4. Ibid. See also " 'Manhattan Project,' 1992," *Newsweek* (November 16, 1992), pp. 36–39.
5. Kelly, "The Making of a First Family."
6. "Manhattan Project," p. 38.
7. William Flanigan and Nancy H. Zingale, *Political Behavior of the American Electorate* (Boston: Allyn and Bacon, 1972), p. 13. See also Chilton Williamson, *American Suffrage from Property to Democracy* (Princeton, N.J.: Princeton University Press, 1960).
8. James MacGregor Burns, *Vineyard of Liberty* (New York, Alfred A. Knopf, 1982), p. 363.
9. August Meier and Elliot Rudwick, *From Plantation to Ghetto* (New York: Hill and Wang, 1966), p. 69.
10. Robert Darcy, Susan Welch, and Janet Clark, *Women, Elections, and Representation* (New York: Longman, 1987).
11. Grandfather clause: *Guinn v. United States,* 238 U.S. 347, (1915); white primary: *Smith v. Allwright,* 321 U.S. 649, (1944).
12. Data on black and white voter registration in the southern states are from the *Statistical Abstract of the United States* (Washington, D.C.: U.S. Bureau of the Census, various years).
13. Richard Limpme, "Mass Mobilization or Government Intervention? The Growth of Black Registration in the South," *Journal of Politics* 57 (May, 1995), pp. 425–42.
14. Bob Benenson, "Arduous Ritual of Redistricting Ensures More Racial Diversity," *Congressional Quarterly Weekly Report* (October 24, 1992), p. 3385. For a very thorough review of the legal and behavioral impact of the Voting Rights Act, see Joseph P. Viteritti, "Unapportioned Justice: Local Elections Social Science and the Evolution of the Voting Rights Act," *Cornell Journal of Law and Public Policy* (Fall, 1994), pp. 210–270.
15. Darcy, Welch, and Clark, *Women, Elections and Representation.*
16. The discussion in this paragraph is drawn largely from Lois Banner, *Women in Modern America* (New York: Harcourt Brace Jovanovich, 1974), pp. 88–90; Glenn Firebaugh and Kevin Chen, "Vote Turnout of Nineteenth Amendment Women," American Journal of Sociology 100 (January 1995), pp. 972–996.
17. Richard Jensen, "American Election Campaigns: A Theoretical and Historical Typology," paper delivered at the 1968 Midwest Political Science Association Meeting, quoted in Walter Dean Burnham, *Critical Elections and the Mainsprings of American Politics* (New York: W. W. Norton, 1970), p. 73.
18. Frances Fox Piven and Richard A. Cloward, *Why Americans Don't Vote* (New York: Pantheon, 1988), p. 30.
19. Daniel Elazar, *American Federalism: A View from the States* (New York: Thomas Y. Crowell, 1972).
20. Piven and Cloward, *Why Americans Don't Vote,* p. 162. See also G. Bingham Powell, Jr., "American Voter Turnout in Comparative Perspective," *American Political Science Review* 80 (March 1986), pp. 17–44.
21. Piven and Cloward, *Why Americans Don't Vote,* pp. 17–18. Data are from 1980.
22. Powell, "American Voter Turnout," p. 30; Piven and Cloward, *Why Americans Don't Vote,* p. 119.
23. George Will, "In Defense of Nonvoting," *Newsweek,* October 10, 1983, p. 96.
24. Richard Morin, "The Dog Ate My Forms, and, Well, I Couldn't Find a Pen," *Washington Post National Weekly Edition,* November 5–11, 1990, p. 38.
25. Curtis Gans, quoted in Jack Germond and Jules Witcover, "Listen to the Voters—and Nonvoters," *Minneapolis Star Tribune,* November 26, 1988. This effect was foreshadowed by Michael J. Robinson, "American Political Legitimacy in an Era of Electronic Journalism," in *Television as a Social Force,* ed. Douglas Cater and Richard Adler (New York: Praeger).
26. Ibid.
27. Priscilla Southwell, "Voter Turnout in the 1986 Congressional Elections," *American Politics Quarterly* 19 (January 1991), pp. 96–108; Stephen Ansolabehere, Shanto Iyengar, Adam Simon, and Nicholas Valentino, "Does Attack Advertising Demobilize the

Electorate," *American Political Science Review* 88 (December, 1994), pp. 829–838.

28. Curtis B. Gans, "The Empty Ballot Box," *Public Opinion* 1 (September/October 1978), pp. 54–57. See also Austin Ranney, *Channels of Power* (New York: Basic Books, 1983); and Richard Boyd, "The Effect of Election Calendars on Voter Turnout," paper presented at the Annual Meeting of the Midwest Political Science Association, April 1987, Chicago, Illinois.

29. Boyd, "The Effect of Election Calendars."

30. Ibid.

31. Piven and Cloward, *Why Americans Don't Vote,* p. 17.

32. Benjamin Ginsberg, *The Consequences of Consent: Elections, Citizen Control and Popular Acquiescence* (Reading, Mass.: Addison-Wesley, 1982), p. 37.

33. See Piven and Cloward, *Why Americans Don't Vote,* pp. 196–97 for illustrations of these kinds of informal barriers.

34. Raymond Wolfinger and Steven Rosenstone, *Who Votes?* (New Haven: Yale University Press, 1980), table 6.1.

35. James A. Barnes, "In Person: Marsha Nye Adler," *National Journal,* February 18, 1989, p. 420.

36. Piven and Cloward, *Why Americans Don't Vote,* pp. 230–31.

37. Peverill Squire, Raymond Wolfinger, and David Glass, "Residential Mobility and Voter Turnout," *American Political Science Review* 81 (March 1987), pp. 45–66. See also Samuel C. Patterson and Gregory A. Caldeira, "Mailing in the Vote: Correlates and Consequences of Absentee Voting," *American Journal of Political Science* 29 (November 1985), pp. 766–88.

38. For review of this literature, see John Petrocik, "Voter Turnout and Electoral Preference," in Kay Schlozman, ed., *Elections in America* (Boston: Allen & Unwin, 1987).

39. Kevin Phillips and Paul Blackman, *Electoral Reform and Voter Participation* (Stanford, Calif.: American Enterprise System, 1975).

40. Kim Quaile Hill, Jan Leighley, and Angela Hinton-Anderson, "Lower-Class Mobilization and Policy Linkage in the U.S. States," *American Journal of Political Science* 39 (February, 1995), pp. 75–86.

41. Anthony Downs, *An Economic Theory of Democracy* (New York: Harper & Row, 1957).

42. Morin, "The Dog Ate My Forms."

43. Kay Lehman Schlozmand, Sidney Verba, and Henry Brady, "Participation's Not a Paradox: The View from American Activists," *British Journal of Political Science* 25 (January, 1995), pp. 1–36.

44. Norman H. Nie, Sidney Verba, Henry Brady, Kay Lehman Schlozman, and Jane Junn, "Participation in America: Continuity and Change," paper presented at the Annual Meeting of the Midwest Political Science Association, Chicago, Illinois, April 1988. The standard work on American political participation is Sidney Verba and Norman Nie, *Participation in America* (New York: Harper & Row, 1972).

45. Ibid.

46. Paul Allen Beck and M. Kent Jennings, "Political Periods and Political Participation," *American Political Science Review* 73 (1979), pp. 737–50; Nie et al., "Participation in America."

47. The following discussion draws heavily from John Aldrich, *Before the Convention* (Chicago: University of Chicago Press, 1980).

48. Ibid. See also David Rohde, "Risk Bearing and Progressive Ambition: The Case of Members of the United States House of Representatives," *American Journal of Political Science* 23 (February 1979), pp. 1–26.

49. "Political Grapevine," *Time,* February 8, 1988, p. 30.

50. "The Fall Campaign," *Newsweek,* Election Extra (November/December 1984), p. 88.

51. Bruce Babbitt, "Bruce Babbitt's View from the Wayside," *Washington Post National Weekly Edition,* February 24–March 6, 1988, p. 24. The 999 days figure is from the *Congressional Quarterly Weekly Report,* February 1, 1992, p. 257.

52. Gerald Pomper and Susan Lederman, *Elections in America* (New York: Longman, 1980), chapter 7.

53. Michael J. Robinson, "Where's the Beef?," in Austin Ranney, ed., *The American Election of 1984* (Durham, N.C.: Duke University Press, 1985).

54. "Squall in New Orleans," *Newsweek,* November 21, 1988, p. 103.

55. "Conventional Wisdom Watch," *Newsweek,* November 21, 1988, p. 18.

56. See *Congressional Quarterly,* July 23, 1988, p. 2015; Thomas Holbrook, "Campaigns National Conventions and U.S. Presidential Elections," *American Journal of Political Science* 38 (November, 1994), pp. 973–98.

57. Benjamin Page and Richard Brody, "Policy Voting and the Electoral Process," *American Political Review* 66 (1972), pp. 979–95.

58. Thomas F. Patterson, *Mass Media Elections* (New York: Praeger, 1980), p. 3.

59. The discussion of the functions of the media relies heavily on the excellent summary found in Stephen Ansolabehere, Roy Behr, and Shanto Iyengar, "Mass Media and Elections," *American Politics Quarterly* 19 (January 1991), pp. 109–39.

60. *Congressional Quarterly Weekly Reports,* July 30, 1971, p. 1622, quoted in Ansolabehere, Behr, and Iyengar, "Mass Media and Elections," p. 109.

61. Martin Schram, *The Great American Video Game: Presidential Politics in the Television Age* (New York: William Morrow, 1987).

62. Patterson, *Mass Media Election,* p. 4.

63. Robert McNeil, *The Influence of Television on American Politics* (New York: Harper & Row, 1968), p. 182.

64. Elisabeth Bumiller, "Selling Soup, Wine and Reagan," *Washington Post National Weekly Edition,* November 5, 1984, pp. 6–8.

65. Paul Taylor, "Pigsty Politics," *Washington Post National Weekly Edition,* February 13–19, 1989, p. 6.

66. Eileen Shields West, "Give 'em Hell These Days Is a Figure of Speech," *Smithsonian* (October 1988), pp. 149–51. The editorial was from the *Connecticut Courant.*

67. Charles Paul Freund, "But Then, Truth Has Never Been Important," *Washington Post National Weekly Edition,* November 7–13, 1988, p. 29.

68. Quoted in Freund, "But Then, Truth Has Never Been Important," p. 29.

69. Freund, "But Then, the Truth Has Never Been Important," p. 29.

70. In her book, *Packaging the Presidency* (New York: Oxford University Press, 1984), Kathleen Jamieson also argued that there are checks on misleading advertising, but later ("Is the Truth Now Irrelevant in Presidential Campaigns?") she argued that these checks did not work well in 1988. See Jamieson, *Dirty Politics: Deception, Distraction and Democracy* (New York: Oxford University Press, 1992).

71. Kathleen Hall Jamieson, "Is the Truth Now Irrelevant in Presidential Campaigns?" *Washington Post National Weekly Edition,* November 7–13, 1988, p. 28.

72. Stanley Kelley, Jr., *Interpreting Elections* (Princeton, N.J.: Princeton University Press, 1983); Stanley Kelley, Jr., Richard Ayres, and William G. Bower, "Registration and Voting: Putting First Things First," *American Political Science Review* 61 (June 1967), pp. 359–79.

73. J. Merrill Shanks and Warren E. Miller, "Partisanship, Policy and Performance: The Reagan Legacy in the 1988 Election," *British Journal of Political Science* 21 (April 1991), pp. 129–97; Eugene DeClerq, Thomas Hurley, and Norman Luttbeg, "Voting in American Presidential Elections," *American Political Quarterly* 3 (July 1975), updated and reported in David B. Hill and Norman Luttbeg, *Trends in American Electoral Behavior,* 2nd ed. (Itasca, Ill.: F. E. Peacock, 1983), p. 50.

74. Lee Sigelman, "If You Prick Us, Do We Not Bleed? If You Tickle Us, Do We Not Laugh? Jews and Pocketbook Voting," paper prepared for presentation at the 1990 American Political Science Meeting: Susan Welch and Lee Sigelman, "The Politics of Hispanic Americans," *Social Science Quarterly,* 1991; *New York Times,* November 5, 1992, p. B9.

75. Paul Abramson, John H. Aldrich, and David Rohde, *Change and Continuity in the 1988 Elections* (Washington, D.C.: CQ Press, 1990), p. 172.

76. Ibid., p. 165.

77. Ibid.

78. Ibid., p. 170.

79. Morris Fiorina, *Retrospective Voting in American National Elections* (New Haven: Yale University Press, 1981).

80. Edward Tufte, *Political Control of the Economy* (Princeton, N.J.: Princeton University Press, 1978); Douglas Hibbs, "The Mass Public and Macroeconomic Performance," *American Journal of Political Science* 23 (November 1979), pp. 705–731; John Hibbing and John Alford, "The Electoral Impact of Economic Conditions: Who Is Held Responsible," *American Journal of Political Science* 25 (1981), pp. 423–39.

81. Benjamin I. Page and Robert Shapiro, "Effects of Public Opinion on Policy," *American Political Science Review 77* (March 1983), pp. 175–90.

82. Abramson, Aldrich, and Rohde, *Change and Continuity.* See also Benjamin Page and Calvin C. Jones, "Reciprocal Effects of Party Preferences, Party Loyalties and the Vote," in Richard Niemi and Herbert Weisberg, *Controversies in Voting Behavior,* 2nd ed. (Washington, D.C.: CQ Press, 1984).

83. Arthur Schlesinger, Jr., *Wall Street Journal,* December 5, 1986.

84. This was the biggest convention bounce since polling began.

85. Maureen Dowd, "A No-Nonsense Sort of Talk Show," *New York Times* (October 16, 1992), p. 1.

86. Kelly, "The Making of a First Family." For scholarly works on the 1992 elections, see Robert Loevy, *The Flawed Path to the Presidency, 1992* (Albany: State University of New York Press, 1995); Robert Steed, Laurence Moreland, and Tod A. Baker, eds., *The 1992 Presidential Election in the South* (Westport, Ct.: Praeger, 1994); Paul Abramson, John H. Aldrich, and David Rhode, *Change and Continuity in the 1992 Elections* (Washington, DC: CQ Press, 1995).

8 The Media

You Are There

Should You Pull Him out of "the Closet"?

You are Michelangelo Signorile, a homosexual activist and a writer for *OutWeek*, a homosexual magazine. It is 1991 and you have to decide whether to publicize the fact that a high-ranking official in the Department of Defense is gay. You think that publication would be newsworthy given the department's stance against homosexuality in the military service. But you also are concerned about the ethical issues involved in publicizing this aspect of the person's private life.

Your own background in the media and in the movement led you to hold these conflicting views. After college you worked for a public relations firm with clients in the entertainment business. When your clients sought publicity for their latest projects, you fed tidbits of information about them to the writers of gossip columns in newspapers. In this way, you planted their names in these columns. When the AIDS epidemic spread in the 1980s, you joined ACT UP (AIDS Coalition To Unleash Power), a group that used protest to gain publicity for its demands that the government invest more resources in the fight against the epidemic.

You know from your public relations work that gossip columnists prattle on about anything in a celebrity's private life except a celebrity's homosexuality. That is taboo. Columnists talk about a straight actor's affairs but not a gay actor's relationships. Sometimes they even pretend that a gay actor is straight by writing that he or she is "dating" someone of the opposite sex. The result, you feel, is to send a message that homosexuality is "so utterly grotesque that it should never be discussed."[1]

This message, you believe, reflects an unconscious conspiracy to keep homosexuals locked in "the closet"—that is, to keep them from revealing their sexual identity, sometimes even to their closest friends and relatives. You think this conspiracy is perpetuated by the government, the media, and the entertainment industry—even including some powerful homosexuals in these institutions who go along out of fear that their power, prestige, and income would plummet if the truth were revealed.

In recent years some gays have tried to reveal the homosexuality of other gays, but the mainstream media normally have not reported the revelations. In 1990 activists held a press conference on the steps of the Capitol and identified three members of the Senate and five members of the House of Representatives as gay. Activists also altered a billboard of an incumbent senator running for reelection—"Closeted Gay. Living a Lie. Voting to Oppress"—and demonstrated outside the homes of some members. But most media did not report these efforts.[2] (In 1989 the media did address the homosexuality of a representative who had a long relationship with a male prostitute who operated out of the member's apartment. The journalists considered this situation scandalous and covered it.)

You were sympathetic with these efforts, and, still disgusted by the gossip columnists' practice of hiding the homosexuality of entertainers, you criticized their practice and implied that two columnists themselves were homosexuals. Your exposé prompted

CONTINUED 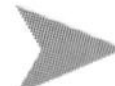

OUTLINE

The Media State
- Roles of the Media
- Concentration of the Media
- Atomization of the Media

Relationship between the Media and Politicians
- Symbiotic Relationship
- Adversarial Relationship
- Relationship between the Media and Recent Administrations
- Relationship between the Media and Congress

Bias of the Media
- Political Bias
- Commercial Bias

Impact of the Media on Politics
- Impact on the Public Agenda
- Impact on Political Parties and Elections
- Impact on Public Opinion

Conclusion: Are the Media Responsive?

another writer to compare you with Senator Joseph McCarthy (R.-Wis.), who shrilly and often falsely accused government employees of being communists in the 1950s.

Other journalists see no sinister motives behind the silence on homosexuality. They deny the existence of any conspiracy to keep homosexuals locked in "the closet." They say they do not publicize a person's homosexuality because of the likely consequences of the public's prejudices.

Now you have information that an assistant secretary of defense in the Bush administration is gay. You have no doubt about the accuracy of the information. Should you report it in *OutWeek*?

The official has a high position and considerable visibility. During the recent Persian Gulf War, he was the primary spokesman for the department.

Since the war the department's policy of discharging gay and lesbian military personnel has come under heavy fire. In the past decade the Pentagon has discharged perhaps 13,000 soldiers, sailors, airmen and women, and marines for homosexuality.[3] This policy rankles you and others in the gay and lesbian community. But you do not know whether the assistant secretary has any influence over the policy or whether he might be working on the inside to overturn it. Do these factors matter?

Although the policy does not apply to civilian officials, such as the assistant secretary, does the situation—being a gay spokesman for a department that discharges gay and lesbian personnel—reflect hypocrisy? If so, is the hypocrisy sufficient for you to reveal his homosexuality?

Or should a concern for privacy override your distaste of hypocrisy? There is no legal right to privacy for one's sexuality, but should there be an ethical right? Many gays think there should be. One called privacy "the central protection" for gays. Forsaking it would cause anguish for people and would ignore the complexities of their lives. Perhaps there are good reasons to allow some to remain in "the closet."[4]

Or do the media routinely disregard privacy to such an extent that it is irrelevant to consider? Reporters already cover out-of-wedlock births, abortions, affairs, and divorces of public figures. Is it pointless to try drawing the line at homosexuality?

Or are the media generally so invasive of people's private lives that their current practices should not serve as a guide for covering homosexuality? Reporting of people's "scandalous" conduct used to focus on their malfeasance or incompetence in public office. Now it has extended to their private behavior, including instances that occurred before they became public officials. Sometimes it has extended to their aides, who were not elected and do not hold public office. In the past decade officials or candidates have been exposed for having a "shotgun" wedding, having affairs while married, smoking marijuana while in college, attending parties where others used cocaine, telling racist or sexist jokes, and a variety of other things.[5] Should people be defined publicly according to the way they lead their private lives or solely according to the way they perform their jobs? If some aspects of their private lives are relevant, is their sexual identity as heterosexual or homosexual relevant?

In this debate, it is not clear whether privacy helps or hurts the lives of gays. Keeping homosexuality secret certainly props up the walls of "the closet." This practice might make life more difficult for gay teenagers, who see few gay adults and who feel isolated. But challenging this practice might complicate the already difficult lives of gay adults still in "the closet."

So what do you do with the information?

Michelangelo Signorile

A "medium" transmits something. The mass media—which include newspapers, magazines, books, radio, television, movies, and records—transmit communications to masses of people.

Although the media do not constitute a branch of government or even an organization established to influence government, such as a political party or interest group, they have an impact on government. In addition to providing entertainment, the media provide political information, sometimes directly through the news, other times indirectly in a program or story addressing a public problem such as crime or drugs. Either way, people obtain most of their information about government and politics from the media.

➤THE MEDIA STATE

The media have developed and flourished to an extent the Founders could not have envisioned. As one political scientist noted, the media have become "pervasive . . . and atmospheric, an element of the air we breathe."[6] Without exaggeration, another observer concluded, "Ancient Sparta was a military state. John Calvin's Geneva was a religious state. Mid-nineteenth century England was Europe's first industrial state, and the contemporary United States is the world's first media state."[7]

Americans spend more time being exposed to the media than doing anything else. In a year, according to one calculation, the average full-time worker puts in 1,824 hours on the job, 2,737 hours in bed, and 3,256 hours exposed to the media (in a day, almost 9 hours exposed to the media).[8] Seventy-seven percent of adults read newspapers; the average person does so for three-and-a-half hours a week. The average person also reads two magazines for one-and-a-half hours a week.[9] Eighty-eight percent of American homes have a radio, and 98% have a television. More homes have a television than a toilet.[10] The average adult watches television three hours a day and the average child four. By the time the average child graduates from high school, he or she has spent more time in front of the tube than in class.[11] By the time the average American dies, he or she has spent one-and-a-half years just watching television commercials.[12]

■ Roles of the Media

American newspapers, which originated in colonial times, were the only regular media in the country for almost two centuries. Although newspapers gained readers, political magazines appeared in the nineteenth century, and newsweeklies began in the 1920s, there were no "mass media" until the advent of the broadcast media. Radio, which became popular in the 1920s, and television, which became popular in the 1950s, reached people who could not or would not read.

People bought television sets to watch entertainment programs, but they also began to watch newscasts. At first the newscasts, lasting only 15 minutes and consisting solely of an anchor and a few correspondents talking, were not compelling. In 1963 the networks expanded the time to 30 minutes and altered the format to emphasize visual interest. That year, for the first time, people said they got more political information from television than from any other source.

As television grew in popularity, newspapers waned. People did not need them for the headlines anymore. Although newspapers began to provide in-depth analysis of news, which television did not, they struggled for readers and advertisers, and some folded.

These trends continued. In the 1970s and 1980s, the number of adults in the country increased 34% and the number of households increased 41%, but the circulation of daily newspapers remained stagnant.[13] The number of young adults (from 18 through 29) who are regular readers of daily newspapers declined the most—50% in the last two decades. Now only one-third are regular readers.[14]

Consequently, television has become the most important of the media for politics. According to surveys, people pay more attention to it and put more faith in it than in other media. This makes positive coverage on television essential for politicians.

Nevertheless, television has not fully eclipsed newspapers. Most people who say they get the bulk of their political information from television admit they do not watch the news daily, whereas more people who get the bulk of their political information from newspapers read the news sections daily. Because newspapers require more effort or provide more depth, they leave a longer-lasting impression; people remember what they read in newspapers better than what they watch on television.[15]

Moreover, national newspapers such as the *New York Times* and *Washington Post,* which blanket the country with in-depth international and national news, influence opinion leaders who, in turn, influence other persons.

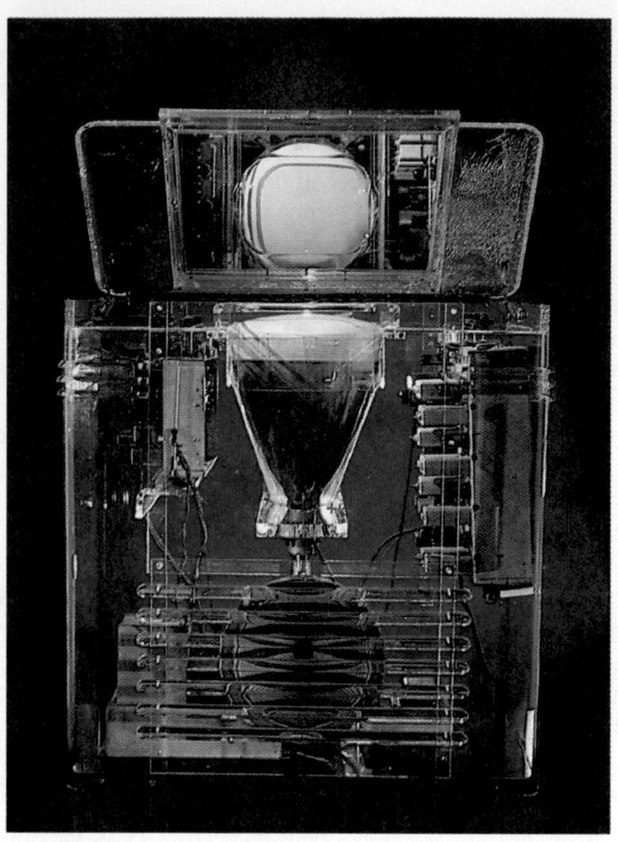

This television (left) made its debut in the Hall of Television at the New York World's Fair in 1939. President Franklin Roosevelt opened the fair by appearing on the tiny screen. Television coverage and programming was limited for years because the equipment, such as this camera in 1938, was so bulky (top).

Coverage of the Persian Gulf War in 1991 reflected the contemporary roles of broadcast and print journalism. Although the networks had little film footage of the war itself, they provided immediacy and drama. When the Scud missile attacks threatened, reporters on the scene announced, "There go the sirens. We'll probably have an attack here in five minutes." Reporters in Israel, where poison gas attacks were feared, broadcast while putting on gas masks or scurrying to sealed rooms. The live reports, beamed via satellite, often were unedited and rough yet compelling, almost hypnotic, for many viewers. But they were also fragmentary and sometimes contradictory. Newspapers presented more complete and accurate accounts the next day.

Concentration of the Media

In the late nineteenth century, journalism started to become big business, and news organizations began to focus less on crusading for their causes and more on maximizing their profits.[16] Although for decades most media remained local media, owned by local individuals or companies, in the middle twentieth century economic pressures forced many organizations to join large chains or conglomerates. These chains and conglomerates came to dominate the business and to constitute a national media.[17]

Although media in this country, compared with those in other Western democracies, remain relatively decentralized—in the United States there are approximately 1,700 daily newspapers, 10,800 radio stations, and 1,600 television stations[18]—these numbers are misleading. Chains own papers that have over 70% of the circulation in the country.[19] Further, in most cities with more than one paper, economic pressures have caused competing papers to merge. As a result, by 1991 only 12 cities had separately owned, fully competitive papers, compared with 35 a decade earlier.[20]

Media conglomerates own newspapers, magazines, radio stations, and television stations. The result is that just 10 corporations control the following:

- 58 newspapers, including the *New York Times, Washington Post, Los Angeles Times,* and *The Wall Street Journal;*
- 59 magazines, including *Time* and *Newsweek;*
- 41 book publishers;

- 3 major radio and television networks;
- 62 radio stations;
- 34 television stations;
- 201 cable television systems; and
- 20 record companies.[21]

Similarly, a small number of businesses garner a disproportionate amount of revenue. Six magazine companies, among 11,000 in the country, account for half the magazine revenue, and 6 book publishers, among 2,500 in the country, account for more than half the book revenue.[22] Fifty radio stations (of 10,800) generate half the radio profits.[23]

These trends are likely to continue because the media business is big business. The media industry is the nation's ninth largest, just below aerospace and just above electronics equipment.[24]

Equally important as the growth of chains and conglomerates is the dominance of a few sources of news. One wire service—AP—supplies the international and national news for most newspapers. Three magazines—*Newsweek, Time,* and *U.S. News and World Report*—control the market of news magazines. Four radio networks—ABC, CBS, NBC, and Mutual—furnish the news for most radio listeners, and four television networks—ABC, CBS, NBC, and CNN—furnish the news for most television viewers. Consequently, the media present quite homogeneous international and national news.

Atomization of the Media

Despite the growing concentration of the media during the twentieth century, a quite different trend—the atomization of the media—also has been developing in recent years. Where concentration of the media led to a national media, atomization of the media is fragmenting the influence of this national media. The major newspapers and broadcast networks are beginning to lose their dominance, while other media, some not even considered news organizations, are starting to play a significant role in politics.

Viewership of network news declined through the 1980s. In 1991 it reached its lowest mark since 1961.[25] The networks offer newsmagazine shows, such as CBS's "60 Minutes," to boost ratings. Yet the networks struggle to retain viewers.

During the same years, viewership of local news increased to a level half again as large as that of network news.[26] Technological innovations enable local stations to present more compelling newscasts than before. Many stations offer combined local and national newscasts by joining a consortium of other stations, spread across the country but linked by satellite, to share coverage of events of national interest.

Expansion of cable television threatens the networks further. Now reaching 60% of American households, cable offers many competing channels and promises more specialized programs. Although much of cable's menu duplicates the networks' (and reflects Bruce Springsteen's complaint, "57 Channels, and Nothin' On"), its offerings will become increasingly focused—"narrowcasting" that will appeal to small segments of the audience, rather that the networks' broadcasting that is designed to appeal to the general audience.

Already CNN, a 24-hour news station on two channels, attracts a large audience, and C-SPAN, which covers Congress at length and with little editing on two channels, has a significant audience. Even MTV, the music channel, offered considerable coverage of the 1992 presidential campaign in a format to attract young viewers.

Other national cable networks cater to blacks and to Hispanics. A cable system in Los Angeles and New York City caters to Jews. A cable channel in California broadcasts in Chinese, one in Hawaii broadcasts in Japanese, while one in Connecticut and Massachusetts broadcasts in Portuguese. Stations in New York City also program in Greek, Hindi, and Korean.

These developments reflect a more diverse country than the one that existed when television was born, and they pose a serious challenge to the networks. "Forty years ago," observed the media critic for *Rolling Stone,* "television news consisted of middle-aged white men reading . . . news into a camera. Today, network news consists of middle-aged white men reading . . . news into a camera.[27]

The popularity of radio and television talk shows also threatens the dominance of major newspapers and broadcast networks. Many radio stations have some talk shows, and about 10% of the stations have an all-talk format, the fastest growing format in the business.[28] According to one 1993 survey, 17% percent of the public say they listen to these shows regularly; 25% more say they listen sometimes. (Eleven percent have tried to call in; 6% have gotten on the air.)[29] According to another 1993 survey, 44% of the public said these shows are their primary source of political information.[30] With millions of people listening, talk radio is a force in politics. It attracts a middle-class audience that serves as a national jury on governmental controversies.

New Populism

Talk Radio

Perhaps no phenomenon more clearly reflects new populism than the rise and popularity of talk radio. Both the hosts and the callers to these shows demonstrate righteous anger toward the government and public officials and an intense desire to change their practices and policies.

Hosts

A survey of 112 hosts in the 100 largest media markets in the country found that a majority of hosts describe themselves as moderates, with a minority of equal numbers of liberals and conservatives. A majority also call themselves independents, with a minority of partisans, slightly more of whom lean toward the Democrats than toward the Republicans. In these ways the hosts are roughly representative of the American public.[1]

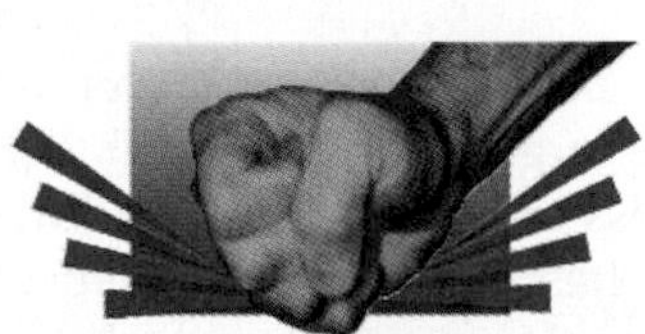

The hosts, however, are more educated and less religious than the public. (Thirty percent of the hosts say they have no religious affiliation, whereas only 10% of the population says this.) The hosts also are more libertarian than the public. They are more likely to oppose restrictions on abortion and on homosexuals teaching in public schools or serving in the military, and they are more likely to oppose banning books from school libraries and reinstating prayers in school classes.

Significantly, the hosts are far more critical of the government and its representatives than the public is. Although more voted for Clinton than for Bush or Perot in 1992, they expressed more criticism of Clinton and of Congress (before the elections of 1994) than the public did.

Thus, the hosts do not fit neatly into the usual liberal and conservative categories. They reflect some attitudes of each.

But these conclusions from the survey are somewhat misleading, because the survey treats all hosts equally. Conservative hosts have a much larger audience, and therefore a considerably greater influence, than liberal hosts.[2] Rush Limbaugh, for example, has the most popular show, with 4.5 million listeners tuning in to 600 stations across the country. (And this does not include his talk television show.)[3]

Callers

The callers are more likely to be conservatives than liberals and more likely to be Republicans than Democrats. In fact, conservatives and Republicans are more than twice as likely to get on the air. (And men are almost twice as likely to get on the air as women.)[4]

Almost all the hosts acknowledge that their callers are not typical of the people in their city. The hosts say that their callers are more critical of Congress, the Democratic party, and President Clinton (and far more critical of Hillary Clinton).[5] They are also more opposed to abortion and more hostile to homosexuals. But, most important, the hosts report that their callers reflect an angrier tone than do most people.

Impact

With these attitudes, the hosts and callers have had a considerable impact on politics in recent years. When Congress voted itself a substantial pay raise in 1988, several hosts decided to coordinate an attack. They sent faxes to other stations, and the hosts urged listeners to phone or fax their representatives and to send tea bags to them. The deluge caused Congress to postpone and scale back the raise.

When *USA Today* reported congressional check kiting in 1992, talk shows turned to the issue. Most people ignored the newspapers' explanation that members who overdrew their checking accounts at the House of Representatives "bank" essentially had borrowed money from each other rather than taken any from the taxpayers. Cued by talk show hosts, people considered these overdrafts from the House "bank" equivalent to overdrafts from their own checking accounts. The vitriol prompted the retirement of some members and the reelection defeat of others.

When it came out that President Clinton's first choice for attorney general—Zoe Baird, a $500,000 a year corporate lawyer—and her husband had hired illegal aliens to provide day care for their children, listeners contacted their senators. As calls mounted, it became clear that she could not be confirmed and her nomination was withdrawn.

For all three incidents, citizens' anger was fueled by talk shows reflecting middle-class indignation that officials were making too much money, getting too many benefits, and not playing by the rules other people had to play by. Although the major media initially had not considered these incidents important and had not covered them prominently, listeners of the talk shows had a different opinion.

Listeners' outrage has also influenced more substantive policies. When a girl was murdered by a career criminal in California, the host of a talk show drafted the outline of the "three strikes and you're out" sentencing policy (which mandates life in prison for persons convicted of three felonies).[6] After the idea caught on in California, it spread to the rest of the country through other talk shows. Although many criminal justice experts said the policy would provide minimal benefit and would cause some harm and considerable expense for society, the torrent of opinion prompted President Clinton and Congress to adopt the policy for the federal courts.

Talk radio might have had an impact on politics in other ways as well. In particular, it might have contributed to Republican victories in the congressional elections in 1994. Voters nationwide favored Republicans by just 2%, but voters who were talk-radio listeners favored Republicans by 28%.[7] Although people who tune in talk radio are disproportionately Republicans (26% of Republicans compared with 14% of independents and 12% of Democrats listen regularly, and 50% of Republicans compared with 41% of independents and 35% of Democrats listen sometimes),[8] the size of this difference suggests that the dynamics of talk radio might have persuaded some listeners to support Republicans or at least galvanized some listeners who already leaned toward Republicans to vote. It is possible that enough listeners did so in close races that they enabled the Republicans to win and wrest control of Congress from the Democrats.

The anger over the airwaves might have a broader impact on society also. "When I started out in 1979," a host in Washington, D.C. recalls, "I believed that talk radio could become a unifying force, a way to help bridge our differences through the sharing of ideas and knowledge." But in recent years, she laments, "talk radio has become one more force to separate rather than unite us.[9] Stations encourage hosts to have strong views and make sharp attacks, rather than to promote full discussion of complex issues, because the former is entertaining—and boosts the ratings for the show—even if it heightens the hostility in society.

Some hosts have followed this approach to the extreme. A Colorado Springs host urged listeners to take their guns to Washington to protest proposals to ban assault weapons. (Not long after, a deranged Colorado Springs man did take his gun to Washington and shot at the White House.) A Phoenix host, in a show about Jim Brady, the press secretary for President Reagan who was wounded when the President was shot, criticized Brady's wife, who has campaigned for gun control. "You know," the host said, "she ought to be put down. A humane shot at a veterinarian's would be an easy way to do it. Because of all her barking and complaining, she really needs to be put down."[10] G. Gordon Liddy, one of the Watergate burglars and now a popular host, advised listeners to shoot for the head of federal agents because they wear bulletproof vests.

Source: *Washington Post National Weekly Edition*, July 19–23, 1993, p. 37.

1. Nationwide sample from May and June, 1993. "The Vocal Minority in American Politics," Times Mirror Center for the People and the Press, Washington, D.C., July, 1993.
2. Richard Corliss, "Look Who's Talking," *Time*, January 23, 1995, p. 22.
3. David Remnick, "Radio Free Limbaugh," *Washington Post National Weekly Edition*, February 28–March 6, 1994, p. 23.
4. "The Vocal Minority in American Politics," pp. 9–10.
5. This survey was conducted before the Whitewater investigation and the proposals for health care reform led to more criticism of Hillary Clinton.
6. Robert Wright, "Hyper Democracy," *Time*, January 23, 1995, p. 16.
7. "Victory by the Numbers," *Time*, November 21, 1994, p. 64.
8. "The Vocal Minority in American Politics," pp. 7–8.
9. Diane Rehm, "Can We Talk about Talk Radio?" *Washington Post National Weekly Edition*, September 19–25, 1994, p. 23.
10. Timothy Egan, "Talk Radio or Hate Radio? Critics Assail Some Hosts," *New York Times* (January 1, 1995), p. 11.

The atomization of the media was especially apparent during the 1992 presidential campaign. *The Star*, a supermarket tabloid, published allegations by Gennifer Flowers, a former nightclub singer, that she had had a 12-year affair with Bill Clinton while he was governor of Arkansas. The major media hesitated repeating the *Star*'s story—they had nothing but scorn for the tabloids which, they insisted, did not practice true journalism—but within days the networks and most newspapers gave in, under the pretense of debating the propriety of reporting personal matters. The Clintons felt obligated to appear on "60 Minutes" to refute the allegations (while sidestepping the question whether he had ever committed adultery). Whereupon Flowers appeared on "A Current Affair," a syndicated television show, rated Clinton as a lover on a scale from 1 to 10, and sang "Stand By Your Man." Thus, Flowers did not need to take her story to the major media; she got the tabloid media to tell it and pay her for it (an estimated $150,000 by the *Star* alone).[31] The continuing coverage precipitated a drop in Clinton's standing during the presidential primaries.

Then Ross Perot announced his candidacy for president on CNN's "Larry King Live," a talk show, rather than through a press conference with the networks. Other candidates followed on various talk shows. Clinton fielded questions on the "Phil Donahue Show" and on MTV, and played the saxophone on the "Arsenio Hall Show." President Bush, who initially called these appearances "weird," eventually courted sports fans on ESPN and country music fans on the Nashville Network.

Candidates saw these shows as ways to communicate with the voters without having their messages "filtered"—that is, condensed, simplified, distorted, or challenged—by the press. Clinton even bought television time for half-hour shows, "electronic town meetings," in which he took questions from voters in several cities.

Because of the expanding role of fringe media, mainstream journalists glimpse a shrinking role for themselves. They no longer monopolize the market of political information; they no longer control the gates through which such information must pass.

In fact, according to one journalism professor, many citizens see no purpose in having journalists intervene in politics. "Max in Seattle feels as well represented by Julie's question from Houston as he would be by Sam Donaldson's inquiry from New York." (Actually, Max might prefer Julie's to Sam Donaldson's. Many citizens are annoyed by the "cult of toughness" among journalists that leads them to challenge public figures with "a level of shamelessness and aggression that ordinary people cannot manage.")[32]

Although the new use of media may be more democratic, in appealing to a broader segment of the population and allowing participation by a portion of the population, it also is less analytical. Most citizens are not versed in issues or knowledgeable about candidates and officials to the extent that professional journalists are. Many citizens are not able to separate the blarney from the gospel truth when candidates and officials open their mouths.

Ross Perot jokes during preparation for the Larry King show.

This problem is aggravated by the fact that some fringe media are less than scrupulous about the accuracy of the information they disseminate. In their quest for an audience, some fringe media pay for stories, possibly encouraging people to lie for the money; many fringe media sensationalize stories, possibly distorting the truth. Of course, the mainstream media also are commercial enterprises subject to the pressures of the marketplace (as will be addressed later in the chapter). However, these established media at the same time are subject to the pressures of tradition. Reporters at major newspapers and broadcast networks often speak of their responsibility to follow certain journalistic norms, while members of the fringe media sometimes reflect the views of a radio talk show host who asserts, "The news isn't sacred to me. It's entertainment . . . designed to revel in the agony of others."[33]

With such views, concern for the accuracy of information is not foremost. For example, when Vince Foster, deputy counsel for President Clinton, apparently committed suicide in a park, a right-wing group sent a fax to news organizations linking the suicide to the Whitewater land deal. The group passed the rumor that Foster died at an administration "safe house" and later was moved to the Washington park. Talk show host Rush Limbaugh reported the rumor. Other talk show hosts repeated it, while some added the rumor that Foster was murdered. A few financial speculators spread the rumors as a way to manipulate the stock market, and the next day newspaper business sections repeated the rumors in articles about their effect on the stock market. Thus, the rumors, through announcement and repetition by the media, came to seem true to many people—yet they remained just rumors.[34]

Relationship between the Media and Politicians

"Politicians live—and sometimes die—by the press. The press lives by politicians," according to a former presidential aide. "This relationship is at the center of our national life."[35]

Politicians and journalists need each other. Politicians need journalists in order to reach the public and to receive feedback from the public. They scan the major newspapers in the morning and the network newscasts in the evening. President Lyndon Johnson watched three network newscasts on three televisions simultaneously. Journalists need politicians in order to cover government. They seek a steady stream of fresh information to fill their news columns and newscasts. Just two days after the election of Bill Clinton, a chorus of reporters complained of a "news blackout" by the incoming administration.[36] A week later the chorus forced the president-elect to call a press conference to pacify the press corps, though he had no news yet and hardly any voice after the long campaign.[37]

The close relationship between the media and politicians is both a **symbiotic relationship,** meaning they use each other for their mutual advantage, and an **adversarial relationship,** meaning they fight each other.

Symbiotic Relationship

President Lyndon Johnson told individual reporters, "You help me and I'll help make you a big man in your profession." He gave exclusive interviews, told outrageous tales, and invited reporters to bunk overnight at his Texas ranch.[38] In return he expected favorable coverage.

Reporters get information from politicians in various ways. Some reporters are assigned to monitor **beats.** Washington beats include the White House, Congress, Supreme Court, State Department, Defense Department, and some other departments and agencies. Other reporters are assigned to cover specialized subjects, such as economics, environmental problems, and energy issues, which are addressed by several branches, departments, or agencies.

The government has press secretaries and public information officers who provide reporters with ideas and information for stories. The number of these officials is significant; in one recent year the Defense Department employed almost 1,500 people just to handle press relations.[39]

The government supplies reporters with a variety of news sources, including copies of speeches, summaries of committee meetings, news releases, and news briefings about current events. Officials also grant interviews, hold press conferences, and stage "media events." The vast majority of reporters rely on these sources rather than engage in more difficult and time-consuming investigative reporting.

Interviews show the symbiotic nature of the relationship between reporters and politicians. During the early months of the Reagan presidency, *Washington Post* writer William Greider had a series of 18 off-the-record meetings with budget director David Stockman. Greider recounted:

> Stockman and I were participating in a fairly routine transaction of Washington, a form of submerged communication which takes place regularly between selected members of the press and the highest officials of government. Our mutual motivation, despite our different interests, was crassly self-serving. It did not need to be spelled out between us. I would use him and he would use me. . . . I had established a valuable peephole on the inner policy debates of the new administration. And the young budget director had established a valuable connection with an important newspaper. I would get a jump on the unfolding strategies and decisions. He would be able to prod and influence the focus of our coverage, to communicate his views and positions under the cover of our "off the record" arrangement, to make known harsh assessments that a public official would not dare to voice in the more formal setting of a press conference, speech, or "on the record" interview.[40]

Interviews can result in **leaks**—disclosures of information some officials want to keep secret. Other officials in the administration, Congress, or bureaucracy use leaks for many reasons. Officials in the administration might leak information about a proposed policy to test the water for it, without committing themselves or their offices to it, in case intense opposition surfaces. Or they might leak to warn their president or fellow officials about the foolishness of a pending policy. Or, engaged in infighting with other officials, they might leak to make the competitors or their policies look bad. Or officials who feel slighted might leak to call attention to their ideas or to force public debates rather than closed-door decisions on issues.

Most presidents get enraged by leaks. Reagan said he was "up to my keister" in leaks, and Nixon established a "plumbers" unit to plug leaks by wiretapping aides and reporters to hear where leaks were coming from. However, despite accusations that leaks are from low-level employees in the opposite party, most are from high-ranking officials in the same party. "The ship of state," one experienced reporter noted, "is the only kind of ship that leaks mainly from the top."[41]

The pervasiveness of the media has increased tremendously. Andrew Jackson was the first president to have his photograph taken. Modern presidents must expect to have their photograph taken almost anywhere at almost any time.

During the Vietnam War, President Lyndon Johnson himself ordered an aide to leak the charge that steel companies were "profiteering" from the war. After an executive complained, Johnson assured him that the statement was inappropriate and that "if I find out some damn fool aide did it, I'll fire the sonuvabitch!"[42]

In the presidential campaign of 1988, there was much speculation about whom George Bush would choose to be his running mate. Bush's campaign manager, James Baker, leaked the fact that Senator Dan Quayle was one of the finalists. Baker saw this as a way to discourage Bush from choosing Quayle; he thought once the press published this fact, there would be so much opposition that Bush would have to select someone else. (Baker's ploy failed because the press did not take the idea seriously enough to criticize it.)[43]

After President Bush nominated Clarence Thomas to the Supreme Court, a Republican leaked the fact that Thomas had experimented with marijuana in college. The purpose was to innoculate Thomas from the greater controversy that might arise if the press discovered and revealed this fact closer to the vote on confirmation.[44] Then a Democrat, presumably, leaked the FBI report on Anita Hill's charges that Thomas sexually harassed her. The report had been secret and Hill had refused to go public before. Once the information came to light, Hill felt forced to go public, and the Senate nearly denied confirmation.

When reporters get information before other reporters, they can **scoop** them. In 1980 NBC correspondent Chris Wallace scooped his colleagues in reporting that Reagan would choose Bush as his running mate. Although Wallace was first by just seconds, this helped him win a promotion to NBC White House correspondent.[45] Usually, however, reporters are reluctant to be out front if their information is controversial. Reporters who are willing to be out front often find their editors reluctant. "There is an institutional reluctance to take on some of these stories," an investigative reporter for a national newspaper said. The editors "don't want to get too far ahead of the curve." Most journalists are more comfortable following the pack than scooping it.[46]

The interdependence between reporters and politicians can result in less news for the public. Reporters who want to continue to receive information and rub shoulders with powerful politicians may feel obligated to treat their sources favorably or at least not as skeptically as they treat others. When the Watergate burglary occurred, most newspapers dismissed it as an inconsequential "caper." With their close ties to high officials, reporters in the Washington press corps did not dig to unearth the story behind the burglary. Instead, two young reporters—Bob Woodward and Carl Bernstein—who covered local news for the *Washington Post* got the story. As one of the *Post's* editors noted, they were not part of "the Establishment"; they did not mind embarrassing administration officials.

Before the Iran-contra affair came to light, some reporters relied on Lt. Col. Oliver North for information. Although many reporters suspected that North was involved in supplying the contras with arms despite congressional restrictions on such aid, North had been a valuable source and, as one reporter remarked, "his romantic derring-do and colorful antics made him more fun to talk to than other bureaucrats."[47] Reporters did not investigate North's involvement until the story broke in an obscure Lebanese magazine. If they had been willing to sacrifice their access to him, they could have publicized the affair far sooner.

Press conferences also show the symbiotic nature of the media-politician relationship. Theodore Roosevelt, the first president who cultivated close ties to correspondents, started the **presidential press conference.**[48] He held irregular and informal sessions while being shaved. Later presidents, uncomfortable with the "cross-examination," offered few sessions and demanded questions in advance.[49] But Franklin Roosevelt realized that the press conference could help him reach the public. Newspaper publishers detested him and criticized him in editorials, but by holding frequent sessions and permitting questions on the spot he provided a steady stream of news, which editors felt obligated to publish. This news publicized his policies and his efforts to implement them.

John Kennedy saw that the press conference could help him reach the public more directly, by allowing the networks to televise it live.[50] Then editors could not filter his remarks.

Televising a press conference seems inherently contradictory. If a president wants to answer reporters, he can do so in private. If he wants to communicate with the public, he can do so in a formal speech, without risking an embarrassing question. So why would a president opt for a televised press conference? He might perform better in the less formal setting of a press conference. Or, like the youthful Kennedy, he might feel a need to demonstrate his competence to the watchful public.[51] With his intellect and wit, Kennedy expected to excel at these, and he did.

As a result, presidents and their aides transformed the conference into a carefully orchestrated media show. Now an administration schedules a conference when it wants to convey a particular message. It might even limit questions to that topic. Aides identify potential questions, and the president rehearses appropriate answers. (Former press secretaries admit that they predicted at least 90% of the questions asked and often the exact reporters who asked them.)[52] Aides prepare a seating chart, and during the conference the president calls on the reporters he wants. Although he cannot ignore those from the major media, he can call disproportionately on those he knows will lob soft questions. Consequently, the conference usually helps the president.

Beaming the conference to the nation results in less news than having a casual exchange around the president's desk, which used to reveal his thinking on programs and decisions. Appearing in millions of homes, the president cannot be as open, cannot commit himself to a policy prematurely, and cannot allow himself to make a gaffe in front of the huge audience.

Televising the conference does not even provide much accountability, because one is scheduled when the administration wants and nearly every aspect is scripted or predicted in advance. For the most part, the conference offers an illusion of accountability.

The transformation of the conference frustrates reporters and prompts them to act as prosecutors. As one press secretary observed, they play a game of "I gotcha."[53] After Clinton's first conference, one reporter criticized him because "he didn't say a single thing he didn't mean to."[54] The reporter considered the conference a game in which the press tries to best the president, and this time the press lost because it could not trick him into saying something imprudent.

Still, reporters value the conference and criticize presidents who hold sessions infrequently. Editors consider the president's remarks news, so the conference helps reporters do their job. It also gives them a chance to bask in the limelight.

Media events also show the symbiotic nature of the media-politician relationship. These events, staged for television, usually pair a photo opportunity and a speech to convey a particular impression of a politician's position on an issue.

The "photo op" frames the politician against a backdrop of things that symbolize clear values—for example, children or flags. Photo ops for economic issues often use factories, whether bustling to represent a success or abandoned to represent a failure. The backdrop is designed to be visually interesting to attract the cameras. The strategy is the same as that for advertisements of merchandise: Combine the product (the politician) with the symbols in hope that the potential buyers (voters) will link the two.[55] In the 1992 campaign, President Bush peered into the Grand Canyon to demonstrate his credentials as an environmentalist, despite his limited record; Governor Clinton appeared at a bowling alley to demonstrate his credentials as an average "Joe," despite his Yale and Oxford education.

When the United States sent troops to distribute food in Somalia in 1992, Pentagon public affairs officials notified news organizations of the landing beach and time. They intended to create a photo op to gain worldwide publicity for this humanitarian mission and national publicity for the military. They hoped to show off the marines' amphibious landing capabilities and demonstrate the military's need for its large budget even with the economy in the dumps and the former Soviet Union falling apart.[56] Officials did not foresee the ridiculous spectacle of troops hitting the beach and sneaking toward the town in camouflage fatigues—while photographers swarmed all around and spotlights lit up the night sky.

The speech in a media event is not a classical oration or even a cogent address with a beginning, middle, and end. It is an informal talk that emphasizes a few key words or phrases or sentences—almost slogans, because television editors allot time only for a short **sound bite.** And the amount of time is less and less. In 1968 the average sound bite of a presidential contender on the evening news was 42.3 seconds, but in 1988 it was just 9.8 seconds and in 1992 7.3 seconds.[57]

Speech writers plan accordingly. "A lot of writers figure out how they are going to get the part they want onto television," a former presidential aide explained. "They think of a news lead and write around it. And if the television lights don't go on as the speaker is approaching that news lead, he skips a few paragraphs and waits until they are lit to read the key part."[58] This does not result in coherent speeches, but the people watching on television will not know and the few watching in person do not matter because they are just props. More significantly, this does not result in adequate explanations for people in either group.

It is tempting to use media events to convey desirable but inaccurate impressions. When polls showed that the public thought Reagan slighted education because he cut federal money for student loans and schools, he traveled across the country to meet with teachers and students in a series of media events. Then, according to an aide, "The polls absolutely flip-flopped. He went from a negative rating to a positive rating [on education] overnight."[59] Yet he did not change his policies at all. Bush unveiled his anticrime package at a police academy, but later it was noticed that his budget proposed cutting funds for this academy.[60]

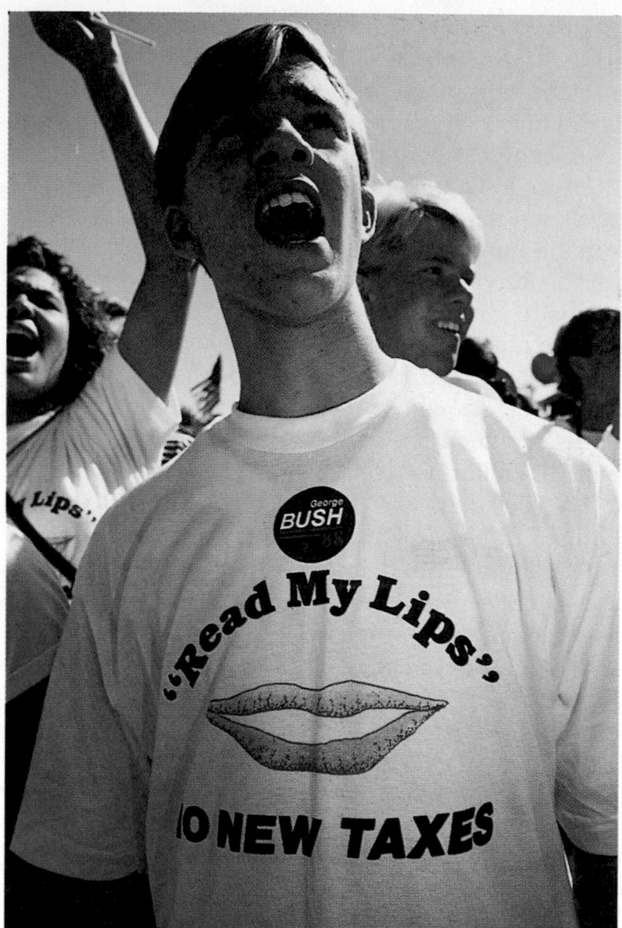

Sound bite journalism leads to sound bite politics.

Perhaps more than any other source of news, media events illustrate the reliance of politicians on television, and of television on politicians. The head of CBS News said, "I'd like just once to have the courage to go on the air and say that such and such a candidate went to six cities today to stage six media events, none of which had anything to do with governing America."[61] Yet television fosters these events, and despite occasional swipes by correspondents, networks continue to show them.

Adversarial Relationship

Although the relationship between the media and politicians is symbiotic in some ways, it is adversarial in others. Since George Washington's administration, when conflicts developed between Federalists and Jeffersonians, the media have attacked politicians and politicians have attacked the media. In John Adams's administration, Federalists passed the Sedition Act of 1798, which prohibited much criticism of the government. Federalists used the act to imprison Jeffersonian editors. Not long after, President Andrew Jackson proposed a law to allow the government to shut down "incendiary" newspapers. Even recently a former press secretary commented, "There are very few politicians who do not cherish privately the notion that there should be some regulation of the news."[62]

The conflict stems from a fundamental difference in perspectives. Politicians want the media to help them accomplish their goals, so they hope the media will pass along their messages to the public exactly as they deliver them. But journalists see themselves as servants not of the government but of the public. They question officials until the public knows enough about a matter to hold the officials accountable. According to correspondent Sam Donaldson, "My job is not to say here's the church social with the apple pie, isn't it beautiful?"[63] But some go beyond skepticism to cynicism. In the eyes of Clinton aide George Stephanopoulos, they walk in the door "assuming that something is wrong" and asking, 'What are you hiding?' "[64]

In contemporary society, information is power. The media and the government, especially the president, with the huge bureaucracy at his disposal, are the two primary sources of information. To the extent that the administration controls the flow of information, it can achieve its policy goals. To the extent that the media disseminate contradictory information, they can ensure that the administration's policy goals will be subject to public debate.

Inevitably politicians fall short of their goals, and many blame the media for their failures. They confuse the message and the messenger, like Czar Peter the Great, who, when notified that the Russian army had lost a battle in 1700, promptly ordered the messenger strangled.

When President Kennedy became upset by the *New York Times* coverage of Vietnam, he asked the paper to transfer the correspondent out of Vietnam. (The paper refused.) When President Nixon became angry with major newspapers and networks, he had Vice President Agnew lash out at them. He also ordered the Department of Justice to investigate some media companies for possible antitrust violations and the Internal Revenue Service to audit a newspaper and a reporter for possible income tax violations.

The wariness between the media and politicians has increased since the Vietnam War and Watergate scandal fueled cynicism about government's performance and officials' truthfulness. Today the media are less trusting of politicians and less trusted by them.[65]

The conflict between the media and politicians also stems from the nature of the modern media. Now there are so many media with so much space to fill that they have a voracious appetite for news. As they cover the same small circle of top officials, reporters are exposed to the same messages and the same policies day after day. Thus reporters get bored, forgetting that the public has not paid as much attention and absorbed as much information. They search for new stories and new angles on old stories. As a result, they often magnify the trivial and distort the important. This is due more to the needs of the media than any desire to conspire against officials.[66]

The rise of the fringe media exacerbates this conflict. This development means more media are seeking news and also more media are deviating from journalistic norms. Once the fringe media publicize an incident, the mainstream media tend to follow, even if the accuracy of the news is in question, because they fear losing their audience. Sometimes the mainstream media follow under the guise of addressing the political ramifications of the incident or the journalistic ethics involved in publicizing it. In this way, charges in the fringe media wind up in the mainstream media as well. Hence an increase in stories about personal shortcomings—sex, drugs, or alcohol—in politicians' lives and questions about their "character."[67]

However, it would be incorrect to think that the relationship between the media and politicians usually is adversarial. In fact, it normally is symbiotic. Although journalists like to think of themselves and try to portray themselves as adversaries who stand up to politicians, most rely upon politicians most of the time.[68]

Thus, despite the impression created by media coverage of Watergate, few journalists engage in investigative reporting. An examination of 224 incidents of criminal or unethical behavior by Reagan administration appointees found that only 13% were uncovered by reporters. Most were discovered through investigations by executive agencies or congressional committees, which then released the information to the press. Only incidents reflecting personal peccadillos of government officials, such as sexual offenses, were exposed first by reporters.[69] Even the $2 billion scandal involving influence peddling at the Department of Housing and Urban Development (HUD) went unnoticed by nearly all reporters until the department's inspector general and a congressional committee probed the payoffs. Yet HUD had been considered "a feeding trough" by Washington insiders for several years.[70]

Relationship between the Media and Recent Administrations

Franklin Roosevelt created the model that most contemporary presidents follow when interacting with the media. Newspaper publishers had no use for Roosevelt and his policies. In fact, a former correspondent recalls, "The publishers didn't just disagree with the New Deal. They hated it. And the reporters, who liked it, had to write as though they hated it, too."[71] Roosevelt saw he was not going to get favorable coverage, but he still wanted to reach the public. He used press conferences to provide a steady stream of news. This tactic enabled him to circumvent the publishers but gain access to their readers. He also used radio—a series of **fireside chats**—to advocate his policies and reassure his listeners in the throes of the Depression. He had a fine voice but, more important, a superb ability to speak informally—he commented about his family, even his dog, in a way to appeal to average people. (He drew so many listeners that he was granted as much air time as he wanted, but he was shrewd enough to realize that too much would result in overexposure.) This tactic enabled him to avoid the filters of reporters and editors and take his case directly to the people.

Reagan Administration

In his younger years, Reagan idolized FDR and developed an imitation of him that included an appropriate accent and even a cigarette holder.[72] As president, Reagan duplicated Roosevelt's success in using the media. Before Reagan lost his effectiveness during his second term, the media dubbed him the Great Communicator for his uncanny ability to communicate his broad themes.

The Reagan administration approached its relationship with the media as "political jujitsu."[73] A jujitsu fighter tries to use the adversary's force to his or her own advantage through a clever maneuver. The administration knew the media would cover the president extensively to fill their news columns and newscasts. Aide Michael Deaver explained the strategy: "The media, while they won't admit it, are not in the news business; they're in entertainment. We tried to create the most entertaining, visually attractive scene to fill that box, so that the networks would have to use it."[74]

Deaver spared no effort or expense to satisfy the demands of television and enhance the image of the president at the same time. Deaver sent advance agents days or weeks ahead of the president to prepare the "stage" for media events—the specific location, backdrops, lighting, and sound equipment. A trip to Korea was designed to show "the commander in chief on the front line against communism." The advance man went to the demilitarized zone separating North and South Korea and negotiated with the army and the Secret Service for the most photogenic setting possible. He demanded that the president be able to use the most exposed bunker, which meant that the army had to erect telephone poles and string 30,000 yards of camouflage netting from them to hide Reagan from North Korean sharpshooters. The advance man also demanded that the army build camera platforms on a hill that remained exposed but offered the most dramatic angle to film Reagan surrounded by sandbags. Although the Secret Service wanted sandbags up to Reagan's neck, the advance man insisted that they be no more than four inches above his navel so viewers would get a clear picture of the president wearing his flak jacket and demonstrating "American strength and resolve."[75]

It did not seem to matter if there was little connection between what the president was doing and what actually was happening. When U.S. planes shot down two Libyan jets, Reagan was helicoptered to the deck of an aircraft carrier—off the coast of California, not Libya—for a triumphant photo op.[76]

On a day-to-day basis, the administration planned its operations around its relationship with the media. In the morning aides met to plan public relations strategy for the day. They determined what "the line of the day"—the message—would be. They considered what questions the president would be asked and what answers he should give, and then they briefed him. Later in the day, after all his appearances, aides called each network to learn what stories about the president or his policies it was going to use on its evening newscast. If aides were not satisfied, they tried to convince the network to change its lineup. At night aides met to evaluate the success of their strategy and often called each network to praise or criticize its coverage.[77]

President Reagan, staged to reflect "American strength and resolve" in Korea.

To set the agenda, and to prevent the media from setting it, the administration tried to control the president's appearances and restrict his comments. Aides especially worried that off-the-cuff comments would reveal Reagan's limited command of the facts and details behind his policies or would result in a blooper, such as the time he said that trees cause most air pollution. To keep such comments from damaging his image or at least overshadowing his message of the day, aides provided few opportunities for reporters to ask questions. When reporters asked questions inside a building, aides frequently demanded the television lights be shut off so any answers could not be televised; outside they often ordered the helicopter's engines revved up so the questions would be drowned out. Aides scheduled few press conferences. Although conferences normally benefit presidents, they are subject to less control than media events and were considered too risky.

Paradoxically, Reagan was highly visible but not very accessible. By alternately using and avoiding the media, his administration succeeded in managing the news more than any other administration.

Bush Administration

Bush rejected some of Reagan's efforts to manipulate the media and, anyway, he lacked most of Reagan's appeal on television. So his administration deemphasized television appearances in favor of frequent press conferences and get-togethers with reporters. Occasionally he telephoned reporters to talk or jog with him. In these settings his grasp of issues came across. He tried to impress reporters and, like Roosevelt, charm them, in hope that he would receive favorable coverage. Journalists did consider Bush more accessible and open than Reagan.

For the invasion of Panama in 1989 and war with Iraq in 1991, however, the Bush administration insisted on strict control and censorship rather than accessibility and openness. When the United States invaded Panama to force General Manuel Noriega from office, reporters were delayed arriving in Panama and then delayed transmitting their dispatches back to the United States. They were prevented from seeing most battles out of fear that they would witness civilian casualties.[78] Despite later indications of many civilian casualties, we may never learn fully what happened in this operation.[79]

Because there were few negative news stories, the Pentagon and Bush administration were satisfied with the results and used a similar system when the United States fought Iraq. About 100 reporters at a time, of 800 on the scene, were escorted to locations where American troops were living or fighting. Reporters were permitted to interview soldiers only when supervised by their officers. Reporters who ventured off on their own were arrested, detained, and threatened with the loss of their credentials (as one who had the temerity to interview Saudi Arabian shopkeepers discovered).[80]

Before dispatches could be sent back to the United States, they had to be cleared by military censors. Though the stated purpose was to prevent release of information that could jeopardize the safety of U.S. troops, sometimes the apparent purpose was to prevent release of information that could put the U.S. military in a bad light. One censor blocked a story that said pilots were watching pornographic movies before bombing missions, while another changed a story that said pilots were "giddy" after a mission. (Instead, the censor described them as "proud.")[81] Yet, according to reporters, censorship was not as much of a problem as lack of access and information.

The Pentagon was most sensitive about casualties, whether American or Iraqi. Officials' concern went far beyond the possibility that television might show a dead soldier before his or her kin could be notified. They worried that pictures of dead or wounded Americans would cause the public to turn against the war. Likewise, they worried that information about injured Iraqi civilians or destroyed homes would weaken support for the war.

As a result of the administration's management of the news, television showed film of one precise bombing attack after another. Commentators lauded the "smart" bombs that were so accurate it was like having them "delivered by Federal Express." Yet after the war one official said only 7% of the bombs were "smart" bombs, and another said only 25% of the other bombs hit their targets. This means that at least 61,000 tons of bombs landed where they were not supposed to.[82]

Polls showed that most Americans approved the military's control of the news, and a majority even thought the military should have more control of the news. Only 19% thought the military was "hiding bad news from the public."[83]

Clinton Administration

Clinton emulates Roosevelt and Reagan in their use of the media. Like Reagan he tries to focus on an issue and highlight a message of the day or week to influence public opinion on that issue. Like Roosevelt, he tries to leapfrog reporters to reach citizens directly. He holds frequent press conferences and periodic question-and-answer sessions with citizens. On television, these sessions are analogous to Roosevelt's fireside chats on radio.

The administration, which considers network television too broad and too unfocused to reach the many groups that contemporary presidents must reach, uses "narrowcasting" to reach groups who have more specific concerns than the national media usually address. For example, when a commission proposed eliminating numerous military bases, press conferences and question-and-answer sessions were held with regional and local media in the three states taking the hardest hits. In Florida additional questions arose about a policy to convert defense plants to domestic factories and about policies concerning Haiti and Cuba.[84] These questions were more specific than ones typically asked by national reporters.

The give-and-take of question-and-answer sessions could be tricky for a president; questions from citizens are less predictable than those from reporters. But Clinton is knowledgeable about issues and com-

fortable when improvising. He also is articulate. As one television critic observed, "We now have a president capable of speaking in complete sentences, each one with a subject, a verb and its various clauses arranged in grammatical order. Not only that, but each sentence . . . progresses logically to the next."[85]

Unlike Roosevelt and Reagan, however, Clinton is not enthralling. He lacks discipline and, as a result, talks too long and gives too many details for most listeners. He strays from his message of the day or week and thus blurs this message. Consequently, he does not effectively communicate his proposals and programs, and many people do not really know what he stands for.

Clinton also has been hampered by a staff that has been inexperienced and incompetent in handling the White House press corps. Too often reporters' calls have gone unanswered or their interview requests have not been granted. Too often reporters' questions have received misleading or false replies. Later the staff would have to acknowledge that certain replies were "misstatements" or were "rendered inoperative," leaving the reporters more cynical than ever.

The youthfulness of the staff has contributed to these problems. At the beginning of the administration, 63 of the 450 members of the White House staff were younger than 24. (A generation gap between the young staffers and the middle-aged reporters also has created tensions. "As a father of a kid in college," one reporter admitted, "I find it somewhat off-putting to talk to male While House aides wearing earrings. It's like coming home and finding your kids got into the liquor cabinet.")[86]

Various slights, whether intended or imagined, have aggravated these problems. Upon taking office Clinton insulted the major media by giving his first interview not to a national reporter, but to the political correspondent from MTV. Other actions were considered direct challenges to the press. The administration closed a White House passageway between the staff offices and the press room. Reporters had hung out in the hallway to buttonhole aides but had clogged the hallway. The administration also revamped the White House travel office, which makes plane and hotel arragements for reporters covering the president on trips. After the administration discovered mismanagement in the office, it scaled back the VIP treatment lavished on reporters. Then reporters complained that they received cold food instead of hot food and cheap domestic champagne instead of the usual expensive imported champagne.

As a result of the administration's bumbling and dissembling and the press corps' overreacting, Clinton has received sharply negative coverage. He had no "honeymoon" from criticism, as new presidents normally have. During his first four months, according to a study of network news, 64% of all references to him were negative, compared with 41% for President Bush at the same point. Some of this coverage was due to Clinton's own missteps, but some was not. According to an analysis of three issues—national service, educational reform, and PAC reform—Clinton received much less favorable coverage than his predecessor, although he did more and fulfilled his campaign promises more fully than Bush did in the same areas.[87]

Most damaging has been the overall charge that Clinton has reneged on his commitments. Although Clinton has kept many promises—like most presidents, he has kept more than he has broken—the media have focused on the ones he has not kept and the ones he has not been able to keep.[88] The media, showing little recognition that bargaining and ultimately compromising are necessary for any president, have characterized Clinton as a "waffler" and a "compromiser." (Serious observers do ask whether Clinton has had to give in as quickly as he has in some disputes, but journalists have gone far beyond questions about tactics.) Thus, the media have reinforced the naive belief of some citizens that politicians need not and should not bargain and compromise. This impression leads to disillusionment with virtually all politicians.

Are reporters as unsophisticated as their coverage suggests? Or are they as alienated from their government and its officials as other citizens now, and as inclined to exaggerate?

Some reporters observed that their colleagues felt "they had blown it" in covering the Reagan and Bush administrations and were determined not to be conned by this administration. Thus, they have looked for manipulation or hypocrisy behind every act.[89] Some political scientists speculated that the media have compensated for favoring Clinton over Bush in the election by being harsher on Clinton in office—perhaps, subconsciously, as a way to prove their critics wrong.[90] Some political scientists speculated that the media have accelerated their normal tendency to oversimplify and overdramatize, to declare "winners" and "losers."[91] In the first weeks of the administration, mistakes led some media to herald "the beginning of the end" and compare Clinton to Carter.

For the congressional elections of 1992, Republicans campaigned against Democrats by linking them to President Clinton and by linking him to former President Carter. Both presidents, they charged, were failures. *Time* magazine reinforced the Republicans' theme by running this series of computer-generated images showing Clinton becoming Carter.

Relationship between the Media and Congress

Members of Congress also use the media but have much less impact. Since 1970 nearly all have hired his or her own full-time press secretary who churns out press releases, distributes television tapes, and arranges interviews with reporters.[92] The Senate and House of Representatives have established recording studios for members, allowed television cameras into committee rooms, and supported creation of C-SPAN. Yet members still have trouble attracting the eye of the media. One president can be the subject of the media's focus, whereas 535 members of Congress cannot. Only a handful of powerful (or, occasionally, colorful) members receive much notice from the national media. Other members get attention from their home state or district media, but those from large urban areas with numerous representatives get little publicity or scrutiny even there.[93]

Since the congressional elections of 1994, Speaker of the House Newt Gingrich (R.-Ga.) has gotten ex-

traordinary coverage, even for a leader of Congress, because he was the point man for the Republican takeover of Congress and has been the leader of the Republican agenda in Congress. With Clinton losing popularity and the next presidential election looming, other powerful Republicans in Congress also have received increased coverage.

➤Bias of the Media

Every night Walter Cronkite, former anchor for CBS Evening News, signed off, "And that's the way it is." His statement implied that the network reported the news exactly the way it happened, that the network held a huge mirror to the world and reflected an image of the world to the viewers—without any distortion. Yet the media do not hold a mirror. They hold a searchlight that seeks and illuminates some things instead of others.[94]

From all the events that occur in the world every day, the media can report only a handful as the news of the day. Even the fat *New York Times,* whose motto is "All the News That's Fit to Print," cannot include all the news. The media must decide what events are newsworthy. When the Wright brothers invited reporters to Kitty Hawk, North Carolina, to observe the first plane flight in 1903, none considered it newsworthy enough to cover. After the historic flight, only seven American newspapers reported it, and only two reported it on the front page.[95]

After the media decide what events to report, they must decide where to report them—on the front page or top of the newscast, or in a less prominent position. Then they must decide how to report them. Except for magazines, most media attempt to be "objective"; that is, they try to present facts rather than their opinions. Where the facts are in dispute, they try to present the positions of both sides. They are reluctant to evaluate these positions, although sometimes they do explain or interpret them.

In making these decisions, it would be natural for journalists' attitudes to affect their coverage. As one acknowledged, a reporter writes "from what he hears and sees and how he filters it through the lens of his own experience. No reporter is a robot."[96]

Political Bias

Historically, the press was politically biased. The party papers, which were established by political parties, parroted the party line. Even the independent papers, which succeeded them, advocated one side or the other. Publishers', editors', and reporters' attitudes seeped—sometimes flooded—into their prose. But papers gradually abandoned their ardor for editorializing and adopted the practice of objectivity to retain as many of their readers as possible.

Yet the public thinks the press is still biased. According to one survey, 41% think the press is "out to get" the groups they identify with: Executives believe the press is out to get businesses, and laborers believe it is out to get unions. Liberals believe it is biased against liberals, and conservatives believe it is biased against conservatives.[97]

Indeed, the public seems more critical today, when most media at least attempt to be objective, than in the past, when they did not even pretend they were. Then, citizens could subscribe to whichever local paper reflected their own biases (without ever recognizing that the paper reflected any biases). Now, as local newspapers have given way to national broadcast networks, and as independently owned media have shrunk and chains and conglomerates have expanded to dominate the business, the public has fewer choices and is more sensitive to perceptions of bias.

Bias for Established Institutions and Values

The media generally do reflect a bias for established institutions and values. This should not come as a surprise. Because the media are major businesses owned by large corporations, and because they need to retain their readers and viewers to make a profit, they consciously or unconsciously mirror the mainstream.

The media have a long history of bias against other ideologies, such as communism or even democratic socialism. The failures of noncapitalist economic systems are played up, the successes played down. In foreign policy matters, the U.S. government line usually is adopted. During the cold war, this meant harsh attacks on the Soviet Union and leftist Latin American countries.[98]

During the Persian Gulf War, this meant embracing the administration's goals and questioning little of its propaganda.[99] Although this was partly due to the administration's manipulation of the news, it was also partly due to the media's own bias. Even when journalists obtained contradictory information, news organizations hesitated reporting it until later.[100] The result was "a frenzy of jingoism" during the fighting.[101]

Correlated with the media's support for established institutions and values is their reliance upon government officials for their news. A study of front-page stories from the *New York Times* and *Washington Post* over two decades found that 74% were based on statements by U.S. government officials.[102] This is striking considering that these papers have far more staffers and resources to do investigative journalism than other papers. Such heavy reliance upon government officials means that the stories are likely to bear their strong imprint. Similarly, a study of ABC's "Nightline," which features news and interviews, found that 80% of the Americans interviewed on the program were from the government or corporate establishment (and 90% of these were white males). The watchdog group Fairness & Accuracy In Reporting (FAIR) found that representatives from peace, environmental, consumer, or labor groups were "hardly visible."[103]

Reporters turn to officials for news because it is easy and because, ironically, they want to avoid charges of bias. Reporters believe their peers, superiors, and the public all consider officials newsworthy. Ignoring them or downplaying them could be interpreted as showing bias against them.[104]

Bias for Particular Candidates and Policies

Most debate about media bias revolves around charges that the media exhibit a preference for particular candidates and policies over others. Conservative groups, in particular, claim that the media are biased toward liberal candidates and policies, and they have gone so far as to mount an effort to buy CBS in order to change its newscasts.

In studying media bias, social scientists have examined the characteristics and behavior of journalists. They have found that journalists are not very representative of the public. They are disproportionately college-educated white males from the upper middle class. Further, they are disproportionately urban and secular, rather than rural and religious. They are disproportionately Democrats or independents leaning to the Democrats, rather than Republicans or independents leaning to the Republicans. Likewise, they identify themselves disproportionately as liberals rather than conservatives.[105]

But journalists do differ among themselves. Those who work for the prominent, influential organizations—large newspaper, wire services, news-magazines, and radio and television networks—are more likely to be Democrats and liberals than those who work for nonprominent organizations—small newspapers and radio and television stations.[106]

Journalists in prominent organizations are more likely than the public to support the liberal position on issues. Large majorities support homosexuals' right to teach in public schools and affirmative action. They are also suspicious of big business, believing it is the sector of society that exerts the most influence but should exert much less.[107] At the same time, they support capitalism. Large majorities think businesses should be owned privately rather than publicly; businesses should be regulated less than they are; and businesses are fair to their workers. According to one study, 73% do not think that our institutions "need overhaul."[108] Thus, although these journalists are likely to be liberals, they are hardly extreme liberals or radicals.

These findings might seem to support the charge that the media are biased against conservatives, but this assumes that journalists' attitudes necessarily color what they report. Several factors mitigate the effect of journalists' attitudes. For one thing, journalists do not seem to have intense opinions. Most did not become journalists because of a commitment to political ideology but because of the opportunity to rub elbows with powerful people and be close to exciting events. "Each day brings new stories, new dramas in which journalists participate vicariously."[109] As a result, most "care more about the politics of an issue than about the issue itself,"[110] which makes them less likely to voice their views about the issue.

In addition, media organizations pressure journalists to muffle their views, partly out of a conviction that it is more professional to do so and partly out of a desire to avoid the headaches that could arise otherwise—debates among their staffers; complaints from their local radio and television affiliates; complaints from their audience; perhaps even complaints from the White House, Congress, or the Federal Communications Commission (FCC), which licenses them.

Sometimes media executives or editors pressure reporters because they have contrary views. Reporters learn not to explore certain subjects, not to ask certain questions. Reporters who pursue the stories regardless might find their copy edited, with the most critical portions deleted. The *New York Times,* despite its liberal reputation, altered reporters' stories on foreign affairs to hew more closely to administrations' conservative policies.[111] CBS toned down correspondents' stories about Reagan's economic policies.[112] Reporters who pursue the stories might find themselves transfered to another beat. One who covered El Salvador for the *New York Times* wrote a series of reports about the government's massacre of nearly a thousand peasants. The reports contradicted Reagan's assertions that the nation was making great strides in human rights. Under pressure, the *Times* pulled the reporter off this beat.[113] Ultimately, reporters who pursue the stories could find themselves fired.[114]

For all of these reasons the media do not exhibit nearly as much **political bias** as would be expected from their journalists' attitudes. Although they do show a bias for established institutions and values, they do not show much bias for particular candidates in elections.

To measure bias, researchers use a technique called "content analysis." They scrutinize newspaper and television stories to determine whether there was an unequal amount of coverage, unequal use of favorable or unfavorable statements, or unequal use of a positive or negative tone. They consider insinuating verbs ("he conceded" rather than "he said") and pejorative adjectives ("her weak response" rather than "her response"), and for television stories they evaluate the announcer's nonverbal communication—voice inflection, eye movement, and body language.

Studies of coverage of several presidential campaigns found relatively little bias. The media typically gave the two major candidates equal attention and rarely made a favorable or unfavorable statement about them or used a positive or negative tone discussing them.[115] The studies did find some bias against incumbents, front-runners, and emerging challengers.[116] For these candidates, the media apparently took their watchdog role seriously.

Overall, then, there is less bias than the public believes or the candidates feel. When candidates complain, they usually are objecting to bad news, and they probably are trying to manipulate the media. The strategy is to put reporters on the defensive so they will be tougher on the candidates' opponents in the future.

Yet the way in which the media cover campaigns can have different implications for different candidates. The media report the facts, and all the details that contribute to the facts: that one candidate is leading while the other is trailing, that one campaign is surging while the other is slipping. This coverage has positive implications for the former—swaying undecided voters, galvanizing campaign workers, and attracting financial contributions—and negative implications for the latter. Such coverage does not benefit one party over the other party in election after election, but it can benefit one party's candidate over the other party's candidate in a particular election. It helped the Democrat Carter in 1976 and the Republican Bush in 1988; it hurt the Republican Ford in 1976 and the Democrat Carter in 1980.[117] Some people, especially supporters of the losers, consider such reporting biased. Journalists, however, consider it a reflection of reality.

There were numerous accusations of bias—for Clinton and against Bush—during the 1992 election, but the media's continuing coverage of the success of Clinton's campaign and the failure of Bush's campaign accounts for most (though not all) of the tilt.[118] During the primaries, Clinton faced much negative news, but during the general election he received more positive coverage. As he climbed in the polls, his characterization by the press changed from "Slick Willie" to a dogged survivor. Meanwhile, Bush presided over a slow economy and ran a hesitant campaign, and he fell in the polls. He was portrayed as an incumbent in trouble, like "a baseball team that was favored to win the pennant but stumbled early and never regained its stride."[119]

The same reporting continues for politicians in office. The press focuses on the extent to which Clinton is "winning"—persuading fellow Democrats or the Republicans to adopt his policies, and getting the public to support him and his policies—or "losing." As Clinton the candidate benefited from these reporting conventions, Clinton the president has suffered from them.

There are two exceptions to the generalization that overt political bias in elections is minimal. First, the media usually give short shrift to third-party candidates. However, the media did pay much attention to Ross Perot's presidential bid in 1992. They took him seriously because he said he would spend $100 million on his campaign and because polls showed he could compete with Bush and Clinton.

Second, newspapers traditionally print editorials and columns that express opinions. In editorials before elections, papers often endorse candidates. Most owners are Republican, and this is one time many seek to influence the content of their papers. Since the first survey in 1932, more papers have endorsed the Republican presidential candidate, except in the election between Democratic President Lyndon Johnson and Republican Senator Barry Goldwater in 1964 and in the election between Clinton and Bush in 1992.[120]

The relative lack of bias in coverage of elections does not necessarily mean there is a lack of bias in coverage of other events. Because elections are highly visible and candidates are very sensitive about the coverage, the media might take more care to be neutral here than elsewhere. Researchers have not examined coverage of other events as much. Some think that journalists' liberal attitudes do surface. A study of coverage of nuclear energy found an evolution from slightly pro- to strongly antinuclear power during the 1970s,[121] while one of school busing found a tilt for busing during the same decade,[122] and one of abortion found a tilt toward choice in the late 1980s.[123] Yet an analysis of news about the Iranian hostage seizure and the Soviet invasion of Afghanistan, both in 1980, revealed a slight conservative bias.[124]

Bias Against All Candidates and Officials

Some critics charge that there is a general bias against all candidates and officials—a negative undercurrent in reporting about government, regardless of who or what is covered. President Nixon's first vice president, Spiro Agnew, called journalists "nattering nabobs of negativism." Critics think this bias increased after the Watergate scandal made reporters more cynical.

There seems to be considerable validity to this charge. Analyses of newspapers, magazines, and television networks show that the overwhelming majority of the stories about government are neutral.[125] However, the rest of the stories are more often negative than positive.[126] Moreover, the number of stories that are negative is increasing. (See Figure 1.)

FIGURE 1
Bad News about Presidential Candidates Increases

In presidential campaigns in the 1960s and '70s, candidates received primarily positive coverage. In the 1980s and '90s, however, they have faced more negative coverage, according to an analysis of articles in *Newsweek* and *Time*.

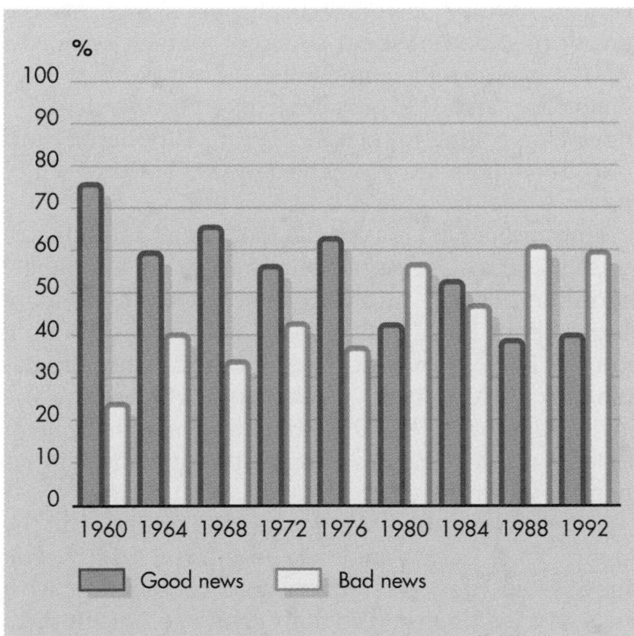

Note: Analysis is based on paragraphs that can be categorized one way or the other. It does not include statements about "the horse race."

SOURCE: Thomas E. Patterson, *Out of Order* (New York: Vintage, 1994), p. 20.

As a result, the media often convey the impression that neither the candidates are worthy of the office they seek nor the officials of the office they hold. They ultimately convey the impression that the political process itself is contemptible.[127]

Despite a tendency toward negativism, the tone appears to vary depending on the medium and the institution covered. Television is more critical than newspapers and magazines,[128] and Congress is more criticized than the president.[129] For example, after reporting that the Supreme Court gave Congress 30 days to revamp an independent regulatory commission, NBC anchor David Brinkley remarked, "It is widely believed in Washington that it would take Congress 30 days to make instant coffee."[130] The tone also appears to vary from the national media to the local media. The national media, whose reporters are better educated and more experienced in national affairs, are far more critical.

The emphasis upon the negative rather than the positive has led some researchers to conclude that newspapers and especially television foster **media malaise** among the public.[131] This is a feeling of cynicism and distrust, perhaps even despair, toward the government and its officials. Although this feeling probably originates among people who are politically unsophisticated, and therefore more easily disillusioned, researchers think this feeling eventually infects others too.

Commercial Bias

Except for public radio and television networks and stations, American media are private businesses run for a profit. They must attract readers and listeners and viewers. With an audience, they can sell advertising. The larger the audience, the higher the price they can charge for advertising. A change of 1% in the ratings of a television news program in New York City, for example, can mean a difference of $5 million in advertising for a station in a year.[132] The opportunity to make a profit is so enormous that CBS's "60 Minutes," the most watched program during some recent years, made more money in its first decade on the air than the entire Chrysler Corporation in the same decade.[133]

The need to attract an audience shapes the media's presentation of the news and leads to a **commercial bias.** Sometimes this means that the media deliberately print or broadcast what advertisers want. At the

WE'RE OUTSIDE THE HOME OF SOME PEOPLE WHO'VE JUST EXPERIENCED A GRAVE PERSONAL TRAGEDY TO BADGER AND HARASS THEM FOR THE SAKE OF A FEW RATINGS POINTS. LET'S WATCH.....
6
PIRARO.
© CHRONICLE FEATURES 1987.
10-7

Source: BIZARRO cartoon by Dan Piraro, reprinted by permission of Chronicle Features, San Francisco, California.

request of the gas company sponsoring the drama "Judgment at Nuremberg," one network bleeped the words "gas ovens" from descriptions of the Nazis' war crimes.[134] Other times the media censor themselves. When the auto industry was pressuring Congress to repeal seat belt and air bag regulations in the 1970s, the *New York Times* publisher urged the editors to present the industry position because it "would affect the advertising."[135] In articles on health numerous magazines avoided references to the dangers of smoking for fear of losing advertising from tobacco companies. *Ms.* magazine, generally attentive to women's health, even avoided references to the increased dangers of smoking during pregnancy (at a time when it still accepted advertising).[136]

Usually, though, commercial bias means that the media must print or broadcast what the public wants, and this means that the media must entertain the public. This creates a "conflict between being an honest reporter and being a member of show business," network correspondent Roger Mudd confessed, "and that conflict is with me every day."[137]

The dilemma is most marked for television. Many people who watch television news are not interested in politics; a majority, in fact, say it covers too much politics.[138] Some watch the news because they were watching another program before the news and left the television on, others because they were going to watch another program after the news and turned the television on early. Networks feel pressure "to hook them and keep them."[139]

Therefore, networks try to make the everyday world of news seem as exciting as the make-believe world they depict in their other programs. One network instructed its staff: "Every news story should, without any sacrifice of probity or responsibility, display the attributes of fiction, of drama. It should have structure and conflict, problem and denouement, rising action and falling action, a beginning, a middle and an end."[140] As one executive says, television news is "info-tainment."[141]

Although television anchors and newscasters help determine the content of their newscasts, they are not hired strictly for their journalistic experience and ability but partly for their appearance and personality. They become show business stars. To enhance their appeal, networks and stations shape their image, ordering them to change their hairstyle and even, with tinted contact lenses, their eye color. They set up clothes calendars so newscasters will rotate their outfits regularly.

Although appearance is important for both men and women newscasters, it is especially crucial for women. While viewers accept men aging on the screen, they do not seem to accept women aging. As one woman anchor commented, "The guys have got white hair, and the girls look like cheerleaders."[142] Indeed, according to one calculation, although a third of local anchors are women, only 3% are past 40; of the men 50% are past 40 and 16% are past 50.[143]

The commercial bias of the media has a number of consequences. One is emphasis on human interest stories. In 1980 UPI and CBS carried seven times more stories about President Jimmy Carter's beer-drinking brother, Billy, than about the Strategic Arms Limitation Talks (SALT) between the United States and the Soviet Union.[144] By 1990, the networks had mentioned President Bush's dog, Millie, in more stories than they mentioned three cabinet secretaries.[145]

In 1988 a pair of whales got trapped under ice in the Arctic. Their plight and rescue efforts, which took three weeks, new technology, and cooperation with the Soviet Union, received daily coverage. Yet efforts to restrict whaling, which results in the slaughter of many whales, receive less attention because they involve more complex policies and less human interest.

The emphasis on human interest also means an emphasis upon crime and sex. During the 1976 presidential campaign, Carter gave an interview to *Playboy* magazine and, in a short portion of the long interview, admitted that he had "looked on a lot of women with lust. I've committed adultery in my heart many times." The media seized upon this quotation and ignored the rest of the interview. During the 1992 presidential primaries, Clinton gave his first major speech on the economy. The same day Senator Bob Kerrey (Neb.), one of his Democratic rivals, was overheard, by a boom mike, telling a lesbian joke to an official next to him. The media focused on Kerry's joke rather than Clinton's speech.

In contrast, during the 1988 presidential campaign, Democratic candidate Michael Dukakis proposed that college graduates repay their college loans by having a percentage of their job salary withheld, so those with a lower salary would pay a lower amount. A television reporter complained that the proposal was "complicated" and "boring."[146]

The emphasis on human interest leads to another consequence of commercial bias—a **game orientation** in political reporting.[147] The underlying assumption is that politics is a game and politicians, whether candidates campaigning for election or officials performing in office, are the players. The corollary to the assumption is that the players are self-centered and self-interested. They are seeking victory for themselves and defeat for their opponents and are not concerned about the consequences of their proposals or the government's policies. Thus, through this game filter, politicians' strategies and tactics are highlighted, and new developments are presented according to how they help some players and hinder others. The substance and impact of the proposals and policies are slighted.

The game orientation appeals to journalists because it generates human interest. It offers new story lines as new information comes to light, much like a board game with "chance" cards injects unexpected scenarios and alters the players' moves and the game's outcomes. This orientation also appeals to journalists because it is easy and relatively free from charges of partisan or ideological bias. (Stories highlight which contestants are winning, not which ones should win or what consequences might result.) Analyzing policy lacks all of these advantages for journalists.

The game orientation attracts an audience, but it creates more public cynicism. The assumption that politics is a game and the corollary that the players are concerned solely with their own interests leads to the conclusion that their strategies and tactics are based mostly on manipulation and deception. Journalists, casting their wary eyes on politicians, look for manipulation and deception and interpret even sincere action in those ways.

For elections, the game orientation results in what is called "horse-race coverage," with "front-runners," "dark horses," and "also-rans." This coverage accounts for much of the total coverage of campaigns.[148] For example, in 1988 one-third of all network television stories about the presidential primaries referred to candidates' poll standings.[149] This is remarkable so early in the campaign, when most citizens know little about most candidates. It is likely that many viewers knew where the candidates were running in the race but not where they stood on the issues.

Horse-race coverage is not new and is not confined to television. An examination of presidential election coverage by metropolitan newspapers from 1888 through 1988 shows that the race was a staple of journalism long before the advent of broadcast media.[150] Yet other research suggests that the proportion of coverage focusing on the race has been increasing in recent decades. (See Figure 2.)

The emphasis upon human interest stories and horse-race aspects of an election led one observer to summarize the 1976 presidential campaign as follows:

> I saw President Ford bump his head leaving an airplane. . . . I saw Carter playing softball in Plains, Georgia. I saw Carter kissing [daughter] Amy, I saw Carter hugging [mother] Lillian. I saw Carter, in dungarees, walking hand in hand through the peanut farm with [wife] Rosalyn. I saw Carter going to church, coming out of church. . . . I saw Ford misstate the problems of Eastern Europe—and a week of people commenting about his misstatement. I saw Ford bump his head again. I saw Ford in Ohio say how glad he was to be back in Iowa. I saw marching bands and hecklers, and I learned about the size of crowds and the significance of the size of crowds. . . .
>
> But in all the hours of high anxiety that I spent watching the network news, never did I hear what the candidates had to say about the campaign issues. That was not news.[151]

Even after elections, the game orientation continues. During Reagan's first term, social programs were cut, income taxes were cut significantly, and military spending was increased sharply, but the main theme of media coverage was whether Reagan was "winning" or "losing" his battles with Congress and the bureaucracy. Similarly, during Clinton's term, the

FIGURE 2
Game Orientation in Presidential Campaigns Increases

In presidential campaigns in the 1960s, policy and leadership issues received approximately equal coverage with the strategies and tactics and the successes and failures that reflect the game orientation. In the 1970s, '80s, and '90s, however, policy and leadership issues have received a much smaller proportion of the coverage, according to an analysis of articles on the front page of the *New York Times*.

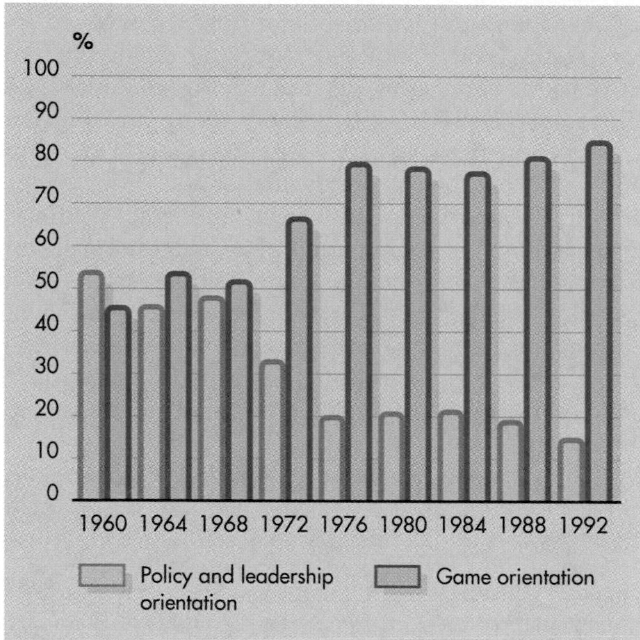

Note: Analysis is based on articles that can be categorized one way or the other. It does note include other orientations, which received about 15% of the coverage.

SOURCE: Thomas E. Patterson, *Out of Order* (New York: Vintage, 1994), p. 74.

main theme is whether Clinton has been "triumphing" or "failing" in his efforts to prod Congress to adopt his policies.

The emphasis on human interest leads to another consequence of commercial bias—an emphasis on controversy rather than agreement. Stories about conflict provide drama. Reporters, one admits, are "fight promoters" rather than consensus builders.[152] Reporters frame disputes as struggles between opposite camps. They depict attack and counterattack, using dueling sound bites from politicians and interjecting metaphors from wars. They talk about politicians who are "targets," who are "under fire," who receive "shots across their bow." They talk about politicians who engage in "search-and-destroy missions" and who "hold back no ammunition." Occasionally they refer to a "cease-fire," but eventually they return to a "war of attrition" with "do-or-die" battles. Ultimately they lament the politicians who "crashed in flames."[153]

With little awareness of a middle ground and with little attention to any nuance, the emphasis on conflict polarizes disputes and at the same time simplifies them. In the 1992 presidential campaign, Vice President Quayle included one sentence about the TV character Murphy Brown in a half-hour speech about poverty, work, and contemporary lifestyles: "It doesn't help matters when prime-time TV has Murphy Brown [who decided to become a single mother] mocking the importance of fathers, by bearing a child alone and calling it just another 'lifestyle choice.' " This sentence became the biggest story in the news for a week. People heard the reactions of representatives of the network and of producers and writers of the show, and they heard the reactions of representatives of civil rights, feminist, pro-choice, and pro-life groups. But people heard little about the main point of the speech—that the breakdown of the family had important consequences for American society.

The commercial bias of the media leads to certain consequences for television specifically. One is emphasis on events, or those parts of events, that have visual interest. The networks have people whose job is to evaluate all film for visual appeal. Producers seek the events that promise the most action; camera operators shoot the parts of the events with the most action; and editors select the portions of the film with the most action.[154] Television thus focuses on disasters, crimes, and protests far more than they actually occur, and when it covers other events, it focuses on the most exciting aspects of them. It distorts reality in order to hold the viewers' attention. In the summer of 1988, fires raged through Yellowstone National Park. Television showed a wall of flame night after night and called the park "a moonscape." As one lifeless scene followed another on the screen, NBC's Tom Brokaw intoned, "This is what's left of Yellowstone tonight." The effect, according to a journalism study, was to create the impression that our first national park was completely burned. Yet three-fourths of the park, including its famed geysers and waterfalls, was nearly unscathed. Further, fire plays a natural and necessary role in the ecosystem of the park.[155]

The emphasis on visual interest often results in coverage of the interesting surface of events over the underlying substance—the protest but not the cause.

When Iranians seized the American embassy and employees in 1980, the demonstrators discovered television's appetite for visual interest and teased it almost every night for more than a year. As the cameras arrived, they erupted with wild chants and threats, hung Jimmy Carter effigies, and shredded American flags. Yet the reasons for the seizure, rooted in Iranian problems, American policies, and superpower conflicts, were only briefly mentioned.[156]

The pressure for visual interest prompts the networks to reenact events that were not originally caught on film. In 1992 "Dateline NBC" broadcast an exposé of General Motors pickup trucks. The show accurately reported that gas tanks on older models were prone to explode upon impact, but the network did not have adequate film, so it staged two crashes.[157] Although the show said the crashes were "demonstrations," it did not admit the trucks were rigged with incendiary devices to guarantee explosions. "NBC had not had a successful magazine show in 17 tries," a veteran employee said, "and here was one that was getting respectable numbers and there was an almost frothing at the mouth to keep that going."[158] Although some journalists consider reenactments legitimate, such dramatizations do blur the line between fact and fiction and make it difficult for viewers to distinguish. And, like the Gennifer Flowers incident, they further blur the line between news shows and entertainment programs.

Another consequence of commercial bias for television is that it covers the news very briefly. In a half-hour newscast, there are only 21 minutes without commercials. In that time, the networks broadcast only about one-third as many words as the *New York Times* prints on its front page alone. Although television conveys visual impressions as well, the contrast in the amount of information these media transmit is striking.

The stories are short—about one minute each—because the time is short and because the networks think viewers' attention spans are short. Indeed, a survey found that a majority of 18- to 34-year-olds who have remote controls typically watch more than one show at once.[159] Thus, networks do not allow leaders or experts to explain their thoughts about particular events or policies. Instead, networks take sound bites to illustrate what was said. Their correspondents usually do not have enough time to explain the events or policies or to provide background information about them.

A network correspondent was asked what went through his mind when he signed off each night. "Good night, dear viewer," he said. "I only hope you read the *New York Times* in the morning."[160]

The networks have tried to expand to a full hour newscast, but local affiliates have resisted because the networks would sell commercials for the extra time and the affiliates would lose revenue they generate during this period. Regardless, there is no guarantee that a longer newscast would be a better newscast. It might be just more of the same.

When the chairman of the board of one network, in conversation with Reagan aide Michael Deaver, asked what the networks could do to provide more responsible reporting, Deaver answered, "Easy, . . . just eliminate ratings for news. You claim that news is not the same as entertainment. So why do you need ratings?" The chairman sighed, "Well, that's our big money-maker, the news."[161]

The same is true for individual stations. One financial analyst estimated that 40–50% of their profits come from news programs.[162]

Overall, commercial bias of the media results in no coverage, delayed coverage, or superficial coverage of many important stories. When members of Congress bounced checks at the House bank, one recalled, there was a "massive scramble to get the list of who bounced checks. . . . It was ya-hoo! . . . Reporters were lusting after it." But few were paying any attention to the "$400 billion worth of hot checks being written by the federal government."[163] The media considered the deficit too difficult to explain to readers and viewers. Not until Perot made it a campaign issue did most media begin to address it.

Even scandals, which might be expected to interest citizens, get limited coverage if they are complicated. When a career civil servant presented evidence of the HUD scandal in the 1980s, a *Washington Post* reporter said it was not worth looking into and a Washington television investigator said it was not "sexy" enough.[164] Although financial publications and business pages of newspapers reported the looming savings and loan scandal of the 1980s, political reporters and editors ignored it for years. They did not understand the substance and were not interested in it. A banking reporter later said, "You would relay this to your editors, but because it involved banking regulations, their eyes would glaze over."[165] The crisis was too complicated and too dull until it could be personalized and sensationalized. Finally, Charles Keating—the chair of a failed S&L and a highflier with three private jets, one with gold-plated bathroom fixtures—was linked to the scandal. Then "looted Rembrandts and party girls on yachts" were discovered, and both the media and the public took notice.[166] Yet by this time, officials estimated, the industry needed a $500 billion bailout from the taxpayers to prevent even more insolvent S&Ls from collapsing (and taking depositors' savings with them).

In sum, the commercial bias of the media, especially television, limits the quality of the news presented. This, more than any political bias, makes it difficult for citizens, particularly those who rely on television, to become well informed.

Impact of the Media on Politics

It is difficult to measure the impact of the media on politics. Different media provide different coverage and reach different though overlapping audiences. Other factors also influence people's knowledge, attitudes, and behavior toward politics. Thus, it is exceedingly difficult to isolate the impact of particular media on particular groups of people. But there is considerable agreement that the media have a substantial impact on the public agenda, political parties and elections, and public opinion.

Impact on the Public Agenda

The most important impact of the media is **setting the agenda**—influencing the process by which problems are considered important and alternative policies are proposed and debated.[167] The media publicize an issue, and people exposed to the media talk about the issue with their fellow citizens. Eventually enough consider it important and expect officials to try to resolve it.[168]

The media's impact is most noticeable for dramatic events that occur suddenly, such as the dismantling of the Berlin Wall. The impact is less noticeable for issues that evolve gradually. Watergate required months of coverage before making it on the public agenda, and AIDS required the death of actor Rock Hudson before making it.[169]

Even for issues that evolve gradually, however, cumulative coverage by the media can have an impact. In 1989 and 1990 people told pollsters that drug use was the "most important problem" facing the country. Although by this time drug use had remained flat, or even had declined slightly, the media lavished attention on it so people assumed it had increased sharply. Once the media's attention was focused on other problems, drug use, which had been cited by a majority of respondents, now was cited by less than a tenth of them. Similarly, in 1993 and 1994 people told pollsters that crime was the "most important problem." Yet the crime rate had been relatively steady (up a bit for some crimes, down a bit for other crimes). Only the amount of media coverage had changed significantly.[170] Between 1992 and 1993 the amount of time devoted to crime on network newscasts had increased 100%.[171]

The impact usually is greatest for stories that appear on the front page of the newspaper or top of the newscast rather than those buried in the back or at the end.[172] Many people who do not follow the news fully check the beginning of the newspaper or newscast for the "important" stories. Without being aware of it, they are accepting the media's role in identifying these stories as the important ones.

And the media's impact usually is greatest on people who are most interested in politics, because they are most likely to follow the news and discuss it with others.[173] Yet the impact varies according to the personal experiences of the audience. For instance, people with recent unemployment in their family will be more sensitive to news about unemployment than other people.

In shaping the agenda, the most prominent print organizations normally are the most powerful. The *New York Times* is preeminent for international politics, the *Washington Post* for domestic politics, and the specialized *Wall Street Journal* for economic matters. The AP wire service is influential, and *Newsweek* and *Time* magazines are also. Other media take their cues from these organizations. Even the television networks get most of their stories from these print media.[174]

However, in recent years radio and television call-in shows set the agenda for some issues. In the 1992 presidential campaign, tabloid newspapers and non-news television programs set the agenda for Clinton's sexual affairs.

For years the major media "controlled the gates through which news passed. If they didn't report it, by and large the rest of us didn't hear about it."[175] But now the mainstream media have no monopoly, the fringe media also can open the gates for some issues.

The media's power to influence the agenda has important implications. The media play a key role in deciding which problems government addresses and which it ignores. They also play a key role in increasing or decreasing politicians' ability to govern and to get reelected. By publicizing some issues, the media create a golden opportunity for politicians with the authority and ability to resolve these issues. At the same time, the media create a pitfall for those who lack the power to resolve these issues. Thus, the Iranian seizure of the American embassy and hostages became the prominent issue in the country in 1980. Every night CBS's Walter Cronkite signed off, "And that's the way it is, the ______ day of American hostages in captivity," as if anyone needed reminding. President Carter's lack of success in persuading Iranian officials to release the hostages or in directing an American invasion to rescue them cost him dearly in his reelection bid that year.

Yet the role of the media in shaping the agenda should not be overstated. Individuals' knowledge and experience lead them to consider some things unimportant even when the media do cover them. And, of course, individuals' interests prompt the media to cover some things in the first place.[176]

Moreover, politicians play an important role in shaping the agenda. For much legislation, such as bills to improve safety in automobiles, workplaces, and coal mines, Congress initiates action and then the media publicize it.[177] For presidential elections, candidates usually establish the agenda of policy issues. By emphasizing issues they think will resonate with the public and reflect favorably on themselves, candidates pressure the media to cover these rather than other issues that might not rebound to their credit. On the other hand, the media usually establish the agenda of nonpolicy issues, involving the candidates' personality and behavior.[178] The media are able to set the agenda for nonpolicy issues because these are more likely to catch the public's fancy.

Impact on Political Parties and Elections

The media have had an important impact on political parties and elections. In particular they have furthered the decline of parties, encouraged new types of candidates, and influenced nominations and elections.

Political Parties

Political parties have declined in power on the national level in large part because of the influence of the media. In the young republic, political parties created and controlled most newspapers. Naturally, the papers echoed the parties' views and the journalists bowed to the parties' leaders. The editor of one Democratic Party paper made sure a pail of fresh milk was left on the White House doorstep for President Andrew Jackson every morning, even if the editor had to deliver it himself.[179] People received much of their political information, however biased, from these papers.

When independent newspapers arose as profit-making businesses, the party papers declined and then disappeared. Eventually, people came to receive most of their political information from independent newspapers, magazines, radio stations, and television stations. Thus, people are no longer dependent upon parties for their political information.

In other ways as well, the media, especially television, have contributed to the decline of parties. In place of selection by party bosses, television allows candidates to appeal directly to the people. If candidates succeed in the primaries, parties have little choice but to nominate them. In place of campaign management by party bosses, television requires new expertise, so candidates assemble their own campaign organization. Television advertising requires substantial amounts of money, so party funds are inadequate and candidates approach other donors. Television also gives voters information so they can make up their own minds about how to vote, rather than rely on the party organization to tell them. Thus, the media have supplanted parties as the principal link between people and their leaders.

Types of Candidates

Television has encouraged new types of candidates for national offices. No longer need candidates be experienced politicians who worked their way up over many years. Celebrities from other fields with name recognition can move into prominent positions even without political experience. It is not coincidental that in recent years the House has had an actor (Fred Grandy, R-Ia.—"Gopher" on "Love Boat"), a professional baseball pitcher (Jim Bunning, R-Ky.), a professional football quarterback (Jack Kemp, R-N.Y.), and a professional basketball player (Tom McMillen, D-Md.) and the Senate has had a professional basketball player (Bill Bradley, D-N.J.) and two astronauts (John Glenn, D-Oh., and Harrison Schmitt, R-N.M.).[180] Nor is it coincidental that the Senate has had a television commentator (Jesse Helms, R-N.C.) and a businessman who appeared in his company's commercials (Rudy Boschwitz, R-Minn.). Alternatively, unknowns with talent can achieve rapid name recognition and move into prominent positions. Jimmy Carter, who had served one term as governor of Georgia, was relatively unknown elsewhere in the country when he ran for the Democratic nomination for president in 1976. People kept asking "Jimmy who?" But through effective use of television, he won enough primaries so the party had to nominate him, even though the leaders were uncomfortable with him.

At the same time that television has allowed newcomers to run, it also has imposed new requirements on candidates for national office. They must demonstrate an appealing appearance and performance on camera; they must be telegenic. President Franklin Roosevelt's body, crippled from polio and often on crutches or in a wheelchair, would not be impressive on television. President Harry Truman's style—"Give 'em hell"—would not be impressive on television either. Although effective in whistlestop speeches, it would be too "hot," too intense, to come into people's homes every day. A "cool," low-key style is more effective.

President Reagan was the quintessential politician for the television age. He was tall and trim with a handsome face and a smooth, reassuring voice. As a former actor he could project his personality and convictions and deliver his lines and jokes better than any other politician. It is not an exaggeration to conclude, as one political scientist did, "Without a chance to display his infectious smile, his grandfatherly demeanor, and his 'nice guy' qualities to millions of Americans, Ronald Reagan, burdened by his image as a superannuated, intellectually lightweight movie actor with right-wing friends and ultraconservative leanings, might never have reached the presidency."[181]

Television has not created the public desire for politicians with an appealing personality. "When candidates shook hands firmly, kissed babies, and handed out cigars, the thrust was not on issues."[182] Yet television has exacerbated this emphasis on the right image.

Washington, Jefferson, and Lincoln in the Media Age

How would three of America's greatest presidents have fared in the media age? George Washington cut an impressive figure, but he had a speech impediment.

Thomas Jefferson was tall—six feet, two inches, when the average American man was about five feet, five inches—but he was shy, even awkward, with people. And apparently he never made a political speech.

Abraham Lincoln was also tall, but he was gangly. According to contemporaries, he was homely in different ways at different times. One newspaper called him "the ugliest man in the Union."[1] He had a "ploughed" face and a "doughnut" complexion, protruding ears, and "spider" legs.[2] He also had a high-pitched voice.

A modern observer speculated how television would cover the Gettysburg Address, which, though brief, would not be brief enough: The cameras would focus on the network correspondent describing the scene and recalling the battle, while in the background Lincoln would be speaking. Finally, the cameras would focus on Lincoln concluding, "government of the people, by the people, for the people, shall not perish from the earth."[3]

Are there contemporary Washingtons, Jeffersons, and Lincolns who might make effective leaders but who would not qualify because they are ineffective on television?

1. Thomas E. Patterson, *Out of Order* (New York: Vintage, 1994), p. 9.
2. Marcus Cunliffe, "What Did Abraham Lincoln Look Like?" *Washington Post National Weekly Edition*, February 27, 1984, p. 35.
3. Thomas Griffith, "Always Articulate on Sunday," *Time*, June 6, 1983, p. 55.

Nominations and Elections

Through their news and commentary and candidates' advertisements, the media shape voters' opinions and affect elections' outcomes. We have already seen that the media help set the campaign agenda. They influence the topics voters believe are important and the weight voters give these topics when they cast their ballots. In addition, the media inform and persuade.

INFORMATION The media provide information about the candidates and the issues.[183] Information about the candidates can have a major impact especially at the nomination stage. In presidential elections, a party without an incumbent president running for reelection might field a dozen candidates. The media cannot cover all adequately, so they narrow the field by considering some "serious" and giving them more coverage. Once the primaries begin, they label some "winners" and others "losers," and they give the "winners" more coverage. In the Democratic race in 1976, Carter finished second to "uncommitted" in the Iowa caucuses. This was enough to give him 23 times more coverage in *Time* and *Newsweek*, and 5 times more coverage on network television, than any of his rivals. Finishing first by just

4% in the New Hampshire primary landed him on the covers of *Time* and *Newsweek* and brought him 25 times more coverage on network television than the runner-up.[184] In the Democratic race in 1992, even before a single primary, the press proclaimed Clinton the front-runner and several magazines put his picture on their cover, although half of the public did not know who he was.[185]

By making these judgments, the media strongly influence the election process at this stage.[186] Because few people have formed opinions about the candidates this early, they are open to impressions from the media. Therefore, when the media declare some candidates winners, they help create a bandwagon effect.[187] When they declare others losers, they make it hard for these candidates to attract contributors and volunteers and eventually supporters in the next primaries.

Information about the issues can have an impact also. In 1988 voters' awareness of Bush's and Dukakis's issue positions increased during the campaign. Those who read newspapers increased their awareness more than those who watched television, but even the latter gained information.[188]

DIRECT PERSUASION The media also can persuade voters directly. This can be seen in several ways.

Televised debates do not sway most viewers because people tend to engage in **selective perception,** which is a tendency to screen out information that contradicts their beliefs. Consequently, most people conclude that their candidate performed better.[189] However, the debates do sway some viewers, usually those who have moderate education and some interest in politics but who are not decided or, if decided, not strongly committed to one candidate. In 1960 the debates might have caused enough voters to cast their ballots for Kennedy that he won the election.[190]

Media commentary about the debates also sways some viewers. In 1976 Ford erroneously said there was "no Soviet domination of Eastern Europe." People surveyed within 12 hours after the debate said they thought Ford won. But the media zeroed in on this slip, and people surveyed later said they thought Carter won (see Table 1). In the first debate in 1984, Reagan appeared tired and confused. By a modest margin, people polled immediately after the debate said Mondale won. But the media focused on Reagan's abilities and age and, by increasingly large margins, people polled in the days after the debate said Mondale won.

Perhaps viewers did not catch Ford's statement or, due to selective perception, notice Reagan's doddering, but the media called attention to them, which prompted many viewers to reconsider and reverse their verdict.

Newspaper endorsements also sway some readers. Many newspapers endorse candidates before elections. Most people do not read editorials, and those who do read them tend to follow politics and make up their mind on the basis of numerous sources of information. Yet even if endorsements sway only a small percentage of voters, this percentage might be enough to determine the outcome of tight races.[191] Endorsements are thought to have little effect on well-publicized races, although one study of the 1964 presidential election concluded that endorsements of President Johnson by monopoly newspapers in 223 counties across the North added about 5% to the vote

TABLE 1 Media Commentary Influenced Perceptions of 1976 Debates

CANDIDATE VIEWERS FELT WON DEBATE	VIEWERS INTERVIEWED WITHIN 12 HOURS AFTER DEBATE	VIEWERS INTERVIEWED FROM 12 HOURS TO 48 HOURS AFTER DEBATE
Ford	53%	29%
Carter	35	58
Undecided	12	13

According to a study of people in Erie, Pennsylvania, and Los Angeles, media commentary on Ford's gaffe caused many to change their minds about which candidate won the debate. A majority of those interviewed before the commentary sunk in thought Ford won, whereas a majority of those interviewed later thought Carter won.

SOURCE: Thomas E. Patterson. *The Mass Media Election* (New York: Praeger, 1980), p. 123.

he would have received in these counties otherwise.[192] Endorsements probably have more effect on relatively unpublicized races, such as for state legislator or local tax assessor, because voters have little other information to guide them. Endorsements apparently have most influence on voters with a ninth- through twelfth-grade education. Voters with less education are less likely to read editorials, while those with more education have more clearly defined ideologies to guide their decisions.[193]

Impact on Public Opinion

Social scientists long thought that the media influenced the things people thought about but not the opinions they held about these things. Some contemporary research, however, demonstrates that the media do have a substantial impact on public opinion. A comparison of the networks' newscasts with the public's policy preferences in a wide variety of foreign and domestic issues for 15 years during the 1970s and 1980s shows that the media influence opinion about issues.[194] Other research shows that the media influence opinion about particular presidents.[195] They affect opinion indirectly—by providing the news and transmitting the views of various opinion leaders—as well as directly—through editorials and commentaries intended to sway opinion.

Conclusion: Are the Media Responsive?

The media have to be responsive to the people to make a profit. They present the news they think the people want. Because they believe the majority desire entertainment, or at least diversion, rather than education, they structure the news toward this end. According to a number of studies, they correctly assess their consumers.[196] For the majority who want entertainment, network television provides it. For the minority who want education, the better newspapers and magazines provide it. Public radio, with its hour-and-a-half nightly newscast, and public television, with its hour nightly newscast, also provide quality coverage. The media offer something for everyone.

When officials or citizens get upset with the media, they pointedly ask, "Who elected you?" Journalists reply that the people—their readers or listeners or viewers—"elected them" by paying attention to their news columns or newscasts.

To say the media are responsive, however, is not to say they perform well. Giving the people what they want most is not necessarily serving the country best. As one reporter lamented, "People seem to 'know' everything now—hearing the same news bulletins repeated around the clock—but they seem to understand precious little of what's really going on."[197] The media personalize and dramatize the news. The result is to simplify the news. Superficial coverage of complex events leaves the public unable to understand these events and, ultimately, unable to force the government to be responsive.

The media reflect a *crisis du jour* mentality in which everything is important but ultimately nothing is important. Almost any political development is important for a day or a week or occasionally a month. But almost no political development is important for long. So the media lurch from a supposed crisis to a real crisis, and back again. In the Clinton years, for example, the media have flitted from the caning of a teenager in Singapore to the making of nuclear weap-

ons in North Korea; from a civil war in the former Yugoslavia to the appropriate commemoration for the fiftieth anniversary of the end of World War II with Japan; from the president's haircut in an airplane, which cost $200, to his first budget bill, which reduced the deficit; from the Clintons' possible corruption in the Whitewater land deal to the effort by a friend of the Clintons to get a White House job in the "Travelgate scandal"; from the secrecy of the health care task force to the substance of health care reform; from the denial of a presidential appointment for Zoe Baird because she hired illegal aliens to the denial of a presidential appointment for Kimba Wood because—well, somebody must remember; it was considered important. The headlines and the stories clamoring for attention go by in such a blur that after awhile they all become a jumble for many people. They leave no sense of what's actually a crisis, what's just a problem, what's merely an irritant, and what's truly trivial.[198]

Thus, most news coverage is episodic—an event is presented as a single, idiosyncratic occurrence—rather than thematic—the event is presented as an example or reflection of a larger pattern. For instance, a story might focus on one hungry person or group of persons rather than on malnutrition as a national problem. Episodic coverage is more common because it is more entertaining—dramatic, with human interest—than thematic coverage. But episodic coverage makes it hard for people to see the connection between problems in society and the actions of government and its officials. Then people do not hold their leaders accountable for addressing or resolving the problems.[199]

Moreover, by bombarding the public with instances of conflict and disagreement, without much coverage on constructive compromises that sometimes flow from that disagreement, and by portraying lobbying and interest groups as evil rather than one way the public is represented, the media contribute to the public's distaste for democratic processes.

The media's shortcomings are aggravated by a declining interest in politics and a decreasing number of people who read newspapers or, to a lesser extent, watch newscasts. Although the public is better educated now than in the 1960s, it is less likely to follow the news and less able to answer questions about the government.[200] People under 35 especially reflect these trends. To keep these vanishing readers, many newspapers have revamped their formats. While some have improved their quality, more have emulated *USA Today* and reduced their substance to hold the attention spans of younger readers weaned on television. This has disturbing implications. Citizens who are not aware of the news or who do not understand it cannot fulfill their role in a democracy.

These trends come at a time when the media, despite their shortcomings, provide more news than ever and—with journalists better educated and better able to address complex topics—more effective news than ever. Because the media are somewhat responsive and effective, they have become powerful enough to serve as a check on government in many situations. This was evident during the major crises of recent decades. During the war in Vietnam, the media stood up to two presidents when Congress and the courts were relatively passive. During the Watergate scandal, the media led Congress and the courts in standing up to a president. The media serve as a check on the government in countless other situations. As a former government official noted, "Think how much chicanery dies on the drawing board when someone says, 'We'd better not do that; what if the press finds out?' "[201]

EPILOGUE

Signorile Revealed Official's Homosexuality

Michelangelo Signorile decided to publish information revealing that the assistant secretary of defense, Pete Williams, was homosexual.[202] Initially the mainstream media refused to report the story. Most reporters on the Pentagon beat did not ask questions about the revelation or write articles about it. Most editors spiked the articles that reporters did write. Eventually one reporter asked Williams directly. He refused to answer: "As a government spokesman, I stand here and I talk about government policy. I am not paid to discuss my personal opinions about that policy or talk about my personal life, and I don't intend to."[203] In subsequent weeks some mainstream newspapers and magazines decided to cover the story and name the official after all.

The brouhaha put the military's policy of discharging homosexuals on the agenda for the 1992 election.

Candidate Bill Clinton criticized the hypocrisy of the situation and promised to change the policy. After Clinton's election, Williams, a political appointee of the Bush administration, left government for the private sector.

"Outing," as the practice of identifying gays and lesbians who remain in "the closet" came to be called, spread. While some activists engaged in outing through their writing, others sent faxes across the country, nailed posters to telephone poles, and confronted persons in public. Supermarket tabloids, always alert for sensational stories, engaged in outing of actors. Unlike the gay activists, these papers were motivated by the desire to boost circulation and increase profits.

Many homosexuals felt threatened by the spread of outing. Signorile remembers, "I was called every name in the book and fended off angry people everywhere I went."[204] Many heterosexuals who felt that the media already were too intrusive into private lives also criticized the practice. One political scientist called it "a despicable new movement."[205]

Signorile acknowledges the media might be too intrusive, but he says if the media cover the private lives of heterosexuals they legitimately can cover the private lives of homosexuals. "Journalists," he adds, "are not in the business of providing comfort or making people feel better. They're in the business of telling the truth, whatever it is, whenever it is pertinent to a story."[206]

But when is a person's homosexuality "pertinent to a story"? Signorile would limit outing to public figures—famous persons who make lots of money from the public or wield considerable power over the public—and to situations that reflect hypocrisy, such as persons in government or the media who act contrary to the interests of homosexuals. Signorile admits these criteria are fuzzy and decisions need to be made on a case-by-case basis.

And he admits he is uneasy about some of what has happened. "I can't say I felt great about all this. It wasn't the outing I had a problem with, but the fact that I was using it as a bludgeoning and blackmailing tool. That wasn't what I originally had in mind. But as has been true in every revolution, there is always a person or group who kicks things off by doing something brutal. . . . We were under siege at the time, and I was operating with a siege mentality."[207]

His goal in outing is "to give courage to millions of gay people who stay in the closet out of fear and shame."[208] He especially wants to show gay teenagers, who are left "feeling alone, like freaks" and who experience more depression and suicide than straight teenagers, that there are gay adults who have made it—like Eddie Murphy and Oprah Winfrey show black kids.[209]

With these words, Signorile indicates that he might be more an activist than a journalist. But in these times, when anyone with a fax machine or an Internet account can be a "journalist," the ethics of reporting have become more blurred.

➤Key Terms

symbiotic relationship	sound bite
adversarial relationship	fireside chats
beats	political bias
leaks	media malaise
scoop	commercial bias
presidential press conference	game orientation
media events	setting the agenda
	selective perception

➤Further Reading

The print media themselves are the primary sources for further reading. A good metropolitan newspaper or a weekly newsmagazine is essential. For political junkies, the *Washington Post National Weekly Edition,* a compilation of the newspaper's best articles and cartoons about politics during the week, is wonderful.

Timothy Crouse, *The Boys on the Bus* (New York: Random House, 1972). *An irreverent account of press coverage of elections by a writer who reported on the reporters rather than on the candidates along the presidential campaign trail in 1972.*

Mark Hertsgaard, *On Bended Knee* (New York: Farrar, Straus & Giroux, 1988). *An indictment of media coverage of the Reagan presidency. The author's thesis is that Reagan turned news hounds into lap dogs.*

Kathleen Hall Jamieson and David S. Birdsell, *Presidential Debates* (New York: Oxford University Press, 1988). *A history of presidential debates and a set of proposals for their reform.*

John R. MacArthur, *Second Front: Censorship and Propaganda in the Gulf War* (Hill and Wang, 1992). *A searing critique of media coverage of the war.*

Joe McGinniss, *The Selling of the President 1968* (New York: Simon & Schuster, 1969). *An account of the often-comical efforts by Richard Nixon's advisers to transform him into a media candidate.*

Nan Robertson, *The Girls in the Balcony: Women, Men, and the* New York Times (Random House, 1992). A history of piggery at the country's most famous newspaper.

Tom Rosenstiel, *Strange Bedfellows: How Television and the Presidential Candidates Changed American Politics, 1992* (New York: Hyperion, 1993). A critical examination of media coverage of the 1992 campaign.

➤Notes

1. Michelangelo Signorile, *Queer in America: Sex, the Media, and the Closets of Power* (New York: Random House, 1993), p. 78.
2. Larry J. Sabato, *Feeding Frenzy: How Attack Journalism Has Transformed American Politics* (New York: Free Press, 1991), pp. 192–93.
3. Signorile, *Queer in America,* p. 138.
4. Ibid., p. 148.
5. Sabato, *Feeding Frenzy,* pp. 1, 8–22.
6. James David Barber, *The Pulse of Politics* (New York: W. W. Norton, 1980), p. 9.
7. Kevin Phillips, "A Matter of Privilege," *Harpers,* January 1977, pp. 95–97.
8. Richard Harwood, "So Many Media, So Little Time," *Washington Post National Weekly Edition,* September 7–13, 1992, p. 28.
9. Thomas R. Dye and L. Hannon Zeigler, *American Politics in the Media Age* (Monterey, Calif.: Brooks/Cole Publishing, 1983), pp. 123–24.
10. Edwin Diamond, *The Tin Kazoo* (Cambridge, Mass.: MIT Press, 1975), p. 13.
11. Doris A. Graber, *Mass Media and American Politics* (Washington, D.C.: Congressional Quarterly, 1980), p. 2.
12. William Lutz, *Doublespeak* (New York: Harper & Row, 1989), pp. 73–74.
13. Richard Harwood, "Nobody Reads Anymore," *Washington Post National Weekly Edition,* December 26, 1988–January 1, 1989, p. 29.
14. Sabato, *Feeding Frenzy,* p. 50.
15. Thomas E. Patterson, *The Mass Media Election* (New York: Praeger, 1980), pp. 58–60, 62–63.
16. Timothy E. Cook, *Making Laws and Making News: Media Strategies in the U.S. House of Representatives* (Washington, D.C.: Brookings Institution, 1989), p. 19.
17. J. Fred MacDonald, *One Nation Under Television: The Rise and Decline of Network TV* (New York: Pantheon, 1991); Lichter et al., *The Media Elite,* pp. 5–7.
18. Otto Friedrich, "Edging the Government Out of TV," *Time,* August 17, 1987, p. 58; Edmund L. Andrews, "A New Tune for Radio: Hard Times," *New York Times,* March 1992.
19. Benjamin M. Compaine, *Who Owns the Media?* (White Plains, N.Y.: Knowledge Industry Publications, 1979) pp. 11, 76–77.
20. Alex S. Jones, "At Many Papers, Competition is at Best an Illusion," *New York Times,* September 22, 1991.
21. Michael Parenti, *Inventing Reality* (New York: St. Martin's, 1986), p. 27.
22. Paul Farhi, "You Can't Tell a Book by Its Cover," *Washington Post National Weekly Edition,* December 5–11, 1988, p. 21.
23. Andrews, "A New Tune for Radio."
24. Harwood, "So Many Media, So Little Time."
25. Elizabeth Kolbert, "For Talk Shows, Less News is Good News," *New York Times,* June 28, 1992, p. E-2.
26. Carol Matlack, "Target Television," *National Journal,* February 1, 1992, p. 263.
27. Judith Miller, "But Can You Dance to It?" *New York Times Magazine,* October 11, 1992, p. 33.
28. Howard Fineman, "The Power of Talk," *Time,* February 8, 1993, p. 25.
29. "The Vocal Minority in American Politics," Times Mirror Center for the People and the Press, Washington, D.C., July, 1993.
30. Richard Corliss, "Look Who's Talking," *Time,* January 23, 1995, p. 23.
31. William A. Henry III, "Handling the Clinton Affair," *Time,* February 10, 1992, p. 28.
32. Richard Harwood, "The Growing Irrelevance of Journalists," *Washington Post National Weekly Edition,* November 2–8, 1992, p. 29.
33. Corliss, "Look Who's Talking," p. 25.
34. Tom Rosenstiel, *The Beat Goes On: President Clinton's First Year with the Media* (New York: Twentieth Century Fund, 1994), p. 35.
35. Dom Bonafede, "Press Paying More Heed to Substance in Covering 1984 Presidential Election," *National Journal,* October 13, 1984, p. 1923.
36. "All Things Considered," National Public Radio, November 5, 1992.
37. "Comment: Take Five," *New Yorker,* November 23, 1992, p. 4.
38. Thomas M. DeFrank, "Playing the Media Game," *Newsweek,* April 17, 1989, p. 21.
39. Charles Peters, "How Washington Really Works (Redding, Mass.: Addison-Wesley Publishing, 1980), p. 18.
40. William Greider, "Reporters and Their Sources," *Washington Monthly* (October 1982), pp. 13–15.
41. Daniel Schorr, "A Fact of Political Life," *Washington Post National Weekly Edition,* October 28–November 3, 1991, p. 32.
42. Howard Kurtz, "How Sources and Reporters Play the Game of Leaks," *Washington Post National Weekly Edition,* March 15–21, 1993, p. 25.
43. Elizabeth Drew, "Letter from Washington," *New Yorker,* September 12, 1988, p. 92.
44. Ann Devroy, "The Republicans, It Turns Out, Are a Veritable Fount of Leaks," *Washington Post National Weekly Edition,* November 18–24, 1991, p. 23.
45. William A. Henry III, "Scrounging for Good Air," *Time,* September 3, 1984, p. 7.
46. Christopher Georges, "Confessions of an Investigative Reporter," *Washington Monthly,* March, 1992, p. 41; Timothy Crouse, *The Boys on the Bus* (New York: Random House, 1972).
47. Jonathan Alter, "When Sources Get Immunity," *Newsweek,* January 19, 1987, p. 54.
48. Samuel Kernell, *Going Public: New Strategies of Presidential Leadership* (Washington, D.C.: Congressional Quarterly, 1986), p. 59.
49. Woodrow Wilson also tried to cultivate correspondents and host frequent sessions, but he did not have the knack for this activity and he scaled back the sessions. Kernell, *Going Public,* pp. 60–61. He did perceive that "[s]ome men of brilliant ability were in the group, but I soon discovered that the interest of the majority was in the personal and the trivial rather than in principles and policies." James Bennet, "The Flack Pack," *Washington Monthly,* November 1991, p. 27.

50. Dwight Eisenhower actually was the first president who let the networks televise his press conferences, but he did not do so to reach the public. When he wanted to reach the public, he made a formal speech. The networks found his conferences so untelegenic that they stopped covering the entire session each time. Kernell, *Going Public,* p. 68.

51. Kernell, *Going Public,* p. 104.

52. Bennet, "The Flack Pack," p. 19.

53. Dom Bonafede, " 'Mr. President,' " *National Journal,* October 29, 1988, p. 2756.

54. Garry Wills, "... But Don't Treat It as a Game," *Lincoln Journal* (Universal Press Syndicate), March 26, 1993.

55. Charles Hagen, "The Photo Op: Making Icons or Playing Politics?" *New York Times,* February 9, 1992, p. H28.

56. "Media Lights' Glare Inhibits Maneuvers," *Lincoln Journal* (AP), December 9, 1992; Jonathan Alter, "Did the Press Push Us into Somalia?" *Newsweek,* December 21, 1992, p. 33.

57. Kiku Adatto, cited in Howard Kurtz, "Networks Adapt to Changed Campaign Role," *Washington Post,* June 21, 1992, p. A19.

58. Lance Morrow, "Time Essay," *Time,* August 18, 1980, p. 78.

59. Steven R. Weisman, "The President and the Press," *New York Times Magazine,* October 14, 1984, p. 71.

60. Ronald H. Brown, "Republican Baloney About Crime," *Washington Post National Weekly Edition,* April 30–May 6, 1990, p. 29.

61. David Halberstam, "How Television Failed the American Voter," *Parade,* January 11, 1981, p. 8.

62. George E. Reedy, *The Twilight of the Presidency* (New York: New American Library, 1970), p. 112.

63. Thomas Griffith, "Winging It on Television," *Time,* March 14, 1983, p. 71.

64. "Talking about the Media Circus," *New York Times Magazines,* June 26, 1994, p. 63.

65. Sabato, *Feeding Frenzy.*

66. Sabato, *Feeding Frenzy,* p. 53.

67. See Sabato, *Feeding Frenzy,* for additional reasons for this increase.

68. W. Lance Bennett, *News: The Politics of Illusion,* 2nd ed. (New York: Longman, 1988).

69. John David Rausch, Jr., "The Pathology of Politics: Government, Press, and Scandal," *Extensions* (University of Oklahoma), Fall 1990, pp. 11–12.

70. Michael Riley, "Where Were the Media on HUD?" *Time,* July 24, 1989, p. 48.

71. William Rivers, "The Correspondents after 25 Years," *Columbia Journalism Review* 1 (Spring 1962), p. 5.

72. James David Barber, *Presidential Character* (Englewood Cliffs, N.J.: Prentice Hall, 1992), p. 238.

73. Hedrick Smith, *The Power Game* (New York: Random House, 1988), p. 403.

74. Timothy J. Russert, "For '92, the Networks Have to Do Better," *New York Times,* March 4, 1990.

75. Smith, *Power Game,* p. 420.

76. Adam Hochschild, "All the President's Patsies," *Mother Jones,* July/August 1988, p. 52.

77. Weisman, "The President and the Press," pp. 71–72; Dick Kirschten, "Communications Reshuffling Intended to Help Reagan Do What He Does Best," *National Journal,* January 28, 1984, p. 154.

78. When Reagan ordered the invasion of Grenada in 1983, the administration excluded reporters. For two days the only news that reached the public came from the administration, and it was uniformly positive about both the need for and the success of the invasion. However, in response to criticism from the media, the Pentagon established a pool system for future wars. Representative groups of reporters would be allowed to cover the action and share their information with other media. The military could transport and protect a few pools more easily than a huge number of individual reporters. But what the Pentagon did not admit was that the military, while appearing to cooperate, could control reporters' access to battles, individuals, and other sources of information more easily as well.

79. Patrick J. Sloyan, "The War the Administration Isn't Going to Let You See," *Washington Post National Weekly Edition,* January 21–27, 1991, p. 23; Vicki Kemper and Deborah Baldwin, "War Stories," *Common Cause,* March/April 1991, p. 18; Stanley W. Cloud, "How Reporters Missed the War," *Time,* January 8, 1990, p. 61.

80. Howard Kurtz, "The Press Pool's Chilling Effect on Covering the War," *Washington Post National Weekly Edition,* February 18–24, 1991, p. 12.

81. Howard Kurtz, "Keeping It All Pretty Quiet on the Mideastern Front," *Washington Post National Weekly Edition,* February 4–10, 1991, pp. 34–35.

82. Calculated from David Sarasohn, "Not So Smart," *Lincoln Journal* (Newhouse News Service), April 2, 1991.

83. Richard Morin, "The New War Cry: Stop the Press," *Washington Post National Weekly Edition,* February 11–17, 1991, p. 38.

84. Sidney Blumenthal, "The Syndicated Presidency," *New Yorker,* April 5, 1993, p. 45.

85. Robert P. Laurence, "Mr. President Proves He Has a Way with Words," *San Diego Union-Tribune,* March 24, 1993.

86. Rosenstiel, *The Beat Goes On,* pp. 8–9.

87. William Glaberson, "The Capitol Press vs. the President: Fair Coverage or Unreined Adversity?" *New York Times,* June 17, 1993, p. A11; Christopher Georges, "Bad News Bearers," *Washington Monthly,* July/August, 1993, pp. 28–34.

88. Thomas E. Patterson, *Out of Order* (New York: Vintage, 1994), pp. 14, 244.

89. Howard Kurtz, "Rolling with the Punches from the Press Corps," *Washington Post National Weekly Edition,* January 24–30, 1994, p. 10; James Fallows, "The Media's Rush to Judgment," *Washington Monthly,* January/February, 1994, pp. 10–11.

90. Mark P. Petracca, "Letters," *Washington Monthly,* September, 1993, p. 2; Larry J. Sabato, cited in Howard Kurtz, "Is It Splitsville for Clinton and the Media?" *Washington Post National Weekly Edition,* February 8–14, 1993, p. 14.

91. Larry J. Sabato, cited in Glaberson, "The Capitol Press vs. the President."

92. Stephen Hess, *Live from Capitol Hill!* (Washington, D.C.: Brookings Institution, 1991), p. 62; Cook, *Making Laws & Making News,* p. 2.

93. Hess, *Live from Capitol Hill!,* p. 102.

94. Edward Jay Epstein, *News from Nowhere* (New York: Random House, 1973), p. 13.

95. Graber, *Mass Media and American Politics,* p. 62.

96. Milton Coleman, "When the Candidate is Black Like Me," *Washington Post National Weekly Edition,* April 23, 1984, p. 9.

97. Roper Organization, "A Big Concern about the Media: Intruding on Grieving Families," *Washington Post National Weekly Edition,* June 6, 1984.

98. Parenti, *Inventing Reality,* chapters 7–11; Charles E. Lindblom, *Politics and Markets* (New York: Basic Books, 1977); MacDonald, *One Nation Under Television.*

99. John R. MacArthur, *Second Front: Censorship and Propaganda in the Gulf War* (New York: Hill and Wang, 1992); James Bennet, "How They Missed That Story," *Washington Monthly,* December 1990, pp. 8–16.

100. E.g., a videotape of Iraqis being killed reached two networks, but they refused to show it. Barber, *Presidential Character,* pp. 481–82.

101. Christopher Dickey, "Not Their Finest Hour," *Newsweek,* June 8, 1992, p. 66.

102. Leon V. Sigal, *Reporters and Officials* (Lexington, Mass.: D. C. Heath, 1973), pp. 120–21.

103. Lucy Howard, "Slanted 'Line'?" *Newsweek,* February 13, 1989, p. 6. See also Stephen Hess, *Live from Capitol Hill!,* p. 50. This tendency is less typical of local news.

104. Cook, *Making Laws & Making News,* p. 8.

105. Lichter et al., *The Media Elite,* pp. 21–25. See also Hess, *Live from Capitol Hill!,* Appendix A, pp. 110–30.

106. John Johnstone, Edward Slawski, and William Bowman, *The Newspeople* (Urbana, Ill.: University of Illinois Press, 1976), pp. 225–26.

107. Stanley Rothman and S. Robert Lichter, "Media and Business Elites: Two Classes in Conflict?" *The Public Interest* 69 (1982), pp. 111–25.

108. S. Robert Lichter and Stanley Rothman, "Media and Business Elites," *Public Opinion* (October/November, 1981), p. 44.

109. Stephen Hess, *The Washington Reporters* (Washington, D.C.: Brookings Institution, 1981), p. 89; Lichter et al., *The Media Elite,* pp. 127–28.

110. James Fallows, "The Stoning of Donald Regan," *Washington Monthly* (June 1984), p. 57. Most individual reporters also probably care more about their career than ideology, but this could lead to bias. In 1976 one media analyst ran into an old friend, an NBC correspondent. When the analyst asked how she was doing, she answered, "Not so great. My candidate lost." That is, the candidate she had covered during the presidential primaries lost his bid for the nomination. Because reporters often follow "their" presidential candidate into office, she lost her chance to become NBC's White House correspondent. Graeme Browning, "Too Close for Comfort?" *National Journal,* October 3, 1992, p. 2243.

111. Parenti, *Inventing Reality,* pp. 38, 56–57.

112. Mark Hertsgaard, "How Ronald Reagan Turned News Hounds into Lap Dogs," *Washington Post National Weekly Edition,* August 29–September 4, 1988, p. 25.

113. Joel Millman, "How the Press Distorts the News from Central America," *Progressive* (October 1984), p. 20.

114. Epstein, *News from Nowhere,* pp. 206–207. This, however is less of a problem than it used to be. Hess, *Washington Reporters.*

115. C. Richard Hofstetter, *Bias in the News* (Columbus, Ohio: Ohio State University Press, 1976); Doris Graber, *Mass Media and Politics* (Washington, D.C.: Congressional Quarterly Press, 1980), pp. 167–68; Michael J. Robinson, "Just How Liberal Is the News?" *Public Opinion* (February/March 1983), pp. 55–60; Maura Clancy and Michael J. Robinson, "General Election Coverage: Part I," *Public Opinion* 7 (December/January 1985), pp. 49–54, 59; Michael J. Robinson, "The Media Campaign, '84; Part II" *Public Opinion* 8 (February/March 1985), pp. 43–48.

116. Clancy and Robinson, "General Election Coverage"; Robinson, "The Media Campaign '84"; Michael J. Robinson, "Where's the Beef? Media and Media Elites in 1984," in Austin Ranney, ed., *The American Elections of 1984* (Durham, N.C.: Duke University Press, 1985), p. 184; Michael J. Robinson, "News Media Myths and Realities: What Network News Did and Didn't Do in the 1984 General Campaign," in Kay Lehman Schlozman, ed., *Elections in America* (Boston: Allen & Unwin, 1987), pp. 143–70.

117. Patterson, *Out of Order,* p. 131.

118. Ibid., pp. 100–07.

119. Ibid., p. 106.

120. "Clinton Gains More Support from Big Papers," *Lincoln Journal-Star* (New York Times), October 25, 1992.

121. Stanley Rothman and S. Robert Lichter, "The Nuclear Energy Debate," *Public Opinion* 5 (August/September 1982), pp. 47–48; Stanley Rothman and S. Robert Lichter, "Elite Ideology and Risk Perception in Nuclear Energy Policy," *American Political Science Review* 81 (June 1987), pp. 383–404.

122. Lichter et al., *The Media Elite,* chapter 7.

123. Sabato, *Feeding Frenzy,* p. 87, and sources cited therein.

124. Robinson, "Just How Liberal Is the News?" p. 59.

125. Hofstetter, *Bias in the News;* Hess, *Live from Capitol Hill!,* pp. 12–13.

126. Robinson, "Just How Liberal Is the News?" p. 58; Arthur H. Miller, Edie N. Goldenberg, and Lutz Erbring, "Type-Set Politics," *American Political Science Review* 73 (1979), p. 69; Patterson, *Out of Order,* p. 6; Charles M. Tidmarch and John J. Pitney, Jr., "Covering Congress," *Polity* 17 (Spring 1985), pp. 463–83.

127. Patterson, *Out of Order,* pp. 25, 245.

128. Michael Baruch Grossman and Martha Joynt Kumar, *Portraying the President* (Baltimore: Johns Hopkins University Press, 1981).

129. Michael J. Robinson and Margaret A. Sheehan, *Over the Wire and on TV* (New York: Russell Sage Foundation and Basic Books, 1983).

130. Michael J. Robinson, "Three Faces of Congressional Media," in Doris A. Graber, ed., *Media Power in Politics* (Washington, D.C.: Congressional Quarterly, 1984), pp. 215–16.

131. Michael J. Robinson, "Public Affairs Television and the Growth of Political Malaise," *American Political Science Review* 70 (1976), pp. 409–432; Miller, Goldenberg, Erbring, "Type-Set Politics."

132. "Anchorwoman Verdict Raises Mixed Opinions," *New York Times,* August 9, 1983.

133. Theodore H. White, *America in Search of Itself* (New York: Harper & Row, 1982), p. 186.

134. George F. Will, "Prisoners of TV," *Newsweek,* January 10, 1977, p. 76.

135. Parenti, *Inventing Reality,* p. 48.

136. David Owen, "The Cigarette Companies: How They Get Away with Murder, Part II," *Washington Monthly* (March 1985), pp. 48–54.

137. Martin A. Linsky, ed., *Television and the Presidential Elections* (Lexington, Mass.: D. C. Heath, 1983).

138. Barry Sussman, "News on TV: Mixed Reviews," *Washington Post National Weekly Edition,* September 3, 1984, p. 37.

139. Bill Carter, "Networks Fight Public's Shrinking Attention Span," *Lincoln Sunday Journal-Star* (New York Times), September 30, 1990.

140. Epstein, *News from Nowhere,* p. 4.

141. William A. Henry III, "Requiem for TV's Gender Gap," *Time,* August 22, 1983, p. 57.

142. Tom Jory, "TV Anchorwoman's Suit Exposes Subtle Bias in Hiring," *Lincoln Journal,* July 31, 1983, p. 1A.

143. Marlene Sanders and Marcia Rock, *Waiting for Prime Time: The Women of Television News* (Urbana, Ill., University of Illinois Press, 1988), pp. 147–48, cited in Hess, *Live from Capitol Hill!,* p. 120.

144. Robinson, "Just How Liberal Is the News?" p. 60.

145. "Tidbits and Outrages," *Washington Monthly* (February 1990), p. 44.

146. Patterson, *Out of Order*, p. 161.

147. Ibid., pp. 53–59 and generally.

148. For 1976 presidential campaign: Thomas E. Patterson, *The Mass Media Election* (New York: Praeger, 1980), p. 24. For 1984 presidential campaign: Henry E. Brady and Richard Johnson, "What's the Primary Message: Horse Race or Issue Journalism?," in Gary R. Orren and Nelson W. Polsby, ed., *Media and Momentum* (Chatham, N.J.: Chatham House, 1987), pp. 127–86. For 1988 presidential campaign: Stephen Ansolabehere, Roy Behr, and Shanto Iyengar, "Mass Media and Elections: An Overview," *American Politics Quarterly* 19 (January 1991), p. 119. For 1992 presidential campaign and in general: Patterson, *Out of Order*. For 1992 congressional campaigns: Charles M. Tidmarch, Lisa J. Hyman, and Jill E. Sorkin, "Press Issue Agendas in the 1982 Congressional and Gubernatorial Election Campaigns," *Journal of Politics* 46 (November 1984), p. 1231.

149. S. Robert Lichter, Daniel Amundson, and Richard Noyes, "The Video Campaign: Network Coverage of the 1988 Primaries" (Washington, D.C.: American Enterprise Institute for Public Policy Research, 1988), p. 65.

150. Lee Sigelman and David Bullock, "Candidates, Issues, Horse Races, and Hoopla: Presidential Campaign Coverage, 1888–1988." *American Politics Quarterly* 19 (January 1991), pp. 5–32. And so was emphasis upon human interest. In 1846 the *New York Tribune* described the culinary habits of Representative William "Sausage" Sawyer (D.-Oh.), who ate a sausage on the floor of the House every afternoon: "What little grease is left on his hands he wipes on his almost bald head which saves any outlay for Pomatum. His mouth sometimes serves as a finger glass, his shirtsleeves and pantaloons being called into requisition as a napkin. He uses a jackknife for a toothpick, and then he goes on the floor again to abuse the Whigs as the British party." Cook, *Making Law & Making News*, pp. 18–19.

151. Parenti, *Inventing Reality*, p. 15, quoting Malcolm MacDougall, "The Barkers of Snake Oil Politics," *Politics Today* (January/February 1980), p. 35.

152. David S. Broder, "Can We Govern?" *Washington Post National Weekly Edition*, January 31–February 6, 1994, p. 23.

153. Kathleen Hall Jamieson, *Dirty Politics: Deception, Distraction, Democracy* (New York: Oxford University Press, 1992), pp. 184–85.

154. Epstein, *News from Nowhere*, pp. 179, 195.

155. T. R. Reid, "Media Wrong about Yellowstone," *Lincoln Journal* (Washington Post), July 24, 1989.

156. David L. Altheide, "Format and Symbol in Television Coverage of Terrorism in the United States and Great Britain," *International Studies Quarterly* 31 (1987), pp. 161–76.

157. NBC did have footage of actual accidents in which the gas tanks exploded and people burned to death, but apparently the footage was not dramatic enough. The staged crashes included a scene, shot by a camera tied to the steering wheel, showing the driver's view moments before impact. Benjamin Weiser, "TV's Credibility Crunch," *Washington Post National Weekly Edition*, March 8–14, 1993, p. 6.

158. Weiser, "TV's Credibility Crunch," p. 7.

159. John Horn, "Campaign Coverage Avoids Issues," *Lincoln Sunday Journal-Star*, September 25, 1988.

160. John Eisendrath, "An Eyewitness Account of Local TV News," *Washington Monthly* (September 1986), p. 21.

161. Michael Deaver, "Sound-Bite Campaigning: TV Made Us Do It," *Washington Post National Weekly Edition*, November 7–13, 1988, p. 34.

162. Hess, *Live from Capitol Hill!*, p. 34.

163. Stanley W. Cloud and Nancy Traver, "Mr. Smith Leaves Washington," *Time*, June 8, 1992, p. 65.

164. "Letters," *Washington Monthly*, May, 1992, p. 2.

165. Howard Kurtz, "Asleep at the Switch," *Washington Post National Weekly Edition*, December 21–27, 1992, p. 6.

166. Larry Martz, "For the Media, a Pyrrhic Victory," *Newsweek*, June 22, 1992, p. 32. See also Hobart Rowen, "Uncle Sam's Underwriter," *Washington Post National Weekly Edition*, May 15–21, 1989, p. 5.

167. Donald L. Shaw and Maxwell E. McCombs, *The Emergence of American Political Issues: The Agenda-Setting Function of the Press* (St. Paul, Minn.: West, 1977). For a review of agenda-setting research, see Everett M. Rogers and James W. Dearing, "Agenda-Setting Research: Where Has It Been, Where Is It Going?" *Communication Yearbook* 11 (Newberry Park, Calif.: Sage, 1988), pp. 555–94.

168. Lutz Erbring, Edie N. Goldenberg, and Arthur H. Miller, "Front-Page News and Real-World Clues: A New Look at Agenda-Setting by the Media," *American Journal of Political Science* 24 (February 1980), pp. 16–49.

169. Michael Bruce MacKuen and Steven Lane Coombs, *More Than News* (Beverly Hills: Sage, 1981), p. 140; Rogers and Dearing, "Agenda-Setting Research," pp. 572–76; G. E. Lang and K. Lang, *The Battle for Public Opinion* (New York: Columbia University Press, 1983), pp. 58–59.

170. Richard Morin, "Public Enemy No. 1: Crime," *Washington Post National Weekly Edition*, January 24–30, 1994, p. 37.

171. Molly Ivins, "Hard Questions, Easy Answers," *Lincoln Journal* (Creators Syndicate), July 7, 1994.

172. Shanto Iyengar and Donald R. Kinder, *News That Matters* (Chicago: University of Chicago Press, 1987), pp. 42–45.

173. Erbring et al., "Front-Page News," p. 38; MacKuen and Coombs, *More Than News*, pp. 128–37.

174. Lichter et al., *The Media Elite*, p. 11.

175. Carl Sessions Stepp, "Establishment Media Have Lost Control of Campaign News Flow," *Lincoln Journal* (Hartford Courant), November 4, 1992.

176. Rogers and Dearing, "Agenda-Setting Research," p. 569; MacKuen and Coombs, *More Than News*, p. 101; Erbring et al., "Front-Page News," p. 38.

177. Rogers and Dearing, "Agenda-Setting Research," p. 577, citing Jack L. Walker, "Setting the Agenda in the U.S. Senate," *British Journal of Political Science* 7 (October 1977), pp. 423–45. See also Cook, *Making Laws & Making News*, pp. 116, 130–31.

178. Robinson and Sheehan, *Over the Wire;* Robinson, "The Media Campaign, '84," pp. 45–47.

179. Thomas Griffith, "Leave Off the Label," *Time*, September 19, 1984, p. 63.

180. After one term, however, Schmitt was defeated by an opponent whose slogan was, "What on Earth has he ever done?"

181. Doris A. Graber, "Kind Pictures and Harsh Words: How Television Presents the Candidates," in Kay Lehman Schlozman, ed., *Elections in America* (Boston: Allen & Unwin, 1987), p. 141.

182. Ibid., p. 116.

183. The discussion of the functions of the media relies heavily on the excellent summary found in Stephen Ansolabehere, Roy Behr, and Shanto Iyengar, "Mass Media and Elections," *American Politics Quarterly* 19 (January 1991), pp. 109–39.

184. David Paletz and Robert Entrum, *Media—Power—Politics* (New York: Macmillan, 1981), pp. 35ff.

185. Patterson, *Out of Order,* p. 44.

186. Ansolabehere et al., "Mass Media and Elections," pp. 128–29; Christine F. Ridout, "The Role of Media Coverage of Iowa and New Hampshire in the 1988 Democratic Nomination," *American Politics Quarterly* 19 (January 1991), pp. 45–46, 53–54; Marc Howard Ross, "Television News and Candidate Fortunes in Presidential Nomination Campaigns," *American Politics Quarterly* 20 (January, 1992), pp. 69–98.

187. Henry Brady, "Chances, Utilities, and Voting in Presidential Primaries," paper delivered at the Annual Meeting of the Public Choice Society, Phoenix, Arizona, cited in Ansolabehere, Behr, and Iyengar, "Mass Media and Elections;" Bartels, *Presidential Primaries,* 1988.

188. Bruce Buchanan, *Electing a President: The Markle Commission Report on Campaign '88* (Austin, Tex.: University of Texas Press, 1990); Montague Kean, *30-Second Politics* (New York: Praeger, 1989). Marion Just, Lori Wallach, and Ann Crigler, "Thirty-Seconds or Thirty Minutes: Political Learning in an Election," paper presented at the Mid west Political Science Association Meeting, April 1987, Chicago, Illinois.

189. Lee Sigelman and Carol K. Sigelman, "Judgments of the Carter-Reagan Debate," *Public Opinion Quarterly* 48 (1984), pp. 624–28.

190. Theodore H. White, *The Making of the President 1960* (New York: Atheneum House, 1961), p. 333.

191. For a review, see MacKuen and Coombs, *More Than News,* pp. 147–61.

192. Robert S. Erickson, "The Influence of Newspaper Endorsements in Presidential Elections," *American Journal of Political Science* 20 (May 1976), pp. 207–33.

193. MacKuen and Coombs, *More Than News,* p. 222.

194. Benjamin I. Page, Robert Y. Shapiro, and Glenn R. Dempsey, "What Moves Public Opinion?" *American Political Science Review* 81 (March 1987), pp. 23–43. Critical news and commentaries about presidents seem to lower their popularity. Darrell M. West, "Television and Presidential Popularity in America," *British Journal of Political Science* 21 (April 1991), pp. 199–214. Even television's "framing" of events, as isolated incidents or parts of patterns, affects viewers' opinions about these events. Shanto Iyengar, *Is Anyone Responsible? How Television Frames Political Issues* (Chicago: University of Chicago Press, 1991).

195. Iyengar, *Is Anyone Responsible?* Chs. 6, 8.

196. Graber, *Mass Media,* p. 244; Doris Graber, *Processing News: How People Tame the Information Tide* (New York: Longman, 1984). A 1993 survey concluded that almost half of Americans over 16 have such limited reading and math skills that they are unfit for most jobs. One task the survey included was to paraphrase a newspaper story. Many people could scan the story but not paraphrase it when they finished it. Paul Gray, "Adding Up the Under-Skilled," *Time,* September 20, 1993, p. 75.

197. Greider, "Reporters and Their Sources," p. 19.

198. Idea for this paragraph from James Fallows, "Did You Have a Good Week?" *Atlantic Monthly,* December 1994, pp. 32, 34.

199. Iyengar, *Is Anyone Responsible?*

200. Stephen Earl Bennett, "Trends in Americans' Political Information," *American Politics Quarterly* 17 (October 1989), pp. 422–35; Richard Zoglin, "The Tuned-out Generation," *Time,* July 9, 1990, p. 64.

201. Peters, *How Washington Really Works,* p. 32.

202. Signorile wrote the article for *Outweek,* but before publication that magazine folded and the article was included in *The Advocate,* another homosexual magazine.

203. Signorile, *Queer in America,* p. 145.

204. Ibid., p. 92.

205. Sabato, *Feeding Frenzy,* p. 192.

206. Signorile, *Queer in America,* p. 149.

207. Ibid., pp. 303–04.

208. Ibid., p. ix.

209. Ibid., p. 81.

9 Money and Politics

You Are There

Quid Pro Quo? Or No?

You are U.S. Senator Dennis DeConcini.[1] A moderate Democrat, you have represented Arizona since 1976. It is now 1987, and you are facing a decision whether to pressure federal savings and loan regulators to go easy on Lincoln Savings and Loan, owned by Charles Keating, your constituent, acquaintance, and campaign donor.

You have known Keating for over a decade. He is a millionaire real estate developer who has, over the years, made generous campaign donations to local, Arizona, and national officeholders. He and his associates gave over $100,000 to campaign funds of Phoenix city council members around 1980, after which they made zoning decisions in his favor. Although Keating is a Republican, he joined your campaign finance committee and raised more than $33,000 for your 1982 campaign. He raised another $48,000 for you between 1985 and 1987 in preparation for your 1988 campaign. You returned the favors. You tried to get President Reagan to appoint Keating ambassador to the Bahamas. Your efforts were rebuffed, probably because Keating earlier had been in trouble with the Securities and Exchange Commission over an alleged bank fraud. And you have called on the president's chief of staff many times to lobby on behalf of a Keating associate for a spot on the Federal Home Loan Bank Board. Now Keating wants you to help him in his fight with the Federal Home Loan Bank Board and its regulators. The board wants to limit the investment activities of Keating's Lincoln Savings and Loan, owned by Keating's Arizona corporation.

Considering this problem, you think about the savings and loan industry. Before 1980, it was a boring business, investing only in houses. It operated according to the 3-6-3 principle: Offer 3% on savings, loan at 6% for home mortgages, and hit the golf course at 3 P.M.[2] But in the 1970s, inflation cut heavily into the industry's profits; other financial institutions offered much higher interest rates on savings, while charging far more on loans. To help the industry, and at the urging of both Presidents Carter and Reagan, Congress stepped in to deregulate. Deregulation allowed savings and loan institutions to pay higher interest, and in order to raise funds to pay that higher interest, Congress allowed them to invest in anything—from junk bonds to real estate. Then, it allowed S&L depositors to have an unlimited number of accounts, each insured up to $100,000. These moves were expected to make S&Ls more attractive to investors and more lucrative for owners. As President Reagan said in signing some S&L deregulation, "I think we've hit the jackpot."[3]

After the deregulation legislation, the Reagan administration was lax in enforcement of the new laws. The S&L regulatory agency, the Federal Home Loan Bank Board, lost half its veteran staff due to budget cuts and poor morale. Those who remained were told by their boss to let S&Ls pretend to be solvent even when they were not, in the hope that they would become stronger eventually.[4]

But two years after deregulation, a new chair of the board feared that insolvent S&Ls were undermining the stability of the whole banking system. The board voted to tighten investment regulations, especially concerning real estate, declaring that only a small proportion of any S&L's investments could be in real

CONTINUED 

The Development of Laws to Regulate Money and Politics

Money in Nineteenth-Century American Politics

Early Reforms

The Role of Money in Election Campaigns

Campaign Finance Laws

Loopholes in the Reforms

How the System Works

The Impact of Campaign Money

Does the Campaign Finance System Deter Good Candidates?

Does Money Win Elections?

Does Money Buy Favorable Policies?

Reforming the Campaign Money System

Conflicts of Interest

Conflict-of-Interest Reforms

Congress

The Executive Branch

Conclusion: Does the Influence of Money Make Government Less Responsive?

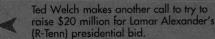

Ted Welch makes another call to try to raise $20 million for Lamar Alexander's (R-Tenn) presidential bid.

estate (most were supposed to be invested in low-risk outlets). This new regulation threatened the stability of S&Ls like Keating's, which had gone overboard in high-risk real estate investments. The board began investigating Keating's S&L, demanding documents and evidence concerning the value of real estate and other investments it had made. By 1987, Keating was complaining that the regulators were harassing his Lincoln S&L.

Keating asks you, along with several other senators, to help him get the regulators off his back. You have mixed feelings about this, though you are basically sympathetic. Helping constituents is part of your job. Keating is not just an average constituent, he is a big fund-raiser and donor to your campaigns. As far as you know, he is an honest businessman. In fact, a managing partner of the prestigious national accounting firm of Arthur Young & Company has written a letter to a fellow senator, John McCain (R-Ariz.), vouching for the Lincoln S&L and charging that it is being harassed by regulators. A respected accountant, Alan Greenspan (later to become chair of the Federal Reserve Bank), has written a letter to several senators also attesting to the S&L's financial health.

On the other hand, there are some warning signals. Your banking aide, an Arizonan whose family is in the S&L business, warns you that Keating takes too many risks. She recommends avoiding him. Others are suspicious too. Senator Jake Garn (R-Utah), for example, has said he will have nothing to do with Keating. Moreover, you are mindful of Senate ethics rules requiring senators not only to refrain from wrongdoing but from conduct giving "the appearance of wrongdoing."[5] While doing favors for constituents is a key element of your job, putting pressure on regulators on behalf of a large campaign contributor could certainly give "the appearance of wrongdoing."

What do you do? Do you help your constituent and campaign donor by trying to get federal regulators to go easy on the Lincoln S&L? That is, do you follow the practice of quid pro quo (tit for tat)? Or do you let the regulatory process work, perhaps closing down the S&L and the parent company in Arizona and angering a rich donor and fund-raiser?

Former Speaker of the House of Representatives Tip O'Neill once said, "There are four parts to any campaign. The candidate, the issues . . ., the campaign organization, and the money. Without money you can forget the other three."[6] Thus, conventional wisdom holds that "money is the mother's milk of politics." But we are not sure if that milk is tainted or pure. On the one hand, without money, candidates or people with new political ideas could never become known in our massive and complex society. Television spreads names and ideas almost instantaneously, so having money to buy television time means your ideas will be heard. In that sense, money contributes to open political debate.

On the other hand, money can be a corrupting influence on politics. At the least, it can buy access to those making decisions. At the worst, it can buy decisions. Money allows some points of view to be trumpeted while others are forced to whisper. Some candidates or groups can afford to spend hundreds of thousands of dollars for each prime time minute of national television or for prestigious Washington law firms to lobby; others can afford only mimeographs and letters. Money increases inequities in political life.

Money, then, leads to a dilemma in politics. In our largely capitalist society, we expect substantial differences in wealth and income. In most cases, we see nothing wrong when those with great income buy goods and services that others cannot afford. But in politics, many people feel uneasy when those with great wealth are able to buy political favors. We feel so uneasy that we have outlawed certain kinds of buying of political favors, such as politicians paying voters for their votes or interest groups paying politicians and bureaucrats for their support.

But we are uneasy about other ways of limiting the influence of money. Many people feel that individuals or groups should be allowed to contribute as much money to candidates as they want, and that candidates should be permitted to buy as much media time to get their point of view across as they want and can afford. This view holds that contributing money and buying media time are forms of constitutionally guaranteed freedom of speech. The opposite view says that this distorts the democratic process.

Over the decades, we have become more explicit in our understandings of the appropriate role of money in politics, but many issues and ambiguities remain. In this chapter, we first focus on the development of laws that regulate how money can influence politics, then we turn to the role and impact of money in elections, and finally we briefly examine conflict of interest on the part of decision-makers in Congress and the executive branch.

➤THE DEVELOPMENT OF LAWS TO REGULATE MONEY AND POLITICS

Concern about the illegitimate influence of money on politics is as old as the Republic. In his campaign for the Virginia House of Burgesses in 1757, George Washington was accused of vote buying. He had given out 28 gallons of rum, 50 gallons of rum punch, 34 gallons of wine, 46 gallons of beer, and 2 gallons of cider.[7] Because there were only 391 voters in his district, he had provided more than a quart and a half of beverages per voter![8]

Obviously, George Washington survived these charges, and his constituents probably survived the effects of the rum and cider. But most discussions of the impact of money on politics were more sober. In his well-known analysis of controlling factions, James Madison, in *Federalist #10,* recognized that "the most common and durable source of factions has been the various and unequal distribution of property." Madison went on to say that although ideally no one should be allowed to make decisions affecting his or her own self-interest, almost any subject of legislation—taxes, tariffs, debts—involves self-interest. For those making laws, "every shilling with which they overburden the inferior number is a shilling saved to their own pockets."[9]

Madison hoped that the design of the new nation, with the power of the government divided among the branches of government and between the nation and the states, would mean that no one interest or faction would overwhelm the others. The interest of one person or group would check the interest of another.

This view of counterbalancing interests is an optimistic one and has not always worked. Over the decades, Americans have found it necessary to make additional rules to restrict the ways that those with money can try to influence policymakers.

■ Money in Nineteenth-Century American Politics

The influence of money on politics has shaped several epochs of American history. For example, from the earliest westward expansion of the nation, charges of graft and corruption surrounded the government's sale and giveaway of land. Indeed, the West was developed by giving land to speculators and railroads, sometimes after bribes. When Congress was debating whether to give federal land to the railroads, the lobbyists "camped in brigades around the Capitol building."[10]

This Puck cartoon mocks President U.S. Grant's involvement in various corrupt activities. Grant (dressed in the flag suit) is shown supporting various political bosses and profiteers.

The impact of money on political life was probably at its peak in the late nineteenth century. The United States grew from a small agrarian society to a large industrialized one. Oil exploration and refining, the growth of the steel industry, the railroad companies that were spanning the nation, and other large corporations produced many millionaires. This was the era

At the turn of the century, rich New Yorkers, wearing vine leaves on their heads, enjoy their wealth.

of "robber barons," when the owners of giant corporations (called "trusts") openly bought political favors.

Business contributions to campaigns and to politicians were routine. One railroad president justified bribery of political officials by noting, "If you have to pay money to have the right thing done, it is only just and fair to do so."[11] Mark Hanna, a Republican fund-raiser in the presidential election of 1896, assessed banks at a fixed percentage of their capital and also collected substantial sums from most insurance companies and large corporations.[12] However, Cornelius Vanderbilt, one of the wealthiest men of his time, refused to contribute to election campaigns, believing it was cheaper to buy legislators after they were elected!

Early Reforms

Around the turn of the century, the Progressive reformers and their allies in the press, called the **Muckrakers,** began to attack this overt corruption. They wanted to break the financial link between business and politicians. In 1907, a law prohibited corporations and banks from making contributions to political campaigns, and a few years later Congress mandated public reporting of campaign expenditures and set limits on campaign donations. Prohibitions against corporate giving to political campaigns were broadened over time to forbid utilities and labor unions from giving as well.

The **Teapot Dome scandal** of 1921 stimulated further attempts to limit the influence of money on electoral politics. The secretary of the interior in the Harding administration received almost $400,000 from two corporations that then were allowed to lease oil reserves in California and Wyoming (one of them was called the "Teapot Dome"). This led to the Federal Corrupt Practices Act (1925), which required the reporting of campaign contributions and expenditures.

Because none of these laws was enforced, each had only a momentary effect. Nevertheless, the reforms did seem to make open graft and bribery less acceptable and less common. Instead of outright bribes, political interests now sought to influence politicians through campaign contributions.

Labor unions, for example, set up **political action committees (PACs)** funded from dues. These committees then raised "voluntary" money from members to support candidates for elections. Then many businesses did the same.

"Honest Graft"

The influence of money on local politics reached a high point in the late nineteenth century. Urban machines used money to cement a complex network of businesses, voters, and political party organizations. Business payoffs to government and party officials for licenses and contracts, and party payoffs to voters for their support, were the norm. Graft was tolerated and even expected.

As we saw in Chapter 6, George Washington Plunkitt was a famous leader of the New York City machine, Tammany Hall. Plunkitt, born in 1842, began life as a butcher's helper and ended up a millionaire through deals made in his role as a party leader and public official. He held a number of state and local public offices; at one point, he held four at the same time. He drew a salary for three of them simultaneously.

Plunkitt's view of graft illustrates the casual attitude about the influence of money on politics common among many of his time:

> There's all the difference in the world between [honest graft and dishonest graft]. There's an honest graft, and I'm an example of how it works. I might sum up the whole thing by sayin': "I seen my opportunities and I took 'em."
>
> Just let me explain. . . . My party's in power in the city, and it's goin' to undertake a lot of public improvements. Well, I'm tipped off, say, that they're going to lay out a new park at a certain place. I see my opportunity and take it. I go to that place and I buy up all the land I can in the neighborhood. Then the board of this or that makes its plan public, and there is a rush to get my land, which nobody cared particular for before. Ain't it perfectly honest to charge a good price and make a profit on my investment and foresight? Of course, it is. Well, that's honest graft.
>
> Tammany was beat in 1901 because the people were deceived into believin' that it worked dishonest graft. . . . [They supposed] Tammany men were robbin' the city treasury or levyin' blackmail on disorderly houses, or workin' in with the gamblers and lawbreakers. . . . Why should the Tammany leaders go into such dirty business when there is so much honest graft lyin' around?
>
> . . . I don't own a dishonest dollar. If my worst enemy was given the job of writin' my epitaph . . . he couldn't do more than write: George W. Plunkitt. He Seen His Opportunities, and He Took 'Em.

SOURCE: William L. Riordon, *Plunkitt of Tammany Hall* (New York: E. P. Dutton, 1963).

The Role of Money in Election Campaigns

In 1971, changed conditions caused new laws to be passed.

Campaign Finance Laws

Prompted by the increasing use of television in campaigns, and the increasing cost of buying television time, in 1971 Congress passed a law regulating spending on advertising. The law limited donations that candidates could pay to their own campaigns and required candidates to disclose the names and addresses of donors of more than $100.

In the course of the Watergate investigations, it became clear that corporations were not abiding by these restrictions. Several corporations secretly funded President Nixon's reelection campaign. For example, Nixon's Justice Department negotiated a settlement favorable to the ITT Corporation in a pending legal dispute soon after an ITT subsidiary gave the Republican National Committee $400,000.[13] Altogether, 21 individuals and 14 corporations were indicted for illegal campaign contributions, mostly but not entirely to the Nixon reelection campaign.

In response to these scandals, Congress again attempted to regulate campaign financing by passing the **Federal Election Campaign Act** in 1974. The following are key provisions of that law, the basics of which, along with individual state laws, regulate campaign finance today:

- Public financing of presidential campaigns. Each candidate is given tax dollars for his or her campaign, as we will see in more detail later.
- Limits on contributions of individuals and committees to campaigns for federal office.
- Limits on overall expenditures by candidates' organizations in presidential campaigns.
- Limits on overall expenditures by national party committees.
- Limits on expenditures by PACs.
- Limits on individual donations to PACs and to individual candidates.
- Prohibitions on cash contributions of more than $100.
- The establishment of a bipartisan Federal Election Commission to enforce the law.

Limits on spending by candidates' organizations in congressional races and limits on so-called **independent spending,** spending by groups not under the control of candidates, were also part of the 1974 act. These limits were ruled unconstitutional and no longer obtain.

Because of the importance of money in campaigns, both elected officials and those who want something from the officials have looked for ways to get around the campaign finance laws.[14]

Loopholes in the Reforms

The objectives of the 1974 law were to make the campaign finance system more open, to limit spending, and to force candidates to be less reliant on a few big donors. The law has not worked as it was intended, however. In 1976, the Supreme Court knocked a hole in it when it ruled that some portions of the act were unconstitutional.[15] In a case brought by an alliance of civil libertarians and conservatives, the Court struck down several spending limits for campaigns that were not publicly funded (in this case congressional campaigns). The Court argued that spending restrictions violated individuals' rights of free speech because spending in a campaign enables candidates to get their message out. Giving money is a form of expression protected by the Constitution.

In addition to the holes knocked into the law by the Supreme Court, it became clear that there were other loopholes in the law. (*Loophole* is a common term for aspects of a law that intentionally or unintentionally limit its effectiveness or restrict its coverage.) One important loophole was created by a little-noticed portion of the law reaffirming the right of unions and corporations to establish PACs using voluntary contributions. Now that there were limitations on the amount of money individuals could give to campaigns, PACs became the vehicle by which individuals could channel more money to their favorite candidates. Individuals could give a limited amount directly to candidates, and then $5,000 to each of several PACs, which in turn could give it to candidates.[16]

PACs quickly sprung up. Business and trade PACs multiplied especially quickly, from around 100 in 1974 to more than 4,700 today. Labor had dominated the PAC game before 1974; now, with fewer than 400 PACs, it finds itself completely outnumbered.

Several other loopholes also have been exploited by candidates, parties, and PACs. Individuals and PACs can avoid most rules and limitations by independent spending. In 1985, the Supreme Court ruled that PACs can spend unlimited amounts working on behalf of issues or candidates, publicly funded or not, as long as they do not give funds directly to parties or candidates.[17]

The Court assumed this spending would be meaningfully independent. However, independent spending often is done by organized groups with indirect links to the candidate. National campaigns are run by a small, interrelated group of pollsters, consultants, and media experts. In other words, independent spending is often a myth. The law presumed that the two candidates would have approximately equal resources, most of them provided by tax dollars. Instead, millions of dollars are now raised and spent "independently."

In addition to the independent spending loophole, there is also the **soft money** loophole. Donors who want to give more than their legal federal maximum can give to national party committees, which channel to state parties, which spend under less stringent state regulations. Soft money need not be reported to the federal government nor, sometimes, to the states.

Soft money is used for such things as voter registration drives, direct mailings, polling, and advertisements for nonfederal party candidates. Soft money, including union dues and corporate funds, also can be used at the federal level by national party committees for capital improvements such as new buildings and computers. Both parties have building funds to which corporations and labor unions contribute freely. And private donors and corporations pay for large proportions of the costs of each party's national convention.

The soft money loophole allows people with money to spend as much as they want on their favorite presidential candidate or party. In 1992, the Democrats received $29 million in soft money from special interests, the Republicans $32 million. These contributions were mostly from business interests, though big labor and a few wealthy individuals also contributed through this loophole. Archer-Daniels-Midland Company gave more than $1 million to the Republicans in the 1992 election cycle; the largest Democratic contributor, the United Steelworkers, gave almost $400,000. Many large corporations give to both parties.[18] As one observer commented, "Soft money is where rich people can play again."[19]

Yet another loophole is sometimes called "back pocket PACS." Members of Congress organize their own PACS and register them only at the state level.

Since many states have lax campaign finance laws, this allows these state-registered PACs to receive contributions that are illegal under federal law, for example, from corporations and labor unions. Charles Keating's corporation gave $200,000 to a back pocket PAC run by John Glenn (D-Ohio).[20]

A final problem with the campaign finance laws is that inflation has changed the real value of the contribution and spending limits. The amount each candidate can spend does increase with inflation, but no other part of the system is indexed to inflation. Thus the maximum $1,000 contribution is now worth only $340 in 1974 dollars. The $1 voluntary checkoff on tax returns that finances the presidential election is now only worth 34¢. Thus the contribution limits are unrealistically low and the checkoff totals increasingly unable to fund the costs of the presidential campaign.

How the System Works

Presidential Elections

Presidential candidates who accept public financing, as most do, may not spend more than $33 million to

PAC Man

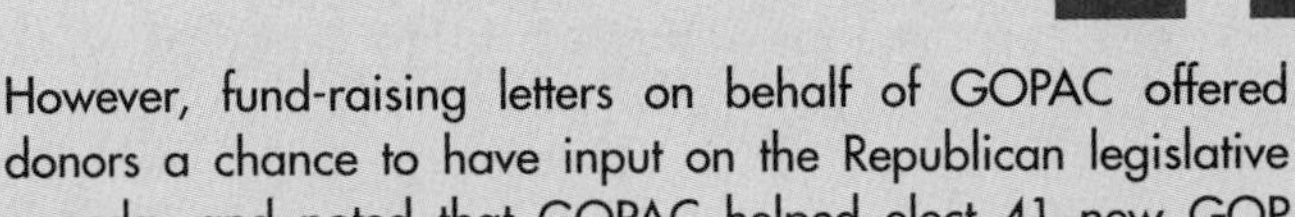

Leadership PACs have mushroomed. These PACs, organized and run by members of Congress, offer a convenient way to avoid some of the campaign finance limits for congressional candidates.

Some of the largest of these PACs are run by candidates for congressional offices such as majority leader, party whip, and committee chair. The founders of these PACS provide funds to lesser known candidates in tacit exchange for support in leadership races. Other personal PACs do not give much money to fellow candidates, but instead use the money to promote the leader's own candidacy and ideologies, using the money for campaign materials and sometimes for travel and luxury items on the campaign trail.

Candidates from both parties have such personal PACs. By far the largest are Campaign America and GOPAC. Campaign America, run by Robert Dole (R-Kan.), raised over $6 million in the 1994 election cycle, but spent only a small fraction of this on candidates. GOPAC, run by Newt Gingrich (R-Ga.), raised nearly $4 million and had spent (as of July, 1994) only $59 on candidates. The largest Democratic leadership PAC, run by Richard Gephardt (D-Mo.), raised about $1 million and spent $200,000 on other Democratic candidates.[1]

All of these leadership PACs have been under attack for being inconsistent with the spirit of the rules governing political action committees, but GOPAC was the subject of major controversy. Because it kept its donor list secret, GOPAC was sued by the Federal Election Commission and was the subject of ethics complaints in two states and in Congress. The *New York Times* labeled it a "stealth PAC."[2] Of the nearly $4 million GOPAC raised, it reported the donors for less than $500,000.[3]

Speaker Gingrich argued that GOPAC was not a political action committee at all, but was an educational institution, and he noted that only 10 percent of its funds went to federal candidates (thus the only part subject to federal regulation). However, fund-raising letters on behalf of GOPAC offered donors a chance to have input on the Republican legislative agenda, and noted that GOPAC helped elect 41 new GOP freshmen in the 1992 elections.

GOPAC activity focuses on providing candidates with training seminars and instructional materials, many featuring Speaker Gingrich. GOPAC was also used to promote Gingrich's college course, "Renewing American Civilization," which is available by video and satellite across the nation. Indeed, corporate donors to GOPAC have been invited to help shape the content of the course and have had their products promoted in the course. Course presentations noted that, for example, "Waffle House is a very highly organized set of habits of behaviors and systems," while McDonald's is "the most successful worldwide seller of food in the history of the human race," and Milliken (carpets) "offers its customers a choice of over 1,000 colors and patterns" (the owner of the latter company gave over $250,000 to GOPAC).[4]

Because Speaker Gingrich had led the attacks on former Majority Leader Jim Wright (D-Tex.) for his questionable ethics practices, Democrats reveled in the opportunity to attack Gingrich for his bad judgment (and possibly illegal actions). After continued Democratic attacks on Gingrich's apparent conflicts of interest and violation of ethics laws, in May, 1995, Speaker Gingrich announced that he was disbanding GOPAC and disclosing the names of donors to it.

---

1. These figures are from Eliza Newlin Carney, "PAC Men," *National Journal* (October 1, 1994), pp. 2272–2273.
2. Ibid, p. 2272.
3. Jonathan D. Salant, "Ethics Spotlight Puts Heat on Speaker Gingrich," *CQ* (March 4, 1995), p. 639.
4. Serge F. Kovaleski and R. H. Melton, "And Now a Word from Our Sponsor," *Washington Post National Weekly Edition* (March 27–April 2, 1995), p. 12.

get the nomination (the money comes from a voluntary checkoff of $1 on individuals' tax returns; the spending limit increases each year to take inflation into account). Candidates who do not accept public funding, such as Ross Perot, can spend as much as they can raise. Once candidates receive their parties' nominations, public funding pays them each about $55 million for the general election campaign (also adjusted each election for inflation), and they can accept several million more from their party's national committee. At this point, fund-raising is officially over for the candidates.

However, money plays a bigger role in practice than in theory. Presidential campaigns cost far more than the amount publicly funded. [21] The discrepancy is due to the independent spending and soft money loopholes. The increasing number of private individuals and corporations donating huge amounts indicates that we have come full circle back to the conditions that led to the campaign finance reforms. As one observer indicated, "The fat cats have returned."[22]

Congressional Elections

Candidates for Congress rely on three sources of funding: PAC contributions, individual donations, and donations from their political parties. PAC contributions make up about half the funds for House seats and a quarter for Senate seats (Figure 1). Over time, PAC funds have grown in importance to candidates.

PACS There are vast differences in the funding activity of PACs. Although there are 4,700 PACs, about one-third do not contribute to any candidates, while about 400 give over $100,000 each (Figure 2). Less than 10% of the PACs give three-fourths of the

FIGURE 1
The Dough Rises: Congressional Campaign Spending

Congressional campaign spending rose sharply in 1992 after slow growth in the 1980s.

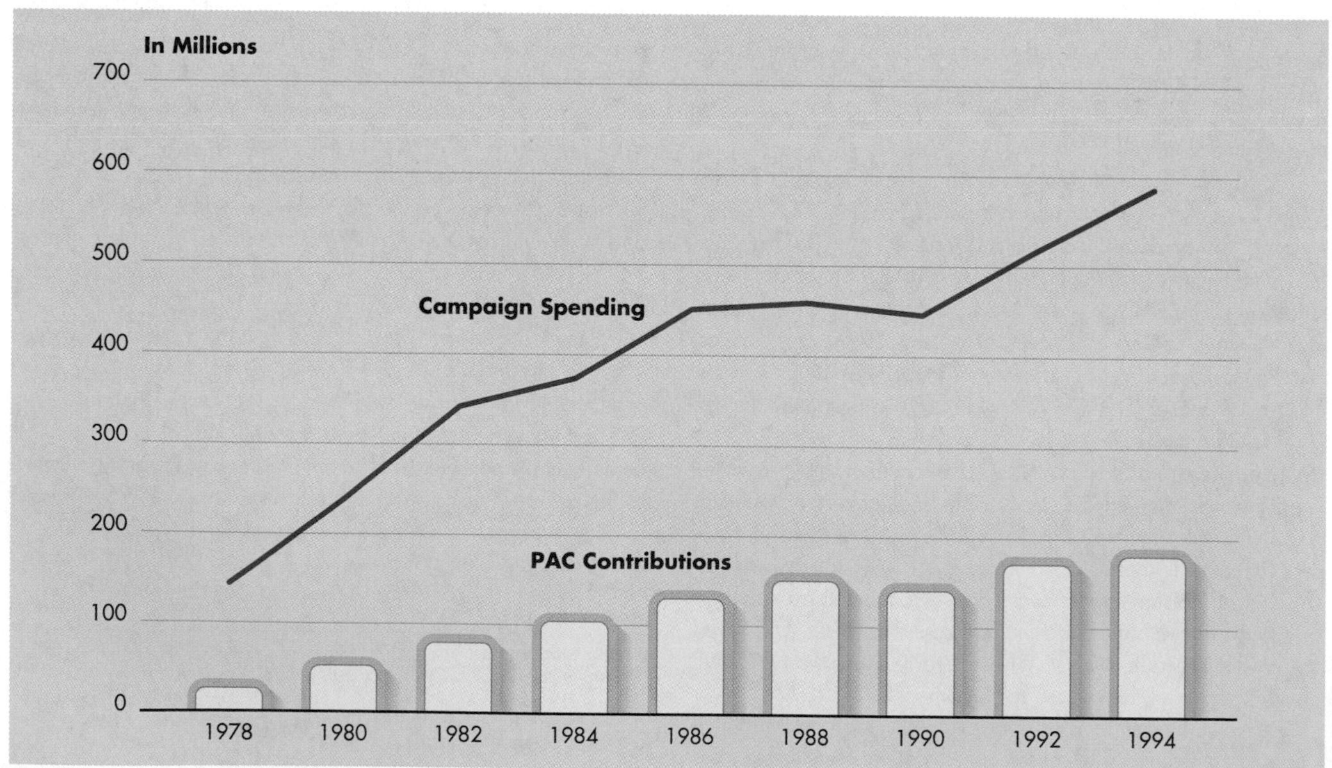

SOURCES: *National Journal*, February 10, 1990, p. 353. We borrowed the title from EMILY's List Newsletter (May 1988).

dollars. Thus, the number of key PACs is relatively small. Some of the biggest spenders include well-known groups such as the National Rifle Association, the Teamsters, and the American Medical Association. But they also include less well-known groups such as the Association of Trial Lawyers, the American Federal-State-County-and-Municipal Employees, and the American Institute of CPAs.[23]

PACs differ in the targets of their donations, but some patterns are clear. PACs show a distinct preference for Republicans in the presidential races, but the pattern in congressional races has been different. PACs usually want to give to the candidate they believe will win so they will have access to a policymaker. Thus, PACs give disproportionately to incumbents. In 1994 more than 90% of all PAC money invested in House races went to incumbents, and, in turn, House incumbents raised nearly half of their campaign funds from PACs. PAC support for Senate candidates also went disproportionately to incumbents.

PACs try to buy access and sometimes votes. PACs buy access with their donations to incumbents and to members of important committees of Congress far beyond what the candidates need to win reelection.

To ingratiate themselves with incumbents, PACs also contribute to winners after the election is over, called "catching the late train." After the surprise Republican victories in the 1994 congressional elections, PACs raced to help winning Republicans pay their campaign debts (Figure 3). As one noted, "We gave to Democrats because they were in control, and we're likely to do the same for Republicans. The balance of power has shifted, and those who affect our company and our customers are in another party."[24] After the election, health care lobbyists paid $1,000 each to attend a breakfast for Republican Senate winner Fred Thompson (Tenn.) although many had contributed to Thompson's opponent before the election. During the election campaign, Newt Gingrich (R-Ga.) warned PACs that if the Republicans took power, those not on board would "suffer the two coldest years in Washington." A Republican fundraiser compiled and circulated a "PAC List of Shame," PACs and lobbyists who had given mostly to Democrats in 1992, to "encourage" PACs to give more to the Republicans in 1994.

FIGURE 2
PAC Spending Levels Vary Greatly

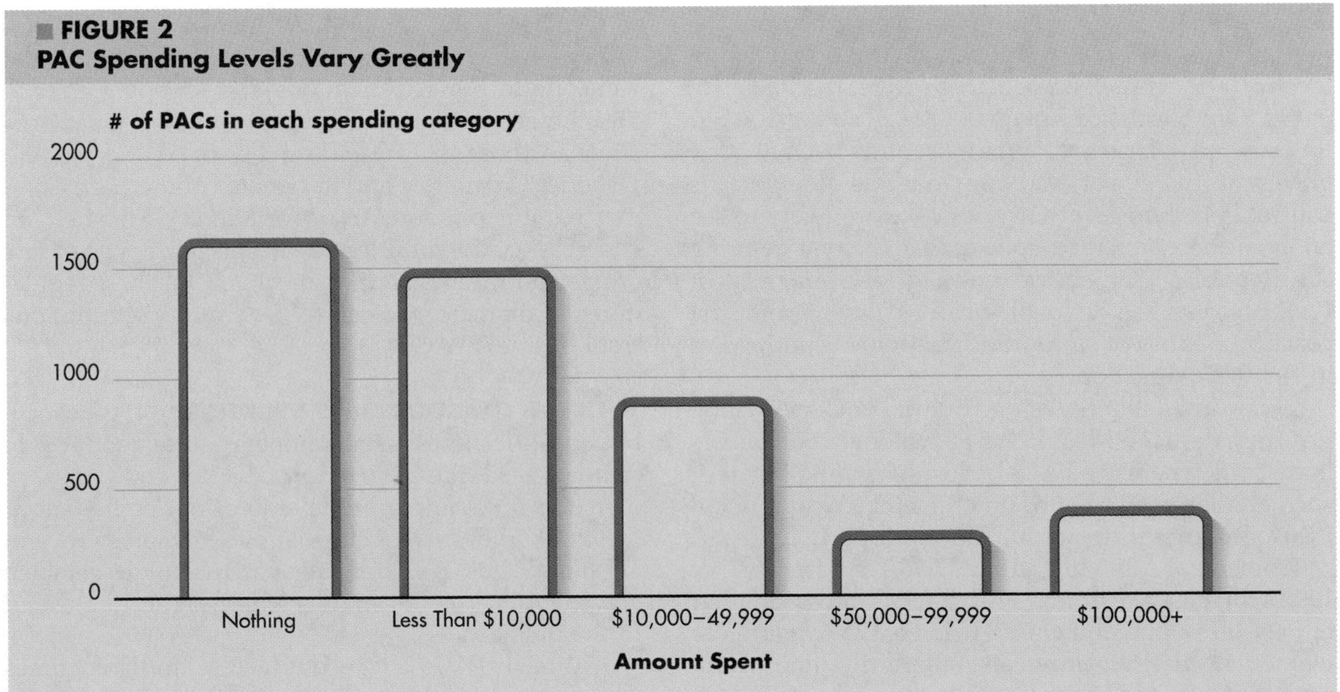

SOURCE: Larry Makinson and Joshua Goldstein, *Open Secrets: The Encyclopedia of Congressional Money and Politics* (Washington, D.C.: Congressional Quarterly Inc. 1994).

FIGURE 3
PACs Give Postelection Donations to Winners

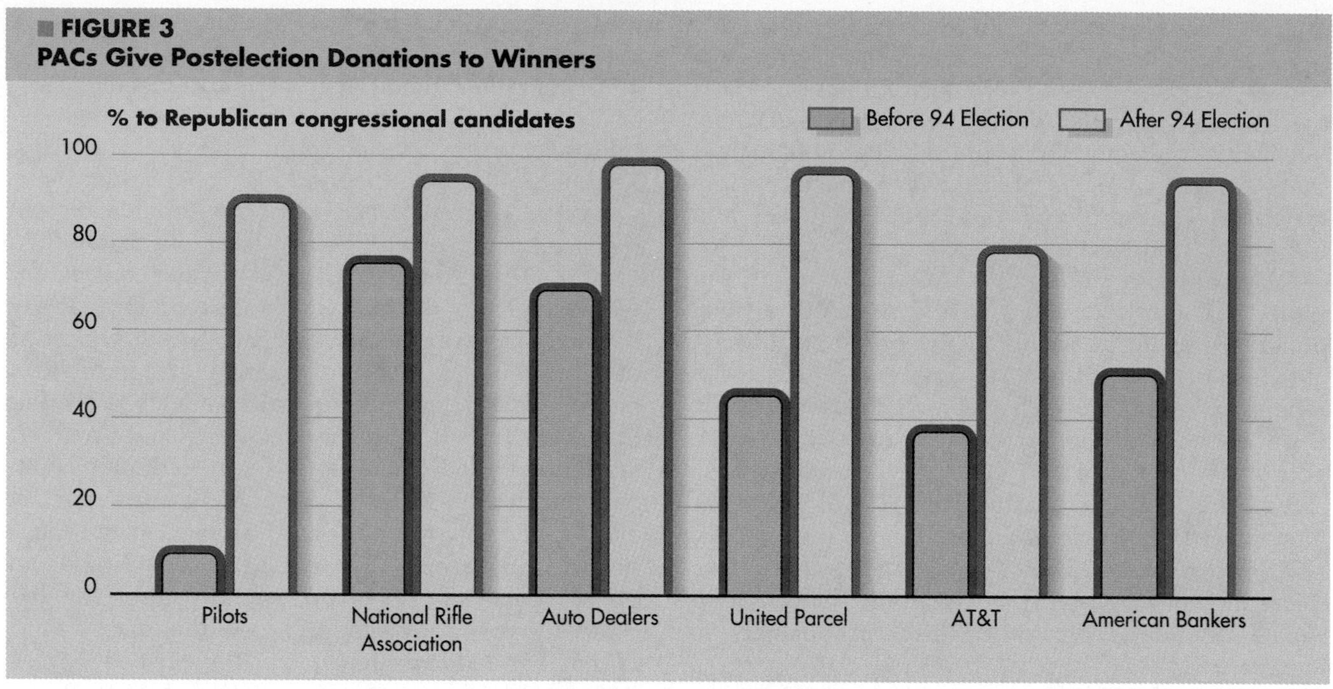

SOURCE: Jonathon Salant and David Cloud, "To the '94 Election Victors Go the Fund Raising Spoils," *Congressional Quarterly* April 15, 1995, p. 1056.

Although the majority of PACs are business related and are ideologically much more sympathetic to the Republicans, before 1994, PACs gave predominantly to the Democrats because they were the majority party. Republicans complained bitterly about this, but PACs were concerned about keeping in the good graces of the majority. Now that the Republicans control both houses of Congress, we are likely to see an even more lopsided split of PAC money favoring the Republicans, because now, for the majority of PACS, conservative ideological sentiment and the practical politics of supporting incumbents both point in the same direction.[25]

What other criteria aside from incumbency guide PAC donations?[26] Most PACs give money to members in districts where the PACs have a substantial interest, such as a large number of union members for a union PAC or a large factory for a corporate PAC.

Women's PACs, including EMILY's List, one of 1992's biggest spending PACs, focus most of their money on nonincumbents. Their goal is to get more women elected, which means supporting nonincumbents with strong chances of winning.

PACs also target contributions to members of key congressional committees. For example, PACs organized by defense contractors give disproportionately to members who serve on the Armed Services Committees, which have a big role in deciding what weapons to purchase. Unions and shipping companies involved in the maritime industry give large sums to those on the House Merchant Marine and Fisheries Committee and its Senate counterpart, Commerce, Science, and Transportation.[27] Members of congressional committees that specialize in tax law (Ways and Means, and Finance) and business regulations (Commerce) receive generous contributions from business PACs.

SPECIAL INTERESTS AS VICTIMS? PAC contributions to congressional campaigns are products of mutual need. PACs need access to and votes of members of Congress, and members of Congress need (or think they need) large sums of money to win elections. Thus, PAC donations are useful to members and to PACs. The question is whether they are useful to the public.

Although PACs try to buy access and sometimes votes, members of Congress are not simply victims of greedy PACs. Indeed, as one recent observer remarked, "There may be no question that the money flowing into campaign coffers is a crime. But there is a question whether the crime is bribery of public officials or extortion of private interests."[28]

Members themselves are increasingly aggressive in soliciting PACs for donations. They fear defeat in the next election and think that raising a lot of money can protect them. Senators, for example, must raise more than $18,000 each week during all six years of their term to fund an average-cost winning reelection campaign. A senator from a high-cost state needs to raise $60,000 a week. On the other hand, many incumbents raise millions even when they face little-known opponents. Phil Gramm (R-Tex.) continued to solicit funds from lobbyists even after he had raised more than $6 million and his opponent had only $20,000.

Thirty years ago most fund-raising by members of Congress was done in their home districts. Members did not want their constituents to think they were influenced by Washington lobbyists. Today, half of the PAC funds raised are raised in Washington.[29] Members of Congress continually hold fund-raisers to which dozens of lobbyists for PACs are invited. Well-known Washington lobbyists and PAC representatives get hundreds of invitations to congressional fund-raisers every year.[30] Indeed, the number of fund-raising events in Washington is so large that a private company sells a special monthly newsletter listing all the events. One Washington insider says of being asked by incumbents to give money, "Unless you give your max [the maximum the law allows], unless you lay out your $5,000 at a fundraiser, you don't have access. . . . If you don't go to these fundraisers, if you don't hit the drum, if you don't 'max out,' you don't get in the door. They [members of Congress] don't ever return your phone calls."[31]

Some attempts to raise money are even more crass than fund-raisers. Former Senator James Abdnor (R-S.D.) hired a courier to go to PAC offices to solicit and succeeded in raising $225,000.[32] Some members keep lists on their desks of which PACs have given to them, an implicit indication that it is those groups that will have access. Others play one PAC off against another. Members might tell a representative of a bank PAC that they received contributions from savings and loan PACs and that the bank PAC should contribute or possibly miss out.[33]

NON PAC SOURCES OF FUNDS Donations from individuals are a second important source of congressional campaign funds. Business interests comprise a much bigger share of individual contributions than of PAC contributions. Donations from members of labor unions are almost nonexistent among individual donors. Individual donors are much less concentrated in the Washington area than are PACs. Particularly well represented among individual donors to congressional races are members of the securities, entertainment, and legal professions.

Party organizations, such as the Democratic Congressional Campaign Committee and its Republican counterpart, and the Republican Senate Campaign Committee and its Democratic counterpart, are the third source of funds. These party groups together gave almost $100 million in the 1994 campaign.

There is no question that the nature of raising money for campaigns has changed. Whatever the problems with the current system, however, we should be careful not to contrast it with an idealized version of the past. After all, almost 100 years ago Mark Twain observed: "It could probably be shown by facts and figures that there is no distinctly native American criminal class except Congress." Big interests always have had influence and access in Washington. The ways in which they exercise that influence are different now. In some ways, this influence is more open because the campaign finance reforms have made public the organizations working for special interests and the money they spend doing it. Thirty years ago we would not have known how much each member of Congress received from each lobbying group; today we do.

➤The Impact of Campaign Money

We have discussed several aspects of money in elections: how much there is, who contributes it, and how they do so. Now we turn to the question of what difference campaign money makes. An obvious question is whether money influences the outcomes of elections. But we also will focus on two other kinds of potential effects of money and the way it is raised: the recruitment of good candidates and the policy decisions of elected leaders.

Does the Campaign Finance System Deter Good Candidates?

When John Glenn, an unsuccessful Democratic candidate in 1984, was asked whether running for president had been worth it despite his defeat, Glenn replied: "My family was humiliated. I got myself whipped. I gained 16 pounds. And I'm more than $2.5 million in debt. Except for that, it was wonderful."[34]

Other presidential candidates have lamented the difficulties and humiliations of having to raise money; Jack Kemp, Richard Cheney, and Dan Quayle, all potential 1996 presidential candidates, bowed out early in 1995 indicating that the magnitude of necessary fundraising was one reason why. The demands for fund-raising have grown because dates for many large state primaries, such as in California, New York, Texas, Florida, and Illinois, have been moved much earlier in the primary season. Thus, candidates no longer have the luxury of hoping to do well in the first small state primary elections and then having some momentum to help in raising large sums of money. They must have the money long before the first primary in order to book and run massive television campaigns.

The necessity of raising a lot of money deters congressional candidates too. As one leading congressional scholar noted, "Raising money is, by consensus, the most unpleasant part of a campaign. Many candidates find it demeaning to ask people for money and are uncomfortable with the implications of accepting it."[35] Senator Brock Adams (D-Wash.), who had served in the House until 1976 and then ran a decade later for the Senate, was shocked at the changes in fund-raising. "I never imagined how much of my personal time would be spent on fund raising. . . . I do not think a candidate for the U.S. Senate should have to sit in a motel room in Goldendale, Washington, at 6 in the morning and spend three hours on the phone talking to political action committees."[36] And, once elected, many new members of Congress are surprised and chagrined to find that they must begin raising funds for their next campaign almost before they are sworn into office.

■ Does Money Win Elections?

Money probably helps win some elections, but other factors also determine election winners. The evidence is mixed as to the impact of money on winning presidential primaries. Some candidates are never considered serious because they do not have sufficient money to mount a large campaign. In that sense, money is crucial. But money alone cannot win. Sometimes the biggest spenders get nowhere. Beyond some point, money might not matter as much. In 1984 and 1988, spending by the major Democratic and Republican presidential primary candidates in each state bore little relationship to whether or not they won that state.[37]

By the time presidential candidates are nominated, they already have spent a great deal. The name recognition achieved during the primaries and at the national conventions carries into the general election campaign. Presidential candidates receive extensive free media coverage in news stories. The amount that they spend after the convention is less likely to be as crucial. This is just as well for the health of the two-party system, because if money determined elec-

Source: Oliphant Copyright 1990 Universal Press Syndicate. Reprinted with permission. All rights reserved.

tions, the Republicans would have won every presidential election since World War II. However, of the presidential elections lost by the Democrats during that time, probably only the election of 1968 between Richard Nixon and Hubert Humphrey was close enough that it might have turned out differently had the Democrats been able to spend more.[38] To the extent that elections are close, as in 1968, the Republicans definitely have the advantage by having more money.[39]

In congressional races, incumbents usually start with a huge advantage. Their name is recognized by many of their constituents. Challengers must buy media to achieve similar recognition. Thus, the ability of the challenger to raise and spend money is crucial. One study showed that every $10,000 spent by a House challenger increases his or her vote total by more than 2%. The amount of money incumbents spend seems unrelated to whether they win or not. As challengers spend more, so do incumbents.[40] That is why big spending by incumbents often means they are in electoral trouble; they have strong, well-financed challengers. However, as Figure 4 shows, challengers to incumbents have a very low probability of winning unless they raise $500,000 or more. In the 1992 election cycle, *no* candidate won who did not raise at least $100,000.

The 1994 election offered contrasting lessons about the impact of money on elections. The biggest two spenders in Senate races, Michael Huffington (R-Cal.) and Oliver North (R-Va.), both lost as did four of the top six House spenders.[41]

On the other hand, on average, money makes a difference. In 1992, a supposedly anti-incumbent year, 26 of 27 Senate incumbents outspent their challengers, and 23 were reelected. In 1994, another anti-incumbent year, over 90% of House incumbents were reelected, and most had a substantial funding advantage. Nonetheless, the Republican successes in knocking off 34 Democratic incumbents is partially due to the much better funding of Republican challengers than most challengers had experienced in the past.

The fact that most challengers cannot raise the amounts of money that incumbents have readily available is probably an important reason most House incumbents get reelected. In 1990, for example, only 35 House incumbents faced opponents who raised as much as half the amount the incumbent did. Even facing these relatively well-financed opponents, almost 80% of the incumbents won.[42]

FIGURE 4
A Challenger's Success is Related to Spending

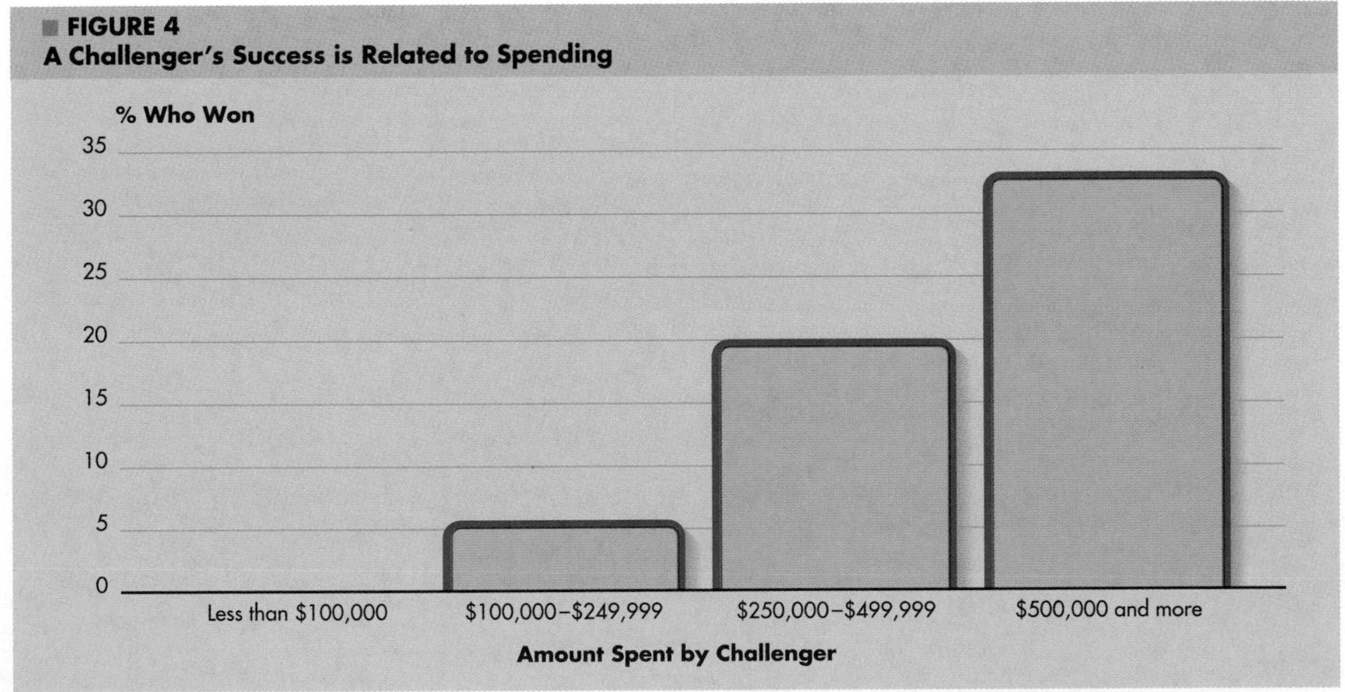

SOURCE: Open Secrets, (See note 23).

Does Money Buy Favorable Policies?

Everyone agrees that money buys access. Both anecdotal and systematic evidence suggests that money also buys votes, although only under some conditions.

There is now a significant amount of research on the impact of PACs on legislators' behavior in committees and in voting. There appears to be a link between campaign contributions and favorable action in legislative committees, where voting patterns are less visible to the public than roll-call votes by the whole Congress. Legislators with PAC support are more active in speaking and negotiating on behalf of positions favored by the PACs and offering amendments favorable to PAC positions.[43]

The research on voting is not completely consistent but suggests that PACs may influence voting, especially on votes that are less visible.[44] Most issues are not of great importance to the public and are not widely publicized. "The plain truth is that most issues before Congress do not involve great moral principles, and the lobbyists understand that a little persuasion will often do the trick."[45] Or more bluntly, "You can't buy a Congressman for $5,000. But you can buy his vote. It's done on a regular basis."[46]

A recent survey of members found that about one-fifth admit the political contributions have affected their votes on occasion, and another one-third are not sure.[47] Analysis of voting has revealed that contributions from the AFL-CIO affected voting on the minimum wage legislation, and contributions

How Congressional Candidates Spend Their Money

Common wisdom suggests that much of the explanation for expensive political campaigns is the high cost of television advertising. A closer look suggests that this common wisdom is somewhat wide of the mark.

The 1988 campaign budgets of two rank-and-file House members, Florida Republican Michael Bilirakis and Virginia Democrat Frederick Boucher, reveal something about how campaign money is used. Most campaign spending goes toward two things: campaign organization and advertising. Campaign organization includes obvious costs such as office space, supplies, phone, and postage, and for incumbents, salaries for key campaign personnel. Challengers, who have fewer funds, often must rely on volunteers to staff their campaign.

Campaign Spending by Three House Candidates

	Bilirakis (Incumbent, unopposed)	Boucher (Incumbent, opposed)	Brown (challenger)
Organization	61%	28%	65%
Advertising	8	44	21
Fund raising	14	5	0
Travel	9	3	5
Consulting	8	20	9
Total spending	$190,000	$600,000	$158,000
% of vote	100%	63%	37%

SOURCE: Sam Miller, "Always Run Scared," *National Journal*, June 16, 1990, pp. 1456–57.

But for many candidates, especially incumbents, organizational expenses can include items that have very little to do with wooing voters. Indeed, a study of congressional campaign spending revealed that half of all campaign spending is unrelated to contacting voters. With little accountability in how money is spent, some candidates run up tens of thousands of dollars worth of food bills, donate hundreds of thousands of dollars to educational institutions, spend days at lavish resorts, and buy decorations for their offices.

Representative Bilirakis's organizational expenses included sending flowers to constituents, treating them to meals at restaurants and clubs, and giving money to local party clubs and charity groups.

Overall, House candidates spend only 23% on television advertising, while Senate candidates who need to reach larger audiences, spend around 30%. Advertising expenses among these three candidates range widely from 8% by Representative Bilirakis who was unopposed, to 44% by Representative Boucher. Boucher did have an opponent, John Brown, but like most congressional challengers, his opponent was underfunded. Boucher had almost four times as much to spend as Brown. Boucher spent almost half of his $600,000 campaign budget on advertising. (Most advertising costs are for television time, though, depending on the locale, candidates might also buy radio and newspaper ads.) Boucher won easily, perhaps discouraging future opponents. In 1990 he had no opposition.

SOURCES: Charles Babcock, "The Big Spenders on the Hill," *Washington Post National Weekly Edition* (September 14–20, 1992), p. 34. Drawn from Sara Fritz and Dwight Morris, *Handbook of Campaign Spending*.

from the trucking interests led senators to vote against deregulation of trucking. Those senators facing reelection the year in which the vote was taken were most susceptible.[48] Voting is also related to donations in such disparate areas as minimum wage legislation, gun control, and regulation.[49]

One classic example concerns used-car legislation. Auto dealers spent $675,000 in the 1980 congressional elections. This investment seemed to pay off when in 1982 Congress voted against a rule requiring dealers to inform prospective buyers of any known defects in used cars. The senators who opposed the measure received twice as much money from the auto dealers' PAC as those who voted for it. In the House, those who opposed the measure received on average five times more money as those who voted for it. Almost 85% of the representatives opposing the legislation had received PAC money.[50]

The relationship between PAC money and votes still existed even when taking into account the party and ideology of the members. For conservatives, who might have voted against requiring auto dealers to list defects anyway, PAC contributions made only a marginal difference in their voting; but for liberals, PAC money substantially raised the probability that they would vote with the used-car dealers.[51] " 'Of course it was money,' one House member said. . . . 'Why else would they vote for used-car dealers?' "[52]

Some Democratic House leaders were surprised when members said they could not vote against a capital gains tax cut (which would benefit the wealthy) because it would anger their business contributors. "I get elected by voters. I get financed by contributors. Voters don't care about this, contributors do."[53]

The relationship between PAC contributions and voting should not be exaggerated, however.[54] Even on these low visibility votes, a member's party and ideology are important. The constituency interests of members are also key factors explaining votes. For example, members with many union workers in their districts are going to vote for those interests regardless of how much or little they get in PAC contributions.[55] Members without these constituents, though, may be more swayed by PAC contributions.

Money not only can help buy votes and access, it can buy congressional influence with federal regulators. This type of influence is well illustrated by the relationship of Charles Keating and Senator DeConcini outlined earlier in this chapter. While this was an extreme case of favor giving, as long as members feel

"I appreciate your offer, but I'm afraid I'm already bought and paid for."

Mailing for Dollars

The Environmental Defense Fund once sent out a mass fund-raising mailing promising new members a copy of the book *50 Simple Things You Can Do to Save the Earth*. The book's number-one suggestion: stop junk mail. Ironically, environmental groups, like others, fill mailboxes with junk mail, which destroys millions of trees a year and eventually amounts to 3% of the volume in our landfills. Yet they persist with the mailings because they bring in new members and new funds.

PACs and political parties soliciting funds send out hundreds of millions of letters annually. For example, the National Rifle Association sends 12 million letters monthly, and the American Association of Retired People (AARP) sends 50 million a year just prospecting for new members.[1]

Because most people look forward to mail more than other daily activities such as television, eating, and hobbies,[2] mail solicitations for money by PACs and other political groups provide an interesting diversion in their day. Many read the letters, are convinced by the arguments, and write checks.

Getting a good response from mail solicitations appears to be both an art and a science. Here are some of the tricks of the trade used by successful PACs.

The *mailing list* is one key to success. Letters are not sent out randomly. Rather, you are likely to receive such mailings if you have already contributed to a candidate or cause or even if you buy goods from mail-order catalogs. One estimate is that average Americans in professional occupations spend eight months of their lives simply opening and sorting political and business junk mail. Mailing lists of potential contributors are shared among like-minded groups.

The *envelope* should be personalized, with real stamps, not metered ones. Often the words URGENT or REPLY REQUIRED stimulate a better response. One PAC sent out a mailing with the words FEDERAL TAX REDUCTION INFORMATION ENCLOSED prominently displayed on the envelope (the PAC letter dealt with the activities of a PAC working to reduce taxes).

The *letter* often is written on expensive-looking paper. The text is written in short paragraphs to capture the reader's attention. A letter from the Independent Action PAC (IAPAC) had about 14 paragraphs per page, many of them just a sentence long. The prose usually is written at the sixth- to eighth-grade level—short, simple language. On the other hand, the letter is often fairly long. Four pages is typical, but many are longer.

The *opening paragraph* is usually an attention grabber such as, "I need your advice," or "This is the most urgent letter I have ever written."[3]

The *language* is usually emotional, overblown, and very negative. One 1995 Democratic fund-raising letter called Newt Gingrich a terrorist (the authors later apologized). The National Rifle Association's labeling of government agents as "jackbooted thugs" caused former President Bush to resign his membership. One NCPAC letter from Jesse Helms warned, "Your tax dollars are being used to pay for grade school courses that teach our children that cannibalism, wife swapping, and the murder of infants and the elderly are acceptable." Campaigning against PACs, IAPAC warned that "money doesn't just talk, it leads many elected officials around on a leash."

Mailers use a personal approach, and their letters are sprinkled with "you"s. A mailing from the National Taxpayers Union offered instructions as to how "you can save America from Washington." Well-heeled PACs sometimes use computers to intersperse your name throughout the letter.

Enclosures are common. Solicitors often promise you something for your membership or send along a small gift, such as a signed picture, stickers, or a pin. "While trying to appeal to you with flattery for your intelligence and compassion, direct mail packages are designed on the assumption you are a self-indulgent idiot," commented one observer of the direct mail scene.

A *donor card* is crucial. Cards are enclosed to make it easy for recipients to give. This card can be pretty emotional, too. For example, one conservative PAC offered recipients two choices on the donor card. If they contributed to the PAC, they could stick a stars and stripes flag on the card. If they refused to contribute, they should stick on the white flag of surrender!

Calvin and Hobbes **by Bill Watterson**

1. Jill Smolowe, "Read This!!!!!!!!" *Time*, November 26, 1990, p. 63.
2. Larry Sabato, "Mailing for Dollars," *Psychology Today* 18 (October 1984), pp. 38–43. This box draws heavily on the Sabato article.
3. Sabato, "Mailing for Dollars." The remainder of the quotations are from this article, unless otherwise noted.

dependent on big donors for campaign funds, these "favors" are likely to remain common.

Although research on the impact of PAC contributions on the behavior of members of Congress is plentiful, we know less about how contributions affect the policies of presidential candidates. Large donations to presidential campaigns may be given in the hopes of buying access, but using money to win influence over presidential candidates is probably less successful than it is with other officials. Presidential candidates tend to have widely publicized views, and their actions as president are subject to intense scrutiny and publicity. Once in office presidents need donors less than donors need them, thus making the leverage of a campaign donation uncertain. Contributors sometimes find, as did one contributor to the campaign of Teddy Roosevelt, "We bought the son of a bitch but he did not stay bought."[56]

Still, analyses of large donors to, and fund-raisers for, the Bush campaign reveal that many were given special favors or benefits from the federal government. The Department of Labor reduced a proposed fine by nearly 90% against a large sugar farmer who gave $200,000 to the campaign.[57] The president proposed incentives for using corn-based ethanol in auto fuels, a proposal that would cost consumers three-tenths of a cent per gallon of gas purchased and yield Archer-Daniels-Midland, which gave the Republican campaign more than $1 million, a profit of $30 to $75 million.

While it is impossible to prove a cause-and-effect relationship in these cases, clearly large donors who expect favorable treatment have plenty of precedents to lead them to that conclusion.

The influence of big money in presidential campaigns probably makes both parties more conservative. The biggest contributors to the Republicans in the last few presidential elections have been some of the most conservative people within that party. The big money contributors to the Democrats are, on the whole, less liberal than the mainstream of the party.

Large contributions to presidential campaigns (including money spent in primaries, soft money, independent spending, and PACs) often lead to appointments to public office. The "spoils system," as it is called, has been with us since at least the time of Andrew Jackson, so it cannot be blamed on modern PACs and soft money. Many times these appointments are to rather minor offices without much significant policy impact. For example, ambassadorships to small nations traditionally have been given to big campaign contributors.

➤Reforming the Campaign Money System

Many believe the current system of raising funds is undesirable. The concentration of congressional fund-raising efforts on Washington lobbyists increasingly gives the appearance, and perhaps the reality, of simply buying elections and then votes. The conservative *Wall Street Journal* colorfully described the system in Washington as "the mutants' saloon in 'Star Wars'—a place where politicians, PACs, lawyers, and lobbyists for unions, business, or you-name-it shake each other down full time for political money and political support ."[58]

We have seen repeatedly that public confidence and trust in government have diminished greatly over time. Some of the reasons for this declining trust have nothing to do with money. But public trust was certainly affected by the Watergate scandal, and it is likely that revelations about big money lobbying activity since then have not improved the public's view of the honesty of public officials.

There is some evidence that the public is reacting against the growth of big money in campaign finance. Though many issues were involved in the defeat of Democratic incumbents in 1994, most of the members of the House who were defeated in the elections of

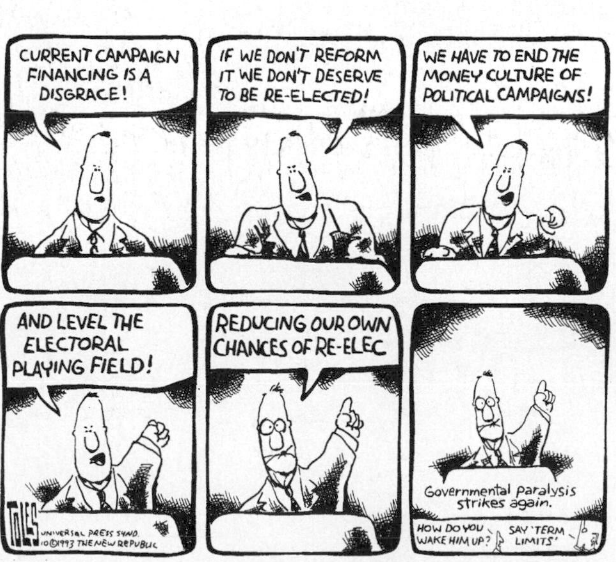

CURRENT CAMPAIGN FINANCING IS A DISGRACE!
IF WE DON'T REFORM IT WE DON'T DESERVE TO BE RE-ELECTED!
WE HAVE TO END THE MONEY CULTURE OF POLITICAL CAMPAIGNS!
AND LEVEL THE ELECTORAL PLAYING FIELD!
REDUCING OUR OWN CHANCES OF RE-ELEC
Governmental paralysis strikes again.
HOW DO YOU WAKE HIM UP?
SAY 'TERM LIMITS'
TOLES
UNIVERSAL PRESS SYND.
10©1993 THE NEW REPUBLIC

Source: By Toles for the New Republic Magazine, Inc.

1990 and 1992 had some conflict-of-interest allegations leveled against them.

Several proposals to reform the system have been offered, most focusing on congressional campaign spending.[59] One of the major proposals, a combination of public financing and limits on spending, is discussed in this chapter's Symbolic Solutions box. Other ideas include strengthening the parties' role in financing elections by allowing them to give more to candidates; raising the amounts individuals can con-

Doctors' Orders

Big money does not always win key congressional votes. One example was the 1982 battle between the American Medical Association (AMA) and a variety of groups including Ralph Nader's Congress Watch, a public interest group.[1] The AMA was fighting to get Congress to overturn a ruling of the Federal Trade Commission (FTC), a federal regulatory agency. The FTC had ruled that doctors could not engage in price fixing, that is, deciding as a group what minimum fees to charge and punishing doctors who charge less. The FTC also had ruled that doctors could advertise their services. In other words, the FTC was applying to doctors the same rules that the Supreme Court had applied to lawyers and that the FTC itself applies to other businesses; automakers, for example, cannot agree to fix the price of cars, nor can they punish other car manufacturers who advertise. If automakers tried to fix prices, they would be in violation of antitrust laws that forbid such collusion.

The AMA wanted to be free to do its own regulating; it wanted Congress to pass a special law exempting doctors from antitrust regulations and from the clutches of the FTC. Given the antigovernment sentiment of the time, the AMA seemed close to achieving a victory. The exemption passed the House and cleared a key Senate committee.

The AMA was thought to be one of the strongest lobbying forces in Washington. It had fought against government regulation of medicine for more than 30 years. Its legitimacy was reinforced by the idea that it was an association of friendly, helpful, lifesaving doctors.

For the anti-AMA forces to win on this issue, they had to challenge the legitimacy of the AMA. To do that, they turned the wealth and power of the AMA against it. The FTC itself unleashed a blitz of public relations pointing out that the AMA was trying to set prices and regulate the economics of medicine. Congress Watch noted that when the FTC permitted advertising of eyeglasses and contact lenses, prices went down and consumers saved $100 million. But most important, Congress Watch, in a well-timed series of press releases, showed that the AMA was trying to buy Congress.

Indeed, the AMA had contributed more money to congressional candidates than any other organization except the National Association of Realtors. It gave $1,700,000 in campaign contributions to the House and Senate cosponsors of the antitrust exemption bill and another $280,000 to members of committees that would hold hearings on the bill. Forty-four members of Congress received $10,000 or more from the AMA.

In its releases, Congress Watch pointed out exactly which members were taking campaign money from the AMA. These names often were picked up by the members' home media, which editorialized against them. A New York representative was narrowly defeated in the primary election after his links with the AMA were exposed. This defeat led the *New York Times* to say: "Opportunistic congressmen who flack for special interests may wind up paying for their jobs."[2] Copies of the editorial were distributed to congressional offices by the anti-AMA lobby.

Gradually, the AMA lost its reputation as a group of selfless individuals interested in the public's health and began to be tagged as a greedy group interested in its own economic health. This perception was helped along by a Congress Watch news release pointing out that the average doctor earned more than $86,000 the year before.

Meanwhile, Congress Watch accompanied its publicity campaign with one-on-one lobbying of members of Congress. Soon, members who originally cosponsored the AMA bill decided to back off.

The Senate vote, which went overwhelmingly against the AMA, was greeted with approval by the press. As one editorial noted: "The vaunted AMA was reeling from severe legislative contusions."

This outcome illustrates a key point about the influence of campaign money. It is more influential when the issue is not well publicized. When AMA foes were able to spotlight the money generously flowing from the AMA to those willing to do its bidding in Congress, the AMA's money began to be seen as a liability rather than an asset. When Congress Watch and other groups were able to focus the debate on the public interest versus the special interest, and to show members that their home constituents were watching, members opted for the public interest.

1. This example is drawn from Michael Pertschuk (former chair of the Federal Trade Commission and now involved in public interest lobbying), *Giant Killers* (New York: Norton, 1986), chapter 4.
2. Ibid, p. 108.

tribute (inflation has eroded the value of the limits set in the early 1970s) and limiting further the amount PACs can give; forcing PACs to disclose more about their operations; or giving tax credits for campaign contributions given only to candidates of one's own state (or to presidential candidates).

Some proposals would allow candidates free media time and prohibit purchase of additional time as is common in other nations (this would also deal with independent spending). Candidates would be given time and must use it in slots of at least 5 or 10 minutes with this proposal. No 30-second slash-and-burn commercials would be allowed. Presidential candidates in 1992 made good use of free media time scheduled, not because of legislative mandates but because of the interests of talk shows hosts and others in interviewing presidential candidates. Interest in congressional candidates is considerably less, however.

Opponents point out the practical difficulties of this kind of reform in a federal system in which each congressional candidate must appeal to his or her own constituency. Unlike Western European nations, where citizens vote primarily for the national party, not for their local candidate, politics in the United States is decentralized. But this roadblock to reform may not be insuperable for, as Senator Robert Dole (R-Kan.) said, "If they can figure out the tax code, they can figure this out."[60]

However, our political leaders have no stake in serious reform. Ideologically, Democrats are more sympathetic to limiting the influence of big money, but practically, Democratic incumbents are heavily dependent upon their PAC "fixes." When a Republican president was in office, Democratic members of Congress could vote their ideological inclinations for campaign finance reform, resting assured that the president would veto any serious reforms. When Clinton took office and indicated his support for reform, Democratic members of Congress presented an interesting spectacle as they found innumerable ways to avoid passing a serious bill. Now that Republicans control Congress, Democrats rue their failure to pass laws regulating campaign financing most tightly. Business interests, ideologically more in tune with Republicans, have begun to move strongly toward supporting them in Congress now that Republicans are in a majority. Democrats are finding their sources of funding drying up.

Walter Lippman, a famous American journalist, once said that American communities govern themselves "by fits and starts of unsuspecting complacency and violent suspicion." We think nothing is wrong, and then we think everything is wrong. So it is with our views of campaign money. For several years after the 1974 reforms, we thought things were going along pretty well. More recently many became convinced that the nation was in terrible jeopardy because of the influence of money. Whether we are overreacting or not, the issue of campaign finance reform is again alive.

➤Conflicts of Interest

In addition to money's influence on political campaigns, it also leads to **conflicts of interest.** This term refers to officials making decisions that directly affect their own personal livelihoods or interests. The campaign contribution system we have just described is certainly a huge conflict of interest. Presidents and members of Congress make decisions about policies affecting those who give them campaign money. But conflicts of interest are not confined to decisions involving sources of campaign money. As Madison noted, almost every decision involves potential conflicts of interest. Decisions made by presidents, bureaucrats, and members of Congress can affect their personal financial interests (including stocks, bonds, or other investments).

■ Conflict-of-Interest Reforms

The 1970s brought about not only reform in campaign finance but also new rules about financial interests within government. Ethics committees had been part of Congress since 1964, when the Senate established

This secretly filmed picture shows the acceptance of money in the Abscam episode. As one of the implicated members said: "I'm gonna tell you something real simple and short. In this business, money talks and b _ _ _s _ _ _ walks."

Members of Congress are barred from accepting gifts worth $100 or more from lobbyists. However, members and PACs show considerable ingenuity in evading this regulation. Members can be reimbursed for travel expenses, so many take themselves and their families to the Caribbean, Europe, and other desirable locations at the expense of lobbyists. These trips are called **junkets** by their critics and "speaking engagements" or "fact-finding tours" by the members. At the invitation of lobbyists, members go to a posh location, give a short speech to a PAC or other interest group meeting there, and then are paid generally for their expenses.

The 1992 check kiting scandal in Congress is another kind of ethical problem. Members of the House set up a bank open only to members. The public was outraged when it became known that some members repeatedly wrote checks without having sufficient funds in their accounts. Even though no public money was involved (members were essentially borrowing each other's money), and no law was apparently broken, the idea of creating these special prerogatives created an outbreak of public anger that caused many of the biggest check kiters to retire rather than face the irate voters.[63] Having many overdrafts also slightly increased the number of well known people who decided to run against incum-

What About Whitewater?

Since 1992, the topic of Whitewater has popped into the news every few weeks. It is an alleged scandal that involves President Clinton, his wife Hillary Rodham Clinton, an obscure savings and loan in Arkansas, and a suicide in Washington, D.C. The story of Whitewater has persisted since 1992, and most people long ago have forgotten, if they ever knew, what the supposed "scandal" is all about. Yet, surfers on the Internet, as well as listeners on conservative talk radio, can read and hear about murders, suicide, and other plots that some people allege are connected to Whitewater.

The facts seem a lot less interesting or exciting than the lurid rumors. The facts appear to be that in the late 1970s, Bill and Hillary Clinton entered into a venture, called the Whitewater Development Company, whose purpose was to sell vacation lots in the Ozarks. The Clintons were a 50% partner in this deal, along with James McDougal, a political supporter of then-Governor Clinton. With an investment of $230,000, the Clintons lost somewhere between $45,000 and $68,000 in this venture, eventually selling their shares to McDougal.

Later, McDougal (but not the Clintons) purchased a savings and loan company, the Madison Guaranty, which, after a time, federal regulators declared to be insolvent. Meanwhile, Hillary Clinton, as a lawyer representing Madison Guaranty, petitioned the new state securities comissioner (who herself had formerly worked for a law firm that represented Madison), to permit the savings and loan to borrow money and remain in operation. But the appeal failed and the savings and loan was finally declared insolvent. It was taken over by the federal government in 1989, as part of the nationwide program to get the savings and loan industry back to financial solvency (see Chapter 18 for more on regulation of savings and loans).

All of this happened long before Bill Clinton was in the White House; and thus has nothing to do with use or misuse of presidential power. Investigations by special prosecutors and Congress have revealed a kind of cronyism that especially affects politics in small towns and small states and can lead to conflicts of interest. There have been charges that funds were siphoned from Madison to Clinton's gubernatorial campaign, but these have not been proven.

The plot thickened, however, when Vincent Foster, another close Arkansas friend of the Clintons, a member of the Clinton White House staff, and the lawyer who had handled the Clinton's sale of their Whitewater holdings to McDougal, committed suicide in a Washington park in 1993.

Immediately rumors spread that Foster had been murdered, or committed suicide because of Whitewater. The motive for a political killing is obscure at best, as is the Whitewater link. Foster was beset by many political problems and despaired of his perceived lack of success in his Washington role. However, White House Counsel Bernard Nussbaum did remove Foster's Whitewater files before the police reached Foster's office, thus adding fuel to the flame. Clinton later fired Nussbaum.

In 1994, Attorney General Janet Reno appointed an independent counsel to investigate the entire Whitewater affair. Republicans in the Congress soon launched an investigation of their own. A year later, several findings have been made that the Clintons did nothing wrong in the Whitewater matter, but congressional inquiries continue to fuel rumors. While new revelations might throw entirely new light on the Clintons, for now it seems like sloppy financial record keeping, cronyism, and a lack of candor about their complicated deals are their major failings. Most of the public seem bored with the continuing story, or non-story, which seems to have taken on a life of its own in the fringes of the news media.

bents, and led to slightly greater probabilities of electoral defeat for those who stayed in the race. The effects in the general election, however, were slight compared to the media focus on this event.

The Executive Branch

In 1986, a high-level executive branch official was the recipient of a $2.5 million loan. His associates purchased a house for him in an exclusive California community. Even though only 2 of the 18 donors' names were revealed and even though the official had more than two years remaining in his term of office, the press and public scarcely commented.[64] The official was Ronald Reagan and the donors were self-described "independently wealthy" individuals. Did this represent a conflict of interest? If the recipient had been anyone else, most people would probably have thought so, but Reagan was so popular that this transaction was largely overlooked (Reagan started paying rent for the house after he left office). The incident does reveal, however, the looseness of the regulations concerning conflict of interest.

Since the Carter administration, all high-level administrative officials have been required to file public financial disclosure statements to allow the public to

Are There Democratic and Republican Kinds of Corruption?

Some observers have pointed out that while both Democrats and Republicans have ethical lapses, the kinds of ethics problems they have are quite different. Corrupt Democrats steal. They accept bribes and improper campaign donations, divert public funds to their own pockets, and in general, engage in personal financial aggrandizement. This style of corruption is reminiscent of the "honest graft" of the big city political machines (see box on Boss Plunkett in Chapter 6). While some Republicans also steal, for example, former Vice President Spiro Agnew, who pleaded no contest to charges of kickbacks, bribery, and extortion, and former Representative Joseph McDade (R-Pa), who has been indicted for bribery and racketeering (but not yet convicted), most of these sorts of scandals involved Democrats. Examples include most of those involved in Abscam, four of the Keating 5, four Democratic members of Congress convicted of graft in the last three years, and most recently Daniel Rostenkowski (D-Ill), former chair of the Ways and Means Committee, indicted (but not yet convicted) for padding his payroll with ghost workers, using his office expense account to buy gifts for friends, and trading stamp vouchers for cash.

Republican ethical failings tend to be related to the use of government for improper means. President Nixon's Watergate scandal involved trying to use the powers of government to punish his personal enemies, and then lying about it. He also ordered Cambodia to be bombed and tried to keep it a secret. President Reagan tried to subvert the constitutional powers of Congress by secretly selling arms to Iran and supplying weapons to rebels in Nicaragua, both expressly against the law. While Democratic presidents have also been guilty of misuse of government power (for example, President Johnson lying about alleged attacks by the North Vietnamese on an American ship in order to justify getting the U.S. more deeply involved in the Vietnamese war and President Kennedy ordering the F.B.I. to wiretap Reverend Martin Luther King), subverting government seems more a Republican style of corruption.

Why do these differences exist? They could be coincidental, of course. But one Democrat argued that these were differences tied to the class basis of the parties: "The lower classes steal, the upper classes defraud." A prominent Republican had a different view: "Most Republicans are contemptuous of government; few Democrats are." Whatever the reason, these examples suggest that partisanship extends to more than presidential preferences.

60. Drew, *Politics and Money*, p. 151.

61. Susan Welch and John Peters, "Private Interests in the U.S. Congress," *Legislative Studies Quarterly* 7 (November 1982), pp. 547–55.

62. John Peters and Susan Welch, "Private Interests and Public Interests," *Journal of Politics* 45 ([illegible] 1983), pp. 378–96.

63. John Alford, Holly Teeters, Daniel Ward, and Rick K. Wilson, "Overdraft: The Political Cost of Congressional Malfeasance," *American Journal of Political Science* 56 (August, 1994), pp. 788–801; Susan Banducci and Jeffrey A. Karp, "Electoral Consequences of Scandal and Reapportionment in the 1992 House Elections," *American Politics Quarterly* 22 (January, 1994), pp. 3–26; Gary C. Jacobson and Michael A. Dimock, "Checking Out: The Effects of Bank Overdrafts on the 1992 House Elections," *American Journal of Political Science* 38 (August, 1994), pp. 601–624.

64. Mark Shields, "[illegible]," *Washington Post National Weekly Edition*, [illegible] 1990.

65. [illegible] 1987, p. 22.

66. "[illegible] Sundry Sidelines," *Time*, May 25, 1987, p. [illegible].

67. Elizabeth Drew, "Letter from Washington," *New Yorker*, May 1, 1989, pp. 99–108. See also Don Beiz, "Tales of Power and Money," *Washington Post National Weekly Edition*, May 1–7, 1989, pp. 11–12.

68. [illegible] "The Campaign Finance [illegible]," *Washington Post National Weekly Edition*, May 11–17, 1992, p. [illegible].

69. "Blowing It All," p. 28.

70. [illegible] p. 14.

71. [illegible]

72. [illegible]

73. [illegible] p. 25.

74. Ibid.

75. [illegible]

76. [illegible]

77. [illegible] pp. 145.

78. [illegible]

were not obscure. Laura Langbein, "Money and Access," *Journal of Politics* 48 (November 1986), pp. 1052–64, shows that those who received more PAC money spend more time with interest group representatives.

45. Drew, *Politics and Money*, p. [illegible].

46. "[illegible] with the PACs," *Time*, October 25, 1982, p. 28. The quotation is from Representative Thomas Downey (D-N.Y.).

47. "Congress Study Links Funds and Votes," *New York Times*, December 30, 1982, p. [illegible].

48. John Frendreis and Richard Waterman, "PAC Contributions and Legislative Behavior: Senate Voting on Trucking Deregulation," *Social Science Quarterly* 66 (June 1985), pp. 401–12. See also W. P. Welch, "Campaign Contributions and Legislative Voting," *Western Political Quarterly* 35 (December 1982), pp. 478–95; Jonathan Silberman and Garey Durden, "Determining Legislative Preferences on the Minimum Wage," *Journal of Political Economy* 84 (April 1976), pp. [illegible].

49. [illegible] "PACs, Lobbies, and [illegible]," [illegible], pp. 254–271; Laura Langbein and Mark Lotwis, "The Political Efficacy of Lobbying and Money: Gun Control in the U.S. House, 1986," *Legislative Studies Quarterly* 15 (1990), pp. 413–40; Janet Grenzke, "Campaign Contributions and Legislative Outcomes," *Western Political Quarterly* 39 (1986), pp. [illegible].

50. [illegible] "PACs Gave More to Senate Winners," *New York Times*, [illegible] p. 12.

51. [illegible]

52. [illegible]

53. [illegible]

54. [illegible]

55. [illegible]

56. [illegible]

57. [illegible]

58. [illegible]

PART THREE

Institutions

Bill Clinton, near his childhood home of Hope, Ark. (right).

Newt Gingrich at 7 (below).

10 Congress

You Are There

Should You Risk Your Career?

It is August 1993 and the House of Representatives is considering Bill Clinton's first budget bill. The bill, which includes a plan to substantially reduce the deficit, has been portrayed as a "make or break" moment in Clinton's presidential term. Failure to get the bill passed will further reduce his persuasive power and stature, perhaps (hyperbolic media pronounced) ruin his presidency, because he is already seen as weak. On the other hand, passage of the bill will be seen by the media and the interested public as a huge victory, the first step in bringing the nation's deficit under control.

You are Marjorie Margolies-Mezvinsky, a freshman Democratic member of Congress from suburban Philadelphia. You are faced with a representative's worst nightmare: On an important, well-publicized vote, you must either stand with the president of your party against the wishes of the majority of your district's voters, or vote with your district but contribute in large part to your president's defeat.

You are not a typical member of Congress. A graduate of Columbia University, you are a television newswoman married to a former Iowa congressional representative. You have eleven children, including biological children, stepchildren, adopted children from Korea and Vietnam, and refugee foster children. After covering the Clarence Thomas-Anita Hill hearings as a journalist, you decided to run for Congress yourself. Your opponent, a former state representative and county commissioner, is well known for his constituency work (called a "zen master of constituency service" by the local paper), but you attacked him for feeding at the public trough and for waffling ("pro-choice, that's me; multiple choice, that's Jon Fox").[1] You supported abortion rights, improved health care programs, and a middle-class tax cut.

You are finishing your first term in office, and like most other members, are greatly concerned about your reelection chances. Your district had been continuously represented by Republicans since 1916(!) before you were elected. But in 1992, the voters of the district gave you a razor-thin majority (you won by only 1300 votes out of 254,000 cast) and a plurality to Bill Clinton, largely because of economic concerns and partly because of an anti-incumbent mood. Since coming to Congress, you have positioned yourself well. You are one of only five freshmen appointed to the powerful Energy and Commerce Committee. A position on that committee has given you access to important interests who have already contributed to your reelection campaign.

Clinton's budget bill calls for a combination of tax increases and spending cuts. It pleases no one entirely, but is the first significant move toward reducing the deficit since the 1960s. But the bill is in jeopardy for two reasons. First, the Republicans, the minority party in the House, are united in opposition. Many Republicans had supported similar budget measures when they were proposed by George Bush. But now that it is Clinton's budget bill, they sensed an opportunity to deal a major blow to his presidency by defeating this key economic package. The Republicans have traditionally positioned themselves as fiscally conservative (even though it was a Republican president, Ronald Reagan, who ran the largest deficits in U.S. history), and they do not wish to relinquish this advantage to the Democrats. But many conservative Democrats are defecting because they oppose the various tax increases, including a proposed tax on fuel as an energy-saving measure.

CONTINUED

OUTLINE

Members and Constituencies
- Members
- Constituencies

Congressional Campaigns and Elections
- The Advantages of Incumbency
- Unsafe at Any Margin?
- Challengers
- Campaigns
- Voting for Congress

The Representative on the Job
- Informal Norms
- Working Privately and "Going Public"
- Voting by Members

How Congress Is Organized
- How Congressional Organization Evolved
- Leaders
- Committees
- Staff

What Congress Does
- Lawmaking
- Overseeing the Federal Bureaucracy
- Budget Making

Conclusion: Is Congress Responsive?

As the Republicans take control of Congress, a staff member for a departing Democrat packs to leave.

You initially voted against the bill because you have told your constituents you will not support the bill. You had mixed emotions when it passed by six votes. The bill has come back to the House after House and Senate representatives reached agreement in a conference committee (when the Senate and House versions of a particular bill are not identical, a committee is set up to negotiate a common version of the bill, which is then sent to each house for ratification). Now the House must ratify the results of that negotiation. You have already prepared a statement explaining your "no" vote on the budget bill. You think it does not go far enough to reduce the deficit. In particular, you believe that it does not pare enough away from entitlements, those programs like Medicare, welfare, and Social Security. As part of your justification for the no vote, you indicate you believe that the president should call a "summit" meeting to discuss entitlement spending.

But now the president has spoken to you at length, pleading for your support. He, and anyone who follows the news, knows the vote is extremely close. He needs every vote, including yours. Given the unanimous opposition of the Republicans, most Democrats must stand firm or the bill will be defeated. You know that a defeat on this bill could have serious repercussions for his entire presidency.

But you do not really favor the bill. It does not go as far as you want on spending cuts, and there are too many tax increases in the bill. Moreover, you think your constituents are not in favor of it either. You want to be reelected, and you fear that because you have told your constituents you will not support the bill, your constituents will think you have sold out. To vote for the bill could mean committing political suicide in your Republican district; even under the best of circumstances you will have an uphill race. To waffle on this key issue could move your reelection chances from marginal to hopeless. What do you do?

Representative Margolies-Mezvinsky with her aides moments before she must vote.

Many Americans are angry at government, and they are most angry at Congress. Americans profess a love for democracy in the abstract, but paradoxically it is the very visibility of democratic processes that makes Congress the least loved branch of government.[2]

The public has the highest level of support for the Supreme Court, the institution that is the least democratic (Figure 1). It, however, is most isolated from the public. Little of the disagreement, negotiation, and compromise that takes place on the Court becomes public. The public gives the president the next highest level of support. The president is certainly the most visible symbol of national government, but within the executive office, disagreement, negotiation, and compromise are somewhat concealed.

The public is least supportive of Congress, where the processes of democracy are exposed for all to see. C-SPAN and news broadcasts bring debate, disagreement, and compromise alive. The media also bring to every American who cares to listen the arguments of lobbyists and special interest groups, each trying to pull Congress in a particular direction. They see Congress as too powerful, impeding the president from carrying out his duties. Too often, for the public's taste, the debate is rancorous rather than calm, and focused on how prospective legislation will affect private interests rather than the public interest. None of this is surprising, of course, in a complex society

■ **FIGURE 1**
Public Perceives Congress as Most Powerful National Institution, and Likes It the Least

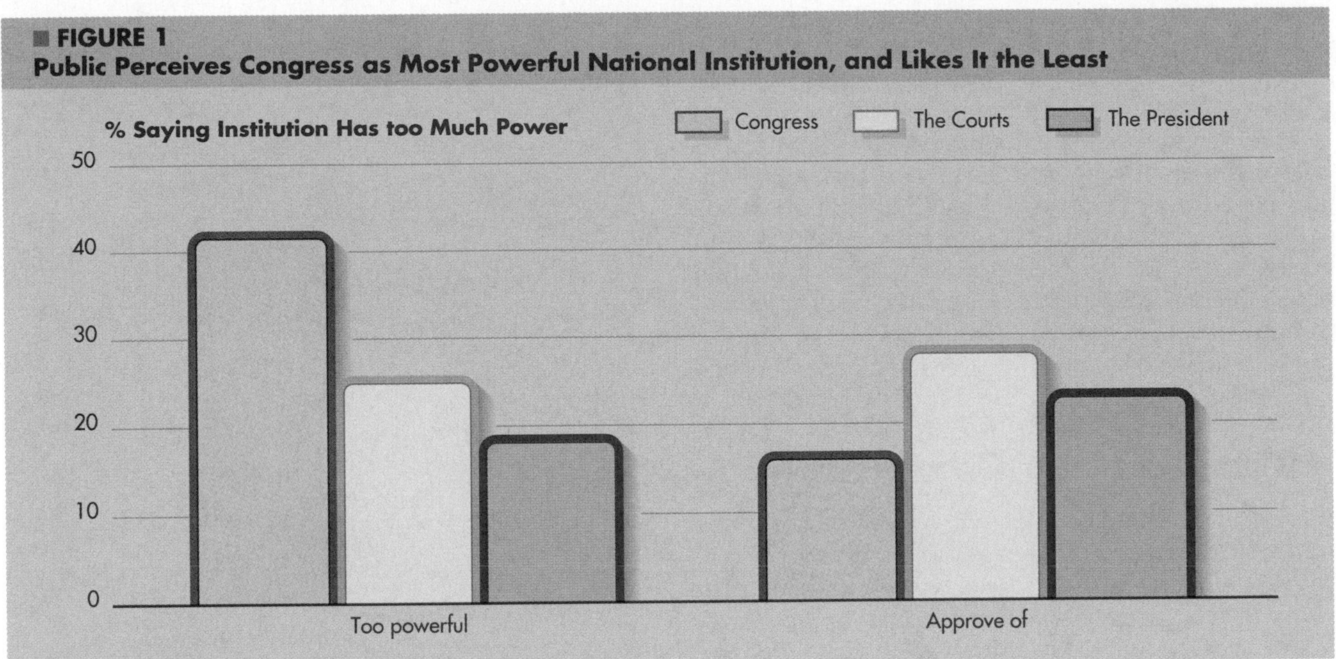

SOURCE: John Hibbing and Elizabeth Theiss-Morse, *Congress as Public Enemy* (Cambridge, Cambridge University Press, 1995). Data are from 1993.

where people and groups do have quite different interests and views of the world. But, as two political scientists recently commented, "The people want democracy without the mess and Congress is a tangible reminder that democracy is messy."[3]

That being said, however, public attitudes about Congress are themselves complex. One famous political scientist once observed that Americans hate their Congress, but love their own member of Congress.[4] This is true, but attitudes are not that simple. Two-thirds of the public approve of their own representative, compared to about one-fourth who approve of the members of Congress as a whole and about the same percentage who approve of congressional leaders.

The public thinks that most members of Congress care more about power than about the best interests of the nation, care more about special interests than the people, and lose touch with the people quickly after being elected. Although almost half think that most members of Congress are doing the best job they can, only 30% believe that members have high personal moral codes and even fewer believe that members care deeply about the problems of ordinary citizens. In other words, the public thinks members of Congress are a rather crass and self-interested group.

Despite all this, nearly 90 percent approve of Congress as an abstract institution, separate from the people in it.[5] The idea of a Congress as enshrined in the Constitution is important and esteemed. It is the people *in* Congress and the way Congress works that the public dislikes.

In addition to the public's dislike for Congress' messy processes, Congress seems to be blamed for the nation's problems, and for taxes and government wastefulness. Conflicts of interest also mar its reputation. Members themselves greatly contribute to the poor image of Congress by belittling the institution and promising voters a change when they campaign for office. They denigrate Congress to get themselves elected.[6]

And if that were not bad enough, the public tends to believe there is one "public interest," and if Congress is not passing legislation to pursue that interest, there must be something wrong. Only a minority of the public, it seems, has a sophisticated understanding that there are many different interests in American society, and that Congress is the focus of controversy over which version of the public interest is adopted.

Individual members seem to be judged by other criteria than the whole Congress.[7] Members who work hard for their constituencies, doing favors for individual constituents and winning economic benefits for the district, usually are reelected. Policy failures of the institution do not seem to hurt them.

In this chapter, we try to understand this paradoxical pattern of citizen attitudes toward their representatives and their Congress by looking at the members of Congress and their backgrounds, elections, and behaviors. What do members of Congress do that makes them so popular back home? Then we look at Congress itself, how it works, and why it is a focus of public criticism.

➤Members and Constituencies

Alexis de Tocqueville was not impressed with the status of members of Congress, noting that they were "almost all obscure individuals, village lawyers, men in trades, or even persons belonging to the lower class." De Tocqueville would still find lawyers and men (and women) in trades, but in the modern Congress he would find few belonging to the lower class.

■ Members

The Constitution places few formal restrictions on membership in Congress. One must be 25 years old to serve in the House, and 30 in the Senate. One has to be a citizen for 7 years to be elected to the House, and 9 to the Senate. Members must reside in the states from which they were elected, but House members need not reside in their own districts.

Social Characteristics

Despite these rather loose requirements, Congress is not very representative of society. The process of recruiting, nominating, and selecting ensures that only certain types of individuals serve in Congress. Members tend to be very high in education, income, and occupational status compared to the rest of the population (see Table 1). Nearly all have college degrees, and a majority have graduate or professional degrees. Members are also quite well-off financially. Over one-fourth of the senators and one-ninth of the representatives are estimated to be millionaires. Although blue-collar workers constitute nearly one-third of the working population, there are no blue-collar workers in Congress. More than half the members of the House have served in their state legislature.[8]

■ TABLE 1 Members of Congress Are Not Representative of the Public in Race, Sex and Class

	POPULATION (%)	HOUSE (%)	SENATE (%)
Lawyer	.6	40	54
Blue-collar	30	0	0
Race & ethnicity			
Black	12	9	1
Hispanic	8	4	0
Asian	2	1	2
American Indian	1	0	1
Women	51	11	8
Catholic	23	26	20
Jewish	4	5	9
Millionaires	**	12	28
Mean age	33	51	58

Data are for 1993-94.

† Does not include nonvoting Hispanic members from Puerto Rico, Guam, Samoa, and the Virgin Islands or the black nonvoting members from the District of Columbia.

**.05% (one-twentieth percent)

SOURCE: *Congressional Quarterly Weekly Report,* November 12, 1994, pp. 7-12; Glenn R. Simpson, "Representative Moneybags," *Washington Post National Weekly Edition,* May 2-8, 1994, p. 25.

By far the most common occupation of both senators and representatives is the law. Over the past decade, about 40% of the members of the House and 60% of the Senate were lawyers. Law and politics are closely linked. Many people enter law specifically because they see it as a stepping-stone to a political career. Lawyers can take time out from a legal practice to pursue a political career whereas most salaried or wage-earning individuals cannot. The personal contacts developed in politics also can be invaluable in obtaining legal clients, and many former members of Congress enter law firms at salaries far higher than they commanded before serving in Congress.

Congress always has been predominantly white, Anglo (that is, not Hispanic), and male. It is only slightly less so today, as Table 1 shows. White, non-Hispanic males, who make up less than 40% of the total population, represent about 80% of the House and 90% of the Senate. Thus, Congress is not very representative in its demographic characteristics.

Opinions and Party Identification

Members of Congress seek to represent their constituencies. Those in districts filled with farmers must represent farmers, whether or not they know anything about farming. Representatives of districts with large universities must be aware of the reactions of university constituents even if they personally think academics have pointed heads. This conception of representation is different and more complex than simply sharing demographic characteristics.

One way members represent their constituents is through shared opinions. The liberalism of districts is reflected in members' votes. Members are more likely to share specific opinions of constituents when the issue is important to constituents and when the opinions are strongly held.[9] However, there is evidence that members are more responsive to the opinions of independent voters than to their own partisans.[10] This is probably because members believe they can count on the support of their own partisans but need to appeal to voters not strongly committed to either party.

Political party loyalties are another route to representation. The party composition of Congress corresponds rather well with the party identification of the public. Just as Democrats have been more numerous than Republicans in the public, Democrats have held majorities in both houses of Congress most of the years since World War II (see endpapers). The Republican victory in 1994 corresponded with the increase in Republican partisans during the 1980s, though there are still more Democrats than Republicans in the population.

■ Constituencies

Senators' constituencies include all the residents of their respective states; each state elects two senators. The number of each state's representatives is based on its population. Most members of the House are elected from districts within states, although six states have only one representative.

Initially, the House of Representatives had 59 members, but as the nation grew and more states joined the Union, the size of the House increased too. Since 1910, it has had 435 members except in the 1950s, when seats were temporarily added for Alaska and Hawaii. Each 10 years, in a process called **reapportionment,** the 435 seats are distributed among the states based on population changes.

Within a constant 435-seat House, states with fast-growing populations gain seats, while those with slow-growing or declining populations lose seats. The 1990 census is the basis for the latest reapportionment.

Since World War II, population movement in the United States has been toward the South, West, and Southwest and away from the Midwest and Northeast. This has been reflected in the allocation of house seats. Since 1950, California has gained 22 seats and New York has lost 12, for example. In the reapportionment after 1990, no Frost Belt state gained and only one Sunbelt state— Louisiana—lost.[11]

States that gain or lose seats and other states with population shifts within the state must redraw their district boundaries, a process called **redistricting.** This is always a hot political issue. The precise boundaries of a district can influence the election prospects of candidates and parties. In fact, districts often are formed with weird shapes to benefit the party in control of the state legislature. The term **gerrymander** is used to describe a district that is designed to maximize the political advantage of a party or a racial group.

Majority parties in state legislatures continue to secure political advantage by drawing districts of bizarre shapes, although the Supreme Court requires all congressional districts to be approximately equal in population. Before 1960, states were often reluctant to redistrict their state legislative and congressional boundaries to conform to population changes within the state. Such redistricting would endanger incumbents and threaten rural areas whose populations were declining. After decades without reapportioning, some legislative districts in urban areas were as much as 19 times the population of rural districts.

When state legislatures, frequently dominated by rural representatives, still refused to reapportion themselves, the Supreme Court in *Baker v. Carr* (1962) issued the first in a series of rulings forcing states to reapportion their legislative districts.[12] The Court required the districts to be approximately equal in population, thus mandating the principle of "one person, one vote."[13] As a result, most states had to redraw district lines, some more than once, during the 1960s. These decisions fueled heated controversy, including a proposed constitutional amendment to overturn them. But after a while the principle of "one person, one vote" came to be widely accepted.

Because of the important role state legislatures play in the redistricting process in most states, both parties

Symbolic Solutions for Complex Problems?

Term Limits

"Throw the rascals out," is the battle cry of the decade. Fed up with politicians and politics, voters are calling for limits to the years that legislators can serve. Members of Congress and state legislators are the focus of voter anger, symbolizing everything that voters do not like about politics.

Over 70% of the public say they favor term limits.[1] Consequently, in 23 of 24 states that allow citizens to vote directly on bills, voters have adopted term limits for their members of Congress and state legislators (Mississippi is the exception; its citizens will vote on limits in 1996). In most states, the limits are twelve years; for Congress, that means a limit of two Senate and six House terms.

The Republican "Contract with America" pledged that Congress would vote on a constitutional amendment to set term limits within the first 100 days of the 1995 congressional session. It did so, rejecting them by a narrow vote.

Despite public support for limits, in 1995, in a 5-4 vote, the Supreme Court held term limits for members of Congress unconstitutional. The majority argued that permitting individual states to have diverse qualifications for Congress would "result in a patchwork of state qualifications, undermining the uniformity and national character that the Framers envisioned and sought to ensure."[2] The Court indicated that state laws added to the qualifications spelled out in the Constitution (age and citizenship), therefore, in effect, "amending" the Constitution. Only a constitutional amendment can amend the constitution, so the state action was not legitimate. The Court ruling does not affect limits placed on terms of state legislators or other state and local officials, but does mean that for limits to be placed on members of Congress, a constitutional amendment to that effect must be passed. Thus supporters of term limits continue to push for such an amendment.

Are term limits merely a symbolic solution, perhaps assuaging the feelings of those who think government is out of control without changing the behavior of legislators at all? Or are term limits a good solution to a real problem of entrenched legislators forgetting about their constituency and building personal empires? Or will term limits actually be a negative factor, exacerbating problems that already exist with government?

Term limits were part of our original governing document, the Articles of Confederation, but were not adopted by the Framers of the Constitution. Why do many people now favor term limits?

Some supporters cling to the mid-nineteenth century image of "citizen lawmakers," who set aside their personal business for a few years to attend to the public's business, and then return home. Most supporters believe that by not having to worry about continuing to be elected, legislators can be free to consider the "public interest," not the "special interests," and will have no desire to build personal empires. Others also see term limits as a way to weaken the power of government by having a more rapid turnover of members of legislatures. Members without experience, this argument holds, could not learn the ropes fast enough to be able to wield power effectively. Still others saw term limits as a way to break the sixty-year-old stranglehold of the Democrats on Congress, a rationale that was undercut by the Republican victories in 1994.

Opponents, including many Republicans, argue that term limits are a very bad, and very radical, idea. Term limits are antidemocratic in that they restrict the ability of voters to elect whomever they please to Congress. If Congressman Smith is not doing a good job, his constituents can elect someone else. Term limits allow Congresswoman Jones to tell Congressman Smith's constituents they cannot elect Smith. Even though the results of democracy are not always ideal, as one commentator remarked, "democracy is like blowing one's nose—you should do it yourself, even if you do it badly."[3]

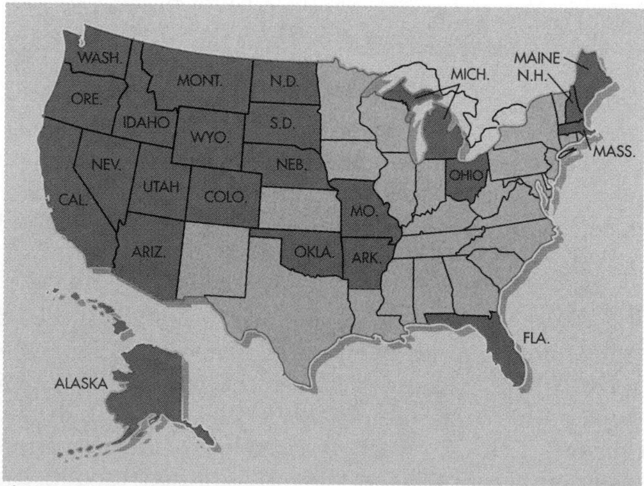

Blue areas show states which have passed term limits.

Opponents also point out that the world is a much more complex place than in the early nineteenth century when many legislators were "citizen legislators." Today, most people want their heart surgery done by "career cardiac surgeons," not by people who sell real estate or teach school for a career and take two years off to try being surgeons. They want their legal problems handled by "career lawyers," their teeth pulled by "career dentists," and their bridges designed by "career engineers." Likewise, opponents of term limits argue, it is appropriate to have laws drafted by "career legislators," or at least legislative bodies with a significant membership of experienced legislators.

Term limits also attack a problem that does not exist. They are a response to the very high-reelection rates of the late 1980s, when the reelection rate of House incumbents was over 90%. However, the elections of 1992 and 1994 show that when voters want change, they can effect change by voting incumbents out. The existing system allows plenty of turnover. In 1995, 45% of the members of the House were first elected in 1992 or 1994 and in the Senate 25% were first elected in these two elections. In other words, there is already considerable turnover in legislatures without term limits.

Term limits also break the tie between citizens and their representatives. If representatives are not responsible to their voters, to whom are they responsible? Opponents of term limits fear that these limits will strengthen the power of lobbyists, bureaucrats, and committee staffs. These unelected officials will have the knowledge about policies and procedures that legislators elected for only a few years cannot possibly have. It is sometimes said that it takes members four years to learn when they are being snookered by lobbyists or bureaucrats; it takes six years to begin to accomplish something.[4] Term limits of six or eight years would ensure a legislature full of individuals with less knowledge than the professional bureaucrats have. As one long-term Republican congressman noted about term limits: "Career politician is an epithet. But pass term limits, and professionals . . . will run this government. Only they will not be elected: they will be the faceless, nameless, try-to-get-them-on-the-phone, unaccountable permanent bureau–cracy."[5] It is unlikely that this is the outcome favored by those who prefer term limits.

Term limits have actually gone into effect in Michigan, where voters limited the members of the lower house in the state legislature to six years and their upper house to eight. As predicted by opponents of term limits, observers believe that lobbyists have more influence than before.[6] Moreover, some newly elected members, knowing they can only serve six years, have already started looking for their next jobs—by currying favor with lobbyists.

1. David Broder, "Dumbing Down Democracy," *Lincoln Journal,* April 5, 1995.
2. Quoted in Kenneth J. Cooper and Helen Dewar, "No Limits on the Term Limits Crusade," *Washington Post National Weekly Edition,* May 29-June 4, 1995, p. 14. The majority of the Court included John Paul Stevens, Anthony Kennedy, David Souter, Ruth Ginsburg, and Stephen Breyer.
3. Garry Wills, "Term Limits Attack Corrupt Electorate," *Lincoln Journal,* March 16, 1992.
4. James J. Kilpatrick, "Cincinnatus' Time Is Past: Term Limits Are a Bad Idea," *Lincoln Journal,* September 3, 1992.
5. Broder, "Dumbing Down Democracy."
6. Arlene Levinson, "Michigan First among 20 States Dealing with Term Limits," *Centre Daily Times,* April 23, 1995, p. 9A.

---

saw the 1990 state legislative elections as crucial. In the early 1980s, Democratic-controlled state legislatures were able to help Democratic candidates in states like California by drawing lines that concentrated Republican strength in a few areas and created districts with small Democratic majorities.[14] After the 1990 state legislative elections, which gave Republicans more clout, many states drew boundaries favoring Republicans.

Another important aspect of redistricting is representation of women and minorities. Inroads into the House by women have been slow because of the large proportion of incumbents and their nearly perfect record of getting reelected. In 1992, however, there were many more open seats than usual, partly due to redistricting, and women were able to win about one-third of open seats.

Different factors influence the impact of redistricting on minority representation. An increase in the proportion of blacks or Hispanics serving in Congress will most likely depend on whether any more majority black or Hispanic districts are created. As we saw in Chapter 7, in 1992, 11 new districts were created with black majorities and 6 with Hispanic majorities; all but 1 were won by blacks and Hispanics. However, much of this redistricting was quite controversial because of the extensive use of gerrymandering to create them. Recent Supreme Court decisions have suggested that using race as a primary basis for creating districts is unconstitutional.[15]

The racial redistricting issue also affects the partisan composition of Congress. In some southern states, several Democratic districts were weakened in order to create one or two new majority black districts;

Democratic black voters were redistricted from newly solid Democratic districts, leaving these districts with fewer Democrats and thereby creating Republican majorities.[16] The exact impact of this change is still being debated, but clearly the overall effect was to substantially weaken Democratic electoral strength in several states.[17]

This outcome was part of a deliberate strategy of the Republican party in several southern states. They often worked in concert with civil rights groups to encourage this type of redistricting, believing that it could result in new conservative Republican districts. Partly as a result, 18 seats were won by Republicans for the first time in 1994. It will be ironic if conservatives on the Supreme Court stifle this development.

➤Congressional Campaigns and Elections

To understand Congress, one must understand the process by which its members are elected.[18] Because reelection is an important objective for almost all members of Congress and *the* most important objective for many, members work at being reelected throughout their terms. Most are successful, though as we have seen, the electoral fortunes of senators are not as secure as those of members of the House. In recent years, as few as 55% and as many as 97% of senators have won reelection, while the success of House incumbents varied only from 88% to 98%.

The Advantages of Incumbency

Before they even take the oath of office, newly elected representatives are given an introduction to the advantages of incumbency. At meetings arranged by the Democratic and Republican leadership and by the House Administrative Committee, new members learn about free mailing privileges, computers and software to help them target letters to specialized groups of constituents, facilities to make videotapes and audiotapes to send to hometown media, and other "perks" designed to keep members in touch with their constituencies and thereby to help win reelection.

Incumbents win because, for a number of reasons, they are better known than nonincumbents and voters evaluate them more positively. Almost all voters can recognize the name of their representatives; they have seen them on television or received mail from them, and they can give a general rating of their performances (see Figure 2).[19] Although most voters can correctly identify their representatives as liberal or conservative, only a small minority know how their representatives voted on any issue.[20] Therefore, representatives have the advantage of name recognition without the disadvantage of having voters know how they really voted.

Representatives' high level of public recognition is not so surprising given that members of Congress spend most of their time and energy looking for and using opportunities to make themselves known to their constituents. Members visit their home districts or states an average of 35 times a year—at taxpayers' expense.[21]

Sometimes members take unusual steps in an attempt to become better known. One member stood on the Capitol steps "dressed in an exterminator's outfit with plastic cockroaches glued to his shoulders." He then jumped up and down, shouting "squash one for the Gipper." This was to endear himself to owners and workers of an insecticide manufacturer in his district.[22]

Franking

Members gain name recognition by free mail privileges called **franking.** In just 6 months during 1989, Senator Alfonse D'Amato (R-N.Y.) sent out nearly 17 million pieces of mail at a cost of $2.65 million. With the exception of 1991, Congressional mailings have increased in volume every election year and fallen in the off-year.

Some restrictions are designed to make franking less blatantly political. For example, mass mailings cannot be sent out close to an election. Regardless, one political consultant estimates that the frank is worth at least $350,000 in campaign funds.[23]

Franking privileges become even more useful when combined with sophisticated word processing systems to target very specific constituency groups with "personalized" letters. Members can maintain incredibly specialized lists, not just of Republicans and Democrats but of those living near federal prisons, small-business owners, veterans, teachers, and government employees, for example. No group is too specialized or ostensibly apolitical to be targeted. Senator Charles Grassley (R-Iowa) even sent a letter to a thousand Iowans with abbreviated intestinal tracts in honor of Ostomy Awareness Month.[24]

FIGURE 2
Senate and House Incumbents Are Well Known to Voters

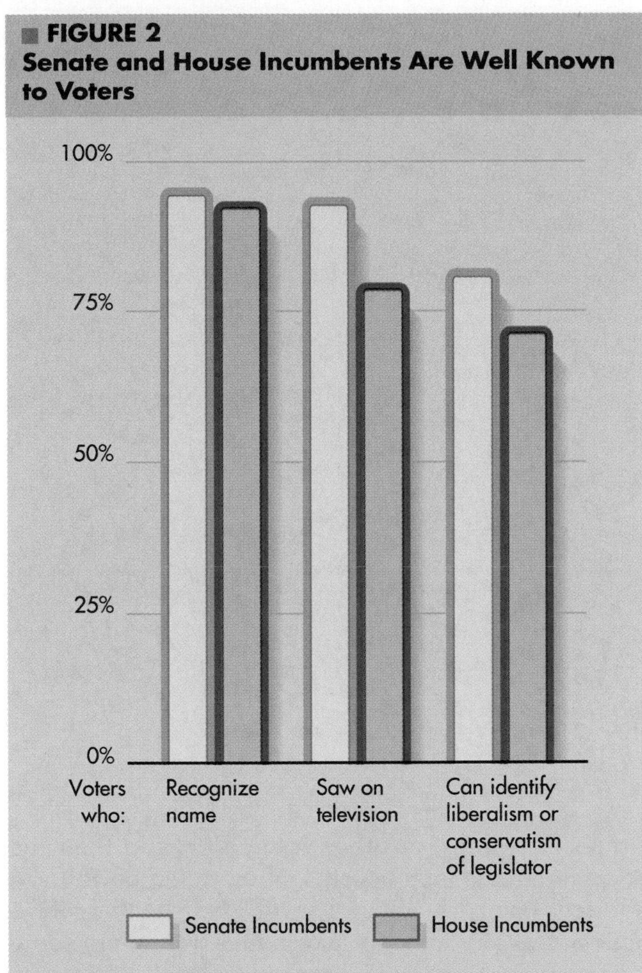

SOURCE: John Alford and John Hibbing. "The Disparate Electoral Security of House and Senate Incumbents," paper presented at the American Political Science Meetings, September 1989, Atlanta, GA.

This system can help improve the representation of constituents. But the frank and the computer together have turned most congressional offices into full-time public relations firms. Their value in reelection is reflected in the fact that members send out much more mail in their reelection year than in other years (see Figure 3).[25]

Media Attention

In addition to "old-fashioned" mail, members use increasingly sophisticated production equipment and technology to make television and radio shows to send home. For example, one evening, on any of three local television news shows, residents of Boise, Idaho, might have seen their congressional representative, Larry Craig (R-Idaho), state in an interview that he was strongly opposed to a pay increase for Congress and would not take it if it were passed. The viewers were not told that the "interviewer" was one of Craig's congressional staffers and that the camera crew was that of the Republican Congressional Campaign Committee, which also paid for the broadcast.[26]

Members also like to tape themselves at committee meetings asking questions or being referred to as "Mr. (or Madam) Chairman" (because many members are chairs of at least a subcommittee). The tape then is edited to a 30-second sound bite to be sent to local television stations. Often stations run these productions as news and do not tell their viewers that they are essentially campaign features prepared by the members. But television is not alone in portraying members' self-publicity as "hard news." Congressional staffers write press releases about accomplishments of the member and fax them to local newspapers, which often print them as written. Local media, whether print or television, are often short of news with a local flavor and eagerly take whatever members give them.

Constituency Service

Members of Congress make themselves known in more routine ways. One is by providing **constituency service:** answering questions and doing personal favors for constituents who write or call for help.

This function, also called **casework,** is crucial for members and their staffs, who function as red-tape cutters for everyone from elderly citizens having difficulties with Social Security to small-town mayors trying to get federal grants for new sewer systems. Members provide information to students working on term papers and citizens puzzled about which federal agency to ask for assistance. Members can provide gifts of calendars, United States flags that were flown over the Capitol, and brochures and publications of the federal government.

Requests for service often come by mail. More than half the congressional office staffs work on the flood of mail that pours in. Members receive nearly 200 million pieces of mail per year, skyrocketing from 15 million in 1970. Much of it simply expresses an opinion about an issue, but some offices get 5,000 to 10,000 requests per year for assistance.[27] In addition to handling casework in Washington offices, most senators and representatives have one or more state or

■ FIGURE 3
Members of Congress Send More Mass Mail in Election Years

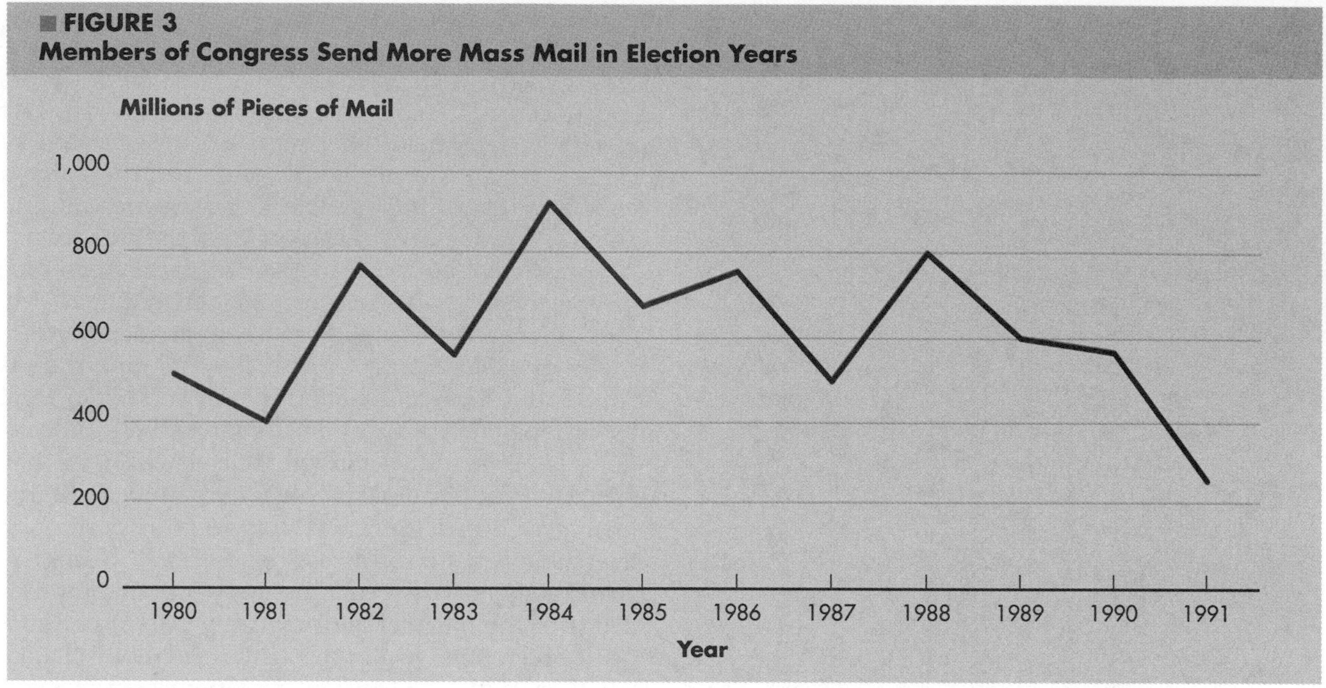

SOURCE: *Vital Statistics of Congress*, 1993–1994. (Washington, D.C.: CQ Press, 1994), p. 163.

home district offices to deal personally with constituents and their casework. More than 35% of senators' staffs and 40% of all representatives' staffs are located in their home state or district.[28]

Citizens turn to their congressional representatives because they see them as allies in their struggles with bureaucracy.[29] Members of Congress, who are in large part responsible for the establishment of the huge Washington bureaucracy, are able to score with voters by helping them cope with the bureaucracy they have created.[30] Individual members may have limited power in trying to get important legislation passed, but in dealing with a constituent's problems, their power is much greater because of their clout with bureaucrats. A phone call or letter to a federal agency will bring attention to the constituent's problem.

Of course, not all casework is directed toward winning reelection. Some members say they enjoy their casework more than their policy roles, perhaps because the results of casework are often more immediate and tangible.

Pork Barrel

Another way members gain the attention of constituents is to obtain funds for special projects, new programs, buildings, or other public works in their districts or states. Such benefits, often called **pork barrel** projects, comprise about a seventh of the budget not devoted to entitlements and interest. They are sometimes defined as "federal spending with a zip code attached."[31] In the final days of one session of Congress, for example, a few of the last-minute pork barrel projects approved included a $3.6 million irrigation project for Maine's potato growers and a $400,000 fuel dock for a Hawaiian hotel.[32] These projects are desired by constituents because they provide jobs and business in the local district.

Because pork barrel projects are considered crucial to reelection chances, there is little support in Congress for eliminating projects known to be unwise or wasteful. Liberals and conservatives, Democrats and Republicans, protect these kinds of projects. Senator Alfonse D'Amato (R-N.Y.) is called "Senator Pothole" for his ability to win highway and transportation projects for New York. One conservative Kentucky Republican, in 1995 argued for a freeway in his district, "This project is not pork, [it is] a vital infrastructure necessity."[33] David Stockman, former President Reagan's director of the Office of Management and Budget, observed, "There's no such thing as a fiscal conservative when it comes to his district."[34]

American Diversity

Women in Congress

Women make up more than 50% of the nation's population but only 9% of the Congress. The first woman in Congress was Representative Jeannette Rankin (R-Mont.), who was elected in 1916 even before women got the right to vote nationally. It was not until 1932 that the first woman served in the Senate. Hattie Caraway (D-Ark.) won the seat after the death of her husband, the former occupant. The first woman elected to the Senate without occupying the Senate seat of a deceased spouse was Margaret Chase Smith, a Republican from Maine who spent a distinguished career in the Senate from 1949 to 1973.

Many called 1992 "The Year of the Woman." Despite gains then and again in 1994 when both the Senate and the House added one woman member, women make up only 8% of the Senate and 11% of the House. These paltry proportions are a large increase from the 1980s when the percentage of women in the House remained around 5% indefinitely. Twenty-three states have at least 1 woman in their delegation.

The women in Congress are racially heterogeneous. One-quarter of the women members of the House and 1 of the 8 women Senators are black, Hispanic, or Asian.

In 1992 the proportion of women increased as much as it did in the House because women targeted the extraordinarily large numbers of open seats available. Indeed, of the 65 open seats in the 1992 election, 22 were won by women. However 6 of these new incumbents were swept out of office in the 1994 Republican landslide.

Although gains were small in 1994, we may expect a growing proportion of women in Congress because more women are being elected to state legislatures and other offices that traditionally have been stepping-stones to Congress. Women fare about as well as men when they run for congressional seats.[1]

Women's problems are not over when they are elected, however. Women feel out of the congressional mainstream in many ways. These include small inconveniences, such as the lack of a women's restroom within 100 yards of the House floor and none at all in the Senate chamber. Only in recent years has the lavish congressional gym been open to women; before that the "ladies' health facility consisted of 10 hair dryers and a ping-pong table." More substantively, the leadership of both houses is all male. Said one woman who has tried for a seat on the prestigious Appropriation Committee three times, "Each time I've been nicely told that the women's slot is already filled on that committee." And in 1993, Nancy Johnson (R-Conn.), one of the Republicans' leading health-care experts, was told by her subcommittee chair at a public hearing that she must have learned about a particular health issue through "pillow-talk" with her physician husband. The chair later apologized, but the incident was not forgotten.[2]

But women do seem to be making a substantive difference. The Congressional Caucus for Women's issues reported that in 1993-94, Congress passed a record 66 bills of special importance to women. That nearly equals the number of such bills passed in the entire previous decade.[3]

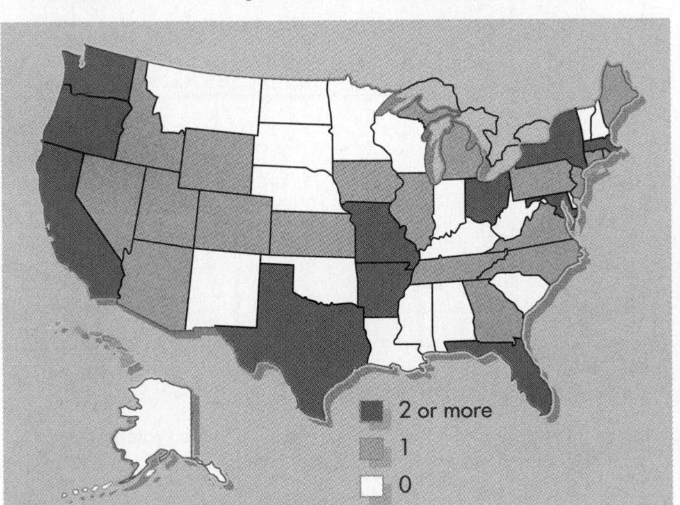

SOURCE: Data from Congressional Quarterly, November 12, 1994; p. 10.

Number of Women Representatives by State.

1. For a recent analysis of Senate voting, see Philip Paolino, "Group-Salient Issues and Group Representation: Support for Women Candidates in the 1992 Senate Elections," *American Journal of Political Science* 39 (May, 1995), pp. 294-313; Barbara Burrell, "Did We Get More than One 'Year of the Woman'?" paper presented at the 1995 Annual Meeting of the Midwest Political Science Association, Chicago, Illinois.
2. Kevin Merida, "A Woman's Place on the Hill," *Washington Post National Weekly Edition* (April 11-17, 1994), p. 15.
3. Leslie Laurence, "Congress Makes Up for Neglect," *Lincoln Journal* (December 5, 1994), p. 8.

Fundraising

Another advantage of incumbency is the opportunity to raise funds from the hundreds of PACs that populate Washington. Eager to gain access to members of Congress, PACs make fund-raising much easier for incumbents than challengers, as we pointed out in Chapter 9.

Unsafe at Any Margin?

Most members are reelected even if they have done relatively little constituency work or have obtained little federal money for their districts (see Figure 4).[35] Indeed, one Republican member remarked, "Let's face it, you have to be a bozo to lose this job."[36] Still, incumbents believe the best way to ensure victory is to be so good at constituency work, so successful in bringing pieces of pork to their districts, and so well known to the voters that no serious rival will want to run. Incumbents hope potential rivals will bide their time and wait for a better year or run for some other office.[37]

Given their advantages, you may wonder why incumbents worry about losing. But worry they do. One political scientist proclaimed that members feel "unsafe at any margin."[38] No matter how big their last victory, they worry that their next campaign will bring defeat. And despite the high reelection rate of incumbents, some are defeated. This fear prompts them to spend even more of their energies preparing for the next campaign.

But this fear is fairly remote, even in recent anti-incumbent elections. In 1994, only 9% of House incumbents lost (all of them Democrats). In 1992, only 7% did. Senators are somewhat more vulnerable. Fifteen percent lost in 1992 and 10% in 1994. Nonetheless, the electoral benefit of incumbency still exists for the great majority of candidates who choose to run for reelection.[39] Turnover in Congress comes primarily from those who decide not to run, sometimes from fear of losing.

Challengers

Another reason for the uneasiness of incumbents is that as their media and public relations sophistication has grown, so has that of challengers. Still, without the advantages of the free frank and other opportunities to become well known to constituents, challengers have a difficult time. The best advice to someone

FIGURE 4
House Incumbents Have Had Secure Jobs in Recent Years

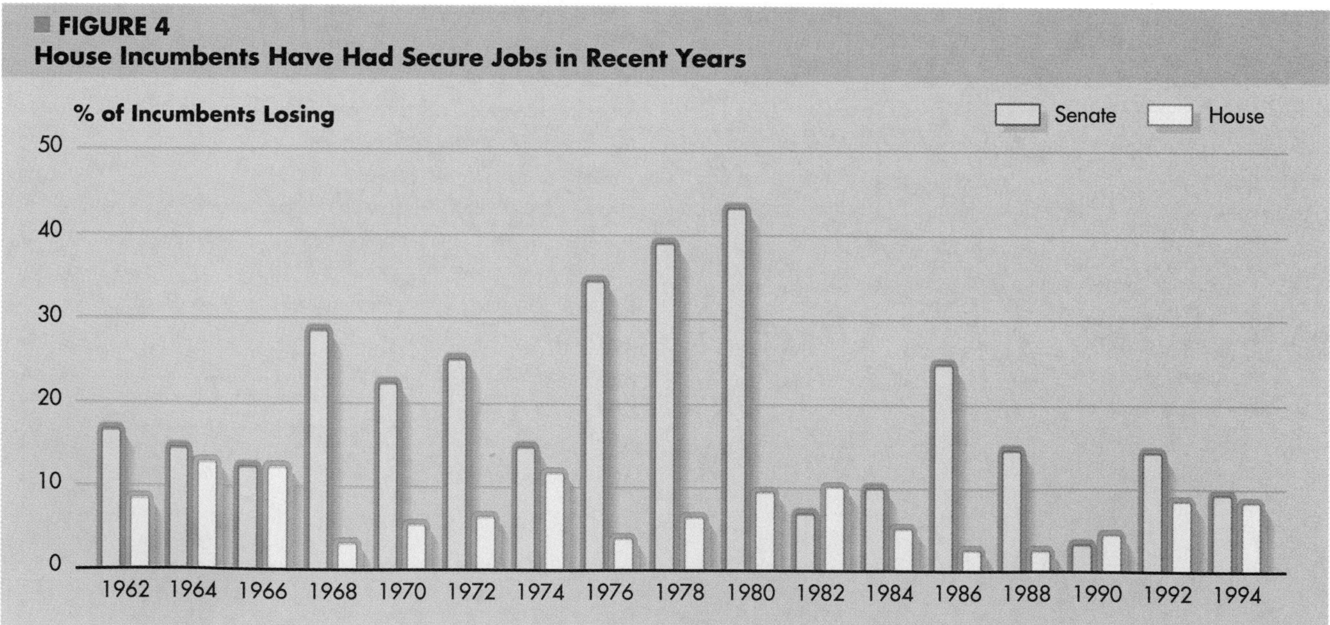

Notice that in the 1980s more House incumbents lost in the reapportionment year of 1982. In the 1970s more lost in the Watergate year, 1974, when many Republican defenders of President Nixon were defeated. In the 1960s reapportionment did not start until after 1962, so the elections of 1964 and 1966 reflected reapportionment.

SOURCE: *Congressional Quarterly Weekly Report*, November 19, 1988, p. 18, and November 10, 1990, p. 3801; "Women, Minorities Join Senate," *CQ Almanac*, 1992 pp. 8A–14A; "Wave of Diversity Spared Many Incumbents," *CQ Almanac*, 1992, pp. 15A–21A, 24A.

who wants to be a member of Congress is to find an open seat.

To beat an incumbent, challengers need money. The more they spend, the more likely they are to win. In recent House campaigns, a challenger needed to spend at least $250,000 to have even a one in four chance of winning—and the cost continues to rise.[40]

Spending is important for challengers because they must make themselves known in a positive way, and they must suggest that something is wrong with the incumbent. Usually challengers will charge incumbents with ignoring the district, being absent from committee hearings or floor votes, being too liberal or too conservative, or voting incorrectly on a key issue. Sometimes, of course, the incumbent has been involved in a scandal, which offers a ready target for the challenger.[41]

Sometimes challengers will try unusual tactics to make themselves known. Tom Harkin (D-Iowa) worked in a series of blue-collar jobs when running

Source: © 1995 Mark Alan Stamaty. Excerpted from "WASHINGTOON" with permission.

New Populism

The 1994 Congressional Elections

"Revenge of the Right," proclaimed one headline. "The GOP Earthquake," declared another. "G.O.P. Celebrates Its Sweep to Power," announced a third. These reports of the 1994 election results suggested their importance and the surprise of many. Overnight, forty years of Democratic control of the House were ended, and almost overnight, President Clinton's legislative agenda lay in ruins. The Republicans, led by Newt Gingrich (R-Ga.), offered a new agenda.

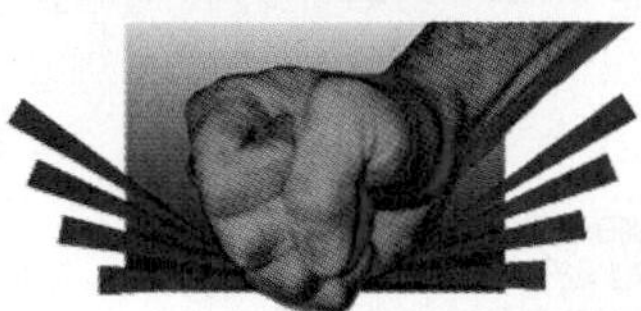

Today, the Republicans control both the House and Senate for the first time since 1954, and some have labeled this a "new populist" revolt. Though Republicanism and populism are certainly not the same, the Republican victory suggested a populist movement to throw out the old elites and try something new. On the other hand, the Republicans, as the party of the better off, represent many of those interests that the original populists fought against: big business and big banks. In that sense, it is ironic that the new populist label has been attached to some of their causes.

The Background

The 1994 election took place in the midst of an economic upturn and in a time when the nation was at peace. Normally these factors lead to high reelection rates for incumbents. But 1994 was different. Voters were angry in 1994, even more angry than in 1992, when they spurned George Bush's bid for a second term. The level of trust in government had plummeted to an all-time low. In 1964, 76 percent of a national sample said they trusted "the government in Washington to do what's right" most or all of the time. By 1992, only 29% said the same.[1]

Fueled by radio and television talk show hosts, Americans said they were fed up with politics as usual: with politicians attuned more to special interest groups than voters, and members of Congress who had been in Washington so long they had forgotten the people back home. Americans were dubious about their economic futures, terrified of crime, and furious at the breakdown in morality. They blamed government for these problems, or at least for not doing something about them, and for not being responsive to the people. They especially blamed Democrats, who had controlled Congress for forty years.

The Democrats, it seems, had grown complacent in power. Democratic congressional leaders quarreled with their president, did not seem inclined to support his key legislative initiative, health care, and grew increasingly dependent on campaign money from large interest groups. Republicans, for their part, had been out of power in Congress so long they seemed to perceive their major goal as obstructionism and had honed attacks on the institution to a fine point.

Voter anger, coupled with redistricting that changed many district lines in 1992, led near record numbers of House and Senate incumbents to retire (48 and 9, respectively). Many were in the South, where the president and Democratic party were very unpopular.

To characterize the 1994 campaign as highly negative is to understate its vitriolic nature. In addition to the usual partisan charges, candidates were commonly portrayed as liars and sometimes even as criminals. Indeed, being an incumbent itself was depicted as nearly a criminal act, as illustrated by a successful Republican Senate candidate from Tennessee who defeated the incumbent: "Bill Frist supports term limits to stop career politicians, and the death penalty to stop career criminals."[2]

Almost every nonincumbent, and even some incumbents, ran against government in general and Congress in particular, a common strategy in recent elections. For example, Fred Thompson (R- Tenn.) argued in his ad that "Congress is more the problem than the solution; they're out of touch and we're out of patience."[3]

The Campaign Results

Even though the election produced dramatic results, it was hardly a landslide. Republicans gained 52% of the contested House votes, 2% increase over 1992.[4] Only 39% of the electorate voted, slightly more than in the 1990 off-year election.[5]

Although the election was not a landslide, Republican candidates got enough votes in enough districts for the party to win a majority in Congress. Before the 1994 election, the Democrats held a comfortable 60% margin in the House.[6] The Republicans gained 74 seats in the election to gain a slimmer, but clear, majority of 53%. The magnitude of the Democratic disaster can be illustrated by the fact that

Thomas Foley (D-Wash.), Speaker of the House, was defeated. This marked only the first time since 1862 (and only the third time in history) that the sitting Speaker was defeated.

The table below shows some of the most important features of the House election results. First, although more Democratic than Republican incumbents won reelection, and although only 9% of all incumbents were defeated, all (35) were Democrats. About half these Democrats were first elected in 1992. *No* Republican incumbent was defeated. Further, Republicans won three-fourths of open seats, those where no incumbent was running. Republicans captured the House, then, because their incumbents who chose to run for election all won, and because they captured a very large majority of seats where no incumbent was running.

Composition of the 1995–96 House of Representatives*

104th Congress (1995–6)	Republicans	Democrats
Incumbents reelected	157	190
Total freshman	74	13
—who defeated incumbents	35	0
—who won open seats	39	13
Total members*	231	203

*One seat is held by an independent.

The Democrats lost seven Senate seats, a seemingly small number, but enough to give Republicans control of the Senate (53-47). Republicans have only controlled the Senate ten years in the past 62, so this new Republican majority is newsworthy too. Not one new Democratic Senator was elected in 1994, a situation that has never occurred before.[7]

Election polls showed that voters had no single reason for their votes. Four of ten voters, for example, listed crime as the issue most affecting their voting; yet about half voted for Republicans and half for Democrats. Republicans claimed the majority of the votes from Republicans, independents, Perot voters, conservatives, males, whites, and those with at least some college education.[8] Democrats claimed a majority of votes from women, those with a high school education or less, blacks, Hispanics, moderates, liberals, and Democrats.

Not surprisingly, those who believed the country is "going in the right direction" voted heavily for the Democrats (76%), and those who believed the country is "off on the wrong track" gave 67% of their votes to the Republicans. About an equal number said their vote was in support of Clinton and against Clinton, while, surprisingly, a plurality of voters (38%) said their vote had nothing to do with Clinton.

Exit (post-election) polls did not find a large turn to the right in this election. Most showed about one-third of the voters claimed to be conservative, about half moderates, and the rest liberals.[9] There was only a slight move toward the Republicans, with about half the public identifying with Republicans, half with Democrats. Moreover, post-election polls showed that most Americans never heard of the Republicans' *Contract with America,* or were unfamiliar with what it said.[10]

The election provides further evidence that Congress, far from being removed from the people, may be too close to the people. While it is certainly true that today's legislators are not "citizen legislators," it is also true that they are responsive to every nuance of public opinion. By being responsive to the tremendous variety of conflicting views, they cannot get much accomplished. One commentator noted that the effect of being in touch with everyone is "to turn a somewhat slow and contemplative system into something more like a 500-channel democracy, with the clicker grasped tightly in the hands of the electorate."[11] In 1992, the voters clicked off Republican George Bush; in 1994, they clicked off the Democratic Congress. Although it is possible that a Republican majority can cool the anger and win the trust of the voters, it seems more likely that voters will continue to have itchy clicker fingers.

1. "The Anger: Ever Deeper," *New York Times Magazine* (October 16, 1994), p. 37. For an analysis of the election, see Everett Carll Ladd, "The 1994 Congressional Elections," *Political Science Quarterly* 110 (1995), pp. 1-23.
2. Robin Toner, "Image of Capitol Maligned by Outsiders, and Insiders," *The New York Times* (October 16, 1994), p. 1.
3. Toner, "Image of Capitol Maligned by Outsiders, and Insiders."
4. Richard Morin, "Myths and Messages in the Election Tea Leaves," *Washington Post National Weekly Edition* (November 21-27, 1994), p. 37.
5. Richard L. Berke, "Victories Were Captured by G.O.P. Candidates, Not the Party's Platform," *New York Times* (November 10, 1994), p. B1.
6. These electoral data are drawn from *CQ* (November 12, 1994), pp. 9ff.
7. Popular election of senators began in 1914, and no freshman class has ever been all Republican.
8. Mitofsky International survey data drawn from "How Groups Divided in the Vote for the U.S. House," *New York Times* (November 10, 1994), p. B4. The following two paragraphs are drawn from these data.
9. Morin, "Myths and Messages in the Election Tea Leaves."
10. Ibid.
11. Wines, "Washington Really Is in Touch: We're the Problem," *New York Times* (October 16, 1994): Section 4, p. 2.

for the House to show people in his district that he understood their problems. Meanwhile he got a lot of free publicity.

Senate challengers have a slightly better chance than House challengers. One reason is that there are stronger candidates to challenge incumbent senators because Senate seats are a bigger prize and because in a statewide constituency there are more potential challengers. Senate challengers are better known than House challengers.[42] They are often former governors or members of the House with a statewide reputation. For example, in 1988, about 80% of voters recognized the name of the person running against their incumbent senator; less than 60% recognized the challenger to their House incumbent.[43] Senate challengers can attract more money because they are better known.

Another reason Senate challengers have greater success is that most incumbents have constituencies (i.e., states) much larger than House districts. The greater population means that senators cannot have personal contact with as high a proportion of their constituents. Also they cannot satisfy as high a proportion since their constituencies are much more heterogeneous than House district constituencies.[44] Evidence indicates that senators from the largest states have about a six- or seven-point electoral disadvantage compared to senators from the smallest states. Senators from the smallest states do about as well as House members from their states.[45]

Campaigns

In the nineteenth century, political campaigns were organized largely by political parties, and the candidates had relatively little to do. Today, however,

Earmarking: How to Pack the Pork

Earmarking is the practice of designating spending for specific projects, outside of any regular formulas or granting processes. Powerful members of Congress use their influence to attach their pet projects, intended to bring funds and jobs to voters in their districts, as footnotes to appropriations legislation. Earmarking has long been one method to serve up pork to the homefolks. (Another method is to quietly pressure bureaucrats to include a particular cut of pork in their recommended projects).

As the pressures of the deficit have left less funding for general public works projects and have decreased bureaucratic discretion over these funds, the practice of earmarking has increased. For example, before 1987, few roads and bridges were earmarked in federal highway legislation. In 1987, the transportation act included 152 "demonstration projects." These, in theory, test something new but in reality are the priorities of influential members of Congress. By 1991, highway legislation included 452 demonstration projects, costing taxpayers more than $6 billion.[1]

Sometimes, the recipient state is not even consulted. In 1991, Senator Robert Dole (R-Kansas) added two home state projects, costing $104 million, to the federal transportation bill. The Kansas secretary of transportation said neither of these projects had been included in the first stage of the state's highway modernization plan. He was "not certain we'd make the same decision at the same time that Sen. Dole would about how and where to spend the money."[2]

There are some signs that the pressures of the deficit and of public disillusionment with such practices may be decreasing the amount of pork served up by Congress. In 1993, Congress killed a Texas project called the superconducting supercollider (SSC) that would have been the world's largest scientific experiment. Although the project had already cost $2 billion and had originally been estimated to cost $4.4 billion, the 1993 estimate had risen to $11 billion. In a lopsided vote in the House, representatives stripped funding for the SSC from the $22.2 billion appropriations bill. The Senate agreed to cancel the SSC, over the objections of many, including Senator Phil Gramm in whose home state of Texas the SSC was being constructed.

There are other signs that earmarking may be on the decline. A review by the House Science, Space and Technology Committee noted that four major appropriations bills in 1993 included only half as many earmarked projects as in 1991. This committee has been holding public hearings on earmarking to bring this practice into public view. "Earmarks" are like mushrooms—they grow best in the dark," noted the former chair of the committee.[3]

1. "Slicing the Pork Isn't Easy," *Governing*, January 1994, pp. 62-63.
2. Dole Shows He's King of the Road," *The Wichita Eagle*, December 14, 1991, pp. 1A, 7A.
3. "A Little Less from the Pork Barrel," *Washington Post National Weekly Edition*, November 8-14, 1993, p. 37.

congressional campaigns are candidate-centered. Most candidates hire workers, raise money, and organize their own campaigns. They may recruit campaign workers from local political parties; single-interest groups they belong to; unions; church, civic, or other voluntary organizations; or simply groups of friends and acquaintances.[46]

Political parties do have a significant role, however. National and local parties also recruit potential candidates. Presidents make personal appeals to fellow party members who they think can run strong races, and national campaign committees also recruit aggressively. Said one Democratic congressional campaign chair, "I'm not looking for liberals or conservatives. That's not my bag. I'm looking for winners."[47] Parties also provide campaign money and assistance to candidates for polling, mailing, issue research, and getting out the vote.[48]

The Media Campaign

To wage a serious campaign, the challenger or a contender for an open seat must wage a media campaign. Candidates hire media consultants and specialists in polling, advertising, and fund-raising.

With candidates establishing their own campaign organizations and hiring media specialists, fears grew that candidates were becoming less closely linked to parties than before and once elected, not as indebted to their party nor as obligated to reflect party views.[49]

Political parties, however, recognized this problem. Since the early 1980s, national parties have increasingly provided useful services to congressional candidates—helping them manage their campaigns, develop issues, advertise, raise money, and conduct opinion polls. National parties also give substantial sums of money to congressional candidates.[50]

Media campaigning has attracted a new type of congressional candidate and hence a new type of congressional incumbent. The old-style politician who might have been effective in small groups but who cannot appear poised and articulate on television has given way to one who can project an attractive television image. Candidates are elected on the basis of their media skills, which may not be the same skills as those of a good lawmaker.

Campaign Money

The old adage says, "Half the money spent on campaigns is wasted. The trouble is, we don't know which half." This bromide helps explain why congressional campaigns are expensive. There is a kind of "campaign arms race" as each candidate tries to do what the other candidate does and a little more, escalating costs year by year.

In 1992, winners of open seats in the House spent $620,000 on average. Successful campaigns against incumbents cost more. Million-dollar campaigns are no longer unusual. Because they are statewide, Senate races are much more expensive than House races. In 1992, winning Senate candidates spent more than $3.5 million, on average.

Voting for Congress

Just as for presidential elections, party loyalties, candidate evaluations, and issues are important factors in congressional elections.[51]

Party loyalties are even more important for congressional than for presidential elections because congressional elections are less visible, so more people

Until this television ad ran, former Senator Walter Huddleston (D-Ky.) was substantially ahead of his opponent. The ad pointed out that Huddleston had a poor attendance record (hence sending out bloodhounds to find him). When the local media focused on this ad, it helped bring victory to his challenger, Mitch McConnell. A result of Senator McConnell's victory in 1984 is that Senate attendance on roll-call votes has been at all-time highs.

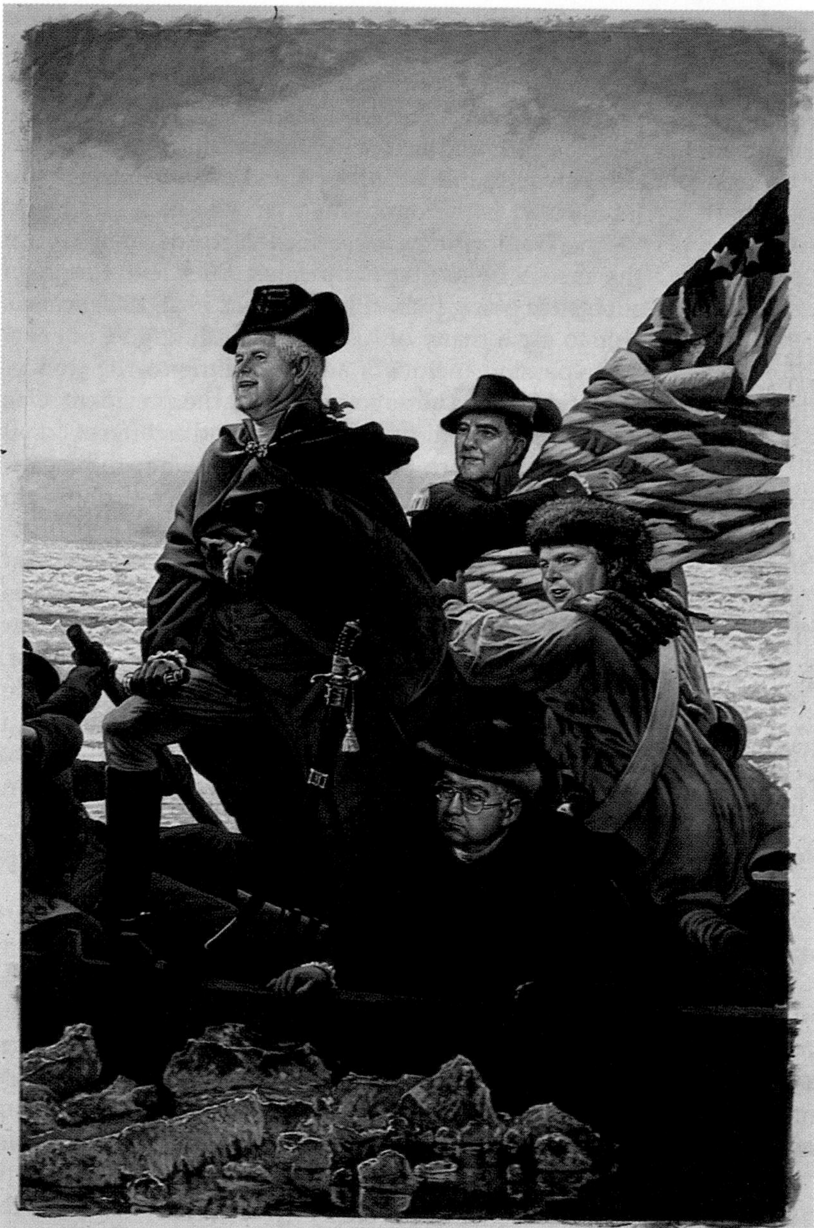

Republican leadership in the style of the classic portrait of Washington crossing the Delaware.

vote. The opinions of constituents do matter, but other influences are also important: the party, the president, the members' ideology, staffers, and other members' recommendations. Members look to these sources for cues as to how to vote.

Party

Forty to 60% of the ballots in Congress are party votes; that is, a majority of one party opposes a majority of the other. In these votes, party members support their party between 70% and 90% of the time. Party support increased during the 1980s and is now at near record highs.

There are several reasons for the continuing importance of party. All members of Congress are elected on a partisan ballot and many receive support from the party. Congress organizes itself on a partisan basis, and party leaders try hard to influence party members to vote the "right" way.

Most of the time this influence is low key, but sometimes party leaders turn on the heat. In a successful vote to override a Reagan veto, Democratic Senate leaders adopted a "baby-sitting" strategy to make sure that wavering Democrats did not get near anyone who might persuade them to uphold the president's veto. These Democrats were accompanied at all times by two other Democrats with the "right" views. For their part, Republicans called on Reagan to make personal appeals to wavering Republicans.

When a member has no strong feelings, it is certainly in the member's interest to go along with party leaders, who have some "perks" to dispense. Then too, members tend to have policy views similar to others in their party, at least more similar than to those in the opposite party. Party votes reflect different constituency needs too, because Democratic and Republican constituencies are different.

Members have several constituencies, including not only their entire district but also constituencies within the district, such as voters of their party, major socioeconomic groups, and their own personal supporters.[62] Sometimes these constituencies may be in conflict. The representatives' personal constituency may be more liberal or conservative than the district as a whole. When members vote in conflict with what seems to be the sentiments of the majority of voters in the district, it may be that they are responding to their own supporters or partisans. Of course, in those rare instances where most of the representative's constituents feel strongly about an issue, the member cannot buck an overwhelming majority and expect to win reelection.

Ideology

The member's own ideology usually reflects both the party and constituency, but it can be an independent influence.[63]

On the whole, Democrats vote for more liberal measures than do Republicans. Traditionally, southern Democrats, often deserted the Democratic leadership and voted with Republicans because they shared the more conservative Republican outlook. Thus, the Democrats, even when a majority in Congress, often did not have a "working majority," as President Clinton learned early in his term.

The tendency of southern Democrats to behave like Republicans has diminished and probably will dwindle further. With the growing strength of southern Republicanism, southern conservatives run as Republicans and have a good chance of winning. Also, many southern districts are increasingly urban and contain voters who are more liberal than they were 30 years ago. The enfranchisement of African Americans also has been an important liberalizing influence on representatives from many southern districts. Many are black and others must pay attention to black voters. Several conservative southern Democrats have switched to the Republican Party.

The President

The president is also a factor in congressional voting, partly due to his role as party leader.[64] The president appeals to fellow partisans to support a program and tries to persuade those in the other party to go along as well. Presidents can win support by granting or withholding favors, such as support for a member's proposed policy or pet project in his or her district.

Interest Groups

Interest group lobbyists are most effective when their interests overlap constituency interests or when the issue is technical or little publicized.

Staffers

Staff can be a very important influence on a member's vote. Staff members are likely to have done the research and briefed the member on an issue. They probably have the greatest influence on technical issues or those the member does not care much about.

Other Members

Members also are influenced by other members of their party or their state's delegation. Members also may turn to colleagues whose judgment or expertise they respect or whose ideology or background they share. In fact, on most routine bills, cues from trusted fellow members are the most important influence on members' votes.

➤How Congress Is Organized

An institution of 535 members without a centralized leadership that must make decisions about thousands of proposed public policies each year is not an institution that can work quickly or efficiently. Each year in the past 10, from 2,000 to 10,000 bills have been introduced in Congress, and 250 to 2,000 have been passed.

Although many of these bills are trivial, such as those proclaiming "National Prom Graduation Kickoff Day" or naming local courthouses, others deal with crucial issues. In addition to these bills, Congress must oversee the performance of the federal bureaucracy in implementing bills previously passed.

How Congressional Organization Evolved

The first House, meeting in New York in 1789, had slow and cumbersome procedures.[65] After discussions by the whole House, a committee was elected to draft each bill, and the House then debated it section by section. To speed things up, permanent committees were eventually created, each with continuing responsibilities in one area, such as taxes or trade.

After a short time the selection of the leader of the House, called the **Speaker of the House,** who appointed members to those committees, became a partisan matter. Beginning about 1811, Henry Clay (Ky.) became the leader of the Jeffersonian-Republicans in the House. As Speaker, he used his powers to appoint committee members and chairs to maintain party loyalty and discipline.

Although in these early years the House was the dominant branch, during the administration of Andrew Jackson its influence declined when it could not cope with the divisiveness of the slavery issue. By 1856 it took 133 ballots to elect a Speaker. In many instances there were physical fights on the House floor and duels outside.[66]

The Senate was a smaller group than the House, less tangled in procedures and more informal and effective in its operation. The influence of the Senate rose as visitors packed the Senate gallery to hear the great debates over slavery waged by Daniel Webster (Mass.), John C. Calhoun (S.C.), and Henry Clay (who had moved from the House). During this era, senators were elected by state legislatures, not directly by the people. Thus they had strong local party ties and often used their influence to get presidential appointments for home state party members.

Despite these more formal norms and party ties, the Senate too became ineffective as the nation moved toward civil war. Senators carried arms to protect themselves as the eloquent debates over slavery turned to violence.

After the Civil War, the House again became an effective legislative body as strong party leadership reemerged. Thomas Reed (Me.), who was chosen in 1889 to be Speaker, assumed the authority to name members and chairs of committees and to chair the Rules Committee, which decided which bills were to come to the floor for debate. A major consequence of the Speaker's extensive powers was increased party discipline. Members who voted against their party might be punished by a loss of committee assignments or chairships.

At the same time, both the House and the Senate became more professional. Prior to the Civil War, membership turnover was high; members of the House served an average of only one term, senators only four years. After the war, the strengthening of parties and the growth of the one-party South made reelection easier. The emergence of national problems and an aggressive Congress made a congressional career more prestigious.

This desire for permanent careers in the House brought about an interest in reform. Members wanted a chance at desirable committee seats and did not want to be controlled by the Speaker. Pressure against the dictatorial practices of House Speaker Reed and his successor Joseph Cannon (Ill.) grew. Cannon was more conservative than many of his fellow Republicans. He used his powers to block legislation he disliked, to punish those who opposed him, and even to refuse to recognize members who wished to speak. In 1910 there was a revolt against "Cannonism," a synonym for the arbitrary use of the Speaker's powers. The membership voted to strip the Speaker of his authority to appoint committees and their chairs and to remove the Speaker from the Rules Committee. The revolt weakened party influence because it meant party discipline could no longer be maintained by the Speaker punishing members through loss of committee assignments.

The Senate also was undergoing a major reform. As part of the Progressive movement, pressure began to build for the direct popular election of senators. The election of senators by state legislatures had made many senators pawns of special interests—the big corporations (called "trusts") and railroads. In a day when millionaires were not as common as now, the Senate was referred to as the "Millionaires Club."

Not surprisingly, the Senate first refused to consider a constitutional amendment providing for its direct election, although in some states popular bal-

Oratory was important in the pre-Civil War Senate. Shown speaking is Henry Clay and standing ready to attack is John C. Calhoun (second from right). Daniel Webster is listening at left with a cupped ear.

loting on senatorial candidates took place anyway. Finally, under the threat of a call for a constitutional convention, which many members of Congress feared might consider other changes in the Constitution, a direct election amendment was passed in the House and Senate in 1912 and ratified by the states a year later.

These reforms of the early twentieth century dispersed power in both the House and Senate and weakened leadership. House members no longer feared the kind of retribution levied by Speaker Cannon on members who deviated from party positions. In the Senate, popular elections made senators responsive to diverse constituencies rather than to party leaders.

Leaders

Members of each party in each house meet to choose their leaders. The Speaker of the House is chosen by the majority party members and presides over the House. Typically someone who has served in the House a long time, the Speaker is usually a skilled parliamentarian and an ideological moderate. The institutional task of the Speaker is to see that legislation moves through the House. His (all speakers have been men so far) partisan task is to secure the passage of measures preferred by his party.

Trying to win partisan support is often difficult. The Speaker has some rewards and punishments to mete out for loyalty and disloyalty, but they are mild compared to the power wielded by Reed and Cannon. The Speaker, however, does have influence on which committees members will be assigned to, on which committees will be given jurisdiction over complex bills, on what bills will come to the House floor, and on how campaign funds are allocated. He also has the sole power to decide who will be recognized to speak on the floor of the House and whether motions are relevant. He has the authority to appoint members to the Rules Committee and to certain special committees, and he controls some material benefits, such as the assignment of extra office space. Despite this formal power, the Speaker's main weapon is persuasion. The current Speaker of the House is Newt Gingrich (R-Ga.).

The party leadership in the House also includes a **majority leader,** a **minority leader,** and majority and minority **whips.** The majority leader is second in command to the Speaker, and the minority leader is, as the name suggests, the leader of the minority party. Whips originated in the British House of Commons, where they were named after the "whipper in," the rider who keeps the hounds together in a fox hunt. This aptly describes the whips' role in Congress. Party whips try to maintain contact with party members, see which way they are leaning on votes, and attempt to gain their support. Both parties have several assistant whips who keep tabs on their assigned state delegations.

The party apparatus in the House also includes committees to assign party members to standing committees, discuss policy issues, and allocate funds to party members running for reelection.

The party organization in the Senate is similar to that of the House except that there is no leader comparable to the Speaker of the House. The vice president is formally the presiding officer but in reality attends infrequently and has relatively little power. He is allowed to cast the tie-breaking vote in the rare instances in which the Senate is split evenly. Vice President Gore had such an opportunity early in his term. The Senate has an elected president pro tempore, a mostly honorific post with few duties except to preside over the Senate when the vice president is absent. Because presiding over the Senate on a day-to-day basis is considered boring, junior members usually do it.

The real leader in the Senate is the majority leader, a position now held by Bob Dole (R-Kan.). The minority party leader is normally in line to assume the majority leadership post when his or her party gains a majority of the Senate.

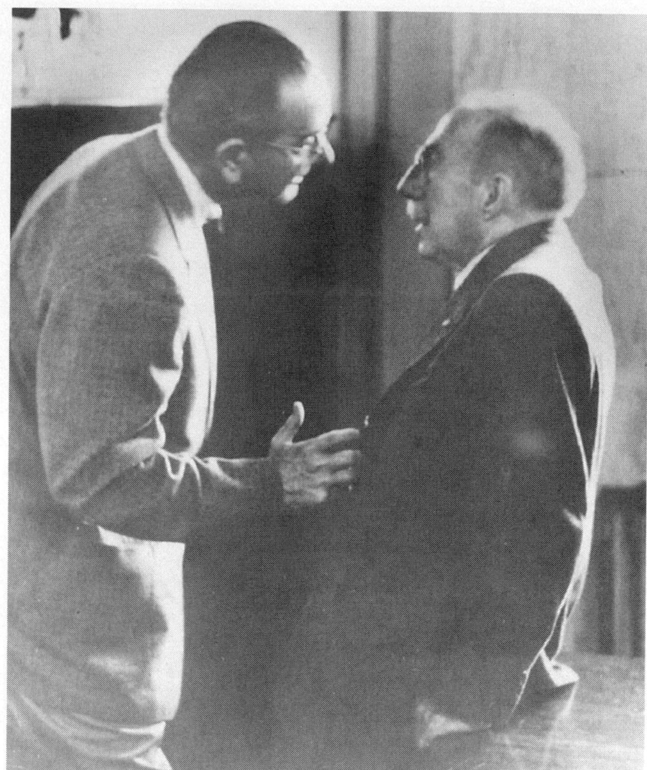

Senate majority leader Lyndon Johnson, persuading. LBJ "used physical persuasion in addition to intellectual and moral appeals. He was hard on other people's coat lapels. If one were shorter than Lyndon he was inclined to move up close and lean over the subject of his persuasive efforts." Here that subject is Senator Theodore Green (D-R.I.). "If a Senator were taller than [Johnson], he would come at him from below, somewhat like a badger." Senator Edmund Muskie (D-Me.), who was taller, "emerged from a meeting with Johnson with the observation that he had not known until this meeting why people had the hair in their nostrils trimmed." Quotes are from Eugene McCarthy, *Up 'Til Now* (New York: Harcourt Brace, 1987).

Committees

Standing Committees

Most of the work of Congress is done in committees. Observers of American politics take this for granted; yet the power of legislative committees is rather rare among western democracies. In Britain, for example, committees cannot offer amendments that change the substance of a bill.

Soon after its establishment, Congress set up four permanent committees; over the years the number slowly grew. Today there are 19 **standing committees** in the House and 17 in the Senate. Each deals with a different subject matter, such as finance or education or agriculture. Each has a number of subcommittees, totaling over 100 in the House and 85 in the Senate. Nearly all legislation introduced in Congress is referred to a standing committee and then to a subcommittee. Subcommittees hold public hearings to give interested parties a chance to speak for or against a bill. They also hold **markup** sessions to provide an opportunity for the committee to rewrite the bill. Following markup, the bill is sent to the full committee, which also may hold hearings. If approved there, it goes to the full House or Senate.

Standing committees vary in size from 11 members to 57. Trying to accommodate members' desires for committee seats that allow them to help constituents has led to ever larger committees. Party ratios—that is, the number of Democrats relative to Republicans on each committee—are determined by the majority party. The ratios are generally set in rough proportion to party membership in the particular house, but the majority party gives itself a disproportionate number of seats on several key committees in order to ensure control. Conflict between the parties flared in 1995, when Republicans offered a seat on an influential committee to a Democrat if he would switch parties. He did, and the extra Republican seat further imbalanced the partisan makeup of the committee.

Committee Membership

New members and those members seeking committee changes express their preferences to their party's selection committee. As a general rule, preferences will be granted, although there is a self-selection process whereby junior members usually do not ask for the most prestigious posts.

Seats on some committees are sought after; others are shunned. The committees dealing with budgets and appropriations are always popular because having money to allocate gives members power and the ability to help their districts. Most members want committees that allow them to tell constituents that they are working on problems of the district. For example, members from agricultural districts strive to get on the agriculture committees.

The practice of filling committees with representatives whose districts have an especially strong economic interest in the subject matter makes committees rather parochial in their outlook and fills them with members who have financial interests in the businesses they make policies for.[67] Most members who sit on the banking committees own bank stock, the agriculture committees agribusiness stock, and the armed services committees stock in military contractors.[68]

In the media age, another criterion has become important for choosing a committee: media coverage. The work of some committees is more likely to be covered by television. In a five-year period, the Senate Foreign Relations Committee had 522 network television cameras covering it, whereas the Indian Affairs Committee had 0.[69] Getting on the right committee is important to those who want to become nationally known. When a journalist once asked Senator Joseph Biden (D-Del.) why he was so newsworthy, Biden replied, "It's the committees, of course." Biden had served on the three most publicized committees.

Committee Chairs

The chair is the leader and most influential member of a committee. Chairs have the authority to call meetings, set agendas, and control the committee staff and funds. In addition, chairs are usually very knowledgeable about matters that come before their committee, and this too is a source of influence. Some chairs have used their power to rule their committee with an "iron hand."

Usually, the member of the majority party with the longest service on a committee becomes its chair—the so-called **seniority rule.** Before the early 1900s, powerful Speakers of the House often would use their authority to reward friends and allies by appointing them as committee chairs. To protect themselves, committee members adopted seniority as the basis for selecting chairs. Chairs might be completely out of touch with most of the party, senile, alcoholic, or personally disliked by every member of the committee, but if they had served the longest and their party had a majority in the House, they were chairs regardless.

Many members believed the custom of seniority led to chairs who were out of step with the rest of the party and dictatorial in their committees. In response to those complaints, in the early 1970s both parties agreed that the seniority rule no longer had to be followed. A Committee on Committees in the Republican party and a Steering and Policy Committee in the Democratic party now recommend chairs. Then the members of the party vote on these recommendations.

In 1975, in a striking break with precedent, the Democratic membership stripped three senior Democrats of their chairs. They did so again in 1985 and 1994. The Republicans also violated the seniority principle in their choice of chairs in 1995.[70] In the House, Speaker Gingrich elevated less senior members who were more conservative over other Republicans on the committees. Still, the seniority principle applies most of the time.

Why does Congress usually follow the seniority rule? It assumes that members with long service on the committee will have expertise in its subject matter, and that is usually true. It also eliminates potentially damaging intraparty fights over who will be chairs of important committees. Some people believe the seniority system is also the best protection for women and minorities as they gain seniority in the institution, although in this white male-dominated institution this is more a side effect than a reason for the system's persistence.

Choosing chairs by means other than strict seniority has ended the days of the autocratic chair. And the reform has brought about an interesting change in the behavior of senior members. Before 1975, committee chairs were much lower in support for their party in roll-call votes than other party members.[71] Since 1975, committee chairs have been much more likely to vote with their party than other members. The same pattern holds true of those who are second, third, and fourth in seniority on each committee. Thus, removing seniority as a sole criterion for choosing committee chairs has meant that senior party members are much less likely to deviate from their party's position. In that sense, the reforms have strengthened party influence in Congress.

Subcommittees

Each committee is divided into subcommittees with jurisdiction over part of the committee's subject. The House Agriculture Committee, for example, has eight subcommittees-one for wheat and soybeans, one for cotton, one for rice, and so on.

Committee chairs traditionally dominated not only their committee but its subcommittees as well. Chairs chose the chairs of the subcommittees and controlled the subcommittees' jurisdiction, budget, and staff. Chairs thus could manipulate the subcommittees' action on proposed legislation as they saw fit. In the 1950s, southern chairs bottled up important civil rights legislation for years.

In another rejection of domineering committee chairs, House Democrats made a number of rules changes in 1973 and 1974, sometimes called the **subcommittee bill of rights.** These measures gave the power of choosing subcommittee chairs to members of the committee (or, for Appropriations subcommittee chairs, to the entire Democratic House membership). The measure also provided a fixed jurisdiction and an adequate budget and staff for each subcommittee. The Senate decentralized power in much the same way.

The subcommittee reforms allow more members, especially newer members, to share in important decisions. In this way they make Congress more democratic. But by diffusing power, they also make it less efficient. Each subcommittee can operate semi-independently of the parent committee. The multiplicity of subcommittees also contributes to government gridlock. Complex legislation might be sent to several subcommittees, each with its own interests and jurisdiction.

With so many committees and subcommittees, the average member is spread pretty thin. The typical senator sits on 11 committees and subcommittees; the average representative about 7. These multiple assignments mean that members have impossible schedules, and committees cannot obtain quorums because members have other committee hearings to attend. This leaves it to the committee chair, a few colleagues, and staff to do the work and make many of the decisions.

Other Committees

There are a few other types of congressional committees. Select or special committees, such as the Senate Watergate Committee, are typically investigative committees organized on a temporary basis to investigate and make recommendations. Joint committees include members from both houses. Another committee is the Conference Committee, which we will discuss later.

Evaluating Committee Government

The division of labor provided by committees and subcommittees enables Congress to consider a vast number of bills each year. If every measure had to be reviewed in detail by each member, it would be impossible to deal with the current workload. Instead, most bills are killed in committee, leaving many fewer for each member to evaluate before a floor vote. Committees also help members develop specializations. Members who remain on the same committee for some time gain expertise and are less dependent on professional staff and executive agencies for information.

But committee government also has disadvantages. In addition to the inefficiencies mentioned already, committees and especially subcommittees are often unrepresentative of Congress as a whole. As a result, they tend to be more responsive to narrow interests and constituencies and less responsive to national objectives.

Over time, members of congressional subcommittees develop close relationships with the interest groups and executive branch agencies affected by their work. These three sets of participants share a concern with a specific policy area. Over the years, the people in these three groups get to know each other, probably come to like and respect one another, and seek to accommodate each other's interests. Personal relationships foster favorable treatment of special interest groups.

The freedom and authority of individual members mean that Congress as a whole often cannot get things done because power is fragmented. Most members of the majority party in the Senate and about half of those in the House chair committees or subcommittees. These centers of power are somewhat independent from party leaders. Thus, Congress often has difficulty mounting a coherent alternative to the president.

On the other hand, the fragmentation of power means it is relatively easy for Congress to block presidential initiatives. In this sense, Congress remains a conservative institution, protecting the status quo. Whether one thinks this is a good idea or not depends on the particular nature of the changes being proposed. Congress has frustrated both conservative and liberal presidents.

Crumbling Committees?

Over the past decade there have been changes in the way Congress deals with important issues. Committee chairs and committees do not always have the power they used to. There is evidence of greater centralization, though not as much as at the turn of the century. Power is gravitating to all members of a few "power" committees, such as the Appropriations, Ways and Means, and Energy and Commerce committees in the House and the Finance Committee in the Senate. The power of these committees lies in their ability to control spending and raise revenue, (as we will see later). As one observer commented, even the most senior member of Public Works finds it difficult to accomplish what the most junior member of Appropriations can do in winning home district pork barrel projects. The former chair of the Senate Appropriations Committee, Robert Byrd (D-W.Va.), was called the "Prince of Pork" for his success in bringing federal money to West Virginia.[72]

Power has also gravitated to party leaders. The formal leader of the House, the Speaker, has gained power, and party unity is on the upswing. Leaders, including some committee chairs, are also more powerful because more and more negotiations over important bills are taking place directly among the leaders of Congress and administration officials. For example, the Senate version of the Clean Air Act was drafted in a series of meetings between the Senate majority leader, other key senators, and Bush administration officials. The bill written in committee was largely ignored. Other issues, such as an anticrime bill, campaign finance legislation, and a congressional ethics package have been developed outside formal committee structures.

These new arrangements have some advantages. They overcome the paralysis that sometimes results from the divided partisan control of Congress and the presidency. Direct negotiations between the White House and congressional leaders can sometimes break long-standing deadlocks.

On the other hand, these new arrangements bypass mechanisms for accountability to the public and to most rank-and-file members. Bills are written without formal hearings and the opportunities to point out potential pitfalls and problems of the legislation. Rank-and-file members often are faced with voting on a huge package of legislation about which they know only what they read in the newspaper.

Moreover, without powerful committees, if the majority leaders are not strong, bargaining over legislation can become a complete free-for-all, with dozens of legislators striking individual deals for their favorite program. Without strong committees or leaders, individual members of Congress, often with no expertise or interest beyond a special interest, can hold a piece of legislation hostage in exchange for a tax loophole or bit of pork.

Thus, many people believe that Congress is still ripe for reform. The Republicans did make several changes when they took over in 1995, including abolishing three House committees and several subcommittees, eliminating proxy committee voters, and planning for a substantial reduction in staff. Despite this modest streamlining, the basic functioning of the Congress is unchanged. However, its burst of legislative energy early in 1995 suggests that when Congress fails to get things done, committee structure is only part of the reason. A cohesive House majority with strong leadership can pass legislation even with a complex committee structure. Conversely, if the public is divided and there is little strong leadership or incentive for members to carry out a legislative agenda, congressional structure only reinforces other impediments to action. As one member remarked,

American Diversity

Black Power in Congress

Special interest caucuses are groups of members united by some personal interest or characteristic. There are more than 60 House caucuses, representing partisan, ideological, policy, or regional interests. One of these, the Black Caucus, was organized in 1969 by black members of Congress determined to gain some clout. This organization, which includes all African-American members of Congress, has grown to 40 members and meets regularly, usually weekly. It also has more than 80 white associate members. Before 1994, the caucus, like other caucuses, had its own small staff. However, the Republican majority eliminated staff support for special interest caucuses, so now the caucus relies on its members to provide support from their staffs.

Paradoxically, at a time when the caucus is at its all-time high in its number of members, it is perhaps the weakest it has been in two decades. The reason is that all but two of its members are Democrats, and now they are the minority party in both houses. When the Democrats controlled the House, many black members had positions of power, chairing, in 1994, 26% of all House committees and many subcommittees too. Now with their party out of power, they chair no committees or subcommittees. Moreover, the caucus has little influence with the Republican majority because of its small Republican membership and the Democratic predispositions of the black constituents of Republican members of Congress.

As we have discussed, the success of blacks in getting several southern states to redistrict to form majority black districts helped weaken Democratic congressional representation in the South and contributed to the Republican majority. One analyst notes that "A lot of people say redistricting was a means to an end of getting more power for black people by getting more blacks in Congress; if redistricting was a means to an end, it turned out to be a dead end."[1] Others, such as Jesse Jackson, urge a continuation of the majority-minority redistricting strategy, arguing that the Democrats did poorly in 1994 partly because of low black turnout, which can be mobilized.

To be influential in these new circumstances, Black Caucus members will have to negotiate and find new allies. Yet they must also continue speaking for their constituency. In today's climate, this is a difficult task. For example, their proposed alternatives to both the Republican and the Clinton budget cuts are getting little publicity, and have even less chance of being seriously considered.

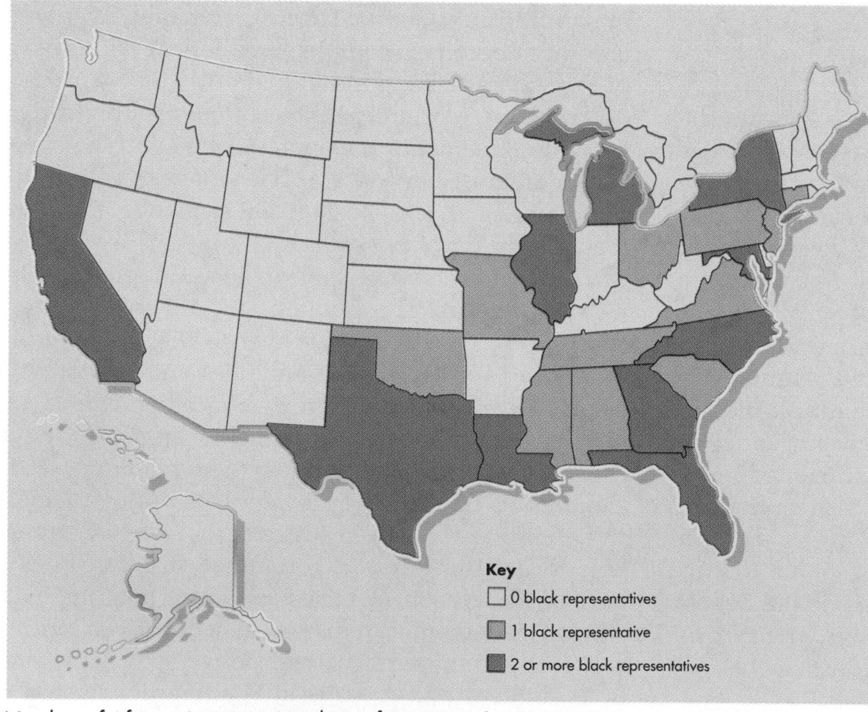

Number of African American Members of Congress, by State.

1. Juan Williams, "How Black Liberal Strategy Failed Its Followers," *Washington Post National Weekly Edition*, November 28-December 3, 1994, p. 25; Steven Holmes "Did Racial Redistricting Undermine Democrats?" *New York Times,* November 13, 1994.

"how is a committee overhaul going to make me more courageous to do things I don't want to do now?"[73]

Staff

The term "Congress" encompasses not only our 535 elected representatives but also their staff of nearly 30,000 people.

Congress hires far more staff members than any other legislative body. Even with recent cuts, it is still by far the largest. The Canadian legislature, which is second in staff size, has only about 3,300 people.[74]

Types of Staff

Congressional staff members include those working in members' Washington and district offices, defined as "personal" staff, those working for congressional committees, those working for the special support agencies of Congress (the Congressional Research Service, Office of Technology Assessment, Congressional Budget Office, and the General Accounting Office), and auxiliary staff such as police.

House members have about 16 personal staff members, and the average senator has more than 40. Senators from states with larger populations have a larger staff than senators from smaller states. Leaders have many more staff than rank-and-file members. By far the largest proportion of members' personal staffs works on constituency service, both in the district offices and in Washington. Other staff members will be assigned to legislative duties, and one or more will do media work.

One of the main reasons for the tremendous growth and size of staff is the increasing demand for constituency service. As more citizens turn to Congress for help with the bureaucracy, Congress hires more staff to take care of them. Another main reason is that Congress has attempted to develop its own expertise and sources of information so it will not have to rely on the executive branch. Thus its committees have staff members who research and draft legislation as well as develop support for it.

Staff in the support agencies of Congress carry out various research functions, again enabling Congress to be independent of the executive branch. The General Accounting Office checks on the efficiency and effectiveness of executive agencies. The Congressional Research Service conducts studies of public issues and does specific research at the request of members. The Office of Technology Assessment provides long-range analyses of the effects of new and existing technology, and the Congressional Budget Office provides the expertise and support for Congress' budgeting job.

Impact of Staff

Some scholars have argued that although increased congressional staff may be necessary, it has created more problems than it has solved.[75] Large staffs create more paperwork and have a tendency to produce ever more research, committee work, and hearings. Information is collected that is impossible for members to digest. Large staffs have made members into executives who need to manage their offices rather than legislators with time to think about policy. Congressional staffs have reduced the amount of discussion members have with one another over policy issues. As former Senator David Boren (D-Okla.) complained, "Very often, I will call on a senator on an issue, and he won't know anything about it. He'll ask me to get someone on my staff to call someone on his staff. It shuts off personal contact between senators."[76]This means the compromises and adjustments necessary to make policy are sometimes made by technicians rather than elected representatives.

What Congress Does

The Founders intended Congress to be the dominant branch of government. The powers and role of Congress are spelled out in Article I of the Constitution, before attention is given to the president. Almost half the Constitution is devoted to a discussion of Congress. The importance of Congress also is reflected in the major, explicit constitutional powers the Founders gave it: to lay and collect taxes, coin money, declare war and raise and support a military, and regulate commerce with foreign governments and among the states. These and other powers specifically mentioned in the Constitution are called the enumerated powers of Congress.

Congress also has implied powers; that is, it can make all the laws "necessary and proper" to carry out its enumerated powers. Although the Founders did not necessarily foresee it, this tremendous grant of power covers almost every conceivable area of human activity.

Lawmaking

High school civics students learn the formal steps by which a bill becomes a law (see Figure 5). Although

■ FIGURE 5
How a Bill Becomes a Law is Not a Simple Story

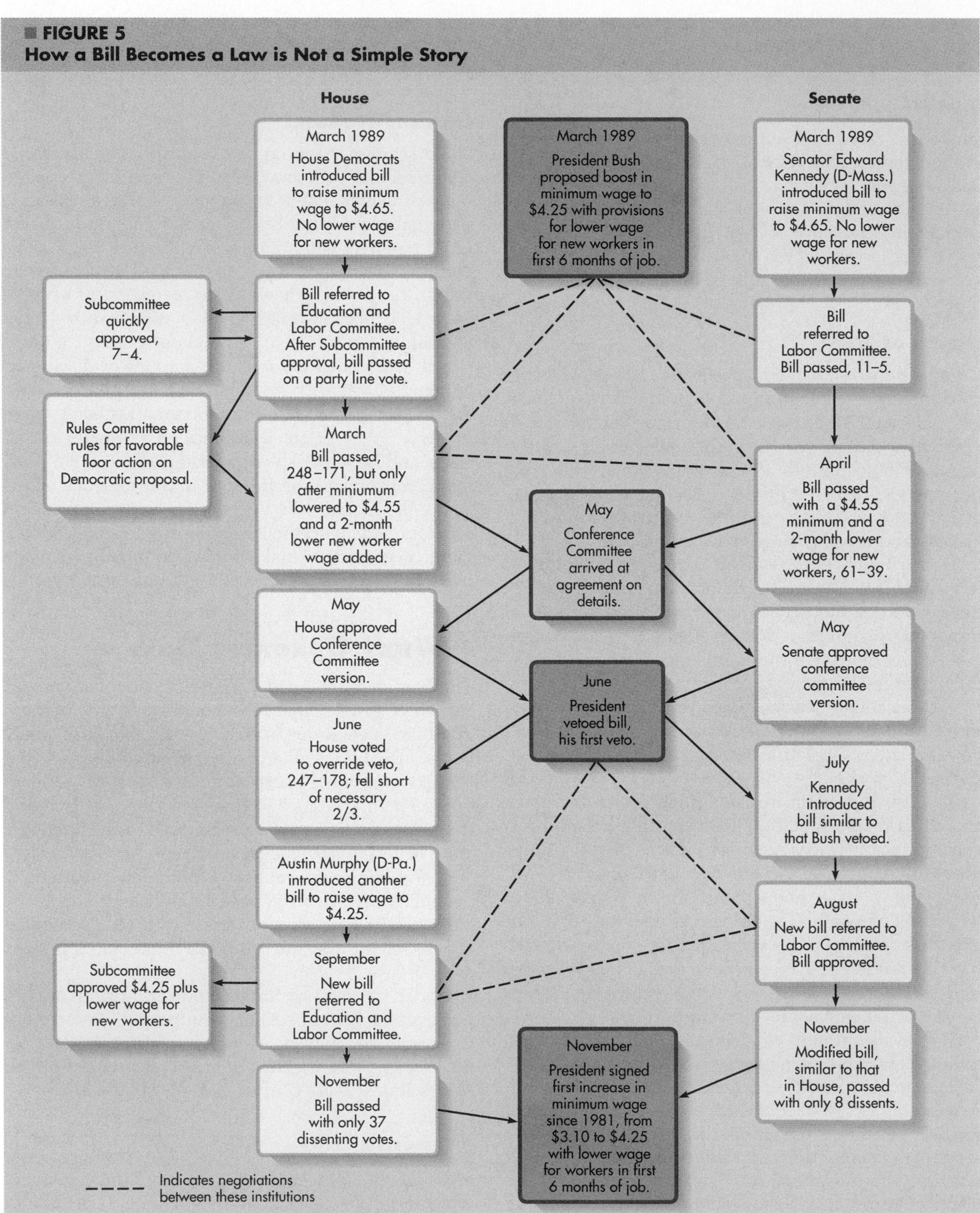

House
Senate
March 1989
House Democrats introduced bill to raise minimum wage to $4.65. No lower wage for new workers.
March 1989
President Bush proposed boost in minimum wage to $4.25 with provisions for lower wage for new workers in first 6 months of job.
March 1989
Senator Edward Kennedy (D-Mass.) introduced bill to raise minimum wage to $4.65. No lower wage for new workers.
Subcommittee quickly approved, 7–4.
Bill referred to Education and Labor Committee. After Subcommittee approval, bill passed on a party line vote.
Bill referred to Labor Committee. Bill passed, 11–5.
Rules Committee set rules for favorable floor action on Democratic proposal.
March
Bill passed, 248–171, but only after miniumum lowered to $4.55 and a 2-month lower new worker wage added.
April
Bill passed with a $4.55 minimum and a 2-month lower wage for new workers, 61–39.
May
Conference Committee arrived at agreement on details.
May
House approved Conference Committee version.
May
Senate approved conference committee version.
June
President vetoed bill, his first veto.
June
House voted to override veto, 247–178; fell short of necessary 2/3.
July
Kennedy introduced bill similar to that Bush vetoed.
Austin Murphy (D-Pa.) introduced another bill to raise wage to $4.25.
August
New bill referred to Labor Committee. Bill approved.
Subcommittee approved $4.25 plus lower wage for new workers.
September
New bill referred to Education and Labor Committee.
November
Modified bill, similar to that in House, passed with only 8 dissents.
November
Bill passed with only 37 dissenting votes.
November
President signed first increase in minimum wage since 1981, from $3.10 to $4.25 with lower wage for workers in first 6 months of job.
---- Indicates negotiations between these institutions

these procedures are important, at every step there are compromises, trade-offs, and understandings. In other words, there is politics.

A bill becomes a law if its supporters can get it through an obstacle course. Approval must be obtained at each obstacle or the bill fails. Those opposing a bill have an advantage because it is easier to defeat a bill than pass it. The need to win a majority at each stage of the process also means that individuals with varying interests must be satisfied. The end result is almost always a compromise.

Introduction

Bills may be introduced in either the House or the Senate, except for tax measures (which according to the Constitution must be introduced initially in the House) and appropriations bills (which by tradition are introduced in the House). This reflects the Founders' perceptions that on tax issues Congress should be especially responsive to the people and that the House would be more responsive than the Senate.

Only members of Congress are permitted to introduce bills. Interest groups or the president must find a congressional sponsor for a proposed bill. About half the legislation passed is initiated by the president.[77]

Referral and Committee Action

After a bill's introduction, it is referred to a standing committee by the Speaker of the House or the presiding officer in the Senate. The content of the bill largely determines where it will go, although the Speaker has some discretion, particularly over complex bills that cover more than one subject area.

Once the bill reaches a committee, it is assigned to a subcommittee. Bills receiving subcommittee approval go to full committee and if approved go to the whole House. Bills that get out of committee usually become law. Most bills, however, die in committee or subcommittee. Indeed, one of the main functions of committees is to screen bills with little chance of passage. (If a committee kills a bill, there are procedures that members can use to try to get the bill to the floor, but these are used infrequently.)

The committee and subcommittee markup stage is legally open yet barely visible to the public. Consequently, lobbyists attend hearings. For critical meetings, lobbyists will hire messengers to stand in line for them, sometimes all night, and then pack the hearing room. Members dependent on particular groups for financial or other support often face intense and direct pressure to vote a particular way in committee, and are sometimes mobbed by lobbyists when they leave the hearing room.

Scheduling and the Rules Committee

Once a bill is approved by committee, it is placed on one of five "calendars," each of which contains a particular type of bill (for example, all bills considered to be noncontroversial are placed on one calendar). Bills from each calendar are generally considered in the order that they are reported from committee. In the House, the **Rules Committee** sets the terms of the debate over the bill by issuing a rule on it. The rule either limits or does not limit debate and determines whether amendments will be permitted. A rule forbidding amendments means that members have to vote Yes or No on the bill; there is no chance to change it. If the committee refuses to issue a rule, the bill dies.

The Rules Committee is not as independent or powerful as it once was. In earlier years the committee was controlled by a coalition of conservative Democrats and Republicans who used the committee to block liberal legislative proposals. It now functions as an arm of the majority leadership.[78] Members are nominated by the Speaker, and the leadership uses the committee to fashion rules to control and expedite floor action.

Debate in the House

Debate on a bill is controlled by the bill managers, the senior committee supporters of the bill. The opposition too has its managers who schedule opposition speeches. "Debates" are hardly a series of fiery speeches of point and counterpoint. They are often boring, given to sparse audiences, some of whom are reading, conversing, or walking around. After the agreed-upon time for debate is over, the bill is reported for final action.

The Senate

Because the Senate is a smaller body, it can operate with fewer rules and formal procedures. It does not have a rules committee. A lot of work is accomplished through the use of unanimous consent agreements, which allow the Senate to dispense with standard rules and limit debate and amendments. As the Senate's workload has increased and its sense of collegiality decreased, unanimous consent agreements are both more desirable and more difficult to gain from opponents of a bill. A few senators can delay or kill important bills. (Table 3 summarizes House and Senate differences.) As one observer remarked, "The Senate has the same procedural rules as you would find on Monkey Island in the San Francisco Zoo."[79]

Without unanimous consent, there is no rule limiting debate and no restrictions on adding amendments. Opponents can add all sorts of irrelevant amendments to pending legislation. One senator held up an antibusing bill for eight months with 604 amendments.

The other major mechanism for delay in the Senate is the **filibuster.** This is a continuous speech made by one or more members to prevent the Senate from taking action. Before 1917, only unanimous consent could prevent an individual from talking. Today a **cloture** vote of three-fifths of the members can limit debate to only 20 more hours.

Like nongermane amendments, filibusters are used by both liberals and conservatives. The filibuster developed in the 1820s when the Senate was divided between slave and free states. Unlimited debate maintained the deadlock.[80] For over a century the filibuster was used primarily to defeat race and civil rights legislation; the 1964 Civil Rights Act was passed only after a cloture vote. Recently, filibusters have occurred on many different types of legislation.

During Clinton's first year in office, Republicans used the filibuster quite frequently. Not only did they use it to work against his economic proposals, but they also used it as a political tactic to embarrass the president. Even though the Democrats had a significant majority, their majority was not large enough to shut off the filibuster unless some Republicans joined them in the antifilibuster vote. Republicans, often picking up some Democratic defectors, used the filibuster to delay or defeat legislation. Now that Repub-

TABLE 3 Important Differences Between the House and Senate

HOUSE	SENATE
Constitutional Differences	**Constitutional Differences**
Must initiate revenue bills	Must give approval to many major presidential appointments
Initiates impeachment and passes impeachment bills	Tries impeached officials
Apportioned by population	Approves treaties
	Two senators from each state
Differences in Operation	**Differences in Operation**
More centralized, more formal:	Less centralized, less formal:
Speaker's assignment of bills to committee hard to challenge	Assignment of bills to committee appealable
Rules Committee fairly powerful in controlling time and rules of debate (works with majority leaders)	No rules committee; limits on debate come through unanimous consent or cloture of filibuster
Nongermane amendments forbidden	Nongermane amendments permitted
Majority party controls scheduling	Schedule and rules negotiated between majority and minority leaders
More impersonal	More personal
Power less evenly distributed	Power more evenly distributed
Members are highly specialized	Members are generalists
Emphasizes tax and revenue policy	Emphasizes foreign policy
Changes In the Institution	**Changes in the Institution**
Power is becoming centralized in the hands of key committees and the leadership	Senate workload increasing and informality breaking down
House procedures are becoming more efficient with less debate and fewer amendments	Members are becoming more specialized; debate and deliberation are less frequent

SOURCES: Louis A. Froman, *The Congressional Process: Strategies, Rules, and Procedures* (Boston: Little, Brown, 1967); Norman Ornstein, "The House and Senate in a New Congress" in Thomas Mann and Norman Ornstein, eds., *The New Congress* (Washington, D.C.: American Enterprise Institute, 1981), pp. 363-84.

licans control the Senate, we may expect Democratic filibusters.

Filibusters protect the rights of congressional minorities and help ensure that controversial issues will get full consideration. On the other hand, they deny the majority the right to legislate, and contribute mightily to gridlock.[81] In the last decade they have been used far more frequently than in the past. In 1991-1992 alone they were used 35 times, compared with only 16 times during the entire nineteenth century. By in effect requiring 60 votes to pass controversial legislation, they make it difficult for a majority to legislate.

Conference Committee

Under the Constitution, the House and Senate must pass an identical bill before it becomes law. Thus the House and Senate versions of the bill must be reconciled. Sometimes the house that passed the bill last will simply send the bill to the other house for minor modifications. But if the differences between the two versions are not minor, a **Conference Committee** is set up to try to resolve them. The presiding officers of each house, in consultation with the chairs of the standing committees that considered the bill, choose the members of the committee. Both parties are represented.

To win approval, majorities of members from each house must agree to the Conference Committee version. Sometimes the bill is rewritten fairly substantially, and occasionally a bill is killed.

Once the Conference Committee reaches an agreement, the bill goes back to each house for ratification. It cannot be amended at that point so Congress must either "take it or leave it." This means the Conference Committee can be very influential.

Presidential Action and Congressional Response

The president may sign the bill, in which case it becomes law. The president may veto it, in which case it returns to Congress with the president's objections. The president also may do nothing, which means the bill becomes law after 10 days unless Congress adjourns.

Presidents infrequently veto legislation, but when they do, they usually are not overridden by Congress. A two-thirds vote in each house is required to override a presidential veto. Congress voted to override only 9 of former President Reagan's 78 vetoes, and only 1 of President Bush's 46.

Overseeing the Federal Bureaucracy

As part of the checks and balances principle, it is Congress's responsibility to make sure the bureaucracy is carrying out the intent of Congress in administering federal programs. This congressional **oversight** has become more important as Congress continues to delegate authority to the executive branch. For a variety of reasons, Congress is not especially well equipped, motivated, or organized to carry out its oversight function. Nevertheless, it does have several tools for this purpose.

One tool is the General Accounting Office, created in 1921, which functions as Congress's watchdog in oversight and is mostly concerned with making sure that money is used properly.

Another tool is the **legislative veto.** Used since 1933, it allows one or both houses of Congress, or on occasion a congressional committee, to block executive action. Congress adds the veto provision to some legislation. In the 1970s, it did much more than in the past in order to restrict agency activities. For example, all Federal Trade Commission rulings were subject to a legislative veto.

In 1983, the Supreme Court declared the legislative veto unconstitutional as a violation of the separation of powers principle. Legislation, the Court ruled, must be passed by both houses and signed by the president. Congress cannot take over executive functions. Even so, since that decision, more than 100 bills have passed with provisions for a legislative veto.[82] Though presumably they could not be enforced, legislative vetoes continue to be honored by federal agencies unwilling to risk congressional wrath by doing something Congress has vetoed.

Yet another method of oversight is committee hearings, although they are not very effective. Members can quiz representatives from agencies on the operation of their agencies, but often they go into great detail about some particular problem of minor importance and neglect broader policy questions. Poor attendance and the pressure of other business mean that members' attentions are usually not focused on congressional hearings.

Nevertheless, officials in agencies view hearings as a possible source of embarrassment for their agency and spend a great deal of time preparing for them.

Political considerations also influence oversight. For example, a year before the Iran scandal hit the front pages in 1986, two congressional committees began investigations of Colonel Oliver North's fund-raising efforts for the Nicaraguan contras. The investigations were dropped in order not to challenge a popular president.

Congress's control over the budget is the major way it exercises oversight. Congress can cut or add to agencies' budgets and thereby punish or reward them for their performance.

Informal oversight is a common tool.[83] This can include requiring reports on topics of interest to members or committees. In a recent year the executive branch prepared 5000 reports for Congress.[84] Moreover the chair and staff of the committee or subcommittee relevant to the agency's mission are consulted regularly by the agency. But one can question whether much actual oversight gets done informally. Members of congressional committee and subcommittees with authority over an agency's budget get benefits for their constituents from that agency. By responding to congressional wishes, agencies get a favorable budget. There are few electoral or other incentives for members to become involved in the drudgery of more thorough oversight.[85]

Overseeing the Pentagon

Congressional monitoring of the Department of Defense (DOD) is a good example of the problems of congressional oversight. It bogs down in details and special concerns but fails to provide critical scrutiny of the big picture.

Forty years ago, Congress engaged in little oversight of the Pentagon. In fact, the Defense Department witnesses at committee hearings actually submitted to the committee the questions that members should ask them. The practice stopped after 1969, however, when a confused committee member read not only the proposed question, but also the proposed answer to this question!

Now Congress has gone to the other extreme. Dozens of committees and subcommittees oversee the Pentagon. Hundreds of Pentagon witnesses spent hundreds of hours testifying before 84 committees and subcommittees. The Pentagon also annually responds to several hundred thousand congressional requests for information. All four congressional support agencies also monitor the department. In its attempts to make the system more responsible, Congress has bogged it down in red tape.

Congress issues detailed requirements for each weapons system or other equipment it orders. Thus a proposal from a contractor for a new military transport jet weighed three tons (the proposal, not the plane!).

Despite all this, Congress spends little time on the "big picture," the overall organization and strategies of our armed forces. Many critics believe these problems are potentially much more damaging to our national security than waste and corruption in weapons purchasing on which congressional oversight focuses. As one military expert noted, "When admirals, officials, and Congressmen gather to examine the Navy in each year's review of the budget, ten minutes of . . . chitchat disposes of the entire question of naval strategy—i.e., the purpose of the Navy, its major tasks . . . before all concerned settle down to many weeks of scrutiny . . . of every single item of expenditure. . . . Debate on each service's chosen operational concepts of war, which actually determine their equipment needs, is almost unknown."

Source: Drawing by Levin, © 1979 The New Yorker Magazine, Inc.

SOURCES: David Morrison, "Chaos on Capital Hill," *National Journal*, September 27, 1986, pp. 2302-7; J. Ronald Fox, *Arming America* (Cambridge, Mass.: Harvard University Press, 1974); Edward Luttwak, *The Pentagon and the Art of War* (New York: Simon & Schuster, 1984), pp. 152-53.

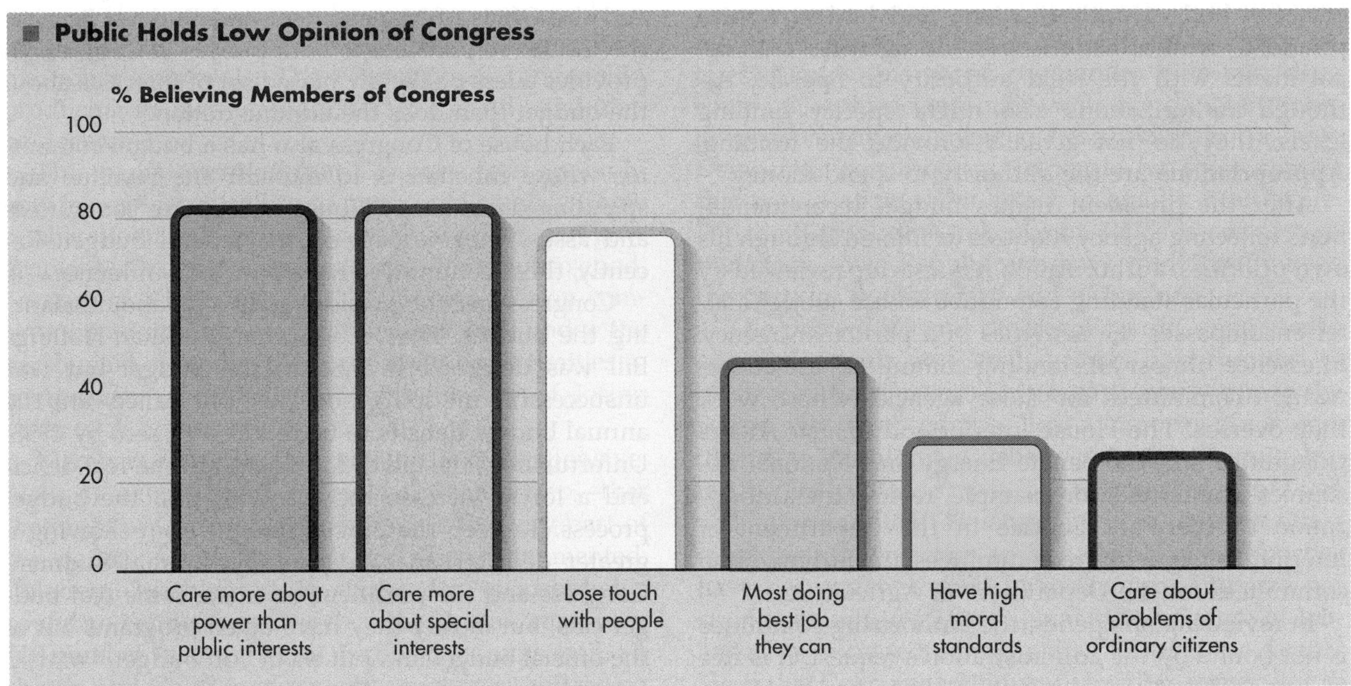

SOURCE: Washington Post-ABC Polls, reported July 11–17, 1994, p. 7.

Budget Making

An increasingly large part of the job of Congress is to produce a budget. The Constitution gives Congress the authority to control the federal purse by collecting taxes and spending money.

The topic of making budgets sounds dull and can be tedious. However, without money to implement laws, laws themselves would mean very little. It is one thing to pass legislation that provides funding for day care, improves Medicare benefits, combats drug addiction, regulates health and safety standards for workers, and provides financial aid to students. But without money in the budget to fund these programs, the programs are empty rhetoric. And in fact, sometimes laws are passed to give the impression that government is really doing something about a problem when in reality it is not doing much. Much of the "War on Drugs" fits this category. In other cases, those who support legislation do see that it is reasonably well funded initially, but later it may lose support and suffer funding cuts. During the Reagan administration, for example, many regulatory programs established during the 1970s, such as the Consumer Product Safety Commission and the Environmental Protection Agency, lost substantial parts of their funding and were forced to cut back their activities. Thus budgets are crucial in determining what government actually does.

There are two major features of congressional spending patterns. First, the process is usually incremental; that is, budgets of one year are usually slightly more than budgets of the past year. Normally, Congress does not radically reallocate money from one year to the next; members assume agencies should get about what they received the previous year. This simplifies the work of all concerned. Agencies do not have to defend, or members scrutinize, all aspects of the budget.[86]

A second feature is that Congress tends to spend slightly more on federal agencies in election years.[87] This tendency increases in times of unemployment and moderates in times of inflation. Members are also more likely to vote for increasing federal payments to individuals (such as veterans' benefits or Social Security) in the years they are up for reelection.[88]

These general tendencies cannot account for every year's budgeting. Reagan's domestic budget cuts and increased military spending in 1981 were clearly an exception to incrementalism. But his failure to win further cuts and increases in succeeding years testifies to the persistence of incrementalism.

Budget legislation goes through a similar but more complicated process as other bills.[89] To grasp the complexity, we have to understand the distinction

11 The Presidency

You Are There

Retreat Again?

It is February 1995, and you are Bill Clinton. Beginning the third year of your presidential term, you are confronted with a tough decision. Should you stick by your nominee for surgeon general, Henry W. Foster, Jr., or should you withdraw the nomination in the face of growing opposition?

This nomination, like many other high-level positions, must be confirmed by a vote of the Senate before the person can take office. Before the Senate votes on the nomination, the candidate must undergo a public hearing before the Senate Labor and Human Resources Committee and win a positive vote from the committee. Because the Republicans are a majority in the Senate, they have a majority on this committee.

You have had trouble with several nominations already. Your first nominee for surgeon general, Joycelyn Elders, was confirmed and served almost two years. But she was controversial throughout her service, speaking out in favor of choice in abortion and the school's role in sex education to prevent teen-age pregnancy and disease. You finally asked for her resignation when she was quoted as saying that children should be taught about masturbation. Your first nominee for attorney general, Lani Guinier, also proved to be controversial, and you withdrew her nomination before she even was able to appear before a Senate committee hearing. She had been an advocate of consideration of different forms of voting (such as multimember districts and proportional representation) in order to promote the electoral strength of minorities. Opponents of affirmative action led the attack on her. Both Elders and Guinier were black women.

You also withdrew other nominees, including a woman attorney general candidate who had hired an illegal alien to do household work. Overall, you and your staff have been highly criticized for slowness in making nominees and having lack of adequate background information on the nominees; having to withdraw nominees gives the impression you are weak and vacillating.

Now the nightmare continues. You are faced with a seemingly no-win situation because of both your political allies and your enemies. Your allies, in particular your own staff, helped cause your problems because of sloppy background work. You choose Dr. Foster because he was a well-known doctor and educator. You believed he could lead a national campaign to reduce teen pregnancy.[1] He had led such a campaign in his hometown of Nashville, Tennessee through his "I have a future" program. In fact, George Bush awarded him his "thousand points of light" award only four years ago for the success of this campaign. Foster, like you born in Arkansas, was the only black in his medical school class at the University of Arkansas. He had been chair of the Department of Obstetrics and and Gynecology at Meharry Medical College in Nashville and later president of the college.

But only a day after you announced his nomination, he became embroiled in the abortion controversy. As an obstetrician, he had delivered over 10,000 babies. But he also performed some abortions. When the question of just how many

CONTINUED 

OUTLINE

Presidential Job Description
- Qualifications
- Tenure
- Succession
- Rewards

Growth of the Modern Presidency
- The Presidency Before the New Deal
- Development of the Personal Presidency

Presidential Power
- Persuading the Washingtonians
- Persuading the Public
- Presidential Popularity
- Limits of Presidential Power

Roles of the President
- Growth of Presidential Staff
- Administrative Leadership
- Domestic Policy Leadership
- Foreign Policy Leadership
- Military Leadership
- Symbolic Leadership
- Party Leadership

Conclusion: Is the Presidency Responsive?

A president's ability to do his job is not always clear. James Garfield was shot in July 1881 and did not die until mid-September. In 1919, Woodrow Wilson had a nervous collapse in the summer and a stroke in the fall and was incapacitated for many months. No one was sure about his condition, however, because his wife restricted access to him. In both cases, the issue of who was or should have been acting as president was unclear.

Another section of the Twenty-fifty Amendment charges the vice president and a majority of the cabinet (or some other body named by Congress) to determine if a president is able to do his job. The vice president becomes "acting president" if they find the president incapacitated. The president resumes his functions after notifying Congress of his recovery. Reagan followed the spirit of this section in 1985. Before undergoing cancer surgery, he sent his vice president, George Bush, a letter authorizing him to act as president while Reagan was unconscious.

Rewards

The president's salary of $200,000 a year is large by most standards but seems almost small compared to the job's other benefits. These benefits include living in one of the world's most famous mansions, a rural retreat (Camp David), fleets of aircraft and cars, and a generous pension after leaving office as well as money for an office and staff.

Many people believed that Edith Galt Wilson, the president's wife, was making the decisions during President Wilson's illness.

No one argues that the president's material rewards should be slight. However, there is some concern that daily life on Pennsylvania Avenue is too isolated from the daily realities of most citizens. Shortly after his inauguration, Bill Clinton described the White House as "the crown jewel in the American prison system" when he found he could not do many everyday things (like jogging on public streets and making unplanned trips to fast-food restaurants). Given daily life in the White House, might a president come to think he is more special than we want him to be, that his views are better than others?

Growth of the Modern Presidency

The Presidency Before the New Deal

Most presidents during the 1800s and early 1900s were "ordinary people with very ordinary reputations."[8] James Monroe, who served from 1817 to 1825, wore outdated knee breeches, silk stockings, ink-spotted clothing, and worn-down shoes. He looked, according to a European diplomat, like an unkempt clerk.[9] The nineteenth century was an age of legislative power. Indeed, Woodrow Wilson wrote a book calling national government in the 1880s "congressional government."

The Founders largely viewed the president as a presiding office. Before 1932, most people saw Congress as the representative and policymaking part of government. They saw presidential leadership as a threat to responsive government. As a result, the office tended to attract individuals of average ability who did not try to be leaders and who regarded administering the law as their primary job. The powerful presidents before the New Deal—Washington, Jackson, Lincoln, Teddy Roosevelt, and Wilson—were the exceptions and not the rule. Washington set many important precedents. For example, he initiated meetings of department heads, or cabinet meetings. Jackson was the first to act assertively to fulfill the popular mandate he saw in his election—the first to veto a bill because *he* did not like it. Lincoln boldly and creatively interpreted the Constitution to say individual states could not legally leave the Union.

Vice Presidency

Job

Vice presidents of private corporations work on matters of importance to their firms. This has only recently been true of United States vice presidents. Historically, the only jobs vice presidents have had were to preside over the Senate and cast tie-breaking votes. Presidents have traditionally given vice presidents little information and few opportunities for involvement. Harry Truman did not know about the atom bomb when he became president after Franklin Roosevelt's (FDR's) death, but within months he had to decide about using it on Japan.

Gerald Ford's vice president, Nelson Rockefeller, called the job "standby equipment." Others have been less charitable. Woodrow Wilson's vice president, Thomas R. Marshall, said holding the job is like being "a man in a cataleptic fit: He cannot speak, he cannot move. He suffers no pain. He is perfectly conscious of all that goes on. But he has no part in it." FDR's first vice president, John Nance Garner, was less elegant in observing that his job was not worth a "pitcher of warm spit."

FDR had told Garner, "You tend to your office and I'll tend to mine." The problem was that there was little to tend. Historically, presidents have had difficulty delegating important jobs to their vice presidents because they themselves have wanted to wield all the power.

Until Jimmy Carter, presidents asked their vice presidents to deal mainly with partisan or ceremonial matters. Vice presidents helped mend party fences and criticized the opposition in harsher terms than the president could use without damaging his image as president of all the people. Spiro Agnew gained considerable attention for calling Nixon's opponents "effete intellectuals," among other things.

Carter was the first president to use his vice president, Walter Mondale, for important work. Carter had no national experience before his election and considered Mondale, a former United States senator, a major asset. Carter gave Mondale a White House office (as opposed to one in the Old Executive Office Building next door), scheduled weekly lunches with him, put him on all White House advisory groups, and had him attend all important meetings, lobby Congress, and read the paperwork that crossed Carter's desk. Ronald Reagan and George Bush did much the same with their vice presidents, and Bill Clinton has added to this new tradition. He has let his vice president, Al Gore, influence his political appointments, review and offer suggestions for many of his speeches, and influence issues related to the environment, advanced technology, and bureaucratic reform.

Although tensions sometimes exist between the vice president's staff and the president's, as a reflection of their separate political careers, there is incentive for cooperation. Given the great public exposure of the White House, it is not to either official's interest to appear on bad terms with the other.

Springboard to the White House?

George Bush was the first incumbent vice president to win a presidential election since Martin Van Buren in 1836. That 34 men after Van Buren failed to win the presidency while serving as vice president led to talk of a "Van Buren Jinx." According to it, a vice president cannot win the White House because he is saddled with the negatives of his president's record without being able to take credit for his successes. Evidence for this are the failed presidential bids of Richard Nixon, Hubert Humphrey, and Walter Mondale. In 1960, Nixon received little help from the popular Dwight Eisenhower, who preferred to avoid partisan battles and did not like Nixon personally. Opposition to the Vietnam War and Lyndon Johnson hurt Humphrey in 1968. And Reagan would not let Mondale escape Carter's shadow in 1984.

However, the "jinx" may be a fiction.[1] Only 7 of the 34 vice presidents from Van Buren to Bush actually ran for president while they were vice president. When Nixon lost in 1960 and Humphrey in 1968 (to former vice president Nixon!), they lost by very little. In fact, recent history shows that vice presidents do become presidential frontrunners. Six of the last nine vice presidents were nominated to be president.

The caliber of recent vice presidents indicates that the office may have become more important. Most have been seasoned public servants with considerable experience and personal records of achievement. That they were willing to take the job suggests it has become more than "standby equipment." Perhaps the furor over the qualifications (or lack of them) of Dan Quayle, Bush's vice president, reflects the fact that the public thinks the vice presidency is worth a highly qualified candidate.

---

1 Michael Nelson, *A Heartbeat Away* (New York: Priority Press, 1988). For more on the vice-presidency, see Paul C. Light, *Vice-Presidential Power: Advice and Influence in the White House* (Baltimore: Johns Hopkins University Press, 1984), and George Sirgiovanni, "The 'Van Buren Jinx': Vice Presidents Need Not Beware," *Presidential Studies Quarterly* 18 (Winter 1988), pp. 61–76.

gives the president a chance to activate public support by recommending budget policies consistent with public expectations. it also allows the president and his staff to initiate the annual budget debate on their own terms.

In addition, the act created the Bureau of the Budget, or BOB. Originally a part of the Treasury Department, BOB was meant to be the president's primary tool in developing budget policy. It was made a part of the newly created EOP in 1939. Nixon changed BOB's name to the Office of Management and Budget (OMB) to stress its function of helping the president manage the executive branch.

Employing hundreds of budget and policy experts, OMB works only for the president and is a powerful presidential resource. It begins evaluating agency

Presidents and Prime Ministers

Most democratic nations have **parliamentary governments,** that is, systems in which the executive is chosen by the legislature. Americans have long admired Britain's parliamentary system. Woodrow Wilson once proposed that members of the president's cabinet sit in Congress and be able to introduce bills like their British counterparts. Many Americans are frustrated by our system's fragmentation and by a lack of accountability among elected officials, as evidenced by the Watergate and Iran-contra scandals. They have looked enviously across the Atlantic where British heads of government, called prime ministers, seem to be better leaders *and* more accountable to the public.

In recent years, we have heard about "gridlock," the inability of our elected officials to agree about how to solve our nation's problems. These differences are exacerbated when different parties control the White House and Congress. Divided control, which has been the case most years since World War II, makes it more likely that the president and congressional leaders will advocate different policies and priorities. It also makes it easier for elected officials to play the "blame game" and avoid taking responsibility for failed policies and inaction. We even have problems when the White House and Congress are controlled by the same party. The president and members of Congress often have different interests because they are elected by different constituencies at different times. And they can use our system's checks and balances to thwart each other's efforts.

In contrast, the British government is marked by a unity of authority. The prime minister, or PM, is an elected member of the House of Commons, the lower house of Britain's national legislature called the Parliament. (Parliament's other house, the House of Lords, is unelected and has very little power.) The PM is elected like other members of the Commons—by the voters of a constituency—and then is chosen by his or her party as its leader. The PM is always the leader of the majority (or largest) party in the Commons and usually decides when elections to the Commons will occur. However, elections must take place within five years of the last election. As members of the Commons, the PM and the cabinet ministers appointed by the PM must argue for their policies and respond to criticism from minority party members in debate.

Rank-and-file members of the Commons have very little independent power and often do not live in the constituencies that elect them. National party organizations have a great deal of influence over who is selected to run for election to the Commons. Members who do not vote the party line sometimes lose their party's support for reelection. This helps explain why 97% of the bills sponsored by the PM and cabinet from 1945 to 1987 were enacted.[1]

Although this is an attractive picture in some respects, the Founders designed our system to represent the diverse interests of a large, heterogeneous population. While more effective leadership in government is appealing, greater centralization can mean less opportunity to accommodate diverse local interests. Many Americans would not like a party organization to have the major influence on nominations for congressional office. Some would also be angry if representatives advocated positions contrary to local majority opinion on an important issue. America is a much more diverse society than Britain, perhaps making centralization less workable.

Diversity in America is also represented by powerful interest groups. Their close ties to congressional committees and subcommittees and executive branch officials give these interest groups considerable power to obstruct government. While these groups might be weakened by parliamentary-style arrangements, the interests they represent would still exist, as would iron triangle relationships and interest group vetoes.

Considering whether parliamentary forms would improve the workings of our government requires us to weigh some difficult trade-offs. Do we want to pay the costs of frequent gridlock and inefficiency to keep a system that is accessible to diverse local and other interests? Or do we want to sacrifice accessibility to government in order to have the efficiency of a stronger, more centralized system?

1. Richard Rose, *Politics in England: Change and Persistence,* 5th ed. (London: Macmillan Press, 1989), p. 113.

budget requests more than a year before the start of each fiscal year and helps defend the president's budget message. OMB also regulates when agencies spend their money, what they do with it, what policy ideas they develop, and how they operate. The budget is a huge document allocating billions of dollars to thousands of programs. It is hard—if not impossible—to read and understand it systematically. Using OMB often gives the president an edge in dealing with Congress on budget issues.

In 1995, each house of Congress voted to give the president another edge in budget matters. Each passed a version of a bill creating a line-item veto to allow the president to kill individual budget recommendations passed by Congress. This veto was also part of Clinton's set of election promises. For example, the president would be able to kill spending for a weapons system without having to veto spending for an entire package of defense-related spending measures. Advocates of the line-item veto used a "good government" argument for it: that it is needed to bring a discipline to budget policy that a fragmented Congress cannot impose on itself. However, the process of reconciling the bill's two versions ran aground. Some observers suspected that the Republican congressional leadership wanted to keep Clinton from having the line-item veto while they were dueling with him over budget issues.

Reorganizing Executive Agencies

Since the 1930s, presidents have had the authority to submit plans to Congress to reorganize parts of the executive branch. Reorganization means redrawing agency boundaries to promote coordination when their actions overlap or duplicate each other. This may involve merging or abolishing offices or creating new ones.

Presidents have also created councils or offices in the White House to oversee departments with overlapping responsibilities. For example, Nixon merged a number of offices to create the Domestic Council to improve White House coordination of domestic programs. Clinton created the National Economic Council to coordinate departments and agencies that shape economic policy and to show that economic issues are a high priority for him.

Domestic Policy Leadership

Polls have consistently shown that Americans consider "leadership" very important in evaluating presidents.[51] Somewhat paradoxically in light of their fear of "big government," most people want a president who can get government to "do" things. Presidents have a difficult position of trying to satisfy popular expectations of executive leadership when popular distrust of government is high.

The Founders, who understood the need for national leadership, required the president to inform Congress and the country of the "State of the Union" and to recommend policies to better it. In the president's State of the Union address at the start of each congressional session, he lists past achievements as well as remaining and new problems.

The Founders' desire to have the president act for the entire nation is also evidenced in his constitutional authority to kill, or veto, bills passed by Congress. Once the president receives a bill from Congress, he can sign it into law, veto it and send his objections to Congress, or not do anything, in which case the bill becomes a law after 10 congressional working days. Congress can enact a vetoed bill if a two-thirds majority in each house votes to override the president's veto. Presidents can avoid override attempts at certain times, however. A bill reaching the president dies if he does not sign it and Congress adjourns within 10 working days. This way of killing a bill is called a pocket veto.

Given expectations of presidential leadership and the presence of White House supporters in Congress, mobilizing two-thirds majorities to override a veto is usually very hard. As a result, presidents can influence Congress to write bills in certain ways by threatening to veto them if they do not conform to presidential wishes.

Only eight presidents never vetoed a bill. Franklin Roosevelt, a very assertive president, holds the record with 635 vetoes in his 14 years in office. That Congress overrode only 9 of his vetoes shows the effectiveness of his leadership. Among more recent presidents, Eisenhower vetoed 181 bills in 8 years. Congress overrode only 2 of them even though his party was in the minority for 6 of those years. Reagan vetoed 78 bills with 9 overridden and Bush vetoed 46 bills with 1 overridden.

Presidents must be careful about using the veto too often to avoid appearing isolated or uncooperative. Vetoes indicate that presidents have failed to win initial support for their positions. Clinton did not use the veto in the first half of his term and still had a number of congressional successes. He used it for the first time in 1995. That presidents are rarely overridden reminds us of their power when they decide they really want something.

Executive orders are another vehicle of presidential leadership. Based on constitutional provisions and congressional acts, they are issued by the president and executive agencies and contain binding policy. Their rationale is that Congress often lacks the expertise and ability to act quickly when technological or other developments require fast action and flexibility. However, recent presidents have used executive orders to make policies opposed by congressional majorities. Thus, Reagan and Bush issued executive orders to ban abortion counseling in federally financed clinics and financial aid to United Nations-sponsored family planning programs. Clinton canceled these orders in his first week in office.

Presidential leadership also includes creating and promoting policy packages such as Teddy Roosevelt's Square Deal, Wilson's New Freedom, Franklin Roosevelt's New Deal, and Johnson's Great Society. In 1981, Reagan had a huge impact on policy although he did not use a catchy label. People often evaluate presidential leadership in terms of the content and impact of these programs.

Reagan's leadership style in dealing with Congress involved going public to pressure it for support. In contrast, Bush used White House staff to negotiate policy matters directly with congressional leaders. Bush lacked Reagan's media skills and, as an insider, already had working relationships with many Washingtonians. This style, as well as a heavy use of the veto to kill bills he opposed, freed him to devote more time to foreign policy.

Clinton tries to generate congressional support by lobbying members himself and by trying to influence opinion in their districts. His aides describe this as combining policy-making and politics. After setting his goals, Clinton tries to influence opinion in those parts of the country and in interest groups most affected by them. One way he and his aides do this is to give interviews to journalists whose work reaches those he wants to influence. Clinton then tries to use popular support to build congressional support by lobbying members of Congress directly and indirectly through intermediaries such as business and union leaders.

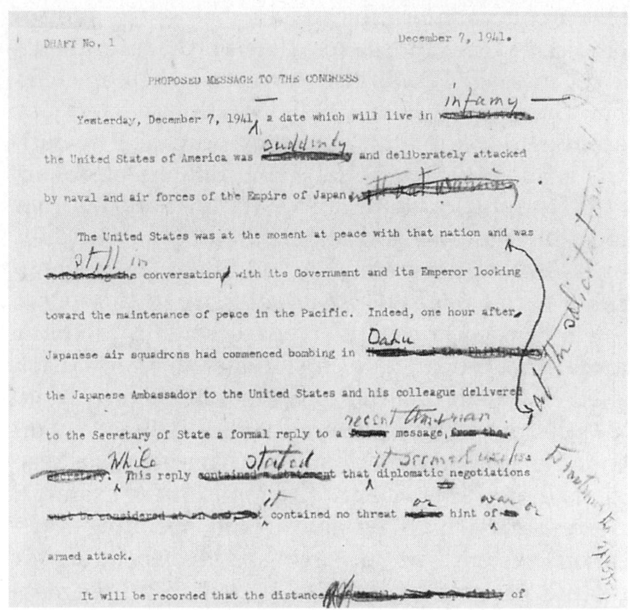
DRAFT No. 1 December 7, 1941.

PROPOSED MESSAGE TO THE CONGRESS

Yesterday, December 7, 1941, a date which will live in infamy the United States of America was suddenly and deliberately attacked by naval and air forces of the Empire of Japan.

The United States was at the moment at peace with that nation and was still in conversation with its Government and its Emperor looking toward the maintenance of peace in the Pacific. Indeed, one hour after Japanese air squadrons had commenced bombing in Oahu the Japanese Ambassador to the United States and his colleague delivered to the Secretary of State a formal reply to a recent American message. While This reply stated that diplomatic negotiations it contained no threat or hint of war or armed attack.

It will be recorded that the distance of

As the nation's foreign policy leader, President Franklin Roosevelt edited his own speech to Congress about the Japanese attack on Pearl Harbor. He added the word that made memorable his phrase, "a date which will live in infamy."

■ Foreign Policy Leadership

Although presidential leadership in domestic policy is important, presidents are even more dominant in foreign policy. Article II of the Constitution gives the president a number of foreign policy powers: to make treaties with other countries, with Senate approval; to appoint ambassadors and consuls to represent us abroad; and to receive ambassadors from other countries. This last power lets presidents recognize or not recognize other governments, an important decision. Recognition may show our approval of a government or a belief that it contributes to our national interest. Recognition is not, therefore, automatic. We did not recognize the Soviet government until 16 years after the Bolshevik Revolution of 1917 and that of the communist government of mainland China until almost 25 years after it took power.

The Constitution also contains implied powers, which were acknowledged by the Supreme Court in a 1936 decision.[52] Congress had authorized Franklin Roosevelt to ban arms sales to warring Bolivia and Paraguay, but a military aircraft manufacturer claimed that Congress lacked the constitutional authority to delegate such power. The Court ruled against the corporation, saying that every nation has implied powers to promote its interests in the world. The Court said there is a logic behind presidential power in foreign policy. A nation's government must be able to speak with one voice; having more than one voice can produce confusion about our ends and actions.

Presidents have their own styles in making foreign policy.[53] Eisenhower preferred using the formal procedures of the National Security Council, Kennedy and Johnson liked face-to-face discussions with many different people, and Nixon isolated himself with staff reports. Bush relied on four or five advisers who had worked together before and knew each other well.

Clinton gave world problems a low priority when he entered office and lacked experience with them. His early attempts at foreign policy leadership produced more criticism than praise, as when he seemed unable to choose between a forceful or hands-off response to bloody "ethnic cleansing" campaigns in Bosnia. By midterm, Clinton found that foreign policy issues can free presidents from the often messy partisan wrangles of domestic politics. He enjoyed higher ratings for a time after a showdown with Iraq and sending troops to Haiti to replace its military leaders with elected civilian leaders in 1994. These and later actions to resolve trade problems with Mexico and China suggest that foreign policy is now a higher priority for him. Success with it can benefit both the nation and his professional reputation.

Over the years, the president has become more powerful than Congress in foreign policy-making, assuming powers that were not explicitly given to either the legislative or the executive branch. As one observer commented:

> The President's normal problem with domestic policy is to get congressional support for the programs he prefers. In foreign affairs, in contrast, he can almost always get support for policies that he believes will protect the nation—but his problem is to find a viable policy.[54]

Sometimes Congress will not support the president. For example, over President Reagan's veto, Congress passed a law detailing policy toward South Africa; it sometimes opposed Reagan's proposed aid to guerrillas fighting the Nicaraguan government; and it overrode President Wilson's desire for the United States to enter the League of Nations and ratify the Treaty of Versailles ending World War I. Usually, however, even ill-conceived presidential foreign policies win congressional support.

Vietnam is a good example of presidential dominance in foreign policy. Kennedy started sending troops there in the early 1960s. By 1968, public opinion polls reported considerable opposition to the war. Nevertheless, American involvement continued until the North Vietnamese victory in 1975. Presidential policy dominated even with demonstrations, mass arrests, opposing editorials, negative opinion polls, and congressional criticism.

President Bush's control of events leading up to the Persian Gulf War is another example of the effectiveness of determined presidential foreign policy leadership. He sent 250,000 troops to the Gulf between August and November 1990 on his own authority. He also delayed announcing his decision to double this number until after the November elections, although he had made the decision in October. This kept the decision that changed our mission from defense (Operation Desert Shield) to offense (Operation Desert Storm) from becoming a campaign issue. And he mobilized United States and world opinion and

Since World War II, one of the president's most important foreign policy tasks has been to develop policy toward the former Soviet Union. Early in his term, President Reagan took a hard line against the Soviet Union. But as pressure in the United States grew for more amicable relations between the superpowers, and as the Soviet Union moved toward a more open political system, Reagan began to negotiate seriously with Soviet leader Mikhail Gorbachev. Here, Gorbachev and Reagan are shown during Reagan's 1988 visit to Moscow.

gained United Nations support. By the time Congress authorized using force in January 1991, the question of whether to do so was, practically speaking, already decided.

One reason for this dominance is that in foreign policy, more than in domestic, the president has more information than others do. He can often stifle debate by saying, "If you knew what I knew, you would agree with me," because of classified or secret information from the CIA, Defense Department, State Department, and other agencies. The president can also share certain information with Congress (and the public) and try to withhold other information. Members of Congress must often rely on the media and are at a distinct disadvantage in dealing with the president. In 1984, the Reagan administration mined harbors in Nicaragua after telling the Senate Intelligence Committee it was not doing so. When the facts became known, the chair of that committee, Barry Goldwater (R-Ariz.), wrote a blistering public letter to the head of the CIA saying, not so formally, "I am pissed off."[55] Later the Iran-contra hearings and the report of the special prosecutor revealed that Reagan administration officials, including Vice President George Bush, deliberately lied to Congress and the press about a whole series of actions taken with respect to Iran and Nicaragua.[56]

The administration also has a large role in shaping the agenda of debate. Alternatives acceptable to the administration are advanced through public statements, background briefings of the press and Congress, and "national" newspapers such as the *New*

Presidential Abuse of Power: The Iran-Contra Affair

During the mid-1980s, eight Americans were kidnapped and held hostage in Lebanon by Moslem extremist groups, some of whom were supported by Iran and its leader, the Ayatollah Khomeini. One hostage, a Central Intelligence Agency (CIA) operative assigned to our Beirut embassy, was killed.

This situation was an embarrassment to President Reagan who, in the 1980 election, belittled his predecessor Jimmy Carter for not being able to free hostages who had been kidnapped from the American embassy in Iran. In 1984, Reagan campaigned for reelection using slogans such as "America is back, and standing tall," and our continuing inability to secure the release of the hostages appeared inconsistent with that message.

In an attempt to free the hostages, President Reagan decided to let the CIA secretly sell weapons to Iran for use in its war against Iraq. He hoped this would convince the Iranians to release the hostages. The sale was opposed by Reagan's secretary of state, George Schultz, and his secretary of defense, Caspar Weinberger, but was urged by national security advisor John Poindexter and his subordinate, Lieutenant Colonel Oliver North.

According to federal law, Reagan was required to notify Congress of the secret arms sale. At the urging of North, and perhaps others, he did not do so.[1]

As a result of Reagan's decision, 2,008 antitank missiles were sent to Iran along with parts for antiaircraft missiles.[2] Everything was kept secret until a pro-Syrian Lebanese publication broke the news in November. This led to more revelations. News surfaced that we had also shipped arms to Iran earlier, in September 1985. Robert McFarlane, then national security adviser, told a congressional committee the president had approved these sales orally. Reagan said he did not remember. And Attorney General Edwin Meese revealed that profits from the sales were used to aid the Nicaraguan contras, again in violation of the law.

Reactions were overwhelmingly negative. Reagan's popularity plummeted.[3] Most did not believe him when he said he did not know what was going on. Media analyses appeared comparing what was being called Irangate to Watergate. The public and Congress asked what the president knew and when he knew it. Comedians asked what he forgot and when he forgot it. At first the president called North a "national hero." Then he fired him.

For the next several years, various investigations tried to find out if the president had authorized breaking the law (and hence violated his constitutional oath) and if Vice President George Bush knew about it. A presidential fact-finding commission reported that Reagan was removed from day-to-day business and that his management of foreign policy was lax and ineffective. Reagan reported to the commission that he could not remember when he authorized arms sales to Iran and that he knew nothing about diversion of funds to the contras. But in 1987, Reagan contradicted his earlier claim by declaring, "I was very definitely involved in the decisions about support to the freedom fighters [i.e., contras]—my idea to begin with."

The congressional hearings investigating the matter suggested that Reagan did know what was going on, and opinion surveys continued to report that most people thought Reagan was lying when he said he didn't remember.[4]

York Times or *Washington Post.* Many reasonable alternatives may never be suggested or receive support. Thus, media outlets did little to initiate discussions of our goals in the Persian Gulf when they covered troop commitments largely as a logistical challenge and human interest story. Media acceptance of Pentagon restrictions on news gathering also helped Bush generate support for his policies by producing news of successful, not unsuccessful, attacks and by concealing information describing casualties on both sides.

Although different presidential advisers sometimes advocate conflicting views publicly, it is much easier for a president to have a coherent policy than for Congress to do so. Thus, another advantage the president has over Congress is that he can act decisively, whereas Congress must talk in order to act and this takes time. President Bush sent American troops to Somalia in December 1992. The House Foreign Affairs Committee met in May 1993 to authorize this action, on the day after the United Nations had assumed responsibility in Somalia and most of our troops had come home.

Because the president is one and Congress is many, the president is usually more effective in appealing for public support. There is almost always a "rally 'round the flag" effect on both Congress and the public when the president takes a strong stance in foreign policy, especially if troops are involved. Our 1989 invasion of Panama is a good example of this. There was very little negative media coverage of the invasion, and public opinion was strongly supportive.

Continued

In well-publicized criminal trials, North and Poindexter claimed they had followed the orders of their superiors, including Reagan. North also said that Bush knew about illegal contra supply efforts and had helped get other countries to assist the contras in return for U.S. aid. Thus, the North and Poindexter trials also became Reagan's and Bush's. Evidence showed that Bush had not been "out of the loop," as he had claimed earlier. Bush regularly attended meetings from 1984 to 1986 dealing with the arms sales, hostages, and contra aid.[5]

Fearing what some of his aides described as a "political witch hunt" after Clinton's victory,[6] Bush pardoned six Reagan-era officials, each of whom had been charged with or convicted of crimes related to the Iran-contra scandal. Bush decried what he saw as the "criminalization of policy differences" and argued that "the common denominator of their motivation—whether their actions were right or wrong—was patriotism. . . . [and] they did not profit or seek to profit from their conduct."[7]

Reactions to the pardons were quick and critical. The special prosecutor declared, "The Iran-contra coverup has now been completed."[8] Some critics charged that Bush had misused his pardon power. Others rebuked him for arguing that the prosecutor had criminalized policy differences when those who were pardoned had been accused or convicted of lawbreaking and lying to congressional and other investigators. A poll found that only 15% of those surveyed thought Bush's main reason for issuing the pardons was "to protect people he felt acted honorably and patriotically from unfair prosecution."[9]

The Irangate incident reveals the temptations offered to presidents to use illegal means to increase their own power. Although presidents have an inherent advantage over Congress in making foreign policy, they cannot legally operate in defiance of Congress.

The Iran-contra affair, like Watergate, raises serious questions about the accountability of the personal presidency. In some ways "Irangate" is more serious than Watergate in that while President Nixon resigned in disgrace rather than face impeachment, the public seemed willing to allow Reagan to serve his full term and then elected Bush to replace him.

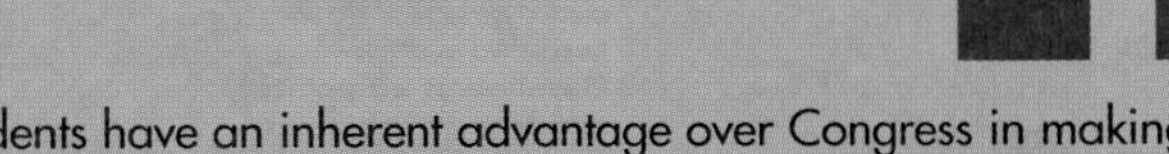

1. Much of the information in this section comes from James M. McCormick and Steven S. Smith, "The Iran Arms Sale and the Intelligence Oversight Act of 1980," *PS* 20 (Winter 1987), pp. 29–37.
2. Robert Pear, "The Story Thus Far: Assembling Some of the Pieces of the Puzzle," *New York Times,* December 14, 1986, Section 4, p. 1. "Reagan's Crusade," *Newsweek,* December 15, 1986, pp. 26–28.
3. Elizabeth Drew, "Letter from Washington," *The New Yorker,* August 31, 1987, p. 72.
4. For a critique of the congressional hearings, see Seymour M. Hersh, "The Iran-Contra Committees: Did They Protect Reagan?" *New York Times Magazine,* April 29, 1990, pp. 46–78; Louis Harris, "Iran-Contra Hearings Erode Faith in Reagan," *Lincoln Star,* May 25, 1987.
5. See Tom Blanton, "Iran-Contradictions: It's Time to Ask Where George Was," *Washington Post National Weekly Edition,* June 18–24, 1990, pp. 24–25; Richard Cohen, "What Did Bush Know?": and Walter Pincus, "Has Bush Come Clean About Iran-Contra?" *The Washington Post National Weekly Edition,* September 28–October 4, 1992, pp. 29 and 31–32.
6. "Pardon Me," *Newsweek,* January 4, 1993, p. 15.
7. Leslie H. Gelb, "Bush's Ethical Manure," *The New York Times,* December 27, 1992, p. E11.
8. Ibid.
9. "Pardon Me." See also George Lardner, Jr., and Walter Pincus, "Dear Diary: Now, About Iran-Contra . . . ," *The Washington Post National Weekly Edition,* January 25–31, 1993, p. 31; see also George Lardner Jr.and Walter Pincus, "The Source of the Iran-Contra Mess Is Tracked to Reagan," *Washington Post National Weekly Edition,* January 24–30, 1994, p. 13.

12 The Bureaucracy

You Are There

Attacking AIDS

You are the surgeon general of the United States, C. Everett Koop. It is 1986 and President Reagan has asked you, the government's top medical officer, to report to him on what has become a major problem, AIDS, or acquired immune deficiency syndrome. AIDS involves a virus that weakens the body's immunity, making it vulnerable to deadly infections.

There have been more than 35,000 cases of AIDS so far in the United States, 493 of them children. Those who contract AIDS inevitably die, as 20,000 Americans have so far. You estimate that 1.5 million people have been exposed to the virus and that 270,000 will develop AIDS by 1991.[1] In the United States, people with the most risk of getting it are intravenous drug users and homosexual men.[2] However, AIDS has begun to appear among heterosexual men and women through contact with intravenous drug users, prostitutes, bisexuals, and those who had multiple blood transfusions before the spring of 1985, when blood banks began testing for AIDS.

As long as the first two groups provided almost all the victims, most people did not worry about AIDS. As it began to spread, however, it became a major issue arousing considerable public anxiety. For example, real estate agents trying to sell Rock Hudson's house found that clients would not enter it because they knew he had died of AIDS. And some parents have tried to bar child victims of AIDS from the schools their children attend.

Now the president has asked for a report advising him what to do. You do not expect an effective vaccine to be available until the mid-1990s at the earliest. A major issue that your report must deal with is whether we should require mandatory testing for AIDS. A blood test can reveal exposure to the AIDS virus, but it cannot predict who will get the disease because some who carry the virus will not contract the disease. Still, finding out who has been exposed to the virus can help limit the exposure of others to it.

Already, military recruits and Foreign Service officers must take a blood test to determine if they have been exposed to AIDS. Proposals have been made to test many others, such as convicted prostitutes and intravenous drug users, hospital patients from 15 to 49 years of age, venereal disease patients, and couples seeking marriage licenses. Secretary of Education William Bennett, whose views often echo the president's, also wants to include prison inmates and people planning to immigrate here. He says the government should notify spouses and past sexual partners if test results are positive—that is, if evidence of exposure to AIDS is found.

Many conservatives view AIDS as a moral issue. They think AIDS is a punishment for homosexuality and drug use. Some charge that public health officials are "intimidated by the homosexual lobby." One called AIDS the "first politically protected disease in the history of mankind."[3] They want you to recommend mandatory testing to identify who is infected so government can quarantine those who will not change their sexual or drug habits to protect society.

Most public health experts reject mandatory testing as unworkable. They argue that many people will go underground to avoid being tested. They also say mandatory testing of huge numbers of people will produce mistakes in test results. Further,

CONTINUED

OUTLINE

Bureaucracy
- Nature of Bureaucracy
- Public and Private Bureaucracies

Federal Bureaucracy
- Growth of the Bureaucracy
- Why the Bureaucracy Has Grown
- Types of Bureaucracy

Bureaucratic Functions
- Making Policy
- Administering Policy
- Other Functions

Expectations About the Federal Bureaucracy
- Responsiveness
- Neutral Competence

Controlling the Bureaucracy
- President
- Congress
- Courts
- Interest Groups and Individuals

Conclusion: Is the Bureaucracy Responsive?

Bureau of Engraving and Printing employees check the quality of $20 bills. The woman at the right is holding $8,000 worth of mistakes.

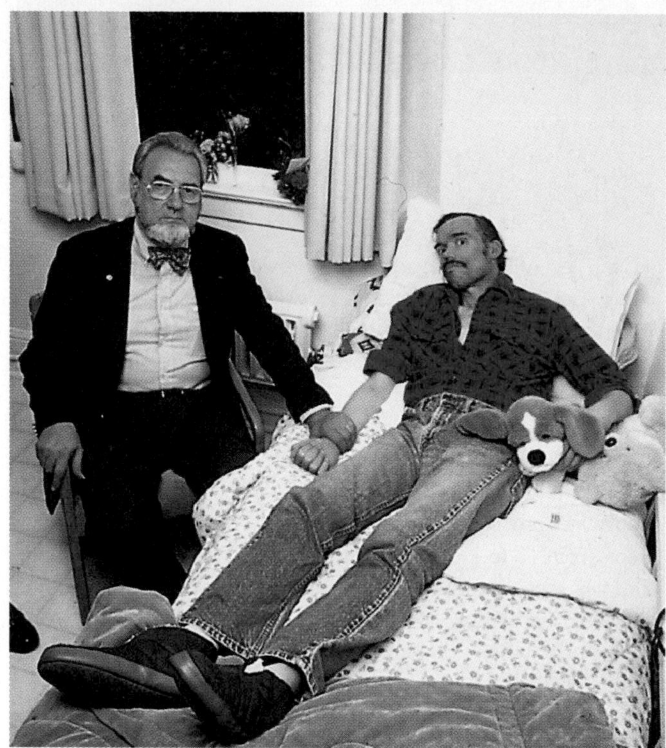
Former Surgeon General Koop visits an AIDS patient.

most experts oppose mandatory testing as a violation of doctor/patient confidentiality and doubt that most people will identify their sexual partners. They add that mandatory testing will only increase discrimination against homosexuals and others who have been exposed to AIDS and who may or may not contract it.

Few experts agree with Secretary Bennett, who argues that the key to stopping AIDS is to teach sexual abstinence to our children. Most experts recommend educating young people about "safe sex" and contraception. They say abstinence as a policy is unrealistic given the emphasis on sex in our society, as illustrated by studies showing that television programming refers to sexual intercourse at least once an hour. Their views reflect Senator Paul Simon's (D-Ill.) remark that, "It's been too long since [Bennett] was a teenager."

Many conservatives object strongly to sex education in schools. Referring to "safe sodomy" instead of "safe sex," they say "condomania" means we have given up trying to raise our children properly.

The president is comfortable with conservative views on AIDS. When he appointed you, you were a surgeon in Philadelphia, known for having pioneered techniques to separate Siamese twins and for being a born-again Christian with conservative views on abortion and birth control. You know your views were more important to the president than your surgical innovations. You agree with him on many issues and want to write a report he will like. Your political instincts push you this way.

On the other side of the coin, and in government there is always another side to the coin, you are a doctor who respects the views of health-care professionals. You want to write a report that will help fight AIDS, without political interference. What should you do?

Americans expect their government to deliver billions of dollars worth of services to them, from highways for fast-moving cars to Social Security payments on time, from clean running water to safe neighborhoods, from protection from foreign enemies to cures for cancer. At the same time, most Americans denigrate their government and its bureaucracy, and some even express hatred toward it. In 1995, in Oklahoma City, scores of people were murdered because they were federal bureaucrats (or happened to be in the same building with bureaucrats).

Despite the strong emotions sometimes directed toward them, federal bureaucrats are ordinary people. But the jobs they are asked to do and the number of different groups to which they are responsible makes them a target for public distress with society's problems.

The federal bureaucracy employs over three million civilians, who work in more than 800 different occupations in 100 agencies, and over two million uniformed military personnel. The bureaucracy executes or enforces policies made by Congress and the president. Because policymakers have given government many different goals, the bureaucracy has many different jobs. It analyzes the soil, runs hospitals and utilities, fights drug abuse, checks manufacturers' claims about their products, and does many other things.

To some, the bureaucracy is the fourth branch of government—powerful, uncontrollable, and often seeming to have a life of its own. As the part of government that carries out the law, the bureaucracy is also political. People disagree about whether it does its job well, largely because they disagree about the goals policymakers set for it. One person's lazy, red tape-ridden, uncaring bureaucracy is another's responsive agency.

➤Bureaucracy

Around the turn of the century, the German social scientist Max Weber predicted that bureaucracy would someday dominate society. That future is now. Bureaucracy affects almost everything we do.

■ Nature of Bureaucracy

Although individual bureaucracies differ in many ways, all share some common features.[4] For example, all have hierarchies of authority; that is, everyone in a bureaucracy has a place in a pyramidal network of jobs with fewer near the top and more near the bottom. Almost everyone in a bureaucracy has a boss and, unless one is at the bottom of a hierarchy, some subordinates.

Individuals with more expertise and experience tend to have more authority. As a result, bureaucracy is not always consistent with democratic principles, which hold that everyone should have the same opportunity to influence events. Indeed, bureaucracy can endanger individual opportunities to express opinions, raise doubts about the value of individual opinions, and jeopardize the availability of information to individuals. In effect, bureaucratic tendencies, if unrestrained, can transform "citizens" into "subordinates."

■ Public and Private Bureaucracies

Many people associate public bureaucracies with monotony and inefficiency. A Virginia company sold a "Bureaucrat" doll, calling it "a product of no redeeming social value. Place the Bureaucrat on a stack of papers on your desk, and he will just sit on them."[5]

While stereotyping the public service can produce some laughs, it misses the similarities shared by

"I'm sorry, dear, but you knew I was a bureaucrat when you married me."

public and private bureaucracies. For example, both involve a good deal of routine. Auditing expense vouchers is as routine in a business firm as in a public agency. Both also have workers who are productive and efficient and others who are not. Executives in the Defense Department bought $600 toilet seats and $650 ashtrays. Their private counterparts at Chrysler, Lockheed, Penn Central, and hundreds of banks and savings and loans ran their businesses into the ground.

To some extent, the distinction between private and public bureaucracies has become blurred.[6] However, Americans typically distinguish public from private bureaucracies by looking at goals and openness.

Goals

Businesses are supposed to make a profit while public agencies are supposed to promote the "public interest." Although people disagree over what the "public interest" is, they know public agencies do not exist to make a profit.

Public and private bureaucratic goals differ in another way too. It is usually easier to measure and put a value on efforts to achieve private goals than public ones. We can identify the value of a chair or a house by computing the cost of building them. Placing a value on such public goals as consumer safety or education is much harder. How many children must die from eating the contents of medicine bottles before government should require pharmaceutical manufacturers to use childproof caps on bottles? How many lives saved make it worthwhile for government to require auto manufacturers to install mandatory seat belts, thereby raising auto prices?

Difficulties in measuring what government agencies do and disagreements over defining the public interest often produce charges that public bureaucracy is wasteful. Indeed, over two-thirds of the American public believes government programs are usually inefficient and wasteful.[7] Of course, private corporations may waste far more than government.[8] But government spending is so great that even if it wastes only proportionally as much money as a typical citizen does, the sums are vast.

Discussions of government "waste" are confusing because they refer to two quite different things. One involves inefficient or corrupt government agencies, those that, for example, do not get competitive bids and therefore pay more than they need to for supplies. Waste also occurs when more employees are hired than are necessary to do a job, when consultants are paid to do little, or when errors are made in making welfare or farm subsidy payments so that recipients are overpaid.

A second kind of government "waste" is a program that some people find objectionable, no matter how well run it is. This meaning of waste has little to do with mismanagement or fraud. Waste in this sense may mean that a particular program serves relatively few people at a large cost. For example, a government commission labeled the operation of hundreds of very small post offices "wasteful." The commission did not allege fraud or mismanagement but said the post offices cost a lot for the small number of people served. However, residents of small communities argued that their post offices were not a waste but an important source of community pride.

Source: CATHY © 1987 Cathy Guisewite. Reprinted with permission of Universal Press Syndicate.

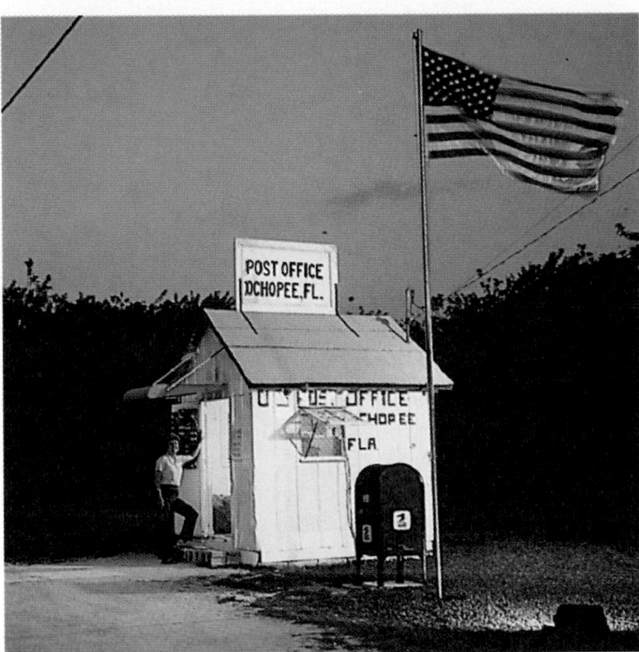

Some local post offices are economically inefficient, but residents of small towns lobby Congress to keep them open.

The average citizen probably does not think much about waste, particularly this second kind, in private bureaucracies. If a business or industry makes a profit, we assume it is not being wasteful. We may not like chocolate-covered raisins, but we do not consider their manufacturer wasteful for making them as long as the product is profitable.

Openness

The openness of public bureaucracy is a second way of distinguishing it from private bureaucracy. Both often have internal disagreements about their goals, but differences about public agency goals are usually more visible. This visibility, or openness, is important to making public agencies responsive.

The Sunshine Act of 1977 recognized the importance of keeping public bureaucracies open. It requires regulatory agencies, such as the Interstate Commerce Commission, to give advance notice of the date, time, place, and agenda of their meetings. Although agencies can close their meetings to protect sensitive information, they must follow certain rules preventing unwarranted secrecy. Citizens can sue agencies in federal courts if they think agencies have unjustifiably closed meetings.

In addition, the Freedom of Information Act of 1966, as amended in 1974, lets people obtain information from agencies, if it is not classified or concerned with sensitive matters. Citizens can sue agencies refusing to cooperate.

Federal agencies get about 500,000 requests for information every year. Approximately 91% of the requests are completely filled.[9] Most are submitted by those who have the time and money to take advantage of the act and who are affected by agency operations: businesses, interest groups, and lawyers. Thus, in 1985, 85% of the requests for information submitted to the Food and Drug Administration came from companies that it regulates. The Freedom of Information Act was intended to make agencies more open to the public, but very few members of the general public take advantage of it.

Efforts to make government agencies more open often run up against a desire to limit the distribution of critical or embarrassing information. It is the rare public or private bureaucracy that wants to reveal its failures. Thus, an evaluation of the Freedom of Information Act in 1972 found that agencies used many tactics to discourage people from seeking information, such as delaying responses to requests, charging high fees for copies of records (the State Department once charged $10 a page for copying records), and requiring detailed descriptions of material in requests for information.[10] In 1993, the Federal Bureau of Investigation (FBI) refused to expedite the release of information to a prisoner on death row who was afraid he would be executed before the information was available. The FBI's judgment that his situation did not show "exceptional need or urgency" was overruled by a federal court.[11]

As the chief executive, a president's views on how open agencies should be has also been important. Until 1982, presidents thought agencies should declassify and give information to the public unless the information would cause harm. Thus President Carter banned the classification of files lacking a clear relation to national security. In 1982, President Reagan took the opposite tack, stopping the routine declassification of files and allowing the reclassification of already released information. Under Reagan, and then Bush, federal agencies adopted a narrow reading of the act, making it more difficult to get information.[12]

On taking office, Clinton assigned an interagency task force to assess agency procedures and make recommendations to promote openness. However, the

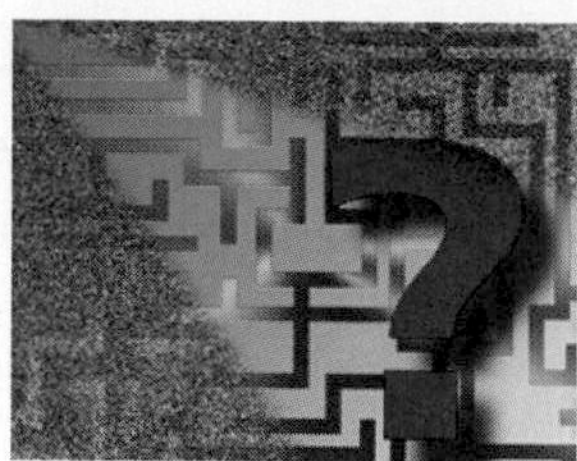

Symbolic Solutions for Complex Problems?

Slashing the Bureaucracy

Government bureaucrats have a long history of getting under Americans' skins (recall that opposition to the king's tax collectors helped to fuel the American Revolution). Despite this perennial irritation, government continues to grow. Most Americans think government is too big, and there are many proposals to cut it. The Clinton administration plans to cut nearly 300,000 federal government positions by 1999. Republicans have proposed the end of the Departments of Education, Commerce, Housing and Urban Development, and Labor, as well as scores of government programs located in other agencies. But is cutting the size of the bureaucracy a real solution to our country's problems? Or is it a symbolic solution?

Cutting the size of the bureaucracy is a real solution if it would make government more efficient, save money, and allow us to direct more resources to attack the nation's problems or to reduce the deficit. For example, Clinton's proposed "reinvention of government," led by Vice President Gore, would cut 2,400 jobs from Health and Human Services by eliminating a layer of management, consolidating dozens of programs, turning some work over to private business, and giving states a bigger role in these programs. The vice president argues that this would create a more "customer friendly" agency.[1]

Some of those who wish to cut some of the federal agencies mentioned above believe that services can be improved by merging programs that duplicate each other, cutting some programs that no longer serve an urgent need, and increasing resources for other, more pressing needs, including deficit reduction.

Other institutions, particularly some large corporations, have found that they can operate more efficiently and serve their customers better by consolidations, cutting, and reducing the layers of management. If government achieves these successes, cutting government could be a real solution.

On the other hand, cries to cut government may be mostly a symbolic solution that does not really help us solve our nation's problems more effectively. Cutting government might not save money. For example, if private firms take over the provision of services, costs could fall, but they could also increase. Those who can pay will get the services, though not necessarily for a lower cost.[2]

Some advocates of cutting the size of government think local government can handle problems more efficiently. This is likely true in some instances but not in others. After all, the federal government got into the programs it did because some constitu-

task force's efforts ran up against the bureaucratic tendency to withhold information. By the end of 1993, his administration had classified more information than Bush's had in 1992. And his appointees had declassified 30% fewer pages of information in 1993 than Bush appointees had in 1992.[13] Clinton issued an executive order in 1995 to turn this situation around. The order directs the declassification of most documents 25 years old or older and puts a 10-year limit on how long documents can remain classified unless a review determines that they should remain so.[14]

Finally, problems with the Freedom of Information Act have surfaced because it was written with the expectation that all information would be on paper. But the federal government, like private businesses, stores an increasing amount of information on computer tapes and disks. The federal bureaucracy now has over 1.25 million microcomputers, compared to only 17,500 in 1985. Retrieving the growing mass of information stored on computer can be easier than finding information on paper. However, the act neither defines when computerized information is in the public domain nor requires agencies to save and release it. Thus the act does not say whether electronic messages used by officials to schedule meetings or exchange opinions are their private property or public records. Reagan and Bush aides used e-mail extensively as do Clinton's now. Bush took his aides' e-mail tapes with him when he left office and argued that the tapes were not public property (see Chapter 11). A federal appeals court ruled that these tapes are public records and must be preserved. The Clinton administration sided with Bush and argued that White House officials have a right to erase the e-mail encies were not satisfied with local or state handling of programs.

And, though we can all point to some agencies that seem ineffective, many agencies do their jobs well, and eliminating them would increase, not decrease, problems—for example, the Social Security Administration, the Securities and Exchange Commission, the air traffic control system, the Secret Service, among others. In fact, there is little evidence that, on the whole, public bureaucracies are less effective than private ones.[3]

Moreover, if we eliminated those agencies the Republicans have targeted, would our nation's problems be closer to solution? Would crime be reduced, more families be intact, our country's defense strengthened, teen-aged pregnancies decreased, or racism ameliorated? Probably not. This is not to suggest that eliminating some federal agencies might not be a bad idea, but only that doing so in and of itself is not a solution to the country's most pressing problems.[4]

Despite years of vociferous debate about whether government is too big, too intrusive, and too expensive, it is difficult to reach a conclusion about what the "right" size of government is. Government has grown considerably over the past 60 years, but so has the size and wealth of the nation. The federal government employs about 2% of all employees in the U.S.; excluding the Department of Defense, it employs 1%. Whether this is too big probably depends on your view of what government should be doing rather than of the size of government itself. That being the case, slashing the bureaucracy is likely to be predominantly a symbolic solution.

After all, if we agree that government is an appropriate agency to solve an important problem, but does it poorly, we should think about fixing the bureaucracy, not eradicating it. For example, if the military slips up (consider Pearl Harbor, the Bay of Pigs, or the bombing of the Marine barracks in Beirut), we do not argue that we should do away with it. We look for ways to make it work better.[5]

This sounds like a sensible approach. But it is easier to agree with than to implement. For example, most Americans criticize the bureaucracy in the abstract but say they are satisfied with the services they receive from particular agencies (e.g., the Postal Service and Social Security Administration).[6] But agreeing to fix the bureaucracy will not work if we do not agree on what government should do and we do not admit that some agencies work well—that government can work—and that our attention must be on agencies that work poorly.

1. For more about "reinventing" government, see: Al Gore, Jr., "The New Job of the Federal Executive," *Public Administration Review* (July/August, 1994), pp. 317–321; Ronald C. Moe, "The 'Reinventing Government' Exercise: Misinterpreting the Problem, Misjudging the Consequences," *Public Administration Review* (March/April, 1994), pp. 111–122; James Q. Wilson, "Reinventing Public Administration," *PS: Political Science & Politics* (December, 1994), pp. 667–673; and "Clinton Team Plans to Redesign HHS," *Omaha World-Herald*, May 12, 1995, p. 5.
2. Rob Gurwit, "Social Services and Reality," *Governing* (May, 1995), p. 13.
3. Nicolas Lemann, "Government Can Work," *The Washington Monthly* (January/February, 1994), p. 37; see also Charles Goodsell, *The Case for Bureaucracy*, 3rd ed. (Chatham, N.J.: Chatham House, 1994).
4. This point is drawn from Herbert Stein, "Shrinking Government May Not Be the Answer," *Washington Post National Weekly Edition*, March 6–12, 1995, p. 28.
5. Lemann, "Government *Can* Work," p. 36.
6. Goodsell, *The Case for Bureaucracy*, Chapter 2.

messages they send to each other.[15] Defining such messages as public helps hold officials accountable. The act also fails to address problems created by the use of incompatible hardware and software and to protect against the loss of data over time because tapes and disks deteriorate. Congress has been trying to remedy computer-related problems for several years without success.

➤Federal Bureaucracy

Growth of the Bureaucracy

The Founders did not discuss the federal "bureaucracy," but they did recognize the need for an administration to carry out laws and programs. They envisioned administrators with only a little power, charged with "executive details" and "mere execution" of the law. But the growing size and complexity of modern society and increasing demands that government do more have dramatically changed the nature of the federal bureaucracy.

George Washington's first cabinet included only three departments and the offices of attorney general and postmaster general, employing a few hundred people. More people worked at Mount Vernon, his plantation, than in the executive branch in the 1790s.[16] The Department of State had just nine employees. By 1800, the bureaucracy was still small, with only 3,000 civil servants. Since then, the bureaucracy has grown continuously, though not always at the same rate. Three eras of especially large growth have occurred.

The first period of rapid growth followed the Civil War. This era of industrialization, westward expansion, and population growth saw increasing demands for government to provide benefits to business, labor, and farmers. So Congress established the Departments of Commerce, Labor, and Agriculture. Worries about abuses by big business also led to the creation of new bureaucracies, such as the Interstate Commerce Commission, and expanded powers for others, such as antitrust law enforcement in the Justice Department.

A second surge of bureaucratic growth took place during the Great Depression. With New Deal programs, such as Social Security and bank deposit insurance, came an expansion of bureaucracy to administer them.

A third era of bureaucratic growth came during the 1960s and 1970s as a response to public demands that government do more to fight poverty, protect the environment, promote civil rights, and ensure consumer and worker safety. During this time Congress created several new cabinet departments (Housing and Urban Development, Transportation, Energy, and Education) and agencies (Environmental Protection Agency [EPA], Occupational Safety and Health Administration [OSHA], and the Equal Employment Opportunity Commission [EEOC]).

Why the Bureaucracy Has Grown

President Reagan once expressed the popular dissatisfaction with big government by noting that he liked flying over Washington because being in the air made government look smaller. Despite Reagan's pronounced feelings about the bureaucracy, it grew by over 200,000 employees during his administration. Although many agencies lost personnel (the biggest loser was the Department of Housing and Urban Development), others such as the Defense, Justice, and Treasury Departments gained. The continued growth of the bureaucracy suggests that powerful forces in society view it as a source of benefits.

One scholar explained the bureaucracy's growth by pointing to Americans' discovery that "government can protect and assist as well as punish and repress."[17] Thus, at the same time we criticize government's growth, we demand educational services, irrigation projects, roads, airports, job training, consumer protection, and many other benefits. Each of us might be willing to cut benefits for someone else, but most of us want government benefits for ourselves.

Sometimes bureaucracies grow in response to external threats. Though World War II was won 50 years ago, our Department of Defense has never returned to

Are Bureaucrats Real People?

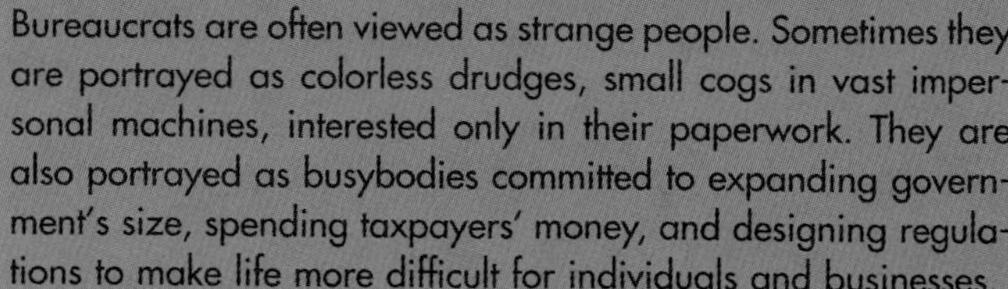

Bureaucrats are often viewed as strange people. Sometimes they are portrayed as colorless drudges, small cogs in vast impersonal machines, interested only in their paperwork. They are also portrayed as busybodies committed to expanding government's size, spending taxpayers' money, and designing regulations to make life more difficult for individuals and businesses.

Are government bureaucrats really like this? Are they different from other citizens? A comparison using a large national sample found that public employees are like everyone else in most ways. They are no more likely to favor raising taxes or government spending; they have about the same confidence in government and other institutions—such as organized religion, business, labor, and the press—as other citizens; and they are about as likely to favor busing and gun control.

When civil servants do differ from other citizens, they seem more open to diversity. For example, they are more likely to say they would vote for a black or woman as president and less likely to accept traditional gender roles. And they are somewhat *less* likely than other Americans to approve government intrusions into people's private lives. They are less likely to approve censoring people with unpopular views or laws banning pornography or interracial marriage. On only one issue are they more liable to favor "big government." They are somewhat more likely to favor wiretapping.

We might conclude, then, that public bureaucrats are mostly different because they are the butt of many jokes. In other respects, they are pretty ordinary people.

SOURCE Gregory B. Lewis, "In Search of the Machiavellian Milquetoasts: Comparing Attitudes of Bureaucrats and Ordinary People," *Public Administration Review,* May/June, 1990, pp. 220–27.

"Then it's agreed. The problem's not *our* fault, because the country's run by *low*-level bureaucrats."

Source: Drawing by Dana Fradon, © 1981 The New Yorker Magazine, Inc.

In its early years Washington was described as "a miserable little swamp." When this photo was taken in 1882, the government was still comparatively small.

its prewar size or scope. The Cold War gave us a new reason to support a massive military establishment. And of course, from the war as well as later ones came demands for services for veterans, another area of government growth.

Because the bureaucracy has grown in response to demands for public services, its growth has not been uncontrolled as some have charged. Every agency needs congressional and presidential approval of its programs, appropriations, staffing, and procedures. In fact, government also grows, ironically, because the president and Congress want it to be more accountable. The number of managerial layers in it has almost doubled in the last 30 to 40 years because of presidential and congressional efforts to control agency rule making and enforcement. This has produced waste, inefficiency, and, ironically, more difficulty in holding agencies accountable.[18] Bureaucrats cannot produce growth on their own. Every agency exists because it is valuable to enough people with enough influence to sustain it.

The growth of the bureaucracy should be seen in the perspective of the overall growth of our economy and population. For example, the number of federal bureaucrats for every 1,000 people in the United States decreased from 16 in 1953 to 11.2 in 1994.[19] This trend will continue. A 1994 law requires cuts of almost 273,000 bureaucratic jobs by 1999. By 1995, 78,000 people had left the bureaucracy as a result of hiring freezes, buyouts, and layoffs. Another 60,000 will follow in 1996. Total personnel costs were only 15% of total federal spending in 1994. If the government fired all its employees and used only volunteers, it would still run a deficit.

The major growth in public employment has been at the state and local levels. Over 37% of all government workers were federal employees in 1953; in 1994 only 14% were. Only 12% of these federal civil servants work in the Washington D.C. metropolitan area.

Some of these trends are illustrated in Figure 1, showing the growth in the size, cost, and regulatory activities of the executive branch. Although the size of the bureaucracy has been relatively stable, its production of regulations has grown more, especially from about 1968 to 1980, and its expenditure of funds has doubled since 1961.

■ **FIGURE 1**
Federal Government Growth: Money, Rules, and People

The numbers listed vertically on the left are percentages, comparing each year with 1961. They indicate the growth of federal regulatory activity, federal spending, and the size of the civil service, each on a per person basis.

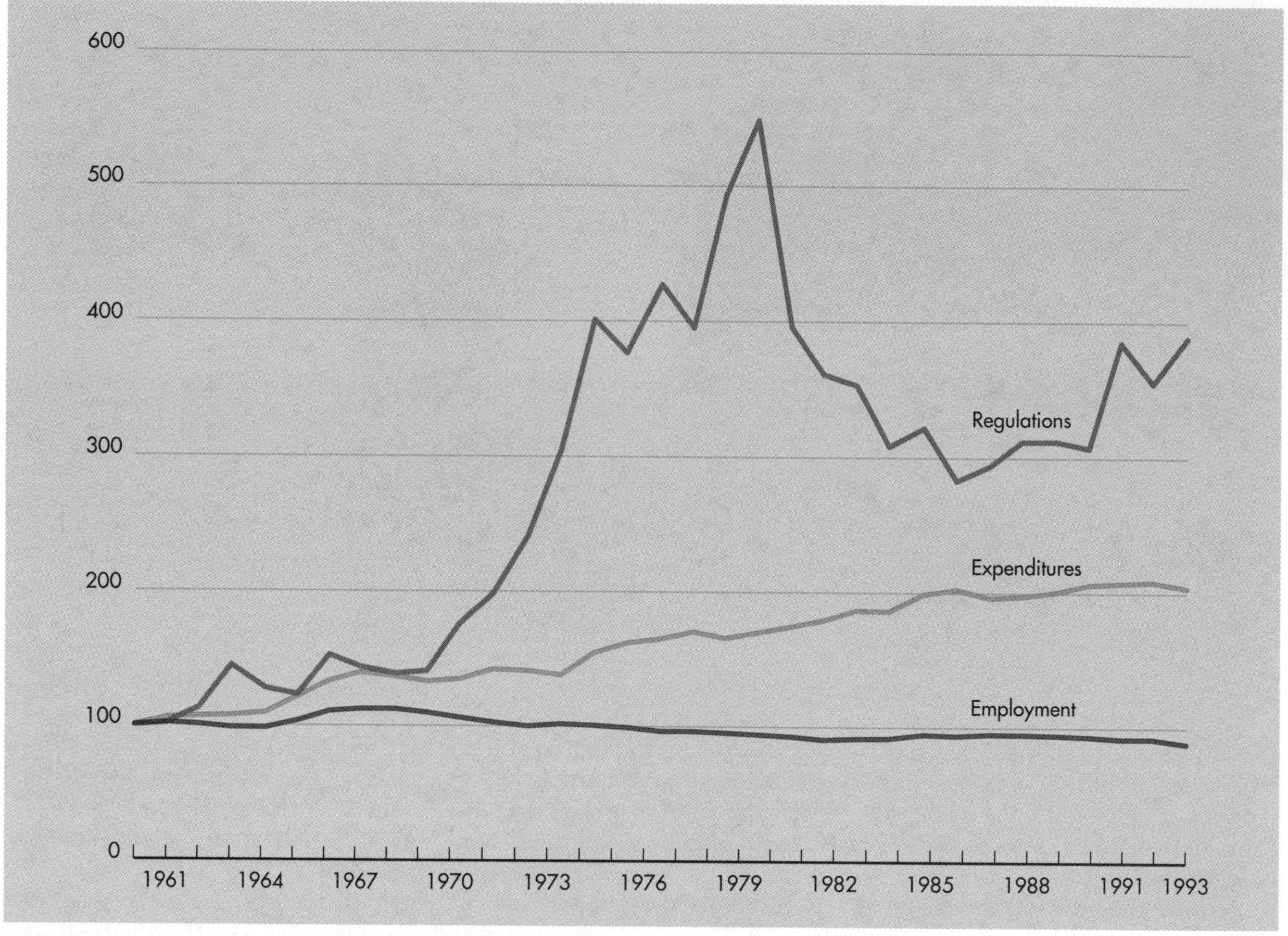

SOURCES: Idea for chart from Hugh Heclo, "Issue Networks and the Executive Establishment," in Anthony King, ed., *The New American Political System* (Washington, D.C.: American Enterprise Institute, 1978), p. 90. Federal employment statistics from *Budget of the United States Government: Fiscal Year 1994,* p. 42; Data on expenditures are from the Bureau of Economic Analysis, Department of Commerce, *Budget of the United States: Fiscal Year 1994* (Washington, D.C.: U.S. Government Printing Office, 1993), p. 101 and *Budget of the United States: Fiscal Year 1995,* p. 251. Federal regulations information is based on the number of pages in *The Federal Register for each year.*

■ Types of Bureaucracy

Although the Constitution says little about the organization of the executive branch, the Founders probably expected all bureaucratic jobs to be included in only a few departments, each headed by one person. Yet the bureaucracy has become much more complex than this. There are several major types of federal bureaucracy.[20]

Departments

Fourteen departments are directly responsible to the president and headed by his appointees (see Figure 2). Thirteen of these appointees, called secretaries, comprise the president's cabinet, along with the attorney general who runs the Justice Department. Departments constitute the lion's share of the executive branch, with over 60% of all civilian workers. The

■ FIGURE 2
The Development and Size of Cabinet Departments

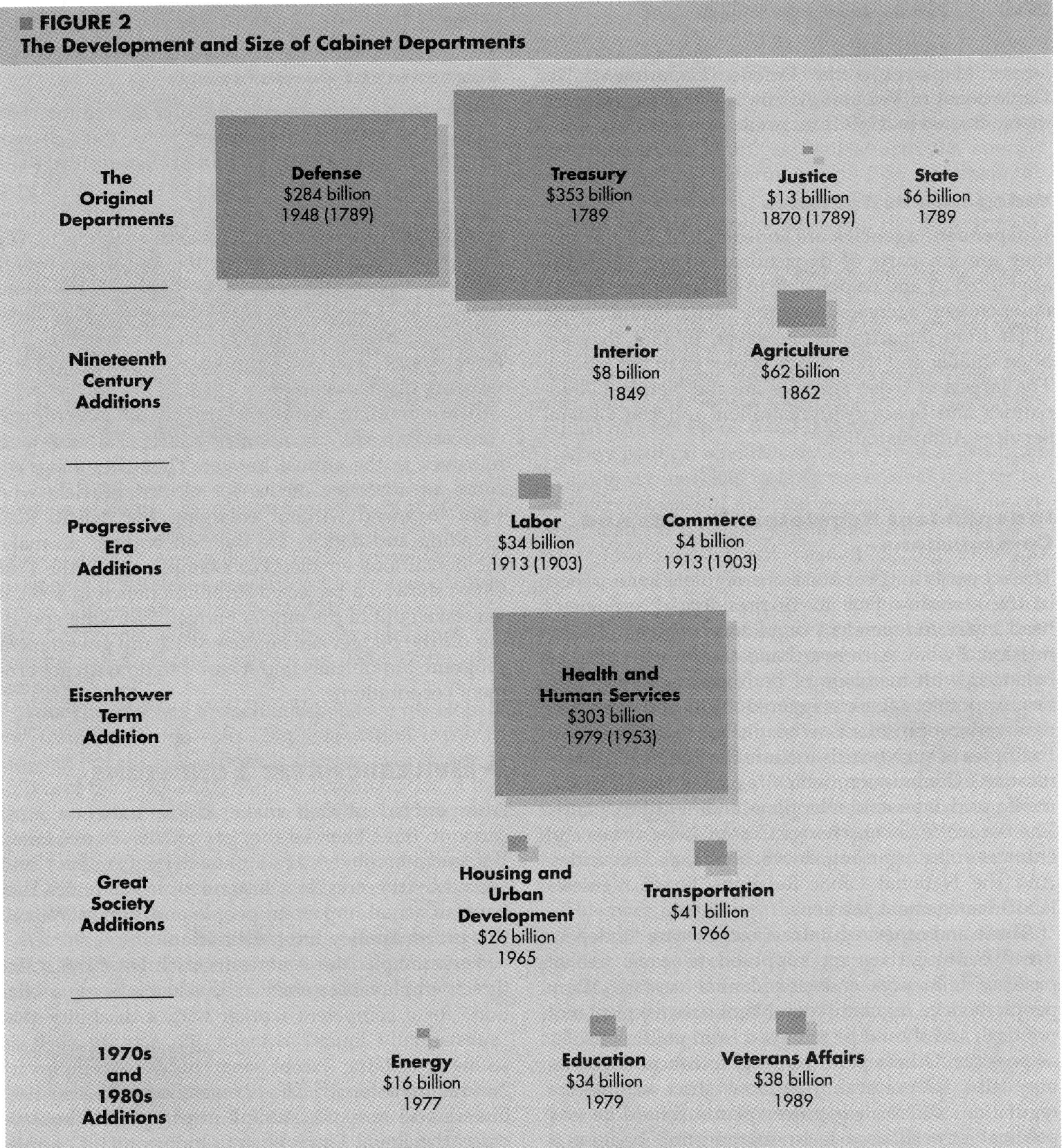

Note: The figures in each box include 1994 budget estimates and year of founding. Some departments have undergone a name change or major reorganization. The date of their initial founding is in parentheses. The modern Defense Department replaced the Departments of War (1789) and Navy (1798); the Justice Department replaced the Attorney General (1789); the Commerce and Labor Departments were first established in 1903 as a joint enterprise; and the Health and Human Services Department and the Education Department replaced the Department of Health, Education, and Welfare (1953).

SOURCE: *Budget of the United States Government: Fiscal Year 1996.* (Washington, D.C.: U.S. Government Printing Office, 1995), p. 215.

Your Hamburger: 41,000 Regulations

Protesting "overregulation" is a popular pastime of Americans. The 41,000 regulations that accompany a hamburger may seem an obvious example of the absurdity of too much regulation. But the issue is more complicated than it seems at first glance. If government does not regulate pesticide use on crops, there is a significant risk of serious illness to consumers who eat the crops. If the government does not inspect to make sure livestock are free of tuberculosis, the incidence of TB bacteria in meat will be higher.

When examined closely, most of the regulations have a plausible rationale. But regulation is not free. The cost of regulating hamburger is about 8¢ to 11¢ per pound. Is this a high cost? It depends on the probability of contracting a serious disease and the value you as a consumer place on having some confidence in the quality of products you buy.

And then, of course, there are some regulations that are mystifying even to those not especially opposed to government regulation. What is the danger in eating a pickle sliced too thin? Only Uncle Sam knows!

SOURCE: *U.S. News & World Report,* February 11, 1980, p. 64.

The hamburger, staple of the quick, inexpensive meal, is the subject of 41,000 federal and state regulations, many of those stemming from 200 laws and 111,000 precedent-setting court cases.

These rules, cited in a three-volume study by Colorado State University, touch on everything involved in meat production—grazing practices of cattle, conditions in slaughterhouses and methods used to process meat for sale to supermarkets, restaurants and fast-food outlets. Here is just a sampling of the rules and regulations governing the burger.

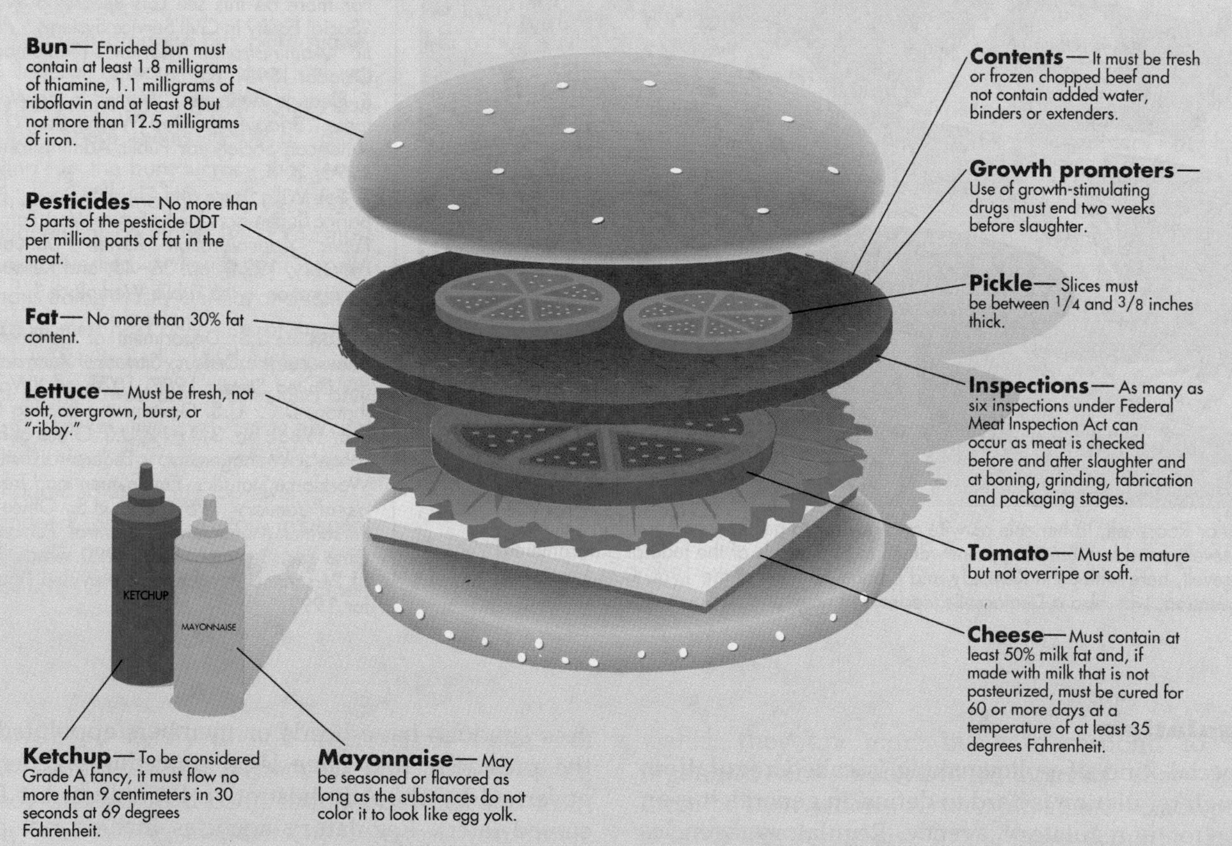
Bun— Enriched bun must contain at least 1.8 milligrams of thiamine, 1.1 milligrams of riboflavin and at least 8 but not more than 12.5 milligrams of iron.
Pesticides— No more than 5 parts of the pesticide DDT per million parts of fat in the meat.
Fat— No more than 30% fat content.
Lettuce— Must be fresh, not soft, overgrown, burst, or "ribby."
KETCHUP
MAYONNAISE
Ketchup— To be considered Grade A fancy, it must flow no more than 9 centimeters in 30 seconds at 69 degrees Fahrenheit.
Mayonnaise— May be seasoned or flavored as long as the substances do not color it to look like egg yolk.
Contents— It must be fresh or frozen chopped beef and not contain added water, binders or extenders.
Growth promoters— Use of growth-stimulating drugs must end two weeks before slaughter.
Pickle— Slices must be between 1/4 and 3/8 inches thick.
Inspections— As many as six inspections under Federal Meat Inspection Act can occur as meat is checked before and after slaughter and at boning, grinding, fabrication and packaging stages.
Tomato— Must be mature but not overripe or soft.
Cheese— Must contain at least 50% milk fat and, if made with milk that is not pasteurized, must be cured for 60 or more days at a temperature of at least 35 degrees Fahrenheit.

mental Protection Agency, and some agencies within cabinet departments, such as the Food and Drug Administration in Health and Human Services and OSHA within the Labor Department.

Some regulatory policies require businesses to meet standards, such as for clean air, safe disposal of toxic wastes, or safe workplaces. Failure to do so results in legal penalties. Other regulations control who can own certain goods. For example, the Federal Communications Commission licenses people to own and operate radio and television stations. Regulations may require businesses to provide information, such as the cancer warnings on cigarette packages and the labels noting sugar, salt, and vitamin content on canned food.

Regulatory actions include two steps: making rules and adjudicating their enforcement. Rulemaking is the establishment of standards that apply to a class of individuals or businesses. For example, the Interstate Commerce Commission sets standards that apply to interstate carriers such as railroads, trucking firms, and bus lines. Adjudication occurs when agencies try individuals or firms charged with violating standards. To do this, they use procedures that are very similar to those of courts.

At J.F.K. International Airport in New York, a Department of Agriculture inspector searches for illegal aliens—insects—in fruits and vegetables that travelers bring into the United States.

Because of the dangers inherent in having one agency be the lawmaker, judge, and jury, in 1946 Congress passed the Administrative Procedure Act (APA) to establish fair and open procedures. For example, agencies must publish a description of their rulemaking procedures in the *Federal Register* and hold open hearings on proposed rules or provide for another means of public input. Those who believe they have been treated unfairly by an agency have the right to take their case to court.

Antiregulation feeling helps to fuel public distrust of government. Surveys report that the number of people who think government controls too much of our daily lives has risen from 57% to 69% since 1987.[25] As Figure 1 shows, regulation has increased since then. This is largely because of the passage of the Clean Air Act, the Civil Rights Act, and the Americans with Disabilities Act during the Bush years and a reversal by Bush and Clinton appointees of the antiregulatory fervor of the Reagan years. Most Americans support the goals of these laws (e.g., 78% of the public says government should do "whatever it takes to protect the environment"[26]). But many also think the regulations produced to implement these and other laws produce wasteful paperwork and more costs than benefits. For example, officials in Madison, Wisconsin report they spend 14% of their transit budget obeying regulations to ensure bus service to the disabled, who make up 1.5% of their users.[27]

Most regulations are based on laws that direct agencies to take certain actions to accomplish certain ends. Thus, Congress gave the Environmental Protection Agency (EPA) authority to tell business to use or not use certain processes to reduce pollution. This "command and control" strategy is expensive because agencies have to employ many experts to design rules to achieve the desired ends and then have to get those they regulate to obey the rules. The strategy also allows little flexibility for the agencies and the people they regulate.

Many people believe there may be better ways to achieve the goals of clean air, fairness to the disabled, and other desirable objectives.[28] Some argue that we should eliminate agency regulations and rely on lawsuits by private citizens to protect public health and safety by proving in court that they have been harmed by something, like pollution. A problem with this idea is that it could pit individuals with limited means against industries with vast resources. It also moves problems to the courts more quickly. Other critics say we should entrust regulation to the states, who would finance their own efforts. Still others call for Washington to give block grants to states to set their own priorities and devise solutions consistent with broad goals set at the federal level. And others argue we should make business and industry comply with goals and standards (for example, in environmental cleanups) but leave them more discretion on how to do it.

Since the 1994 elections, some change, perhaps significant, in the regulatory process seems certain. Congress signalled its opposition to command-and-control regulation by threatening to pass bills to stop the making of new regulations for one year and to force agencies to give greater weight to the costs of new regulations (to kill those based on "minute or exaggerated risks"[29]). And Clinton issued an executive order to cut paperwork, void many regulations, and create a pilot program to give business more flexibility to comply with clean air and water requirements. These actions indicate that less regulatory activity is likely now given the influence of policymakers' preferences. However, titanic political battles lie ahead because advocates of a cleaner environment, more rights for the disabled and other interests protected by regulations point out that giving businesses more flexibility and weakening regulations is likely to erode progress toward goals they desire.

Administering Policy

Public bureaucracy's oldest job is to administer the law. To "administer" is to execute, enforce, and apply the rules that have been made either by Congress or the bureaucracy itself. Thus if policymakers decide to go to war, they must empower an agency to acquire weapons, recruit and train soldiers, and lead them in

The Politics of Breast Implants

Bureaucracies affect most things in life, including sometimes the shape of one's body. The debate over how government should regulate silicone-gel breast implants illustrates the pervasiveness, slowness, and political responsiveness of the regulatory process.

Breast surgery is a $300 million industry and accounts for more than 130,000 surgical operations annually. It is one of the most frequently used forms of plastic surgery in the United States. Some plastic surgeons obtain more than 50% of their income from this operation.[1] Fifteen to 20% of these operations involve replacing breast tissue lost to cancer surgery. The rest are elective surgeries to augment the size and change the shape of the breasts of women who are not pleased with their natural shape.[2]

When silicone-gel implants were introduced in the 1960s, the Food and Drug Administration (FDA), which has the regulatory responsibility for food and drugs, did not have specific legislative authority to regulate medical devices such as implants. Thus manufacturers did not have to obtain FDA approval before marketing implants. In 1976, Congress gave the FDA responsibility for regulating the safety of medical devices but exempted more than 100,000 existing medical devices. The FDA could, however, ask manufacturers to submit safety data on existing devices for the purpose of deciding if regulation was needed.[3]

In 1987, the FDA asked silicone-gel implant manufacturers to provide evidence of their safety by 1991. If the devices were found safe, the FDA would allow them to be sold and used as in the past.[4] If not, the FDA could impose restrictions on their use or even ban them all together. The FDA requested this safety information after the medical literature began to report that the implants did not always perform as advertised (they sometimes leaked or became lumpy or hard). Even more seriously, silicone from leaky or ruptured implants appeared to be causing arthritic conditions and autoimmune diseases.

In 1991, three of the four manufacturers of the implants submitted millions of pages of documentation on implant safety

Karen Berger holds a silicone-gel breast implant. Berger, an author of a book on implants, testified at an FDA hearing on the safety of implants.

battle with a winning strategy. Policymaking without administration is usually tantamount to having no policy at all.

Administration involves thousands of different kinds of activities. It involves writing checks to farmers who receive payments for growing—or not growing—crops, providing direct services to the public, evaluating how well programs are working, prosecuting those who try to defraud the government, and maintaining buildings and offices. For forest rangers, administration involves helping backpackers in the Grand Canyon or putting out a forest fire in northern Minnesota. For postal employees, it includes delivering the mail or repairing an automatic sorting machine.

Other Functions

In the course of policymaking and administration, the bureaucracy performs other functions. It collects data, such as in the census, and makes information available to us. Much of what we know about ourselves comes from the government's collection of data on births and deaths, occupations and income, housing and health, crime, and many other things.

The bureaucracy does research too. A prime example is the Department of Agriculture, which for over 100 years has conducted research on how to grow bigger and better crops, raise healthier animals, and transport and market products more effectively.

In addition, providing continuity is an important offshoot of the bureaucracy's activities. Presidents and members of Congress come and go, and political appointees in the bureaucracy stay an average of two years. Many barely learn their jobs by the time they leave. Career civil servants tend to know more about government's past and current efforts, which can make government more productive. At the same time, the presence of careerists can make the bureaucracy less responsive.

Continued

(the fourth manufacturer discontinued the product). They argued that these studies of patients' medical records and their other research found silicone-gel implants harmless. The American Society of Plastic and Reconstructive Surgeons reported that over 90% of breast implant patients were happy with the results.[5]

Critics presented a different picture. They pointed out that despite the documentation presented, manufacturers had not studied many patients. Dow Chemicals, one of the largest manufacturers, had studied only about 1,000 women. More important, the patients had not been studied over a long time period. Most were followed only a year or two after the operation, a time that would not begin to reveal long-term effects. Only one-third of the subjects in the biggest test had been studied more than 2 years, and only 46 women were checked after 7 years. Even without long-term studies, the companies' data showed problems with one-third of the implants.[6] And there were many personal accounts from women who told stories of pain and serious disease after implant surgery.[7]

When it was apparent that serious regulation was contemplated, the American Society of Plastic and Reconstructive Surgeons launched a multimillion-dollar lobbying initiative to fight proposed regulations. Each member was assessed $1,050 to pay for the campaign, which included recruiting 400 women to travel to Washington to state how important the breast implants were to their health and well-being.[8] On the other side, a network of women whose implants were unsuccessful formed a group called Command Trust Network to continue to publicize the negative aspects of implants.

After committee hearings highlighting these disagreements and in the context of a larger discussion over whether government agencies were giving women's health concerns equal weight to those of men, the FDA commissioner decided that silicone-gel breast implants would be restricted while additional safety data were collected. Implants will be limited to women who are part of FDA-approved safety studies. The studies will be open to all women seeking implants following breast cancer surgery, but the number of implants for cosmetic purposes will be drastically reduced until safety questions are answered.[9]

1. Jean Seligmann, Mary Hager, and Karen Springen, "Another Tempest in a C Cup," *Newsweek,* March 23, 1992, p. 67.
2. Diana McLellan, "Rethinking Big," *The Washingtonian* (June 1991), pp. 57–59; Laura Shapiro, Karen Springen, and Jeanne Gordon, "What Is It with Women and Large Breasts?" *Newsweek,* January 20, 1992, p. 57.
3. Malcolm Gladwell, "FDA Set to Begin Hearings on Silicone Breast Implants," *Washington Post,* February 17, 1992, p. A1.
4. Malcolm Gladwell, "Silicone Breast Implants," *Washington Post* (Health Supplement), March 3, 1992, p. 10.
5. McLellan, "Rethinking Big," p. 57.
6. Philip Hilts, "Under Pressure, US Weighs Ban on Use of Breast Implants," *New York Times,* October 21, 1991, p. 1.
7. "Reprieve for Breast Implants," *Time,* November 25, 1991, p. 81.
8. Hilts, "Under Pressure . . ."
9. Malcolm Gladwell, "FDA Will Allow Limited Use of Silicone-Gel Breast Implants," *Washington Post,* April 17, 1992, p. A2.

13 The Judiciary

You Are There

Friend or Foe?

You are Justice William Douglas of the Supreme Court facing a decision in the case of ***Korematsu v. United States.*** Fred Korematsu, a Japanese American, was born and raised in California. He was working as a welder when Japan bombed Pearl Harbor and forced the United States into World War II. As an American citizen, he tried to enlist in the army but was rejected because of ulcers. A few months later President Franklin Roosevelt issued an executive order, which Congress ratified, that allowed the secretary of war to exclude persons of Japanese ancestry from the three West Coast states and part of Arizona to prevent espionage and sabotage. Under the order, these persons were required to report to assembly centers—often fairgrounds, racetracks, or stockyards, from which the animals had been removed days before.[1] Allowed to take only what possessions they could carry, 120,000 persons were then relocated to camps in deserts and swamps further inland for, presumably, the duration of the war. Enclosed by barbed wire and patrolled by armed guards, these camps resembled prisoner-of-war camps.

Korematsu did not leave with the others. He had fallen in love with an Italian American woman, and they planned to marry. He had had plastic surgery to look Spanish Hawaiian instead of Japanese. But the surgery was not successful, and while walking down the street in his hometown, he was identified and arrested for violating the order. At trial he was convicted, and on appeal his conviction was upheld. On further appeal his case has reached the Supreme Court.

On one hand, the government claims the order is justified. Although officials do not expect an invasion of the West Coast, they do fear espionage and sabotage. Before the war some Japanese Americans supported Japan's efforts to expand its territory in Asia. Some contributed money, tinfoil, and scrap metal, while a few formed an espionage ring. Intelligence officials crushed the ring but now fear renewed attempts. Already Japanese submarines have attacked American merchant ships off our coast, sinking two and damaging another. Officials speculate that Japanese Americans were signaling Japanese ships (The *Los Angeles Times* even reported that local

Los Angeles police frisk Japanese Americans who did not report for relocation.

CONTINUED

OUTLINE

Development of the Courts' Role in Government
- Founding to the Civil War
- Civil War to the Depression
- Depression to the Present

Courts
- Structure of the Courts
- Jurisdiction of the Courts

Judges
- Selection of Judges
- Tenure of Judges
- Qualifications of Judges
- Independence of Judges

Access to the Courts
- Wealth Discrimination in Access
- Interest Group Help in Access
- Restrictions on Access
- Proceeding Through the Courts

Deciding Cases
- Interpreting Statutes
- Interpreting the Constitution
- Restraint and Activism
- Following Precedents
- Making Law

The Power of the Courts
- Use of Judicial Review
- Use of Political Checks Against the Courts

Conclusion: Are the Courts Responsive?

Japanese farmers were guiding Japanese airplanes to their targets: "Caps on Japanese Tomato Plants Point to Air Base."[2])

Officials question Japanese Americans' loyalty. Most, born here, are U.S. citizens, but they have been granted citizenship by Japan as well because of their ancestry. And they have formed semiclosed communities and adhered to Old World cultural patterns. The army general in charge of evacuation expressed the prevalent attitude toward them: "There isn't such a thing as a loyal Japanese."[3]

Many groups characterized the Japanese as rats. West Coast restaurants placed signs in their windows: "This Restaurant Poisons Both Rats and Japs." Groups distributed pamphlets—"Slap the Jap Rat"—and put stickers with pictures of a rat with a Japanese face on their cars. A patriotic parade in New York City included a float the crowd reportedly "loved"—an eagle leading a squadron of American bombers toward a herd of yellow rats trying to escape.[4]

On the other hand, Korematsu claims the order discriminates against him on the basis of his race and thereby violates his Fifth Amendment right to due process of law. As evidence, Korematsu notes that the order does not apply to persons of German or Italian ancestry. (Although the order was general, the military-commander was told not to remove the many persons of Italian descent on the West Coast. The mayor of San Francisco was Italian, and baseball star Joe DiMaggio, whose parents were aliens, was a national idol. Anyway, President Roosevelt said he was not worried about the Italians. "They are a lot of opera singers. . . ."[5])

Korematsu also notes that there has been widespread discrimination against Asians on the West Coast. For decades there has been talk of the "yellow peril." In 1913 Congress refused to allow more Japanese to become citizens and in 1924 refused to allow more to immigrate. The discrimination has resulted in segregated neighborhoods and schools and, in at least one city—Bakersfield—even the omission of their names from the telephone directory. The hostility has fueled efforts to drive Japanese Americans off their productive farmland. Many Japanese, brought over as cheap laborers, worked hard enough to become successful owners. At the outbreak of the war, according to some estimates, they grew about half the fruits and vegetables in California, and an acre of their land was worth more than seven times the average value of farmland on the Coast. Competitors covet their land.

You are torn. You were appointed by President Roosevelt, yet you are strongly committed to individual rights. What do you decide?

Most people assume that courts are nonpolitical and that judges are objective. People say we have "a government of laws, not of men." This is a myth. At any time in our history, "It is individuals who make, enforce, and interpret the law."[6] When judges interpret the law, they are political actors and courts are political institutions.

As political institutions, courts make policy, although not all make policy to the same degree. Among the federal courts, the Supreme Court makes national policy in most of its cases. As the highest court, it decides difficult legal questions and resolves important national controversies that the lower courts could not settle to the litigants' satisfaction. The lower courts make regional and local policy in some of their cases, although most of their cases are routine because the law is clear and the decisions are of little consequence except to the litigants.

That the judiciary is part of the political process can be seen in the history, structure, jurisdiction, composition, operation, and impact of the courts.

➤Development of the Courts' Role in Government

The Founders expected the judiciary to be the weakest branch of government. In the *Federalist Papers,* Alexander Hamilton wrote that Congress would have power to pass the laws and appropriate the money; the president would have power to execute the laws; but the courts would have "merely judgment," that is, only power to resolve disputes in cases brought to them. In doing so, they would exercise "neither force nor will." They would not have any means to enforce decisions, and they would not use their own values to decide cases. Rather, they would simply apply the Constitution and laws as written. Consequently, the judiciary would be the "least dangerous" branch.[7]

This prediction was accurate for the early years of the Republic. The Supreme Court was held in such low esteem that some distinguished men refused to accept appointment, or they accepted appointment but refused to attend sessions. The first chief justice thought the Court was "inauspicious,"[8] without enough "weight and dignity" to play an important role.[9] So he resigned to be governor of New York. The second chief justice resigned to be envoy to France. To add insult, when the capital was moved to Washington in 1801, the planners overlooked the Court and forgot to provide a place for it to hold sessions. It had to meet in the office of the clerk of the Senate for some years.

However, the status of the Court changed after the appointment of the third chief justice—John Marshall. Under the leadership of Marshall and later chief justices, the Court gradually developed "weight and dignity" and came to play an important role in government. The lower courts eventually did as well.

The development of the courts' role in government can be shown by dividing the courts' history into three eras—from the Founding to the Civil War, from the Civil War to the Depression, and from the Depression to the present.

Founding to the Civil War

The primary issue for the courts in the era from this country's founding to the Civil War was the relationship between nation and state. In addressing this issue, the Supreme Court established judicial review and national dominance.

Judicial Review

Judicial Review is the authority to declare laws or actions of government officials unconstitutional. The Constitution does not mention judicial review, but the Founders apparently expected the courts to exercise it. In the *Federalist Papers,* Hamilton said the courts would have authority to void laws contrary to the Constitution,[10] and at the time some state courts had such authority. Yet the Founders did not expect the courts to exercise it vigorously.

Chief Justice John Marshall.

The Supreme Court asserted itself to exercise judicial review in the case of ***Marbury v. Madison*** in 1803.[11] The case had its origins in 1800, when President John Adams was defeated in his bid for reelection by Thomas Jefferson, and Federalist members of Congress were defeated by Jeffersonians. With both the presidency and Congress lost, the Federalists tried to ensure continued control of the judiciary. The lame duck president and Congress added more judgeships to which they appointed Federalists, working feverishly to install these "midnight judges" before the new president and Congress took over. Adams named his secretary of state, John Marshall, to be chief justice. Although Marshall, still secretary of state, was responsible for delivering the commissions to the new judicial appointees, he failed to deliver 17 of the 42 commissions for District of Columbia justices of the peace. He assumed that his successor would deliver the rest. But Jefferson, angry at the Federalists' efforts to pack the judiciary, told his secretary of state, James Madison, not to deliver the commissions. Without the signed commissions, the appointees could not prove that they had in fact been appointed.

William Marbury and three other intended appointees petitioned the Supreme Court for a writ of mandamus, a writ that orders government officials to do something they have a duty to do. In this case it would order Madison to deliver the commissions.

As chief justice, Marshall was in a position to rule on his own negligence. Today this would be considered a conflict of interest and he would be expected to disqualify himself. But at the time people were not as troubled by such conflicts.

Marshall could issue the writ, but surely Jefferson would tell Madison to disobey it and the Court would be powerless to enforce it. Or he could not issue the writ, and the Court would appear to cave in to Jefferson. Either way the Court would demonstrate weakness rather than strength. But Marshall, in his genius, found a way out of the dilemma.

Marbury had petitioned the Court for a writ of mandamus under the authority of a provision of the Judiciary Act of 1789 that permitted the Court to issue this type of writ. But Marshall maintained that the Court could issue the writ only in cases that came to it on appeal from a lower court rather than in ones, like Marbury's, that started at the High Court. The Constitution gives the Court original jurisdiction over cases involving a state or foreign ambassador, which Marbury's case did not. By expanding the Court's original jurisdiction, Marshall argued, the Judiciary Act contradicted the Constitution. This interpretation was questionable because the Constitution does not say that the Court shall have original jurisdiction *only* over cases involving a state or foreign ambassador. Many of those who had drafted and voted for the Judiciary Act had been delegates to the Constitutional Convention, and it is unlikely they would have initiated a law that contradicted the Constitution. But this interpretation allowed Marshall a way out of the dilemma.

This portrait of William Marbury reflects the importance of *Marbury v. Madison*. It is the only portrait of a litigant owned by the Supreme Court Historical Society.

Speaking for a unanimous Court, Marshall insisted that Marbury had a right to the commission. But Marshall concluded that the Court could not order the administration to give the commission because the provision of the act was unconstitutional. Thus, Marshall exercised judicial review. He wrote, in a statement that would be repeated by courts for years to come, "It is emphatically the province and duty of the judicial department to say what the law is."

Marshall justified judicial review this way: The Constitution is the supreme law of the land. If other laws contradict it, they are unconstitutional. So far, few of his contemporaries would quarrel with his reasoning. Marshall continued: Judges decide cases, and to decide cases they have to apply the Constitution. To apply it they have to say what it means. They can be trusted to say what it means because they take an oath to uphold it. Here many would quarrel with his reasoning. Other officials who have to follow the Constitution and who take an oath to uphold it could interpret it as appropriately as judges could.

But Marshall was persuasive enough to convince many people. A sly fox, he sacrificed the commissions—he could not have gotten them anyway—and established the power of judicial review instead. In doing so, with one hand he gave the Jeffersonians what they wanted, while with the other he gave the Federalists something much greater. And all along he claimed he did what the Constitution required him to do.

Jefferson saw through this. He said the Constitution, in Marshall's hands, was "a thing of putty."[12] But the decision did not require Jefferson to do anything, so he could not do anything but protest. Most of Jefferson's followers were satisfied with the result. They were not upset that the Court invalidated a Federalist law or concerned with the means used to do so.

Of course, they were shortsighted because this decision laid the cornerstone for a strong judiciary. Thus, the case that began as a "trivial squabble over a few petty political plums"[13] became perhaps the most important case the Court ever decided.

National Dominance

After *Marbury* the Court did not declare any other congressional laws unconstitutional during Marshall's tenure, although it did declare numerous state laws unconstitutional.[14]

The Court also furthered national dominance by broadly construing Congress's power. In *McCulloch v. Maryland* (see Chapter 3), the Court interpreted the "necessary and proper clause" to allow Congress to legislate in many matters not mentioned in the Constitution. The Court also furthered national dominance by narrowly construing states' power to regulate commerce.[15]

When President Andrew Jackson named Roger Taney to replace Marshall, proponents of a strong national government worried that Taney would undo what Marshall had done. But, although Taney did not further expand national power, he upheld national supremacy and thus solidified most of Marshall's doctrine.

Even so, in one case Taney severely undermined the Court's reputation and effectiveness. In the Dred Scott case,[16] the Court jumped into the thick of the slavery conflict and declared the Missouri Compromise of 1820, which controlled slavery in the territories, unconstitutional.

This was only the second time the Court had declared a congressional law unconstitutional, and it could not have come in a more controversial area or at a less opportune time. The slavery issue had polarized the nation, and the ruling polarized it further. Southerners were disenchanted with the Court because of its emphasis on a strong national government. Now northerners became disenchanted too. The Court's prestige dropped so precipitously that it could play only a weak role for two decades. President Abraham Lincoln refused to enforce one of its rulings,[17] and Congress withdrew part of its jurisdiction.[18] As a result, the Court avoided important issues.

The Taney Court naively thought it could resolve the clash over slavery and thereby resolve the conflict between nation and state. But no court could achieve this. It took the Civil War to do so.

Civil War to the Depression

With the controversy between nation and state dampened, the next primary issue for the courts was the relationship between government and business in cases involving regulation of business.

After the war, industrialization proceeded at a breakneck pace, bringing not only benefits but many problems. Some corporations abused their power over their employees, their competitors, and their customers. Some legislatures passed laws to regulate these abuses, but the corporations challenged the laws in court. The Supreme Court, dominated by justices who had been lawyers for corporations, reflected the views of corporations and struck down laws regulating them.

Beginning in the 1870s, intensifying in the 1890s, and continuing in the 1900s, the Court invalidated laws that regulated child labor,[19] maximum hours of work,[20] and minimum wages for work.[21] It also discouraged employees from joining unions and striking,[22] and it limited antitrust laws.[23] In just one decade, the Court invalidated 41 state laws that regulated railroads.[24]

In 1935 and 1936, the Court struck down 12 congressional laws,[25] nearly nullifying President Franklin Roosevelt's New Deal program to help the country recover from the Depression.

The Court's action precipitated another major crisis. Roosevelt was reelected resoundingly in 1936.

Although many children worked long days in unhealthy conditions, the Supreme Court declared initial laws prohibiting child labor unconstitutional. This boy worked in coal mines at the turn of the century.

Heady from his victory and frustrated by the Court's decisions and his lack of opportunities to appoint new justices in his first term, he retaliated against the Court by proposing what was soon labeled a **court-packing plan.** The plan would have authorized the president to nominate and the Senate to confirm a new justice for every justice over 70 who did not retire, up to a total of 15. At the time, there were 6 justices over 70, so Roosevelt could have appointed 6 new justices and assured himself a friendly Court. Roosevelt claimed the plan was to help the Court cope with its increasing caseload, but virtually everyone could see through this. Even many of his supporters criticized him for tampering with the Court.

Before Congress could vote on the plan, two justices who often sided with four conservative justices against New Deal legislation switched positions to side with three liberal justices for the legislation. Chief Justice Charles Evans Hughes and Justice Owen Roberts apparently thought the Court would suffer if it continued to oppose the popular president and his popular programs. Their "conversion" tipped the scales from votes of 6 to 3 against New Deal legislation to 5 to 4 for similar legislation. As a result, Roosevelt's plan became unnecessary, and Congress scuttled it. Hughes's and Roberts's switch was dubbed "the switch in time that saved nine."

Thus the Court resolved this issue in favor of government over business. Since then it has permitted most efforts to regulate business.

Depression to the Present

With the controversy between government and business subdued, the next primary issue for the courts has been the relationship between government and the individual in cases involving civil liberties and rights.

Especially since the 1950s, individuals have demanded an expansion of the rights in the Bill of Rights and the guarantees of due process and equal protection in the Fourteenth Amendment.

Chief Justice Earl Warren, flanked by Justices Hugo Black (*left*) and William Douglas.

Traditionally the Supreme Court had not supported civil liberties and rights very much. But in 1953 President Dwight Eisenhower appointed Earl Warren to be chief justice. For the rest of the 1950s and 1960s, Warren led the Court more effectively than any chief justice since Marshall. The **Warren Court** completely overhauled doctrine in three areas—racial segregation, criminal defendants' rights, and reapportionment. It also significantly altered doctrine in other areas—libel, obscenity, and religion. In the process it held many laws unconstitutional. It was more activist in these areas than the Court had ever been (see Figure 1).

Because its decisions generally favored a minority or unpopular individual, such as an alleged subversive or a criminal defendant, over government, the Court brought about a backlash by the majority that peaked in the late 1960s. President Richard Nixon vowed to change the direction of the Court, and in 1969 he appointed Warren Burger to be chief justice. Then Nixon and the next Republican president appointed four more justices. They wanted to slow, halt, or even reverse the Warren Court's actions. They expected the **Burger Court** to make a "constitutional counter-revolution."

But the Court did not. Although it eroded some of the Warren Court's doctrine, particularly in the area of criminal defendants' rights, it left most of the doctrine intact. Further, it overhauled doctrine in two areas where the Warren Court was silent—sexual discrimination and abortion. In these and other areas, the Burger Court held numerous laws unconstitutional. Although not as committed to civil liberties and rights as the Warren Court, the Burger Court was more committed to them than any earlier Court.

President Reagan sought to erode the Warren Court's doctrine further by appointing three more conservatives to fill vacancies and in 1986, when Burger retired, by naming William Rehnquist, the most conservative associate justice, to be chief justice. President Bush also had an opportunity to erode the Warren Court's doctrine further by appointing two more conservatives when the only two consistent liberals retired. By the end of his administration, Republican presidents had named 10 straight justices and the **Rehnquist Court** had seven conservatives. Yet conflicts among the conservatives—some are willing to uphold precedents they would not have agreed to set in the first place, while others vote to sweep them away—have splintered the bloc. In some terms, the former group dominates, but in other terms the latter group dominates. Overall, the Rehnquist Court, though markedly more conservative than the Burger Court, has not overturned most of the Warren Court's doctrine.

The election of President Clinton, a Democrat, in 1992 probably will keep the Court from tilting any more to the right as long as he is in office.

In sum, throughout its history the Court's role in government has been that of a policymaker—in relationships between nation and state, government and business, and government and the individual. In the first and second eras, the Court was a solidly conservative policymaker, protecting private property rights and limiting government regulation of business; in the third era the Court has been a generally liberal policymaker, permitting government regulation of

FIGURE 1
Number of Laws Regulating Economic Activity and Restricting Civil Liberties and Rights Declared Unconstitutional by the Supreme Court Since 1900

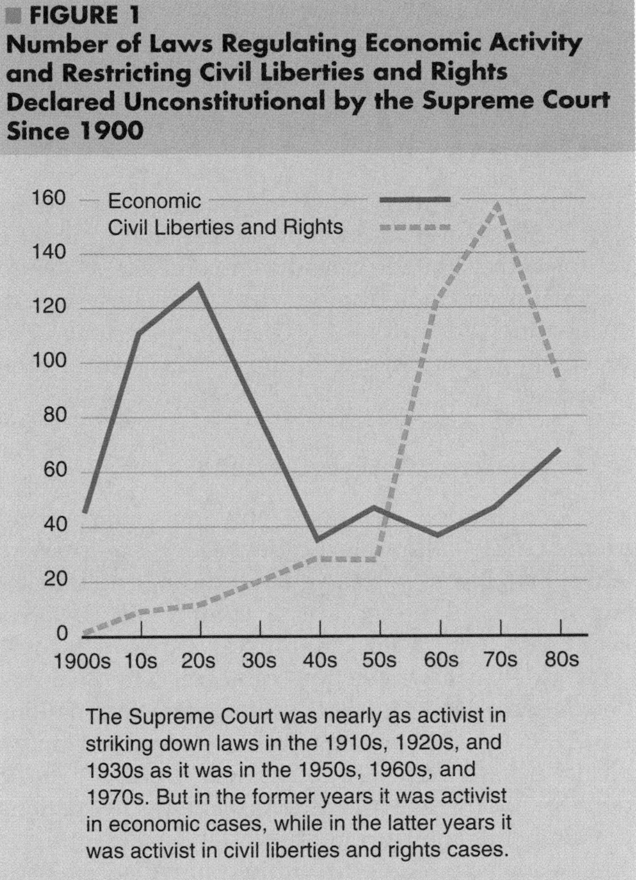

The Supreme Court was nearly as activist in striking down laws in the 1910s, 1920s, and 1930s as it was in the 1950s, 1960s, and 1970s. But in the former years it was activist in economic cases, while in the latter years it was activist in civil liberties and rights cases.

SOURCES: Congressional Research Service, *The Constitution of the United States: Analysis and Interpretation* (Washington, D.C.: U.S. Government Printing Office, 1973 and 1982); Lawrence Baum, *The Supreme Court*, 3rd ed. (Washington, D.C.: CQ Press, 1989), p. 188.

business and supporting civil liberties and rights for individuals. The third era, however, might be coming to a close.

➤Courts

Most countries with a federal system have one national court over a system of regional courts. In contrast, the United States has a complete system of national courts side by side with complete systems of state courts, for a total of 51 separate systems. This makes litigation far more complicated than in other countries.

■ Structure of the Courts

The Constitution mentions only one court—a supreme court—although it allows Congress to set up additional, lower courts, which it did in the Judiciary Act of 1789. The act was a compromise between Federalists, who wanted a full system of lower courts with extensive jurisdiction—authority to hear and decide cases—in order to strengthen the national government, and Jeffersonians, who wanted only a partial system of lower courts with limited jurisdiction in order to avoid strengthening the national government. The compromise established a full system of lower courts with limited jurisdiction. These courts were authorized to hear disputes involving citizens of more than one state but not disputes relating to the U.S. Constitution and laws. The state courts were permitted to hear all these.

In 1875, Congress granted the federal courts extensive jurisdiction. Sixteen years later Congress created another level of courts, between the Supreme Court and the original lower courts to complete the basic structure of the federal judiciary.

The **district courts** are trial courts. There are 94, based on population but with at least 1 in each state. They have a number of judges, although a single judge or jury decides each case.

The **courts of appeals** are intermediate appellate courts. There are 12, based on regions—"circuits"—of the country. A group of three judges decides their cases.

The Supreme Court is the ultimate appellate court. Although it can hear some cases (those involving a state or diplomat) that have not proceeded through the lower courts first, in practice it hears nearly all of its cases on appeal. A group of nine justices decides its cases.

The district courts conduct trials. The courts of appeals and Supreme Court do not; they do not have juries or witnesses to testify and present evidence—just lawyers for the opposing litigants. Rather than determine guilt or innocence, these courts evaluate arguments about legal questions arising in the cases.

The state judiciaries have a structure similar to the federal judiciary. In most states, though, there are two tiers of trial courts. The lower tier is usually for criminal cases involving minor crimes, and the upper tier is for criminal cases involving major crimes and for civil cases. In about three-fourths of the states, there are intermediate appellate courts, and in all of the states there is a supreme court (although in a few it is called another name).

■ Jurisdiction of the Courts

Jurisdiction is the authority to hear and decide cases. According to the Constitution, the federal courts exercise jurisdiction over cases in which the subject involves either the U.S. Constitution, statutes, or treaties; maritime law; or cases in which the litigants include either the U.S. government, more than one state government, one state government and a citizen of another state, citizens of more than one state, or a foreign government or citizen. The state courts exercise jurisdiction over the remaining cases. These include most criminal cases because the states have authority over most criminal matters and pass most criminal laws.

Despite this dividing line, some cases begin in the state courts and end in the federal courts. These involve state law and federal law, frequently a state statute and a federal constitutional right. For these cases there are two major paths from the state judiciary to the federal judiciary. One is for the litigant who lost at the state supreme court to appeal to the U.S. Supreme Court.

The other path, available only in a criminal case, is for the defendant who has exhausted appeals in the state courts to appeal to the local federal district court through a writ of **habeas corpus.** Latin for "Have ye the body!" this writ demands that the state figuratively produce the defendant and justify his or her incarceration. If the district court decides that the state courts did not grant the defendant's federal constitutional rights, it will reverse the conviction. From the district court's decision, the losing side can try to appeal to the courts of appeals and Supreme

FIGURE 2
Federal and State Court Systems

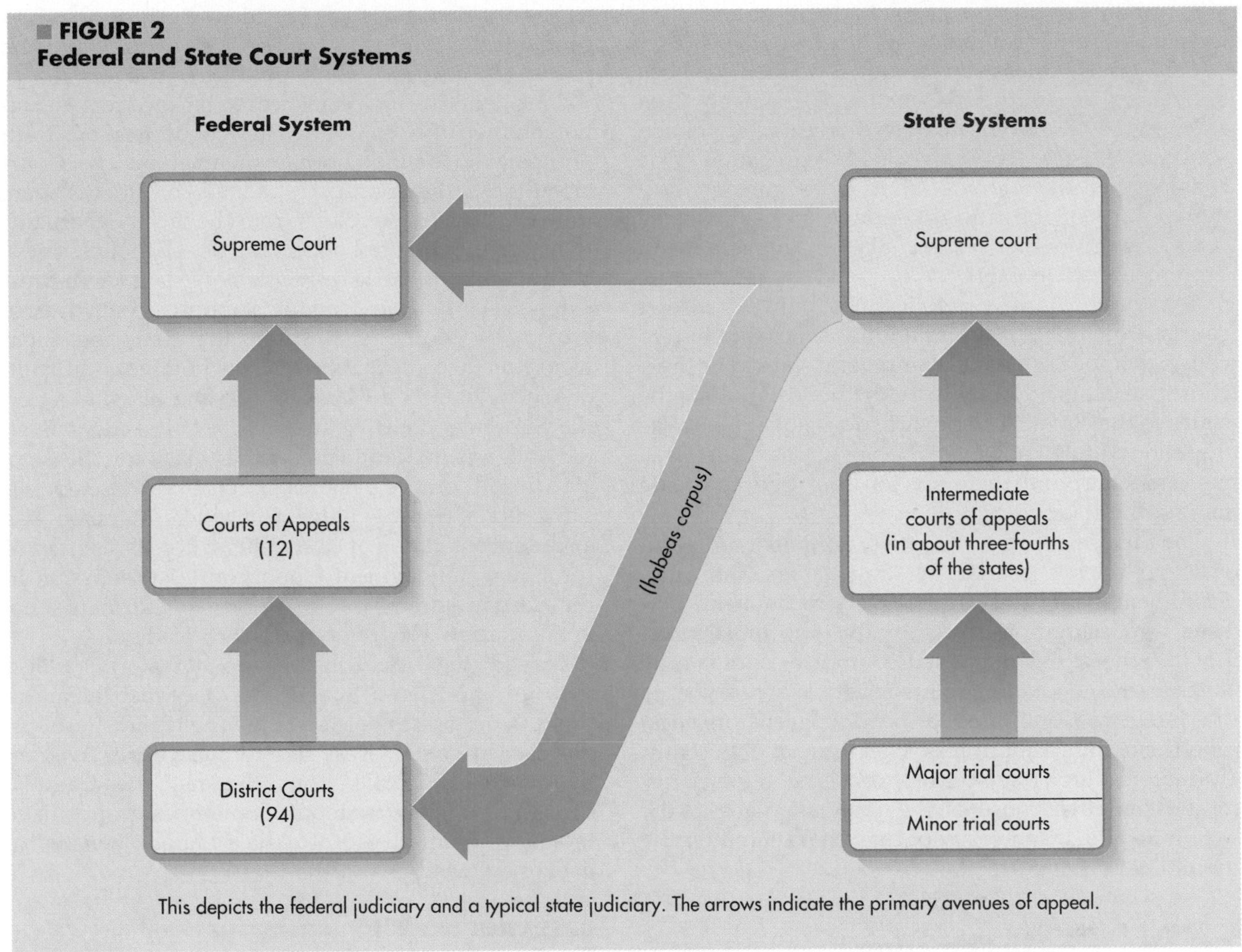

This depicts the federal judiciary and a typical state judiciary. The arrows indicate the primary avenues of appeal.

Court. Jurisdiction in these cases is complicated, and appeals may be numerous (see Figure 2).

JUDGES

Selection of Judges

Benjamin Franklin proposed that judges be selected by lawyers because lawyers would pick "the ablest of the profession in order to get rid of him, and share his practice among themselves."[26] The Founders rejected this unique idea in favor of a plan whereby the president nominates judges and the Senate confirms them. There are no other requirements in the Constitution, although there is an unwritten requirement that judges be lawyers and an expectation that they be members of the president's political party. Most have been active party members who have served in office or contributed to candidates. In this century presidents nominated members of their party from 82% of the time (Gerald Ford) to 99% of the time (Woodrow Wilson). Thus the process of selecting federal judges is highly political.

Mechanics of Selection

For lower court vacancies, administration officials recommend candidates, but senators also play a key role through the practice of senatorial courtesy. This tradition allows senators of the president's party to veto candidates for positions in their state and to recommend other candidates instead.

Senatorial courtesy can tie the president's hands. In deference to southern senators, President John Kennedy, who advocated civil rights, appointed southern judges who advocated segregation. One characterized the Supreme Court's desegregation ruling as "one of the truly regrettable decisions of all time," and another called blacks "niggers" and "chimpanzees" in court.[27]

Senatorial courtesy applies not only to district courts, which lie within individual states, but also to courts of appeals, which span several states. For these courts, senators informally divide the seats among the states in the circuit. The practice does not apply to the Supreme Court, however, because this court is a national court and there are too few seats to divide among the states.

For Supreme Court vacancies, administration officials conduct a search for acceptable candidates. Prominent politicians and lawyers recommend persons, and interest groups lobby for their preferences.

Once the president has settled upon a candidate, he submits the nomination to the Senate, where it goes to the Judiciary Committee for hearings. Senators question the nominee about his or her judicial philosophy, and interest groups voice their concerns. If a majority of the committee consents, the nomination goes to the whole Senate. If a majority of the Senate consents, the nomination is confirmed.

Criteria Used in Selection

The Founders expected judges to be selected by merit; they did not foresee the policymaking role of the courts or the development of political parties and senatorial courtesy, which have thrust political criteria into the process of selection.

CRITERIA USED BY PRESIDENTS Although presidents prefer judges with merit, usually they select them on the basis of other factors—friendship, favors, political experience, or ideological views. President Reagan emphasized ideology in an effort to mold the bench more than any president since Franklin Roosevelt. His administration screened candidates for conservative views on controversial issues. For example, the administration looked for those who, in the language of the Republican party platform, "respect the sanctity of innocent human life"—code words for opposition to Supreme Court decisions allowing abortion. President Bush also sought candidates with conservative views, although he tried to avoid those who would be controversial.

Presidents also select justices to balance representation on the Supreme Court. They choose persons from groups who do not have a member on the Court already. As the country expanded, presidents were urged to nominate persons from the West. Eventually, they were pressured to nominate Catholics, Jews, blacks, and women. Presidents bowed to these pressures because they sought support from diverse groups of people and feared that ignoring them would make confirmation of their nominees difficult.

When Thurgood Marshall, the first black to sit on the Supreme Court, retired in 1991, President Bush felt obligated to nominate another black for this seat. He chose Clarence Thomas, a conservative Republican court of appeals judge. But where Marshall was an ardent champion of civil rights, Thomas, as head of the Equal Employment Opportunity Commission in the Reagan administration, criticized affirmative action and drew the ire of most black leaders.

Indeed, individual justices do not always reflect their group's views. In abortion cases Justice Sandra Day O'Connor has voted against the feminist groups' position in some cases, and former Justice William Brennan, a Catholic, voted against the Catholic Church's policy consistently. Sometimes groups have to satisfy themselves with the symbolic benefits of having a "member" on the Court.

CRITERIA USED BY SENATORS Although senators normally confirm presidential nominations to the lower courts, occasionally they refuse to confirm Supreme Court nominations. Because the high Court is more important and appointments to it are more visible, these nominations are more likely to become embroiled in politics. Since the late 1960s senators have rejected six nominations to the Court—two of President Lyndon Johnson, two of President Nixon, and two of President Reagan.

Senators decide whether to confirm a nomination primarily on the basis of the qualifications and ideology of the nominee.[28] If the qualifications are good, they usually approve, regardless of the ideology. But if the qualifications are questionable, they often consider how closely the nominee's ideology matches theirs. (However, they are reluctant to admit this because doing so would reveal the politics involved, and most of the public thinks politics is not or at least should not be involved.)

American Diversity

Do Women Judges Make a Difference?

Some argue that there should be more women judges because women are entitled to their "fair share" of all governmental offices, including judgeships. Others argue that there should be more so that women as well as men would feel that courts represent them and, therefore, would believe that courts' decisions are fair and legitimate. Still others argue that there should be more because women, compared to men, have somewhat different views and would make somewhat different decisions.

A study of Justice Sandra Day O'Connnor's behavior shows that although she generally votes on the conservative side of issues, she usually votes in a liberal direction in sex discrimination cases. Moreover, her presence on the Court apparently sensitizes her male colleagues to gender issues. All but two of them began to vote against sex discrimination more frequently after she joined the Court (and one of these two already had voted against sex discrimination regularly).[1]

Some studies reflect similar results for women justices on state supreme courts. These justices tend to support a broad array of women's rights in cases ranging from sex discrimination to child support and property settlement. On these issues even women justices from opposing political parties tend to agree.[2]

But studies that compare voting patterns on issues less obviously related to gender have less clear findings. Women judges appear more liberal than men in cases involving employment discrimination and racial discrimination. Perhaps the treatment they have experienced as women has made them more sympathetic to the discrimination others have faced. On the other hand, women judges do not appear more liberal or conservative than men in cases involving criminal rights or obscenity.[3]

A study of the sentences of state trial court judges found that compared to male judges, women judges sentenced men defendants the same way, but they sentenced women defendants to prison more frequently. That is, in borderline cases, women judges ordered women defendants to prison, while men judges gave them probation. Where women judges treated men and women defendants equally, men judges treated women defendants more leniently and more paternalistically, permitting them to avoid prison.[4]

In addition, women judges seem to make a difference in a less direct way. They help protect the credibility of women lawyers and witnesses. In court some men judges and lawyers refer to women lawyers and witnesses by their first names or by such terms as "young lady," "little girl," "sweetie," or "honey." Or the men, in the midst of the proceedings, comment upon the women's perfume, clothing, or appearance. "How does an attorney establish her authority when the judge has just described her to the entire courtroom as 'a pretty little thing'?"[5] Even if the men consider their remarks harmless compliments rather than intentional tactics, their effect is to undermine the credibility of women lawyers and witnesses in the eyes of jurors. Women judges have attempted to squelch such remarks.[6]

1. Karen O'Connor and Jeffrey A. Segal, "Justice Sandra Day O'Connor and the Supreme Court's Reaction to Its First Female Member," in Naomi B. Lynn, ed., *Women, Politics and the Constitution* (New York: Haworth Press, 1990), pp. 95–104.
2. David W. Allen and Diane E. Wall, "Role Orientations and Women State Supreme Court Justices," *Judicature* 77 (November/December, 1993), pp. 156–65.
3. Sue Davis, Susan Haire, and Donald R. Songer, "Voting Behavior and Gender on the U.S. Courts of Appeals," *Judicature* 77 (November/December, 1993), pp. 129–33; Thomas G. Walker and Deborah J. Barrow, "The Diversification of the Federal Bench," *Journal of Politics* 47 (1985), pp. 596–617.
4. John Gruhl, Cassia Spohn, and Susan Welch, "Women as Policymakers: The Case of Trial Judges," *American Journal of Political Science* 25 (May 1981), pp. 308–22.
5. William Eich, "Gender Bias in the Courtroom: Some Participants Are More Equal Than Others,' *Judicature* 69 (April–May 1986), pp. 339–43.
6. Georgia Dullea, "Women on the Bench Increase," *New York Times*, April 26, 1984.

When Nixon chose Court of Appeals Judge G. Harold Carswell, law scholars familiar with his record were dismayed. At Senate hearings they testified that he was undistinguished, as well as opposed to civil rights. Nixon's floor manager for the nomination, Senator Roman Hruska (R-Neb.), blurted out in exasperation, "Even if he is mediocre there are a lot of mediocre judges and people and lawyers. They are entitled to a little representation, aren't they and a little chance? We can't have all Brandeises, Cardozos, and Frankfurters, and stuff like that there."[29] This was the kiss of death. Once Carswell's supporters admitted his mediocrity, senators who objected to his views on civil rights could vote against him more freely, and his nomination was doomed.

Yet when Nixon and Reagan nominated conservatives with unquestioned qualifications, they rarely faced a problem. One exception was Reagan's nomination of Robert Bork in 1987. Bork had criticized Court doctrine in his writings and speeches, and the debate focused on his ideology. In addition to rejecting a right to privacy, which is the basis of Court decisions allowing birth control and abortion, he had criticized Court decisions and congressional laws advancing racial equality. Bork's positions struck many Americans as extreme, and his nomination was voted down.

This battle prompted some observers to ask whether anyone with a record could be nominated again. Indeed, when Bush had his first vacancy, he chose a man who had left no trail of controversial writings and speeches. David Souter, though a former New Hampshire attorney general and then state supreme court justice, was called the "Stealth candidate" (after the bomber designed to elude radar).[30] Souter was a private person, living alone in a house at the end of a dirt road and not answering his neighbors' phone calls some nights. He had expressed few positions and made few decisions reflecting his views on federal constitutional doctrine. Even in his confirmation hearings he refused to reveal his views. It was assumed that he was another conservative, because of his lifestyle and because of his support from conservative aides to the president, yet he offered a small target and won confirmation easily.

When Bush had his second vacancy and chose Thomas, he realized that the nomination could be controversial (even before the charges of sexual harassment surfaced) but saw that it would split the Democratic coalition: some Democrats would be sympathetic because of his race, while others would be critical because of his views. For insurance the administration instructed Thomas to soft-pedal his views. Thomas told senators he made his previous statements as a representative of the administration but would be impartial as a justice. On abortion he insisted, incredibly, that he had no position and, in fact, he had never discussed the issue with anyone.

Both Souter and Thomas said they could not reveal their views because they would have to decide these issues and so would need to preserve their impartiality. Yet both stated their support for capital punishment, although they would also have to decide these cases. The difference is that their view on capital punishment coincided with that of three-fourths of the public, whereas their views on other issues probably did not.

When Clinton had his first vacancy, he was wary because the Senate had forced him to withdraw several nominations to other positions and because Republicans had vowed to avenge Bork's defeat. The president chose Ruth Bader Ginsburg, a court of appeals judge for 13 years. The nomination satisfied Republicans because Ginsburg had often voted with Republicans on the bench, yet it also pleased some Democratic constituencies. Women's groups, of course, expected more seats, and Jews, who had not had a representative on the Court since 1969, also wanted a seat.

Ginsburg refused to discuss doctrine at her hearings, but her record showed a commitment to abortion rights and sexual equality. Although she had tied for first in her graduating class from Columbia Law School in 1959, she was turned down for a clerkship by Justice Felix Frankfurter and for a job by New York City law firms. The firms, just beginning to hire Jews, were not ready to hire mothers with young children. She taught law and then served as an attorney for the American Civil Liberties Union (ACLU). In the 1970s she argued six sex discrimination cases before the Supreme Court and, with an innovative approach, won five.

When Clinton had his second vacancy, he was still wary of a confirmation fight. Instead of the people he most desired, he chose Stephen Breyer, a court of appeals judge with a reputation as a moderate.

Nominations to the Court, which were contentious during the nineteenth century but not during the first half of the twentieth century, have become contentious again partly because of the Court's activism—both liberals and conservatives saw what the Court can do—and partly because of the struggle for control of the divided government since the late 1960s. In most years Republicans have dominated the presidency while Democrats have dominated Congress, so both have fought over the judiciary to tip the balance. Republicans, especially, have been frustrated by their inability to push their civil liberties and rights policies through Congress, so they have hoped that their appointees to the Court would do what their members in Congress have not been able to do.

Results of Selection

Judges are drawn primarily from the lower federal and state courts, the federal government, or large law firms. These established legal circles are dominated by white men so, not surprisingly, most judges have been white men. Before President Jimmy Carter took office, only eight women had ever served on the federal bench.[31] Carter, however, made a concerted effort to appoint more women and racial minorities. Sixteen percent of his appointees were women, and 21% were racial minorities. President Reagan, despite the impression he created by naming a woman to the Supreme Court, named mostly white men to the lower courts. Eight percent of his appointees were women, and 6% were racial minorities. Seventeen percent of President Bush's appointees were women, and 11% were racial minorities.[32]

President Clinton, in his first two years nominated 30% women, 21% blacks, and 8% Hispanics among 143 vacancies.[33]

Most judges have been wealthy. Most of Bush's appointees were worth more than a half million dollars; a fourth of Reagan's and a third of Bush's appointees were millionaires.

Despite some efforts to balance representation on the Supreme Court, presidents have not sought actual representatives of all socioeconomic groups. Throughout history, justices have come from a narrow, elite slice of society. Most have been born into families of Western European stock (especially English, Welsh, Scotch, and Irish), profess the Protestant religion (especially Episcopalian, Presbyterian, Congregational, and Unitarian), and are upper middle or upper class. Moreover, they have been born into families with traditions of political or even judicial service, families with prestige and connections as well as expectations for achievement.[34]

With the power to nominate judges, presidents have a tremendous opportunity to shape the courts and their decisions. By the time Carter finished his term, he had appointed about 40% of the lower court judges, although he had no opportunity to appoint Supreme Court justices. By the time Bush finished his term, he and Reagan had appointed about 65% of the lower court judges and five Supreme Court justices (in addition to elevating Rehnquist from associate to chief justice). Most of Carter's appointees were moderates or liberals, whereas most of Bush's and Reagan's were conservatives (see Tables 1 and 2).

In addition to ideological differences in broad categories of cases, appointees of recent presidents also reflect differences in the narrower categories of abortion and the environment. Carter's appointees to the district courts voted against abortion rights in just 13% of their cases, whereas Reagan's appointees voted against abortion rights in 77% of their cases.[35] Carter's appointees to the appellate courts sided more

TABLE 1 Appointees of Democrats and Republicans Think Differently

	PERCENT WHO AGREE		
	Democratic Appointees	**Republican Appointees**	**Difference**
Big corporations should be taken out of private ownership.	10%	2%	8%
U.S. institutions need complete restructuring.	24	13	11
The more able should earn more.	86	98	12
America would be better off if it moved toward socialism.	19	4	15
Private enterprise is fair to workers.	70	87	17
The poor are such due to circumstances beyond their control.	50	33	17
America offers an opportunity for financial security to all who work hard.	59	85	26
Government should ensure a good standard of living.	57	27	30
Less regulation of business is good for the country.	54	85	31
Government should not guarantee jobs.	36	70	34
Government should reduce the income gap between rich and poor.	78	44	34

A survey of the economic attitudes of federal lower court judges shows that most hold opinions accepting the economic status quo. Even so, there are significant differences according to the political party of the appointing president. Judges appointed by Republican presidents tend to think individuals are largely responsible for their financial success or failure and that government should do less to equalize conditions.

SOURCE: Althea K. Nagai, Stanley Rothman, and S. Robert Lichter, "The Verdict on Federal Judges." Public Opinion (November/December 1987). p. 54.

TABLE 2 Appointees of Democrats and Republicans Vote Differently

Issue	PERCENT LIBERAL* VOTES BY APPOINTEES OF Nixon (R)	Ford (R)	Carter (D)	Reagan (R)	Bush (R)
Criminal justice	27%	37%	39%	28%	26%
Civil rights and civil liberties	40	40	53	31	23
Labor and economic regulation	49	52	61	47	48

A study of the votes of federal district court judges appointed by President Nixon through President Bush shows marked differences according to the political party of the president. The study also shows some differences, especially in civil rights and liberties cases, among appointees of Republicans. Compare the appointees of Bush and Reagan with those of earlier Republicans. These results reflect the effort that the Bush and Reagan administrations made to nominate candidates who held conservative views on these issues.

*Liberal votes were defined as ones in favor of criminal defendants' or prisoners' rights in criminal justice cases; individuals' rights, involving freedom of expression or religion and equality between the races or sexes, in civil rights and liberties cases; and workers' or economic underdogs' interests, rather than businesses' or economic upper-dogs' interests, in labor and economic regulation cases. Cases through 1991 are included.

SOURCE: Robert A. Carp, Donald Songer, C. K. Rowland, Ronald Stidham, and Lisa Richey-Tracy, "The Voting Behavior of Judges Appointed by President Bush," *Judicature*, 76 (April–May, 1993), pp. 298–302.

Racial and Sexual Stereotypes in Thomas versus Hill

With a combustible mixture of politics, race, and sex, the battle over the nomination of Clarence Thomas to the Supreme Court was enticing theater; it was bound to play on television. In this medium, which oversimplifies complex issues, dividing competitors into two camps—pro and con—and then encouraging them to attack and counterattack, perhaps it was inevitable that the key participants would be assigned roles that were not nearly as subtle and complex as the real people were. But these roles, actually stereotypes, would determine the outcome of the battle.[1]

Bush administration officials began with a nonracial stereotype—the heroes of nineteenth-century writer Horatio Alger, the boys who overcame insurmountable odds (for example, *From Canal Boy to President*). In interviews with reporters, officials emphasized, and Thomas stressed, how he began life in Pin Point, Georgia, and overcame poverty and injustice along the way. Thomas, in fact, had far more to say about prejudice against him when young than about any prejudice against blacks today. But officials did not stop with Horatio Alger. They also invoked Booker T. Washington, the late-nineteenth-century black educator who urged blacks to become self-reliant rather than dependent on the government for help. Like Washington, officials said, Thomas had pulled himself up by his own bootstraps. Although he had benefited from affirmative action to gain admission to Yale Law School, Thomas later had rejected affirmative action and other vigorous government initiatives and instead had called for more self-reliance. Thomas had even used the stereotype of the "welfare queen" to deride his sister, who for a time received welfare, and to distance himself from many blacks and their leaders.

Blacks critical of the nomination thought the stereotypes did not stop with Horatio Alger and Booker T. Washington. Some believed that the whites were looking for an "Uncle Tom" (without, of course, using the phrase), a loyal and trustworthy, even compliant, black man who was willing to cater to white prejudices.

During the first round of confirmation hearings, blacks critical of the nomination saw another stereotype—"Sambo," a grinning, mindless minstrel who could remember nothing without his master's help.[2] Thomas did come across as affable and, under the coaching of his handlers, refused to divulge his views on judicial doctrine.

After Anita Hill's charges of sexual harassment, and all their sordid details, became public, blacks cringed as another stereotype surfaced—"Buck," an oversexed black male who has casual sex with black women but who lusts after white women.[3] According to Hill, Thomas talked about the size of his penis and scenes in pornographic movies, and he pressured her to go out with him before he eventually married a white woman.

During the second round of confirmation hearings, after the charges of harassment, Thomas himself invoked the stereotype of the "uppity black." Characterizing himself as rebellious, because he disagreed with black leaders and liberal activists about the role of government in civil rights, he angrily proclaimed that the country was witnessing a "high-tech legal lynching" of an "uppity black man." The image of lynching an uppity black man, seared into the black consciousness for generations, was calculated to arouse the sympathy of African Americans. Indeed, this particular stereotype was decisive in persuading most of the black public to support Thomas and, in often with environmental groups, whereas Reagan's and Bush's appointees sided more often with businesses.[36] Reagan's appointees to the appellate courts voted to narrow existing air and water pollution laws and to resist recognizing new environmental obligations.[37]

Tenure of Judges

Once appointed, judges can serve for "good behavior." This means for life, unless they commit "high crimes and misdemeanors." These are not defined in the Constitution but are considered serious crimes or, possibly, political abuses. Congress can impeach and remove judges as it can presidents, but it has impeached only 13 and removed only 6.[38] The standard of guilt—"high crimes and misdemeanors"—is vague, the punishment drastic, and the process time consuming, so Congress has been reluctant to impeach judges.

As an alternative, Congress established other procedures to discipline lower federal court judges in 1980. Councils made up of district and appellate court judges can ask judges to resign or can prevent them from hearing cases, but they cannot actually remove them. The procedures have been used infrequently, although their existence has prompted some judges to resign before being disciplined.

Continued

turn, persuading the undecided senators to vote for confirmation. Senators, especially those with large black constituencies, did not want to be accused of racism.

Hill was also the beneficiary and victim of stereotypes. Feminist critics of the nomination rallied around Hill, with some calling her the "Rosa Parks of sexual harassment," after the woman whose refusal to accept segregation on the bus sparked the Montgomery boycott. Yet Hill waited many years to air her charges and even then did so reluctantly. And, like Thomas, she had worked in the Reagan administration and supported the Bork nomination that so many of her new champions had assailed.

Although white professional women were impressed with Hill, many black workers were not. Some lower-class black women distrusted her because of her Yale education and her standard English diction. Neither the "nurturing mammy" nor the "surly black wife with the frying pan in her hand," according to one black writer, she was not recognizable as a black woman to some of them.[4] Others criticized her for airing the dirty laundry of the African American community in front of the larger white society.

Hill was also the target of sexual stereotypes promoted by Republicans on the Senate Judiciary Committee. Worried that her charges would cause senators to abandon Thomas, they characterized her as a "scorned and vengeful woman" who was attracted to Thomas and who sought revenge when he did not return her feelings. They also characterized her as a "whiny and weak woman" who wanted to do traditional male jobs but who could not put up with common problems in the workplace; a woman who complained about minor things but was not strong enough to voice her objections at the time.

Most of these stereotypes were promoted, not by Thomas and Hill, but by the warring forces—Republicans and Democrats, conservatives and liberals—who were using them as the weapons of their opposing agendas.

And all of these stereotypes were effective because they played off sharp divisions in society—between blacks and whites, women and men, feminist women and traditional women, the professional classes and the working classes. Finally, black observers lament that the battle reflected another metaphor—blacks as "crabs in a barrel" who will fight, even destroy each other, over a few crumbs.[5]

---

1. See, generally, Robert Chrisman and Robert L. Allen, eds., *Court of Appeal: The Black Community Speaks Out on the Racial and Sexual Politics of Thomas vs. Hill* (New York: Ballentine, 1992), an extensive collection of essays by black writers reflecting on the confirmation battle.
2. Llenda Jackson-Leslie, "Tom, Buck, and Sambo or How Clarence Thomas Got to the Supreme Court," in Chrisman and Allen, *Court of Appeal*, p. 106.
3. Jackson-Leslie, "Tom, Buck, and Sambo," in Chrisman and Allen, *Court of Appeal*, p. 108; Henry Vance Davis, "The High-Tech Lynching and the High-Tech Overseer," in Chrisman and Allen, *Court of Appeal*, pp. 59–62.
4. Rosemary L. Bray, "Taking Sides Against Ourselves," in Chrisman and Allen, *Court of Appeal*, p. 53. See also Melba Joyce Boyd, "Collard Greens, Clarence Thomas, and the High-Tech Rape of Anita Hill," in Chrisman and Allen, *Court of Appeal* pp. 43–46.
5. Maulana Karenga, "Under the Camouflage of Color and Gender," in Chrisman and Allen, *Court of Appeal*, p. 131. See also David J. Dent, "The Clarence Thomas Hearings and the Entertaining of America," in Chrisman and Allen, *Court of Appeal*, pp. 63–66.

The Supreme Court Decides a Case

When the Supreme Court agrees to hear a case, it asks the litigants to submit written arguments. These "briefs" identify the issues and marshall the evidence—statutes, the Constitution, precedents—for their side. After the Court receives the briefs, it sets a date for oral arguments.

On that date the justices gather in the robing room behind the courtroom. They put on their black robes and, as the curtains part, file into the courtroom and take their places at the raised half-hexagon bench. The chief justice sits in the center, and the associate justices extend out in order of seniority. The crier gavels the courtroom to attention and announces:

> The Honorable, the Chief Justice and Associate Justices of the Supreme Court of the United States! Oyez, oyez, oyez! [Give ear, give ear, give ear!] All persons having business before the Honorable, the Supreme Court of the United States are admonished to draw near and give attention, for the Court is now sitting. God save the United States and this Honorable Court.

The chief justice calls the case. The lawyers present their arguments. Those who read from a prepared text find the justices bored or even hostile; those who speak extemporaneously find them willing to engage in a lively dialogue. They interrupt with questions whenever they want. When Thurgood Marshall, as counsel for the NAACP, argued one school desegregation case, he was interrupted 127 times. Some lawyers are so unnerved by this practice that occasionally one faints on the spot.

The chief justice usually allots half an hour per side. When time expires, a red light flashes on the lectern, and the chief justice halts any lawyer who continues. Chief Justice Hughes was so strict he reportedly cut off one lawyer in the middle of the word "it."

The Court holds Friday conferences to make a tentative decision and assign the opinion. The decision affirms or reverses the lower court decision; it indicates who wins and who loses. The opinion explains why. It expresses principles of law and thereby establishes precedents for other cases, so it is very important.

A portrait of Chief Justice Marshall presides over the conference. To ensure secrecy, no one is present but the justices. They begin with handshakes. (During his tenure Chief Justice Marshall suggested that they begin with a drink anytime it was raining anywhere in the Court's jurisdiction. Perhaps this accounts for his extraordinary success in persuading his colleagues to adopt his views.) Then the justices battle. The chief justice initiates the discussion of the case. He asserts what he thinks the issues are and how they ought to be decided, and he casts a vote. The associate justices follow in order of seniority. The discussion might become heated. When the justices reach a

Law clerks of the Supreme Court, recent law school grads who ranked high in their classes, are chosen by the justices each year to help read petitions for review, research statutes and precedents, and draft opinions. Here two clerks meet with Justice John Paul Stevens.

Continued

tentative decision, if the chief justice is in the majority, he assigns a justice to write the opinion of the Court. If not, the most senior associate justice in the majority assigns one to write it.

These procedures reveal the chief justice's power. Although his vote counts the same as each associate justice's vote, his authority to initiate the discussion and assign the opinion is significant. The former can influence what the other justices think about the case; the latter can determine what the opinion expresses.

Before Marshall became chief justice, each justice wrote his own opinion. But Marshal realized that one majority opinion would have more clout. He often convinced the other justices to forsake their own opinions and subscribe to his; he authored almost half of the Court's approximately 1,100 opinions during his years. Chief Justices Warren and Burger assigned more than 80% of the Court's opinions during their years, though they wrote only some of them.[1] Burger reportedly used his authority to punish several colleagues who voted opposite him in other cases. Justice Powell told another justice, "I'm resigned to writing nothing but Indian affairs cases for the rest of my life."[2] Chief Justice Rehnquist is so conservative that he has dissented more than most chief justices and consequently has left the most senior associate to assign numerous opinions.[3]

After the conference the Court produces the opinion. This is the most time-consuming stage in the process. Because the justices are free to change their vote anytime until the decision is announced, there is much maneuvering and politicking. The justice assigned the opinion tries to write it to command support of the justices in the original majority and possibly even some in the original minority. The writer circulates the draft among the others, who suggest revisions. The writer circulates more drafts. These go back and forth, as the justices attempt to persuade or cajole, nudge or push their colleagues toward their position. Justice Brennan was especially adept at this and is considered by some scholars "the best coalition builder ever to sit on the Supreme Court."[4]

If the opinion does not command the support of some of the justices in the original majority, they write a concurring opinion. This indicates that they agree with the decision but not the reasons for it. Meanwhile, the justices in the minority write a dissenting opinion. This indicates that they do not agree even with the decision. Both concurring and dissenting opinions weaken the force of the majority opinion. They question the validity of it, and they suggest that at a different time with different justices there might be a different ruling.

The Court's own print shop in the basement prints the opinions. Then the Court announces the decision and opinions in the hushed courtroom.

"My dissenting opinion will be brief: "You're all full of crap."

1. David W. Rhode and Harold J. Spaeth, *Supreme Court Decision Making* (San Francisco, W. H. Freeman, 1976), p. 177; Harold J. Spaeth, "Distributive Justice: Majority Opinion Assignments in the Burger Court," *Judicature* 67 (December/January 1984), pp. 299–304.
2. Nina Totenberg and Fred Barbash, "Burger's Colleagues Won't Be Sorry to See Him Go," *Washington Post National Weekly Edition*, July 7, 1986, p. 8.
3. Al Kamen, "The Scalia Surprise," *Washington Post National Weekly Edition*," March 23,1987, p. 6.
4. Michael S. Serrill, "The Power of William Brennan," *Time*, July 22, 1985, p. 62.

polls on the same issues found that the rulings mirrored the polls in 62% of the cases.[78]

But when court rulings do not reflect the views of the public, opinion toward the courts can turn negative. Although research shows that citizens know little about the cases, they do remember especially controversial decisions, and they do recognize broad trends in decisions. A study of opinion toward the Supreme Court from 1966 to 1984 found that opinion became more negative when the Court struck down more congressional laws and when it upheld more criminal rights. (On the other hand, opinion grew more positive immediately after Watergate; people saw the Court as the bastion of law in the face of the Nixon administration's efforts to circumvent the law.)[79]

Yet opinion toward the courts retains a reservoir of support. In recent years, for example, attitudes about the Supreme Court have been more positive than attitudes about the presidency or Congress.[80] Because the public believes in the myth that courts are nonpolitical or because the public does not see the ways in which the courts are political—the inner workings of the courts, and the politicking among the judges, are not as visible as such processes are in the other branches—the public has not gotten as disgusted with the justices as it has with presidents and members of Congress.

However, when opinion toward the courts turns negative, the president or Congress is more likely to impose checks on the courts. This possibility has made the courts wary. As one political scientist concluded, the Supreme Court has "learned to be a political institution and to behave accordingly." It has "seldom lagged far behind or forged far ahead" of public opinion.[81] When it has, notably in the Dred Scott case and in the business regulation cases in the 1930s, it has lost some of its support and consequently some of its power.

In response to the occasional checks threatened or imposed on them, the courts have developed a strong sense of self-restraint to ensure self-preservation. This, more than the checks themselves, limits their use of judicial review.

➤Conclusion: Are the Courts Responsive?

The judiciary, appellate court judge Learned Hand said, stands as a bulwark against "the pressure of public panic." It provides a "sober second thought."[82] The Founders did not intend the judiciary to be responsive. They gave judges life tenure so courts would be independent to a large extent.

Indeed, the judiciary is more independent of pressures from the rest of the political process than the other branches are. Consequently, courts sometimes act on behalf of the relatively powerless individuals and small groups that lack clout with the executive and legislative branches. Courts have extended important civil liberties and rights to these individuals and groups.

Although relatively independent, the judiciary is part of the political process and is sensitive to others in the process. It is responsive to the president and Congress—or at least to one of these. Ultimately, it is responsive to the majority of the public. Even when courts act on behalf of nonelites, they rarely challenge the fundamental principles of society. They ordinarily uphold "the system." They simply give nonelites a place in it. Thus, in most cases, decisions by the courts reflect the attitudes of society.

EPILOGUE

Exclusion of Japanese Upheld

In *Korematsu v. United States,* the Supreme Court, by a six-to-three vote, upheld the order excluding Japanese Americans from the West Coast.[83] Justice Douglas voted against the order in conference but switched to the majority just before the Court announced its decision.[84] The Court noted that the president and Congress agreed that the order was necessary, and it emphasized that the government could take precautions to prevent espionage and sabotage during wartime.

Thus the majority was restrained, deferring to the combined force of the other two branches. These justices did not question the validity of officials' fear

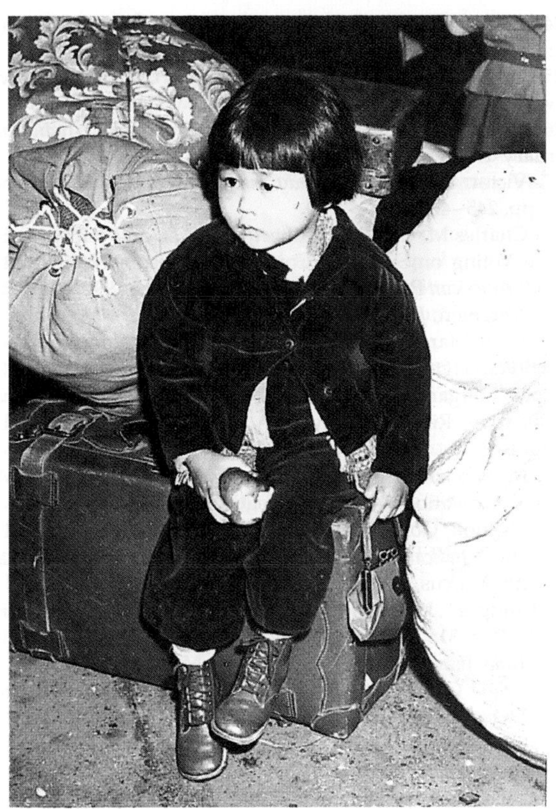

This three-year old awaits relocation to a detention camp in northern California. Yukiko Llewellyn is now an assistant dean of students at the University of Illinois.

of espionage or sabotage or the scanty evidence of such acts by Japanese Americans. Nor did they question the discrimination against these persons. In contrast, the minority was activist, challenging the other two branches. These justices disputed the charges of disloyalty and suspected that discrimination against these persons led to the order.

The minority raised the specter that the Court's ruling would set a dangerous precedent. "A military order, however unconstitutional, is not apt to last longer than the military emergency," Justice Robert Jackson wrote. "But once a judicial opinion rationalizes such an order . . . the Court for all time has validated the principle of racial discrimination . . . and of transplanting American citizens. The principle then lies about like a loaded weapon ready for the hand of any authority that can bring forward a plausible claim of an urgent need."

In December 1944—two-and-a-half years after it began the evacuation and one day before it heard the Court's decision—the military ordered release of all "loyal" Japanese Americans.

Upon release they discovered that the government had failed to keep its promise to protect their property. Many of their possessions stored in warehouses had been vandalized or stolen. Some of their homes had been taken over by strangers, and some of their land had been seized for unpaid taxes.

"They did me a great wrong," Korematsu said. But he returned to live in the same town where he was arrested. "I love this country and I belong here."[85]

Near the end of his career, Justice Douglas expressed regret that he and others in the majority went along with the government. The case "was ever on my conscience."[86] Douglas did not live long enough to learn about research that revealed that the War Department had presented false information to the Court. The department had altered some reports and destroyed others demonstrating the loyalty of the Japanese Americans.[87] From Pearl Harbor until the end of the war, the government had no record of a single incident of sabotage by a Japanese American citizen or alien in this country.

With help from the lawyer who discovered the false information, Korematsu reopened his case through a rarely used procedure available only when the original trial was tainted with prosecutorial misconduct and fraud. In 1983 a federal judge reversed his conviction.[88]

In 1988 Congress passed a law offering a public apology for the internment and $20,000 compensation to each surviving internee.[89]

➤Key Terms

Korematsu v. United States
judicial review
Marbury v. Madison
court-packing plan
Warren Court
Burger Court
Rehnquist Court
district courts
courts of appeals
jurisdiction
habeas corpus
criminal cases
civil cases
standing to sue
writ of certiorari
restrained judges
activist judges
stare decisis

67. Abraham, *Judicial Process*, p. [illegible]

68. William O. Douglas, "Stare Decisis," *Columbia Law Review* [illegible] (1949), pp. 735–[illegible]

69. *U.S. v. Butler*, 297 U.S. 1 (1936), at 79.

70. Murphy and Pritchett, *Courts, Judges and Politics*, [illegible]

71. Baum, *The Supreme Court*, p. [illegible]

72. 110 U.S. 110 [illegible]

73. [illegible] Robert L. Dudley, "Federalism, State Judges and Presidential Power," paper presented at the Midwest Political Science Association Meeting, April, 1983.

74. Baum, *The Supreme Court*, p. 158.

75. Sheldon Goldman, "How Long the Legacy?" *Judicature* 76 (April/May 1993), p. 295.

76. [illegible] (1966).

77. William K. [illegible] "[illegible] Supreme Court [illegible] [illegible] Law Journal 101 (1991), p. [illegible]

78. [illegible]

79. [illegible]

80. John [illegible] and [illegible]

81. [illegible]

82. Abraham, [illegible]

Bill of Rights (Madison, Wis.: University of Wisconsin Press, 1981), p. 282.

49. *Weston v. Illinois*, [illegible] U.S. [illegible] (1951).

50. *Poe v. Ullman*, 367 U.S. 497 (1961).

51. *Griswold v. Connecticut*, 381 U.S. 479 (1965).

52. C. K. Rowland and Bridget Jeffery Todd, "Where You Stand Depends on Who Sits," *Journal of Politics* 53 (February 1991), pp. 175–85.

53. Although the court accepted about 150 cases for oral argument and written opinions (and about an equal number to decide summarily without oral argument and written opinions) each term during the mid-1980s, the Rehnquist Court, [illegible] the docket, heard only 84 cases in the 1993 term.

54. Fred Barbash and Al Kamen, "Supreme Court Is Rushing Way to Form a [illegible]," *Washington Post National Weekly Edition*, October [illegible], 1984, p. [illegible]

55. Robert H. [illegible] (Simon & Schuster, 1990).

56. Lawrence Tribe, *On Reading the Constitution* [illegible] University Press, 1991).

57. *Edwards v. U.S.* [illegible]

58. [illegible]

59. [illegible]

60. [illegible]

61. "[illegible] Moves [illegible]" April [illegible]

62. [illegible]

PART FOUR

Civil Liberties and Rights

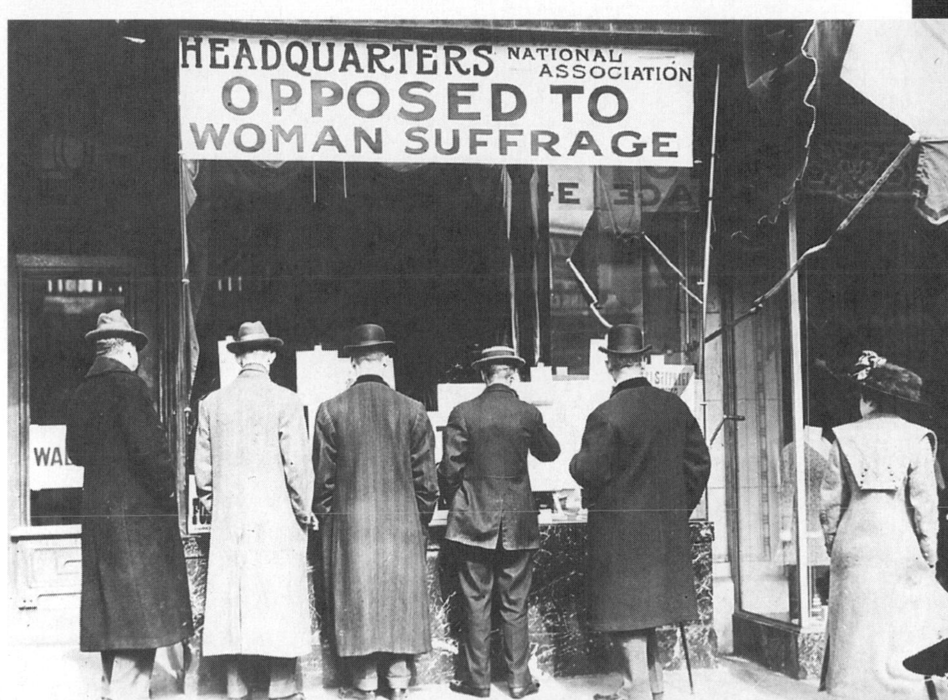

14 Civil Liberties

You Are There

Does Religious Liberty Include Animal Sacrifice?

You are Justice Anthony Kennedy of the U.S. Supreme Court facing an unusual case from Hialeah, Florida. The Church of the Lukumi Babalu Aye has brought suit against the city because of ordinances that restrict the church's practices.

The church follows the Santeria religion, which originated in Nigeria 4000 years ago. The religion spread to Cuba when Nigerians were brought as slaves and eventually to Florida when Cubans fled their communist government. Santeria now blends ancient African rites and Roman Catholic rituals, but its distinguishing and most provocative practice is animal sacrifice. Adherents believe animal sacrifice is necessary to win the favor of the gods, and they practice it at births, marriages, and deaths, and at initiations of new members and priests. Chickens, ducks, doves, pigeons, sheep, goats, and turtles are killed by knife, their blood is drained into pots, and their meat is prepared for eating.

Santeria long existed underground, but the church decided to bring it into the open in 1987, leasing a used-car lot and announcing plans for a church building, cultural center, museum, and school in the Miami suburb. Then "the neighborhood went ape," according to one resident.[1] The city council held an emergency session, at which one council member stated that devotees "are in violation of everything this country stands for," while another quoted the Bible in opposition. The council president asked, "What can we do to prevent the church from opening?"

The city attorney's office drafted a series of ordinances, which the city council passed, that essentially deny adherents the opportunity to practice their religion. Although the ordinances do not explicitly refer to Santeria, they prohibit ritualistic animal sacrifice. They make exception for kosher slaughter for persons who follow Jewish dietary laws.

The church filed suit, claiming that the ordinances impinge on members' free exercise of their religion guaranteed by the First Amendment of the Constitution. The free exercise clause allows individuals to practice their religion as they see fit. Governments cannot restrict a particular religion or practice, unless there is a compelling reason to do so. The city countered that there were compelling reasons: First, animal sacrifice presents a health risk to the adherents, because the animals are uninspected and might be unsanitary, and to the public, because the carcasses sometimes are found rotting in the streets and floating in the canals. (The church responded that it properly disposes of the remains but adherents of Santeria who are not members of the church might not.) Second, animal sacrifice entails cruelty to animals. (The church responded that it humanely kills the animals by slicing their carotid artery, as kosher slaughter does.) Third, animal sacrifice results in emotional injury to children who witness it.

The church's priest, Ernesto Pichardo, suggested that town officials were hypocrites. "You can kill a turkey in your backyard, put it on the table, say a prayer, and serve it for Thanksgiving. But if we pray over the turkey, kill it, then eat it, we violated the law."[2]

CONTINUED 

OUTLINE

The Constitution and the Bill of Rights
- Individual Rights in the Constitution
- The Bill of Rights

Freedom of Expression
- Freedom of Speech
- Freedom of the Press
- Libel and Obscenity
- Freedom of Religion

Rights of Criminal Defendants
- Search and Seizure
- Self-Incrimination
- Counsel
- Jury Trial
- Cruel and Unusual Punishment
- Rights in Theory and in Practice

Right to Privacy
- Birth Control
- Abortion
- Homosexuality
- Right to Die

Conclusion: Are the Courts Responsive in Interpreting Civil Liberties?

Ernesto Pichardo, priest of the Santeria church.

But the federal district court ruled for the city, and the federal court of appeals affirmed. Now it is 1993, and the Supreme Court is deciding the case.

You were appointed by President Reagan because of your conservatism. Actually, you were not Reagan's first choice for this seat. Robert Bork was, but he was denied confirmation because of his more extreme conservatism. Eventually you were nominated because you were less flamboyant and less likely to antagonize the groups and senators who opposed Bork. But in most cases you have voted the way observers predicted Bork would have voted—generally against individual rights and for government authority.

You are a Roman Catholic—you even served as an altar boy—and you seem inclined to accommodate people's religious desires or demands, yet your views appear uncertain. A year ago, for instance, you wrote the majority opinion that invalidated prayers at graduation ceremonies for public elementary, middle, and high schools.[3] In cases involving minority religious practices, you voted to allow Hare Krishnas the right to distribute literature at public airports, yet you voted to deny members of the Native American church the right to use peyote, a hallucinogen, in worship ceremonies.[4] In this case you joined an opinion that could make it difficult for members of minority religions to adhere to their practices.

So how do you decide this case?

Americans value their "rights." Eighteenth-century Americans believed that people had "natural rights" by virtue of being human. Given by God, not by government, the rights could not be taken away by government. Contemporary Americans do not use this term, but they do think about rights much as their forebears did.

Yet Americans have a split personality about their rights. As Chapter 4 described, most people tell pollsters they believe in various constitutional rights in the abstract, but many do not accept these rights when applied to concrete situations. For example, most people say they believe in free speech, but many would not allow Communists, socialists, or atheists to speak in public or teach in schools.

Surveys in the 1990s show that Americans remain divided over their support for civil liberties. Thirty-one percent say freedom of expression should not apply to network television; 28% say it should not apply to newspapers; and 26% say it should not apply to art, film, or music. Fifty-five percent think songs with sexually explicit lyrics should be barred from radio and television, and 50% think books with "dangerous ideas" should be banned from school libraries.[5] Forty percent believe police should be able to search homes of suspected drug dealers without search warrants.[6]

Conflicts over civil liberties and rights have dominated the courts since the Depression. This chapter, covering civil liberties, and the next, covering civil rights, describe how the courts have interpreted these rights and tried to resolve these conflicts. We will explain the most important rights and recount the struggles by individuals and groups to achieve them. We will see how judges act as referees between litigants, brokers among competing groups, and policymakers in the process of deciding these cases.

The Constitution and the Bill of Rights

Individual Rights in the Constitution

Although the term *civil liberties* usually refers to the rights in the Bill of Rights, a few rights are granted in the body of the Constitution. The Constitution bans religious qualifications for federal office and guarantees jury trials in federal criminal cases. It bans **bills of attainder,** which are legislative acts rather than judicial trials pronouncing specific persons guilty of crimes, and **ex post facto laws,** which are legislative acts making some behavior illegal that was not illegal when it was done. The Constitution also prohibits suspension of the writ of habeas corpus, except during rebellion or invasion of the country. These rights are significant, but they by no means exhaust the rights people believed they had at the time the Constitution was written.

The Bill of Rights

Origin and Meaning

The Constitution originally did not include a bill of rights, but to win support for ratification, the Founders promised to adopt amendments to provide such rights. James Madison proposed 12, Congress passed them, and in 1791 the states ratified 10, which came to be known as the Bill of Rights.[7] Of these, the first 8 grant specific rights. (The Ninth says the listing of these rights does not mean they are the only ones the people have; and the Tenth clarifies the relationship between the federal and state governments.)

The Bill of Rights provides rights against the government. According to Justice Hugo Black, it is "a collection of Thou shalt nots" directed at the government.[8] Essentially, the Bill of Rights provides rights for minorities against the majority, because government policy concerning civil liberties tends to reflect the views of the majority.

As Chapter 2 explained, the Founders set up a government to protect property rights for the well-to-do minority against the presumably jealous majority. Separation of powers, checks and balances, and various specific provisions of the Constitution were intended to limit the ability of the masses to curtail the rights of the elites. However, as Americans became more egalitarian and got more opportunity to participate in politics, the importance of property rights has declined while the importance of other rights has increased. At the same time, the role of the Bill of Rights has increased to protect the "have-nots" of society—the unpopular, powerless minorities in conflict with the majority.

Responsibility for interpreting the Bill of Rights generally falls on the courts, especially the federal courts. Because their judges are appointed for life, they are more independent from majority pressure than are elected officials. The Supreme Court, as the highest federal court, is most responsible for defining and protecting these rights.

Application

For many years the Supreme Court applied the Bill of Rights only to the federal government—not to state governments (or local governments, which are under the authority of state governments). The Court ruled that the Bill of Rights restricted only what the federal government could do.[9]

The Founders thought that states, being closer to the people, would be less likely to violate their liberties. Also, they knew that many states had their own bills of rights, and they expected the rest to follow.

The Founders did not realize that states would come to violate people's liberties more frequently than the federal government. State governments, representing smaller, more homogeneous populations, tended to reflect majority sentiment more closely than

Civil Liberties in the Bill of Rights

- First Amendment
  freedom of religion
  freedom of speech, assembly, and association
  freedom of the press
- Second Amendment
  right to keep and bear arms (for individuals in a militia at a time when there was no standing army to protect the country)
- Third Amendment
  forbids quartering soldiers in houses during peacetime
- Fourth Amendment
  forbids unreasonable searches and seizures
- Fifth Amendment
  right to grand jury hearing in criminal cases
  forbids double jeopardy (more than one trial for the same offense)
  forbids compulsory self-incrimination
  right to due process
  forbids taking private property without just compensation
- Sixth Amendment
  right to speedy trial
  right to public trial
  right to jury trial in criminal cases
  right to cross-examine adverse witnesses
  right to present favorable witnesses
  right to counsel
- Seventh Amendment
  right to jury trial in civil cases
- Eighth Amendment
  forbids excessive bail and fines
  forbids cruel and unusual punishment

the federal government, and they often rode roughshod over criminal defendants or racial, religious, or political minorities. When disputes arose, state courts tended to interpret their bills of rights narrowly.

However, starting in 1925[10] and continuing through 1972,[11] the Supreme Court gradually applied most provisions of the Bill of Rights to the states, using the Fourteenth Amendment's due process clause as justification. This clause, adopted after the Civil War to protect blacks from southern governments, reads, "Nor shall any state deprive any person of life, liberty, or property, without due process of law." The clause refers to states and "liberty." it is ambiguous, but the Court interpreted it to mean that states also have to provide the liberties in the Bill of Rights.

The Court has applied all but two provisions of the First and the Fourth through the Eighth Amendments to the states: guarantee of a grand jury in criminal cases and guarantee of a jury trial in civil cases. In addition, the Court has established some rights not in the Bill of Rights, and it has applied these to the states too: presumption of innocence in criminal cases, right to travel within the country, and right to privacy. Thus, most provisions in the Bill of Rights, and even some not in it, now restrict what both the federal and state governments can do.

To see how the Court has interpreted these provisions, we will look at three major areas—freedom of expression, rights of criminal defendants, and right to privacy.

"Let me give you a lesson in American history: James Madison never intended the Bill of Rights to protect riffraff like you."

➤Freedom of Expression

The First Amendment provides freedom of expression, which includes freedom of speech, assembly, and association;[12] freedom of the press; and freedom of religion.

The amendment states that "Congress shall make no law" abridging these liberties. The language is absolute, but few justices interpret it literally. They cite the example of the person who falsely shouts "Fire!" in a crowded theater and causes a stampede that injures someone, and they say the amendment does not protect this expression. So the Court needs to draw a line between expression the amendment protects and that which it does not.

■ Freedom of Speech

Freedom of speech, Justice Black asserted, "is the heart of our government."[13] First, by allowing an open atmosphere, it maximizes the opportunities for every individual to develop his or her personality and potential to the fullest. Second, by encouraging a variety of opinions, it furthers the advancement of knowledge and discovery of truth. Unpopular opinions could be true or partially true. Even if completely false, they could prompt a reevaluation of accepted opinions. Third, by permitting citizens to form opinions and express them to others, it helps them participate in government. It especially helps them check inefficient or corrupt government. Fourth, by channeling conflict toward persuasion, it promotes a stable society. Governments that deny freedom of speech become inflexible; they force conflict toward violence.[14]

Seditious Speech

The first controversies to test the scope of freedom of speech involved **seditious speech,** speech that encourages rebellion against the government. The government historically prosecuted individuals for seditious speech during or shortly after war, when society was most sensitive about loyalty.

Numerous prosecutions came with World War I and the Russian Revolution, which brought the Communists to power in the Soviet Union in 1917. The

Russian Revolution prompted a "Red Scare," in which people feared conspiracies to overthrow the U.S. government. Congress passed the Espionage Act of 1917, which prohibited interfering with military recruitment, inciting insubordination in military forces, and mailing material advocating rebellion; and the Sedition Act of 1918, which prohibited "disloyal, profane, scurrilous, or abusive language about the form of government, Constitution, soldiers and sailors, flag or uniform of the armed forces." Many states passed similar laws. In short, government prohibited a wide range of speech.

During the war the federal government prosecuted almost 2,000 and convicted almost 900 persons under these acts, and the states prosecuted and convicted many others. They prosecuted individuals for saying that war is contrary to the teachings of Jesus, that World War I should not have been declared until after a referendum was held, and that the draft was unconstitutional. Officials even prosecuted an individual for remarking to women knitting clothes for the troops, "No soldier ever sees those socks."[15]

These cases gave the Supreme Court numerous opportunities to rule on seditious speech. In six major cases, the Court upheld the federal and state laws and affirmed the convictions of all the defendants.[16] The defendants advocated socialism or communism, and some advocated the overthrow of the government to achieve it. Except for one—Eugene Debs, the Socialist party's candidate for president—the defendants did not command a large audience. Even so, the Court concluded that these defendants' speech constituted a "clear and present danger" to the government. Justice Edward Sanford wrote, "A single revolutionary spark may kindle a fire that, smouldering for a time, may burst into a sweeping and destructive conflagration."[17] In reality, there was nothing clear or present about the danger; the defendants' speech had little effect.

More prosecutions came after World War II. Congress passed the Smith Act in 1940, which was not as broad as the World War I acts because it did not forbid criticizing the government. But it did forbid advocating overthrow of the government by force and organizing or joining individuals who advocated overthrow.

The act was used against members of the American Communist party after the war. The uneasy alliance between the United States and the Soviet Union had given way to the Cold War between the countries. Politicians, especially Senator Joseph McCarthy (R-Wis.), exploited the tensions. McCarthy charged various government officials with being Communists. He had little evidence, and his tactics were called "witch-hunts" and, eventually, **McCarthyism.** Other Republicans too accused the Democratic administration of covering up Communists. They goaded it into prosecuting members of the Communist party so it would not appear "soft on communism."

In 1951 the Court upheld the Smith Act and affirmed the convictions of 11 top-echelon leaders of the Communist party.[18] These leaders organized the party and the party advocated overthrowing the government by force, but the leaders had not attempted overthrowing it. (If they had, they clearly would have been guilty of crimes.) Even so, the Court majority concluded that they constituted a clear and present danger, and Chief Justice Fred Vinson wrote that the government does not have to "wait until the putsch is about to be executed, the plans have been laid and the signal is awaited" before it can act against the party. The minority argued that the Communist party was not a danger. Justice William Douglas said that the party was "of little consequence. . . . Communism has been so thoroughly exposed in this country that it has been crippled as a political force. Free speech has destroyed it as an effective political party."

Following the Court's decision, the government prosecuted and convicted almost 100 other Communists.

But the Cold War thawed slightly, the Senate voted to condemn McCarthy, and two new members, including Chief Justice Earl Warren, joined the Court. In a series of cases in the 1950s, the Court made it more difficult to convict Communists,[19] thereby incurring the wrath of the public, Congress, and President Eisenhower. In a private conversation, Warren asked Eisenhower what he thought the Court should do with the Communists. Eisenhower replied, "I would kill the S.O.B.s."[20]

The government took other action against Communists. The federal government ordered Communists to register, and then some state governments banned them from public jobs such as teaching, or private jobs such as practicing law or serving as union officers. Legislative committees held hearings to expose and humiliate them. The Court heard numerous cases involving these actions and usually ruled against the government.

The Vietnam War did not prompt the same fears that World Wars I and II did. Congress did not pass comparable laws, perhaps because many "respectable" people opposed this war and also because the

Eugene Debs, the Socialist party's candidate for president, criticized American involvement in World War I and the draft. He was convicted for violating the Espionage Act and sentenced to 10 years in prison. When President Harding pardoned him early, Debs commented, "It is the government that should ask *me* for a pardon."

Court in the 1950s and 1960s increasingly allowed seditious speech.

The Court developed new doctrine for seditious speech in 1969. A Ku Klux Klan leader said at a rally in Ohio that the Klan might take "revengeance" on the president, Congress, and Supreme Court if they continued "to suppress the white, Caucasian race." The leader was convicted under a statute similar to those upheld after World War I, but this time the statute was unanimously struck down by the Court.[21] The justices said people can advocate—enthusiastically, even heatedly—as long as they do not incite illegal action. This broad protection for seditious speech remains in effect today.

Thus, after many years and many cases, the Court concluded that the First Amendment protects seditious speech as much as other speech. Justice Douglas noted that "the threats were often loud but always puny."[22] Even the attorney general who prosecuted the major Communist cases later admitted that the cases were "squeezed oranges. I didn't think there was much to them."[23] Nevertheless, the Court had permitted a climate of fear to overwhelm the First Amendment for many years.

Public Forum

People usually communicate with each other in private. But sometimes speakers want more listeners and they use public places where people congregate. This means speakers will be heard by some listeners who do not like their message or their use of public places to disseminate it, and it also means speakers might disrupt the normal purposes of these places.

The Court holds that individuals have a right to use public places, such as streets, sidewalks, and parks, to express their views on public issues. These places constitute the **public forum** and serve as "the poor person's printing press."

When speakers seek to use other public facilities, the Court has to determine which ones are also part of the public forum. It decided that federal and state capitol grounds,[24] Supreme Court grounds,[25] and public school grounds[26] are part of the forum. It decided that blacks could protest library segregation at a public library[27] and promoters could show the rock musical *Hair* at a public theater[28] because these too are part of the forum.

On the other hand, the Court decided that civil rights activists could not demonstrate against jail segregation outside a jail because of the need for security,[29] and Dr. Benjamin Spock—the baby doctor—and other antiwar activists could not encourage opposition to the Vietnam War at an army base because of the need for discipline in the army.[30]

Normally only publicly owned facilities are considered part of the public forum, but the proliferation of shopping centers and malls prompted speakers to use

At congressional hearings Senator Joseph McCarthy identified locations of alleged Communists and "fellow travelers."

these privately owned facilities to reach crowds of shoppers. The Warren Court permitted them to do so, saying that shopping centers and malls are similar to downtown shopping districts where streets and sidewalks are part of the public forum.[31] But the Burger Court overruled the Warren Court, emphasizing property rights rather than First Amendment rights in this situation.[32]

Even in public forums people cannot speak whenever and however they want. The Court has divided speech into three kinds—pure speech, speech plus conduct, and symbolic speech—and established doctrine for each.

Pure Speech

Pure speech is speech without any conduct (besides the speech itself). Individuals can say what they want as long as they do not cause a breach of the peace or a riot, or hurl "fighting words" at specific persons, except at police officers, who are supposed to be trained and disciplined to take abuse.[33]

Before the Court's ruling in 1972, arrests for swearing were common. In the District of Columbia, for example, more than half of the 15,000 to 20,000 arrests for "disorderly conduct" each year involved swearing, usually at police.[34]

Individuals can use offensive language in many situations.[35] During the Vietnam War, a man walked through the corridors of the Los Angeles County courthouse wearing a jacket with the words "Fuck the Draft" emblazoned on the back. Police arrested him. The Court reversed his conviction, and 72-year-old Justice John Harlan remarked that "one man's vulgarity is another's lyric."[36]

The media, however, cannot broadcast some offensive language. A California radio station broadcast a monologue by comedian George Carlin. Titled "Filthy Words," it lampooned society's sensitivity to seven words that "you couldn't say on the public airwaves . . . the ones you definitely wouldn't say, ever." The seven words, according to the Federal Communications Commission report, included "a four-letter word for excrement" repeated 70 times in 12 minutes. In a close vote, the Court ruled that although the monologue was part of a serious program on contemporary attitudes toward language, it was not protected under the First Amendment because people, including children, tuning the radio could be subjected to the language in their home.[37]

Yet the Court struck down a Utah law restricting "indecent material" on cable television. The difference apparently is that people choose to subscribe and pay for cable television.[38]

Speech Plus Conduct

Speech plus conduct is speech combined with conduct that is intended to convey ideas—for example, a demonstration in which protesters chant slogans or carry signs with slogans (the speech) and march, picket, or sit-in (the conduct).

Individuals can demonstrate, but they are subject to some restrictions. Places in the public forum are used for other purposes besides demonstrating, and individuals cannot disrupt these activities. They cannot, Justice Arthur Goldberg remarked, hold "a street meeting in the middle of Times Square at the rush hour."[39] To avoid this, governments can require them to obtain a permit, which can specify the place, time, and manner of the demonstration. However, officials cannot allow one group to demonstrate but forbid another, no matter how much they dislike the group or its message. They cannot forbid the group even if they say they fear violence, unless the group actually threatens violence. In short, officials may establish restrictions to avoid disruption, but they may not use these restrictions to censor speech.

Accordingly, lower federal courts required the Chicago suburb of Skokie to permit the American Nazi party to demonstrate in front of the town hall in

1978.[40] About 40,000 of Skokie's population of 70,000 were Jews. Of these, hundreds had survived the German Nazi concentration camps during World War II, and thousands had lost relatives who died in the camps. The city, edgy about the announced demonstration, passed ordinances that prohibited wearing "military-style" uniforms and distributing material that "promotes and incites hatred against persons by reason of their race, national origin, or religion." These ordinances were thinly disguised attempts to bar the demonstration, and the courts threw them out. One quoted Justice Oliver Wendell Holmes's statement that "if there is any principle of the Constitution that more imperatively calls for attachment than any other it is the principle of free thought—not free thought for those who agree with us but freedom for the thought we hate."[41]

The Rehnquist Court, however, did uphold a Milwaukee suburb's ordinance that prohibited picketing at a residence.[42] The city passed the ordinance after antiabortionists had picketed, six times in one month, the home of a doctor who performed abortions. Although protesters can march through residential neighborhoods, the Court said, a city can prohibit them from focusing on a particular home. Thus the Court emphasized the right to privacy at home over the right to demonstrate in this situation.

The Rehnquist Court addressed another potential restriction on demonstrations when homosexual groups demanded to be included in the St. Patrick's Day parade in Boston. The parade, though not as political as most demonstrations, was a form of expression, and the Court unanimously concluded that the private sponsors cannot be forced to include an unwanted message—recognition or acceptance of gay groups.[42a] These groups could hold their own parade.

Symbolic Speech

Symbolic speech is the use of symbols, rather than words, to convey ideas.

During the Vietnam War, men burned their draft cards to protest the draft and the war. This was powerful expression, and Congress tried to stifle it by passing a law prohibiting destruction of draft cards. The Supreme Court was uncomfortable with symbolic speech and reluctant to protect it. Even Chief Justice Warren worried that this would mean that "an apparently limitless variety of conduct can be labeled 'speech.' " The court upheld the law.[43]

One year later, however, the Court was willing to protect symbolic speech. A junior high and two senior high school students in Des Moines, Iowa, including Mary Beth Tinker, wore black armbands to protest the war. They were suspended, and they sued school officials. Public schools, Justice Abe Fortas said, "may not be enclaves of totalitarianism." They must allow students freedom of speech, providing students do not disrupt the schools.[44]

In the 1960s and 1970s, many students wore long hair or beards in violation of school policy. Some claimed they did so to protest "establishment culture." Blacks and Indians claimed they wore Afros and braids to show racial pride. Federal courts of appeals split evenly as to whether this was symbolic speech. The Supreme Court refused to hear any of these cases, so there was no uniform law across the country.

Some individuals treated the American flag disrespectfully to protest the Vietnam War. A Massachusetts man wore a flag patch on the seat of his pants and was sentenced to six months in jail. A Washington student taped a peace symbol on a flag and then hung the flag, upside down, outside his apartment. The Court reversed both convictions.[45]

When a member of the Revolutionary Communist Youth Brigade burned an American flag outside the Republican Convention in Dallas in 1984, the justices faced the issue of actual desecration of the flag. The Rehnquist Court surprisingly permitted this symbolic speech.[46] Two Reagan-appointed conservatives, Jus-

Mary Beth Tinker, here with her mother and brother, wore a black armband at school to protest the Vietnam War.

tices Anthony Kennedy and Antonin Scalia, joined the three most liberal members of the Court to forge a bare majority. The foremost free speech advocate on the bench, Justice William Brennan, wrote that the First Amendment cannot be limited just because this form of expression offends some people. "We do not consecrate the flag by punishing its desecration, for in doing so we dilute the freedom that this cherished emblem represents." The ruling invalidated laws of 48 states (not Alaska or Wyoming) and the federal government.

Chief Justice Rehnquist emotionally criticized the decision. He said the First Amendment should not apply because the flag is a unique national symbol. He recounted the history of the "Star-Spangled Banner" and the music of John Philip Sousa's "Stars and Stripes Forever"; he quoted poems by Ralph Waldo Emerson and John Greenleaf Whittier that refer to the flag; and he discussed the role of the "Pledge of Allegiance."

Civil liberties advocates praised the decision. One lawyer for the defendant said, "If free expression is to exist in this country, people must be as free to burn the flag as they are to wave it." Another said veterans should cheer the decision because it shows that the values in the Bill of Rights that they fought for are intact. Yet veterans groups were outraged.

After administration officials assessed public opinion by monitoring talk shows, President Bush stood in front of the Iwo Jima Memorial and proposed a constitutional amendment to override the decision.[47] Members of Congress, always anxious to appear patriotic, lined up in support. But some, especially Democrats, later came out in opposition. They criticized the proposal for creating an unprecedented exception to the First Amendment. Instead of the proposed amendment, Congress passed a statute prohibiting flag desecration. Apparently a majority felt that this less permanent substitute would be an adequate shield against the public's wrath. Yet in 1990, the justices, dividing the same way, declared the statute unconstitutional for the same reasons they reversed the Dallas conviction.[48] President Bush, this time waving a model of the Iwo Jima Memorial, proposed another constitutional amendment, and Senate Republican Leader Robert Dole (Kan.) warned Democrats that their opposition to the amendment "would make a good 30-second spot" for the upcoming elections, but Congress rejected the amendment. Members sensed less pressure from the public. By this second year of debate on this issue, the initial emotional reaction of the public had ebbed. More voices had spoken out against dilution of the First Amendment.

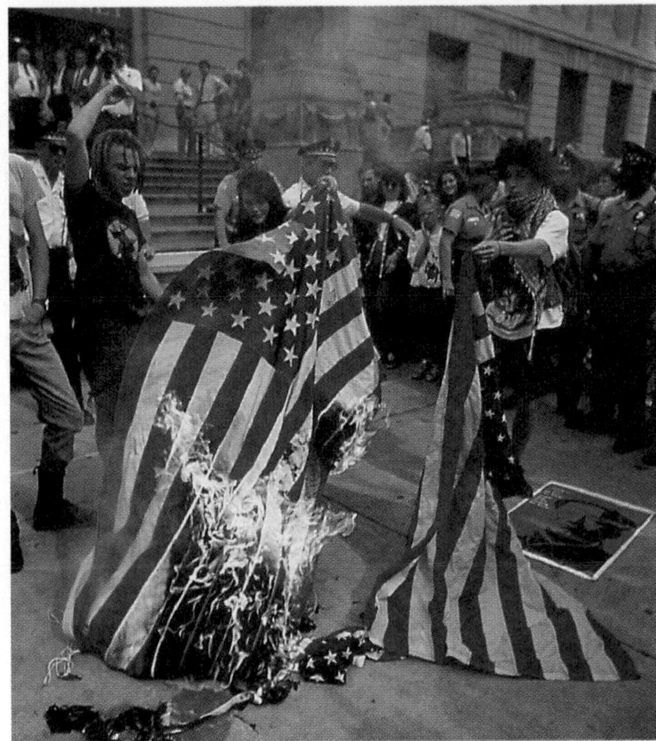

Protestors torch flags in Chicago.

Freedom of the Press

Unlike most civil liberties cases, which pit a relatively powerless individual or group against the government, freedom of press cases usually feature a more powerful publisher or broadcaster against the government. Even so, these cases still involve rights against the government.

Prior Restraint

The core of freedom of the press is freedom from **prior restraint**—censorship. If the press violates laws prohibiting, for example, libelous or obscene material, it can be punished after publishing such materials. But freedom from prior restraint means the press at least has the opportunity to publish what it thinks is appropriate.

Freedom from prior restraint is not absolute. At the height of the Vietnam War, the secretary of defense in the Johnson administration, Robert McNamara, became disenchanted with the war and ordered a thorough study of our involvement. The study, called "The Pentagon Papers," laid bare the reasons the country was embroiled—reasons not as honorable as the ones officials had been giving the public—and it questioned the effectiveness of military policy. The study was so revealing that McNamara remarked to a friend, "They could hang people for what's in there."[49] He printed only 15 copies and classified them "Top Secret" so few persons could see them. One of the 36 authors, Daniel Ellsberg, originally supported the war but later turned against it. In 1971 he photocopied the papers and gave them to the *New York Times* and *Washington Post*, which published excerpts.

The Nixon administration sought injunctions to restrain the newspapers from publishing more excerpts, but the Supreme Court refused to grant them.[50] Most justices said they would grant injunctions if publishing the papers clearly jeopardized national security. But information in the papers was historical; it did not directly hinder the war effort. Thus, the rule remained—no prior restraint—but exceptions were possible.

The Rehnquist Court did approve prior restraint in a situation far removed from national security. When journalism students at a St. Louis high school wrote articles for their newspaper about the impact of pregnancy and of parents' divorce on teenagers, the principal deleted the articles and three of the students sued. The Court, noting that students below the college level have fewer rights than adults, decided that officials can censor school publications.[51]

The chief of the presses of the *Washington Post* hails the Supreme Court's decision allowing publication of the Pentagon Papers.

Principals have exercised their authority typically over articles covering school policies or social issues. A Colorado principal blocked an editorial criticizing his study hall policy while allowing another editorial praising it. A Texas principal banned an article about the class valedictorian who succeeded despite the death of her mother, the desertion of her father, and her own pregnancy. An editorial urging students to be more responsible about sex was censored by a Kentucky principal, who feared it could be interpreted as condoning sex, while a survey on AIDS was censored by a Maryland principal, who prohibited students from defining the term "safe sex." A North Carolina high school newspaper was shut down and its advisor was fired because of three articles, including a satirical story about the "death" of the writer after eating a cheeseburger from the school cafeteria.

High school newspaper advisers, according to a 1994 survey, said principals have tightened their control in recent years. Over a third of the advisers reported that principals have rejected articles or required changes in articles for their paper.[52]

Despite these exceptions to freedom from prior restraint, the press in the United States is freer than that in Great Britain, where freedom from prior restraint began. Britain has no First Amendment and tolerates more secrecy. In 1987 the government barred publication of controversial and embarrassing memoirs by a former security service agent, even though they were being published in the United States at the time. A year later the government banned radio and television interviews with all members of the outlawed Irish Republican Army (IRA) and its political party, including its one representative in Parliament.[53] The government even banned broadcast of a song by a popular folk group because the lyrics supported people convicted of IRA bombings. During the Persian Gulf War, the French government banned sale of a song—"Go For It Saddam"—that criticized the West. After neo-Nazi violence in 1992, the German government banned the sale of music by skinhead groups.

Restrictions on Gathering News

Although prior restraint is an obvious limitation on freedom of the press, restrictions on gathering news in the first place are less obvious but no less serious. They also keep news from the public.

Leanne Tippell and Leslie Smart, two of the St. Louis high school students who sued their school for suppressing their student newspaper story, meet with their attorney, Leslie Edwards (left).

The Burger Court was not vigilant in guarding the press from these restrictions. Most important, it denied reporters a right to keep the names of their sources confidential. In investigative reporting, reporters frequently rely on sources who demand anonymity in exchange for information. The sources might have sensitive positions in government or relations with criminals that would be jeopardized if their names were publicized. A Louisville reporter was allowed to watch persons make hashish from marijuana if he kept their names confidential. But after publication of the story, a grand jury demanded their names. When the reporter refused to reveal them, he was cited for contempt of court, and his conviction was upheld by the Supreme Court.[54] The majority said reporters' need for confidentiality is not as great as the judicial system's need for information about crimes. So either reporters cannot guarantee potential sources anonymity, or reporters might have to choose between breaking their promise or being cited for contempt and jailed for an indefinite period of time.

Invasion of Privacy

The right to a free press can conflict with an individual's right to privacy when the press publishes personal information. The Supreme Court has permitted the press to publish factual information. For example, although a Georgia law prohibited the press from releasing names of crime victims to spare them embarrassment, an Atlanta television station announced the name of a high school girl who was raped by six classmates and left unconscious on a neighbor's lawn to die. The girl's father sued the station, but the Court said the press needs freedom to publish information that is a matter of public record so citizens can scrutinize the workings of the judicial system.[55]

In 1975 a man in a crowd of people watching President Gerald Ford noticed a woman pull out a gun. He grabbed the gun and prevented the assassination. Reporters wrote stories about this hero, including the fact that he was a homosexual. This caused the man embarrassment and some practical problems and he sued. The courts sided with the press again. The man's good deed made him newsworthy, whether he wanted to be or not.[56] Persons who become newsworthy are permitted little privacy. Justice Brennan said this is a necessary evil "in a society which places a primary value on freedom of speech and of press."[57]

Libel and Obscenity

Despite broad protection for the press overall, courts grant much less protection for libelous and obscene material. Traditionally, they considered such material irrelevant to the exposition of ideas and search for truth envisioned by the framers of the First Amendment. Whatever benefit such material might have was outweighed by the need to protect persons' reputations and morals. Courts thus allowed states to adopt and implement libel and obscenity laws as they saw fit.

Libel

Libel consists of printed or broadcast statements that are false and that tarnish someone's reputation. Victims are entitled to sue for money to compensate them for the damage.

The Warren Court decided that traditional state libel laws infringed on freedom of the press too much and forced radical changes in these laws. Its landmark decision came in *New York Times v. Sullivan* in 1964.[58]

The *Times* ran an ad by black clergymen who criticized Montgomery, Alabama, officials for their handling of racial protests. The ad contained some trivial inaccuracies. It did not mention any officials by name, but the commissioner of police claimed it referred to him implicitly, and he sued. The local jury ordered the *Times* to pay him a half million dollars! The Court could see that the law was used to punish a detested northern newspaper for an ad that criticized the handling of controversial civil rights protests. And the Court could not ignore the size of the award or the fact that another jury had ordered the *Times* to pay another commissioner a half million dollars for the same ad. It was apparent that libel laws could be used to wreak vengeance on a critical press.

The Court ruled against the police commissioner and made it harder for public officials to win libel suits. It said officials must show not only that the statements about them were false but also that the statements were made with "reckless disregard for the truth." This provides the press some leeway to make mistakes and print false statements, as long as the press is not careless to the point of recklessness.

This protection for the press is necessary, according to Justice Brennan, because "the central meaning of the First Amendment" is that individuals should have the right to criticize officials' conduct. This statement prompted one legal scholar to herald the decision "an occasion for dancing in the streets."[59]

In later cases the Court extended this ruling to public figures—persons other than public officials who have public prominence or who thrust themselves into public figures: candidates for public office,[60] a retired general who spoke for right-wing causes,[61] a real estate developer,[62] and a university athletic director.[63] The Court justified making it harder for public controversies. The court held several persons to be public figures to win libel suits by saying that they sometimes influence public policy as much as public officials do. They also are newsworthy enough to get coverage to rebut any false charges against them.

The Burger Court was less inclined to consider various persons public figures,[64] but it maintained the core of the Warren Court's doctrine, which shifted the emphasis from protection of personal reputation to protection of press freedom.

Hate Speech on Campus and the First Amendment

A student puts a sign on her dorm room door that announces, "People who will be shot on sight—preppies, bimbos, men without chest hair, and homos."

A fraternity holds a "slave auction" as a fund-raiser. White pledges in blackface and Afro wigs perform skits. Afterward, audience members bid on the performers.

Two black students find the letters "KKK" carved into their dorm room door and a note saying, "African monkeys, why don't you go back to the jungle."

After a class discussion of media treatment of African Americans, a black woman receives a card asking her to have "a very bad Christmas" and calling her a "nigger."

Such incidents have forced members of college and university communities—students, faculty, and administrators—to consider in a real and personal way the meaning of the First Amendment. Many conclude that hate speech should be prohibited and that students who engage in it should be punished. They argue that students who hurl epithets or slurs at others, especially anonymously, are more interested in intimidating than in initiating a dialogue about issues. They also argue that civility and tolerance must be maintained. Otherwise, victims of such speech are made to feel unwelcome on campus and in some cases are kept from concentrating on their studies. A student who was jeered nightly by students taunting "Faggot!" said, "When you are told you are not worth anything, it is difficult to function."[1]

Some legal scholars believe hate speech could be a violation of the Fourteenth Amendment's equal protection clause—which guarantees "equal protection of the laws" and restricts discrimination in society—if it creates a hostile and intimidating environment for minority students.[2]

However, other scholars believe such speech is protected by the First Amendment. Precedents described in this chapter emphasize that even repulsive speech is allowed. Indeed, the First Amendment would be meaningless if only speech acceptable to everybody were protected.

Critics of speech codes point to history: The First Amendment has helped minorities make their case against discrimination. By thwarting southern law enforcement officials' efforts to censor and intimidate the media, the amendment helped the civil rights movement gain national support. On the other hand, censorship has been used against minorities. It is shortsighted to expect new censorship to be used primarily for minorities against majorities. New censorship could be directed at students and speakers who say the sorts of things Malcolm X once said.

Critics also say the codes could be directed at students who make relatively innocuous comments. A Brown University student was the first casualty. He was expelled for shouting "nigger" and "faggot" to no one in particular while drunk. A University of Pennsylvania student faced disciplinary action for yelling, "Shut up, you water buffalo. If you're looking for a party, there's a zoo a mile from here," to a dozen sorority sisters singing loudly outside his dorm window while he was writing a paper one night. It turns out that the women were black and the remark was considered a racial slur.[3] (The women who filed the grievance later dropped it.)

This shift in emphasis has aided the press tremendously at a time when its coverage of controversial events has angered much of the public. Increasingly since the 1960s, individuals and groups have sued the press not primarily to win compensation for damage to personal reputations but to punish it. A lawyer for a conservative organization admitted that the organization sought "the dismantling" of CBS by suing the network for its depiction of the army general commanding the U.S. military in Vietnam.[65]

Although the press has an advantage in the law when public officials or figures bring suits, lawsuits are expensive to defend against. A recent case cost the *Washington Post* more than a million dollars in defense expenses at the trial court level alone.[66] The expense puts pressure on the press to refrain from publishing controversial material. Large news organizations can withstand most of this pressure, but many small ones cannot. After 12 libel suits in as many years, the publisher of 6 weekly newspapers in suburban Philadelphia halted his papers' investigative reporting. "I found myself vigorously defending the First Amendment and watching my business go to hell," he said. "Now the communities our papers serve no longer learn about the misconduct of their officials."[67]

Obscenity

Obscenity also pits conservative groups against the media, albeit a small and specialized part of the media. Yet there are important differences. Whereas it is relatively clear what libel is and who the victim is, it is not at all clear what obscenity is and who, if anyone, the victim is. It is not even clear why the law needs to deal with it. Some say it is necessary because

Continued

Critics observe that more than any other institutions, colleges and universities traditionally have fostered free inquiry and free expression. They have allowed, even encouraged, a variety of views so the views could be debated.

The answer to the problem, these critics contend, is more, not less, speech. According to the theory of free expression, the remedy for bad ideas is more speech to demonstrate why the ideas are wrong. Four black women at Arizona State University passed a dorm room door with a "job application form" for minority applicants. The form asked for:

- Sources of income: (1) theft, (2) welfare, (3) unemployment;
- Marital status: (1) common law, (2) shacked up, (3) other;
- Number of legitimate children (if any).

Although ASU had a speech code, the women did not try to invoke it or even approach the administration. First they knocked on the door and told one of the occupants what they thought of the form. Then they organized an open meeting in the dorm. Eventually there was a news conference, a rally, and a program on African American history in the dorm. All along there was a lively exchange in the campus newspaper. The women accomplished more, and in the process kept the focus on racism rather than on a speech code.[4]

Many schools enacted speech codes, but federal district courts struck down codes at the Universities of Michigan and Wisconsin on grounds that they were overly broad and inherently vague.[5] The Supreme Court has not ruled on the constitutionality of these codes, but it struck down a St. Paul, Minnesota, ordinance that prohibited people from writing graffiti and displaying objects such as a Nazi swastika or a burning cross on public or private property.[6] This ruling probably means that the Court would invalidate campus speech codes as well.

However, the Court did say that illegal *conduct* associated with the speech can be punished. A person who erects a burning cross on private property can be prosecuted for trespassing, starting an open fire, and littering, or for such major crimes as arson and making terroristic threats. Similarly, students who engage in hate speech in some situations might be punished for defacing public property or making terroristic threats.

1. Mary Jordan, "Free Speech Starts to Have Its Say," *Washington Post National Weekly Edition*, September 21–27, 1992, p. 31.
2. Mary Ellen Gale, "On Curbing Racial Speech," *The Responsive Community* (Winter 1990–91), pp. 53, 57.
3. Mike Littwin, "Penn's Water Buffalo Debate," *Lincoln Journal* (Baltimore Sun), May 13, 1993.
4. Nat Hentoff, "The Right Thing at ASU," *Washington Post National Weekly Edition*, July 1–7, 1991, p. 28.
5. *Doe v. University of Michigan*, 721 F.Supp. 852 (E.D. Mich., 1989); Jordan, "Free Speech Starts To Have Its Say." A California court also struck down Stanford University's antiharassment code, which was similar to a speech code.
6. *R.A.V. v. St. Paul*, 120 L.Ed.2d 305 (1992). Yet the Court has upheld state laws that provide longer sentences for violent crimes motivated by bias than for the same crimes without evidence of bias. *Wisconsin v. Mitchell*, 124 L.Ed.2d 436 (1993).

obscenity is immoral; others say it is necessary because obscenity leads to improper behavior (although this link is uncertain). The justices themselves have disagreed, perhaps more than in any other area, and their decisions reflect this. They have been neither clear nor consistent.

The Warren Court decided that state obscenity laws restricted publication of sexual material that should be allowed. While maintaining that the First Amendment does not protect obscenity, the Court narrowed the definition of obscenity in a series of cases in the 1950s and 1960s.[68]

The Burger Court, however, thought the Warren Court went too far. When a man and his mother received an ad for a book entitled *Orgies Illustrated,* their suit gave the justices an opportunity to broaden the definition of obscenity somewhat.[69] Now the Court defines obscenity as sexual material that is patently offensive to the average person in the community and that lacks any serious literary, artistic, or scientific value. The Court generally permits state legislatures and local juries, in passing statutes and deciding cases, to determine if this definition applies to certain types of material.

But some local officials got carried away. A prosecutor in Charlottesville, Virginia, announced that he would prosecute persons who sold *Playboy* magazine. Jurors in Albany, Georgia, convicted a theater manager who showed the movie *Carnal Knowledge.* The movie, which featured explicit language and occasional nudity, was nominated for an Academy Award as the best film of the year. The Burger Court reversed the conviction and announced that local communities have discretion but not "unbridled discretion."[70]

In 1990 a prosecutor in Cincinnati put the director of an art gallery on trial for an exhibit of photographs by Robert Mapplethorpe. The homoerotic pictures, which the director called "tough, brutal, sometimes disgusting," included three showing penetration of a man's anus with various objects. Yet the prosecutor could not prove that they lacked serious artistic value, because the photographer has received praise from art critics and the pictures, of course, were displayed in an art gallery, so the jury acquitted the director.

The Burger Court did not succeed in its efforts to reduce the availability of sexual material. A survey asking prosecutors across the country to compare the years immediately before the Burger Court redefined obscenity with those immediately after found, surprisingly, that they prosecuted fewer cases. Prosecutors said the public is less concerned about obscenity, so jurors are less likely to convict.[71]

The continuing flow and increasing violence of pornography prompted some radical feminists, in alliance with religious fundamentalists, to advocate new antipornography statutes. They maintain that pornography discriminates against women by degrading them and portraying them as willing targets for violent sex. In response, Indianapolis passed a statute that defined pornography as "the sexually explicit subordination of women"—material in which women were "sexual objects for domination . . . or use" or depicted in "positions of servility or submission or display." The statute allowed women who believed themselves victims of pornography to sue for a court order banning such material and, possibly, for monetary damages. The proponents' aim was to encourage enough women to sue to drive the purveyors out of business.

A coalition of book and magazine publishers, distributors, and sellers challenged the law. They said it was so broad and vague it could apply to many nonpornographic books and magazines. The American Civil Liberties Union (ACLU) maintained that it could apply to books such as Ian Fleming's James Bond stories and movies like *Last Tango in Paris.* Some feminist writers said it could apply to feminist literature.

The federal district court judge, a woman, ruled the statute unconstitutional. She said its breadth and vagueness would prohibit much sexual material now permitted by the Supreme Court and would severely restrict the First Amendment. The Supreme Court affirmed the decision.[72]

Despite the Court's refusal to broaden its definition of obscenity further, it does allow cities, through zoning ordinances, to scatter "adult" theaters and bookstores to avoid seedy districts that might attract criminals, or to concentrate them to avoid location in neighborhoods where they might offend residents or passersby.[73] The Court acknowledged that such ordinances help preserve the quality of urban life.

Overall the court seems close to saying, in the words of one scholar, "If people want it, they can have it. But they shouldn't subject everyone else to it."[74]

Freedom of Religion

Some people came to America for religious liberty, but once they got here many did not want to allow others this liberty. Some communities here were as intolerant

American Diversity

Can They Be "As Nasty as They Wanna Be"?

When the rap group 2 Live Crew released its album "As Nasty As They Wanna Be," a Florida lawyer who is a born-again Christian and a crusader against pornography sent copies of the lyrics to the governor and every sheriff in the state. The lawyer likens himself to Batman—he wears a Batman watch and distributes copies of his driver's license with Batman's photograph pasted over his own—and says he needs to help law enforcement officials. The Cuban-born Broward County sheriff, who as a public official has a history of flamboyant actions that attract publicity, mobilized his deputies to protect citizens against the album. They arrested a record store owner for selling the album and then arrested members of the group for singing lyrics from the album in an adult nightclub in Fort Lauderdale.[1]

Is the album obscene? According to current doctrine, it is obscene if it is patently offensive to the average person in the community and if it lacks serious artistic value. This doctrine from the Burger Court differs from that of the Warren Court primarily in its emphasis on the local community. Where the Warren Court based the definition on the views of the average person in the country, the Burger Court spoke of the average person in the community. The Warren Court reasoned, "It is, after all, a national Constitution we are expounding."[2] But the Burger Court countered that the Constitution should not require "the people of Maine or Mississippi [to] accept public depiction of conduct found tolerable in Las Vegas or New York."[3] So the decision in these cases would be made according to the views of the average person in Broward County.

Is the album patently offensive? The songs are about sex, and they feature explicit lyrics, including descriptions of oral sex, group sex, and masturbation, moans at appropriate moments, and a beat that mimics sexual passion. According to an evangelical group, the 79-minute album refers to genitalia 117 times (1.4 times per minute).[4] In addition, the songs are mean-spirited and sometimes violent; they exhibit, in the words of one critic, "a knuckle sandwich approach to women."[5] The rappers, who use the word "bitch" 163 times, speak of rape and ripping open women's vaginas.

Does the album lack serious artistic value? According to some students of African American culture, the album reflects the vernacular tradition of this culture.[6] In particular, it reflects the oral tradition of inner-city speech, with its profanity, satire, and exaggeration. This tradition includes pretense—acting out the folklore of the streets. Other African Americans, however, are offended by the lyrics and the depiction of women in them.

The residents of the county were called upon to decide. In a civil suit preceding the criminal cases, a Hispanic male judge found the album obscene, making it the first musical recording ever banned by a court in this country. Then a jury of six whites, mostly women, convicted the record store owner. Just two weeks later a jury of five whites and one black, also mostly women, acquitted the members of the group for their live performance. These jurors said they thought the album had artistic value.

These decisions have implications for the Court's obscenity doctrine. Is it possible to define a single "community standard" anywhere, let alone in cities or counties with ethnically and religiously diverse populations? Who or what determines the community standard? Men or women? Whites or blacks or Hispanics? Middle-class norms or those of the ghetto? When the jury convicted the record store owner, he yelled, "They don't know nothing about the . . . ghetto! . . . The verdict does not reflect my community standards as a black man in Broward County."[7] Even assuming it is possible to define a single "community standard," is it reasonable to expect laypersons to assess the artistic value of material they find offensive? Is it reasonable to ask a Hispanic judge and white jurors to gauge the artistic merit of black rap music?

Meanwhile, the controversy propelled the album toward the two-million sales mark.

1. Laura Parker, "How Things Got Nasty in Broward County," *Washington Post National Weekly Edition,* June 25–July 1, 1990, p. 10.
2. *Jacobellis v. Ohio,* 378 U.S. 184 (1964).
3. *Miller v. California,* 413 U.S. 15 (1973).
4. Paul Gray, "Grapevine," *Time,* July 2, 1990, p. 13.
5. Richard Lacayo, "The Rap Against a Rap Group," *Time,* June 25, 1990, p. 18.
6. For a good discussion, see David Mills, "The Judge vs. 2 Live Crew," *Washington Post National Weekly Edition,* June 25–July 1, 1990, pp. 9–10.
7. "Which Community's Standards?" *Lincoln Journal,* October 10, 1990.

The country's religious diversity has led to demands for some exotic exemptions. Inspired by the Bible's statement that Jesus' followers "shall take up serpents" and "if they drink any deadly thing, it shall not hurt them," members of the Holiness Church of God in Jesus' Name handle snakes and drink strychnine. Some become enraptured and entranced to the point of hysteria, and occasionally some die. In 1975 the Tennessee Supreme Court forbade such practices, saying that the state has "the right to guard against the unnecessary creation of widows and orphans." However, the practices continue in some places.

Early decisions by the Supreme Court usually reflected the first of these traditions. In 1892 Justice David Brewer smugly declared that "this is a Christian nation."[88] But as the country became more pluralistic, the Court moved toward the second of these traditions. Since the early 1960s, the Court generally has interpreted the establishment clause not only to forbid government from designating an official church, like the Church of England in England, but also to forbid government from aiding one religion over another or even from aiding religion over nonreligion.

Courts have used the clause to resolve disputes about prayer in public schools. In 1962 and 1963, the Supreme Court issued its famous, or infamous, prayer rulings. New York had students recite a nondenominational prayer at the start of every day, and Pennsylvania and Baltimore had students recite the "Lord's Prayer" or Bible verses. The Court, with only one justice dissenting, ruled that these practices violated the establishment clause.[89] The prayers technically were voluntary; students could leave the room. But the Court doubted that the prayers really were voluntary. It noted that nonconforming students would face tremendous pressure from teachers and peers, and that leaving the room usually connotes being bad and being punished. Thus, the Court said the prayers fostered religion. According to Justice Black, "Government in this country should stay out of the business of writing and sanctioning official prayers and leave that purely religious function to the people themselves and to those the people choose to look to for religious guidance." Schools could teach about religion, but they cannot promote it.

Many people sharply criticized the rulings. A representative from Alabama lamented, "They put the Negroes in the schools, and now they've driven God out."[90] Actually, the justices had not driven God out because students could pray on their own anytime they felt the need.

A survey of teachers two years after the rulings found that prayers and Bible readings had decreased but by no means disappeared. Schools in the West, East, and, to a lesser extent, the Midwest generally complied with the rulings, but schools in the South overwhelmingly refused to.[91] For example, just 1 of 121 districts in Tennessee fully complied. A local official said, "I saw no reason to create controversy," and another asserted, "I am of the opinion that 99% of the people in the United States feel as I do about the Supreme Court's decision—that it was an outrage. . . . The remaining 1% do not belong in this free world."[92]

Despite the passage of time, periodic news reports indicate that many schools, especially in the rural South, still use prayers or Bible readings in violation of the Court's rulings.

Congress considered a constitutional amendment to overturn the rulings but did not pass one for several reasons. Some people support the rulings. Others support the Court and do not want to challenge its authority and thereby set a precedent for other groups on other matters. Some religious leaders doubt that groups would ever agree about specific prayers. America's religious diversity means that the prayers would offend some students or parents. Prayers that suit Christians might not suit Jews; those that suit Jews might not suit persons of other faiths. Recent immigrants from Asia and the Middle East, practicing Buddhism, Shintoism, Taoism, and Islam, have made the country even more pluralistic. Now, according to one researcher, America's religious diversity is greater than that of any country in recorded history.[93] Thus, asking students in this country to say a prayer would be like "asking the members of the United Nations to stand and sing the national anthem of one country."[94] Other religious leaders expect that officials anxious to avoid controversy would adopt the religious equivalent of canned peas—bland and watered-down prayers. And they expect that prayers would become rote exercises while students were daydreaming or checking out their classmates. In either event, the prayers would trivialize religious faith.

In lieu of an amendment, about half the states have passed laws providing for a "moment of silence" to begin each school day. Although the laws ostensibly are for meditation, some legislators admit they really are for prayer. In 1985 the Supreme Court invalidated Alabama's law that authorized a moment of silence "for meditation or voluntary prayer" because the wording of the law endorsed and promoted prayer.[95] Yet a majority of justices indicated that they would approve a moment of silence if students were not encouraged to pray.

Although the Rehnquist Court's support for the prayer rulings was uncertain, the Court did reaffirm them and even extend them in 1992. It held that clergy cannot offer prayers at graduation ceremonies for public elementary, middle, and high schools.[96] The prayers in question were brief and nonsectarian, but the majority reasoned, "What to most believers may seem nothing more than a reasonable request that the nonbeliever respect their religious practices, in a school context may appear to the nonbeliever or dissenter to be an attempt to employ the machinery of the state to enforce a religious orthodoxy." Although attendance at the ceremony was voluntary, like participation in school prayers, the majority did not consider it truly voluntary. Justice Kennedy wrote, "Everyone knows that in our society and in our culture high school graduation is one of life's most significant occasions. . . . Graduation is a time for family and those closest to the student to celebrate success and express mutual wishes of gratitude and respect. . . ." The Court decided this case by a bare majority, but its wording was very emphatic.

Yet later that year the Court refused to review a federal court of appeals ruling that allowed student-led prayers at graduation ceremonies.[97] When a Texas school board faced a lawsuit for planning to include an invocation and benediction during graduation ceremonies, it modified its policy to permit the senior class to decide whether to have a prayer and, if so, which student to give it. The appellate court held that

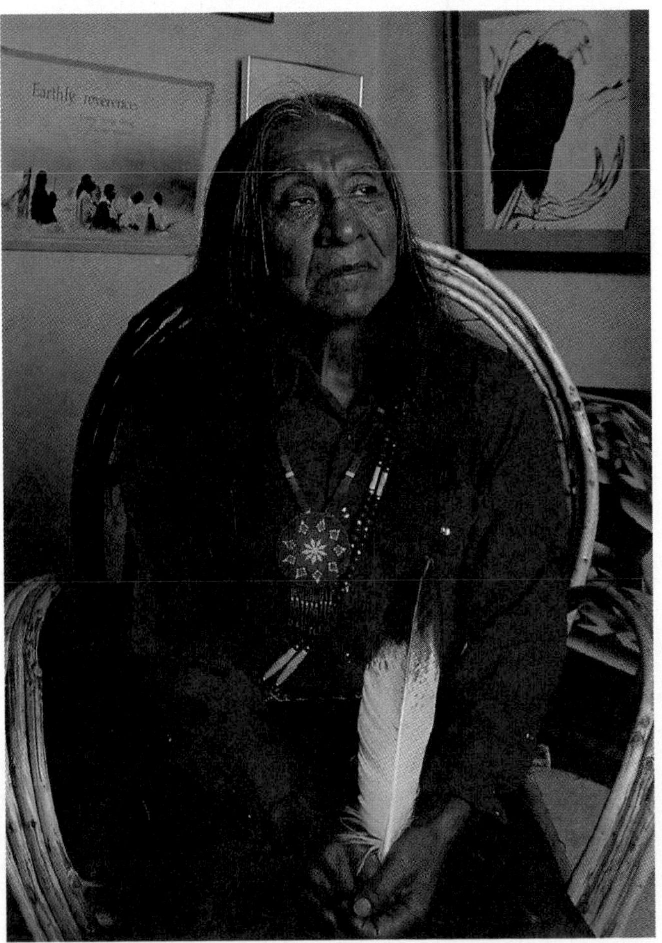

Alfred Smith, fired for using peyote in religious ceremonies, challenged Oregon's law.

Source: Don Wright, *The Miami News*.

this policy was not precluded by the Supreme Court's ruling, because the decision was not made by officials and the prayer was not given by a clergy member, so there would not be any official coercion. Of course, there would be a great deal of peer pressure. Yet the court said a majority of students could do what the state could not. But graduation would still be an official event sponsored by the state, and the opportunity to include a prayer would be offered by the state. Thus, the legality of this policy is in doubt.

Such doubt, however, did not prevent the American Center for Law and Justice, a conservative religious organization funded by televangelist Pat Robertson, from sending bulletins to 15,000 administrators and 500,000 parents and students advising them that graduation prayers, if led by students, were lawful after all. This mailing prompted the American Civil Liberties Union to notify administrators that the issue was not really resolved after all.[98] Meanwhile, confused school boards reached contradictory conclusions and made varying decisions.

The appellate court's holding encouraged opponents of the Supreme Court's school prayer rulings to use the same approach to circumvent these rulings as well. A high school principal in Jackson, Mississippi, let students vote whether to have a daily prayer and then he let them give it over the intercom. After ignoring a warning from the school board, he was suspended, prompting thousands of students in 15 counties to walk out of their schools in protest. Then the legislature passed a law allowing students to initiate and give prayers. Several other southern states followed Mississippi. The legality of these laws is in doubt.

The public demand is fueled by the symbolism of school prayer and a nostalgia for the less troubling times before the 1960s. As one writer perceived, the demand "doesn't have much to do with prayer anyway, but with a time, a place, an ethos that praying and pledging allegiance at the beginning of school each day represent."[99] Many people echo the feelings of a Pennsylvania school board member who said, "The country has certainly gone downhill since they took it out."[100] For these people, reinstitutionalization of school prayer would be a symbol that our society stands for appropriate values. For some religious leaders, however, calls for school prayer are "a cynical exploitation" of the public by politicians who imply that "two-minute pieties" will make up for the decline of values in society.[101]

In a related matter, the Court said that the University of Missouri at Kansas City had to make its meeting rooms available to students' religious organizations on an equal basis with other organizations, even if the religious organizations used the rooms for prayer or worship.[102] Otherwise, the university would be discriminating against religion. After this decision, Congress passed a law that requires public high schools as well to allow meetings of students' religious, philosophical, or political groups outside class hours. The Court accepted this law in 1990.[103] Justice O'Connor said high school students "are likely to understand that a school does not endorse or support student speech that it merely permits on a nondiscriminatory basis." Students have established 12,000 Bible clubs in public schools, according to an estimate in 1994.[104]

The Rehnquist Court also said that the University of Virginia had to provide financial aid, from students' fees, to students' religious organizations on an equal basis with other campus organizations, even if a religious organization sought the money to print a religious newspaper.[104a]

Despite its prayer rulings, the Court has been reluctant to invalidate traditional religious symbols. It has not questioned the motto "In God We Trust," on our money since 1865, or the phrase "One nation under God," in the Pledge of Allegiance since 1954.

The Rehnquist Court upheld the display of a nativity scene on government property, at least if it is part of a broader display for the holiday season.[105] Pawtucket, Rhode Island, had a creche, Santa Claus, sleigh with reindeer, Christmas tree, and talking wishing well. Although the nativity scene was an obvious symbol of Christianity, the Court said it was a traditional symbol of a holiday that has become secular as well as religious. Moreover, the presence of the secular decorations diluted any religious impact the nativity scene would have. A creche by itself, however, would be impermissible.[106]

Courts also have used the establishment clause to resolve disputes about teaching evolution in schools. In 1968 the Supreme Court invalidated Arkansas' 40-year-old law forbidding schools from teaching evolution.[107] Arkansas and Louisiana then passed laws requiring schools that teach evolution to also teach "creationism"—the biblical version of creation. In 1987 the Court invalidated these laws, because their purpose was to promote the fundamentalist Christian view.[108]

Courts also have used the establishment clause to resolve disputes about aid to parochial schools, most of which are Catholic. Millions of students attend, and their parents pay tuition and other expenses. In recent decades, costs have risen and enrollments have dropped. Schools have asked legislatures to provide money to defray part of the costs of their nonreligious activities. Courts have had to decide whether providing the money helps religion or whether denying it hinders religion. In addition, courts have had to determine if providing the money leads to excessive entanglement of church and state because of the monitoring required to ensure that the money is not spent for religious purposes.

In its first modern case, in 1947, the Court upheld New Jersey's program to reimburse both public and parochial students for bus fares to school.[109] Then the Court upheld New York's and Pennsylvania's programs to furnish textbooks to both public and parochial students.[110] Because the government already provided textbooks to public schools, the programs basically aided parochial schools, allowing them to use more of their scarce resources for religious purposes. But the Court said providing transportation and textbooks for all students is little different than providing police and fire protection for all schools.

The Court has struck down most other forms of aid, however.[111] Because these kinds of assistance have entailed sizable sums of money, the Court has said they could help Catholicism significantly and entangle church and state excessively. Yet the Court, reflecting shifting coalitions of justices, has not been consistent. The Burger Court, for example, struck

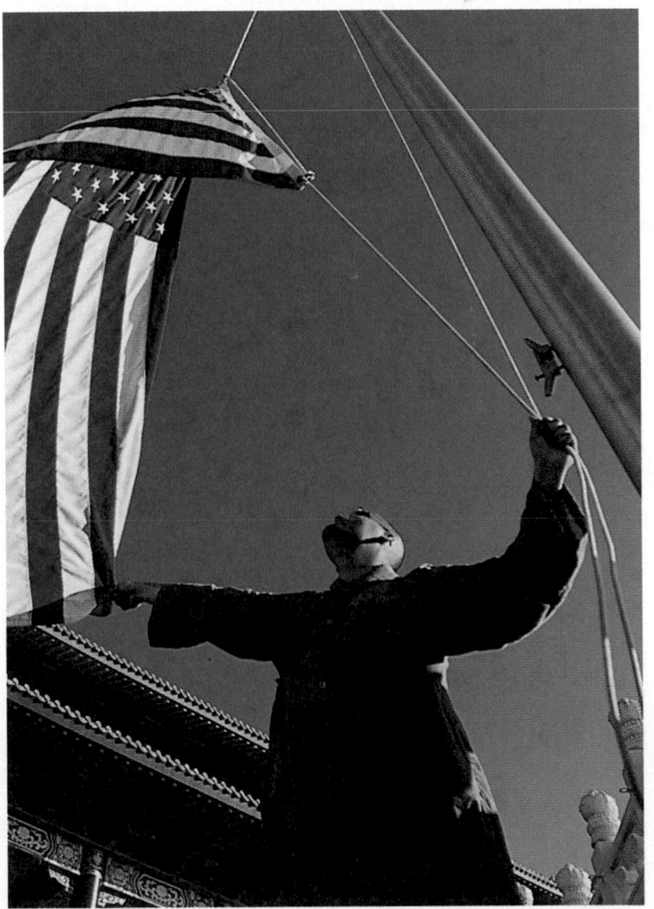

A Buddhist priest in California lowers the American flag at the end of the day.

down tax credits but upheld tax deductions to reduce tuition costs for parents.[112]

At the same time the Court struck down most forms of aid to parochial schools, it permitted aid to church-related colleges.[113] The Court noted that colleges are less likely to be under direct control of church officials and are less likely to try to indoctrinate their students, who are less impressionable than younger students.

Rights of Criminal Defendants

The Fourth, Fifth, Sixth, and Eighth Amendments provide numerous **due process** rights for criminal defendants. When the government prosecutes defendants, it must give them the process—that is, the procedures—they are due; it must be fair and "respect certain decencies of civilized conduct,"[114] even toward uncivilized people.

One defense attorney said many of his clients "had been monsters—nothing less—who had done monstrous things. Although occasionally not guilty of the crime charged, nearly all my clients have been guilty of something."[115] Then why do we give them rights? Partly we do so to avoid convicting innocent defendants. But mostly we do so because defendants are citizens, and we give all citizens rights. As Justice Douglas observed, "respecting the dignity even of the least worthy citizen ... raises the stature of all of us."[116]

Search and Seizure

England fostered the notion that a family's home is its castle, but Parliament made exceptions for the American colonies. It authorized writs of assistance, which allowed customs officials to conduct general searches for goods colonists had imported without paying taxes to the crown. The English tradition combined with the colonists' resentment of the writs of assistance led to adoption of the Fourth Amendment, which forbids **unreasonable searches and seizures.**

One type of seizure is the arrest of a person. Police must have evidence to believe that a person committed a crime. Another type of seizure is the confiscation of illegal contraband. The general requirement is that police should get a search warrant from a judge by showing evidence that a particular thing is in a particular place.

However, the Court has made exceptions to this requirement that complicate the law. These exceptions account for the vast majority of searches. If persons consent to a search, police can conduct one without a warrant. If police see contraband in plain view, they can seize it; they do not need to close their eyes to it. If police have suspicion that persons are committing a crime but lack evidence to arrest them, they can "stop and frisk" them—give them a pat-down search. If police have evidence to arrest them, they can search them and the area within their immediate control. If police face an emergency situation, they can search for weapons. And if police want to search motor vehicles in some situations, they can do so because vehicles are mobile and could be gone by the time police get a warrant.

Customs and border patrol officials can search persons and things coming into the country to enforce customs and immigration laws. Airport guards can search passengers and luggage to prevent hijackings. And prison guards can search prisoners to ensure security.

In defining reasonable and unreasonable searches and seizures, the Court has tried to walk a fine line between acknowledging officials' need for evidence and persons' need for privacy.

Exclusionary Rule

To enforce search and seizure law, the Court has established the **exclusionary rule,** which bars from court any evidence obtained in violation of the Fourth Amendment. The rule's goal is to deter police from illegal conduct.

Although the Court issued the rule for federal courts in 1914,[117] it did not impose the rule on state courts until 1961. Even so, the Warren Court's decision, in the case of *Mapp v. Ohio*,[118] was one of its most controversial. Until this time, police in many states had ignored search and seizure law.

The decision still has not been widely accepted. The Burger Court in 1984 created an exception to it. In a pair of cases, the justices allowed evidence obtained illegally to be used in court because the police had acted in "good faith."[119] The Rehnquist Court probably will define the scope of this exception more fully.

Electronic Surveillance

The Fourth Amendment traditionally applied to searches involving a physical trespass and seizures producing a tangible object. Electronic surveillance, however, does not require a physical trespass or result in a tangible object.

This posed a problem for the Supreme Court when it heard its first wiretapping case in 1928. Federal prohibition agents tapped the telephone of bootleggers by installing equipment on wires in the basement of the bootleggers' apartment building. The majority of the Court rigidly adhered to its traditional doctrine, saying this was not a search and seizure so the agents did not need a warrant.[120]

In a classic example of keeping the Constitution up to date, the Warren Court overruled this precedent in 1967.[121] Because electronic eavesdropping might threaten privacy as much as traditional searching, officials must get judicial authorization, similar to a warrant, to engage in such eavesdropping.

Self-Incrimination

The Fifth Amendment provides that persons shall not be compelled to be witnesses against themselves, that is, to incriminate themselves. Because defendants are presumed innocent, the government must prove their guilt.

This right means that defendants on trial do not have to take the witness stand and answer questions, and neither prosecutor nor judge can call attention to their failure to do so. Neither can suggest that defendants must have something to hide and thereby imply that they must be guilty. (But if defendants do take the stand and testify, this constitutes a waiver of their right, so the prosecutor can cross-examine them and they must answer.)

This right also means that prosecutors cannot introduce into evidence any statements or confessions from defendants that were not voluntary. However, the meaning of "voluntary" has changed over time.

For years law enforcement officials used physical brutality—"the third degree"—to get confessions. After 1936, when the Supreme Court ruled that confessions obtained this way were invalid,[122] officials resorted to more subtle techniques. They held suspects incommunicado, so the suspects could not notify anyone about their arrest, and delayed bringing them to court, so the judge could not inform them of their rights.[123] They interrogated suspects for long periods of time without food or rest, in one case with alternating teams of interrogators for 36 hours.[124] They tricked suspects. In one case, they told a man they would jail his wife if he did not talk, although they knew she was not involved, and in another they told a woman they would take away her welfare benefits and even her children if she did not talk, although they did not have authority to do either.[125] The Court ruled that these techniques, designed to break the suspects' will, were psychological coercion, so the confessions were invalid.

The Warren Court still worried that many confessions were not truly voluntary, so it issued a landmark decision in 1966. Arizona police arrested a poor, mentally disturbed man, Ernesto Miranda, for kidnapping and raping a woman. After the woman identified him in a lineup, police interrogated him for two hours, prompting him to confess. He had not been told that he could remain silent or be represented by an attorney. In *Miranda v. Arizona,* the Court decided that his confession was not truly voluntary.[126] Chief Justice Warren, himself a former district attorney, noted the tremendous advantage police have in interrogation and said suspects needed more protection. The Court ruled that officials must advise suspects of their rights before interrogation. These came to be known as the **Miranda rights:**

- You have the right to remain silent.
- If you talk, anything you say can be used against you.
- You have the right to be represented by an attorney.
- If you cannot afford an attorney, one will be appointed for you.

The Burger and Rehnquist courts have not required police and prosecutors to follow *Miranda* as strictly as the Warren Court did but, contrary to expectations, have not abandoned *Miranda.*

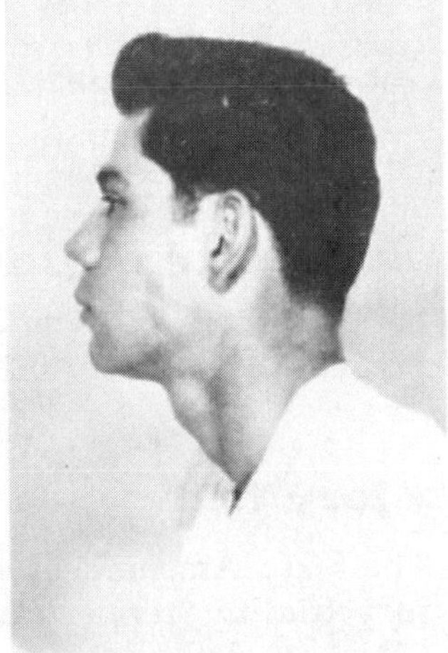

Ernesto Miranda.

Counsel

The Sixth Amendment provides the **right to counsel** in criminal cases. Historically, it permitted defendants to hire an attorney to represent them in court, but it was no help to most defendants because they were too poor to hire one.

Consequently, the Supreme Court required federal courts to furnish an attorney to all indigent defendants as long ago as 1938.[127] But most criminal cases are state cases, and although the Court required state courts to furnish an attorney in some cases, it was reluctant to impose a broad requirement on these courts.[128]

In 1963 the Warren Court accepted the appeal of Clarence Earl Gideon. Charged with breaking into a pool hall and stealing beer, wine, and change from a vending machine, Gideon asked the judge for a lawyer. The judge refused to appoint one, leaving Gideon to defend himself. The prosecutor did not have a strong case, but Gideon was not able to point out its weaknesses. He was convicted and sentenced to five years. On appeal, the Warren Court unanimously declared that Gideon was entitled to be represented by counsel.[129] Justice Black explained that "lawyers in criminal courts are necessities, not luxuries." The Court finally established a broad rule: State courts must give an attorney to indigent defendants in felony cases.

Gideon proved the Court's point. Given a lawyer and retried, he was not convicted. The lawyer did the effective job defending him that he had not been able to do himself.

In 1972 the Burger Court expanded the rule: State courts must give an attorney to indigent defendants in misdemeanor cases too, except those that result in no incarceration at all,[130] because even misdemeanor cases are too complex for defendants to defend themselves. In addition, the Court decided that courts must provide an attorney for one appeal.[131]

Receiving counsel does not necessarily mean receiving effective counsel, however. Some assigned attorneys are inexperienced, some are incompetent, and most are overworked and have little time to prepare the best possible defense.

When a Court Reverses a Conviction . . .

. . . the defendant does not necessarily go free. An appellate court normally only evaluates the legality of the procedures used by officials; it does not determine guilt or innocence. Therefore, when it reverses a conviction, it only indicates that officials used some illegal procedure in convicting the defendant—for example, they may have used evidence from an improper search and seizure. Then the prosecutor can retry the defendant, without this evidence, if the prosecutor thinks there is enough other evidence. Often prosecutors do retry the defendants, and in about half the cases judges or juries reconvict them.[1]

1. Robert T. Roper and Albert P. Malone, "Does Procedural Due Process Make a Difference? A Study of Second Trials," *Judicature* 65 (1981), pp. 136–41.

Jury Trial

The Sixth Amendment also provides the **right to a jury trial** in "serious" criminal cases. The Supreme Court has defined "serious" cases as those that could result in more than six months' incarceration.[132]

The right was adopted to prevent oppression by a "corrupt or overzealous prosecutor" or a "biased . . . or eccentric judge.[133] It also has served to limit governmental use of unpopular laws or enforcement procedures. Regardless of the extent of evidence against a defendant, a jury can refuse to convict if it feels the government has overstepped its bounds.

The jury is to be "impartial," so persons who have made up their minds before trial should be excluded. It also is to be "a fair cross section" of the community, so no group should be systematically excluded.[134] But the jury need not be a perfect cross section and, in fact, need not have even one member of a particular group.[135] Most courts use voter registration lists to obtain names of potential jurors. These lists are not truly representative because poor people do not register at the same rate as others, but courts have decided that the lists are sufficiently representative. And Congress passed and President Clinton signed the "motor voter bill," which requires drivers' license and welfare offices to offer voter registration forms. Presumably more poor people will register and be eligible for serving on juries.

Cruel and Unusual Punishment

The Eighth Amendment forbids **cruel and unusual punishment** but does not define it. The Supreme Court had defined it as torture or any punishment grossly disproportionate to the offense, but the Court had seldom used the provision until applying it to capital punishment in the 1970s.

Because the death penalty was used at the time the amendment was adopted and had been used ever since, it was assumed to be constitutional. In fact, in the nineteenth century the Court ruled that two methods of execution—the firing squad and the electric chair—were not so inhumane as to be torture.[136]

But in 1972 the Burger Court, albeit with Chief Justice Burger and the other three Nixon appointees in dissent, held that capital punishment as it was then being administered was cruel and unusual.[137] The Court said the laws and procedures allowed too much discretion for those who administered the punishment and too much arbitrariness and discrimination for those who received it. It was imposed so seldom, according to Justice Potter Stewart, that it was "cruel and unusual in the same way that being struck by lightning is cruel and unusual." Yet when imposed, it was given to blacks disproportionately to their convictions for murder.

The decision invalidated the laws of 40 states and commuted the death sentences of 629 inmates. But because the Court did not hold capital punishment cruel and unusual in principle, about three-fourths of the states adopted new laws that permitted less discretion in an effort to be less arbitrary and discriminatory.

These changes satisfied a majority of the court. In 1976 and 1977, the Court said capital punishment is not cruel and unusual for murder if the punishment is administered fairly.[138] But the punishment cannot be imposed automatically for everyone convicted of murder, for the judge or jury must consider any mitigating factors that would call for a lesser punishment.[139] Also, the punishment cannot be imposed for rape, because it is disproportionate to that offense.[140]

Clarence Earl Gideon, convinced he was denied a fair trial because he was not given an attorney, read law books in prison so he could petition the Supreme Court for a writ of certiorari. Although he had spent much of his life in prison, he was optimistic. "I believe that each era finds an improvement in law each year brings something new for the benefit of mankind [*sic*]. Maybe this will be one of those small steps forward."

DIVISION OF CORRECTIONS No. 890 Misc.

CORRESPONDENCE REGULATIONS OCT. TERM 1961

MAIL WILL NOT BE DELIVERED WHICH DOES NOT CONFORM WITH THESE RULES U.S. Supreme Court

No. 1 -- Only 2 letters each week, not to exceed 2 sheets letter-size 8 1/2 x 11" and written on one side only, and if ruled paper, do not write between lines. *Your complete name* must be signed at the close of your letter. *Clippings, stamps, letters from other people, stationery or cash must not be enclosed* in your letters.

No. 2 -- All *letters* must be addressed in the *complete prison name* of the inmate. *Cell number*, where applicable, and *prison number* must be placed in lower left corner of envelope, with your complete name and address in the upper left corner.

No. 3 -- *Do not send any packages without a Package Permit.* Unauthorized *packages* will be destroyed.

No. 4 -- *Letters* must be written in English only.

No. 5 -- *Books, magazines, pamphlets,* and *newspapers* of reputable character will be delivered *only if* mailed direct from the publisher.

No. 6 -- *Money* must be sent in the form of *Postal Money Orders* only, [illegible] complete prison name and prison number.

RECEIVED JAN 8 1962 OFFICE OF THE CLERK SUPREME COURT, U.S.

INSTITUTION CELL NUMBER

NAME NUMBER

In the Supreme Court of The United States
Washington D.C.
Motion for leave to proceed in Forma Pauperis
Clarence Earl Gideon, Petitioner
vs.
H. G. Cochran Jr, Director, Divisions of corrections State of Florida Respondent

Petitioner Clarence Earl Gideon, who is now held in the Florida state penitentiary, asks leave to file the attached petition for a Writ of Certiorari To The United States Supreme Court, directed to The Supreme Court of The State of Florida, without prepayment of costs and to proceed in Forma Pauperis. The petitioner's affidavit in support is attached hereto.

Clarence Earl Gideon
counsel for Petitioner

Affidavit in support of petition for leave to proceed in Forma Pauperis
Clarence Earl Gideon, petitioner
vs.
H. G. Cochran Jr, Director, Divisions of corrections State of Florida, Respondent.

I, Clarence Earl Gideon, being duly sworn according to law, depose and say that I am

The new laws apparently have reduced but not eliminated discrimination. Although past studies showed discrimination against black defendants, recent studies show discrimination against black or white defendants who murder whites. People who affect the decision to impose capital punishment—prosecutors, defense attorneys, judges, and jurors—appear to value white lives more. Despite evidence that in Georgia those who kill whites are more than four times as likely to be given the death penalty as those who kill blacks, the Rehnquist Court, by a five to four vote, upheld capital punishment in the state in 1987.[141] The majority, in part reflecting the views of lawyers untrained in and uncomfortable with social science, expressed reluctance to use such evidence in reaching decisions. They acknowledged that the study showed discrimination but said it did not show that this particular defendant, a black man who killed a white cop, was a victim of the discrimination.

Rights in Theory and in Practice

Although the Supreme Court has interpreted the Bill of Rights to provide an impressive list of rights for criminal defendants, not all rights are available for all defendants in all places. Some trial court judges, prosecutors, and police do not comply with Supreme Court rulings. If defendants appeal to a high enough court, they probably will get their rights, but most defendants do not have the knowledge, the resources, or the perseverance to do this.

When rights are available, most defendants do not take advantage of them. About 90% of all criminal defendants plead guilty, and many of them do so as part of a **plea bargain.** This is an agreement between the prosecutor, the defense attorney, and the defendant, with the explicit or implicit approval of the judge, to reduce the charge or the sentence in exchange for a plea of guilty. A plea bargain is a compromise. For officials it saves the time, trouble, and uncertainty of a trial. For defendants it eliminates the fear of a harsher sentence. However, it also reduces due process rights. A plea of guilty waives defendants' rights to a trial by a jury of their peers, in which defendants can present their own witnesses and cross-examine the government's witnesses, and in which they cannot be forced to incriminate themselves. A plea of guilty also waives the right to counsel to some extent because most attorneys appointed to represent defendants are overworked and inclined to pressure defendants to plead guilty so they do not have to prepare a defense. Despite these disadvantages for due process rights, the Court allows plea bargaining because of its practical advantages.[142]

Right to Privacy

Neither the Constitution nor the Bill of Rights mentions "privacy." Nevertheless, the **right to privacy,** Justice Douglas noted, is "older than the Bill of Rights,"[143] and the framers undoubtedly assumed that people would have it. The framers did include amendments that reflect a concern for privacy: The First Amendment protects privacy of association, the Third privacy of homes from quartering soldiers, the Fourth privacy of persons and places where they live from searches and seizures, and the Fifth privacy of knowledge or thoughts from compulsory self-incrimination.

So far the Court's right-to-privacy doctrine reflects a right to autonomy—what Justice Louis Brandeis called "the right to be left alone"—more than a right to keep things confidential. As noted earlier in the chapter, the Court has been reluctant to punish the press for invasion of privacy.[144]

Birth Control

The Warren Court established the right to privacy in 1965 when it struck down a Connecticut law that prohibited distributing or using contraceptives.[145] To enforce the law the state would have had to police people's bedrooms, and the Court said the very idea of policing married couples' bedrooms was absurd. Then the Court struck down Massachusetts and New York laws that prohibited distributing contraceptives to unmarried persons.[146] "If the right of privacy means anything," Justice Brennan said, "it is the right of the individual, married or single, to be free from unwarranted governmental intrusion into matters so fundamentally affecting a person as the decision whether to bear or beget a child."[147]

Abortion

When 21-year-old Norma McCorvey became pregnant in 1969, she was divorced and already had a 5-year-old daughter, and she sought an abortion. But Texas, where she lived, prohibited abortions unless the mother's life was in danger. She discovered, "No

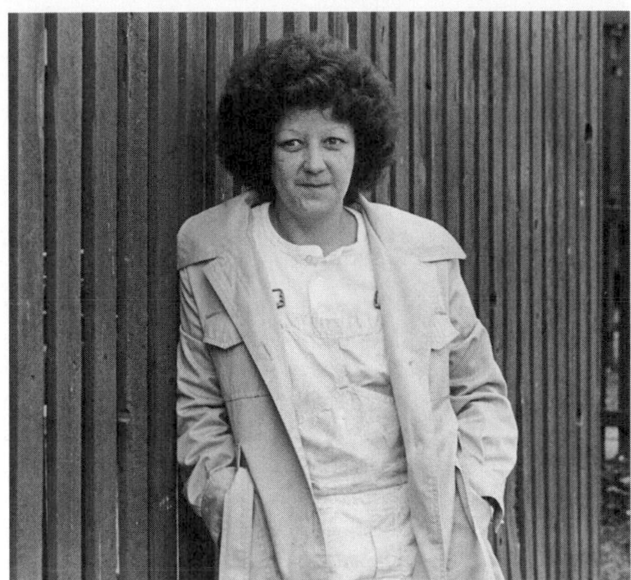

Norma McCorvey, alias "Jane Roe," whose suit prompted the landmark abortion ruling.

legitimate doctor in Dallas would touch me. . . . I found one doctor who offered to abort me for $500. Only he didn't have a license, and I was scared to turn my body over to him. So there I was—pregnant, unmarried, unemployed, alone, and stuck."[148]

Too poor to go to a state that permitted abortions, McCorvey decided to put her baby up for adoption. But the state law still rankled her. With the help of two women attorneys recently out of law school, she used her case to challenge Texas's law. She adopted the name Jane Roe to conceal her identity.

In *Roe v. Wade* in 1973, the Burger Court extended the right to privacy from birth control to abortion. The majority concluded that because doctors, theologians, and philosophers cannot agree when life begins, judges should not assert that life begins at conception, thus deeming a fetus a person and abortion murder. Amidst such uncertainty, the majority decided that a woman's right to privacy of her body is paramount.

The Court ruled that women can have an abortion during the first three months of pregnancy and, subject to reasonable regulations for health, during the middle three months. States can prohibit an abortion during the last three months. Thus the right is broad though not absolute.

The justices, as revealed in memos discovered years later, acknowledged that their division of pregnancy into trimesters was "legislative," but they saw this as a way to balance the rights of the mother in the early stages of pregnancy with the rights of the fetus in the later stage.[149]

The Court's ruling invalidated the abortion laws of 45 states (see Figure 1). Far from settling the issue, however, it stimulated more controversy. The right-to-life movement, spearheaded initially by Catholics and later by fundamentalist Protestants, organized to pro-

FIGURE 1
The Number of Abortions Has Leveled Off

The number of abortions in the United States was already increasing before the Supreme Court's *Roe* decision because some states had liberalized their laws. After the *Roe* decision, the number increased sharply but leveled off in the 1980s. The rate of abortions is about 29% of all pregnancies (excluding miscarriages and stillbirths). This compares with 13% for West Germany, 14% for Canada, 27% for Japan, and 68% for the former Soviet Union.

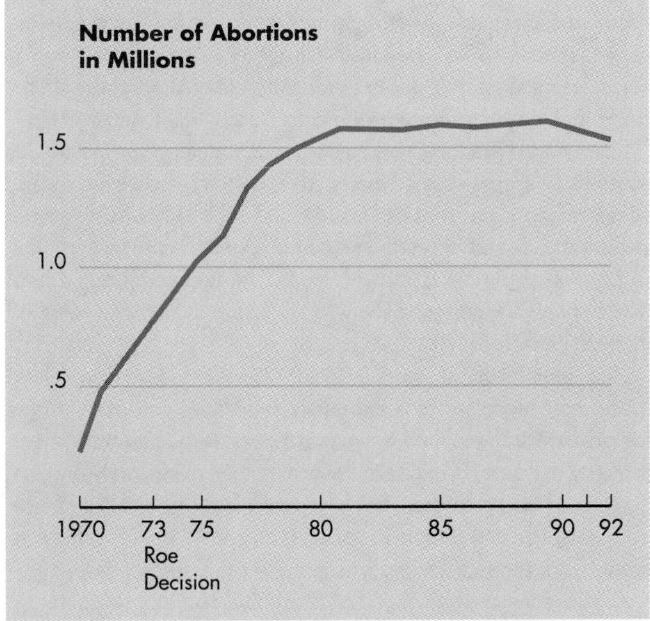

SOURCES: 1970–1972: Susan Hansen, "State Implementation of Supreme Court Decisions: Abortion Rates since *Roe v. Wade*," *Journal of Politics* 42 (May 1980), pp. 372–95; 1973–1981: Stanley K. Henshaw and Ellen Blaine, *Abortion Services in the United States, Each State, and Metropolitan Area, 1981–1982* (New York: Alan Guttmacher Institute, 1985), p. 64; 1982–1983: Stanley K. Henshaw, "Characteristics of U.S. Women Having Abortions, 1982–1983," *Family Planning Perspectives* 19 (1987), pp. 6–7; 1984–1985: Stanley K. Henshaw, Jacqueline Darroch Forrest, and Jennifer Van Vort, "Abortion Services in the United States, 1984 and 1985," *Family Planning Perspectives* 19 (1987), p. 64; 1986–1988: *Abortion Fact Book*, (New York: Alan Guttmacher Institute, 1992); "Number of Abortions at Lowest Level Since '79," *Lincoln Journal* (AP), June 16, 1994.

Symbolic Solutions for Complex Problems?

Capital Punishment

Public opinion, which opposed capital punishment in the 1960s and early 1970s, flip-flopped as the crime rate soared. Since the early 1970s, 70–80% of the people have supported this punishment. Many people see it as one solution to the crime problem, especially to the homicide rate. That is, they consider the death penalty a deterrent.[1] Others believe the death penalty is only a symbolic solution.

The theory of deterrence rests on the assumption that people are rational actors who weigh the costs and benefits of their actions. They try to avoid unpleasant or painful consequences. If society does not want them to do something, society imposes such consequences. If these do not work, society increases the consequences. Thus, because almost no one wants to die, capital punishment in theory ensures that almost no one will take a life. But does capital punishment actually deter murder?

The death penalty, of course, does deter the killer who receives it from killing again. This penalty, however, is not necessary to deter most killers. Studies of killers who were not executed and who were eventually paroled show that they rarely kill again. And those released in states without capital punishment are no more likely to kill again than those released in states with it.[2]

But does the death penalty deter potential killers from killing in the first place? This is extremely difficult to measure. Many factors contribute to the homicide rate—poverty, unemployment, brutality at home, brutality in the community, availability of guns, number of males in their teens or early 20s (the most criminal- and violent-prone people in society), and so forth. It is difficult to identify, let alone take into account, all of the relevant factors.

Social science studies do not prove that capital punishment is a deterrent.[3] (Nor do they conclusively prove that it is not.) Comparisons of neighboring states with and without the death penalty found that the murder rates are similar and increase or decrease at about the same time, suggesting that the rates reflect broad social trends rather than official executions.[4] Examinations of states that abolished or reinstated the death penalty and comparisons with neighboring states that did not change their punishment found that the murder rates seem unaffected by the changes.[5]

Numerous studies looked at the possibility of deterrence in the murder of police officers. These murderers have a high rate of apprehension, and because their victims are officers, they have a good chance of facing the death penalty. And these crimes and their punishment receive much publicity. Thus, if capital punishment is a deterrent, it should be seen here. Yet the studies found no higher murder rates of police officers in states that have abandoned capital punishment.[6]

Some proponents of capital punishment have hypothesized that it would also deter crimes beside murder by educating people in general to obey the law or face the consequences. Yet a study found no such impact on other serious crimes.[7]

Some proponents acknowledge that capital punishment is not a deterrent now because it is not used soon enough after arrest or conviction. There are, on average, delays of 8 years between a murder and the execution. These are due to additional appeals afforded defendants who face this ultimate and irrevocable punishment. Although most convicted criminals do not take advantage of their appeals, those facing the death penalty have the most incentive to do so. Because the punishment is irrevocable—and reports of new evidence exonerating inmates on death row periodically surface—it is unlikely that society would tolerate much reduction in these safeguards.

There are good reasons why we should not expect capital punishment to be a deterrent. Before defendants can be given this sentence, they must be arrested and convicted. Otherwise, the sentence on the books is irrelevant.

Further, the alternative sentence—life in prison, with or without the possibility of parole—already is steep. Perhaps it already provides as much deterrence as possible. Capital punishment presumably would be a deterrent only to the extent that a potential killer thought life in prison was acceptable but execution was not.

Moreover, consider the typical killers. "Professional" killers are rare and are rarely caught. When caught, they are usually offered leniency in exchange for information about those who employ them.[8] Unlike professionals, most killers do not plan their crimes. Murders frequently occur in a fit of rage, as an outgrowth of an argument with an acquaintance, often a partner or ex-partner in a sour domestic relationship. The killers normally do not calculate their eventual punishment; they do not even think of getting caught and being convicted. Often they are high on alcohol or drugs so they are even less rational. Murders also frequently occur in the drug trade. Drug dealers realize that rivals, wannabes, or others might kill them for drugs, money, territory, or "respect" any day, yet the the dealers continue to traffic in drugs and sometimes commit violent acts. If their immediate fears do not prompt them to quit, the remote possibility of capital punishment is not likely to, either. If capital punishment is not a deterrent, then it is a symbolic rather than a real solution to crime.

There is actually some evidence that official executions slightly increase the homicide rate in the month or two afterward.[9] Perhaps executions convey the message that violence is an acceptable solution to problems—just enough to push people already on the brink. Or perhaps executions show potential killers that they, too, can get public attention by committing such acts.

Many people also consider the death penalty just retribution. The theory of retribution is the secular equivalent of the biblical phrase, "an eye for an eye." It is a payment to society, to satisfy the moral indignation of society, for the act the defendant committed. If the act was taking a life, the payment should be forfeiting one's life. (Taken literally, the execution should be performed in the same manner as the murder was committed.)

Opponents of retribution say society, rather than being more moral for using the death penalty, is less moral. Society is supposed to reflect appropriate standards of behavior, not imitate the lowest standards of its worst members. They also maintain that society is less moral because the death penalty, unlike the typical murder, is undertaken in a rational and cold-blooded way. Essentially, in response to "an eye for an eye," opponents say that "two wrongs don't make a right."

As a moral, rather than a pragmatic argument, the theory of retribution cannot be refuted by studies the way the theory of deterrence can be.

If the death penalty is accepted as retribution, it is a symbolic reflection of society's morality and as such is also a symbolic solution to crime. This might be a sufficient basis to persuade many people to support capital punishment. Indeed, polls find that many people who support capital punishment do not want it used much. Apparently they want it on the books as a symbol. But these people should not expect it to reduce the homicide rate, let alone the overall crime rate.

Regardless of one's own preference for or opposition to capital punishment, this issue reflects the inherent problems of symbolic solutions in our politics. Some sponsors of such solutions are merely trying to score political points, pointing out their stand in favor, or their opponent's stand against, the penalty. Other sponsors are sincerely hoping to do some good. Either way, the debate about symbolic measures usually takes precedence over and interferes with efforts to adopt more substantive solutions. Mario Cuomo, who as governor of New York vetoed capital punishment and lost reelection in part as a result, called it "the ultimate political cop-out." It lets legislators convince constituents that they are doing something about the crime problem. When Congress adopted the death penalty for federal courts in 1994, sponsors claimed that they made the country safer by allowing the penalty for 50 different crimes. But one crime was murder of egg inspectors, another was murder of poultry inspectors, and so on. Many members privately conceded that they voted for the penalty only to avoid appearing "soft on crime."[10] Yet many legislators who claim to be so worried about the crime problem refrain from proposing substantive solutions. Such programs would cost more money, require more taxes, and take years to reap the benefits. Instead, Cuomo said, "It is easier to hold out a quick fix, the idea that all will be well if we just burn people."[11] But the crime problem did not develop quickly, and it will not be resolved quickly.

---

1. K. M. Jamieson and T. J. Flanagan, *Sourcebook of Criminal Justice Statistics, 1988* (Albany, NY: Hindelang Criminal Justice Research Center, 1989), p. 229.
2. Hugo Adam Bedau, ed., *The Death Penalty in America,* 3rd ed. (New York: Oxford University Press, 1982), p. 180.
3. Victor E. Kappeler, Mark Blumberg, and Gary W. Potter, *The Mythology of Crime and Criminal Justice* (Prospect Heights, IL: Waveland, 1993), pp. 213–22; Samuel Walker, *Sense and Nonsense about Crime and Drugs,* 3rd ed. (Belmont, CA: Wadsworth, 1994), pp. 103–108.
4. Thorsten Sellin, *The Penalty of Death* (Beverly Hills, CA: Sage, 1980).
5. Hans Zeisel, "The Deterrent Effect of the Death Penalty: Facts v. Faith," in Philip B. Kurland, ed., *The Supreme Court Review, 1976* (Chicago: University of Chicago Press, 1977).
6. See numerous sources cited in Kappeler, et. al., *Mythology of Crime and Criminal Justice,* p. 218. Isaac Ehrlich claimed that every execution from 1930 to 1969 deterred 7 or 8 murders. Although he took into account some variables that could affect the homicide rate, such as the probabilities of apprehension, conviction, and execution, there were flaws in the study that led later researchers to dismiss his conclusions. See Ehrlich, "The Deterrent Effect of Capital Punishment," *American Economic Review* 65 (1975): 397–417; and numerous sources cited in Kappeler, et. al., *Mythology of Crime and Criminal Justice,* pp. 220–21.
7. William C. Bailey, "The General Prevention Effect of Capital Punishment for Non-Capital Felonies," in R. M. Bohm, ed., *The Death Penalty in America: Current Research* (Cincinnati: Anderson Publishing and Academy of Criminal Justice Sciences, 1991).
8. John Kaplan, "The Problem of Capital Punishment," *University of Illinois Law Review* 31 (1963): p. 565–70.
9. W. J. Bowers, G. L. Pierce, and J. F. McDevitt, *Legal Homicide: Death as Punishment in America, 1864–1982* (Boston: Northeastern University Press, 1984), p. 284.
10. Helen Dewar, "It's Better to Look Good Than to Do Good," *Washington Post National Weekly Edition,* December 2–8, 1991, p. 12.
11. Michael Kramer, "Cuomo, the Last Holdout," *Time,* April 2, 1990, p. 20.

test the ruling. The movement also pressured legislators to overturn or circumvent the ruling. Although Congress failed to pass a constitutional amendment banning abortions or allowing states to regulate them, many state legislatures did pass statutes restricting abortions in various ways.

The Burger Court invalidated most of these laws.[150] It held that states cannot require abortions to be performed in hospitals rather than clinics, where they are cheaper.[151] They cannot require consent by either the parents of unmarried minors[152] or the husband of married women (Table 1).[153]

The Burger Court, however, upheld a major restriction on the right to abortion. It allowed laws that bar the use of government funds to pay for abortions for poor women. The Medicaid program, financed jointly by the federal and state governments, had paid for abortions for poor women. Before these laws, the program had paid for about one-third of the abortions in the country each year.[154] These laws put a safe abortion, by a doctor in a clinic or hospital, beyond the financial reach of some women. Regardless, a majority of the Burger Court ruled that governments have no obligation to finance abortions, even if this means that some women cannot take advantage of their right to have them.[155]

Congress and over half the states now prohibit use of their funds to pay for abortions for poor women, except for those whose pregnancy threatens their life or whose pregnancy is the result of rape or incest. (Although Congress had voted to allow funds for those whose pregnancy is the result of rape, President Bush vetoed this extension. After Bush lost his reelection bid, Congress passed this extension again and broadened it to cover incest, and President Clinton signed the bill.) However, about a fifth of the states do provide funds for all poor women who want abortions.[156]

One effect of the laws barring use of government funds is to delay abortions, making them more risky and expensive, while the women search for the money.[157] Another effect is to deny abortions to an estimated 20% of the women who cannot obtain the money. The women, then, bear their unwanted children. As a result, state medical and welfare expenditures for the additional children increase. According to one analysis of states that do provide funds for poor women, the states incur the cost of the abortions initially but save money in the long run. For every $1 spent for the abortions, $4 is saved in medical and welfare expenses in what would have been just the first two years of the child's life.[158]

Presidents Reagan and Bush sought justices who opposed *Roe* and, after they filled their fifth vacancy on the Court, pro-life advocates expected the Court to overturn it. Yet the Rehnquist Court, while narrowing *Roe,* has not overturned it.[159] In *Planned Parenthood of Southeastern Pennsylvania v. Casey* in 1992, a bare majority of five justices reaffirmed the right to abortion.[160] At the same time, the majority signaled a willingness to allow more restrictions on the right—as long they do not place an "undue burden" on women seeking abortions.

The majority upheld Pennsylvania's 24-hour waiting period between the time a woman indicates her desire to have an abortion and the time a doctor can perform one. Although a 24-hour waiting period will not be much burden for many women, it will for some. Poor women who live in rural areas and must travel to cities to obtain abortions will have to make one trip, turn around and go home, then turn around and come back the next day. Or they will have to spend the night and pay for food and lodging. One woman in Mississippi hitch-hiked and planned to sleep on outdoor furniture in the K Mart parking lot across the street (until the clinic offered to pay for her motel room).[161]

Teenagers will also be affected. Pro-life groups often note the license numbers of cars driven to clinics by teenagers. They look up the name and address of the family and then inform the parents in hope the parents will pressure the daughter to change her mind during the waiting period.

TABLE 1 Why Women Have Abortions

Reason	Percent
Child would change life (job, school)	76%
Cannot afford child	68
Problems with husband or partner, or do not want to be single parent	51
Do not want people to know I had sex or am pregnant	31
Too young, or cannot handle the responsibility	30
Husband or partner wants me to	23
Concerned for fetus's health	13
Concerned for own health	7
Pregnancy was due to rape or incest	1

Women gave these reasons for having abortions. Because many gave more than one, the percents total more than 100.

SOURCE: 1985 data from Alan Guttmacher Institute, published in *Lincoln Sunday Journal-Star*, April 30, 1989.

The majority struck down Pennsylvania's requirement that married women notify their husband before having an abortion. This was an undue burden because women who fear physical abuse from their husbands would be deterred from seeking an abortion. Justice O'Connor said a state "may not give to a man the kind of dominion over his wife that parents exercise over their children."

The Rehnquist Court upheld various states' requirement that unmarried minors notify their parents before having an abortion.[162] If a daughter does not want to tell her parents, she can try to get permission from a judge. She must convince the judge that an abortion would be in her best interest or that she is mature enough to make the decision herself. If she is not mature enough, she must become a mother. These laws, Justice Marshall wrote in dissent, force "a young woman in an already dire situation to choose between two fundamentally unacceptable alternatives: notifying a possibly dictatorial or even abusive parent or justifying her profoundly personal decision in an intimidating judicial proceeding to a black-robed stranger."

Pro-life groups advocated these laws with the expectation that they would result in fewer abortions. They believed many teenagers would go to their parents rather than face the forbidding atmosphere of a court hearing and their parents would persuade or pressure them not to have the abortion. Some evidence indicates that the laws have had this effect.[163] When teenagers do go to court, they routinely get waivers in some states, such as Pennsylvania, but do not in others, such as Indiana. There they are advised to go out of state.[164]

Despite the dissatisfaction of some people, it is worth noting that the unelected, nonmajoritarian Supreme Court has come closer to forging a policy reflective of public opinion than have most politicians. Polls show the majority of the people want to keep the right to abortion but would like to discourage it somewhat.[165] The Court's doctrine now essentially articulates this view.

Another type of restriction on the right to abortion was the policy of the Reagan and Bush administrations banning family planning clinics (for example, Planned Parenthood) that receive any federal funds from telling pregnant women where they can get an abortion or even from discussing with them the option of abortion. In 1991 the Rehnquist Court dismayed operators and supporters of family planning clinics by voting five to four to uphold the ban.[166] However, upon taking office President Clinton rescinded this "gag rule."[167]

The pro-life movement, growing increasingly frustrated in recent years, has adopted more militant tactics. Organizations such as Operation Rescue engage in civil disobedience, blockading clinics and harassing workers and patients as they come and go. Some organizations spray chemicals inside clinics, ruining carpets and fabrics and leaving a stench that makes the clinics unusable. Such incidents occurred 50 times in one recent year alone.[168]

Protestors in Charleston, South Carolina, distributed fliers in the city's poorest neighborhood encouraging residents to rob an abortion clinic: "The killers accept only cash! They kill about 60 babies each week. That is $16,500 of CASH taken to the bank each week. That means that an average of $5,500 is waiting there each day of business in cash before closing hours."[169]

Organizations also target doctors, nurses, and other workers of the clinics. Operation Rescue runs a training camp in Florida that instructs members how to use public records to locate personal information about employees, how to tail them to their homes, and how to organize demonstrations at their homes. Organizations put up "Wanted" posters, with a doctor's picture, name, address, and phone number. They encourage others to harass the doctor, his or her spouse, and even their children. (One 13-year-old was confronted in a restaurant and was told that he was going to burn in hell.)[170] Some activists go further. They have come out in favor of killing abortion doctors. One organization released a "deadly dozen" list of abortion doctors—a quasi-hit list. One minister wrote a book—*A Time to Kill*—and markets a bumper sticker—"EXECUTE ABORTIONISTS-MURDERERS."[171]

In this climate, two doctors, two clinic receptionists, and one clinic volunteer have been killed, and seven other doctors, employees, and volunteers have been wounded.[172] Numerous clinics have been firebombed. The tactics have had their intended effect on doctors. Although surveys show that most gynecologists and obstetricians are pro-choice, fewer do abortions now than a decade ago.[173] While many doctors consider abortions routine work that pays little, others worry about the consequences.

Abortions remain available in most metropolitan centers but not in most rural areas. Eighty-three percent of U.S. counties have no doctor who performs abortions. Some states have only one or two places where women can obtain abortions.[174]

15 Civil Rights

You Are There

Compromise or Continue to Fight?

You are Fannie Lou Hamer, a leader of the Mississippi Freedom Democratic Party (MFDP), a group of mostly African Americans challenging the seating of the regular state Democratic Party delegates at the national Democratic Party Convention in 1964. You have to decide whether to accept a compromise offered by national party officials.

You have come a long way.[1] You were born the youngest in a family of 20 children in the small town of Ruleville, located in the heart of the Mississippi Delta. Like many other African Americans, your parents were sharecroppers, picking cotton on a white family's plantation in exchange for housing and a little money for food.[2] At the age of 6, after the owner enticed you with treats from the plantation store, you began picking cotton too.

You were resigned to your life but never satisfied with it because you had little control. For instance, the owner of the house you lived in refused to fix the indoor toilet, saying you did not need it. When you cleaned his house, you discovered that his family had a separate bathroom for their dog. And when you entered the hospital to have a small tumor removed, you were sterilized without your knowledge or permission.

So when the civil rights movement reached Ruleville in 1962, you were ready. You were 44 years old, yet you could not vote. At a meeting at church, a leader of the Student Non-Violent Coordinating Committee (SNCC) and a minister with Martin Luther King's Southern Christian Leadership Conference (SCLC) spoke. When they asked who would try to register to vote, you raised your hand. Two weeks later you and 17 others were driven to the county seat where the courthouse was located. You were confronted by many people, you recalled, "and some of them looked like the Beverly Hillbillies . . . but they wasn't kidding down there; they had on, you know, cowboy hats and they had guns; they had dogs."[3] The registrar pulled out a copy of the state constitution and asked you to explain one section. You could not, so he would not register you.

On the way back to Ruleville, the civil rights workers' bus was stopped and the driver was arrested. The charge? The bus was too yellow. (Police said it looked like a school bus.) Once home, the owner of the plantation where you had toiled for 18 years told you to go back and take your name off the registration forms or leave the plantation. You told him, "I didn't go down there to register for you. I went down to register for myself."[4] You left your house on the plantation and moved in with friends in town (and after the cotton season, your husband also was evicted from the plantation).

It was clear that getting your rights would not be easy. But you are deeply religious, and you told people, "Whether I want to do it or not, I got to. This is my calling. This is my mission."[5]

With help from the SNCC workers, you studied the state constitution and several months later returned to register again. This time you passed the "test." At the next election, however, you were not allowed to vote because you had not paid polltaxes in the previous years when you were not allowed to register or vote.

You were determined to get your right to vote and to help others get theirs. You attended an SCLC training course in

CONTINUED 

OUTLINE

Race Discrimination

- Discrimination Against African Americans
- Overcoming Discrimination Against African Americans
- Continuing Discrimination Against African Americans
- Discrimination Against Hispanics
- Discrimination Against Native Americans

Sex Discrimination

- Discrimination Against Women
- Discrimination Against Men

Affirmative Action

Are Civil Rights Enough?

Conclusion: Is Government Responsive in Granting Civil Rights?

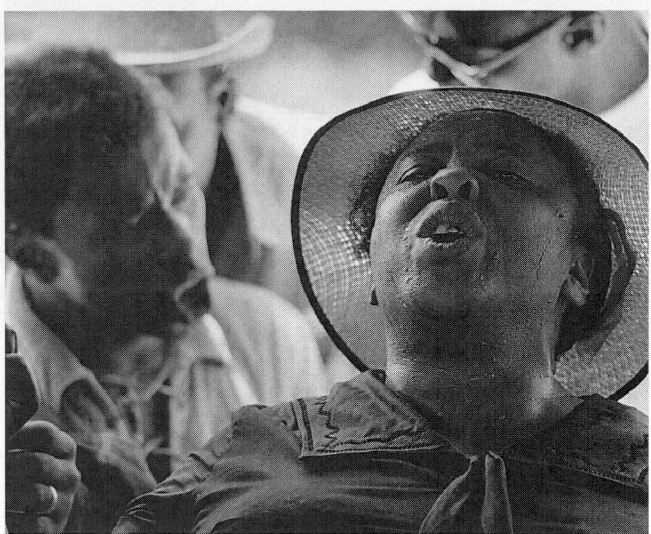

Fannie Lou Hamer leads marchers in song.

Georgia. While returning through Mississippi, you and others in the group sat at a whites-only lunch counter in a bus station and then complained when a white girl was moved ahead of you in line to board the bus. The driver explained that "niggers are not to be in front of the line."[6] When the bus reached the next town, the sheriff arrested members of your group and had them severely beaten. For the rest of your life, you would be plagued by ailments from this beating.[7]

Yet you continued. You organized throughout the Delta, inspiring your neighbors to be strong and mocking those, such as the "chicken-eating preachers," who were less courageous. You traveled throughout the country to help raise funds for civil rights organizations. Although you are short and overweight and you have little education, you are a charismatic figure in the movement—a rousing speaker, perhaps more than anyone except King, and you are a beautiful singer. After your speeches, you lead the audience in religious hymns and movement songs, breaking down the barriers between strangers.

"We're tired of all this beatin', we're tired of takin' this," you say to anyone who will listen. "All my life I've been sick and tired. Now I'm sick and tired of being sick and tired."[8]

In 1964 you were permitted to vote for the first time in your life, but most blacks were still shut out of the regular political process, shut out of the regular Democratic Party in Mississippi. The state party, whose platform endorsed segregation, controlled the state legislature, which passed the laws making voting by blacks nearly impossible. So you and a few others decided to organize your own party.[9] The MFDP would be the voice of the poor blacks in the state.

The Freedom Democrats' immediate goal is to challenge the regular Democrats chosen as delegates to the national convention this year. The Freedom Democrats' claim is that the delegates are unlawful representatives of the state because they were chosen by unlawful means.

The MFDP held its own precinct, county, and state conventions, and allowed whites as well as blacks to participate. You were elected as one of the delegates.

In August your upstart delegation loaded onto buses for the long trip to Atlantic City, New Jersey. Yet when you arrived you learned that national party officials, though sympathetic to your cause, did not want you to challenge the regular delegation.

President Johnson, who took office after President Kennedy was assassinated, is running for his own term. Although a southerner—a Texan—he favors civil rights. He plans to tap Minnesota Senator Hubert Humphrey as his running mate. At the 1948 convention Humphrey gained attention by calling for government to open the door to people of all races. His speech caused many white southerners to walk out in protest.

Johnson will face the Republican, Arizona Senator Barry Goldwater, whose positions are much closer to most white southerners' views. The Democrats are worried, with the civil rights movement and the combination of Humphrey's liberalism and Goldwater's conservatism, that southerners will not vote solidly Democratic this year as they have historically. Now Johnson and other officials are vexed that a challenge by the MFDP, even if unsuccessful, would attract publicity that would upset southerners still more.

So Johnson sent word that he might not pick Humphrey if the Freedom Democrats persisted. Clearly, you would prefer Humphrey to anyone else mentioned as a possible vice presidential candidate, and you would prefer Johnson to Goldwater.

If you gave up your challenge, officials said you could sit as honored guests in the balcony. You rejected this offer; it was too much like the segregated seating in the movie theaters back home. Then officials made their final proposal: You could have two seats as at-large delegates. The regular delegates could keep their seats but would have to pledge loyalty to the national ticket. (It was likely that many would refuse and would leave.) Further, officials promised that in the future delegates would not be seated if their state party did not allow full participation by blacks.

Do you accept this compromise? Some national civil rights leaders urge you to. They have stressed that you are now involved in politics, not protest, and that politics is the art of compromise.[10]

Civil rights refer to equality of rights for persons regardless of their race, sex, or ethnic background. The Declaration of Independence proclaimed that "all men are created equal." The author, Thomas Jefferson, knew all men were not created equal in many respects, but he sought to emphasize that they should be considered equal in rights and equal before the law. This represented a break with England where rigid classes with unequal rights existed; nobles had more rights than commoners. The Declaration's promise did not include nonwhites or women, however. Thus, although colonial Americans advocated equality, they envisioned it only for white men. Others gradually gained more equality, but the Declaration's promise remains unfulfilled for some.

Virtually all minority groups in this country have suffered discrimination. Some religious groups, such as Catholics and Jews, and many ethnic groups, such as the Irish, Italians, and Poles, have made enormous progress against discrimination, but other groups have not. This chapter focuses on the struggle by racial minorities and women to overcome discrimination.

Race Discrimination

African Americans, Hispanics, and Native Americans all have endured and continue to face much discrimination.

Discrimination Against African Americans

Slavery

The first blacks came to America in 1619, just 12 years after the first whites. The blacks, like many whites, initially came as indentured servants. In exchange for passage across the ocean, they were bound to an employer, usually for 4 to 7 years, and then freed. But later in the seventeenth century, the colonies passed laws requiring blacks and their children to be slaves for life. Once slavery was established, the slave trade flourished, especially in the South.

As a result of compromises between northern and southern states, the Constitution accepted slavery. It allowed the importation of slaves until 1808, when Congress could bar further importation, and it required the return of escaped slaves to their owners.

Shortly after ratification of the Constitution, northern states abolished slavery. In 1808 Congress barred the importation of slaves but did not halt the practice of slavery in the South. Slavery became increasingly controversial, and abolitionists called for its end.

The Supreme Court tried to quell the antislavery sentiment in the **Dred Scott case** in 1857.[11] Dred Scott, a slave who lived in Missouri, was taken by his owner to the free state of Illinois and the free territory of Wisconsin and, after five years, was returned to Missouri. The owner died and passed title to his wife, who moved but left Scott in the care of people in Missouri. They opposed slavery and arranged to have Scott sue his owner for his freedom. They argued that Scott's time in a free state and a free territory made him a free man even though he was brought back to a slave state. The owner, also opposed to slavery, had the authority to free Scott, so the purpose of the suit was not to win his freedom. Rather, she and others sought a major court decision to keep slavery out of the territories. Scott, who desperately wanted to be free, was just a pawn in the contest.

In this infamous case, Chief Justice Roger Taney stated that no blacks, whether slave or free, were

Dred Scott.

citizens, and that they were "so far inferior that they had no rights which the white man was bound to respect." Because Scott was not a citizen, he could not sue in federal court. This ruling could have ended the case, but Taney continued. He declared that Congress had no power to control slavery in the territories. This meant that slavery could extend into the territories Congress already had declared free. It also raised the possibility that states could not control slavery within their borders.[12]

By this time, slavery had become the hottest controversy in American politics, and this decision fanned the flames. It provoked vehement opposition in the North and prompted further polarization, which eventually led to the Civil War. Meanwhile, Scott got his freedom from his owner.

The North's victory in the Civil War gave force to President Lincoln's Emancipation Proclamation ending slavery. But blacks would find short-lived solace.

Civil War Amendments and Reconstruction

After the war, Congress passed and the states ratified three constitutional amendments. The Thirteenth prohibited slavery (Mississippi became the last state to ratify the amendment—in 1995.). The Fourteenth granted citizenship to blacks, thus overruling the Dred Scott decision, and also granted "equal protection of the laws" and "due process of law." The Fifteenth provided the right to vote for black men. The **equal protection clause** eventually would become the primary guarantee that government would treat people equally.

Congress also passed a series of civil rights acts to reverse the "Black Codes" that southern states had enacted to deny the newly freed slaves legal rights. These civil rights acts allowed blacks to buy, own, and sell property; to make contracts; to sue; and to be witnesses and jurors in court. They also allowed blacks to use public transportation, such as railroads and steamboats, and to patronize hotels and theaters.[13]

Even so, most freed blacks faced bleak conditions. Congress rejected proposals to break up plantations and give former slaves "40 acres and a mule" or to provide aid to establish schools. Without land or education, they had to work for their former masters as hired hands or sharecroppers. Their status was not much better than it had been. Landowners designed a system to keep them dependent. They allowed sharecroppers to sell half their crop and keep the proceeds, but they paid so little, regardless of how hard the farmers worked, that the families had to borrow to tide them over the winter. The next year they had to work for the landowner to pay off their debt. The following year the cycle continued. And, lacking education, most sharecroppers did not keep records of how much they owed and how much the landowner owed them, and many were cheated.

During the period of Reconstruction, the Union army was supposed to enforce the new amendments and acts. To some extent it did. But in state after state, the South resisted and the North capitulated. After a decade, the two regions struck a deal to end what was left of Reconstruction. The 1876 presidential election between Republican Rutherford Hayes and Democrat Samuel Tilden was disputed in some states. To resolve the dispute, Republicans, most of whom were northerners, and Democrats, many of whom were southerners, agreed to a compromise: Hayes would be named president, and the remaining Union troops would be removed from the South.

Segregation

In both the South and North, blacks came to be segregated from whites.

SEGREGATION IN THE SOUTH The reconciliation between Republicans and Democrats—northerners and southerners—was effected at the expense of blacks. Removing the troops enabled the South to govern itself again, and this enabled the South to reduce blacks to near-slave status.

Slavery itself kept blacks down, and segregation would have been inconvenient when blacks and whites needed to live and work near each other. There was no residential segregation—not in rural areas, where former slaves' shacks were intermixed with plantation houses, and not in urban areas, where few blocks were solidly black. But after slavery, southerners established segregation as another way to keep blacks down. Initially, they did so haphazardly—one law here, another there. By the early 1900s, however, there was a pervasive pattern of **Jim Crow laws.**

Jim Crow laws segregated just about everything. Some segregated blocks within neighborhoods, others neighborhoods within cities. Laws in some small towns excluded blacks altogether. Some did so explicitly; others by setting curfews that required blacks to be off the streets by 10 P.M. Laws also segregated schools, which blacks had been allowed to attend during Reconstruction, and even textbooks (black

American Diversity

Black Masters

Although most slaveowners were white, some were black. William Ellison of South Carolina was one. Born a slave, he bought his freedom and then his family's by building and repairing cotton gins. Over time he earned enough to buy slaves and operate a plantation. With 60 slaves, Ellison ranked in the top 1% of all slaveholders, black or white.

Ellison was unusual, but he was not unique. In Charleston, South Carolina, alone, more than 100 African Americans owned slaves in 1860. Most, however, owned fewer than 4.

Although part of the slave-owning class, black slaveholders were not much more acceptable to whites. Ellison's family was granted a pew on the main floor of the local Episcopal church, but they had to be on guard at all times. Failure to maintain the norms of black-white relations—acting deferentially—could mean instant punishment. And as the Civil War approached, free blacks, even slaveholders, were seen as a growing threat by whites trying to preserve the established order. Harsher legislation regulated their lives. For example, they had to have a white "guardian" to vouch for their character, and they had to carry special papers to show their free status. Without these papers, they could be sold back into slavery.

Some black slaveowners showed little sign of shared concerns with black slaves. Indeed, Ellison freed none of his slaves.

SOURCE: Michael P. Johnson and James L. Roark, *Black Masters* (New York: W. W. Norton, 1984).

schools' texts had to be stored separately from white schools' books). Many laws segregated public accommodations, such as hotels, restaurants, bars, and transportation. At first they required the races to sit in separate sections of streetcars; eventually they required them to sit in separate cars; finally they also forced them to sit in separate sections of waiting rooms. They segregated parks, sporting events, and circuses. Laws segregated black and white checkers players in Birmingham and there were districts for black and white prostitutes in New Orleans. They segregated drinking fountains, restrooms, ticket windows, entrances, and exits. They segregated the races in prisons and in hospitals and in homes for the blind. They even segregated the races in death—in morgues, funeral homes, and cemeteries.

Blacks were forced to defer to whites in all informal settings as well, and failure to do so could mean punishment or even death. They were "humiliated by a thousand daily reminders of their subordination."[14]

Meanwhile, northern leaders, who had championed the cause of the slaves before and during the Civil War, abandoned blacks a decade after the war; Congress did not pass new laws, presidents did not enforce existing laws, and the Supreme Court gutted the constitutional amendments and civil rights acts. All acquiesced in "the southern way."

The Supreme Court struck down the civil rights act allowing blacks to use public accommodations, including transportation, hotels, and theaters.[15] Where the Fourteenth Amendment said that "no state" shall deny equal protection, the Court interpreted this to mean that "no government" shall, but private individuals—owners of transportation, hotels, and theaters—could. The Court's interpretation might seem plausible, but it was clearly contrary to Congress's intent.[16]

Then the Court upheld segregation. Louisiana passed "an Act to promote the comfort of passengers," which mandated separate accommodations in trains. New Orleans black leaders sponsored a case to test the act's constitutionality. Homer Adolph Plessy bought a ticket and sat in the white car. When the conductor ordered him to move to the black car, Plessy refused. He maintained that the act was unconstitutional under the Fourteenth Amendment. In ***Plessy v. Ferguson*** in 1896, the court disagreed, claiming that the act was not a denial of equal protection because it provided equal accommodations.[17] Thus the Court established the **separate-but-equal doctrine,** which allowed separate facilities if they were equal. Of course, government required separate facilities only because it thought the races were not equal, but the Court brazenly commented that the act did not stamp "the colored race with a badge of inferiority" unless "the colored race chooses to put that construction on it." Only Justice John Harlan, a former Kentucky slaveholder, dissented: "Our Constitution is color-blind, and neither knows nor tolerates classes among citizens."

Three years later the Court accepted segregation in schools.[18] A Georgia school board turned a black high school into a black elementary school. Although the board did not establish a new high school for blacks or allow them to attend the ones for whites, the Court did not object. This set a pattern in which separate but equal meant separation but not equality.

SEGREGATION IN THE NORTH Although Jim Crow laws were not as pervasive in the North as in the South, northerners imitated southerners to the point where one writer proclaimed, "The North has surrendered!"[19]

Job opportunities were better in the North. Southern blacks were sharecropping—by 1930 80% of those who farmed were still working somebody else's land[20]—and northern factories were offering jobs. Between 1915 and 1940 more than a million southern blacks headed north in the "Great Migration." But they were forced to live in black ghettos because they could not afford better housing and because they could not escape discrimination in the North, either.

Denial of the Right to Vote

With the adoption of the Fifteenth Amendment, many blacks voted and even elected fellow blacks to office during Reconstruction, but southern states began to disfranchise them in the 1890s (as explained in Chapter 7). Thus, they were unable to elect black representatives or even pressure white officials to oppose segregation.

Violence

To solidify their control, whites engaged in sporadic violence against African Americans. In the 1880s and 1890s, whites lynched about 100 blacks a year. In the 1900s vigilante "justice" continued (Table 1). For example, a mob in Livermore, Kentucky, dragged a black man accused of murdering a white man into a theater. The ringleaders charged admission and hanged the man. Then they permitted the audience to shoot at the swinging body—those in the balcony

Lynching occurred not only in the South but also in northern cities such as Marion, Indiana, in 1930.

TABLE 1 Why Whites Lynched Blacks in 1907

Whites gave the following reasons for lynching blacks, who may or may not have committed these acts.	Number
Murder	5
Attempted murder	5
Manslaughter	10
Rape	9
Attempted rape	11
Burglary	3
Harboring a fugitive	1
Theft of 75¢	1
Having debt of $3	2
Being victor over white man in fight	1
Insulting white man	1
Talking to white girls on telephone	1
Being wife or son of rapist	2
Being father of boy who "jostled" white women	1
Expressing sympathy for victim of mob	3
	56

SOURCE: Adapted from Ray Stannard Baker, *Following the Color Line* (New York: Harper & Row, 1964), pp. 176-77. Copyright 1904, 1905 by S. S. McClure Co. Copyright 1907, 1908 by the Phillips Publishing Company. Copyright 1908 by Doubleday & Company, Inc.

could fire once; those in the better seats could empty their revolvers.[21] In 1919 there were 25 race riots in six months. White mobs took over cities in the North and South, burning black neighborhoods and terrorizing black residents for days on end.[22]

The Ku Klux Klan, which began during Reconstruction and started up again in 1915, played a major role in inflaming prejudice and terrorizing blacks. It was strong enough to dominate many southern towns and even the state governments of Oklahoma and Texas. It also made inroads into some northern states.

Federal officials said such violence was a state problem—presidents refused to speak out and Congress refused to pass legislation making lynching a federal offense—yet state officials did nothing.

For at least the first third of the twentieth century, white supremacy reigned—in the southern states, the border states, and many of the northern states. It also pervaded the nation's capital, where President Woodrow Wilson instituted segregation in the federal government.[23]

Overcoming Discrimination Against African Americans

African Americans fought white supremacy primarily in three arenas—the courts, the streets, and Congress. In general, they fought in the courts first and Congress last, although as they gained momentum they increasingly fought in all three arenas at once.

The Movement in the Courts

The first strategy was to convince the Supreme Court to overturn the separate-but-equal doctrine of *Plessy v. Ferguson*.

THE NAACP In response to white violence, a group of blacks and whites founded the **NAACP,** the National Association for the Advancement of Colored People, in 1909. In its first two decades, it was led by W. E. B. DuBois, a black sociologist. In time it became the major organization fighting for blacks' civil rights.

Frustrated by presidential and congressional inaction and its own lack of power to force action, the NAACP devised a winning strategy—to converge on the federal courts, which were less subject to pressures from the majority. The association assembled a cadre of lawyers, mainly from Howard University Law School, a black university in Washington, D.C., to bring lawsuits attacking segregation and the denial of the right to vote. In 1915 they persuaded the Supreme Court to strike down the grandfather clause (which exempted persons whose ancestors could vote from the literacy test),[24] and two years later they convinced the court to invalidate laws prescribing residential segregation.[25] But the Court continued to allow most devices to disfranchise blacks and most efforts to segregate.

In 1938 the NAACP chose a 30 year-old attorney, Thurgood Marshall, to head its litigation arm.[26] In the next two decades, presidents appointed more liberals to the Supreme Court. These two developments led to the NAACP's success in the courts.

DESEGREGATION OF SCHOOLS Seventeen states and the District of Columbia segregated their schools (and four other states allowed it by local option). The states gave white students better facilities and paid white teachers more. Overall, they spent from 2 to 10 times more on white schools than on black ones.[27] Few of these states had graduate schools for blacks: As late as 1950 they had 15 engineering schools, 14 medical schools, and 5 dental schools for whites, and none for blacks; they had 16 law schools for whites and 5 for blacks.

The NAACP's tactics were first to show that "separate but equal" really resulted in unequal schools and then to attack "separate but equal" head on, arguing that it led to unequal status.

The NAACP began by challenging segregation in graduate schools. Missouri provided no black law school but offered to reimburse blacks who went to out-of-state law schools. In 1938 the Supreme Court said the state had to provide a black law school.[28] Texas established a black law school clearly inferior to the white law school at the University of Texas in size of faculty, student body, library, and opportunities for students to specialize. In 1950 the Court said the black school had to be substantially equal to the white school.[29] Oklahoma allowed a black student to attend the white graduate school at the University of Oklahoma but designated a separate section of the classroom, library, and cafeteria for the student. The court said this too was inadequate, because it deprived the student of the exchange of views with fellow students necessary for education.[30] The Court did not invalidate the separate-but-equal doctrine in these decisions, but it made segregation almost impossible to implement in graduate schools.

The NAACP continued by challenging segregation in grade schools and high schools. Marshall filed suits in two southern states, one border state, one northern state, and the District of Columbia. The suit in the northern state was brought against Topeka, Kansas, where Linda Brown could not attend the school just 4 blocks from her home because it was a white school. Instead, she had to go to a school 21 blocks away.

When the cases reached the Supreme Court, President Eisenhower pressured his appointee, Chief Justice Earl Warren, to rule in favor of segregation. Eisenhower invited Warren and the attorney for the states to the White House for dinner. When the conversation turned to the segregationists, Eisenhower said, "These are not bad people. All they are concerned about is to see that their sweet little girls are not required to sit in schools alongside some big overgrown Negroes."[31]

However, Warren not only voted against segregation but persuaded other justices, some of whom had supported segregation, to vote against it too.

In the landmark case of ***Brown v. Board of Education*** in 1954, the Court ruled unanimously that school segregation violated the Fourteenth Amendment's equal protection clause.[32] In the opinion, Warren asserted that separate but equal not only resulted in unequal schools but was inherently unequal because it made black children feel inferior. In overruling the *Plessy* doctrine, the Court showed how revolutionary the equal protection clause was—or could be interpreted to be. The Court required the segregated states to change their way of life to a degree unprecedented in American history.

After overturning laws requiring segregation in schools, the court overruled laws mandating segregation in such places as public parks, golf courses, swimming pools, auditoriums, courtrooms, and jails.[33]

Linda Brown's kindergarten class. Brown is in the back row, fourth from right.

Outside the Supreme Court, NAACP attorneys George E. C. Hayes, Thurgood Marshall, and James M. Nabrit celebrate the *Brown v. Board of Education* decision.

In *Brown* the Court ordered schools to desegregate "with all deliberate speed."[34] This was a compromise between those who wanted schools to do so immediately and those who wanted schools to do so gradually.[35] The ambiguity of the phrase, however, allowed them to take years to desegregate. The ruling prompted much deliberation but little speed.

The South engaged in massive resistance. The Court needed help from the other branches of government to implement its ruling but failed to get any cooperation for some time. President Eisenhower, who had desegregated the military and also public schools and public facilities in Washington, D.C., was reluctant to tell the states to change. In fact, he joined their representatives in Congress in criticizing the decision. With his position and popularity, the president could have speeded implementation by speaking out in support of the decision, yet he did not do so for more than three years. When nine black students tried to attend a white high school under a desegregation plan in Little Rock, Arkansas, the governor's and state legislature's inflammatory rhetoric against desegregation had encouraged local citizens to take the law into their own hands. Finally President Eisenhower acted; he sent federal troops and federalized the state's national guard to quell the riot.

A few years later President Kennedy used federal marshals and paratroopers to quell violence after the governor of Mississippi blocked the door to keep James Meredith from registering at the University of Mississippi. Kennedy again used force when the governor of Alabama, George Wallace, proclaiming "segregation now, segregation tomorrow, segregation forever," blocked the door to keep blacks from enrolling at the University of Alabama.

After outright defiance, some states attempted to circumvent the ruling by shutting down their public schools and providing tuition grants for students to use at private schools, which at the time could segregate. They also provided other forms of aid, such as textbooks and public recreation facilities, for private schools. These efforts hindered desegregation and hurt black education because the black communities seldom had the resources to establish their own schools.

The states also tried less blatant schemes, such as "freedom of choice" plans, that allowed students to choose the school they wanted to attend. Of course, virtually no whites chose a black school, and, due to strong pressure, few blacks chose a white school. The idea was to achieve desegregation on paper, or token desegregation in practice, in order to avoid real desegregation. But the Court rebuffed these schemes and even forbade discrimination by private schools.[36]

The Court's firm support gave blacks hope. Thurgood Marshall said, "Chief Justice Warren became the image [of the Court] that allowed the poor Negro sharecropper to say, 'Kick me around Mr. Sheriff, kick me around Mr. County Judge, kick me around Supreme Court of my state, but there's one person I can rely on.' "[37]

Nevertheless, progress was excruciatingly slow. If a school district was segregated, a group like the NAACP had to run the risks and spend the time and money to bring a suit in a federal district court. Judges in these courts reflected the views of the state or local political establishment they came from, so the suit might not be successful. If it was, the school board had to prepare a desegregation plan. Members of the school board reflected the views of the community and the pressures from the segregationists, so the plan might not be adequate. If it was, segregationists would challenge it in a federal district court. If the court upheld the plan, segregationists would appeal to a federal court of appeals. Judges in these courts came from the South, and they sat in Richmond and New Orleans. However, they were not as tied to the state or local political establishment, and they usually decided against the segregationists. But then segregationists could appeal to the Supreme Court. Segregationists knew they would lose sooner or later. But

The Movement in Congress

As the civil rights movement expanded, it pressured presidents and members of Congress to act. Presidents Kennedy and Johnson supported civil rights but felt hamstrung by southerners in Congress who through the seniority system had risen to chair key committees and dominate both houses. As a result, the presidents considered civil rights leaders irritating nuisances pushing measures that would alienate the southerners upon whom they had to rely. But once the movement demonstrated its strength, it was able to prod officials to act. After 200,000 blacks and whites marched in Washington in 1963, President Kennedy introduced civil rights legislation, and President Johnson, with his consummate legislative skills, forged a coalition of northern Democrats and northern Republicans to overcome southern Democrats and pass the Civil Rights Act of 1964. After 1,000 blacks and whites had been arrested and many had been attacked in Selma, the public outcry led Johnson to introduce and Congress to pass the Voting Rights Act of 1965.

Within a span of four years, Congress passed legislation prohibiting discrimination in public accommodations, employment, housing, and voting.

DESEGREGATION OF PUBLIC ACCOMMODATIONS The **Civil Rights Act of 1964** prohibits discrimination on the basis of race, color, religion, or national origin in public accommodations. This time, unlike after the Civil War, the Court unanimously upheld the act.[52]

The act does not cover private clubs, such as country clubs, social clubs, or fraternities and sororities, on the principle that the government should not tell people with whom they must associate in private. (The Court has made private schools an exception to this principle to help enforce *Brown*.)

DESEGREGATION OF EMPLOYMENT The Civil Rights Act of 1964 also prohibits employment discrimination on the basis of race, color, religion, national origin, or sex and (as amended) physical handicap, age, or Vietnam-era veteran status. The act covers employers with 15 or more employees and unions.[53]

In addition to practicing blatant discrimination, some employers practiced more subtle discrimination. They required applicants to meet standards unnecessary for their jobs, a practice that hindered blacks more than whites. A high school degree for a manual job was a common example. The court held that standards must relate to the jobs.[54] However, the Court held that standards that hindered blacks more than whites are not necessarily unlawful. Washington, D.C., required applicants for police officer to pass an exam. Although a higher percentage of blacks failed to pass, the Court said the exam related to the job.[55]

When the Burger Court held that standards must relate to the job, it placed the burden of proof on employers. In a dispute, employers had to show that their requirements were necessary. The Rehnquist Court overruled this precedent and interpreted the legislation in a way that shifted the burden of proof to workers.[56] This technical change had a substantial impact; it made it hard for victims to win in court. In 1991 Congress passed new legislation to override the ruling and clarify its intent that employers should bear the burden of proof.

The Court has allowed employers to reduce their work force by laying off workers with less seniority, even though these workers often are disproportionately black due to past discrimination.[57] The principle of "last hired, first fired" means that, in hard times, blacks face even harder times.

DESEGREGATION OF HOUSING Although the Supreme Court had struck down laws that prescribed segregation in residential areas, whites maintained segregation by making **restrictive covenants**—agreements among neighbors not to sell to blacks if they sell their house. In 1948 the Court ruled that courts could not enforce these covenants because doing so would involve the government in discrimination.[58]

Realtors also played a role in segregation by practicing **steering**—showing blacks houses in black neighborhoods and whites houses in white neighborhoods. Unscrupulous realtors practiced **blockbusting.** After a black family bought a house in a white neighborhood, realtors would warn white families that more blacks would move in. Because of prejudice and fear that their houses' values would decline, whites would panic and sell to realtors at a low price. Then realtors would resell to blacks at a higher price. In this way neighborhoods that might have been desegregated were instead resegregated—from all white to all black.

Banks and savings and loans also played a role. They were reluctant to lend money to blacks who wanted to buy a house in a white neighborhood.

Some engaged in **redlining**—refusing to lend money to those who wanted to buy a house in a racially changing neighborhood. The lenders worried that if buyers could not keep up with their payments, the lenders would be left with a house whose value had declined.

The government also played an important role. The Veterans Administration and the Federal Housing Authority, which guaranteed loans to some buyers, were reluctant to authorize loans to blacks who sought to buy houses in white neighborhoods. And the federal government planned low-income housing, which local governments located in ghettos. By approving these sites, the governments helped perpetuate segregation.

But the **Civil Rights Act of 1968** bans discrimination in the sale or rental of housing on the basis of race, color, religion, national origin, and (as amended) on the basis of sex, having children, or being disabled. The act covers about 80% of the available housing and prohibits steering, blockbusting, and redlining.

RESTORATION OF THE RIGHT TO VOTE After years of skirmishing with the states, the Supreme Court and Congress barred measures designed to keep blacks from voting. The Voting Rights Act of 1965 permitted large numbers of blacks to vote for the first time (as explained in Chapter 7).

Continuing Discrimination Against African Americans

African Americans have overcome much discrimination but still face continuing discrimination. Most overt laws and practices have been struck down, but more subtle manifestations of old attitudes and habits persist—and in ways far more numerous and with effects far more serious than this one chapter can convey.[59] Further, of course, blacks must cope with the legacy of generations of slavery, segregation, and discrimination, and for many of them the effects of generations of poverty.

Discrimination in Education

Although de jure segregation of schools has been eliminated, widespread de facto segregation, especially in big cities, remains. In fact, school segregation is getting worse. Despite progress since the mid-1960s, the trend of desegregation slowed and then reversed itself in the 1980s. "For the first time since the *Brown v. Board* decision," according to one study, "we are going backwards."[60] (See Table 2.)

The reversal is due to massive residential segregation that is exacerbated by the flight of whites to the suburbs and, in the largest cities, the removal of whites from the public schools. In our 47 largest cities, only 1 of 4 students in public schools is white. In Detroit, for example, the number of whites in public schools fell from 98,000 in 1970 to 14,000 today; in

How Much Is White Skin Worth?

"You will be visited tonight by an official you have never met. He begins by telling you he is extremely embarrassed. The organization he represents has made a mistake, something that hardly ever happens.

"According to their records, he goes on, you were to have been born black—to another set of parents, far from where you were raised.

"However, the rules being what they are, this error must be rectified, and as soon as possible. So at midnight tonight, you will become black. And this will mean not simply a darker skin, but the bodily and facial features associated with African ancestry. However, inside, you will be the person you always were. Your knowledge and ideas will remain intact. But outwardly you will not be recognizable to anyone you now know.

"Your visitor emphasizes that being born to the wrong parents was in no way your fault. Consequently, his organization is prepared to offer you some reasonable recompense. Would you, he asks, care to name a sum of money you might consider appropriate? He adds that his group is by no means poor. It can be quite generous when the circumstances warrant, as they seem to in your case. He finishes by saying that their records show you are scheduled to live another 50 years—as a black man or woman in America.

"How much financial recompense would you request?"

A professor who puts this parable to white college students finds that most feel $1 million per year—$50 million total—would be appropriate. This much would protect them from, and reimburse them for, the discrimination and danger they would face if they were perceived as black. In acknowledging that white skin is worth this much, the students also are admitting that treatment of the races, even today, is not nearly equal.

SOURCE: Andrew Hacker, *Two Nations: Black and White, Separate, Hostile, Unequal* (New York: Charles Scribner's Sons, 1992), pp. 31–32.

■ TABLE 4 School Segregation of Hispanics Is Greatest in North and Southwest

States with the largest percentages of Hispanic students attending schools with 50% or more minority enrollment.	
New York	86%
Illinois	85
Texas	84
New Jersey	84
California	79
Rhode Island	78
New Mexico	74
Connecticut	72
Pennsylvania	67
Arizona	57

SOURCE: Gary Orfield and Franklin Montfort, "Status of School Desegregation: The Next Generation," a report to the National School Boards Association, reprinted in Karen De Witt, "The Nation's Schools Learn a 4th R: Resegregation," *New York Times,* January 19, 1992, p. E5.

One generation later, per-pupil spending in Texas ranged from about $2,000 in the poorest districts to $19,000 in the wealthiest ones. Yet the 100 poorest districts had a property tax rate more than 50% higher than the 100 wealthiest ones.[109] Faced with these figures, the Texas Supreme Court held in 1989 that state law requires the state to equalize funding.[110] Some other states also have decided to reform financing of schools.

Even where Hispanics attend desegregated schools, often they are segregated within the schools. They face "second-generation discrimination," though not as much as blacks. Hispanics are more likely than Anglos to be put in EMR classes and less likely to be placed in gifted classes.[111] Some Hispanics also face a language barrier because of their inability to speak English. These children are often grouped in bilingual education classes.

Bilingual education gives instruction in substantive subjects such as math in students' native language for those who do not speak English. (It also provides instruction in English itself.) In 1968 Congress encouraged bilingual education by providing funding, and in 1974 the Supreme Court, in a case brought by Chinese parents, held that schools must teach students in a language they can understand.[112] This can be their native language, or it can be English if they have been taught English. These federal actions prompted many states to establish bilingual education programs.

Now more than 150 languages, from Chinese to Yapese, are offered nationwide. With almost three-fourths of the students who do not speak English being Hispanic, Spanish is the most common.[113]

In any event, Hispanic parents want their children to learn English, and to learn it well, as chapter 2 explains.

These programs are controversial, and the debate revolves around politics as much as education. Some proponents of bilingual education, especially Hispanic groups, see it as a way to preserve the students' native language and heritage. So they want it not as a temporary bridge until students learn English but as a permanent fixture for them through high school. These proponents consider it a necessary component of multiculturalism. They say that students with another native language tend to fail in school not solely or primarily because they cannot speak English but because they feel shame for not being part of the dominant group in society. Bilingual education, then, becomes a symbol of rebellion against the dominance of Anglo-Americans.[114]

Many opponents of bilingual education dismiss the need for multiculturalism and resent challenges to the dominance of traditional values. Other opponents acknowledge the benefit of maintaining students' native language and culture but say this is not as important as helping them succeed in the broader society.

Meanwhile, it remains unclear whether bilingual education helps or hinders students in their efforts to learn English or other subjects in school. Bilingual education might help older students already accustomed to speaking their native language, where intensive English instruction might frustrate them and cause them to drop out. As it is, over a quarter of Hispanics drop out of high school, a rate higher than that for blacks.[115] Intensive English instruction might help younger students more.[116]

Bilingual education is expensive and impractical in some places because it requires many extra teachers. For example, "It's hard to find someone who can teach math in Korean," one educator in Virginia explained.[117]

In contrast to the difficulty Hispanics historically had getting into public schools, in 1982 the Supreme Court ruled, by a close vote, that children of illegal aliens have the right to attend public schools.[118] The majority assumed that most of these children, although subject to deportation, would remain in the United States, given the large number of illegal aliens who do remain here. Denying these children an education would deprive them of the opportunity to fulfill their potential or contribute fully to our society.

Partly because of discrimination and low-quality schools, but mainly because of the continuing influx of poorly educated Mexican immigrants, Hispanics have less education than blacks. Nearly one out of five is illiterate. Proportionately fewer Hispanics go to college than non-Hispanics, although the gap shrinks each year.

Combating Discrimination Against Hispanics

Hispanics have had some political success at the local level in places where they are heavily concentrated, but they have had less success at the national level. Except for Cesar Chavez, who led a coalition of labor, civil rights, and religious groups to bring better working conditions for migrant farm workers in California in the 1960s, Hispanics have not had highly visible national leaders or organizations.

Hispanics are more diverse and less cohesive than blacks. Most do not even consider themselves part of a large group of Hispanics.[119] They profess strong loyalty to people of their national origin and have little contact with Hispanics with other ancestry. Thus, most do not call themselves "Hispanics" or "Latinos," but "Mexican Americans," "Puerto Ricans," or "Cuban Americans."[120] Also, they have different legal statuses. Puerto Ricans have American citizenship by birth, but many Hispanics do not have it at all. And they lack a common defining experience in their background, such as slavery for blacks, to unite them.

Hispanics are gradually improving their status. This woman toils as a migrant farm worker, but her son graduated from college and now runs personnel management programs for farmers.

Discrimination Against Native Americans

About one and a half million Native Americans live in the United States. Although some are Eskimos and Aleuts from Alaska, most are Indians, representing more than 300 tribes with different histories, customs, and languages. More than half live off reservations, mostly in urban areas.

Although Native Americans have faced some discrimination similar to that against blacks and Hispanics, they have endured much discrimination of a different nature.

Government Policy Toward Native Americans

The government's policy toward Native Americans has varied over the years, ranging from forced separation at one extreme to forced assimilation at the other.

SEPARATION Initially the policy was separation. For many years people believed the continent was so vast that most of its interior would remain wilderness, populated by Indians who would have ample room to live and hunt. The Constitution reflects this belief. It grants Congress authority to "regulate commerce with foreign nations, and among the several states, and with the Indian tribes." In early cases Chief Justice John Marshall described the tribes as "dependent domestic nations."[121] They were within U.S. borders but outside its political process.

Early treaties reinforced separation by establishing boundaries between Indians and non-Indians. These boundaries were ones the government thought necessary for its growth, the Indians for their survival; they were intended to minimize conflict. White hunters or settlers who ventured across the boundaries could be punished as the Indians saw fit.

But as the country grew, it became increasingly difficult to contain settlers within the boundaries. Mounting pressure to push Native Americans further west led to the Indian Removal Act of 1830, which authorized removal of tribes east of the Mississippi River and relocation on reservations west of the river. At the time people considered the Great Plains to be the great American desert, unfit for habitation by whites but suitable for Indians. At first, removal was voluntary, but eventually it became mandatory for most and was supervised by the U.S. cavalry.

ASSIMILATION As more settlers moved west, the vision of separate Indian country far enough beyond white civilization to prevent conflict faded. In the 1880s the government switched its policy to assimilation. Prompted by Christian churches, officials sought to "civilize" the Indians, that is, to incorporate them into the larger society, whether they wanted to be incorporated or not. In place of their traditional means of subsistence, rendered useless once the tribes were removed from their homeland, the government subdivided reservation land into small tracts and allotted these tracts to tribe members in hopes that they would turn to farming as white and black settlers had. (In the process, the government reclaimed "surplus" land and sold it to white settlers. Ultimately, the Indians lost about two-thirds of their reservation land.)[122] Bureau of Indian Affairs agents, who supervised the reservations, tried to root out Native American ways and replace them with white dress and hairstyles, the English language, and the Christian religion. Government boarding schools separated Native American children from their families to instill these new practices.

CITIZENSHIP Native Americans were not considered citizens but members of separate nations early in the history of the United States. Treaties made exceptions for those who married whites and for those who left their tribes and abandoned their tribal customs. But in 1890, after government policy switched to assimilation, Congress permitted some who remained with their tribes on reservations to become citizens by applying to the U.S. government. Citizenship was sometimes marked by a formal ceremony. In one the Indian shot his last arrow and then took hold of the handles of a plow to demonstrate his assimilation.[123] After World War I, Congress granted citizenship to those who served in the military during the war, and finally in 1924, Congress extended it to all those born in the United States.

Citizenship enabled Indians to vote and hold office, though some states effectively barred them from the polls for decades. Arizona denied them the right to vote until 1948, Utah until 1956.[124]

TRIBAL RESTORATION By the 1930s, the government recognized the negative consequences of coerced assimilation. Most Indians could speak English, but they were poorly educated in other respects. And with their traditional means of earning a living gone,

Tom Torlino, before and after his transformation at a boarding school in Carlisle, Pennsylvania. Native Americans were shorn of their hair and clothes and trained to adopt white ways.

most were poverty stricken. The policy led to destruction of Native American ways without much assimilation in white society. Consequently, Congress implemented a new policy of tribal restoration in 1934 that recognized Indians as distinct persons and tribes as autonomous entities encouraged to govern themselves once again. Traditional cultural and religious practices were accepted, and children, no longer forced to attend boarding schools, were taught some Indian languages.

Reflecting the new policy as well as the efforts by other minorities, Indian interest groups became active in the 1960s and 1970s. Indians tried to take over Alcatraz Island, the former federal prison in San Francisco Bay, which they claimed was their land. Others marched to Washington on the "Trail of Broken Treaties" and occupied the Bureau of Indian Affairs (BIA) building. The BIA, controlled by whites, implemented federal policy for Indians. In 1973 members of the American Indian Movement (AIM) seized the village of Wounded Knee, South Dakota—site of the last massacre of Indians by the U.S. cavalry—and demanded review of treaties between native Americans and the government.

Indian law firms pursued varied interests in court, seeking to protect not only tribal independence and traditional practices but also land, mineral, and water resources. Some filed claims for restoration of tribal territory.

In 1975 the Indian Self-Determination Act gave tribes more authority to administer their own educational and social programs. Now they control about 40% of the BIA's budget.[125]

In recent years Indians have fought for an end to digging up old gravesites and for a return of bones and artifacts unearthed from them. With little regard for Native American culture, "pothunters" have searched for artifacts to sell to collectors. Such looting raises the ire of archaeologists who say, "We'll never know what's been taken or how it relates to what remains in the ground. Everything has been scrambled." But digging for scientific purposes itself enrages some Indians, who say that archaeologists are "hardly any better than grave robbers themselves; only difference is they've got a state permit." Until recent years, in fact, many laws about exhumation of bones applied only to those of whites.[126]

Overall, Native Americans enjoy renewed pride. From 1970 to 1990, according to birth and death records, the Indian population increased by 760,000. Yet, according to people's self-identification for the census, this population rose by 1.4 million.[127] Evidently, many people, including those with only distant Indian ancestry, who did not wish to identify themselves as Indians in 1970, did by 1990.

Collectors of ancient Native American artifacts prompt "pothunters" to dig up gravesites.

The tribes also enjoy renewed vitality. Although the diversity of tribes—divided by geography and culture and located in many of the remotest and poorest parts of the country—makes it difficult to present a united front, they have been able to wrest some autonomy from the government. They have become a more integral part of American federalism. Some have become wealthy from revenue from gambling casinos and mineral rights. As one activist sees the situation, "You have a federal government, state governments, and tribal governments—three sovereigns in one country. This is . . . the civil rights movement of Native Americans."[128]

"Kemo sabe, I want you to be official greeter at my new casino."

Individual Rights of Native Americans

Despite citizenship, many Indians do not have equal rights with whites. Due to tribal self-government, Indians who remain on reservations are subject to tribal laws, and those who break the laws, except the most serious ones, are tried in tribal courts rather than in federal courts where the U.S. Constitution and Bill of Rights would apply.

Tribal courts are not as adversarial as federal and state courts. They reflect the traditional purpose of Native American justice, which is to mediate disputes to the parties' satisfaction rather than to determine guilt and levy punishment. Trials, therefore, are casual, with few professional attorneys. Even judges seldom are attorneys, because they act less as a referee settling legal questions than as the head of a family resolving problems.

Some defendants complained that this system of justice denied them various individual rights. In response, Congress passed the Indian Civil Rights Act of 1968, which applied most provisions of the Bill of Rights to tribal courts. Thus, Congress, which had encouraged the development of autonomous tribal courts, decided the courts were too autonomous and too unlike non-Indian courts.

Yet the act did not apply one major provision of the Bill of Rights, as interpreted by the Supreme Court—the right to counsel for defendants too poor to hire their own. Congress made this exception to limit the adversarial quality that attorneys would inject into tribal courts. This means most defendants get no attorney. Moreover, tribal courts do not apply the provisions of the act strictly, so most defendants do not get their rights consistently. Nevertheless, the act provides more rights than Indians had in the past.

As with other policies, granting individual rights in tribal courts is an effort to balance the demands of the federal government for what it considers justice and the needs of native Americans for self-government.

➤Sex Discrimination

Discrimination Against Women

Unlike blacks, Hispanics, and Native Americans, women are not a minority—in fact, they are a slight majority—but, like minorities, they were not considered equal. Thomas Jefferson, the most egalitarian of the Founders, insisted, "Were our state a pure democracy there would still be excluded from our deliberations women, who, to prevent deprivation of morals and ambiguity of issues, should not mix promiscuously in gatherings of men."[129] That is, women are too moral—they would be corrupted by politics—and too muddleheaded—they would confuse the issues.

Indeed, women were not considered equal. In 1824 the Mississippi Supreme Court acknowledged a husband's right to beat his wife, and some other state courts followed.[130] According to the "rule of thumb," a husband could not beat his wife with a weapon thicker than his thumb.

Before the Civil War, women were not admitted to public high schools. Because they were being prepared for motherhood, education was considered unnecessary, even dangerous. According to the *Encyclopaedia Britannica* in 1800, women had smaller brains than men.[131] Education would fatigue them and possibly ruin their reproductive organs. Similarly, women were not encouraged to hold jobs. Women who did seek employment were shunted into menial and industrial jobs, mostly in sewing shops and textile mills, where they worked long hours for low wages. (Apparently people were not concerned that such jobs would ruin these women's reproductive organs.)

Women were denied the right to vote in most places, and married women were denied other legal rights. They did not have the right to manage property they owned before marriage, to manage wages they received from jobs, to enter into contracts, or to sue. Beginning in 1839, some states legislated these rights, but when disputes arose, male judges hesitated to tell other men how to treat their wives. Often, then, the rights did not exist in practice. Other states did not even adopt such rights until well into the twentieth century.

The Women's Movement

Early feminists were determined to remedy these inequities. Many had gained political and organizational experience in the abolitionist movement. It was not considered "unladylike" for women to campaign for the end of slavery, because the movement was associated with religious groups. Yet women were barely tolerated by the male leaders of the movement and not allowed to participate fully in the major antislavery society. They formed their own antislavery society, but when they attended a convention of antislavery societies, they were not allowed to sit with the male delegates.

Angry at such treatment, the women held a meeting to discuss the "social, civil and religious rights of women." This first Women's Rights Convention in 1848 adopted a declaration of rights based on the Declaration of Independence. It said, "We hold these truths to be self-evident: that all men and women are created equal." The convention also passed a resolution in favor of women's suffrage.

Following the Civil War, women who had worked in the abolitionist movement expected that women, as well as blacks, would get legal rights and voting rights. When the Fourteenth and Fifteenth Amendments did not include women, they felt betrayed and they disassociated themselves from the black movement. They formed their own organizations to campaign for women's suffrage. This movement, led by Susan B. Anthony and Elizabeth Cady Stanton, succeeded in 1920, when the Nineteenth Amendment gave women the right to vote.

Then dissension developed within the women's movement. Many groups felt the passage of the Nineteenth Amendment was but a first step in the struggle for equal rights. They proposed the Equal Rights Amendment to remedy remaining inequities. Other groups felt the battle had been won. They opposed the Equal Rights Amendment, arguing it would overturn labor laws recently enacted to protect women. Because of this dissension and the conservatism in the country, the movement became relatively dormant.[132]

The movement reemerged in the 1960s. As a result of the civil rights movement, many women recognized their own inferior status. Numerous writers sensitized more women to this. A group of middle-class, professional women formed the National Organization for Women (NOW) in 1966 and installed Betty Friedan as its first president. They resolved "to bring women into full participation in the mainstream of American society now."

Other women, also middle class but veterans of the civil rights and antiwar movements, had developed a taste for political action and gained political experience. They formed other organizations. Where NOW fought primarily for women's political and economic rights, the other organizations fought more broadly for women's liberation in all spheres of life. Together these organizations pushed the issue of discrimination against women back onto the public agenda.

The Movement in Congress

Under pressure from the women's movement, Congress adopted legislation to prohibit discrimination against women in employment, education, and credit. Congress also passed the Equal Rights Amendment, though the states failed to ratify it.

EMPLOYMENT The Civil Rights Act of 1964 forbids discrimination on the basis of sex as well as race in hiring, promoting, and firing. The original bill did not cover sex discrimination, and its inclusion was the result of a joke. Eighty-one-year-old Representative

During World War II, women were urged into the labor force to replace men called to war. "Rosie the Riveter" became a symbol of women working in the war effort. Following the war, they were told that it was patriotic to go home and give their jobs to returning veterans. This 1955 magazine cover depicts the stereotypical women's role in this postwar era before the beginning of the modern women's movement.

Howard Smith (D-Va.) proposed an amendment to add sex discrimination to the bill. A foe of equal rights for blacks, Smith thought his proposal so ludicrous and radical that it would help defeat the entire bill. Indeed, during debate on the amendment, members of Congress laughed so hard that they could barely hear each other speak.[133] But the joke was on them, because the amendment, and then the entire bill, passed. Unlike other legislation prohibiting discrimination against women, Congress adopted this provision without pressure from women.

The act prohibits discrimination on the basis of sex, except where sex is a "bona fide occupational qualification" for the job. The Equal Employment Opportunity Commission (EEOC), which enforces the act, interprets it broadly and accepts sex as a legitimate qualification for very few jobs. For example, employers can seek a man or woman to be a restroom attendant, lingerie salesclerk, model, actor, or performer in the entertainment business where sex appeal is considered necessary. On the other hand, employers cannot seek a male for jobs men traditionally held, such as those that entail heavy physical labor, unpleasant working conditions, late-night hours, overtime, or travel.

Some employers are reluctant to comply. For matched pairs of men and women, resumes were sent to 65 Philadelphia restaurants in 1995. The men were more than twice as likely to get an interview and more than five times as likely to get the job at the higher-priced restaurants than the equally qualified women.[134]

An executive of a Fortune 500 company, in a conversation with business professors at a southwestern university in a recent year, admitted that his company prefers to hire men married to traditional housewives.[135] The men are dependent upon their own job for all their family's income, and they are relieved of most of the household chores. It is not coincidental that executives who reach the higher rungs of management, according to one research organization, are "almost always men from what used to be the traditional family—men with wives who don't work outside the home."[136]

The **Equal Pay Act** of 1963 requires that women and men receive equal pay for equal work. The act makes exceptions for merit, productivity, and seniority. Yet more than a quarter century after passage of the act, working women earn only 75¢ for every $1.00 working men earn (although young women, from 16 through 24, earn more than 90¢ for every $1.00 young men earn).

Women make less partly because they have less education and experience than men in the same jobs; many stopped their schooling or working to marry and have children (see Table 5). But they make less primarily because they have different jobs than men, and these jobs pay much less.

Traditionally, women have been shunted into a small number of jobs; currently 80% are squeezed into 20 of the 427 jobs identified by the Department of Labor.[137] These "pink-collar" jobs include secretaries (99% are women), household workers (98%), child care workers (97%), nurses (96%), waiters (88%, although waiters in fancy restaurants, who get larger tips, are mostly men), librarians (87%), health technicians (84%), elementary school teachers (83%), and bank tellers (81%).[138] In contrast, few women are plumbers (less than 1%), truck drivers (2%), butchers (7%), or mail carriers (12%).[139]

Although the Equal Pay Act mandates equal pay for essentially equal work, it does not require equal pay for comparable work—usually called **comparable worth.** According to a personnel study in Washington State, maintenance carpenters and secretaries performed comparable jobs, but the carpenters, mostly men, made about $600 a month more than the secretaries, mostly women. Overall, the study found that "men's jobs" paid about 20% more than comparable "women's jobs." These findings prompted unions representing government employees in the state to file a suit and demand an increase in pay for jobs held mostly by women. The federal court of appeals, in an opinion by Judge Anthony Kennedy, now on the Supreme Court, rejected comparable worth. Nevertheless, some state and city governments have begun to implement comparable worth plans for their employees after prodding by unions and women's groups. Most private companies, however, have not adopted comparable worth because it would require them to pay most of their women employees more.

TABLE 5 Women with Children Earn Less

FEMALE-TO-MALE EARNINGS PERCENT	
With Children	Without Children
72%	91%

These figures are for whites, ages 20-44, in 1987. The figures control for age, education, skill level, labor force turnover, and region.

SOURCE: Current Population Survey, 1988. Reprinted in June O'Neill, "Women & Wages," *The American Enterprise*, November-December, 1990, p. 32.

EDUCATION The Education Amendments of 1972 (to the Civil Rights Act of 1964) forbid discrimination on the basis of sex in schools and colleges that receive federal aid. The amendments were prompted by discrimination against women by undergraduate and graduate colleges, especially in admissions and financial aid.

The language of the amendments, often referred to as "Title IX," is so broad that the Department of Education, which administers them, has established rules that cover more aspects of education than their congressional supporters expected.[140] The department has used the amendments to prod institutions into employing and promoting more female teachers and administrators, opening vocational training classes to women and home economics classes to men, and offering equal athletic programs to women. If institutions do not comply, the government can cut off their federal aid.

The amendments have had a substantial impact on athletic programs in particular. Before the amendments, schools and colleges provided fewer sports for women than for men, and they spent far fewer dollars—for scholarships, equipment, and facilities—on those they did provide. Now institutions offer more sports for women and allocate more money for them, although institutions do not provide equal resources, primarily because of the size and cost of men's football programs and the lack of a women's counterpart. To offset this disparity somewhat, more schools are establishing women's teams in sports where they do not have a men's team. The number of schools that offer women's soccer, for example, increased from 133 to 445 during the 1980s and 1990s.[141]

An unintended consequence of the amendments, however, has been a reduction in the number of noted, are not as private as traditional men's clubs, which still may discriminate against women.[158]

Only occasionally did the Court go in the opposite direction. Most important, the Court ruled that government may give military veterans a preference over nonveterans in obtaining civil service jobs.[159] Because most veterans are men, this benefits many men who seek government jobs at the expense of almost all women who seek them. Nevertheless, the Court said government may adopt this policy to thank veterans for their service.

Although formal restrictions against women have been struck down, informal discrimination continues. Women get hired, but some find it more difficult to get promoted than comparable men. They hit a "glass ceiling."

Many women in masculine workplaces feel pressure to submerge feminist beliefs. "You're not a feminist, are you?" is a familiar query. Women who seek career advancement say they would commit "professional suicide" if they spoke up for their rights or beliefs as women.[160]

Some women also face sexual harassment. "In college, they lied to us twice," one disillusioned young woman said. "They said it would be equal. And they said it would be safe."[161]

Mothers with young children confront more obstacles. Their male employers and co-workers think women should be responsible for child rearing, but these men do little to accommodate the demands of child rearing. Most companies do not provide paid maternity leaves, flexible schedules, or on-site day

Sexual Harassment at Work

Although the Supreme Court had ruled that sexual harassment was a form of job discrimination prohibited by the Civil Rights Act of 1964,[1] and Congress had passed a law allowing victims to collect monetary damages from employers for distress, illness, or loss of their job due to harassment, there was little public awareness of the law until Clarence Thomas' confirmation hearings for appointment to the Supreme Court in 1991.

The hearings propelled sexual harassment to the forefront of societal debate. For seven days the public was riveted to the televised hearings. Anita Hill's charges—that Thomas, as her supervisor at the Equal Employment Opportunity Commission, made lewd comments about her, about sex, about finding pubic hairs on Coke cans and watching animals have sex in films—led to many discussions around workplace water coolers.

The hearings illustrated that sexual harassment includes more than just physical acts, such as unwanted touching, or propositions in which sex is demanded in exchange for a job or promotion. It also encompasses other conduct and comments that create a "hostile working environment."

Although some men fear that innocent comments will be construed as harassment by women, other men who do not want women as co-workers intend their behavior to upset women. Sometimes they turn the workplace into a locker room and then say, "What's the matter, you can't handle it? You wanted equality—you got it." For example, the first female skilled crafts worker for Santa Clara County, California, found that in the yard the men kept the women's restroom locked and on the road they refused to stop to let her use a restroom. "You wanted a man's job," a superior told her, "you learn to pee like a man."[2]

The dynamics of sexual harassment do not revolve around sex as much they reflect abuse of power. A supervisor, or a co-worker in a position to cause problems, makes a woman feel vulnerable. Thus, the supervisor or co-worker demonstrates psychological dominance or economic dominance ("You need this job? Then keep quiet.").

Surveys show that a third of female workers say they have been sexually harassed on the job.[3] After 23 women acknowledged in 1992 and 1993 that they had to fend off sexual advances by Senator Bob Packwood (R.-Ore.), the *Washington Post* conducted a survey of women who worked as aides to

Do You Think It Is Sexual Harassment If a Man Who is a Woman's Supervisor . . .

	YES
Insists on discussing pornographic acts with her	91%
Makes remarks to her that contain sexual references or double meanings	80
Pressures her to go out to dinner with him	77
Insists on telling sexual jokes to her	74
Frequently puts his arm around her shoulders or back	64
Flirts with the woman	41

SOURCE: A nationwide survey of men and women by Yankelovich Clancy Shulman for *Time* and CNN. *Time*, October 21, 1991, p. 64.

care. The United States lags far behind many other countries, 98 of which grant partly paid maternity leaves for at least three months.[162]

When Congress passed a bill requiring employers to grant unpaid maternity leaves, President Bush vetoed it, but then President Clinton signed a similar bill. Companies must allow leaves for up to three months for workers with newborn or recently adopted children or with seriously ill family members. The act applies to companies that have 50 employees and to workers who work 25 hours a week for a year. This covers about 40% of American workers.

So far, however, few workers have taken advantage of maternity leaves or flexible schedules where they are available. Researchers have concluded that managers often do not support such measures, so employees are reluctant to take advantage of them. At a time when many companies have laid off workers to cut costs, "If you look like you are not career-oriented, you can lose your job."[162a]

Discrimination Against Men

Although nearly all sex discrimination has been against women, some has been against men. However, laws discriminating against men often have reinforced negative stereotypes about women and in this sense have perpetuated discrimination against them as well.

The Burger Court struck down Oklahoma's law that allowed women to drink beer at 18 but required men to wait until 21.[163] Prior to the law, men 18 through 20 were arrested for drunk driving 10 times

Continued

members of Congress or staffers for congressional committees. It found the same results: A third of them had been sexually harassed in the hallowed halls of Congress, and a third of these had been harassed by a member of Congress. (The others had been harassed by supervisors, co-workers, or lobbyists.)[4]

Yet few victims file formal complaints, let alone bring lawsuits, because they need their jobs. According to several studies, only 3% of women who have been harassed have filed formal complaints.[5] On Capitol Hill, 80% of the women surveyed said they would lose their job if they did; 80% said they would never find another job there if they did; and 70% said nothing would be done to the harasser anyway.[6]

Sexual harassment can be directed toward men as well. About 15% of male workers say they have been sexually harassed by men or women on the job.[7]

While the public expressed disgust with the Thomas hearings—because of the way they were conducted and the charges they revealed—people were sensitized to sexual harassment. After the hearings, more women recognized that behavior they had dismissed as merely annoying was actually harassment. More workers filed complaints with the EEOC—nearly twice as many annually.[8] And more employers adopted written policies and held training sessions to educate their employees.

The new awareness of sexual harassment apparently affected attitudes toward Thomas and Hill as well. After the hearings, the public thought Thomas had told the truth (40% to 24% for Hill), but a year later the public thought Hill had told the truth after all (44% to 34% for Thomas).[9]

In 1993 the Supreme Court sent a signal to lower courts and employers to take harassment seriously. It ruled unanimously, just 27 days after oral arguments, that victims do not have to prove a severe psychological injury to collect damages.[10] Teresa Harris, the rental manager of an equipment company, had endured repeated comments by her boss—"You're a woman; what do you know?"—and suggestions to accompany him to the Holiday Inn to negotiate her raise. Harris and other female workers also had been asked to retrieve coins from his pants pockets. Although Harris did not suffer any concrete psychological injury, she did feel compelled to quit the job. Justice O'Connor wrote that the law applies if a reasonable person would consider the workplace a hostile environment. (On the other hand, the law does not apply to "merely offensive" conduct short of creating an abusive environment.)

1. *Meritor Savings Bank v. Vinson,* 91 L.Ed.2d 49 (1986).
2. Nancy Gibbs, "Office Crimes," *Time,* October 21, 1991, p. 53.
3. Richard Morin, "Think Twice Before You Say Another Word," *Washington Post National Weekly Edition,* December 28, 1992–January 3, 1993, p. 37.
4. Richard Morin, "Jack and Jill Went Up the Hill," *Washington Post National Weekly Edition,* March 1–7, 1993, p. 37.
5. Daniel Goleman, "Sexual Harassment: About Power, Not Sex." *New York Times,* October 22, 1991, p. B8.
6. Morin, "Jack and Jill Went Up the Hill."
7. Janice Castro, "Sexual Harassment: A Guide," *Time,* January 20, 1992, p. 37.
8. Kara Swisher, "Corporations Are Seeing the Light on Harassment," *Washington Post National Weekly Edition,* February 14-20, 1994, p. 21.
9. Jill Smolowe, "Anita Hill's Legacy," *Time,* October 19, 1992, p. 56.
10. *Harris v. Forklift Systems,* 126 L.Ed.2d 295 (1993).

In 1995 about 13% of white males told pollsters they think they lost a job or promotion at some time because of their race, while about 10% think they did because of their sex.[6] Many others claim they "heard about" someone else who was a victim of affirmative action. Yet often persons do not know the worker hired or promoted instead of them or do not know the qualifications of this worker (which may have been better than those of the white male).

One analyst concluded that white males' beliefs that they are at a disadvantage come from a concern that "the category I belong to, the group I'm in, doesn't have the same access we used to."[7] This perception is correct though exaggerated, given the limited scope of affirmative action.

Does Affirmative Action Result in Less Merit?

It is difficult to assess merit. The concept means different things to different people, and its characteristics cannot be measured precisely. For example, assume one applicant for a social work position has more years of experience, another has the highest score on the exam, while another seems better able to understand and communicate with the people who are the agency's clients. Which applicant is more qualified? Some people would emphasize the first applicant's experience, others would focus on the second applicant's score—these can be measured—while still others would emphasize the third applicant's ability to understand and communicate—these cannot be measured easily.

The Supreme Court's decision approving affirmative action for women reflects the problems in assessing merit. A woman who applied to be a dispatcher for the transportation agency of Santa Clara County, California, was one of nine considered qualified for the job. She scored 73, and a white man scored 75, on a subjective oral exam administered by a panel of men who had never hired a woman for a skilled position. The county decided that the two-point differential was inconsequential and hired the woman for affirmative action. The man sued for reverse discrimination, but the Court upheld the hiring.[8]

In addition, opponents of affirmative action tend to compare it with an idealized picture of traditional employment practices. Opponents assume these practices were based squarely on merit. In reality, these practices were based only partly on merit.

For government employment, many jobs were open only to those who already worked for that government. Other jobs were open to those who took exams and performed well, but the jobs did not necessarily go to the person who scored highest. Typically they went to the person among the three or five who scored highest and who had the desired political connections, personal connections, personality, or area of residence, or to the person who was a military veteran.

For faculty positions in colleges and universities, the "old boy network" of fellow faculty at other schools was the primary means of hiring. Departments seldom advertised their positions widely.

For private employment, vacancies were advertised by word of mouth to relatives or friends. Union membership was necessary for many skilled blue-collar jobs, and places were reserved for sons and brothers—rarely daughters and sisters—of members. Even when jobs were advertised, usually no effort was made to canvass the locality or region for the most meritorious candidate.

For both public and private employment, jobs often went to persons of particular ethnic groups when members of these groups reached positions of power. Italians and Irish in New York and Boston, for example, hired other Italians and Irish.

Nevertheless, there is a legitimate concern that affirmative action might result in lower standards and lower quality employees or students. Affirmative action probably pressures some employers and schools into choosing some

Source: Clay Bennett, North America Syndicate.

minorities or women who lack adequate education, training, or experience because of past discrimination. At the same time, affirmative action provides a larger pool of talent to choose from. According to one executive, before affirmative action, "We were not using all the talent available." With affirmative action, the company found a "goldmine" of untapped talent.[9]

Does Affirmative Action Result in Reverse Discrimination?

By compensating for past discrimination against some, does affirmative action constitute new discrimination against others? If the number of jobs or places in schools are limited and if more are offered to minorities or women, fewer are available for white men. To determine if this is reverse discrimination, consider four possible outcomes of affirmative action: (1) Choosing a minority or woman who is more qualified than a white man. Although the principle of nondiscrimination, rather than affirmative action, should have led to this outcome, often it did not. In fact, the greatest accomplishment of affirmative action may have been to prod employers to hire or promote minorities and women who should have been hired or promoted all along. (2) Choosing a minority or woman who is as qualified as a white man. This occurs frequently in less specialized jobs, where candidates do not differ clearly in qualifications, but rarely in more specialized jobs, where candidates do differ significantly. (3) Choosing a minority or woman who, though qualified, is less qualified than a white man. Here affirmative action is similar to past practices in that both select persons from among qualified candidates but according to some factor other than merit. (4) Choosing a minority or woman who is unqualified. Employers or schools are not required to choose unqualified persons, but undoubtedly they do occasionally.

Of these four outcomes, only the last two result in reverse discrimination. When they occur white men pay for the sins of their fathers and grandfathers. Yet the first two probably occur more often. White men dominate public and private institutions and, as the personnel director of a Fortune 500 company observed, "People tend to hire people like themselves."[10] If reverse discrimination were widespread, minorities and women would hold more jobs, at higher levels, than they do now.

Does Affirmative Action Result in Less Fairness?

When affirmation action prods employers to hire or promote minorities or women who are more qualified than white men (see outcome 1 above), it results in more fairness. When affirmative action prompts employers to hire or promote minorities or women who are as qualified or less qualified than white men (outcomes 2 and 3 above), it appears to result in less fairness. A Chicago police officer complained, "I didn't own slaves, and I shouldn't be penalized for what happened hundreds of years ago."[11]

But, of course, whites benefited from hundreds of years of slavery, segregation, and discrimination. Whites increased their wealth and improved their position in society and then passed these gains on to their descendants. (Sometimes whites gained at the direct expense of blacks. Other times they gained because of the lack of competition from blacks—from a sizable portion of the population.) For instance, after World War II, Levittowns in New York and Pennsylvania developed suburban tract housing and made it available to white GIs—for just $100 down—but not to black GIs. In the 1990s, these houses are worth about $180,000. This wealth will continue to accrue to these white families but never to any black families.[12]

Although many individual whites today are not responsible for the status of blacks today, they continue to benefit from the discrepancy. Without affirmative action or some comparable policy to redress past discrimination, they will continue to benefit from it. The advantages will be locked in. (Even with affirmative action, which is only a modest effort to compensate, most advantages will remain.)

This problem is compounded by society's view that slavery was not just bad luck—one of life's misfortunes that seem to befall people randomly—or even a shortsighted or inefficient policy, but that it was morally wrong behavior. As a black Birmingham, Alabama, firefighter observed: "Say your father robs a bank, takes the money and buys his daughter a Mercedes, and then buys his son a Porsche and his wife a home in the high-rent district. Then they discover [his crime]. He has to give the cars and house back. And the family starts to cry: 'We didn't do anything.' [But] sometimes you have to pay up. If a wrong has been committed, you have to right that wrong."[13] Seen in this light, it is not clear that affirmative action results in less fairness.[14]

Still, the analogy becomes less valid in an increasingly diverse society, with many newcomers whose ancestors were not here during the era of slavery or even Jim Crow, and who may not be white. The recent discussions of affirmative action in the California university system, for example, reveal that the biggest beneficiaries of removal of affirmative action admittances would be Asians, not whites.

Why, if affirmative action has made only modest differences, is there is so much opposition to it? Many people are limited in their historical knowledge. They assume the Civil War not only abolished slavery but also leveled the playing field for blacks and whites. Many people are affected by the pervasive racism in society. Although such feelings are considered socially unacceptable now, at least in some circles, the feelings exist still.[15] In focus groups (which, as

Chapter 6 explained, are designed to make participants feel comfortable and free to express their opinions), the racism comes out. Researchers who tried to discover why middle-class whites in a Michigan county were leaving the Democratic Party found that the main reason was the racial policies of the Democratic Party juxtaposed with the racial feelings of the whites. The participants considered affirmative action a threat to their livelihood and the city of Detroit, with its black majority, a sinkhole for their tax dollars. These concerns, by themselves, would not necessarily be evidence of racism, but prejudicial attitudes emerged. When researchers had participants listen to a quotation from Robert Kennedy challenging whites to honor their "special obligation" to blacks, almost all participants reacted angrily. One even remarked, "No wonder they killed him."[16]

Many people feel that affirmative action is just not fair, that America should try to be a colorblind society. Some feel that affirmative action distributes benefits in a way that does not take into account need, effort, or any characteristics except skin color or gender. (Ironically, these are the very points used by civil rights advocates against segregation laws.)

This feeling of unfairness is exacerbated by the economic problems that have prevailed since the 1970s. During the 1960s and 1970s, the economy was robust and affirmative action was not so threatening. But during the 1980s and 1990s, the economy has been sluggish, with more competition for good jobs and decent paychecks. The real earnings (adjusted for inflation) of white men have declined, and the economic status of white men without a college degree has dropped the most. As a result, affirmative action has become very threatening.

Politicians could explain that major economic trends, not affirmative action, account for the precarious position of many workers: corporations have computerized and automated many functions, downsized their workforce, hired part-time employees to whom they do not have to pay benefits, and moved their factories to Third World countries to minimize their payroll. It is easier, however, to blame affirmative action. Some Republicans see affirmative action as a "wedge issue"—an issue that enables them to drive a wedge between the constituencies of their opponents. By focusing on affirmative action, they hope to drive white men, especially laborers, from the Democratic Party, and by emphasizing minorities (rather than women) as the beneficiaries of affirmative action, they hope to drive some white women from the Democratic Party as well.[17]

The debate over affirmative action shows how the parties are trying to be responsive to the voters and to their members. When Republicans discovered that opposition to the policy was intense, they tried to capitalize on it. When Democrats saw that the issue could splinter their party, some called for reform of the policy to retain white men, while others called for continuation of the policy to satisfy minorities and women who constitute key groups in the party. Yet the parties have framed the issue for their own short-term gains rather than to have a true discussion where the rights and wrongs of both sides could be considered and the polarization of the races could be minimized. Thus, the debate also has reflected the downside of being responsive to the people.

---

1. Richard Lacayo, "A New Push for Blind Justice," *Time,* February 20, 1995, p. 39.
2. Richard Morin and Sharon Warden, "Poll Says Americans Angry about Affirmative Action," *Washington Post,* March 24, 1995, p. A4. There appears to be majority support for the vague concept of "affirmative action," undefined, but the support evaporates when the questions use language indicating or implying any preference for minorities or women. Richard Morin, "No Place for Calm and Quiet Opinions," *Washington Post National Weekly Edition,* April 24–30, 1995, p. 34.
3. Morin and Warden, "Poll Says Americans Angry about Affirmative Action."
4. Louis Jacobson, "A Speak-No-Evil Veil Lifted," *National Journal,* April 1, 1995, p. 836.
5. Peter Eisinger, *Black Employment in City Government* (Washington, D.C.: Joint Center for Political Studies, 1983).
6. Donald Kaul, "Privilege in Workplace Invisible to White Men Who Enjoy It," *Lincoln Journal-Star,* April 9, 1995.
7. Richard Morin and Lynne Duke, "A Look at the Bigger Picture," *Washington Post National Weekly Edition,* March 16–22, 1992, p. 9.
8. *Johnson v. Transportation Agency,* 94 L.Ed.2d 615 (1987).
9. Douglas B. Huron, "It's Fashionable to Denigrate Hiring Quotas—But It's Wrong," *Washington Post National Weekly Edition,* Aug. 27, 1984, p. 23.
10. Robert J. Samuelson, "End Affirmative Action," *Washington Post National Weekly Edition,* March 6–12, 1995, p. 5.
11. Thomas B. Edsall, "A Political Powder Keg," *Washington Post National Weekly Edition,* January 14–20, 1991, p. 6.
12. Juan Williams, "White Man's Burden," *Washington Post National Weekly Edition,* April 10–16, 1995, p. 24.
13. Edsall, "A Political Powder Keg."
14. For an extended analysis, see Ronald J. Fiscus (ed. Stephen L. Wasby), *The Constitutional Logic of Affirmative Action* (Durham, NC: Duke University Press, 1992).
15. Jacobson, "A Speak-No-Evil Veil Lifted."
16. Elizabeth Kolbert, "Test-Marketing a President," *New York Times Magazine,* August 30, 1992, p. 18.
17. Rochelle L. Stanfield, "The Wedge Issue," *National Journal,* April 1, 1995, pp. 790–93.

➤Are Civil Rights Enough?

Although minorities and women have advanced toward legal equality, judicial decisions and legislative acts have not guaranteed economic equality. Expansion of civil rights has opened doors for minorities and women, but those in the middle class were better positioned to pass through the doors. The percent of black professionals nearly tripled, from 1.7% of all professionals in 1966 to about 5% in 1993.[176] The number of black families able to leave the inner cities for the suburbs dramatically increased. One-third of all blacks live in the suburbs now. The majority of blacks in the Washington, D.C., area, for example, live not in the District of Columbia, but in the suburbs.[177]

But other blacks lag far behind whites in education, employment, income, housing, and longevity, Blacks have illiteracy and poverty rates three times those of whites, a college graduation rate one-half that of whites, and unemployment and infant mortality rates twice those of whites. Their life expectancy is six years less than that of whites because of poorer living conditions and health care and greater drug use and violence in their communities.

The plight of young black men is worse than that of any other group in society. Almost one of every four black men between 20 and 29 is in prison or on probation or parole.[178] And a black man in Harlem has less chance of living past 40 than a man in Bangladesh.[179]

Although blacks overall made gains in the 1960s and 1970s, they lost ground, according to some measures, since then. Economic stagnation and economic changes, beginning in the mid-1970s, hit the poor the hardest. Good-paying manufacturing jobs in the cities—the traditional path out of poverty for immigrant groups—declined, while service jobs in the suburbs increased. Blacks, especially men, lost their manufacturing jobs. Most service jobs were too far away or they required too much education or paid too low wages to compensate. Black men found it hard to support a family. The result was a decrease in the number of "marriageable" black men and an increase in the number of households headed by black women. These households are among the poorest in the country.[180]

Although the success of the civil rights movement has enabled some blacks to escape, others are trapped in the poverty and pathologies of the ghetto.

A sudden surge in drugs and crimes in inner cities compounded the deleterious effects of the changes in the economy. Crack, a cheap form of cocaine, was new in the mid-1980s and became epidemic in the late 1980s in some cities. Entire neighborhoods became overwhelmed by drug use and drug trafficking. Crack ravaged the lives of users in ways that other drugs did not. And crack created steady demand by users and huge profits for dealers, which stimulated an increase in violence. As drug gangs multiplied and tangled with each other for control of turf, drug executions and drive-by shootings became commonplace.[181]

Meanwhile, middle-class blacks left the inner cities for the suburbs. Their migration left those in the ghettos with fewer healthy businesses, strong schools, or other institutions to provide stability and fewer role models to portray mainstream behavior.[182]

Many who live in the ghetto face a bleak future. After the riots in the 1960s, the Kerner Commission, appointed by President Johnson to examine the cause of the riots, concluded, "What white Americans have never fully understood—but what the Negro can never forget—is that white society is deeply implicated in the ghetto. White institutions created it, white institutions maintain it, and white society condones it." After the riots, however, governments did little to improve the conditions that precipitated the riots. Now, over a quarter of a century later, the conditions are the same—except for the drug epidemic and the AIDS epidemic, which have combined to make life in the ghetto even more grim and dangerous than before.

After the riots that followed the first trial of the Los Angeles police officers who beat Rodney King, there was more talk about improving the conditions in the ghetto. But a columnist who had heard such talk before commented, "My guess is that when all is said

Source: Steve Ansul, for The Washington Post.

and done, a great deal more will be said than done. The truth is we don't know any quick fixes for our urban ills and we lack the patience and resources for slow fixes."[183]

To make these problems more difficult to resolve, the cities have lost political power as they have lost population, due to white flight and black migration. In 1992, for the first time, more voters lived in the suburbs than in the cities. These voters do not urge action on urban problems. Sometimes, in fact, they resist action if it means an increase in their taxes or decrease in their services.

A woman in Simi Valley, the suburb where the first trial of the Los Angeles police officers was held, unintentionally revealed a common attitude when she shouted at inner city blacks who came to picket the courthouse, "Why do you bother us? Let us go on with our lives, like you are down there."[184]

Hispanics, too, remain disadvantaged. They earn considerably less than white non-Hispanics, though more than blacks.[185] But they are moving up the ladder. More attend college and become managers and professionals. At least those who speak educated English appear to be following the pattern of Southern and Eastern European immigrants—arriving poor, facing discrimination, but eventually working their way up.

Native Americans, with a legacy of discrimination and coerced assimilation, continue to suffer extreme poverty and unemployment, which are exacerbated by high rates of alcoholism.

Women also have suffered. Although popular stereotypes associate poverty with racial minorities, women, like minorities, are more likely than others to be poor. Increasing proportions, now almost 40%, of all female-headed families are below the poverty line (see Figure 1).

Despite the value of civil rights, it should be apparent from the current status of minorities and women that civil rights alone are not enough. As one black leader said, "What good is a seat in the front of the bus if you don't have the money for the fare?"[186]

■ **FIGURE 1**
Men Earn More than Women at Each Educational Level

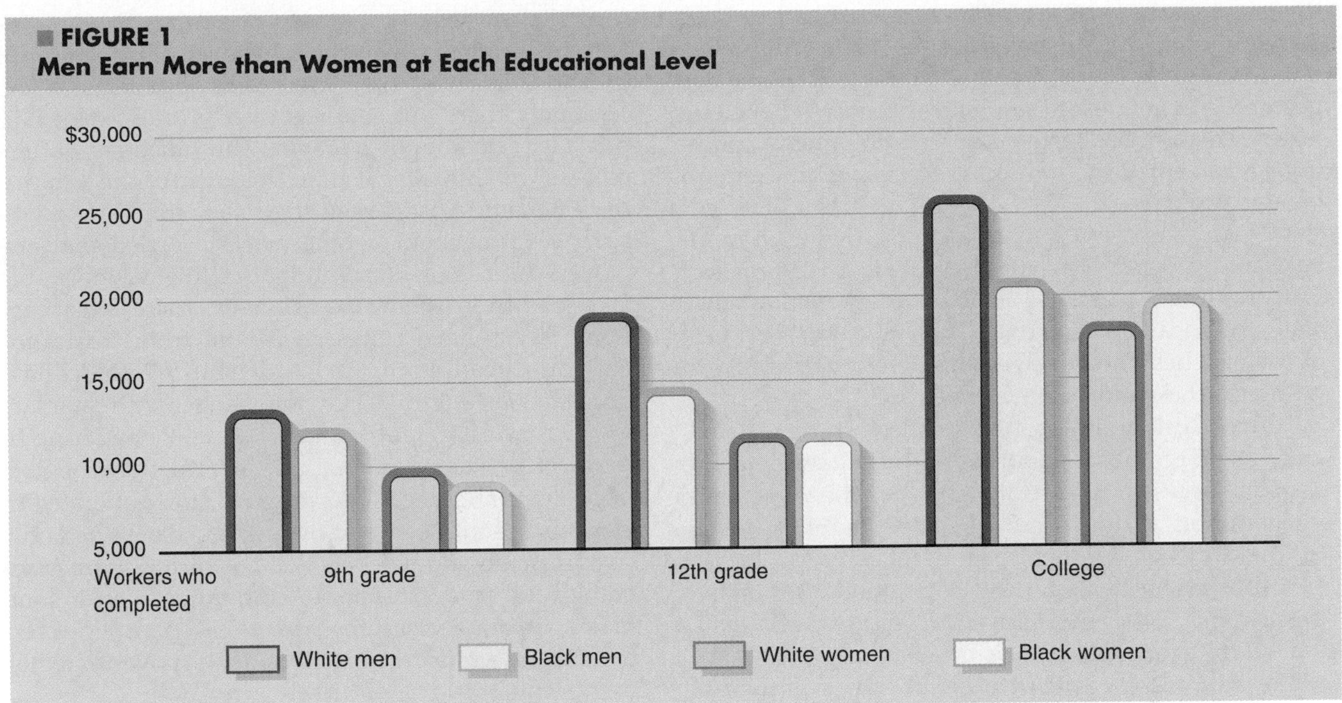

These data are for adults employed full time and are adjusted for years of labor market experience and southern residence. 1986 data.
SOURCE: Reynold Farley, "After the Starting Line: Blacks & Women in an Uphill Race." *Demography* 25 (November 1988), pp. 477–95.

➤Conclusion: Is Government Responsive in Granting Civil Rights?

Blacks and women have made tremendous progress in obtaining civil rights since the time when a federal official who fired competent blacks could insist, "A Negro's place is in the cornfield,"[187] or employers who refused to hire women could insist, "A woman's place is in the home." The black movement and the women's movement initiated the changes. They protested legal inequality and put the issue on the public agenda. As they grew and garnered support, they pressured the government. Finally, approximately one century after the first significant agitations for change, the government responded.

Within the government, the Supreme Court exercised decisive leadership. Historically, the Court was both activist and restrained toward blacks—whichever was necessary to deny their rights—while it was restrained toward women. Then in the 1950s and 1960s, the Warren Court was activist in striking down segregation. In the 1970s and 1980s, the Burger Court was somewhat less activist in upholding limited busing and affirmative action. At the same time, it was activist in striking down sex discrimination. As with the Warren Court's decisions against race discrimination, the Burger Court's decisions against sex discrimination may go down in history as its major achievement.

But the Court's rulings themselves did not guarantee the rights. Because the Court lacks the means to enforce its decisions, the president and Congress had to help overcome the resistance. The history of the government's efforts to grant civil rights, especially to blacks, shows the limits of the Supreme Court.

The changes in policy illustrate the responsiveness of government. In its subjugation of minorities until the 1950s and treatment of women until the 1970s, government was responding to the majority view. When minorities and women organized to protest their status, government began responding to them and to shifts in the majority view that their protest prompted.

In pressuring government to respond, blacks have benefited from being numerous, visible, and, with their common legacy of slavery, segregation, and discrimination, relatively cohesive. Their concentration in large northern cities and some southern states has helped them exercise political power. Their long legacy, though, has fostered debilitating ghetto conditions and denied them resources to make quicker and greater progress.

Hispanics are less numerous but growing in number rapidly. Their concentration in some western and southwestern states has enabled them to influence state and local governments. Their diversity and lack of cohesiveness, however, has hindered their ability to influence the national government.

Native Americans are the smallest, most isolated, and least organized minority, so they have had the poorest success in pressuring government to respond.

As minority groups grow in size, they will be able to pressure governments more effectively. In the 1980s, blacks increased their population 13%, native Americans 39%, Hispanics 53%, and Asians 108%, while whites increased their population just 6%.[188]

But as minority groups expand, they will increasingly come into conflict with each other, especially if economic conditions remain stagnant. Competition for scarce resources will widen the cracks in the coalition. Already there are tensions. Some blacks resent the faster progress of Hispanics and Asians. Blacks say they were here before most Hispanics and Asians, they suffered more and struggled more, and so they should reap the rewards sooner. On the other hand, some Hispanic leaders resent the reluctance of black groups to help them with their civil rights problems.[189] Occasionally there are conflicts over issues. When Hispanic leaders sought to repeal the sanctions on employers who hire illegal aliens, because of concern that these penalties discourage employers from hiring Hispanic legal residents, some blacks worried that employers once again would hire legal aliens who would take jobs from them. Occasionally, there have been riots. Blacks have rioted in Miami from frustration with the Cuban-dominated leadership. Hispanics have rioted in Washington, D.C., out of anger with their lack of city services and jobs and with gerrymandering by the black power structure. In the aftermath of the Rodney King trial, some blacks targeted stores operated by Koreans in south central Los Angeles. Blacks had criticized Korean shopkeepers for not hiring more black employees from the local community. And some blacks apparently had resented the Korean shopkeepers' success amidst the black residents' poverty in their own community.

Nonminority women were never subjugated as much as minority men and women, so they have had less to overcome. Moreover, women are a majority, they vote as frequently as men, and they have well-organized and well-funded interest groups. Consequently, since the 1970s they have made the greatest gains toward equality.

EPILOGUE

Hamer Continues to Fight

Fannie Lou Hamer was not one to back down from a challenge, especially since that fateful day when she first tried to register to vote. Indeed, a frequent criticism levied against her, by supporters as well as opponents, was that she was unwilling to compromise. At the Democratic convention in 1964, she and two other women leaders of the Mississippi Freedom Democratic Party urged the delegation to reject the compromise offered by the national Democratic Party officials. "We didn't come all this way for no two seats," she declared.[190] They were also miffed by the party officials' proposal that the seats be given to two middle-class representatives of the delegation—a professor and a druggist—rather than to any of the poor sharecroppers who formed the bulk of the delegation. The MFDP voted to press its case before the credentials committee of the convention.

But the FBI had infiltrated the MFDP and had wiretapped the phones in its hotel to determine the delegation's plans, and then had forwarded this information to President Johnson. When the credentials committee began its hearing, the president called a press conference to preempt the hearing from television. Without the presence of cameras, the committee voted to seat the regular Democrats.

Furious, the Freedom Democrats entered the convention hall, using their tickets as "guests," and stood silently in a circle to call attention to their issue. The sergeants-at-arms tried to remove them but gave up when officials realized that the effort would cast the

36. *Griffin v. Prin*
(1964); *Norwood v. Ha*
ery, 417 U.S. 556 (197
U.S. 430 (1968).
37. James F. Simo
1974), p. 70.
38. William Cohe
N.Y.: Foundation Pre
39. *Swann v. Char*
(1971).
40. *Columbus Boa*
Dayton Board of Educ
School District 1, Den
41. *Milliken v. Bra*
42. Lee A. Danie
Magazine, April 17, 1
43. Daniels, "In D
44. Ibid., p. 97; Su
tion," *New York Times*
45. Rob Gurwitt, '
pp. 30–36.
46. *Board of Educat*
(1991).
47. Gurwitt, "Gett
48. Chira, "Housi
49. J. Harvie Wilki
University Press, 197
Study Says," *Lincoln J*
50. Woodward, *St*
51. *Norris v. Alaba*
128 (1940); *Avery v. G*
52. *Heart of Atlant*
53. For discussion
enactment and enfo
the act, see Herbert
Title VII of the 1964
Litigation Record," i
America (Madison: U
263–341.
54. *Griggs v. Duke*
55. *Washington v. L*
56. *Wards Cove Pac*
57. *Firefighters Loc*
58. *Shelley v. Kraen*
59. For more exte
Nations: Black and W
Charles Scribner's So
60. Gary Orfield, q
try from the *Brown*
Edition, December 20–
61. Mary Jordan, '
ington Post National W
62. Jordan, "Separ
63. Jonathan Koz
Schools (New York: Ha
64. Kozol, *Savage I*
65. Ibid., p. 35.
66. "That's Quite a
67. In addition, cit
colleges, museums, ho
do not pay property t

wrong image on television. The protest did bring the press coverage that had been denied at the hearing.

Meanwhile, all but three of the regular Democrats left for Mississippi. They apparently went to the convention just to keep the Freedom Democrats from getting the seats.

When Johnson wrote his memoirs after retiring, he omitted any mention of the Freedom Democrats' challenge. "Atlantic City in August 1964," he wrote, "was a place of happy surging crowds and thundering cheers. To a man as troubled as I was by party and national divisions, this display of unity was welcome indeed.[191]

Hamer continued to fight. Following the election she and two other Freedom Democrats challenged the seating of all five white men elected to the House of Representatives from Mississippi. Hamer claimed they were elected illegally because officials refused to put the Freedom Democrats' candidates on the ballot. The House sent 150 lawyers to the state to collect information about violations of election laws. The findings of widespread discrimination prompted enough support to force a roll call vote, but the challenge was defeated.

Change did come, however. In 1965 President Johnson pushed the Voting Rights Act through Congress, and in 1968 the Democratic Party propounded rules against seating delegations that denied full participation to blacks.

Yet Mississippi's regular Democrats refused to change. In 1968 a coalition calling itself the "Loyal Democrats," including Hamer, other Freedom Democrats, and moderate whites, challenged the seating of the regular Democrats at the national convention. This time Vice President Humphrey, running for president after Johnson retired, backed the challenge and it succeeded. Finally, an integrated delegation represented Mississippi.

Fannie Lou Hamer, with her boundless energy, still had battles to fight. She brought lawsuits to broaden interpretation of the Voting Rights Act, reconfigure electoral districts in the state, and desegregate schools in her town.

As African Americans began to overcome discrimination, she believed the next step was for the poor, blacks and whites alike, to overcome poverty. She arranged financing for 70 new homes in town, and she helped organize a farm co-op and a "pig bank." (She bought 40 pigs and loaned them to families who would care for them and keep the new piglets—the "dividends"—and then return the pigs—the "principal"—to the bank for other families the next year.)

In her declining years, she felt frustrated because she had not accomplished more and forgotten because people had not come to see her as often once she no longer had the energy for their cause. In 1977 she died.

Yet Fannie Lou Hamer had achieved much. With the increased participation of black voters in Mississippi, black candidates ran for office, and many won; and white candidates began to court black voters as well. In 1986 the first black member of the U.S. House of Representatives was elected from Mississippi since Reconstruction.

Fannie Lou Hamer would not be forgotten. She showed people that although she had much to fear, her oppressors were the ones who came to fear her because she would not be silenced and could not be controlled. "She owed them nothing, and she gave them hell. . . ."[192]

➤Key Terms

Dred Scott case
equal protection clause
Jim Crow laws
Plessy v. Ferguson
separate-but-equal doctrine
NAACP
Brown v. Board of Education
de jure segregation
de facto segregation
Civil Rights Act of 1964
restrictive covenants
steering
blockbusting
redlining
Civil Rights Act of 1968
bilingual education
Equal Pay Act
comparable worth
Equal Rights Amendment (ERA)
affirmative action

➤Further Reading

Paul Berman, ed., *Blacks and Jews: Alliance and Arguments* (Delacorte Press, 1992). *Essays about the "love-hate" relationship between these two peoples who have suffered prejudice and embraced in the civil rights era but tangled in recent decades.*

Taylor Branch, *Parting the Waters: America in the King Years, 1954–63* (New York: Simon & Schuster, 1988). *Extremely readable account of Martin Luther King, Jr., and the first decade of the civil rights movement.*

Seth Cagin and Philip Dray, *We Are Not Afraid: The Story of Goodman, Schwerner, and Chaney and the Civil Rights Campaign for Mississippi* (New York: Macmillan, 1988). *An American crime in the steamy summer of 1964.*

Audrey K. Edwards
Dream: The Psych
Doubleday, 1992). *I*
als who came of ag
decision and Martin
Melissa Fay Greene, *I*
Addison-Wesley, 19
between "good old bo
county in the 1970s.
Andrew Hacker, *Two*
Hostile, Unequal (N
1992). *Perceptive ins*
Jonathan Kozol, *Sava*
Schools (New York:
school financing upo
tunately) real schools
Jane Kramer, "Whose
1992, pp. 80–109. *A*
between a white arti
models for his lifelik
officials in New York
the controversial scul
Susan Ware, *Still Miss*
Modern Feminism (I
pilot, who disappear
reflection of America

➤Notes

1. The information fo
Light of Mine: The Life of F
2. In the Delta, as in
cotton or cleaned or cook
some status, but they w
white officials of the segre
ers and funeral directors
3. Mills, p. 36.
4. Ibid., p. 38.
5. Ibid., p. 18.
6. Ibid., p. 57.
7. This incident rec
reporters were present.
leaders to seek help fro
rectly, that if any of the
coverage of the repressi
recruitment of northern
drives during the summe
8. Mills, p. 93.
9. The Republican Pa
time. There was a black wi
but its only role was to h
Republican president. In f
Tans was an attorney who
10. Ibid., p. 128.
11. *Scott v. Sandford*, 1
12. Despite the ruling,
national character," and t

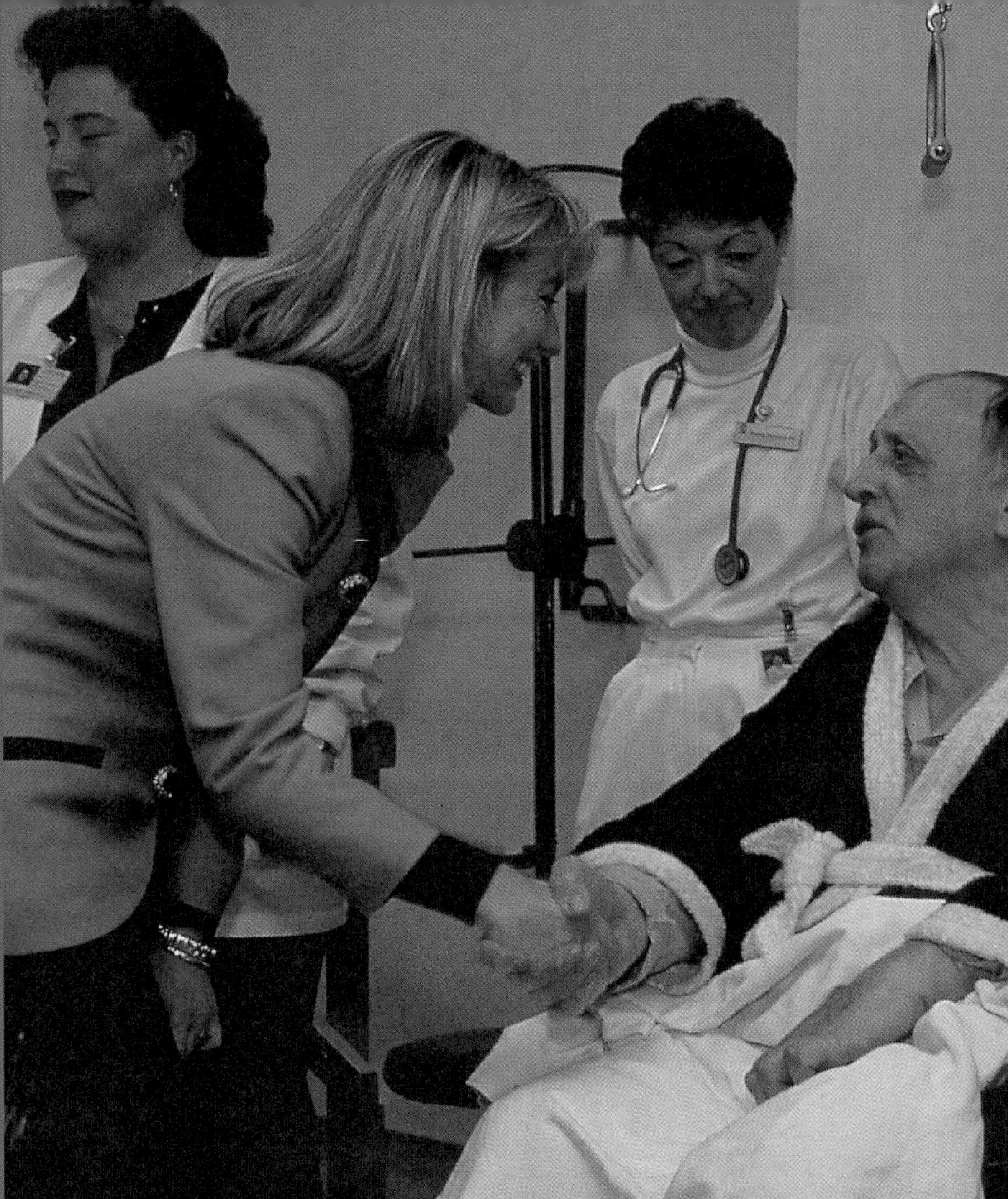

16 Social Welfare Policy

You Are There

Can This Bill Be Saved?

You are President Bill Clinton. It is January 1994, and you are drafting your State of the Union speech. You are trying to decide what to say about the pending legislation to reform American health care. Making sure that no American is without adequate health care was one of your campaign themes. One of the first actions you took after being elected was to appoint Hillary Rodham Clinton, your wife, to head a large task force to study and recommend changes in the nation's health care system. Their report recommended far-reaching and complex changes in the way Americans pay for health insurance, changes that are being fought by those who benefit from the current system, especially insurance and drug companies. Congress is deeply split over the issue, and even many Democrats do not support your proposals. You are now faced with the decision whether to stick with your original plan or to offer compromises to those who do not want such a far-reach reform as you do.

Everyone agrees that the problems facing America's health care system are daunting. Most people think the health care system is in a crisis, perhaps even in its death throes. Most agree that the crisis is produced by two factors: rocketing costs and diminishing access to quality health care. But opinions differ wildly as to the right prescription for the problem.

Health care costs have increased an average of 10% per year for three decades, far outpacing inflation. We spend more on health care, whether measured per person or as a proportion of our national income, than any country in the world. Over 14% of our entire economy goes toward health care, twice the rate in most nations. The soaring costs are a major drain on the economy. Half of the projected increase in budget deficits in the next few years reflect the growth of health care costs. You have stated, "If we don't do something on health care, it's going to bankrupt the country."[1] And another observer commented, "We are offering the health industry each year an unlimited budget and they are exceeding it.[2]

The spiraling costs of health care are dragging down businesses too. In one recent year, General Motors paid more for health care benefits than for the steel to make its products.[3] During the Bush presidency, 1.2 million new jobs were created in the American economy, but *all* of that growth was accounted for by the health care system. In the rest of the economy new jobs were canceled out by jobs lost. Businesses pay increasing amounts for health care packages for their workers and retirees. Keeping up with ever higher medical insurance costs leaves little for wage increases for workers. If businesses drop these benefits, as many do, their workers are left without insurance coverage. Many major corporations, including many with relatively generous health care benefits, have been cutting jobs to reduce their costs. During the first three months of 1994, the U.S. economy lost more than 3,000 jobs daily on average. Many of the newly unemployed workers then found themselves without health care coverage.[4]

While government and business are suffering from escalating health care costs, individuals suffer the most. About 20 million people covered by private insurance lack sufficient coverage and should be considered "underinsured." Between 48 and 58 million Americans can no longer afford health

CONTINUED 

OUTLINE

What Are Social Welfare Policies?

Evolution of Social Welfare Policies

Social Welfare for Everyone
- How Social Security Works
- Problems with the Program
- The Future of Social Security
- Federal Health Care Programs
- Health Care Reforms

Social Welfare for the Poor
- How Many Are Poor?
- Who Is Poor?
- The Causes of Poverty
- Basic Programs for the Poor
- Reforming Welfare for the Poor

Social Welfare for the Well-Off
- Tax Breaks
- Farm Subsidies
- Other Programs for the Rich

Conclusion: Are Social Welfare Programs Responsive?

FIGURE 3
Significant Numbers Are Uninsured

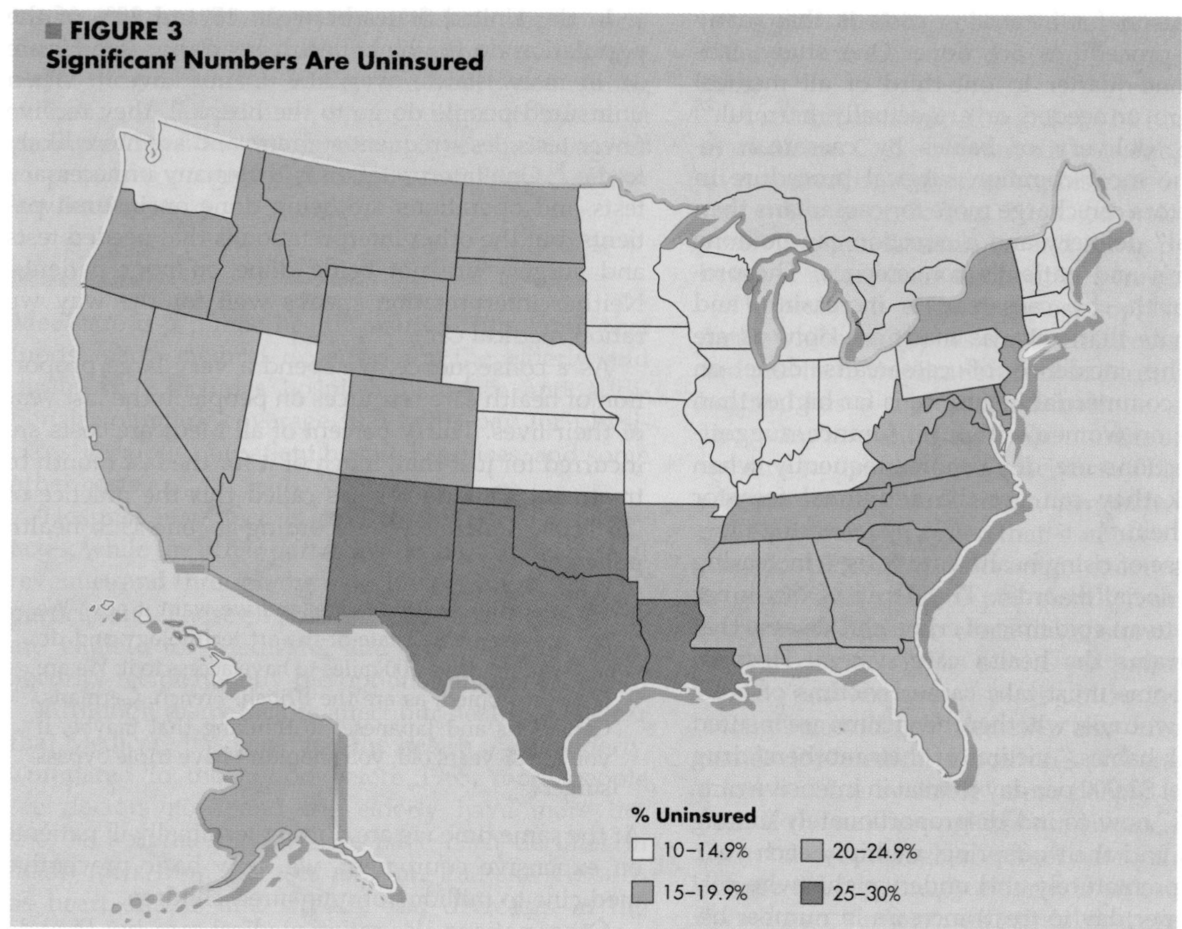

SOURCE: "How the States Have Expanded Health Coverage" *New York Times* July 2, 1995, p. 20.

plan for 40% of all Americans (compared to only 10% in 1988). Most employees have a limited choice of doctors and hospitals if they want insurance to cover their bills. Medicare sets limits on what it will pay for each procedure. New health care organizations have sprung up to challenge the old fee-for-service practice and can account for 20% of all health care. Called **health maintenance organizations (HMOs),** these groups of doctors agree to provide full health care for a fixed monthly charge. This system provides direct incentives for doctors to keep costs low, avoid unnecessary hospitalization and procedures, and emphasize preventive medicine. Private insurers try to limit unnecessary operations and provide incentives for outpatient care rather than hospital stays.

States are trying their own reforms. Maryland is attempting to standardize health insurance billing forms. Oregon decided it will not use Medicaid funds to pay for certain expensive kinds of procedures and will target more funds to preventive medicine, such as prenatal care. Hawaii requires employers to provide insurance benefits for all workers and regulates insurance costs (consequently almost everyone in Hawaii has health insurance). Several other states considered such legislation but backed off.

The federal government has tried to cut costs by tightening access to Medicaid and by limiting the amount it pays on amounts doctors and hospitals bill Medicare and Medicaid. But these are stopgap solutions, as Medicare and Medicaid costs spiral at the same time that increasing numbers of Americans cannot afford private health care and are not eligible for either Medicare or Medicaid.

Our existing system has been called "lemon socialism." Private enterprise insures those at least risk—the young, the well, and the well-off; government—ultimately the taxpayer—pays for many of those most likely to be sick—the elderly and the poor.

There seem to be two main alternatives. One is to adopt some type of national health insurance system as all other industrial democracies have done. Another alternative is to force private insurance companies to share the risk of insuring those most likely to be ill. Managed competition incorporates this idea.

The public is unsure what it wants.[34] While over two-thirds believe the system needs significant change and almost everyone believes it needs *some* change, there is little consensus on what kind of change. The public is divided on whether government or private insurers should cover costs. They are split over whether government regulation should limit choice if cost savings could be found. Most want to regulate doctors' salaries, but that is only a small part of the cost problem. Other versions of health-policy reform would make smaller changes in the present system.

The Canadian Way

The quality of, and access to, health care in the United States are often compared unfavorably to that in Canada. In fact, one noted British publication joked that "a Canadian is an American without a gun and with health care.[1]" The **Canadian health care plan** provides everyone free health care—rich and poor. A tax supports the system, and government pays doctors for the services they perform. It is called a *single-payer system*. Individuals choose their own doctors, but the provincial (what are called "states" in the U.S. are called "provinces" in Canada) governments pay doctors for services performed. Fees are strictly regulated. Consequently doctors' incomes are about one-third lower than in the U.S., but in exchange doctors are free from most of the burdensome red tape that is making the practice of medicine so unpleasant for many U.S. doctors.

The administrative costs of the Canadian system are much lower than in our system. Here, hospitals and doctors must cope with both government regulation and oversight by insurance companies. For example, Johns Hopkins Medical Center is required to keep track of 18,000 different charge categories for 500 different insurance plans. At this one hospital alone, billing insurance companies, government, and patients costs $13 million.[2] It is not surprising that, in the U.S., administrative costs are almost 25% of all health costs, compared to administrative costs of only 9% in Canada. Overall, costs are about 22% less in Canada. Where studies have been done, it appears that the quality of medical care is equal in the two systems, though Canadians may have to wait longer for surgery that is not urgent.[3]

When Canadians and Americans are asked in surveys to compare the two systems, almost all Canadians (91%) and a plurality (43%) of Americans say Canada has a better health system. Barely one-quarter of Americans and almost no Canadians think the U.S. system is better.[4]

But powerful interest groups in the U.S. are opposed to the Canadian system. In general, Americans dislike "socialized medicine," fearing they will lose their ability to choose their own physician (in the Canadian system patients do choose their physicians, however). Some doctors are opposed to the Canadian system, though others think it might be the best alternative to meet the crisis. Insurance companies are strongly against the Canadian system because it would remove them as major parts of the health care system.

Because of the complexity of the health care issue and the volatility of public opinion on it, one newspaper sponsored a "Citizens Jury" to weigh the evidence to find the best health care program. In contrast with opinion polling, which asks for views based on whatever information the public has, the Citizens Jury takes a different approach. The jury, chosen to be representative of the country on all aspects of race, age, gender, geography, and so forth, studied various health care reform proposals, heard presentations of varying perspectives, asked their own questions, and, at the end of their study and deliberation, chose the single-payer plan, which is similar to the Canadian system. This plan, according to one of the jurors, "offers just one bureaucracy, the federal government. Tax it, pay it, and get it over with."[5] Many observers think that the Clinton health care proposals would have been more successful if they had adopted this Canadian, single-payer approach.

1. *The Economist*, quoted in the *Lincoln Journal*, October 25, 1993.
2. Spencer Rich, "Trimming Waste Will Help, But It's Not a Cure-all," *Washington Post National Weekly Edition*, May 17–23, 1993, pp. 8–9.
3. "Study: Canadian Care Cost Efficient," *Champaign-Urbana News Gazette*, March 18, 1993, p. D–1; Watzman.
4. Larry Hugick, "American Unhappiness with Health Care Contrasts with Canadian Contentment," *Gallup Poll Monthly* #311 (August 1991), pp. 2–3.
5. William Raspberry, "The Single-Payer Plan," *Washington Post National Weekly Edition*, October 25–31, 1993, p. 29.

This ambivalence, coupled with unhappiness about the expense of the current system, suggests that support for a coherent, well-explained program could certainly be found.

United States Lags Behind in Infant Mortality

Infant mortality rates are one measure of the quality and availability of health care. If either the mother or the child fails to receive adequate care, the child may suffer and, in the worst case, die. Measured by infant mortality rates, as on other measures, the U.S. lags behind all other western democracies and many other nations too. At the same time, the U.S. spends more on health care than any other nation. The table provides a sampling of comparisons. One might reasonably expect that the more a country invested in health care spending, the fewer infants would die. But this does not always appear to be the case. Japan spends 6.6% of its gross domestic product on health and has only 5.0 infant deaths per 1,000 live births. Switzerland spends 7.9% of its gross domestic product on health care and has 6.8 infant deaths per 1,000 live births. In contrast, the U.S. spends 13.4% of gross domestic product on health and has a considerably higher rate of deaths than Japan. Further, even with this high level of health care spending, the infant mortality rate for U.S. blacks is higher than for any other country shown, and nearly double that for U.S. whites. In this area, at least, health care spending has not produced the desired results.

COUNTRY	DEATHS PER 1,000 LIVE BIRTHS	% OF GROSS DOMESTIC PRODUCT SPENT ON HEALTH
Japan	5.0	6.6
Switzerland	6.8	7.9
Canada	7.3	10.0
U.S. (whites)	7.3	
France	7.7	—
United Kingdom	8.8	6.6
U.S. (total)	8.9	13.4
China	12.0	—
Nigeria	13.8	—
U.S. (blacks)	17.6	

SOURCES: Statistical Office of the United Nations; National Center for Health Statistics; data on spending from Peter Passell, "Health Care's Fever," *New York Times*, May 16, 1993, p. E3; *Statistical Abstract of the United States, 1994*, Table 120.

Social Welfare for the Poor

How Many Are Poor?

We think of the United States as a rather egalitarian society, but in fact income is very unevenly distributed (Table 1). The poorest 20% of families earn only 4% of all income, and the richest 20% earn almost half of the income. The gap between rich and poor widened noticeably in the 1980s, as the proportion of income earned by the upper middle class increased.

Distribution of wealth, which includes homes, land, savings, and stocks and bonds, as well as cash, is even more skewed. One percent of Americans own 40% of all wealth and over half of all income-producing wealth, such as business investments, farms, and so forth. The bottom half of Americans own only 4% of the nation's wealth.[35]

The Census Bureau defines as poor anyone beneath a certain income. In 1992, this was about $14,300 for a family of four. Due to the booming economy and the Great Society programs of the 1960s, the proportion of poor people dropped from 22% in 1959 to 11% in 1973, the lowest point ever achieved in the United States. Since then, it has increased, peaking at over 15% in 1983. It is now about 14%.

Not everyone agrees with the Census Bureau's estimates. Some conservatives argue that it overstates the number of poor because it does not take into account many "in-kind" benefits poor people receive, such as food stamps, housing, and medical care. If we considered this income, about 4% fewer would be considered poor. Others think the census understates the amount of poverty, because they believe the standard is based on costs for food, housing, and fuel that are inadequate.[36]

Not surprisingly, those who believe government should do relatively little to increase income equality tend to minimize the extent of the poverty problem; those who favor a more activist government usually have a higher estimate. What is beyond dispute, however, is that a sizable minority of the American population—anywhere from 10% to 25%—does not have enough money to live at a decent standard. By all measures, the number living in poverty increased in the 1980s.

Many observers are quite concerned about the growing gap between rich and poor in America. Until 1979, that gap had stayed fairly steady since World War II. Between the war and the late 1970s, the rich grew richer, but so did the middle class. The amount

TABLE 1 Income Distribution Is Becoming More Lopsided

% OF POPULATION	% OF INCOME EARNED					
	1970		1980		1992	
Lowest fifth	4%		4%		4%	
Next lowest	11	53	10	52	11	51
Middle fifth	17		17		17	
Next highest	25		25		24	
Highest fifth	43		44		45	
Top 5%	17		17		18	

SOURCE: Bureau of the Census, Current Population Reports, Series P-60, no. 180, *Money Income of Households, Families, and Persons in the United States: 1991* (U.S. Government Printing Office, 1992), Table 13-3. U.S. Department of Commerce *Statistical Abstract of the United States 1994,* Table 716. Data are for households.

of poverty shrank. But during the 1980s, the gap opened. The poorest 20% saw their income drop 3%, while the richest 20% experienced an income gain of 32%. The richest 1% gained over 80%. The most recent data, for the 1989–93 period, indicate that income inequality continued to grow until about 1992, then began to reverse a tiny bit.[37] Reasons for the widening gap include the loss of manufacturing jobs, unemployment, and declining real wages for workers; the lack of child support paid by fathers to an increasing number of divorced and unwed mothers; and the Reagan tax and spending policies, which redistributed the wealth upward by reducing taxes for the better-off and reducing spending for the poor.

Who Is Poor?

The *Wall Street Journal* commented on the growing gulf between rich and poor: "At the top is a growing overclass of well-educated two-income families. At the bottom is a growing underclass of single mothers, Baby Boomers stuck in low paying jobs, and children who inherited poverty from their parents."[38] With the important omission of race, the *Journal* description accurately depicts those most vulnerable to poverty.

Race, Family Status, and Sex

Race, family status, and sex are important predictors of poverty. Whites and Asians are less likely to be poor than blacks and Hispanics. In 1993, about 31% of all blacks and 27% of Hispanics, but only 9% of all whites and 14% of Asians, were poor. Families headed by a married couple are much less likely to be poor than are single-parent families, especially those headed by a woman (see Table 2). Individuals living alone or with other nonfamily members are also more likely to be poor.

Women and their dependent children are the single largest group of poor people in the United States. Female-headed families make up 25% of families with children. Yet they comprise 80% of people on Aid to Families with Dependent Children (AFDC), and over 50% of food stamp users. Half of all poor people in the United States live in female-headed families. This has been called the **feminization of poverty.**

The number of people in female-headed families who are poor has grown for several reasons. The rate of poverty among female-headed families is actually much smaller than in the early 1960s before the Great Society programs. But the proportion of families headed by women has doubled since 1960.

About half of black and Hispanic female-headed families fall beneath the poverty line, and over one-quarter of white female-headed families do so. For whites, the primary reason for the growth in poor female-headed families is divorce. When divorce occurs, even between a middle-class couple, often the women and children fall into poverty. The woman cannot earn enough to support a family, and child support from the man is typically erratic and inadequate. Less than half the children of divorced white women receive support payments.[39]

TABLE 2 Poverty Is Much More Common Among Female-Headed and Minority Families

	PERCENT IN POVERTY
All families	12
White	9
Black	31
Hispanic	27
Asian	14
Married-couple families	7
White	6
Black	12
Hispanic	19
Female-headed families, no husband	36
White	29
Black	50
Hispanic	52

SOURCE: U.S. Bureau of the Census, Current Population Reports, *Income, Poverty, and Valuation of Noncash Benefits, 1993,* Series P-60-188, Table C.

than 60% of poor pregnant women can receive food supplements and prenatal care, even though it is clear that the relatively cheap food supplements and prenatal care would save thousands of dollars in treatment for each child born with problems because of the mother's poor health and nutrition.

Can Welfare Work?

Despite these successes, most agree that welfare programs for the poor do not achieve their objective of helping most poor achieve better lives. Indeed, some believe welfare programs have actually worsened the condition of the poor, particularly the black underclass. They argue that our welfare system discourages the poor who try to work by making government assistance too easy to obtain and too lucrative.[53] Thus, critics charge, the welfare rolls continue to grow, even when the economy is relatively good. Many people stay on the welfare rolls for large parts of their lives and pass on their welfare dependence to their children.

Like many stereotypes, this stereotype of the welfare system has some validity, but the true picture is much more complex. Though the number of recipients was fairly stable from the mid-1970s to the late 1980s, it zoomed up in the recession of the late 1980s and early 1990s. In contrast to the common stereotype, however, the increase in welfare recipients is not tied to the growth in welfare benefits, which have dropped steadily since the 1970s. The purchasing power of the average monthly AFDC benefit declined by 43% between 1970 and 1993;[54] even in the past three years, the actual dollar grant per recipient decreased, even before taking into account inflation.

The number of recipients increases fastest when economic times are hard; but when the economy is good, the rolls do not fall back to their previous level. Part of the reason is that, even in years when the economy was growing, job growth has not been in well-paying blue-collar jobs. Job prospects for people without college degrees have deteriorated over the past 15 years, even in good years.

Another reason for the continuing growth in welfare rolls is that the proportion of births to unmarried women has skyrocketed in the black community and risen dramatically among whites (Figure 5). One-quarter of all births are to women without husbands, many of them teenagers. (The number of births to unwed white teenagers has almost doubled since 1970; the number to unwed black teenagers has in-

FIGURE 5
Births to Unmarried Mothers Are Increasing

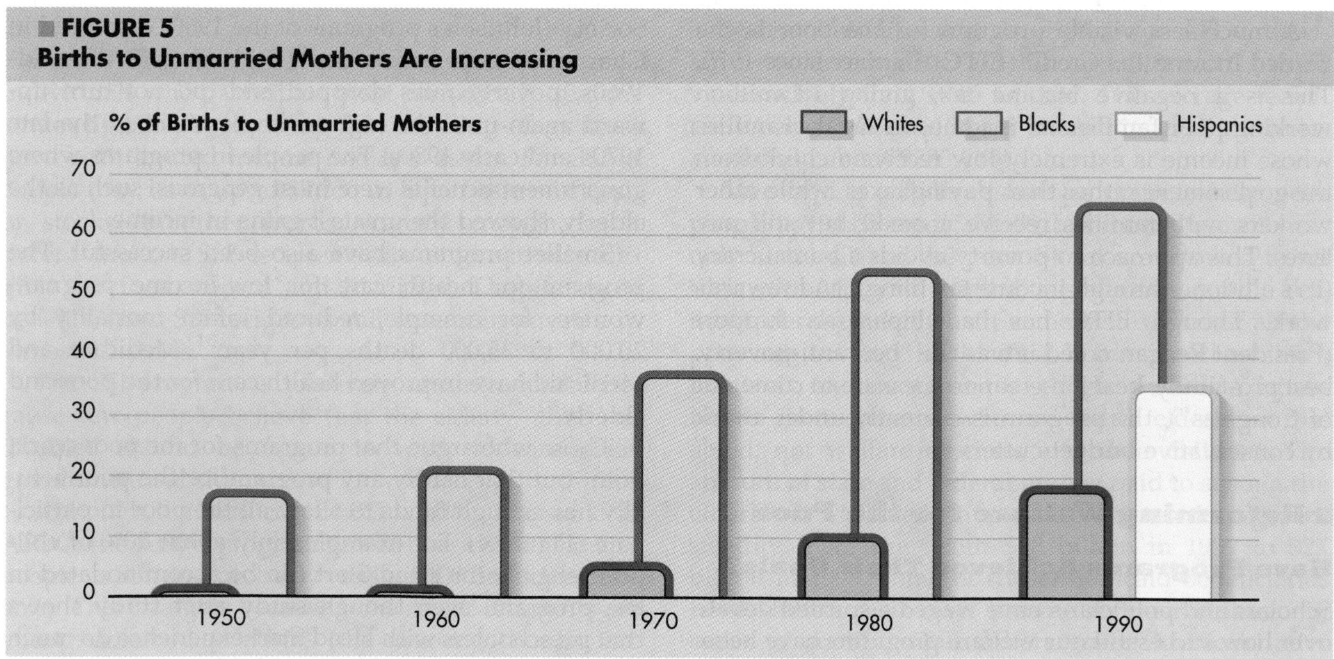

SOURCE: National Center for Health Statistics, reported in the *New York Times*, July 26, 1992, p. 12.

creased slightly, while the overall number of births to teenagers has declined by about one-third.) Over 80% of unwed mothers go on the welfare rolls for at least some time.

Most people who collect welfare do so for a relatively short time.[55] They find a job, marry someone who earns more than a poverty income, or both. However, nearly one-quarter of women who go on welfare stay for ten years or more, and another 20% stay for six to nine years. Those who stay on welfare are more likely to be teenaged mothers with no high school degree, no husband, and who are black or Hispanic. As one commentator remarked, "An 18-year-old girl from a broken family with two babies, no high school degree, no work experience, and no husband is going to have serious trouble supporting herself."[56] That difficulty does not usually to go away with a few months on AFDC.

Figuring out who are the primary welfare recipients reveals a paradox. At any one time, blacks and whites are about equal numbers of people on welfare. Yet most (86%) whites but only a minority (28%) of African Americans grow up in homes where the family was never on welfare. Of those on welfare, most whites stay on welfare for only a relatively short time and then leave. Looking at young white adults, age 18, we find that only 2% have lived in homes receiving welfare for as many as 13 years, and only another 2% in homes receiving welfare from 7 to 12 years. Among black 18-year-olds, however, 14% have been on at least 13 years, and another 28% from 7 to 12 years. For most whites on welfare, then, the system is a relatively short-term stopgap until they are able to support themselves. For most blacks on welfare, it is a longer-term means of support.[57]

There is no evidence that welfare causes fathers to leave their homes or unwed mothers to have babies, but neither does welfare provide any incentive to do otherwise.[58] Moreover, the system discourages work. Women who choose low-paid work over welfare are economically worse off because they must pay child care and they usually lose their medical benefits. Thus, for the last 25 years, almost everyone agreed that the welfare system needed to be reformed. But, serious reform attempts have bogged down in debates over what causes poverty and whether the system should maximize the carrot or the stick in getting people off welfare.

There is no simple answer for explaining existing patterns of welfare dependence. Clearly racism is an important contributor. Racism perpetuates housing segregation patterns that make it nearly impossible for blacks with working-class incomes to escape neighborhoods with high levels of crime and poor school systems. Racism also limits the ability of working-class blacks to get decent jobs. But other factors are also at work: the changing economy resulting in the loss of tens of thousands of factory jobs held by unskilled and semi-skilled workers, the altered societal norms of sexual behavior that have led to acceptance of unwed motherhood (and fatherhood), and the decay of the social institutions and-norms within lower-class black communities that tied them to the larger society.

A New Welfare Structure

In 1993, President Clinton took office promising to end welfare "as we know it." In the 1994 elections, the Republican "Contract with America" promised even more dramatic reform. After heated debate throughout 1995, Congress passed, and the president signed, a welfare reform bill that abolished the previous system whereby welfare was an entitlement to all those who met federal guidelines. Instead, states were mandated to set up their own welfare systems, under loose federal guidelines. The federal government is to give block grants to states to run these programs, but the states can decide who is eligible and (as in the previous system) how much to pay them. States can limit the amount of time that an individual can stay on welfare, and whether stipends are to increased for women who have children while on welfare. Some federal funds are available for child care to encourage women to go to work, but these fall far short of the realistic needs.

The legislation allows great discretion to the states. This is both an advantage and disadvantage. The advantage is that is allows each state an opportunity to create new policies; ideally, in a few years we can compare the successes and failures of different kinds of policies. This is an example of the "states as laboratories of democracy," discussed in Chapter 3. The disadvantage of the new policy is that states have strong incentives to do very little about the poverty problem. By doing little, they can save tax money and perhaps encourage poor people to leave the state. Observers have commented on the possibility of a "race to the bottom," where states vie with each other to cast off responsibility for the poor.

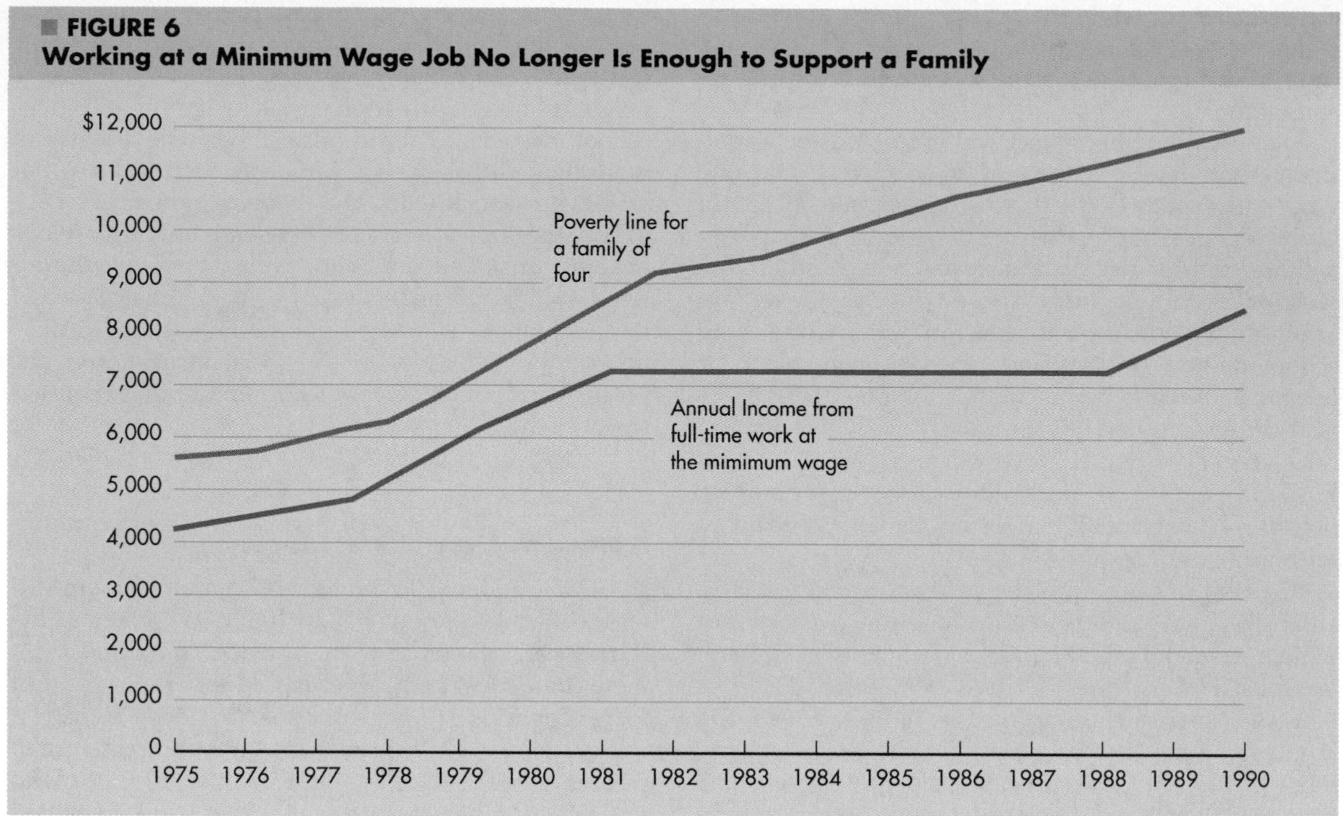

Although the minimum wage was increased in 1990, even working full time at minimum wage provides far less than a minimum standard of living.

The new policy has other advantages and disadvantages. From the perspective of many people, its main advantage is that it is something new. Most agreed that the old policy was a failure; conceivably this new approach will be more successful by allowing states more discretion. On the other hand, the great disadvantage is that by forcing families off welfare even when no responsible adult in the family has an income may mean forcing tens of thousands more children into poverty.

The program also does not address the problems of the unemployed fathers of children on welfare. In the black community, among those aged 25 to 34, the number of "marriageable men," those who are employed, decreased from 68 per 100 black women in 1954 to only 60 per 100 black women in 1982. Consequently, marriage is becoming less common. Over 20% of black women never marry during their childbearing years, compared to 10% of white women. Fully 23% of births to whites and 68% of births to blacks are to unmarried couples.[59] This declining number of employed black men is unfortunate in many ways, including the fact that one important way a family on welfare can leave the rolls is when the mother gets married. Relatively few intact husband and wife families, of any race, are poor. If this is so, one solution is to find jobs, not just for welfare women, but also for the fathers of their children.[60]

The new legislation ignores other possible reforms. Some have argued that a better way to diminish welfare is to provide state funding for abortions. When Michigan banned the use of state Medicaid funds for abortions in 1988, the number of abortions dropped by over 10,000, and the number of children enrolled before birth for welfare rose by 3,000 (31%).[61] Of course, cutting off benefits to welfare mothers is considerably more politically palatable than trying to help them avoid becoming mothers in the first place.[62] Pro-life advocates are nervous, however, about discussions of removing benefits when additional children are born because of the abortion incentive it would provide.

In sum, after years of debating welfare reform, in 1995 government did act. New welfare legislation reflected conservative thinking that government is helping poor people too much and thus eroding personal responsibility. It also reflected conservative thinking that states should be responsible for social welfare policies. It largely ignored liberal solutions, which are based on the idea that poor people are poor largely through lack of opportunity. Thus, the legislation neglects job training, shuns any effort to help people find jobs, and nearly ignores child care.

The most compelling reasons for a better welfare system are probably not financial. We need to stop the loss of human potential for the benefit of the poor themselves and for the larger society, which is denied the benefits of their productivity. In America, we like

Food Stamps and Hunger in America

In 1991, one out of every eight American children went hungry each day because their families could not afford to buy enough food. An equal number did not get enough to eat some of the time. These children, not surprisingly, tended to be sick, have trouble learning and paying attention, and miss school often. Poverty is taking its toll on America's children. But what can be done about it?

The major federal programs to combat hunger are federally supported, free and reduced-price school lunches for poor children and the **food stamp program.** The food stamp program, for families and individuals, gives poor people coupons redeemable in grocery stores for food. The stamps may be used only to purchase unprepared food and cannot be used for eating out or for toilet or kitchen items, liquor, or tobacco. The only eligibility requirement for food stamps is to be poor. In recent years, one of every ten Americans received food stamps.

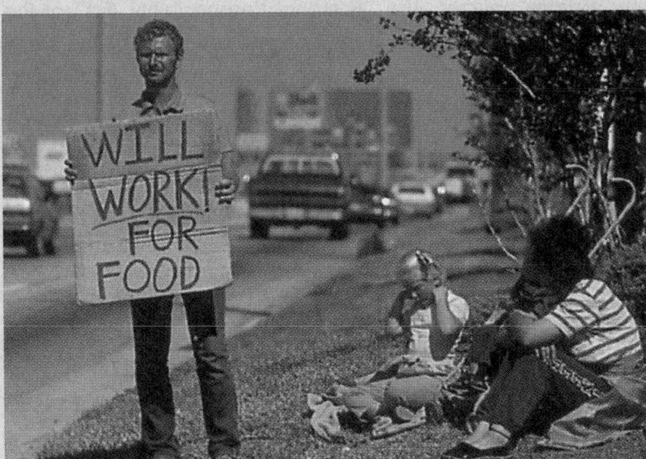

A jobless breadwinner in Texas.

The program, established nationwide in 1971, was spurred by an investigation of hunger in America demonstrating that tens of thousands of Americans were malnourished and many suffered from retarded growth, anemia, protein deficiencies, high rates of infant mortality, scurvy and rickets (from inadequate vitamin D and milk), and an impaired ability to learn. In other words, this "other nation" of the poor was subject to the same diseases and conditions that most Americans thought affected only poor people in Africa or Asia.

The establishment of a food stamp program also had support from those who saw it as one way to deal with the food surplus problem. Food stamps would allow more people to buy more food, and this would ultimately increase farm prices. For this reason the program was given to the Department of Agriculture to administer.

The food stamp program grew tremendously, but like the school breakfast and lunch programs it was cut back during the 1980s.

Despite public stereotypes that many food stamp benefits go to the nonpoor, analyses of the program have shown that most of the recipients are the poorest of the poor. (A study in 1985 showed the average household income of users was $6,200.) Most of the recipients did not own a car, a home, or any other assets.

There is little doubt that food stamps helped raise the level of health and nutrition among the very poor and that cutbacks are creating more hungry people. In the first six years of the program, malnutrition among the poor decreased, and they had far fewer diseases caused by poor nutrition. Still, sufficient hunger exists that nearly 26 million Americans turn, at least occasionally, to soup kitchens and food pantries. For some, the food stamp allotment never lasts until the end of the month.

SOURCES: "How Hungry Is America?" *Newsweek,* March 14, 1994, pp. 58–59; "10% Rely on Food Aid," *Lincoln Star,* March 9, 1994, pp. 1, 9; Guy Gugliotta, "Bare Cupboards in the Golden Years," *Washington Post National Weekly Edition,* November 19–December 5, 1993, p. 37;Martina Shea, *Dynamics of Economic well Being: Program Participation, 1990 to 1992.* U.S. Bureau of the Census, Current Population Reports, P 10–41, U.S. Government Printing Office, Washington, DC, 1995.

more economically elsewhere, such as alfalfa, cotton, pasture for cows and sheep, and rice, which normally is only grown in very wet climates. These crops use far more water than the grapes, nuts, oranges, strawberries, and tomatoes we associate with California farming.[71]

At a cost of $26 billion annually, military pensions cost considerably more than AFDC payments. David Stockman, former President Reagan's budget director, called them a "scandal," partly because the typical beneficiary starts collecting at age 41. More than 60% of these benefits are paid to individuals in the richest 20% of the population. The bottom 20% get only 2% of the pension benefits.[72]

➤Conclusion: Are Social Welfare Programs Responsive?

Our social welfare system is extremely complex. The major beneficiaries of direct income support programs are the elderly of all classes, while programs for the poor are a much smaller part of all social welfare payments. Many programs also provide support for middle- and upper-income groups, including direct income supplements, tax breaks, and support for services largely used by the nonpoor.

Getting Off Welfare—and Staying Off[1]

Even though many welfare recipients stay on the rolls for years, most do not. Indeed, 70% leave the system within two years.[2] But getting off welfare is not easy, and staying off is even harder. About half those who leave welfare return,[3] unable to support their families without public aid. The *Washington Post* featured a welfare success story that illustrates the difficulties of getting off the rolls. Lisa Childress was forced to rely on welfare after a divorce left her with four children and no child support. With a high school diploma and intermittent work experience as a real estate agent, she began studying for an associate's degree in computer technology, preparing for a time when she could leave AFDC. With that training, and a lot of persistence, she found a job paying almost $12 an hour. Even though she is doing well at her job and expects a substantial merit raise, she still considers herself only one crisis away from falling back on ADFC.

Her circumstances illustrate why many assumptions about getting people off welfare are unrealistic. Even with an uncommon amount of persistence in trying to find a job, and even though her job is better than 108 of the 109 other welfare recipients placed in jobs in her county during a nine-month period, she can still barely make it.

When her $488 per month AFDC check stopped, so did $300 in food stamp aid. Her rent-free housing, Medicaid benefits, and child-care subsidy also came to an end. Earning, after taxes, about $1500 a month, she pays $385 a month rent. In the summer she pays a neighbor to baby-sit, but knows once summer ends she cannot afford the $800 a month day care for her three children, the standard rate in her area. She can afford a $300 a month car payment for a used van only when her husband pays child support. Most of the time he does not, and she plans to give the car back to the bank. Thus, even though her paycheck on the job is much better than her AFDC check, the other parts of the AFDC safety net are crucial.

Ms. Childress is a success story, but as her employment counselor observed, "She was smart and got an education, and she was willing to put forth the effort. But she's just a car breakdown away from being back in the system." Childress herself states, "I know I'm going to make it, but I know I'm going to have to struggle."

If getting off welfare is a struggle for a woman with a post-high school education and a work history, what about women with less education and no regular work history? Working 30 hours at the jobs former welfare mothers typically get brings them only about $900 a month and no health benefits.[4] It seems likely that providing a transition safety net for families like this—some health insurance and child care subsidies—might greatly improve the success rate in getting people off welfare and keeping them off.

1. Drawn from a case study presented by Patricia Davis and Robert O'Harrow, Jr., "A Tough Climb from Welfare," *Washington Post National Weekly Edition* (July 10–16, 1995), p. 7. Unattributed quotes are from this source.
2. Ways and Means Committee, 1994 Green Book, reported in "Welfare Booby Traps," *Newsweek*, December 12, 1994, p. 34.
3. Ibid.
4. "Up From Welfare: It's Harder and Harder," *New York Times* (April 16, 1995), p. 4.

These programs reflect the responsiveness of government to different groups. Most taxpayers define themselves as middle income, and they support services for themselves and others like them. Benefits to the upper classes are tolerated to a large extent because many of them go unnoticed or because the groups receiving them are powerful and respected in society. Those that do not go unnoticed, such as tax breaks, are resented, however.

Programs for the poor are both obvious and unpopular. The poor, although a sizable proportion of the population, do not have the status or organization to win public support for programs benefiting them. In recent hard times, when support was most needed, programs for the poor took the brunt of budget cuts.

Not all Americans view politics only in terms of what they get. In the past, many religious, labor, civic, and business groups have rallied to the side of the poor. Now, some of these groups and others of the nonpoor are working to solve current problems. The nonpoor are finding out that the growth of the urban underclass harms not only those in it but also other citizens, who must pay for new jails, who are increasingly unable to buy reasonably priced health insurance, whose children are exposed to drug sellers, who see homeless on their way to work and in their neighborhoods, and who, in many cities, have become afraid to walk in their own neighborhoods or take public transportation. Businesses are discovering that the decay of public services, particularly schools, increases their costs when workers are ill educated and trained. Extreme inequality is exacerbating our racial problems too. Some blacks believe the failure of government to deal with drugs and crime in inner-city ghettoes is part of a genocidal plot, while some whites see these same problems and use them to denounce civil rights and welfare. Increasing economic inequality seems to undermine our ability to deal with either poverty or racial issues.

But can we generate the will to act to save a generation of millions of children whose environments now provide them with little chance of developing into productive citizens? So far, we have not. We seem to have stopped trying to solve domestic problems. The problem is not money. We spent more in the first 28 hours of the Persian Gulf War than the federal government spends in a year for maternal and child health; we spent more in four days of that war than for Head Start in an entire year.[73] Current cuts in welfare and medicare are accompanied by proposals for increased tax breaks for the wealthy. The money is there for programs we think are important. Thus our social welfare policies illustrate the popular, if ungrammatical, saying: "Them that has, gets." Social welfare policies illustrate again that government is most responsive to those who are most organized and have the most resources.

Source: © 1995 Mark Alan Stamaty. Reprinted with permission.

17 Economic Policy

You Are There

Stand by Your Man?

You are Senator Bob Kerrey and in March 1993 you face an important decision—whether to support President Clinton's economic stimulus package. You represent Nebraska, a conservative farm state that votes overwhelmingly Republican in presidential elections and supported Bush in 1992. Although a Democrat, you are a popular politician because of your background as a highly decorated Vietnam veteran, successful businessman, and fiscal moderate.

You opposed Clinton for the Democratic nomination for president and tried to win party moderates by portraying him as a traditional "tax and spend" Democrat. Like many members of your party, you believe Clinton was elected in part because he claimed to be "a new kind of Democrat" and you want him to offer a legislative program that will convince the public this tag was accurate. It is important not only to his reelection but to the campaigns of all those congressional Democrats who will face voters before 1996.

To your dismay the new president gives high priority in his first months in office to passage of a bill authorizing $16 billion in new spending to stimulate the economy. It would create 200,000 temporary jobs in construction of roads, bridges, highways, and other infrastructure projects as well as for the building or repair of community facilities. It also includes provisions for child immunizations and extension of unemployment compensation. Clinton has argued that funding for infrastructure projects, health, and education are necessary investments, and should not be thought of in the same way as spending for consumption.

You are not convinced; although these programs might be useful, you think the public will only see new spending. Already your Republican colleagues are attacking the plan's authorization of community projects, such as recreational facilities, as little different from the pork-barrel provisions of past spending bills. Senate Minority Leader Dole grabs evening news headlines portraying Clinton as another tax-and-spend Democrat.

You believe Clinton's high approval ratings during his first two months in office were bolstered by the State of the Union message in which he emphasized the need for sacrifice and a new approach to government in dealing with the budget deficit and economic stagnation. You argue that the president should follow through by emphasizing spending cuts and deficit reduction rather than advocating increased spending to create jobs. Yet as a Democrat you want to see Clinton succeed. He had worked hard to heal the rifts among his primary opponents and put together one of the party's most unified nominating conventions. What good would that party unity be if it could not get behind the policies of the man it helped elect?

Should you support your party and give the president a chance to enact his economic proposals? Or, since you believe he is wrong, both politically and economically, should you vote your conscience? A No vote is probably more in tune with your state, but it risks the wrath of party leaders and the president, whose goodwill will make it easier for you to get things you want later.

OUTLINE

Types of Economic Systems
- Capitalism
- Socialism and Communism
- Mixed Economies
- Economic Systems and Political Systems

Regulating the Economy
- Economic Problems
- Government's Economic Tools
- Managing the Economy for Political Purposes

The Budget in the Economy
- Our Tax Burden
- Income Tax Policy
- Where the Money Goes
- Discretionary and Mandatory Spending
- Budget Forecasting
- Deficits and Debt

Government and the Economy in the 21st Century
- The American Quarter Century
- Age of Diminished Expectations
- What Can Government Do?

Conclusion: Is Our Economic Policy Responsive?

Millions of middle-income American families, like this one, have flattened or declining real incomes and hold jobs that are not secure. Secretary of Labor Robert Reich has called them "The Anxious Class."

Americans pride themselves on their free, private economy. Yet when economic problems occur, they want government to do something. The degree to which government should be involved in the economy is a perennial source of conflict.

Only a few people believe government should not be involved at all. Most agree, for example, on the following:

1. Government, not volunteer efforts, must pay for a military force. Thus government must tax. We cannot individually decide whether to contribute to maintaining our nation's defense. If we did, some citizens would become "free riders."[1] Without paying, they would benefit from the voluntary contributions of others.

2. The market cannot determine which television or radio company should have the right to broadcast at a specific frequency. If broadcasting companies competed on the same frequency, none would be intelligible to listeners.

3. Market forces alone cannot regulate supply and cost of food and lifesaving medicine. Deaths from malnutrition and treatable illnesses would be much more frequent than they already are without government aid to the poor, disabled, and elderly.

Despite broad consensus on points such as these, there is much honest disagreement about how far government should go in regulating the economy and altering the distribution of wealth.

➤Types of Economic Systems

Capitalism

The role of government in the economy largely determines the kind of economic system we have. An economy in which individuals own businesses, factories, and farms is called a free market, free enterprise, or **capitalist economy.**

In a pure capitalist economy, prices, profits, working conditions, and wages would be totally determined by the market. Manufacturers would sell goods at what the market could bear, pay workers as little as possible, and manufacture products as cheaply as possible, concerned with health and safety only to the extent dictated by individual morality and the necessity to maintain consumer loyalty.

The idea that a capitalist economy would promote prosperity was popularized in 1776 by the British economist Adam Smith in *The Wealth of Nations.*[2] In his view, as each person seeks to maximize his or her own economic well-being, the collective well-being is enhanced. Businesses become more efficient, sell more at lower cost, hire more workers, and hence promote the economic well-being of the workers as well as the owners.

Socialism and Communism

Socialism is another kind of economic system. In theory it refers to collective ownership and control by the people of a country's productive capacity, its factories, farms, land, and capital. But in practice it commonly refers to a system in which government owns the businesses and farms and has the power to control wages and supply and demand for goods.

There have been many well-known theorists of socialism but none so famous as Karl Marx. He was even better known for his writings on communism; perhaps this is why socialism is often used interchangeably with communism. But in theory communism is a more advanced form of economic organization than socialism. Collectively owned economic units would also become self-governing, and the need for formal government or "the state" would disappear. No country that called itself communist ever came close to achieving this utopian goal. In fact, in those countries labeled communist, the state grew in size and became increasingly more invasive in the economy and private lives.

The core of the struggle between leaders of capitalist and socialist countries is an intense disagreement about how much control government should have over the economy and the consumption and work habits of its citizens. Sometimes in American public debate one candidate will accuse another of supporting "socialism"; in this context, socialism is often just a synonym for something a person does not like, especially bigger government.

Mixed Economies

In practice, there are no pure capitalist systems in the world and no pure socialist ones. In the United States, for example, government owns power-generating dams, some railroads, and much land. It loaned money to the Chrysler Corporation to save it from bankruptcy and has bailed out several large banks in danger of failing. In other modern societies, such as Britain, France, Sweden, Germany, and the former

Communist nations of Eastern Europe, government owns airlines, television networks, and telephone systems.

Just as all capitalist nations have socialist components, socialist nations have capitalist aspects. Even before the reforms of the late 1980s, which led to Communist governments being swept away across Eastern Europe, most of these nations found it useful to tolerate or even encourage some private enterprises, and some, such as Hungary, had quite large private economies.

Most countries, then, have a **mixed economy.** Some are more capitalist, others more socialist, but all have elements of both.

Government plays a large role in the economies of most mixed systems. For example, government directly influences the behavior of business and industry through regulation and taxation. Even Adam Smith believed there was always some role for government in a capitalist system, such as to stop one business from dominating the market and to protect the nation against external threats.

Our own system is a mixture of private enterprise and government ownership combined with considerable government intervention through taxation and regulation.

Adam Smith believed that a free, but not completely unregulated, market would best promote efficiency and individual economic well-being.

In nineteenth-century America we had much less government involvement than we do today. We have moved toward a more active government economic role largely because of abuses by big business in the late nineteenth century: Child labor was widely used; workers were paid a pittance; filthy and unsafe working conditions (as suggested by the term sweatshop) led to thousands of workers' deaths from industrial accidents; foods and drugs were often unsafe; and markets came to be dominated by a few large producers who controlled prices and wages. Public anger led to increased government regulation of wages, working conditions, content of foods and drugs, and more.

Government also intervenes in the economy by taxing and spending. Budget policies can make the rich richer and the poor poorer, or it can make the poor better off at the expense of the rich. Most Western democracies have fairly elaborate social welfare systems that redistribute some wealth from the rich to the poor in order to provide them with a minimal standard of living. In the United States, we do less of this than do most other industrialized nations.

Despite our mixed economy, we have a very individualistic, capitalistic ethic. The idea that individuals, not government, should provide services and that government should be small influences a wide range of public policies. The belief that individuals are poor because of their own failings limits our sense of responsibility to provide support for low-income families. The idea that private business is inherently self-regulating makes it difficult to enact higher standards for worker health and safety. The belief that private profit is not only the most important goal of business, but perhaps the only one, means that those fighting to protect the environment from abuse by industry have a difficult time.

Economic Systems and Political Systems

Our Constitution specifies only a little about the nature of our economic system. It emphasizes private property rights and gives government taxation and regulatory powers. By contrast the governments of most other mixed and socialist economies, whether democracies or dictatorships, have constitutions that link their political system to a form of economic organization and give government major responsibilities for achieving economic goals.

Economic distinctions between capitalism and socialism are not necessarily linked to gradations in democracy. Capitalist systems are not inevitably democratic. The most democratic systems in the world are mixed economies with strong elements of capitalism (such as Sweden, Britain, and Denmark), but many capitalist systems are undemocratic (the most blatant example being South Africa under white rule). Indeed, there is an inevitable tension between capitalism and democracy. The capitalist marketplace rewards and encourages inequities that, if unchecked, threaten democratic beliefs about individual equality.

For example, capitalist systems place no upper limits on the accumulation of wealth, even though wealth can be used to buy greater access to decision makers. The potential for greater exercise of influence by the wealthy weakens the concept of one person, one vote.

Socialist systems promote equality in wages, but in practice most socialist systems have tolerated significant disparity in overall standard of living. Socialist theory also advocates democratic control by workers, but in countries such as the former Soviet Union and China, the Communist party has used its dictatorial powers to deny individual freedom. Today in Eastern Europe and the independent republics formed from the old Soviet Union, many of the political parties working to establish democratic governments hope to retain some elements of socialism in their economies.

➤Regulating the Economy

Economic cycles of boom and bust have been one of the constants of human history. Good times with rising living standards are followed by bad times when harvests are poor, people go hungry, unemployment is rife, and living standards decline. Until modern times, governments did little to regulate these cycles, although some tried to ease the consequences of the bad times by distributing grain to people who were starving or providing temporary shelters for the homeless. Only recently have governments tried, through economic policies, to prevent these cycles from occurring.

The idea that government intervention could ease the boom and bust cycle of the economy was revolutionary. Classical economists had argued that the market would adjust itself without government action. But in democratic societies, as government became larger and more powerful, people expected government to "do something" to alleviate economic problems.

Economic Problems

One of the familiar economic problems that modern government is expected to "do something" about is unemployment. Even in a "full employment" economy several percent of the labor force will be out of work—people who quit their jobs to look for others, those just entering the work force, those unable to work, and those who do not want to work for one reason or another. But most Western countries experience periods when there are many people unemployed because the economy does not create enough new jobs. During the peak of the recession in 1981–1982, over 10% of the American work force was unemployed, and many others had only part-time work or had simply quit looking for work. This did not approach the level of the Great Depression (1929–1935), when over one-quarter of the working population were without jobs. (A **depression** is a period of prolonged high unemployment.)

A second recurring economic problem is **inflation**—a condition of increasing prices during which wages and salaries do not keep pace with the price of goods. As a dollar becomes worth less, there is little incentive to save and great incentive to borrow. In the late 1950s and early 1960s, inflation in the United States was quite low, as little as 2% or 3% a year, but the Vietnam War and the high cost of imported oil during the early 1970s stimulated a sharp rise. It was not until the early 1990s that inflation returned to pre–Vietnam War levels.

Though some economists believe moderate inflation is not a bad thing,[3] many people feel threatened by it. It erodes the value of savings and gives people an incentive to consume rather than save. Bankers hate inflation because the dollar paid back to them in the future is going to be worth a lot less than the dollar they lend today. Inflation drives interest rates up as banks charge higher and higher interest to compensate for the declining value of the dollar. Credit becomes more expensive, which makes it difficult for businesses and industries to expand. And, of course, inflation is bad because people think it is bad—they worry about it getting out of control.

A third economic problem is stagnant production, that is, the failure of the economy as a whole to produce increasing amounts of goods and services.

In Germany in 1923 inflation was so high that a basket of money barely sufficed to buy a few groceries. The inflation was caused by the German government's printing ever more money to repay the victors of World War I the penalties they had assessed. The government finally ended the inflation by issuing new currency, one unit of which was equal to one trillion of the old. This made the lifetime savings of many people worthless.

Two or more consecutive quarters (a quarter is three months) of falling production are termed a **recession.**

Productivity, one measure of the country's economic health, is the ratio of the total hours worked by everyone in the labor force to the total amount of goods and services they produce (that is the Gross National Product, or GNP). When businesses and industries discover new ways to produce goods and services using less labor, productivity rises. To achieve improvement in the overall standard of living without increasing inflation, productivity must steadily rise. Productivity is also a measure of competitiveness; businesses must become increasingly more efficient to be competitive at home and abroad.

For decades the United States had the highest productivity rates in the world. Although in the 1980s Japan and Germany began to close the gap, the American labor force, when measured by worker output per hour, is still the most efficient in the world. As businesses began streamlining and cutting back their labor forces in the early 1990s, the U.S. economy registered sharp increases in productivity.[4]

The ultimate goal in any economy is to have low unemployment, low inflation, and increasing productivity while total economic output grows steadily. Achieving all of this simultaneously is rare, however. Inflation is usually at its lowest when unemployment is high and production sags. Increasing employment often brings high levels of inflation. This means there usually is some trade-off among these three goals.

Depression, inflation, and recession all affect people's standard of living. Today, when the standard of living stagnates or begins to decline, most people expect government to take action to stimulate or slow the economy. But they do not agree on which are the most appropriate or effective responses.

■ Government's Economic Tools

Government has two primary tools to help achieve its economic goals: fiscal policy and monetary policy.

Fiscal Policy

Government decisions on how much money it will spend and how much tax it will levy determine **fiscal policy.** Increased spending stimulates the economy and increases employment; lower government spending helps slow the economy and decreases inflation. How great an impact government has depends on how much it spends in relation to the size of the economy.

Tax policy can also help regulate economic cycles. Tax cuts can be used to leave more money in the hands of the consumer, thus stimulating private spending and reducing unemployment. Increased taxes take more money out of the hands of the consumer, slow the economy, and thus reduce inflation.

Government's ability to regulate economic activity through spending and taxation is limited, however. Sometimes the economy responds to government changes too quickly, other times not quickly enough. International trends also affect our economy, as we shall see in the last section.

Who makes fiscal policy? In the United States, laws regarding taxation and spending are passed by Congress and approved by the president. In making his recommendations to Congress about taxes, spending, and other economic matters, the president is advised primarily by three people: the secretary of the treasury; the head of the Office of Management and Budget (OMB), who is responsible for preparing the annual budget message; and the chair of the Council of Economic Advisers, a group of economists who are specialists in fiscal policy matters. Sometimes, of course, these three advisers to the president are at odds with each other or uncertain their advice is sound. Indeed, Harry Truman once said he was in search of a one-armed economist so that the person could never make a recommendation and then say "on the other hand. . . ."[5] Economics, like political science, is an inexact science!

To improve communication and policy coördination among his economic advisers, President Clinton created the National Economic Council, a new office within the White House. Its members include the vice president and the heads of Labor, Commerce, Treasury, OMB, and the Council of Economic Advisers. The Council's chair was charged with briefing the president daily and translating the needs and demands of executive branch agencies into workable policies.

Congress has its own fiscal specialists on committees such as Appropriations and Budget and relies heavily on the director of the Congressional Budget Office.

Approaches to Fiscal Policy

That government can have a substantial impact on the economy through its fiscal policy has been accepted wisdom since the British economist John Maynard Keynes published *A General Theory of Employment, Interest and Money.*[6] In 1935 Keynes argued that government could stimulate the economy by increasing spending in a time of high unemployment. This would put more money into the economy, thus stimulating the demand for goods and services and, in turn, causing factories to produce more and hire more workers. Therefore, even if government had to borrow to increase spending, the deficit could be justified because eventually higher employment rates would increase tax revenue.

Keynesian economics ran counter to the conventional wisdom of the time. During the Great Depres-

John Maynard Keynes's ideas revolutionized economics.

sion, President Hoover believed that if the government went into debt it would make the depression worse, not better. His opponent in the 1932 election, Franklin Roosevelt, also ran on a pledge of a balanced federal budget. It was only after he was elected that Roosevelt adopted the Keynesian idea that government itself could help the nation get out of the depression by borrowing and spending money.

Keynesian thinking dominated fiscal policy for several decades. Well into the 1960s economists were optimistic that government could successfully regulate the economy to maintain high levels of employment and reasonable inflation. But by the 1970s this confidence disappeared due to simultaneous high unemployment and high inflation. No government policies coped well with **stagflation,** the word created to describe this combination of economic stagnation and inflation. This dealt a blow to Keynesian economics, which predicts that high unemployment and inflation cannot exist simultaneously (because, historically, higher levels of unemployment had driven prices down). The arrival of stagflation signaled a new era in the development of the American economy and led to increasing dissatisfaction with existing fiscal policy.

In 1981, the Reagan administration came to the White House with a new policy, **supply-side economics,** that promised to reduce inflation, lower taxes, increase military spending, and balance the budget simultaneously. The basic premise of this theory is that as government taxes less, more money is freed for private investment. Therefore, when the economy is sluggish, supply-siders advocate tax cuts to stimulate growth. They believe people will save some of the money they would have paid in taxes, thus making more money available to lend to businesses for expansion and modernization. Taxpayers would also be left with more money to spend on consumption; and to satisfy the increased demand, businesses would hire more workers. With increased employment fewer people collect unemployment compensation and more pay taxes. So, according to supply-side economics, even though the tax rate is lower, government revenue increases.

These ideas appealed to conservatives because they offered an economic rationale for smaller government. They also have broad appeal to Republicans who, since the Great Depression, have drawn substantial electoral support from the wealthiest Americans. Whereas Keynesian economics has been used to endorse across-the-board tax cuts to stimulate consumer spending, the supply-side approach puts more emphasis on tax cuts for the highest income groups as a means of encouraging private investment.

The extent to which government should regulate the economy is one key to understanding differences between Keynesians and supply-siders over fiscal policy. Keynesians believe that government intervention can be effective both in steering the economy and in cushioning the blow to consumers of a sluggish or overheated economy. Supply-siders believe that taxing and spending for this purpose is an inappropriate and inefficient use of governmental powers. They believe it is better to leave as much money and as many decisions on spending and investing as possible in the hands of consumers.

Supply-side economics, as implemented by Reagan's economic team and continued by the Bush administration (even though Bush had once labeled it "voodoo economics"), led to disillusionment with the policy. Dramatically increased spending for the military combined with small cuts in spending for social programs and the loss of billions of dollars in tax revenues left the country with $2.5 trillion dollars of new debt.

Perhaps due to the association of supply-side policies with the huge deficits of the Reagan-Bush years, few Republicans in the 104th Congress identified themselves as supply-siders. Still, the fiscal policies of the Republican leadership that assumed control of Congress in 1995 had much in common with supply-side thinking, especially its emphasis on tax cuts for the wealthy and the belief that government attempts to redistribute wealth through tax and spending policies are a misuse of power. Post-Reagan leaders of the Republican Party, however, have been less patient with deficits and have assumed an aggressive posture toward coupling tax and spending cuts.

Monetary Policy

Whereas fiscal policy affects the economy through spending and taxation decisions, **monetary policy** attempts to regulate the economy through control of short-term interest rates and the supply of money. Monetary policy is made by the seven-member Federal Reserve Board (Fed) and an advisory council comprised of the heads of the 12 regional banks in the Federal Reserve System. Fed members are appointed by the president for 14-year terms in order to minimize the effect of short-term political considerations on their decisions. The position of chair, however, is held for only four years, opening the door to greater influence by Congress and the president. The role of

Recognizing the importance of the chair of the Federal Reserve Board to his economic recovery program, President Clinton asked Alan Greenspan, the current chair, to sit with Mrs. Clinton in the House gallery while he delivered his first State of the Union message.

the Fed as governing body of the nation's central banking system is crucial. As Will Rogers once said, "There have been three great inventions since the beginning of time: fire, the wheel, and central banking!"

The Fed controls the supply of money in several ways. It can buy and sell hundreds of millions of dollars of treasury notes and bonds. When it buys, it pumps money into other banks; when it sells, it depletes the money reserves of the banks and thus takes money out of the economy. The Fed also changes the interest rates it charges banks to borrow its money. Low interest rates stimulate borrowing and put more money into the economy. As a last resort, the Fed can increase or decrease the amount of reserves it requires banks to have. If the reserve requirement is increased, banks take money out of circulation to build up their reserves. If the reserve requirement is decreased, banks take money out of the reserve and lend it to customers, thus increasing the money supply.

When the Fed makes money scarce, interest rates go up and businesses and industries find it harder to borrow money for plant expansion. As a result, production and inflation may slow. When the Fed allows more money into the economy, interest rates go down, making it easier for businesses to borrow for expansion.

Monetary policy is a dry subject, but its effects can be dramatic. In the nineteenth century when fiscal policy was not yet a major factor in the economy, "tight" money was often the main issue in elections. In 1982, when the Fed tightened the money supply, forcing interest rates, unemployment and bankruptcies up, one man entered the offices of the Fed and tried to kill its chair.[7] Other groups drew up "wanted" posters for the board members. And still others, thrown out of work or off their farms, killed themselves.

Today, the chair of the Federal Reserve Board is one of the most powerful people in the country. His influence has grown as huge budget deficits have limited the options available to the president and Congress to stimulate or slow the economy through taxing and spending. With so little flexibility left in fiscal policy, some economic observers look to monetary policy as the principal means for fine-tuning the economy in the 1990s. This development is seen as favorable by monetarists, who have always believed that if government has to tinker with economic cycles it should be done through monetary and not fiscal policy.

Monetary policy is made primarily to protect the value of currency and ultimately to protect investors. Fiscal policy is geared much more toward protecting the average consumer against unemployment and the effects of inflation (rather than in *preventing* inflation). While many people are both investors and consumers, and while fiscal and monetary policy should be complementary and not at odds, at times they may seem to be at cross-purposes.

To see how this works we can look at the fiscal policy of the Clinton administration and the monetary policy of the Fed under the chairmanship of Alan Greenspan. Clinton came into office with the goal of "growing" the economy and increasing the real wages of workers. Primarily a politician, his eye was on the earning and buying power of the average voter. As protector of the currency, Greenspan did not want to see Clinton achieve his goals through a too-rapid expansion of the money supply, nor by wage increases that were too quick or precipitous. Primarily a banker, his eye was on the saver/investor.

During Clinton's first two years in office the growth rate soared, five and a half million new jobs were created, and inflation stayed at or below 3%. But as the unemployment rate fell toward 6% (a rate many at the Fed consider as close to full employment as we can get without an increase in inflation) and then below it, the Fed began imposing a series of interest rate hikes—six in 1994 alone (five before the mid-term election). Greenspan also started jawboning (see below), trying to slow the economy and offset a rise in inflation. Although it is arguable whether the impact of monetary policy can be felt so quickly, by early 1995, the rate of growth did slow and unemployment rose for the first time in two years.

To a large extent the concerns of the Fed and the Clinton administration should overlap: In an era of flat wages, workers do not want higher prices, and Clinton certainly would not want to take the rap for high inflation and a devalued dollar. On the other hand (remember that expression?), most workers would rather have a job and higher prices than have no job and stable prices, especially in an era of decreased spending for welfare. And while no politician may claim to favor it, the devalued dollar can lead to more exports, and more exports can mean more jobs.

In addition to the difference in the priorities of fiscal and monetary policy makers, accountability is also an issue. If greater power to regulate the economy *has* gravitated toward monetary policy makers, it has passed into the hands of men and women whom most Americans cannot identify and who are not directly accountable to voters.

Jawboning or Persuasion

The government, and the president in particular, has an informal means for affecting the economy—trying to persuade businesses or individual consumers to behave in a certain way. Jawboning or persuasion can make a difference because psychological factors affect economic behavior. For example, economists recognize the importance of consumer confidence, that is, the degree of optimism individuals have about the economy. Confidence is rooted in the real performance of the economy but sometimes there is a lag between the economy's performance and consumers' perception of its health. A president can try to persuade businesses to expand or consumers to spend, for example, by expressing his confidence in the country's economic direction. Lyndon Johnson was extremely skillful in persuading business and labor leaders to accept his economic policies, and Presidents Kennedy and Reagan were remarkably adept at persuading both business and the public. In contrast, Carter's calls for sacrifice to meet economic problems seemed to decrease consumer confidence, and Bush was unsuccessful in trying to talk the country out of recession in 1992.

Managing the Economy for Political Purposes

Policymakers use knowledge of fiscal and monetary policy to improve the economy in election years by trying to increase the income of individual citizens and reduce inflation and unemployment. In his 1978 book, *Political Control of the Economy,* Edward Tufte finds that there is an observable relationship between trying to win elections and the kind of economic policy a president pursues.[8] Real changes in disposable income available to voters tend to be larger in election years than in other years. Unemployment tends to decrease in presidential election years, although not in off-year election years.

This suggests that presidents consciously work to manipulate the economy in ways that will benefit them at the polls. The timing of policies therefore is crucial. Cuts in government spending and increases in taxes reduce real personal income, so presidents usually do not make budget cuts or raise taxes in election years. Congress, too, responds to an electoral cycle. Spending on selected benefit programs has tended to increase somewhat in election years although there are indications this may be changing.[9]

Making no adjustments in fiscal policy can also have an electoral impact, as President Bush found out in 1992. In spite of evidence to the contrary, Bush claimed the economy was on the road to recovery and he need take no further action. He believed he had already interfered too much and apologized to voters throughout the campaign for raising taxes early in his term. He presented the outlines of a new fiscal plan only two months before the election, when it was clear Clinton's lead in the polls was related to the state of the economy. But by then it was too late. In November 1992, 43% of all voters said the economy and jobs were the issues that most affected their vote, and 53% of them voted for Clinton.[10]

There are partisan differences in the management of the economy. Conservatives and Republicans tolerate higher unemployment more easily than do liberals and Democrats, whereas liberals and Democrats are more tolerant of inflation.[11] The business and middle-class supporters of the Republican party are more concerned about inflation, whereas the working class has more to fear from unemployment and other attempts to "cure" inflation. Thus Republicans first try to bring down inflation, while Democrats first try to stimulate the economy.[12]

The Federal Reserve Board, although not under the direct control of the president, is capable of acting in a partisan way in dealing with inflation and unemployment. During an election campaign when the economy is the central issue, there is enormous potential for politicization of the Fed. In the summer before the 1992 election, following a jump in the unemployment rate, the Fed lowered its prime lending rate (in an attempt to increase borrowing and thus consumer and business spending). President Bush had publicly demanded such a reduction just several days earlier. Although Bush denied it, his Secretary of the Treasury was accused of pressuring the Fed's chair to lower rates even further as a condition of his renomi-

Source: KAL, Cartoonists and Writer's Syndicate.

nation for another term.[13] The Fed chair does not have to listen to the president, even when there is a close working relationship, as there was between Clinton and Alan Greenspan. In 1994, when Clinton was hoping to benefit in the mid-term elections from a period of strong economic growth, Greenspan was arguing that the economy was growing too rapidly and warning of an inflationary spiral.

The economy has an impact on the vote, although it is not as simple as we might suspect. Those who have studied the impact of economic hard times on individual vote choices have reported that how people feel they are doing compared to a year or two before does have some mild influence on their presidential and congressional voting choice. If they feel things are improving, they are somewhat more likely to favor the incumbent; if they believe their financial situation is eroding, they are somewhat more likely to vote against the incumbent. There is evidence that voters respond to changes in real per capita income in the few months before the election.[14] Voters are more concerned, however, with the state of the overall economy than with their own family's situation. But they do not seem to respond to changes in unemployment or inflation levels. There was evidence for this in the 1994 election. With the economy strong and unemployment low, voters were strongly anti-status quo and, while claiming their own economic situation was better than the previous year, expressed deep pessimism over the country's future.[15]

THE BUDGET IN THE ECONOMY

The size of the annual federal budget tells us government's share of the domestic economy and indicates the potential for fiscal policy to affect the nation's economy. Since 1980, the federal budget's share of gross domestic product (GDP) has hovered between 22 and 23%; that is, more than one-fifth of all the goods and services produced in the country are accounted for by federal spending.[16] (This does not include spending by state and local governments, which would put total government spending closer to 43% of GDP, or on a similar level with government spending in Germany and France.)

The federal budget also reflects the country's political goals and values, because who is taxed, at what rates, and what government spends the money on, tell us something about national priorities. Government spending is often discussed within the larger debate over fundamental political values and disagreements on taxation have always been linked to the debate over the proper size and role of government in both a democracy and a free market economy.

Our Tax Burden

We often believe our tax rates are high, yet our tax burden is the smallest in the industrial world (Figure 1). Reasons for this include our aversion to taxes and big government, our less than comprehensive social welfare system, and the low percentage of government ownership of economic enterprises. Still, by 1992 the total tax burden amounted to $6,000 a year for every man, woman, and child in the country. The average person needed 35% of his or her paid labor to meet federal, state, and local tax obligations; in other

FIGURE 1
U.S. has Smallest Tax Burden in Industrial World

The United States Government's total tax revenues as a percentage of gross domestic product were less than those of other wealthy nations in 1990, the latest year for which figures are available.

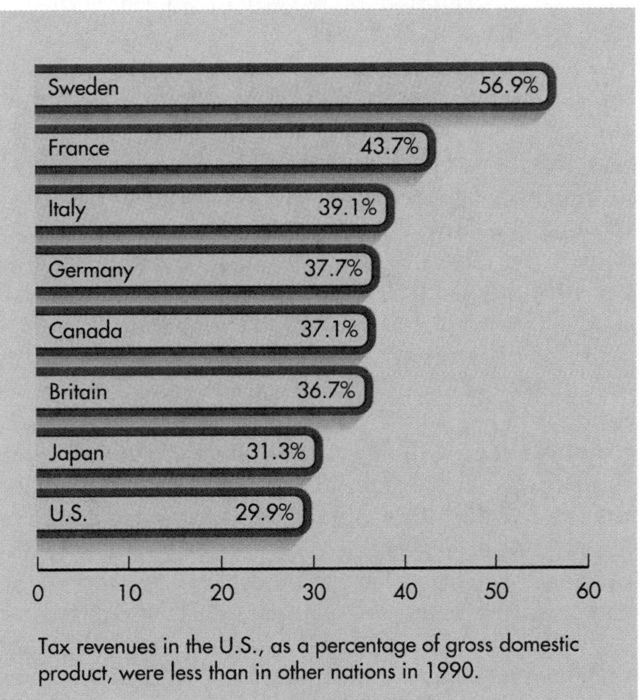

Tax revenues in the U.S., as a percentage of gross domestic product, were less than in other nations in 1990.

SOURCE: Organization for Economic Cooperation and Development.

words more than four months of each year are spent working to pay taxes.[17]

The distribution of this tax burden across the population differs from that in other industrial democracies, in part because the U.S taxes its wealthiest citizens at a much lower rate, including those countries with substantially higher savings rates. (The U.S. has the fourth lowest tax rates of the 24 countries in the Organization for Economic Cooperation and Development.)[18] In addition, even though personal and corporate income taxes account for a smaller share of government revenue than in earlier decades, they still form a higher percentage of total government revenues than in Japan and the nations of Europe. Those countries rely more heavily on taxing goods and services, which means, relative to the U.S., a larger share of the tax burden falls on consumption than on income. By placing greater emphasis on Social Security and personal income taxes, our tax policy allows the average worker to keep a smaller part of a paycheck than his or her counterpart in Europe or Japan. At the same time, the wealthiest Americans have a double advantage over their counterparts in that both their incomes and their consumption are taxed at substantially lower levels. This helps to explain why the United States now has the most unequal distribution of wealth of all the industrial democracies.

As Figure 2 shows, the government does raise small amounts of revenue by taxing consumption through the levies it places on the sale or manufacture of some luxury and nonessential items such as liquor and cigarettes, as well as on a few essential products such as gasoline. These excise taxes—also sometimes called "sin taxes"—are designed not only to raise revenue but to limit or discourage use of scarce or dangerous products.

In 1996 personal and corporate income taxes will account for 49% of all federal revenue, and Social Security taxes paid by workers and their employers for another 32%. The proportion of revenue coming from corporate income tax is still dramatically below the level of the 1950s and 1960s, when it accounted for about 25% of all federal revenue (or about the same proportion paid by Japanese corporations today). Social Security taxes, in contrast, have increased, accounting for 12% more of federal revenues in 1996 than in 1960. This is another example of how the tax burden, as measured by proportion of disposable income, has fallen more heavily on the average worker than on upper income groups.

FIGURE 2
Estimated Federal Revenue Sources, 1996

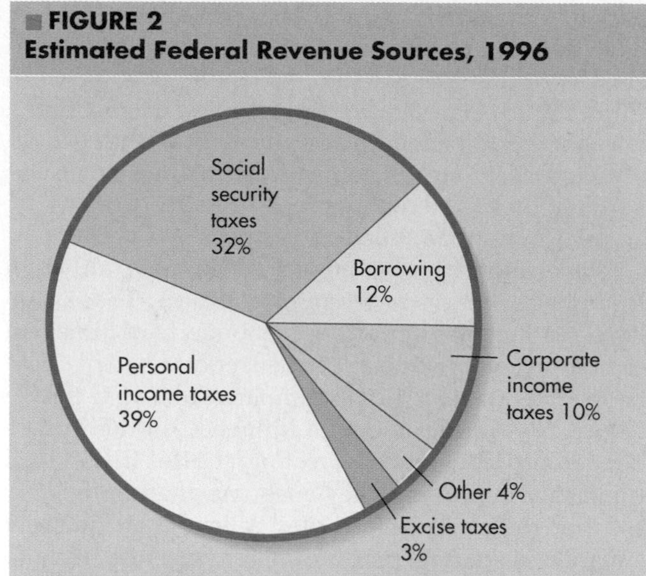

SOURCE: Budget of the U.S. Government, 1996, p.2.

The other major source of government revenue, 12% in 1996, is borrowing. This too adds to the tax burden, since everything the government borrows must be repaid from future revenues. By one estimate, with our nation's current debt load, the average American will pay about $100,000 in taxes over his or her lifetime just to pay interest on the debt.[19]

Income Tax Policy

Our tax code is complex. President Franklin Roosevelt once stated that the tax code "might as well have been written in a foreign language," and the laws are dozens of times more complex now.[20] The complexity is because Congress and the president have designed a tax code to achieve a variety of social goals. Congress wants to encourage families where both parents work to have adequate care for their children, so it allows credits for child care; it wants to encourage business growth so it gives credits and deductions for investment. (A deduction is the amount taxpayers have spent for some item, such as mortgage interest or business equipment, that they are allowed by law to subtract from their income when filing their income tax reports.) Congress believes that voluntary giving to charitable organizations is good, so it creates deductions for that too. Congress wants to help people buy homes and stimulate new housing construction, so deductions are allowed for interest on mortgage

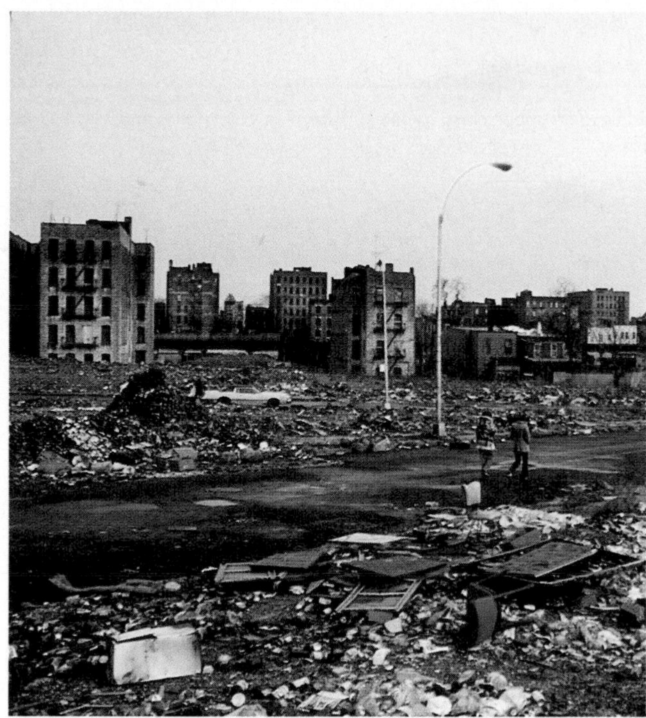

Tax credits can be used for constructive social purposes. For example, federal tax credits stimulated private and community investment in this burned out section of South Bronx. Photos show before (1981) and after (1994) this investment, in what was one of the most bleak central city areas in the United Sates.

payments. Though these and hundreds of other exemptions and deductions may individually be desirable, together they create a tax code that is difficult to understand and favors wealthier Americans who are able to take advantage of more loopholes. Every taxpayer, however, receives at least one deduction, (the personal exemption), for a total cost in lost revenue of $5,000 per filee each year.[21]

In 1986 Congress passed major income tax reform in an effort to make the tax structure fairer, simpler, and more efficient. The code's definition of fairness is spreading the tax burden among households according to their ability to pay. A tax structure based on the principle of wealthy and middle-income households paying higher percentages of their income in taxes than poorer households is called **progressive.** A tax that requires the poor to pay proportionately more than those middle- and upper-income brackets is a **regressive tax.**

The 1986 tax law tried to achieve greater fairness by reducing deductions and exemptions, and lowering the number of tax rates from 15 to 4 (counting the zero rate for low-income households). These simplifications in turn were to make the system more efficient. Taxes should have been easier to calculate and the forms less time-consuming to complete. However, in a test of the new code's simplicity and efficiency, a mythical family's income and expenses for 1989 were sent to 50 tax experts to calculate their tax liability. They arrived at 50 different answers ranging from a tax bill of $12,500 to nearly $36,000.[22]

One of the reasons the tax code remains so complex is that the reform did not go far enough in reducing deductions and loopholes. That so many exemptions and special provisions were retained is testimony to the power of a variety of interests. For example, middle-income Americans along with housing construction and real estate lobbies ensured that mortgage interest on first and some second homes would remain deductible. Part of the cost of travel, meals and entertaining for business purposes is still deductible, as is interest on business loans. The cost in lost federal revenue of tax breaks for American businesses has been estimated as high as $100 billion a year.[23] In addition, loopholes in the tax code have made it possible for a majority of foreign corporations to pay few or no taxes.[24] (The cost of some of the major deductions are given in Figure 3.)

FIGURE 3
Tax Deductions Mostly Benefit Middle and Higher Income Families

Billions of dollars of tax revenue are lost through deductions benefitting middle and upper class families. Shown in color for comparison is the spending on the food stamp program, most of which goes to low income families.

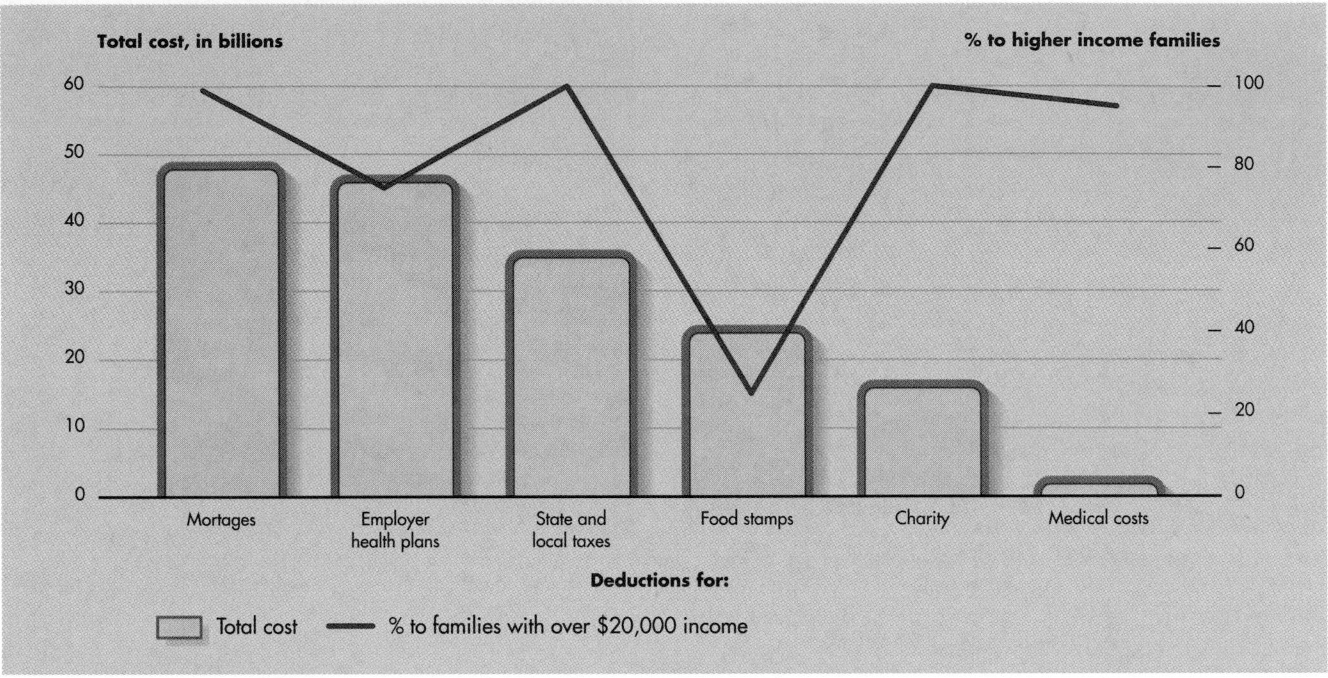

SOURCE: New York Times, November 20, 1994, p. E–5.

Because Social Security taxes rose sharply for most Americans during the 1980s and because they are withheld from paychecks just as income tax is, few middle-income people felt any tax relief from the 1980s tax cuts. Furthermore some Americans faced hikes in state and local taxes as well to compensate for reduced federal funding for social services.

Current Tax Issues

The Reagan tax cuts and the 1986 tax reform have been blamed for the increasing gap between rich and poor in the United states as well as the burgeoning budget deficits. Although they do not explain all of the redistribution of wealth that has occurred since the 1980s, the benefits did go lopsidedly to the wealthy, and the loss in federal revenues from the lower tax rates certainly added to the budget deficit. The top fifth in income level continued to pay the greatest share of taxes, but with allowable deductions and income that grew more rapidly than that of other Americans they paid a smaller portion of their income in taxes. Thus income tax was somewhat more regressive after the reform than before it.

These factors led the Clinton administration to submit legislation designed to make the income tax more progressive by forcing the wealthiest Americans to carry a larger share of the burden. In 1993 Congress increased the highest tax rate on ordinary income from 31% to 36%. When income exceeds $250,000 a 10% tax surcharge applies, making the effective rate 39.6% for those in the highest income group. The top corporate tax rate rose from 34 to 35%. The law eliminated some business deductions and reduced the deduction for business meals and entertainment, but overall the cost to the Treasury of annual tax breaks remained near the $400 billion level.[25] The purpose of the Clinton bill was to raise more revenue by making the tax structure more progressive; it did little to make it simpler or more efficient.

Achieving a tax policy that is both fair and simple is difficult given our complex occupational and income structure, and perhaps impossible without a total overhaul of the system of deductions.

The heavier tax burden for middle-income Americans, the high marginal tax rate for the wealthy, and the complexity of the tax code led to renewed calls for further reform. The most conservative proposals came from Republicans who wanted to undo the Clinton tax hike on the highest earners, and from Clinton, who asked Congress to pass a tax cut for middle-income Americans. Others called for abolishing our present tax code and replacing it with a **flat tax,** that is, a single rate for all income groups.

A flat tax bill submitted by House Majority Leader Dick Armey in 1995 would eliminate almost all deductions other than the personal exemption, greatly simplify the present 9,400-page tax code, cut millions for administering the IRS from the federal budget, and reduce the present U.S. 1040 to a single page, or postcard-sized form. Opponents of the bill argue that a flat tax promotes simplicity and efficiency over fairness. The tax code historically has defined fairness as requiring a multirate structure, so tax burdens would increase in proportion to one's ability to pay. Although most agree that this principle has been deeply compromised by a system of deductions favoring wealthier Americans, supporters of progressive taxation would rather reform and simplify the present code.

Flat tax advocates believe that a progressive tax policy punishes people for earning more and creating wealth. They argue that fairness can be better achieved by requiring all Americans to pay the same proportion of their income (in the range of 10–20%) to the government. Under plans allowing large personal exemptions, lower income individuals could pay a smaller percentage of their income in taxes than under the present system. Moreover, under a proposal such as Armey's, with an exemption of $26,000 per couple, there would be a de facto zero tax rate for an estimated 10 million of the poorest Americans.

Others advocate a move toward taxing consumption by eliminating the personal income tax in favor of a 16–18% national sales tax. But unless the tax exempted basic necessities such as food and clothing, on which the lowest income groups spend a high proportion of their earnings, it would be an extremely regressive tax.[26]

Where the Money Goes

Although it expects to raise more than $1.4 trillion in revenue, the government will spend over $1.6 trillion in 1996. A very large proportion of the budget is consumed by a few (Figure 4) categories of expenditures. Military spending, Social Security, interest on the national debt, Medicaid, and Medicare make up almost three-quarters of the national budget. Spending for education, conservation of natural resources, farm subsidies, transportation and road construction and income support for the poor are dwarfed by these budget items.

Discretionary and Mandatory Spending

Recent legislation designed to bring the budget deficit under control divides federal spending into two categories: discretionary, and direct or mandatory. **Discretionary spending** is set by annual appropriations bills passed by Congress, and as the label suggests, amounts are established at the discretion of members of Congress in any given year. Included in this category of spending are such items as government operating expenses and salaries for many federal employees. Spending on each item is limited by the

FIGURE 4
Estimated Federal Spending, 1996

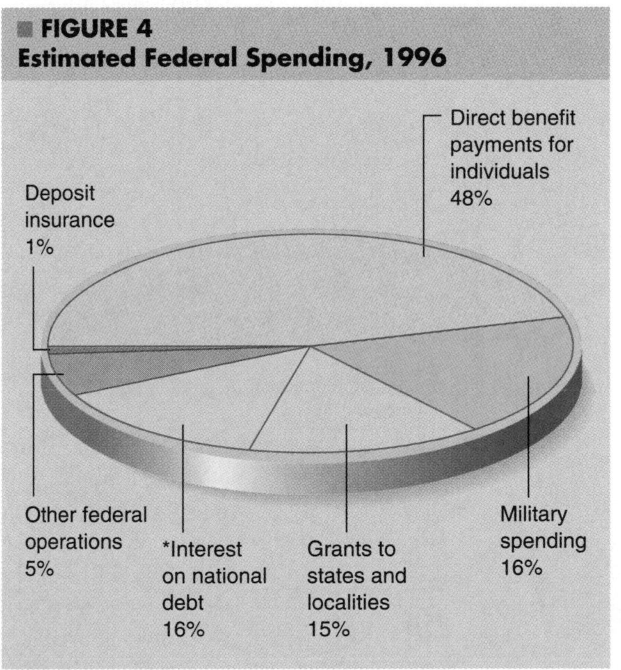

*Does not include interest paid on government securities held by the Social Security Trust Fund.
SOURCE: Budget of the United States Government, 1996, p. 1. Direct payments to individuals include primarily Medicare and Social Security, but also AFDC and other support for the poor.

dollar ceilings, or caps, that Congress authorizes for the year.

Direct or mandatory spending, in contrast, is mandated by permanent laws. Even though some of these outlays are provided for by annual appropriation bills, Congress *must* appropriate the money because there are laws that order it to do so. Examples of mandatory spending are payments made for Medicare and Medicaid, various government subsidies such as farm price supports, and unemployment insurance.

As its name implies, mandatory spending is harder than discretionary spending for Congress to control. Yet mandatory spending is not uncontrollable in every instance. In considering the president's budget, Congress cannot simply refuse to fund Medicaid, for example, nor can it decide to drastically lower its funding level. But it can amend the law to change eligibility, or it can repeal the law and remove any need for appropriations. This type of spending, therefore, while not controllable through the budgetary process alone, can be altered through legislation. An expenditure such as interest on the national debt, however, is truly mandatory and can be reduced only by paying down the debt.

In 1996, discretionary spending was expected to account for 34% of all budgetary outlays and mandatory spending for 66%.[27] Clearly any serious effort to reduce the budget deficit requires reductions in direct spending. Therefore when Republicans committed to balancing the budget assumed leadership of Congress in 1995, they immediately introduced legislation to alter the permanent laws that created, and which order spending for, welfare, farm subsidies, and other programs.

Budget Forecasting

Deciding how large the budget should be and how much should go to each government activity are part of the political process. Because the amount the government can spend is supposed to be a function of the revenue it collects, revenue projection is crucial to budget making.

Predicting revenue is not a science, as much as we would like to think otherwise; it is rooted in political as well as economic considerations. To estimate accurately what revenues are likely to be and what outlays will be needed, budget writers have to estimate future rates of economic growth, inflation, unemployment, and productivity. With economic growth comes greater revenue. If factories are idle, workers are laid off and more money will be needed for unemploy-

"WHY, YES, I AM AN ECONOMIC FORECASTER. HOW DID YOU GUESS?"

Source: © 1982 Albuquerque Journal. Reprinted by permission of John Trever, Albuquerque Journal.

ment insurance, welfare support, crime control, and even mental health care.

Small errors in predictions make an astoundingly large difference. For example, underestimating unemployment by 1% can mean a $17 billion difference in the budget—it reduces revenue by $12 billion and increases expenditures (for unemployment compensation and welfare) by $5 billion.[28]

Presidents usually rely on estimates of economic growth, inflation, and unemployment that are most favorable to their own economic program. President Reagan's projections were especially far off the mark. David Stockman, Reagan's first budget director, described how such estimates were made for his first budget. In order to justify a huge tax reduction, and show a balanced budget, significant economic growth and low inflation had to be projected. The administration's initial figures included a 2% projected inflation rate, a figure far below the existing rate. The chair of the Council of Economic Advisers, Murray Weidenbaum, said "Nobody is going to predict 2% inflation on my watch. We'll be the laughingstock of the world."[29] So Stockman and Weidenbaum bargained over what the forecasts would be; Weidenbaum selected an inflation figure he could live with and Stockman raised the economic growth projections. Of course, both were horribly wrong, and that is why the real deficit was 100 times bigger than the projected one.

The projections made by the Congressional Budget Office (CBO) are usually more reliable than those of the White House. The CBO, because it serves both parties, accepts neither the most nor the least rosy estimates of economic performance.

Deficits and Debt

Politically-driven economic forecasting, tax cuts unmatched by spending cuts, dramatically increased health care costs for the poor and elderly, and huge outlays for unforeseen events such as the savings and loan bailout have all contributed to deficits in the federal budget. A budget deficit occurs when federal spending exceeds federal revenues. This has happened every fiscal year since 1969. The accumulation of money owed by the government from all budget deficits is the **national debt.** Between 1980 and 1995, our national debt quadrupled to more than 4.6 trillion dollars.

Despite the widespread conviction that moderate deficits are sometimes needed to stimulate the economy, most experts today fear that the huge recurring deficits have impaired the long-term health of the country. When government borrowing reaches a high level it crowds out private borrowing and therefore private investment. And the intense competition for investment dollars drives up interest rates. Budget deficits, coupled with private debts, mean there is not enough money in the United States to finance this mass borrowing. We must borrow from foreign as well as domestic sources.

The fact that we are the world's largest debtor nation makes us increasingly vulnerable to the uncertainties of international markets. The outflow of interest and other payments made by our government to foreign investors also contributes to our trade deficit. Whereas 25 years ago foreign investors held less than 5% of our public debt (i.e., debt not owned by government agencies), in 1994 they held closer to 19%.[30]

The economy also suffers from government's reduced flexibility in fiscal policy. With 16¢ of every tax dollar designated for interest payments, there is less money for spending to meet urgent needs in education, health care, research, and infrastructure improvements necessary to economic growth. Our spending has been largely for the military, for social insurance programs for the middle class, and for interest on the debt rather than for investments that lay the basis for future economic growth. This means our children and grandchildren will be stuck with paying for goods and services consumed today.

Another serious problem is the huge amount of the national debt owned by government agencies. Although the public (domestic and foreign institutions and individual investors) holds $3.5 trillion of the debt, state, local and federal government agencies hold the remainder. The Social Security Trust Fund, for example, is required by law to invest its surplus (money paid in each year by workers and employers in excess of what is needed to meet outlays to Social Security recipients) in government securities. Just as you, a private investor, might loan the government money by buying a Treasury bond, so does the Social Security Trust Fund. The interest paid on these securities stays in the Trust Fund along with the bonds. The government uses the cash received from the Trust Fund purchase of securities, just as it uses the cash you spend to buy a bond, to offset the budget deficit. It means less money has to be borrowed from banks and other institutions.

The Trust Fund's annual surpluses are projected to begin dwindling in 2001 and to disappear within twenty-five years as baby boomers retire en masse. A worst case scenario projects a $5.5 trillion deficit for

Symbolic Solutions for Complex Problems?

Balancing the Budget by Constitutional Amendment?

President Reagan once said, "Balancing the budget is like protecting your virtue: you have to learn to say no."[1] If this is the case, America has been suffering from persistent promiscuity: balancing the budget has been easy to talk about but nearly impossible to do. Despite his admonition, President Reagan ran up the largest deficits in our country's history. Neither Congress nor the president has yet put together enough spending cuts or tax increases to bring the budget into balance.

One solution that has been offered periodically since the early nineteenth century, and persistently during the past twenty years, is a constitutional amendment to require a balanced budget. Republicans, acting on their *Contract with America,* have pushed hard to pass the amendment, thus far without success.

The public appears to favor strongly such an amendment, with 80% typically saying they support it. However, when faced with the possibility of higher taxes or cuts in social insurance programs as conditions for erasing the deficit, the support falls to far less than a majority.[2] Therefore, opponents of the amendment argue that what is needed more than a constitutional mandate is that legislators have the political will and the backbone to face the anger of groups whose favorite programs or tax deductions are cut. Reducing the deficit requires unpopular choices: higher taxes, spending cuts, or both.

Backers of the proposed amendment argue that only a constitutional requirement will give big spenders in Congress and the White House the courage they need to enact big spending cuts. In support of this claim, Senator Nancy Kassebaum (R.–Kan.) pointed out that when an earlier version of the amendment had been introduced in the Senate in 1982, it received 69 votes. Yet two years later only 33 senators had supported her bill to freeze all federal spending for one year.[3] Amendment supporters argue that unless members of Congress can say, "The Constitution made me do it," most will not take the political risk of voting for cuts in popular programs.

By itself the amendment offers no solution to the problems that have contributed to the deficit, such as spiraling health care costs, waste and fraud, and Cold War military spending. However, supporters argue that an amendment would provide an imperative for finding solutions.

Opponents of an amendment argue that it would remove the fiscal flexibility Congress needs to respond to emergencies. What would happen if huge unforeseen expenditures were needed for a war or natural disaster or an economic downturn, for example? The Gulf War, sending troops to Somalia and Haiti, the flooding of the Mississippi River, and the Northridge earthquake all required special budget authorizations. By some estimates, government insistence on a balanced budget during the recession of the early 1990s would have led to an unemployment rate of 9% instead of 7.7%, and $5,000 less per year in unemployment benefits for a laid-off worker.[4] Would Congress refuse to buffer the effects of a recession if the amendment passes? Or, if government-insured pension funds or savings accounts were to fail, would Congress refuse to cover these losses as it is required to do by law? The 1995 amendment bill responded to this concern by including a provision that in the event of war, or if three-fifths of Congress agreed there was a need for spending beyond revenues, the balanced budget requirement could be waived.

Both opponents and supporters of the amendment have also expressed concern over a possible loss of budgetary powers to the federal courts. Even with an amendment in place, Congress

---

the Fund by 2050.[31] The question is whether the government will have the money to pay off the securities held by the Trust Fund when they mature, and if not, who will meet benefit obligations to retiring workers.

Today there is little disagreement that the current debt level has become a drag on the government and the economy. For some the solution to the recurring deficits is amending the Constitution to require a balanced budget (see the Symbolic Solutions box above.) The most recent call for a constitutional convention won support in 32 states by 1990, just 2 short of the minimum needed. But changing the constitution is usually regarded as a last-ditch alternative, and shepherding an amendment through to ratification can take years. Therefore many in Congress have

"A billion is a thousand million? Why wasn't I informed of this?"

Source: Drawing by Mankoff © 1995 The New Yorker Magazine, Inc.

still may not be able to agree on a combination of taxes and outlays that balances the budget. In this case, who but the federal courts would be in a position to review the budget and resolve the imbalance? To prevent an unwanted strengthening of the judiciary, the Senate version of the bill denied budgetary review powers to the federal courts.

If the amendment forbids the courts to step in and includes a waiver option allowing an unbalanced budget in emergency situations, and if interest groups continue to demand support for their favorite programs, then will an amendment prevent Congress from engaging in the same kind of budgetary gimmickry used to meet the requirements of the Gramm-Rudman-Hollings Act? Moreover, requiring a balanced budget will not make budget forecasting any more of a science than it is. It will be just as difficult with an amendment as without to discourage wishful thinking by politicians and to prevent budgetmakers from making errors in estimating economic growth and revenues. For example, most of President Reagan's early budgets predicted surpluses. The magnitude of error was huge as year after year rosy estimates of revenue were not realized. A constitutional amendment could encourage such optimistic forecasting in order to make estimated federal revenues match outlays.

The CBO has estimated that, without additional taxes, it would take $1.2 trillion in spending cuts to eliminate the deficit by 2002. This is a huge sum, but for the first time there appears to be a commitment—if not agreement on how to do it—in both Congress and the White House to cut spending and reduce the size of government. In addition in 1995 Congress passed legislation requiring that tax cuts had to be matched dollar for dollar by spending cuts.

When the 1995 balanced budget amendment bill was narrowly defeated in the Senate, budget plans were submitted containing a combination of spending cuts, changes in the permanent laws creating entitlements, and elimination of federal agencies that met or surpassed CBO requirements for balancing the budget. Winning legislative support for these measures will be enormously difficult, but in the absence of new or higher taxes, many of the program changes would be necessary to balancing the budget, with or without an amendment to the Constitution.

Once the budget is balanced, there will still be the matter of paying off close to $5 trillion of accrued debt. The figure sounds staggering but the picture is not all gloom and doom. By 1790 the fledgling U.S. government had run up a national debt of $75.4 million, mainly from the costs of the Revolutionary War. This figure was fifteen times greater than the new government's annual revenues, whereas in 1995 our national debt was "only" four times larger than the $1.4 trillion in revenues. It took almost 50 years to pay off that first debt, but by 1835 the U.S. was virtually debt free.[5] And during that period of steady debt reduction the country continued to grow and prosper.

1. Quoted in "The Deficit: Out of Control?" *Newsweek,* December 12, 1983, p.36.
2. David E. Rosenbaum, "In Loss, Republicans Find Seeds of Victory," *New York Times,* March; 5, 1995, p. E16; George J. Church, "Hard Going for the Easy Part," *Time,* January 23, 1995, p. 34.
3. Senator Nancy Kassebaum, quoted by William Rasberry, "Mandating a Destination Without a Hint of How to Get There," *Lincoln Star-Journal,* December 19, 1994.
4. Louis Uchitelle, "The Pitfalls of a Balanced Budget," *New York Times,* February 21, 1995, p. C1.
5. Thomas K. McCraw, "Deficit Lessons: Hamilton the Hero," *New York Times,* May 2, 1993, p. F13.

SOURCES: Paul Krugman, *Age of Diminished Expectations* (Cambridge, Ma: MIT Press, 1992), pp. 35–78; *U.S. Budget for Fiscal Year 1996.*

looked to legislative action as a quicker and surer route to deficit reduction.

Because the Treasury Department cannot borrow beyond limits set by Congress, Congress could just refuse to approve an increase in the debt ceiling and force the Treasury Department to stop borrowing money. Congress has actually threatened to do this a few times, raising the specter of closed offices and millions of bureaucrats and military personnel out of work. When the government runs out of operating funds it must shut down. This is why such threats have never lasted more than a few days: Everyone knows government cannot simply come to a halt.

Why doesn't the government just print more money or stop making interest payments until the budget is brought under control? Defaulting would destroy the government's financial credibility at home and abroad with the banks and corporations who help finance the debt, and it would betray millions of private citizens who invest in government bonds individually or through their pension plans. If the Treasury Department simply printed more money the market would be flooded with dollars, setting off an inflationary spiral.

In 1985 Congress tried to force spending reductions by passing the Balanced Budget and Emergency Deficit Control Act, more commonly referred to by its co-sponsors' names—Gramm-Rudman-Hollings. This act was supposed to trigger automatic cuts in most programs if annual goals for deficit reduction were not met.

The experience of Gramm-Rudman-Hollings is in some ways rather frightening. It led to even more playacting about the budget than usual. The deficit was artificially reduced by selling off public land and public enterprises, a one-shot infusion of money that does nothing to solve any long-range spending problems (it is like selling your house to pay off a vacation) and by gimmicks like delaying military pay raises for a day. Spending items were put into an "off-budget category" and not counted in the estimate of the deficit. Had the items been included in the budget, the deficit would have doubled.

Investments from the surplus in the Social Security Trust Fund were used to offset part of the deficit while interest paid on Trust Fund investment was put off-budget. More dangerously, to make the budget look more balanced, balances in accounts created to maintain and improve roads and air traffic were not spent even though the funds were desperately needed. Senator Rudman, a co-sponsor of the budget bill, got so sick of these games, he decided not to run for reelection.

After the failure of Gramm-Rudman-Hollings, no serious effort to deal with the deficit through budgetary reform came until the Clinton administration's 1993 proposal. It called for substantial tax increases in combination with reductions in spending increases for domestic programs and the military. The bill was offered as one part of a larger package designed to bring mandatory spending under control. This required sweeping reforms in the permanent laws governing spending for health care and welfare.

Although Congress did pass Clinton's deficit reduction plan, it refused to consider a national health insurance bill designed to reduce the deficit by restraining runaway health care costs. In addition, most Republicans and some fiscally conservative Democrats opposed new categories of spending proposed by the Clinton administration for worker training, infrastructure projects, and education. Clinton argued that such spending was essential to the country's economic competitiveness and therefore should be seen not as consumption, but as an investment that would show a return in economic growth. Opponents of the Clinton plan countered that decisions on investment and provision of health services are best left in the private sector.

Although the size of the deficit fell during Clinton's first two years in office (Figure 5), Congress, under Republican control in 1995, advocated a new and more drastic approach to deficit reduction. The House leadership proposed tax cuts for the wealthy-coupled with huge cuts in domestic spending and passage of the balanced budget amendment.

FIGURE 5
The Deficit Begins to Shrink

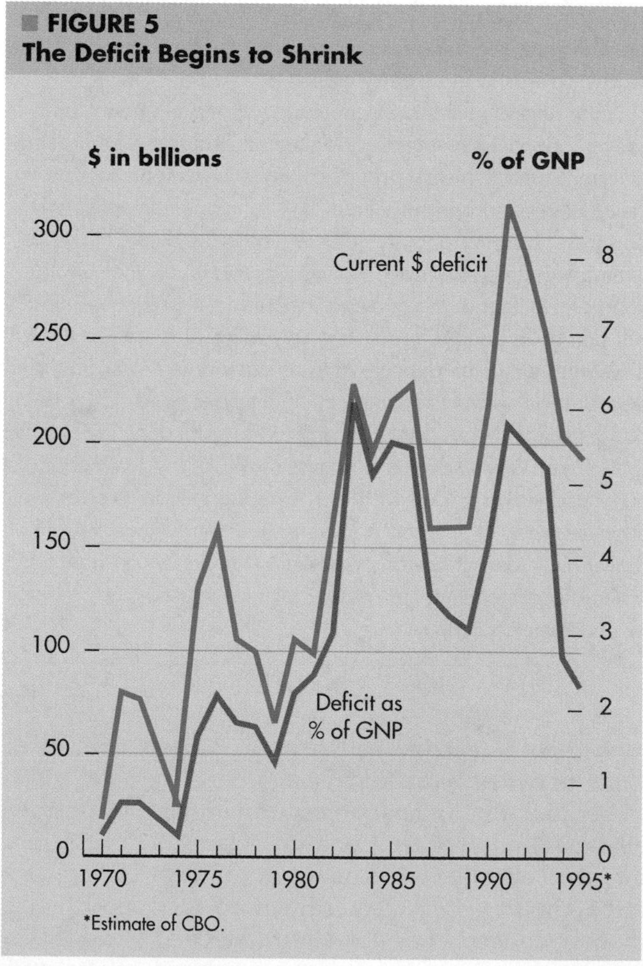

The process of writing and passing the federal budget remains a major staging ground for the debate over fundamental American values. When the Republicans gained control over Congress the debate was carried to a new intensity, and not simply because the 1994 election resulted in a divided government. Ever since the 1992 election both Republicans and Democrats have been struggling to find new economic policies to guide their parties. Many Republicans are unhappy with the supply-side economics of the Reagan-Bush era, believing it did not deliver the level of growth in the national economy that was promised when taxes were cut for the well-off. Without growth to create new jobs and increase tax revenues, and with increased spending on the military and social programs, supply-side administrations created the worst deficit problem in the history of the country. Democrats are unhappy with traditional Keynesian policies that encouraged government spending to stimulate the economy and downplayed the impact of the deficit on the health of the economy. With a volatile electorate looking for new candidates and solutions, both parties are rethinking their commitments to old policies.

➤Government and the Economy in the 21st Century

The health of any economy depends on many factors, only some of which government can influence and none of which it can completely control. But the role of government has to change over time if it is to be responsive to public needs and to structural changes in the economy. As we head into the twenty-first century, the relationships between governments and economies are everywhere in flux.

In the United States after the Great Depression, the Keynesian-influenced activist role of the government was not seriously challenged until the Reagan years, and even then without great impact. But the collapse of one-party socialist systems in Eastern Europe and a relative decline in U.S. economic strength revived the debate over government's role in a free market economy. Before looking to the future, we look back briefly at the U.S. economy since World War II and government's contributions to current problems and successes.

■ The American Quarter Century

In the late 1940s, following World War II, we were the undisputed economic power of the world. Optimistic (and perhaps jingoistic) Americans talked of the "American century," in which America would dominate the world much as Britain had done in the nineteenth century and other powers had done in earlier eras. The economies of World War II allies and enemies alike (Britain, France, the Soviet Union, Germany, and Japan) were shattered by the expense and human loss of the war, the dislocation of populations in some nations, and the destruction of factories, businesses, and public facilities such as highways and railroads in others. In these circumstances our economy boomed, and we produced goods for the entire world.

The economic good times continued, fueled in part by our growing population, for 25 years. Slow-downs in economic growth and increases in unemployment were temporary, inflation was not serious, and productivity marched steadily upward. Our standard of living zoomed as Americans bought cars, new homes, household appliances, and luxury items in quantities unheard of before. Most people could anticipate being better off in the future than in the present and felt sure that their children would be even better off. Economic improvement seemed inevitable, not for everyone, of course, but for most people.

The late 1960s brought the first obvious signs of trouble as inflation rose along with spending on the Vietnam War. Then in 1973 the bottom fell out of our economic machine. A group of oil-producing nations (called OPEC), which controls much of the world's known reserves, forced a large price increase in oil. Dependent on foreign oil, Americans found prices skyrocketing, not only for gas for their cars but for almost everything else. Petroleum products ran our factories and our farm machinery and were essential ingredients in the manufacture of goods ranging from plastics to pesticides, petrochemicals to Chapstick. The United States was not alone in its distress. All of the industrialized and much of the developing world also experienced rampant inflation. But the United States, used to being "on top of the world," may have been shaken more deeply.

The oil price shock was not the only blow to our economy. During the 1970s, the baby boom generation—those born in the late 1940s and early 1950s—entered the work force in record numbers. As a consequence, unemployment increased because the economy was unable to handle these millions of new workers. To add to our woes, other industrial nations of the world had long since recovered from the devastation of World War II and were giving us stiff competition in the international marketplace. Developing nations of Asia were also beginning to industrialize and, with low wage rates for their workers, were underselling us in international markets. Many of our heavy industries shriveled as U.S. and foreign manufacturers discovered they could buy steel and machinery cheaper in Japan, Korea, or Germany, and consumers at home and abroad decided they preferred energy-efficient foreign-made cars to those produced by the American auto industry. These developments increased unemployment as workers in declining industries were laid off.[32]

Despite these woes and the fact that inflation made the dollar worth less in 1979 than in 1970, real income in the 1970s increased by over one-fourth, and the distribution of income between the rich and poor changed little.[33] The average person was better off but felt worse off because of the specter of rising inflation, which reached "double digit" figures during some months of the late 1970s. During the decade, inflation totaled 112%, compared to only 31% in the 1960s and 20% in the 1950s. Economists could not agree on any solution to inflation that would not increase unemployment. Pessimists, looking at the shattered U.S. economy, noted that the "American century" had lasted only 25 years.

The Reagan-Bush Years

During his eight years in the White House, Ronald Reagan succeeded in reviving public confidence in the economy. As promised, he reduced income taxes, increased military spending, and lowered inflation. Inflation rates after 1982 were the lowest since the early 1970s, due in part to a big drop in oil prices. However, most of the decrease in inflation was due to the Federal Reserve Board's policies of taking money out of the economy by raising prime interest rates and making it very expensive for businesses to borrow money. This tight money policy slowed growth, and with it inflation, but it also contributed to a severe recession in 1981 and 1982. High unemployment drove down wages as workers threatened with layoffs agreed to forego pay increases and in some cases even to accept pay cuts and reduced fringe benefits.

With the Fed's tight money policy and the sharp drop in inflation, farm land plummeted in value, deflating even more than wages. Having borrowed amounts for expansion far in excess of the new value of their land, farmers were unable to sell the land at prices equal to their debt when banks called in their loans. Thousands of farmers lost their land and homes and were thrown into an uncertain job market.

In 1982, unemployment reached 11%—its highest level since the Great Depression—but then began to fall as an economic recovery took hold. Higher levels of consumer spending, stimulated by the tax cut, and record levels of government spending increased the demand for goods, which in turn fueled more production and employment. Moreover, the economy had grown in response to the baby boom generation; but then in the latter part of the 1980s, the smaller number of children born during the "baby bust" era (the mid to late 1960s) entered the work force, leaving many parts of the country with labor shortages. By the time Reagan left office, the unemployment rate was around 5%.

Unfortunately the boom in our economy was built in large part on a foundation of debt. Supply-side economics did not work; though production increased, new business did not generate enough tax revenue to make up for the lower rates. Individuals borrowed heavily too. Buying on credit became such a way of life for Americans that, in 1990, 90% of all bankruptcies were filed by individual consumers unable to pay their debts.[34]

During the Reagan years we did not save or invest for the future. We consumed about as much as we earned. Indeed, if it were not for pension funds and the Social Security Trust Fund, collectively as consumers we would have spent all we earned. Most public borrowing paid for consumption rather than modernization of our nation's industries, or improvement of our rapidly deteriorating infrastructure of roads, bridges, and water treatment plants. By the time President Bush took office, 42% of America's highway bridges were closed or restricted to light traffic; a bridge failed every two days.[35]

President Bush rode into office on the Reagan administration's successes in reducing inflation and unemployment and building up the military. Due to the growing deficit Bush did agree to new taxes but otherwise veered little from the Reagan economic path, despite his earlier rejection of supply-side policies.

As Bush turned his attention to foreign policy and the end of the Cold War, economic conditions at home deteriorated. Inflation rose and more than one million private sector jobs were lost in 1990–1991. Corporate profits fell by almost 6% and economic growth slowed almost to a halt. The nation was declared to be in recession as unemployment rose to 7.5% (2.5% higher than when Reagan left office). With the budget and trade deficits soaring, Bush could not turn to the supply-side cure of further tax reductions to stimulate the economy. Yet government continued to spend. By the time Bush left office another trillion dollars had been added to the national debt.

Age of Diminished Expectations

By the time Clinton entered the White House, Americans were pessimistic about the country's economic future. We now live in an era of diminished expectations; many of us have declining real wages and living standards.[36] Indeed, "America's families today find themselves on a treadmill. They must run as fast as possible—work harder than ever—to sustain a living standard no greater than that which prevailed in 1973."[37] This statement summarizes much about changes in our standard of living. In real dollars (that is, dollars adjusted for inflation), the average family today earns only about as much as it did in 1975, even though most families now have two wage earners, rather than one (see Figure 6).

From the post–World War II decades into the 1970s, family income grew over 3% a year.[38] Indeed, in 1966, a 50-year-old man could look back over a 10-year period in the work force and see that his income had risen over 30%. At the end of the 1980s he could look back over the same number of years and find his income had risen only 10%.[39] Today's workers earn less, in real terms, than their parents did at a comparable age and growth in living standards has nearly stopped.

Today's families are divided between those who are moving ahead and those who are falling behind. In the first group are middle-aged and older Americans and those with college educations. Falling behind are younger people, families headed by only one wage earner, and those whose education ended with high school.

Americans tolerate wide disparities in income, as this scene from LaJolla, California illustrates.

■ **FIGURE 6**
Inequality in Wealth is Higher in the U.S. than in Other Developed Nations

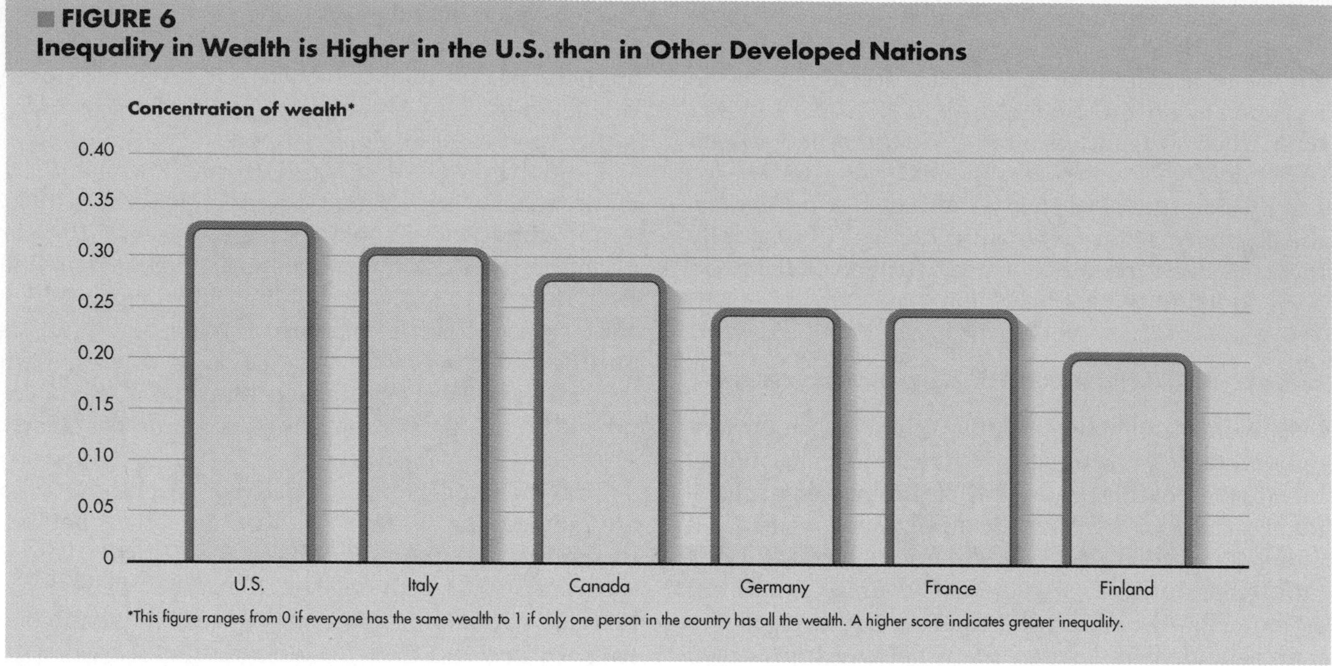

SOURCE: *New York Times,* April 17, 1995, p. c4.

Most middle-aged and older people established themselves in a job and bought a house (by far the biggest investment most families make) years ago, when economic times were good. These Americans saw their homes increase in value and their wages rise steadily into the 1980s. Most are pretty secure.

Younger Americans entered the work force when the economy was faltering. By 1995, of all men between the ages of 25 and 34, 32% earned "less than the amount necessary to keep a family of four above the poverty line. Mothers have to work longer hours if the family is to have the old standard of living."[40] Opportunities have knocked for most college-educated young adults, but there are fewer well-paying jobs for blue-collar workers than there were 20 years ago. Heavy industries that traditionally paid high wages to unionized workers have fallen on hard times. Many lost their highly paid jobs (sometimes upwards of $14 per hour) for positions that barely pay minimum wage ($4.25 per hour in 1995).

The well-paying jobs are largely for people with college educations, but getting a college education is increasingly difficult for students from poor families. The proportion of students from poor families attending college dropped by 4% between 1976 and 1986.[41] Nearly 68% of high school graduates from families with incomes in the top quartile go to college, but only 29% of these in the bottom quartile do so. Today's anger at government is fueled in part by frustration at the lack of economic opportunity for those without a college education.

Real wage rates in many nonservice jobs have decreased too. Wage concessions made by workers worried about job security mean that even a unionized job in industry has not provided protection against income declines. However unionized workers in almost all job categories still fare better than non-unionized workers, especially in fringe benefits.[42]

The 1990s are a time of taking stock of what the 1980s' private and public spending binge has wrought. The president and Congress reigned in spending and businesses that had overexpanded in the 1980s began cutting back their labor forces, eliminating unnecessary jobs and computerizing clerical work. Even when economists pronounced the recession over in 1993, factories relied on temporary employees or on overtime work to meet increasing demand rather than bear the expense of recruiting, training, and picking up fringe benefits for new workers. By one estimate money spent on overtime pay rather than on wages for new workers cost the economy 1.3 million jobs and accounted for most of the lost jobs in the manufacturing sector in the late 1980s.[43] With fewer employees turning out more goods and services, productivity began to increase sharply in 1992–1993.

Even in the strong economic recovery of 1993 and 1994, wages remained flat. In 1995 the Secretary of Labor reported, "More than 11% of working families with at least one full-time wage earner have fallen into poverty—up from 7% in the 1970s. Nearly one out of five workers who lost a full-time job between 1991 and 1993 was still without work [in 1994]. And among those who landed new jobs, almost half are earning less than before."[44]

There is some evidence that the middle class in America is declining in numbers. From 1980 to 1993 the share of total household income going to the middle three-fifths of households fell by 3.6%, while the share going to the top fifth rose by 4.1%. While real income for the middle one-fifth of households rose on average by less than $200 in that thirteen-year period, the income of the top 5% grew by $41,200.[45] The concentration of wealth and privilege (especially access to higher education in elite institutions) has become so pronounced that one observer refers to the formation of an "overclass."[46]

The United States is now the most economically stratified country in the modern industrial world. One percent of the population controls almost 40% of the country's wealth and America's children are among the poorest in the industrialized world (ranking 16th out of 18).[47] And proposed solutions to the federal budget deficit—tax cuts for the wealthy and reduced spending for social programs, including worker training, college loans, and welfare—are likely to add to the maldistribution of income. If the middle class is declining, this is clearly a danger sign because democratic stability rests in part upon a large middle class. A society of haves and have-nots with relatively

The American postwar economy lifted millions of families into middle-class status and comfort. Above is a poverty-stricken family in 1936. Victims of the drought and depression, they had left Oklahoma, where they were homeless with little to eat, to find a better future in California. Below is the same family 43 years later in front of the daughter's home in Modesto. Is such dramatic improvement in family fortunes probable today?

few in the middle is not likely to be very stable.[48] Moreover, when many people believe their standard of living is slipping, we can expect hostility to increase between young and old, poor and rich, black and white, those with limited educations and those with college degrees.

What Can Government Do?

The problems Americans are facing are not the result only of government policies or our own consumption and saving habits. We are part of a world system in which the fastest growing economies are no longer in

Industrial Policy

The United States economy is still the largest in the world in terms of total output of goods and services. But in many sectors it has lost is competitive advantage to other industrial nations, especially the European Community, Germany and Japan. The manufacturing sector, a prime source of high-paying jobs, is disappearing into developing countries where wages are much lower. Everyone is aware that the economy is undergoing structural change but there is no agreement on what government's role should be in this transition period.

One way government can help nudge the economy in new directions, some argue, is by having an **industrial policy.** This policy would specify a set of actions government would take to encourage the development of industries and technologies—fiber optics, high-speed computing, clean-fuel cars, and biotechnology, for example—of central importance in the future economy. Specific actions the government could take include giving tax credits to businesses doing research and development in these fields, redirecting government research and development to critical technologies, and encouraging collaboration among research scientists in universities, private businesses and government agencies.

The Bush administration was officially opposed to industrial policy but took actions consistent with having one. For example, it adopted a National Technology Initiative to facilitate research collaboration between business and government and it created a Critical Technologies Institute whose staff was to identify technologies deserving of government support.

Clinton has spoken much more forcefully about industrial policy, although like Bush he sometimes prefers to call it a technology initiative. Shortly after taking office Clinton traveled to Silicon Valley to win support for his plan to redirect government R&D spending from the defense sector to development of products with commercial applications. His first budget called for "All Federal R&D agencies . . . to act as partners with industry wherever possible."[1]

Clinton's Secretary of Labor proposed government support for the retraining of workers for high tech industries and for government encouragement of those high tech industries in which the U.S. is already on the cutting edge of international competition. Vice President Gore became an outspoken advocate of a government-built electronic superhighway that would serve as a database for every business, institution and home that uses computers. He likened the information superhighway to other government-supported infrastructure projects, such as the building of the railway system, and saw it as just as essential to moving the economy into the future as railroads were in the nineteenth century.

Proponents of industrial policy cite the support given to critical industries by the governments of all leading industrial nations and claim it has contributed to the competitive edge they have gained against the United States. They point out the German government spends 14.5 percent of its R&D money on industrial development while we have spent less than 1%. Japan's government spends 50% more (as a percentage of GDP) than ours on nonmilitary R&D.[2]

Opponents of industrial policy are most concerned about who will decide which industries and technologies should be targeted for government support. They believe politicians do not have the necessary knowledge and that who gets R&D money may be determined by pork barrel politics. Other critics have cited businesses which have put taxpayer-funded technologies to work in factories they build abroad or who share the technology with foreign businesses that may be competitors of U.S.-based industry.

Both the Bush and Clinton administrations agreed with these critics that government alone should not make decisions on which industries and technologies are to be singled out for support. But with economic restructuring, high trade deficits, and a gap between the educational system and industrial needs, they believed that the time for the government to have an industrial policy had arrived. The Republican leadership in the 104th Congress did not agree, however. Labeling such cooperation between government and business as inappropriate, they eliminated Clinton's R&D proposal from the 1996 budget.

---

1. Budget of the United States Government, 1994, p. 43. 2. Steven Greenhouse, "The Calls for Industrial Policy Grow Louder," *New York Times,* July 19, 1992, p. F.3. *Other sources:* Paul Krugman, *The Age of Diminished Expectations,* Cambridge, Mass..; MIT Press, 1992, pp. 15-17; Robert Reich, *Work of Nations,* New York: Vintage Books, 1992, Chapters 14, 15, and 18; Bill Clinton, "Putting People First," economic plan issued June 20, 1992; John Markoff, "Building the Electronic Superhighway," *New York Times,* January 24, 1993, Section 3, p. 1.

North America and Europe but in Asia. In addition to Japan, Germany and the rest of the European Union, China, Taiwan, Hong Kong, South Korea, Singapore, and several Latin American countries are now major rivals in world trade. We cannot dominate markets with our manufactured or agricultural products, and we cannot keep jobs within our borders when it is much more efficient and therefore profitable for businesses to operate elsewhere. Actions taken by government, business leaders, and ourselves as consumers have certainly contributed to the seriousness of some of our problems, but we could not have prevented other countries from developing into major competitors. The competition can be good in that it forces us to become more efficient and brings greater prosperity to the citizens of other countries (who are potential consumers of goods and services we produce).

As the U.S. economy's position in the global economy has changed, so has the government's ability to effect economic change. The question has been raised whether today there is even such a thing as an American economy.

Robert Reich, Secretary of Labor in the Clinton administration, maintains there are no longer separate national economies to manage.[49] The days when the board chairman of General Motors could say "What is good for GM is good for the country and what is good for the country is good for GM" are over. The American economy is now simply a region of the global economy, and both business and labor must compete in an international market. We may still jealously guard our territorial boundaries but today no border can contain financial and intellectual activities.

A revolution in technology—computers, telecommunications, and transportation—brought us to this new era. Money can be transfered to foreign banks instantaneously through computerized accounts, making competition for investment international. The most highly paid workers—scientists, systems planners and analysts, lawyers, and artists, for example—are very mobile; modern transportation makes it feasible to travel to employment opportunities anywhere in the world, and telecommunications makes easy the transmission of their ideas. They are part of an international labor pool.

Blue-collar workers too compete in an international market, not just against available labor in the United States. Manufacturers relocate where low overhead and wages ensure higher profits, and highly paid North Americans lose jobs to poorly paid Latin Americans and Asians.

Businesses do not make decisions on relocating to another city or country based on how their departure will affect the local economy. Workers do not worry (unless restricted by national security laws) about whether the company they sell their invention, new software, or design idea to is an American-based or a foreign company as long as they get the highest possible price for their services or product.

Therefore Reich says we should not be preoccupied with revitalizing an "American" economy because it no longer exists. Instead we should do a much better job than we have been doing of preparing the American labor force to compete in the global economy.

In today's world, Reich argues, national competitiveness no longer depends on the amount of money a nation's citizens save and invest in building more factories on American soil. It depends instead on the skills and insights workers can contribute to the global economy. Given our great university system and leadership in high technology, Reich believes the U.S. has a greater potential than almost any other country to train workers for the economy of the twenty-first century. But it will mean upgrading the educational system so that it does an equally good job for people in all income groups. In today's global economy, Reich says, that is what economic nationalism means.

Even if an "American economy" no longer exists, there is not much evidence that Americans, except perhaps those in the highest income groups, have stopped thinking that there is an economy contiguous with the country's borders and that their government is responsible in some way for its performance. This creates a set of expectations that government officials may be increasingly less able to meet.

While our government cannot control developments in the global economy or dictate to corporations where they will do business or how many or what kind of jobs they will create, there are actions government can take to encourage economic recovery. For example, it can reduce the deficit, thus freeing more money for private borrowing and investment, and it can support programs for retraining workers who have lost their jobs.

Government has a special responsibility for the dislocation created by the redirection of public spending from defense to the civilian sector because it created the problem. From 1988 to 1993, 450,000 defense-related manufacturing jobs were lost, and 594,000 more are projected to disappear by 1997 under Clinton's proposed defense cuts.[50] In addition active military ranks will be pared by one half million

TABLE 1 The Proportion of Workers Holding Low Paid Jobs Increased During the 1980s.

	'90	'79
Men	14%	8%
Women	24	20
18 to 24	43	23
35 to 54	13	10
H.S. dropouts	36	21
H.S. grads	22	13
Whites	17	11
Blacks	25	19
Hispanics	31	20

In 1992, 14 million Americans held low-paying jobs, almost double the number in 1982. A low-paying job was defined as one that paid less than $12,195 a year or $6.10 an hour (1990 dollars).

SOURCE: U.S. Census Bureau, cited in *Champaign-Urbana News-Gazette,* May 12, 1992.

men and women; many who planned to make the military their career will now have to look to the civilian labor market. Middle-aged missile scientists and engineers have nowhere to market their skills while many of the lower-skilled manufacturing personnel will never find jobs as well paid as those in defense industries.

With the closing of hundreds of military bases many cities face substantial revenue losses in a time of diminished federal aid. The Clinton administration promised a defense conversion program to retrain workers and find civilian markets for former Pentagon contractors but a successful outcome is dependent upon continued growth in the economy.

The federal government can also monitor trade practices to see foreign markets are open to American products, encourage reform of the educational system, fund repair and upgrading of the country's infrastructure; and target new technologies and industries for government support (see box on industrial policy). Government can also do nothing and wait for some kind of market readjustment, but this option has not been chosen by any modern industrial country.

➤Conclusion: Is Our Economic Policy Responsive?

If we can draw one lesson from the performance of the American economy during the 1970s and 1980s, it is that economic policymakers, both government and private, were living for the short term. In the 1980s, corporate America improved its profit margin at the expense not only of investment but also of workers, many of whose real wages fell significantly. Government policymakers preferred politically popular tax cuts to either balancing the budget or investing in programs to improve our nation's infrastructure, promote research, or upgrade human capital through education and training. Moreover, government was content to let income inequalities grow and even exacerbated them by cutbacks in social programs.

In the mid-1990s the U.S. still had the largest and most productive economy on earth. It also had the greatest income disparity of all the industrial democracies, fostered in part by public policy—a tax structure that placed the heaviest burdens on middle- and lower-income groups—and in part by private policies—market changes in the job and wage structure—that government was less and less willing to ameliorate.

The mid-nineties saw a movement away from policy geared toward short-term electoral results and toward long-term solutions to the problem of maintaining the country's economic vitality, in part because the electorate in 1992 and 1994 signaled its support for a change in fiscal policy. Congress and the

"The poor are getting poorer, but with the rich getting richer it all averages out in the long run."

Source: Drawing by Mirachi; © 1988 The New Yorker Magazine, Inc.

White House, however, were divided over how government should respond to this signal. The Clinton administration argued that a responsive government is one that uses fiscal policy both to foster economic growth and to regulate the distribution of income generated by that growth. Congress under Republican leadership argued that the country's economic difficulties stemmed precisely from this overresponsive, interventionist, Keynesian approach. In their view the most responsive government is that which leaves an unfettered market to "grow" the economy and distribute its wealth. This is the essence of the long-standing debate in American political life over the proper relationship of government to the economy. Only after the effects of a shift away from post–World War II fiscal policies is felt will it be known whether the electorate agrees that government has been responsive.

EPILOGUE

Kerrey Opposes the President

Senator Kerrey tried to distance himself from Clinton's Republican critics by defending the president's commitment to improving the economy and his willingness to negotiate with Congress to eliminate spending for noninfrastructure projects. But Kerrey joined Republicans and four other Democrats in an unsuccessful attempt to strip the president's stimulus package of $100 million in spending for community projects. On national television he argued that the bill would have at best a marginal impact on the economy and, at the same time, would send a signal to special interests that Congress is willing to continue spending increases. Kerrey said if he supported the bill it would undermine his capacity to say No to special interests who wanted him to vote for additional new spending.

Senator Kerrey voted on his political conviction that the first and best way to improve the economy was by spending down the deficit, not through old-fashioned Keynesian policies of stimulating the economy. He did not accept Clinton's position that spending on infrastructure was really an investment. But Kerrey did not agree with the supply-siders either because he supported tax increases. He argued that there was a popular mandate for tax increases linked to deep spending cuts and that the government had "to seize that moment." Only when the deficit was eradicated, Kerrey maintained, would the economy grow and generate real, permanent jobs.

Clinton and the fiscal rebels in his party were struggling to redefine the Democrats' position on the appropriate role for government in regulating economic performance. The 1992 election turned on this issue and seemed to be a rejection of both supply-side economics and the do-nothing approach. But there was no mandate for traditional Keynesian policies either. Clinton understood this in running as a "new" Democrat but was unable to convince the public or enough key members of Congress that his stimulus package was a new or necessary kind of spending.

➤Key Terms

capitalist economy
socialism
mixed economy
depression
inflation
recession
productivity
fiscal policy
Keynesian economics
stagflation
supply-side economics
monetary policy
progressive tax
regressive tax
flat tax
discretionary spending
mandatory spending
national debt
industrial policy

➤Further Reading

General

Robert Heilbroner and Lester Thurow, *Economics Explained* (New York: Random House, 1982). *A readable discussion of major economic concepts and issues.*

Hibbs, Douglas. *The American Political Economy* (Cambridge, Mass.: Harvard University Press, 1987).

Edward Tufte, *Political Control of the Economy* (Princeton, N.J.: Princeton University Press, 1978). *An interesting, sophisticated, but readable account of the relationship between trying to win elections and economic policymaking.*

Topical

Donald L. Barlett and James B. Steele. *America: What Went Wrong?* (Kansas City, Mo.: Andrews and McMeel, 1992). *A compilation of a series of articles from the* Philadelphia Inquirer *which explains in nonacademic language some of our major economic problems: the national debt, the cost of deregulation and health care, junk-bond dealing, loss of jobs through foreign investment, and the growing tax burden on middle and lower income groups. These articles produced the greatest public response in the newspaper's history.*

Benjamin Friedman, *Day of Reckoning* (New York: Random House, 1988); and Murray Weidenbaum, *Rendezvous with Reality* (New York: Basic Books, 1988). *Two economists, a liberal (Friedman) and a conservative, critique Reaganomics. Both believe something must be done about the biggest Reagan legacy—the deficit—but they disagree about what that something should be.*

William Grieder, *Secrets of the Temple* (New York: Simon & Schuster, 1988). *It is hard to imagine a book about the Federal Reserve Board being interesting, but this one is. Reveals the human face behind this most technical institution.*

Robert Heilbroner, *The Worldly Philosophers*, 6th ed. (New York: Simon & Schuster, 1986). *A readable account of the lives and ideas of famous economists throughout history.*

Paul Krugman. *Peddling Prosperity in the Age of Diminished Expectations: U.S. Economic Policy in the 1990s* (New York: W.W. Norton and Co., 1995). *An economist from MIT writing for a general reading audience explains the trade and budget deficits, inflation, unemployment, Fed policies, devaluation, and the S&L scandal in terms of their costs to the nation's overall economic health and concludes we are not in as much trouble as the public mood suggests.*

Frank Levy, *Dollars and Dreams* (New York: W.W. Norton, 1988). *Explains why families today have less chance of achieving middle-class status than they did 20 years ago.*

Michael Lind. *The Next American Nation: The New Nationalism and the Fourth American Revolution* (New York: The Free Press, 1995). *This study of American identity by an editor of* The New Republic *includes two chapters (4 & 5) on the social and political consequences of the growing concentration of wealth and privilege in the United States.*

Katherine S. Newman, *Declining Fortunes: The Withering of the American Dream.* (New York: Basic Books, 1994). *An anthropologist describes the economic fortunes of the baby boom generation.*

Peter G. Peterson, *How to Rescue the Economy from Crushing Debt and Restore the American Dream.* (New York: Simon and Schuster, 1994). *A former secretary of commerce gives his plan for saving Social Security and Medicare while balancing the budget.*

Kevin Phillips, *The Politics of Rich and Poor* (New York: Random House, 1990). *A conservative political analyst argues that the 1990s will bring a populist revolt against the greed of the 1980s.*

Robert Reich, *The Work of Nations* (New York: Knopf, 1991). *Argues that we must see ourselves as part of a world economy and be prepared to compete internationally.*

David Stockman, *The Triumph of Politics: Why the Reagan Revolution Failed* (New York: Harper & Row, 1986). *Reagan's budget director tells all.*

➤Notes

1. Mancur Olson, *The Logic of Collective Action* (New York: Schocken, 1971).

2. Adam Smith, *An Inquiry into the Wealth of Nations* (1776; Reprinted in several editions including Indianapolis: Bobbs Merrill, 1961).

3. James Galbraith, *Balancing Acts* (New York: Basic Books, 1988); Robert Heilbroner and Lester Thurow, *Five Economic Challenges* (Englewood Cliffs, N.J.: Prentice-Hall, 1981), p. 62.

4. Sylvia Nasar, "Cars and VCRs Aren't Necessarily The First Domino," *New York Times,* May 3, 1992, p. E6; Steven Prokesch, "Service Jobs Fall As Business Gains," *New York Times,* April 18, 1993, p. 1

5. Quoted in *Time,* January 30, 1989, p.46.

6. John Maynard Keynes, *The General Theory of Employment, Interest and Money* (1936).

7. William Grieder, *Secrets of the Temple* (New York: Simon & Schuster, 1988), p. 461. Grieder's analyses of the Reserve Board's anti-inflation policies in the early 1980s are revealing and compelling.

8. Edward Tufte, *Political Control of the Economy* (Princeton, N.J.: Princeton University Press, 1978).

9. William Keech and Kyoungsan Pak, "Electoral Cycles and Budgetary Growth in Veterans Benefit Programs," paper presented at the Midwest Political Science Association Meeting, April 1988; John Hibbing, "The Liberal Hour," *Journal of Politics* 46 (August 1984), pp. 846-65.

10. *National Journal,* November 7, 1992, p. 2544.

11. Douglas Hibbs, "Political Parties and Macroeconomic Policy," *American Political Science Review* 71 (December 1977); Paul Peretz, *The Political Economy of Inflation* (Chicago: University of Chicago, 1983).

12. Henry Chappell and William Keech, "The Economic Conservations of the Reagan Administration," paper presented at the conference on the Resurgence of Conservatism in the Anglo-American Democracies, May 1986; Douglas Hibbs, *The American Political Economy: Macroeconomics and Electoral Politics* (Cambridge, Mass.: Harvard University Press, 1987).

13. Steven Greenhouse, "Brady Sought Greenspan Policy Pledge," *International Herald Tribune* (NYT), September 25, 1992, p. 13.

14. There is a huge literature, well summarized in Peretz, *Political Economy of Inflation.* For a sampling see, James Kuklinski and Darrell West, "Economic Expectations and Voting Behavior in U.S House and Senate Elections," *American Political Science Review* 75 (June 1981), pp. 436-47; John Owens and Edward Olson, "Economic Fluctuations and Congressional Elections," *American Journal of Political Science* 24 (August 1980), pp. 469-93; John Hibbing and John Alford. "The Electoral Impact of Economic

Conditions," *American Journal of Political Science* 25 (August 1981), pp. 423-39; Douglas Hibbs, "The Dynamics of Political Support for American Presidents Among Occupational and Partisan Groups," *American Journal of Political Science* 26 (May 1982), pp. 312-32; Robert Erikson, "Economic Conditions and the Presidential Vote," *American Political Science Review* 83 (June, 1989), pp. 567-73.

15. "Poll: Citizens OK About Money, Glum on Future," *Champaign-Urbana News-Gazette,* April 12, 1995, p. B8.

16. David E. Sanger, "Republicans Want to Renew Vision of Reagan," *New York Times,* January 15, 1995, p. 10.

17. "The Demographics of Taxes," *The American Enterprise,* March/April, 1992, p. 94.

18. Figures from Organization of Economic Cooperation and Development cited by David Broder, "Tax Load Toward the Light Side," *Lincoln-Star Journal,* April 23, 1995.

19. Marcia Stepanek, "Debt: America Awash in Red Ink," *Champaign-Urbana News-Gazette,* March 27, 1994, p. B1.

20. Robert J. Samuelson, "The True Tax Burden," *Newsweek,* April 21, 1986, p. 68.

21. Michael Wines, "Taxpayers Are Angry. They're Expensive, Too," *New York Times,* November 20, 1994, p. E5.

22. "Don't Feel Alone if Tax Confusing: 50 Experts Differ over Family Return," *Lincoln Star* (AP Report), February 18, 1989, p. 2.

23. Donald L. Barlett and James B. Steele, *America: What Went Wrong?* Kansas City, Mo.: Andrews and McMeel, 1992, p. 41; Robert D. Hershey Jr., "A Hard Look at Corporate 'Welfare'," *New York Times,* March 7, 1995, p. C1-C2.

24. Barlett and Steele, pp. 92-93.

25. Michael Wines, "Using Taxation in a Good Cause Often Backfires," *New York Times,* June 6, 1993, p. E3.

26. Paul Starobin, "The New Abolitionists: No Returns," *National Journal,* March 18, 1995, p. 666; Rep. Dick Armey, letter to *New York Times,* April 23, 1995, p. E16.

27. *The Budget System and Concepts* (Washington, DC: U.S. Government Printing Office, February, 1995), pp. 5–8; *U.S. Budget for Fiscal Year 1996* (Washington, DC: Government Printing Office), pp. 33–60.

28. John Gist, "The Reagan Budget," PS (Fall 1981), pp. 738-47.

29. David Stockman, *Triumph of Politics* (New York: Harper & Row, 1986).

30. "Federal Borrowing and Debt," *U.S. Budget for Fiscal Year 1996: Analytical Perspectives* (Washington, DC: U.S. Government Printing Office, 1995), p. 195.

31. Peter G. Peterson, "The Budget Buster," *New York Times,* April 9, 1995, p. E5. Peterson is a former secretary of commerce.

32. See John Schwartz, "America's Hidden Success, rev. ed. (New York: W.W. Norton, 1988) and Bennett Harrison and Barry Bluestone, *The Great U-Turn* (New York: Basic Books, 1988) for analyses of the economy in the 1970s.

33. Paul Peretz and Raymond Ring, "Variability of Inflation and Income across Income Classes," *Social Science Quarterly 66* (March 1985), pp 203-9.

34. *New York Times,* April 18, 1991, p. C18.

35. George Will, "Good Roads, Robust Economy Linked," *Lincoln Star,* March 12, 1990.

36. Paul Krugman, *Age of Diminished Expectations: U.S. Economic Policy in the 1990s* (Cambridge, Mass.: MIT Press, 1992), p. x.

37. Harrison and Bluestone, *The Great U-Turn.*

38. John Berry, "The Legacy of Reaganomics," *Washington Post National Weekly Edition,* December 19-25, 1988; Spencer Rich, "Are You Really Better Off Than You Were Thirteen Years Ago?" *Washington Post National Weekly,* September 8, 1986, p. 20; Levy, "We're Running Out of Gimmicks."

39. *New York Times,* January 8, 1989.

40. Lester C. Thurow, "Companies Merge; Families Break Up," *New York Times,* September 3, 1995, p. E11.

41. Barbara Vobejda, "Class, Color, and College," *Washington Post National Weekly Edition,* May 15-21, 1989, p. 6.

42. Louis Uchitelle, "For Employee Benefits, It Pays to Wear Union Label," *The New York Times,* July 16, 1995, pf10.

43. Louis Uchitelle, "Fewer Jobs Filled as Factories Rely on Overtime Pay," *New York Times,* May 16, 1993, p. 15.

44. Robert B. Reich, "Drowning in the Second Wave," *New York Times,* April 16, 1995, p. E16.

45. *U.S. Budget for Fiscal Year 1996,* p. 13.

46. Michael Lind, *The Next American Nation: The New Nationalism and the Fourth American Revolution* (New York: The Free Press, 1995), pp. 139-216.

47. Keith Bradsher, "Gap in Wealth in U.S. Called Widest in West," *New York Times,* April 17, 1995, p. C4.

48. See, for example, Charles F. Cnudde and Deane E. Neubauer, eds. *Empirical Democratic Theory* (Chicago: Markham Publishing Company, 1969).

49. Robert B. Reich, *Work of Nations: Preparing Ourselves for 21st-Century Capitalism* (New York: Vintage Books, 1992).

50. "Study: Defense Job Crisis Just Beginning," *Champaign-Urbana News-Gazette* (AP), May 10, 1993, p. A5.

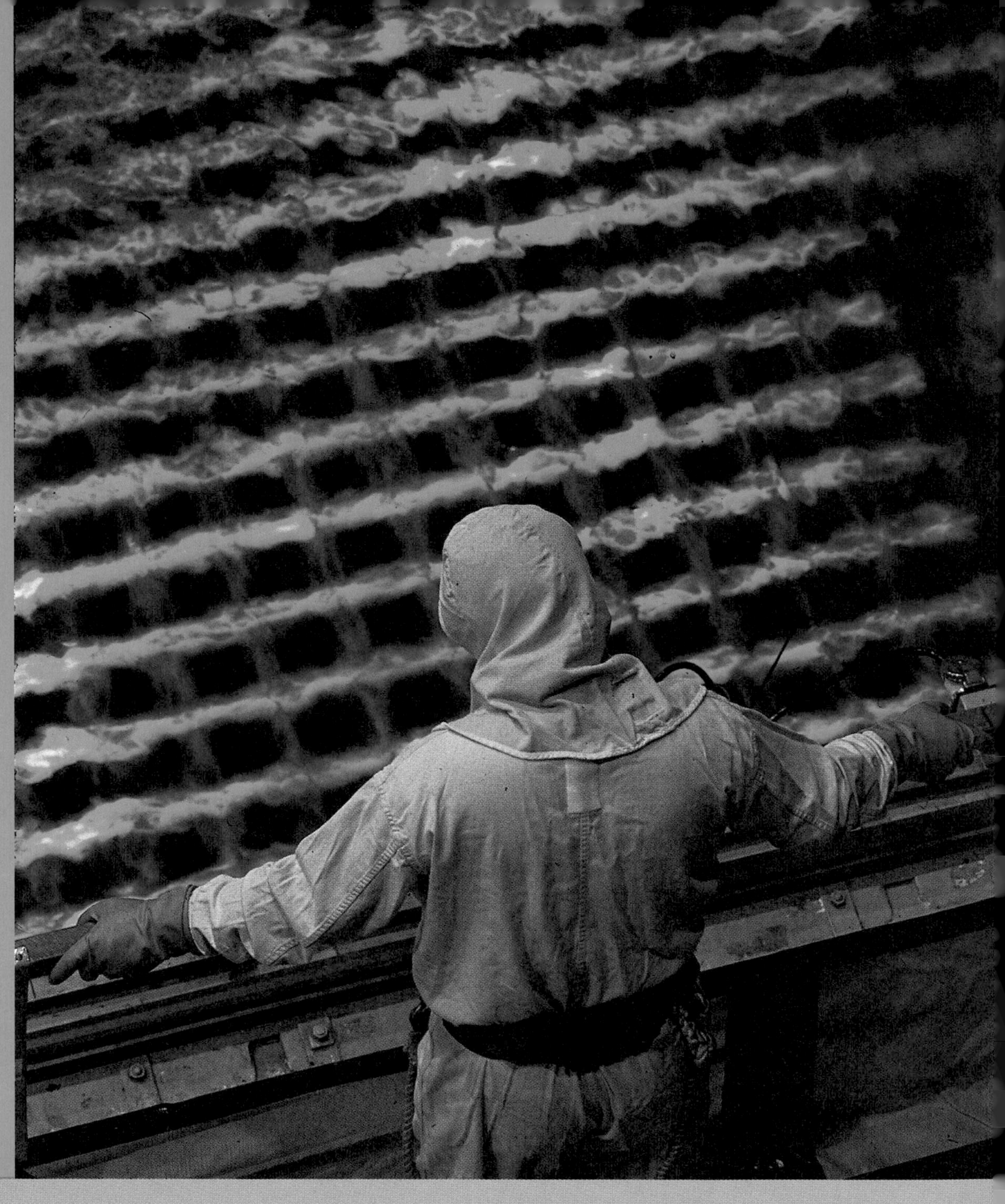

18 Regulation and Environmental Policy

You Are There

Endangered Species or Endangered Jobs?

You are Bruce Babbitt, President Clinton's newly appointed Secretary of the Interior. In office only a month, you are already facing a decision that you have labeled a "test case" for the new administration's enforcement of the Endangered Species Act. You must make a recommendation to the president on how to resolve the conflict between environmentalists demanding protection of virgin, or natural-growth, forests in Oregon, Washington, and California and a timber industry fighting for increased access to government land.[1]

You are a former governor of Arizona, another state with large parts of its land under federal control. You have experience in negotiating land use with the federal government and are considered knowledgeable on natural resource management issues. You grew up near the Grand Canyon, hiking and camping on protected lands, and see yourself as a committed environmentalist.

Clinton said he wanted to be the environmental president that Bush only promised to be, but his record as governor was widely criticized during the campaign. You were appointed to Interior to beef up his image and to provide, along with Vice President Gore, an expertise the president does not have.

You share with the president the view that environmental and other interest group politics have been too adversarial and that an attempt must be made to find a middle ground. And like him, you know what it is like to be a governor facing a business slowdown, rising unemployment, and the increasing costs of complying with federal regulations.

You have been handed a very difficult situation, one in which the differences between militant environmentalists and angry loggers have led to violence. The issue came to a head when environmentalists sued the U.S. Forest Service to stop what they claimed was excess logging in the old-growth forests of the Northwest. They said it violated the Endangered Species Act by threatening to destroy the habitat of the spotted owl. A federal judge agreed and ordered the Forest Service to stop the logging until an acceptable plan for protecting the owl's habitat was drawn up.

It is not only the owl which is at stake; an estimated 600 additional plants and animals are dependent upon the particular habitat provided by old-growth forests. Their preservation is seen as essential to maintaining biodiversity and the planet's ecological balance. Ninety percent of our virgin timberland has already been destroyed. Even though loggers plant trees where they cut, new trees on timber farms cannot replace the role of old-growth forests as wildlife habitats. Environmental activists want a permanent ban on logging on 7 million acres in the three states and want the old-growth forests left to take their natural course.

The 30,000 loggers whose jobs are on the line want to know why protecting a rare owl is more important than safeguarding their ability to support their families. Many believe there is no proof that the endangered species could not adapt to life in newly planted forests. They say the timber is there to be used, and if they are not allowed to cut it they will lose their homes and jobs.

Conservationists argue that if we do not protect our ecosystem, eventually no one will have a job. They are worried not just about endangered species but about air and water pollution,

CONTINUED 

OUTLINE

Development of Regulation
- Reasons for Regulation
- Kinds of Regulation
- Writing Regulations
- Enforcing Regulations

Cycles of Regulation
- Deregulation
- Reregulation
- Deregulation: The Cycle Continues

Regulatory Politics and Environmental Protection
- Evolution of Government's Role
- Implementing Environmental Regulations
- Reforming Environmental Regulations

Benefits and Costs of Regulation

Conclusion: Is Regulation Responsive?

soil erosion, and long-term damage to the fishing and timber industries from bad land management practices. They criticize the timber industry for complaining that it does not have enough logs to keep mills open while it exports 20% of its cut overseas and receives a tax break from the government for doing it. They say it is better to save jobs by halting timber exports and diverting logs to domestic saw mills. As new studies are done and logging is suspended without any final resolution in sight, positions on both sides harden.

During his campaign for the White House, President Clinton promised if elected to hold a conference in the Northwest to hear all sides in the debate. He committed himself to finding a permanent answer to the conflict between logging and preservation, one that would both protect the owl's habitat and revitalize the timber industry. You are sent to tour the area, meet with all parties to the dispute, and make a policy recommendation to the president before he holds his promised conference on timberland use.

Your visit reinforces your belief that a middle ground must be found. You are awed by the timberland and understand the environmentalists' drive to preserve it. But you are also deeply affected by saw mills without timber to process and logging families in danger of losing their homes. You tour an experimental forest where loggers are allowed to cut but required to leave some of the trees standing on each acre. When you offer this as an example of a middle road it is rejected by environmentalists who say the method cannot preserve habitat and by loggers who say their profits are significantly reduced when they leave trees standing in cut areas.

Environmentalists think our very existence is at stake, but whatever the scale of some future ecological disaster it is difficult for it to seem as threatening to loggers as the present-day loss of their jobs. How do you weigh the interest of the environment against the demands of the loggers? Allowing logging to proceed or banning it in all old-growth forests are two options. Or you could recommend banning logging in some but not all forests. You could also recommend more study, but this just postpones a decision that must be made. What do you recommend?

"...FOLLOWING UP ON THAT RUMOR THAT THE SPOTTED OWL WAS BOUGHT OFF BY THE LUMBER INTERESTS..."

Source: North American Syndicate Orlando Sentinel.

Americans have paradoxical attitudes about regulation. We call on government to protect us from unsafe workplaces, unclean air and water, fraudulent advertising, hazardous highways and drunk drivers, dangerous drugs, and many of life's other perils. But then we want government "off our backs"; we resent regulations, rules, and red tape. We want government involved in protecting us, but we are uncertain about how, when, and how much.

The extensive rule-making authority of the executive branch (Chapter 12), Congress's oversight functions, and its power to regulate foreign and interstate commerce have an enormous influence on the behavior of both business and consumers.

In a true free market economy, there would be no forced saving for retirement, no minimum wage or child labor laws, no bankruptcy protection for businesses and individuals, no farm subsidies or tariffs on imports that compete with domestic goods, no regulated public utility rates, no government-run corporations like Amtrak, the post office, and the TVA, no laws protecting workers' safety or the quality of the air and water, and no redistribution of wealth through progressive taxation and welfare programs. This is so because a basic principle of capitalism is that unrestricted competition in the marketplace gives us the best chance to obtain the economic goals we desire.

Adam Smith believed the "invisible hand" of the marketplace works to increase production and make individual firms more efficient.[2] Although each individual firm does not intend to work toward the greater good of society, the greater good is in fact achieved as each firm tries to maximize its own profit. If the economy did work this way, we would have little regulation. But unfortunately it goes awry in ways that threaten the public good because individuals and businesses do not always behave honestly, cautiously, and considerately. So government regulates to limit or correct these effects.

But how much risk should government protect us from? How should the benefits of regulation be weighed against the costs to business and industry of those regulations?

The public gives no clear-cut answer to these questions. Americans often condemn regulation in the abstract but support specific kinds of regulations. Regulation that is seen as beneficial by one group is regarded by another as wasteful and unnecessary red tape. This is why there is continuing controversy over what should be regulated, how much regulation is needed, and the regulatory mechanisms that should be used.

Source: Dana Fradon—The New Yorker Magazine, Inc.

Corporate leaders gather in a field outside Darien, Connecticut, where one of them claims to have seen the invisible hand of the marketplace.

Development of Regulation

Reasons for Regulation

Damage to Common Property

One reason for regulation has been called the **tragedy of the commons.**[3] The air we breathe and the water we drink are common to all of us. Yet individuals may seek to exploit them for their own uses to the detriment of the common good. To maximize their profits, farmers pump as much irrigation water as they need from rivers or aquifers, even in water-short areas, and industries spew toxic chemicals into the air or bury them in the soil. They are acting in accord with the profit motive. Indeed, each individual who exploits the "commons" fares better, so has no incentive not to do so. But when many people exploit the commons, the community as a whole suffers.

Consider the case of Los Angeles and General Motors. Los Angeles once had a pollution-free electric railway system. In the 1930s, General Motors bought the system and then destroyed it, because GM wanted to sell cars, trucks, and buses. The company replaced the electric system with noisy, polluting diesel buses, so uncomfortable and unreliable that Los Angelenos were given a great incentive to rely on private autos.

In 1949, after buying and destroying electric railway systems in more than 100 cities, GM was fined a paltry $5,000 by the government for illegally conspiring to replace municipal services with its own. Meanwhile the company made millions of dollars. Now, due in large part to the reliance on cars, smog in Los Angeles is a major health hazard. Some studies claim that children who grow up in Los Angeles lose up to 50% of their lung capacity from breathing in the polluted air.[4] Obviously, it is absurd to charge GM with creating the entire automobile culture of Los Angeles, but clearly its drive for private profits did not contribute to the common good.

When GM or any other entity imposes a cost on people for actions or decisions for which they are not responsible, economists call it an **externality.** The auto industry has created a major externality in air pollution, as have chemical companies who dispose of their toxic wastes in unsafe ways. Students living in dorms who play their stereos very loudly create less serious externalities.

Although almost everything we do affects others, government does not regulate all externalities that impose costs. It cannot make you buy a new car, paint your house, or use deodorant. Appropriate levels of

The nation's foulest air is in Los Angeles. Ozone concentrations have exceeded EPA standards by as much as 300%, though the air is better than it used to be.

government must decide what externalities it wishes to eliminate and then how best to eliminate them, whether through setting standards, taxation, or other means of regulation.

Inefficient Competition

Government intervention is also desired when competition is inefficient. Adam Smith believed goods and labor would be used in a way to maximize profit and limit cost. Because of competition among firms desiring to sell their products to consumers, manufacturers would make goods as cheaply as possible. But sometimes competition is not efficient. For example, because it is not cost effective (due to large capital outlays) for each community to have more than one company laying gas pipelines or generating electric power, competition cannot work to drive down prices or increase efficiency. Thus utilities (such as gas and electric producers) are controlled monopolies in most countries; in the United States the regulating is done largely by state governments. The government allows a utility to be the only provider of a service in a given geographic area (that is, allows only one power company to operate), but it regulates prices because people do not have a choice of sellers of electricity or gas. Smith himself agreed that this form of government intervention was appropriate.

Lack of Necessary Coordination

Another reason for regulation is that sometimes the free market produces an unacceptable lack of coordination. An obvious example is regulation of airline flights. The free market is not well suited to determine which planes shall have priority to take off at 2:00 P.M. on a certain runway at J.F.K. International Airport in New York. Competition could lead to disaster. Thus the Federal Aviation Administration (FAA) has been empowered to coordinate air traffic patterns.

We could let the market make decisions about takeoff and landing priorities by selling takeoff rights for a fee. But regulation would still be needed to make sure that all the planes authorized to take off at a given time did so in a way to maximize safety.

Unacceptable Inequities

Another reason for regulation is to promote equity. Equity in this context does not refer to equality in outcome but to ensuring fair conditions for participation in the marketplace. Sometimes individuals or groups are severely disadvantaged by the private marketplace. For example, legislation setting minimum wages, banning child labor, protecting workers' rights to organize, and defining minimum standards for workplace health and safety recognizes that there is an inequity in power between individual workers and employers.

Regulations forbidding race and gender discrimination are also designed to enhance equity. Consumer protection laws, such as those forbidding false advertising, and laws licensing pharmacists, physicians,

Children work in a vegetable cannery. At the turn of the century, many young children worked 12-hour days in unhealthy conditions. New Deal era regulations outlawed most child labor but abuse of child labor laws is increasing in some urban areas.

lawyers, and public accountants are based on the assumption that consumers will often not have sufficient information to evaluate the competence of those selling the service or product. Government seeks to remedy an inequity in information between the buyer and the seller of a product or service.

Antitrust regulation reduces inequity by prohibiting monopolies. A **monopoly** is a company that controls a large share of the market for its goods and is therefore able to fix prices. If one or a few firms control the supply of a product, they can set prices at a high level or sell products below cost to drive small businesses out of the market.

One firm may use antitrust laws to sue others, or the government itself may initiate antitrust actions. The enforcement of antitrust legislation has waxed and waned over the years. The breakup of AT&T, which formerly controlled all the long-distance telephone service in the United States, is the result of antitrust legislation. It opened the door for other firms to compete with AT&T to sell telephones and telephone services. More recently, the government took antitrust action against Microsoft, accusing the company of trying to corner the market in computer software.

Regulation to correct inequities is one of the most controversial types of regulation. Conservatives often argue that this type of regulation is inappropriate. They believe the free market can solve problems: Unsafe or ineffective products will sooner or later end up unwanted; pizza eaters can stop buying pizza with artificial cheese; unions can protect workers from unreasonable demands of corporations. (But some oppose unions too, believing unions interfere with the free market for labor.)

Defenders of equity-based regulations point out that the workings of the market to provide vital information are too slow. People have been killed and injured before information about defective products became widely known. In the mid-1960s, many children were born with serious deformities because of the prescription drug thalidomide, which their mothers took during pregnancy. This incident caused Congress to set higher standards for drug safety and the Food and Drug Administration (FDA) to tighten its drug-testing rules. And before 1972, 20 million consumers were injured each year by consumer products, and of those 30,000 were killed and more than 100,000 permanently disabled. This prompted Congress to establish the Consumer Product Safety Commission (CPSC), an independent regulatory agency mandated to establish safety standards for consumer products.

Some people have a good deal of faith in "educating" the public about risks. They believe education campaigns, not regulation, are the best way to protect people. But education campaigns are not cheap, especially over a long period of time, and not always effective either. The government's campaign to educate the pubic about the health hazards of smoking has had a significant impact, but millions of Americans still smoke, and the campaign has cost tens of millions of dollars.

Congress does not regulate to remedy the effects of every inequity. Sometimes the costs are seen as higher than the gains; in other cases, resistance by politically powerful groups is stronger than lobbying by potential beneficiaries of regulation.

Kinds of Regulation

There are several types of regulation:

1. *Requiring information.* Government may regulate by requiring that an employer, lender, or other entity provide certain kinds of information to employees or consumers. For example, credit card companies must provide cardholders with information about how to appeal charges they think are not really theirs. Manufacturers of many food products must tell on the label how much salt, sugar, vitamins, and various ingredients their products contain. This allows consumers to see if their peppermint ice cream, for example, is colored with beet juice or red dye number 2, a potentially dangerous additive. This requirement is called **truth in labeling.**

Manufacturers sometimes oppose labeling the contents of their goods. The manufacturers of juice beverages resisted FDA pressure to label the contents of their drinks more accurately.[5] "Fruit punch," "fruit blend," and "fruit drink" may in fact have no fruit; only for orange juice are there requirements for minimum amounts of juice to be in a "juice" product. The FDA and some public interest groups believe shoppers have a right to know if they are buying real juice or sugar water for their children.

The FDA also requires that when information *is* provided it be accurate. Many manufacturers have taken advantage of a new public awareness of the relationship between health and nutrition by labeling their products as "health" foods. The FDA is forcing manufacturers to remove words such as "fresh" from processed juices and "no cholesterol"

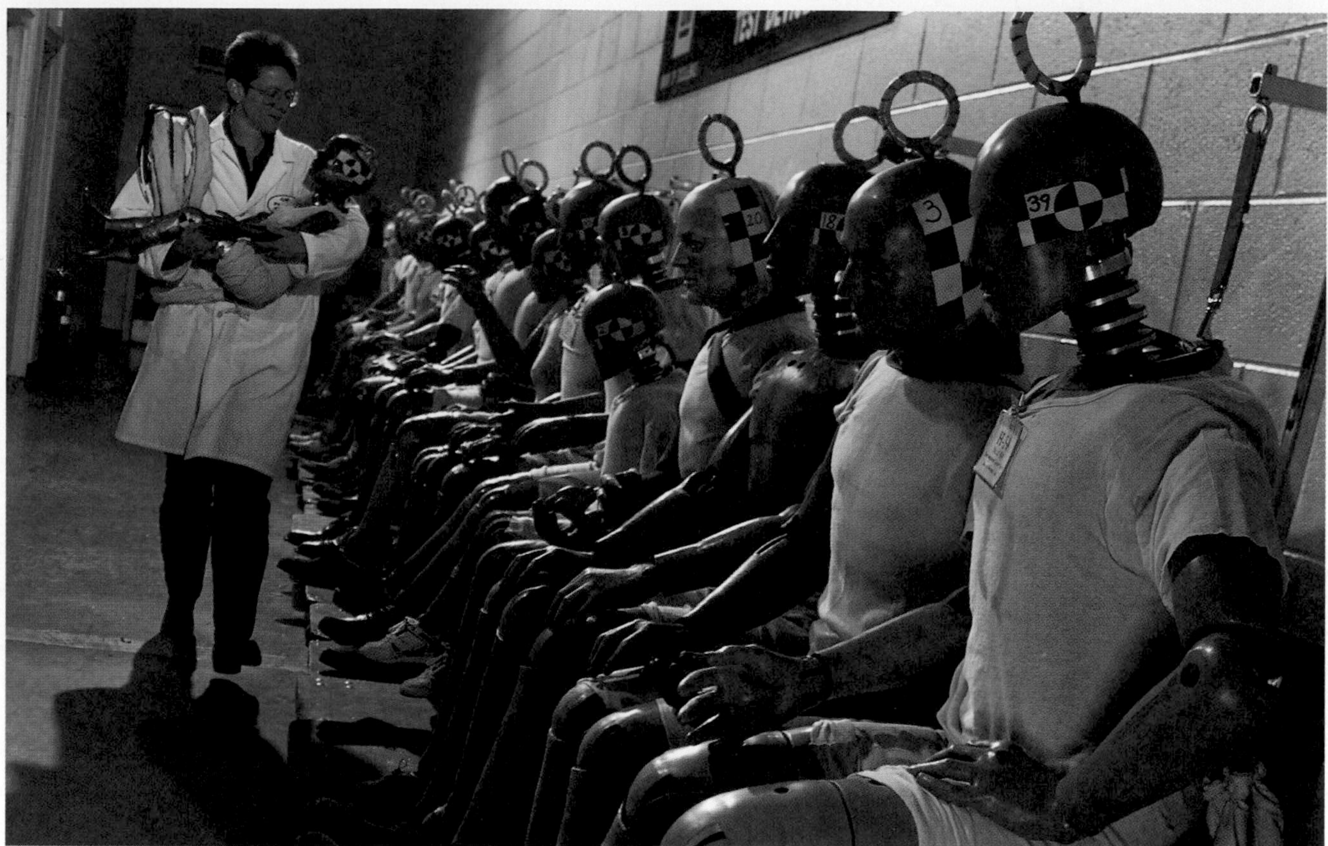

In order to save lives, federal regulations mandate testing autos for safety. These dummies allow simulation of the impact of crashes on humans.

from food products that are high in vegetable fats that could contribute to heart disease. It is also demanding that manufacturers remove false claims that their products are "biodegradable" or in other ways "environmentally safe." Such consumer come-ons are called "green fraud."

2. *Licensing.* Government may regulate by requiring people to obtain licenses to practice certain trades, or professions, or to operate certain businesses. For example, the federal government licenses radio and television stations, and states license doctors, beauticians, dentists, and many others. Licensing is economically valuable for those receiving a license because it allows them to make money while keeping others out.

3. *Setting standards.* Manufacturers must meet certain standards of content, quality, environmental cleanliness, workplace safety, and employee wages and working conditions. Failure to maintain the standards results in legal penalties if convicted. A product called chicken soup must have a minimum of chicken in it, and hot dogs cannot include more than a certain proportion of bone, hair, insects, and other extraneous material. The FDA requires condoms to be tested for leaks. Manufacturers must destroy an entire batch of 1,000 if more than 4 are defective.

4. *Providing economic incentives.* Higher taxes may be imposed on goods or activities viewed as less beneficial than on those deemed more beneficial. In this way, the less desirable are penalized. An example is a tax on cars that use fuel inefficiently. Some people, particularly conservatives, believe taxation is a better way to achieve regulatory goals than setting mandatory standards because it gives individuals or businesses an incentive to comply and the choice not to.

5. *Limiting liability.* Some regulations are designed to discourage legal actions against individuals or firms. Congress has passed a law limiting the

Steve Kelley, San Diego Union-Tribune, Copley News Service.

liability of nuclear power plants in case of a nuclear accident. Taxpayers, not the industry, pick up the cost of claims above a certain amount.

Writing Regulations

The benefit of even the most needed regulation will be felt only if it is effectively implemented. Executive branch agencies must make the rules necessary to implement and enforce regulatory activity authorized by Congress, and Congress must exercise its oversight function to see that regulatory agencies write rules capable of achieving the goals it has established. But writing effective regulations requires guidelines beyond the policies and goals stated in the authorizing legislation.

One of the standards by which the effectiveness of any regulation is judged is whether it has a net benefit for society. It is easy for both the average citizen and bureaucrat to see that it is not cost-effective to enforce a rule requiring all workplace toilet seats to be horseshoe-shaped. No one fought to prevent the rule's abolition. But in most cases it is far more difficult to decide if a rule has more negative than positive effects. How do we decide whether the risk involved in using a particular chemical or product, or working in a hazardous environment is great enough to regulate? There is no agreement on this.

In authorizing new regulations, Congress uses different standards of risk. One is the "no-risk" standard: If there are any risks at all, a substance is not to be used. Sometimes called the better-safe-than-sorry rule, it is often applied to regulations concerning safety in food or drugs: If a substance is found to cause cancer, it cannot be used.

In other cases the "margin of safety" criterion is used. The regulatory agency establishes a reasonable standard and then allows an extra margin of safety. For example, standards for clean air mandate the Environmental Protection Agency to declare how much lead, sulfur, and other materials can be in the air before it is unsafe. Then the agency is supposed to set the standards a little higher to allow the extra margin of safety.[6]

Sometimes Congress mandates a standard whereby cost of the regulation is to be weighed against the risk. The process of making this evaluation is called **cost-benefit analysis.** Many consumer product safety regulations apply this risk standard. A product is not to be regulated unless the benefits outweigh the costs. Generally, proregulation groups prefer the no-risk or

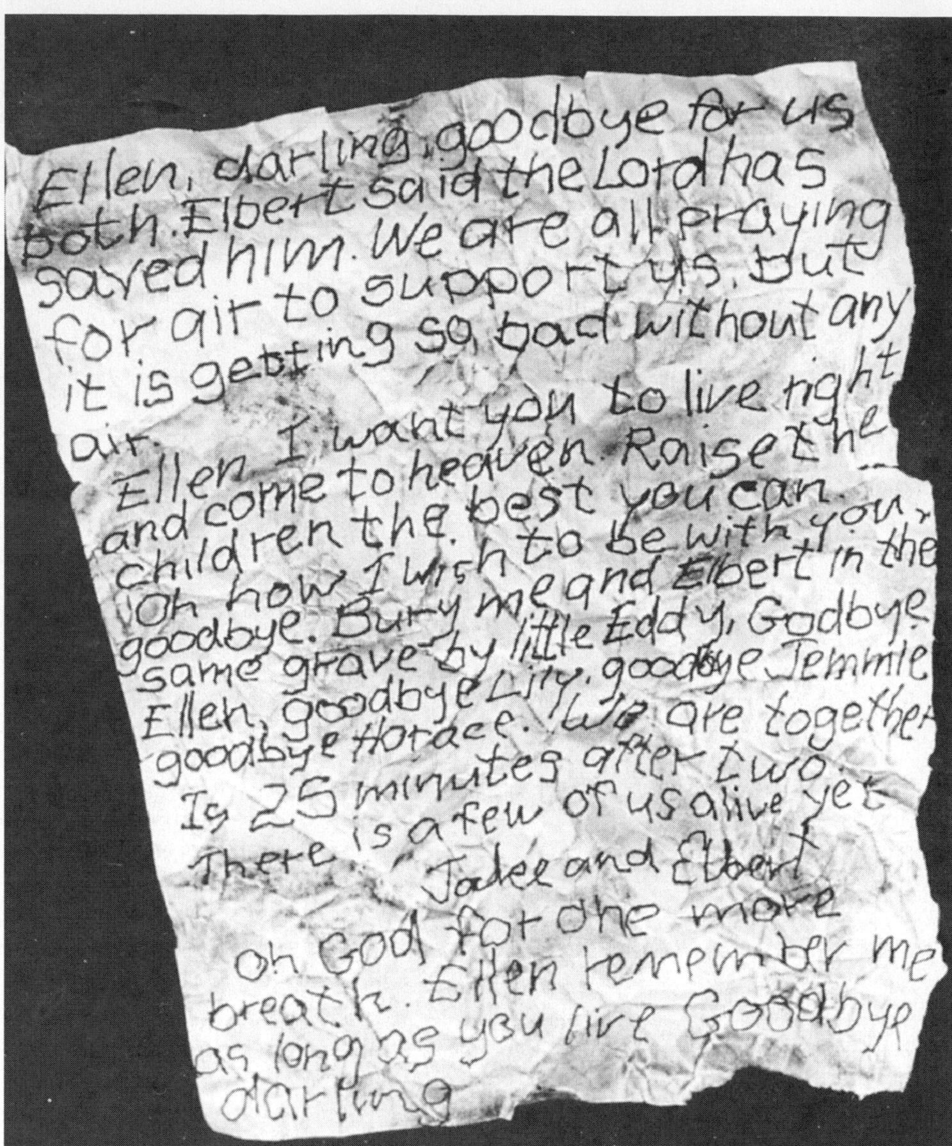

Ellen, darling, goodbye for us
both. Elbert said the Lord has
saved him. We are all praying
for air to support us, but
it is getting so bad without any
air.
Ellen I want you to live right
and come to heaven. Raise the
children the best you can.
Oh how I wish to be with you,
goodbye. Bury me and Elbert in the
same grave by little Eddy. Godbye
Ellen, goodbye Lily, goodbye Jemmie
goodbye Horace. We are together
Is 25 minutes after two.
There is a few of us alive yet
Jake and Elbert
Oh God for one more
breath. Ellen remember me
as long as you live Goodbye
darling

Jacob Vowell wrote this letter shortly before dying of suffocation in a mine disaster in Fraterville, Tennessee, in 1902. Such disasters eventually prompted government regulation of mining.

extra margin standards, while antiregulation forces prefer cost-benefit analysis.

Deciding which standard to apply and assigning values to these standards inevitably involves both science and politics. For example, critics of the Reagan and Carter administrations' reliance on cost-benefit analyses have charged that these analyses are not done fairly or competently.[7] They believe that costs are concrete and easily calculated, while benefits are often more difficult to put in dollar terms. How do you quantify saving human lives? If a particular rule is likely to save five lives per year at a cost of $5 million, does the regulation offer a net cost or a net benefit? It ultimately depends on a value judgment, which, critics charge, can be obscured by a cost-accountant mentality (see Figure 1).

For example, in their cost analyses, the Occupational Safety and Health Administration (OSHA) figures a human life is worth $2 million, the CPSC $1 million, and the FAA $650,000.[8] Thus, using the $1 million estimate, the CPSC told manufacturers of reclining chairs they need not fix a problem with the chairs that had resulted in several children being strangled unless fixing it cost less than $.25 per chair. The CPSC's economists figured out that at more than $.25 for each of 40 million chairs manufactured, the

FIGURE 1
How Much Is a Saved Life Worth?

How Much is a Saved Life Worth?

Here are estimates of the value of a life that are built into some government regulations. Figures do not include benefits of the regulations, other than lives saved, such as prevention of property damage and injuries that do not result in death.

		Estimated Cost of Regulation per Life Saved
Automobiles	Reduce lead content of gasoline from 1.1 to 0.1 grams per gallon	No net cost
	Child restraints in cars	$1.3 million
	Dual master cylinders for car brakes	$7.8 million
Ejection system for the B-58 bomber		$22 million
Flashing lights at railroad crossings		$730,000
Asbestos	Banned in brake linings	$230,000
	... in automatic transmission parts	$1.2 billion
Radiation	Safety standards for X-ray equipment	$400,000
	... for uranium mine tailings	$190 million

Source: Harvard Center for Risk Analysis, cited in Peter Russell, "How much for a Life?" *New York Times,* January 29, 1995, p. F3.

SOURCE: Harvard Center for Risk Analysis. Cited in Peter Passell, "How Much for a Life?" *New York Times,* January 29, 1995, p. F3.

cost of fixing the problem would be more than the lives of the children were worth.[9]

Enforcing Regulations

Regulatory agencies must also oversee the implementation of the rules they write by monitoring the behavior of potential rule violators. Agencies also are authorized to assess penalties for noncompliance, although their enforcement powers are negligible. The political and technical difficulties of carrying out such a large mandate are discussed in greater detail in the section on environmental regulation.

Implementation of rules by regulatory agencies is overseen both by Congress and the Office of Management and the Budget (OMB). The OMB authority to review agency rules derives from an executive order issued by President Reagan as part of his efforts in administrative deregulation. This innovation was designed to give OMB the authority to identify and eliminate duplicate rules and to develop procedures for cost-benefit analyses.

Many strongly oppose this power of OMB, arguing that it erodes the independence of regulatory agencies. Regulations developed by agencies under formal rules and according to due process have been killed by OMB without any public hearings or advance notification. This violates the spirit of the Administrative Procedure Act, which requires openness in rule making, and it diminishes governmental responsiveness. For example, EPA rules for limiting the amount of toxic chemicals that industries could dump in municipal sewage systems were killed three months after they were issued. This undoing of the rules followed extensive lobbying of OMB by chemical manufacturers and other producers of toxic wastes.[10]

One of the first regulatory reforms initiated by the Clinton administration was to limit the monitoring role of OMB and therefore the ability of the White House to intervene in the regulatory process. This in turn would make it less worth the effort for lobbyists to pressure the White House to eliminate or alter rules. The Republican-controlled House, however, objected to the reversal in policy and introduced bills that would, alternatively, concentrate the oversight function in either the OMB or the House Ways and Means Committee.[11]

Every phase of the regulatory process is open to influence by parties affected by the content of regulations. Those with a direct stake in a particular type of regulation can give testimony and lobby legislators, especially members of the relevant House and Senate subcommittees, while legislation is being written. They can lobby bureaucrats who write the rules enforcing legislation, agency heads responsible for implementation of rules, or members of congressional committees with oversight functions. Rules, and the way they are or are not enforced, can be appealed to the agencies issuing them, and in some cases challenged in federal courts. For powerful interest groups there are opportunities to pressure the White House on the appointment of agency heads and the content of specific rules. This can be especially effective if the president has a strong position on regulation, as Reagan did.

Cycles of Regulation

Like other government activity, the push for government regulation comes in fits and starts. The first spurt came in the late 1800s, when a poor economy

The Electreat, a device first sold in 1918, could (so its manufacturers claimed) cure everything from headaches to tonsillitis and get rid of dandruff as a bonus. It was the first device outlawed by the FDA.

led to charges, especially by farmers, that the large corporations of the day were exploiting the public. In 1890 Congress prohibited firms from conspiring to set prices or in other ways to restrain trade. It also declared monopolies illegal and established the Interstate Commerce Commission to regulate the railroads.

The next burst of regulatory activity came after the turn of the century, in the Progressive Era. Demands for consumer protection arose largely because industrialization and railroad transportation created national markets for goods formerly produced and consumed locally. In these new national markets, consumers had little recourse if the products they bought from distant companies were not safe or reliable. Consumer fraud became endemic. Business engaged in deceptive advertising, food products often contained harmful substances (Coca-Cola contained cocaine; formaldehyde was used to preserve milk), and popular patent medicine usually contained alcohol or addictive drugs, such as opium.[12] Reformers also pointed to unsafe and unsanitary conditions in the meat-packing industry. After the media and so-called muckrakers highlighted these scandals, Congress banned certain food additives, prohibited false claims about products, and gave the Department of Agriculture power to inspect meat sold in interstate commerce.

The New Deal era spurred further regulatory activity. After 100 people died from an unsafe drug, Congress passed an act mandating that the FDA declare a drug safe before it could be marketed.

In the activist 1960s and 1970s reformers were again influential in pressuring Congress to undertake new regulatory activity. New agencies were established to regulate consumer product safety (Consumer Product Safety Commission), the environment (the EPA), and industrial safety (OSHA). The powers of older agencies, such as the Federal Trade Commission (FTC), were strengthened.

Beginning in 1976 with the Carter administration and continuing into Reagan's second term, there was strong bipartisan support for slowing regulatory activity. The Bush years saw a flurry of new rule-making, but the Clinton-Gore administration took a special interest in regulatory reform as part of its reinventing government initiative. However, the 1994 election brought to Congress many new members whose objective was to dismantle rather than to reform or slow government's rule-making powers.

Deregulation

As long as there has been regulation there have been demands for **deregulation,** that is, ending regulation in a particular area. One kind of deregulation is to eliminate unnecessary rules. Both Presidents Carter and Reagan promoted this type of regulatory reform. During the Carter administration OSHA abolished more than 1,100 of its 10,000 rules; many, such as the horseshoe-shaped toilet seat rule, had been severely criticized as nitpicking. OSHA paperwork requirements, particularly for small businesses, were reduced, and safety inspections were concentrated on the industries with the worst safety records. The Reagan administration continued this pattern.

Proponents of deregulation argue that it is not enough to streamline, eliminate the more trivial rules, and make regulators more accountable; in many cases regulators simply should not be regulating at all.

Although deregulation has had broad bipartisan support since the 1970s, there have been some partisan differences in the nature of this support. The Carter administration and Democrats in general tended to support deregulation to the extent that it made business activity more efficient and less cumbersome and when it eliminated rules that were not beneficial to the public. Many Republicans have gone further by opposing in principle some kinds of regulation as interference with market competition.

Deregulation can be carried out legislatively, that is, by act of Congress, or administratively, by executive orders and new appointments. The Carter administration, which deregulated the trucking, airlines, and banking industries, relied mainly on legislation. Reagan, the president most ideologically committed to deregulation, tried to enact many of his reforms through administrative action. One method was to

"I've deregulated Arthur, but he still doesn't run very efficiently."

Source: Handelsman—The New Yorker Magazine, Inc.

strip regulatory agencies of personnel and budgets. Agency budgets decreased 8% during Reagan's first term, with some agencies taking much larger cuts. On the whole, agencies regulating consumer and environmental interests were hardest hit; those regulating health and safety were cut less.[13] Not until 1988 did regulatory agencies reach the level of funding they had in 1980.

Another deregulation technique used by President Reagan was to appoint people to regulatory posts who favored either little regulation or self-regulation by industry. This meant that the number of regulations proposed and enacted decreased, and enforcement slowed too.

Critics point out that these attacks on regulation made some problems worse; understaffed agencies meant longer delays, larger backlogs, and inadequately researched decisions—the very problems that antiregulation forces complain about.

Work-related injuries began to increase in 1983, and in 1987 and 1988, 21,000 people died in workplace accidents, not counting those who died of work-related illnesses such as black lung. In a 1989 survey, workers listed safety as their highest job priority, above salary, benefits, and day care.[14] By Reagan's second term, a backlash against the effects of deregulation emerged and regulatory activity increased.[15]

Administrative deregulation did continue in the Bush administration. Vice President Quayle headed the Council on Competitiveness, a White House group devoted to making American businesses more competitive. The Council frequently asked Bush to override rules written by regulatory agencies. After supporting the Clean Act, for example, Bush allowed its provisions to be undercut by a Council-backed rule that lets industries exceed their permitted pollutions level simply by notifying the EPA of their intent.[16] Clinton abolished the Council shortly after taking office.

While deregulation brought lower rates or fares and greater competition in some industries, it also brought new problems, as in the airline industry.

Before 1978, commercial airlines were heavily regulated. Under a 1938 law an airline had to gain the approval of the Civil Aeronautics Board (CAB) in order to fly any particular route and to set its fares. Originally this procedure was designed to help the struggling airline industry by protecting it from competition.

In the years after the 1938 law was passed, the airline industry grew in size and economic strength. By the middle 1970s the oil crisis had caused airline rates to skyrocket and put many in economic difficulties. Many felt that the time was right for deregulation.

In 1978 President Carter signed a bill phasing in deregulation. Airlines were allowed to enter new routes without CAB approval and were permitted flexibility in setting their rates. However, airlines serving certain routes between small communities were given subsidies in order to ensure that these communities would be served for at least 10 years. The CAB itself was abolished, and regulation of airlines was left to the Federal Aviation Administration (FAA), which oversees safety matters.

One reason for deregulation was to make the industry more competitive. By opening up competition among the airlines, it was hoped they would seek ways to become more efficient and then lower fares.

At first it appeared that deregulation would increase competition. The number of airlines nearly tripled between 1978 and 1983. But in the following decade many airlines folded or were bought out by larger carriers. By 1990, the eight largest airlines controlled about 90% of all commercial air travel in the United States. A fare war in the summer of 1992 brought deeper financial trouble as two more large carriers, USAir and TWA, threatened to go under. In the first three years of the 1990s, the industry lost almost $10 billion and three huge carriers—United, American, and Delta—dominated the market. United survived only after an employee buyout was approved in 1994.

Competition has been further diminished because the airlines have divided up the nation into regional turfs. In 10 major cities, two-thirds of the air traffic is controlled by one airline, such as TWA in St. Louis and Northwest in Minneapolis. Even in huge airports such as Chicago and Atlanta, two airlines control three-fourths of the traffic. One GAO study showed that at concentrated hubs the fares of the dominant airlines were 27% higher than the fares at other airports.[17] The system is what economists call an oligopoly, a market condition in which a few firms dominate an industry.

Domination by the major carriers contributes to congestion at major airports. These carriers have special 20- to 30-year leasing arrangements with large airports where they control much of the traffic. At over half of the largest airports these long-term leases give a single airline a veto over airport expansion. Thus the dominant airline can stop an expansion project that would provide new gates for potential competitors.[18] Denver's International is the first new airport to have been built since 1976.

In addition to delays, passengers now have to contend with a byzantine system for setting fares. On one 1990 United Airlines domestic flight, five passengers with identical coach accommodations paid five different fares, ranging from $124 to $586.

In the struggle to be competitive and profitable, airlines may have increased their efficiency at the expense of passenger safety. Given the higher volume of air traffic, jets built in the 1960s have been kept in service beyond their planned life span. In addition there has been a decline in the number of experienced mechanics available to service them. Pilots are being pushed harder by their airlines to fly more hours, sometimes in excess of the legal limits. Because of the increased stress, more pilots are quitting. Commuter airlines are having a difficult time finding any experienced pilots. Although the overall accident rate for 1980–1990 was half that for the previous 10 years[19] there were 293 domestic airline crashes between 1988 and 1994 and U.S. airlines are no longer the world's safest.[20]

President Reagan may have contributed to safety problems by getting rid of thousands of experienced air traffic controllers (whose job it is to monitor air traffic and communicate with pilots, telling them when it is safe to take off and land and what traffic pattern they must follow). In 1981, in order to break their strike, he fired about two-thirds of the nation's 16,000 air controllers. Even though thousands of new controllers have been hired since then, they work many hours a week overtime at major airports. Most believe their workloads are probably a danger to air safety, as are the outmoded computers still in many airports. For example, air traffic control at Chicago's O'Hare, one of the nation's largest and most congested airports, was operating in 1995 with 1960s computer technology.

When deregulation of the airline industry was approved, no one imagined a time when the industry's very existence would be threatened. Air transportation is an important part of the country's infrastructure and essential to a healthy economy. It is so crucial that federal law does not allow foreigners to buy voting stock in American airlines. But overexpansion and the recession left some airlines with such huge debts that foreign investment was the only hope for survival.

Early in his administration, Clinton gave approval for British investment in USAir but held up the purchase of voting stock. He threatened reregulation of landing and takeoff rights at major airports and a reallocation of international routes. Dismayed by the state of the industry after 15 years of deregulation, Clinton appointed a 26-member panel to investigate ways to revitalize it. The jury, therefore, is still out on the success of airline deregulation.

DEREGULATION GIVES CONSUMERS GREATER CHOICES
... AND WOULD YOU FOLKS LIKE MAINTENANCE OR NO MAINTENANCE?
ROULETTE AIR
LET US TAKE YOU FOR A SPIN

Source: 1987, Boston Globe. Distributed by Los Angeles Times Syndicate. Reprinted by permission.

Reregulation

In politics as in physics, actions usually produce reactions. Actions to deregulate bring cries for some **reregulation,** a resumption of regulatory activity. Banking provides a good example of how deregulation led to reregulation. Traditionally banks and savings and loan (S&L) institutions were heavily regulated and protected from competition. But during the 1970s and early 1980s interest rates were rising rapidly, and banks and S&Ls were competing fiercely to retain their depositors and attract new ones. They were also in competition with the federal government for investors' money as interest rates on treasury notes continued to rise. In the bipartisan deregulatory mood of the time Congress adopted a series of measures, beginning in 1980, to deregulate many aspects of the banking industry. To help S&Ls be more competitive, the cap was lifted on the interest they could pay depositors; at the same time Congress raised the maximum level of federal deposit insurance allowable on each account. Both banks and S&Ls were given more freedom to decide what financial services to offer. Within days, interest was being paid on checking accounts; credit card companies raised their interest rates; brokerage, insurance firms, and even department stores got into the banking business; and S&Ls offered a new range of services and made new types of investments formerly prohibited.

With the cap removed on interest rates some S&Ls attracted new depositors by paying interest rates that were more than double the interest rates their mortgage holders were paying. With these policies it was only a matter of time before the S&Ls would go broke, unless they made windfall profits from their investments. As a result, many S&Ls, big and small, made increasingly risky investments in order to survive and profit in the now highly competitive atmosphere. Banks too made high-risk loans to foreign governments and domestic farmers, while some S&Ls made shaky real estate investments, then saw the bottom drop out of their investments when real estate prices plummeted.

During this period, federal scrutiny of bank and S&L activities fell off drastically, even though the government, through its deposit insurance program, guaranteed each deposit (of up to $100,000) that the banks and S&Ls used for their risky investments. Charles E. Schumer (D-N.Y.) has said the government "behaved like a fire insurance company that said to its customers: 'Go ahead, play with matches. We'll cover you if anything goes wrong'. "

The Federal Home Loan Bank Board, which regulates S&Ls, was repeatedly denied its requests for more examiners and auditors. In the last half of the 1980s, 1,000 banks failed, including the nation's eighth largest, Continental Illinois. Thanks to the federal deposit insurance program few individuals lost their savings, but it took an additional $4 billion loan from the government to restore Continental Illinois to solvency.

The S&L crisis has proven much more costly; 27% of all thrifts failed. Covering the losses, the federal insurance company for S&Ls, the Federal Savings and Loan Insurance Corporation (FSLIC), went broke. As a consequence, the FDIC took control of more than 200 of the institutions, trying to put them on a sounder financial base. By 1995, more than $190 billion of taxpayer money had been committed to the bailout.

In short, deregulation in the financial industry led to disaster. Proponents of deregulation argue that a truly free market would be more efficient because consistently bad business decisions would bring failure without benefit of a taxpayer rescue. But in the case of Continental Illinois and the hundreds of insolvent S&Ls, the government believed the nation could not afford to let them go under. Huge banks defaulting and millions of people losing their savings would send shock waves throughout the nation, so the federal government stepped in to save them. Thus critics of banking deregulation argue that since banks have the luxury of Uncle Sam's pocketbook when things go wrong, they should be forced by Uncle Sam to conduct themselves in a prudent manner. The S&L bailout reflected this, by imposing tougher new regulations that S&Ls must now meet.

Reregulation has also involved the states. After years of lax federal regulatory activity during the 1980s, many states became "regulatory Rambos."[21] Faced with new state regulation of their activities, pesticide manufacturers, credit card and insurance companies, auto manufacturers, used-car dealers, and other business and trade groups appealed to the federal government for regulation. If there has to be regulation, businesses and industry usually would rather have one federal regulation, especially if it is not too strong, than 10 or 30 or 50 separate state rules.[22]

Deregulation: The Cycle Continues

At the end of the Bush administration, as the country faced huge budget and trade deficits and an economy that was barely growing, most officials were looking

Symbolic Solutions for Complex Problems?

Deregulating to "Get Government Off Our Backs"

The 1990s saw the coming together of a variety of interests advocating smaller government. Demands included ending regulation in specific areas, freezing all regulatory activity, abolishing major regulatory agencies such as the EPA, FDA, FAA, and the Department of Energy (DOE), selling government corporations like the TVA and Amtrak, and privatizing government functions such as air traffic control, the National Weather Service, and the naval petroleum reserves.

Candidates in the 1994 elections played to this sentiment by promising both the average citizen and the local official greater freedom from federal rule-makers. Deregulators emphasized the burden and aggravation of red tape and the sheer cost of enforcement—as much as a half-trillion dollars a year to government and industry for all forms of regulation, with estimates as high as $1500 per household annually just to pay for environmental protection.[1] Regulation opponents also stressed the rigidity of the command-and-comply system of federal rule-making in comparison to the flexibility and greater cost-effectiveness of local or company-specific solutions to health and safety problems.

In Congress, the Republican-led deregulation effort was written into three bills. One would freeze the writing of new rules to enforce existing legislation pending broader regulatory reform (with exemptions for rules favored by industry). Another would put in place the risk assessment guideline for writing new regulations and prohibit any new rule whose cost of implementation would be greater than the estimated benefits from its enforcement. And the third would authorize the federal government (i.e., taxpayers) to compensate landowners when regulatory restrictions placed on use of their property (such as for wetlands or endangered species protection) led to a decline in its value or a loss of income.

Some deregulators went even further by calling for a system in which assessing risks and calculating their costs would be taken away from federal bureaucrats and turned over to insurance companies. Industries would be held responsible in the private sector for risks imposed on the public and, like home or car owners, would purchase liability insurance to cover claims for damage. Presumably the price of these premiums, and the knowledge that government would not share in the cost of cleaning up industrial pollution as it now does, would provide a market incentive to avoid actions that endangered the public.

Such alternatives have been proposed by those deregulation advocates who, in almost every instance, place individual and private property rights above those of common property (i.e., mineral resources, waterways, and parklands) and the public good. They assume that the marketplace is the only arena for resolving what is rational and appropriate economic behavior. But the marketplace is no more nor less than the people who operate within it, precisely because it is a place where individuals and businesses pursue private gain. There is no guarantee that the cumulative effect of these actions will benefit the common good.

Most Americans do share the belief that the private sector can do many things better than government and have a general distaste for red tape and in-your-face government. But it was the federal government, not industry, that took the initiative on environmental protection and workplace health and safety. Federal regulations have resulted in a multitude of benefits for the American public. Workers are safer on the job, endangered species have been saved, large-scale reforestation has taken place, recycling has become commonplace, and progress is being made in cleaning up hazardous waste sites. Smog has

---

for ways to cut spending and encourage economic growth. The new wave of reformers stressed the need to make greater use of economic incentives to encourage desired behavior and to reduce the cost of enforcing regulations.

Many people also criticized the command and control approach to regulatory policy which lays down rules and orders people to comply.[23] To force compliance with rules requires monitoring by a large, expensive, and unwanted bureaucracy. When rule-breakers are caught they are assigned penalties that cannot realistically be enforced, even after huge sums are spent on legal fees to force them to comply. Critics argue that, instead of trying to control behavior after the fact, government should make individuals and businesses "face up to the full costs and conse-

decreased by a third, even though there are more cars being driven more miles than ever before. And, whereas in 1972 only a third of our rivers and lakes were safe for swimming and fishing, in the 1990s, two-thirds are safe.[2]

Despite the enormous benefits of regulatory activity, the costs continue to be great. State and local governments and private industries have spent millions on compliance with rigid rules when much cheaper methods might have achieved the same results had there not been one-size-fits-all federal rules. Stories are legion of citizen groups waiting years for federal action on cleanup of a toxic waste site and of small businesses going under because they cannot cope with regulatory red tape.

Business has complained for decades, for example, that the FDA hurts their ability to compete with foreign firms by causing long delays in the marketing of their products while testing for safety. Research indicates that American firms are often slower than their European counterparts in marketing new drugs, for example, but the same studies also show that the overwhelming majority of drugs removed from the market for health risks are European-made. Of the nine American-made drugs removed from the market between 1990 and 1992, three involved criminal withholding of evidence of risk by the manufacturers.[3] This raises questions about the practicality of abolishing the FDA or privatizing some of its functions, as some deregulators advocate.

Not every supporter of regulatory reform is an advocate of blanket deregulation. Many believe it is appropriate, and possible, for the government to provide for the general welfare by setting standards for health and safety and environmental protection while limiting its role in rule-writing. This view was expressed in a best-selling book by Philip Howard on regulatory law much cited by both Republicans and Democrats.[4] Howard argues that the federal government has gone too far in its belief that science and technology make it possible to protect against every public danger. This has led to an excessive number of rules that try to anticipate every eventuality and in the process produced a country suffocating under the weight of law. One often-cited example is that of the progression in air quality legislation. Whereas the 1970 Clean Air Act was forty-seven pages long, its renewal (the Clear Air Act Amendments of 1990) took five years to write and was two hundred pages long. And, while the initial act had almost unanimous support, the second had substantial opposition.

Howard's solution is to decentralize the rule-writing process while leaving federal standards in place. This would allow businesses and localities more flexibility in findings ways to meet the mandated standards, greatly reduce the oversight bureaucracy, and result in more cost-effective rules.

Before wiping away the rules that improved public health, worker safety, and ecosystem management and turning risk assessment over to the private sector we should consider these questions. Does private industry have the same stake in preserving the commons or protecting the general public against shoddy or dangerous products or toxic waste as does the general public through its representatives in government? How well does any group—doctors, lawyers, professors, or business executives—police itself? How reliable has the tobacco industry been, for example, in reporting product risk to the public? Do individual citizens want to take on private industries and their insurance companies in the courts to stop pollution or seek compensation for damages without benefit of federal laws and enforcement agencies? Do businesses want to contend with fifty different sets of state regulations?

1. Glenn Collins, "What If Congress Reforms the FDA?" *New York Times,* March 26, 1995, p. F5; Rep. Thomas Ewing, "Bill Brings Common-sense Update to Clean Water Act," *Champaign-Urbana News-Gazette,* June 4, 1995, p. B3.
2. Gregg Easterbrook, "Here Comes the Sun," *The New Yorker,* April 10, 1995, pp. 39–40.
3. Peter H. Stone, "Ganging Up on the FDA," *National Journal,* February 18, 1995, pp. 412–413.
4. Philip K. Howard, *The Death of Common Sense: How Law Is Suffocating America* (New York: Random House, 1994). Howard's book has been criticized as well as praised, especially for its undocumented examples. See Richard Lacayo, "Anecdotes Not Antidotes," *Time,* April 10, 1995, pp. 40–41.

OTHER SOURCES: Margaret Kriz, "A New Shade of Green," *National Journal,* March 18, 1995, pp. 661–665; Margaret Kriz, "Risky Business," *National Journal,* February 18, 1995, pp. 417–421; John H. Cushman, Jr., "Republicans Plan Sweeping Barriers to New U.S. Rules," *New York Times,* December 25, 1994, pp. 1, 12; Linda Greenhouse, "Blowing the Dust Off the Constitution That Was," *New York Times,* May 28, 1995, pp. E1, E6.

---

quences" of harmful actions at the time they make their decisions."[24]

The objective of this reform is to discourage environmentally or other socially harmful behavior by driving up its cost and thereby putting the individual or business engaging in it at a competitive disadvantage in the marketplace. Disincentives could take the form of high-cost pollution permits for companies that decide to pollute, and taxes on manufacturing or purchasing environmentally harmful products, waste disposal processes, and energy use. Environmental groups support heavy "green" taxes on "products and activities that pollute, deplete or otherwise degrade natural systems."[25] Such taxes would help pay for mounting cleanup costs and at the same time encourage environmentally sound practices.

The bank failures of the 1930s, which wiped out the life savings of ordinary and wealthy citizens alike, led the government to provide insurance for depositors at banks and savings and loans. This program meant that the taxpayers in general, and not individual depositors, paid the bill when reckless and sometimes illegal actions of banks and savings and loans caused a new round of failures after deregulation in the 1970s.

President Clinton supported these reforms and in his first budget tried to link revenue-raising to market incentives for conservation by asking for a broad-based energy tax. The projected costs to business, especially the oil industry, and the complications of enforcement, brought the proposal to a quick end in the Senate.

Market-based reform to achieve greater efficiency and cost-effectiveness was only the first phase in the latest round of deregulation. Although a majority of Americans continued to support some forms of federal regulatory activity, especially environmental protection, deregulation was a major campaign issue for Republicans in 1994. Shortly after assuming control of Congress, they submitted new legislation in both the House and Senate. (see the Symbolic Solutions box entitled 'Deregulating to "Get Government off our Backs" ').

Rather than trying to repeal existing regulation, the Republicans' approach has been to suggest replacing existing health-based regulatory standards with "risk assessment." This is a more stringent calculation of cost against benefits based on rigid standards of scientific proof that a particular product or act being regulated is harmful to the public. If risk assessment were to replace the health-based standards that currently guide rule-writing in eleven departments and agencies that monitor pollution control, worker safety, the manufacture and sale of foods and drugs, and consumer safety, it would drastically alter the number and type of regulations issued.

The proposed legislation would also open the process of rule-writing to peer as well as judicial review, processes that could kill proposed regulations by tying them up in administrative and court challenges. Deregulators saw in this measure a kind of retribution for the lengthy litigation industry had been subjected to from interest groups challenging compliance with federal regulations.

Critics have called it a paralysis approach to deregulation: "Its cleverness lies not in streamlining the regulatory process but in adding 31 new steps, two additional years of review, and $700,000 in additional cost to every rule issued by the [EPA] and other federal agencies. . . . In case that doesn't work, [the bill] also creates 267 new opportunities to sue at every step of agency rule-making." The process was likened to injecting Arnold Schwarzenegger with steroids, "in hopes he soon will be so muscle-bound he can't move at all."[26]

Deregulators particularly targeted landmark environmental legislation such as the Clean Water Act, which is extremely costly to implement, and the Endangered Species Act, which many western farmers and ranchers believe interferes with their property rights. One observer said that the Republican tactic of bringing regulatory activity to a halt without actually repealing the legislation was "the equivalent of a neutron bomb: a tactical weapon that leaves the legal edifice of environmental laws standing but kills all the bureaucrats."[27] This is a much more extreme form of deregulation than advocated by the Clinton administration, whose reforms focused on prevention through economic incentives but retained a commitment to regulate to achieve health-based standards.

➤Regulatory Politics and Environmental Protection

The benefits of regulation are produced at a cost. Some are trivial, such as depriving hunters of the satisfaction of shooting eagles. But some are significant. The cost of environmental regulation to industry was estimated to be $150 billion in 1994. This and every other estimate is controversial, although it is indisputable that regulation requires industry to increase its costs to relieve the larger community of the burden of pollution,[28] unsafe products, hazards to workers, or other negative aspects of business. Because regulation incurs costs as it bestows benefits, it is inevitable that those who sustain the costs will compete with those seeking benefits to influence the process of writing rules. In this section we use the example of one area of government regulation—environmental protection—to illustrate how legislators, regulators, and interest groups have contributed to the politicization of the regulatory process.

Government action to set standards for protection of the environment has had more bipartisan legislative, and broader public, support than almost any area of regulation. For a quarter-century the importance of this type of regulatory activity has been proclaimed by leaders from Richard Nixon—who called a clean environment the "birthright" of every American—to Al Gore, who wrote a best-selling book based on the notion that safeguarding the environment should be "the central organizing principle for civilization."[29]

A majority of the public supports spending for environmental protection, even when agreeing with the statement that government should regulate less. For example, a 1995 poll in which a majority of respondents agreed that "government regulation of business usually does more harm than good" showed 78% of the same respondents also agreeing with the statement that "this country should do whatever it takes to protect the environment."[30] Nevertheless, neither widespread support for regulatory activity nor its real achievements were able to prevent a strong backlash from developing against environmental activism by government and interest groups.

The crucial question in the debate over government's role can be stated simply, but it cannot be answered simply. How can we define regulations and standards that protect society's interest in having a clean and healthy environment and at the same time not unreasonably handicap business and individual producers of pollution? Historical and current debates over environmental policy revolve around that issue.

Evolution of Government's Role

Eighteenth-century Americans did not worry about harming the environment. The continent, largely unsettled, was graced with resources that seemed almost infinite: "A fertile, widespreading country . . . blessed with a variety of soils . . . and watered . . . with innumerable streams, for the delight and accommodation of its inhabitants."[31]

The Constitution contains no hint of concern about preserving and protecting the environment. Indeed, the Founders' and our own orientation to the environment is rooted in the Western, Judeo-Christian tradition that the physical world exists to serve human needs.[32] This sentiment was reinforced during the eighteenth-century period known as the Enlightenment, which led people to believe that through science and learning, we could conquer almost any obstacle to human progress.[33] The possible negative consequences of science and technology for the environment were a long way away.

But in the nineteenth century, concern grew about the effect that the industrial revolution, coupled with rapid population growth, might have on the environment. Late in that century, a conservationist movement to preserve some of the natural environment from farmers and loggers who were clearing the land resulted in the creation of the national forests and a national park system.[34]

Along with concern about saving some forests and other areas of scenic beauty came an awareness of pollution. The first effort to combat water pollution was an 1899 law requiring that individuals dumping waste into navigable waters get a permit from the

In the 1870s, Congress appropriated money to survey, map, and photograph the previously uncharted West. The photographs, like this 1871 shot of Mammoth Hot Springs in Yellowstone, helped convince unbelievers that reports of glorious scenery in places like Yellowstone and the Tetons were true. In 1872, Yellowstone became the first national park.

Army Corps of Engineers. And in 1924, Congress banned oceangoing ships from dumping oil in coastal waters. Neither of these acts was enforced very well, but the legislation did indicate an embryonic concern with pollution.

The modern environmental movement probably stems from a book, *Silent Spring*, published in 1962 by Rachel Carson. Carson showed that pesticides used in agriculture find their way into the air and water and harm crops, animals, and people. Moreover, she demonstrated that scientists and engineers did not know the extent of these harmful effects, nor did they seem particularly concerned. The chemical industry immediately attacked Carson, accusing her of hysteria and misstatement of facts. The industry's attacks created widespread publicity for her views and raised the environmental consciousness of millions of Americans.

An Earth Day celebrant illustrating a possible future scenario if air pollution is not curbed.

The decade and a half following the publicity over Carson's book was characterized by a burst of new regulatory activity. Beginning in 1964 and continuing through 1977, Congress passed a series of laws designed to protect the air and water from pollution and to deal with hazardous waste.

Public concern peaked too. Huge oil spills, rivers catching fire, and the growing impact of the automobile on air quality lent substance to these concerns. By 1970, opinion polls showed that the most frequently cited public problem was protecting the environment, surprising in light of the continuing protest against the Vietnam War.[35] The environmental movement had its protest too. In April 1970 Earth Day was inaugurated and hundreds of thousands of citizens across the nation demonstrated to show their concern about the environment. Every year since, one day in April has been set aside to celebrate the planet's resources and to heighten environmental awareness.

In 1970, Congress gave citizens a more formal way to affect environmental policy. New legislation, the National Environmental Policy Act, mandated government agencies to prepare **environmental impact statements** for their projects or projects they fund. These analyses were to detail the effect, including any negative consequences, a project or other activity would have on the environment. No new buildings, dams, sewers, pipelines, or highways were to be built nor any research or other government projects initiated until this statement had been filed.

Not only did the law give federal agencies the power to comment on each other's environmental impact statements, but it also gave citizens access. Added almost as an afterthought, this provision would become an important device for organizations interested in protecting the environment, giving them real opportunity to influence environmental policies. Within a few years, more than 400 legal suits were filed to force the government to comply with the act's provisions, and by 1980, thousands had been filed.[36] Strictly enforced by the courts, the act affected the activities of dozens of federal agencies.

Another landmark move marking the growing federal involvement in environmental protection was the 1970 creation of the **Environmental Protection Agency (EPA)** by President Nixon.[37] Recognizing that responsibilities for pollution control were spread throughout the executive branch, Nixon, with congressional approval, brought them together in one regulatory agency with a single head who reported to the president.

During the EPA's first years three foundational pieces of environmental protection legislation were passed by Congress: the Clean Air Act (1970), the Clean Water Act (1972), and the Endangered Species Act (1973). During the 1970s the EPA received extensive new mandates to regulate hazardous waste, pesticides, and noise pollution. By 1980, the EPA administered, under the watch of 70 congressional committees and subcommittees, 16 major environmental statutes.[38] (Figure 2)

FIGURE 2
Spending for Environmental Protection in the Regulatory-Deregulatory Cycle

From almost nothing, federal spending rose steadily after 1973 as Congress passed legislation to control air, water, and hazardous waste pollution. Deregulation brought a sharp drop in environmental spending between 1980 and 1984 and threatened to do so again in 1996, when the Republican leadership called for cutting the EPA's budget by one-third. Figure for 1996 is an estimate.

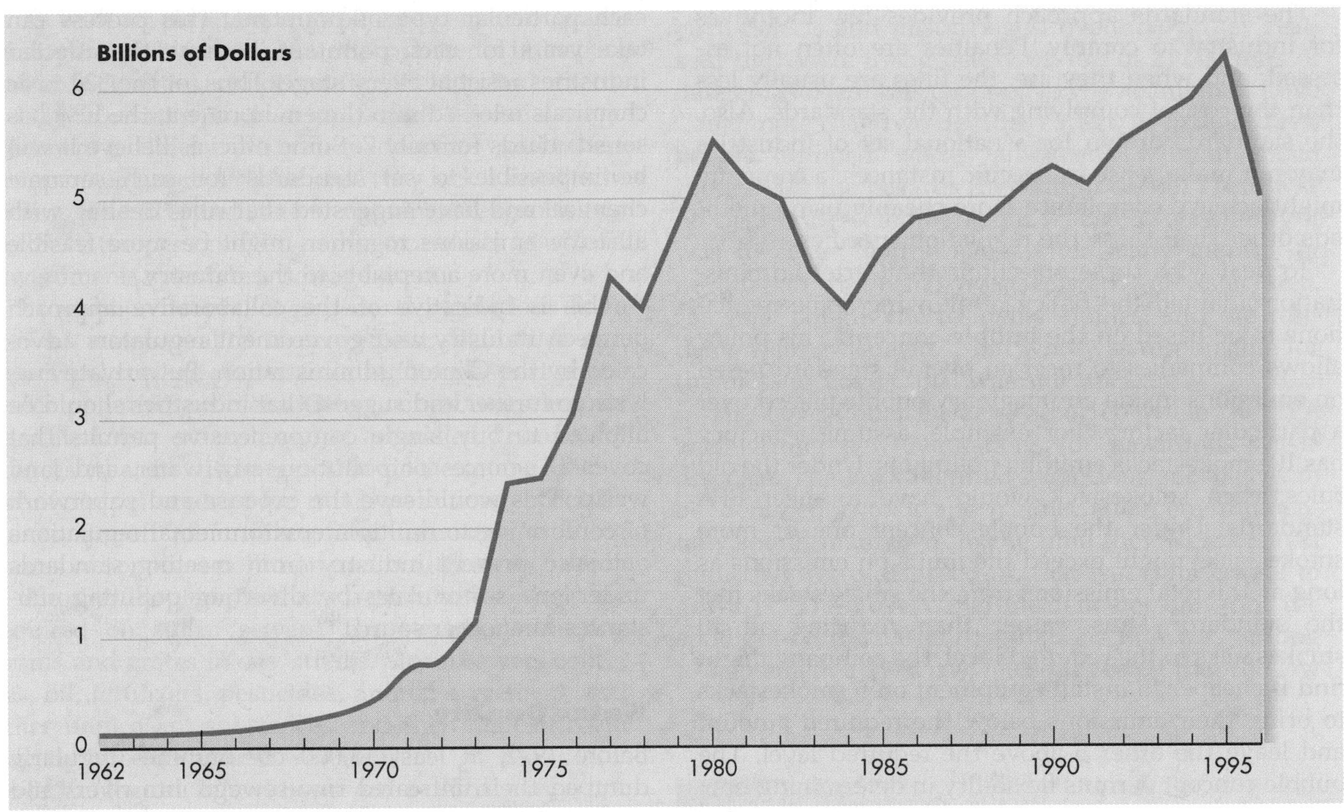

SOURCE: *Budget of the United States 1996.* Historical Tables, Table 4.1, pp. 58–62.

Implementing Environmental Regulations

Passing laws is one thing, enforcing them another. Congress mandated the EPA to achieve certain goals, but the EPA had to write the rules for reaching them, then monitor their implementation. This process is vulnerable at all stages to influence by affected parties. For example, under the Clean Air Act the EPA was ordered to establish air quality standards for major pollutants and states to produce acceptable air pollution control plans. The act also permitted citizens to sue to enforce its provisions.[39]

Auto manufacturers who had to reduce auto emissions or face fines, immediately asked for more time to reduce emissions, claiming they could not meet the standards. After the price hike in oil in 1973 brought financial difficulties to auto manufacturers in the mid-1970s, several extensions were granted. However, it became apparent that, counter to U.S. auto manufacturers' claims, the standards were technologically feasible since foreign manufacturers were able to meet them. Consequently, by the end of the 1970s, the standards had been restored, only to be partly rolled back during Reagan's deregulation campaign.

Enforcing air quality standards for industries has been difficult. Though in theory the EPA can have a noncomplying company closed down, this is simply not politically feasible or particularly wise. Generally, the agency is reluctant to enforce standards against

Who Will Regulate Government?

While the EPA struggles to collect restitution from private businesses and industries for environmental cleanup, who will hold the nation's worst polluters—the Departments of Defense and Energy—responsible for unsafe activities? The problems of accountability are even more formidable than for the private sector. The Department of Justice does not want to sue other federal agencies; the EPA can impose fines but has no power to collect them; and citizens' right to sue the federal government has been restricted where national security activities are at issue. Charges can be brought against the private industries who pollute while fulfilling DOD or DOE contracts, but they can claim they were just following orders from federal agencies. States left with huge toxic waste problems by weapons or energy plants have been told by the Supreme Court that they cannot collect civil penalties from a federal agency. How can government be made accountable for damage to the environment and the health of its citizens? Who will regulate the regulators?

Much of the government's polluting is tied to the development of nuclear weapons and nuclear power. These projects have already exacted enormous health costs. In the 1940s when government engineers recruited Navajo men and boys living near Cove, Arizona, to mine the uranium necessary for new atomic weapons programs, no one mentioned the dangers of radon exposure. And no one warned the citizens of Nevada about radioactivity, even though the government exploded more than 1,000 bombs in their state. Atomic Energy Commission documents refer to people living in the fallout area as "a low-use segment of the population."[1]

Source: Reprinted by permission, Tribune Media Services.

It was not until the 1990s that Congress appropriated money to compensate for injuries and deaths to uranium miners, participants in nuclear testing, and victims of radioactive fallout. By that time Congress was also facing the massive cost of cleaning up toxic waste and other pollution at the nation's military bases and nuclear weapons plants. One person has called them "virtual museums of environmental misbehavior."[2] Plants that built nuclear bombs focused on national security and gave little attention to safety procedures or to the effects their actions might have on surrounding communities. Leaking earthern pits were used as dumps for industrial chemicals and radioactive wastes. Sewage systems, some built when the plants opened, leak pollutants into the ground. Inadequate or nonexistent air pollution control devices allowed toxic and sometimes radioactive emissions into the air. Other radioactive waste is discharged into streams and rivers.

The nuclear weapons plant in Hanford, Washington knowingly released into the air massive amounts of radioactive materials, including iodine, for test purposes. Downwind, near Mesa, Washington, in an area known as the "death mile," 14 of 108 residents have become ill with, or died of cancer, and several children have died or were born handicapped.[3] Researchers from the Centers for Disease Control believe that 20,000 children in eastern Washington may have been exposed to unhealthy levels of this iodine by drinking milk from cows grazing in contaminated pastures.[4]

In Fernald, Ohio, a red and white checkerboard design on a water tower and the name "Feed Materials Production Center" led some residents to believe a local firm produced animal feed. Instead it made uranium rods and components for warheads. Residents were stunned to find out that, for 35 years, the plant had dumped radioactive refuse into pits in the ground that regularly overflowed when it rained. The plant also discharged 167,000 pounds of wastes into a local river and released about twice that much into the air. Though these actions were taken by the private company that ran the plant, they were approved and even encouraged by the supposed regulators, the Atomic Energy Commission. As Senator John Glenn (D-Ohio) commented ironically, "We are poisoning our people in the name of national security."[5]

Continued

After federal courts ruled that the EPA has the authority to regulate waste disposal at federal weapons plants, the agency fined the Department of Energy $300,000 for delays in implementing a cleanup plan for the Fernald plant. But it had no way to collect the fine, any more than it could force the Department of Energy to carry through on plans to clean up the Hanford Nuclear Reservation. However, after receiving some bad press coverage, the Department of Energy agreed to pay a much smaller fine and negotiated a new 40-year cleanup schedule. Perhaps this was on the mind of Clinton's Energy Secretary when she replaced pictures of nuclear submarines and power plants in her new office with photos of wind-energy farms and solar power units.

Cheerleaders at Hanford, Washington, High School, whose teams are named the "Bombers," illustrate the civic pride in the nuclear weapons plant located nearby.

From 1990 to 1993 the DOE spent $12 billion on plant cleanup and estimates run as high as $200 billion for completion of the work. But cleanup will slow with the department's new budgetary restrictions. Under threat of elimination by deregulators, and ordered by the Clinton administration to cut more than $10 billion from its budget within five years, the DOE cut $4.4 billion from its cleanup programs at 39 nuclear weapons plants.

Like the DOE, the Defense Department is also facing huge cleanup problems. Its domestic military installations produce more hazardous waste each year than the top U.S. chemical companies. There are now studies or cleanup underway at more than 10,000 sites at 800 military installations.[6] This includes many bases being closed to reduce military spending. None of these bases can be sold or converted to any civilian use until they are detoxified and made safe from such hazards as unexploded artillery and mortar shells. Environmental cleanup is now the fastest growing item in the military budget. In the 1990s, the bill for carelessness and neglect is coming due.

---

1. Carole Gallagher, *American Ground Zero: The Secret Nuclear War* (Cambridge, Mass.: MIT Press, 1993), p. xxiii.
2. Cass Peterson, "A Monumental Cleanup Job," *Washington Post National Weekly Edition,* December 12–18, 1988, p. 11.
3. "Nuclear Danger and Deceit," *Newsweek,* October 31, 1988, pp. 20–30.
4. "They Lied to Us," *Time,* October 31, 1988, p. 64.
5. Ibid, p. 61.
6. U.S. Budget for Fiscal 1996, p. 88.

OTHER SOURCES: John Hanrahan, "Testing Ground," *Common Cause,* January/February 1989; Mathew Wald, "When the Government Runs Afoul of Its Own Regulators," *New York Times,* March 10, 1991, p. E16; Keith Schneider, "A Valley of Death for the Navajo Uranium Miners," *New York Times,* May 3, 1993, p. A18; Bill Turque and John McCormick, "The Military's Toxic Legacy," *Newsweek,* August 6, 1990, p. 20; Bruce van Voorst, "A Thousand Points of Blight," *Time,* November 9, 1992, pp. 62–69.

costly standards and to eliminate unnecessary rules.[58] She said the issues of risk assessment, property rights, and unfunded mandates "cast a shadow over environmental legislation" and had to be "addressed head-on" before any new regulations could be written.[59]

The EPA's attempts to control pollution and hazardous substances are undermined by fast-changing technology, inconsistent goals of political leaders, and of course, resistance by regulated groups. But they are also frustrated by the public. We want clean air and water, but we do not want to give up gas-guzzling cars, plastic containers, energy-consuming conveniences, and other pollution-causing aspects of our life-styles. We use far more energy per person than

Drilling and Spilling

The discovery of huge reserves of oil in Prudhoe Bay, Alaska, in 1968 set off an equally huge political controversy.[1] How was the United States going to get the oil from "up there" down here? Very quickly, a group of seven oil companies, including Exxon, Atlantic Richfield, Mobil, and Phillips Petroleum, joined together to propose constructing a huge pipeline from Prudhoe Bay in northern Alaska to Valdez on Alaska's southern coast. From there, the oil would be taken by tanker to West Coast ports for distribution across the United States.

The pipeline had many proponents. Oil producers saw huge profits from this rich new source. The Nixon administration wanted to increase the amount of oil produced in the United States. In 1973, when Middle Eastern and other foreign oil producers raised prices dramatically, the public, facing huge increases in the price of gas for their cars and oil to heat their homes, demanded more and cheaper oil. To government officials, and much of the public, the Alaska pipeline seemed like a good deal.

Most pipeline opponents were environmentalists. Environmental groups filed suit against the oil companies, charging that the pipeline and its construction would destroy much of the virgin timber and animal life in America's last frontier and, in places, destroy forever the fragile ecology of the tundra. Environmentalists were also concerned about the damage that might result from oil spills when oil from the pipeline was loaded and shipped from Valdez.

Despite these concerns, the secretary of the interior approved the pipeline. The courts then blocked it, noting that some of the provisions of the plan violated federal law.

But after extensive debate, Congress overrode the courts. The majority believed that the concerns expressed by environmental groups were outweighed by the need for more domestic oil. Proponents argued that having the Alaska pipeline was a matter of national security. Moreover, by declaring the pipeline in compliance with provisions of the National Environmental Policy Act, a slim majority in Congress barred more suits and further court review of the pipeline.

The pipeline opened in 1977, and for a dozen years no major catastrophe occurred. Nearly 300 billion gallons of oil were carried from the port of Valdez with relatively little spilling.[2]

Alaskan government officials, lured by the millions of dollars flowing into state businesses and tax coffers, relaxed their concern about possible accidents. Oil companies cut back on safety measures and standby emergency crews and blocked efforts to increase state inspections and safety regulations. Local communities that volunteered storage space for cleanup equipment were spurned by the companies.

In 1989, an Exxon tanker ran aground spilling, 11 million gallons of crude oil into one of the most beautiful areas in North America, Prince William Sound. A few days after the spill, high winds dispersed the oil throughout the sound so that the gooey slick covered 900 square miles and contaminated 1,500 miles of coastline. Though it had an 1,800-page contingency plan that assured the government it could take care of any spill in a few hours, Exxon was unable and unprepared to clean up such a massive spill. Eleven thousand workers were hired to break up and disperse the oil using high-pressure hoses.

The spill killed thousands of birds, sea otters, and other marine animals, but the jury is still out on the extent of long-term ecological damage to the region. In the first years after the spill, for example, salmon and herring catches were not significantly affected. But by the third and fourth years their populations had dropped off drastically, due to genetic damage according to marine scientists, temporarily shutting down the herring industry. By the fifth year both salmon and herring catches were on the rebound.

By 1993, 97% of the oil was gone from the beaches but scientists claim that nature, in the form of storms and wave action, did more than the hoses to disperse the oil. Moreover, the high-pressure, hot-water treatment killed billions of tiny organisms and created a toxic crude oil mist which may have affected the health of the cleanup crew. Hundreds of workers reported cases of respiratory infections, dizziness, and other health problems.[3]

Perhaps the disaster could have been avoided; certainly the magnitude of the disaster should have been avoidable. But the Prince William Sound scenario is repeated frequently on a does any other nation, and with energy use comes pollution. Part of this heavy consumption is due to our wealth, but part is due to our wastefulness. High oil prices in the 1970s curbed energy use for awhile, but we have returned to our more wasteful ways. To ask the EPA to control pollution, then, is to ask it to protect us from ourselves.

Changing human behavior is at the center of the current debate over how much progress has been made in environmental protection and how much remains to be done. The optimists point to real achievements in improving air and water quality, reforestation, and cleaning up toxic waste and believe it is possible to control or limit ecological damage through adjust-

Continued

Workers disperse oil from the spill with hot water from high-pressure hoses.

smaller scale and with less severe consequences. Business and industry bent on making a profit with new technologies or new projects always assure government and the public that there will be "no problem." Critics are accused of being "antigrowth" or, as in the case of the pipeline, "environmental extremists." Often government is eager to accept these assurances because of the influence of business and sometimes because government policymakers believe the project is in the interests of national security (like the pipeline). Later, when an accident happens, government officials and business leaders appear to be shocked, though few others are. In this case, a year after the spill Congress passed a bill, first proposed in the 1970s, that specifies tanker safety measures and increases owners' liability if accidents occur. This law has been credited with the reduction of spills in American waters since 1990.

In 1991, Exxon pleaded guilty to four misdemeanor violations of pollution laws and agreed to pay a $100 million fine, plus $1 billion in compensation (not counting the $2.1 billion it spent on cleanup). Shortly after the settlement was announced it was thrown out by a federal judge, who ruled that the fine, the largest ever assessed for criminal violation of federal pollution laws, was too lenient. In a combination of state and federal rulings and out-of-court settlements in 1994, Exxon agreed to pay $306 million in compensatory damages. About a third went to commercial fisherman for loss of income and $20 million to native villagers for damage to their food supply.

In addition to compensation, Exxon was ordered to pay $5 billion in punitive damages for reckless behavior. Almost a billion dollars is earmarked for purchase of timber and coastal land for wilderness perservation and for marine research. Lawyers for the plaintiffs had asked for $15 billion on the grounds that a company with annual gross receipts of $111 billion would not be sufficiently motivated to change its behavior by a smaller fine.

Exxon did change its behavior however; it began divesting itself of its oil shipping operation, and now subcontracts with a separate company to carry much of its oil. Should that company have a spill, Exxon would not be liable. The Exxon Valdez was transferred to this company and renamed. Barred from Alaska waters, it is now used in international shipping, where its owners say it runs at a loss. They have applied to a federal subsidy program to keep the ship in operation. And in 1995 Exxon filed papers challenging the verdict and requesting a new trial.

1. David Heard Davis, *Energy Politics* (New York: St. Martin's Press, 1982), pp. 90–91; *Congressional Quarterly Almanac,* 1973, pp. 596–614.
2. Cass Peterson and Jay Mathews, "A Crude Awakening For Alaska," *Washington Post National Weekly Edition,* April 10–16, 1989, p. 7.
3. McNeil-Lehrer Report, "Update: Toxic Legacy," PBS broadcast, March 30, 1993.

OTHER SOURCES: Jay Mathews, "The Sound and the Easing Fury," *Washington Post National Weekly Edition,* March 4–10, 1991, p. 33; *New York Times,* March 17, 1991, p. E5; "Oil Trustees Back a Land Deal," *New York Times,* May 16, 1993, p. 16; "Big Drop Found in U.S. Oil Spills," *New York Times,* August 23, 1992, p. 17; MacNeil/Lehrer Newshour, August 30, 1994 (transcript #5041 pp. 6–8); "Former Exxon Valdez Seeks Federal Subsidy," *Champaign-Urbana News-Gazette* (AP), April 12, 1995, p. B-8; Keith Schneider, "Dispute Erupts on Settlement in Valdez Spill," *New York Times,* October 16, 1994, p. 12.

19 Foreign Policy

You Are There

Trade Rights, or Trading Rights for Jobs?

You are Rep. Nancy Pelosi (D.-Calif.), one of the most outspoken congressional critics of human rights abuses in China.[1] In 1993, as in each year since the Chinese government's violent suppression of pro-democracy demonstrators in Beijing's Tiananmen Square, you cosponsor a resolution to use trade relations to pressure China to improve its human rights record. You believe this is one area in which we have real leverage with China; trade between our two countries has grown so rapidly that by 1992 only Japan had a larger trade surplus with us. You argue that we should not be rewarding China by opening our markets on the most favorable possible terms, but demanding political concessions in exchange for access. Your resolution would make the renewal of China's trade status as a **most favored nation (MFN)** conditional on improvements in human rights and compliance with international agreements on export of missile and nuclear technology.

When our government grants MFN status to a country, as it has to almost all of our trading partners, it permits the export of goods to our markets under the most advantageous tariff agreements. When China sells us clothing or tennis shoes or fishing rods, for example, the tariff or import duty set on these products can be no higher than that placed on similar goods imported from other countries granted MFN status. If China lost this status the average tariff on its exports to the U.S. could increase by as much as 40-60 percent of the value of the goods. This might drive the price so high the goods would no longer be competitive with other imports or with domestically made products.

This is exactly what you hope for—that the threat of the loss of favored access to American consumers will pressure Chinese leaders into providing greater political freedoms at home. A majority of your colleagues agree; ever since the Tiananmen assault Congress has been in a mood to revoke China's MFN status, both as punishment and as a means of encouraging political reform. The issue is reviewed each June on a date that coincides with the Tiananmen anniversary, which makes the appeal to human rights even more emotional. President Bush consistently opposed revoking MFN, and while the House overrode his veto the Senate was unwilling to do so.

Critics of your resolution to attach conditions to renewal of MFN argue that the U.S. has far more leverage with Chinese leaders on human rights and other issues by maintaining strong diplomatic and economic ties. The deeper and more visible our economic and diplomatic presence, the greater the exposure of Chinese to alternative cultural and political values, and the better able we are to pressure Chinese leaders to release political prisoners. In this sense, Bush said that renewing, not revoking, MFN status was the "moral" thing to do.

Other critics stress the practical aspects of trade with China and say it should never be used to achieve political objectives. They claim that as many as 150,000 American jobs will be lost

CONTINUED

OUTLINE

Foreign Policy Goals

Making Foreign Policy in a Democracy

- The Inner Circle
- Specialists
- Congress
- Interest Groups and Lobbyists
- Public Opinion

Changing Approaches to U.S. Foreign Policy

- Isolationism
- The Cold War
- Containment in the Nuclear Age
- Vietnam
- Detente
- Cold War Revival
- End of the Cold War
- Merchant Diplomacy and Multilateralism

Military Instruments of Foreign Policy

- Military Intervention
- Military Alliances
- Military Aid

Economic Instruments of Foreign Policy

- Trade
- Economic Sanctions
- Foreign Aid

Conclusion: Is Our Foreign Policy Responsive?

President Clinton's effort to normalize relations with Vietnam reflects the importance of trade in our current foreign policy.

public confusion over what the U.S. role would be in the post–Cold War era.

Specialists

The process of formulating long-term policy usually involves more people than the number involved in decision making in crisis situations. The State Department has experts on every region of the globe and on substantive policy issues such as economic assistance, trade, political affairs, and arms control.

Political officers in Washington and in our embassies and consulates abroad write daily summaries of important political and economic events in the countries to which they are assigned. This information is used to provide daily briefings for higher-level officials, but almost none of it ever reaches the president's desk and only a small portion of it can be read even by the secretary of state.

Important background work is also done by specialists in other cabinet departments and independent agencies, such as Defense, Treasury, Commerce, Agriculture, Justice, the Arms Control and Disarmament Agency, and the CIA. Their work can be crucial to the negotiation of arms control and law of the sea treaties, trade agreements, and immigration policy, for example.

We should not assume that these experts present neutral information that is somehow mechanically cranked out as public policy. Even if the experts do their best to provide the most accurate information and comprehensive policy alternatives possible, this information is used by top policymakers who see it through their own perceptual and ideological lenses. So, for example, information on human rights violations in Argentina received by President Reagan led to very different policy recommendations than the same information presented to President Carter. Nevertheless, issue and area specialists are crucially important in providing accurate information and the historical context for current policies.

Our Vietnam policies failed in part because many of our best Asian experts had been purged from the State Department during the McCarthy era. The Reagan administration ignored advisors who cautioned against his covert policies in Nicaragua and Iran and replaced State Department experts who disagreed with his Central America policies. More than most presidents, Reagan made appointments to key positions in the State Department based on political considerations rather than on career expertise.

Bush's appointments included both members of the foreign policy establishment who had held high positions in previous administrations and several associates from his tenure as CIA director, an organizational tie that made many in Congress uncomfortable.

Clinton appointed many foreign policy officials who had served in the Carter administration. His choices from the pool of experienced policymakers were somewhat limited, since the Democrats had held the White House and thus had controlled these appointments for only four of the preceding twenty-four years.

High turnover in specialist positions puts us at a disadvantage relative to our adversaries and allies. For example, the former Soviet Union had much the same team of arms control negotiators for many years. Our negotiating teams change, on average, every three to four years. Since arms control is an extremely complex field, our negotiators are continually in the process of learning.

Also sometimes influential in foreign policymaking are experts outside government who are associated with various "think tanks." Primarily located in Washington, close to decision makers and the national media, these institutions—including the Institute for Policy Studies on the left of the political spectrum, the Heritage Foundation on the right, and the Brookings Institute, the American Enterprise Institute, the Center for Strategic and International Studies, and the Council on Foreign Relations in the middle—conduct and publish research on policy issues. These think tanks offer a home for foreign policy experts whose party is out of office and a place for academic foreign policy experts to get Washington experience and become more visible. By writing articles for national newspapers and journals and being interviewed on news and public affairs programs, experts in these institutions "wage perpetual war against each other" trying to determine the course of American foreign policy.[3]

Congress

The leading members of congressional committees on foreign affairs and armed services and of the oversight committees for intelligence agencies play a larger role in foreign policy than the average member. But Congress as a whole has specific constitutional authority to act as a check on the president's policies through its power to declare and fund wars and the requirement for Senate ratification of treaties and confirmation of ambassadorial and high-level State Department officials. Because Congress appropriates all money for carrying out foreign policy, the president is limited in the actions he can take without congressional approval.

Rivalry between the White House and Congress in foreign policy-making intensifies or diminishes with the issue in question. Nowhere is conflict greater than over the use of the military to achieve foreign policy goals. (This subject is discussed in greater detail in Chapter 11).

Politicians and scholars have been arguing for more than 200 years about how Congress's constitutional authority to "declare war" limits the president's authority as commander in chief. The Founders, believing it too dangerous to give war powers to the president alone, were also unwilling to accept wording that would have given Congress the power to "make war." Instead they gave Congress the power to "declare war," leaving the president "the power to repel sudden attacks."[4] This left Congress and the president to struggle over what constitutes an attack on the United States and in which cases a military intervention is a war.

During the debate in Congress over the War Powers Act in 1973, former Senator Jacob Javits (R-N.Y.) compiled a list of more than 200 occasions when the president had sent troops into combat situations without congressional approval. In fact Congress has exercised its power to declare war only five times, and on only one of those occasions, the War of 1812, did it conduct a debate before issuing the declaration. Yet the two undeclared wars in Korea and Vietnam alone produced in excess of 100,000 American deaths, more than the combined losses of all of our declared wars, except for World War II.[5]

Figuring Out How U.S. Foreign Policy Is Made

One insight into U.S. foreign policy-making was offered by Nizar Hamdoon, Iraqi ambassador to the United States from 1983 to 1987, years when we supported Iraq in its war with Iran and before the Persian Gulf War. Hamdoon lived through what he calls "every ambassador's nightmare" when, during his term, the Iraqi Air Force mistakenly attacked a U.S. ship. Dealing with this tragedy, he believed, confirmed several lessons he had learned about how Americans make foreign policy. Here are some of his insights:

1. Washington is driven by crises and expectations of crises. To influence policy, one needs to seize opportunities that arise during these crises.
2. Make contact with media and give them access. Don't be afraid of them. They shape public opinion, and public opinion is what matters, especially during a crisis. Be honest with the media, and when they call, be available.
3. Don't ignore the bureaucracy. A diplomat watches the internal debates of, and listens to gossip about, the middle-level bureaucracy. By the time policy pronouncements are made from the top, it may be too late to influence them.
4. Cultivate good relations with the "desk officer" at the State Department, that is, the official who is in charge of policy-making and information about your particular country. Also cultivate congressional staff. Hamdoon reported that the Iraqi Embassy held a lunch or dinner for congressional staff every few weeks.
5. Never feel secure about any issue. Things can happen quickly in Congress, the executive branch, or the media, and you had better be ready.
6. Take the long-range view of issues.
7. Reach out to all Americans, no matter what their position on issues. Be prepared to debate rationally and refute stereotypes of your country.
8. Get away from Washington. As Hamdoon said, "If you stick too long in the capital, you begin to think that America is a nation of opportunists, and that nobody cares about you unless you are a power broker in a business suit." But, he concluded, people outside Washington are not so influenced by the media and not so caught up in what's happening today.
9. Watch out for checks and balances. Washington is different from other capitals because in Paris, London, or Moscow there are central governments in charge of foreign policy. In the United States, you may deal with a State Department official today, only to find that the policy has been reversed by Congress tomorrow. The positive side of this, however, is that you can affect policy because it is so changeable. "Nothing is ever final in Washington. . . . Everything and everyone is workable."

SOURCE: This box is summarized from Nizar Hamdoon, "The Washington Education of an Arab Diplomat," *Washington Post National Weekly Edition,* September 14, 1987, p. 24.

tices. He and his advisors must be able to calculate just how much retaliation will be accepted by the trading partner without setting off a new round of trade restrictions.

The difference in responsiveness of the president and Congress on trade issues was made clear in the legislative battle over the North American Free Trade Agreement (NAFTA). This agreement between the U.S., Canada, and Mexico (soon perhaps to include Chile) will phase out tariffs, duties, and other trade barriers during the decade after ratification and create near total market access for agricultural products. It creates the world's largest and richest trading bloc.

The agreement, negotiated by the Bush administration, was strongly supported by Clinton and had bipartisan support. But organized labor argued that the removal of tariffs on goods made in Mexico would make these products so much cheaper than U.S.-made goods that American businesses would rush to relocate in Mexico to take advantage of cheaper labor. They joined environmental groups, who opposed the removal or lowering of environmental protection and quality control regulations on imported goods, to pressure Congress to reject the agreement. Many members of the Democratic Party deserted the president on this issue, fearing electoral retaliation from angry workers and environmentalists. Yet by the end of his first year in office, Clinton could count the NAFTA battle among his successes with Congress, as the legislation passed narrowly.

A Barbie doll and a G.I. Joe fighter plane from China. A baseball mitt from South Korea and another from the Philippines. Adidas running shoes from South Korea and Nikes from Taiwan. Teapots and china from England, cognac and crystal from France. A suburban Los Angeles family of five was asked to identify all their possessions made in foreign countries or in the U.S. by foreign companies. The family also located products from Colombia, Denmark, Germany, Hong Kong, Italy, Malaysia, Mexico, Singapore, Sweden, and Switzerland. By far the most, however, were from Japan—two cars, three motorcycles, and one bicycle; cameras, binoculars, and a telescope; a TV, VCR, Nintendo, stereo, and tape player; a clock, watch, and calculator; a microwave; and a lawn mower.

There is no doubt that Europe is gearing up for economic competition with the rest of the world. In 1992 the **European Union (EU)** removed all internal economic barriers and customs posts for member nations. Formerly called the European Economic Community, or Common Market, the EU was formed in 1957 to foster political and economic integration in Europe. Within the decade it hopes to have a common currency and monetary system. The membership of the EU has expanded from its original six members to encompass all of the European members of NATO, except Norway and Turkey, plus the Republic of Ireland. With the breakup of the Warsaw Pact, some countries of Eastern Europe, too weak to compete with it as exporters, have petitioned to join the EU. This raises the possibility for the twenty-first century of an even broader European economic integration.

The U.S. is particularly concerned about EU competition in the export of agricultural goods. Although much is made of farm subsidies in the United States, European farmers are among the most highly subsidized in the world. The removal of import quotas and fees within the EU and a unified policy on price supports for European farmers will make it even harder for us to export our agricultural products to Europe.

Trade problems in East Asia also loom large in our foreign policy. This region has some of the fastest growing economies in the world, including Taiwan, South Korea, Hong Kong, and Singapore, which are often referred to as the four little dragons. Furthermore, Japan and China now count as the world's second and third largest economies, after the U.S. In 1992 the two countries' $68 billion trade surplus with us accounted for almost 80% of that year's total trade deficit. Developing export and investment opportunities in the massive Chinese market will continue to receive priority in our relations with the People's Republic, as is evidenced by the token actions taken against that government for its brutal repression of the prodemocracy movement in 1989, and Clinton's decision not to revoke China's MFN status (the topic of this chapter's "You Are There"). Our relations with China demonstrate how difficult it is in a world of powerful trading nations to use trade to achieve political goals such as promotion of human rights or internal reform. (We have pressured China far more on the issue of protecting the copyrights of American artists, musicians, and writers than on human rights.) It is hard enough, as our relations with Japan have shown, just to negotiate fair trade agreements with our allies.

The Clinton administration made Japan a special target of trade negotiations, hoping to force it to remove restrictions on U.S. agricultural products, auto parts, color film, and other goods. Clinton's emphasis on managed trade created a hostile reaction in Japan, which was in recession and suffering large budget deficits. This led to an increase in anti-U.S. sentiment among the public; in 1993, 64 percent of all Japanese viewed relations with the United States as "unfriendly."[36]

The very countries that have served as our staunchest military allies are at the same time among our strongest economic competitors. And they are about to become even stronger, threatening to make worse our already record-setting trade deficits. Indeed, containment may take on a new meaning in this era as we try to limit the economic reach of Japan, China, and the European Union.

Economic Sanctions

Economic sanctions are policies designed to get a state to change its behavior, or to take some action or set of actions, by refusing to engage with it in the conventional range of international economic relations (for example, trade, aid, loans), or by denying it access to specific economic goods or services. Economic sanctions are generally regarded as middle-of-the-road measures.[37] They are stronger than talking diplomacy but weaker than military confrontation. The United States has used sanctions to try to force internal political reforms, improve human rights, end trade barriers, change military and weapons policies, and destabilize governments. Countries currently targeted by the U.S., in some cases in concert with other countries or the U.N., include Cuba, Iran, Iraq, Libya, Bosnia, Serbia, and the Sudan.

When the United Nations voted to place economic sanctions on Iraq for its invasion of Kuwait in August 1990, it set off another round in an old debate on the usefulness of such measures. There is a widespread belief that economic sanctions are not effective in getting governments to change their behavior. The argument against sanctions is that they require unrealistic amounts of time and international cooperation to bring about the desired results. The longer the sanctions are in effect, the argument continues, the greater the temptation for nations to pursue their own economic interests by trading or selling prohibited goods to the targeted nation.

Those who believe that under the right circumstances economic sanctions can work point to their use against the government of South Africa. South Africa, one of the largest countries in Africa, was governed by a white minority of 5 million in a nation of about 30 million. Due to the system of apartheid, the huge black majority had no say in government and lacked basic civil rights, including the right to vote, the right to marry a person of another race, equal opportunities for good jobs and pay, and the right to live in most areas of the country. All black adults had to carry identification cards, and thousands were arrested each year for not having proper identification. Most public facilities were segregated. Both black and white critics of the regime were subject to arbitrary arrest and indefinite imprisonment.

The Reagan administration, a supporter of the white government of South Africa, developed a policy called "constructive engagement." The idea of constructive engagement was to keep good relations with South Africa and try to persuade its government slowly to move toward democracy, a policy similar to that now pursued toward China.

In 1985, however, increased black protest and demonstrations in South Africa focused world attention on apartheid. In the United States, college students and others around the nation also staged demonstrations in cities and on campuses. Corporations were pressured to remove their businesses from South Africa, and colleges, churches, cities, and foundations were pressured to "divest," sell stocks in companies that had investments in South Africa, and to refuse to do business with companies that operated in South Africa.

In 1985, in the face of public opinion and a Congress threatening to impose severe restrictions on U.S. economic involvement with South Africa, Reagan dropped the policy of constructive engagement and imposed some mild economic sanctions. In this case it might be said that government policy was coopted by the private sector. The actions taken by corporations, under shareholder and public pressure, to divest their holdings in the South African economy had a greater impact than the limited action taken by the U.S. government. Divestiture occurred on an international scale, with corporations from all parts of the world pulling out of South Africa. These actions, coupled with sanctions placed on South Africa by the United Nations, undoubtedly played a role in the elimination of all remaining apartheid laws and the end of white minority rule.

In situations where the international community cannot achieve such widespread consensus as that which developed in the South African case, economic sanctions have not been as effective in attaining their objectives. One study of 103 instances of economic sanctioning dating from World War I found a success rate of 36%. It concluded that sanctions were most effective when the goals were modest or were used to destabilize a government; they were least effective in damaging a country's military capacity or in effecting some major change in a state's behavior.[38] Sanctions are much more likely to be successful when a large state targets a much smaller, weaker state, but even then there is not a high likelihood of success if the goals are too ambitious.

Rarely does the U.S. target a large or powerful country, unless it is to achieve a very limited objective, such as by using trade sanctions to force the former Soviet Union to allow the emigration of Jews. As discussed in "You Are There," the U.S. elects not to take sanctions against China, even though democracy and human rights are at the very least as scarce as in Cuba, against whom we have had a trade embargo for more than thirty years. China is a large and economically powerful country and the last two administrations decided that sanctions would achieve nothing while hurting the U.S. economically.

The Cuba example shows that even against a much smaller country, which was once quite dependent on the U.S. as a trading partner, sanctions will not necssarily be effective. Even the most severe form of sanction, a trade embargo, has not achieved its goal of effecting significant political and economic reform or destabilizing the Castro government. Sanctions may have contributed to a lower standard of living for Cubans, but they did little to change the leadership's policies or lifestyle. There have been many other countries willing to trade with Cuba and meanwhile the Cuban government was able to use the U.S. embargo to deflect criticism from its own economic failures. Failed domestic policies and the withdrawal of foreign aid by Russia are likely to have a far greater impact on political change in Cuba than an embargo supported by a single nation, however powerful.

Even though the U.N. joined the U.S. in sanctions against Haiti, they too were unsuccessful in hitting the targeted group. Sanctions caused widespread unintended suffering among the general population while doing little to topple the military dictatorship. In this case, the U.S. waited not decades but a single year before committing to a military invasion to achieve what sanctions could not do. This was not a serious option in Cuba which, although also a small country, has a large, well-trained and equipped army and a population (less emigrants) that historically has been supportive of the government. An invasion would be too costly and probably politically unwinnable.

Sanctions may be continued despite evidence of their ineffectiveness simply as a way to exact punishment for behavior other states cannot change. A senior Clinton aide has said, "Sanctions are not a precision-guided instrument that can bring a solution to every problem. But they are effective at their fundamental purpose of exacting a cost for behavior that's repugnant, dangerous, and destabilizing."[39] In cases like Iraq where the cost to the population is very high and the allegiance to the leadership much weaker than in Cuba, economic sanctions may eventually achieve their goals.

On the cover of a popular Japanese business magazine, Uncle Sam points threateningly at Asia.

Foreign Aid

Extending economic assistance to other countries is another tool of American foreign policy. Aid can take the form of grants, technical assistance, or guaranteed loans, for example. The primary object of the aid is to promote development and stability, but indirectly it is a means for influencing the direction of other countries' development, expanding export markets for U.S. goods, and in general spreading our sphere of influence. The grants and loans are often used to purchase American goods, or to repay loans from American banks or public agencies.

In the fifty years since the end of World War II the United States has spent $436 billion on foreign aid, about two-thirds of which was given in military assistance. Most of the money earmarked for economic assistance has been channeled through USAID. Whereas economic sanctions operate by *denying* a state goods or services until it changes its behavior, foreign aid is used as an *incentive* to change behavior or as a reward for actions taken. In recent years, for example, the United States has paid millions in aid to the Ukraine and Russian Republics to destroy nuclear weapons inherited from the Soviet arsenal, and promised hundreds of millions to North Korea to pay for denuclearization and the development of alternative energy sources. And in each year since 1976, when they signed the U.S.-brokered peace treaty, Israel and Egypt have received nearly half of our annual aid budget.

The greatest success ever achieved with foreign aid was the rebuilding of Europe after World War II under the Marshall Plan. Since that time major successes have been rare, and in recent years there has been great disillusionment with economic aid as an effective means for achieving our goals. Too often the money ended up in the bank accounts of corrupt leaders, as in Haiti, Zaire, and Panama, for example, or was spent on showy construction projects that did little to further development.

Such failures have led to congressional and public disillusionment with the effectiveness of foreign aid, both as a tool of foreign policy and as a spur to economic development. In response to criticism, USAID has closed its missions in 23 countries, and in 1995 Congress cut its budget and threatened to eliminate it. The attack on foreign aid was politically popular in an era of budget-cutting, but the program accounts for a tiny proportion of the federal budget and costs the average taxpaying family just $44 per year.[40]

The Israeli-Palestinian Conflict: The Limits of Foreign Aid and Superpower Diplomacy

In 1993 the world was stunned to hear that Israel and the Palestinian Liberation Organization (PLO) had reached agreement on mutual recognition and a plan to negotiate Palestinian self-rule. For more than twenty-five years the United States acted as intermediary in peace negotiations between Israel and its Arab neighbors. But it was relegated to a secondary role in the final round of talks that led to the Israeli-PLO agreement. By looking at our role in mediating the Arab-Israeli conflict we can learn something about the uses and limitations of superpower diplomacy.

The United States has multiple economic and security goals in the Middle East, including maintaining access to that region's immense oil reserves. Thus we want to have good relations with the Arab governments that control most of those reserves. Some Mideastern monarchies, such as Saudi Arabia, Jordan, and Kuwait, which feared leftist challenges to their rule, also cooperated with the United States during the Cold War. In return we helped equip and train their armies. In more recent years these states have also shared U.S. opposition to the rise of fundamentalist Islamic movements (such as seized power in the non-Arab state of Iran), movements that have sponsored international terrorist actions and that want to topple the more moderate Arab governments.

In spite of these shared interests with Arab countries, the United States has always had far closer ties to the state of Israel. Israel is the only democracy in the Middle East and it was our staunchest ally in that region throughout most of the Cold War. Israel provided military and intelligence support for U.S. activities against the growing Soviet presence in the Mediterranean. In return the United States government provided billions of dollars in economic and military aid to Israel, most of it after 1967.

In addition to strong state relations with Israel, there are the deep cultural and religious ties of millions of Jewish and Christian Americans. Private citizens have given additional billions in aid and have supported pro-Israel lobbies in Washington. Until the 1980s American public opinion overwhelmingly favored Israel's claims in the conflict over land rights in the Middle East.

Despite military and economic ties to most of the states involved in the Arab-Israeli conflict, the United States had only limited success in its attempts to broker a peace agreement. To Palestinians and Israelis the issues at stake are a matter of life and death and the United States had nothing to use as leverage to force them into actions they believed would jeopardize their survival.

The crux of the problem is that Israel was created from territory to which both Arabs and Jews laid claim. All the pages in this textbook could not document the claims and counterclaims to the land, but both Arabs and Jews have a special identity with this territory. It is the birthplace of Judaism and the location of many shrines sacred to Muslim Arabs. Creation of a homeland for Jews in Palestine was first recommended to the League of Nations during World War I. But it was not until 1947, when under pressure to resettle survivors of the Holocaust, that the United Nations voted to partition Palestine into two territories: one for Jews and one for Palestinians. The decision was denounced by Arabs as an attempt to use their land to solve a European problem.

In 1948, when Israel declared itself a state, Palestinians and neighboring Arab states attacked. The Israelis inflicted the first of a series of defeats on the Arab nations, largely because the Arabs were divided. Jordan, Egypt, Syria, and Lebanon all had expansionist ideas and were almost as opposed to other Arab nations gaining territory as they were to Israel's existence.

This first defeat left hundreds of thousands of Palestinians homeless. They fled or were driven from Israel during the war and would not or could not return. Thousands of Jews also fled or were driven from the Arab nations when the war began, but they were welcomed to Israel. The Arab nations were reluctant to resettle the Palestinians, however, believing that they, as refugees, would constitute useful and continuing evidence of the rightfulness of Arab claims to Israeli territory.

The fate of these Palestinians and their descendants is at the heart of the Arab-Israeli problem. Hundreds of thousands still live in refugee camps, while others have settled elsewhere in the Middle East and around the world. Many Palestinians were brought under Israeli control in 1967 when, during the third Arab-Israeli war, the Israelis captured the Golan Heights from Syria, the Gaza Strip and the Sinai Peninsula from Egypt, the West Bank from Jordan, and the eastern part of Jerusalem.

After the fourth Arab-Israeli War in 1973 (Yom Kippur War) the United States took an increasingly active role in trying to promote a peace accord between Israel and its Arab neighbors. The Carter administration was instrumental in negotiating a peace settlement between Egypt and Israel, with President Carter personally serving as a go-between for Egyptian president Anwar Sadat and Israeli prime minister Menachim Begin. In these Camp David Accords, Israel agreed to evacuate the Sinai Peninsula and return control to the Egyptians in return for Egypt's diplomatic recognition of Israel. This was very important to Israel because until then no Arab state had recognized Israel's right to exist.

Continued

The Camp David agreements left the Palestinian question unsettled and the situation continued to fester. After 1967 Israel built Jewish settlements on the West Bank and in many ways incorporated the area into its economic and political life. But the international community, including the United States, continued to regard these areas as occupied territory.

This issue has been a continuing source of unrest. Palestinians formed a variety of political organizations, some of them terrorist, to work for the liberation of Palestine. But the Palestinian leadership has been deeply divided over strategy and tactics, including the role of terrorism.

The conflict developed some new twists in 1988, when the militance of Palestinians in the West Bank increased. In a movement called the *intifada,* meaning uprising, Palestinians, often children, stoned Israeli soldiers. In retaliation, the Israelis bulldozed the houses of Palestinians engaged in anti-Israeli activity. These actions in turn, created Palestinian martyrs, intensified Palestinian hatred of the Israelis, undermined Israel's image abroad, and fostered the Peace Now movement in Israel that called for negotiations with the Palestinians.

During the Persian Gulf War, Saddam Hussein tried to link his invasion of Kuwait to the Palestinian question. This won strong support for him from the PLO and from Jordan, but few others in the international community believed that Hussein's takeover of Kuwait was motivated by a desire to see the Palestinian question resolved.

The PLO's support for Saddam Hussein ended any progress it had made in improving its public image in the United States during the *intifada.* More seriously, it cut off a major source of funding as Saudi Arabia and Kuwait, which had bankrolled PLO activities, broke with Arafat over his support for Iraq. In addition the wealthy Arab oil states have had serious financial setbacks from the costs of the war and the drop in oil prices. With his political and economic position weakened, surrounded by critics in his own organization, and threatened by Islamic fundamentalists who regard him as a secularist, Arafat was in a position where he had no choice but to negotiate.

Israel too was in a mood to deal. Its economy was not growing rapidly enough to assimilate all of the Russian Jews who were immigrating, and it had a new prime minister, one less opposed to trading land for peace. Furthermore, Israel lost some of its leverage in the United States when its role as dependable Cold War ally disappeared with the demise of the Soviet Union.

These conditions made it possible for President Bush to pressure both Israel and those Arab governments whom United States' forces had defended in the Gulf War to support a new round of peace talks. Through personal mediation, Secretary of State James Baker was successful in initiating several rounds of highly publicized talks between Israelis and non-PLO Palestinians in Europe and the United States. But as frequently happens when negotiations on politically volatile issues are hashed out in the daily press, little progress was made.

Israel and its Neighbors

The West Bank and Golan Heights, parts of Jordan and Syria, respectively, were captured by Israel in 1967 and have been partially settled by Jewish Israelis who live in villages separate from the Arab population. The West Bank was the site of the *intifada.*

Continued

Meanwhile the negotiations crucial to a settlement, those involving direct meetings between Israelis and PLO representatives, were being held in strict secrecy in Norway. At this stage in the process the United States could no longer serve as an effective mediator. This was in part because U.S. diplomacy is very vulnerable to press leaks, but more important, our role as mediator was limited by the fact that we were not a neutral party in this dispute. Carter's role at Camp David was possible because the United States was on very friendly terms with Egypt as well as Israel, and a major aid donor to both countries. But we had very hostile relations with the PLO and did not even recognize its existence. In contrast, Norway has strong relations with both Israel and the PLO, is a small country without a major international press contingent in residence, and provided a completely unexpected setting for the talks.

The agreement was only a first step authorizing Israeli withdrawal from the West Bank and the Gaza Strip and limited Palestinian self-rule. Most major issues remain unresolved, but more was accomplished in the Norway talks than at any time since the Camp David meetings. Why did it take so long?

In diplomacy, timing, finesse, and the attitudes of the negotiating parties count for more than raw power. The United States' role as a major military and economic partner does not give it the power (or right) to dictate peace terms to Israel any more than the wealthy Arab states that bankrolled the PLO can impose peace terms on Palestinians. But under the right circumstances third-party mediation can lead to results.

In 1993, the timing was right for Israel and the PLO to talk and Norway provided an isolated and neutral setting in which they could do it. In light of Norway's role in hosting such historic talks it might seem more appropriate to have had the signing ceremony in Oslo rather than Washington. But symbolism is extremely important in diplomacy. Norway had already played out its role in the process. In a ceremony televised worldwide, the United States was seen giving full support to the agreement and equal diplomatic treatment to both Israelis and Palestinians. Clinton provided the final touch by persuading Prime Minister Rabin to appear in public and shake hands with PLO head Arafat.

President Clinton invites Yitzak Rabin and Yassir Arafat to make peace.

One of our most perplexing foreign policy problems is how to use aid to help the developing nations of Africa, Asia, and Latin America whose economies are poor and rural and whose populations are often inadequately fed and housed and sometimes even starving.

Despite relief assistance in times of crisis, such as the Ethiopian famine and our Somalian intervention in 1992–93, the West has not done much to aid these countries. In the 1980s, the four largest recipients of U.S. aid in Africa (other than Egypt)—The Sudan, Somalia, Liberia, and Ethiopia—were targeted because of their geopolitical importance, not for their ability to use aid wisely.

In the past decade, the economic growth and standard of living of many poor nations have declined. This is especially true for Africa, which has 28 of the world's 42 poorest countries and where per capita incomes fell for 12 consecutive years.[41] One reason is the ever-mounting interest on debt owed by these nations. During the recessions and hard times of the 1970s and early 1980s, many oil-importing countries went deeply into debt. Other oil- and gas- producing countries such as Brazil and Mexico borrowed large amounts during boom periods, often encouraged to do so by Western banks looking for places to invest. Unlike the United States, which is also heavily in debt, the economies of poor nations are not growing fast enough to provide the means to repay the debt or even keep up with the interest payments. Some countries have debts that far exceed the value of the goods they export annually.[42] Paying the interest on the debt leaves no money for investment in the economy; the money flows to banks and lenders outside the country, many of them in the United States.

The reasons for the lagging progress in education, income, and development of stable political institutions are complex. Western leaders blame the developing nations themselves especially for turning their backs to private enterprise. They claim these nations have neglected their own agricultural base; unable to feed their people, they must spend scarce money on food imports. Western leaders also charge that many of these governments have been corrupt and that few have made an effort to improve the lot of the average person. Other criticisms focus on the high birth rate of some developing nations, a situation that causes improvements in economic output and food production to be offset.

Leaders of poorer countries do not accept these charges. They believe they are as exploited now as they were in colonial days, partly because they are dependent upon the markets of the West, which buy their raw materials and sell them finished goods. They argue that Western powers "stack the deck," buying raw materials cheap and selling finished products dear, leaving them in perpetual poverty.

Our relations with developing countries are important, yet in most cases military aid, military intervention, and economic aid have not worked very well in promoting economic progress, democratic government, or positive attitudes toward the United States. Some may ask why we should come to the aid of governments with poor human rights records who are sometimes militantly anti-American in their foreign policy rhetoric. Putting aside the humanitarian issues and looking at these problems in terms of our national interests, the fact remains that it is not in our interest that three-quarters of the world's population are unable to buy the agricultural and industrial goods we export. For many years the world's largest economies have been one another's principal trading partners. With the populations of these countries stabilizing, can their economies continue to grow without parallel growth in developing economies?

Another foreign aid problem that has emerged since the collapse of communism is the extent to which our government should be involved in the economic reconstruction of Eastern Europe and the former Soviet Union. Most of these countries are in desperate need of foreign investment, loans and credits, and technical assistance. Opponents of extending aid point out the high risk of making grants to countries that are politically unstable. Russia has raging corruption, a huge black market, and a homegrown mafia that is deeply involved in the private sector economy. And large sectors of its economy are still under state ownership and managed by the same former party officials who were responsible for its inefficiency. Why, critics of aid ask, should the U.S. entrust these officials with billions of aid dollars?

Those who support aid believe it is in our interest to encourage economic growth as quickly as possible in order to defuse public unrest with the current reforms—unrest that threatens to slow the move toward privatization of the economy. Supporters of aid say it is a good investment that will pay off in stability and friendly governments that translate into reduced defense spending for us. And higher standards of living for the public mean new markets for our exports.

➤Conclusion: Is Our Foreign Policy Responsive?

Our foreign policy reflects our conflicting values and goals. We pride ourselves on our strength and power and have spent billions of dollars to build a strong military, yet since Vietnam we have been uncertain how to use that power. We desire a strong alliance system and have entered into treaties with many nations around the world, but are reluctant to get involved in "their affairs."

The Persian Gulf War clearly boosted American morale and caused a rush of patriotic fervor, so much so that some claim it laid to rest the so-called Vietnam syndrome. Some even thought that this renewed belief in America's ability "to get the job done" would lead us to look for new jobs for our armed forces to take on. But domestic problems and lack of public support for new foreign ventures constrained policy makers.

Is the direction of our foreign policy responsive to the public? Public attitudes can constrain the general policy directions of the president and Congress, but presidents can do a lot to shape these attitudes. Over the long term, as in Vietnam, the administration must be somewhat responsive to public sentiment that intensely opposes administration policy. In most specific foreign policy decisions, the public has little influence because it is not well-informed. Most people are more concerned about domestic issues, particularly those affecting their pocketbooks. Ordinarily the public will support a president, at least in the short run, especially if he can convince them that our national security is threatened. But the 1990s have not been ordinary times; the public is more aware of the convergence of domestic and foreign policy issues and feels more threatened by the economy at home than by foreign powers. That has made it more difficult for the president to justify policies on grounds of national security.

In the mid-1980s, the Reagan administration tried to escape the constraints of responsiveness by engaging in private activities in pursuit of its own foreign policy objectives. We saw "a shadowy new world," where "retired military men lead supposedly private organizations to intervene in foreign military operations."[43] Such operations weaken democratic government and responsibility to the people. Although the public generally gives the president wide discretion in carrying out foreign policy, the president cannot be above the law in this or in any other aspect of governing.

As the head of the world's largest military and economic power and a partner in major military and trade alliances, the president has a constituency larger than the American public. He is often called upon to be responsive to the needs of other people or countries: victims of famines, civil wars, natural disasters, and human rights abuses, or countries in need of military and economic assistance. In such cases the president and Congress have to weigh external demands against the needs and wishes of the American people. But if the United States is to continue to act in a leadership role in international politics, as the American public has long wanted it to, it must demonstrate some measure of responsiveness to the needs of other countries.

EPILOGUE

Pelosi Goes Along

Pelosi decided to accept the executive order renewing China's MFN status, saying the president's action would achieve what her resolution would if passed.

Although he renewed China's favorable trading relationship without winning concessions on human rights or the arms trafficking issues, Clinton did go further than the Bush administration in attaching formal written restrictions on any subsequent renewal. For Pelosi, challenging a Republican president was quite different from going against the leader of her party, especially if it appeared to be on a matter of degree and not principle. If in a year's time the administration offered no evidence that it had held China accountable for the conditions attached to renewal, Pelosi could reintroduce her resolution to revoke MFN.

The Chinese government expressed its satisfaction with Clinton's "wise decision" to renew MFN but also its extreme displeasure with what it called interference in Chinese domestic affairs and violations of

YOU OWE ROYALTIES ON THE SHIRT!
CHINA
POLITICAL DISSENT
JOEL PETT 2/7/95 LEXINGTON HERALD-LEADER

Joel Pett, the Lexington Herald-Leader, North America Syndicate.

existing agreements between the two countries. The criticism of Clinton was probably intended in part to defuse MFN opponents like Pelosi by suggesting that Clinton had already taken punitive measures instead of just threatening to do so.

It takes great skill, clear goals, and substantial leverage to promote human rights through foreign policy, and it is almost impossible to do so without antagonizing other governments for interfering in their domestic affairs. If trade can be used to pressure another government to take some action we favor, it will most likely be in situations where we have a distinct advantage over the trading partner as, for example, when it has no other export markets for its products, or when it cannot find another supplier for goods it needs to import. In today's world, where we are in stiff competition for export markets with Japan and the countries of Europe and Latin America, our trade leverage has diminished.

By new international standards of measurement, China now has the third largest economy in the world. Per capita income is rising rapidly in major urban and some rural areas, so the consumer market of 1.2 billion people that the U.S. business community has long coveted is each day more accessible. Jeopardizing access to this market in a period of a depressed domestic market in order to get the Chinese government to seek goals no Chinese government has ever sought was a risk bigger than Clinton was willing to take.

Therefore, in May 1994, Clinton announced his decision to renew China's MFN status despite a worsening of the human rights situation. He also declared his intention to delink human rights issues from trade policies—even though just days earlier he had announced renewed support for the economic embargo on Cuba. Pelosi was furious, accusing the president of deserting Chinese dissidents and adopting the Bush administration policy of "trickle-down liberty." She and her congressional allies, however, decided not to try to override the president's decision.

Clinton's argument for retaining MFN status for China—that the U.S. would have its greatest impact on China by maintaining close ties—was indeed virtually identical to the Bush policy. But it also had a great deal in common with the position of Chinese President Jiang Zemin: In the hierarchy of human rights issues, job security comes first.

➤Key Terms

most favored nation (MFN)
isolationism
Monroe Doctrine
containment
NATO
Cold War
domino theory
mutual assured destruction (MAD)
Vietnam syndrome
detente
glasnost
protectionism
free trade
European Union (EU)

➤Further Reading

Kevin Buckley, *Panama: The Whole Story* (New York: Simon and Schuster, 1991). *An account of how the United States got Noriega on its payroll, of how he fell out of favor, and of the U.S. invasion to overthrow him.*

James Chace, *The Consequences of the Peace: The New Internationalism and American Foreign Policy* (New York: Oxford/Twentieth Century Fund, 1992). *Describes the United States' loss of superpower status in the face of the rising power of Europe, but argues that the post-Cold War era is a time for increased foreign involvement, especially in Latin America and the Pacific.*

Louis Fisher, *Presidential War Power* (Lawrence, Kan.: University of Kansas Press, 1995). *A staff member of the Congressional Research Service reviews presidential use of the military from the first days of the republic to the present and concludes congressional war-making powers have been usurped by the executive branch.*

David Forsythe, *Human Rights and American Foreign Policy,* 2nd ed. (Lincoln, Neb.: University of Nebraska Press, 1989). *How human rights issues affect the making of foreign policy.*

Gary Clyde Hufbauer and Jeffrey J. Schott, with Kimberly Ann Elliott, *Economic Sanctions Reconsidered: History and Current Policy* (Washington, D.C.: Institute for International Economics, 1985). *Three economists abstract and evaluate 103 applications of economic sanctions, beginning with the economic blockade of Germany in World War I, and specify the conditions that make success most likely.*

Walter Isaacson and Evan Thomas, *The Wise Men: Six Friends and the World They Made* (New York: Simon & Schuster, 1986). *An insight into the foreign policy-making establishment that dominated the postwar era into the early 1960s.*

Charles W. Kegley and Eugene R. Wittkopf, *American Foreign Policy,* 3rd ed. (New York: St. Martins Press, 1987). *A comprehensive text on the making of American foreign policy.*

Robert S. McNamara, *In Retrospect: The Tragedy and Lessons of Vietnam* (New York: Times Books, 1995). *A former secretary of defense and principal architect of Vietnam War policy gives eleven reasons why he thinks the Vietnam War was a mistake, rejecting the domino theory and placing a preponderance of blame on the incompetence of South Vietnamese forces and U.S. underestimation of the North Vietnamese.*

James Nathan and James Oliver, *United States Foreign Policy and World Order,* 4th ed. (Boston: Little, Brown, 1989). *An introduction to U.S. foreign policy after World War II.*

David Remnick, *Lenin's Tomb: The Last Days of the Soviet Empire* (New York: Random House, 1993). *A chronicle of the demise of the Soviet Union.*

Barry Rubin, *Secrets of State: The State Department and the Struggle over U.S. Foreign Policy* (New York: Oxford University Press, 1985). *After learning about conflicts among those charged with making foreign policy, readers will finish the book surprised we have a foreign policy at all.*

Neil Sheehan, *A Bright Shining Lie* (New York: Random House, 1988). *The Vietnam War as seen through its effect on a young American officer.*

Gaddis Smith, *The Last Years of the Monroe Doctrine, 1945–1993* (New York: Hill and Wang, 1994). *A distinguished scholar of American foreign policy argues that the goals of the Monroe Doctrine were a fantasy and that U.S. policymakers and the American public finally have come to accept them as unachievable.*

Kenneth Timmerman, *The Death Lobby: How the West Armed Iraq* (New York: Houghton Mifflin Co., 1992). *An account of how the United States and its allies built up the war machine of Saddam Hussein during the Iran-Iraq war. The author accuses intelligence agencies of being so focused on preventing an Iranian victory that they overlooked or ignored Iraq's nuclear weapons program.*

Richard H. Ullman, *Securing Europe* (Princeton, N.J.: Princeton University Press, 1991). *Describes the breakup of military alliances in Europe, possibilities for restructuring, and the future of NATO.*

Bob Woodward, *The Commanders* (New York: Simon and Schuster, 1991). *An examination of military policy making in the Bush administration, with a special focus on the invasion of Panama and Operation Desert Storm.*

➤Notes

1. Sources for this "You Are There" include: *Congressional Record,* April 26, 1993, p. E1023; May 20, 1993, pp. S6204–5; May 26, 1993, pp. S6600–1; May 28, 1993, pp. S6812–3 and S6855–7; June 10, 1993, pp. H3437–8; Nicholas D. Kristof, "China is Making Asia's Goods, and the U.S. is Buying," *New York Times,* March 21, 1993, p. E3; Bruce Stokes, "Not-So-Favored China," *National Journal,* May 15, 1993, p. 1204; Keith Bradsher, "China Trade: Cash or Care?" *New York Times,* May 14, 1993, pp. 1, 6; David C. Morrison, "Capitalist Roaders," *National Journal,* May 29, 1993, pp. 1282–4; Calvin Sims, "China Steps Up Spending to Keep U.S. Trade Status," *New York Times,* May 7, 1993, pp. A1, C2; *MacNeil/Lehrer NewsHour,* transcript for May 26, 1994, pp. 3–12.

2. Walter LaFeber, *New York Times,* July 3, 1983. "Diplomatic Subcontracting's Fine If You Get Good Help," *New York Times,* September 25, 1994, p. E6.

3. I.M. Destler, Leslie H. Gelb and Anthony Lake, *Our Own Worst Enemy: The Unmaking of American Foreign Policy* (New York: Simon & Schuster, 1984), pp 115-116.

4. Joan Biskupic, "Constitution's Conflicting Clauses Underscored by Iraqi Crisis," *Congressional Quarterly,* January 5, 1991, p. 34.

5. Ronald D. Elving, "America's Most Frequent Fight Has Been the Undeclared War," *Congressional Quarterly,* January 5, 1991, p. 37.

6. Rep. Toby Roth (R-Wis.), quoted in Katharine Q. Seelye, "House Defeats Bid to Repeal 'War Powers'," *New York Times,* June 11, 1995, p. A7.

7. Barry B. Hughes, *The Domestic Context of American Foreign Policy* (San Francisco: W. H. Freeman, 1978), chapter 5.

8. Robert Weissberg, *Public Opinion and Popular Government* (New York: Prentice-Hall, 1976).

9. Raymond Bonner, "Azerbaijanis Try to Learn English Under U.S. Handicap," *New York Times,* February 19, 1995, p. 6.

10. Information in this paragraph is based on Jeff Gerth with Sarah Bartlett, "Kissinger and Friends and Revolving Doors," *New York Times,* April 30, 1989, p. 1ff.

11. For a discussion of the foreign policy establishment, see Walter Isaacson and Evan Thomas, *The Wise Men: Six Friends and the World They Made* (New York: Simon & Schuster, 1986).

12. Bruce Russett, *The Prisoners of Insecurity* (San Francisco: W. H. Freeman, 1983).

13. See James Nathan and James Oliver, *United States Foreign Policy and World Order,* 2nd ed. (Boston: Little Brown, 1981), pp. 359–61.

14. Robert S. McNamara, *In Retrospect: The Tragedy and Lessons of Vietnam* (New York: Times Books, 1995).

15. Robert Weissberg, *Public Opinion and Popular Government,* pp. 144–48.

16. Ole Holsti, "The Three-Headed Eagle," *International Studies Quarterly 23* (September 1979), pp. 339–59; Michael Mandelbaum and William Schneider, "The New Internationalisms," in Kenneth Oye, Donald Rothchild, and Robert J. Lieber, eds., *The Eagle Entangled: U.S. Foreign Policy in a Complex World* (New York: Longman, 1979), pp. 34–88.

17. For an analysis of U.S.-Soviet relations in the Reagan era, see Alexander Dallin and Gail Lapidus, "Reagan and the Russians," in Kenneth Oye, Robert Lieber, and Donald Rothchild, eds, *Eagle Resurgent?* (Boston: Little Brown, 1987); Kenneth Oye, "Constrained Confidence and the Evolution of Reagan Foreign Policy," in Oye, Lieber, and Rothchild, eds., *Eagle Resurgent?;* John Newhouse. "The Abolitionist," Parts 1 and 2, *New Yorker,* January 2 and 9, 1989.

18. See George F. Kennan, "After the Cold War," *New York Times Magazine,* February 5, 1989, pp. 32ff.

19. Bill Clinton, "A Democrat Lays out His Plan," *Harvard International Review,* Summer, 1992.

20. Quoted in Thomas Friedman, "What Big Stick? Just Sell," *New York Times,* October 2, 1995, p. E3.

21. Ibid.

22. Elaine Sciolino, "Monroe's Doctrine Takes Another Knock," *New York Times,* August 7, 1994, p. E6. For a discussion of the U.S. turn to multilateralism see Stanley Hoffmann, "The Crisis of Liberal Internationalism," *Foreign Policy* 98 (Spring, 1995) pp. 159–177.

23. Mathew I. Wald, "Today's Drama: Twilight of the Nukes," *New York Times,* July 16, 1995, p. E5. A slightly lower estimate of the costs of nuclear preparedness can be found in David C. Morrison, "Putting a Price Tag on the Arms Race," *National Journal,* May 13, 1995, p. 1171.

24. Lawrence J. Korb, "The Readiness Gap. What Gap?" *New York Times Magazine,* February 26, 1995, pp. 40–41 (Korb was an assistant secretary of defense in the Reagan administration); David C. Morrison, "Ready for What," *National Journal,* May 20, 1995, pp. 1218–1222.

25. Rep. David R. Obey, quoted by Eric Schmitt, "Pentagon's Bargains (Extra Cost for War)," *New York Times,* February 12, 1995, p. 12; David C. Morrison, "Defense Deadlock," *National Journal,* February 4, 1995, p. 279.

26. *U.S. Budget for Fiscal 1996* (Washington, DC: Government Printing Office, 1995) p. 121.

27. Daniel Williams, "Clinton Stretches Partnership to Fit All," *Washington Post National Weekly Edition,* January 24–30, 1994, p. 17; "Russia, NATO Make History with Accord," *Lincoln Star,* June 23, 1994, p. 1.

28. Quoted in David E. Sanger, "Corrosion at the Core of Pax Pacifica," *New York Times,* May 14, 1995, Sect. 4, p. 1; Nicholas D. Kristof, "Drawing a Line in the Pacific," *New York Times,* July 16, 1995, p. E4; James Sterngold, "Some Leaders in Japan Begin to Question U.S. Bases," *New York Times,* August 28, 1994, p. 7.

29. Cited in "Still No Policy on Arms Sales," *New York Times,* April 3, 1994, op-ed page.

30. David E. Sanger, "Foreign Relations: Money Talks, Policy Walks," *New York Times,* January 15, 1995, Sect. 4, p. 1.

31. Joan Spero, an undersecretary of state, quoted in David E. Sanger, "How Washington Inc. Makes a Sale," *New York Times,* February 19, 1995, Sect. 3, p. 1.

32. Alan Binder, *Hard Heads, Soft Hearts* (New York: Addison-Wesley, 1988).

33. "What Am I Bid for This Fine Quota?" *Time,* March 16, 1987, p. 59; "The Battle Over Barriers," *Time,* October 7, 1985, pp. 22–35.

34. For a concise summary of the advantages and disadvantages of protectionism and free trade, see Paul Krugman, *The Age of Diminished Expectations* (Cambridge, Mass.: MIT Press, 1992), pp. 101–113.

35. David E. Sanger, "64% of Japanese Say U.S. Relations are 'Unfriendly,' " *New York Times,* July 6, 1993, pp. 1, 6.

36. Sanger, p. 6.

37. Gary Clyde Hufbauer and Jeffrey J. Schott, with Kimberly Ann Elliot, *Economic Sanctions Reconsidered: History and Current Policy.* (Washington, DC: Institute for International Economics, 1985), p. 10.

38. Ibid, p. 80.

39. Quoted by Steven Greenhouse, "U.S. View of Sanctions: Turn Up Heat Half Way," *New York Times,* July 3, 1994.

40. *MacNeil/Lehrer Newshour,* December 26, 1994, transcript #5127, pp. 2–3.

41. Steven Greenhouse, "Poor Nations Get Unspecified Pledge of More Aid," *New York Times,* September 16, 1990, p. 4.

42. See Pedro-Pablo Kuczynski, "Latin American Debt," *Foreign Affairs* 61 (Winter 1982–83), pp. 344–64.

43. Anthony Lewis, "Reagan Doctrine is Corrupting Institutions," *Lincoln Star,* April 27, 1987.

APPENDIX A

The Declaration of Independence*

In Congress, July 4, 1776.

A Declaration by the Representatives of the United States of America, in General Congress assembled.

When in the Course of human Events, it becomes necessary for one People to dissolve the Political Bonds which have connected them with another, and to assume among the Powers of the Earth, the separate and equal Station to which the Laws of Nature and of Nature's God entitle them, a decent Respect to the Opinions of Mankind requires that they should declare the causes which impel them to the Separation.

We hold these Truths to be self-evident, that all Men are created equal, that they are endowed by their Creator with certain unalienable Rights, that among these are Life, Liberty, and the Pursuit of Happiness—That to secure these Rights, Governments are instituted among Men, deriving their just Powers from the Consent of the Governed, that whenever any Form of Government becomes destructive of these Ends, it is the Right of the People to alter or to abolish it, and to institute new Government, laying its Foundation on such Principles, and organizing its Powers in such Forms, as to them shall seem most likely to effect their Safety and Happiness. Prudence, indeed, will dictate that Governments long established should not be changed for light and transient Causes; and accordingly all Experience hath shewn, that Mankind are more disposed to suffer, while Evils are sufferable, than to right themselves by abolishing the Forms to which they are accustomed. But when a long Train of Abuses and Usurpations, pursuing invariably the same Object, evinces a Design to reduce them under absolute Despotism, it is their Right, it is their Duty, to throw off such Government, and to provide new Guards for their future Security. Such has been the patient Sufferance of these Colonies; and such is now the Necessity which constrains them to alter their former Systems of Government. The History of the present King of Great Britain is a History of repeated Injuries and Usurpations, all having in direct Object the Establishment of an absolute Tyranny over these States. To prove this, let facts be submitted to a candid World.

He has refused his Assent to Laws, the most wholesome and necessary for the public Good.

He has forbidden his Governors to pass Laws of immediate and pressing Importance, unless suspended in their Operation till his Assent should be obtained; and when so suspended, he has utterly neglected to attend to them.

He has refused to pass other Laws for the Accommodation of large Districts of People, unless those People would relinquish the Right of Representation in the Legislature, a Right inestimable to them, and formidable to Tyrants only.

He has called together Legislative Bodies at Places unusual, uncomfortable, and distant from the Depository of their Public Records, for the sole Purpose of fatiguing them into Compliance with his Measures.

He has dissolved Representative Houses repeatedly, for opposing with manly Firmness his Invasions on the Rights of the People.

He has refused for a long Time, after such Dissolutions, to cause others to be elected; whereby the Legislative Powers, incapable of Annihilation, have returned to the People at large for their exercise; the State remaining in the mean time exposed to all the Dangers of Invasion from without, and Convulsions within.

He has endeavoured to prevent the Population of these States; for that Purpose obstructing the Laws for Naturalization of Foreigners; refusing to pass others to encourage their Migration hither, and raising the Conditions of new Appropriations of Lands.

He has obstructed the Administration of Justice, by refusing his Assent to Laws for establishing Judiciary Powers.

He has made Judges dependent on his Will alone, for the Tenure of their offices, and the Amount and payments of their Salaries.

He has erected a Multitude of new Offices, and sent hither Swarms of Officers to harass our People, and eat out their Substance.

*The spelling, capitalization, and punctuation of the original have been retained here.

into different degrees of activity, according to the different circumstances of civil society. A zeal for different opinions concerning religion, concerning government, and many other points, as well of speculation as of practice; an attachment to different leaders ambitiously contending for pre-eminence and power; or to persons of other descriptions whose fortunes have been interesting to the human passions, have, in turn, divided mankind into parties, inflamed them with mutual animosity, and rendered them much more disposed to vex and oppress each other than to cooperate for their common good. So strong is this propensity of mankind to fall into mutual animosities that where no substantial occasion presents itself the most frivolous and fanciful distinctions have been sufficient to kindle their unfriendly passions and excite their most violent conflicts. But the most common and durable source of factions has been the verious and unequal distribution of property. Those who hold and those who are without property have ever formed distinct interests in society. Those who are creditors, and those who are debtors, fall under a like discrimination. A landed interest, a manufacturing interest, a mercantile interest, a moneyed interest, with many lesser interests, grow up of necessity in civilized nations, and divide them into different classes, actuated by different sentiments and views. The regulation of these various and interfering interests forms the principal task of modern legislation and involves the spirit of party and faction in the necessary and ordinary operations of government.

No man is allowed to be a judge in his own cause, because his interest would certainly bias his judgment, and, not improbably, corrupt his integrity. With equal, nay with greater reason, a body of men are unfit to be both judges and parties at the same time; yet what are many of the most important acts of legislation but so many judicial determinations, not indeed concerning the rights of single persons, but concerning the rights of large bodies of citizens? And what are the different classes of legislators but advocates and parties to the causes which they determine? Is a law proposed concerning private debts? It is a question to which the creditors are parties on one side and the debtors on the other. Justice ought to hold the balance between them. Yet the parties are, and must be, themselves the judges; and the most numerous party, or in other words, the most powerful faction must be expected to prevail. Shall domestic manufacturers be encouraged, and in what degree, by restrictions on foreign manufacturers? are questions which would be differently decided by the landed and the manufacturing classes, and probably by neither with a sole regard to justice and the public good. The apportionment of taxes on the various descriptions of property is an act which seems to require the most exact impartiality; yet there is, perhaps, no legislative act in which greater opportunity and temptation are given to a predominant party to trample on the rules of justice. Every shilling with which they overburden the inferior number is a shilling saved to their own pockets.

It is in vain to say that enlightened statesmen will be able to adjust these clashing interests and render them all subservient to the public good. Enlightened statesmen will not always be at the helm. Nor, in many cases, can such an adjustment be made at all without taking into view indirect and remote considerations, which will rarely prevail over the immediate interest which one party may find in disregarding the rights of another or the good of the whole.

The inference to which we are brought is that the *causes* of faction cannot be removed and that relief is only to be sought in the means of controlling its *effects.*

If a faction consists of less than a majority, relief is supplied by the republican principle, which enables the majority to defeat its sinister views by regular vote. It may clog the administration, it may convulse the society; but it will be unable to execute and mask its violence under the forms of the Constitution. When a majority is included in a faction, the form of popular government, on the other hand, enables it to sacrifice to its ruling passion or interest both the public good and the rights of other citizens. To secure the public good and private rights against the danger of such a faction, and at the same time to preserve the spirit and the form of popular government, is then the great object to which our inquiries are directed. Let me add that it is the great desideratum by which alone this form of government can be rescued from the opprobrium under which it has so long labored and be recommended to the esteem and adoption of mankind.

By what means is this object attainable? Evidently by one of two only. Either the existence of the same passion or interest in a majority at the same time must be prevented, or the majority, having such coexistent passion or interest, must be rendered, by their number and local situtation, unable to concert and carry into effect schemes of oppression. If the impulse and the opportunity be suffered to coincide, we well know that neither moral nor religious motives can be relied on as an adequate control. They are not found to be such on the injustice and violence of individuals, and lose their efficacy in proportion to the number combined together, that is, in proportion as their efficacy becomes needful.

From this view of the subject it may be concluded that a pure democracy, by which I mean a society consisting of a small number of citizens, who assemble and administer the government in person, can admit of no cure for the mischiefs of faction. A common passion or interest will, in almost every case, be felt by a majority of the whole; a communication and concert results from the form of government itself; and there is nothing to check the inducements to sacrifice the weaker party or an obnoxious individual. Hence it is that such democracies have ever been spectacles of turbulence and contention; have ever been found incompatible with personal security or the rights of property; and have in general been as short in their lives as they have been violent in their deaths. Theoretic politicians, who have patronized this species of government, have erroneously supposed that by reducing mankind to a perfect equality in their political rights, they would at the same time be perfectly equalized and assimilated in their possessions, their opinions, and their passions.

A republic, by which I mean a government in which the scheme of representation takes place, opens a different prospect and promises the cure for which we are seeking. Let us examine the points in which it varies from pure democracy, and we shall comprehend both the nature of the cure and the efficacy which it must derive from the Union.

The two great points of difference between a democracy and a republic are: first, the delegation of the government, in the latter, to a small number of citizens elected by the rest; secondly, the greater number of citizens and greater sphere of country over which the latter may be extended.

The effect of the first difference is, on the one hand, to refine and enlarge the public views by passing them through the medium of a chosen body of citizens, whose wisdom may best discern the true interest of their country and whose patriotism and love of justice will be least likely to sacrifice it to temporary or partial considerations. Under such a regulation it may well happen that the public voice, pronounced by the representatives of the people, will be more consonant to the public good than if pronounced by the people themselves, convened for the purpose. On the other hand, the effect may be inverted. Men of factious tempers, of local prejudices, or of sinister designs, may, by intrigue, by corruption, or by other means, first obtain the suffrages, and then betray the interests of the people. The question resulting is, whether small or extensive republics are most favorable to the election of proper guardians of the public weal; and it is clearly decided in favor of the latter by two obvious considerations.

In the first place it is to be remarked that however small the republic may be the representatives must be raised to a certain number in order to guard against the cabals of a few; and that however large it may be they must be limited to a certain number in order to guard against the confusion of a multitude. Hence, the number of representatives in the two cases not being in proportion to that of the constituents, and being proportionally greatest in the small republic, it follows that if the proportion of fit characters be not less in the large than in the small republic, the former will present a greater option, and consequently a greater probability of a fit choice.

In the next place, as each representative will be chosen by a greater number of citizens in the large than in the small republic, it will be more difficult for unworthy candidates to practice with success the vicious arts by which elections are too often carried; and the suffrages of the people being more free, will be more likely to center on men who possess the most attractive merit and the most diffusive and established characters.

It must be confessed that in this, as in most other cases, there is a mean, on both sides of which inconveniencies will be found to lie. By enlarging too much the number of electors, you render the representative too little acquainted with all their local circumstances and lesser interests; as by reducing it too much, you render him unduly attached to these, and too little fit to comprehend and pursue great and national objects. The federal Constitution forms a happy combination in this respect; the great and aggregate interests being referred to the national, the local and particular to the State legislatures.

The other point of difference is the greater number of citizens and extent of territory which may be brought within the compass of republican than of democratic government; and it is this circumstance principally which renders factious combinations less to be dreaded in the former than in the latter. The smaller the society, the fewer probably will be the distinct parties and interests composing it; the fewer the distinct parties and interests, the more frequently will a majority be found of the same party; and the smaller the number of individuals composing a majority, and the smaller the compass within which they are placed, the more easily will they concert and execute their plans of oppression. Extend the sphere and you take in a greater variety of parties and interests; you make it less probable that a majority of the whole will have a common motive to invade the rights of other citizens; or if such a common motive exists, it will be more difficult for all who feel it to discover their own strength and to act in unison with each other. Besides other impediments, it may be remarked that, where there is a consciousness of unjust or dishonorable purposes, communication is always checked by distrust in proportion to the number whose concurrence is necessary.

Hence, it clearly appears that the same advantage which a republic has over a democracy in controlling the effects of faction is enjoyed by a large over a small republic—is enjoyed by the Union over the States composing it. Does this advantage consist in the substitution of representatives whose enlightened views and virtuous sentiments render them superior to local prejudices and to schemes of injustice? It will not be denied that the representation of the Union will be most likely to possess these requisite endowments. Does it consist in the greater security afforded by a greater variety of parties, against the event of any one party being able to outnumber and oppress the rest? In an equal degree does the increased variety of parties comprised within the Union increase this security. Does it, in fine, consist in the greater obstacles opposed to the concert and accomplishment of the secret wishes of an unjust and interested majority? Here again the extent of the Union gives it the most palpable advantage.

The influence of factious leaders may kindle a flame within their particular States but will be unable to spread a general conflagration through the other States. A religious sect may degenerate into a political faction in a part of the Confederacy; but the variety of sects dispersed over the entire face of it must secure the national councils against any danger from that source. A rage for paper money, for an abolition of debts, for an equal division of property, or for any other improper or wicked project, will be less apt to pervade the whole body of the Union than a particular member of it, in the same proportion as such a malady is more likely to taint a particular county or district than an entire State.

In the extent and proper structure of the Union, therefore, we behold a republican remedy for the diseases most incident to republican government. And according to the degree of pleasure and pride we feel in being republicans ought to be our zeal in cherishing the spirit and supporting the character of federalists.

APPENDIX D

Federalist Paper #51

To what expedient, then, shall we finally resort, for maintaining in practice the necessary partition of power among the several departments as laid down in the Constitution? The only answer that can be given is that as all these exterior provisions are found to be inadequate the defect must be supplied, by so contriving the interior structure of the government as that its several constituent parts may, by their mutual relations, be the means of keeping each other in their proper places. Without presuming to undertake a full development of this important idea I will hazard a few general observations which may perhaps place it in a clearer light, and enable us to form a more correct judgment of the principles and structure of the government planned by the convention.

In order to lay a due foundation for that separate and distinct exercise of the different powers of government, which to a certain extent is admitted on all hands to be essential to the preservation of liberty, it is evident that each department should have a will of its own; and consequently should be so constituted that the members of each should have as little agency as possible in the appointment of the members of the others. Were this principle rigorously adhered to, it would require that all the appointments for the supreme executive, legislative, and judiciary magistracies should be drawn from the same fountain of authority, the people, through channels having no communication whatever with one another. Perhaps such a plan of constructing the several departments would be less difficult in practice than it may in contemplation appear. Some difficulties, however, and some additional expense would attend the execution of it. Some deviations, therefore, from the principle must be admitted. In the constitution of the judiciary department in particular, it might be inexpedient to insist rigorously on the principle: first, because peculiar qualifications being essential in the members, the primary consideration ought to be to select that mode of choice which best secures these qualifications; second, because the permanent tenure by which the appointments are held in that department must soon destroy all sense of dependence on the authority conferring them.

It is equally evident that the members of each department should be as little dependent as possible on those of the others for the emoluments annexed to their offices. Were the executive magistrate, or the judges, not independent of the legislature in this particular, their independence in every other would be merely nominal.

But the great security against a gradual concentration of the several powers in the same department consists in giving to those who administer each department the necessary constitutional means and personal motives to resist encroachments of the others. The provision for defense must in this, as in all other cases, be made commensurate to the danger of attack. Ambition must be made to counteract ambition. The interest of the man must be connected with the constitutional rights of the place. It may be a reflection on human nature that such devices should be necessary to control the abuses of government. But what is government itself but the greatest of all reflections on human nature? If men were angels, no government would be necessary. If angels were to govern men, neither external nor internal controls on government would be necessary. In framing a government which is to be administered by men over men, the great difficulty lies in this: you must first enable the government to control the governed; and in the next place oblige it to control itself. A dependence on the people is, no doubt, the primary control on the government; but experience has taught mankind the necessity of auxiliary precautions.

This policy of supplying, by opposite and rival interests, the defect of better motives, might be traced through the whole system of human affairs, private as well as public. We see it particularly displayed in all the subordinate distributions of power, where the constant aim is to divide and arrange the several offices in such a manner as that each may be a check on the other—that the private interest of every individual may be a sentinel over the public rights. These inventions of prudence cannot be less requisite in the distribution of the supreme powers of the State.

But it is not possible to give to each department an equal power of self-defense. In republican government, the legislative authority necessarily predominates. The remedy for this inconveniency is to divide the legislature into different branches; and to render them, by different modes of election and different principles of action, as little connected with each other as the nature of their common functions and their common dependence on the society will admit. It may even be necessary to guard against dangerous encroachments by still further precautions. As the weight of the legislative authority requires that it should be thus divided, the weakness of the executive may require, on the other hand, that it should be fortified. An absolute negative on the legislature appears, at first view, to be the natural defense with which the executive magistrate should be armed. But perhaps it would be neither altogether safe nor alone sufficient. On ordinary occasions it might not be exerted with the requisite firmness, and on extraordinary occasions it might be perfidiously abused. May not this defect of an absolute negative be supplied by some qualified connection between this weaker department and the weaker branch of the stronger department, by which the latter may be led to support the constitutional rights of the former, without being too much detached from the rights of its own department?

If the principles on which these observations are found be just, as I persuade myself they are, and they be applied as a criterion to the several State constitutions, and the federal Constitution, it will be found that if the latter does not perfectly correspond with them, the former are infinitely less able to bear such a test.

There are, moreover, two considerations particularly applicable to the federal system of America, which place that system in a very interesting point of view.

First. In a single republic, all the power surrendered by the people is submitted to the administration of a single government; and the usurpations are guarded against by a division of the government into distinct and separate departments. In the compound republic of America, the power surrendered by the people is first divided between two distinct governments, and then the portion allotted to each subdivided among distinct and separate departments. Hence a double security arises to the rights of the people. The different governments will control each other, at the same time that each will be controlled by itself.

Second. It is of great importance in a republic not only to guard the society against the oppression of its rulers, but to guard one part of the society against the injustice of the other part. Different interests necessarily exist in different classes of citizens. If a majority be united by a common interest, the rights of the minority will be insecure. There are but two methods of providing against this evil: the one by creating a will in the community independent of the majority—that is, of the society itself; the other, by comprehending in the society so many separate descriptions of citizens as will render an unjust combination of a majority of the whole very improbable, if not impracticable. The first method prevails in all governments possessing an hereditary or self-appointed authority. This, at best, is but a precarious security; because a power independent of the society may as well espouse the unjust views of the major as the rightful interests of the minor party, and may possibly be turned against both parties. The second method will be exemplified in the federal republic of the United States. Whilst all authority in it will be derived from and dependent on the society, the society itself will be broken into so many parts, interests and classes of citizens, that the rights of individuals, or of the minority, will be in little danger from interested combinations of the majority. In a free government the security for civil rights must be the same as that for religious rights. It consists in the one case in the multiplicity of interests, and in the other in the multiplicity of sects. The degree of security in both cases will depend on the number of interests and sects; and this may be presumed to depend on the extent of country and number of people comprehended under the same government. This view of the subject must particularly recommend a proper federal system to all the sincere and considerate friends of republican government, since it shows that in exact proportion as the territory of the Union may be formed into more circumscribed Confederacies, or States, oppressive combinations of a majority will be facilitated; the best security, under the republican forms, for the rights of every class of citizen, will be diminished; and consequently the stability and independence of some member of the government, the only other security, must be proportionally increased. Justice is the end of government. It is the end of civil society. It ever has been and ever will be pursued until it be obtained, or until liberty be lost in the pursuit. In a society under the forms of which the stronger faction can readily unite and oppress the weaker, anarchy may as truly be said to reign as in a state of nature, where the weaker individual is not secured against the violence of the stronger; and as, in the latter state, even the stronger individuals are prompted, by the uncertainty of their condition, to submit to a government which may protect the weak as well as themselves; so, in the former state, will the more powerful factions or parties be gradually induced, by a like motive, to wish for a government which will protect all parties, the weaker as well as the more powerful. It can be little doubted that if the State of Rhode Island was separated from the Confederacy and left to itself, the insecurity of rights under the popular form of government within such narrow limits would be displayed by such reiterate oppressions of factious majorities that some power altogether independent of the people would soon be called for by the voice of the very factions whose misrule had proved the necessity of it. In the extended republic of the United States, and among the great variety of interests, parties, and sects which it embraces, a coalition of a majority of the whole society could seldom take place on any other principles than those of justice and the general good; whilst there being thus less danger to a minor from the will of a major party, there must be less pretext, also, to provide for the security of the former, by introducing into the government a will not dependent on the latter, or, in other words, a will independent of the society itself. It is no less certain than it is important, notwithstanding the contrary opinions which have been entertained, that the larger the society, provided it lie within a practicable sphere, the more duly capable it will be of self-government. And happily for the *republican cause,* the practicable sphere may be carried to a very great extent by a judicious modification and mixture of the *federal principle.*

Contras Rebels who have fought to overthrow the Sandinista government of Nicaragua.

Cost overruns The amount by which the cost of a certain project exceeds the expected cost.

Cost-plus project A project for which the contractor is reimbursed for all of its costs in addition to a set, agreed-upon profit rate.

Credentials committee A body responsible for examining the credentials of political convention delegates.

Cuban Missile Crisis The 1962 stand-off between the United States and the Soviet Union over an offensive missile build-up in Cuba. The Soviets finally agreed to remove all the missiles from Cuban soil.

Deficit A condition in which expenditures exceed revenues.

Demagogue A leader who obtains political power by appealing to the emotions and biases of the populace.

Departments Executive divisions of the federal government, such as the Departments of Defense and Labor, each headed by a cabinet officer.

Direct lobbying Direct personal encounters between lobbyists and the public officials they are attempting to influence.

Dixiecrat A member of a group of southern segregationist Democrats who formed the States' Rights Party in 1948.

Education Amendments of 1972 These forbid discrimination on the basis of sex in schools and colleges that receive federal aid.

Empirical approach In political science, the attempt to describe politics and government as they are, rather than how they should be. Compare **normative approach.**

Equal Credit Opportunity Act This act forbids discrimination on the basis of sex or marital status in credit transactions.

Equal Employment Opportunity Commission (EEOC) The EEOC enforces the Civil Rights Act of 1964, which forbids discrimination on the basis of sex or race in hiring, promotion and firing.

Exit polls Election-day poll of voters leaving the polling places, conducted mainly by television networks and major newspapers.

Federal Communication Commission (FCC) A regulatory agency that controls interstate and foreign communication via radio, television, telegraph, telephone, and cable. The FCC licenses radio and television stations.

Federal Election Commission Created in 1975, the commission enforces federal laws on campaign financing.

Federal Register A government publication describing bureaucratic actions and detailing regulations proposed by government agencies.

Federal Reserve Board Created by Congress in 1913, the board regulates the lending practices of banks and plays a major role in determining monetary policy.

Felonies Crimes considered more serious than misdemeanors, and carrying more stringent punishment.

Fifteenth Amendment An amendment to the Constitution, ratified in 1870, which prohibits denying voting rights on the basis of race, color or previous condition of servitude.

Fixed-cost project A project that a contractor has agreed to undertake for a specified sum.

Frontrunners Candidates whom political pros and the media have portrayed as likely winners.

Fundraiser An event, such as a luncheon or cocktail party, hosted by a legislator or candidate for which participants pay an entrance fee.

Gender gap An observable pattern of modest but consistent differences in opinion between men and women on various public policy issues.

GOP Grand Old Party or Republican Party, which formed in 1856 after the Whig Party split. The GOP was abolitionist and a supporter of the Union.

Grace Commission A special commission established by President Reagan to recommend ways of cutting government waste.

Grand jury A jury of citizens who meet in private session to evaluate accusations in a given criminal case and to determine if there is enough evidence to warrant a trial.

Grass roots lobbying The mass mobilization of members of an interest group to apply pressure to public officials, usually in the form of a mass mailing.

Honoraria Legal payments made to legislators who speak before special interest groups or other groups of citizens.

ICBM Intercontinental ballistic missiles, or land-based missiles.

Impeachment and removal A two-step process by which Congress may remove presidents, judges, and other civil officers accused of malfeasance. The House decides questions of impeachment; if a majority favors impeachment, the Senate decides whether to remove the accused from office.

Imperial presidency A term that came into use at the end of the 1960s to describe the growing power of the presidency.

Impoundment A refusal by the president to spend money appropriated by Congress for a specific program.

Incrementalism A congressional spending pattern in which budgets usually increase slightly from year to year.

Independent A voter who is not aligned with any political party.

Independent expenditures Campaign contributions made on behalf of issues or candidates, but not made directly to candidates or political parties.

Indirect lobbying Attempts to influence legislators through such non-traditional means as letter-writing campaigns.

Individualistic political culture One of three primary political cultures in the United States. One in which politics is seen as a way of getting ahead, of obtaining benefits for oneself or one's group, and in which corruption is tolerated. See **moralistic** and **traditionalistic** political cultures.

Industrial policy A strategy that calls for an active government role in improving a nation's economy and its competitiveness in world markets.

Injunction A court order demanding that a person or group perform a specific act or refrain from performing a specific act.

Inquisition A medieval institution of the Roman Catholic Church used to identify and punish heretics.

Institutional approach An investigation of government that focuses on institutions, such as Congress or the civil service, and their rules and procedures.

Investigative reporting In-depth news reporting, particularly that which exposes corruption and wrongdoing on the part of government officials and big institutions.

Issue consistency The extent to which individuals who identify themselves as "liberal" or "conservative" take issue positions that reflect their professed leanings.

Issue voting Refers to citizens who vote for candidates whose stands on specific issues are consistent with their own.

Jeffersonian Republicans (Jeffersonians) Opponents of a strong national government. They challenged the **Federalists** in the early years of the Republic.

Joint resolutions Measures that have the force of law and must be approved by both houses of Congress and signed by the president.

Justices of the peace Magistrates at the lowest level of some state court systems, responsible mainly for acting on minor offenses and committing cases to higher courts for trial.

Kitchen cabinet A group of informal advisers, usually longtime associates, who assist the president on public policy questions.

Know-Nothing Party An extreme right-wing party in mid-nineteenth-century America that opposed Catholics and immigrants.

Lame duck An officeholder, legislature or administration that has lost an election but holds power until the inauguration of a successor.

Landslide An election won by a candidate who receives an overwhelming majority of the votes, such as more than a ten-point gap.

Legislative calendar An agenda or calendar containing the names of all bills or resolutions of a particular type to be considered by committees or either legislative chamber.

Line-item veto A proposal that would give a president the power to veto one or more provisions of a bill while allowing the remainder of the bill to become law.

Litigation Legal action.

Mandamus, writ of A court order demanding government officials or a lower court to perform a specified duty.

Marble cake federalism The idea that different levels of government work together in carrying out policies; governments are intermixed, as in a marble cake.

McGovern-Fraser Commission A commission formed after 1968 by the Democratic Party to consider changes making convention delegates more representative of all Democratic voters.

Minimum tax A proposed tax that would require corporations and individuals with high incomes to pay a certain minimum amount in federal taxes.

MIRV Stands for multiple independently targeted reentry vehicles; an offensive missile system that uses a single rocket to launch a number of warheads, each of which could be aimed at a different target.

Misdemeanors Crimes of less seriousness than felonies, ordinarily punishable by fine or imprisonment in a local rather than a state institution.

Missouri Compromise of 1820 A set of laws by which Congress attempted to control slavery in the territories, maintaining the balance between slave and nonslave states.

Mixed economies Countries that incorporate elements of both capitalist and socialist practices in the workings of their economies.

Moralistic political culture One of three political cultures in the United States. One in which people feel obligated to take part in politics to bring about change for the better, and in which corruption is not tolerated. See **individualistic** and **traditionalistic** political cultures.

Nader's Raiders The name given to people who work in any of the "public interest" organizations founded by consumer advocate and regulatory watchdog Ralph Nader.

National chair The head of a political party organization, appointed by the national committee of that party, usually at the direction of the party's presidential nominee.

National Organization for Women (NOW) A group formed in 1966 to fight primarily for political and economic rights for women.

New Deal Coalition The broadly based coalition of southern conservatives, northern liberals and ethnic and religious minorities that sustained the Democratic Party for some 40 years.

News release A printed handout given by public relations workers to members of the media, offering ideas or information for new stories.

Nineteenth Amendment An amendment to the Constitution, ratified in 1920, guaranteeing women the vote.

Normative approach An approach by which political scientists consider how people *should* behave with regard to political matters, as opposed to an **empirical approach.**

Nullification A doctrine advocated by supporters of state-centered federalism, holding that a state could nullify laws of Congress.

Obstruction of justice A deliberate attempt to impede the progress of a criminal investigation or trial.

Occupational Safety and Health Administration (OSHA) An agency formed in 1970 and charged with ensuring safe and healthful working conditions for all American workers.

Office of Management and Budget (OMB) A White House agency with primary responsibility for preparing the federal budget.

Overlapping membership The term refers to the tendency of individuals to join more than one group. This tends to moderate a group's appeals, since its members also belong to other groups with different interests.

Parliamentary democracy A system in which voters elect only their representatives in parliament; the chief executive is chosen by parliament, as in Britain.

Party boss The head of a political "machine," a highly disciplined state or local party organization that controls power in its area.

Party convention A gathering of party delegates, on the local, state or national level, to set policy and strategy and to select candidates for elective office.

Pendleton Act of 1883 This act created the Civil Service Commission, designed to protect civil servants from arbitrary dismissal for political reasons and to staff bureaucracies with people who have proven their competence by taking competitive examinations.

Pentagon Papers A top-secret study, eventually made public, of how and why the United States became embroiled in the **Vietnam War;** the study was commissioned by Secretary of Defense Robert McNamara during the Johnson administration.

Platform committee The group that drafts the policy statement of a political party's convention.

Plebiscite A direct vote by all the people on a certain public measure. Theodore Lowi has spoken of the "Plebiscitary" presidency, whereby the president makes himself the focus of national government through use of the mass media.

Pocket veto A legislative bill dies by pocket veto if a president refuses to sign it and Congress adjourns within ten working days.

Political equality The principle that every citizen of a democracy has an equal opportunity to try to influence government.

Political trust The extent to which citizens place trust in their government, its institutions and its officials.

Precedents In law, judicial decisions that may be used subsequently as standards in similar cases.

Precinct The basic unit of the American electoral process—in a large city perhaps only a few blocks—designed for the administration of elections. Citizens vote in precinct polling places.

Pressure group An organization representing specific interests that seeks some sort of government assistance or attempts to influence public policy. Also known as an "interest group."

Pretrial hearings Preliminary examinations of the cases of persons accused of a crime.

Probable cause In law, reasonable grounds for belief that a particular person has committed a particular crime.

Professional association A **pressure group** that promotes the interests of a professional occupation, such as medicine, law or teaching.

Prohibition Party A political party founded in 1869 that seeks to ban the sale of liquor in the United States.

Public interest A term generally denoting a policy goal, designed to serve the interests of society as a whole, or the largest number of people. Defining the public interest is the subject of intense debate on most issues.

Quorum calls Often used as a delaying tactic, quorum calls are demands that all members of a legislative body be counted to determine if a quorum exists.

"Red Scare" Prompted by the Russian Revolution in 1917, this was a large-scale crackdown on so-called seditious activities in the United States.

Reelection constituency Those individuals a member of Congress believes will vote for him or her. Differs from a geographical, loyalist or personal constituency.

Religious tests Tests once used in some states to limit the right to vote or hold office to members of the "established church."

Responsiveness The extent to which government conforms to the wishes of individuals, groups or institutions.

Right against self-incrimination A right granted by the Fifth Amendment, providing that persons accused of a crime shall not be compelled to be witnesses against themselves.

Sandinistas The name of the group that overthrew Nicaraguan dictator Anastasio Somoza in 1978 and which now governs Nicaragua.

Scientific polls Systematic, probability-based sampling techniques that attempt to gauge public sentiment based on the responses of a small, selected group of individuals.

Senior Executive Service The SES was created in 1978 to attract high-ranking civil servants by offering them challenging jobs and monetary rewards for exceptional achievement.

Sharecroppers Tenant farmers who lease land and equipment from landowners, turning over a share of their crops in lieu of rent.

Shield laws Laws that protect news reporters from having to identify their sources of information.

Social choice An approach to political science based on the assumption that political behavior is determined by costs and benefits.

Social issue An important, non-economic issue affecting significant numbers of the populace, such as crime, racial conflict or changing values.

Special prosecutor A prosecutor charged with investigating and prosecuting alleged violations of federal criminal laws by the president, vice president, senior government officials, members of Congress or the judiciary.

"Star Wars" The popular name for former President Reagan's proposed space-based nuclear defense system, known officially as the Strategic Defense Initiative.

States' rights The belief that the power of the federal government should not be increased at the expense of the states' power.

Statutes Laws passed by the legislative body of a representative government.

Structural unemployment Joblessness that results from the rapidly changing nature of the economy, which displaces, for example, auto and steel industry workers.

Subgovernment A mutually supportive group comprising a **pressure group,** an executive agency and a congressional committee or subcommittee with common policy interests that makes public policy decisions with little interference from the president or Congress as a whole and little awareness by the public. Also known as an iron triangle.

Subpoena A court order requiring someone to appear in court to give testimony under penalty of punishment.

Super-delegates Democratic delegates, one-fifth of the total sent to the national convention who are appointed by Democratic Party organizations, in order to retain some party control over the convention. Most are public officials, such as members of Congress.

Tariff A special tax or "duty" imposed on imported or exported goods.

Tax deductions Certain expenses or payments that may be deducted from one's taxable income.

Tax exemptions Certain amount deductible from one's annual income in calculating income tax.

Third party A political party made up of independents or dissidents from the major parties, often advocating radical change or pushing single issues.

Trade association An interest or **pressure group** that represents a single industry, such as builders.

Traditionalistic political culture One of three political cultures in the United States. One in which politics is left to a small elite and is viewed as a way to maintain the status quo. See **individualistic** and **moralistic** political cultures.

Treason The betrayal of one's country by knowingly aiding its enemies.

Turnout The proportion of eligible citizens who vote in an election.

Unanimous consent agreements Procedures by which a legislative body may dispense with standard rules and limit debate and amendments.

Underdogs Candidates for public office who are thought to have little chance of being elected.

United Nations An international organization formed in 1945 for the purpose of promoting peace and world-wide cooperation. It is headquartered in New York.

Unscientific polls Also known as "straw polls," these are unsystematic samplings of popular sentiments.

Weber, Max German social scientist, author of pioneering studies on the nature of bureaucracies.

Whigs Members of the Whig Party, founded in 1834 by National Republicans and several other factions who opposed Jacksonian Democrats.

Wire services News-gathering organizations such as the Associated Press and United Press International that provide news stories and other editorial features to the media organizations that are their members.

Yuppies Young upwardly mobile professionals.

NAME INDEX

A

Abdnor, James, 263
Abraham, Henry J., 426n, 427n
Abramowitz, Alan I., 325n
Abramowitz, Michael, 519n
Abramson, Paul R., 105n, 107n, 211n
Adams, Abigail, 27
Adams, Brock, 264
Adams, Bruce, 393n
Adams, Charles Francis, 27
Adams, John, 27, 32, 146, 225
  campaign of 1796, 202
  communication with the public, 339
  and development of political parties, 145
  reelection bid, 1808, 400
Adams, John Quincy, 146
  election by the House of Representatives, 84, 196, 198
Adams, Sherman, 343–344
Adatto, Kiku, 246n
Aftergood, Steven, 393n
Agnew, Spiro, 275
  attempt to control the press, 225, 234
  resignation of, 331
Ailes, Roger, 200
Alba, Richard D., 20n
Aldrich, John, 210n, 211n
Alford, John, 211n, 324n, 325n, 584n
Allen, David W., 407n
Allen, Robert L., 411n
Allen, W. B., 48n
Almond, Gabriel A., 20n, 105n, 107n, 138n
Alter, Jonathan, 246n
Altheide, David L., 249n
Altman, Lawrence K., 394n
Alumbaugh, Steve, 426n
Ambrosius, Margery, 73n
Amy, Douglas, 174n
Anderson, Gary, 427n
Anderson, James, 617n
Anderson, John, 155, 195
Anderson, Martin, 552n
Andrews, Edmund L., 246n
Ansolabehere, Stephen, 209n, 210n, 248n, 249n
Anthony, Susan B., 175, 497
Anton, Thomas J., 394n
Apple, R. W., 58n
Appleby, Joyce, 393n
Arafat, Yassir, 655
Archibald, Sam, 393n
Arden, Harvey, 518n
Aristotle, 15
Armey, Richard, 141, 569, 585n
Arterton, F. C., 105n
Asher, Herbert, 106n, 325n
Ashford, Nicholas, 618n
Ayres, Richard, 210n

B

Babbitt, Bruce, 190, 210n, 587–588, 615–616
Babchuk, N., 138n
Babcock, Charles, 266n, 280n
Babson, Jennifer, 280n
Bailey, William C., 459n
Bailyn, Bernard, 48n
Baird, Zoe, 218n
Baker, James, 222, 655
Baldwin, Deborah, 247n
Balz, Dan, 21n, 107n, 139n, 166n
Banducci, Susan, 281n
Banfield, Edward, 552n
Banner, Lois, 209n
Barbash, Fred, 48n, 423n, 427n
Barber, James David, 246n, 247n
Barger, Harold M., 361n
Barlett, Donald L., 585n
Barnes, James A., 210n
Barnet, Richard J., 362n
Barone, Michael, 72n, 324n
Barr, Stephen, 379n
Barrera, M., 518n
Barrett, Laurence I., 154n
Barringer, Felicity, 518n
Barrow, Deborah J., 407n
Barry, Colleen, 517n
Barry, John M., 362n
Bartlett, Sarah, 660n
Baum, Lawrence, 426n, 427n
Bazelon, David, 419
Beard, Charles, 37, 48n
Beaumont, Enid F., 73n
Beck, Paul Allen, 210n
Beckerman, John, 553n
Beckley, Gloria T., 466n
Beeson, Peter, 519n
Begin, Menachim, 654
Behr, Peter, 138n
Behr, Roy, 210n, 248n, 249n
Belknap, Jeremy, 31
Bell, Derrick, 518n
Benenson, Bob, 209n
Benesch, Susan, 519n
Bennet, James, 246n, 247n
Bennett, Linda L. M., 21n
Bennett, Stephen Earl, 21n, 250n
Bennett, W. Lance, 247n
Bennett, William, 365–366
Bentley, Arthur F., 21n
Bentsen, Lloyd
  "faithless elector" vote for, 198
  as Secretary of the Treasury, 648
  as vice-presidential candidate, 194
Berch, Neil, 73n
Berke, Richard L., 183n, 299n
Berkman, Michael, 324n, 325n
Bernstein, Carl, 23, 222
Bernstein, Marver, 394n
Bernstein, Richard, 518n
Berry, Jeffry M., 138n, 139n
Berry, John M., 393n, 585n
Berry, Mary Frances, 518n
Bickel, Alexander, 427n
Biden, Joseph, 309, 330
Bilirakis, Michael, 266
Binder, Alan, 661n
Birkby, Robert H., 467n
Birnbaum, Jeffrey H., 138n, 139n
Biskupic, Joan, 394n, 660n
Black, Earl, 189n
Black, Eric, 48n
Black, Hugo, 433, 434, 448, 454
Black, Merle, 189n
Blackman, Paul, 210n
Blaine, Ellen, 457n
Blake, Robert, 48n
Blanton, Tom, 353n
Bledsoe, Timothy, 20n
Blessing, Tim, 340n
Bluestone, Barry, 585n
Blumberg, Mark, 459n
Blumenthal, Sidney, 139n, 247n
Bobo, L., 106n
Boggs, Thomas H., 129
Boles, Janet, 518n
Boller, Paul F., Jr., 361n
Bollier, David, 618n
Bolz, Don, 281n
Bonafede, Dom, 246n
Bonner, Raymond, 660n
Boodman, Sandra G., 139n, 468n
Booth, William, 467n
Boren, David, 313
Bork, Robert, 24, 427n, 432
  nomination to the Supreme Court, 408
Borrelli, S., 107n
Bosso, C. J., 139n
Boswell, Thomas, 44n
Boucher, Frederick, 266
Boulard, Gary, 517n
Bouvier, Leon, 12n
Bowen, Terry, 427n
Bower, William G., 210n

Bowers, W. J., 459n
Bowman, Carol, 393n
Bowman, William, 247n
Boxer, Barbara, 127, 177
Boyd, Melba Joyce, 411n
Boyd, Richard, 210n
Boyer, E. L., 105n
Bozeman, Barry, 393n
Bradley, Bill, 240
Bradley, Joseph, 501
Bradsher, Keith, 585n, 660n
Brady, David, 617n
Brady, Henry E., 210n, 248n, 249n
Brady, Jim, 219
Branch, Taylor, 135n, 390n
Brandeis, Louis, 419, 456
Brandes, Sara L., 325n
Brandes-Crook, Sara, 326n
Brannon, Laura A., 362n
Bray, Rosemary L., 411n
Brennan, William, 406, 423, 439, 441, 442, 456
Breslin, Jimmy, 279n
Brewer, David, 448
Breyer, Stephen, 291n
  appointment to the Supreme Court, 408
Brezhnev, Leonid, 637
Brinkerhoff, David, 20n
Brinkley, David, 234
Brinkley, Joel, 618n
Broder, David S., 21n, 106n, 138n, 139n, 166n, 167n, 249n, 280n, 281n, 291n, 326n, 585n
Brody, Richard, 210n
Brokaw, Tom, 237
Brown, C., 138n
Brown, Jerry, 90, 169
Brown, John, 266
Brown, Kirk, 281n
Brown, Linda, 478
Brown, R. E., 48n
Brown, Ronald H., 247n, 346
Browner, Carole, 610, 611, 618n
Brownstein, Ronald, 394n
Bruce, Willa, 379n
Bryan, William Jennings, presidential campaign of, 148, 189
Buchanan, Bruce, 249n
Buchanan, Patrick, on immigration, 1991, 11
Buckley, Christopher, 325n
Bullock, Charles, 617n
Bullock, David, 249n
Bumiller, Elisabeth, 210n
Bunning, Jim, 240
Burger, Warren, 24, 46, 403, 423, 455
  appointment of, 480
  decision in Watergate tapes case, 412
Burke, John P., 362n
Burnham, Walter Dean, 166n
Burns, James MacGregor, 48n, 166n, 209n
Burrell, Barbara, 295n
Burstein, Paul, 466n
Bush, Barbara, 90
Bush, George, 52, 90, 92, 102, 124, 185, 220, 298, 329, 336, 352–353, 439, 460, 564–565, 576–577, 625
  campaign of 1988, 196, 200, 201
    debates, 242
  campaign of 1992, 3, 208
    televised debates, 203
  campaign promises, 336
  court appointments of, 406, 409
  economic policy of, 563
  foreign policy style of, 625
    Somalia, 353
  on gays, 185
  knowledge of Ira-Contra, 352
  lobbying Congress during administration of, 337
  nomination of Clarence Thomas to the Supreme Court, 109–110
  Persian Gulf War policy, 351–352
  professional reputation of, 338
  public support for Persian Gulf War policy, 341
  relationship with the media, 227–228
  support of the Clean Air Act (1990), 597
  talk show appearances of, 220
  union support for 1988, 1992, 118
  vetoes by, 349
  as vice-presidential candidate, 194
  vote for, 1988, 199
  on war powers of the president, 628
Byrd, Robert, 311

■ C

Cahalan, Don, 106n
Cain, Bruce E., 174n, 324n
Caldeira, Gregory A., 210n, 427n
Calhoun, John C., 58, 306
Califano, Joseph, 326n
Calle, Jim, 279n
Calvin, John, 215
Cameron, Charles M., 426n
Campagna, Janet, 324n
Campbell, James, 325n
Canassatego, Iroquois chief, 36
Cannon, Angie, 426n
Cannon, Joseph, 306
Cantril, A., 105n, 106n
Caplan, Nathan, 44n
Caplan, Theodore, 72n
Caraway, Hattie, 295
Cardozo, Benjamin, 420
Carlin, George, 437
Carlson, Margaret, 44n, 426n, 467n
Carmines, Edward, 106n
Carney, Eliza Newlin, 259n
Carson, Rachel, 604
Carswell, G. Harold, 407
Carter, Bill, 248n
Carter, Jimmy, 65, 149, 235, 237, 504, 649
  campaign of, 189
    debate with Ford, 242
    debate with Reagan, 203
  on classified documents, 369
  communication with the public, 339
  court appointments of, 409
  and deregulation, 596, 597
  election of, 149
  foreign policy of, 625, 638
  and the Iran crisis, 352
  post-presidential activities of, 625
  Southern vote for, 151
  use of the media, 240
Carville, James, Clinton campaign manager, 1992, 201
Castro, Janice, 503n, 551n
Catt, Carrie Chapman, 176
Chafee, Zechariah, Jr., 465n
Chappell, Henry, Jr., 281n, 584n
Chase, Harold W., 427n
Chavez, Cesar, 493
Chen, Kevom, 209n
Childress, Lisa, 548
Chira, Susan, 517n
Choy, Marcella H., 44n
Chrisman, Robert, 411n
Church, George J., 552n
Cigler, A. J., 138n
Citrin, J., 105n
Clancey, M., 106n
Clancy, Maura, 248n
Clark, Janet, 209n
Clark, Michelle A., 551n
Clark, Tom, 516n
Clarke, Michael, 617n
Clausen, A. R., 105n, 106n
Clawson, Dan, 139n
Clay, Henry, 84, 306
Claybrook, Joan, 618n
Cleveland, Grover, staff of, 343
Clift, Eleanor, 326n
Clinton, Bill, 8, 9, 45, 77, 88, 90, 155, 207–208, 219–220, 223, 235, 274, 299, 329, 332, 336, 460, 461, 468n, 523–525, 577, 583, 642, 661n
  appointments to foreign policy positions, 625
  appointments to the Supreme Court, 408
  campaign, 3–4
    of 1992, 3, 196
    of 1992, strategy, 201, 203
  campaign promises, spending proposals, 555
  on classified documents, 369–370
  communications strategies of, 340
  court appointments of, 409
  deficit reduction plan, 580n
  economic policy, 563
  environmental protection actions of, 615

executive order, on lobbying by former government employees, 386–387
foreign policy of, 351
on the Foster nomination, 360–361
on gays, 185
health care plan, 549–550
health care proposals of, 18
moderation as stance of, 153
National Economic Council of, 349
packaging of, 169–170
popularity of, 341
proposals on health care, 1994, 18
professional reputation of, 338–339
relationship with the media, 219–220, 228–230
responses of Congress to proposals of, 157
support by
for environmental issues, 587–588
for human rights, 622
support for, by gender, 102
vetoes by, 349
Clinton, Hilary Rodham, 127–128, 169, 274, 345, 524–525
Cloud, Stanley W., 249n, 326n
Cloward, Richard A., 209n, 210n
Clymer, Adam, 281n, 340n
Cnudde, Charles F., 585n
Cochran, Clarke E., 552n
Cohen, Felix, 36n
Cohen, Jeffrey, 394n
Cohen, R. E., 325n
Cohen, Richard, 59n, 353n, 517n
Cohen, Steven A., 617n
Cohen, William, 517n
Cohn, Bob, 465n
Coleman, Milton, 247n, 519n
Collins, Glenn, 601n
Compaine, Benjamin M., 246n
Connell, R. W., 105n
Connor, Eugene "Bull", 483
Converse, P. E., 105n
Cook, Timothy E., 105n, 246n, 247n, 249n
Cooke, Alistair, 162n
Coolidge, Calvin, 358
Coombs, Steven Lane, 249n, 250n
Cooper, Kenneth J., 174n, 291n
Copeland, Gary, 552n
Corliss, Richard, 219n, 246n
Cortner, Richard C., 427n
Cose, Ellis, 518n
Costain, A. N., 138–139n
Costain, W. D., 138–139n
Couglin, Charles, on ethnicity and race, 1930s, 11
Cover, Albert D., 426n, 427n
Coverdell, Paul, 124
Cox, Archibald, 24
Crain, W. Mark, 325n
Cranford, John R., 279n
Cranston, Alan, 277
Crawford, William H., 84
Crespi, I., 106n
Crigler, Ann, 249n
Crockett, H. H., Jr., 107n
Cronin, Thomas E., 362n
Cronkite, Walter, 230, 239
Crossette, Barbara, 641n
Crouse, Timothy, 246n
Cruzan, Nancy, 463–464
Cunliffe, Marcus, 241n
Cuomo, Mario, 459
Curran, Tim, 139n
Curtis, James, 44n
Cushman, John H., Jr., 601n, 617n
Cushnie, Peter, 467n

■ D

Dahl, Robert A., 21n
Daley, Richard, 160
D'Amato, Alphonse, 294
Dana, James, Jr., 198n
Danforth, John, 109
Daniels, Lee A., 517n
Danzo, Andrew, 617n
Darcy, Robert, 209n
Dart, Justin, 128
David, Sue, 407n
Davidson, Roger, 324n, 326n
Davis, C., 518n
Davis, David Heard, 613n
Davis, Henry Vance, 411n
Davis, John W., 192
Davis, Patricia, 548n
De Montesquieu, Charles, 37
De Parle, Jason, 552n
de Tocqueville, Alexis, 14, 138n
on Congress, 288
on foreign policy in a democracy, 624
on litigation in the United States, 420
De Witt, Karen, 518n
Dearing, James W., 249n
Deaver, Michael, 226, 238, 249n, 276, 346
Debs, Eugene, 435
Deckard, Barbara Sinclair, 518n
DeClerq, Eugene, 211n
DeConcini, Dennis, 253, 268–269, 277–278
DeCrow, Karen, 518n
Deering, Christopher, 326n
DeFrank, Thomas M., 246n
DeLay, Tom, 141
Delli Carpini, M. A., 105n, 106n
Deloria, Vine, Jr., 518n
Dempsey, Glenn R., 105n, 250n
DeMuth, Jerry, 517n
Dennis, Jack, 105n, 166n
Dent, David J., 411n
Denton, Nancy, 517n
DePauw, Linda Grant, 27n
Desky, Joanne, 379n
Destler, I. M., 660n
Devroy, Ann, 201n, 246n
Dewar, Helen, 281n, 291n, 459n
Dewey, Thomas, election of 1948, 86
Diamond, Edwin, 246n
Dickey, Christopher, 247n
Dimock, Michael A., 281n
Dionne, E. J., Jr., 9n, 21n, 394n
Disraeli, Benjamin, 47–48n
Dockser, Amy, 280n
Dolbeare, Kenneth M., 48n, 466n
Dole, Robert, 259, 271, 300, 360–361, 439, 555
Dometrius, Nelson C., 519n
Donahue, James P., 117n, 553n
Donaldson, Sam, 220
Douglas, William O., 397, 419, 425, 427n, 435, 436, 452, 456
Douglass, Frederick, 177
Dowd, Ann Reilly, 362n
Dowd, Maureen, 211n, 362n
Dower, John W., 426n
Downey, Thomas, 326n
Downs, Anthony, 184, 210n
Drew, Elizabeth, 139n, 246n, 273n, 280n, 281n, 353n, 362n
D'Souza, Dinesh, 505n
DuBois, W. E. B., 477
Ducat, Craig R., 427n
Dudley, Robert L., 427n
Dukakis, Michael, 188, 195–196, 236
campaign of 1988, 201
debate, 242
loss of early lead, 208
vote for, 1988, 199
Duke, Lynne, 44n, 510n, 518n
Dullea, Georgia, 407n
Duncan, Greg J., 552n
Dunn, Patricia, 551n
Durden, Garey, 281n
Duston, Diane, 326n
Duverger, Maurice, 166n
Dye, Thomas R., 21n, 246n

■ E

Eads, George C., 394n, 617n
Eagleburger, Lawrence, 629
Easterbrook, Gregg, 601n, 617n, 618n
Easton, D., 105n
Eckholm, Erik, 552n, 553n
Edsall, Thomas B., 139n, 166n, 205n, 280n, 326n, 510n
Edwards, George C., III, 362n
Edwards, J., 138n
Egan, Timothy, 219n, 617n
Ehrenhalt, Alan, 325n, 326n
Ehrlich, Isaac, 459n
Eich, William, 407n
Eichel, Larry, 617n
Eisendrath, John, 249n

Eisenhower, Dwight D., 63, 246n, 333
on the Communist party, 435
elections of, 149
foreign policy style, 351
on his appointment of Warren to the Supreme Court, 412
on segregation, 478, 479
Supreme Court appointments, 403
vetoes by, 349
Eisinger, Peter, 510n, 519n
Eismeier, Theodore, 280n
Elazar, Daniel, 72n, 209n
Elders, Jocelyn, 329, 330
Elinson, Elaine, 44n
Elliot, Jonathan, 48n
Elliot, Kimberly Ann, 661n
Ellis, David, 394n
Ellison, William, 475
Ellsberg, Daniel, 440
Elving, Ronald D., 660n
Emerson, Thomas J., 465n
England, Robert E., 517n, 518n
Entrum, Robert, 249n
Epstein, Edward Jay, 247n, 248n, 249n
Epstein, Lee, 63n, 139n, 427n
Erbring, Lutz, 249n
Erickson, Robert S., 250n
Erikson, Robert, 324n, 584n
Eskridge, William N., Jr., 427n
Espenshade, Thomas, 12n
Espy, Mike, 276, 330, 346
Estrich, Susan, 467n
Eubanks, Cecil L., 48n
Evans, P. M., 139n
Evers, Medgar, 133
Evers-Williams, Mrylie, 133
Ewing, Thomas W., 601n, 618n
Exon, James, 546
Ezorsky, Gertrude, 519n

F

Fairhall, John, 326n
Fallows, James, 247n, 248n, 250n
Falwell, Jerry, 130
Farhi, Paul, 246n
Farley, Christopher John, 64n, 416n
Farrand, Max, 48n
Feinberg, Lotte E., 393n
Feinstein, Dianne, 177
Feldman, Paul, 325n
Feldman, S., 107n
Fenno, Richard, 324n, 325n, 326n
Fenster, Mark J., 181n
Ferraro, Geraldine, 177, 188
as vice-presidential candidate, 194
Fine, Donald I., 390n
Fineman, Howard, 20n, 246n
Finkelman, Paul, 48n
Fiorina, Morris, 159n, 211n, 325n, 326n
Firebaugh, Glenn, 209n
Fiscus, Ronald J., 510n
Fisher, Louis, 48n, 326n
Fiske, John, 174
Fitzgerald, Ernest, 391, 394n
Fix, Michael, 394n, 617n
Flanagan, T. J., 459n
Flanigan, William, 209n
Fleron, F., Jr., 105n
Foerstel, Herbert N., 390n
Foley, Thomas, 299
Ford, Gerald, 46
attempted assassination of, 441
naming as vice president, 331
presidential debate, 1976, 203, 242
tactics of, in persuading Congress, 337
use of presidential pardon, 357
Foreman, Christoper H., Jr., 138n
Forer, Lois G., 427n
Forrest, Jacqueline Darroch, 457n
Fortas, Abe, 438
Foster, Henry W., Jr., 329, 360–361
Foster, Vincent, 220, 274
Fowler, Linda L., 325n
Fox, J. Ronald, 318n
Fox, Jon, 323
Fraga, Louis R., 518n
Fraley, Colette, 361n, 362n
Frank, Barney, 185
Franklin, Benjamin, 28, 29, 30, 32, 405
Franklin, R. D., 105n
Frantz, Douglas, 468n
Frendreis, John, 281n
Freund, Charles Paul, 210n
Friedan, Betty, 497
Friedman, Thomas, 661n
Friedrich, Otto, 44n, 246n, 468n
Frist, Bill, 298
Fulbright, J. William, 98

G

Gaebler, Ted, 617n
Galanter, Marc, 517n
Galbraith, James, 584n
Gale, Mary Ellen, 443n
Gallagher, Carole, 609n
Gallicchio, Salvatore, 551n
Gallup, George, 86
Gandhi, Mahatma, 482
Gans, Curtis, 209n, 210n
Garay, Ronald, 325n
Gardner, John, 124
Gardner, Robert, 12n
Garfield, James, disability and death in office, 332, 385
Garn, Jake, 254
Garner, John Nance, vice president, 333
Garraty, John A., 426n
Garreau, Joel, 519n
Gelb, Joyce, 518n
Gelb, Leslie H., 353n, 660n
Genaci, Lisa, 519n
Geoghegan, Thomas, 326n
Georges, Christopher, 246n, 247n
Gephardt, Richard, 259
Germond, Jack, 281n
Gerry, Elbridge, 31, 37, 174
Gerth, H. H., 20n, 393n
Gerth, Jeff, 660n
Gibbs, Lois, 617n
Gibbs, Nancy, 503n, 617n
Gideon, Clarence Earl, 454, 455
Gilder, George, 552n
Gilmour, Robert, 393n
Gingrich, Newt, 9, 88, 141, 161, 164–165, 230, 259, 267, 298, 303, 309
Ginsberg, Benjamin, 210n
Ginsburg, Ruth Bader, 291n, 518n
nomination of, 408
Gist, John, 585n
Glaberson, William, 247n, 466n
Gladstone, William, 31
Gladwell, Malcolm, 383n, 468n, 552n
Glaser, J. M., 107n
Glass, David, 210n
Glassman, James, 281n
Glendon, Mary Ann, 73n
Glenn, John, 240, 259, 263–264, 277–278, 608
Goff, Brian, 325n
Goldberg, Arthur, 437
Goldenberg, Edie N., 248n, 249n, 325n
Goldenson, D., 105n
Goldman, Sheldon, 426n, 427n
Goldstein, Amy, 551n
Goldstein, Joshua, 280n
Goldstein, Robert Justin, 390n
Goldwater, Barry, 234, 472
Southern vote for, 151
vote for, 1964, 199
Goleman, Daniel, 503n
Goodman, Ellen, 72n
Goodman, Matthew, 518n
Goodsell, Charles, 371n
Gopoian, J. David, 280n
Gorbachev, Mikhail, 351, 638–641
Gordon, David, 552n
Gordon, Jeanne, 383n
Gore, Albert, Jr., 308, 370, 371n, 580, 587, 617n, 618n
on the environment, 614
as vice president, 333
as vice-presidential candidate, 195
Gorham, Nathaniel, 26
Gorney, Cynthia, 468n
Goshko, John M., 394n
Gould, Stephen Jay, 393n
Graber, Doris A., 246n, 247n, 248n, 249n, 250n
Gramm, Phil, 263, 300, 360
Granat, Diane, 280n
Grandy, Fred, 240
Gray, Edward, 277

Gray, Paul, 250n, 446n, 518n
Grebler, Leo, 518n
Green, D. P., 105n
Green, Donald, 280n
Green, John C., 139n, 166n
Green, Mark, 138n, 393n
Green, Theodore, 308
Greene, Melissa Fay, 517n
Greenfield, Meg, 280n
Greenhouse, Linda, 601n
Greenhouse, Steven, 580n, 584n, 661n
Greenspan, Alan, 254, 279, 562–563, 565
Greenstein, Fred I., 105n, 362n
Greider, William, 221, 246n, 250n
Grenzke, Janet, 280n, 281n
Gress, D. P., 107n
Grieder, William, 584n
Grier, Kevin, 280n
Griffin, Elisabeth, 177n
Griffith, Thomas, 241n, 247n, 249n
Grossman, Michael Baruch, 248n
Grove, Lloyd, 167n
Gruhl, John, 407n
Grundman, Hermann, 551n
Gugliano, Guy, 543n
Guinier, Lani, 174n, 329, 330
Gurian, Paul-Henri, 166n
Gurwitt, Bob, 371n, 517n
Guth, James L., 139n
Guy, Mary E., 379n
Guzman, Ralph C., 518n

■ H

Haas, Lawrence J., 394n
Hacker, Andrew, 485n, 517n, 518n
Hagen, Charles, 246n
Hager, Mary, 383n
Haire, Susan, 407n
Halberstam, David, 247n, 361n
Haldeman, H. R., 344
Hall, Richard L., 280n
Hamdoon, Nizar, 627
Hamer, Fannie Lou, 471, 514–515
Hamilton, Alexander, 28, 29, 37, 56, 72n
  Federalist Papers, 398
  Federalist #69, 354, 362n
  support for strong national government, 146
Hamilton, Martha, 617n
Hammond, Phillip E., 466n
Hand, Learned, 424
Handler, Edward, 280n
Hanna, Mark, 256
Hanrahan, John, 609n
Hansen, J. M., 138n
Hansen, Susan, 457n
Harbeson, Winfred, 72n
Harding, Warren, mandate of, 207
Harkin, Tom, 169, 190, 297
Harlan, John, 437, 476
Harrington, Michael, 536–537, 552n
Harris, Louis, 353n
Harris, R., 139n
Harris, Teresa, 503
Harrison, Benjamin, election of, electoral votes for, 198
Harrison, Bennett, 585n
Harrison, William Henry, death in office, 331
Hart, Gary, 189
Hartz, Louis, 20n
Harvey, Lynn, 552n
Harwood, Richard, 246n
Hatcher, Richard, 172
Haub, C., 518n
Havemann, Judith, 394n
Hawke, David, 48n
Hawkins, R. P., 105n
Hayes, Denis, 617n
Hayes, M. T., 138n
Hayes, Rutherford B., 474
  electoral vote for, 198
  nomination of, 172
Heilbroner, Robert, 584n
Helms, Jesse, 240, 267, 507
Henry, Patrick, 28
Henry, William A., III, 246n, 248n, 466n, 517n
Henshaw, Stanley K., 457n
Hentoff, Nat, 443n
Hernandez, Debra Gersh, 393n
Herrnson, Paul, 167n, 325n
Hersey, John, 426n
Hersh, Seymore M., 48n, 353n
Hershey, Robert D., Jr., 585n
Hertsgaard, Mark, 248n
Hertzke, Allen D., 9n, 20n, 139n
Hess, R. D., 105n
Hess, Stephen, 247n, 248n, 249n, 326n
Hibbing, John R., 20n, 105n, 107n, 211n, 324n, 325n, 326n, 361n, 362n, 427n, 584n
Hibbs, Douglas, 211n, 584n, 585n
Hill, Anita, 137, 222, 410–411, 502
Hill, David B., 211n
Hill, Herbert, 205n, 517n
Hill, Kevin A., 324n
Hill, Kim Q., 324n
Hill, Kim Quaile, 210n
Hilts, Philip J., 383n
Hinckley, Barbara, 325n
Hinton-Anderson, Angela, 210n
Hirsch, H., 105n
Ho Chi Minh, 633
Hobbes, Thomas, 13
Hochschild, Adam, 247n
Hoffman, Stanley, 641n, 661n
Hofstadter, Richard, 31n, 48n, 166n, 280n
Hofstetter, C. Richard, 248n
Holbrook, Thomas, 210n
Holmes, Oliver Wendell, 412, 438
Holmes, Steven, 312n, 324n
Holsti, Ole, 661n
Holton, Sean, 130
Hooks, Benjamin, 109, 137
Hoover, Herbert, 561
Hoover, J. Edgar, 390
Horn, John, 249n
Hoskin, M., 105n
Hout, M., 107n
Hovey, Harold, 73n
Howard, Lucy, 247n
Howard, Philip K., 601n
Hruska, Roman, 407
Huddleston, Walter, 301
Hufbauer, Clyde, 661n
Huffington, Michael, 265
Hughes, Barry B., 660n
Hughes, Charles Evans, 402, 418, 422
Hugick, Larry, 533n
Humphrey, Hubert, 191, 194, 472, 515
  election of 1968, 265
  vice president, 333
Hunt, Albert R., 129n
Hunt, Conover, 27
Huntington, Samuel, 394n
Hurley, Patricia, 324n
Hurley, Thomas, 211n
Huron, Douglas B., 510n
Hussein, Saddam, 341, 655
Hwang, H., 106n
Hyman, Lisa J., 248n

■ I

Inglehart, Ronald, 20n
Ingram, Helen, 617n
Irons, Peter, 426n, 427n
Isaacson, Walter, 466n, 660n
Ivins, Molly, 249n
Iyengar, Shanto, 209n, 210n, 248n, 249n, 250n, 362n

■ J

Jackman, M., 106n
Jackman, R. W., 107n
Jackson, Andrew, 84
  campaign of 1832, 202
  and civil service changes, 378
  and founding of the Democratic party, 146–147
  governmental innovations of, 332
  informal advisers of, 345
  proposed censoring of news, 225
  Supreme Court appointment by, 401
Jackson, Jesse, 9, 51, 123, 154, 187, 312, 625
  campaign for nomination, 188–189
Jackson-Leslie, Uenda, 411n
Jacobs, Lawrence, 552n
Jacobson, Gary, 280n, 281n, 325n
Jacobson, Louis, 510n, 618n

Jamieson, K. M., 459n
Jamieson, Kathleen Hall, 210n, 249n
Janofsky, Michael, 517n
Jaros, D., 105n
Javits, Jacob, 627
Jaworski, Leon, 24
Jay, John, 72n, 617n
Jefferson, Thomas, 33, 48n, 400, 401, 473, 623
  campaign of 1796, 202
  and development of political parties, 146
  on freedom for women, 496
  potential of, in the media age, 241
  view of the presidency, 334
Jellstedt, Lyman A., 139n
Jencks, Christopher, 545n
Jennings, M. Kent, 105n, 210n
Jensen, Richard, 209n
Jillson, Calvin C., 48n
Job, Brian I., 362n
Johansen, Bruce E., 36n
Johnson, Andrew, threatened impeachment, 331
Johnson, David, 519n
Johnson, Frank, 419
Johnson, Haynes, 279n, 280n
Johnson, J. Bennett, 337
Johnson, Loch, 326n
Johnson, Lyndon B., 109, 275, 336, 514–515
  and civil rights legislation, 472, 484
  communication with the public, 339
  effect of newspaper endorsements on vote for, 242
  interest in polls, 91
  leadership skills, 308
  mandate of, 207
  newspaper endorsement of, 234
  presidential style of, 359
  use of the media, 221
  Vietnam policy, 187, 242, 634–635
  vote for, 1964, 199
Johnson, Michael P., 475n
Johnson, Nancy, 295
Johnson, P. E., 138n
Johnson, Paul, 641n
Johnson, Richard, 248n
Johnstone, John, 247n
Jones, Alex S., 246n
Jones, Calvin C., 211n
Jones, Jacqueline, 516n
Jones, James E., 519n
Jones, Woodrow, 280n
Jordan, Barbara, 12
Jordan, Hamilton, 4
Jordan, Mary, 443n, 517n
Jory, Tom, 248n
Judson, George, 618n
Junn, Jane, 210n
Just, Marion, 249n

■ K

Kalish, Susan, 20n
Kalven, Harry, 466n
Kamen, Al, 423n, 426n, 427n, 468n
Kaplan, David A., 465n
Kaplan, John, 459n, 517n
Karenga, Maulana, 411n
Karp, Jeffrey A., 281n
Kassebaum, Nancy, 330, 360, 572, 573n
Katz, Jeffery L., 69n
Kaufman, Herbert, 393–394n
Kaufman, Jonathan, 517n
Kaul, Donald, 281n, 510n, 519n
Kayden, Xandra, 167n
Kazin, Michael, 9n
Kean, Montague, 249n
Kearney, John, 551n
Keating, Charles, Jr., 238, 253–254, 268, 277–279
Keech, William, 584n
Keim, Gerald, 280n
Keiser, K. Robert, 280n
Kellerman, Donald S., 393n
Kelley, Joseph J., 177n
Kelley, Stanley, Jr., 203, 210n
Kellough, J. Edward, 379n
Kelly, Alfred, 72n
Kelly, Brian, 325n
Kelly, Michael, 209n, 211n
Kemp, Jack, 240
Kempe, Vicki, 552n
Kemper, Vicki, 247n
Kennan, George, 661n
Kennedy, Anthony, 291n, 431–432, 449, 464–465
  on comparable worth, 499
  on symbolic speech, 439
Kennedy, Edward, 12
Kennedy, John F., 187, 188, 189, 275, 330, 479
  attempt to control the press, 225
  and civil rights legislation, 484
  court appointments of, 406
  death in office, 331
  foreign policy, Vietnam, 351
  press conferences, 223
  television debates with Nixon, 202–203
Kennedy, Robert, 90
Kenny, Christopher, 280n
Kenworthy, Tom, 64n, 281n
Kenyon, Cecilia M., 48n
Kernell, Samuel, 139n, 246n, 325n, 339, 362n
Kerrey, Bob, 169, 235, 555, 583
Kessel, John H., 362n
Ketchum, William, 129
Kettl, Donald F., 394n
Key, V. O., 106n
Keynes, John Maynard, 560, 584n
Khomeini, Ayatollah, 352
Kiewiet, D. Roderick, 326n
Kilborn, Peter T., 394n, 551n
Kilpatrick, James J., 291n
Kim, Pan Suk, 379n
Kinder, Donald R., 106n, 249n
King, Martin Luther, Jr., 13, 134–135, 275, 390, 482, 486
Kingdon, John, 326n
Kirkpatrick, James J., 291
Kirschten, Richard, 12n, 20n, 247n, 362n, 519n
Kissinger, Henry, 629, 637–638
Klapper, J., 106n
Klemmach, D., 138n
Klobus-Edwards, P., 138n
Kluger, Richard, 516n, 519n
Knight, Jerry, 517n
Kohl, Herbert, 153
Kohut, Andrew, 393n
Kolbert, Elizabeth, 90n, 246n, 510n
Konigsberg, Eric, 468n
Koop, C. Everett, 385–386, 392, 394n
Koppler, Victor E., 459n
Korb, Lawrence J., 661n
Korematsu, Fred, 397–398, 425
Kosterlitz, Julie, 72n, 394n, 552n
Kotkin, Joel, 44n, 154n
Kovaleski, Serge F., 259n
Kovatit, William E., 426n
Kozol, Jonathan, 517n, 518n
Kraft, Michael, 617n
Kramer, Michael, 459n
Kranowsky, Marc, 553n
Krasno, Jonathan, 280n
Kristof, Nicholas D., 660n, 661n
Kriz, Margaret, 394n, 601n, 617n, 618n
Krosnick, John A., 362n
Krugman, Paul, 573n, 580n, 585n, 661n
Kuczynski, Pedro-Pablo, 661n
Kuklinski, James, 584n
Kumar, Martha Joynt, 248n
Kuntz, Phil, 279n
Kurtz, Howard, 201n, 246n, 247n, 249n, 325n

■ L

Lacayo, Richard, 105n, 394n, 426n, 446n, 466n, 468n, 510n, 519n, 552n, 601n
Ladd, Everett Carll, 105n, 166n, 299n
LaFeber, Walter, 660n
LaFraniere, Sharon, 553n
Lake, Anthony, 641n, 660n
Landau, Martin, 48n
Landon, Alfred, election of 1936, 85
Lang, G. E., 249n
Lang, K., 249n
Langbein, Laura, 280n, 281n
Langton, K., 105n
Lardner, George, Jr., 353n, 362n, 393n
Larew, John, 505n
Lasch, Christoper, 9n

Laudicina, Eleanor, 379n
Laurence, Leslie, 295n
Laurence, Robert P., 247n
Leach, Richard H., 48n, 72n
Lederman, Susan, 210n
Lee, Gary, 394n
Leeman, Nicolas, 371n
Leibeck, Stella, 414
Leighley, Jan, 210n
Lemann, Nicolas, 371n
Less, G., 138n
Levine, Adeline Gordon, 617n
Levine, Jeffrey, 519n
Levinson, Arlene, 291n
Levy, Frank, 585n
Lewis, Anthony, 661n
Lewis, Gregory B., 372n, 379n, 394n
Lewis, I. A., 106n
Lewis, Martin W., 618n
Lichter, Linda S., 246n
Lichter, S. Robert, 246n, 247n, 248n
Liddy, G. Gordon, 219
Lieber, Robert J., 661n
Light, Paul C., 333n, 393n
Limbaugh, Rush, 218, 220
Limpme, Richard, 209n
Lincoln, Abraham, 14, 401
  interpretation of the Constitution, 332
  nomination of, 148
  potential of, in the media age, 241
  presidential pardon used by, 357
  staff of, 343
  suspension of habeas corpus, 355
Lind, Michael, 585n
Lindblom, Charles E., 247n
Line, A. E., 105n
Linsky, Martin A., 248n
Lippman, Walter, 271
Lipset, S. M., 105n, 107n
Littwin, Mike, 443n
Livingston, William, 31
Lloyd, Gordon, 48n
Locke, John, 13, 37
Loevy, Robert, 211n
Longley, Lawrence, 198n
Loomis, B. A., 139n
Lott, Trent, 337
Lotwis, Mark, 281n
Lowi, Theodore J., 21n, 48n, 72n, 107n, 166n, 334, 361n, 394n
Luttbeg, Norman, 211n, 324n
Luttwak, Edward, 318n
Lutz, Donald S., 48n
Lutz, William, 246n
Lytle, Clifford M., 518n

■ M

McAllister, Bill, 185n, 379n, 617n
McAneny, Leslie, 551n
MacArthur, John R., 247n
McBurnett, Michael, 280n
McCain, John, 254, 277–278
McCarthy, Eugene, 187
  Up 'Til Now, 308
McCarthy, Joseph, 214, 435
McCarthy, K. F., 12n, 44n
McCloskey, Robert G., 48n, 427n
McClosky, H., 107n
McCombs, Maxwell E., 105n, 249n
McConnell, Mitch, 301
McCormick, James M., 353n
McCormick, John, 609n
McCorvey, Norma, 456–457, 462
McCraw, Thomas K., 573n
McCubbins, Matthew, 326n
McDade, Joseph, 275
McDaniel, Antonio, 20n
McDevitt, J. F., 459n
MacDonald, J. Fred, 246n
MacDonald, Stuart, 166n
McDougal, James, 274
McFarlane, Robert, 352
McFarland, A. S., 138n
McGovern, George, campaign of 1972, 207
McGregor, Molly, 553n
McKibben, Bill, 618n
McKinley, William, 178, 640
  campaign style of, 189
MacKuen, Michael Bruce, 249n, 250n
McLarty, Thomas, 344–345
McLellan, Diana, 383n
McMillen, Tom, 240
McNamara, Robert, 440, 635, 661n
McNeil, Neil, 326n
McNeil, Robert, 210n
MacPherson, Peter, 361n
Madison, James, 13, 14, 28, 31, 32, 33, 37, 38, 42, 48n, 56, 72n, 110, 146, 279n, 416–417, 433
  on factions, and distribution of property, 255
  on interest groups, 136–137
  on political parties, 146
Mahtesian, Charles, 174n
Makinson, Larry, 280n
Malbin, Michael J., 325n, 326n
Malone, Albert P., 454n
Mandelbaum, Michael, 661n
Mangy, Michael, 280n
Mann, Dean, 617n
Mann, Thomas E., 167n, 324n, 325n, 545n
Mansbridge, Jane, 518n
Mao Zedong, 632
Mapplethorpe, Robert, 444
Marbury, William, 400
Marcus, Eric, 139n
Marcus, G., 107n
Marcus, Ruth, 426n
Margolies-Mezvinsky, Marjorie, 285–286, 322–323
Margolis, Richard, 552n
Markoff, John, 580n
Markowitz, Laura M., 518n
Marshall, John, 58, 399, 417, 422–423, 493
  Constitutional interpretations as chief justice, 400–401
Marshall, Paul, 280n
Marshall, Thomas R., 427n
  vice president, 333
Marshall, Thurgood, 109, 406, 422, 461, 477, 478, 479
Martin, Philip, 12n
Martz, Larry, 249n
Marx, Karl, 556
Mason, Alpheus T., 48n
Mason, George, 31
Massey, Douglas, 517n
Masters, Marick, 280n
Mathews, Jay, 613n
Matlack, Carol, 246n, 324n
Matlock, Carol, 280n
Mayhew, David R., 159n, 324n
Maynard-Moody, Steven, 394n
Medcalf, Linda J., 48n
Meese, Edwin, 346, 352
Meier, August, 209n
Meier, Kenneth J., 517n, 518n, 552n, 617n
Melton, J. Gordon, 467n
Melton, R. H., 259n
Mencimer, 552n
Mendelsohn, H., 106n
Meneimer, Stephanie, 467n
Meredith, James, 479
Merelman, R., 105n
Merida, Kevin, 295n
Merriman, W. R., 106n
Michels, Robert, 16, 21n
Milk, Jeremy L., 518n
Miller, A., 107n
Miller, Arthur H., 248n
Miller, Judith, 246n
Miller, Merle, 426n
Miller, Tim, 324n
Miller, W., 105n
Miller, Warren E., 211n, 324n
Miller, William Lee, 466n
Millman, Joel, 248n
Mills, C. Wright, 16, 20n, 21n, 393n
Mills, David, 446n
Mills, Kay, 516n, 519n
Miranda, Ernesto, 453
Mitchell, G., "Voter Registration Laws and Turnout", 181n
Mitgang, Herbert, 390n
Moe, Ronald C., 326n, 362n, 371n
Moe, Terry, 394n
Mondale, Walter
  union support for, 1984, 118
  vice president, 333
Monroe, James, 332, 630
Moore, David W., 551n
Moore, Donna M., 518n

Moore, Joan W., 518n
Moore, S. W., 105n
Moore, W. John, 394n, 518n
Morgan, Dan, 552n
Morganthau, Tom, 20n
Morin, Richard, 69n, 85, 87, 104n, 105n, 106n, 167n, 201n, 205n, 209n, 210n, 247n, 249n, 280n, 281n, 299n, 326n, 361n, 362n, 465n, 503n, 510n
Morris, Gouverneur, 29
Morrison, David C., 318n, 394n, 660n, 661n
Morrow, Lance, 246n
Moynihan, Daniel Patrick, 528, 552n
Mudd, Roger, 235
Mueller, John, 362n
Mulkern, John, 280n
Muller, Thomas, 12n
Murphy, Walter F., 426n, 427n
Murray, Charles, 552n
Murray, Sylvester, 379n
Muskie, Edmund, 189, 308

■ N

Nadeau, Richard, 519n
Nader, Ralph, 120–121
Naff, Katherine C., 379n
Nasar, Sylvia, 584n
Nast, Thomas, 146
Nathan, James, 660n
Navasky, Victor, 426n
Nejelski, M., 426n
Nelan, Bruce, 12n
Nelson, Michael, 333n
Neubauer, Deane E., 585n
Neustadt, Richard E., 48n, 337, 361n, 362n
 on the monarchial presidency, 359
Neustadtl, Alan, 139n
Newton, Isaac, 37
Ngo Dinh Diem, 634
Nice, David, 280n
Nie, Norman H., 21n, 106n, 107n, 210n
Niemi, R. G., 105n
Niemi, Richard G., 519n
Nisbet, Robert, 617n
Nixon, Richard, 47–48n, 257, 330, 480
 attempt to control the press, 225
 campaigns of, 187
 communication with the public, 339
 detente, 637–638
 Domestic Council of, 349
 election of 1968, 265
 foreign policy style of, 625
 interest in polls, 91
 mandate of, 207
 new federalism of, 65
 resignation of, 331
 response to limitations on presidential power, 336
 role in Watergate scandal, 24, 46–47
 Supreme Court appointments, 403
 television debate with Kennedy, 202–203
 vetoes, War Powers Act, 355
 vice president, 333
 Vietnam War strategy, and recognition of China, 635
Nore, Ellen, 48n
Noriega, Manuel, 645
Norpoth, Helmut, 166n
North, Oliver, 92, 223, 346, 353
 campaign of 1994, 265
Noyes, Richard, 248n
Nunn, C. Z., 107n

■ O

Obey, David R., 643, 661n
O'Brien, Robert, 617n
O'Connor, Karen, 407n, 427n
O'Connor, Sandra Day, 406, 407, 450, 461, 503
Ogul, Morris, 326n
O'Harrow, Robert, Jr., 548n
O'Leary, Rosemary, 362n
Oliver, James, 660n
Olson, Edward, 584n
Olson, Mancur, 584n
O'Neill, Tip, 254, 303, 528
Ophuls, William, 617n
Oppenheimer, Bruce, 326n
O'Reilly, Kenneth, 390n
Orfield, Gary, 517n
Ornstein, Norman, 325n
Orren, Gary R., 280n
Ortiz, Alfonso, 518n
Osborne, David, 617n
Oshinsky, David, 9n
Ostberg, Cynthias, 426n
Ostrom, Charles W., Jr., 362n
Overby, Peter, 280n
Owen, David, 248n
Owens, John, 584n
Oye, Kenneth, 661n

■ P

Packwood, Bob, 502
Page, Benjamin I., 105n, 107n, 210n, 211n, 250n, 326n
Paine, Thomas, 171
Pak, Kyoungsan, 584n
Paletz, David, 249n
Palley, Marian Lief, 518n
Panetta, Leon, 127
 as Clinton's chief of staff, 345
Paolino, Philip, 295n
Parenti, Michael, 246n, 247n, 249n
Parker, Glenn, 325n
Parker, Laura, 446n
Parker, Suzanne, 325n
Parks, Rosa, 134–135, 482
Passell, Peter, 12n
Patterson, Samuel C., 210n
Patterson, Thomas E., 210n, 241n, 246n, 247n, 248n, 249n
Paul, Alice, 176
Paxon, Bill, 141
Peak, G. W., 138n
Pear, Robert, 353n, 519n, 551n
Peirce, Neal R., 519n, 617n
Pelosi, Nancy, 621–622, 658–659
Peretz, Paul, 584n, 585n
Perot, Ross, 19, 88, 102, 195, 220, 260
 on ban on gays in the military, 185
 campaign, 3–4
 media attention to, 233
 percentage vote for, 1992, 19–20, 154
 use of television, 220
Pertschuk, Michael, 270n
Peters, Charles, 246n, 250n, 394n, 551n, 552n
Peters, John G., 280n, 281n, 326n
Peterson, Cass, 325n, 609n, 613n
Peterson, M. A., 138n
Peterson, Paul, 73n
Peterson, Peter G., 585n
Petrocik, John R., 106n, 166n, 210n
Phillips, Kevin, 9n, 20n, 89n, 139n, 166n, 167n, 210n, 246n
Pichirallo, Joe, 426n
Pierce, G. L., 459n
Pierson, J., 107n
Pincus, Walter, 353n, 362n
Pingree, S., 105n
Pious, Richard, 362n
Pitney, John J., Jr., 248n
Piven, Frances Fox, 209n, 210n
Planin, Eric, 326n
Plessy, Homer Adolph, 475
Plunkitt, George Washington, 162, 257
Poindexter, John, 346, 353
Pollock, Philip H., 280n
Polsby, Nelson, 280n
Pomper, Gerald, 210n
Ponessa, Jeanne, 361n
Postrel, Virginia I., 394n
Potter, Gary W., 459n
Powell, Colin, 189, 625
Powell, G. Bingham, Jr., 209n
Powell, Lewis, 423, 462
Press, Eric, 414n, 466n
Priest, Dana, 551n
Pritchett, C. Herman, 48n, 426n, 427n, 466n, 516n
Prokesch, Steven, 584n
Putnam, Robert D., 138n

■ Q

Quayle, Dan, 222, 237, 597
 as vice president, 333
 as vice-presidential candidate, 194–195
Quindlen, Anna, 467n

■ R

Rabe, Barry, 73n
Rabinowitz, George, 166n
Rakove, Milton L., 167n
Randolph, Edmund, 25, 29
Rangel, Charles, 126
Rank, Mark, 552n
Rankin, Jeannette, 177, 295
Ranney, Austin, 167n, 210n
Raspberry, William, 518n, 533n
Rauch, Jonathan, 552n
Rausch, John David, Jr., 247n
Reagan, Michael D., 617n
Reagan, Ronald, 93, 100, 155, 187, 189, 247n, 303, 330, 352, 460, 572, 576, 597, 598, 626, 649
  administrative agency appointments of, 128
  appointments of Clarence Thomas, 109
  on classified documents, 369
  communication with the public, 339–340
  court appointments of, 406
  deregulation under, 595
    of savings and loans, 253
  foreign policy of, 351, 625, 638
  growth of bureaucracy under, 372
  informal advisers of, 345
  mandate of, 207
  new federalism of, 65
  persuasive tactics in administration of, 338
  relationship with the media, 226–227
  response to limitations on presidential power, 336
  Supreme Court nominations of, 403
  televised debates with Carter and Mondale, 242
  union support for, 1984, 118
  use of media, 241
  vetoes by, 349
Reed, Christine, 379n
Reed, Ralph, 122
Reed, Thomas, 306
Reedy, George E., 247n
Rehm, Diane, 219n
Rehnquist, William, 137, 403, 423, 439
  decision in special prosecutor case, 412
  dissents by, 423
Reich, Robert, 580n, 581, 585n
Reid, T. R., 249n, 618n
Reinhold, Robert, 20n
Remmers, H. H., 105n
Remnick, David, 48n, 219n
Reno, Janet, 274
Reston, James, 362n
Rhode, David W., 166n, 210n, 423n
Rich, Spencer, 72n, 139n, 533n, 551n, 552n, 585n
Riche, Martha Farnsworth, 388n
Ridout, Christine F., 249n
Riegle, Donald, 277–278
Riley, Michael, 247n
Ring, Raymond, 585n
Ringquist, Evan J., 618n
Riordon, William L., 257n
Rivers, William, 247n
Roark, James L., 475n
Robbins, William, 552n
Roberts, Bill, 279n
Roberts, D., 105n
Roberts, Owen, 402, 419
Robertson, Pat, 9, 122, 450
  campaign of, 187
Robinson, J. P., 105n
Robinson, Jo Ann, 134
Robinson, Michael J., 106n, 209n, 210n, 248n, 249n, 280n, 325n
Roche, John P., 48n
Rock, Martha, 248n
Rockefeller, Nelson
  naming as vice president, 331
  as vice president, 333
Rodgers, Harrell, 551n, 552n
Rogers, Everett M., 249n
Rogers, Will, 562
Rohde, David, 211n
Rohr, John A., 362n
Roll, C., 105n, 106n
Rollins, Edward, 4
  Reagan campaign manager, 1984, 201
Roosevelt, Franklin Delano, 240, 561, 566
  appointment of the Brownlow Committee, 387
  banning of arms sales, Bolivia and Paraguay, 350
  court-packing plan of, 401–402
  creation of the Executive Office, 343
  death in office, 331
  election in 1932, 148–149
  election of 1936, 85
  election of, 1932, 61
  internment of Japanese-Americans, 355, 398
  mandate of, 207
  and power of the presidency, 334–335
  press conferences, 223, 226
  professional reputation of, 337–338
  use of radio, 194–195
  vetoes by, 349
Roosevelt, Theodore, 19, 269, 272
  communication with the public, 339
  use of presidential power, 334
  views on the Supreme Court, 412
Roper, Robert T., 454n
Rose, Richard, 348n
Rosenbaum, David E., 573n
Rosenbaum, Walter A., 617n, 618n
Rosenbloom, David H., 394n
Rosenstiel, Thomas B., 161n, 166n, 246n, 247n
Rosenstone, Steven, 181n, 210n
Ross, Marc Howard, 249n
Rossiter, Clinton, 343, 362n
Rostenkowski, Daniel, 275
Ros-Lehtinen, Ileana, 51, 71
Rotello, Gabriel, 139n
Roth, Toby, 660n
Rothchild, Donald, 661n
Rothman, Stanley, 247n, 248n
Rowen, Hobart, 249n
Rowland, C. K., 139n, 426n, 427n
Rubin, Alissa, 139n, 468n
Rubin, Barry, 73n
Ruckelshaus, William, 611
Rudwick, Elliot, 209n
Rusk, Jerrold, 166n
Russell, Benjamin, 174
Russett, Bruce, 660n
Russett, Timothy J., 247n

■ S

Sabato, Larry J., 245n, 246n, 247n, 248n, 250n, 267n, 273n, 280n
Sadat, Anwar, 654
Safire, William, 362n
St. John, Kelly, 280n
Salant, Jonathan D., 259n
Salholz, Eloise, 44n, 518n
Salisbury, Robert H., 138n
Samuelson, Robert J., 510n, 552n, 585n
San Miguel, Guadaloupe, 518n
Sanchez, Rene, 21n, 105n
Sanders, Marlene, 248n
Sanford, Edward, 435
Sanger, David E., 585n, 661n
Sarasohn, David, 166n
Sawhill, Isabel, 552n
Sawyer, William, 249n
Scalia, Antonin, 137, 447
  on symbolic speech, 439
Schattschneider, E. E., 113, 136n, 138n, 139n, 143, 164, 166n
Scheb, John M., II, 427n
Schick, Alan, 325n
Schick, Allen, 326n
Schlafly, Phyllis, 72n
Schlesinger, Arthur, Jr., 211n, 361n, 641n
Schlozman, Kay Lehman, 138n, 210n
Schmaltz, Jeffrey, 139n, 185n
Schmidhauser, John R., 426n
Schmitt, Harrison, 240
Schneider, Jerrold E., 326n
Schneider, Keith, 609n, 613n, 618n
Schneider, William, 106n, 107n, 661n
Schorr, Daniel, 246n
Schott, Jefrey J., 661n
Schram, Martin, 210n
Schroedel, Jean Reith, 280n, 281n
Schultz, George, 352
Schuman, H., 106n
Schumer, Charles E., 599

Lipp, Melinda, 551n
Uslaner, Eric M., 139n, 325n

V

Valdez, R. Burciaga, 12n, 44n
Valentino, Nicholas, 209n
Van Buren, Martin, [illegible]
Van Voorst, Bruce, [illegible]
Van Vort, Jennifer, [illegible]
Vanderbilt, Cornelius, 256
Verba, Sidney, 20n, [illegible], 105n, 107n, 139n, 210n
Verdugo, Naomi, 519n
Verdugo, Richard, 519n

W

Wall, Diane E., 402n
Wall, James M., 465n
Wallace, Chris, 222
Wallace, George, [illegible]
Warren, [illegible]
Warren, [illegible]
Washington, Booker T., [illegible]
Washington, George, [illegible]
cabinet of, 373
communication with [illegible]
and political parties, [illegible]
potential of, in the media age, 341
precedents for governing set by, 332
staff of, 343
Wasserman, Gary, 280n
Waterman, Richard, 281n
Watzman, Nancy, 552n
Wayman, Frank, 260n
Weber, Max, 397n
Webster, C., [illegible]
Webster, Daniel, 279, 306
Weidenbaum, Murray, 593
Weinberger, Caspar, 342n
Weinstein, Michael, [illegible]
Wilson, Charles, 17
Wilson, Edith Galt, 632
Wilson, G. K., 138n, 139n
Wilson, J. Q., 138n, 371n
Wilson, William Julius, 519n, 532n
Wilson, Woodrow, 42, 248n, 344, 394n, 479, 516n, 630
communication with the public, 339
Congressional opposition to, 501
disability and death in office, 332
and neutral competence, 388
staff of, 343
view of the presidency, 334
Wines, Michael, 21n, 286n, 299n, [illegible]

SUBJECT INDEX

A

Abington School District v. Schempp, 466n
Abortion
  opinions about
    and group membership, 7
    survey, 83
  and the right to privacy, 456–457, 460–462
Abortion Rights Action League, 125–126
Abrams v. United States, 465n
Abscam scandal, 271, 273
Access
  to the courts, 412–415
    restrictions on, 413, 415
  to health care, 531
  to members of Congress, and PAC contributions, 263, 269
  to natural resources, in international trade, 623
  to the president, and campaign contributions, 269
Accountability, of the bureaucracy, 387–391
Acquired immune deficiency syndrome. *See* AIDS
Activism, judicial, 419
Act Up, 123, 213
Adair v. United States, 426n
Adarand Constructors v. Pena, 519n
Adderley v. Florida, 466n
Adkins v. Children's Hospital, 426n
Administrative Procedure Act (APA)(1946), 381
Administrative reform, as a tool for controlling the bureaucracy, 387–388
Adversarial relationship, between politicians and journalists, 221, 224–226
Advertising
  government subsidies for, 117
  in presidential campaigns, 200–202
  revenue from, and media bias, 234–235
Advisers, presidential, on foreign policy, 624–626
Affirmative action, 504–510
Africa
  immigration from, 6
    and slavery, 5
African Americans. *See* Blacks
Age
  and campaign participation, 186
  and gender, of newscasters, 235
  interest groupings by, 119–120
  and poverty, 536
  and the right to vote, 176–177
  and voter turnout, 179, 183
Agency for International Development (USAID), 648
  economic assistance through, 653
Agents of political socialization, 79
Agriculture
  competition with European, 651
  interest groups representing, 118
  problems of, under state law and the Articles of Confederacy, 26
Agriculture Committee, House, subcommittees of, 310
Aid. *See* Subsidies
AIDS, 365–366
  costs of caring for people with, 531
  impact in the gay community, 123, 185, 511
  surgeon general's policy on prevention, 365–366, 392
Aid to Families with Dependent Children (AFDC), 62, 68, 538
  cost of, 1994, 117
  long-term recipients of, 544–545
Air quality standards, 605–606
  benefits of, 614
Air traffic controllers, 598
Akron v. Akron Center for Reproductive Health, 467n
Alaskan pipeline, 612–613
Albania, independence of the Soviet policy, 633
Aliens. *See* Immigrants
Allegheny County v. ACLU, 467n
Alliances, military, 645–647
Amalgamated Food Employees v. Logan Valley Plaza, 466n
Amendment
  of bills in committee, 315
  of bills in the Senate, 316
  of the Constitution, 40, 42, 290, 315, 316
    need for, to limit congressional terms, 290
    to require a balanced budget, 572–573
Amendments, Constitutional
  Eighth, 40, 433, 454
  Equal Rights Amendment (ERA), 193, 358, 497, 500–501
  Fifteenth, 42, 171, 476, 673–674
  Fifth, 40, 416, 433, 453, 456
  First, 40, 44, 416, 431–432, 433, 434–452, 456, 464–465
  Fourteenth, 42, 417, 434, 474, 475, 478, 673
  Fourth, 40, 416, 433, 452, 456
  Nineteenth, 42, 497, 674
  Ninth, 40
  Second, 40, 433
  Seventeenth, 33, 42, 674
  Seventh, 40, 433
  Sixth, 40, 433, 454
  Tenth, 40, 56, 59–60, 72
  Third, 40, 433, 456
  Thirteenth, 42, 474, 673
  Twenty-fifth, 331, 676
  Twenty-fourth, 42, 173, 675–676
  Twenty-second, 331, 675
  Twenty-seventh, 42, 676
  Twenty-sixth, 42, 177, 183, 676
  Twenty-third, 42, 675
  See also Bill of Rights; Constitution
American Agriculture Movement (AAM), 118
American Association of Retired Persons (AARP), 112, 119–120
  mass mailing by, 267
American Bar Association (ABA), 119
American Center for Law and Justice, 450
American Civil Liberties Union (ACLU), 124, 128, 408, 450
  access to the courts, 413
American Enterprise Institute, 626
American Farm Bureau Federation, 118. *See* Farm Bureau Federation
American Federal-State-County-and-Municipal Employees, political action committee of, 261
American Federation of Labor-Congress of Industrial Organizations, as an interest group, 113
American Indian Movement (AIM), 495
American Institute of CPAs, political action committee of, 261
American Medical Association, 119, 130, 133–134, 524
  lobbying in challenge to the Federal Trade Commission, 270
  political action committee of, 261
American Political Science Association, 119
American Public Welfare Association, 66
Americans for Generational Equity, 120
American Society of Plastic and Reconstructive surgeons, on breast implants, 383
Americans with Disabilities Act, 376, 381
Amnesty International, 120
An Economic Interpretation of the Constitution (Beard), 37
"Angry white male", role in elections, 114, 205
Antiballistic missiles, limitations on, under SALT, 637

Antifederalists, 39
Antitrust regulation, 591
Appointments, by the president, control of bureaucracy through, 387–388
Appropriations, budget, 320
Appropriations Committee, House and Senate, 320
Argersinger v. Hamlin, 465n, 467n
Arizona Governing Committee v. Norris, 519n
Armenian Americans, as an interest group, 629
Army. *See* entries for Military
Articles of Confederation, 25–26
Articles of Confederation, term limits in, 290
Ashcraft v. Tennessee, 467n
Asia, immigration from, 6, 11
  present-day, 8
Asian Americans, size of population, 6–7
Assimilation, of Native American, negative consequences of, 494
Associated Press v. Walker, 466n
Association of Trial Lawyers, political action committee of, 261
Atomic Energy Commission, pollution under programs of, 608
Attorney general, executive of the Justice Department, 374
Authorization, budget, 320
Automobile Workers v. Johnson Controls, 518n
Auto Safety Act (1965), 120–121
Avery v. Georgia, 517n

■ B

Back pocket PACs, 258–259
Baker v. Carr, 289
Balance, in appointments to the Supreme Court, 406
Balanced Budget and Emergency Deficit Control Act (1985), 574
Balance-of-power approach, to foreign policy, 637–638
Balancing the budget, 320
Baldwin v. New York, 467n
Baltimore versus Dawson, 516n
Bandwagon effect
  of media coverage, in primaries, 241–242
  of polls, 91
Banking, results of deregulation, 599
Bank of the United States, 58–65
Barron v. Baltimore, 465n
Beal v. Doe, 467n
Beats, of reporters, 221
Benefits
  mandatory, health and retirement, 537
  welfare, cutting off, 544–545
Berea College v. Kentucky, 516n
Berlin Wall, fall of, 639
Bias
  of the media, 230–238
  political, of the media, 231
  urban, in the Electoral College system, 198
  See also Discrimination
Bill, process of becoming a law, 314–315
Bill of Rights, 40
  for congressional subcommittees, 310
  emphasis on liberty, 13
  origin and meanings of, 433–434
  text of, 671–672
Bills of attainder, 432
Birth control, and the right to privacy, 456
Birth rate, to unmarried men and women, 539–540
Black Caucus, 312
"Black Codes", 474
Blacks
  continuing discrimination against, 485–490
  death penalty for, in murder convictions, 455
  discrimination against, 473–490
  employment opportunities for, in the North, 476
  feminization of poverty among, 536
  National Bar Association, 119
  officeholders, 172
    since the Voting Rights Act, 175
  perceptions of racism, poll results, 97
  power of, in Congress, 312
  presidential race potential, 188
  relative life expectancy, education, and employment rates, 511
  right to vote, 171–173, 485
  as slaveowners, 475
  support for Jesse Jackson in churches, 123
  vote of, presidential elections, 203–204
  on welfare, 541
Blame game, 17–18
Blanton v. North Las Vegas, 467n
Blockbusting, 484
Block grants, 65
Board of Education v. Allen, 467n
Board of Education v. Mergens, 467n
Board of Education of Oklahoma City v. Dowell, 517n
Board of Directors of Rotary International v. Rotary Club, 519n
Book Named John Cleland's Memoirs ... v. Attorney General of Massachusetts, 466n
Bosnia, American policy in, 351
Boston Tea Party, 48
Bowers v. Hardwick, 468n
Boycott, bus, Montgomery, Alabama, 482
Bradwell v. Illinois, 518n
Brady v. United States, 467n
Brady bill, 124
Branches of government, establishing at the Constitutional Convention, 29
Brandenburg v. Ohio, 466n
Branzburg v. Hayes, 466n
Breast implants, 382–383
Britain
  censorship in, 440
  immigrants from, 5
  rights of the Constitution derived from law of, 13
Brookings Institution, 626
Brown v. Board of Education, 109, 478–479, 516n
Brown v. Louisiana, 466n
Brown v. Mississippi, 467n
Brownlow Committee, 387
Bubble concept, 606
Buchanan v. Warley, 516n
Buckley v. Valeo, 280
Budget, balancing by Constitutional amendment, 572–573. *See also* Appropriations; Authorization, budget
Budget and Accounting Act (1921), 347–348
Budget bill, Clinton's, 1993, 285–286
Budget deficit
  balancing with Social Security Trust Fund monies, 528
  Clinton bill reducing, 285–286
  Perot on, 3
  sources of, 571–575
Budget forecasting, 570–571
Budget making, 319–320, 347–349
  and the economy, 565–575
Bureaucracy, 365–392
  federal, 371–376
  lobbying of, 128
  overseeing, 317–319
  policymaking by, 18
    effects of term limits on, 291
  reducing the size of, 370–371
  size of, relative to population size, 373
Bureau of Indian Affairs, 494
Bureau of Land Management, 64
  subsidy of dairy farming, 547
Bureau of the Budget (BOB), 348
Burger Court, 403
  on abortion, 457, 460
  on capital punishment, 455
  on civil rights, 513
  on confidentiality of reporters' sources, 441
  on demonstrations in shopping malls, 437
  on discrimination against women, 501
  on freedom of religion, 445
  on laws discriminating against men, 503–504
  on obscenity, 444
  on right to counsel, 454

on tax benefits for private religious school tuition, 451–452
versus the Warren Court, on obscenity, 44
Burnet v. Coronado Oil and Gas, 427n
Bus boycott, Montgomery, 134–135
Business, commercial bias in the media, 234–238. *See also* Corporations
Business-Industry Political Action Committee (BI-PAC), 132
Business organizations, as interest groups, 113, 115
Business Roundtable, 115
Busing to desegregate schools, 480–482

■ C

Cabinet, departments represented in, 374–376
Calendars, of bills reported from committees, 315
California, "Save Our State" initiative, limiting rights of illegal immigrants, 12
California Central Valley Irrigation Project, subsidy of agriculture through, 547
Cambodia, immigration from, 6
Campaign America, personal PAC, 259
Campaign promises, Clinton's record, 230
Campaign Reform Act (1974), 124
Campaigns
congressional, 292–302
contributions to, 254
finance laws, 257–258
impact of money on, 263–269
negative, 141–142, 201
packaging of, 169–170, 207–208
presidential, general election, 195–203
spending on, examples, by category, 266
and voter turnout, 180–182
See also Elections
Campaign support, by interest groups, 128
Camp David Accords, 654
Canadian health care plan, 533
Candidates
bias in media coverage of, 231–234
evaluation of, and vote in presidential elections, 204
impact of the media on selection of, 240–241
negative media bias against, 234
quality of, and campaign financing, 263–264
recruiting of, by party organizations, 158–159, 358
Capitalism, 556
journalists' support of, 232
Capital punishment, 458–459
Captured agencies, 389
Carnegie Commission, survey of college faculty, political outlook, 82
"Catching the late train" (post-election PAC contribution), 261
Catholics, vote of, presidential elections, 203–204
Caucus, 161
presidential, 190
Celebrities, as politicians, 240
Censorship, freedom from, 439–440
Center for Strategic and International Studies, 626
Centers for Disease Control, 65–66
estimate of radioactive iodine exposure in Washington state, 608
Centralization
through Constitutional amendment, 42
and federalism, 56
of media control, 216–217
of power in Congress, 311
Certiorari, writ of, 41
Challengers, for Congressional seats, 296–300
Chamber of Commerce, 115
Change, growth of government, and federalism, 58–65
Checkbook members, of interest groups, 113
Checks and balances, 33–34, 37
Cherokee Nation v. Georgia, 518n
Chief of state, the president's role as, 357
Child care, government provisions for, 51–52, 71–72
Children's Defense Fund (CDF), 120, 124
as a memberless interest group, 113
China
diplomatic relations with, 637–638, 658–659
growth of, 659
immigration from, 6
independence of Soviet policy, 633
linking human rights and trading rights, 621–622
People's Republic of, immigrants from, 6
China lobby, 629
Christian Coalition, 122–123
Christian right, 187
Church of Holy Trinity v. United States, 466n
Church of the Lukumi Babalu Aye v. Hialeah, 464–465
Church of the Lukumi Babalu Aye, 431–432, 464–465
Citizenship
of Native Americans, 494
teaching, 81
Civil Aeronautics Board (CAB), 597
Civil cases, 413
Civil disobedience, 132–133
Civil liberties, 431–465
Civil rights, 471–515
court actions on segregation, 45
Civil Rights Act (1964), 381, 480, 484
authorization of bureaucratic rules to end discrimination, 504
on discrimination in employment, against women, 497–498
on discrimination in public accommodations, 487–488
Education Amendments of 1972, 499–500
Civil Rights Act (1968), 485, 489
Civil Rights Cases, 109 U.S. 3 (1883), 516n
Civil servants, characterization of, 372–376
Civil service. *See* Public service
Civil Service Commission, 385
Civil Service Reform Act (1978), 388
protection of whistleblowers under, 391
Civil suits. *See* Law
Class. *See* Socioeconomic characteristics
Classical democracy, 15
Classified information, 369–370
Clean Air Act (1970), 135, 381, 597, 604
amendments of 1990, 601
Clean Water Act (1972), 602, 604
cost to municipalities, estimated, 614–615
Cleveland Board of Education v. LaFleur, 518n
Closed primary, 162
Cloture, 316
CNN, 321
audience of, 217
Coalitions, 131–132
building of, by the president, 337
Code words. *See also* Bias; Discrimination
Cohen v. California, 466n
Cohens v. Virginia, 426
Coker v. Georgia, 467n
Cold war, 631–632
after detente, 638
Collin v. Smith, 466n
Columbus Board of Education v. Penick, 517n
Commerce, and bias in the media, 234–238
Commerce Department, "Advocacy Center" for businesses, 648
Commercial bias, 235
Committee for Public Education and Religious Liberty v. Nyquist, 467n
Committee on Committees (Republican party), recommendation on committee chairs, 309
Committee on Political Education (COPE), 116
Committees
Conference Committee, 317
of Congress, 308–311, 313
referral of bills to, 315
Common Cause, 112, 124, 128
Common property, regulation to protect, 589–590
Communism, 556
international, as a threat after World War II, 631–632

Communist party, 155, 435
Comparable worth, 499
Competition
inefficient, 590
among interest groups, 134–136
interstate, 69–70
Competitive federalism, 65
Compromise
and civil rights, 471–472
and fragmentation of power, 45
and health care proposals of the Clinton administration, 550
Computer files, and the Freedom of Information Act, 370
COMSAT, 376
Confederal governments, 32, 54
Conference Committee, 317
Confidentiality, taping conversations, 23–24
Conflict
drama of, and bias in media coverage, 236–237
federal-state, 66–67
managing in a system of checks and balances, 34
between the media and politicians, 225
among minority groups, 514
at national nominating conventions, 194
in politics, 10
Conflicts of interest, 271–276
Congress, 285–323
amendment to the Constitution by, 40
under the Articles of Confederation, 25–26
civil rights legislation, 484
conflicts of interest in, 273–275
control over the bureaucracy, 388–389
relationship of, with the media, 230
sexual harassment by members of, 503
support of the president, 338
women's rights legislation, 497–501
Congressional Budget Office (CBO), 313, 320
budget projections of, 571
Congressional Caucus for Women's Issues, 295
Congressional Research Service, 313
Congress Watch, 113
challenge to the AMA over Federal Trade Commission regulation, 270
Connecticut Compromise (Great Compromise), 29
Consensus, and checks and balances, 45
Conservatives, 93
explanations for poverty, 536
opinions about government action, 95
trust in government, 101
Conspiracy theories, 114, 114n
Constituents
influence on congressional votes, 303–304
interest of, and Congressional votes, 268, 286, 323
of members of Congress, 289, 291–292
Constituent service, 293–294, 296, 321
controlling the bureaucracy through, 389
and size of congressional staffs, 313
Constitution, 23–47
acceptance of slavery, limited, 473–474
Article I
powers and role of Congress, 313
Article II, powers of the president, 350
emphasis on liberty, 13, 432–434
interpreting in court, 416–418
interstate relations defined by, 67, 69–70
text of, 665–676
See also Amendments; Bill of Rights
Constitutional Convention, 26, 28–31
Constitutions, written, 31
Constructive engagement, in South Africa, 652
Consumer confidence, 563
Consumer groups, 120–121. *See also* Interest groups
Consumer Product Safety Commission (CPSC), 591
funding of, 319–320, 596
Consumption tax, proposed, 569
Containment policy, 631
and nuclear weapons, 633
Content analysis, to measure bias, 232–233
Continental Congress, 25
"Contract with America", 125, 141–142
details of, 164–165
effect on election, 207
and perception of presidential power, 343
on personal responsibility, 544–545
validation of, and poll results, 91
on welfare reform, 68, 541
Control
concentration of the media, 216–217
over information, 225
Convention bounce, in presidential polls, 194
Conventions
and caucus outcomes, 190
for nominating candidates, comparison with primary system, 163
political party, 161, 192–195
Cooper v. Pate, 466n
Cooperation
federal-state, 65–66
through government, 10
interstate, voluntary, 69
Cooperative federalism, 57
Coordination, regulation involving, 590
Corporations
government, 376
as memberless interest groups, 113
Corruption
kinds of, by political party, 275
by money for campaigns, 254
and patronage, 384
Progressive reforms to eliminate, 178
See also Conflicts of interest
Costa Rica, constitution of, 42
Cost-benefit analysis, in setting product safety standards, 593–594
Costs
of health care, increasing, 530–531
of nuclear preparedness, as an instrument of foreign policy, 642–643
Costs and benefits
of environmental damage regulation, 614–615
of voting, 184
Council of Economic Advisers, 560
Council on Competitiveness, 597
Council on Foreign Relations, 626
Counsel, right to, 45
Court cases
347 U.S. 483 (1954), 516n
369 U.S. 186, 324n
376 U.S. 1, 324n
376 U.S. 254, 466n
376 U.S. 643, 467n
384 U.S. 436, 467n
418 U.S. 683 (1974), 48n
Court decisions, 415–420
Court-packing plan, Franklin Roosevelt's, 402
Courts, 404–405
changing the Constitution by judicial interpretation, 42
control over the bureaucracy, 389
development of the role of, 398–404
on discrimination against women, 501–503
lobbying of, 128
tribal, Native Americans subject to, 496
using to enforce civil rights, 477
See also Judiciary; Supreme Court
Courts of appeals, 404, 415
Coverage, superficial, by television, 237–238
Cox Broadcasting v. Cohn, 466n
Cox v. Louisiana, 466n
Craig v. Boren, 519n
Credentials committee, national conventions, 193
Credit, consumer, 576
Crib safety standards, 614
Criminal cases, 413
Criminal defendants, rights of, 452–456
Cruel and unusual punishment, 454
Cruz v. Beto, 466n
Cruzan v. Missouri Health Department, 468n
C-SPAN, 303, 321
audience of, 217
as a campaign tool, 141–142, 161

Culture
and artistic value, 446
assimilation of Native American
negative aspects, 494–496
policy of, 494
See also Political culture
Cumming v. Richmond County Board of Education, 516n
Cumulative voting, 174
Curtis Publishing v. Butts, 466n

■ D

Day care, for working families, 51–52
Dayton Board of Education v. Brinkman, 517n
Dealignment, 151
Death penalty, 455
Debates
on bills reported out of committees, 315
limitation of, in the Senate, 316
presidential election, televised, 202–203
Debs v. United States, 465n
Debt, of developing nations, 657
Debt ceiling, 573–574
Decentralization, under the Articles of Confederation, 25–26
Declaration of Independence
emphasis on equality, 473
emphasis on liberty, 13
text of, 663–664
Declaration of war, by Congress, 627
Deductions, tax, as social welfare, 546
De facto segregation, 480
Defense Department, 376
hazardous waste of, 609
Deficits, budget, 571–575
Delaware, ratification of the Constitution, 39
Delegated legislative authority, 377
Democracy
American, 3–20
and bureaucracy, 367
characteristics of, 13–14
classical, 14–15
and economic system, 558
foreign policy in a, 624–631
versus republic, 32
Democratic party, 148–149
characterization of members, 150, 156
convention delegate selection, 191
on gay rights, 185
members as talk-show listeners, 219
origin of, 146
style of corruption, 275
Demographic characteristics, of joiners, 113
Demographics
age distribution of the American population, 528
distribution of population by immigrant group, 9–10
Dennis v. United States, 465n
Departments. *See* specific entries, e.g. Defense Department
Depression, 558
Deregulation, 596–598
cycle of, 599–602
of savings and loans, 253–254
Desegregation, 484. *See also* Integration
Detente, 637–638
Deterrence, and punishment for crimes, 458–459
Developing nations, effects of aid in, 657
Diminished expectations, economic, 577–580
Dioxin, standards for, 611
Diplomats, private, 625–626
Direct democracy, 14
rejection of, Constitutional Convention, 32
Direct primary, 161–162
Disabled individuals, Social Security coverage of, 527
Discretionary spending, 569–570
Discrimination
against Asian-Americans, 6–7
economic, in access to the courts, 413
effect of, on voting patterns, 204
by ethnicity/race, 473–496
against Japanese Americans, 425
cultural and physical characteristics, 7
skin color, language or religion, 6
job, against immigrants, 8
overcoming with education, 6–7
poverty resulting from, 537–538
in sentencing after criminal conviction, 456
by sex, 496–504
unintended, from affirmative action, 509
See also Bias
Distortion, from television's focus on action, 237
District courts, 404
appeal from, 415
Diversity
cable networks catering to specific groups, 217
ethnic and economic, 5–12
federalism as a way of managing, 54
among Hispanics in the United States, 491, 493
in legislative bodies, 172
polls indicating changing opinions about, 97
in the United States, 5–12
Divestiture, pressure on South Africa from, 652
Divided government, 159
Divorce, discrimination in court settlements, 504
Doe v. Commonwealth's Attorney, 468n
Doe v. University of Michigan, 443n
Domino theory, 632
Dothard v. Rawlinson, 518n
Douglas v. California, 467n
Drama, and reporting the news, 235
Dred Scott case, 401, 473
Drugs, 511
health care costs of users, 531
Dual federalism, 57, 60
and laws covering the workplace, 61
Due process, 452
Duncan v. Louisiana, 467n

■ E

Earmarking, 300
Earned Income Tax Credit (EITC), 539
Earth Day 1970, 123–124
Earth First!, 124
East Asia, trade with, 651
Economic diplomacy, 642, 648–657
Economic diversity, 5–12
Economic interests
and congressional committee membership, 309
and the Constitution, 37–38
and vote for presidential candidates, 206
Economic policy, 555–583
regulation through incentives, 592
sanctions as a tool in foreign policy, 651–653
stimulus package, Clinton administration, 555
Economic security, 623
Economy, as a campaign issue, 3–4
Ecosystem mapping, 615–616
Editors, newspaper, support for political candidates, 233–234
Education
affirmative action in admission to colleges and universities, 505
of the Founders, 36–37
overcoming discrimination barriers with, 6–7
and political participation, 81–82
public, level of spending on, 486
and voter turnout, 179
Edwards v. Aguillard, 467n
Edwards v. South Carolina, 466n
Eighth Amendment
guarantees of, 433
protection against cruel and unusual punishment, 40, 454
protection against excessive bail and fines, 40
Eisenstadt v. Baird, 467n
Elderly. *See* Age
Elections, 170–208
of bureaucrats, 384
Congressional, 260–263
effect of money on outcomes, 264–265

impact of the media on, 240–242
presidential, 259–260
public funding for, proposed, 272
role of money in, 257–263
Electoral College, 30, 33, 196–197
role of, 198
Electoral security. *See* Incumbents
Electorate
characteristics of, 1990s, 150
See also Voters
Electronic surveillance
Fourth Amendment applied to, 452
Elitism, 16–17
at the Constitutional Convention, 38
and influence in foreign policy, 629
tolerance of, 99
Emancipation Proclamation, 474
EMILY's List, 262
Employer of last resort, opposition to plans providing, 545
Employment
affirmative actions requirements, 505
discrimination in, 484, 488–489, 497–498
laws forbidding, 501–502
and education, 578
versus environmental protection, 587–588
and immigration, 9
from international trade, 621–622
and marriage prospects, 542
from meeting federal regulatory standards, 614
Employment Division v. Smith, 466n
Endangered species, 587–589
Endangered Species Act (1973), 587–588, 602, 604
enforcement of, 615–616
Endorsements, newspaper, effect on voters, 242
Energy, Department of, pollution cleanup by, 609
Energy and National Resources Committee, Senate, review of Park Service authorization, 320
Engel v. Vitale, 466n
English language, in the colonies, 5
Entertainment, media function as a source of, 235
Environmental Defense Fund, mass mailing by, 267
Environmental groups, 123–124
Environmental impact statements, 604
Environmental policy, 587–616
Environmental Protection Agency (EPA), 381, 604
actions of, in minority communities, 490
funding of, 319–320
standards set by, 593
Epperson v. Arkansas, 467n
Equal Credit Opportunity Act (1974), 500
Equal Employment Opportunity Commission (EEOC), 376–377, 489
on affirmative action, 504
on discrimination in employment, by sex, 498–499
harassment within the agency, 502–503
Equality, political, 13
Equal Pay Act (1963), 499
Equal protection clause, 474
Equal Rights Amendment (ERA), 193, 358, 497, 500–501
Espionage Act (1917), 435
Establishment, media bias toward, 231
Establishment clause, 447
Ethics
check kiting in the congressional bank, 274–275
codes of conduct, congressional, 272
lapses characteristic of particular ideologies, 275
of lobbying by former government employees, 629
of testing for AIDS, 365–366
Ethics Committee, Senate, hearings on the Keating 5, 278–279
Ethics in Government Act (1978), 272, 276, 386
Ethnic diversity, 5–10
Ethnicity, and economic diversity, 5–12
Europe
eastern, immigration from, 6
western, immigration from, 5
European Economic Community. *See* European Union
European Union (EL), 651
Evaluation, of committee government, 310
Everson v. Board of Education of Ewing Township, 467n
Excise taxes, 566
Exclusionary rule, 452
Executive branch
administrative departments of, 374–376
checks on the courts by, 421
ethical standards of, 275–276
reorganizing agencies of, 349
Executive leadership, presidential, 387–388
Executive Office of the President (EOP), 343, 387
Executive orders, 350
Executive privilege, 24
Ex parte McCardle, 426n
Ex parte Merryman, 426n
Expenditures. *See* Money
Expertise
as a lobbying tool, 127
Ex post facto laws, 432
Externality, 589
Exxon oil spill, 612–613

■ F

Factions, parties and interest groups as, 145–146
Fair Government Foundation, 124
Fairness
and affirmative action, 509–510
in taxation, 569
Faithless elector phenomenon, 198
Family, political socialization in, 80–81. *See also* Aid to Families with Dependent Children; Women
Family status, and poverty, 535
Farm Bureau Federation, 112
Farmers Home Administration, subsidies to farmers through, 546–547
Farm subsidies, 546–547
FCC v. Pacifica Foundation, 466n
Federal aid, for students, 71. *See also* Aid; Subsidies
Federal Aviation Administration (FAA), 597
Federal Bureau of Investigation (FBI), 369
excesses of, 390
Federal Communications Commission, 376
broadcasting industry's influence on, 389
Federal Corrupt Practices Act (1925), 256
Federal Election Campaign Act (1974), 257–258
Federal Election Commission, suit over GOPAC, 259
Federal Home Loan Bank Board, 599
Federal Housing Authority (FHA), limitation of loans to blacks, 485
Federalism, 32, 51–72
Constitutional bases of, 55–56
Federalist Papers, 41, 48n, 354, 398, 399, 416–417, 677–680, 681–683
on nation-centered federalism, 56–57
#10, 48n, 57, 145, 255
#47, 48n
#51, 48n
#78, 426n
Federalists, 39
Federal Register, 381
Federal Reserve Board, 387, 561–563
partisan actions of, 564–565
study of mortgage discrimination, 489
Federal Savings and Loan Insurance Corporation (FSLIC), 599
Federal system, reinforcement of, by Electoral College elections, 197
Federal Trade Commission, 596
limitation on, by Congress, 388–389
rule for practice of law and medicine, 270
rulings subject to legislative veto, 317
Feminization of poverty, 535
Fifteenth Amendment
right to vote, black men, 42, 171, 476
text of, 673–674
Fifth Amendment
due process of law, 40, 416
guarantees of, 433
protection against self-incrimination, 40, 453, 456

Filibuster, 316
over the Foster nomination for Surgeon General, 360
Firefighters Local Union v. Stotts, 517n
Firefighters v. Cleveland, 519n
Firefighters v. Stotts, 519n
Fireside chats, 226, 335
First Amendment
and criticism of public officials, 442
freedom of expression, 40, 416, 434–452
freedom of religion, 445, 464–465
religious expression, 431–432
guarantees of, 433
and privacy, 456
and state official language laws, 44
First-among-equals position, in NATO, 647
Fiscal policy, 560
Flag, symbolic speech involving, 438–439
Flat tax, 569
Fletcher v. Peck, 426n
Focus groups, 90
Clinton campaign use of, 170
for determining campaign tactics, 141–142
Reagan administration use of, 340
Food and Drug Administration, 601
on breast implants, 382–383
funding for, 386
on thalidomide, 591
Food stamps, 543
cost of, 1994, 117
Foreign Intelligence Advisory Board, 629
Foreign policy, 621–659
aid as a tool in, 653–657
bipartisan support in, 337
presidential leadership in, 350–354
Forest Service, 64
Founders, views of political parties, 145–146
Fourteenth Amendment
due process clause, 434
equal protection of the law, 42, 417, 474, 475, 478
text of, 673
Fourth Amendment
guarantees of, 433
protection against unreasonable searches and seizures, 40, 416, 452, 456
Fragmentation of power
and congressional committee work, 311, 321
within political parties, 152
France, constitution of, 44
Franking, 292
Freedom. *See* Rights
Freedom of choice plans for school desegregation, 479
Freedom of expression, 434–452
through campaign contributions, 258
and hate speech, 442–443
Freedom of Information Act (1966), 369
Free exercise clause, 445
Free trade, 649
Frisby v. Schultz, 466n
Frohwerk v. United States, 465n
Full faith and credit clause, 69
Fullilove v. Klutznick, 519n
Fundamentalism. *See* Christian right
Funding
for schools attended by blacks, 486–487
for schools attended by Hispanics, 491
Furman v. Georgia, 467n

■ G

Game orientation, 236
Garcia v. San Antonio Metropolitan Transit, 72n
Gay Men's Health Crisis, 123
Gay rights organizations, 123, 438
outing by, ethical dilemma, 213–214, 244–245
power of, 185
Gender, and campaign participation, 186
General Accounting Office, 313, 317
General revenue sharing, 65
Geography. See Demographics
Germany
constitution of, 42
Germany, immigration from, 6
Gerrymandering, 289
racial, 174
Gertz v. Robert Welch, 466n
Gibbons v. Odgen, 426n
G.I. Bill of Rights, as a social welfare measure, 526
Gideon v. Wainwright, 467n
Gitlow v. New York, 465n
Glasnost, response to, 639
Glass ceiling, 502
in the bureaucracy, 378–379
See also Discrimination; Equality
Goals
of bureaucrats, public and private, 368
common, of Americans, 9
of economic sanctions, 652–653
of foreign policy, 623–624
of military interventions, 645
of the Vietnam policy, 635
Going public
by members of Congress, 302–303
by the president, 339
Goldman v. Weinberger, 427n, 466n
Gooding v. Wilson, 466n
GOPAC, 141–142, 161, 259
Government
federal-state relations, 65–66
negative bias in media coverage of, 234
polls used by, 86
role in mixed economies, 557
state-local relations, 70
trust in, results of opinion polls, 99–103
units of, in the United States, 66
See also States
Graft, honest, one politician's view, 257.
See also Conflicts of interest; Corruption; Political machine
Gramm-Rudman-Hollings bill, 574
effects of, 320
Grandfather clause, 172
invalidation of, 173, 477
Grand Old Party (GOP), 148
Grants-in-aid, 61, 66
Grassroots lobbying, 130–131
Gray lobby, 119–120
Grayned v. Rockford, 466n
Great Compromise (Connecticut Compromise), 29
Great Depression, end of, 62
Great Law of Peace (Iroquois), 35–36
Great Society, 63–64, 350
successes of, 539
Green v. New Kent County School Board, 517n
Greenbelt Cooperative Publishing v. Bresler, 466n
Greenpeace, 124
civil disobedience as a tactic of, 132
Greenpeace (ship), 132
"Greens", 124
Gregg v. Georgia, 467n
Grenada, invasion of, 643
news coverage, 247n
Gridlock, and unity in government, 159, 348
Griffin v. Prince Edward County School Board, 517n
Griggs v. Duke Power, 517n
Griswold v. Connecticut, 427n, 467n
Gross domestic product (GDP), government's share of, 565
Gross National Product (GNP), 559
Groups, formation of, 111–113
Guerilla warfare, in Vietnam, 635–636
Guinn v. United States, 516n
grandfather clause, 209n
Gulf of Tonkin Resolution, 634
repeal of, 635
Gun control, regional controversy over, 64

■ H

Habeas corpus, 404–405
Haiti, American policy in, 351, 642
Hamburger, regulations covering, 380
Hammer v. Dagenhart, 426n
Handgun Control (interest group), 124
Harassment, at work, 502–503
Harns v. Forklift Systems, 503
Harris v. Forklift Systems, 503n
Harris v. McRae, 467n
Harrisburg Pennsylvanian, origination of straw polls by, 84
Hatch Act (1939), 386
Hate speech, 442–443
Hawaii, universal health insurance in, 532

Hazardous waste, 607–610
Hazelwood School District v. Kuhlmeier, 466n
Head Start, 51
rate of participation in, 539
Health
and malnutrition, 543
teenage pregnancy rate, 51
Health care
coalitions built around debate over, 131
current debate and action on, 18, 523–525, 549–550
federal programs, 529–530
Health insurance, percentage of population covered by, 531
Health maintenance organizations (HMOs), 532
Heart of Atlanta Motel v. United States, 517n
Henry, Prince of Prussia, offer to rule America, 26
Heritage Foundation, 626
Hispanics
discrimination against, 490–493
integration into American society, 6
languages of, 44
officeholders, 172
relative employment and education patterns, 512
vote of, presidential elections, 204
Hodgson v. Minnesota, 467n
Holmes v. Atlanta, 516n
Homelessness, prevalence of, among children, 51
Homosexuality, 462–463
Homosexual rights. *See* Gay rights organizations
"Horse-race coverage"
and commercial bias in the media, 236
House of Representatives
blacks in, nineteenth century, 171
comparison with the Senate, 316
size of individual representatives' staffs, 313
Housing
desegregation laws affecting, 484–485
discrimination in, 489–490
Hoyt v. Florida, 518n
Hudnut v. American Booksellers Association, 466n
Human interest stories, 235
Human rights, as a criterion in foreign policy, 621–622, 658–659
Human Rights Campaign Fund, 123
Hunt v. McNair, 467n
Hurley v. Irish-American Gay, Lesbian and Bisexual Group of Boston, 466n
Hyperpluralism, 17

I

Ideology
and congressional voting patterns, 305
of court appointees, 409–411
of judges, and access to the courts, 415
and participation in party conventions, 193
and public opinion, 93–94
as a reason for running for president, 187
Illegitimacy rates, inverse correlation with welfare benefit level, 545
Image
fashioning for a campaign, 170, 196
of presidential leadership, 341
Immigrants
job discrimination against, 8
resentment toward, 6
Immigration
control of, current concerns, 11–12
history of, 5–6
illegal, 6, 8
state policies affecting, 12
Impeachment
of judges, 411, 426n
of the president, 331
Imperial presidency, 330, 359
Implied powers clause, 56, 313, 350
Income taxes, 61
as a percentage of federal revenue, 566
and public policy, 566–569
See also Taxes
Incompetence, and patronage, 384
Incumbents
advantages of, 292, 295–296
effects of public financing on campaigns of, 272
losses in 1994, 298
PAC support for, 261, 296
spending by, and reelection, 265
terms limits and, 291
Independence Hall, 26
Independent Action PAC (IAPAC), 267
Independent agencies, 376
Independent counsel, for investigation of the Whitewater affair, 274
Independents
characterization of, 150
importance of, in presidential elections, 203
nominees for president, 195
presidential elections determined by, 199
responsiveness of congressmen to, 289
as talk-show listeners, 219
Independent spending, for campaigns, 258
Indian Civil Rights Act (1968), 496
Indian Removal Act (1830), 494
Indians. *See* Native Americans
Indian Self-Determination Act (1975), 495
Indirect democracy, 14, 32
Individualism, in political cultures, 54
Individuals
as contributors of congressional campaigns, 263
influence on state government policy, 59
influence on the bureaucracy, 391
interactions among members of Congress, 305
value of, democratic philosophy, 13
Industrialization, after the Civil War, 60–61
Industrial policy, 580
Inequity, government action to reduce, 590–591
Infant mortality
as a measure of health care, 534
reduction in, through health care for low-income women, 539
Inflation, 558
in the 1980s, 574
Influence peddling, 276
Information
assessing accuracy of, 220
classified, public policy based on, 352
and effects of campaign advertising, 202
lobbying by offering, 127
from media coverage of candidates, 241–242
power and, 22
public opinion based on, 92–93
reluctance of bureaucratic agencies to provide, 369
Insider. *See* Washingtonians
Institute for Policy Studies, 626
Institutional loyalty, in the House, 302
Insurance, discrimination in, 489
Integration. *See* Desegregation
Intercontinental ballistic missiles (ICBMS), 633
Interest groups, 109–137
access to the courts, 413
and foreign policy, 628–629
influence with bureaucracies, 389, 391
representation through, 16, 305
and presidential government, 348
use of the court system by, 416
Interests, counterbalancing, 255
Interior and Insular Affairs Committee, House, review of Park Service authorization, 320
Interior Department, policy for managing jobs-versus-environment issues, 615–616
Intermediate-range nuclear forces (INF), removal from Europe, 639
International economy, 581
International Society of Krishna Consciousness v. Lee, 468n
Internet, effect on group formation, 112
Interstate Commerce Commission, 386
origin of, 596
proposal to eliminate, 389
rules and standards of, 381
Intifada, in Palestine, 655
Investigative reporting, 225–226
"Invisible hand" of the marketplace, 589

Iran-contra
as an abuse of presidential power, 352–353
and congressional oversight, 318
effect of public opinion on policy, 630
presidential management style and, 344
press response to rumors about arms, 223
Iraqi ambassador, view of U.S. foreign policy, 627
Ireland, immigration from, 6
Iron law of oligarchy, 16
Iron triangles, 348, 388, 389, 391
Iroquois Confederacy, 35
Isolationism, 630–631
return of, 640
Israel, interest groups representing, 122
Israeli-Palestinian conflict, 654–656
Issues
association with political parties, 144
ethnic values shaping opinions on, 7
information from media coverage of, 241–242
journalists' positions on, 232
in presidential campaigns, 196, 204, 206
Republican and Democratic stands on, 159
See also Social issues
Italy, immigration from, 6

J

Jacobellis v. Ohio, 446n
Japan
immigration from, 6
peace treaty terms limiting military establishment, 647
Jawboning, by the Federal Reserve system, 563
Jeannette Rankin Brigade v. Chief of Capital Police, 466n
Jeffersonian Republicans, 146
Jenkins v. Georgia, 466n
Jews
immigration of, 6
vote of, presidential elections, 203
Jim Crow laws, 474
Job discrimination, against immigrants, 8
Jobless rates, and immigration, 11
Johnson v. Virginia, 516n
Johnson v. Zerbst, 467n
Joint Chiefs of Staff, role as foreign policy advisors, 625–626
Joint committees of Congress, 310
Jones v. Clear Creek, 467n
Journalists
characterization of, 232
mutual dependency with politicians, 220–221
Judges, 405–412
characterization of, 409–411
federal, nomination and confirmation of, 33
Judicial review, 399–401
and power of the courts, 420–421
Judiciary, 397–425. *See also* Courts
Judiciary Act (1789), 400, 404
Judiciary Committee, House
impeachment
Richard Nixon, 46–47
impeachment proposal, Watergate, 24
Junkets, 274
Jurisdiction of the courts, 404–405
Jury trial, right to, 45

K

Katz v. United States, 467n
Keating 5, 253–254, 277–279
Kenya, constitution of, 42
Kerner Commission, on the black ghettos, 511
Keyes v. School District 1, Denver, 517n
Keynesian economics, 560
Kitchen cabinets, 345
Knowledge, as a resource for interest groups, 134
"Know-Nothing" party, 6, 7, 155
Korea, North, nuclear capability of, 647
Korematsu, Fred, 425
Korematsu v. United States, 397–398, 425, 427n
Ku Klux Klan, 477
right to free speech, 436

L

Labor, as an interest group, 115–118
Lake Erie, success of water improvement program, 614
Land control, and regional political cultures, 64
Land grants, support for the states through, 61
Language
bilingual education, 492
making English the official language, 43–44
regulation by law, 7
and school performance, 491
Latin America, immigration from, 6, 8, 11
Latinos. *See* Hispanics
Lau v. Nichols, 518n
Law. *See* Lawmaking; Statutes
Lawmaking
in the courts, 419–420
Lawmaking, federal, 313–317
Leadership
administrative, by the president, 345–349
chairs of committees in the House and the Senate, 309–310
in the House and the Senate, 307–308
of political parties, 358–359
presidential
in domestic policy, 349–350
in foreign policy, 350–354
image of, 341
symbolic, 357–358
Leadership Conference on Civil Rights, coalition, 131–132
League of Nations, refusal of the United States to join, 630
League of Women Voters, 124
Leaks, of news from government, 221
Lee v. Washington, 516n
Lee v. Weisman, 465n, 467n
Legislation, during Franklin Roosevelt's first term, 63
Legislative veto, 317
Legislature, checks on the courts by, 421
Lemon v. Kurtzman, 467n
"Lemon socialism", in health care, 532
Lesbians, interest groups representing, 123
Liability, limitation on, as regulation, 592–593
Libel, 441–443
Liberals, 93
explanations for poverty, 536–538
opinions about government action, 95
trust in government, 101
Liberty, religious, 431–432. *See also* Civil liberties; Civil rights; Rights
Licensing, regulation through, 592
Life Dynamics, malpractice suits as a tool in abortion controversy, 416
Limited government, 37
Line-item veto, 346–347
Literacy
rates of, 493
tests for voting, 172
Literary Digest, polling by, 85
Litigation
example, hot coffee burn, 414
by interest groups, 128
Lloyd v. Tanner, 466n
Lobbying
and campaign contributions from outside Congressional districts, 263
by corporations, 117
direct, by interest groups, 126–128
by foreign governments, 120, 629
about foreign policy, 628–629
by former government employees, restrictions on, 272, 386–387
indirect, 129–132
by interest groups, 110
by memberless interest groups, 113
by the president, to control bureaucrats, 387
by state and local governments, 66
and term limits, 291
Local political parties, big-city, 160–161
Lochner v. New York, 426n
Log Cabin Federation, 123

Logrolling, 302
Loopholes
in campaign financing reform, 258–259
defined, 258
in hazardous waste reduction, 610
in tax policy, reducing, 567
in water quality improvement, 607
Looting, of Native American gravesites, 495
Los Angeles Department of Water and Power v. Manhart, 519n
Love Canal incident, 607
Lynch v. Donnelly, 467n
Lynching, of blacks, 477

M

McCarthyism, 435
Magnet schools, 482
Maher v. Roe, 467n
Mail solicitations, rules for success, 267
Majority leader, House of Representatives, 308
Majority rule, 14
curbing, 57
and natural rights, 37
Mallory v. United States, 467n
Malnutrition, health costs of, 543
Managed care, 550
Managed competition, 524, 531–532
Mandate, presidential, 206
Mandatory spending, 570
Manual Enterprises v. Day, 466n
Mapp v. Ohio, 452
Marbury v. Madison, 400
Marketplace, rational behavior in, 600
Market share, as a resource in lobbying by interest groups, 133–134
Markup session, 308, 315
Marshall Plan, 631, 653
Martin v. Hunter's Lessee, 426n
Massachusetts v. Feeney, 519n
Massachusetts v. Sheppard, 467n
Mass media, effect on political socialization, 84. *See also* Media
Maternity leave, law requiring, 503
Mayflower Compact, 24, 31, 48
McCleskey v. Kemp, 467n
McCulloch v. Maryland, 58, 72n, 401
McLaurin v. Oklahoma State Regents, 516n
McNabb v. United States, 467n
Means test programs, 538
Media, 213–245, 293
blaming for failures, 341
congressional campaign in, 301
coverage of congressional committees, 309
effect of, on presidential power, 335
freedom of the press, 439–440
impact on public policy, 321
and party conventions, 193–194
presidential campaign in, 199–203
restriction on freedom of expression, 437
staging of events for, 221, 223–224, 226
See also Television
Media malaise, 234
Medicaid, 538–539
abortion provision under, 460, 542
costs of, 550
Medicare, 119, 527, 530
costs of, 550
Melting pot, 6
America as, 7
Membership, on congressional committees, 309
Men
"angry white male" phenomenon, 114, 205
discrimination against, 503–504
marriageable, 542
Merchant diplomacy, 641–642
Merit system, 385
versus affirmative action, question of, 508–509
Mexico, Hispanic citizens originating in, 6, 8
Michael M. v. Sonoma County, 519n
Michigan, ratification of Twenty-seventh Amendment, 42
Military
discrimination against women in, 504
as an instrument of foreign policy, 642–648
pensions of, costs, 548
Military aid, as an instrument of foreign policy, 647–648
Military diplomacy, link with economic diplomacy, 648
Military intervention, 643–645
and foreign policy, 641
in Vietnam, 634–635
Military leadership, and foreign policy, 354–357
Milk Wagon Drivers Union v. Meadowmoor Dairies, 465n
Miller v. California, 446n, 466n
Miller v. Johnson, 324n
Milliken v. Bradley, 517n
Minimum wage laws, 537
Mining
government subsidy for, 547
on public lands, dollar value of, 117
Minorities
in the civil service, 378–379
rights of, in a democracy, 14
size of, and influence on government, 514
voting rights of, 175
Minority leader, House of Representatives, 308
Minor parties, role in American politics, 155
Miranda v. Arizona, 453
Miranda rights, 453
"Mischiefs of faction", 57, 110–111
Mississippi University for Women v. Hogan, 519n
Mississippi Freedom Democratic Party (MFDP), 471, 514–515
Missouri ex rel. Gaines v. Canada, 516n
Mixed economy, 557
Moderation, in American political parties, 153–155
Monetary policy, 561–563
Money
for challenging an incumbent in Congress, 297
impact on campaigns, 263–269
congressional, 301
and politics, 253–279
as a resource for interest groups, 134
See also Campaign financing; Expenditures
Monitor Patriot v. Roy, 466n
Monopoly, 591
Monroe doctrine, 630, 642
Moralism
and divisive opinions, 83
in political cultures, 54
Most favored nation (MFN) status, 621–622
for China, 658–659
Muckrakers, 256
Mueller v. Allen, 467n
Muller v. Oregon, 518n
Mutual assured destruction, 633, 642

N

Narrowcasting, 228
Nashville Gas v. Satty, 518n
National Association for the Advancement of Colored People (NAACP), 128, 477
access to the courts, 413
on the Thomas nomination, 109–110, 137
National Association of Evangelicals, 122
National Association of Manufacturers, 115
National Audubon Society, 123–124, 611
National Bar Association, 119
National Cancer Institute, on environmental causes of cancer, 611
National committee, political party, 158
National Conference of State Legislatures, 66
National Council of Churches, 122
National Council to Control Handguns, 134–135
National debt, 571. *See also* Budget deficit
National dominance, 401
National Economic Council, 560
National Education Association, 119
National Environmental Policy Act, 604

National Farmers' Union, 118
National Federation of Independent Business, 115, 130
National Highway Traffic Safety Administration, 128
National Labor Relations Board (NLRB), 117, 376
  sensitivity to court decisions, 389
National League of Cities, 66
National League of Cities v. Usery, 72n
National Organization for Women (NOW), 121, 497
National party chair, 158
National party committees, gifts to, campaign reform loophole, 258
National Policy Forum, 158
National Rifle Association (NRA), 113
  effective lobbying by, 130
  mass mailing by, 267
  political action committee of, 261
  as a single-interest group, 124
National Right to Life Committee, as a single-interest group, 125
National Security Council, 351, 625–626
National Small Business Association, 115
National Taxpayers Union, 120
  mass mailing by, 267
National Technology Initiative, 580
National Women's party, 176
Nation-centered federalism, 61–62
Native Americans
  counting for representation, Constitutional Convention, 29
  discrimination against, 493–496
  Iroquois Confederacy, 35–36
  origins of, 5–6
  poverty and unemployment among, 512
Naturalist Society, 112
Natural Resources Defense Council, 123–124
Natural rights, 37. *See also* Rights
Nazi party, 437–438
Necessary and proper laws, 56
Neutral competence, 384–387
  and AIDS, 392
New York Times v. Sullivan, 441–442
New York Times v. United States, 466n
New Deal, 61–62, 350
New Deal coalition, 149
New federalism, 64–65
New Freedom, 350
New Hampshire, ratification of the Constitution, 39
News, sources of, 217
Newspapers, importance in politics, 215
News programs, television, commercial importance of, 238
Newsweek, 239
"New World Order"
  fear of, by angry Americans, 114
  reference to, in the Bush Administration, 641
New York, ratification of the Constitution, 39–40
New York Herald, straw polls by, 91
New York Times, 239, 321, 352–353, 440
Nicaragua
  American policy toward, 351
    effect of public opinion on, 630
Nineteenth Amendment
  right to vote, women, 42, 497
  text of, 674
Nineteenth century, money in politics, 255–256
Ninth Amendment, 40
Nominations
  effect of the media on, 241
  presidential, 329–330, 345–346, 360–361
  process of, 161–164
    presidential campaigns, 186–195
    reforming, 191–192
Nonpoint sources of pollution, 607
Norris v. Alabama, 517n
North American Free Trade Agreement (NAFTA), 77, 340, 650
  opposition to, within the Democratic party, 153
  role in containment, 631
North Atlantic Treaty Organization (NATO), 623, 645–647
  origin of, 631–632
Norway, role in Arab-Israeli talks, 656
Norwood v. Harrison, 517n
Nuclear capability, North Korea's, 647
Nuclear deterrence versus conventional capability, 642–643
Nuclear development, pollution resulting from, 608
Nuclear weapons, as a foreign policy tool, 633
Nursing homes, cost of, to Medicaid, 539

■ O

Obscenity, 443–444
Occupational Safety and Health Administration (OSHA)
  benefits calculations of, 594
  on safety versus religious expression, 447
Ocean Dumping Act, 610
Office of Management and Budget (OMB)
  power of, 345
  preparation of the president's budget message, 560
  review of regulations by, 595
Office of Technology Assessment, 313
Office of Trade Assistance, 120
Oligopoly, in the airline industry after deregulation, 598
Olmstead v. United States, 467n
O'Lone v. Shabazz, 466n
Open meetings, of bureaucratic agencies, 369
Open primary, 162
Operation Rescue, as a single-interest group, 125
Opinion polls. *See* Polling
Opinions
  stability of, 78
Oregon, health care rationing in, 532
Organization
  of Congress, 305–311
  of the courts, 404
  for presidential campaigns, 195
Organizational structure. *See* Party organization
Organization for Economic Cooperation and Development
  report of tax rates in developed countries, 566
Orr v. Orr, 519n
Osborn v. U.S. Bank, 427n
Outsiders, presidential strategies of, 339–340
Override of a veto, 317
  War Powers Act, 356
Oversight, congressional, of the bureaucracy, 317

■ P

Packaging in campaigns, 207–208
Palestinian Liberation Organization (PLO), 654–656
Panama, invasion of, 643
  management of the media during, 227
Paranoia in American politics, 114
Pardon, presidential power of, 357
Parliamentary governments, 348
Participation
  Constitutional provisions for, 45
  political, and socioeconomic status, 15
  in political campaigns, 184–186
  teledemocracy, 89
Partnership for Peace, 647
Party identification, 155
  of congressional committee chairs, 310
  in congressional elections, 301–302
  and congressional votes, 304–305, 322–323
  family influence on, 81
  of members of Congress, 289
  political implications of, for a member of Congress, 555, 583
  of the president, 358–359
  and vote for president, 203–204
Party in government, 143, 156–158
Party in the electorate, 143, 155–156
Party organization, 143
Party politics
  Democratic, and populism, 9
  Republican, and populism, 9
Party system
  development of, 144–151

ratios of members on congressional committees, 309
responsibility of, in American politics, 157
Patronage, 160–161
and bureaucratic responsiveness, 384
See also Spoils system
Peers, political socialization by, 82–83
Pendleton Act (1883), 385
Pentagon, overseeing, 318
Pentagon Papers, 440, 634
Perks, of the president, 332
Persian Gulf War, 355, 655
building support for in the media, 341
Bush's leadership during, 351–352
management of the media during, 227–228
media coverage of, 216, 231
popularity of Bush during, 338
public opinion and, 630
Personal contacts, for lobbying effectively, 126–127
Personal presidency, 334–336
responsiveness of, 359
Persuasion, by media coverage, 242
Peyote, religious use of, 445
Pharmaceutical Manufacturers Association, 130
Pharmaceuticals, subsidy for development of, 117
Phillips v. Martin-Marietta, 518n
Pierce v. Society of Sisters, 466n
Pittsburgh Press v. Pittsburgh Commission on Human Relations, 518n
Planned Parenthood of Missouri v. Danforth, 467n
Planned Parenthood, 125–126
Planned Parenthood of Southeastern Pennsylvania v. Casey, 460
Plea bargain, 456
Plessy v. Ferguson, 475, 516n
Pluralism, 16
excesses in, 17–18
Plyler v. Doe, 518n
Poe v. Ullman, 427n
Poelker v. Doe, 467n
Poland, immigrants from, 6
Policy
effect of elections on, 207
implementation of, by bureaucrats, 376
making of, by bureaucrats, 377–378
Political action committees (PACs), 256, 259
as checkbook interest groups, 113
in Congressional elections, 260–263
coordination among, 132
loophole in campaign financing, 258
mass mailing by, 267
back pocket, 258–259
Political bias, 232
Political consultants, 129. *See also* Lobbying
Political Control of the Economy (Tufte), 563
Political culture, 54–55
changing the Constitution through practices of, 42
and economic system, 557
Political machine, 160–161
typical leader of, 162
Political participation. *See* Voter participation
Political parties, 141–165
convention delegates, characterization of, 193
convention delegate selection, 191
donations to congressional campaigns, 263
fate of, under Progressive reforms, 178
impact of the media on, 240–242
organization participation in presidential elections, 196
presidential leadership of, 358–359
role in congressional campaigns, 301
role in mobilizing voters, 183–184
role in presidential nominations, 187–190
Political socialization, 79–84, 105n. *See also* Socialization
Political tolerance, 98–99
Politicians
compromise by, Constitutional Convention, 37
public agenda shaped by, 240
public view of, 5
Politics, 10
and the economy, 563–565
impact of the media on, 238–243
and principle, dilemmas, 472
of regulation, 602–603
of the Vietnam policy, 635–636
See also Political culture
Polling
convention bounce effect, 194
factors affecting accuracy of predictions, 86
wording, 85
impact on politics, 89–91
phony, 91
predictions and outcomes, recent elections, 86–87
scientific, 85–86
uses of, 87–89
See also Opinion polls
Poll tax, 172–173
Popularity, of presidents, 341–342
Popular sovereignty, 14
Populism, new, 9, 64
angry while males, 114, 205
attitudes about affirmative action, 507–510
congressional elections of 1994, 298–299
controlling immigration, 11–12
and political parties, 154
return of isolationism, 640–641
and talk radio, 218–219
and teledemocracy, 88–89
Populism, traditional, 8–9
Populist party, 155
Pork barrel, 294
and committee structure, 311
earmarking to defend, 300
effect of a line-item veto on, 346–347
Poverty
defined, Census Bureau, 534
among the employed, 579
and rising demand for health care, 531
and Social Security, 527–528
social welfare to alleviate, 534–546
Powell v. Alabama, 467n
Power
of the courts, 420–424
distribution of, in Congress, 311
fragmentation of
under the Constitution, 32–34
within political parties, 152–153
and information, 225
presidential, 336–343
abuse of, 352–353
limits of, 342–343
to persuade, 337
of special interest caucuses, 312
Preamble to the Constitution, 30
Precedent, and judicial decisions, 419
Prejudice
against Americans of Japanese descent, 397–398
against Germans, during World War I, 7
Presidential preference primaries, 190–191
Presidential press conference
Eisenhower's, 246n
origin of, 223
Presidential Succession Act (1947), 331
President/presidency, 329–361
actions of, on a bill passed by congress, 317
characterization of candidates for, 186–187
control over the bureaucracy, 387–388
criteria of, for nominating judges, 406
election of
decided in the House of Representatives, 84
nominating campaigns, 186–195
foreign policy role, 624–626
general election campaigns, 195–203
influence of, on congressional votes, 305
voting for a candidate for, 3–4
See also Executive branch
Press, management of relationships with, Defense Department, 221. *See also* Media
Primaries, 161–164
presidential, game of, 189

Prime minister, comparison with the president, 348
Prior restraint, 439–440
Privacy, and revelation of homosexuality, 214. *See also* Rights, to privacy
Private interest groups, 113, 115
Productivity, measuring competitiveness and economic health in terms of, 559
Professional reputation, of the president, 337–338
Professions, interest groups representing, 119
Progressive management, and labor union support, 117
Progressive party, 148
Progressive reforms, 178
  attacks on corruption through campaign expenditures, 256
  direct election of senators, 306–307
  See also Reform
Progressive taxes, 567
Prohibition party, 155
Property, Constitutional provisions protecting, 39
Proportional representation, 152
Proposition 187 (California), 12
Protectionism, 649. *See also* Trade
Protestants, vote of, presidential elections, 204
Protest by interest groups, 132–133
  Montgomery bus boycott, 134–135
Public accommodations
  desegregation of, 484–485
  discrimination in, 487–488
Public agenda, impact of the media on, 239-240
Public Citizen (consumer interest group), 120–121
Public employment, growth in, twentieth century, 373–376
Public forum, 436–437
Public funding, for Congressional campaigns, 272–273
Public image, as a resource for interest groups, 134
Public interest
  and diversity, 9–10
  and immigration, 8–10
Public interest groups, 120
Public opinion, 77–104
  about affirmative action, 507
  as a check on the courts, 421, 424
  of the cold war, 638
  effect on congressional votes, 303–305
  about foreign policy, 629–630
  about health care, 533
  impact of the media on, 242–243
  influencing, as a lobbying technique, 131
  measuring, 84–91
  about members of Congress, 287
  about presidents, 336
  about South Africa, 652
  about the war in Vietnam, 635–636
Public policy
  impact of money on, 266, 268–269
  impact of the media on, 321
Public service. *See* Civil service
"Publius", author of the *Federalist Papers*, 41
Pure speech, 437
Push polls, 91

■ Q

Qualifications
  of judges, 411
  for membership in Congress, 288
  for the presidency, 331
Queer Nation, 123

■ R

Race
  and campaign participation, 186
  gerrymandering to assure election outcomes, 174
  and immigration, 9–10
  and opinions about affirmative action, 507
  and poverty, 535
  public opinion about issues around, 96–98
  self-identification with, 7
  of women in Congress, 295
Radio, talk radio, and the new populism, 218–219
Rally events, effect of, on presidential popularity, 341
Ratification
  of amendments to the Constitution, 40
    time limits, 42
  of the Constitution, 38–40
Ratings
  by interest groups, 131
  of presidents, 340
Rationing, of medical care, 531
R.A.V. v. St. Paul, 443n
Realignment, of political parties, 144
Reapportionment, 289
Recession, 559
Reciprocity, in the House, 302
Reconstruction period, 171
Redistributive policies, New Deal, 62
Redistricting, 289, 291
  and retirements, 1994 election, 298
Reed v. Reed, 518n
Reform
  of the campaign money system, 269–271
  of environmental regulation, 610–614
  See also Progressive reforms
Region
  and influence of interest groups, 133
  and poverty, 536
Regional political cultures, 54–55
  and campaign participation, 186
  and school prayer, 448
  the South
    primaries on Super Tuesday, 191
    realignment in, 151
    subcultures and voting rights, 173
  the West, 64
Registration. *See* Voter registration
Regressive taxes, 567
Regulation, 379–382
  of the economy, 558–565
  and environmental policy, 587–616
  of government programs, 608–609
  of immigration, 8
  of money in politics, 255–257
  under the New Deal, 62
  See also Deregulation; Reregulation
Regulations
  congressional influence on, 268–269
  enforcing, 595, 605–610
Regulatory boards, independent, 376
Regulatory reform, interest of Clinton administration in, 596
Rehnquist court, 403
  on abortion, 460
  on busing to desegregate schools, 481–482
  on capital punishment, 456
  on establishment of religion, 449, 451
  on freedom of religion, exemptions from laws involving, 445
  on prior restraint, 440
  on the right to privacy, 438
  right to refuse medical treatment, 463–464
  size of docket, 427n
Reid v. Covert, 465n
Religion
  and abortion rate, survey, 462
  Amish, 445
  Catholic
    interest groups representing, 122
    "Know-Nothing" fear of, 7
  Christian right, interest groups representing, 122
  diversity of, and political action, 8–9
  establishment of, 447–452
  freedom of, 444–452, 464–465
  interest groups representing, 122–123
  Jewish, interest groups representing, 122
  Judeo-Christian, equality in, 13–14
  Native American church, 445, 447
  and the right to vote, 171
  Santeria, 431–432, 464–465
  Seventh-Day Adventist, 445
  See also Christian Right
Religious Freedom Restoration Act (1993), 447
Religious right, 152
Redlining, 485
Reporters, restraints on, 232

Representation, compromise over, Constitutional Convention, 29
Representatives, jobs of, 302
Republic, 14
  consensus on form, Constitutional Convention, 29
  versus democracy, 32
Republican party
  characterization of members, 150, 156
  convention delegate selection, 191
  on gay rights, 185
  members as talk-show listeners, 219
  origin of, 148
  style of corruption, versus Democratic style, 275
Reregulation, stage in the regulation-deregulation cycle, 598–599
Resource Conservation and Recovery Act of 1976, 618n
Resources
  allocation of, in presidential campaigns, 199
  financial, for political campaigns, 203, 253–279
  of successful interest groups, 133–134
Responsible party government, 156
Responsiveness
  of the bureaucracy, 391
  of Congress, 320–322
  of the Constitution, 42–45
  of the courts, 424
    in interpreting civil liberties, 464
  of economic policy, 582–583
  of the federal bureaucracy, 384
  of federalism, 70–71
  of foreign policy, 658
  of government, 18
    in civil rights provision, 513–514
    effect of elections, 206–207
    effect of political parties, 164
    effects of interest groups on, 136–137
    impact of money on, 276–277
    to public opinion, 103–104
  of the media, 243–244
  of the president, 359, 361
  of regulation of the environment, 615
  of social welfare programs, 548–549
Restraint, judicial, 418
Restrictive covenants, 484
Retirement, income after, 528
Retribution, as a function of the legal system, 459
Retrospective voting, 206
Revenues, government. *See* Taxes
Reynolds v. United States, 466n
Rhode Island, lack of representation, Constitutional Convention, 28
Richmond v. Croson, 519n
Rights
  to counsel, 454
  of criminal defendants, 454–456
  free speech, and campaign giving, 258
  individual, provision in the Constitution, 39
  to a jury trial, 454
  natural, 432
    Locke's concept of, 37
  to privacy, 438, 441, 456, 460–462
  property, 38
  to vote, 171, 485
    black men, 42, 476
    demonstration in Selma, Alabama, 483
    women, 42, 175–176
  See also Civil rights; Freedom; Natural rights; Voting rights
Right to die, 463–464
Risk assessment, for setting regulatory standards, 602
Ritual, patriotic, 81
Roberts v. United States Jaycees, 519n
Rochin v. California, 467n
Roe v. Wade, 420, 457
Roemer v. Maryland Public Works Board, 467n
Rogers v. Richmond, 467n
Rosenberger v. University of Virginia, 467n
Rosenfeld v. New Jersey, 466n
Rostker v. Goldberg, 519n
Roth v. United States, 466n
Rulemaking, 381
Rules Committee (House), 315
Runoff primaries, 162–163
Russia, Jewish immigration from, 6
Rust v. Sullivan, 467n

■ S

Safe Drinking Water Act (1974), 607
Salary, of the president, 332
"Saturday Night Massacre", Watergate investigation, 24
Savings, in Social Security and retirement funds, 576
Savings and loans, 253–254
  cost of Lincoln Savings and Loan collapse, 278–279
  results of deregulation of, 599
Scales v. United States, 465n
Scheduling, of hearings on bills, 315
Schenk v. United States, 465n
Schiro v. Bynum, 516n
Schools
  desegregation of, 477–480
  discrimination in, against Hispanics, 491–493
  political socialization in, 81–82
  prayer in, 448
  private, religious, 451–452
  professional and graduate, desegregating, 478
  segregation in, 476, 485–486
  See also Desegregation
Science, Space and Technology Committee, House of Representatives, 300
Scoop, 222
Scott v. Sandford, 426n, 516n
Sea Shepherds, 12
Second Amendment
  guarantees of, 433
  right to bear arms for a militia, 40
Secretary of defense, foreign policy advisory role, 625–626
Secretary of state, 625–626
Securities and Exchange Commission, 376
Security, and foreign policy, 623
Sedition Act (1798), 225
Seditious speech, 434–435
Segregation
  in the federal government, 477
  of Native Americans, 493–494
  in the North, 476–477
    impatience with, 483
  residential, of Hispanics, 491
  in the South, 474–476
Select committees, of Congress, 310
Selective perception, 242
Self-identification, with political labels, 93–94
Self-incrimination, 453
Self-selected listener opinion polls (SLOP), 87
Senate
  blacks in, nineteenth century, 171
  comparison with the House of Representatives, 31
  confirmation of presidential appointments, 345–346
  criteria of, for confirming judicial appointments, 406–408
  election of members, by state legislatures, 33
  processing of bills by, 315–317
  reform of, early twentieth century, 306–307
  size of individual senator's staffs, 313
  success of challengers in races for, 300
Senatorial courtesy, 345–346
  and selection of judges, 405–406
Sendak v. Arnold, 467n
Senior Executive Service (SES), 388
Seniority rule, for assigning committee chairs, 309
Separate-but-equal doctrine, 475, 478
Separation of powers, 32–33
Setting the agenda, 239
Seventeenth Amendment
  election of senators, 33, 42
  text of, 674
Seventh Amendment
  guarantees of, 433
  right to trial by jury in civil cases, 40
Sex, and poverty, 535
Shadow cabinet (Great Britain), 628

Shays's Rebellion, 26
Sheet Metal Workers v. EEOC, 519n
Shelley v. Kraemer, 517n
Sherbert v. Verner, 466n
Sierra Club, 123–124, 128
  access to the courts, 413
Silent Spring (Carson), 604
Silicone implants, safety of, 382–383
Single-issue groups, 124–126
Single-member districts, 152
Single-parent homes, demographic distribution of, 51
Sit-ins, to desegregate public facilities, 482–483
Sixth Amendment
  guarantees of, 433
  right to counsel and jury trial, 40, 454
Slavery
  Constitutional provisions regarding, 30
  counting slaves, in determining representation in Congress, 29–30
  history of, 473–474
Smith v. Allwright, white primary, 209n
Smith v. Goguen, 466n
Smith v. Texas, 517n
Smith Act (1940), 435
Social contract, 31
  for establishing limited government, 37
Social insurance, 527
Socialism, 556
Social issues, public opinion on, 95–96. *See also* Values
Socialization, in adulthood, and political opinions, 84. *See also* Political socialization
Social Security
  benefits of, 71
  the future of, 528–529
  as a social welfare measure, 525–526, 527
  taxes for, as a percentage of federal revenue, 566
Social Security Trust Fund, investment in government securities, 571–572
Social welfare
  cost of, services to illegal immigrants, 9t
  policy for, 523–550
  role of government in, 94–95
  for the well-off, 546–548
    tax breaks, 568
Socioeconomic characteristics
  of the "angry white male", 205
  of campaign participants, 186
  of conservative factions, 152
  of judges, 409–411
  of members of Congress, 288
  of voters
    in presidential elections, 203–204
    versus nonvoters, 179
Soft money, for political campaigns, 258
Somalia, media event of landing at, 224
Sound bites, 224
  presidential use of, 340
  See also Media
South Africa
  American policy toward, 351
    effect of public opinion, 630
  economic sanctions against, 652
Southeastern Promotions v. Conrad, 466n
Southern Christian Leadership Conference (SCLC), 471, 482
Soviet Union, foreign policy toward, after World War II, 631
Spano v. New York, 467n
Speaker of the House, 306
Special education, second-generation discrimination in, 487, 492
Special interest caucuses, 312
Special interests, 117
  influence on the Senate, early twentieth century, 306–307
  as victims of the PAC system, 262–263
  See also Interest groups
Specialists, government, advising the President on foreign policy, 626
Specialization, in Congress, 302
Speech, freedom of, 434–441
Speech plus conduct, protection of, 437–438
Spence v. Washington, 466n
Sphere of influence, 623–624
Spoils system, 269. *See also* Patronage
Spotted owl, 615–616
Sputnik, 633
Square Deal, 350
Staff members
  congressional, 313
  impact of, 313
  influence of, on congressional votes, 305
  presidential, 343–345
Stagflation, 561
Stamp Act, 36
Standards
  air quality, 605–606
  setting, no-risk or margin of safety, 592
  See also Regulation
Standing committees, of Congress, 308–309
Standing to sue, 413
Stanton v. Stanton, 518n
Stare decisis, 419
State Department, 648
States
  Constitutional convention called by legislatures of, 40
  conventions in, to ratify the Constitution, 38
  enlargement of powers, by the Supreme Court, 62
  government by, under the Articles of Confederacy, 26
  interstate relations, 67, 69–70
  official language adopted by, 43
  prohibition of powers to, 56
  public trust of, 52
  state-centered federalism, 57, 60
Statutes, interpreting, 415–416
Steering, in real estate, 484, 489
Steering and Policy Committee (Democratic party), recommendation on congressional committee chairs, 309
Stein v. New York, 467n
Stereotypes
  affecting relationships between blacks and whites, 490
  about food stamp recipients, 543
  of men's and of women's roles, 501
  in the Thomas versus Hill hearings, 410–411
  of welfare recipients, 539
Stone v. Powell, 468n
Strategic Arms Limitation Treaties (SALT), 637, 639
Strategy
  media events, staging in presidential campaigns, 200
  negative campaigns, 201
  for presidential campaigns, 197–199
Straw polls, 84
Stress, and formation of groups, 111–112
Strict construction, of the Constitution, 416
Structure, of political parties, 158–161
Student Non-Violent Coordinating Committee (SNCC), 471
Subcommittee bill of rights, 310
Subcommittees
  congressional committees, 310
  referral of bills to, 315
Subgovernments. *See* Iron triangles
Subsidies
  agricultural, as social welfare, 546–547
  for airlines serving small communities, 597
  dollar value of, 117
  for the Exxon Valdez, application for, 613
  See also Aid
Succession, to the presidency, 331–332
Suffrage, 171
  for women, 175–176
Sunbathing Association, 112
Sunshine Act (1977), 369
Superdelegates, to Democratic presidential nominating conventions, 191
Superfund, 610
Superfund Act, amendment of 1986, 610
Super lobbyists, 129
Super Tuesday, 191
Supplemental Security Income (SSI), 528, 538
Supply-side economics, 561, 576
Supremacy clause, 56

Supreme Court
appeal to, 415
decisions of
on criticism of public officials, 442
on executive privilege, 24
on the grandfather clause, 477
on Interior Department ecosystem management plan, 616
on the legislative veto, 317
on poll taxes, 173
on the power to remove presidential appointees, 347
on prior restraint, the Pentagon Papers, 440
on public accommodations, 475
on residential segregation, 477
on school funding equalization, 491–492
on segregation in buses, 135
on segregation in the schools, 476
on segregation in the schools, reversal of, 478
on term limits, 290
effect of attempted packing of, 207, 402
nomination of Clarence Thomas to, 109–110
process of deciding a case, 422–423
Woodrow Wilson on, 42
Surgeon General, nomination and confirmation of, 329–330
Survivors benefits, Social Security, 527
Swain v. Alabama, 467n
Swann v. Charlotte-Mecklenburg Board of Education, 517n
Sweatt v. Painter, 516n
Symbiotic relationship, 221–224
Symbolic speech, 438–439
Symbolism
of an amendment requiring a balanced budget, 572–573
in the death penalty, 458–459
in deregulation, 600–601
of the Equal Rights Amendment, 500–501
fall of the Berlin Wall, 639
in language, 44
of the line-item veto, 346–347
patriotic, 81
of public funding for campaigns, 272
in reducing the size of the bureaucracy, 370–371
in state-administered welfare, 69
in term limits, 290
in voter registration proposals, 181

■ T

Talk shows, characterization of hosts and callers, 218–219
Tariffs, controversy over, Constitutional Convention, 30
Taxation
under the Articles of Confederacy, 25–26
and freedom of religion, 445
John Marshall on the power of, 58
and poverty, 535
Taxes
cost of tax breaks, 568
"green", 601
origin of, in the House, 315
per capita burden, 565–566
regulation of economic cycles using, 560
Social Security, 527
as a percentage of federal revenue, 566
on Social Security benefits, 528
tax breaks for the well-off, 546
Tax Reform Act (1986), 377, 568
Taylor v. Louisiana, 467n, 518n
Teamsters, political action committee of, 261
Teapot Dome scandal, 207, 256
Technology
and the cost of health care, 530–531
as a source of pollution, 607
Teledemocracy, 88–89
Television
broadcasting presidential press conferences, 223
cable, and atomization of the media, 217
importance to politics, 215, 303
See also Media
Tennessee, right of women to vote, school board elections, 175–176
Tennessee Valley Authority, 376
Tenth Amendment, 56
application to minimum wage and hour laws, 72
in the pre-Civil War period, 59–60
reserving to the states powers not enumerated, 40
Tenure
of judges, 411
of presidents, 331
on welfare, 541
Terms
of members of the House of Representatives, 33
of the president, 33
proposals for limiting, 290–291
of senators, 33
Testimony, at hearings, by lobbyists, 127–128
Texas v. Johnson, 466n
Third Amendment
guarantees of, 433
right to not quarter soldiers in peacetime, 40, 456
Third parties, 154
media coverage of, 233
presidential nominees of, 195
See also Minor parties
Thirteenth Amendment
abolition of slavery, 42, 474
text of, 673
Thornton v. Calder, 466n
Three-fifths Compromise, 30
"Three strikes and you're out" legislation, 77–78
origin of, 218–219
Ticket splitting, 149
Tight money policy, effects of, 1980s, 576
Tileston v. Ullman, 427n
Tilton v. Richardson, 467n
Time, 239
Time v. Firestone, 466n
Time v. Hill, 466n, 467n
Tinker v. Des Moines School District, 466n
Title IX enforcement, 499–500
Tolerance, political, 98
Torcaso v. Watkins, 466n
Tort, defined, 414
Tort reform, 414
focus in lobbying over, 131
Town meeting
direct democracy of, 14
electronic, as a campaign tool, 220
Toxic Substances Control Act of 1976, 618n
Trade, Constitutional protection of, 30
Trade policy
and foreign policy, 648–651
interest groups influencing foreign policy through, 629
nonisolationist trend in, 641
Traditionalism, in political culture, 54
Tragedy of the commons, 589
Transportation, federal aid for, 71
Treasury Department, role in economic diplomacy, 648
Treaties, ratification by Congress, 628
Truman Doctrine, 631
Truth in labeling, 591–592
T.W.A. v. Hardison, 466n
Twenty-fifth Amendment
naming a vice-president in case of vacancy, 331
text of, 676
Twenty-fourth Amendment
abolition of the poll tax in federal elections, 42, 173
text of, 675–676
Twenty-second Amendment
limiting the terms of the president, 331
text of, 675
Twenty-seventh Amendment
restriction on midterm pay raises for Congress, 42
text of, 676
Twenty-sixth Amendment
text of, 676
voting age of eighteen, 42, 177, 183

Twenty-third Amendment
right to vote, residents of the District of Columbia, 42
text of, 675
Two-party system, 152

■ U

Underdog effect, of polls, 91
Unemployment
government intervention to manage, 558–559
rate of, 1980s, 576
Unfunded mandates, 66
Unitary governments, 32, 53–54
United Steelworkers v. Weber, 519n
United States v. American Friends Service Committee, 466n
United States v. Curtiss-Wright Export Corp., 362n
United States v. E.C. Knight Co., 426n
United States v. Grace, 466n
United States v. Lee, 466n
United States v. Leon, 467n
United States v. Nixon, 24, 46–47
United States v. O'Brien, 466n
United States v. Paradise Local Union, 519n
United States v. Reynolds, 48n
United Nations
backing for American involvement in Haiti, 642
as a confederal system, 54
United We Stand (Perot party designation), 19–20
University of California Regents v. Bakke, 506, 519n
Unreasonable searches and seizures, 452
Unsafe at Any Speed (Nader), 120–121
U.S. v. Butler, 427n
U.S. v. Eichman, 466n
U.S. v. Schwimmer, 466n
Utilities, regulation of, to limit inefficient competition, 590

■ V

Values
common, of Americans, 9
conflicting, over social issues, 95–96
reflection by the media, 231
Veterans Administration, limitation of loans to blacks, 485
Veterans Affairs, Department of, 376
Veto
legislative, 317
presidential, 317
power of, 349
of the War Powers Act, 356
Vice president
office of, 333
selection of candidates, 194–195
Vietnam
American policy toward, 351, 633–637
immigrants from, 6
Vietnam syndrome, 637
Vietnam War, foreign policy and, 356
Violence, against blacks, 476–477
Virginia, ratification of the Constitution, 39
Voter participation, 5, 178–184
Voter registration
barriers to, 182–183
same-day, proposed, 181–182
Voters, characterization of, 179
Voting
for Congress, 301–302
effect of party loyalty on, 206
Congressional, 303–305
effect of political contributions on, 266, 268
effect of issues on, 206
evaluating the candidates, 3, 19–20
historic limitations on right of, 171
patterns of, 1994, 299
in presidential elections, 203–206
residential patterns of, 512
turnout, 5, 178–184
Voting Rights Act (1965), 172, 173, 175, 209n, 485, 515
amendments of 1982, 174

■ W

Wages, effect of immigration on, 9
Wallace v. Jaffree, 467n
Wall Street Journal, 239, 269, 535
Wards Cove Packing v. Atonio, 517n
War Powers Act (1973), 356, 627
Warren Court, 403
versus the Burger Court, on obscenity, 446
on civil rights, 513
on demonstrations in shopping malls, 437
on electronic eavesdropping, 453
on freedom of religion, 445
on obscenity, 444
on right to counsel, 454
on self-incrimination, 453
Washington v. Davis, 517n
Washingtonians, 337, 359
Washington Post, 239, 353, 440, 548
Waste, by government, 368
Watergate scandal, 23–24, 80, 344
press response to, 222
Water quality, 606–607
Wealth of Nations, The (Smith), 556
Webster v. Reproductive Health Services, 467
Wedge issues, affirmative action, 510
Weeks v. United States, 467n
Welfare
federal versus state responsibility for, 68–69
individual costs of getting off the rolls, 548
reform of, 539–546
Whig party, split over slavery, 147–148
Whips, House of Representatives, 308
Whistleblowers, protection of, 391
"White flight" from cities, 480, 512
White primary, 173
Whites
perceptions of racism, poll results, 97
vote of, presidential elections, 204
on welfare, 541
White supremacy, overcoming, 477–485
Whitewater affair, 274, 276
Whitney v. California, 465n
Widmar v. Vincent, 467n
Wilkerson v. Utah, 467n
Wilkinson v. Jones, 466n
Winner-take-all elections, 152
of Electoral College delegates, 196–197
Wisconsin v. Mitchell, 443n
Wisconsin v. Yoder, 466n
Women
appearance of, and newscasting jobs, 235
in the civil service, 378–379
in Congress, 295
exclusion from political equality, history of, 13
interest groups representing, 121
as judges, 408
as officeholders, 177
PACs representing interest of, 262
political opinions of, 102
and poverty, 512, 535
right to vote, 175–176
roles in the Revolution, 27
selection of Iroquois Confederacy chiefs by, 35
statistics on abortion, 462
Women's Rights Convention, 1848, 497
Woodson v. North Carolina, 467n
Worcester v. Georgia, 518n
World Policy Institute, study of expenditures on military aid, 648
World War II
entry of the United States, 630–631
losses during, 631
Writ of certiorari, 415
Writ of mandamus, 400
Wygant v. Jackson Board of Education, 519n

■ Y

Yates v. United States, 465n
Young v. American Mini Theaters, 466n
Youngstown Sheet and Tube Co. v. Sawyer, 362n
Yugoslavia, independence of the Soviet policy, 633

■ Photo Credits—*Continued*

328 Associated Press; **332** Historical Pictures Chicago/Stock Montage; **334** The Granger Collection; **335** Edward Clark; **344** George Tames, New York Times Pictures; **350** FDR Library; **351** AP/Wide World Photos; **355** National Archives; **357** © 1990 Wally McNamee, Woodfin Camp & Associates; **358** New York Times; **360** AP/Wide World Photos; **364** Ted Thai/Time Magazine; **366** © Rick Browne/Photoreporters; **369** Ted Thai/Time Magazine; **373** National Archives; **377** AP/Wide World Photos; **379** UPI Photo; **381** Charles Krebs; **382** Reuters/Bettmann; **384** The Granger Collection; **385** The Granger Collection; **390** Fred Ward Prod, Inc./Black Star; **392** Courtesy of New York City Department of Health; **396** Lynn Johnson; **397** UPI/Bettmann; **399** Bettmann; **400** Supreme Court Historical Society; **402 (top) Courtesy of the Utah State Historical Society; 402** (bottom) Dennis Brack, Black Star; **414** Photoreporters; **417** Ken Regan/Regan Pictures, Inc.; **422** © 1986 Ken Heinen; **425** Courtesy of National Archives; **429** (top) Photo by Harris & Ewing, Courtesy of Library of Congress; **429** (bottom) © 1993 David Burnett/Contact Press; **430** Tom Salyer; **436** (top) UPI/Bettmann; **436** (bottom) UPI/Bettmann; **438** UPI/Bettmann; **439** Bob Kusel/Sipa Press; **440** AP/Wide World Photos; **441** © 1994 Bob Sacha; **447** Tom Defeo © 1965, The Des Moines Register and Tribune Co.; **448** Courtesy of National Archives; **449** © Phil Schofield; **451** Gamma Liaison; **453** Mark Solomon/Time Magazine; **455** (left) National Archives; **455** (right) National Archives; **457** Bill Janscha; **470** Arthur Grace/Sygma; **472** © Charmian Reading 1966; **473** The Granger Collection; **476** AP/Wide World Photos; **478** AP/Wide World Photos; **479** AP/Wide World Photos; **481** Stanley R. Forman Pulitzer Prize, 1977; **482** Charles Moore/Black Star; **483** AP/Wide World Photos; **488** © Mark Heckman; **493** ©Mario Pignata-Monti; **494** (left) Courtesy of Smithsonian Institute; **494** (right) Courtesy of Smithsonian Institute; **495** © 1989 Steve Wall **498** (left) Printed by the permission of The Estate of Norman Rockwell; **498** (right) Printed by the permission of the Estate of Norman Rockwell **500** UPI/Bettmann; **511** Rick Rickman/Black Star; **521** (top) S. Ferry Ciai; **521** (bottom) National Archives; **522** Bill Luster, Matrix/Sipa; **526** Mary Ellen Mark/Library; **527** Indiana University Photographic Services; **529** © 1991 Lester Sloan, Woodfin Camp & Associates, all rights reserved; **536** © Jacques Chenet, Woodfin Camp & Associates; **537** (left) Library of Congress; **537** (right) Robert Ferrone; **543** Dan Ford Connolly/Mercury; **546** Richard Ross; **554** Doug Knutson; **557** Bettmann Archive; **559** Bettmann Archive; **560** UPI/Bettmann Newsphotos; **562** AP/Wide World Photos; **567** (left) Camilo Jose Vergara; **567** (right) Camilo Jose Vergara; **577** Courtesy of John Gruhl; **579** (left) Library of Congress; **579** (right) Bill Ganzel, University of Nebraska Press; **586** Michael Melford, Inc.; **590** (top) Lester Sloan, Woodfin Camp & Associates; **590** (bottom) The Granger Collection; **592** Brad Trent; **594** United Mineworkers Association; **596** O'Lindan Collection, FDA History Room; **602** Paula Nelson/The Dallas Morning News; **603** American Heritage Center, University of Wyoming; **604** AP/Wide World Photos; **607** UPI/Bettmann Newsphotos; **609** Doug Menuez, Reportage; **613** Michael Kienitz; **616** Woodfin Camp & Associates; **620** Agence France-Presse; **631** Courtesy Tatiana Baltermants & Paul Harbaugh; **632** (top) Sygma; **632** (bottom) Sygma; **633** Paul S. Conklin; **634** Jack Kightlinger/Lyndon Baines Johnson Library; **636** (left) AP/Wide World Photos; **636** (right) Joe McNally; **637** Courtesy of National Archives; **638** Andy Hernadez/Sipa Press; **639** Alex MacLean; **650** Henry Groskinsky © Time Warner Inc.; **653** Tomohillo Taniguchi of Nikkei Business Pub.; **656** AP/Wide World Photos sues may have been vague, but individuals were able to understand the issues enough to define their own general positions.

Also, for voters to cast issue votes, candidates must have detectable policy differences. A substantial minority of voters are able to detect some differences among presidential candidates. In recent elections the percentages able to identify correctly general differences between the major party candidates varied between 36 and 62%.[76]

In the 1972 through 1988 elections, more than 70% of those who could correctly identify the positions of the candidates as well as their own position on an important issue cast a vote consistent with their own position.[77] We call this issue voting. Issues with the highest proportion of issue voting were those that typically divided Republicans and Democrats, such as government spending, military spending, and government aid to the unemployed and minorities. However, because only one-third to two-thirds of the electorate was able to define both their own and the candidates' positions on each issue, the proportion of the total electorate that can be said to cast an "issue vote" is usually less than 40%, and for some issues it is much less.[78]

Some scholars have suggested that issue voting is really more of an evaluation of the current incumbents. If voters like the way incumbents, or the incumbent's party, have handled the job in general or in certain areas—the economy or foreign policy, for example—they will vote accordingly, even without much knowledge about the specifics of the issues.

Voting on the basis of past performance is called **retrospective voting.** There is good evidence that many people do this, especially according to economic conditions.[79] Voters support incumbents if national income is growing in the months preceding the election. Since World War II, the incumbent party has won a presidential election only once when the growth rate was less than 3% (Eisenhower in 1956) and lost only once when it was more than 3% (Ford in 1976). Unemployment and inflation seem to have less consistent effects on voting, and economic conditions two or three years before the election have little impact on voting.[80] The recession in the early Reagan years hurt Republicans in the congressional elections of 1982, but the recovery helped Reagan get reelected in 1984 and helped put Bush in the White House in 1988.

Parties, Candidates, and Issues

All three factors—parties, candidates, and issues—clearly matter. Party loyalties are especially important because they help shape our views about issues and candidates. However, if issues and candidates did not matter, the Democrats would have won every presidential election since the New Deal. Republican victories suggest that they often have had more attractive candidates (as in 1952, 1956, 1980, and 1984) or issue positions (in 1972 and in some respects in 1980). However, , the Democrat's partisan advantage shrank throughout the 1980s. Though there are still more Democrats than Republicans, the margin is modest and the number of independents is growing.

Party loyalties have been even more important in congressional voting. The Democrats controlled the House continuously between 1954 and 1994, and controlled the Senate most of those years. However, the Democratic lock on the House was broken in the 1994 election which found the Republicans winning control in a sweeping victory. Clearly, issues overcame traditional partisan habits in that election. Exactly which issues, however, were less than clear.

Conclusion: Do Elections Make Government Responsive?

Although election campaigns are far less successful in mobilizing voters and ensuring a high turnout today than they were in the past century, in a democracy, we expect elections to allow us to control government. Through them we can "throw the rascals out" and bring in new faces with better ideas, or so we think. But other than to change the party that controls government, do elections make a difference?

In the popular press, we hear a lot about "mandates." A president with a **mandate** is one who is clearly directed by the voters to take some particular course of action—reduce taxes or begin arms control talks, for example. George Bush had a substantial majority in his 1988 victory. But did he have a mandate? If so, what for? The campaign hardly talked about the budget deficit even though the election-day polls showed that this was the issue of concern to the largest group of voters. They, in turn, gave an overwhelming majority of *their* votes to Dukakis. On other issues, such as protecting the environment, Bush portrayed himself as a liberal. On many issues, ranging from abortion to day care to defense policy, the two candidates clearly differed. But did Bush's victory mean that he was to limit abortions, leave it to the states to fund day care, or continue the Reagan defense policy? Did he have a mandate on any of these issues?